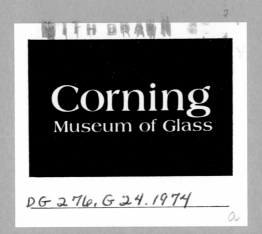

FROM TIBERIUS
TO THE ANTONINES

ALBINO GARZETTI

FROM TIBERIUS
TO THE ANTONINES

A History of the Roman Empire
AD 14-192

Translated by J. R. Foster

METHUEN & CO LTD
LONDON

First published as
L' Impero da Tiberio agli Antonini
by Istituto di Studi Romani, Rome
© *1960 Istituto di Studi Romani, Rome*
This English translation, including
author's revisions and additions, first published 1974
by Methuen & Co Ltd, 11 New Fetter Lane, London EC4
© *1974 Methuen & Co Ltd*
Printed in Great Britain by
Butler & Tanner Ltd, Frome and London

ISBN 0 416 16800 0

Distributed in the USA by
HARPER & ROW PUBLISHERS INC.
BARNES & NOBLE IMPORT DIVISION

CONTENTS

A*

CONTENTS

TRANSLATOR'S PREFACE

I should like to thank Dr R. P. Duncan-Jones of Gonville and Caius College, Cambridge, Mr R. W. Howorth, my colleague at the Civil Service Commission, and Mrs Gillian Wright of Methuen's editorial staff for many felicitous suggestions. I alone am responsible for the deficiencies that remain.

In the difficult matter of names, I have elected to use the anglicized forms – those likely to be the most familiar to the majority of English readers – but I doubt if I have been absolutely consistent. In any inconsistencies that I have overlooked – and indeed also for inadequacies in the translation as a whole – I beg the reader's – and, of course, Professor Garzetti's – indulgence.

J.R.F.
March 1973

PART I

THE JULIO-CLAUDIAN DYNASTY

I

TIBERIUS

THE SUCCESSION AFTER AUGUSTUS

The death of Augustus, after forty-five years of personal power and fifty-seven years from the day when he had accepted the legacy of Caesar, was not to pose any problem of succession from a practical point of view. The care he had taken during his lifetime, right from the earliest days of his principate, to put a member of his family constantly in the limelight, with the clear implication that this person was marked out to succeed him, shows how he himself regarded it as natural both that the system he had founded should continue – notwithstanding the provisional character with which he deliberately endowed it by clothing it in legal fictions – and in particular that the principate should remain in his own family. More-over, it must have appeared natural to the Senate and people of Rome, to Italy and to the provinces. After almost half a century of the new régime, the mere fact that people were now accustomed to it was sufficient to remove it from the realm of discussion, if only because it was a lesser evil than the troubled conditions prevailing previously. If we add to this the advantages of a peaceful life in an order of things in which the prestige and personal tact of Augustus had managed to overcome mistrust and satisfy sensibilities, it is easy to see why a solid base of universal consent henceforth sustained the Augustan principate, even in its evolution to-wards the revelation of its own true nature, that of an ever more clearly marked despotism. That the régime should revert to a struggle between factions, thus renouncing the very element which had finally reduced the latter to silence, was quite unthinkable and far from anyone's wish. We must not fall into the error of introducing into this context of facts and judgements the concept of freedom as we understand it today. Cicero (*De Rep.*, II, 43) had said, it is true, that 'a people which is under a king lacks many things, *in primis* freedom, which does not consist in being under a just lord, but in being under no lord at all': but in Cicero's eyes Augustus would not have ranked as a king. In the political atmosphere officially promoted by Augustus, with its resurrection of republicanism and rehabilitation of Pompey, Cato's freedom could be commemorated and honoured with impunity by anyone who wished to do so. The great families who now made their influence felt in the state by serving the monarchy, as they had made it felt before – with bigger risks – in the framework of the oligarchy, were not going to exchange the certainty of present dignity for the uncertain return to a situation which would have only been the starting-point of a new struggle for supremacy. As for the population of Rome and the empire as a whole, the problem did not even arise. The principate was henceforth firmly established, both in form and substance, as the product of the long process of development which had led it, under the shrewd and attentive eye of its founder, from the original usurpation of power to a *de facto* legitimacy founded in the unanimous view of all on the superhuman primacy of the *auctoritas*, and to the *de jure* legitimacy of the restoration of the republic. But apart from its constitutional characteristics the structure built up by Augustus was made to last because, realistically, its architect had seen it as an essentially administrative structure. The remote but fundamental cause of the Roman revolution, at any rate from the period of the great Mediterranean conquests onward, had been the inadequacy of the government of the city-state when confronted with the demands of a world empire. Hence the republic's evolution – governed by the needs that arose on the way, guided by the typically Roman law of empiricism and checked by the powerful rein of tradition – into the principate and the régime of Augustus, who, with his genius for practical organization, utilizing all the preceding experiences and devoting to the business of government a constant personal attention which to us seems wonderful and is in fact the principal aspect of his greatness, completed and concluded the long process after his final victory in the Civil War.

In fact, the Augustan structure, through the very solidity of its administrative framework, did last, and delayed by some centuries the end of the Roman state. And the backbone of the Augustan administration really consisted of the republican nobility, against whose authority the struggle for innovation had developed; it now became the hierarchical corps, proud and revered, of the empire's highest officials: magistrates, generals, governors of provinces. From this point of view, too, it would have been difficult, after decades of happy experience, to suppress the instrument created specially for the demands of empire and to go back to the beginning again. Material interest – which for the richer classes counselled loyalty to the principate as the restorer of tranquillity in economic life and of security of credit and landed property, and for the poorer classes signified the advantages and distractions of munificence – formed another powerful reason for the continuation of the régime. Other factors certainly leading in the same direction, less visibly but no less efficaciously, were the innumerable tiny relationships between persons, families and parties – the relationships through which the real and sovereign power of the Princeps was effectively exercised behind the façade of legal fictions. These relationships were furthered by the strengthening of his own party – the party which had given him victory in the Civil War – by the subtle manœuvres, to which Augustus was always most attentive, of political marriages, by his position as patron of individuals and communities both in Italy and abroad, and by the favour he showed his friends in the exercise of the two fundamental elements of everyday Roman public life, the *clientela* and political *amicitia*.

If one can envisage the self-annihilation at one stroke of the power of a man to whom, at the end of the still uncertain and confused period of the Civil War, Rome, Italy and the western provinces had sworn a personal oath of loyalty outside any constitutional framework and who, on the *consensus* revealed by this act, whether it had been voluntary or extorted, based the real and practical legality of his position when, *potentiae securus*, he established the system through which succeeding generations enjoyed peace and a Princeps[1]; a man who was also 'father of his country', son of a god, a god himself in the eastern provinces, and confidently expecting to become one, like his 'father', throughout the empire (though this presupposed the continuation of the principate); who controlled the elections, the armies and the treasury; who was still in a word head of the party, and hence the wielder of a power all the more fearful because it was hidden; only if the abolition of all this can be imagined is it also thinkable that the principate as an effective reality could begin and end with Augustus.

Consequently it was beyond dispute that there had to be a successor to Augustus. Theoretically this successor could be chosen from outside the family of Augustus, for according to the legal fiction which from the start placed all questions relating to the principate on two different planes, those of formal authority and real power, it was a matter for the Senate and people to choose their protector and prince. The nobility, however, which accepted the confirmed supremacy of the Julio-Claudian family because it was based on the immense personal prestige of Augustus and also because this nobility felt itself incorporated in the system without any damage to its pride, would have hardly accepted the supremacy of

[1] TAC., *Ann.*, III, 28, 2.

any other family chosen from its own ranks – quite apart from the wishes of the army and the feelings of the provinces. Augustus himself had brought this out in the quiet speech addressed to L. Cinna, who wanted to kill him: 'Do you think that, if you become prince in place of me, Paulus and Fabius Maximus, the Cossi and the Servilii will remain peaceful and content?'[1]

The successor could only be Tiberius, for two reasons. First, in the final stages of Augustus's physical decline Tiberius happened to be governing the empire already; in other words, he was deeply involved in an administrative system which he more than anyone else was bound to endorse because of his own character, and he was also equipped from the formal point of view with the powers to govern, having been placed in this very position by Augustus himself through the implicit procedure of veiled but effective designation, a distinction so often conferred on various people and just as often frustrated by fate. Second, on any objective estimate, no better candidate for the succession could be found. And even if the position of indispensability that he had by now achieved was still only a makeshift[2] solution to the dynastic design constantly pursued by Augustus, it certainly also represented the results of Livia's secret efforts in favour of her son and of those of his friends or of people more friendly disposed to the Claudii, with their lofty and ancient patrician nobility, than to any others.

Tiberius had not had an easy life. His father, Tiberius Claudius Nero, was an honourable man whom Cicero would have liked to have had as a son-in-law instead of the dissolute Dolabella. Although a supporter of Caesar, after the Ides of March he had nevertheless proposed honours for the tyrannicides; then he had become involved in the Perugian War against Octavian and when the latter's side was victorious, at the end of the winter of 41–40, had fled first to Sextus Pompeius in Sicily and later to Mark Antony in Achaea. He had taken with him his wife Livia Drusilla, who was herself a Claudius by blood, since she was the daughter of the Pompeian Appius Claudius Pulcher, who fell at Philippi. Appius Claudius had become M. Livius Drusus Claudianus, having been adopted in infancy by M. Livius Drusus, the famous tribune of 91 B.C. With his parents, in the romantic circumstances described by Suetonius, was the little Tiberius, who had been born less than two years before, on 16

---

[1] SENEC., *De Clem.*, I, 9, 10.

[2] If the preamble to the will preserved by Suetonius is authentic (*Tib.*, 23: 'Since adverse fortune robbed me of my sons Gaius and Lucius, Tiberius Caesar is to inherit two-thirds of my property . . .'), it cannot be denied that Augustus did not even try to save appearances.

November 42, in the house on the Palatine. When the triumvirs were reconciled at Brundisium, it became possible for the couple, before the end of the year 40 B.C., to return to Rome, where their erstwhile persecutor fell in love with the young and attractive Livia. Although she was about to give birth to her second son, Drusus, he married her on 17 January 38, with the more or less forced concurrence of her husband and after repudiating his own wife Scribonia, who had borne him Julia, his only daughter. The marriage was naturally also a political match (as can be seen from the family and party connections sketched above) as well as a romantically happy union.

When his father died, the nine-year-old Tiberius pronounced the funeral oration. From this moment onward he and his little brother became more closely attached to the house of Octavian, who had been named by the dying father as the guardian of his sons. Continuing his practice of arranging marriages of convenience, Octavian at that point promised Tiberius to little Vipsania, the daughter, then hardly a year old, of M. Agrippa, his faithful collaborator and future son-in-law, and of Caecilia Attica, the daughter of T. Pomponius Atticus, Cicero's rich equestrian correspondent, a friend of Octavian and no less of Antony. Atticus died a little later (in 32 B.C.), after a life notable chiefly for its perfect equilibrium. On 7 August 29, at Octavian's triumph, Tiberius, now a boy of thirteen, rode on the outer left-hand horse of the quadriga, the second position of honour, since the first – on the right-hand horse – was occupied by M. Claudius Marcellus, who was his coeval but also, as the son of Octavia, the nephew of the man celebrating the triumph. He enjoyed a position of distinction at the games held on the same occasion, and considerable prominence was also given to his assumption of the toga virilis, on 24 April 27. The young man's own public displays were likewise encouraged by Augustus and Livia, who provided the means for the funeral games in honour of his father Ti. Claudius Nero and his grandfather M. Livius Drusus.

Thus the position of Tiberius, both in the household of the Princeps and in the public eye, was from the start a leading one, and it subsequently became even more prominent when he was also dispensed from the age qualifications. For example, in 24 he was allowed to anticipate by five years the entry to the magistracy and as a result in 23 became a quaestor at the age of nineteen. Moreover, among all the relations and kinsmen whom Augustus was accustomed to appoint from preference to the highest posts in the government, Tiberius swiftly distinguished himself by the talents, especially the military ones, with which he was

endowed. But from the practical point of view of the dynastic programme
there were still other people ahead of him. First of all there was Marcellus,
who had Augustus's blood in his veins and whose designation had been
made crystal clear if not official (and these designations could never be
made official without destroying the fiction of the restoration of the
republic) by his marriage to Julia, the Princeps's only daughter (25 B.C.).
Next, when Marcellus died in 23, came Agrippa, to whom it fell in his
turn to marry Julia; but when Agrippa also died in 12 B.C. Tiberius's
hour struck at last. In 11 B.C. he was constrained to give up his beloved
Vipsania, by whom he had had one son, Drusus, and from whom he
awaited another, and to marry Julia, now the mother of five children
fathered by Agrippa. Augustus's flights of imagination in pursuing his
own matrimonial combinations were equalled only by the tyranny with
which he insisted on their execution. They were nothing new or marvellous
to the high society of the age, but Tiberius was embittered by them.

The son whom Julia bore him at Aquileia soon died. In the year 9 his
brother Drusus died in Germany. The dissolute conduct of Julia and the
excessive satisfaction with which Augustus regarded Agrippa's young
sons Gaius and Lucius Caesar, born in 20 and 17 respectively and both
already adopted by Augustus in this same year, provided Tiberius with
new motives for resentment. Whether it was these motives alone or
others as well that caused his disguised exile in Rhodes from 5 B.C. to
A.D. 2, it is impossible to say for certain. He returned to Rome in A.D. 2;
three years earlier Julia had been banished, and just at that time Lucius
Caesar died. In A.D. 4, on the death of Gaius Caesar (as well), adoption
by Augustus came at last, and Tiberius Claudius Nero became Tiberius
Julius Caesar, or more simply and more frequently, Tiberius Caesar.
However, on the same occasion Augustus also adopted Agrippa Postumus,
Agrippa's youngest son (whom he caused to be banished, however, in
A.D. 7), and in addition made Tiberius adopt, that is, put on an equal
footing with his own son Drusus, his nephew Germanicus, son of the
elder Drusus. But Germanicus was also the son of Antonia, the second of
the daughters of Mark Antony and Octavia, and was thus of the blood of
Augustus; he was bound even more closely to the family of the Princeps
by his marriage (probably in A.D. 5) to Agrippina, one of Agrippa's and
Julia's daughters. Nevertheless, it was Tiberius alone whom Augustus at
this point made his partner in the *tribunicia potestas*, for ten years; and from
this time onwards he collaborated in the government of the empire, involved almost continually, by virtue of his proconsular authority, in the
hard military campaigns which marked the last period of Augustus's

principate. His *tribunicia potestas* was renewed in A.D. 13. In the same year a law conferring on him powers equal to those of Augustus over the provinces and the armies made him effectively co-ruler; and it was as 'collega' of Augustus with 'consular imperium'[1] that in May of A.D. 14 he carried out the census. He then set out for Illyria, whence in August he was recalled by his mother to the side of the dying Augustus. He hastened to Nola, 'and the news that Augustus was dead and that Tiberius had assumed power was simultaneous'.[2]

In fact the personality of Tiberius, at that time fifty-five years old, must for years have impressed itself on the Roman state and the Roman world as that of an outstanding individual. Today, through the veils of the equivocal verdict of the ancients, largely caused by incomprehension and malicious interpretation of a character far removed from any stereotype (and far removed from that of Augustus), the true countenance of Tiberius can be discerned fairly clearly by dint of deeper study. Equipped not only with the normal rhetorical culture of the age (as a young man he had followed Theodorus of Gadara's courses in oratory in Rhodes) but also with original interests of his own, if of an erudite and somewhat formalistic character, he was a lover of painting and sculpture, a connoisseur of the Greek language and Greek literature, yet a purist and an archaizer with regard to Latin, an admirer of the Alexandrine lyric poets of the preceding age, the friend of poets and a poet himself, and on easy terms with philosophers and mathematicians. These stern intellectual pursuits were in harmony with the fundamental tendencies of his austere character. Averse to popularity and intolerant of adulation, as he demonstrated by his dislike for shows in general, reserved and independent, he could seem proud, like all the Claudii, and misanthropic. Heavily involved in the service of the state, with the consciousness of duty characteristic of Roman aristocrats of the old stamp, he had had the experience until now of seeing at close quarters the operation of the first principate. However, his devotion to duty had made obedience easy for him and had also allowed him, like the other nobles in the new political organization, to satisfy his pride and personal ambition without offence to his traditionalism and republican sympathies, which in any case were not regarded as blameworthy in anyone during the reign of Augustus. On one occasion only had he rebelled, when Augustus, by revealing too openly his monarchical and dynastic intentions in regard to his young nephews and adoptive sons Gaius and Lucius Caesar, had offended in Tiberius the consciousness of his own merit and the republican principles preserved by the very

---

[1] *Res gestae divi Augusti*, C.8, 4. [2] TAC., *Ann.*, I, 5, 4.

fiction of the Augustan principate. On that occasion Tiberius showed, by his withdrawal to Rhodes, the tenacity of his decisions and also many other sides of his character: his sensitivity, his mystical tendencies, and his liking for the pleasures – the ones most liable to be misinterpreted – of solitude.

Cautious and shrewd, full of positive good sense, rough, fonder of deeds than of words, as stern with himself as he was with others, scrupulous in carrying out the business of government, he could seem mistrustful and suspicious, yet also proud and haughty, as well as in-humanly cold and rigid in his self-control, and pedantic and oppressive in his attitude to administration; but the soldiers, whose blood he conserved with the greatest possible care, respected him for this and at the crucial moment preferred him to more brilliant and more popular leaders. Above all, the vicissitudes of his life had given him a sense of the tragic serious-ness of things human and a modesty, *moderatio*, learnt from the often bitter adaptations necessary in his long period of obedience and preserved ever after as a general mode of conduct, which could be combined quite easily with stoic fatalism in the position of voluntary subordination of himself and of his principate before the memory of the divine Augustus. This attitude, too, was one difficult to appreciate, though for a man outwardly so different from Augustus – whose affability, used with such tact and attention, had managed to conciliate and transform into props of the system created by himself all the elements of Roman society, from the most illustrious patricians to obscure quartermasters – there was no alternative way of neutralizing the difference destined to impress his contemporaries. Augustus must have been alive to the problem of this great difference between himself and his successor, and his hesitations about designating him may not have been due solely to the lack of con-sanguinity. Suetonius attributes to the dying Emperor an expression of pity for the Roman people, about to be masticated by such slow jaws.[1] Yet this story also reveals the superficiality of the difference so far as the real business of governing was concerned: Tiberius's administrative experience, based on his own serious and scrupulous character, constituted the best guarantee for the continuation of the central element of the Augustan régime, the new administration. As an administrator, Augustus had himself been precise and meticulous, so that Tiberius's succession, as was later demonstrated by events, was among other things the most natural one so far as continuity of real and concrete direction was con-cerned.

[1] SUET., *Tib.*, 21, 2.

Certainly from this point of view no one else could boast Tiberius's length of service, or more titles to the task of conserving and continuing the great work of the architect of the empire. All that his official public career owed to privilege was simply an exceptionally – but not absurdly – early start; for the rest, it had developed in the same way as that of any member of the old aristocracy could have developed under Augustus. But his military services had made him through his own personal talents into the greatest general of the age, while his accession to the *tribunicia potestas* and the extraordinary and unlimited *imperia* (in what concerned the formal expression of power) and his proximity to the *auctoritas* of the Princeps (in what concerned its substance) had officially involved him, more deeply and variously than all the others, in the central life of the new order of things. Tiberius had begun his military career at the age of sixteen, as *tribunus militum* in the Cantabrian campaign of 26–25. These were the *stipendia prima*, required to initiate a career; and the oratorical performances at Rome in the following year – the defence of King Archelaus of Cappadocia, of the citizens of Tralles and of the Thessalians, and the speech to the Senate requesting a remission of tribute for the people of Laodicea, Thyatira and Chios, who had been afflicted by an earthquake – had also possessed the character of a parade-ground exercise. More serious, certainly, was Tiberius's assumption in 23 or 22 of the task of prosecutor in the trial of Fannius Caepio and Varro Murena for treason. He had already been *quaestor Ostiensis* (in 23) and as such, in a year particularly critical for the principate, had contributed to remedying a scarcity of corn. In 20, after successfully pacifying Armenia, he obtained from the Parthians the restitution of the standards lost at Carrhae. In 19 he was already back in Rome, *ornamentis praetoriis ornatus*; in 16, as praetor, he accompanied Augustus to Gaul and remained there to pacify and govern it. Now came the start, for both Tiberius and his brother Drusus, of a period of more intense military activity. In 15 he subdued the Raetians and the Vindelicians, and he may also have operated in the same year in Macedonia and Moesia. In 15 he was received into the college of priests and in 13 he reached the consulate, his colleague being P. Quintilius Varus, another relation of Augustus. From 12 to 9 B.C. he went on to acquire fresh honours. In 12, as governor of Illyria, he won the Pannonian War, partly by enlisting, in accordance with his shrewd policy of sparing Roman blood, the help of the Scordisci of northern Macedonia. For this the Senate awarded him a triumph, which was reduced by Augustus to the mere insignia of a triumph. In 11 he subdued the Dalmatians and Pannonians, who had rebelled again, and was saluted by his soldiers as *imperator*, a title which Augustus forbade him to use. In 10 he was back in Dalmatia, after accompanying Augustus to Gaul, and then once again in Rome, accompanying Augustus. From there he soon returned once more to Pannonia, where fresh successes won him the *ovatio* (probably in the early part of 9 B.C.). In the same year he had to hasten to Germany, to the side of the dying Drusus, and then accompany the corpse to Rome, where he pronounced the funeral *laudatio*. It now became his duty to continue the German war. In 8, consul designate for the second time, he won victories in Germany, a fresh salute as *imperator*, and finally a triumph, which he celebrated in 7 B.C. at Rome, as consul (his colleague was Cn. Calpurnius Piso). He set off at once for another expedition into Germany. Then came the eclipse. In the year 6 B.C. at Rome, after receiving the *tribunicia potestas* for five years and the task of pacifying Armenia again, he retired from public life. He left the city, but only to shut himself up in Rhodes, 'quasi legatus', as Suetonius puts it,[1] to lessen scandal. The reasons for this move have already been indicated, and they are not ones unworthy of him. He came back to Rome in A.D. 2, but the return to public service did not take place until 4 and was very much in accord with his taste: the soldiers of the German and Danubian legions were delighted to see their experienced leader again. From A.D. 4 to 6 he fought in Germany, always returning to Rome in the winter; in 6 he was hailed as *imperator* for the third time. From now onwards war followed war without respite; from 6 to 9 the terrible Illyrian war raged. During the course of it Tiberius was hailed twice more as 'imperator' and at the end of it was awarded a triumph; this had to be postponed, however, as a result of the *clades Variana* of A.D. 9, to repair the effects of which he had to go on fighting for three hard years (10–12) in Germany. He finally celebrated his Pannonian and Dalmatian triumph on 23 October of the year 12. He was hailed twice again as *imperator*, for the sixth and seventh times, in 11 and 14. In fact, in the year 14, when he was summoned to the side of the dying Augustus, he was once again in restless Illyria. Nine times, he himself wrote later, Augustus had sent him to Germany.[2]

Thus it was as the logical outcome of a lifetime of service in which he had no equals, at any rate in substance if not in popularity (the young Germanicus was in fact already ingratiating himself), that Tiberius inherited the legacy of Augustus; and he was worthy of it.

---

[1] *Tib.*, 12, 1. A dedication by the people of Rhodes dating from the period of his sojourn among them has come to light (G. PUGLIESE CARRATELLI, in *Studi offerti a E. Ciaceri*, 1940, p. 254 f. = *AE*, 1948, 198).
[2] TAC., *Ann.*, II, 26, 3.

In terms of practical reality the matter is simple and natural. Modern scholars, on the basis of prosopographical considerations, seek in ties of kinship and friendship new reasons for confirming the inevitability of Tiberius's succession. This research is useful for the correct interpretation of the sequence of his activities, but it is secondary in character. Tiberius must undoubtedly have had friends and enemies, but the former could certainly not have granted him the empire – or the latter refused it – had it not already been firmly in his hands. It is also difficult to draw general inferences about Tiberius's policy before his accession from the position of his friends. At any rate, working on the numbers of *homines novi* and of old-established aristocrats present in the consular *fasti* after A.D. 4 – and hence presumably appointed partly through the influence of Tiberius – some scholars have arrived at the conclusion that he favoured a rejuvenation of the aristocracy, and hence that his policy was innovatory and anti-aristocratic, while others, with the very same data, have arrived at the opposite conclusion of a traditionalist and philo-aristocratic policy.[1] In practice, the support of friends and the symptoms of opposition by enemies can only be noted in general as indications of tendencies – tendencies which merge with the very origins, certainly murmurs more than openly expressed views, of the historical tradition about Tiberius. It would also be naïve to seek, in the reality of the principate, declared dispositions for and against the prince and despot. The very character of Tiberius, his resemblance to Agrippa in devotion to hard work, must have won him the sympathy of the strictest old Caesarians. We have already seen some of his ties with the Pompeians. In addition, as head of the Claudian family, he certainly had, in accordance with Roman custom, an extensive body of clients. He could naturally count on Livia's relations. The innumerable ramifications of the network of women and freedmen – the embryo of the future court –, subtle and powerful if sometimes dubious links, must also have served him in good stead. Names of friends are rare: P. Sulpicius Quirinius, who honoured him in Rhodes when everyone else disdained him, his colleagues in the consulate in 13 and 7 B.C., P. Quintilius Varo and Cn. Calpurnius Piso respectively; and probably people praised by Velleius Paterculus, men like L. Calpurnius Piso, mentioned in connection with the Thracian War of 12–10 (or 11–9) B.C., and M. Lepidus, Vibius Postumus, L. Apronius, Aelius Lamia and A. Licinius Nerva Silianus, who distinguished themselves in the Illyrian War of A.D. 6–9.[2]

[1] Cf. especially R. SYME, *The Roman Revolution*, Oxford 1939, p. 434, and F. B. MARSH, *The Reign of Tiberius*, Oxford 1931, p. 43 ff.
[2] VELL., II, 98, 114–16.

The majority of the personages known to us present relationships which can be interpreted one way or the other. The same is true of enemies: Julia's lovers, perhaps, especially Iullus Antonius, the son of Mark Antony; and M. Lollius, the counsellor of Gaius Caesar on his trip to the East; the former had all died in 2 B.C. and the latter in A.D. 2. It is a fact that during Tiberius's period of eclipse in Rhodes we characteristically lack information about the military campaigns which nevertheless continued in Germany and Pannonia; we glimpse only a few names of men, who, being in the public eye while the Claudii were in low water, may presumably not have been on the best of terms with them. An example is L. Domitius Ahenobarbus, husband of Antonia, elder daughter of the triumvir and Octavia, and hence a relative of Augustus. Yet we also have news during the same period of M. Vinicius, praised by Tiberius's admirer, Velleius Paterculus, and of P. Sulpicius Quirinius, who favoured Tiberius; and we know that the disgrace of Lollius and his obscure death in the East also date from the period of the withdrawal to Rhodes. As can be seen, there are few conclusions to be drawn from the actual names, and this is in any case natural. There are no reports of any concrete opposition at the moment of succession; nor are we permitted to know the true significance of the assassination of Agrippa Postumus, the responsibility for which it will always be possible to toss to and fro between Augustus and Tiberius (and also Livia? Cf. SUET., *Tib.*, 22): 'primum facinus novi principatus', according to Tacitus (*Ann.*, I, 6, 1), or perhaps the last of Augustus's principate. In the year 14 Julia, Augustus's daughter, also died in exile. Scribonia, who had accompanied her, still lived on.

Thus the actual succession was accomplished with the greatest spontaneity, just as it had been prepared by a whole carefully arranged and inevitable complex of circumstances. It was a perfect succession from the point of view of policy, too. The most recent numismatic research has confirmed strikingly all that was already known about the scrupulous care taken by Tiberius to continue the policies of Augustus, right from the start, in every field. But when it comes to the formal side of the succession the uncertainties begin, uncertainties that accompany the legal interpretation of the Augustan principate itself and, quite simply, of the principate in general. What was the position of Augustus's successor in the carefully conserved republican fiction? What were the official terms of the succession? What were the powers legally conferred on him? Tacitus, though distorting it later with his moral conclusion, accurately divined the distinction between the two levels always present in the story of the principate: 'At Rome consuls, senators and knights hastened to serve him. . . . The oath of loyalty to Tiberius Caesar was sworn first by the consuls, Sextus Pompeius and Sextus Apuleius, then immediately afterwards by Seius Strabo and Gaius Turranius, the former being the prefect of the praetorian cohorts and the latter of the corn supply; and finally by the Senate, army and people'.[1] It was the oath that reconstituted round his successor the *consensus* once proclaimed in favour of Augustus, in accordance with the practice of the *clientela*, as the champion of the West in the war against the East; this was the concrete and effective basis of the Princeps's power, even though it was outside any legal framework. Tacitus continues in these words: 'Tiberius left the initiative in every action to the consuls, as if the old republic still endured and he were uncertain of his own power; he even issued the edict summoning the senators to the senate house simply by virtue of the tribunician power which he had received under Augustus. . . .Yet, on Augustus's death, he had given the pass word to the praetorian cohorts as *imperator*; he arranged the guards, the weapons and every other palace duty; he had himself escorted by soldiers in the forum and the Senate; he sent letters to the army as if he were already Princeps; he never hesitated about anything except when he was speaking in the Senate'.[2]

Tacitus really has no equal in his capacity for applying to one person, and transforming into the characteristic features of hypocrisy, the contradiction inherent not in the position of this or that emperor, but in the principate as such, in all the principates, including those of Nerva and Trajan; the contradiction between effective power and formal powers, between the practical exercise of an undisputed predominance, covered by the concept, in itself indefinite, of *auctoritas*, which was nevertheless the real, practical, legitimizing source of the initial revolutionary usurpation, and the official parade-ground powers – features still belonging to tradition, if transformed and freed of their limits – such as the proconsular imperium and the tribunician authority; in a word, between the profound reality of autocracy and the republican façade. Nevertheless, even this formal aspect possessed an importance of the first order, because the Roman mentality demanded respect for forms, with which it was in fact content. Augustus had been most careful to meet this demand; that is the most remarkable side of his political masterpiece.

From a specifically formal point of view the situation had no precedents. If Tiberius, though strengthened by the *consensus* of all those who had sworn allegiance to him personally in the practical sphere of *auctoritas*,

[1] *Ann.*, I, 7, 1–2.   [2] *Ann.*, I, 7, 3–5.

that is, of the real substance of power, also simply continued to exercise without further ado in the formal sphere the powers which he already possessed as Augustus's co-ruler, namely the tribunician authority and the consular and proconsular *imperia* (those which he held previously and the special one conferred on him, as we have seen, only the year before), he would clearly be acting at variance with the theory, formal but intangible, of the Augustan principate itself, according to which the position of the Princeps was always provisional and dependent on the will of the Senate and people. To follow in the steps of Augustus, therefore, and not pass directly, at the first change of ruler, to the simple, declared reality of domination, some kind of ceremony was required which should make it clear that the new Princeps had been invested with his own formal powers by the Senate and people. Hence the famous sittings of the Senate (especially the second, on 17 September) described in the most carefully composed sections of Tacitus's *Annals* (I, 8, 11–13), from which springs complete the figure of the hypocritical Princeps. In an atmosphere still marked by freedom of speech – which should not surprise us, since it was normal practice in senatorial discussions under Augustus and Tiberius – the latter refuses, then declares himself ready to accept, part of the immense burden offered to him by the Senate, basically the part also accepted by Augustus (the armies and the imperial provinces; always, it is understood, under the legal and formal aspect of things); finally he yields to the entreaties, accepting in such a way as to make it clear that his acceptance is purely provisional. The parallelism with the sessions of the Senate in 27 B.C. dealing with Augustus is clear. In both cases it is a question only of observing the constitutional fictions, as they are still observed today in connection with resignations. That the constitutional play-acting was protracted for a certain period of time (on 17 September Augustus had been dead for almost a month) is demonstrated, among other things, by the fact, recently brought to light, that in Egypt the beginning of Tiberius's principate was placed, and remained, on a date later than the official Roman beginning (19 August). For the rest, the hesitations of Tiberius, more scrupulous and more sincere in his republican ideals than Augustus and conscious of the difficulties that awaited him, may also have been real and justified.

At all events, after the sittings of the Senate, which were followed by some form of acclamation by the assemblies, Tiberius was effectively and formally Princeps, Augustus's successor. That is, on the one hand, he was the inheritor by adoption and by the popular will, expressed in private oaths, of Augustus's *auctoritas*, in which he had obviously not shared during his period as co-ruler, since it was by its nature the specific attribute of the Princeps, the personal and semi-private sign of his domination as head of party and of his body of clients; and on the other hand he was confirmed in and invested with his official powers by the Senate and people. The exact nature of these powers has been finally disentangled by the most recent research from the somewhat confused information provided by the sources: confirmation of the *tribunicia potestas* for life (the previous annual numbering of which in fact continues), extension for life of the *imperium proconsulare maius et infinitum*, and cessation of the *imperium consulare*. Through renouncing this last power, which he had still exercised in the spring of 14 in the census carried out with Augustus, Tiberius, who had previously sat between the consuls, now as Princeps rose in their presence. The Augustan republic was thus in the hands of the man best suited to preserving its delicate fictions.

So far we have concentrated on the protagonist in this first imperial succession. Other men were naturally also in the limelight at such an important moment, and other measures accompanied the event. Of Agrippa Postumus, the victim of 'reasons of state', we have already spoken. The splendour of Augustus's funeral and of his apotheosis, debated at a sitting naturally devoted to this theme alone, made people forget this and other deeds. The reading of the will, which had been deposited according to custom with the Vestal virgins, disclosed that the principal legatees were Tiberius (who inherited two-thirds of the estate) and Livia (one-third). The latter, however, by another instalment of the family combinations constantly devised by Augustus's tireless imagination (whether the aim in this case was to please Tiberius or to create difficulties for him is uncertain), was adopted into the Julian family, thus becoming the daughter of her own husband, with his *nomen* and even his *cognomen, Julia Augusta*, as she was to be known for the rest of her long life. Other relations and notabilities were also remembered, in accordance with usage; nor were the *congiarium* and the *donativum* omitted, the former going to the *plebs urbana*, the latter to the soldiers. They formed a strong support for the beginnings of the new principate, since it fell to Tiberius to execute these wishes, just as Octavian had once executed the wishes of Divus Julius, drawing tremendous political advantage from the act. Thus the ashes of Augustus, after being honoured in the ways of which we are amply informed by Suetonius in particular (*Aug.*, 100, 2–4), were taken from the pyre in the Campus Martius and deposited in the mausoleum which he himself had begun to build in 28 B.C. 'There was even one person of praetorian rank who swore that he had seen the spirit of the deceased soar up from the pyre towards the sky' (SUET., *ibid.*).

Augustus dead, deified and honoured by a temple with a priesthood of over 20 members, thus gave rise even at Rome to the real imperial cult. As for Augusta, on whom the Senate wished to confer the titles of 'Genitrix' and 'Mother of her country', proposing in addition that she should figure in the official title of her son through the formula 'son of Julia', Tiberius did not wish her to accept any of these marks of honour. The moderation in the matter of honours practised by Augustus towards himself he now observed, and with more justification, with regard to his mother, refusing her even the concession of a lictor and forbidding the erection of an altar in honour of her adoption. Numismatic research has in fact confirmed that Julia Augusta's official position was always solely that of priestess of the cult of the divine Augustus. Right from the start Tiberius's relations with his mother, in spite of her conspicuous participation in the inheritance of Augustus's estate, were clear: deference, concessions in secondary questions, but firmness and independence in the business of government. Another problem was posed by Germanicus, the young son of Drusus, born in 15 B.C. and thus now twenty-eight, married, perhaps since A.D. 5, to Agrippina, the daughter of Agrippa and Julia, and already father of three sons, Nero, Drusus and Gaius Caesar. He had been consul in A.D. 12, held a proconsular *imperium* similar to that conferred by Augustus on Agrippa, Tiberius and his own father, Drusus, and commanded the army of Germany. Germanicus was the adoptive son of Tiberius and already, by the wish of Augustus, successor designate since A.D. 4, taking precedence over Drusus Caesar – the only son of Tiberius and his first wife Vipsania Agrippa – who was only two years younger than his cousin. Although until now, and even later, relations between the two young men were excellent, the situation was certainly delicate. Moreover, Germanicus was endowed with the qualities most likely to win popularity: he was generous, brilliant and daring, so that the contrast with the elderly general and administrator, cautious, deliberate and fond of solitude, was only too obvious. It is quite natural that Tacitus and Suetonius, well aware in their day of the *arcanum imperii* – revealed for the first time at the fall of Nero – 'that the Princeps could be made elsewhere than at Rome',[1] should speak of the dissatisfaction of the Rhine legions at not being consulted about the succession, which had taken place completely at Rome, and immediately afterwards of their offering the principate to Germanicus.[2] Probably none of this occurred, at any rate in

[1] TAC., *Hist.*, I, 4.   [2] SUET., *Tib.*, 25, 2; TAC., *Ann.*, I, 35, 3; cf. CASS.D., LVII, 5, 1.

this particular form and with the precise aim – which only became the fashion later – of putting up a rival to the reigning Princeps. In any case, Tiberius, as if hastening here as well to underline his loyalty to the wishes of Augustus, assigned to Germanicus the proconsular *imperium* for life, having requested it on Germanicus's behalf from the Senate. On the other hand, he did not confer it on his own son Drusus because, says Tacitus (*Ann.* I, 14, 3), the latter was consul and present in Rome; but the differentiation, which was noted, certainly had an object. That he then pretended to be ill, so that Germanicus should remain quiet in the hope of succeeding him quickly or at any rate of becoming his colleague, is a rumour due either to Suetonius (*Tib.* 25, 3) or to the tradition on which he drew, founded on the motive of simulation.

Tiberius thus embarked on his principate with the effective, even energetic, exercise of power and at the same time with obsequious respect for the republican tradition, making a conscious effort to follow the line marked out by Augustus.

THE EARLY STAGES AND THE PROGRAMME OF TIBERIUS'S REIGN

A division is indicated automatically by the circumstances, even if we recognize the presence of the same basic problems throughout the reign of the already elderly Princeps and do not wish to lay an exaggerated emphasis on the difference between the verdicts passed by tradition on the two principal periods. It is an undeniable fact, directly experienced by contemporaries, that in a first period Tiberius was obstinately reluctant to go far from Rome, so much so as to provoke criticism for his alleged inaction,[1] and that in a second period, after the withdrawal to Capri, he was just as obstinate about not returning to Rome, thus furnishing the principal ground for the widely unfavourable interpretation of his conduct. Beyond this first big division, which is in fact more apparent than real so far as the aims of Tiberius's administration were concerned, there seem to emerge other moments marked by the presence of men who stand out in particularly sharp relief, such as Germanicus and later Sejanus. These moments can help us to put some kind of order into the vast mass of historical material at our disposal for these years, but it is not right to use them to create breaks and contrasts in the fabric of a story which shows from beginning to end the presence of a firm, unified direction.

Although Tiberius's succession was secure, in the early days of his reign he displayed in practice some uncertainty. According to Tacitus this was

[1] TAC., *Ann.*, I, 46.

simulation; according to Suectonius it was due to fear. In reality the uncertainty proceeded from the objective situation. On the one hand there was the difficulty for any successor of emerging victorious from the inevitable comparison with Augustus; this could be overcome by the adoption of the pose of moderation and obsequious devotion to the instructions of his predecessor, a pose which fitted in perfectly with Tiberius's character and intentions and was evident even in the modesty of his title, which was always just 'Tiberius Caesar Augustus', with his own praenomen rather than the imperial epithet. On the other hand there were also the difficulties presented by the circumstances of the moment. Tiberius's remark that 'he was holding a wolf by the ears',[1] was basically true.

However, the situation at Rome was not his biggest worry; greater preoccupations were provided by the Rhine and the Danube. On the Rhine the legions were commanded by Germanicus; those of Pannonia were under the orders of the legate Junius Blaesus. Tiberius could recall years of hard battles in those sectors against external enemies, but now the very instrument of the struggle was in a state of crisis. The settlement after their service of men discharged from the legions had already been a problem under Augustus and one not completely resolved by the insti- tution in A.D. 6 of the *aerarium militare*. Among the soldiers, men tested in campaigns as hard and long as they were poor in booty, dissatisfied with their pay, detained with the colours beyond their period of service, envious of the comfortable, shorter engagement of the praetorian cohorts, full of hatred for the centurions – the officers nearest to them and those of whom they had the most direct experience – rebellions broke out, inspired by the hope of obtaining better conditions of service from the new Princeps. Tiberius faced the situation with prudence and firmness. Rightly he did not move from Rome, where he was engaged, in accordance with his severely constitutional views, in consolidating relations between the Princeps and the Senate and, on the practical plane, his own personal relations with the members of the governing class, which were certainly still in too delicate a state for him to risk a prolonged absence from the capital. He sent to Pannonia his own son Drusus, escorted by two praetorian cohorts and the corps of Germans employed as the Princeps's personal guard and accompanied by a number of notable persons, includ- ing one of the two praetorian prefects, L. Aelius Sejanus, who had just been appointed colleague to his father, L. Sejus Strabo. On the Rhine Germanicus could look after himself. The revolt of the three legions in

[1] SUET., *Tib.*, 25, 1.

Pannonia (VIII, IX, XV) – an event partly due to their commanding officer, Junius Blaesus, who by suddenly relaxing discipline had given the troops the impression that with the death of the Princeps something exceptional had occurred – had grown rapidly, with serious outbreaks of violence and looting. It was quelled by the intervention of the young Drusus, who, profiting by the fear aroused in the soldiers by an eclipse of the moon, began to make their solidarity crumble and then, while a delegation including the governor himself was on the way to Rome to present the legions' requests to Tiberius, promptly punished those responsible for the revolt. This firmness, and the torrential downpours of an exceptionally rainy autumn, interpreted by the soldiers as divine punishment, induced the three legions to return to their winter quarters completely repentant and calm.

The situation was more serious on the Rhine, where there were eight legions under the supreme command of Germanicus, who was engaged at the time in carrying out the fiscal organization of Gaul. Four of these eight legions were on the Lower Rhine, probably on the left bank a little downstream from Colonia (I, V, XX and XXI), under the orders of Aulus Caecina. These were already in revolt. The other four (II, XIII, XIV, XVI), under Gaius Silius, were on the Upper Rhine and still undecided, waiting to see how the rebellion of the first four developed. It was likely that there the proximity of the successor designate, Augustus's favourite, the husband of Agrippina – Agrippa's daughter – and the nephew of Augustus, would give the revolt a wider political significance; in reality it was essentially the same in character as the Pannonian rebellion – a pure and simple demand for better conditions of service. Germanicus could do nothing but yield to the requests of the soldiers, assuming the heavy responsibility of reading out the concessions from a message drawn up in the name of Tiberius: an absolute discharge for those who had completed the twenty years' service; transfer to the reserve, without any obligation to serve except in the case of enemy attack, for those who had done sixteen years; and payment of double the promised bounties. These concessions, put into effect immediately by calling on the funds of Germanicus and his retinue, succeeded only in inducing two legions to follow Caecina into the winter camp at Vetera (near Xanten), whither they betook themselves, still rioting, in a disgracefully disorderly procession, escorting the boxes of money snatched from the general. Germanicus paid a quick visit to the legions of the Upper Rhine; from three of them he secured the oath of allegiance to Tiberius without further ado, but from the fourth only after granting discharges and bounties. On the Lower Rhine the legions, though divided, remained in a state of unrest. A commission of senators sent from Rome was very nearly lynched. Once again Germanicus used emotional methods, playing on the men's feelings and reviving their sense of military honour by letting them see Agrippina departing with her little son Gaius Caesar – affectionately known in the camp, where he had been born, as Caligula – sorrowful and unescorted, to seek safety, away from the quarters of the Roman legions, in the foreign city of the Treviri. When the rebellion was on the decline he changed to subtler methods, so that the soldiers, cleverly divided and set against each other, took it upon themselves to execute summary justice. On the results of this indiscriminate massacre he then shed tears of sorrow, and the army, repentant and anxious to blot out the shame with some glorious enterprise, crossed the Rhine full of enthusiasm, although winter had set in, before the end of A.D. 14 – for the first time since the year 11 – and followed into Germany the leader whom they had treated so badly a little while before.

The rebellions had no other sequel and in practice secured no result, since, apart from the donative obtained, the pay remained (and was to remain until the time of Domitian) what it had been under Augustus, 225 denarii a year for the legionaries; and in the very next year the period of service was extended again by Tiberius to twenty years. Nor were there at that time any other legionary revolts. We are explicitly informed by Velleius about the Spanish legions, under M. Lepidus, which remained quiet, and about those of the Illyrian coast, under P. Cornelius Dolabella. The régime emerged intact from the crisis, which in any case was not a serious one. The gloomy colours used by Velleius (II, 125) serve naturally only to throw into relief the merit of Tiberius in resolving the situation; they are as conventional as the rosy tints employed immediately afterwards to describe the happiness of his reign. The army was still solidly in the hands of the Princeps. Assured of the instrument of effective power, Tiberius could pursue with complete peace of mind, once the first uncertainties had been overcome, his programme of soliciting the collaboration of the Senate in the government of the state, not only in the shape of the already numerous contributions of individual members of it to the service of the Princeps but also as a body.

This side of Tiberius's activity is not easy to illustrate, because it naturally implies consideration of the much wider problem of his relations with the nobility, which were determined not only by general political factors but also to a large extent by psychological and personal ones; and this in turn brings us close to the problem of the interpretation of the

figure of Tiberius as it is presented by the tradition, for which relations
with the aristocracy are the central point. Nevertheless, if we make
allowance for the fatal incomprehension which was to arise during the
course of time in the development of these relations, it will suffice for the
initial period to point to the concrete measures by which Tiberius sought
to put into effect his programme in this field and to the facts which,
right from the beginning, revealed points of friction and resistance and
made the collaboration chequered and difficult, in spite of the most
sincere intentions. We have already seen that it does not seem possible to
establish with any certainty in Tiberius's policy either a philo-aristocratic
line in the conservative sense or a clearly innovatory line designed to
create a new nobility. The sources say nothing on this subject and statistics
about the composition of the Senate provide data which can be interpreted
whichever way one likes. In these circumstances there is no point in
following ingenious but bold theories about alleged struggles between
old and new nobility and favours shown by the Princeps to the one rather
than the other, with reflections on the formation of parties based on the
dynastic succession, the party of Drusus and the party of Germanicus.
There certainly were struggles and rivalries, and in the name of the two
young princes too,[1] but amid the infinite possibilities for friendship and
hatred, alliances and oppositions, that existed in the society of Tiberius's
age, as they exist in every age, it seems futile to go looking, beyond the
established facts, for precise deployments of men and parties. Tiberius, as
a Claudius and a stern traditionalist, must have had – apart from the wish
to pursue the Augustan programme of utilization of the existing governing
class – the same feelings of sympathy as Augustus, or even stronger ones,
for the old aristocracy, which was his own class; and at the same time,
following in the footsteps of Augustus and also the revolutionary tradition
of his own house, he must have appreciated the merits of the new men.
Neither the admiration of the *municipalis* Velleius Paterculus and the
ennobling of the knight Aelius Sejanus on the one hand nor the independence of language and behaviour of an Asinius Gallus or a Calpurnius
Piso on the other should lead us to draw general conclusions. The only
conclusion that is legitimate, because it is supported by the convergence of
all the evidence, is that Tiberius's policy, in this respect as in all others,
continued that of Augustus.

The first act recorded by tradition is the transference of the elections of
magistrates from the comitia to the Senate, which thus became an electoral
body. A recent epigraphical discovery has brought us interesting particulars

[1] TAC., *Ann.*, II, 43, 5-6.

about the mechanism of the elections at the stage of *destinatio*, allowing us to glimpse how far these elections had already passed from the
comitia to the Senate under Augustus. It was in any case known that
Tiberius did no more than put into effect a project of his predecessor.[1]
The senators were spared, among other things, the expenses of the
electoral campaign; the Princeps was able to give a more regular appearance
to his official recommendatory intervention; the people grumbled a bit
and then accepted the situation. In legislative activity, too, the Senate
had already collaborated under Augustus with the Princeps through its
senatusconsulta; the legislative function of the comitia remained in existence
but was exercised more and more rarely. Tiberius pursued the same path,
promoting a large number of *senatusconsulta*. Augustus had relieved the
comitia of their judicial functions; the abolition of trial by the comitia
had been the most serious and brutal step in the harsh process of transforming the régime and suppressing the effective sovereignty of the
Roman people, but perhaps no one noticed this. Now, alongside the ever
growing importance of the judge, whether the Princeps himself or one of
his delegates, in the somewhat more discretionary process of the *cognitio
extra ordinem* or inquisitorial trial – a procedure in natural conformity
with the autocratic tendency even though guided by the great jurisprudence of the imperial age, which already had its champions – the
Senate became a court of justice, under the presidency of the consuls, for
trying offences committed by its own members or by knights, or else a
court of appeal superior to the *quaestiones* and inferior only to the final
appeal to the Princeps. The establishment of this court, adumbrated in
the last years of Augustus's principate, became definitive with Tiberius,
and the functioning of the Senate as a criminal tribunal, as seen in the
dramatic accounts of the big trials left us by Tacitus, represents one of the
best known and most characteristic aspects of the second principate, and
also one which provided most material for the general distortion of
judgement on this principate.

From the beginning of his reign, Tiberius had the closest relations with
the Senate as an electoral, legislative and judicial body. Like Augustus,
he did not see why he could not claim from the Senate as a whole,
without prejudice to his own position as autocrat, the collaboration which
he asked for in the government of the provinces, the command of the
armies and the assumption of trusteeships from individual senators. It
was a fundamental principle of the principate that the old organs should
all function in conformity with the new reality. The members of the

---

[1] TAC., *Ann.*, I, 15, 1; VELL., II, 124, 3.

great families, the *principes viri*, friends and rivals of the Princeps in the social ambit of the old aristocracy, could think individually as they pleased of the new situation in the course of their private relationships or sitting in the Senate; but they could not refuse a collaboration necessary for the proper functioning of the constitutional system and made in every way to look spontaneous and hence devoid of humiliation. Tiberius showed great, even anxious, deference to the senators; so as not to give too much weight to his position as Princeps in comparison with them, he continued in his private capacity to maintain polite relations with the families of the nobility on a footing of equality, even amid the receptions of his mother and the ladies of the court. Similarly, in his official capacity he refused some titles of honour, such as the name *imperator*,[1] the title *pater patriae*, the mode of address *dominus*, the *corona civica* on his house and the annual renewal of the oath of loyalty sworn to him spontaneously immediately after the death of Augustus. He had no wish to intrude on the senatorial career and assumed the consulship only three times more, and only then with the object of doing honour to others; above all, he declined the offer of divine honours for himself and his relations, rejecting the proposal that his name should be given to the month of September and Livia's to October, and refusing temples, statues alongside those of the gods, and flamens and priests. This has been confirmed by a recent epigraphical discovery, the letter written by Tiberius himself on the subject to the inhabitants of Gizio, a town in Laconia. He used to enter the Senate unescorted, paid homage to the consuls, the presidents of the assembly, and allowed matters to be discussed freely, not giving his own views too quickly, so as to avoid influencing the deliberations, and voting in his turn like the other senators. His interventions in the debates, however Tacitus may have judged them, were aimed at the most at correcting deviations from what was expedient, at encouraging greater freedom of decision, or, in enquiries into cases of treason, at containing indignation and zeal within the strict limits of the law. For example, in A.D. 16 he joined forces with Asinius Gallus to throw out a sumptuary law,[2] and when the Senate proposed to take action about defamatory pamphlets and verses he said that if that window were opened neither he nor the Senate would have time for any other business, since every dispute and piece of idle tittle-tattle would be submitted to their lofty jurisdiction.[3]

---

[1] There is confirmation of this in the oath taken by the Cypriots on Tiberius's accession in an inscription discovered recently (*AE*, 1962, 248): the space for *imperator* is left blank.

[2] TAC., *Ann.*, II, 33, 4.   [3] SUET., *Tib.*, 28.

He demonstrated his desire for collaboration in even more concrete ways than by mere outward deference to the Senate. He helped, with generosity but also with discernment, families that belonged to the nobility but had fallen from the richest census rating; he made abundant use of senators for commissions of enquiry and other similar tasks; he delegated to the Senate full powers of decision on important questions (for example, in A.D. 22, that of the right of asylum in the temples of Asia), yet always kept it informed of all his own decisions, even in fields like relations with foreign kings and peoples, and the administration of the imperial provinces, the army and religion, which under Augustus had been tacitly regarded as outside even the theoretical competence of the Senate as a body. And out of regard for the Senate he, like Augustus, struck gold and silver coins at Lyon and avoided issuing from the Capitoline mint, the old mint of the republic, the currency which, being traditionally connected with the *imperatores* of the civil wars, particularly recalled the illegal origins of the principate. After this we cannot doubt the sincerity of his sentiments when, shaken in his belief that he was confronted by the Senate of other days after seeing that his exhortations to decide freely fell on deaf ears and that the Senate sought to saddle him with the responsibility for every decision, he came out of the Curia exclaiming in Greek, 'O men made to serve!'[1]

The already effective reality of the autocracy continually tended to tear away the thin veil of legal fictions, against the will of a man who sincerely wanted to preserve them and despite the more or less sincere deference of a man who had to accept them and play his part in them. Thus the less he wished to look like an autocrat, the more others made him into one and even gained him a reputation for personal hypocrisy, while all the time the ambiguity resided in the system itself, which Tiberius, animated by the firm and as yet undisappointed hopes of his early days as successor to the principate, loyally wanted to keep on the lines laid down by Augustus, with an even more modest share of the honours for himself. On the other hand, the legions on the Rhine, with their near-lynching of the senatorial commission, had made it quite clear what they thought about the situation. There was no constitutional illusion that could stand up to the force of reality. Tiberius, besides his constitutional scruples, fortunately also inherited from Augustus, and in large measure, a sense of reality; spontaneously, without being seriously impeded in the exercise of his power by the preoccupations we have described, 'principem exseruit, praestititque'[2] ('revealed the Princeps and really behaved like one'), continuing to operate

---

[1] TAC., *Ann.*, III, 65, 3.   [2] SUET., *Tib.*, 33, 1.

above all in the field in which the genius of Augustus had chiefly exercised itself, that of administration.

From this point of view the principate of Tiberius represents the development and consolidation of Augustan institutions, especially in the bureaucratic structure, the financial system and the organization of the provinces. Tiberius, who continued without interruption the work of the last decade of close collaboration with Augustus, must have made a considerable contribution, in the way of work, to this systematization, which was to assume the lines more or less preserved throughout the first two centuries of the Empire. Here, in the field of the effective, working reality of the Empire, lay his greatest accomplishments, even if they are the most difficult for us to learn about from the ancient witnesses, who bothered little about such things, and when they did, only in order to make them yield fresh grounds for denigration. Recent studies, based above all on epigraphical material, have illuminated Tiberius's organizational achievements, especially in the administration of the provinces and the finances, and this in the midst of economic difficulties unknown in the age of Augustus. Under him the equestrian order, renewed by Augustus and conceived as a reinforcement for the hereditary aristocracy still represented by the senatorial families, progressed towards its definitive rôle in the service of the state, that of receiving into its ranks the military, municipal, provincial and intellectual *élites* of the Empire. Under him the organization of the financial hierarchy began and the process of the substitution of direct management for the contract system in the collection of taxes was carried further. The foundation of colonies went on, both in Italy (Tifernum) and abroad (Emona), and especially in Illyricum and Pannonia; so did the inevitable tendency, initiated in the time of Augustus, to intervene paternally in municipal life. New provinces were set up and organized right at the beginning of Tiberius's reign: for example, Moesia (in A.D. 15), Raetia (date uncertain, but probably in the first few years of the reign) and Cappadocia (in A.D. 17). The last two were made procuratorial provinces, that is, they were given the form in which – since every person of senatorial rank was excluded – close dependence on the Princeps was particularly apparent.

Outside the frontiers Tiberius pursued the policy of client states and even extended it for the first time to certain areas of the Rhine and Danube, thus anticipating by a happy intuition a practice that became normal later on, and in any case securing at least fifty years of relative peace in Rome's troubled relations with the German peoples. For the rest, right from the start of the principate all the provinces felt the strong hand that ruled them from the centre. The senatorial provinces felt it through the controls exercised more and more, if not officially (sometimes they were even disavowed, as in the case of Lucilius Capito, TAC., *Ann.*, IV, 15), by the procurators of the patrimonium and through the justice firmly done to the claims of the provincials against embezzling proconsuls. (Well known cases are those of M. Granius Marcellus, governor of Bithynia, accused in A.D. 15 of treason and extortion, and cleared of the first charge but sent for trial on the second, and C. Junius Silanus, proconsul of Asia, prosecuted in 21 for embezzlement by his subjects and for high treason by his enemies in Rome, as was Caesio Cordo, proconsul of Crete and Cyrene, between 21 and 22.) There were also the emperor's direct interventions by letter – a practice already adopted by Augustus – in disputes with cities; for example, the letter to the citizens of Cos in A.D. 15[1] and the one to the people of Aezani in Phrygia.[2] The imperial provinces felt the strong hand of the central government through its direct control of the governors, who were also the military commanders, and the procurators; Tiberius left them in office for a long time, longer than Augustus, but watched and disciplined them carefully.

By ordered administration he made the provinces produce a good yield in taxes without being oppressive; he took the view that the good shepherd shears his flock but does not flay it.[3] A shrewd administrator, generous but also economical and capable of making good use of money – a virtue that even Tacitus recognizes that he lost after all the rest –,[4] he was stern where the finances of the state were concerned. The situation in this respect was not easy because expenditure tended to increase while income remained static; wars against bellicose but poor peoples devoured money without producing any compensation in the way of rich booty. We have already seen how the concessions made to the army by Germanicus were suddenly cancelled for financial reasons; and on the very same occasion Tiberius refused demands for the abolition of the *centesima rerum venalium* (1 per cent on sales), pointing out that it financed the *aerarium militare*, the treasury which paid gratuities to the soldiers when they were discharged. He was only induced to reduce it by half when, in 17, with the annexation of Cappadocia, he found an income that to a certain extent replaced it. But in 31 the tax went back again to the old percentage.

[1] *IGRR*, IV, 1042 = EHRENBERG & JONES, *Documents Illustrating the Reigns of Augustus and Tiberius*, No. 318.

[2] *ILS*, 9463 = EHRENBERG & JONES, No. 319.

[3] SUET., *Tib.*, 32, 2; CASS. D., LVII, 10, 5 (referred explicitly to the early days of Tiberius's principate).

[4] TAC., *Ann.*, I, 75, 2.

As for the ordinary and extraordinary bounties that had now become the custom, Tiberius could certainly not think of abolishing them; but he tried to keep them within the limits gradually fixed, after successive increases, during the time of Augustus. The *frumentationes*, that is, the distribution at regular intervals of free corn to those entitled to it, continued, still organized directly by the Senate, though naturally with interventions by the Princeps arising out of the fact that he was responsible for the general grain supply (*cura annonae*) – not an easy task but one which he performed with his usual diligence. The *congiaria* and *donativa* did not exceed the usual limits. It is known that he found it difficult to pay immediately not only the *donativum* specified in Augustus's will, as we saw in connection with the revolt of the German and Pannonian legions,[1] but even the *congiarium* to the people, if we are to trust the evidence of the story recorded by Suetonius and Cassius Dio.[2] According to this story, a humorist requested a corpse, while the funeral was passing, to inform Augustus that his successor had not yet paid his bequests; seized by Tiberius and given what was due to him, he was then killed so that he could go and tell Augustus that his wishes had been carried out. However, this *congiarium* was paid in 15 and the difficulty encountered must have discouraged the too frequent repetition of this kind of expenditure. In fact, throughout the long reign of Tiberius we find only three more *congiaria*: in 17 for the triumph of, and in the name of, Germanicus, and in 20 and 23 on the occasions of the *tirocinia* of Nero and Drusus, the two elder sons of Germanicus. Thus they were always connected with political tactics. That of 31, for the assumption of the *toga virilis* by Gaius, was only promised. The bequests made by Tiberius in his will were not much bigger than those of Augustus (45 million sesterces against 43·5 million); and the task of implementing them was in turn the concern of his successor.

We also find signs of a policy of restricting expenditure, though never to the point of overturning the directives of Augustus, in the fields of games and theatrical shows, which Tiberius personally did not like, and of public works. As early as A.D. 15, in fact, he did not attend the games at which his son Drusus presided in his own name and in that of Germanicus as well; he deplored the disorder to which these shows gave rise and it was only thanks to his customary deference to the arrangements of his predecessor that he did not abolish the exemption from corporal punishment granted by Augustus to actors. But he could not tolerate

---

[1] *Ibid.*, I, 35 ff.: CASS. D.. LVII, 5 ff.
[2] SUET., *Tib.*, 57, 2; CASS. D., LVII, 14, 1–2.

something else that Augustus had permitted, that Roman knights should make an exhibition of themselves in the arena. He caused actors' pay to be limited and finally in 23 he had them all ejected from Rome. Outside Rome, too, he tried to ensure that money was employed for better purposes than the bloodthirsty pleasures of the circus; for example, at Trebiae (Trevi) he attempted without success to deflect to the repair of a road a legacy intended for the construction of a new theatre,[1] and at Pollentia (Pollenzo) he prevented *manu militari* the extortion by the populace of a sum which it was demanding from the relatives of a deceased local dignitary for the purpose of mounting a gladiatorial show.[2] In practice these diversions must have subsequently been discouraged in every way at Rome, for in 27 the people hastened to Fidenae to see the shows of a private impresario in a wooden theatre which collapsed and killed twenty thousand spectators.[3] Tiberius's attitude was undoubtedly very laudable, but it provided contemporaries with a fresh reason for incomprehension. Nor did he make use of the other classic means of acquiring popularity, big public works. Since he was as parsimonious with his own money (under the Empire new works were a charge on the munificence of the Princeps and other important people) as with the state's, and since, in the footsteps of Augustus, the maintenance of existing works was assured (this being the concern of and a charge on the *aerarium*, the state treasury, through the *curae*), he profited by the fact that his predecessor – furnished with more abundant means and out of political opportunism rather than practical necessity – had restored all that could be restored and built lavishly, leaving a marble Rome in place of the brick one he had found, and contented himself with erecting only a few new buildings: the temple of *Divus Augustus* (finished by Gaius), the stage of Pompey's theatre, the so-called arch of Tiberius, the principal part of the *domus* on the Palatine which was his own residence and that of his successors up to the Flavians, and the *castra praetoria*, that is, the barracks for the praetorian guards and the urban cohorts outside the city. Only rarely does his name appear on public works, so that it is difficult to specify his restorations. However, it was found on milestones of the road running from the Dalmatian coast (Salonae) towards Pannonia and on those of the road in Africa (Leptis Magna) leading into the interior, as well as on a *cippus* at Nicopolis in Syria recording the construction of an aqueduct: significant pieces of evidence.[4]

---

[1] SUET., *Tib.*, 31.   [2] *Ibid.*, 37.
[3] TAC., *Ann.*, IV, 62–3.
[4] EHRENBERG & JONES, Nos. 292–3; 291 (= Inscr. of Rom. Tripolitania, 930), 284.

As for the administration of justice, Tiberius was extremely diligent – which was both praiseworthy and dangerous: praiseworthy in the sincere concern for justice inspired by his rectitude, and dangerous, even against his will, through the natural tendency to conceive measures character- istic of authoritarian régimes. Tiberius participated not only in all the sessions in which the Senate met as a court of justice but also in all the sessions of the ordinary tribunals, positioning himself in a corner so as to leave the presidential seat to the praetor. It is true that his mere presence frustrated attempts at deceit and favouritism, but it may well also have been true that the presence, sometimes silent, of this stern and reserved man influenced justice in the opposite direction and in any case robbed the discussion of freedom, through no fault of his own. It is also a fact that verdicts contrary to his own view were passed, and without consequences for anyone, as our sources record,[1] but it should be noted that this was not the normal outcome; not through the imposition of an unjust will, but simply through force of circumstances. Naturally Tiberius was not burdened by any tradition: another ground for incomprehension, and on the face of it one of the least unjustified ones.

As for religion, we have already seen the limits imposed on the imperial cult. So far as the practice of the traditional cult was concerned, we have reason to believe that it was protected in every way by Tiberius's con- servatism, even beyond what was required of him by his position as *pontifex maximus* (since 10 March 15). His stern reminders of religious ritual and taboos are well known. For example, in 15 he reproved Ger- manicus because, while augur, he had sullied himself with the obsequies of the men who had fallen in the Teutoberg forest, and in 22 he contested the right of the *Fetiales* to preside over certain votive games in company with the other priests; and the only case so far known to us of a meeting of the *Fratres Arvales* under the presidency of the Emperor as *magister* of the college and not simply in his presence as an honorary observer belongs in fact to the reign of Tiberius (the year 16). On the question of foreign religions, a noteworthy facet of the activity of the man in whose principate the Passion of Christ took place, we find simply the continuation of the traditional criteria and in particular of the attitude of Augustus. Just as Augustus had been tolerant, but inexorable in repression (though only in the city of Rome) when exotic rites posed a threat to public order, so Tiberius, on uncovering a scandal among the priests of Isis in A.D. 19, had those responsible crucified and the statue of the goddess, with all the trappings of the cult, thrown into the Tiber. Similarly, when a plot among

[1] CASS. D., LVII, 7, 3.

the Hebrews came to a head he persuaded the Senate to expel them from Italy; he sent four thousand of the youngest and most robust of them to Sardinia as a police corps. The same anxiety to keep religious practices within the bounds counselled by the demands of general security was behind the regulations, the formulation of which was left to the Senate, on the right of asylum.

In view of this programme of excellent government, carried into effect from the beginning, as we have seen, in the most promising manner, with firm adherence to the policies of Augustus both in handling the practical realities of the principate and in respect for tradition (and if there were modifications, they were improvements), we should be surprised at the unpopularity of Tiberius (not at the misrepresentation, which is a consequence of it, subsequently exploited in the literary tradition but springing from his unpopularity with his contemporaries, even before the withdrawal to Capri), if the examination of his character, of the nature of his achievements and finally of certain external circumstances did not provide the explanation. He himself never sought popularity; he said expressly that he aimed only at the esteem of posterity (TAC., Ann., VI, 46, 2; cf. IV, 38). Men intent only on doing their own duty, and consequently on making others do theirs, are never very entertaining. It was only too easy for seriousness to seem like hardness, austerity like meanness, prudence like perfidy and reserve like contempt. Not even a joke was permissible with men whom he wanted to be his equals but who, for the first time since the advent of the principate, were suspicious through his own alienating manner of having in the Princeps a master. The witty old aristocrat's response to the proposal to call November 'Tiberius', 'What will you do if there are thirteen emperors?,[1] only aroused a murmur of resentment. Nor did he win any great approval for replying to an embassy from Ilium which had arrived rather late to express their condolences on the death of his son Drusus, 'Thank you, and condolences to you on the death of your fellow citizen Hector'.[2] This may have been witty, but it was hardly diplomatic. Fatal developments on the home and foreign fronts, with a close degree of interconnection between them, did the rest.

---

[1] CASS. D., LVII, 18, 2: this proposal was evidently distinct from the one to give September and October the names of Tiberius and Livia respectively, see above, p. 25.
[2] SUET., Tib., 52, 2, who quotes it, however, only to underline the inscrutability of a father who could make a joke out of the death of his son.

GERMANICUS

Scarcely had the revolt of the Rhine legions been quelled in the manner described when Germanicus, still in the autumn of 14, made an incursion into the territory of the peoples on the other side of the Rhine opposite Vetera. He launched a surprise attack on the Marsi, the first tribe he encountered, and massacred them, then withdrew when the neighbouring tribes, the Bructeri, Tubantes and Usipetes, hastened to their assistance. The aim of creating a distraction for the troops was attained, but the unexpected and gratuitous provocation was not to remain without consequences; it could only be the prelude to a large-scale resumption of operations against the Germans, something which was in any case ardently desired by the young generalissimo. But the conquest of Germany no longer formed part of Tiberius's plans, especially since after succeeding Augustus he had made it a point of honour to respect his directions in all things, including therefore the advice not to enlarge the empire any further. Moreover, it is legitimate to doubt whether Tiberius, as a seasoned and expert soldier, had a very high opinion of the military capabilities of his nephew and adoptive son; Germanicus himself certainly did nothing to raise it, either earlier, in the Illyrian war of 6–9, or later by the way in which he handled the mutinous legionaries and subsequently carried out the thrusts into Germany of 15 and 16, which were semidisasters. Not that Tiberius was meanly jealous of the young man's fame, as the sources – all favourable to Germanicus – insinuate; but, seriousminded as he was, he must have been disgusted at the fame somewhat artificially fabricated for the youth ever since the days when, cherished and valued beyond his due, he had assumed in Augustus's affections the place left vacant by the young Gaius and Lucius Caesar.

Tiberius himself was now constrained to pay this fame, *pro bono pacis*, a tribute which he felt was by no means deserved. The triumph which he caused the Senate to vote Germanicus early in the year 15 for the deeds of 14, and which was out of proportion to the minor successes achieved, was political in significance. So were the words which he wrote[1] to Germanicus and Agrippina before the end of 14 praising their loyalty, the thanksgivings to the gods voted at that time in honour of Germanicus and Drusus for the repression of the revolt of the legions, and finally the reception of Germanicus and Claudius, together with his own son Drusus, into the *Sodales Augustales*, a college – to which Tiberius himself belonged – for the worship of *Divus Augustus*, of whom Germanicus was

[1] Only according to CASS. D., LVII, 6, 2–3.

also *flamen*. In the difficult dynastic situation left by Augustus's arrangements, in which a fatal family rivalry was bound to develop, Tiberius's
main task was to maintain an equilibrium rendered difficult by the shifting ties of friendship and party. It was easy for feeling against Tiberius
(which was bound to build up, granted his character and aims) to polarize
in ostentatious favour of his heir and rival; and there were too many
powerful ladies at the court – one of the foremost being Agrippina, who
enjoyed an ample share of her husband's popularity – for intrigue not to
flourish there. Thus when in 17 Tiberius thought it best to interrupt his
nephew's command in Germany and to send him on a diplomatic-cum-
military mission to the East, this in particular was seen as an outburst of
envy. In reality it was a measure taken in the interests of the empire and,
in point of fact, of Germanicus himself. If he wanted glory, glory was
traditionally to be won in the East. In Germany, with Tiberius's policy,
only forays could be made, it is true; but Germanicus had behaved in
such a way that, in spite of some successes, it was difficult to avoid the
impression that his retreats were not planned but imposed by the enemy.

Tacitus's account of these operations in Germany is somewhat perplexed. After the short campaign of 14, in the year 15 Germanicus, still
profiting from internal discords among the enemy, had advanced with
powerful forces into the interior of Germany and arrived in the neighbourhood of the Teutoberg forest, where he had paid the last honours to those
who had fallen in the calamitous defeat of Varus. However, shortly
afterwards, while proceeding with the aim of avenging Varus by defeating
Arminius and massacring his Cherusci, he had been in danger of coming
to the same end, surrounded in the maze of woods and marshes, from
which he fought his way out with some difficulty in a battle that ended
manibus aequis.[1] He then hastily gained the River Ems and sailed down it
back to the mouth of the Rhine with four legions, two of which, disembarked and ordered to proceed on land in order to lighten the ships,
were very nearly overwhelmed by the tide. Meanwhile, on the road
leading through forests and bogs straight to the Rhine and raised for
long stretches on an embankment built some fifteen years earlier, Caecina,
the capable commander of the legions of the Lower Rhine, had fallen
into an ambush laid for him by Arminius and only succeeded in saving
himself and the army by dint of his courage and the skill bred of long
experience. Agrippina, on the other side of the bridge at Xanten, which
she herself had saved when, a little earlier, the news from Germany had
almost induced people to destroy it, had welcomed and comforted the

[1] TAC., *Ann.*, I, 63, 2.

legions as they returned, badly knocked about. The campaign of 16 was supposed to achieve the decisive success which would re-establish the prestige of the Romans among the German peoples. In fact the two battles actually fought, the first against the Cherusci at Idistaviso on the Weser – whither Germanicus had transported in a thousand boats his eight legions with all the auxiliaries and the cavalry – and the second in the borderland between the Cherusci and the Angrivarii to escape (once again!) from the encircling movement attempted by all the German tribes, who had risen as a consequence of the discomfiture of the Cherusci, were indeed favourable to the Romans. But Arminius remained free and the return journey was once again disastrous, for a storm blew up and destroyed a large number of the boats, which had left the Ems and were coasting along the Frisian Islands. A fresh incursion, in this same summer of 16, into the territory of the Chatti and Marsi sought to neutralize the impression of disaster and to stifle any desire among the Germans to profit by it. It seemed to Germanicus that to attain the aim of reconquering the province lost with the defeat of Varus he needed one more year. At this point came the order to halt operations; it was accompanied by the offer of a triumph and a fresh consulship.

As a responsible statesman, Tiberius calculated the debits and credits of the enterprise: the serious losses inflicted by the elements were scarcely outweighed by the victories gained; the prestige of the Roman name had been re-established; let the Germans abandon themselves to their internal strife; he himself, who had been in Germany nine times, had achieved more by diplomacy than by force of arms; and if force of arms was needed again, Drusus could go to Germany:[1] the presence of Germanicus, who ranked next to the Princeps, was required elsewhere. All these reasons were valid ones: between the intangible guide-lines of the foreign policy fixed by Augustus (no further conquests; diplomacy preferable to force of arms) and in the context of the local and general situation, Tiberius could not have acted otherwise. Moreover, it must be emphasized that he was concerned to rid Germanicus's recall of any appearance of dismissal and that he showed this concern by the expediently amplified recognition of his merits. Yet the general situation justified Tiberius's foresight, in which it is time we saw only the political act, divorced from any psychological colouring. After years of war Tiberius, who had no equal as an expert on German affairs, knew that the moment had come to gather the fruits of the seeds of discord sown among the proud Germanic tribes. Arminius was free, but his wife and son were under guard at

[1] *Ibid.*, II, 26.

Ravenna. The great Germano-Danubian state put together by Maroboduus, king of the Marcomanni – a state already gradually reduced under
Augustus to Bohemia alone and subsequently, within these boundaries,
a faithful friend of Rome during the Illyrian crisis of A.D. 6–9 and even
after 9, when Arminius had sent Varus's head to the king as an invitation
to unite with him – was in full decline, remaining henceforth only as
a proof of the inability of the Germans to achieve national unity. Between
17 and 19, after struggles in which Tiberius's wisdom saw that the
Romans acted only as spectators, Maroboduus and Arminius, the leaders
most to be feared, came to blows. Maroboduus succumbed, after calling
in vain on the impassive Romans to help (Drusus, Tiberius's son, happened
to be in Illyria at the time, but made no move). He was expelled from
the kingdom by the new leader of his own people, Catualda, sought
refuge inside the Empire and lived peacefully at Ravenna, the city of
illustrious prisoners, for eighteen years. Arminius was killed by his own
people. Catualda, after quarrelling with the Hermunduri, another powerful German people, also quit the scene and ended up by being interned
by the Romans at Forum Julii (Fréjus) in Gallia Narbonensis, while his
own tribes, settled with other Germans to the north of the Middle Danube
under Vannius, king of the Quadi, formed the first example of a client
kingdom on the northern frontier. Fifty years of peace on the whole
Rhine-Danube sector were the proof of the soundness of Tiberius's policy,
which was certainly not inspired by quietism or worse, but by an acute
sense of reality and by a comprehensive vision of the Empire's needs and
the means available to meet them.

Action, both military and diplomatic, was in fact required elsewhere.
In Africa at the beginning of 17 headway was being made among the
native Musulamii and Mauri by a revolt led by Tacfarinas, a Numidian
who had served in the Roman *auxilia*. On the Lower Danube, in Thrace,
still in the hands of a client dynasty, the jealousy between Rhescuporis
and his nephew Cotys, between whom Augustus had divided the kingdom
of Rhoemetalces – assigning to the former the wilder western regions
and to the latter the eastern plains, with the Greek cities – had been giving
rise for some years to acts of provocation and violence and a situation
which Tiberius was bound to watch attentively, not just for the sake
of a quiet life, 'ne composita turbarentur'.[1] Here too in fact a crisis was
to erupt a little later, with the assassination of Cotys by his uncle, who
was subsequently taken off to Rome to answer for his crime (in A.D. 19).
Above all, the eastern frontier called for a new settlement, and one based

[1] TAC., *Ann.*, II, 65, 1.

on the same criteria, to restore the stable situation achieved by Augustus. In the very first year of Tiberius's reign the distant regions of the Cimmerian Bosporus had been definitively organized as a client kingdom, with the recognition granted, without much regard for delicacy, to a certain Aspurgus, who had participated in the elimination of King Polemo, placed on the throne by Augustus. However, Aspurgus, after obtaining the title of *amicus Caesaris populique Romani* and Roman citizenship, adopted the names *Tiberius Julius* which were handed down to his descendants for centuries, and for his part remained a faithful ally until his death, which occurred in the same year as that of Tiberius: another proof of the soundness of the system. In the East manifold problems awaited a solution on the same lines, and Tiberius enumerated them in the Senate, recommending that the task of dealing with them should be entrusted to Germanicus. According to Tacitus (Ann., II, 42, 1), these problems were mere pretexts intended solely to remove far from Rome the young man who on 26 May had ascended to the Capitol on the triumphal car, with his five living children, amid delirious applause. In reality it was a question of concrete facts; and after the precedents of Agrippa, Gaius Caesar and Tiberius himself, who in 20 B.C. had placed Tigranes III on the throne of Armenia, it ought not to have caused surprise that the heir to the principate should be employed on a mission of this kind. However, it was not in Tiberius's power, for all his circumspection, to anticipate and prevent every possible interpretation of his actions, and on this occasion misinterpretation was rendered fatally easy by the unfortunate choice, made just at the same time, of Cn. Calpurnius Piso as the new governor of Syria.

The client kingdom of Armenia was once again the centre of attention. The Parthian kingdom was henceforth of less direct interest to the Romans; any idea of conquest having been abandoned, as in the case of Germany, internal strife sufficed to render it, like Germany, innocuous. In the period since the year 11 Vonones, king of the Parthians – one of the sons of Phraates IV sent to Rome for their education and a friend of Augustus – had been driven out by Artabanus IV and had subsequently been accepted as king by a section of the Armenian nobility, without however being recognized either by the Romans or by the Parthians. In 16 Artabanus was preparing to drive him out of Armenia, too, and Tiberius, thinking that it was pointless to make war on the Parthians to defend a worthless character, had him interned by the governor of Syria, Q. Caecilius Metellus Creticus Silanus, at Antioch, where he could live peacefully, enjoying the wealth he had brought with him from Parthia and retaining nominally the title of king of Armenia. In practice, however, Armenia was without a king and it was essential to forestall the Parthians in setting one up; there could be no question of direct annexation in the context of a 'good neighbour' policy with the Parthians. On the other hand, still in accordance with Augustus's directives and the precedents he had himself set – for example, in the cases of Galatia (25 B.C.) and Judaea (A.D. 6) – there were also regions ripe for annexation: Cappadocia, whose king, Archelaus, was giving grounds for suspicion, Commagene, and a little Cilician state to the north of Syria. The rulers of these regions had died in that very year (17), leaving their respective peoples divided between a majority that wanted direct rule by Rome and a minority that still wanted native monarchs. To these eastern problems was added the request from the provinces of Syria and Judaea for a reduction in the tribute they paid.

Germanicus therefore received from the Senate an extraordinary command, one superior to those of the individual proconsuls and governors, over the overseas provinces. He was in Rome from the end of the winter of 16–17 and it could not really be said that consideration for him was lacking. Tiberius heaped honours on him; he enjoyed brotherly relations with his cousin Drusus, and neither he nor Tiberius was responsible for the disputes between their womenfolk and for the partisan attitudes of the gossips who frequented the court. If Tiberius stifled his natural preference for Drusus and behaved towards Germanicus as Augustus had not behaved towards him, that only does him credit. We must think ourselves back to those days and consider the significance of a triumph, of the distribution of a *congiarium*, of the festivities for the dedication of a temple and of holding the ordinary consulship in company with the emperor; our conclusion will surely be that a man could not remain in the limelight for a whole year, enjoying such high distinctions, just because under cover of these honours the pangs of jealousy could be subtly manifested. It was probably on the occasion of the triumph, at the end of May, that the distribution of seventy-five denarii per head was made; next are recorded the solemn dedication, by Germanicus, of the restored temple of Spes, a venerable sanctuary dating back to the First Punic War, and the victorious participation of a quadriga of Germanicus's in the Olympic games. Consul designate for the second time as colleague of Tiberius, whose third consulship it would be, he was extremely active as a patron, both on behalf of private individuals and communities; his name figures in many places among those of the municipal magistrates, a sign that this great popularity was not displeasing to the Princeps, to whom he dedicated, almost certainly in the same year, his by no means contemptible translation of the *Phenomena* and *Prognostica* of Aratus, thus crowning his recognized greatness as the man of the day with fame as a poet.

If the scene on the so-called 'grand camée de Paris' really does refer to his departure for the East, this curious artistic relic would reflect exactly the measure of his glory in the atmosphere of enthusiasm which surrounded his person in that brief period of the year 17, when much was expected of his new Eastern enterprise. He set out in the autumn of 17 with his wife, little Gaius and a large band of *comites*. His unhurried progress was attended by the theatrical pomp which was customary on such missions and also in accord with his own taste. On his way through Dalmatia he exchanged greetings with his cousin Drusus, who had arrived there shortly before, as we have seen, to keep an eye on the activities of Maroboduus. On 1 January he insisted on assuming the consulship at Nicopolis, the city founded by Augustus on the isthmus near which the battle of Actium had been fought. Passing on thence to Athens, and having received there, in exchange for his own compliments to a city that lived on memories, the exaggerated homage known to us from many inscriptions, he sailed, via Euboea, to Lesbos, where Agrippina gave birth to Julia Livilla, the ninth and last of Germanicus's children. This was naturally the occasion of exceptional celebrations, which in any case all the cities visited hastened to stage, with all the adulation and prodigal splendour characteristic of the East. The traces of Germanicus's journey were long preserved in the temples and altars erected all over the place, in the coinage, and in the cities which changed their names (Caesarea Germanica in Bithynia, Germanicopolis in Cilicia). Germanicus for his part paid homage to the memory of ancient times, making sacrifices on the tombs of the heroes of the *Iliad* and visiting oracles and sanctuaries.

He was followed at a few days' interval by the new governor of Syria, Cn. Calpurnius Piso, appointed in place of Caecilius Creticus Silanus, whose replacement, since his daughter was promised in marriage to Nero Caesar, Germanicus's eldest child, had certainly attracted attention, coming as it had just before this journey. Now no one could deny to Tiberius – who was almost too scrupulous in fulfilling the duty of granting the formal honours to the heir to the principate – the right to take the precautions suggested to him by his real esteem for Piso's political qualities. An energetic man like Piso in charge of Syria could make good any possible deficiencies on the part of Germanicus. Piso did not lack ability and seemed to be an independent sort of man. The friend first of Augustus, then of Tiberius, whose colleague he had been in the consulship in 7 B.C., he was nevertheless no obsequious courtier; according to Tacitus (*Ann.*, II, 43, 2), he found it difficult to give precedence to Tiberius and looked upon his children with disdain. Apart from the Senate's responsibility in suggesting such a man as Germanicus's colleague,[1] it was certainly inadvisable to employ a person who, given to alternating firmness with the extravagances of excessive rigour,[2] would have committed fatal imprudences if he had ever gained the idea that he had been placed in the post to carry out a special task; in this case the task, which Tiberius had certainly never dreamed of entrusting to him,[3] of putting a spoke in the wheel of Germanicus. Then there was his wife, Munatia Plancina, niece of Munatius Plancus, the friend of Augustus; one can well believe that she was encouraged by Julia Augusta, whose friend she was, possibly through the social relations existing in Augustus's time, to enter into feminine rivalry with Agrippina. In his last letter to the Princeps, at the end of the whole disastrous business, Piso recommended his innocent children to him and did not expend one word on Plancina; for she was the principal cause of his ruin. Arriving in Athens with a great uproar some time after Germanicus, he made a wild speech bitterly attacking the motley crowd that usurped the name of the ancient Athenians and criticized Germanicus for paying honour to it and thus humiliating the majesty of Rome. Proceeding on his journey, and after being saved from a shipwreck near Rhodes with the help of Germanicus himself, who happened to be in that area, he rushed on to Syria without waiting for Germanicus and caused confusion there, introducing greater liberality into the army and the public life of the cities, while Plancina rode like a daredevil with the cavalry units and took part in the manœuvres of the cohorts, in competition with Agrippina.

However, Germanicus too finally arrived and personally assumed the task of settling Armenia, while his lieutenants looked after the other regions. The pacification was rapid and in Artaxata, the old capital on the Araxes, Germanicus crowned as king of the Armenians the candidate preferred by the Armenians themselves, Zeno, son of Polemo, the king of Pontus and Bosporus who had been killed by the people of Bosporus. This prince also adopted the Armenian name of Artaxias, and the felicity of the choice was proved by the sixteen years of peaceful rule which

---

[1] TAC., *Ann.*, III, 12, 1: '. . . datum a se auctore senatu'.

[2] SENEC., *De ira*, I, 18, 3.

[3] The reports in TAC., *Ann.*, II, 43, 4; 55, 6; III, 16, 1 etc. are always given only as 'rumores'.

followed. For this success, which had not really demanded much effort, the Senate at Rome granted Germanicus an *ovatio* at the same time as they granted one to Drusus for the pacification of Maroboduus's Germans. Cappadocia was organized into a province under a procurator by Q. Veranius, a step which indicates the financial importance attributed to this rich region; however, the start of direct Roman rule was sweetened by a reduction in taxes. Part of the dominions of Archelaus (eastern Lycaonia and Cilicia Trachea) was left to his son of the same name, who reigned there till 36. Commagene became a province for the time being, with the propraetor who had organized it, Q. Servaeus, remaining there as governor; but it was to be incorporated very soon afterwards in Syria. We hear nothing about the little Cilician kingdom that had been without a king; a new dynasty may have been installed there,[1] even though simple incorporation in Syria would seem more natural and more in line with the other provisions made. As for meeting the complaints of Syria and Judaea, Germanicus would have certainly dealt with these (and he must have done so, though we hear nothing further about them) during his stay in Syria, whither he necessarily had to go to complete his mission. In fact he moved into the province even before the winter of 18–19; at Cyrrhus, in the camp of Legion X, came the first cool encounter with the governor, while his friends, as Tacitus recognizes (*Ann.*, II, 57, 2), also fomented with slanders the already open enmity.

Soon the two men were at daggers drawn. Piso, who had disobeyed, for good political reasons certainly, but without bothering to preserve appearances, when Germanicus had ordered him to send part of the legions into Armenia, now either sat with an angry expression at the assizes held by his superior or else did not let himself be seen at all. Meanwhile Germanicus was receiving, at Antioch no doubt, the representatives of the provinces and of the client or allied states, among them those of Palmyra, the important caravan city, which he may have subsequently visited, and those of Artabanus, king of Parthia, who, while offering friendship and alliance and renewing the invitation to a meeting on the Euphrates like the one offered sixteen years earlier by Phraataces and accepted by Gaius Caesar, called for a more secure internment of the dethroned Vonones. The latter, who was among other things a friend of Piso, was in fact moved to Pompeiopolis in Cilicia and killed while attempting to escape. In the winter of 18–19, Germanicus decided to do some travelling and ventured as far as Egypt. He stayed there for several months, playing the part of the dilettante and man of letters and performing

[1] Cf. *Cambr. Anc. Hist.* X, p. 621 (Charlesworth) and p. 746 (Anderson).

acts and receiving applause which, though they may have appealed to his taste for the theatrical, were not in line with the special form of government which Augustus had established in Egypt and which Tiberius intended to preserve. Tiberius did not conceal his official disapproval any more than he had when his nephew had transgressed the dictates of religion by the funeral rites in the Teutoberg forest. When Germanicus returned to Syria he found that Piso had demolished the arrangements he had made, substituting clients of his own for those of Germanicus. The situation was no longer tolerable and Piso, if he had not already thought of doing it on his own account, probably received from his superior the order to leave the province. But soon after returning from Egypt Germanicus had fallen ill, and after lingering on for some time in the langours of a fever similar to the one to which Alexander the Great had succumbed (the comparison is made in the ancient tradition and can be easily developed), oppressed by the conviction that he was the victim of poisoning and witchcraft on the part of Piso and in particular Plancina, died at Antioch at the age of thirty-three, on 10 October 19, after calling on his friends and his wife Agrippina to avenge him. She, although the season was already far advanced, set sail soon after the hasty funeral, taking back with her to Rome her husband's ashes.

In spite of the dying man's exhortation to prudence, it was foreseeable that a wife of such strong character and uncontrolled passions would turn the cult of her husband's memory into a sort of banner. The spontaneous and general sympathy for her misfortune now gave the support of the humble to the political faction that had already crystallized in the upper classes close to the seat of power. The reticences, the murky sides of the event, the hidden manœuvres, the facile inferences drawn from the relations – known to everyone – between the dead man and Piso, and between Piso and Tiberius, sowed suspicion and rendered conjecture morbid. In this sense the disappearance of Germanicus, who had died young like many other gilded and vicious scions of the Julio-Claudian house, had fatal consequences, though not because of the loss of a mediocre general and an incautious statesman. Henceforth a motive for division, never again eliminated, was lodged in the laborious edifice of Tiberius's programme of government. The mourning for Germanicus naturally corresponded with the degree of popularity he had enjoyed during his life, from the effusive displays of the peoples and ruling families of the East to the honours paid to him in Rome.[1] At the beginning of the year 20

---

[1] The *iustitium* announced on 8 December 19 for the death of Germanicus is recorded in the *Fasti Ostienses* (*I. It.*, XIII, I, pp. 185, 216).

Agrippina landed at Brindisi, to be welcomed by a large and sorrowing crowd. Two praetorian cohorts sent by Tiberius escorted the urn, which was carried to Rome on the shoulders of tribunes and centurions through municipalities and colonies all in mourning. Drusus and Claudius travelled out as far as Terracina, as did Germanicus's children, who had stayed in Rome during his mission, and numerous senators came out to meet the procession as it passed. The funeral ceremonies reached their climax on the day of the interment in the mausoleum of Augustus. Tiberius, Livia and Antonia, Germanicus's mother, did not let themselves be seen in public; the Princeps wished to keep the mourning within the bounds of moderation, but this time too succeeded only in causing himself to be misunderstood.

THE TRIALS

'Adolescebat interea lex maiestatis': the sentence used by Tacitus[1] as a substitute for evidence to introduce his account of the trial of Appuleia Varilla in 17, with its echo of infinite implications which has gone on resounding down the centuries, is a measure of the fatal distortion of a reality which was much more modest and which can be reconstructed from Tacitus himself. Tiberius was not the author of the treason law and it did not disappear with him; he did not demand a more rigorous application of it; indeed, at any rate up to his last few years, he did not invoke it in the case of direct verbal attacks on his person; and not all the trials which took place in his reign, and which are reported by Tacitus or other sources, were for treason. Yet through a concatenation of events this particular aspect of public life in Rome made a notable contribution to the formation of the tragically equivocal verdict on Tiberius's home policy, inherited and adopted by the tradition. In reality the imputation of this offence, by its very nature ill-defined, or the facile reduction to this offence of other crimes like treachery to the state, was inseparable from the emergence of the principate, which was itself, as we have seen, an ill-defined constitutional entity. Ever since the beginning of the first century before Christ, laws on treason, such as the *Varia* of 90 and the Sullan *Lex Cornelia* of 81, had begun to signal both the first concrete experiments in the use of legal means to enable some citizens to oppress others and also the approach of the inevitable monarchical solution to the crisis of the republic. Under Augustus – besides the innumerable interferences of a private and confidential nature in the lives of the most

---

[1] *Ann.*, II, 50, 1, at the start of the chapter and of the argument.

highly respected families – laws like the *Papia Poppaea* and the *Iulia de maiestate*, which were not only harmful to personal liberty, henceforth somewhat disregarded, but also formally vague in content and subject in their application to the whims of informers, investigators and judges, permitted all kinds of legal persecution. The deficiencies of the judicial system, particularly the absence of a public prosecutor, which encouraged unscrupulous persons, since they shared in the confiscation of the condemned man's goods, to launch prosecutions even with little or no foundation, increased the already serious dangers to personal freedom.

Augustus's sense of 'fair play' had not entirely avoided trials of this sort, but it had ensured that the echo of them in the tradition was much more subdued. If we leave aside the case of Salvidienus Rufus, found guilty of treachery while the Civil War was still in progress, the same thing happened to Lepidus and Servilia immediately after Actium. They and the numerous adherents of Antony were all put to death. In 27 B.C. the obscure trial of the prefect of Egypt, Cornelius Gallus, was left to the Senate and ended with the suicide of the accused; in 23 there was the trial of M. Primus, proconsul of Macedonia, found guilty of treason, and in the same year that of Fannius Caepio and Varro Murena, a consul in office, which ended with the death penalty for both. In 19 B.C. the ex-praetor Egnatius Rufus was tried and condemned on some charge which is not very clear, and about the same time an attitude of honest independence cost one of the most eminent jurists of the time, M. Antistius Labeo, the consulship. The business of those implicated in the scandal of Julia (2 B.C.), which ended in the execution of various notable persons, certainly took a more mysterious and arbitrary course than any of the dark machinations attributed to Tiberius; and the same is true of the obscure affair of the younger Julia, whose husband, L. Aemilius Paullus, had lost his life after being implicated in a charge of conspiracy at an unknown date; she too, with her lovers, came to a miserable end, like her mother (A.D. 8), in an exile that lasted until A.D. 28. We know[1] that there were many other cases, and that where conspiracy or supposed conspiracy was concerned the treatment (capricious in any case) employed with L. Cinna[2] was the exception; usually even Augustus had not wasted any words.

The introduction, encouraged by Tiberius, of greater regularity and more system into the functioning of public life was bound nevertheless in this field to provoke a less favourable impression, giving the appearance of malevolence to what was simply greater seriousness, of organized terror to the merely episodic, and of zeal for persecution to a scrupulous

---

[1] SENEC., *De Clem.*, I, 9, 6.   [2] See above, p. 6.

feeling for justice; all the more so in view of Tiberius's character and the long period already spent by society in the habit of obedience. But if we examine, as has been done, the hundred or more cases zealously recorded by tradition for the reign of Tiberius, and if we look at the details of the charges and the defences, the arguments and the verdicts, especially with regard to the highly controversial matter of treason, basing ourselves on the specific facts contained in the fundamentally honest narrative of Tacitus rather than on the generalizations of Suetonius and Cassius Dio, we are forced to correct the view commonly held on the subject and to note at the same time how it could have arisen, as the result of a fatal concatenation of circumstances in which Tiberius did not play the deciding part. He did not purposely extend the law of treason to cover trifling cases and the mere expression in words of criminal thoughts; if anything, he restricted the application of the law. Personally he had no wish to exert his authority in the debates; if anything – granted the now accepted reality of the principate and of the consequent law of responsibility deriving from the Princeps, the absolute master – he could reproach himself with not having done so, with having placed too much confidence in the Senate, henceforth the normal court for such cases, and – always out of excessive formal deference to this venerable body, symbol of the old Republic – of not having made himself clear enough in his words, or, worse, in writing, if he did decide to intervene. With his sensible ideas about religion, he would not even hear of connecting the concept of the offence against his person with that of impiety, the element which was to become predominant in the charge of *maiestas* in later times, even under emperors with a better reputation. Numismatic research has given clear confirmation of this aspect of Tiberius's sane and realistic attitude.

We could already read something of this in Tacitus, in connection with one of the first trials he mentions as launched by informers and quashed at once by the intervention of the Princeps, that of the knights Falanius (or Faianius) and Rubrius, charged in A.D. 15 with offences against *divus Augustus* and of perjury in his name: 'His father had not been granted divine status in order that it might be turned to the ruin of the citizens . . . the perjury should be regarded in the same light as an offence against Jupiter; and offences against the gods were the concern of the gods' (TAC., *Ann.*, I, 73, 3–4). That, in some trials, too much weight seems to have been given to magical causes may be attributed to the temper of the times; it was also inevitable that, with the passage of the administration of justice from the free regimen of the *comitia* to the more discretionary one of the tribunals and judges of the autocracy, the death penalty should appear for the crime of treason, as for many other crimes,[1] though it is doubtful whether under Tiberius, at any rate until the last few years, anyone was executed for the crime of treason *alone*. As for the refusal to abolish in certain cases the remuneration of informers,[2] one must ask oneself whether Tiberius, preoccupied with ensuring that the laws were fully effective, could have substituted institutions unknown to antiquity for ones that were defective but still functioning regularly under an emperor like Trajan.

To confine ourselves to the most sensational cases, let us look at the trial of M. Scribonius Libo Drusus, a man related to the family of the Princeps through the still living Scribonia, Augustus's first wife and mother of Julia. In A.D. 16 Drusus was accused by the senator Fulcinius Trio and others of obscure revolutionary intrigues (not specifically of *maiestas*). The case was heard by the Senate, and Drusus evaded condemnation by committing suicide, but the Senate, even after his death, went on unperturbed with the proceedings until it reached a verdict. If one reads the extensive account of Tacitus (*Ann.*, II, 27–32) attentively and without letting oneself be influenced by the colour spread over it superficially to maintain the general thesis of Tiberius the hypocrite, it is impossible not to feel convinced, without rejecting as false any of the facts reported, that the young man, probably a weakling, was the victim of the Senate's search for opportunities to display its own zeal, not of an arbitrary action on the part of the Princeps. On the contrary, Tiberius showed moderation, first by taking no account for almost two years of any imputation against the suspect (just as in general he rejected systematically any charge of using treasonable language), then by preserving an attitude of absolute impartiality in the debate and finally by the declaration that he would have pardoned Libo if the latter had not anticipated the sentence by killing himself, a declaration confirmed with an oath the sincerity of which there is no reason to doubt once we abandon the thesis of hypocrisy. Tiberius's behaviour in this episode, which was certainly the first of real importance, even if the details are obscure, only confirmed the line which he had followed the year before in the case of Granius Marcellus, ex-proconsul of Bithynia. Marcellus was charged with extortion, and was also belaboured by his accusers with the imputation of treason, among other things because he had had a statue made for himself bigger than that of the Princeps and because he had cut the head off a statue of Augustus and substituted the head of his successor. Tiberius set aside with disdain this piece of fatuity but allowed the charge of

[1] CASS. D., LVII, 9, 3.   [2] TAC., *Ann.*, IV, 30, 2–3.

extortion, which touched the administration of the empire, to go forward, just as, in 17, in connection with the already mentioned Appuleia Varilla, accused of treason and adultery, the first charge was dropped by the express intervention of the Princeps but the second was pressed. In the case of Clemens, a slave who from 15 to 16 had claimed that he was Agrippa Postumus returned to life again, had created disturbances, not without support in high quarters, and had been dealt with in the palace, the procedure followed was the one normal with slaves; moreover, Tacitus says that Tiberius had thought of letting things take their course and of waiting for vain credulity to fade away with the passage of time. He had decided to act only when serious danger seemed to be threatened and even then he had forbidden any search for accomplices (*Ann.*, II, 40, 1–3).

The year 20 saw the big trial of Cn. Calpurnius Piso. When Germanicus died, Piso and his wife Plancina were at Cos, on the way back to Italy. Continuing their mad behaviour, the pair did not hide their joy at the event, thus lending colour to the accusations already being made against them in connection with the young prince's suspicious death. Blinded by their hatred of him, they probably persisted in the error of believing themselves the champions of loyalty to the Emperor in face of the alleged traitor Germanicus, and did not doubt that Tiberius was on their side. There would still have been time to abandon this illusion had not Piso, adding crime to pride, returned against the advice of his son from Cos to Syria to recover his command by force from Cn. Sentius Saturninus, one of the *comites* of Germanicus, who had temporarily assumed the functions of governor. When this enterprise failed there was nothing left for Piso to do but to return to Rome and face the charges against him. In the meantime Agrippina had arrived in Rome with the ashes of Germanicus and had been accorded a triumphant welcome. Piso found himself marked out as the victim of the blind popular fury. He was accused principally of poisoning Germanicus; however, the proceedings took place not before the *quaestio de veneficiis* but, because of the importance of the case and the status of the persons involved, before the Senate, to which Tiberius had referred without prejudice the investigation of the accusations. He had done this because, since the ultimate target of the prosecution, for Agrippina and the party of Germanicus, was himself, the Princeps, it would have been embarrassing for him to grant an acquittal and perfidious to pass sentence on an innocent man. Nevertheless, Tiberius presided over the debate, with impartiality, and there was no lack of senators to defend the accused effectively, so that Tacitus's own account gives the impression that the affair was treated with great care and concern for justice. The charge of poisoning could not be proved; and in reality not even Tacitus seems to believe that Germanicus was in fact poisoned. The same thing happened with the charge of insubordination, which was victoriously countered with an accusation against Germanicus over his behaviour in the East. But there remained the attempt to recover the province by force of arms. On this point even Tiberius, indeed Tiberius in particular, could not compromise, and it would have been the reason for a verdict of 'guilty', which was demanded in any case by the political situation, had not Piso, after himself recognizing this as his only crime and recommending his innocent children to the Princeps, anticipated the judgement by committing suicide.

Tiberius assumed the protection of the children, allowed Livia to take Plancina to a place of safety and opposed the suggestion that Piso's name should be erased from the *Fasti Consulares*. Thus there was nothing unusual about his scrupulous and humane conduct. But the fact that this time the delicate matter of trials had encountered an obscure event, in which the tacit but ever-present reality of the dynastic problem and the political passions it generated were bound to inspire every sort of interested interpretation of an episode never entirely clarified, undeniably cast a shadow over the rest of Tiberius's reign. The hatred and intrigues of Agrippina and her party, and an ever more defamatory interpretation of the Emperor's work, particularly in the field of justice, which moreover formed a shocking experience for the upper classes, who were after all the people who moulded tradition, were to be the dominant factors in the years of tragic events which followed. Nevertheless, after this fatal conjuncture of circumstances, which was bound to disappoint and embitter Tiberius's already closed mind, the Emperor's personal attitude was always to remain one of moderation and admonition to justice, even when the Senate's habit of opportunistic behaviour in trials and the thriving body of informers produced by the defective procedural system enabled a man like Sejanus to flourish.

In 21 two knights who had accused a praetor of treason were punished when the charges turned out to be false, and one Antistius Vetus, a prominent Macedonian, charged with adultery but prosecuted instead for sedition because he had plotted with Rhescuporis, the king of Thrace already mentioned, against the security of the Empire, was sentenced to no more than the penalty anciently provided for a crime of this sort, namely *interdictio aquae et ignis*. Towards the end of the same year, during the Emperor's first absence from Rome, Clutorius Priscus, author of a much-praised poem on the death of Germanicus, was accused by an informer of having also written one for Drusus, who had fallen ill, and was summarily judged and condemned to death by the Senate and executed immediately. Tiberius openly praised a senator who had proposed a lighter punishment and himself instigated a decree by which at least ten days had in future to elapse between sentence and capital punishment. In 22 two provincial governors, C. Junius Silanus and Caesius Cordus, were condemned, but for extortion, ·and so far as the former is concerned we know that Tiberius intervened to reduce the sentence, while in the case of the knight L. Ennius, accused of treason because he had melted down a silver statue of the Princeps into plate, he would not even allow the prosecution to be brought. He thus offered the great jurist Ateius Capito the opportunity for the protest[1] which may have seemed then (and to Tacitus) adulatory, but for us is packed with significance as a sign of the now explicit recognition of the new imperial reality, of the incipient identification of the state with the person of the Princeps. In 25 Vibius Serenus, found guilty of corruption, was exiled to Amorgos; on the other hand, two other persons, accused of supplying wheat to the rebel Tacfarinas, were acquitted, Tiberius yielding in the case of one of them to the pleas of influential senators – which is significant in itself. In the same year he requested that Lucilius Capito, one of the procurators of his own *patrimonium*, who had interfered improperly in the proconsul's administration in the province of Asia, should be judged by the Senate without any consideration. Even from 24 onwards, when it seemed to Tacitus that the reign of Tiberius deteriorated irretrievably and in fact the greater frequency of trials did mark – with the schemes of Sejanus, the sharpening of the opposition and a proportionate number of conspiracies – the period of the sordid struggle unfortunately provoked by the dynastic problem – a problem which causes Tacitus's narrative itself to drop its tone of passion and familiar general colouring – even then, if we look at the facts alone, these show that the part played by Tiberius always corresponded with rectitude of intention and that, if there was a departure from strict justice, this was rather in the direction of clemency than in that of cruelty. And the specific imputation of *maiestas* was still not by itself a deciding factor in the verdicts.

In 24 C. Silius, his wife Sosia Galla and Titius Sabinus were accused: Tacitus, while stressing the implication of treason, recognizes nevertheless that without any doubt they could not clear themselves of the charge of

---

[1] TAC., *Ann.*, III, 70, 2: 'Sane lentus in suo dolore esset: reipublicae iniurias ne largiretur'.

extortion, while the diligence employed at that time by Tiberius in recovering for the state treasury their ill-gotten gains lent itself only too easily to being interpreted by the historian as chronologically the first proof of avarice. Similarly, in the same year no further conclusions can be drawn from the trials of L. Calpurnius Piso, Cassius Severus and Plautius Silvanus, while in that of Vibius Serenus, accused by his son together with Caecilius Cornutus, the only figure to rise above the vile surroundings is that of the Princeps, anxiously searching out the truth and counselling clemency. Even in this he did not act without discernment: for example, C. Cominius was completely pardoned for his crime of 'probrosum carmen', unlike the exile P. Suillius – wretched tool whom Tiberius did well to keep at a distance, as Tacitus himself agrees, for when he returned under Claudius he was mixed up in everything – and Firmius Cato, a senator who, in his passion for informing, had not spared his own sister. Again, in 25, the notorious trial of the historian Cremutius Cordus seems to be no more than one of the usual manœuvres of the informers, assisted by Sejanus; the actual charge is not very clear. Nor is it clear in the case of Votienus Montanus, which also developed in such a way that either an acquittal or an act of clemency would have been gravely prejudicial to the dignity of the Princeps.

And so things went on, even with the recrudescence of the opposition, which gave him the right to exercise greater severity. Nor was Tiberius's moderation displayed only in personal acts of clemency; just as informers were several times dismissed with contempt, so counsel for the defence was never deprived of the right to speak. Manius Aemilius Lepidus, who was among the men marked out by Augustus as fit to rule, retained until Tiberius's last years both his boldness and frankness of speech and the friendship of the Princeps, so that Tacitus himself could only account for a fact so contrary to his view of the period by the consideration that with good sense it was still possible to follow the right middle path between obstinate opposition and shameful servility without running into trouble[1] The historian may have thought perhaps to justify in this way his own regular career under Domitian.

From this long survey (resulting from the need to follow the sources over the ground where they themselves lead us) the figure of Tiberius thus emerges in a different light, at any rate up to the last few years, when we do in fact meet a number of events which leave us perplexed, precisely in what the tradition was to see as a chapter of infamy. In fact, it is now fairly easy for modern research to conclude that the light concentrated by

[1] TAC., *Ann.*, IV, 20, 3.

the ancient historians on the tragic central figure, through the process of personalization natural to them in general and through the addition of the power of psychological and artistic transfiguration peculiar to Tacitus alone, must be redistributed over the manifold elements which go to make up the complexity of that age as of every other: the atmosphere of the principate, indeed of every despotic principate, the baseness of opportunists, the shame of informers, the interests in conflict in a society that was not free, the need for adulation and the temptation to conspiracy. Tiberius saw, together with the beneficial results, the first bitter consequences of the new reality.

THE DYNASTIC CRISIS AND THE SEJANUS AFFAIR

The element of uncertainty introduced into the objective situation, and even more into subjective appreciations of it, by the death of Germanicus, and continually intensified by the constant misinterpretation, partly through bad faith, partly through mere chance, of Tiberius's actions (the most obvious aspect of these being the trials) accordingly surrounded his figure with a sinister light. Other elements were added in the course of time, not so much through external difficulties – for under Tiberius the state of the empire was excellent and it suffered little from the crisis, which was a decidedly urban, 'palace' one – as through the flaring up of dissensions in his own family and through the growth, largely favoured precisely by these dissensions, of an affair that can be regarded as the first example of serious hypertrophy in the development of a particular organism forming the apex of the Augustan structure of the principate, with repercussions – though their extent must not be over-estimated – on the whole system. A complete and consecutive reconstruction of events is naturally impossible because, apart from the lacuna in the fifth book of Tacitus's *Annals* (years 30–31), the account in the sources, though it extends to so many years of events, is nevertheless episodic and fragmentary, and presents, besides its notoriously tendentious colouring, many obscure points, as indeed is natural with historiographical material of this sort, already reflecting to a large extent in the very moment of its formation only indications, interpretations and suppositions.

The principal elements in the course of events are nevertheless clearly recognizable: they are the activity of those who, taking advantage of the feelings of Agrippina, upheld the dynastic claims of the household of Germanicus; the natural reaction of Tiberius, who at one time must have felt really worried by such intrigues; and the patient execution on the part of Sejanus, who made use in his operations of both the above factors, of the mad plan of winning for himself, a mere knight, the position of Princeps or, what was equivalent, that of the Princeps's regent. In this tragic episode we can still grant Sejanus the role of protagonist justly assigned him by the ancient tradition, without exaggerating, however, the importance of the affair in the vast context of imperial politics. Tiberius's blindness in the affair can in fact only be explained if we remember that he could hardly suspect the presence of such ambitious aspirations in a prefect of the praetorian guard, an official still considered not particularly important,[1] notwithstanding the prophetic hesitation about the post already displayed by Augustus. Thus the Sejanus affair is confined to the personal sphere of his own mad dream, played out against the background of family plots in the household of the Princeps and of the struggles between the factions in the bosom of the aristocracy. It is in this context that we must see the career of this curious character, though without sharing the unjust contempt of Tacitus (*Ann.* IV, 3, 4) for the person of this knight of municipal origin. One has only to think of the importance of the equestrian order in the Augustan social scheme, and of some knights in particular, the advance guard of a new nobility arriving on the scene – encouraged by the opportunities for service and the prompt reward for merit offered by the principate – to put fresh blood into the old aristocracy.

Sejanus's father, L. Seius Strabo, a native of Volsinii who after arriving in Rome had allied himself by marriage to the old noble family of the Cornelii Lentuli but had remained a knight, was prefect of the praetorian guard at the death of Augustus; at that point Tiberius had given him as colleague his son, who was already at least thirty years of age and whose quality Tiberius certainly appreciated. This son had become L. Aelius Sejanus, through adoption by another knight, probably L. Aelius Gallus. When (in 15) his father was appointed prefect of Egypt, where he died soon afterwards, Sejanus had remained sole prefect of the praetorian guard; and he never received a colleague. He had long been close to the family of the Princeps (in A.D. 1–2 he had been in the retinue of Gaius Caesar on the latter's mission to the East; and in 14, as we have seen, he accompanied Drusus to Pannonia), and after winning Tiberius's confidence he took pains to transform his growing actual power, derived from this semi-private relationship of personal esteem, into a position of greater formal strength as well. The construction – which he organized, probably in 23 – of one single barracks for all the

---

[1] TAC., *Ann.*, IV, 2, 1.

praetorian cohorts, which had been concentrated in Rome by Augustus but quartered in various different parts of the city, and the care he put into disciplining them and binding them to himself, were in themselves provisions intended to increase the power of the post and his own personal authority. The Senate, conscious of the favour with which the Princeps regarded the energetic prefect, did not spare flattery and through practical necessity became more and more dependent on him, not only in the sphere of prosecutions but also in the small change of political life: the nomination of centurions and tribunes, manœuvres for the distribution of jobs and provincial commands, and all the operations characteristic of life under a despotism, however enlightened it may wish to be at the summit. To crown the first stage of his ascent he was able in 20 to draw a step nearer to the family of the Princeps by betrothing his little daughter to a son of Claudius, Germanicus's brother, and probably in the same year he obtained the praetorian insignia; soon afterwards statues were dedicated to him in public and even in the legionary shrines.

Dynastic affairs gave him the opportunity to take the decisive step. The death of Germanicus in 19 had only on the surface resolved the situation in favour of Drusus, Tiberius's son. There remained the sons of Germanicus, who had strong rights if, as seemed indubitable from the very conditions surrounding the succession of Tiberius, the wish of Augustus that the principate should return to his direct descendants by blood was to prevail. They were also favoured by reasons of expediency if no further credence was desired for the supposition, which Agrippina's hatred already inclined her to regard as a certainty, that Germanicus had been eliminated to clear the way for Drusus. Thus, even if we can assume, as a pure hypothesis and a dubious one, that, in associating Drusus with himself by conferring the *tribunicia potestas* on him in the spring of 22, Tiberius obliged him to assume explicitly, vis-à-vis Germanicus's sons, the position of *locum tenens* that he himself had occupied with regard to Germanicus – with Drusus too setting aside his own children – it is clear from the facts that Tiberius himself had considerable regard for Germanicus's sons, and that even Drusus behaved in quite a friendly fashion with them, that it was too risky to eliminate them without further ado from the succession, and that on the contrary they continued to be kept prominent. The presentation to the Senate of Nero Caesar, the eldest, by Tiberius in 20 on the occasion of his assumption of the *toga virilis*, was a very solemn event, and the family bonds seemed to become even tighter when, immediately afterwards, this same Nero married Julia, the daughter of Drusus. Nevertheless, these events, as can be seen, did not change the situation, which still presented the same fundamental uncertainty, while at the Court, underneath the appearance of harmony, Agrippina did not lay down her arms; she now also felt bitter towards the Augusta for saving Plancina. Such was the terrain on which Sejanus worked.

The first obstacle in his path was Drusus, who did not hide his antipathy for his father's powerful adviser and once, during an argument, had even struck him. Quite apart from any question of usurpation, Sejanus could see only too clearly what his fate would be if Drusus one day came to reign. But on 14 September 23[1] the young prince, who had already been seriously ill two years earlier, died. That he had been poisoned by his wife Livilla, sister of Germanicus, widow of Gaius Caesar and now mistress of Sejanus, who must of course have been the instigator of the crime, was revealed eight years later by Apicata, Sejanus's own wife, in a letter she sent to Tiberius before committing suicide after the ruin of her husband and the murder of her eldest son. If it seems surprising that no trace of the crime ever leaked out (even though Sejanus had banished his wife Apicata) and if it is obscure why Livilla, already destined in the normal course of events to reign with Drusus, should have preferred the merely possible and risky alternative of reigning instead with Sejanus – so risky in fact that in modern times the whole episode has sometimes been questioned – the fact remains that the ancient tradition is unanimous in accepting the story of the crime. Moreover, it is difficult to see what objection can be made to the clear and decisive account given by Tacitus, who indicates that he had evaluated the various different versions with special care and says explicitly that he had rejected one that was too complicated.[2]

The death of Drusus, his only son, was a blow that Tiberius felt keenly, even if, as usual, he did not make a big outward show of grief. Not that Drusus was a man of exceptional merit from the point of view of the succession; his bloodthirsty tastes, his perfect accord with Germanicus and his friendship with the Jewish prince Julius Agrippa were not qualities or circumstances calculated to recommend him as different or better in comparison with the other young scions of the family. But politically his disappearance from the scene signified the revival of the party supporting Germanicus's family, which seemed henceforth to be certain

---

[1] The date is preserved by the *Fasti Oppiani maiores*, *CIL*, VI, 32493 (cf. *Not. d. Sc.*, 1894, p. 245). The reference is certainly to Drusus the son of Tiberius since the name is given complete (*inferiae Drusi Caesaris*), while previously the mutilated name *infer. Dr* in the *Fasti Antiates* (*CI–*, 12, p. 249) for the same date was generally referred to Drusus the elder, Tiberius's brother (*CIL*, 12, p. 329).

[2] *Ann.*, IV, 10–11.

of the succession, even officially, after Tiberius, in a solemn speech, had recommended to the Senate Germanicus's two eldest sons, Nero and Drusus. The latter had assumed the *toga virilis* only a few months before, but was now accorded all the privileges granted to his brother three years earlier. The designation was clear, and Tiberius's request to the senators to act 'parentum loco' to the young great-grandsons of Augustus[1] robbed Sejanus of the hope, if he had ever entertained it, of quickly making himself regent for them. But he was in no hurry. Now that the direct line of descendants of Tiberius had been eliminated (of Drusus's twin sons, one, little Germanicus, died in that same year and the other, Tiberius Gemellus, was four years old), Sejanus was confronted with the family of Germanicus, and in the first instance with Agrippina.

In some ways the struggle became easier: Agrippina, with her passionate and incautious character, must have worked to his advantage; the precedents and the complexity of the situation must have lent an air of credibility to all the cabals organized by Sejanus to convey to Tiberius the dangers that threatened him from Agrippina's party and to constrain him to act for his immediate safety. In actual fact Agrippina, surrounded by a numerous group of friends, adopted an openly provocative attitude in her meetings with the Princeps and thus gratuitously played Sejanus's game. However, it was a slow game that lasted a long time, at any rate as far as we can tell, for although Tacitus says that as early as 24 Sejanus was putting heavy pressure on Tiberius and saying that the city was divided into factions, as in a civil war, that many people were openly-declared supporters of Agrippina, and that it was necessary to teach them a sharp lesson, the narrative from then onwards is fragmentary; we glimpse only a few episodes, some of them not very significant, or else explicable in other ways, of a struggle that certainly existed but took some years to enter an acute phase. In fact, so far as the prosecutions are concerned, which Tacitus here says were launched against friends of Germanicus or Agrippina with the aim of indirectly inculpating the latter, prosecutions such as the ones already mentioned of C. Silius and Sosia Galla, of Vibius Serenus and Caecilius Cornutus (in 24), and of P. Suillius and Fonteius Capito (in 25), together with that of Claudia Pulchra (in 26), one must recognize that they were all based on real charges of which the defendants were convicted independently of any prejudice against them, even if it seemed to Agrippina's party (and hence to the tradition inherited by Tacitus) that in their cases special severity was employed. In the matter of the reproof addressed to the *pontifices* by Tiberius because at the

[1] *Ibid.*, IV, 8, 5.

beginning of 24, in formulating the prayers for the well-being of the emperor, they had included in the invocation to the gods the names of Nero and Drusus Caesar, nothing more can be discerned than a characteristic and not unprecedented trait in the mentality of the old Princeps, worried in case such an honour should go to the heads of easily excitable young men. Still, it must be presumed that the steady drip of provocations on the part of Agrippina and her party, certainly utilized and regulated by Sejanus, provoked a reaction in Tiberius, even if he confined himself within the limits of strict justice. Other episodes are known to us and give us a number of indications that are interesting, if fragmentary and insufficient to enable us to reconstruct a continuous line in the development of the intrigue. A good example is Sejanus's request in 25 for permission to marry Livilla; Tiberius replied with a refusal that was quite definite though mildly worded. Evidently he did not wish, by agreeing, to make the divisions that rent his family irreconcilable. In fact, if Sejanus, at the height of his favour and power, entered the imperial family, his position could only be that of guide to the young prince – whoever this might be – who was to succeed the old emperor; and it was only too clear that Sejanus would have arranged that it should be Livilla's son (and also his own? – but this hypothesis rests only on Cassius Dio, LVII, 22, 4b, LVIII, 23, 2), little Tiberius Gemellus, not Agrippina's eldest son, now an adult. Tiberius was not yet in such open conflict with the family of Germanicus; another push in this direction was required on the part of Sejanus. His activities in the years that followed were directed precisely to this end; and they were favoured by Tiberius's withdrawal to Capri. In 26 Claudia Pulchra, a cousin of Agrippina, was tried and condemned for adultery and the practice of magic. Agrippina was furious; regarding the affair as an affront to herself, she heaped abuse on Tiberius. Shortly afterwards, when she was ill and Tiberius visited her, she expressed the desire, amid tears and lamentations, to marry again, at which Tiberius went off without saying a word; he hardly needed a complication of this sort! A husband for Agrippina meant a regent for her sons; if Agrippina had planned the move to strike at Sejanus, having guessed his secret plans, it was a master stroke. But nothing came of it. Another episode deepened the hostility between the emperor and the proud matron. Invited by Tiberius at a dinner to try some apples, and having been warned in advance (by agents of Sejanus, says Tacitus) to be on her guard against her father-in-law's banquets, since he wanted to poison her, she ostentatiously gave the fruit first to the slaves to sample; Tiberius, turning to the Augusta, said that people could now hardly be surprised if he was forced to be severe with some one who considered him a poisoner.[1] Henceforth life at the court, with its perpetual quarrels, must have been intolerable to him and it is not surprising if episodes of this sort finally exhausted his long-tried patience. The man who had withdrawn when he was still young into solitary retirement now yielded once again to the temptation to seek seclusion. The longing for peace, the possibility of guarding himself better if he really did have to fear conspiracies against his life, the growing intrusiveness of his mother, which he wished to avoid without offending her, perhaps the hope that in his absence Agrippina would tone down her hatred and Nero Caesar would learn, without his help, to cope with government affairs, and finally the wish to hide from view his own face, which was disfigured by herpes, may have pushed him to the decision to leave Rome for ever and take refuge on the island of Capri, in the company of Greek literary men and philosophers, of a lawyer, M. Cocceius Nerva, the future emperor's grandfather, and of one other knight besides Sejanus, for even in the peace of his retreat he did not intend to give up, and never did give up, the government of the state. Going into Campania in 26 on the pretext of dedicating a temple to Jupiter near Capua and one to Augustus at Nola, he then (in 27) crossed over to the island, after receiving proof of Sejanus's devotion to him in an incident near Fondi: while he was dining in a natural cave there was a fall of rock on his guests and, while everyone else fled, the praetorian prefect, who was a big, robust man, shielded the Princeps from danger with his own body. From then onwards the people of Rome believed that Tiberius was completely in the power of his favourite. In fact distance in itself did make it look as if Sejanus's power was now unlimited; and in practice his hands were still freer to pursue his designs, whether he was with the Emperor on Capri or, even better, in Rome, whither he must have soon returned. For if the withdrawal of Tiberius was a fatal error from the point of view of political expediency in general, in so far as it caused him a loss of prestige with the people and hatred on the part of the Senate, which trembled when his letters were opened and in its constant uncertainty began to have the feeling of humiliating dependence on an inaccessible despot, for Sejanus it provided the decisive impetus to carry his operations through to their goal. However, in 26, when Tiberius was still in Campania, they were confined to covert intrigue. Nero Caesar in particular was the object of attention: surrounded by spies and *agents provocateurs* who encouraged him to adopt an arrogant attitude to Tiberius and Sejanus, he gave vent to threats which the latter made it his task to

[1] *Ann.*, IV, 54, 2.

convey to the ear of the Princeps, while Nero's own private utterances, passed on by his wife Julia to her mother Livilla, were at once known to Sejanus. The prefect had also succeeded in sowing discord in the very family of Germanicus by setting Drusus Caesar, a violent and impulsive character like his mother, against his elder brother, who was Agrippina's favourite.

When Tiberius crossed over to Capri and Sejanus was able to regulate at will the news which he wished to reach Tiberius, his operations became more open. Agrippina and Nero Caesar were kept under surveillance in such a way that they noticed it, so that, pushed to desperation, they should yield to the pressure of crafty suggestions to take refuge with the armies of the Rhine or utter in the Senate or the forum a clamorous denunciation of the dangers by which they felt threatened. But they did not take the bait. The next attack was another indirect one, via the person of one of their friends, a knight called Titius Sabinus, who was prosecuted in 28 at the request of Tiberius after being accused of conspiring in favour of Nero Caesar. The charge had been prepared with patience and furnished with evidence procured in a somewhat romantic fashion. There must certainly have been some substratum of fact in it, and Tiberius felt insecure. He saw that it was possible to conspire against him, and that there were friends of Germanicus's family ready to take the risk. Sabinus had already been accused in 24, with Silius and Sosia Galla, but nothing had come of the charge. Tiberius now revealed his anxieties to the Senate and Asinius Gallus, a relative of Agrippina and a man already noted for his frankness of speech, challenged him to name Agrippina and Nero openly. But he did not yet dare to do so.

In 29 Livia died at the age of eighty-six, and the disappearance of this intelligent and imperious woman whose influence had made itself felt for sixty years in the family of the Caesars and also, discreetly, in public life, seemed to remove the last obstacle to the prosecution of Sejanus's schemes. It was certainly he who pushed the Princeps to take the ultimate step. As late as the end of 28 Tiberius still arranged amicably the wedding of the eldest of Germanicus's daughters, Agrippina, who was to be the mother of the emperor Nero, to Cn. Domitius Ahenobarbus, son of Antonia, the elder daughter of Antony and Octavia, and thus already of the blood of Augustus and cousin of Germanicus. Tiberius did not attend the funeral of his mother and, in accordance with his custom, wrote enjoining moderation in the honours which people wished to pay her; but the funeral oration was pronounced by Gaius Caesar, the third son of Germanicus. A few days later the Senate received a letter from

Tiberius, written before his mother's death, containing a general accusation of Agrippina and Nero; in it Tiberius denounced the arrogance of the former and the unpleasant habits of the latter. The Senate, caught unawares, evaded the issue by postponing any decision; but when the people rioted and carried round statues of Agrippina and Nero Caesar, simultaneously praising Tiberius and declaring that his letter was a forgery, and at the same time voices hostile to Sejanus were raised, the latter had to warn Tiberius that a less circumstantial accusation was necessary, as seemed required by the popular demonstrations in favour of the accused. If these demonstrations were not encouraged by Sejanus himself to illustrate the dangerous nature of the situation and to induce the Princeps to act, he certainly exploited them very skilfully. Tiberius repeated the charge and the Senate declared Agrippina and Nero public enemies. Sentence was passed by Tiberius; Agrippina, after a violent scene with him, was exiled to the island of Pandataria and Nero to Pontia.

Succeeding events become more difficult to follow, especially from the chronological point of view, since our sources of information are reduced – thanks to the big lacuna in Book V of Tacitus's *Annals* – to the anecdotal and highly coloured narratives of Suetonius and Dio and the epitomists. Nevertheless, the main lines can be traced. The elimination of the imprudent Drusus Caesar, induced to come from Capri to Rome, was an easy matter for Sejanus: accused – we do not know of what – by L. Cassius Longinus, one of the consuls of the year 30 and the man who three years later was to marry Drusus' sister Julia Drusilla, Drusus finished up as a prisoner in the cellars of the palace. Sejanus was at the summit of his success. The numerous names that figure first among those of the partisans of Germanicus and his family and then reappear among those of the victims swept away in the downfall of the praetorian prefect show that the latter had secured a following even among the members of the party that he had destroyed. Although still a knight, he must have had many friends and adherents in the Senate, and he could also count by and large on the flattery of the Senate as a whole, which had come to render the same honours to him as to the Princeps. If many of its members also suspected his intrigues, they certainly did not care to make curious enquiries at the expense of the man whom the assent of the Princeps caused to be regarded for all practical purposes as his *alter ego*. With his command of the nine cohorts he effectively dominated the city; and in all the big provincial commands he had succeeded either in placing his own friends, or at any rate in preventing the posting of his enemies. Thus Cn. Cornelius Lentulus Gaetulicus was already related to Sejanus and his daughter had just been promised to the latter's son when in 29 he was appointed to command the four legions of Upper Germany; the four legions of Lower Germany had been entrusted shortly before to Gaetulicus's father-in-law, L. Afronius, whose son was a friend of Sejanus's. Poppaeus Sabinus, governor of Moesia, Macedonia and Achaea, had already been in this post some time; but he was the father-in-law of one T. Ollius, also a friend of Sejanus. And, *vice versa*, we seem to be justified in supposing that L. Arruntius, who was governor of Spain from 24 or 25 to 35 but never arrived in his province, and L. Aelius Lamia, who was governor of Syria but always stayed in Rome, of which he became *praefectus* in 32 – soon enough after the fall of Sejanus to rule out his being one of the latter's friends – were kept far from their commands through his manœuvres.

In the end the Princeps's intentions about the succession seemed to coincide with the plans of his adjutant. Some ten years after his fourth consulate, held in 21 with his son Drusus and clearly meant to designate Drusus as successor – an intention confirmed in 22 by the conferment on him of the *tribunicia potestas* – Tiberius stated in 30 that he wished to be consul in 31 with Sejanus; and it seems that the latter had the designation confirmed by means of a popular election on the Aventine, the 'inprobae comitiae' of a curious epigraphical fragment (*ILS*, 6044). The marriage to Livilla (more probably than to her daughter Julia, perhaps already the widow of Nero Caesar, although the only source that furnishes the information, Cassius Dio in Zonaras, names the latter) was now permitted by Tiberius, and this seemed to confirm his preference for the succession of the little Tiberius Gemellus and to eliminate any real hope for the sons of Germanicus. Proconsular power was also granted to Sejanus. The only thing lacking to make him co-regent and successor designate was the conferment of the *tribunicia potestas*. But this never took place; instead came unexpected and terrible downfall.

The chronological uncertainty affecting the years 30–31 does not allow us to establish when Tiberius's first suspicions were born, and above all at what precise moment to insert events of primary importance like the death of Nero Caesar and the trap set for the young Gaius. However, it appears that these events must have formed part of the operations conducted with some anxiety by the favourite who – feeling near the coveted goal and quickening the tempo when faced with the slowness, harmless though it may still have seemed, of the Princeps – now precipitated the course of events which he had plotted. It seems fairly logical to suppose that the death of Nero – who killed himself in his place of exile at the false news that he was to be executed, passed on to him to induce this act of desperation – must be attributed to Sejanus, who certainly had his faithful followers among the young prince's gaolers. In fact Tiberius had not yet arrived at the point of putting to death his own relations. Agrippina was still alive, and so were all her children. Did Sejanus sense the danger of a reconciliation in the family? In the case of Nero he probably did, and so he got rid of him. Drusus was safely in prison. Sejanus had his fears confirmed through Gaius. He was in the process of plotting against Gaius, too, and the accuser stood ready, as was subsequently discovered. But when he asked Tiberius to send Gaius to Rome, Tiberius – either because he was already preparing the plan to get rid of Sejanus or else, as seems more probable, because he was intending to draw closer to his great-nephews (as Sejanus must have thought, for we know that he had no fears for himself right up to the fatal session of the Senate on 18 October 31) – began just at that point to employ Gaius, making him assume the *toga virilis* (two years later than usual), appointing him pontifex and keeping him with him on Capri.

Other facts indicate that Tiberius was now taking the case of his favourite very seriously. Probably warned – by Antonia, the mother of Germanicus, so it is said, though there was no lack of other informers, such as the Satrius Secundus named retrospectively by Tacitus (*Ann.* VI, 47, 8) – of the secret manœuvres of the man whom he believed to be a loyal collaborator in the government of the state and on whose behaviour, which he attributed to outward ambition, he was disposed to turn a blind eye precisely because of his very real services, he sought to repair the mistake he had made. There was no question of forestalling a conspiracy against his own life; Sejanus could not desire the death of Tiberius so long as his own succession was not assured. All that was required was to put an end, now that the truth about his intentions had come to light, to the unexpected and intolerable experiment of a praetorian prefect who had so far exceeded his functions and, profiting from the really excessive trust of the Princeps, meddled in the thorny dynastic question in order to deflect its course in favour of his own mad dream. Cautiously, in the letters he sent to Rome, Tiberius began to create the impression that he was still the Princeps and that Sejanus was not as powerful as people thought. One day he wrote that his health was poor, then, immediately afterwards, that he was better and on the point of returning to Rome and wished Sejanus to stay there. The result was a situation of uncertain expectation, perhaps indirectly attested by episodes such as the dedication to *Concordia* made by the notorious L. Fulcinius Trio, *consul suffectus* from 1 July 31. In his letters to the Senate Tiberius would at one moment put all the honorific titles of his prefect and praise him, and at the next would omit them (as for example in the letter in which he announced the death of Nero – a significant point) and criticize him. One day he wrote forbidding the conferment of any honours on Sejanus, thus blocking the preparations of the Senate to bestow some on him; and he recalled the prohibition against offering sacrifices on altars dedicated to living men. Such a reminder was very much in character, but it was significant coming at that particular moment. The proceedings against the above-mentioned L. Arruntius, proceedings engineered by Sejanus, were suspended on the orders of Tiberius and the accusers punished. Before the end of 31 Sejanus was not even consul any longer, since he had naturally been bound to follow the example of his august colleague and yield his position to a *suffectus*. And the *tribunicia potestas* still failed to arrive. Already, on the other hand, it could be sensed that the partial restoration of the fortunes of Germanicus's family, with the favour bestowed on the young Gaius, had been in general well received. When this too had given Tiberius the feeling that he could act with success, he precipitated the crisis, preparing at the same time for every eventuality; for in fact the direction from a distance of a stroke of this sort, at a time when Tiberius was being constantly watched by agents of the intended victim and did not know who could be trusted, was a difficult enterprise. Its successful execution has something miraculous about it. Just in case anything went wrong Tiberius had ships ready in which he could flee to one of the provincial armies, and he had given orders that in this case Drusus was to be pulled out of the dungeons of the Palatine and presented to the people. But this was not necessary. The new praetorian prefect whom he had secretly appointed, Naevius Sutorius Macro, together with the *praefectus vigilum*, Graecinius Laco, and one of the *consules suffecti*, P. Memmius Regulus, who had taken office on 1 October 31, carried out the operation superbly and with such great secrecy that Tiberius's 'verbosa et grandis epistula',[1] read out in the Senate on the day on which Sejanus expected to have the *tribunicia potestas* conferred on him, and containing instead the list of charges against him, took him completely by surprise. What followed – the consternation of the accused and the unanimity of the senators, both friends and enemies, in trampling on the fallen favourite; the popular fury against statues representing him; the condemnation and swift execution in the evening of that same 18 October which had begun with the highest hopes; the corpse abandoned on the

[1] JUVENAL, *Sat.*, X, 71.

Gemonian Steps, reviled and eventually thrown into the Tiber; the execution six days later of Sejanus's innocent eldest son; the suicide of Apicata after she had revealed to Tiberius the responsibility, real or presumed, of her husband and Livilla for the death of Drusus; the slaughter in December, in horrifying circumstances, of Sejanus's other son and of the daughter promised in marriage to the son of Claudius; and finally the summary justice liberally meted out to anyone who had been a friend of the unfortunate wretch – all this belongs to the history of political tragedies as it does to the story of human vileness. 'Dum iacet in ripa, calcemus Caesaris hostem'.[1] The fact remains that his elimination was also necessary in order to restore the equilibrium of the principate, which had been compromised by the abnormal development of one of its administrative organs; though one must always remember the manifold personal elements present in this curious episode.

However, it was now highly desirable that Tiberius should settle clearly once for all the problem of the succession, return to Rome and renew his collaboration with the Senate. But, as we shall see, human and personal considerations prevailed in the mind of the deluded old monarch. Although he continued, as far as he could, to govern the empire with a firm hand, he was unwilling to leave his island refuge, or, if he did leave it, he never again went as far as Rome. He thus offered public opinion, already inclined to misinterpret his actions and intentions and to let imagination run riot in exact proportion to the amount of circumspection and concealment he employed, an apparently well justified reason for stamping his memory with the seal of condemnation.

DIFFICULTIES ABROAD

In the long period under consideration internal events are completely predominant. The state of the empire finds a smaller echo in the sources, not only because it held less attraction for chroniclers primarily interested in the vicissitudes of individual human beings, but also because there was in fact little out of the ordinary to record. It is well known that day-to-day administration seldom finds a place in history. The empire was henceforth secure within its frontiers, thanks largely to the military and diplomatic successes of Tiberius himself in the period when he was co-ruler and subsequently in the first few years of his own principate. On the other hand, there were still internal disturbances in Africa, Gaul and Thrace; not such as to compromise the general security, but of some importance

[1] *Ibid.*, 86.

nevertheless. It took some time to settle them, and it is certainly not Tiberius's smallest claim to fame and praise that an empire which at the death of Augustus was still in many ways in a precarious condition was left on the whole at peace and organized for a long future of peace and prosperity. From this angle, too, the principate of Tiberius represented the laborious – and worthy – complement to that of Augustus.

We have already mentioned that during the settlement of the East by Germanicus and Tiberius's interventions to depose Archelaus of Cappadocia (who had to answer in a court of law, at Rome, for his suspicious activities and, as it happened, died at Rome, in obscure circumstances in 17) and G. Julius Laco, who held as a historical curiosity the position of tyrant of Sparta, a post abolished in 18 or 19 (but restored, with the reinstatement of this same Laco, by Gaius), there had been disturbances in Africa and Thrace. Tacfarinas had put himself at the head of the semi-nomadic Numidian tribes' resistance to the progressive occupation of their territory by Roman capitalists and by 17, supported by powerful peoples such as the Musulamii and even by the Moors, he had become formidable. Defeated by the proconsul, M. Furius Camillus, in 20, he had renewed the attack, which was contained by the new proconsul, L. Apronius. But to finish off the war, which was seriously damaging the Roman landowners, another legion – from Pannonia – had to be sent to Africa. Tiberius would have liked these military reinforcements to mark the limit of his direct intervention in this senatorial province, which – predisposed as he was to take literally the division of jurisdiction established on Augustus's map – he wished to leave as the exclusive concern of the Senate, especially in a war in which senatorial interests were particularly at stake. However, when it came to selecting the new proconsul, the Senate, in view of the gravity of the local situation, did not trust itself to leave the appointment to the drawing of lots and looked for the nomination to Tiberius, who, annoyed, suggested two names. The post was accepted by Q. Junius Blaesus, Sejanus's uncle and in fact a very good general, who after three years of energetic fighting reduced Tacfarinas to such straits that the next proconsul, P. Dolabella, was able to defeat him once and for all in the same year, 23. Tacfarinas fell on the field of battle and Africa was henceforth at peace; the province co-existed happily for a long time with the neighbouring client kingdom of Mauretania and the construction of roads and cities could proceed undisturbed. The legion sent as a reinforcement returned to Pannonia.

In Gaul, which had been organized from an administrative point of view by Augustus and where, with the construction of the great roads marked out by Agrippa and the beginnings of urbanization, the powerful, still fresh forces tamed by Caesar remained largely in the phase of transformation and settlement, the first revolt since the time of Vercingetorix occurred. It does not seem to have been a very serious affair, to judge from Tacitus's account – extensive though this is – and from the hyperbolical verdict of Velleius on the dangers involved and the great merit of Tiberius in averting them.[1] Not even the reasons for the rising are clear, nor the connexions between the various revolts, particularly those between the rebellion of the Treviri under Julius Florus and that of the Aedui under Julius Sacrovir. The excessive burden of tribute is adduced by Tacitus, together with other minor reasons, among them – significantly – the opportunity to profit from the discontent of the Rhine legions after the death of Germanicus. But the tribute was not such a heavy burden as the perpetual state of war existing before the Roman conquest. Perhaps it was simply a question of episodes which triggered off a certain response in the surviving aspirations of Celtic nationalism, though the practical initiatives were not shared by the majority of the Gallic population; the aristocracy in particular seems to have remained outside the rebellion. The first episode, in 21, was a rising among the Andecavi and the Turones on the middle Loire, easily subdued with the assistance of other Gauls. The second was the revolt of the Treviri, led by Julius Florus and suppressed mainly by one of his fellow-citizens loyal to the Romans, Julius Indus, whose name was afterwards perpetuated in the empire as a mark of honour in the title of the *ala Indiana*, an auxiliary unit of Gallic cavalry. The third and most serious episode was the rising of the Aedui, headed by Julius Sacrovir. The poorly armed and half-hearted crowd of new townsmen dragged into the field by their enthusiastic leader was routed near Augustodunum (Autun) by C. Silius with just half of his army of Upper Germany, after he had won the day in the rivalry between himself and his colleague of Lower Germany to gain the easy success. Florus and Sacrovir disappeared from the scene dramatically, and Tiberius announced the victory of his armies without over-valuing it. For his own part, in the provisions which he made subsequently and also in the last few years of his reign with regard to Gaul, he did not forget the lesson furnished by the events of 21.

The difficulties in Thrace lasted longer and the present state of our knowledge does not allow us to say how they ended. The disturbances in this important region had not been settled by the removal of Rhescuporis, who in 18, as we have seen, had eliminated his nephew and rival Cotys

[1] TAC., *Ann.*, III, 40–7; VELL. PAT., II, 129, 3.

and, after being taken to Rome to answer for his crime and found guilty by the Senate, had been banished from his kingdom and forced to live at Alexandria, where he was soon afterwards put to death for attempting flight. Tiberius, respecting the partition introduced by Augustus, assigned Rhescuporis's share of the kingdom to his son Rhoemetalces II and the other half to Cotys's sons who, being too young, were kept in Rome, where they were brought up with the young Gaius in the house of Antonia, a relation of their mother. Their kingdom was governed on their behalf by the ex-praetor T. Trebellenus Rufus. However, neither the native king nor the Roman regent was acceptable to the local peoples, who probably suspected in this arrangement a stage on the road to direct annexation, and in 21 several tribes rebelled, besieging Rhoemetalces himself in Philippopolis. The intervention of P. Vellaeus, who commanded the troops in neighbouring Moesia, sufficed to quash the revolt, which was badly organized and without any unified direction. The year 26 saw the outbreak of a more serious war, caused by the mountain tribes' objection to the conscription which carried off their young men to serve far away in the Roman auxiliary units. The governor of Moesia, Macedonia and Achaea, the experienced general Poppaeus Sabinus, intervened in person, first keeping these high-spirited peoples at bay and only going over to the offensive when a legion arrived from Moesia and he could also count on the auxiliary troops of Rhoemetalces. Tacitus's fairly extensive account shows how hard the struggle was and the importance assigned to it by the tradition. In the end the rebellion was suppressed and Sabinus was awarded triumphal insignia for the victory. We know no more about Thrace under Tiberius, except that piracy flourished again on its coasts – possibly a sign of unsettled conditions in the hinterland – and that in 35 Trebellenus Rufus, accused of treason, killed himself in Rome; but we do not know if and to what extent the charge concerned his period of administration in Thrace. In fact, we do not even know how long this period lasted.

In comparison with the hard years at the end of the reign of Augustus and with the upheavals which later shook the foundations of the empire, these troubles all seem to amount – as far as we can see – to very little; nevertheless they were not negligible, and certainly not so in the eyes of Tiberius, from the point of view of that activity on behalf of the provinces which, given only a secondary place by the tradition, has been revealed to modern research by evidence of other kinds, particularly inscriptions, as his main concern in the obscure years of decline. It was precisely in these years that he had to deal with fresh difficulties in the

Parthian-Armenian sector settled in the time of Germanicus and sub-sequently at peace for some fifteen years. These difficulties will be dis-cussed in the section devoted to the close of the reign, not only for chronological reasons but also because the shrewdness of Tiberius's actions in this case demonstrates how vigilant his attention to more serious problems still was in a phase of his life described by the tradition as one of total abandonment to cruelty and depravity.

THE LAST YEARS

It is hardly surprising that, after the fall of Sejanus and the revelations, true or imaginary (but certainly believed), about the death of Drusus, Tiberius should shut himself up in proud grief. And that this human reaction to hard and sudden blows should influence his conduct as a ruler seems perfectly logical and only too vividly confirmed by the tradition. The question remains just how far this tradition exaggerated in regarding the last part of Tiberius's reign as a period of pure terror. Certainly there was something different about these last years, for the tradition, in-fluenced though it was by all the subjective elements we have noted, persists unanimously in pointing to these years in particular as the worst of a principate which, as this tradition itself allows, had begun reasonably enough, if only out of hypocrisy. The defence à outrance of all the acts of Tiberius the man in this last tired and disillusioned phase of his life is in fact a difficult enterprise. Statistical attempts to construct comparative percentages of people executed, impelled to commit suicide, banished and acquitted, and considerations such as the one that allowing some one to die of hunger (as was done with Drusus Caesar) was regarded as a merciful form of execution,[1] echo in our minds with a false and macabre ring. Even the critical principle so felicitously utilized as a basis for the rehabilitation of Tiberius – that of looking for the bare facts underneath the interpretative colouring laid on them by a hostile tradition for political motives and, in good faith, by chroniclers influenced by moral considerations – cannot quite overcome the reality of facts which remain errors and faults even in origin, before undergoing any kind of distortion or interested interpretation. It is impossible to justify everything, nor is it necessary, unless we wish to do violence to the sources and to substitute for the figure systematically altered for the worse by the tradition another figure just as untrue, a Tiberius systematically presented as a man without blemish. But much certainly can be explained.

[1] Cf. MARSH, *The Reign of Tiberius* p. 208.

After the death of Sejanus the Senate had voted for the erection of a statue of *Libertas*, declared 18 October a public holiday and begged the Princeps to accept the title of *pater patriae*, which he refused. The provinces followed Rome in commemorating the danger averted, as inscriptions and coins testify. Meanwhile the reaction against the fallen favourite's partisans raged violently, through the desire of these same senators to remove suspicion from themselves or to forestall accusations by accusing others. Of the early days of this senatorial terror, to which Tiberius appears a stranger, we learn nothing from Tacitus, whose narrative resumes (on 31 December) with an account of the forty-fourth speech in a trial relating to the deeds of Sejanus.[1] If it really is the trial for the poisoning of Drusus and was willed by Tiberius, forty-four speeches hardly suggest that the justice done was summary. However, from this point to the death of Tiberius, throughout what remains of the fifth book of the *Annals* and for the whole of the sixth book, the narrative concentrates, with short respites, on a sequence of trials, and even if it is true that Tacitus's interest is particularly focused on these and that he certainly omitted very few of them, as he himself declares,[2] it is undeniable that they are rather too numerous to be regarded as normal, especially in comparison with the preceding period, in which they had certainly not been rare. And even if there was no resurgence of severity on the part of the Princeps, since the very situation consequent on the tragedy of Sejanus and the logic of despotism were bound to lead to an increase in trials, it cannot be denied that sometimes – so far as we can judge from the not always exhaustive account of Tacitus – Tiberius no longer troubled, as he had earlier, to avoid the arbitrary exercise of power. Animosity against the aristocracy, which had not responded to his appeals to collaborate – appeals that were sincere, if also utopian in the reality of the principate – fear of new plots, loss of faith in men, the pangs of misfortune, of old age and of solitude certainly exerted their influence. Yet even here an examination of the dates in fact explains almost everything, and in Tiberius's favour.

Before the end of 31 there were proceedings, as a resut of denunciation by informers, against P. Vitellius and Pomponius Secundus. The former killed himself, convicted of misappropriation in connection with the 'militaris pecunia';[3] the latter was acquitted. Then came the execution of Sejanus's younger children – victims of the Senate, still borne along on the wave, now almost spent, of reaction against Sejanus, as Tacitus clearly gives us to understand; he says that their removal was pointless, since the

---

[1] TAC., *Ann.*, V, 6, 1.   [2] *Ibid.*, VI, 7, 5.   [3] *Ibid.*, V, 8, 1.

anger of the people was now placated.[1] In 32 it was the turn of Sextius Paconianus and Latinius (or Lucanius) Latiaris. Both of them were informers; the former (who had been Sejanus's tool in the plot being hatched against Gaius) tried to save himself by accusing the latter; and the Senate, which detested them both, was delighted to support the charges each made against the other. Latiaris, the man responsible for the downfall of Titius Sabinus in 28, paid for his crimes immediately; Sextius Paconianus was put to death in prison three years later for the satires that he was accused of composing there against Tiberius. Here the will of the Princeps certainly came into play to set the seal on senatorial justice. Haterius Agrippa next tried to rekindle the strife between Memmius Regulus and Fulcinius Trio, the consuls at the time of the death of Sejanus, who had already quarrelled in the previous year because Trio, once a friend of Sejanus, accused his colleague, who had been hostile to him, of being lukewarm in pursuing the fallen favourite's supporters. This activity of Agrippa's simply followed the usual deplorable pattern of senatorial intrigue and for the time being led to nothing. Immediately after this came the significant case of Cotta Messalinus, who was accused of uttering words disrespectful to the Princeps and members of his family; Tiberius intervened directly and recommended the Senate not to make a criminal charge out of tavern gossip. The accuser was punished. We do not know the final fate of Q. Servaeus and Minucius Thermus, who were tried as friends of Sejanus at the wish of the Princeps and, when convicted, involved Julius Africanus and Seius Quadratus in the charge. In the midst of the general cowardice a knight, M. Terentius, defended his friendship with Sejanus in a courageous speech; his accusers were punished.

Then came a resurgence of accusations: Sextus Vistilius, after losing the friendship of the Princeps and swaying tragically between hope and despair, killed himself; and Annius Pollio and his son Vinicianus, Mamercus Scaurus, Appius Silanus and Calvisius Sabinus were prosecuted *en masse* for treason. The last two were acquitted; the Princeps himself took over the investigation of the other three and did nothing. Scaurus came to a bad end two years later, but on another charge, and Vinicianus was still alive in 42. A woman, Vitia, was executed on the orders of the Senate, and two old friends of Tiberius from his Rhodes days, Vescularius Flaccus and Julius Marinus, were sentenced to death by the Princeps himself. The last trials of 32 were those of three more friends of Sejanus – the knights Geminius, Celsus and Pompeius – and of one Rubrius Fabatus, who had asserted that he wanted to leave Rome and seek peace

[1] *Ibid.*, 9, 1.

among the Parthians; he was condemned but left alive, forgotten, in prison. At the beginning of 33 we hear of a number of trials conducted with severity, such as those of Considius Proculus, accused of treason and executed; of his sister Sancia, who was exiled; of Pompeia Macrina, who, however, was only exiled, while her father and brother killed themselves; and of Sextus Marius, thrown from the Tarpeian Rock. Finally there was the indiscriminate massacre without trial, on the orders of Tiberius, of all those in prison on the charge of complicity with Sejanus, an act which is inexplicable at this distance in time, except perhaps as the precipitate effect of fear of some new plot. In any case, this drastic liquidation put an end to the most intense phase of trials.

There was still to be, in 33, the suspicious death of Asinius Gallus after three years of imprisonment and the suicides of the blameless Cocceius Nerva and the guilty Plancina. And the beginning of 34 witnessed an absolute epidemic of suicides: those of Pomponius Labeo and his wife Paxaea, actuated by the wish to forestall conviction for mis-appropriation (Labeo had been governor of Moesia) and thus to preserve the efficacy of the will – a course of action adopted henceforth by many people; then those of the above-mentioned Mamercus Scaurus and his wife Sextia, victims of the machinations of Macro. But the same year also saw the accusers of Scaurus suddenly banished, and this fate also overtook the accuser of Lentulus Gaetulicus who, although a relative of Sejanus, had remained in command of the legions of Upper Germany (he was to stay there until 39) and had saved himself, as M. Terentius had done two years earlier with his frank speech, by writing a courageous letter to the Princeps. In 35 Fulcinius Trio, the accuser with the longest career in the reign of Tiberius, after escaping in 31 and 32, decided to forestall charges against himself by committing suicide, not without first drawing up a will in which he revealed the scoundrelism of Macro and other men of the court and reproached the Princeps with being softened by old age and to blame through his absence from Rome (here he hit the target): charges which Tiberius calmly caused to be read out to him in public. Shortly afterwards, two senators, Granius Marcianus and Tarius Gratianus, were accused of treason; the former killed himself and the latter was executed. In the same way Trebellenus Rufus, whom we met as administrator of eastern Thrace on behalf of the sons of Cotys, now committed suicide and Sextius Paconianus, in prison since 32, was put to death. In 36 there were the deaths of L. Aruseius and others, the tragic one of Vibulenus Agrippa, executed when he had already taken poison on his own account, and that of the ex-king of Armenia, Tigranes IV,

who must have been in Rome for some thirty years and was now put to
death for some unknown reason. In addition, there were the voluntary
deaths of the ex-consul C. Galba and the two Blaesi, whose father, the
famous Junius Blaesus, had been among the first victims of the anti-
Sejanus reaction in 31; and finally the death, also voluntary, of Aemilia
Lepida, once betrothed to Drusus Caesar, then denounced by him, and
now ending her life in miserable circumstances. The year 37, the last of
the reign, again saw a number of trials and, according to Tacitus (*Ann.*,
VI, 47, 1), it also saw the sowing of the seeds of future bloodshed.

Such are the facts; their interpretation is naturally a difficult matter
owing to the quantitative unevenness in the reports of the circumstances
furnished by Tacitus. But considered in themselves, and if we set aside
evident generalizations, such as those of Suetonius,[1] they do not suffice to
make Tiberius into a bloodthirsty tyrant. Terentius's speech and Gaetulicus's letter, the repudiation of the charges against Cotta Messalinus
and the good sense shown in connection with the proposals of Junius
Gallio, who after all that had happened conceived the strange idea of
recommending an increase in the privileges granted to discharged members
of the praetorian guard, privileges which in practice would have rendered
them equal to knights, lead us to think that here too the blame attributed
to the old Princeps should to some extent be shared out among all the
factors helping to produce the unhappy situation of a principate torn at
the centre by ambiguity and by family and party passions.

By far the most important of these factors was the dynastic problem.
Far from being resolved, as it might seem to have been by the ruin of
Germanicus's family, it dominates these last years too. After the death
of Sejanus, officially explained by the Princeps as necessitated by his
persecution of the relatives of Germanicus, Agrippina's exile nevertheless
continued and so did Drusus's imprisonment. Gaius was practically left
to himself; in 33 he was quaestor, with the privilege of holding the
office five years early, but Tiberius did not initiate him in the responsibilities of government. Agrippina, still on terms of sharp hostility with
the Princeps, died in exile in 35 and Tiberius did not spare her memory
the bitterest insults. Drusus was allowed to die of hunger in the same
year, in the dungeons of the Palatine, and he too was heaped with abuse.
Did Tiberius still feel the threat of some sort of danger from this direction?
In 31 an impostor had appeared in Greece claiming to be Drusus escaped

---

[1] See Chapter 61 of the *Life* of Tiberius, where the procedure is obvious. Even Tacitus
  often refers artificially with apposite expressions to an atmosphere of blood which
  would not follow in such a dreadful form from the facts: see *Ann.*, VI, 29, 1; 40, 1, etc.

from prison, and he had had a certain following, sufficient to provoke the intervention of the governor himself, Poppaeus Sabinus. This is a sign that a party favouring Germanicus's family still survived even in the provinces; but it is not enough to justify acts much more easily explicable as due to family feuds and the weariness of having to endure a tenacious hatred largely based simply on hurtful suspicion. Misfortunes in other directions had also embittered him; Livilla, the unhappy lover of Sejanus, had been tried and handed over in 31, according to a somewhat suspect tradition, to her mother Antonia, who had let her die of hunger.[1] In these family circumstances, Tiberius must now have been wondering who could succeed him. As in his relations with the Senate, with which he had never succeeded in establishing the dialogue he desired, so in this atmosphere of domestic disillusionment he seemed to be leaving to the course of events the solution of the most serious problem of all. In any case there was little room for choice. The wishes of Augustus were still law to him. So Gaius, the surviving son of Germanicus, was the predestined heir, taking precedence over Claudius, Germanicus's brother, who was regarded as feeble-minded, and over Tiberius Gemellus, the child – still only a boy – of his own son Drusus. Tiberius made no deliberate choice and allowed Gaius, amid the not entirely healthy popularity which had also surrounded his father, to proceed towards the throne as though by the most natural path. In his will (made in 35) he named as heirs on an equal footing Gaius and his grandson, thus contradicting his own experience; but this had the savour of a pure formality.

One can well say that the old Princeps was weary of facing these problems that had tormented him for so long, that he had given up the struggle. There was a resurgence of fatalism (Stoic fatalism?) in him, and his life, henceforth divided between painful alternatives, passed in gloomy abandonment to uncertainty and inaction and in frenzied bursts of energy. These attitudes were for the most part not understood. 'If I know what I should write to you at this time, senators, or how to write it, or what I should not write, may the gods destroy me, and with a crueller fate than the one I feel overtaking me day by day!' That is how he began a letter to the Senate in 32, in which he rejected as ridiculous the accusation against Cotta Messalinus. Madness and remorse consequent on his crimes, says Tacitus; and it is not surprising that this last misunderstanding of the tormented decline of a mind which had seen disastrous effects spring from the best intentions, and scrupulous regard for justice create infinite injustices, should give rise to the charge of con-

[1] CASS. D., LVIII, II, 7.

cealed iniquities, carefully collected and preserved by the anecdotal tradition. This charge must certainly be rejected, or considered, in so far as it can be accepted at all, from the point of view of the man's strictly private responsibility. Unfortunately Tiberius's most serious fault – and one that was also culpable by the standard of his own very lively sense of duty as Princeps – was the obstinate fixation not to return to Rome. The thing must certainly have tormented him; in 32, crossing over from Capri to the mainland, he made a start towards keeping the promise, so often given, to return, and he was in correspondence with the Senate about the details of his escort; it was the same in 33 and 35. He did get as far as his villas within sight of Rome, and in his last few years he frequently changed his place of residence, which was always on the mainland; death overtook him near Misenum, in a villa which had once belonged to Lucullus. But he never set foot again in Rome. When he finally did return there, dead, the people wanted to throw him into the Tiber. His behaviour was thus a culpable and inexplicable error.

Yet even in the midst of this uncertainty it is possible to discern the signs of energetic and shrewd governmental activity. The administration of the empire does not reveal any notable trace of relaxed attention, and we are tempted to wonder whether the tragedy of Tiberius was not a private one and limited in its consequences to his personal relations with his own family, with the circle of the nobility at Rome, and whether the – so to speak – police problem of security, which occupies the chief place in the tradition, was not just one part – the most interesting to Rome, and therefore the most sensational at the time and in the tradition, but nevertheless still only a part – of a complex of activities that are impressive in a quite different way. Examples of wise conduct are not lacking in any field. In his own family he did not yield to his prejudices when it came to arranging marriages for the younger children of Germanicus. In 33 Julia Drusilla was given in marriage to L. Cassius Longinus, who belonged to a family of ancient but not first-rank nobility, and Julia Livilla to M. Vinicius, a man of municipal origin. In the same year he caused Gaius to marry Junia Claudilla, the daughter of his friend M. Junius Silanus, and still in the same year he gave as husband to Julia, daughter of Drusus and widow of Nero Caesar – not without incurring criticism, reported by Tacitus (*Ann.*, VI, 27, 1) – Rubellius Blandus, grandson of an ordinary knight of Tibur. That by these steps he wished to bring into the family, without paying any heed to the greater or lesser nobility, men of proved worth whom he could use at the opportune moment seems to be proved by the membership of the commission recorded by Tacitus under the year 36 (*Ann.*, VI, 45, 2) and set up to estimate the compensation to be paid to those who had suffered losses in the serious fire on the Aventine. This commission consisted precisely of the three persons named, together with Cn. Domitius, already married earlier to Agrippina, the elder sister of Drusilla and Livia, and a fifth member nominated by the consuls. As for Gaius, it must be recognized that Tiberius's capitulation to ineluctable dynastic necessity was nevertheless modified, to judge by the episodes recorded by Tacitus (*Ann.*, VI, 46, 3–5), by an ironic awareness of the present and a vivid prevision of the future. With regard to the central administration, he kept a man of high quality, L. Calpurnius Piso, in office as *praefectus urbi* until his death (in 32); he energetically reminded the magistrates of their duty to maintain public order on one occasion when they had let the populace riot about the *annona*, for which he demonstrated, dates in hand, that he had made better provision than at any previous time; and Macro, who could have become another Sejanus and in fact was no stranger to plots, was never trusted too far. Even when the praetorian prefect's attentions were transferred from himself, near death, to Gaius, the rising star, he showed that he was aware of it and said as much in public. Interventions characteristic of his realistic temperament occurred in 32, for example, when he reproached the Senate for its light-heartedness in accepting a prophetic book that claimed to be the work of the Sibyl;[1] and again in the next year, when he met the economic crisis provoked through the rigorous application of the laws on usury by putting down a hundred million sesterces of his own money for three-year interest-free loans, to restore confidence; and once more in 36, when the exact provisions for the fire on the Aventine – provisions also recorded in the *Fasti Ostienses*[2] – were carefully settled.

But the administration of the provinces and foreign policy continued to be his greatest concern; and fortunately on this subject we have not only the already favourable literary testimony but also the evidence of the inscriptions, which completely rehabilitate Tiberius as the administrator of the empire, showing him to have been the loyal follower of Augustus precisely in his principal field of activity, the great work of organization. This zeal, still present in his last years, is proved not only by the re-proofs administered in 33 to the nobility for avoiding provincial commands – an attitude which suggests that with the serious approach to administration advocated by Tiberius these were among other things not very profitable – but also by his positive achievements on various occasions, particularly when the Eastern crisis flared up again, and finally by the

---

[1] TAC., *Ann.*, VI, 12.   [2] *CIL*, XIV, 4535 = *I. It.*, XIII, 1, pp. 189, 219.

many pieces of testimony to concern for the practical needs of the people of the empire furnished by the inscriptions. Indeed from this point of view all the evidence is far from leading us to see the close of Tiberius's reign as a unique period of unrelieved terror.

The new settlement of Armenia, after the death, in 34 or 35, of Zeno Artaxias, was a masterpiece of diplomacy, the credit for which must go to Tiberius, even if he was intelligently assisted by the governor of Syria, L. Vitellius, who in any case had been put in charge of this most important province just at that time by the emperor himself, although he was among the youngest ex-consuls (he had been *consul ordinarius* in 34). Obviously the age of theatrical missions by young princes of the blood was over. Artabanus III, king of the Parthians, grown arrogant after long years of prosperous rule, had issued an open challenge to Rome by placing on the throne of Armenia his own son Arsaces and sending Tiberius an ultimatum in which he demanded the restitution of the treasure left in Syria seventeen years earlier by Vonones and quite simply the evacuation by the Romans of all the territory which had belonged to the Seleucids. But Tiberius had already secretly received a deputation of Parthian notables asking for the speedy return of the youngest of the sons of Phraates IV, also called Phraates and perhaps now the only survivor of the four brothers sent to Rome by their father in 10 B.C., as recorded in the *Res Gestae* of Augustus (Chap. 32). Phraates was to be set up in opposition to Artabanus, and Tiberius gladly let him go; but soon after his arrival in Syria, while he was re-accustoming himself to Parthian ways of life, the elderly pretender died. He was immediately replaced by another Arsacid, Tiridates. As for Armenia, Tiberius avoided setting up a Roman candidate in direct opposition to the one already installed by Artabanus – which would have meant war with Parthia – and supported instead the Iberian Mithridates, who, after being reconciled with his brother Pharasmenes and having Arsaces removed from the scene by poison, succeeded in leading into Armenia a powerful army of Iberians, Albanians and Sarmatians, vainly opposed by Artabanus, who sent his son Orodes against them. Thus the Parthians and Iberians fought among themselves while the legions, under L. Vitellius, looked on. Tiberius's great principle in foreign policy, 'consiliis et astu res externas moliri, arma procul habere',[1] had once again been applied with success.

The Iberians in fact defeated first Orodes's army in Armenia and then Artabanus himself, who withdrew from the area thanks also to the rumour that the Roman legions were about to invade Mesopotamia. This

---

[1] TAC., *Ann.*, VI, 32, 1.

withdrawal was fatal to him, for he was abandoned by his own people, who had already been won over by the diplomacy of Vitellius, and he was forced to take refuge in the depths of Hyrcania and live the life of a hunter. Tiridates, after receiving the homage of the great nobles of Parthia and after being escorted across the Euphrates by the legions, which returned from there to Syria, marched to Ctesiphon, where he was crowned. But because he did not listen to the request of two governors for a brief postponement of the ceremony these people turned back again to Artabanus, who came down to their assistance from his refuge on the borders of Scythia and very soon succeeded, thanks to the fickleness of his people and the irresolution of his adversary, in reconquering the throne. Tiridates fled to Syria and the Romans did not judge it expedient to help him; having achieved the settlement they wanted in Armenia, a settlement recognized also by Artabanus, they made no difficulty about leaving him undisturbed, hoping that he had been tamed by the lesson which he had received. Whether it was still in Tiberius's reign, as would appear from Flavius Josephus (*Ant. Iud.*, XVIII, 101–5 [4,5]), that the meeting on the Euphrates between L. Vitellius and Artabanus took place, a meeting similar to that of Gaius Caesar with Phraataces in A.D. 1, or in the reign of Gaius, as is implied by the silence of Tacitus in the sixth book of the *Annals*,[1] is of no great importance in the assessment of this brilliant success, the effects of which, though briefly disturbed by the wild interventions of Gaius, were durable. Mithridates, exiled under Gaius, nevertheless returned to Armenia, where he ruled until 51, and Parthia, very soon torn again by fresh internal feuds, was for some time no longer a danger to the empire.

So far as this same Eastern sector is concerned, Flavius Josephus (*Ant. Iud.*, XV, 405–7 [11,4]; XVIII, 88–95 [4,2–3]), provides us with further details, not recorded by Tacitus, of Tiberius's shrewd administration through the agency of L. Vitellius. For example, there were the interventions in Palestine to incorporate in the province of Syria, in conformity with the principles laid down by Augustus, the tetrarchy of Philip, who had died in 34, and subsequently to dismiss the ill-famed procurator Pontius Pilate who, alternating between weakness ('I am innocent of the blood of this just man!', Matth. 27: 24) and cruelty (massacre of the Samaritans on Mount Gerizim) had exasperated the difficult people he had been sent to govern. Vitellius, on the other hand, respecting the mentality and customs of the Jews, avoided entering Jerusalem with the legions when he returned to Judaea in 37 to help Herod Antipas against

---

[1] Supported by CASS. D., LIX, 27, 3 and SUET., *Calig.*, 14, 3.

Aretas, king of Nabataea – an operation cut short by the news of the death of Tiberius. Tacitus himself on the other hand informs us here (*Ann.*, VI, 41, 1) of a short expedition by one of Vitellius's generals, M. Trebellius, against the Cietae of Cappadocia, who had revolted for fiscal reasons and were soon reduced to order. Vitellius's administration in general is an example of good provincial government; and it lies in the last period of Tiberius and under his direct influence. It should be noted that the very same Vitellius, recalled to Rome by Gaius in 39 and constrained by continual fear to commit every kind of vileness, subsequently left behind him a detestable memory.

If to this we add the inscriptions, not only those containing the homages paid to the Princeps immediately after the victory over Sejanus,[1] but also those which in the most distant regions, from the Iron Gates on the Danube[2] to Spain,[3] from Gaul[4] to Africa,[5] bear witness, even after the numerous works of the preceding period, to the continuation of an attentive care particularly for the improvement of roads and the increase of public building, and in general for the well-being of all the provinces, we may conclude that while the Tiberius of the last years may have seemed a cruel despot to the circles nearest to him – the nobility involved in the emotional events of the court and the urban populace exasperated by his absence and his parsimony – he did not seem so to the empire, which saw in him an enlightened monarch.

In these last months the now seventy-eight year old emperor must nevertheless have shown signs of failing health and may well have seen that the end was very near, in spite of his capacity to remain stoically

---

[1] e.g., *CIL*, XI, 4170 = *ILS*, 157 (Interamna, A.D. 32); *CIL*, III, 12036 = *ILS*, 158 (Gortyna, Crete); *CIL*, XI, 3872 = *ILS*, 159 (Capena, A.D. 32/33); *AE*, 1922, 40 (Oneum, Dalmatia, A.D. 33).

[2] *CIL*, III, 1698 (= *ILS*, 2281); 13813b (A.D. 33/34).

[3] *CIL*, II, 4778, 4904, 4945, 4947 (A.D. 32/33); 4883 (A.D. 33/34); 4712, 4715 (A.D. 35/36). See MARSH, *op. cit.*, p. 210.

[4] *CIL*, XII, 5445, 5449, 5557, 5558, 5600, 5619, 5665 (A.D. 31/32).

[5] *CIL*, VIII, 25844 (Membressa, A.D. 32/33); *CIL*, VIII, 25516 (Bulla Regia, A.D. 34/35); *AE*, 1914, 172 (= *Inscr. Lat. d'Afr.*, 558, Thugga, A.D. 36/37); ROMANELLI, in *Afr. Ital.*, VII, 1940, pp. 87 ff. (= *AE*, 1948, 1 = *Inscr. of Rom. Tripolitania* 330, 331): the monumental inscription repeated twice on one arch and once on another at Leptis Magna (A.D. 35/36) to record the restoration of all the streets of the city carried out by the proconsul C. Rubellius Blandus, the husband of Julia, daughter of Drusus and widow of Nero Caesar, 'ex reditibus agrorum quos Lepcitanis restituit'. The proconsulship of Rubellius Blandus, of which we already knew, is thus now shown to have been the proconsulship of Africa. In the same years 35–36 Rubellius Blandus restored the theatre at Leptis (*Inscr. Rom. Trip.*, 269 = *AE*, 1951, 84). Cf. *Inscr. Rom. Trip.*, 332, 333, 540 (Leptis); and also I. GISMONDI, 'Il restauro dello strategheion di Cirene', in *Quad. Arch. della Libia*, II, 1951, pp. 7–25.

imperturbable in the face of death – the ultimate proof, in Tacitus's view (*Ann.*, VI, 50, 1), of his habitual hypocrisy. On 16 March 37 he passed away in the villa near Misenum that had once belonged to Lucullus. It was stated officially that his death was due to natural causes, but there were all kinds of rumours, traces of which remain in the different versions preserved by the tradition. According to one story he was poisoned or strangled by Gaius;[1] according to another he was refused food when he called for it as he was recovering from an attack of fever;[2] and according to a third he was suffocated under a mound of cushions by Macro. This last tale alleged that when everyone thought Tiberius was already dead and people were rushing to pay homage to Gaius, it was announced that he had regained consciousness; amid the general consternation the embarrassing situation was swiftly resolved by the enterprising praetorian prefect.[3] The story of natural death, according to which Tiberius fell lifeless to the floor near his bed, from which he had risen to look for something when the servants did not answer his call – a version given only by Seneca the Rhetorician[4] and written moreover in the reign of Gaius (Seneca died before 41) – may well nevertheless be the most authentic one.

Such was the end of Augustus's successor. Examination of his work, illuminating as it does virtues and defects, merits and faults, leads us to a clearly favourable verdict on the imperial administrator and to a partly adverse one – if we look at the results more than at the intentions – on the man as head of the family and repository of the concept of the principate. A conscientious executor of Augustus's plans, in foreign affairs Tiberius was completely successful in carrying out his task; the system was not only shown to be viable but also reinforced in such a way that it was able to survive unimpaired through moments of crisis at the centre under Gaius and Nero and beyond. But at home the attempt to follow the same line of deference to Augustus's programme turned out – in spite of good intentions – to be a difficult enterprise. This was partly because Tiberius was a very different person from his predecessor and partly because there had been objective changes in some of the circumstances. The result was that a Senate which he wished to be more independent was left still more servile and the principate which he strove to render even more like the free Republic assumed for the first time the aspect of a tyranny.

[1] SUET., *Tib.*, 73; *Calig.*, 12.   [2] SUET., *Tib.*, 73.
[3] TAC., *Ann.*, VI, 50, 4–5, and, with some differences of detail, SUET., *Tib.*, 73 and CASS. D., LVIII, 28, 1–3.
[4] Cited by SUET., *Tib.*, 73.

We have already underlined how much in this fatal evolution was due to his own fault and how much to adverse interpretation, which then passed into the work of the historians and obliges us even today, when we try to reconstruct Tiberius's reign, to follow events over terrain, such as that of the trials, which in other circumstances would not have been made the object of such acute attention. And we have seen how Tiberius the man, acquitted of the most serious accusations of a moral nature – those of hypocrisy, of suspiciousness, of dissoluteness, of encouraging informers and of deliberate cruelty to innocent people – does not all the same escape other charges which, while morally irrelevant and indeed from this point of view even possibly claims to merit, were in the context of the period politically serious – the charges of lack of tact and of contempt for popularity and the conventions dear to his contemporaries. In addition, there were all the mistakes provoked by his hesitations – mistakes like the withdrawal to Capri and the consequent appearance of tyranny in his written interventions in the Senate; the continual uncertainty in solving the problem of the succession, and hence the sometimes too yielding, sometimes too energetic attitude to the family of Germanicus; the excessive trust reposed in Sejanus and then the inevitable chain of reprisals against his friends after he had fallen; and finally the failure to initiate Gaius into the business of governing. These mistakes not only helped to damn his memory in the judgement of his own age and in that of a posterity seeking the origins and most terrible examples of the degeneration of the principate into tyranny, but were also in actual fact the cause of undeniable damage. But even if we grant the effect of Tiberius's personal weakness on his political behaviour, the honesty of his intentions still remains intact. If we add to this the acknowledged excellence of his imperial administration, in which he himself nurtured the seed which, maturing in Flavian society and carrying to the top fresh forces from the *municipia* and the provinces, was to compensate even for the urban tyranny which also developed in his reign out of the tragic ambiguity of his relations with the dynasty and the nobility, enough is left, not just to dismiss Tiberius with a verdict of 'not guilty', but to place him among the better emperors.

II

GAIUS

EARLY DAYS

The succession of Gaius, an easy and undisputed one, must have produced a clear sense of reaction in comparison with the reign of Tiberius. The new Princeps brought back the memory of Germanicus and represented the recovery of his family, encircled by the halo of martyrdom as a result of the unhappy ends of Agrippa and of Nero and Drusus Caesar. In the eyes of Tiberius's opponents, who had become ever more numerous because of his fatal errors, this was sufficient guarantee of a radical change. Now at last they would see the inauguration of the régime that would have been that of Germanicus and still earlier might have been that of Gaius and Lucius Caesar. No one really knew Gaius, but his family's popularity, based not only on its direct descent from Augustus but also on its supposed inheritance of the particular gifts of tact and munificence which had adorned the architect of the empire but had not been among those of his successor, may have raised hopes of the advent of a régime of generosity at the centre, in which the understanding and gentlemanly indulgence of the Princeps would correspond with gilded society's demand for freedom of movement, even though the principate continued to remain a now established reality.

Instead, the reign of Gaius was a wild tyranny (whatever view we take of the mental condition of the Princeps himself), which already revealed in the third holder of the position of princeps the most dangerous aspects of the system, that is, 'quid summa vitia in summa fortuna possent',[1] and that what was henceforth in effect a monarchy, whenever it was 'unius vitio praecipitata',[2] could become the worst of régimes, thus provoking the need for tyrannicide as the only remedy in the absence of any other constitutional guarantee against the excessive powers of the princeps, with the intervention of the factor which was to become the usual and indispensable one in such cases, namely the alliance of the defenceless Senate with the praetorian cohorts and the palace ministers. Fortunately

[1] SENECA, *Dial.*, XII (*Ad Helv. Matr.*), 10, 4.   [2] CIC., *De Rep.*, II, 23, 43.

the solid foundations laid by Augustus and consolidated by Tiberius for the substantial reality of administering the empire ensured that its structure felt little of these mad interludes, which were in any case of brief duration.

Born at Antium on 31 August A.D. 12, Gaius was not yet twenty-five at the moment of his accession, a point which he had reached almost effortlessly thanks to Tiberius's lukewarm interest in the dynastic problem. There was no competition – thanks to the series of circumstances already mentioned – either from Germanicus's surviving brother Claudius, who had always remained in the shadow of a tacit disdain because he seemed to be psychologically abnormal, or from the feeble son of Drusus and grandson of Tiberius, Tiberius Gemellus, now at least seventeen but not yet wearing the *toga virilis*, although he had been named heir in the will on an equal footing with Gaius and thus designated to a certain extent to succeed to the principate with him. The decisive action of Macro also helped to eliminate any uncertainty. Scarcely was Tiberius dead when the praetorian prefect went from Misenum, where he had already made the soldiers and the sailors of the fleet swear allegiance to the new Princeps, to Rome with the will, and as early as 18 March induced the Senate, through the consuls, to confer on Gaius, who so far had never received the imperial salutation, the title *imperator* and to recognize his position as sole princeps. Tiberius's will was declared null and void. It was from this day, the anniversary of which, it was decided, was to be celebrated under the name of *Paliliae*, as if Rome were celebrating its re-foundation, that Gaius counted the years of his *tribunicia potestas*; the other titles, such as *Augustus, pontifex maximus* and finally *pater patriae* – the last a title adopted officially by Augustus only after repeated requests in 2 B.C. and always refused by Tiberius – were assumed soon afterwards.

Gaius arrived in Rome on 28 March, after accompanying the body of his predecessor in a solemn procession the whole length of the Appian Way, amid wild applause for the new Princeps; on the night of 28/29[1] the corpse was carried into the city by the soldiers and the ashes were deposited in the mausoleum of Augustus. Apotheosis was requested, but the matter was allowed to drop; thus Tiberius never became 'divus'. Animated by the vague feelings of good will and general benevolence excited in him by the enthusiastic welcome he had received, the young Princeps, calling himself the son and pupil of the Senate,[2] declared that it was his aim to make it his

---

[1] This is how DEGRASSI, *Inscr. Ital.*, XIII, 1. p. 220, reconciles the date *IIII K. Apr.* (29 March) in the *Fasti Ostienses* with the *V.K. Apr.* of the Acta of the *Fratres Arvales*, *CIL*, VI, 2028.   [2] CASS. D., LIX ,6, 1.

close collaborator in the work of government. At the same time, in a speech to the praetorian guards, he promised to pay in double measure the legacy of Tiberius (that is, 500 denarii per head), thus considering the will valid so far as gifts were concerned. This promise was punctually kept, among other things with the apposite minting of coins for the occasion. The *donativum* to the urban cohorts, the *cohortes vigilum* and the legions was paid in the same fashion, while the *congiarium* to the populace of 60 denarii per head was raised – by a precedent going back significantly to Julius Caesar[1] – a further 15 denarii by way of interest (1 June 37). The basis for the interest was the *congiarium* promised by Tiberius in 31 on the occasion of the assumption of the *toga virilis* by Gaius himself and never paid out; this *congiarium* was subsequently repeated without any apparent reason and in the same measure on 19 July.[2] Similarly, Julia Augusta's legacies, disregarded by Gaius's predecessor, were also paid, and so too were Tiberius's own bequests, down to the last sesterce. These beginnings were naturally well calculated to confirm in the soldiers and the urban populace hopes of a golden principate, hopes also shared by the provinces, where the oath of allegiance was sworn as soon as Gaius's accession was announced and preparations were put in hand to despatch the delegations which came thronging to Rome in the early months of the new reign to honour the 'New Sun'.[3] As for the oath, which Gaius later wished to be renewed every year, it was an expression of the *consensus*, the semi-private basis of the *auctoritas* (there was thus no change constitutionally in the essence of the Augustan principate); besides the mention in Josephus (*Ant. Iud.*, XVIII, 124 [5,3]) of the one sworn by the Jews and the reference to that of the Boeotians in an inscription from Acraephiae,[4] we can still read the precise formula in the inscriptions from Aritium in Lusitania[5] and from Assus in the Troad.[6] Still in the early atmosphere of exaltation, Gaius also performed the pious duty of visiting the islands where his mother and his brother Drusus had ended their lives in exile and bringing back their ashes to the mausoleum of Augustus's family, where the inscriptions on their urns can still be read today.[7] This episode, too, contributed to his reputation and to the definitive triumph of the ideal of government symbolized by the memory of Germanicus.

---

[1] SUET., *Caes.*, 38. 1.

[2] The *Fasti Ostienses* (*Inscr. It.* XIII, 1, pp. 191, 220) confirm SUET., *Calig.*, 17, 2.

[3] DITTENBERGER, *Syll.*³, 798, 2 (decree of 37).

[4] *Inscr. Gr.*, VII, 2711, 21 ff. = *ILS*, 8792.

[5] *CIL*, II, 172. Cf. p. 810 = *ILS*, 190 and addend.

[6] *Inscr. Gr. ad res Rom. pertinentes* IV, 251 = DITTENBERGER, *Syll.*³, 797.

[7] *CIL*, VI, 886, 887. Cf. 31192, 31193 and 3777 = *ILS*, 180, 183.

Tiberius was more than ever forgotten, even though his name was bound to recur in certain ceremonies. The family of Germanicus reached the zenith of its fortunes: Antonia, the grandmother, became *Antonia Augusta*, and priestess of Divus Augustus, as Livia had been; public tributes and commemorative games in honour of the family's dead multiplied; Gaius's sisters – Julia Agrippina, Julia Drusilla and Julia Livilla – enjoyed with Antonia the status of Vestal virgins and the privilege of being mentioned with the Princeps in the sacred ritual and the prayers for the new year; the month of September was called Germanicus; in Egypt Drusieus and Neroneus[1] also appeared as names of months. So did Drusilleus,[2] probably after the death of Drusilla. The empire supported these marks of favour, as is clear from local coins and inscriptions in both East and West. Tiberius Gemellus, the only person who could remind people of a different line of counterpoint in the dynastic concert and possibly present a different centre of attraction, was adopted by Gaius when he put on the *toga virilis*, named *princeps iuventutis* and for the time being left in peace. The neglected Claudius was taken by Gaius as his colleague in his first consulship, which, out of respect for the consuls already in office, was modestly assumed only on 1 July, although the Senate had already offered it to him earlier and also granted a repetition for all succeeding years. When he took up office as consul Gaius crowned his munificent conduct with an explicit statement of policy; his mode of government was to be the reverse of that of Tiberius. In particular, he had already emptied the prisons of those accused of treason under his predecessor; he had destroyed, so he said, the records of the trials of Agrippina and his brothers without reading them, thus ridding anyone possibly implicated of the fear of reprisals; he had paid no attention to the denunciation made to him of a conspiracy; he had permitted the circulation of the historical works forbidden under Tiberius; he had forbidden the erection of statues to him; and he had invited people not to put themselves out to pay homage to him in the street. In short, here we have the whole series of laudable actions which the ancient anecdotists were pleased to collect in preparation for the time when Gaius, too (like Tiberius in 23, on the death of Drusus), reached the unforeseen point of breakdown and transformation, after which there would be nothing but perversity and folly. However, from 19 August, the anniversary of the death of Augustus, to 31 August, the birthday of Gaius, festivals for the dedication of the divine Augustus's temple, now completed, still

[1] *Ryl. Pap.*, II, 149.
[2] Papyrus in *Journ. of Egypt. Arch.*, XIII, 1927, p. 185 (A. E. R. BOAK).

demanded the unanimous and joyous participation of the whole people in the splendid celebrations, which were replete with every kind of show, largesse and splendour. We also possess evidence of displays of modesty with regard to the empire, such as the expression of thanks to the *koinòn* of the Achaeans, Boeotians, Locrians, Phocians and Euboeans, on 19 August 37, for their message of congratulations; with the thanks went permission to erect statues to him in the principal places, provided that this did not involve heavy expenditure.[1]

On 1 September Gaius, together with Claudius, laid down the consulship.[2] In October came the illness which aroused apprehensions everywhere and caused prayers that were certainly sincere to rise for his recovery. Even if some people may have begun to note the essential vacuity of the new ruler, he was still preferable, with his easy-going attitude, to possible struggles over the succession. We are not informed about the nature of the illness, and what is reported about the insomnia from which Gaius suffered and the epilepsy to which he had been subject since childhood,[3] and what we learn from various episodes about the delicacy of his health,[4] is not necessarily more closely related to this illness than to the general disposition of his physique, no doubt tainted like that of the other young men of the family and subjected in addition to the strain of unremitting intemperance. The illness itself was probably a result of this intemperance. That people should have subsequently seen in it the immediate cause of a mental derangement is only too easy to explain, granted the apparent change which they wished to detect in his outward behaviour. But perhaps the difference between the periods before and after the illness should be minimized and attributed not so much to a mental disturbance as to the build-up of a sort of exasperation with his sense of unlimited authority in a weak man devoid of moral principles and ill prepared for the responsible use of the immense power with which he had been invested more by chance than through any real merits.

Just as afterwards he was not to lack wit and intervals of generosity, so even before the illness he had revealed some extremely disquieting signs, including a thirst for blood and shows. In reality he had not carried out, as we have seen, any real act of government; the promise of deference to the Senate had soon taken the concrete shape of asking it for permission to exceed the legal number of pairs of gladiators in the games, and a

[1] Inscr. cited above, p. 82, n. 4, from Acraephiae, containing in fact a letter from Gaius.
[2] *Fasti Ostienses, Inscr. It.*, XIII, 1, pp. 191, 219, which support SUET., *Calig.*, 17, 1, *Claud.*, 7, against CASS. D., LIX, 7, 9.
[3] SUET., *Calig.*, 50, 2–3. It is well known that Julius Caesar too was an epileptic.
[4] *Ibid.* He was indisposed even on the day when he was murdered, *ibid.*, 58, 1.

popular measure dating probably from this first period consisted in permitting people to take off their shoes in the theatre.[1] A pure piece of
ostentation, if it is to be assigned to the beginning of the reign, was the
transportation from Egypt of an obelisk (the Vatican obelisk) for the
entrance to the temple of Augustus and the construction for this purpose
of a gigantic ship. This quest of the spectacular as an end in itself – a sure
sign of megalomania – characterizes all Gaius's enterprises, from the
ships floating on the Italian lakes (the famous ones of Lake Nemi) to the
order for the rebuilding of the palace of Polycrates of Samos and the
projected canal across the Isthmus of Corinth, just so that he could sail
through it when he went to the East. In the same way, any positive intention to further the interests of the empire was certainly absent from
his assignation of the tetrarchies already belonging to Philip and Lysanias
to his dearest friend, the Jewish prince Julius Agrippa,* and of Commagene to Antiochus, contrary to the principles of the eastern policy
followed not only by Tiberius but also by Augustus. And if we can accept
the stories of cruelty and insensibility recorded by the sources in connection
with his behaviour to Antonia, honoured a little earlier in the fashion we
have seen and then, so it is said, poisoned by him or driven to suicide,[2]
stories which the recent discovery of the date of Antonia's death, 1 May
37,[3] force us to refer to the period before the illness, then here are further
reasons for doubting the validity of a simplistic contrast between early
days of unalloyed happiness and a sequel of gloomy tyranny, ushered in by
the affliction of an unexpected bout of madness. Probably the illness
brought nothing more than the confirmation of a young man intoxicated
with power in a dream of complete absolutism inspired by the very
tradition of the family in the figure of his great-grandfather Mark
Antony and nourished in his boyhood by the Egyptian slaves he had encountered in the house of Antonia. So far as methods of putting the
dream into practice were concerned, these had been conveyed to him in little
bits of advice from the eastern princes who had grown up with him and
from that Julius Agrippa who, though now endowed with a kingdom
after spending the last period of Tiberius's reign in chains, must have
certainly continued to remain by the side of the new Princeps until the
end of 37. In any case, Gaius was still surrounded by eastern slaves and
freedmen, especially Egyptians.

Whatever the truth of the matter, the first act of Gaius after his

---

[1] CASS. D., LIX, 7, 7.   [2] *Ibid.*, 3, 6; SUET., *Calig.*, 23. 2.

[3] *Fasti Ostienses, CIL*, XIV, 4535 = *Inscr. It.*, XIII, 1, pp. 191, 220.

* Usually, but wrongly, known in England as Herod Agrippa (Trans.).

recovery, which was hailed with as much enthusiasm as his accession to the throne, was to send orders to Tiberius Gemellus to kill himself, on the grounds that during Gaius's illness he had certainly, as heir, desired his death. In reality it was nothing but the application of the oriental despot's normal practice of eliminating any possible competitor. Claudius was spared because he was regarded as nothing more than a buffoon.[1] No account of the deed was given to the Senate, to whose members their real or presumed behaviour during the illness was however a source of woe, with a savage punishment, though one not devoid of wit, for those who had offered – out of flattery or hope of reward – to die to save the Princeps were now required to keep their promises. Next it was the turn of the Emperor's ex-father-in-law, M. Junius Silanus, whose daughter Junia Claudilla had been given in marriage to the twenty-one year old youth by Tiberius in 33. She had died in 36 or early in 37. The old ex-consul, highly regarded by Tiberius but relentlessly persecuted by the young Princeps, was reduced to despair and committed suicide. These arbitrary acts could still be ascribed, in the optimism of the moment, to the sphere of private caprice, like the marriage, which took place at the end of 37 or the beginning of 38 and lasted only a few days, to Livia (or Cornelia) Orestilla, snatched on the very day of her wedding from her legitimate husband C. Calpurnius Piso – the friend who had invited Gaius to the ceremony – with the witty justification that both Romulus and Augustus had done the same. But these acts had only to be multiplied and to touch more closely and more widely the various different aspects of public life for the threatening nature of this despotic régime to be revealed in its true colours. The rest of Gaius's reign, with its attempt, pursued not without logic, at total absolutism, finally opened everyone's eyes. But another three years were needed to achieve this result, three years during which a number of curious details, such as the fact that the decision to embark on the German and British expeditions was taken seriously by the armies and their commanders, and the behaviour at Rome of men like the future emperor Vespasian, always make one ponder about the real nature of the reactions to a state of affairs which largely escapes any kind of definition but was certainly not uninterruptedly a disordered medley of the results of pure madness, as the tradition asserts.

ABSOLUTISM AND SELF-DEIFICATION

The mystique of power absorbed by the crude and unbridled mind of the young Princeps was soon translated into acts which, however alien at that

---

[1] SUET., *Calig.*, 23, 3.

time to Roman custom, were to be accepted as the route to the formation of the new kind of imperial cult. At the beginning of 38, as already indicated, the names of his three sisters were included with that of the Princeps in the formula of the prayers for the new year, while the oath on the acts of Tiberius was omitted; evidently the memory of the latter continued to grow fainter. At once the Senate put on its bronze coins the likenesses of the princesses, under the guise of goddesses: *Securitas, Concordia* and *Fortuna*.[1] A new element was introduced by the death, towards the middle of 38, of Gaius's favourite sister, the twenty-two year old Drusilla, at that time wife of M. Aemilius Lepidus (no longer of L. Cassius Longinus, assigned to her in 33 by Tiberius). She was probably the only person with any kind of influence over Gaius, who was morbidly attached to her and in the previous year had named her his heir in his will, taking in return for the succession the legacy of her husband M. Aemilius Lepidus. His grief (he even thought of suicide) was comforted by the decree that she should be deified and by the inauguration at Rome, where a college of twenty priests was set up, in Italy and in all the provinces (as can be observed from inscriptions and coins[2]) of the cult of the new goddess, who was equated with Aphrodite. The usual senator who saw her – like Augustus once before – ascending into heaven received a reward of a million sesterces. But the repetition of the comedy for a mere member of the Princeps's family underlined the novelty and enormity of the event. Moreover, if the institution of the new cult is to be connected with the official favour granted to the Egyptian rites of Isis and with the foundation of the *Isaeum* in the Campus Martus, we also have here a relaxation of Tiberius's severity towards eastern religions, although Gaius also showed himself a conservative with regard to the traditional religion, to the point of reviving barbarous old customs in the succession of the *rex Nemorensis*.

Soon afterwards (autumn 38) Gaius rid himself of the influence of Macro, the mainstay of the early days of his principate. He transferred Macro to the prefectship of Egypt and then ordered him to kill himself before he had left the city. The powerful praetorian prefect was followed in death by his wife and many others, condemned on the basis of the documents dealing with the trials of his mother and brothers – the documents which Gaius had declared a year earlier he had burnt without reading – or for their behaviour during the illness or for offending the

[1] M. GRANT, *Rom. Imp. Money*, London 1954, p. 141.
[2] *Inscr. Gr. ad res Rom. pert.*, IV, 78, 145, 1098, 1721; *ILS*, 196–7; coins from Miletus, etc.

divinity of Drusilla. The need to stifle a probably incipient opposition brought back the plague of trials, for which there was also a further motive, now dominant for the first time, namely, lack of money. The squandering of wealth on the continual shows and distributions of largesse, by means of which Gaius retained an unhealthy popularity and the only kind of prestige which he considered appropriate to the sovereign majesty of the Princeps, had absorbed in little more than a year the extensive personal resources accumulated under Tiberius Thus from the end of 38 onwards the effort to acquire money by any possible means was the most odious aspect of the now declared autocracy. There was also a repetition (still in 38, if the event unexpectedly interrupted, as it seems to have done from its place in Cassius Dio's chronological narrative – LIX, 12, 1 – the mourning for Drusilla, and is to be related to the presence in Rome during September and October, attested by the *Acta* of the *Fratres Arvales*, of the governor of Macedonia, P. Memmius Regulus) of the episode of a marriage dictated by caprice, this time one with much wider political echoes in view of the calibre of the persons involved and of the attendant circumstances. This marriage was to Lollia Paulina, Memmius Regulus's wife, whom Gaius recalled from Macedonia with her husband, wedded and soon dismissed, though he forbade her to return to her previous husband or to marry anyone else. Similarly, soon after this, he banished Livia Orestilla as well as C. Calpurnius Piso because after the adventure of the brief marriage with the Princeps she had been reunited with her first husband. These incidents too provide characteristic testimony to what Gaius thought of his own divine person.

We can say that by the end of 38 the effects of misgovernment were already perceptible, and we should be surprised that the situation nevertheless continued, did we not know that the administration of the empire – paradoxical though it may seem – remained for its part largely immune from the interventions of the Princeps, who in any case up to then had not shown much interest in it. The measures he took were for the most part theatrical and provoked by sudden opportunities. Whether he happened to put out a fire personally with the *vigiles* or whether, in contrast to Tiberius, he resumed the useless publication of the accounts, restored some aspect of the electoral functions of the *comitia*, drew up a fresh *lectio* of the senators and knights, instituted a fifth *decuria* of judges, thus making himself popular among the middle class inscribed on that list (as already among those on the third and fourth), demagogically abolished some taxes, or ordered work to start on the aqueduct of the *Anio Novus*, all these actions had for the most part limited echoes within the urban area of Rome alone.

In 39 he was consul for the second time, for the whole month of January, showing, both in assuming and in laying down office, respect for the strictest legal norms. But soon afterwards he gave the most odious displays of senseless caprice, again corresponding with the ever more pressing scarcity of money, which was nevertheless still squandered without restraint. 'And there was nothing but massacres',[1] especially in the circus, by now an important centre of public life, where the victims of a new wave of trials were forced to fight and condemned to die as gladiators, in addition to the usual shows of unparalleled ferocity and the bloodthirsty reprisals against spectators who rioted or who had simply seemed to differ from the Princeps in their choice of circus faction to support. This period of more intense and quarrelsome contact with the urban mob was interrupted by Gaius's unexpected departure for Campania. From there he went on as far as Sicily where, presiding at Syracuse over the games in honour of Drusilla, he rewarded the city for its adroit homage by restoring its walls and temples. On the way to Sicily he had ordered the construction at Rhegium of an emergency port for the ships employed in bringing corn supplies from Egypt – the only useful thing he ever did in the view of the ancients,[2] although it is not known whether he subsequently completed it or whether, as in the case of the aqueduct of the *aqua Virgo*, which he caused to be demolished and forgot to rebuild, the first enthusiasm was never followed by any concrete action. In fact neither at the start of his reign nor later was he much interested in works of real public utility; or at any rate the very few of his milestones known to us do not suffice to show that he was. The milestone found recently in Spain is a real rarity.[3] Returning to Rome, he celebrated the festivals in honour of Drusilla's birthday; he had an ivory statue of the goddess driven round the circus and once again began holding games and distributing money with mad prodigality. From now onwards no one's money was any safer from the Princeps's favour than from his anger; it was exposed not only to the danger of confiscation through the owner's conviction, or through fines and reprisals of every kind, but also to that of having to be used for the hasty acquisition, at exorbitant prices fixed by the Princeps, of the surviving gladiators at the end of the games (this duty was imposed on the senior magistrates). There was also the threat of testamentary spoliation. This was partial if the Princeps was included among the heirs,

[1] CASS. D., LIX, 13, 2.   [2] JOSEPH., *Ant. Iud.*, XIX, 205 (2, 5)
[3] *AE*, 1952, 112.

total if he had been forgotten; bachelors were obliged by law to make the Princeps their sole heir – and Gaius did not disdain to become the legatee of mere centurions.

The Senate as a whole was threatened. The reversal of his initial goodwill towards it was in any case brutally asserted in a speech in which Gaius, who in his previous moods had constantly criticized Tiberius, declared that from then onwards he regarded the latter as his model. So far as the formal re-introduction of trials for treason was concerned, he reproved the senators, not without a certain rough logic, for criticizing Tiberius about trials in which they themselves had been prosecutors and judges, as emerged from the documents which he caused to be read out by the freedmen. He added a rhetorical tirade to increase the fear of his dismayed audience and, after ordering that his speech should be posted up, hurriedly left the senate house and retired first to a villa on the outskirts of the city and then once again to Campania. The senators responded on the following day by voting praises for his sincerity and piety and thanks for not having had them all put to death; in commemoration of this a sacrifice was to be celebrated in future on the anniversary of the speech and during the *Ludi Palatini*, and a golden statue of Gaius was to be carried up to the Capitol amid choirs of maidens. Meanwhile Gaius was granted an *ovatio*, that is, the lesser sort of triumph. But he was already far away and disdained the honour offered him, procuring for himself instead a triumph, which was the clearest outward manifestation of the chaotic medley of emotions and of historical and mythological reminiscences of every kind that lay at the base of his own theory of absolute power. Like Xerxes at the Hellespont, he built a bridge some three miles long from his villa at Bauli to Puteoli with the aid of merchant ships from the corn trade, requisitioned at the cost of letting Rome go hungry, and rode over it on horseback, wearing a crown of oak-leaves and the cuirass believed to have belonged to Alexander the Great. He then made a sacrifice to Neptune, whose personification he believed himself to be on this occasion, and to Invidia. The next day he crossed the bridge again in a chariot, wearing a tunic embroidered with gold and taking with him Darius, son of Artabanus III of Parthia, who had been sent to Rome as a hostage. He was accompanied by friends, soldiers and a big crowd, which stayed on the bridge feasting all through the day and late into the night, amid the myriad lights which glittered in the gulf, turning 'night into day' just as Gaius, with a more than human design, had wanted to 'turn the sea into land',[1] until finally many drunks fell into the water and the Princeps

[1] CASS. D., LIX, 17, 9.

allowed himself the fun of pushing some of them in. This spectacular feast left a profound impression on people. Suetonius heard about it from his grandfather, who, rejecting the explanation, which he regarded as feeble, that it was a sort of display of force designed to frighten the Germans and Britons just before the campaign planned against them, maintained, having heard it stated by Gaius's own courtiers,[1] that the real motive of the display had been to fulfil and at the same time refute Thrasyllus's prophecy to the old Tiberius, that Gaius had as much chance of reigning as of riding across the gulf of Baiae on horseback, that is, no chance at all. It was a refutation which could be reconciled perfectly with his pretensions to omnipotence, asserted to annoy the envious; the sacrifice to Invidia is a significant clue.

Returning to Rome to recoup his expenses, he proceeded with enthusiasm to keep his promise of a systematic revival of trials for treason; his own court and that of the Senate sat simultaneously to carry out the great task. Among the illustrious victims who anticipated conviction by committing suicide were C. Calvisius Sabinus, governor of Pannonia, and his wife Cornelia, who was probably the sister of Cornelius Lentulus Gaetulicus, the able governor of Germany, himself very near to ruin; Titius Rufus, for an imprudent remark; Julius Graecinus – father of Agricola, Tacitus's father-in-law – already disliked for some time by Gaius because he had refused to support the charge against M. Junius Silanus; Junius Priscus, whose death Gaius later regretted when it turned out that he was not as rich as the Emperor had thought; and others too. At that time both Cn. Domitius Afer, the orator, and Seneca ran the risk of being killed because the Princeps did not tolerate competition in the field of oratory; however, one escaped through his readiness of speech and the favour of the powerful freedman Callistus, the other through his poor health, which made his death from natural causes seem close at hand. Some days later Domitius was suddenly made consul. It happened in this way: the consuls having strangely forgotten to announce the feast of 31 August, Gaius's birthday – when only the praetors presided over the games – and having on the other hand inaugurated in the regular way the feast of 2 September for the victory of Actium, the angry Princeps forbade the celebration of the defeat of his great-grandfather Antony (out of hatred for Agrippa, the victor, and in conformity with his own ideas of dynastic mystique, he preferred to accept without demur the rumour that his mother Agrippina was not the daughter of Agrippa but of an incestuous union between Augustus and Julia) and made the consuls break the rods, that is to say,

[1] SUET., *Calig.*, 19, 3.

he cancelled their consular authority. One of the consuls immediately killed himself. Three days after this act of unparalleled arbitrariness Gaius demanded the appointment of the new consuls by comitial election in the form restored by himself, but seeing that it did not work (the consuls were his own nominee, Domitius Afer, and Cn. Domitius Corbulo, probably one of the two previous consuls, a man who enjoyed Gaius's favour for advice tendered on the subject of making money), he withdrew the popular concession. But this exercise of open tyranny, which reflected at home his attempt to put fully into effect his programme of absolutism and self-deification, when extended to foreign policy on exactly the same lines, with the forcible imposition of worship of himself and the search for the military glory which he still lacked, was soon going to produce developments dangerous to the empire precisely in the two most delicate sectors, ones treated with the shrewdest political care by his predecessors, namely Germany and the East.

EXTERNAL AFFAIRS

We know too little about the situation on the far side of the Rhine at that particular moment to be able to decide whether or not there was a real necessity for a campaign in Germany, but it is easy to see how Gaius, wishing to gain military glory, should recall the tradition associated with his father. However, the decision to make the expedition was not taken on the spur of the moment, as one might be led to believe by the hasty departure from Rome in the middle of September 39 – a time of year when campaigns usually came to an end – and by the swift journey across Gaul. Arrangements for the preparation of the army and for the levies in Italy and Narbonese Gaul must have been made previously if, as seems likely, we should attribute to Gaius the raising of the two new legions XV and XXII *Primigeniae* which would have brought the strength of the army of the Rhine up to ten legions, a powerful force. Moreover, anticipation of the coming campaign must have played a large part in the exaltation of the new Alexander in the display at Bauli. Another point to be borne in mind is the fact that even in this field the orders of the Princeps were still carried out to the letter, although what we know of the part played by Gaetulicus, powerful governor of Germany for some ten years, in the attempt to get rid of the despot, leads us to think that at bottom the reinforcement of the army of the Rhine was regarded by him as also advantageous to his own ends.

However, the days before the departure also witnessed an episode of great interest, not only in itself and because it is vouched for directly by a contemporary, but also in the context, of which it forms a part, of Gaius's political and, more generally, religious and cultural relations with the East. Above all, it more or less coincides with the official beginning, so far as the Roman Empire is concerned, of the phenomenon of anti-Semitism. The delegation of Jews from Alexandria, led by the famous neo-Platonic philosopher Philo, which had been trying for months (it had arrived in the winter of 38/39) to present its views to the Princeps, but had only succeeded – once at the entrance to the suburban villa where he had retired after the famous speech in the Senate and a second time at Bauli – in meeting him fleetingly and in handing over memoranda to his freedmen, finally managed to obtain an audience, in the adventurous and picturesque fashion described so vividly by its leader in the *Legatio ad Gaium*.[1] Gaius's relations with the East had always been governed more by personal feelings than by general political considerations. This may have been due first to the effect of the impressions he brought back with him when, as a child, he accompanied his parents on Germanicus's mission of 17–19, then to his close contact with the various eastern princes brought up with him at Rome, some of whom were also related to him through Mark Antony, and finally to the part that the East played in his excitable mind as the model for a theocratic monarchy. Thus where the diplomacy of Augustus and Tiberius had created at relatively small expense a fairly secure settlement, which just at the beginning of the new reign, so it seems, even Artabanus of Parthia had brought himself to accept, a few interventions by Gaius were sufficient not only to cause financial loss to the state but also to stir up dangerous ferments and to leave the general situation indubitably worse than he had found it.

Ever since he came to the throne he had been generously distributing kingdoms. To the three sons of King Cotys of Thrace and Antonia Trifena (grand-niece of Antony), namely Cotys, Polemo and Rhoemetalces, who had grown up with him, he assigned respectively lesser Armenia; Pontus and the kingdom of Bosporus (in the latter of which, however, Polemo probably never succeeded in setting foot); and that eastern half of the kingdom of Thrace over which his father had reigned and which under Tiberius had been administered by T. Trebellenus Rufus. C. Julius Laco was reinstated as lord of Sparta. A certain Sohaemus, otherwise unknown to us, was made tetrarch of some of the Ituraean Arabs residing in the Lebanon to the north-west of Damascus; and Damascus itself was given to Aretas, king of the Nabataeans, against whom the

[1] 349–67.

governor of Syria, L. Vitellius, had been on the point of marching in the last days of Tiberius in support of Herod Antipas, tetrarch of Galilee and Peraea.[1] C. Julius Antiochus, son of Antiochus III of Commagene, who had died in 17, received back his father's kingdom, enlarged by a part of the coast of Cilicia, together with an indemnity of a hundred million sesterces for the taxes not received during the twenty years of direct Roman rule.

But the man most in Gaius's good graces, and one who knew how to keep himself there, was the astute Jewish prince Julius Agrippa. Flavius Josephus has left us a vivid description of his picturesque career.[2] Son of Aristobulus and nephew of Herod the Great, he spent almost all his childhood and youth at Rome, where his father had also been brought up. A friend of Tiberius's son Drusus, after the latter's death (A.D. 23) he had returned to Palestine. There his uncle Herod Antipas – who had deserted his first wife, the daughter of the Nabataean Aretas (one of the distant causes of the war), and married Agrippa's sister (and hence his own niece) the celebrated Herodias, with whom he had fallen in love during a visit to Rome round about 14 or 15,[3] snatching her away from his brother Herod – came to the assistance of his destitute nephew and brother-in-law by giving him a post in Tiberias. But the restless and ambitious prince quarrelled with his uncle and after a series of adventures re-appeared in 36, pursued by his creditors, at Rome, where he became a friend of Gaius. He exerted a strong influence on the character of the young man, who was over twenty years younger and looking for just the sort of tuition that the oriental adventurer could give him. Just to be on the safe side, Tiberius kept Agrippa in prison during the last few months of his reign for allegedly uttering a remark disrespectful to himself. Gaius recompensed Agrippa for this by freeing him immediately after Tiberius's death and presenting him with a gold chain of the same weight as the iron one he had worn during his six months in prison. For the moment he assigned to him the former tetrarchies of Philip (Gaulonitis and Trachonitis, incorporated in Syria after the death of Philip in 34) and Lysanias (Abilene, that is, the principal part of the old realm of the Ituraeans), with the title of king, finally having the praetorian insignia conferred on him by the Senate. Agrippa did not proceed at once to take possession of his kingdom, but only set out in the course of the year 38.

[1] See above, p. 76. St Paul, in connection with his escape from Damascus in 39, mentions an ethnarch of Aretas as the authority exercising jurisdiction over the city. 2 Cor. 11: 32; cf. Acts 9: 25. Damascene coins of Gaius and Claudius are in fact missing.

[2] *Ant. Iud.*, XVIII, 143–204 (6, 1–7); 228–39 (6, 10–11).

[3] According to the very probable dating of W. Otto, in *Real-Encyclopädie* Suppl. II (1913, cc. 181–4).

When he was passing through Alexandria, an incident provoked by himself irritated the already latent discord between the Greeks and the Jews, who formed quite a large element in the great city.

The final result was the outbreak of serious disorders, in which the Greeks, backed by the prefect, A. Avillius Flaccus – who, feeling that he was in disgrace with the new Princeps, thought he had found the chance to rehabilitate himself – employed the easy advantage they enjoyed through having no prejudices against the imperial cult in the particular form desired by Gaius to blame the Jews, who rejected it. They demanded that the synagogues should be turned into temples of Gaius and responded to Jewish resistance with destruction and massacre. Although the prefect, who must have already been replaced by Macro, was taken to Rome under arrest in October 38 and, swept up in the wave of trials which followed the fall of the powerful praetorian prefect, was condemned to exile, the Jews, and not only those of Alexandria, offended in the sensitive area of their religion and ancestral customs, never forgave Gaius for this, although they had hailed his accession with joy like the rest of the empire. The Princeps for his part, who until then had had no particular reason for disliking the Jews, began to hate them and to provoke them with imprudent levity. Thus while Augustus and Tiberius had sometimes been hard on the Hebrews in Rome, expelling them and subjecting them to police regulations, but had treated them with respect in their own country, Gaius offended them as a people in their most sensitive spot. He thus fanned the dangerous fire which, spreading over all the East and flaring up now here, now there in succeeding years, was only with difficulty held in check by the skill of the local organs of government. In fact so long as the whole affair was limited to the Alexandrian episode it was not yet of irreparable gravity.

The particular question of the Alexandrian Jews, which had been submitted – as we have seen – to Gaius, had from the start very little chance of being resolved favourably, not only because of the Princeps's general disposition but also because the court freedmen, especially Helicon, were hostile to the Jews for other reasons and therefore favoured the counter-delegation of Alexandrians also present in Rome. This other delegation was led by Apion, the pedantic charlatan whom Josephus was to attack in a piece of writing that has come down to us. The mockery of an audience held in September 39 – when Gaius rushed from one room to another of two villas that he was furnishing and forced the ambassadors to run after him – emphasized as it was by the laughs of the Jews' opponents and concluded by the Princeps with the admission that these Jews seemed to be worthy people but incapable of understanding his own divine nature, only exasperated the local situation. It also had wide repercussions because the support given to the Alexandrians presented the enemies of the Hebrews with a weapon with which to persecute them. Worst of all, Gaius became blinded by the desire to overcome an obstinacy all the more irritating because it was isolated (the Christians were certainly not yet an independent political entity or in any case one socially and ethnically differentiated from the Hebrews) and also courageous, as was shown, probably in the spring of 39, by the destruction of an altar erected to Gaius by the Greek population of the imperial domain of Iamnia, on the coast of Palestine – an affair which the procurator, Herennius Capito, referred immediately to the Princeps. Thanks to this blindness, Gaius sent orders to P. Petronius, who had now succeeded Vitellius as governor of Syria, to put up in the actual temple of Jerusalem a statue of Zeus in his own likeness, smashing any resistance, if necessary, with the legions. Petronius, a man of good sense and a diplomat 'of the school of Tiberius',[1] while giving orders for the construction of the statue at Sidon and posting himself with his troops first at Ptolemais, then at Tiberias, tried to drag out the affair, also profiting no doubt from the absence from Rome of Gaius, who was occupied from the autumn of 39 to the late spring of 40 with the German and British campaigns. However, in the spring of 40 he had to take some sort of action again. The Jews besieged him with proposals and supplications and then turned to acts of desperation such as abandoning the harvest, so that in the end he returned to Antioch, succeeding for the moment in justifying himself to Gaius who, soon after returning to Italy (at the end of May 40), accepted the excuse but repeated the order. However, summer saw the arrival in the neighbourhood of Rome, where Gaius was residing, of his friend Julius Agrippa, now king of the greater part of the old kingdom of Herod the Great, since in the previous year he had also been given Galilee and Peraea. Herod Antipas and Herodias had been exiled to Lyon; envious of the fortunes of their relative and especially of his royal title, they had come to Baiae and taken the false step of accusing him to the Princeps, consequently succumbing themselves to a counter-accusation with which the astute adventurer had forestalled them. Agrippa now succeeded in persuading Gaius, after a long discussion according to Philo,[2] or more probably with a sumptuous banquet, as Josephus states,[3] to revoke the order about the statue in the case of the temple of Jerusalem only. The governor was to take stern action

---

[1] MOMMSEN, Röm. Gesch., V, p. 518.
[2] Leg. ad Gaium, 261 ff.   [3] Ant. Iud., XVIII, 289–301 (8, 7–8).

against disobedience in other places and the destruction of other statues. But later on Gaius turned inflexible; dreaming, after the German expedition, of the glory of an eastern one, which was to start from Egypt, now his favourite spot, he planned to go in person and proclaim himself God in the temple of Jerusalem, taking with him a statue ordered, for greater security, in Rome itself. Meanwhile, now convinced that Petronius's tergiversations had been intentional, he sent him the order, at the end of December 40, to kill himself; but by some mysterious chance or other the order reached Petronius a good twenty-three days after the news of the murder of the Princeps and thus remained unfulfilled. Judaea too could breathe again, but if the statues of the despot-god fell for ever, the consequences of his mad policy had a long-term effect, especially in the nourishment given to the seeds of discord germinating between the Hebrew and non-Hebrew elements.

As for the German expedition, at the beginning of October 39 Gaius was already on the Rhine, probably at Mogontiacum (Mainz). There the first trap laid by senators awaited him. That he had to expect conspiracies on the part of the Senate was natural, even if he scarcely realized that conduct like his own was bound to provoke a natural reaction in the class most directly exposed to danger. Shortly before, profiting from the assumption of the proconsulship of Africa by L. Calpurnius Piso, the son of his father's enemy, he had stripped the post of the legion which Augustus had left, exceptionally, in this senatorial province and put it under the command of a separate officer (this was also the germ of the province of Numidia). Even if one is unwilling to take the view that the whole German expedition was a pretext for a big recruitment exercise really intended to break the power of Gaetulicus[1] – which would put the action of the Princeps in a totally different light – this power must certainly have given rise to fears. The facts fully confirmed the identity of the possible suspects, for the conspiracy frustrated immediately after the arrival on the Rhine (was Gaius already aware of it when he left Rome, and was this one of the reasons for his haste?) showed that in the web the governor of Germany represented the strength of the legions. However that may be, Cn. Cornelius Lentulus Gaetulicus and M. Aemilius Lepidus, Drusilla's husband and already successor-designate of Gaius in the will when Drusilla was still alive (and now among the conspirators in case they should be successful) were executed in October. Gaius's sisters Agrippina and Julia Livilla, also parties to the conspiracy, were banished, and Agrippina, who had become Lepidus's mistress, was forced to carry

[1] R. SYME, in Camb. Anc. Hist., X, p. 788.

his ashes to Rome in an urn, thus parodying to her shame the journey made twenty years before by her mother with her father's ashes; after this came the veto on paying honours to members of the imperial house. A donative and a severe purge preserved the loyalty of the army, command of which on the Upper Rhine was entrusted to Ser. Sulpicius Galba, the future emperor. Galba did actually launch some operations against the Germans, during which Gaius was saluted as *imperator* seven times, although his own share in the activities was limited to carrying out a raid across the river in which he did not meet anyone. The report on the conspiracy sent to the Senate provoked measures of thanks for the danger escaped, tokens of homage, among them a fresh *ovatio*, and the despatch of a deputation led by Claudius and poorly received by the ill-humoured despot. Later on, the news of the victories was the cause of further honours paid both in Rome and throughout the empire, as is attested by inscriptions.

Meanwhile Gaius had returned for the winter to Gaul and was holding splendid court in Lyon. With him were probably the ill-famed Julius Agrippa – who may have arrived at Baiae the previous summer (39) shortly after Antipas and who, as we have seen, was once again with Gaius in the summer of 40 – and also Antiochus of Commagene, 'the tutors in tyranny'.[1] A third prince, Ptolemy of Mauretania, nephew of Antony and Cleopatra, was sent for by Gaius and then put to death, probably still at Lyon; according to the sources, for no other reasons than his wealth and splendid bearing. This left in Mauretania – previously quiet but now a prey to rebellion because a loyalist faction led by Aedemon was unwilling to accept the status of procuratorial province – another avoidable conflagration. The reason given by Cassius Dio (LIX, 21, 1–2) for the whole expedition, namely that Gaius, having pillaged Italy, was casting glances at the wealth of the Gauls and Iberians, may have originated in the indelible memory left in the province by his lavish expenditure and odious acts of plunder during that winter. All the previous pretexts for confiscation, forced purchases and the most disgraceful expedients were called into play in order to make money; in addition, the order was given to execute all exiles, with the object of laying hands on their property. The freshly discovered conspiracy provided yet further opportunities. On 1 January, at Lyon, the Princeps assumed his third consulship, without a colleague, since the man designated had just died on 31 December. This constitutional anomaly, which the Senate at Rome, meeting without being convoked by anyone, took good care not to repair – it confined itself to

[1] CASS. D., LIX, 24, 1.

paying homage to the empty throne – lasted until 13 January, the day on which Gaius laid down his office and the *consules suffecti* took up theirs. Among the innumerable episodes of this sojourn in Lyon, many of them certainly embroidered by the anecdotists, particular importance is to be attached to Gaius's fourth marriage, this time to one Milonia Caesonia, who was neither young nor beautiful and was already the mother of three daughters; the fourth, born a month after the wedding, was recognized by Gaius and called Julia Drusilla.

But the warlike enterprises were not over yet: in the spring of 40 Gaius marched to the Channel for the projected expedition to Britain. This operation was probably ripe for execution, as is shown by the arrival among the Romans – in contrast with the behaviour of his father Cunobelinus – of the British prince Adminius. This was an indication of the existence of a philo-Roman movement even in the island probed by Julius Caesar and then left outside the limits assigned to conquest by Augustus and respected by Tiberius. But here too Gaius remained content with the surrender of Adminius as if it were a famous victory. Newly hailed *imperator* with the title of Britannicus, he paid a donative of one hundred denarii per head to the soldiers without even attempting the crossing (although he had had the ships prepared), started the construction of a lighthouse on the coast, at Boulogne, and turned back. He went first to the troops on the Lower Rhine, then to Galba on the Upper Rhine, and finally to Italy, where he arrived again by the end of May and stayed in the outskirts of Rome, ostentatiously at loggerheads with the Senate.

We have in fact already mentioned the sort of welcome which he gave to the senatorial deputation the previous autumn at Lyon. The insults and reproaches continued; already, if the start of the imperial coining of gold and silver at Rome is to be placed in the reign of Gaius, another important mode of respect for the Senate, one scrupulously preserved by Augustus and Tiberius, had fallen by the wayside. Yet the Senate now only functioned to anticipate the despot's wishes in the way of honours to his living self and to the dead of his family. Even in this, however, it had been placed to a certain extent in a position of serious embarrassment through the Princeps's veto on voting him honours of any kind. Thus when it was a question of fixing the usual festivities for the British victory, the Senate restricted itself to a deputation requesting his speedy return. This irritated him so much that he complained as if the Senate wanted to defraud him of his triumph, and issued an edict saying that he no longer regarded himself as either the Princeps or fellow citizen of the senators, but that he would return only for the knights and the rest of the people; as for the triumph, he would celebrate it later where his divine nature was fully understood, namely in Egypt, where he dreamed of going to receive the adoration of his loyal subjects. His notions of absolutism and self-deification, resulting henceforth in a sort of permanent delirium, had gone far beyond the limits of tolerance. Abroad, the consequences – fortunately still not too serious – of an ill-considered policy were now manifest. Judaea was in a ferment, Mauretania was in revolt, his friend Antiochus, by falling into disgrace and losing his kingdom, was leaving fresh scope for disorder, and in Armenia the equilibrium, always unstable, was once again rudely and unnecessarily disturbed by the expulsion of Mithridates, who was taken to Rome and then exiled, without any attempt to replace him, so that the way was left open for the reoccupation of Armenia by the Parthians. Meanwhile at home the reaction which would soon put an end to the first attempt at open despotism was mounting steadily.

THE END

On 31 August 40 Gaius solemnly entered Rome, claiming that he was celebrating a mere *ovatio*, but displaying a splendour and prodigality never seen before; still angry with the Senate, he wanted to flatter the people and soldiers. But soon he was to fall out with everyone, and for more practical reasons than the demand that his divinity should be recognized. This was in fact now a *fait accompli* in the East, as is clearly shown by coins and numerous inscriptions. At Didyma, near Miletus, in the precinct sacred to Apollo from the most remote times, there rose, at the expense of the province of Asia, the temple of Gaius. Even at Rome – perhaps as a sign of reconciliation and loyalty after the discovery of the new conspiracy of Sextus Papinius and Betilienus Bassus, a conspiracy betrayed by Anicius Cerealis, adoptive father of the former, and crushed with a horrifying cruelty calculated to discourage further attempts – the Senate finally brought itself in the autumn of 40 to recognize the unparalleled but basically innocuous claim and decreed the erection of a temple, possibly on the Capitol, to the still living Princeps. Gaius, for his part, delighting more than ever in dressing up in the style of the divinities both masculine and feminine which he continued to fancy he embodied, and in having sacrifices of rare birds made to him, had created a temple for himself in the palace. In addition, he regarded as a vestibule to the palace itself, considerably enlarged by the huge substructures still visible, the venerable temple of Castor and Pollux, between whose statues he was accustomed to sit to be adored. He had also joined the Palatine to the Capitol by a bridge, so that he could proceed more quickly to his conversations with Jupiter. He naturally also had priests, who had to pay dearly for the honour; even Claudius and Gaius's wife Caesonia had each to disburse two million sesterces, for his periods of mystical exaltation had not entirely dulled his need for money or hindered him from thinking out every possible means of obtaining it. He now loaded even the common people with taxes, especially taxes on commerce and handicrafts, on the Egyptian model, taking particular care to catch the unwary in contraventions, since then he made even bigger profits; and one day when the people protested in the theatre he sent in soldiers to massacre them. He thus incurred the enmity of the urban populace as well. All he needed to do now was to alienate the only support for his tyranny still loyal to him, the soldiers, whose attachment to the son of Germanicus and the nephew of Augustus had not yet grown less in spite of the punishments inflicted on them, sometimes without motive, and of the gradual diminution of his generosity. By the mad behaviour of his last months he succeeded not only in increasing the hatred of the rest but also in offending the praetorians and in convincing them that violent suppression was the only way left to put an end to a state of affairs now intolerable to everyone.

After the conspiracy of Bassus relations with the Senate were resumed amid the sort of scenes of terror and abject servility which can only be furnished under a tyranny by the collective baseness of bodies composed of men still worthy as individuals. Examples of such scenes were the summary execution, in the senate house itself and by colleagues, of the distinguished senator Scribonius Proculus as soon as he had been named by the freedman who accompanied the Princeps and who carried, in accordance with the oriental practice adopted by Gaius, the book containing the names of the condemned; the flattery of L. Vitellius, who had shown himself to be a man of merit in the governorship of Syria but was now reduced by fear to the role of buffoon and to a state of mind in which he found no difficulty in rendering to the Roman *imperator* the *proskinesis* of the oriental monarch; and the humiliation, all the more bitter to the formalistic Roman conscience, inflicted by the Princeps when he put out his foot to kiss to anyone who thanked him. Then there were his wild commands and the threats of death he hung for the most futile reasons over men like Petronius, of whom we have spoken; Memmius Regulus, governor of Macedonia, who, when ordered to send to Rome the statue of Zeus at Olympia, had pointed out the impossibility of the plan and now awaited punishment; and Cassius Longinus, proconsul of Asia, recalled and put in chains simply because an oracle had warned Gaius to beware of a Cassius (or so the sources tell us, naturally playing *post eventum* on the name of the man who actually killed Gaius, Cassius Chaerea). People had certainly not forgotten the end of a man of the worth and wide connections of Gaetulicus, nor the execution of figures like Calvisius Sabinus, the governor of Pannonia, and Avillius Flaccus, the prefect of Egypt – indications, among others, and ones certainly noted and feared, of Gaius's particular mistrust of provincial governors. Nor is it surprising that among the illustrious victims of the tyranny there were also philosophers like Julius and Rettus, and that it is under Gaius that we must place the start not only of open anti-Semitism but also of the long struggle between the principate and the philosophers.

The conspiracy that finally removed Gaius arose in the circles best adapted to ensure its success; it included not only members of the Senate and the equestrian order but also, as an essential element, praetorian guards and the ministers of the palace. It was the model for the conspiracies which eliminated Domitian and Commodus in strikingly similar combinations of circumstances. According to the account of Flavius Josephus (*Ant. Iud.*, XIX, 1–211 [1–2]), who has most to say about the whole series of events, the senators were represented principally by L. Annius Vinicianus, a relative of the M. Vinicius who had married Julia Livilla, Gaius's sister, and a friend of Lepidus, put to death the previous year. He was joined by the rich senator Valerius Asiaticus, a favourite of the Princeps, who in these last days of folly could no longer distinguish between friends and enemies and had brutally insulted Asiaticus in public. However, the principal part was played by two tribunes of praetorian cohorts, Cornelius Sabinus and Cassius Chaerea, who was angry with Gaius for sneering at his woman's voice (though he was the 'adulescens animi ferox' who in 14 had cut a path with his sword through the rebellious soldiers on the Rhine, T A C., *Ann.* I, 32, 3). Other tribunes were behind these two and so were the prefects themselves, only one of whom, M. Arrecinus Clemens, is known by name (after the fall of Macro, Gaius had restored the collegiality of the praetorian command). From the palace the powerful freedman Callistus – grown too rich to be safe – participated, together with other highly placed ministers, including Narcissus. On 1 January of the year 41 Gaius assumed his fourth consulship, with Cn. Sentius Saturninus as his colleague, but laid down office again on 7 January. On 24 January, the last day of the *Ludi Palatini*, which Gaius had prolonged that year by three days, when the Princeps, in an interval between the shows, was walking through one of the galleries of the palace on the way to take some refreshment and, having paused to admire some Asian boys who were waiting to appear before the public, had been left alone for a moment, the conspirators with Chaerea at their head came on him and felled him to the ground under a hail of blows. The plot had succeeded, but the situation was not devoid of danger, for the German bodyguards immediately tried to avenge their master, and some senators were killed in the confusion. The tyrannicides had at first to take refuge in the house of Germanicus. However, on the same day the Germans were induced to see the futility of their attempts at revenge, the praetorian troops backed their leaders, and even the populace, which at first had assembled in a threatening way in the forum, was persuaded by the Senate, particularly by the abolition of the hated taxes, to stay quiet and wait. In the evening the tragedy concluded with the brutal killing, on the orders of Chaerea, of Caesonia and the little Julia Drusilla, wife and daughter of the dead tyrant.

So ended the experiment in oriental absolutism, a very premature one in the story of the principate. However, it showed that the framework established by Augustus could hold, without any constitutional modification, even oriental despotism; which in turn gives us a fresh piece of evidence about the nature of the principate. The difference between the reign of Augustus and that of Gaius is the difference between the two men concerned. Augustus's tact and moderation made him see the laws of the Republic as the voluntary, not the constitutional, limit to his will; Gaius made his will law and, tearing away all legal fictions, became the first undisguised master of the Roman state. His concept of omnipotence, complicated by an obscure belief in his own natural divinity, impelled him to regard every wish of his own as a necessary manifestation of his position as Princeps, which would have had limits if subordinated to laws or even if only directed by a sense of responsibility or just of paternalistic function. It was natural in any case that to be princeps should signify for completely amoral men like those already appearing in the last days of the Republic (Clodius can stand for them all) the exclusive and egoistic affirmation of their own personalities and the satisfaction of all their desires, with that systematic exercise of free will which in the case of Gaius led to the results described. As for the attempt at self-deification, Gaius only wanted to speed up an inevitable process which would lead one day to a situation in which no one felt any surprise that emperors whose mental condition was never even open to discussion should be equated with gods, and in which these emperors themselves were perfectly content to be regarded as such.

When it comes to making a judgement on Gaius as a person, the recognition that his conduct was based on a unified and systematic concept removes in itself the possibility of accepting the thesis of pure and simple madness, in the sense of a pathological alteration in the organism resulting from the illness of October 37. In any case, there have been many madmen like Gaius in history. Certainly he must have borne the physical burden of hereditary weaknesses and a neurasthenic temperament and the moral burden of the bad examples given him in childhood and adolescence in place of a good education. This is how we must interpret the testimony on his character of those who knew him, namely his successor Claudius (in allusions contained in documents that have been preserved), Philo and Seneca. This testimony is influenced by hatred, but not distorted by later anecdotal embroidery like that of Flavius Josephus and in particular that of Suetonius and Cassius Dio, whose common source was almost certainly Cluvius Rufus. Rufus must therefore have been responsible in the first place for the interpretation of Gaius's striving towards an oriental monarchy as 'ostentatious demoniacal madness'.[1] This interpretation does not present us with the figure of a sick man who today would have been kept away from contact with his fellow men but with that, up to a certain point not unattractive, of the gifted megalomaniac endowed with a bizarre wit and with the prodigal, extravagant quality of the *grand seigneur* best appreciated by the classes most distant from the centre of power. There is no other explanation for the constant attachment of the soldiers and of the populace, who were still ready, even after the hard taxation and repression of the last period, to go up to the forum and avenge him on the day of his death. His skill at oratory, his refinement of taste and greed for pleasure, his delight in cruel shows, the passion for the bloodthirsty games of the circus and the amphitheatre, and for everything connected with them – gladiators, dancers, horses – were not so much personal characteristics as ones common to his age, in the context of which (and this is not the last point to consider) he must after all be placed. Augustus had enjoyed shows, Tiberius had despised them; but it was Tiberius who was the exception, not Augustus or Gaius. Gaius's own personal qualities were much rather arrogance, especially towards the great, insistence on having his own way, a mad lack of regard for anyone at all and a resourceful rapacity; and since the victims certainly did not see in his oppressive rule the effort to activate the power of the god-king, but only tyranny, they dug its grave. With the disappearance at the age of twenty-nine of this tall, pallid, awkward young man – he had a big body with a slender neck

---

[1] A. MOMIGLIANO, 'Osservazioni sulle fonti per la storia di Caligola, Claudio, Nerone', in *Rend. Acc. Lincei*, ser. VI, vol. VIII, 1932, p. 307.

and legs, sunken eyes and hollow temples, a wide forbidding forehead, thin hair, and a sombre face twisted by exercises before a mirror into a frightening expression (such is the portrait, naturally touched up to look worse, provided by Suetonius, *Calig.*, 50), the empire's first experience of government by a descendant of Augustus came to an end.

III

CLAUDIUS

THE CONTINUATION OF THE PRINCIPATE

The solidarity of interest among heterogeneous elements only lasted a few hours after the aim of eliminating Gaius had been achieved. The Senate, which had had the rôle of protagonist in the conspiracy, took the first outward steps to reactivate the Republic by occupying the Capitol, taking control of the treasury, and giving the watchward 'Libertas' to the armed forces, but soon itself destroyed the dream of restoration, first by simply discussing at length if and how the republican régime should be renewed and then by advancing from its own ranks new candidates for the principate – Annius Vinicianus, Valerius Asiaticus and others. The military – that is, the praetorians – made a rapid decision: regarding a return to the Republic as impossible and in any case not even advantageous to themselves, and conscious on the other hand of the need to forestall the Senate in the choice of the new princeps if, as seemed likely, the Senate itself had decided to continue the principate, they chose the person already indicated by circumstances as the only one compatible with their feeling of dynastic loyalty. The uncle of the dead Gaius, old Tiberius Claudius Nero Germanicus, son of the elder Drusus and brother of Germanicus, never adopted into the *gens Julia* and thus still a Claudius, should be emperor. He was taken to the praetorian camp and acclaimed as such.

Everyone knows how the tradition introduces at this point the figure of Claudius. Always regarded as abnormal and now discovered by chance trembling in a corner of the palace, he was dragged half dead from fear to the *castra praetoria*, where he expected to be killed and received instead the purple. Even after this, so the story goes, he remained incredulous about what was happening to him, and was at the mercy of whoever suggested to him how he should behave in the negotiations with the Senate. This tradition is embellished in the versions coloured by Jewish national pride with the story of a decisive intervention by the astute Julius Agrippa. However, it is not difficult (less difficult in practice with Claudius than with Tiberius, for example) to make out the truth at the bottom of a tradition hostile to the whole dynasty, and in particular of a tradition springing round Claudius from the usual incomprehension or distortion of facts and intentions and from the caricaturing of traits in his character shown nevertheless to be true and real by contemporary testimony. The most obvious consideration suggested by good sense is that while more illustrious men, who could point to the achievement of suppressing the tyrant, were putting forward their own candidature to the principate, while the soldiers themselves were divided (for the urban cohorts were with the Senate) and when the proposal of an opposition candidate by the praetorian camp could mean civil war, the praetorian guards could hardly put forward a candidate from the family whose very memory people wanted to forget if this candidate was just the simpleton depicted by tradition. Moreover, that Claudius was not such a person emerges from the way in which, compromised precisely by his kinship with the dead tyrant and without the advisers – women and freedmen – whom tradition usually puts at his elbow, he mastered the situation – provided that we take the facts at their face value and apply to this moment too the innumerable later pieces of evidence that Claudius was a person who was perfectly well aware of what he was doing. It is sufficient in fact to transfer to Claudius even just the credit for initiating the negotiations conducted with the Senate in the two tragic days of 24 and 25 January. These negotiations are only too explicably attributed by Flavius Josephus in the *Antiquitates Iudaicae* (XIX, 212 ff.) to the Jewish prince, characteristically with an accentuation of this aspect of the matter in comparison with the version he had given twenty years earlier in the *Bellum Iudaicum* (II, 204 ff.), when he was evidently less subject to the influence of a certain tradition when it came to seeing things as they really were.

So Claudius accepted the principate offered to him. His own firmness made the rest easy, since it was simply a question of seconding a spontaneous movement. If we confine our attention simply to the confines of the city, the populace of Rome did not know what to make of a republican restoration of whose utility not even all the senators themselves were convinced. We have seen how the praetorian guards felt about it. It is difficult to imagine that the news of such a project could have reached the provincial armies without provoking an uproar. When the Senate, on the very evening of the day on which freedom had been regained, sent two tribunes of the people to the camp to tell Claudius to return to private life or at any rate, if he wished to be princeps, to induce him to recognize that he owed his position to the authority of the Senate, the situation was to all intents and purposes resolved. Claudius's reply, transmitted through

Julius Agrippa, was disarming in its moderation: he had certainly not
sought the principate, he said, but from the moment that it had been
offered to him and he had accepted it, he neither would nor could turn
back; in any case the Senate had nothing to fear from government by him,
schooled as he was to expect the worst by the fresh lesson of the killing
of the tyrant. The second response, sent the day after the refusal to accept
servitude proclaimed boldly if platonically by the few senators who had
not by now melted away and had even declared that they were ready to
fight, communicated the firm decision that he would oppose arms with
arms. In the meantime the urban cohorts had certainly been informed of
the distribution to each soldier of 15,000 sesterces (a piece of liberality
which was probably intended simply to make up for the missing testamentary donative of Gaius, but undeniably revealed, notwithstanding
complaints at the initiation of a dangerous practice, considerable ability
in the moment chosen to announce it), and at this response of Claudius's
they abandoned the senators, who were left with no choice but to hasten
to the camp and pay homage to the new Princeps, though at the risk of
being cut to pieces by the praetorian guards who were in an angry mood
and only kept in check by Claudius with difficulty.

So the man who the day before could easily have been involved in the
massacre of the Emperor's family now moved to the palace and made his
first task the execution of Gaius's murderers. Even the senators had to
agree that the assassination of the Princeps was not a deed that could be
left unpunished, if only as a warning for the future, and the principal
actors in the elimination of the tyrant, headed by Chaerea, were put to
death at once. But Claudius's political sense did not need the advice of
Julius Agrippa, as Josephus would have us believe, to persuade him to
effect a reconciliation with the senators. Apart from caste feeling (which was
certainly very strong in Claudius – a man already well on in years in the
time of the Augustan régime – thanks to his own character and to the respect
for tradition deriving from his historical studies), expediency too was bound
to lead him to renew the dialogue with the aristocracy already rendered
difficult by the inevitable force of events in the reality of the principate
and of late violently interrupted by the tyranny of Gaius. If only in
contrast to this tyranny and to the memory, still alive, of the last few years
of Tiberius's reign, he was bound to proclaim the return to Augustus. The
fact that he did not succeed in his aim was not his fault, as the abundant
evidence about his intentions illustrates; the hatred of the aristocracy
dogged him right from the start of the reign. He did not permit the
formal proclamation of the *damnatio memoriae* of Gaius, but he allowed his

name to be erased from inscriptions and took down the statues, giving the bronze to the Senate for their mint. He recalled exiles, though with some discrimination, and by means of a *senatusconsultum* he restored property that had been confiscated, even handing it over to the children where the person involved was dead; but he required restitution of money given away by Gaius without good reason. He punished slaves and freedmen who had testified in the courts against their masters; he destroyed a box of poisons kept in reserve by Gaius (it infected for a long time the water round the spot in the sea where it was thrown); and he also destroyed the documents relating to Gaius's trials, getting rid of two of the freedmen most seriously compromised by them, Protogenes and Helicon. All these measures must certainly have had the effect of enabling the upper classes to breathe more freely, as did also the abolition of treason charges and the veto on the torturing of free men. A favourable impression must also have been created by the imposition of the requirement for entry into the Senate of free birth since the great-grandfather's generation. The speeding-up of the public proceedings and ceremonial, with the abolition of the obligatory commemorative readings from speeches of Augustus and Tiberius at sittings of the Senate, the abolition of festivals and New Year's gifts and other similar measures must also have been intended to establish greater simplicity in relations with the Senate. This promising beginning was hailed with the usual official homages; in 41 the senatorial mint issued coins with the legend 'Libertas Augusta'.

But in Claudius we find from the very beginning (and it was to be the germ of the contradiction inherent in his work, which aimed at being loyal to the urban, aristocratic tradition but in reality was more faithful to the technical needs of the empire's administration) a more lively awareness and a more explicit manifestation, even in outward details, of the effective rule of the Princeps. No historical experience disappears without leaving behind it some sort of effect on the future; the experience of Gaius's despotism, not repeated, indeed even deplored by Claudius, nevertheless clarified in him – harassed as he was by the situation of the empire, which had been launched by Augustus on the path of centralization and bureaucratic organization – the notion of what the monarch had to be, namely the effective vertex of the governmental edifice. After Gaius's violent assertion of authority the reality of despotism cloaks itself once again, in Claudius's programme, in legal and formal respect for tradition, though a great deal less than under Augustus and Tiberius. In particular, Claudius did not repeat the theoretical scrupulosity of Tiberius. A freshness of attitude is clearly visible in Augustus's third successor as soon as he comes to the throne, and it is certainly in the direction of a more open display of monarchical power. Such a display was demanded by events. He appeared in the Senate for the first time thirty days after his accession, accompanied by the praetorian prefects and the military tribunes, and both then and subsequently he made no bones about taking security measures; he had those who attended meetings and banquets searched. He was just as frank with the urban populace, letting it understand clearly right from the start, without the peevishness of Tiberius, that he would look after its needs and cater for its tastes (especially in the matter of shows), but would not tolerate its rioting. He removed most of Gaius's crushing taxes, though not all of them; he made good the deficiency of corn left by Gaius and restored regularity to the circulation of money, but he would not permit people, once the days immediately following the tragic 24 January were past, to go on fishing in troubled waters; and if he was generous with largesse he nevertheless abolished a good number of the festivals and pro-hibited distributions of wine and the sale of cooked meat and hot water, things which must have been regarded as implying excessive refinement. As for the image which he wished to create of his own person as Princeps and of the imperial house, it is worth noting that he preferred to remain outside the Julian clan but assumed the name Caesar, which was dear to the armies, the provinces, the urban proletariat and the Italians. He also adopted the name Augustus, as a sort of guarantee that his régime would be modelled on that of the first Princeps. However, he did not take the title *imperator*, to avoid emphasizing formally the military nature of his power, though in reality he was particularly attached to it (yielding in this point to the natural course of events), as is clear from his foreign enter-prises and from the twenty-seven salutations as *imperator* which he accepted during the course of his comparatively brief reign. He did not wish the name Augustus to be extended to his wife (at any rate at first) and his children, but it was he who finally carried out the consecration of Julia Augusta, who had died in 29, and he commemorated with honours and festivals all his relatives, including his grandfather Mark Antony and his sister-in-law Agrippina, as is attested by coins. And in the field of dynastic alliances to which Augustus had devoted so much attention, his accession was soon followed by the marriage of his daughter Claudia Antonia to Cn. Pompeius Magnus, a descendant of Pompey the Great, and the betrothal of the little Claudia Octavia to L. Junius Silanus Torquatus, a grandson of Julia, herself a grandchild of Augustus.

CLAUDIUS THE MAN – THE FAMILY – THE COURT – THE NOBILITY

The difficulty, already noted in the case of Tiberius, in the way of giving a strictly chronological account of Claudius's activity as Princeps is that even the ancient sources devote most of their attention to his legislation. This, consisting by its nature largely of measures of an enduring kind, throws little light on chronology, which is more applicable to the politically not very relevant details of private life, especially marriages and court events. But this very feature of the sources constitutes a claim to merit for Claudius, whose true countenance could already be glimpsed – even before the many important discoveries of documentary evidence about his reign – through the distortions of the literary tradition, especially in Suetonius's 'Life', considerably shorter than the 'Life' of Gaius (although Claudius's reign was longer) and considerably poorer in anecdotes, but richer in those administrative and institutional details which Suetonius never overlooked because they particularly interested him. For us, Claudius is no longer the stupid monster of the official ancient tradition – a picture in any case at variance with most of the facts preserved by this very tradition. Nor is he the mystery that Tiberius partly remains, but a clear figure whose work, especially for the empire, can be gauged and appreciated. It was opportune for the empire that, just at the moment when the still largely empirical arrangements of the Augustan organization must have been taking firm shape through the first official attempts to crystallize them, it should have had as Princeps a man who had spent much of his life studying the Roman tradition.

In fact Claudius, born in 10 B.C. at Lyon to Drusus and Antonia the Younger, was variously regarded by his relatives and cautiously kept out of the limelight by both Augustus and Tiberius, who were evidently perplexed by this incomprehensible mixture of temperamental oddness and physical infirmity. Since there were other more brilliant young men in the family, he had spent his youth more or less on the sidelines. In particular, it seems that he was precluded from a public career. Under Augustus and Tiberius he did not enter on the senatorial career, simply holding some posts of a ceremonial character and provoking a mixture of favourable and unfavourable verdicts on his ability. The latter were determined, as appears from a letter of Augustus to Livia, by concern 'lest he should do something that could be seen and laughed at',[1] and the former by recognition of his intelligence in matters of business – when he was not overcome by absent-mindedness – and of his oratorical ability. Most of his contacts

[1] SUET., *Cl.*, 4, 3.

were with knights, to which order he belonged up to the reign of Gaius, with those of his relatives less in the public eye, with the slaves and freedmen belonging to the family, with tutors – about the choice of whom he himself complained – and with eastern princes staying in Rome as guests or hostages. It was only in 37, with Gaius, that he had attained the honour of the consulship, but even his nephew, once his first kind feelings had evaporated, had pushed him to one side. Of course, it is difficult to judge how far his second-rank position was due to the wishes of other people and how far it was the result of his own free choice. On the one hand, his marriages and plans for marriage from his earliest youth with women of the most illustrious families (that they were not personally of the highest character and sometimes positively ignoble is of no significance) testify to his recognized normality as an individual and to his eminent position in the family; and on the other, his love of study adequately justifies his personal desire for retirement. Thus Claudius, removed from the active life, formed in study the habit of thoughtfulness and the feeling for the large view of historical developments that he later characteristically infused into his activity as a ruler.

Suetonius (*Cl.*, 41–2) tells us about his activity as a writer and it is worth mentioning this to complete our picture of the man. It was continued even when he became Princeps and was both notable for its bulk and characteristic in the scope of the interests it revealed. It ranged from the projected history of the civil wars from the death of Caesar onward – a subject abandoned after two books because the open-minded treatment did not meet with the approval of his mother, a daughter of Antony, or of his grandmother Livia, the wife of Octavian, and taken up again in another less controversial work, the history *A Pace Civili* in forty-one books – to the eight books *De Vita Sua*, the defence of Cicero against Asinius Gallus (this too was a work of political topicality) and finally the histories, written in Greek, of Etruria (twenty books) and Carthage (eight books). The last two works corresponded with his really scholarly interests. We cannot judge any of these books at first hand since they have all been lost, but the esteem of Pliny the Elder among others is a sufficient guarantee of the excellence of work begun under the guidance of Livy.

So Claudius brought to the business of government the historian's habits of disturbing curiosity and inexorable precision, together with the lack of balance characteristic of other members of the family and the almost inevitable clumsiness of the scholar who leaves his study and turns to action. The result was that, understandably enough, his diligence was taken for pedantry and his legal scruples for lunatic obstinacy. And this is only part of the distorted verdict on him current at the time. The principal part of the traditional verdict derives from the internal history of the family and the court as reflected in their direct relations with the urban aristocracy.

When Claudius came to the throne he had been married for at least a year to the sixteen-year-old Valeria Messalina, daughter of his cousin M. Valerius Messalla Barbatus. He had previously been married to Plautia Urgulanilla, who had borne him the two children Drusus (the one who in 20 had been promised to the daughter of Sejanus) and Claudia, both now dead; and also to Aelia Paetina, who had borne him Claudia Antonia – still alive and the husband of Cn. Pompeius Magnus. Messalina had already produced Claudia Octavia and in 41 she presented him with Tiberius Claudius, who became Britannicus after the triumph of 44, so that dynastic hopes were represented by three children of the Princeps, including a male. Aside from the personal ambitions of Messalina, the tendency to give a privileged position to members of the imperial family already apparent with Gaius and now continuing, though against Claudius's initial intentions, accentuated the process which was transforming the Princeps's house into a 'court'. Such indeed it must already have seemed to the senators, through the presence of the powerful ministers, the ex-slaves of the household, the private procurators of the *patrimonium*, who had gradually become officials of the state. For it was part of the logic of autocracy that those nearest to the despotic power, however lowly their origins, should participate by the force of events in that power, ever more centralized and paternalistic as it tended to become by another of the ineluctable laws of absolutism, even when enlightened. The Princeps himself, right from the time of Augustus, must have been carried along by the palace bureaucracy, which had become indispensable for enabling him to deal not only with the administration of his own estate but with that of the empire. Claudius, who took note, as we shall see, of this unavoidable necessity and accepted and organized the bureaucracy that had developed spontaneously, may even have provided wisely for the empire; but Roman senators who, returning from the command of groups of legions on the frontiers, or going as consuls or praetors to confer with the Princeps, were obliged, apart from having to suffer the arrogance of an empress, to pass through the offices and anterooms of Greek and oriental freedmen, must have felt offended. Even if these omnipotent officials were well disposed, the senators certainly hated them and hated the state of affairs which had raised them up; they felt more and more what they had not felt under Augustus, but had begun to feel, though for other reasons, under Tiberius, namely that above the Roman aristocracy there was not only a Princeps but a despot. Claudius's good intentions towards the nobility, sincere though they were thanks to his own instinct as an old aristocrat, his cultured training and the vision present to him of the structure of the imperial government according to the Augustan model, came to nothing when they were confronted with this situation, which he himself encouraged and fixed in a definitive form with the frank inconsistency of the zealot.

Thus after the initial idyll, itself somewhat lukewarm, the story of the contacts between Claudius and the Senate became, as in the days of Tiberius, that of a difficult and painful relationship, in which Claudius also had to bear the weight of other people's guilt. For Messalina and the freedmen, profiting each time from his indifference, his credulity and superstition, or his hasty decisions in moments of anger, secured in the execution of their greedy and ambitious plans (which even included a trade in the granting of citizenship and privileges) the ruin of noble characters. Claudius's reign too is spangled with trials and condemnations, which tradition itself ascribes largely to court intrigues, directly assisted by obliging senators such as L. Vitellius, who had nevertheless started so well under Tiberius. Thirty-five senators and about three hundred knights perished in the thirteen years of Claudius's reign according to the statistical summary of Suetonius (*Cl.*, 29, 2), who does not go into details. These abound on the other hand in Tacitus, whose narrative happens to resume again, after the long lacuna of books VII–X of the *Annals*, in the year 47 with a string of trials (XI, 1–5). The most illustrious victims were the senator from Narbonese Gaul, Valerius Asiaticus, sentenced in the palace itself, and the beautiful Poppaea Sabina, daughter of Poppaeus Sabinus, the able governor of Moesia under Tiberius. Poppaea perished because she was hated by Messalina; others were condemned even for dreaming things of bad augury for the Princeps.

What was exploited above all by Claudius was the fear of conspiracies, reports of which – whether true or alleged – are certainly not lacking in his reign. In 42, as a sequel to the dreamed-of senatorial take-over of 24 January 41, there was the attempted rising by the governor of Dalmatia, L. Arruntius Camillus Scribonianus, who, having rebelled, was abandoned by his two legions when he proclaimed the restoration of the Republic and was killed at Issa (Lissa), where he had taken refuge, after a revolt lasting five days. Suetonius calls it a *bellum civile* (*Cl.*, 13, 2), and it is an interesting episode in the context of the general history of the empire – a prelude to, and an indication of, possibilities of a very different scope. For the moment, however, with the devotion of the armies to the Julio-Claudian house still unimpaired, it would be an irrelevant episode were it not for the fact that the collapse of the revolt swept away other senators who had played leading parts in the crisis of the preceding year – Annius Vinicianus, a possible candidate for the succession, Q. Pomponius Secundus, first an enthusiastic admirer of Gaius, then one of the restorers of the Republic, and A. Caecina Paetus and his wife Arria (the elder), the couple who came to be regarded as models in the tradition of opposition to the Caesars. In 43 there was the attempted coup by a knight, who suffered the ancient traitor's penalty of being thrown from the Tarpeian Rock; in 46 came the conspiracy of the senators Asinius Gallus and Statilius Taurus Corvinus; and in 47 there were yet further plots. In 48 there was the conspiracy of Silius and Messalina and in 52, if it is right to infer an aversion nourished since the downfall of his father, the plot of L. Arruntius Furius Camillus Scribonianus, son of the rebel of 42. In fact Scribonianus seems to have contented himself with questioning Chaldean astrologers about the death of the Princeps.[1] Many illustrious ladies of the imperial house itself met their end, obviously victims of the jealousy and hatred of Messalina. For example, Julia Livilla, the youngest daughter of Germanicus, after first being recalled with her sister Agrippina from the exile imposed on both by Gaius, was then condemned in 42 and put to death for no particular reason (though Seneca's exile in Corsica was connected with her fall). Julia, daughter of Drusus (Tiberius's son), unhappy widow of Nero Caesar, then married to C. Rubellius Blandus, was accused and put to death in 43 without any reason. In 42, still within the circle of relatives of the Princeps, who was evidently kept in a state of anxiety by the threats posed by possible rivals, C. Appius Junius Silanus had been put to death; he had shortly before married Domitia Lepida and was thus Messalina's stepfather. In 47 the same fate overtook Cn. Pompeius Magnus, husband of Claudia Antonia, Claudius's daughter by Aelia Paetina; with him went his father M. Licinius Crassus Frugi – who in 41 had received the *ornamenta triumphalia* with the Princeps himself, probably for the Mauretanian campaign – and his mother Scribonia, while Antonia had to move on hastily to a fresh marriage with Faustus Cornelius Sulla Felix, a half-brother of Messalina. A close collaborator in the government of the empire like the praetorian prefect Catonius Justus was a direct victim of this terrible woman, who was afraid that he would denounce her crimes to Claudius when the latter returned from Britain. The tragic end to her deeds is recorded in Tacitus's narrative, where we

[1] TAC., *Ann.*, XII, 52. 1–2.

read (*Ann.*, XI, 26–37) how, attracted by a young senator, Gaius Silius, and profiting by Claudius's absence, she dared in October 48 to marry him with full ceremonial before an astounded Rome; the act signified revolution, since it was clear that Silius would not have lent himself to such a fantastic deed to satisfy a whim but because the logical consequence was that he was to become Princeps in place of Claudius. The rash pair succumbed to the energy of the freedman Narcissus, who was rewarded by the Senate with the *ornamenta quaestoria*. The memory of the wretched Messalina was officially condemned and the problem arose once again of finding a wife for Claudius and an empress for the court.

The problem was resolved by choosing from the various candidates supported by the ministers of the palace Claudius's niece, Agrippina. Backed by Pallas, who now became the most influential of the freedmen, she had the better both of Aelia Paetina, proposed by Narcissus as the most appropriate person because she had already been Claudius's wife and was the mother of Claudia, and of Lollia Paulina, wife of Memmius Regulus (from whom Gaius had snatched her for a few days), who was supported by Callistus. Agrippina, the last surviving daughter of Germanicus, was the mother of a boy of eleven, L. Domitius Ahenobarbus, the son of her first husband, who had been given to her by Tiberius and had died in 40. She had recently become the widow, not without suspicion of crime, of one Passienus Crispus. The obstacle of too close relationship was overcome through the intervention of L. Vitellius, who obtained a *senatusconsultum* giving a general sanction for marriages between paternal uncle and niece, a dispensation utilized, according to Tacitus (*Ann.*, XII, 7, 2), only (apart from Claudius) by one knight, who wanted to ingratiate himself with Agrippina, and according to Suetonius (*Cl.*, 26, 3) only by one freedman and one leading-centurion. At the beginning of 49 the wedding was celebrated and Agrippina entered the Princeps's house as his consort. Energetic and violent like her mother, and possibly shrewder, more coldly calculating and more practical, this woman of thirty-three wanted to be in both substance and form a queen. Although the choice made was on the whole the best one, since the fact that Agrippina was the only direct descendant of Augustus made her dangerous if she was outside the family and the union with Claudius also kept within the family circle the inevitable conflict between her son and Messalina's children, nevertheless the 'adductum et quasi virile servitium' (TAC., *Ann.*, XII, 7, 3) to which she subjected the court and the city, not just to satisfy sensual whims, like Messalina, but from the serious desire to rule, helped to put the finishing touch to the traditional figure of a Claudius subservient to the wishes of women and ministers, just at the time, as we shall see, when a relaxation of attention even to the problems of the empire lead us to think that a certain decline was in fact apparent in the old Princeps, and that the caricature of Seneca's *Apocolocyntosis* was not so far from the real figure of the Claudius in slippers known to his acquaintances, with the defects malignantly enlarged.

THE PRINCEPS: ACTIVITY ABROAD

But this is not the true Claudius, or at any rate the importance of his reign is not exhausted in circumstances of this kind. Modern research has achieved a new balance in the story of Claudius, which was once no more than the repetition, entertaining if you like, of Tacitus's account, supplemented by Suetonius and Dio Cassius. In fact, the abundance of epigraphical and papyrus material, which conclusively supplements the literary sources and corrects the traditional image, makes the rehabilitation relatively easy.

Claudius's activity, as we see it today, suggests a reincarnation in a fresh and original form of the characteristic image of the typical political man of the Roman tradition, an image that is both traditionalist and innovatory, in conformity with the empirical process of conservation and bold innovation at the base of the whole expansion of Rome. Augustus was like this; that is why in his work Claudius is so like Augustus, taking in his footsteps the path of expansion and progressive organization of the empire, after the phase of settlement and consolidation desired even by Augustus in the second period of his long principate and continued by Tiberius, and after the wild experiment of Gaius, which had however indicated the necessity for a renewal of dynamism. Thus Claudius, accentuating in the Princeps the image of head of the armies and the administration, of supreme protector of the empire, in other words disclosing a little more clearly the true nature of his real power, in contrast to the care taken by Augustus and Tiberius to preserve for the monarchy the appearance of a civil principate in the formal context of an aristocratic republic, yielded to the requirements of the despotic régime's development, requirements which seemed all the more natural as social conditions in the empire became more equal in comparison with its apex. Yielding, too, to the evidence of the facts, he also abandoned, where it seemed advisable, the defensive principate of Augustus and Tiberius and added new territories to the Roman domains.

We have seen what problems the thoughtlessness of Gaius had provoked in various parts of the empire – in Mauretania, in the direction of Britain, in the East and among the Jews. It fell to Claudius to solve them. Other problems also appeared during the course of his reign. The war already in progress in Mauretania was brought to an end in two campaigns, in 41 and 42, under the direction of C. Suetonius Paulinus and Cn. Hosidius Geta. The ancient kingdom of Juba, already considerably Romanized by its princes, was brought under direct rule and divided into two provinces, Mauretania Tingitana in the west and Mauretania Caesariensis in the east, both under procurators. Claudius continued the work of civilization begun by the native kings. Some cities, such as Tingis (Tangier) and Iol-Caesarea (the capitals of the two Mauretanian provinces), Tipasa, Lixus and others were populated with colonists (*coloni*) and were granted certain privileges, so that they should become centres of Romanization in the middle of less advanced populations. Among them was Volubilis in the interior (A.D. 44), and recently discovered inscriptions concerned with this city[1] provide significant evidence of Claudius's largeness of view where the provincials were concerned. The African provinces gave no further cause for concern, apart from some threats of attack by desert peoples, probably the Musulamii, for which reason in 44 Claudius, in-stead of leaving the appointment to be settled by lot, appointed the pro-consul of Africa directly, in the person of one of his best generals, Ser. Sulpicius Galba, possibly in the same way as in the year 20 Tiberius had put forward two names in similar circumstances for the very same post (the step is also of interest for the history of the evolution of the relations between Princeps and Senate). Galba was also authorized to stay for two years instead of the one year usual in senatorial provinces, and it is clear that he had at his disposal the legion transferred by Gaius to Numidia.

In the meantime Britain had been conquered. It fell to Claudius to carry out, in direct continuation of Gaius's not very serious attempt, an enterprise which was bound to be undertaken sooner or later once Gaul had been conquered. In fact the immediate reason for intervention flowed from a situation that had already arisen under Gaius – the flight of British nobles to the Romans and their protection by the latter. The prince who had reigned ever since the time of Augustus in a relatively unified Britain, the famous Cunobelinus (Shakespeare's Cymbeline), King of the Trino-bantes, who had his capital at Camulodunum (Colchester) on the east coast, had managed to contain hostility to the Romans within reasonable limits; but his sons Togodumnus and Caratacus, when their father died

---

[1] *Inscr. Lat. du Maroc*, 116 (= *Inscr. Lat. d'Afr.*, 634), 56, 57.

about 42–43 and their brother Adminius and other important Britons were still in Roman territory, gave the hostility a fanatical character and succeeded in challenging the empire with raids on the Belgian coasts, without pausing to think that the Romans, now firmly established in Gaul, would no doubt accept the challenge. Four legions were disembarked in Britain in 43 under the command of Aulus Plautius, the able ex-governor of Pannonia, whose subordinate commanders included Cn. Osidius Gaeta, back from the victorious campaign in Mauretania, and T. Flavius Vespasianus. In spite of the fierce resistance encountered first at the River Medway, where Togodumnus fell, and then at the Thames, where they had to mark time for a little while, the Roman troops found little difficulty in overthrowing the British kingdom. From the Thames to the capital, Camulodunum, the army, led by Claudius himself (he had left L. Vitellius in Rome as his representative and joined his troops while they were halted), carried out a triumphal march. On the whole, the petty kingdoms which had obeyed Cunobelinus and his sons did not view the Roman victory unfavourably. Having stayed in Britain for sixteen days altogether, Claudius returned to Rome at the beginning of 44 after an absence of six months (the outward journey in particular had taken a long time) and celebrated the conquest with a spectacular triumph and a festival subsequently repeated every year (in 45 it was accompanied by a *congiarium*). The Senate voted him and his son the name 'Britannicus' (it was in fact adopted only by the son), the erection of an arch at Gesoriacum[1] and another in Rome, and finally honours for Messalina as well. The Princeps for his part granted the legionaries, out of gratitude, citizenship with *conubium*. His own position was certainly strengthened by the successful enterprise, and the impression left by the conquest and triumph is widely reflected in literature, inscriptions and coins. It was at this time that the cult of *Victoria Britannica*, with its own priests, began in the empire.

Britain was made a province, naturally under a *legatus Augusti pro praetore*; the first of these, until 47, was the same Aulus Plautius who had led the conquest. However, some years of fighting were still required before total submission was obtained. Intensive operations to extend the conquest towards the western parts of the island continued in 45 and 46, directed mainly by Vespasian. In 47 the new governor, P. Ostorius Scapula, had to repulse a strong attack, and soon afterwards he began the construction of a permanent system of fortifications; but because he included within it the Iceni, a friendly client tribe which was nevertheless not disposed to submit to direct rule, he provoked a rebellion on their

---

[1] Boulogne (*Trans*).

part which was not finally repressed until 49. In 50 Scapula's victorious advance westward reinforced the conquest; in the mountains of Wales the family of Caratacus was captured. In the following year Caratacus himself fell into the hands of the Romans and was sent to Rome, where Claudius showed mercy to him. In 52 Scapula died, and the war, now concentrated against the Silures of Wales, was continued on a reduced scale first by the officers of A. Didius Gallus and then by Q. Veranius and C. Suetonius Paulinus, until the great revolt of Boudicca in 61. What was especially remarkable in Britain was the speed of Romanization. It was at this time that the colony of Camulodunum, where the governor resided, was established, and soon after came a temple to Divus Claudius. Other places were repopulated about the same time or soon afterwards and received the status of Roman cities; among them were Verulamium (St Albans), possibly Glevum (Gloucester) and the great market at the Thames crossing, Londinium, which soon became, thanks to the intensity of its trade, the principal centre of the province.

In the East too there were many problems, some of them already raised by Gaius, others on the point of arising as a result of his policy. In general, so far as Gaius's distribution of kingdoms to his friends was concerned, Claudius wisely abided by the existing situation, but he had to intervene in numerous matters of detail. Polemo, who besides Pontus had also received the kingdom of the Bosporus, had never taken possession of the latter, where Claudius recognized the effective rule of one Mithridates. He was therefore compensated as early as 41 with the cession of some cities in Cilicia Trachea, while his brother Cotys kept Lesser Armenia. Antiochus IV, who had fallen into disgrace with Gaius, received back Commagene, with the addition of parts of Cilicia. Sohaemus was confirmed in his Ituraean tetrarchy, which was subsequently incorporated in Syria on his death in 49. A Herod, brother of Julius Agrippa, was given the city of Chalcis in Lebanon and the *ornamenta praetoria*.

The fortunes of Julius Agrippa are particularly interesting. Whatever the part he played in the succession of Claudius, the latter was grateful to him for it, for apart from the conferment of the *ornamenta consularia* voted by the Senate he added to his dominions Judaea and Samaria, which since A.D. 6 had been under direct rule, and also some lands in the Lebanon and the city of Abila, sealing the alliance with a pact made in the forum according to the ancient ritual. Thus the year 41 saw the reconstitution under the sceptre of Julius Agrippa of the kingdom of his grandfather, Herod the Great. The first effects were extremely good, for Agrippa, returning to Jerusalem in the autumn of 42, succeeded in being at the same time welcome to the Jewish population and the priests, acceptable to the gentiles and devoted to the empire, so that the solution of interposing between the Roman dominion and the Jewish people the shock-absorber of a native dynasty may well still have seemed the wisest course; it had favourable repercussions throughout the Hebrew diaspora, which had been severely tested under Gaius. However, Agrippa's ambition and his passion for intrigue subsequently caused clouds to appear on the horizon; the governor of Syria, Vibius Marsus, had to keep his eyes open and even to intervene to halt the fortification of Jerusalem (in 42) and to break up the conference of kings convoked at Tiberias in 43, a conference possibly connected with the contemporaneous threat by the Parthian Vardanes to Armenia. At this conference almost all the client kings mentioned above were present; and they were all related to Agrippa, or on the way to becoming related. However, in 44 Agrippa died. That Claudius had been somewhat worried by his dangerous initiatives, all the more since he knew the strength of the dynastic and religious bonds on which the astute monarch counted, is proved by the fact that Agrippa's young son, the future Julius Agrippa II, then in Rome, was not placed on his father's throne. He had to wait until 50 to receive just the principality of Chalcis, the property of his uncle Herod, who had died in 48. Then in 53 he was given other lands on the other side of the Jordan and also Abilene, but not Judaea, which thus in 44, after only three years of monarchy, returned to government by procurator. On the whole, in this delicate sector Claudius preferred the security of direct control, even with the odium it provoked, to the experiment of indirect rule, successful though this had been from one point of view. He stuck to this view in spite of the troubles which soon arose again thanks to the misgovernment of the procurators Ventidius Cumanus and Antonius Felix, the brother of Pallas.

Claudius did not have Gaius's blind aversion for the Jews; on the contrary, he sought to repair the consequences of his nephew's imprudence by issuing, soon after he came to the throne, a special edict in favour of the Jews of Alexandria and a general one guaranteeing Jews throughout the empire the undisturbed practice of their religion.[1] Nevertheless, distrust of this proselytizing people, 'which came down the rivers of Syria and Egypt' and flowed into Alexandria, a phenomenon liable to arouse serious suspicions and to raise thoughts of measures against those who seemed to be 'fomenters of a plague now infecting the whole world', must have been present in his mind and is revealed both in the phrase quoted and in other passages of the letter to the Alexandrians which came to light

[1] JOSEPH., *Ant. Iud.*, XIX, 280–5 [5,2].

some years ago in a papyrus.[1] This important document, dated 10 November 41 in the Prefect of Egypt's copy, contains not only the response to certain deliberations on the subject of honours (interesting for the history of the imperial cult, Claudius's attitude to which was the same as that of Tiberius) and the skilful but definite rejection of the request for the institution at Alexandria of a civic senate, but also – and it is the most important section – a long reproach for the riots between Greeks and Jews which had erupted again at the death of Gaius. The Princeps exhorts both sides impartially to keep the peace, calling on the Greeks to respect the customs of the Jews and the privileges granted to them by Augustus and confirmed by himself, and the Jews to be content with these and not to demand others. He then goes on to threaten that, if they continue to litigate and to send delegations to him, he will show 'what a benevolent Princeps can become when he is impelled by righteous anger'. What the rights of the Jews were in Alexandria is a subject for discussion; but it is clear that the difficulties encountered in the great city and in Egypt as a whole by the already hated and numerous Jewish element in living together with the Greek and Egyptian elements, difficulties recently exacerbated by Gaius, permitted no other attitude than that adopted by Claudius. It was an attitude characteristic of his genius and of his paternalism which was even more openly displayed in detailed local interventions co-ordinated to the general aim of assuring the indivisible peace and order of the empire.

Other interventions, all of them dictated by a solidly unitary vision of the Roman state and of its security requirements, followed in due course, whether it was a question of making different arrangements for lands already included within the frontiers or of facing the big problems of relations with the peoples and states beyond the Augustan frontiers – the Rhine, Danube and Euphrates.

In 43 Lycia, which had preserved its free cities thanks to its cordial relations with the Caesarian party in the last days of the Republic, was reduced to a province under a governor, Q. Veranius, as a result of continuous discord. Veranius conducted some operations against the peoples of the interior. In 44 Rhodes, always treated with consideration because of its glorious past, was deprived of its freedom after riots in which some Roman citizens were killed and did not regain it again until 53. In 46 Thrace suffered the same fate as Mauretania; on the death of Rhoemetalces

---

[1] *Pap. Lond.*, 1912, published by H. I. BELL, *Jews and Christians in Egypt*, London 1924, pp. 23–37; cf. HUNT and EDGAR in *Select Papyri*, II, No. 212, with Eng. tr. (Loeb Classical Library).

III, murdered by his wife, Claudius turned the country into a pro-curatorial province, and this step finally guaranteed the peace of an important strategic area, where in any case national resistance had already faded away, so much so that by 44 neighbouring Macedonia and Achaea no longer needed the protection of the legions controlled by the governor of Moesia. Since the last days of Augustus the latter had also ruled, precisely because of possible threats from Thrace and the Danube, the old province, which was now handed back to the Senate.

The provinces instituted by Claudius were thus six – the two Maure-tanias, Britain, Lycia, Thrace and Judaea (which had already been a province once before) – and the preference accorded to government by procurator is significant in connection with what has been said above and what will be said later about the tendency to administrative centralization in the development of the empire. Frontier policy, except in the case, already discussed, of Britain, continued more or less on Augustan lines but with a greater dynamism imposed by the changed circumstances. However, it was still coloured by the feeling of superiority and benevolent protection symbolized by the episode, recorded in Suetonius (*Cl.*, 25, 4), of the German envoys who in the theatre at Rome were permitted to sit in the orchestra by Claudius, 'simplicitate eorum et fiducia commotus': taken into the seats for the common people and seeing Parthians and Armenians sitting among the senators, they had gone to sit in the same place, saying that they were not inferior in rank or services rendered.[1]

In Germany, incursions by the Chauci and Chatti had already been repelled at the very beginning of the reign; later, in 47, Claudius imposed as king on the Cherusci the son of Flavus and grandson of Arminius, one Italicus, who was in Rome. But he was unwilling to do more than this; indeed, he brusquely halted the campaign which the great Cn. Domitius Corbulo, then governor of the Lower Rhine, had started against the Frisii and the Chauci as a sequel to his victorious operations against Gannascus, who had made raids on the coast of Gaul with his Canninefates. The garrisons were all withdrawn to the left bank of the Rhine and Corbulo, awarded the insignia of a triumph, contented himself with digging a canal between the Meuse and the Rhine. In 47 the triumphal insignia were also conferred on Curtius Rufus, governor of the Upper Rhine, for opening a silver mine in the territory of the Mattiaci. Other interventions, mainly of an administrative nature, took place in 50: another attack by the Chatti was repulsed by P. Pomponius Secundus, the tragic poet, now the new governor of the Upper Rhine; and after disturbances among the

---

[1] The episode is referred by TACITUS (*Ann.*, XIII, 54, 3) to Nero.

Suebi, Vannius who had been set up with his Quadi and Marcomanni by
Tiberius as a client king on the far side of the middle Danube, was moved
inside the empire to Pannonia, while under the supervision of Sextus
Palpellius Hister, governor of this province, Vangio and Sido, Vannius's
nephews and successors, acknowledged the patronage of Rome.

Of particular interest was the campaign waged by Didius Gallus,
governor of Moesia, and by Julius Aquila, prefect of the auxiliary cohorts,
in the steppes of Sarmatia; it was provoked by the need to intervene in the
struggles of the client dynasty of the Bosporus. There, on the death of
Aspurgus (A.D. 37), the throne was claimed by his widow and his stepson
Mithridates. Mithridates was not recognized by Gaius, who assigned the
kingdom to Polemo. As we have seen, Claudius did recognize Mithridates, who however succeeded by his intrigues in losing the throne, which
passed to Cotys, installed in 45–46 by the legions of Moesia led by
Didius Gallus (the future governor of Britain). For this exploit Gallus
received the triumphal insignia when he returned to Rome. Mithridates,
who returned to the charge with the help of Sarmatian tribes, was
defeated (in 49) by Cotys and Julius Aquila, supported by tribes of the
hinterland, in a series of big operations which extended to the vast areas
between the Caspian, the valley of the Kuban and the estuary of the Don.
Mithridates himself was taken prisoner and finished up in Rome, where
he lived in peace until the reign of Galba. Roman prestige was strengthened
in those distant regions, while the old Greek cities on the coast of the
Black Sea gratefully saw in the Romans – and we have epigraphical
evidence of this precisely for the reign of Claudius – their natural
protectors against the barbarous peoples of the interior.

Claudius naturally also found himself faced with the problem of Parthia
and Armenia, and the solution he tried to provide for it followed in its
general lines, apart from the gradual decline of interest and activity in his
last years, the diplomatic method of Augustus and Tiberius, in other
words that of encouraging internal discord among the Parthians and
keeping Armenia under control. The two activities were, as always, inter-
dependent; and in fact the internal strife that tore Parthia after the death
of Artabanus III, which probably occurred not later than 38, made it
easy for Claudius to put back on the throne of Armenia in 42, through
the agency of the Iberian Pharasmanes and with the help of Roman
forces which subsequently remained in the fortress of Gorneae, near
Artaxata, that Mithridates who had been driven from it by Gaius.
Gotarzes, Artabanus's successor, who had initiated his reign with a series
of crimes, including the murder of his step-brother Artabanus and all his

family, had not been able to keep himself on the throne and had been replaced, as early as 42, by another step-brother, Vardanes. Retiring as usual to the distant recesses of Hyrcania, he returned to the charge the following year. But when he arrived on the borders of Bactriana, whither Vardanes had moved to meet him, and battle was about to be joined, a conspiracy to eliminate both of them was discovered and the two were reconciled; Vardanes remained on the throne of Parthia and Gotarzes returned to Hyrcania as his vassal. At this point Vardanes, now at the zenith of his fortunes, thanks to the submission, after seven years of rebellion, of the great city of Seleucia, wished to reconquer Armenia; however, nothing came of this since the governor of Syria, Vibius Marsus, threatened to invade Mesopotamia. Soon afterwards Vardanes had to resist a new assault by Gotarzes; he succeeded in repelling it, but this made him so arrogant that he became intolerable to his own followers, who killed him in 45. Gotarzes then seized the throne, but in 49 his cruelty impelled the leading Parthians to request from Claudius the despatch of Meherdates, the son of Vonones, the king who had been expelled in 11 by Artabanus. There was a repetition of the situation of 35, when Tiberius sent first Phraates and then Tiridates as rivals of Artabanus; and the similarity in the situation is paralleled by an almost word-for-word echo in Tacitus.[1] Claudius sent Meherdates, entrusting him to the advice and support of Vibius Marsus's successor as governor of Syria, the worthy individual and eminent lawyer C. Cassius Longinus, just as fourteen years earlier Tiberius had used the services of L. Vitellius. The fate of the Romanized claimant was also similar to that of Tiridates, for between the advice of real friends and the trickery of false friends he met disaster: defeated by Gotarzes, he escaped with the amputation of his ears (A.D. 50).

In 51 Gotarzes died and was succeeded by Vonones, king of Media Atropatene, who was replaced in the very same year by his son Vologaeses. But Claudius, like his predecessors, was not so much interested in imposing his own candidate on Parthia as in maintaining anarchy there. However, in Vologaeses an able prince had come to the throne and the anarchy was then transferred to Armenia, which had remained at peace during the struggles of the Parthians, and led in due course, not without disgrace and damage to the name of Rome, to the great war of Nero's time. A son of the Iberian Pharasmanes, Radamistus, with the connivance of his father, succeeded by trickery in snatching the kingdom from his

---

[1] *Ann.*, VI, 31, 2 (Artabanus): 'regem saevum in pace et adversis proeliorum exitiosum'; XII, 10, 1 (Gotarzes): 'socors domi bellis infaustus'.

uncle and brother-in-law Mithridates, who, after taking refuge with the Roman garrison of Gorneae, was betrayed for money by the commander of the garrison, Caelius Pollio, a prefect of auxiliary cohorts, in spite of the opposition and attempt at personal intervention with Pharasmanes of the centurion Casperius, his subordinate. Mithridates and his family were put to death (A.D. 51) and the governor of Syria, now C. Ummidius Durmius Quadratus, on the advice of his councillors and without instructions from Claudius, confined himself to telling Pharasmanes to recall his son. Now (52) came the intervention, without any contact with the governor of Syria, of the procurator of Cappadocia, Julius Paelignus, who perhaps interpreting in his own way the wishes of the Princeps, whose favour he enjoyed, had the idea of reconquering Armenia on his own, with some forces that he had gathered on the spot. But abandoned by these and corrupted by Radamistus, he finished up by setting the crown on his head. Quadratus then sent a legion to put a stop to this disgraceful performance, but it was swiftly withdrawn as soon as the threat of a war with the Parthians appeared on the horizon. However, in the same year Vologaeses easily drove out Radamistus and put his own brother Tiridates on the throne. When Claudius died, Tiridates had just started to reign again in Armenia after a brief return by Radamistus in 53. Such is Tacitus's account, which seems to echo the gossip and mutual reproaches which arose under Nero when the eastern situation was tackled with energy and there were perhaps recriminations about the torpor of the closing period of the previous reign. Certainly, apart from the responsibility of the local organs of government, it is difficult to discern any personal action by the Princeps in these last few years to salvage the prestige of Roman honour. There was no need to punish the crimes committed by foreigners among themselves, for in fact the principles applied in the eastern sector called for the seeds of discord to be directly sown among them.[1]

These policies may well in fact represent a final decline on the part of Claudius, and we shall see how this is reflected in home affairs as well. But it does not detract much from the imposing amount of work accomplished in the empire on top of the military enterprises and major pieces of provincial organization already mentioned, to which must be added others of lesser importance. As a sequel to the reduction of the legions stationed in Hither Spain (in 46 there were two in place of the three of Tiberius's reign), there was a regrouping of the 'dioceses' into which this province had been divided by Augustus. It was probably now that the province of the *Alpes Graiae et Poeninae* was constituted, with the addition

[1] TAC., *Ann.*, XII, 48, 2.

of the Valais, taken away from Raetia, the definitive organization of which as a province some modern scholars attribute to Claudius, together with that of Noricum. Noricum had been annexed by Augustus, but we know that it was at first administered by a *praefectus civitatum* and only went over to regular procuratorial rule at a later stage. In 44 M. Julius Cottius acquired an increase in his Alpine territory and the title of king. Other episodes that should be mentioned are the victory in 52 of Antiochus IV of Commagene, reinforced by Roman units, over the Cietae, restless again, and in the same year the suppression by Quadratus, the governor of Syria, of disorders that had broken out between the Jews and the Samaritans and which the two procurators of Judaea had not succeeded in mastering. This operation also contained reflections of internal politics, for the price for it was paid by Ventidius Cumanus alone, and Antonius Felix, Pallas's brother, remained sole procurator of Judaea, Samaria, Galilee and Peraea.

Romanization was encouraged not only by a generous and original attitude in the matter of citizenship, of which more will be said further on, but also by the repopulation of old cities with colonists, the foundation of new colonies and the granting of municipal status where a civic tradition already existed, as in Narbonese Gaul (*Vienna*), in Mauretania, with its towns organized in days gone by on the Punic model, and in the Alpine areas nearest to Italy, sometimes with provisions leading to the use of the honorary concession of the title of *colonia*, as seems to be the case, for example, with Narbonne, *Colonia Julia Paterna Claudia*. For Claudius, too, colonization and 'municipalization' were the two sides of the work of urbanizing the empire which was pursued with success by Augustus, continued under Tiberius, and destined to have such importance for the social and political future of the Roman state. The settlement of veterans in colonies was vigorously resumed in Italy itself (*Teanum Sidicinum, Iulium Carnicum*, possibly *Opitergium* and *Misenum*) and especially of course in the imperial provinces: in Gaul, particularly favoured by Claudius, who was born at Lyon on the day (1 August B.C.) on which the altar of Rome and Augustus was inaugurated there (reinforcement of *Lugudunum*, foundation of *Colonia Claudia Ara Augusta Agrippinensium*, the modern Cologne, in 50, of *Colonia Vellavorum*, the modern Le Puy on the Upper Loire, of *Colonia Augusta Treverorum*, now Trier); in Mauretania and Britain, as already described; in Dalmatia (*Colonia Claudia Aequum*, today Sinj, in the hinterland of Split); in Pannonia (*Claudia Savaria*, near Szombáthely in Hungary); in Thrace (*Apri* or *Colonia Claudia Aprensis*); in Cappadocia (*Archelais*); possibly *Iconium* in Lycaonia (more probably founded by

Hadrian) and in Syria (*Ptolemais Ace*, the old Akko of the Phoenicians) (Acre).

The granting of municipal government in its various gradations of legal status and of treatment for taxation purposes is a still more interesting indication of a work that was adapted to local situations. We have already mentioned *Volubilis*, which received immunity and privileges as well as Roman citizenship. The Alpine centres like *Forum Claudii Vallensium* (previously *Octodurus*, now Martigny) and *Forum Claudii Ceutronum*, in Savoy, had Latin rights, while among the *municipia* with full Roman rights were the cities of Noricum, which were also equipped by Claudius with a magnificent network of roads joining them to Italy, of which he considered them an appendage: *Aguntum* (Lienz), *Teurnia* (near Spittal in Carinthia), *Virunum* (to the north of Klagenfurt), *Celeia* (Celje, between Ljubljana and Zagreb) and finally *Iuvavum*, the modern Salzburg. All were preceded by the epithet *Claudia*, which recorded their origin. And it is possible that the series of municipalities strung out along the Alpine roads of the area began on the Italian side of the Alps with a centre in the neighbourhood of the present Bolzano. Apart from the urban settlements proper, Claudius's activity in encouraging provincial centres seems to be attested, especially in the East, by the numerous towns called *Claudiopolis* still remembered, while traces of tiny interventions are continually being brought to light, as with Tiberius, by epigraphical finds in every part of Italy and the empire recording building operations, restorations and delimitation of boundaries, and expressing gratitude for concessions and gifts. These finds range from the pillars of aqueducts and milestones, which are extremely numerous, to monumental inscriptions, the most recent examples of which have appeared in the excavations at *Leptis*, in Tripolitania.

Claudius's concern for the roads, which were built for military purposes but turned out to be powerful aids to the economic development and political cohesion of the empire, is visible everywhere: in Italy, where the *Via Claudia Nova* (A.D. 47) and its continuation, the *Via Claudia Valeria* (48), improved communications between the Sabine region and the Adriatic; in Sardinia and the rugged mining regions of north-western Spain, as well as in Baetica and Lusitania; in Gaul, where, apart from the reorganization of the road system as a whole, the new road along the Rhine between *Mogontiacum* and *Colonia Agrippinensis* formed an excellent line of communications for the legions behind their defences and a useful commercial route; and in the Alps, traversed at the Resia pass by the *Via Claudia Augusta*, from Altinum to the Danube, which was opened in 46 and completed in 47, with an important branch leading to Pannonia via the Claudian cities of Noricum. In Dalmatia and Asia Minor, too, important roads were built – in the north of Asia Minor the road along the coast of Bithynia and Pontus and in the south a more inland one through Caria and Pisidia to Cilicia and also one along the coast of Lycia and Pamphylia. Roads were also built in Cyrenaica, where only recently some milestones of Claudius's have been dug up, and even in Crete.

As for the defence of the frontiers, units were shrewdly moved every so often and skilful attention was given to the morale of the army, with the result that Claudius, although not brought up in a military atmosphere like Tiberius, was nevertheless among the Julio-Claudian emperors most popular with the troops (the conferment of the title *Claudia pia fidelis* on legions VII and XI, which in 42 had declined to rebel with Scribonianus, is an example of Claudius's skill in this sphere and also the start of a custom). In addition, the defences were reinforced by the establishment of the *classis Britannica*, based at Gesoriacum, and of two flotillas on the Danube; it was also the reign of Claudius that saw the erection of the big stone camps in places such as Bonn, Mainz and Vindonissa where legions were normally stationed. Disorders and brigandage were dealt with severely, both inside the empire and on its borders.

Claudius treated the governors of the senatorial provinces with the deference generally shown to members of the Senate and called them collaborators in his work of government,[1] but in reality he wanted them to be rather less the successors of the old pro-magistrates of the Republic and rather more his own officials. For example, he required them to set out punctually for their provinces and punished them without mercy if they made a mistake. As for the governors of the imperial provinces, the example quoted above, that of Corbulo, is significant; for the rest, we find among them men of the first rank, leading actors in subsequent events, whose utilization does credit to Claudius. It shows that the balance between senatorial and equestrian commands was tipped, for the Princeps as a traditionalist, at any rate in intention, in favour of the senatorial class, in spite of the advance of procuratorial posts, also favoured by the Princeps as an innovator. The fundamental contradiction was always present.

On the whole, the now stable organization of the empire (of the newest part of this organization, the central and peripheral equestrian bureaucracy, more will be said below) was helpful to the provincials, who also benefited from the direct interventions of a Princeps acting in accordance

[1] CASS. D., LX, 11, 7.

with the paternalistic tendency to interfere already described as an inevitable trend right from the start of the principate. It was a trend
particularly congenial to the character of Claudius, who made the proper
running of even the smallest things into a scruple and even a worry. His
general programme of good government for the provinces is alluded to in
an edict of the proconsul of Asia, Paulus Fabius Persicus, who, in laying
down principles for the elimination of certain abuses in the finances of the
temple of Diana at Ephesus, asserts that he wishes to provide for the
well-being of his subjects not only for his own year of office as governor
but for always, 'following the example of the valiant and truly just
Princeps who, having gathered under his protection the whole human race,
has granted, among the principal benefits welcome to all, that everyone
should be assured of the enjoyment of his own property'. Appearing as it
does in an official document of a Roman magistrate, the reference is too
curious not to allude to a widely recognized aspect of Claudius's attitude
to the provinces.[1] Numerous even for him are the known cases of a small-
scale activity which it would take too long to illustrate in detail, though
it would be interesting to do so, for these cases would take us down to the
lowest level of daily public life in the empire. There was Bononia,[2]
granted a sum of money to repair damages caused by a fire; Delphi,[3]
where the Princeps intervened in civic questions; Cibyra,[4] in Phrygia,
where he dismissed a local official for exacting too much money; Apamea,
also in Phrygia, Ephesus, Smyrna, Crete,[5] where he granted the usual remission of taxes for five years after an earthquake; Byzantium,[6] exhausted
by resistance to pressure from the Thracians and also relieved of taxes;
Ilium and Cos,[7] honoured for the glory of their past; and other places,
especially in the East, always readier than the West to perpetuate in stone
or bronze the memory of benefits received. Finally there was Claudius's
intervention at Alexandria. The original document, which has already
been quoted, is characteristic of Claudius's mentality, as are other similar
documents – the speech requesting the *ius honorum* for the Gauls, the edict
granting citizenship to the Anauni.

[1] *Suppl. Epigr. Gr.*, IV, 516 (c. 44).
[2] TAC., *Ann.*, XII, 58, 2 (A.D. 53).
[3] DITTENBERGER, *Syll.²*, 801, D (A.D. 52).
[4] *Inscr. Gr. ad res Rom. pert.*, IV, No. 914.
[5] TAC., *Ann.*, XII, 58, 2 (Apamea, A.D. 53); MALAL., X, p. 246 (Ephesus and Smyrna).
[6] TAC., *Ann.*, XII, 62–3 (A.D. 53).
[7] *Ibid.*, 58, 1; 61; SUET., *Cl.*, 25, 3 (Ilium, A.D. 53); TAC., *Ann.*, XII, 61, 2 (Cos, A.D.
    53).

THE STATESMAN AND REFORMER

But the clearest light on Claudius's activity abroad is provided by an examination of the general principles governing his activity at the centre. Within the limits of the paradox that tradition and progress were championed with equally good faith, the same concepts of citizenship, of the principate's functional nature and of religious policy were applied at home and to the empire. Consequently one can speak of them as the basic features of a unified programme, put into effect through the channel of the actual republican magistracies assumed by Claudius – and not just *honoris causa*, for the consulships (the second in 42, the third in 43, the fourth in 47 and the fifth in 51) were held for at least two months, the last for a good part of the year. Similarly, the censorship, exercised with L. Vitellius for the usual period of eighteen months – April 47 to October 48 – in its traditional functions and with old-fashioned severity, was the instrument for a vast systematic work.

But these conservative forms, fruit of a deliberate respect for tradition, were only an outward show, for every detail of Claudius's activity is coloured by the quirks of his own character. He was led by the habit of study to rigour in classification, that is, to organize in practice an apparatus spontaneously created by the needs of government into a hierarchy and a bureaucracy. The same habit, combined with a temperament attentive to the smallest needs and keen to study the measure appropriate to each, produced Claudius's copious legislative activity, while the concern to check the working of his legislation gave rise to his passion for legal proceedings.

Thus in the matter of citizenship, although the above-mentioned edict of 44 which granted certain privileges to the people of Volubilis, and the one that in 46 ended an anomalous situation by conceding full citizenship to some Alpine tribes – the Anauni, the Tulliassi and the Sinduni – who thought they possessed it already, may be sporadic measures (though indicative of wider thinking on the subject than that current in the programmes of Augustus and Tiberius), the assumption of the censorship signified the application to citizenship of a plan, and a fully developed one, destined to mark out the line taken by Rome in this question at any rate until the edict of Caracalla. In a programmatic speech which we can read in part in an inscription, the *tabula Claudiana* from Lyon, as well as in Tacitus's paraphrase (*Ann.*,XI, 23–5,1), Claudius pleads the justice of the claim by the leading men of Gallia Comata – descendants of the first Roman citizens created by Caesar and Augustus – to be admitted to the senatorial career. He demonstrates with historical arguments that Rome had grown, unlike the Greek cities, by the shrewd and generous incorporation of élites, even foreign ones, and that therefore by proceeding along the same path he was only continuing the genuine Roman tradition. The *lectio senatus* and the *recognitio equitum*, operations of the censorship, had shown officially the need to inject fresh blood into the old nobility, and the advanced degree of Romanization of some of the provinces must have excluded the possibility of doing this – as had been done until now (in practice there were very few non-Italian senators under Augustus and Tiberius), and as the jealous Senate wished – from the resources of Italy alone (and even this extension was regarded by some as superfluous). Thus a *senatusconsultum* established the concession first of all for the Aedui, but Claudius certainly availed himself for others of his power of *adlectio*, just as at the same time, again with the aim of reinvigorating, but according to the religious tradition and for religious ends, the body of the Roman aristocracy, he availed himself of the power to create *patricii*, making use of it even outside his term of office as censor.

The colonial policy which we have looked at and the relative generosity in granting Latin rights, the preparation for full citizenship, belonged to the same order of ideas; so did the numerous individual grants of citizenship – even, indeed especially, in the East – as a reward for services rendered, particularly military service in the auxiliary units. The first military diplomas drawn up in the customary terms appear under Claudius; a typical example is the one for the trierarchs and sailors of Misenum, dated 11 December 52.[1] However, this generosity did not lower the value of citizenship, for Claudius, having conceded what he was bound to concede to the march of time and to his own personal view of what was just, kept a strict check, as usual, on the established state of affairs. He punished severely any overstepping of the bounds by non-citizens who illegally acquired citizenship, by citizens who did not speak Latin and by people who falsely pretended to be knights. In this he preserved Augustan strictness and even emphasized it with explicit provisions, such as those designed to restore the efficacy of the bond between former master and freedman (*senatusconsultum Ostorianum*, probably of 46; and in the same year the veto on official support in law courts for freedmen who accused their former masters), to avoid the mixture of free blood with slave blood (*senatusconsultum* of 52) and to maintain the decorum appropriate to Roman citizens. Regulations were issued, especially during his censorship, on behaviour in the theatre, against luxury and celibacy, against the limitation

[1] *CIL*, XVI, 1 = *ILS*, 1986.

of births and against the abuse of putting statues of private persons in public places. The equestrian order, cared for and promoted with particular care by Claudius, who gave it more clearly defined duties and privileges in the administration of the state, assumed the role of second pillar of the Roman social order. It was probably thanks to the Senate's resistance and Claudius's traditionalism, prevailing this time over his programme of innovation, that the equestrian order did not acquire still greater importance in the military field. Here too there was a foretaste of times to come, with the experiment – planned and tried, but not retained – of inserting in the 'militiae equestres' command of a legion after that of a cohort or a squadron of cavalry.[1] As a result, the tribuni angusticlavii, that is, genuine knights who had passed on to the command of a legion after the experience gained in the hard apprenticeship of leading auxiliary troops, proved far superior to the tribuni laticlavii, the young sons of senators, who moreover, thanks in fact to another innovation of Claudius's, could even be dispensed from actual service and enter on the senatorial career after the militia imaginaria. But the experimental reform remains, like others, to indicate a tendency already in force, the tendency to substitute competence for birthright, real job for sinecure; that it was withdrawn is explained by the fundamental contradiction in Claudius's activities. When the census was taken in 48 and the operations of the censorship were concluded with the ancient ceremony of the lustrum, the number of citizens turned out to be almost six million, about a million more than at the last census taken by Augustus and Tiberius in A.D. 14.

The rest of Claudius's activity simply amounts to the search for, and the consistent application of, the most suitable means to secure the functioning, in conformity with the demands of the moment and with due respect for tradition, of a state consisting of a citizen body, so organized legally and socially, and of a mass of subjects in the provinces. The notion of the functional character of the Princeps, already clear but limited to the sense of personal duty in Augustus and Tiberius (hence the ease with which Gaius was able to divest himself of it), acquires in Claudius a little of that sense of constitutional duty which it was to possess in full measure with the Antonines. We can see this in the main, characteristic categories into which his work can be divided: the organization of the imperial chancellery, with consequent modifications to the senatorial career and to the regulations of the Senate itself; legislation; the administration of justice; the policy of social welfare and public works; and religious policy.

Claudius gave official recognition to the state of affairs already prevailing

[1] SUET., Cl., 25, 1.

under Augustus, namely that his own private procurators, assigned to the *patrimonium*, had become in practice officials of the state. He therefore took further steps towards the organization into a real imperial state treasury, alongside the old *aerarium Saturni*, of the *fiscus* that had come into being out of the empirical switch to the state finances of the efforts of the officials assigned to the *patrimonium* of the Princeps. Furthermore, as well as effecting this important separation of functions, which meant that in the reign of Claudius a clear distinction was made between the *aerarium Saturni*, the *fiscus Caesaris* and the private purse, a distinction typical of the central financial organization in later principates (it was to be the concern precisely of the 'good' emperors to preserve the distinction against the constant and understandable tendency to fusion), Claudius wanted these financial officials, and all the others who attended in the palace to the various aspects of the complex direction of affairs of every kind, to head officially the administration of the empire. This arrangement had useful effects from the point of view of unity and of greater speed of government, but the other side of the medal was a new network of connivances, and, what is more, one run by people of the lowest social and moral antecedents. A case in point is the above-mentioned Jewish procuratorship of Antonius Felix, known as 'the husband of three queens',[1] for he had repeatedly allied himself with client dynasties, while in the palace he had the powerful protection of his brother Pallas. Proper departments were created at the centre, each with a freedman at its head and a troop of subordinates – slaves and freedmen of the Princeps's household. There was the *ab epistulis*, that is, the general secretary, in the person of Narcissus, the most influential of Claudius's freedmen until the advent of Agrippina; and the *a rationibus*, or financial secretary, M. Antonius Pallas, on whom all the procurators of the imperial provinces depended, themselves increased in authority by the conferment on them by Claudius, through a *senatusconsultum* of 53, of jurisdiction in fiscal matters. Also dependent on Pallas, in the sense of being inferior to him, was the central *procurator patrimonii*, who in his turn was head of all the procurators of the *patrimonium* scattered throughout the provinces, including senatorial ones. Then there was the *a libellis* or freedman in charge of petitions, C. Julius Callistus; the *a cognitionibus*, whose task it was to prepare the papers for law cases heard by the Princeps; and the *a studiis*, Polybius, who may have been Claudius's cultural adviser. It was natural that with the establishment of this imperial general staff, whose members also enjoyed outward distinctions such as the *ornamenta quaestoria* (granted to Narcissus after the

---

[1] SUET., *Cl.*, 28.

murder of Messalina) and *praetoria* (granted to Pallas in 52 for suggesting the *senatusconsultum* on unions of free persons with slaves), the Senate should lose a little more of its special status, which had already been affected, as we have seen, by the relatively greater importance accorded in general to the equestrian class.

However, there were also some modifications to the functions of the old senatorial magistrates. Two quaestors, nominated by the Princeps for three years and then passing on without a break to the praetorship, replaced (in 44) the praetors in the management of the *aerarium Saturni*; in return the praetors received some of the functions of the consuls in the matter of trusteeships and the consuls were given back their old prerogatives in the field of guardianship. As early as 42 three praetors had been entrusted with the task of looking after the collection of monies for the treasury. But just at this time there is an explicit report of the suppression of two of the four *quaestores classici*, venerable survivals of a situation now overtaken. These were the *quaestor Gallicus*, resident at Rimini or Ravenna, and the *quaestor Ostiensis* (there is no news of the other two posts; one of them was sited at Cales in Campania, but the site of the other is unknown; probably they had disappeared some time before). The *praefecti* of the fleets of Ravenna and Misenum, who were knights, now sufficed for the policing of the Italian seas. At Ostia, the grain emporium, there appeared a *procurator portus Ostiensis*, also a knight. The *praefecti frumenti dandi ex senatusconsulto*, who were senators, still existed, but the tendency to transfer the financing of expenditure from the *aerarium* to the *fiscus* diminished still further their status – which must already have been more or less honorary – in the matter of the distribution of corn. For the same reason imperial officials were put alongside the *curator aquarum*, and the maintenance of the city streets was taken away from the quaestors, who were entrusted instead with the task, possibly involving more expense than honour, of organizing gladiatorial games. All this helps to explain the further changes, even in matters of form (apart from the mutual relations of outward deference), in the relative position of the Senate as compared with the Princeps, who was elevated even higher in the solitary splendour of the despot and was now surrounded by a proper official court.

In fact, in spite of the easements granted to the senatorial career and the abundance of legislation through *senatusconsulta*, Claudius controlled the Senate rigidly, making attendance at its sessions obligatory and fixing rules about absence, simplifying the ceremonial and abolishing holidays, and subsequently intervening in various ways. In 46, for example, he assumed the power, through a *senatusconsultum*, of granting senators permission for journeys outside Italy, an arrangement modified in 49 when senators returning to Narbonese Gaul were dispensed from the need to obtain such permission. All this was naturally done with the object, already pursued by Tiberius, of making the assembly function seriously, but it was now carried out without any further attempt to save appearances (apart from the rendering of mere formal respect), especially in the matter of the elimination of those who no longer possessed the requisites for membership. In the *lectio* of 48 Claudius in fact included without distinction in the same list those struck off by himself and those who after a personal examination of conscience had told him that they could no longer remain senators. For this they offered him the title, which he refused, of *pater senatus*; and in 52, in a speech in the Senate, he exhorted those who no longer possessed the minimum wealth required to leave of their own accord.

So far as his legislation is concerned, which according to tradition was positively ridiculous in its abundance and minuteness (during his censorship he is supposed to have managed to issue twenty edicts a day), a few indications will suffice. His eagerness to look after everything did not make him renounce all traditional forms of legislative procedure. From this point of view he is the only Princeps apart from Augustus and Tiberius to figure among the 'constitutional' emperors cited in Vespasian's *lex de imperio*. Out of archaeological enthusiasm he resurrected comitial laws and the plebiscite (the latter was used, for example, to introduce into the alphabet the famous three new Claudian letters!); more frequently he used *senatusconsulta*; but his customary form of legislation was the edict, limited in validity to the life of the Princeps but perfectly legal in the context of the principate. His legislation is particularly interesting from the point of view of the rights of the private individual. It has been noted how in his reign the jurists remained in the background; but whether he enjoyed competing with them, preferred the advice of his freedmen, or more probably had something of his own to put into his legislation, one cannot fail to notice in it a novelty of concept and a sense of humanity which were certainly original and which herald times to come. The *senatusconsultum Ostorianum* (A.D. 46), which bound freedmen more closely to their former masters, possibly the earlier *senatusconsultum Largianum* (42), which laid down that on the death of the master the goods of individuals holding the particular degree of citizenship known as that of the *Latini Iuniani* should be inherited by the sons, and again, later on, the already cited *senatusconsultum* of 52, which stipulated that a free woman who married a slave should become a slave if she acted without the master's knowledge and a freedwoman if he did know the facts, certainly showed an attitude of greater strictness in the social field; but apart from these concessions to the ideal of conserving the traditional citizen body Claudius's other arrangements represent a step forward. By means of a *lex Claudia* (laid before the *comitiae* by virtue of his *tribunicia potestas* and approved by them, like the *leges Iuliae* of Augustus) he freed women from the tutelage of their male relations, so that for the first time a mother could be the natural heir of any of her sons who died intestate. Repeating an Augustan regulation, he made it illegal, probably by an edict, to call on a woman to guarantee bail granted to the husband; and this prohibition was subsequently extended at an uncertain date by the *senatusconsultum Vellaeanum* to cover any kind of pecuniary guarantee given by women. The object was to protect dowries. Both these measures indicate the same care for the weak and imprudent that we also meet in the veto, imposed by a comitial law of 47, on loans made by usurers to young men with a view to the death of the father. Claudius also excluded from confiscations property belonging to the children; opposed the bad habit of naming the Princeps in wills to the disadvantage of the legitimate heirs; devised a milder form of disgrace which did not involve confiscation or loss of citizen rights and consisted of forced residence in Rome or within a radius of three miles; and, as for slaves, made it obligatory (in 47, it seems, by a comitial law) for masters to look after them when they fell ill. If a master evaded the obligation and caused the slave's death, he was charged with homicide; if on the other hand he put the slave in the temple of Aesculapius on an island in the Tiber, he could not regain possession of the slave if he recovered.

A scrupulous concern for justice also inspired right from the start his passion for law and the law courts; but, as with Tiberius, this was the most risky aspect of his activity for, though the excellence of his intentions is beyond question, it was inevitable that the more authoritarian character conferred on the legal system by the growth of the jurisdiction of the procurators and the greatly increased role of legal proceedings in the field of administration, outside the rules of the *ordo iudiciorum*, should in itself cause a weakening of safeguards. Moreover, the direct exercise of justice on the part of the monarch, with the abuse of the procedure known as *'intra cubiculum principis'* – in spite of the Princeps's use of 'assessors', a practice which had lapsed since Tiberius's departure for Capri in 26 – seemed to provide good grounds for suspicion about the reliability of the administration of justice. And in fact Claudius's zeal in this field is depicted in the tradition – when it is not adding further touches to the caricature of a mean and stupid Princeps – as the exercise of cruelty and caprice. In reality we know of fair and mild judgements, and Claudius's concern to ensure the speed of the proceedings and to protect the due rights of the weak against arrogance, exploitation and legal trickery can be noted in a piece of direct testimony preserved in a papyrus.[1] This is a speech which he made in the Senate in 41 or 42, in which we find, together with regulations lowering the age of judges so as to augment their numbers and thus speed up the despatch of business, at any rate in the minor courts, the proposal, aimed against the bad habit of adjourn- ments, that cases should continue in the vacations when they had not been concluded in the regular session. What is still more interesting as a statement of principle is the ruling that cases should continue even in the absence of one of the parties. Then in 47, by a *senatusconsultum*, Claudius fixed the maximum fee for advocates at 10,000 sesterces, a figure that remained unchanged until the time of Diocletian. But the whole principle of justice had been profoundly impaired as compared with republican times and Claudius could not do anything about that. He must be credited with having encouraged, thanks to his enthusiasm for the administration of justice, a better organization of the courts and with having called into being a considerable amount of legislation, which remained part of the corpus of Roman law.

Social welfare and public works were naturally given a special impetus by Claudius's concern for the smooth running of everything. His measure to relieve private individuals of the expenses of the *vehiculatio*, that is, of services rendered to the state postal service, the *cursus publicus*, a measure known to us from an edict mentioned in an inscription of A.D. 49 from Tegea in Arcadia,[2] is a precursor of the similar one of Nerva. The veto on the acquisition of houses and villas in Rome and Italy, because the purchaser 'diruendo plus adquireret quam quanti emisset', enforced by the *senatusconsultum Hosidianum*,[3] possibly of 45 (the veto was to be repeated in 56 by the *S.C. Volusianum*), was perhaps intended to combat the ex- tension of luxurious *horti* and big estates. The measure was reinforced, possibly in the same year, by the concession to private persons of the privilege of putting up statues of themselves only if they built something. The corn supply was always in the forefront of Claudius's thoughts and it certainly was an extremely formidable problem, for the grain needed to feed the huge city came almost entirely from overseas. Just to meet this grave responsibility Claudius had already started work, in 42, on the new port of Ostia, with its lighthouse and the canal regulating the flow of the

---

[1] *Berl. Griech. Urkunden*, 611.   [2] *ILS*, 214.   [3] *ILS*, 6043.

lower Tiber – a gigantic operation only completed under Nero. He made alterations in the mechanism for distributing corn in Rome and from 43 introduced into the city a kind of list of controlled prices for the principal foodstuffs. Nevertheless, in 52 famine was once again at the gates, and Claudius, under pressure from the threats of the mob, granted privileges in the field of citizenship to the builders of ships destined for the transport of grain, and personally insured against loss from storms seamen who would carry grain to Rome even in winter. These privileges were still in force when Suetonius was writing (*Cl.*, 19). He was responsible for many other useful works besides the port of Ostia; some were completely new, others restorations of already existing ones and others again continuations of those begun but not finished by Gaius. Good examples are the aqueducts known as the *aqua Claudia* and the *Anio Novus*, which were started in 47 and brought into use in 52. Many other aqueducts were substantially improved or almost entirely rebuilt between 44 and 45, especially the *aqua Virgo*. A boundary post found in the nineteenth century attests that Claudius, too, was concerned with the completion of the embankments of the Tiber[1] and there is a record of *horrea* in the Campus Martius. It is difficult to follow down to the smallest details building activities that were certainly intense at Rome and in the provinces, both eastern and western, but one operation that should be mentioned, for it also had political repercussions, is the colossal work of digging a subterranean outlet from the Fucine Lake. This tunnel was begun in 42 and opened in 52.

Claudius's religious policy was more or less the same as that of Augustus and Tiberius. So far as the imperial cult was concerned, Claudius soon made his own views clear, and these were that divine honours were the privilege of the gods alone. In fact, things went just as they had for Augustus and Tiberius, since the East regarded him as a god when he was still alive and traces of this irresistible tendency are not missing in the West; for example, there are records of a *sacerdotium* of the Princeps at Puteoli in 46.[2] He had a vast and systematic programme for the restoration of traditional religion, as was to be expected from a man of his character and intellectual background. Like Augustus, he grafted it on to the trunk of patriotism. The resurrection of divination (by a *senatus-consultum* of 47 authorizing the priests to reorganize the college of *haruspices*, with an increased membership of sixty) and of archaic forms of expiation, the reorganization of the priesthoods and the related creation of patricians, the modifications to the calendar and the restoration of old

[1] *Not. d. sc.*, 1887, p. 323.   [2] *CIL*, X, 1558.

sanctuaries such as that of Venus Ericina in Sicily may well correspond to a taste for antiquity in itself, but there is a deeper significance in the fact that he assumed the censorship, in abeyance for sixty years, in the year 47, just after the celebration, with the repetition of the *ludi saeculares*, of the eighth centenary of the foundation of the city. The same is true of his enlargement in 49 of the *pomerium*, 'auctis populi Romani finibus',[1] and his celebration, also after a very long interval, of the *augurium Salutis*, both of them ceremonies connected with the political facts of the completion of conquest and the restoration of a state of peace. The traditional religion was fitted into the political theology of the eternity of Rome and the empire: this is Claudius's particular brand of mysticism as compared with those of his predecessor and successor. The dedication in 43 of the altar of *Pietas Augusta*, voted by the Senate in 22, is also significant.

As a corollary came the action against foreign cults, which were viewed from the angle of the security of the empire and of possible competition with the traditional religion. We have already looked at relations with Judaism in the provinces, as defined in the edicts recorded by Josephus and by the letter to the Alexandrians; to this evidence we can add, if it is to be regarded as dating from the reign of Claudius, as seems likely, the rescript or edict on the violation of tombs from the inscription at Nazareth. At Rome, apart from an alleged veto in 41 on assembling in synagogues, recorded, perhaps erroneously, by Cassius Dio alone (LX, 6, 6) and not very likely in view of Claudius's recent cordial relations with Julius Agrippa, there took place in 50 the famous expulsion of the Jews, 'impulsore Chresto adsidue tumultuantes' (SUET., *Cl.* 25, 4), a phrase in which the allusion to the Christians is clear. Then came, in 52, by *senatusconsultum*, the banishment of the astrologers, competitors of the restored haruspicy; and in Gaul there was the final prohibition of the barbarous cult of the Druids, which was also dangerous because of its nationalist content. The attempt recorded by Suetonius (*Cl.*, 25, 5) to introduce the Eleusinian mysteries was not inconsistent with this general policy, for Greek religion was certainly not considered foreign, even if some exaggerations, like those of the Pythagorean rites, provoked a repressive intervention from Claudius. There is nothing to prove that he recognized the cult of the Phrygian Attis in a form different from the one that had been traditional since the introduction, during the war against Hannibal, of the cult of Cybele, the Great Mother of Mt. Ida. That the motive of security was still in general the dominant one, as with Augustus, so much so as to dictate a kind of impartiality of treatment in the matter of

[1] *ILS*, 213.

repression for religious or politico-religious reasons, is also proved by the fact that the Alexandrian Greeks themselves could feel persecuted and the victims of obscure connivances between the Jews and the central power. That they did so is clear from the trial before Claudius and Agrippina of the Alexandrians Isidorus and Lampo, who were condemned to death in 53 – the first important incident recorded in a curious collection of material known as the 'Acts of the Pagan Martyrs'.

Such was the sum total of the activity of Claudius as Princeps. It justifies our favourable verdict on him and at the same time explains the misunderstanding of those of his contemporaries who did not approve of this activity because they did not understand it, and opposed it out of self-interest or denigrated it out of hatred, handing down a distorted and ridiculous picture of it. In the basic context of the reality of despotic government, and within the limits fixed by that context, Claudius had political intuitions that are not to be despised; he put into action a conscientious programme of measures providing for the empire's welfare and – as a minimum on which everyone can agree – his aim was the general good. The figure of the old man allowed to live by Clotho 'so that he could grant citizenship to the few who still did not possess it' (SENEC., *Apocol.* 3, 3) and ending in the after-life as clerk *a cognitionibus* to a freedman of Aeacus, the judge of the infernal regions (*ibid.*, 15, 2), is nothing but a caricature based on the most distasteful points in a programme which, like almost all the programmes of emperors, was inevitably bound to be hopelessly at variance with the surviving ideals of the aristocratic opposition.

THE DECLINE AND END

In the last few years of Claudius's reign a slackening of his personal attention has been remarked, particularly in his eastern policy. Although it can be conceded that this may also have been partly due to the even more invasive interposition between him and the empire of the shock-absorber of his bureaucracy, which may have been interested in suspicious manœuvres in the fruitful field of eastern affairs, this in itself and his declining resistance to the plots that dominated the court make it undeniable that he was on the irreversible path to his unhappy fate.

The aim of putting her son forward for the succession was pursued energetically by Agrippina as soon as she was married to Claudius. Her own wedding was followed by the betrothal of the twelve-year-old Domitius to Octavia, whose previous fiancé, L. Junius Silanus Torquatus, opportunely ruined a little earlier by a charge of incest adroitly handled as usual by L. Vitellius, had killed himself on the very day of Claudius's marriage to Agrippina. Then came the recall from exile of Seneca, who was entrusted with the education of the young man. On 25 February A.D. 50, after a series of manœuvres by Agrippina and intrigues by Pallas, her favourite and at that point the most powerful of the freedmen, Domitius was adopted by Claudius, 'lege curiata apud pontifices', and became Nero Claudius Drusus Germanicus Caesar. This was an extraordinary achievement, for it involved overcoming not only the legal difficulty that the adopter already had a son of his own but also the serious obstacle posed by the family tradition, of which Claudius must by temperament have been a jealous guardian: no one had ever been adopted by the Claudian family. The whole episode seems to show both the power of Agrippina and an effective decline of energy in the old Princeps. Octavia naturally had to be adopted by another family in order to continue as Nero's betrothed; Agrippina assumed the title of Augusta; and just at this time the city of the Ubii, on the Rhine, where she had been born, took its name from her. In 57 Nero, then fourteen, put on the *toga virilis*; he was marked out to be consul in his twentieth year and was given the proconsular imperium outside Rome, as well as the title of *princeps inventutis*. The knights dedicated a shield of honour to him, the priests vied with each other in co-opting him to their colleges; in his name a *congiarium* was distributed to the people and a *donativum* to the soldiers, he received the praetorian guards in person and thanked his father with a speech in the Senate.

The next few years, the last ones of Claudius, saw the growing power of Agrippina, who acted like a genuine empress: invested with extraordinary privileges, she was present at public audiences, had her interventions recorded in the official papers, and participated, on a throne by her husband's side, in all the festivals and ceremonies. In the East she received divine honours and her effigy appeared on coins – and not only provincial ones. Above all, she took care to put faithful followers of hers in the key posts. In 51 she had Afranius Burrus, who was devoted to her, appointed praetorian prefect; and her creatures surrounded the unfortunate Britannicus. In 52, when the outlet from the Fucine Lake was opened, she took advantage of certain defects in the work to accuse Narcissus, who, though no better morally than his colleagues, was extremely loyal to Claudius and thus the principal obstacle to the fulfilment of this ambitious woman's designs. For the time being she had no success, but the following year, while Claudius was ill, she made no further secret of her intention to put

Nero on the throne and hastened his marriage to Octavia. At the same time, to make him popular in the provinces as well, she made him recite in the Senate the speeches composed by Seneca in favour of certain eastern cities (Ilium, Rhodes). Britannicus was systematically discredited, in spite of the fact that he had many partisans working on his behalf, enlisted by Narcissus even though he had killed Britannicus's mother. These supporters also gained some success, even as early as 51, when the Senate put the effigy of Britannicus on its coins, L. Vitellius was attacked and a certain Tarquitius Priscus, a creature of Agrippina's, was expelled from the Senate. In 54 Britannicus's cause seemed close to victory: Claudius let slip the remark that it was his fate to put up with the wickedness of wives and then to punish them;[1] and in a speech to the Senate he recommended his two sons equally and named them on equal terms in his will. Finally he made up his mind to give the *toga virilis* to Britannicus.

Agrippina quickened the tempo. First she got rid of Domitia Lepida. Thanks to her position in the imperial family, this ambitious and violent woman was, even more than her sister Domitia, who was also hated, the natural rival of Agrippina, much as Plancina had been the rival of Agrippina's mother. She was a cousin of Claudius, since she was the daughter of Antonia the elder and the sister of Cn. Domitius Ahenobarbus, Nero's father; thus she was Agrippina's sister-in-law and Nero's aunt. Furthermore, she was Messalina's mother, since her first husband had been M. Valerius Messalla Barbatus; Claudia Antonia's mother-in-law, since the latter's husband, Faustus Cornelius Sulla, was the son of her second husband; and her third husband had been the Appius Junius Silanus murdered in 42 at the instigation of Messalina. It can be imagined what a network of relations she could call on to weave her intricate web, thus arousing Agrippina's suspicions, especially when, competing with the latter to capture the affections of the young Nero, whom she had looked after during his mother's exile in the reign of Gaius, she came up against Agrippina's morbid desire to be the sole influence on her son; for it is clear that, through her son, she meant to reign herself. Accused of 'devotiones' against her sister-in-law and of stirring up sedition on her estates in Calabria, Domitia was found guilty. But this was not enough for Agrippina; she had to make sure that Britannicus was not preferred to Nero and that the latter was not removed from her influence, as was in fact being attempted. Taking advantage of the absence of Narcissus, on 13 October 54 she got rid of Claudius by sprinkling a dish of mushrooms with poison. The details of his death are variously reported, but the

[1] TAC., *Ann.*, XII, 64, 2; cf. SUET., *Cl.*, 43.

sources are almost unanimous in accepting the criminal version, which is indeed the most likely one, for even if it is true that 'rumour always deals more savagely with the death of the great',[1] the fact remains that the death of Claudius certainly did not happen just by chance to complete a carefully laid plan and that Agrippina was not the woman to be deterred by scruples from putting the finishing touch to her work. The death was kept hidden for some hours, through some difficulty in the auspices, until all necessary preparations had been made to secure the succession of Nero, who was finally presented by Burrus to the praetorian guards; he promised them 15,000 sesterces per head – the very donative granted to them by Claudius in 41 – was accepted without any protest, and hailed as *imperator*. The Senate, before which Nero appeared the same evening, conferred on him the insignia and the usual imperial powers, and also offered him the title of *pater patriae*, which he refused. Claudius's will was not even read, but his apotheosis was resolved upon, together with public tributes of the sort paid to Augustus, for Agrippina 'did not wish to fall behind her great-grandmother Livia'.[2] She did in fact become *flaminica*, and the priests of the divine Augustus also attended to the worship of the new emperor-god, while on the Caelian hill a start was made on the construction of the temple of the divine Claudius. This enterprise was subsequently abandoned by Nero, who soon completely gave up the worship of his deified father. Vespasian revived both the cult and the temple, with the same idea of revaluing a principate in so many ways exemplary that we meet again in the coins of Trajan commemorating the reign of Claudius.

Disappearing silently from the scene amid hopes of the dawn of an age of happiness under the aegis of the wise counsellors of the new young Princeps, the pedantic administrator cannot in fact have been much regretted, any more than Tiberius was at the promising advent of Gaius. Moreover, the Roman nobility, as we can infer from the promises made to them by Nero, hoped that the disappearance of Claudius would mean the end of trials, especially trials *intra cubiculum principis*; the decline of the power of the freedmen; and the return of full authority to the Senate. But Claudius had taken the decisive step towards open despotism, realistically, and along the path of natural evolution. What seemed exaggerations in the eyes of the aristocracy – and to some extent were indeed such owing to the zealous enthusiasm which the Princeps devoted to their execution – were only isolated aspects of the new reality. There could be no turning back, nor would this have been useful to the empire, unified and consoli-

---

[1] 'Atrociore semper fama erga dominantium exitus', TAC., *Ann.*, IV, 11, 2.
[2] *Ibid.*, XII, 69, 3.

dated by the beneficent radiation of an attentive and far-sighted pater-nalism. It is Claudius's greatest claim to honourable fame, that, following in the footsteps of Augustus and preserving respect for tradition, he con-verted into an enlightened force to be used in the service of the empire the absolute power which Gaius had interpreted as something quite arbitrary to be used merely for his own ends. Claudius the man may have possessed the venial failings which might even have lent a certain attrac-tion to the figure of a sincere and tractable person, quick to laughter and anger, a great glutton and relentless joker, an incautious person who talked to everyone about everything in anyone's presence, an adminis-trator who personally supervised the execution of his directives, thus overloading himself with work and complaining about it, just as he lamented the human wickedness which put spokes in the wheel and kept forcing him to intervene to the detriment of his imperial majesty. He may have been a naïve student with his head always in the clouds – the *oblivio* and *inconsiderantia* of which he is accused by Suetonius (*Cl.*, 39, 1). He may even have possessed the more serious defects of weakness with those near to him, superstition, cruelty, suspiciousness, and in general a certain lack of balance. Nevertheless, he made up for his defects and faults with qualities which in the end turned out to be the most useful ones in the man who, given the development of the principate, held henceforth in his hands alone, and showed by his deeds that he felt it keenly, the tremendous responsibility of ruling the world.

IV

NERO

The famous phrase attributed to Trajan by Aurelius Victor (*De Caes.*, 5, 2) is to be understood as a late attempt to repeat, for the reign of the last Julio-Claudian emperor, the split into two parts – the good start and the degeneration – already applied by a much more authoritative tradition (Tacitus and Suetonius) to the reigns of Tiberius and Gaius. In reality Nero's principate displays the same characteristics from start to finish so far as the personal activity of the protagonist is concerned, and it is difficult to avoid the impression that what concrete good there was in it, such as some wise pieces of legislation and the smooth running of the administration, were the fruits of the organization consolidated principally by Tiberius and Claudius and functioning now through the work of men perfectly suited to fill its posts and shoulder its burdens: senators adapted to the now century-old reality of the principate and the new officials continually rising from every class and flocking in from every region, even the peripheral ones, to serve the imperial state. In this situation, in which, as we have already seen with Gaius, the automatic functioning of the state was largely sheltered from the whims of the Princeps himself, we must nevertheless note the efforts of the latter to impose his own personality and will in confrontations with officials closer to the machinery. The story of Nero is the story of the emancipation pursued and gradually achieved by the young man – who for base motives grew more and more intolerant of restraint and was at the same time carried away by awareness of his own mystical and sovereign superiority – in the confrontations with his counsellors and assistants in government, even when these were his mother and his wife. Thus the first period of Nero, when his impatience was held in check by the still effective influence of his teachers and ministers, if only by dint of various expedients, may easily have appeared the better one and could also be distinguished from the following one by the memory, reflected in literature, of the expectations of a golden age with which people hailed the advent of the new Princeps and of the programme he announced of deference to the Senate, justice and liberality. There was also the tardy homage rendered by the tradition to the rule of philosophy as represented by Seneca, the chief of the 'rectores imperatoriae iuventae'.[1] But if the figure of Nero, already in many ways difficult to interpret, is not to become unreal or to remain completely unintelligible, the presence of his concept of the Princeps's power, a concept certainly more refined than that of Gaius but nevertheless similar, and of the policy of exploiting despotism, in the particular form he had chosen – that of pseudo-cultural excellence – must be noted right from the beginning, when we know that it was encouraged, imprudently and deceitfully, by his counsellors themselves.

Born at Antium (Anzio) on 15 December, in all probability in the year 37, amid the blackest omens recorded by tradition for events of this kind, at the age of three Nero had lost his father, Cn. Domitius Ahenobarbus, and also his inheritance, confiscated by Gaius. Separated from his mother too, who was banished, he had been looked after by his aunt, Domitia Lepida. The boy was able to return to a more comfortable mode of life on the accession of Claudius, who returned his father's estate to him and recalled his mother from exile. He inherited another estate from his mother's husband, Passienus Crispus. The good fortune that befell the boy through Agrippina's marriage to the Princeps has already been described, as has also this terrible woman's clear determination to gain the throne for her son and to rule through him. The characteristic aspect of Agrippina's plan in comparison with any vulgar scheme of usurpation was the care she took over the education of the heir designate. She must have known her son and remembered her brother Gaius clearly enough not to want any repetition of the experiment in crude profligacy which he had tried. Nero's despotism, though no less complete, was to be guided in conformity with the ideals of the age, which were continually loading the superhuman concept of *auctoritas*, the basis of the principate, with all the elements of messianic expectation elaborated by spiritual and cultural developments. Apart from the real intention of Agrippina to exercise the effective power herself, and the rival and no less real intentions of Seneca and Burrus in the same direction, official aims were bound to lie precisely in this direction, granted that the Princeps had to be, and was, in the eyes of Rome and the empire, Nero. His education was therefore directed by Seneca and other philosophers such as the Peripatetic Alexander of Aegae and the Stoic Chaeremon of Alexandria, a

[1] TAC., *Ann.*, XIII, 2, 1.

notable figure in the Hellenistic culture of the period. But the teachers'
limits and guide-lines were probably laid down by Agrippina herself, who
did not want too much philosophy, 'harmful to anyone who had to rule';[1]
and the young man himself, having learnt the customary rules of academic
oratory, developed as a result of his initiation into the liberal arts only an
immoderate passion for the theatrical exhibitions of reciting poetry,
singing, music and horse-racing. He probably also developed a fanatical
feeling of his own 'primacy' in a field which he thought a new and sublime
one for the display of the true greatness of the Princeps. Thus the culture
and poetic inspiration which had not been lacking in the Julio-Claudian
dynasty but had always been cultivated only as private occupations and
personal pleasures were to become for Nero the greatest explanation of his
quality of superiority to all men, and what could have been the first reign
of philosophy was nothing more than one long comedy ending in tragedy,
thanks to the uncompromising opposition of the Roman tradition, which
was not disposed to take theatrical greatness seriously.

With this preparation and these ideas, to be developed just as soon as it
should be possible, Nero at the age of seventeen became Princeps; and he
was not only accepted – for no one now thought that the empire could be
ruled otherwise than by the principate and in particular by the Julio-
Claudian dynasty – but hailed with general enthusiasm. However, the
password given to the soldiers on the very first night was significant:
'optima mater'. The funeral oration for Claudius and the statement of
policy delivered in the Senate were put into his mouth by Seneca, who
made him declare that his only model was Augustus (all the successors of
the first Princeps had begun like this) and that he bound himself to
respect the rights of the Senate, not to interfere in the administration of
justice and to keep the *domus* and the *res publica* separate:[2] promises which
were welcomed with the decision that they should be engraved on silver
and read out whenever new consuls took office. In these first steps, whatever the youth's degree of personal commitment to what he was made to
say and do, we can detect the two separate influences, already at variance
with each other, of Agrippina on the one hand and of the two mentors,
Seneca and Burrus, on the other. Agrippina in particular thought she had
fully achieved her programme of dominion, and supported by Pallas, who
was as interested as she was in defending the position of the Claudian
bureaucracy, she opposed the resolutions which the Senate, only too
eager to avail itself of the concessions suggested to the Princeps by Seneca,
had passed to abolish various measures of Claudius such as the one

[1] SUET., *Ner.*, 52, 1.   [2] TAC., *Ann.*, XIII, 4, 2.

concerning gifts and fees to advocates and the one laying on quaestors designate the heavy burden of giving gladiatorial shows. The tradition also ascribes to Agrippina sole responsibility, without any intervention on Nero's part, for the death of Narcissus, who fell a victim to the powerful woman's hatred and to the rivalry between the freedmen, and for that of M. Junius Silanus, struck down by hired assassins in his province of Asia. But limits were set to her extraordinary power and a counterpoise provided by Seneca and Burrus, who, with the administration of the empire effectively in their hands, fought against her and certainly gained some victories – and not merely in questions of etiquette like that involved in the episode of the reception of the Armenian ambassadors. On this occasion, when Agrippina entered the room and walked towards the throne to sit beside her son, Seneca suggested to Nero that he should go to meet his mother, so that filial respect should conceal the shame of feminine rule.[1] In this way they also succeeded in weakening the mother's influence on the son and possibly in turning him against her, an attitude he was probably already inclined to adopt on his own account so as to eliminate any obstacles to the satisfaction of his private wishes and through the consciousness, fed by natural pride and the exhortations of others, that it was he who was Princeps. This consciousness, still guided by his counsellors in the direction of an almost constitutional collaboration with the Senate, gave rise towards the end of 54 to fresh manifestations of an idyll whose essential emptiness indicated that its duration would be brief. To the Princeps's request for a statue to his father and the consular insignia for his guardian, the Senate responded with the offer of statues to himself, which were declined if they were of gold and silver, and the proposal, also rejected, to move the beginning of the year to December, the month in which he had been born. He also refused to entertain two charges of treason. Then on taking up the consulship on 1 January 55 with L. Antistius Vetus, he asked to be put on an equal footing with his colleagues, whom he exonerated from swearing allegiance to the imperial acts; and he readmitted to the Senate Plautius Lateranus, who had been expelled from it on the grounds that he had compromised himself with Messalina. As a result of these actions, of the famous 'vellem litteras nescire!'[2] uttered as he was signing a death sentence, and of the episodes, not really very numerous, recorded by Suetonius (Chap. 10), there came the development, with how much assistance from propaganda we do not know,[3] of the theme of *clementia*, officially proposed to singers of the

---

[1] *Ibid.*, 5, 2; CASS. D., LXI, 3, 3–4.
[2] SENEC., *De Clem.*, II, 1, 1 ff.; SUET., *Ner.*, 10. 2.   [3] TAC., *Ann.*, XIII, 11, 2.

returning age of gold and made the subject of a philosophical treatise which the great theatrical director was just then in the process of writing.

All these displays probably cost Nero no more than a growing sense of boredom. The year 55 cannot have been far advanced when he laid down the consulship, summoned the lyre-player Terpnus to the court and fell in love with a freedwoman, Claudia Acte. His teachers and advisers immediately changed their tune. Abandoning the young man to his natural tendencies, which his mother on the other hand persisted in opposing, they succeeded in detaching him from her and possibly from any interest in the business of government, which no doubt was carried on more and more effectively by them. So things continued, with benefit to the empire, so long as the young man's caprices, now subject to no check of any sort, did not exceed the bounds of forays through the city. By 55 the figure of the traditional Nero – dissolute, histrionic, stained with crime – was completely formed. He sought to profit from the lyre-player's teaching and made various sacrifices to cultivate his 'exigua et fusca'[1] voice; but he also wanted to marry Acte, having completely lost interest in Octavia. Agrippina, supported by Pallas, opposed this with all her might; she even threatened to take away the throne which she had given him, forgetting that power, once it has slipped from one's hands, cannot be regained.[2] Nero for his part threatened to withdraw to Rhodes, but the theatrical quarrel was patched up for the moment by Seneca and Burrus: they introduced a screen in the shape of Annaeus Serenus, the *praefectus vigilum*, who was to act as Acte's official lover and also, as chief of police, protect the Princeps on his nocturnal expeditions. These were another of Nero's favourite diversions; he and his friends would roam the city robbing, pillaging and committing acts of violence, until he was induced by the risk which he ran – once in 56 he got a bigger thrashing than he had bargained for – to surround himself with a more efficient apparatus of protection, namely soldiers and gladiators ready to intervene in case of need.

However, Pallas was removed from office and the conflict between mother and son soon broke out again. Agrippina unwisely showed favour to Britannicus; the only result she achieved was that the unfortunate boy was coldly poisoned. Nero sought by munificence to erase the memory of his crime from the minds of the senators, who in the enduring euphoria of the golden age were already trying to explain it away as justified by reasons of state; meanwhile Agrippina once again started to utter threats and transferred her signs of affection to Octavia. This time the result was

[1] SUET., *Ner.*, 20, 1; cf. CASS. D., LXI, 20, 2.   [2] CASS. D., LXI, 7, 3.

that her own guards were taken away from her and she was forced to
leave the palace and go to live in the house of her grandmother Antonia,
more or less as a private citizen. But the intrigues were not over, for a pile
of charges fabricated against Agrippina by Junia Silana, once her friend,
and energetically rebutted by the accused, led to a number of condemnations, some of them death sentences. Burrus himself was accused, with
Pallas, of having thought of replacing Nero with Faustus Cornelius Sulla,
Claudia Antonia's husband and son-in-law of Claudius. This was a
dangerous charge and, together with the fact that in Junia Silana's plot
the name of another descendant of Augustus, Rubellius Plautus, had been
mentioned as a planned fourth husband for Agrippina, it formed the
prelude to the hunting-down of possible claimants to the throne, another
sport that was subsequently to reach a high degree of development.
Burrus and Pallas easily extracted themselves from trouble, but Agrippina
too registered a success with the appointment of some of her followers to
important posts, especially that of Faenius Rufus as prefect of the corn
supply. However, her power remained impaired and a year after her
pointless crime she found herself in a position considerably weaker than
the one she had enjoyed as Augusta alongside her husband. As for Nero,
in his outward display of authority (towards the end of 55 he carried out a
solemn *lustratio* of the city after lightning had struck the temple of
Jupiter and about the same time received honours for the operations in
Parthia) and in the arrangements, more in conformity with his genius,
which he made for shows (in this same year he gave a huge *venatio* with four
hundred bears and three hundred lions, and towards the end of the year he
abolished the guard normally present at public spectacles), he tolerated no
further interference from his mother; and the directors of the serious life
of the state, Seneca and Burrus, drew nothing but a gain in their effective
power from the family quarrel. In fact Sejanus's plan was being put into
effect, if less openly, for the progress accomplished in the organization of
the central administration now allowed for, almost as part of the structure
of the state, such figures of all-powerful ministers. The praetorian and
(from 56) consular Annaeus Seneca and the praetorian prefect Afranius
Burrus in practice ran the state, applying an economic and foreign policy
of their own, to which must be attributed, as we have said, all the blessings
of the famous 'quinquennium'.

The sources tell us little about the next two years, 56 and 57. So far as
the personal activity of Nero is concerned the reports are all of much the
same sort (in 56, continuation of the nocturnal revelries, participation in
the brawls in the theatre and restoration of the guard abolished the previous

year, when these brawls became too dangerous for Nero himself; in 57, construction of a wooden amphitheatre in the Campus Martius and a sea battle in the theatre), but with regard to the interests of the state they indicate a notable legislative activity, and one quite independent of Nero. When he did want to take the initiative himself, in 58, with his own wild plan for the abolition of indirect taxes, the fact signified, together with the appearance on the horizon of Poppaea Sabina, that the Princeps's arbitrary behaviour was about to overflow the bounds of that private, urban display of power which had so far avoided damage to the empire and pass into the phase of total despotism.

In 56 and 57, however, some legal questions could be dealt with in relative freedom by the Senate. One such was the proposal concerning the power of masters to revoke the liberation of slaves, a question which the Senate finally left the Princeps to settle; he replied that each case should be judged on its merits. And in the 'imago reipublicae'[1] which still remained, there was even a conflict of competences between a praetor and a tribune of the people, which was promptly followed, on the resolution of the Senate itself, by a limitation of the jurisdiction of tribunes and aediles. More important was the reform of the administration of the *aerarium*; in place of the quaestors, two *praefecti aerarii Saturni* were put in charge of it. These two were appointed by the Princeps for three years, and were chosen from the ranks of the senators of praetorian rank and thus from the ranks of older and more experienced men. The sufficiently autonomous functioning of the Senate is also proved by the occurrence of a number of prosecutions, all for embezzlement. In 56 a proconsul of Crete and Cyrene was acquitted, while a procurator in Sardinia and even a prefect of the Ravenna fleet, both of them close to the personal staff of the Princeps, were found guilty. In 57 there were charges against P. Celer, procurator of the *res privata* in Asia and one of the murderers of M. Junius Silanus; against Cossutianus Capito, governor of Cilicia; and against Eprius Marcellus, governor of Lycia. In the same year, 57, the accusation against the noblewoman Pomponia Graecina, 'superstitionis externae rea',[2] a charge which may well have covered – so it has been conjectured – adhesion to Christianity, although there is absolutely no proof of this, gave rise to the revival of the ancient custom of trial by one's own kinsmen. Also in 57, from the first to the last day of which Nero held his second consulship, the development of the policies of Seneca and Burrus towards Italy and the provinces can be glimpsed in measures such as the settlement of veterans at Capua and Nuceria, a plan intended to compensate for (not

---

[1] TAC., *Ann.*, XIII, 28, 1.   [2] *Ibid.*, 32, 2.

without difficulty, for three years later the veterans assigned to Tarentum
and Antium did not want to go there) the decline in the number of
Italian citizens. A *congiarium* of 400 sesterces per head to the urban
populace appeased the first possible disappointments and revived the
atmosphere of continual expectation of benefits, a necessary outward
concomitant of the principate in the view of the author of the *De Clementia*.
The allocation to the treasury of Saturn of the sum of forty million
sesterces, 'ad retinendam populi fidem',[1] was a measure of the same order,
with more appearance than substance to it, for since the time of Augustus
deference and generosity to the old treasury had been simply formal
gestures. The modification which followed in the application of the tax of
4 per cent on the sale of slaves may have been nothing more than a case,
preserved in the record, of an ordinary administrative measure; and police
considerations, made acceptable to the touchiness of the Princeps as
precautions against the dangers of gatherings of the lower strata of the
provincial population, may have been at the bottom of the prohibition on
the holding of games and shows by magistrates and procurators in the
provinces. The problem of the mass of freedmen and slaves must have been
a thorny one in a society now shaken by fresh tremors. This is clear from
the important Claudian legislation, already noted, on this subject, from
the long discussion in the Senate the previous year, and from the savage
application in 61, not without lively opposition in the Senate and among
the people, of the old law of interrogation with torture and of the execution *en masse* of the whole *familia* when a slave had killed his master. This
same problem also provoked a *senatusconsultum* which, based on a similar
one of A.D. 10, gave free persons an increased degree of protection against
slaves.

On 1 January 58, with his second consulship hardly over, Nero
assumed his third, which however he laid down after four months. In the
early days of 58, by granting subventions to various people, including his
colleague M. Valerius Messalla Corvinus, a man belonging to a family
of considerable renown but now in somewhat straitened circumstances, he
continued to keep up official relations with the nobility on the lines
postulated by the plans of Seneca and Burrus. Otherwise, just at this time
Nero, now twenty-one, was trying to escape from tutelage in matters
more substantial than the outward trappings of his official position and in
a wider sphere than that of private activities, where his guardians had
already made sure that he could do whatever he liked. He was now to
display in a vaster arena, in fact in the whole area embraced by his official

---

[1] *Ibid.*, 31, 2.

majesty – in other words, the entire world – his passion for grandeur and popularity in his own chosen form of the cult of art and Greek manners. This was in complete conflict with the Roman tradition represented above all in his infatuated mind by his family acquaintances – his mother, his wife and his ministers – who must have seemed to him like ever-present obstacles to the realization of his own splendid dream. During this year, in the course of which, in the Senate, there were the usual trials, with acquittals and condemnations, but also, significantly, with more frequent personal interventions by the Princeps and the disclosure by one defendant, P. Suillius, of things which cannot have sounded welcome to the ears of Seneca – it is at this point that Cassius Dio (LXI, 10, 1–6), moralizing, pronounces the indictment subsequently repeated down the centuries of the contrast between Seneca's philosophical pretensions and his behaviour – Nero began among other things to exercise more authority in the field of imperial legislation. But the first idea that occurred to him, the one already mentioned of abolishing all customs duties and indirect taxes (Tacitus, *Ann.* XIII, 50, 1, regarded it as evidence of megalomania and a tendency to indulge in demagoguery, and we have no reason today to take a different view from Tacitus), was withdrawn without even being officially proposed. Nero had been convinced by the advice of the *seniores* of its inopportuneness, and the state of affairs which had given rise to his impulse, namely discontent and the rapacity of the tax collectors, provoked legislation which no doubt forms one of the measures produced by the beneficent administrative activity of these years and one owing no more than usual to the Princeps himself. A regulation on the *publica* was published at this time and steps were taken to prevent abuses by the tax collectors and at the same time to encourage businessmen, for example by exempting ships assigned to the transport of grain from the tax on property. Fundamentally there was nothing in all this that was not a continuation in all essentials of the legislation and methods of the preceding years. For instance, just at this time the disputes of the people of Puteoli were heard in the Senate and men appointed by the Senate were sent to the spot to take appropriate measures; and the Senate also permitted the Syracusans to increase the number of their gladiators, not without causing Tacitus, who mentions the matter in connection with Thrasea Paetus (*Ann.*, XIII, 49), to emphasize the triviality of some of the subjects discussed at this period.

In fact the Princeps's urge to assert his despotic power was still displayed primarily in the field of private caprice, but in such a way as to involve the destiny of the state. The tradition does not omit the prodigies announcing the turning point in the development of Nero's principate: a flame sprang from the ground at Colonia, Agrippina's city, and the fig-tree called 'Ruminalis' withered and then revived again. The 'magnorum rei publicae malorum initium'[1] was set in motion by Poppaea Sabina, daughter of T. Ollius, the friend of Sejanus, but known by the name of her mother – the Poppaea Sabina who had been Messalina's rival and victim – in memory of her grandfather, the great Poppaeus Sabinus. Beautiful, intelligent and unscrupulous, like her mother, she had first been the wife of one Rufrius Crispinus, by whom she had had a son, but had just married M. Salvius Otho, for years the intimate friend and drinking companion of the Princeps. It may well be that when Poppaea married Otho she was already aiming at a higher conquest and the enterprise did not turn out to be difficult, favoured as it was by Otho's incautious praising of his wife to Nero, who fell madly in love with her. Although Otho had not yet been praetor he was sent off as governor to Lusitania, where he remained until the Civil War, ruling with unexpected wisdom.[2] Thus the end of the year found the Princeps furiously pursuing, against the wishes of Agrippina and his ministers, his new plan of marriage to Poppaea who, saturated in oriental mysticism, must have implanted heaven knows what new ideas about the essence of power in his mind. Nero was probably carried away just at this time by the special honours voted by the Senate for the victory won in the East by Corbulo, who had captured the capital of Armenia, Artaxata. Henceforth he would tolerate neither advisers nor rivals. Faustus Cornelius Sulla, whose slaves clashed with those of the Princeps on one of the usual nocturnal expeditions, could not avoid the charge of attempted assassination and was banished to Marseilles. Then it was his mother's turn. Poppaea succeeded in con-vincing Nero that the only obstacle to the divorce of Octavia and their own marriage was Agrippina, and matricide was decided upon early in 59. Because it was one of the most famous crimes in ancient history our sources are in substantial agreement in their account of it, from the horrifying details of Agrippina's attempts to retain her hold on her son to those of the execution of the plan engineered by the freedman Anicetus, commander of the fleet based at Misenum.

Agrippina's death had to look like an accident and to this end, after a banquet given for her by her son at Baiae on the occasion of the *Quin-quatria* (on 19 March and the days following it), she was embarked at dead

---

[1] TAC., *Ann.*, XIII, 45, 1.
[2] *Ibid.*, 46. The slightly different version of *Hist.*, I, 13, 3 is to be explained by the adoption of another of the 'rumores' which were certainly numerous in matters of this sort.

of night for the trip back to Antium on a ship tampered with in such a way that it was bound to sink soon after it had put to sea. This in fact happened before it had rounded Cape Misenum; but the sturdy woman, although injured, swam to safety and took refuge in a villa on the Lucrine lake. Thinking it best to pretend that she did not understand the significance of what had happened, she sent a messenger, the freedman Agerinus, to her son to inform him of the danger which she had escaped. Since Nero himself was overcome by fear, Anicetus once again resolved the situation, not without the intervention of Seneca and Burrus, though the latter refused for his own part and that of the praetorian guard to do violence to a daughter of Germanicus. The commander of the fleet, with a ship's captain and a centurion, found Agrippina in her refuge and murdered her brutally. The official version of the affair, that Agrippina's messenger had been an assassin sent by her to kill her son, and that she had killed herself when the attempt failed, must have been universally accepted. The matricide, at first racked by remorse, finished by believing this story himself when it was repeated to him by the centurions and tribunes of the praetorian cohorts at Burrus's instigation, by his flattering friends and by delegations from the towns of Campania, which promised festivals and sacrifices. The praetorian guards received a donative. Nero went off to Naples and from there sent the Senate a message, probably written by Seneca, containing the public version of the episode and violent recriminations against Agrippina. The Senate voted thanksgivings in all the temples, the addition of games to the *Quinquatria*, the erection of a gold statue of Minerva in the senate house, with a statue of the Princeps beside it, and in addition that Agrippina's birthday (6 November) should be regarded as a day of ill omen. Thrasea Paetus alone walked out of the Senate. There followed the recall of exiles banished through Agrippina and other acts of clemency. However, Nero did not yet dare to return to Rome; but when, feeling reassured, he did so, he found the populace marshalled as if to watch a triumph, and like a triumphing general he went up to the Capital to render thanks to the gods. Agrippina's power must certainly have been hated and her disappearance seemed to signify the end of an influence regarded as sinister. In reality it simply meant the destruction of the balance of influences and restraints on which the business of governing had rested and which had resisted, if more and more feebly, the Emperor's restless longing to forge ahead to the imposition of his own absolute will.

THE ASSERTION OF DESPOTISM

The programme that Nero wanted to impose on the empire was more humane and practicable than that of Gaius but possibly in more irreconcilable opposition to Roman tradition, readier as it was to recognize the divinity of the living Princeps than to adapt itself to a change of custom and to find itself forced to translate into reality the splendid and heroic life of the most admired masterpieces of Greek literature. Nero's logic did not find it strange or unseemly that the senators of his own time should be obliged to compete in public like the princes of Greek cities or the heroes of the fifth book of the *Aeneid*. He himself gave the lead, and the story of his reign after the assassination of his mother is filled *ad nauseam* in the sources with the episodes and enactments in which he exerted, in his dealings with a Roman society amazed and hurt by his behaviour, especially in the upper classes, his own characteristic form of despotic will. It may be that the sources, preserving mainly the voice of hatred, have concentrated on this activity alone and concealed or minimized others in which he must nevertheless have interested himself to some extent, but it remains undeniable that this particular activity was preeminent as the deliberately willed manifestation of the emperor's genuine majesty. The rest could be looked after by the organs of government, which fortunately still functioned on their own account. So already in 59, while the incipient weariness of his subjects was being expressed anonymously in *graffiti* alluding to the matricide, Nero began to engage in chariot racing and musical contests. Seneca and Burrus, once again indulgently yielding to what they believed to be the expression of a caprice and themselves giving the signals for applause, could only insist that the exhibitions should take place in the private stadium of the Vatican valley and at first before an audience of friends. But soon the whole populace was admitted and senators whose names Tacitus omits out of respect for their glorious ancestors (Cassius Dio,[1] with an eye for rhetorical effect, chooses them from the most famous of the old Roman families – the Furii, the Horatii, the Fabii, the Porcii, the Valerii) were forced to make an exhibition of themselves in the arena, in the presence of provincials who pointed out to each other, thus cheapened, the descendants of their conquerors.

To be accurate, the final shame of appearing on the stage was avoided, in the view of the Princeps, by the character he assigned to these displays, which were supposed to be Greek games, like the famous ones of Olympia

---

[1] TAC., *Ann.*, XIV, 14, 3; CASS. D., LXI, 17, 4.

and the Isthmus; and such in fact were the *Iuvenalia*, dramatic and musical games introduced just at this time, and also the *Neronia*, instituted at the beginning of 60 and scheduled to be repeated every five years, with contests in music, singing, poetry, oratory, athletics and chariot racing, and the consequent distribution of oil to senators and knights. But Roman society was not persuaded of the reality of these distinctions and the pitiful sight of the eighty-year-old noblewoman Aelia Catella being forced to dance in the *ludi iuvenales* must have justified the feelings of those who thought the dead were fortunate.[1] The Princeps took part in the competitions, preferably as a lyre-player, and in the *Neronia* of 60 he was also given the first prize for oratory, even though he had not entered his name for the contest. In any case he thought of nothing else. Even at table he practised with the poets and after dinner he spent his time with the philosophers, enjoying their controversies. Propaganda and flattery had already formed an authoritative current of official opinion on the timeliness and excellence of the games he had established. Their permanent success was assured by the institution of the *Augustiani*, a quasi-military body of young knights, five thousand in number, forming a genuine 'claque' organized in companies assigned to the various kinds of applause – 'Hornets', 'Roof-tiles', 'Flat-tiles'[2] – and commanded by leaders who were generously paid. Nor should we be surprised that just at this point the tradition begins to speak of the rapacity which – rendered ever more necessary by his mad prodigality – became a characteristic feature of Nero's tyranny, as it had been of Gaius's. For even if there is some doubt about the report of the murder in 59 of his aunt Domitia, his father's surviving sister (the other, Domitia Lepida, had fallen a victim to Agrippina in 54), a report given by Suetonius and Cassius Dio – the motive alleged being his desire to gain possession of her property – but omitted by Tacitus,[3] the expenses incurred and about to be incurred in inaugurating and continuing the 'new development' of his displays of sovereign power must have made it obvious that once supplies had been exhausted money would be procured by any means that lay to hand.

Such was the course of the years 59 to 62 in home affairs, which were still influenced by Seneca and Burrus so far as real acts of government were concerned, but less and less effectively. Our sources do not in fact record many events for these years, apart from those abroad like the great

[1] CASS. D., LXI, 19, 2–3.

[2] SUET., *Ner.*, 20, 3. Evidently distinguished by their mode of applauding: by buzzing; by clapping with hands hollowed like roofing tiles; and by clapping with hands spread out like flat tiles.

[3] SUET., *Ner.*, 34, 5; CASS. D., LXI, 17, 1; cf. TAC., *Ann.*, XIII, 19, 4.

revolt in Britain and the operations in the East, in which one can trace an interest on the part of the Princeps different from the basic one described above. In 59 he charged the Senate with the measures to be taken after a bloody quarrel that had broken out in Pompeii between Nucerians and Pompeians during the games: and in a controversy concerning the recovery of state lands usurped by private individuals in Cyrenaica he gave judgement in favour of the accused official, Acilius Strabo, who had been given the job of recovering the lands by Claudius, but he allowed the occupiers to retain the estates, with the evident aim of making himself more popular than his predecessor. In 60, a year in which for six months Nero held his fourth consulship, the appearance after the *Neronia* of a comet excited expectations of something new and all eyes turned to the nearest possible claimant to the throne, Rubellius Plautus, who managed to avoid trouble for the moment by accepting the Princeps's advice to retire to his possessions in Asia. In the same year the case of Laodicea – a city in Asia which was struck by an earthquake and rose again out of its own resources – was cited as a proof of the empire's happiness under Nero; Puteoli was given, as a title of honour, the status of *colonia* (Colonia Claudia Neronensis Puteolana); and veterans were settled, without much success, at Tarentum and Antium. At Antium noteworthy work was also carried out on the harbour. Two interventions by Nero are also recorded in 60, one to eliminate a competitive situation in the election of praetors and the other in the matter of trials. The year ended with the condemnation of the procurator Vibius Secundus, who had been accused by his Mauretanian subjects. In the year 61 the figure of the Princeps can hardly be glimpsed in the sources, except for one act in complete conformity with his ideals, the foundation of a gymnasium, on which occasion oil was once again distributed to senators and knights 'Graeca facilitate';[1] for the rest, the year was marked at home solely by a number of crimes. The senator Valerius Fabianus forged a will, abetted by, among others, Antonius Primus, who here makes his first and dishonourable appearance in history. The *praefectus urbi*, Pedanius Secundus, was murdered by one of his slaves and as a result all his four hundred slaves were executed *en masse*. In addition, there was the condemnation, welcome to the senators, of the Tarquitius Priscus who under Claudius had accused Statilius Taurus.

In 62 the young despot's struggle to emancipate himself seemed to have reached a victorious conclusion. The year opened with the trials of Antistius Sosianus, who was accused by Cossutianus Capito, the son-in-law of Tigellinus, and Fabricius Veiento; these were the first trials for

[1] TAC., *Ann.*, XIV, 47, 2.

treason under Nero. Then came the death of Burrus, a decisive event, which was bound to raise the suspicion, not supported by any evidence, that it was not natural but engineered by the Princeps. Of his two successors – Faenius Rufus, until then prefect of the corn supply, and Ofonius Tigellinus, a Sicilian of low birth already banished by Gaius in 39 for intrigues with Agrippina, neglected under Claudius, prominent again under Nero as counsellor in vice and already appointed *praefectus vigilum* – one was evidently appointed to throw dust in the eyes of the people, who liked him for his good administration of the corn supply, and the other was to continue in a higher post his collaboration with the Princeps. The effects were soon felt. First came Seneca's retirement, inevitable sooner or later once the collaboration with Burrus had come to an end. Marked on both sides by the amplest displays of courtesy and deference, the departure of the teacher and minister signified the end of the compromise, beneficial to the empire, of effective and realistic rule behind the façade of imperial majesty, and the defeat of a system of government. With the help of Tigellinus, who had become in practice the new factotum, while the weak Faenius Rufus was kept in order with continual reminders of his old devotion to Agrippina, there now followed the elimination of the possible claimants to the throne, Faustus Cornelius Sulla and Rubellius Plautus. They were accused of revolutionary intrigues and put to death, one at Marseilles, the other in Asia. Nero informed the Senate of the danger, and it struck the two men off its roll and voted thanksgivings. Encouraged by the attitude of the Senate, which took his criminal activities for glorious deeds,[1] he then repudiated his wife on the pretext that she had not borne him any children; he made her the ill-omened gifts of Burrus's house and the estates of Rubellius Plautus and then sent her under guard into Campania. Twelve days later he married Poppaea Sabina. Not content with repudiating Octavia, at the instigation of Poppaea he tried to disgrace the unhappy woman with a charge of adultery; when this came to nothing and the populace welcomed with joy the news that Nero had repented and was going to recall Octavia, Anicetus was given the job of finally ruining her. Declaring that he was the adulterer, he was given a comfortable exile in Sardinia and Octavia was imprisoned on the island of Pandataria where, possibly on 9 June, a day which was to be a fateful one for Nero too,[2] she was put to death. She was just over twenty when she died and, alone among all the Julio-Claudian ladies, she left behind her a long echo of compassionate sympathy in the tradition.

By the end of the year, with the suppression of the freedmen Doryphorus

---

[1] TAC., *Ann.*, 60, 1.   [2] SUET., *Ner.*, 57, 1.

and the already powerful Pallas, on whose wealth – not the smallest advantage – the Princeps could also lay his hands, none of the old circle of advisers and administrators was left. In name and in fact the Princeps had attained the full measure of his absolute power. At the beginning of 63, when Poppaea gave birth at Antium to the little Claudia, the whole Senate (only Thrasea Paetus was prevented from attending) went to congratulate him, and mother and child received the title of Augusta. A few months later the baby died and was beatified as *diva Claudia*. Significantly, Tacitus, in the brief and not entirely clear report of a denunciation of Seneca for seditious activities with which Book XIV of the *Annals* closes (65, 2), puts as early as 62 the first hint of the Pisonian conspiracy. Whether or not he was right in his chronology, the complete collapse of the principate just at that time made the solution of tyrannicide, employed in the case of Gaius, once again topical.

The senatorial nobility must have been at daggers drawn with Nero, exposed as it was to his exotic demands, which hurt its dignity, and also to the more concrete perils of greed and suspicion. The praetorian guard must have been divided between the honourable weakness of Rufus and the shameless servility of Tigellinus. The years of Nero's unimpaired personal power, from 63 to 66, rested at home on these unstable elements; but the armies were still loyal, and the provinces, which knew only that they had an emperor, one more splendid than the previous ones, and that some among their numbers – the eastern provinces, to be accurate – were the object of his predilection, made no move beyond displaying the veneration appropriate to the imperial cult, which had now become normal practice. On the purely human plane they were also disposed to attribute to the personal merit of the emperor the beneficial fruits of the anonymous good government. In 62 the power of the Princeps, now asserted without further let or hindrance in public life and government as well as in the private sphere, was displayed in the directive to continue the erection of the trophies and arch on the Capitol voted by the Senate for the victories over the Parthians, in spite of the arrival of bad news from Armenia. With the same ostentatious assurance Nero ordered a large quantity of corn that had gone bad to be thrown into the Tiber and did not increase the price of grain, although two hundred ships had been destroyed by a storm in the port of Ostia and another hundred by fire while they were sailing up the Tiber. He also set up a commission of three ex-consuls to inspect revenues and was able to boast of putting into the treasury every year from his own resources a good sixty million sesterces – something, so he said, that his predecessors had not done. Naturally he maintained official relations with the Senate for ordinary administrative business; in this he differed from Gaius, whose wild mentality did not admit half measures in the implementation of a programme of crude, total, personal power. Nero pursued what he believed to be the lofty ideal of the regeneration of mankind through the beneficent influence of his own virtues; he pursued it tyrannically, but he had to devote some interest to everyday political realities – the questions debated in the Senate, the demands of the provinces, which had to be considered if only to gain popularity, and the reports from the East. He would then intervene, if only with contradictory and harmful decisions (as we shall see in connection with the eastern campaigns) or else would let things take their course and depart to attend to his own whims or to the programme that dominated his thoughts above all else. But traces of continuous collaboration in this sense are always visible, and if the few good qualities – among so many shameful ones – recorded by Suetonius (*Nero*, 15, 1), such as that of calling on his advisers for their individual opinions in writing and then drawing his own conclusions from them after careful reflection, are to be regarded as holding good for the whole duration of his reign, we must recognize that appearances at least were not trampled upon by Nero with the brutal disregard shown by Gaius.

In 62 the Senate passed more resolutions: one intended to prevent fictitious adoptions by people wishing to qualify, with election to magistracies in mind, for the preference granted by the Lex Papia Poppaea to those with a certain number of children; and another forbidding thanksgivings by provincials to governors. Neither regulation was of much interest to the Princeps, who was certainly more concerned about the destruction by lightning of his barely completed gymnasium and with the work, just starting then, on the baths in the Campus Martius. In 63 the one recorded measure of his not connected with his favourite field of activity – shows – is the granting of the *ius Latii* to the Maritime Alps; apart, of course, from his interest in events in the East. He removed the Euripus or trench round the Circus Maximus to make new places for the knights, and put up instead a palisade of wood clad with ivory to protect the spectators from the wild beasts, the function previously fulfilled by the ten-foot-wide trench. He made senators and matrons take part in the gladiatorial games staged that year. This passion of his grew in 64. But although he was obsessed with the idea of his own artistic merits and longed to display them, he did not dare to exhibit them on the stage at Rome and instead chose Naples, 'quasi Graecam urbem';[1] in fact at this

[1] TAC., *Ann.*, XV, 33, 2.

time he conceived the plan of going straight from Naples to Greece and of only presenting himself to the people of Rome after he had won the glorious old crowns and was at last worthy of its applause. At Naples, the audience had hardly left the theatre in which he had been singing when it collapsed, probably thanks to an earthquake (the previous year Pompeii had been almost completely destroyed by an earth tremor; these seismic disturbances may have been the prelude to the forthcoming re-awakening of Vesuvius). At Beneventum, on his way to Greece, he watched a gladiatorial show and at the same time sent orders for the death of D. Junius Silanus Torquatus, who had been consul in 53 and was one of the last survivors of an unhappy family whose misfortune it was to have a few drops of the blood of Augustus in its veins. Then, unexpectedly giving up the idea of a trip to Greece, he returned to Rome, possibly to announce with due solemnity a still more grandiose plan, that of visiting the whole East, and Egypt in particular. But he abandoned this journey too, 'amore patriae';[1] he could not bear to see the citizens looking so sad at the news of his departure. To demonstrate his love for them he arranged banquets all over Rome and lived among the populace, using the whole city 'quasi domo' and causing Tigellinus to organize the orgies which passed into popular legend as the salient events of the whole reign. Then he retired to Antium, where he was staying when he received the news of the greatest calamity to befall Rome since the days when it was captured by the Gauls.

Ten of the fourteen Augustan districts, that is, more than two-thirds of the city, were burnt down in the great fire which, starting in the night of 18/19 July at the end of the Circus Maximus adjoining the Palatine and Caelian hills, raged for six days and then flared up again for several more. The balanced account of the fire given by Tacitus (*Ann.*, XV, 38–41), from which it appears that when Nero was informed he returned to Rome, exerted himself to put the fire out, opened even private buildings and gardens to those without a roof over their heads and made sure that corn was available at a low price, is also the best evidence that the disaster was an accident. But Tacitus also records the 'rumor', which was certainly current, that the fire was criminal in origin and had been arranged by Nero himself. It was said that the Princeps had been seen to walk on to the stage at his own house and there to recite to the accompaniment of the lyre, while all around was in flames, his own *Sack of Troy*. The grandeur of the rebuilding that followed and the extent of the area embraced by Nero's private residence subsequently seemed a decisive argument for his

[1] *Ibid.*, 36, 2.

guilt. For Suetonius (*Nero*, 38) and Cassius Dio (LXII, 16–18), who present him singing from the top of the tower of Maecenas, this is indubitable: slaves of the Princeps, even the watchmen, were seen feeding the flames and impeding the efforts of anyone trying to halt them. But Nero may well have improvised the recitation while carried away by the horror and fascination of the spectacle, which translated into reality his exalted literary imaginings; and he may have taken advantage of the destruction of the city to rebuild it on better lines without having set fire to it on purpose with this aim in mind. As for the people seen feeding the flames, this kind of phenomenon is always reported in calamities. Nevertheless, the rumour did circulate and it is significant in itself that such a story should have arisen and assumed such menacing consistency that the Princeps had to remedy the situation by looking for a scapegoat. He found it in the Christians, who now make their first important appearance in the history of the empire as people quite distinct from the Jews. They were blamed for the fire and many of them were sacrificed to the popular hatred. Some were torn to pieces by dogs, some were crucified, and some were impaled and burnt like human torches, so that their sufferings served at the same time as a spectacle in the games staged day and night in the Princeps's own gardens. That Nero chose this particular distraction makes it clear that the Christians must already have been disliked by the urban populace; but the savagery of the punishment gave rise to a feeling of pity for the unhappy victims, whose horrible fate really did no more than satisfy the cruelty of one man. On this subject, too, as on the question of the emperor's responsibility, the judgement of Tacitus, if silent about the hatred for the Christians from which he himself was not exempt, allows the truth to emerge: the Christians were innocent and the 'rumor' about Nero's guilt persisted. However, the episode introduced into the story of the empire's relations with foreign religions a harshness undeniably exercised in a special way where Christianity was concerned. The martyrdoms of the apostles Peter and Paul, who arrived in Rome during the aftermath of the terrible mass execution, may have been episodes in the period of attention focused in this direction by Nero for purely political reasons.

Meanwhile Rome was in the process of being rebuilt. The ships which sailed up the Tiber laden with corn sailed down it again loaded with rubble, which was dumped in the marshy parts of Ostia. The new buildings rose in accordance with regulations which prescribed the amount of material to be employed and limited their height. They faced wide, straight roads, were provided with porticos and furnished with water more rationally distributed from the aqueducts (the *aqua Claudia* was now extended to the Caelian hill and the *Marcia* to the Aventine). There were people who missed the cool shade of the narrow old streets, but on the whole the city must have become a more agreeable place to live in. The most grandiose works were those directed by Severus and Celer, who had already pandered to Nero's megalomania by suggesting the excavation of a navigable canal from Ostia to Lake Avernus in Campania – a project that was actually started – and who were now given the task of rebuilding the Emperor's palace. Even before the fire these two had tried to enlarge the palace by using the slopes of the Esquiline and linking the buildings on the Palatine with the *horti* of Maecenas by means of the *domus transitoria*. There now arose, running in this same direction, the *domus aurea*, with its splendidly decorated halls, its porticos, temples and shrines, while the gardens, woods, lakes and pavilions also occupied the valley between the Palatine, Esquiline and Caelian – subsequently to become the site of the Colosseum – and a good part of the Caelian hill itself. On the Velia rose a colossal statue of the sun in the likeness of Nero, whose glory as the builder of all this naturally had to be commemorated and inflated to divine proportions. But the glory was expensive; to rebuild Rome, Italy and the provinces were pillaged and the treasures of their temples impounded. To adorn the imperial palace, works of art and even the statues of the gods were brought from the temples of Greece and Asia. These acts of plunder, together with the rapacious extortions of the tax-collectors, certainly provoked in the minds of the provincials – not merely in the scrupulous conscience of Seneca, who just at this time began to talk more about retiring – feelings of resentment and anxiety for the future.

Other disasters, such as a revolt of gladiators at Praeneste, which for a moment caused people to fear a renewal of the terror produced by Spartacus, and the shipwreck on the shore at Cumae of a large part of the fleet based at Misenum, are recorded by the sources in this same year of 64, together with a long list of prodigies, obviously intended to establish the atmosphere for the following year – rendered famous by the big Pisonian conspiracy – and for the now not far distant catastrophe. In fact what remains of Tacitus's narrative, which breaks off in the year 66 with the death of Thrasea Paetus, and those of Suetonius and Cassius Dio are the story of one long orgy of excitement, absolutism and terror, in which it will be as well to distinguish, as usual, the moments of more normal activity, such as the recruitment carried out in Narbonese Gaul to put fresh blood into the armies of Illyricum and the ordinary business of administration. Nevertheless, the form taken by the reaction which finally arose out of the certainly exacerbated state of affairs and involved the city of Rome itself, Italy, the armies and the provinces, the last two of which had never before been provoked to general revolt, indicates the extent to which confusion reigned in the last years of the Neronian tyranny.

However, the first attempt at organized resistance to the Princeps, the big Pisonian conspiracy, failed miserably at the beginning of 65. Named after C. Calpurnius Piso, the man chosen by most of the conspirators to replace Nero, it had gathered together in too vast a network people discontented for the most various reasons, particularly members of the upper classes – senators and knights – but also soldiers of the praetorian guard. The nobles were tired of living in a continual state of fear and of being constantly humiliated, especially since Nero – probably yielding more to the spontaneous development of the bureaucracy established by Claudius than with any deliberate intention of belittling the Roman ruling classes – had begun to make extensive use of officials of eastern origin. The soldiers could not tolerate the excessive power of Tigellinus. Then there was the philosophical opposition to tyranny in itself, an opposition inspired by Stoicism; while the opposition of the poets was probably expressed in the anonymous *Laus Pisonis*. All these people longed for a change; some few – the idealists – hoped to restore the Republic; most would have been content with a Princeps with some respect for tradition and the rights of the aristocracy. To judge from Tacitus's not very flattering portrait (*Ann.*, XV, 48), the candidate selected does not seem to have been the man best fitted to satisfy these aspirations, for this friend of Gaius (who had snatched his wife from him on his wedding day), a ranter, poet and singer in tragic costume, might even have been expected to produce a repetition of Nero's ostentation. Perhaps precisely because Piso fell outside his own moralistic categories, Cassius Dio does not even name him, and tells the story – one that seemed more rational but was certainly not in accord with the facts – of a noble plot by philosophers, headed by Seneca and Musonius Rufus and followed by the martyrdom of the principal participants – Seneca himself, Barea Soranus and Thrasea Paetus (LXII, 24–7). People must certainly also have thought of Seneca as a possible candidate for the throne, granted the extensive nature of the conspiracy, which no doubt embraced several different currents of opinion; but Piso, apart from the personal ambitions and the interplay of interests which we are not in a position to judge, must have been the man most acceptable to the majority, which in the age of Nero must after all have assimilated the cultural tastes and aspirations carried to a mad, tyrannical extreme by the Princeps. In the event, the failure of the plot made any further discussion or choice superfluous.

The plot was first revealed by a freedwoman called Epicharis to a captain in the fleet at Misenum, Volusius Proculus, in an attempt to win him over to the cause. He told the whole story to Nero, but since Epicharis had prudently not mentioned any names the matter finished there, though not without alerting the already suspicious emperor and forcing the conspirators to hasten the execution of their plan. Nero was to be attacked during the games in the circus on the feast of Ceres (19 April). But on the very eve of the appointed day the senator Flavius Scaevinus, one of the most resolute of the conspirators, was denounced by his freedman, Milicus, along with another of the principal assassins-designate, the knight Antonius Natalis. The latter, subjected to torture and having extracted the promise (subsequently kept) of a pardon, named Piso and Seneca; Scaevinus named others, including Lucan, persecuted by Nero out of literary jealousy. There followed scenes of vileness and heroism: senators denounced friends and relations (Lucan is said to have denounced his own mother), Faenius Rufus participated with bitterness in the trials so that he should not be unmasked, and praetorian colonels not concerned in the conspiracy carried out the sentences of death on colleagues whose complicity had been discovered; on the other hand Epicharis, a woman and an ex-slave, died under torture without revealing one name. Altogether a score of well-known people were put to death or obliged to commit suicide either at once or in the following months, among them Seneca, Lucan, Piso and Claudia Antonia, the last surviving daughter of Claudius. Nero, emerging from this narrow escape as if from a military victory, distributed military rewards: to the praetorian guard, two thousand sesterces a head and free grain for life; to Tigellinus and two loyal senators, the ex-consul P. Petronius Turpilianus and the praetor-designate M. Cocceius Nerva (the future emperor), who had distinguished themselves in the repression of the conspiracy, the triumphal insignia, with the special distinction for Tigellinus and Nerva of having their portraits put up on the Palatine as well as in the forum; and to Nymphidius Sabinus, Faenius Rufus's successor as joint commander of the praetorian guard, the consular insignia. But he must have been frightened by the plot, which made him see how widely hated he was by the Roman aristocracy. He too had now arrived at the stage, inevitably reached by all Augustus's successors, of a complete break with the nobility, even though the Senate officially voted thanksgivings for his escape from danger and suggested that the name of the fateful month, April, should be changed to Neroneus. Other measures included the proposal, made by the consul-designate Anicius Cerealis, to build a temple to the 'god' Nero, as a recognition of his sovereign supremacy. This suggestion was abandoned because so far people had only become 'gods' after their death and the honour could also be a presage.

After the conspiracy the terror did not slacken. Tigellinus was given *carte blanche* to eliminate anyone who might represent a danger to the Princeps, while Nero himself grew more and more frenzied in the assertion of absolutism in accordance with his concept of omnipotent and omnipresent majesty. He also grew more and more isolated and blinded in an atmosphere of extravagant expectations and forced festivity which could produce an episode like that of the illusions aroused by the alleged discovery of the treasure of Dido, illusions cultivated by the whole of Rome in a sort of collective hallucination. This episode also took place in the context of real financial difficulties, which just at this time provoked, in conjunction with the repression of the conspiracy, still greater harshnesss in the field of confiscations. These had been intensified, at any rate since 64, even where no semblance of guilt existed, as in the case of the six African landowners who were disposed of so that their extensive farms could pass into the hands of the imperial treasury. Nero also revived the obligation to name the Princeps in wills, and Piso himself left a wretched document full of self-abasement and flattery in order to save what could be saved for his family. A genuine monetary reform, with the reduction in the weight of the aureus from $\frac{1}{40}$ to $\frac{1}{45}$ of a pound and in that of the silver denarius from $\frac{1}{84}$ to $\frac{1}{96}$ of a pound, together with an experimental extension of minting in orichalc, had been put into effect since 64; but even if it was also recommended for technical reasons – so much so that the weights, thus stabilized, of gold and silver coins remained unchanged until Caracalla – the reduction in weight could easily seem to have been devised with a view to the benefit of the issuing authority. On the other hand, Nero gave no thought at all to the idea of reducing expenditure. Still in 65 he started giving performances in the theatre again. As the time for the repetition of the quinquennial *Neronia* approached, the Senate vainly sought to forestall Nero by voting him in advance the first prize in singing and oratory. However, he complained that he had no need of such subterfuges in order to be victorious,[1] and, appearing on the stage, sang in accordance with all the rules for artists not only before throngs of the urban proletariat but also in the presence of austere, old-

---

[1] TAC., *Ann.*, XVI, 4, 2.

fashioned Italians and of senators, who ran a tremendous risk if they stayed at home and a fairly serious one even if they merely looked sad at this shameless behaviour or were absent-minded and bored, like Vespasian, who nodded off and nearly lost his life. Tradition also connects with these goings-on the death of Poppaea, who was pregnant and did not survive the blows she received from Nero when he returned rather late to the palace after a chariot-race and was reproached by her. Her body, embalmed and not burnt on a pyre, was placed in the Mausoleum of Augustus after the *laudatio* pronounced from the rostrum by Nero himself and the *consecratio* voted by the Senate.

The conflict with the nobility continued with the accusation by the Princeps and condemnation by the Senate – how freely the verdict was given can be imagined – of the jurist C. Cassius Longinus, banished to Sardinia, and of his nephew L. Junius Silanus Torquatus, the last of his unhappy family, banished to Barium and killed there. Then came, still in 65, the deaths of L. Antistius Vetus, Nero's colleague in the consulship of 55, of his daughter Pollitta, the widow of Rubellius Plautus, and of Sextia, Vetus's mother-in-law. The year 66 saw the deaths of Anteius Rufus and M. Ostorius Scapula, son of the governor of Britain, of Annaeus Mela, Anicius Cerealis, Rufrius Cripinus – the son of Poppaea's first husband – of Petronius, Barea Soranus and Thrasea Paetus. There were so many deaths that Tacitus says explicitly that he records only some of them (*Ann.* XVI, 16, 1); and it is well known that with the death of Thrasea Paetus, dramatically presented as the death of a wise man, fate determined that what is preserved of the *Annals* should come to a stop. A lively conflict was thus in progress, and if the quality of the victims and their previous relations with Nero lead us to think that it must have still been confined to the urban nobility or to limited circles of ostentatious opposition, it must have spread, as it easily could, until it affected, with fatal consequences, those nobles serving as military commanders.

But before we come to this conflict and to the final breakdown it is worth mentioning an event at Rome, the coronation of Tiridates in 66, that marked the zenith of Nero's façade of power. Suetonius (*Nero*, 13, 1) is quite right to place it 'inter spectacula', for this theatrical display was the natural outward manifestation of the essence of the 'lord and saviour of the world',[1] as the Princeps was henceforward called in the East. Indeed, he was already identified with still greater deities, with Jupiter, Apollo, Hercules and the Sun; and names of cities were changed in his

---

[1] DITTENBERGER, *Or. Gr. Inscr. Sel.*, 668; *Syll.*³, 814.

honour (even Rome was to become Neropolis), as were names of months: April had already become 'Neroneus', May was to become 'Claudius' and June 'Germanicus'. The Parthian prince, who had been recognized as king of Armenia as a result of a compromise, was given a splendid welcome at Naples after a journey of nine months made overland with a big retinue. Passing from feast to feast with a daily allowance of eight hundred thousand sesterces paid to him by the Roman state, he was accompanied to Rome by Nero himself and there, in the forum, he knelt before Nero – who was seated on a throne and dressed in triumphal regalia – worshipped him as Mithras and received the crown from his hands. The homage thus rendered to the Roman power, the subsequent closing of the temple of Janus, the splendid feasts, at which Nero showed his prowess as a lyre-player and charioteer, the exchange of gifts, the commissioning of architects by Tiridates to rebuild Artaxata, which was naturally to be renamed Neroneia, and the pomp connected with the presence of the eastern prince at Rome must have made a great impression. But the whole affair was basically superficial and while it provided fresh food for Nero's megalomaniac dreams it did not resolve the real difficulties of the internal situation. Even in the specific field of foreign affairs, this spectacular conclusion to the eastern problem, though it secured years of relative peace, represented, in the homage paid by an Arsacid prince to the Roman Emperor, only a formal success, compared with the concrete success achieved by Parthia, which had secured effective possession of Armenia.

EXTERNAL AFFAIRS: PARTHIA AND BRITAIN, THE RHINE AND THE DANUBE

The important activity abroad that took place under Nero seems to have been largely unaffected by any direct personal intervention on his part, especially in the early years, since the system of imperial government, organized – mainly by Claudius – in a central administrative body, must naturally have shared, in the field of foreign policy as well, in the examination of situations and must have influenced the decisions taken. Measures dictated by caprice are indeed perceptible; they help to explain oscillations in the line pursued on the Armenian problem and are reflected in the contradictory reports we are given about Nero's intention to abandon Britain,[1] and about the grandiose plans for expansion in the East with which he toyed in his last few years. He must certainly have made his

[1] SUET., Ner., 18.

will felt more and more as he achieved his personal emancipation and asserted his despotic power, and foreign dynasties and peoples must always have seen in him, in accordance with their own experience of absolute monarchy, the holder of the power with which alone they dealt. But foreign policy in general was conducted according to a fixed tradition which was on the whole, with some oscillations possibly exaggerated by modern interpretations, that of Augustus and Tiberius. What was new since the wars of the Augustan age was the length – and complexity – of the operations in the East, which lasted more or less throughout Nero's reign, and the assertion in them of the personality of a general like Domitius Corbulo, whose loyalty, taken in conjunction with the forces he controlled and the quality of the emperor he served, seems to have provoked wonder not least in his enemies themselves, even if we make allowances for the large degree of fabrication in the anecdotes retailed by Cassius Dio (LXII, 23, 5–6; LXIII, 6, 4). But already there were men who, in command of military forces, would do what he did not do and thereby give the signal – in a new way, from the periphery to the centre – for the revolt of the armies and the first great turning-point in the history of the principate.

At the end of 54 the news arrived in Rome that the Parthians were overrunning Armenia, having driven out Radamistus, and that Tiridates, brother of the Parthian king Vologaeses, was firmly established on the throne. There is also mention of a delegation of Armenian notables, who had certainly come to ask Rome to intervene. Appropriate measures were taken at once, by Seneca and Burrus, as Tacitus (*Ann.* XIII, 6) gives us clearly to understand. A recruiting drive was ordered in the neighbouring provinces, to reinforce the eastern legions, which were to be moved up to the Armenian frontier. King Julius Agrippa II and King Antiochus of Commagene were instructed to build bridges over the Euphrates and to move into Parthian territory with their forces. Lesser Armenia was given to Aristobulus, another prince of the Herodian house, and Sophene to Sohaemus, a prince of the house of Emesa, not the man of the same name appointed tetrarch of the Ituraean Arabs by Gaius in 38. But meanwhile Vologaeses withdrew from Armenia because a rival to himself had appeared. The retreat of the Parthian king was hailed in the Roman Senate as a victory and the Princeps was voted special honours. Nevertheless, the general chosen to settle eastern affairs, the talented and austere Cn. Domitius Corbulo, appointed governor of the provinces of Cappadocia and Galatia, hastened to take up his post, and in the spring of 55 he must have already been in Cilicia, where Ummidius Quadratus, who had remained governor of Syria, had come to meet him to hand over to him, in accordance with his orders, two of his four legions. In fact, being jealous of the fame which preceded the new arrival and fearful of seeing his own decline, he wanted to avoid carrying out the transfer in his own province, especially since the client and allied princes, who were to put themselves under the orders of one or the other governor according to military requirements, did not conceal their liking for Corbulo. However, the first step in the confrontation with Vologaeses – the exhortation to resume good relations with Rome – was taken in common. Vologaeses, certainly still involved in the struggle with the pretender, accepted the suggestion and sent a number of important Parthians as hostages, probably taking the opportunity to rid himself of some of his enemies in the process. The handing over of the hostages led to a dispute, for the centurion sent by Quadratus to receive them was unwilling to resign himself to being set aside by the cohort commander (and thus his superior in rank) sent by Corbulo with the same orders. When the choice was left to the hostages they opted for Corbulo. The generals continued the altercation and the matter was only settled in Rome, with the command that the imperial fasces should be wreathed in laurel 'ob res a Quadrato et Corbulone prospere gestas'.[1]

Thus the first intervention ended in 55, to all appearances inconclusively, since Tiridates was left undisturbed on the throne of Armenia. The orders had certainly been to repair the slackness of the last years of Claudius's reign by more energetic demonstrations of military power, but not to exceed the usual limits of the traditional eastern policy. In any case, it was impossible to undertake active operations with the soft and undisciplined troops then forming the Syrian garrisons, and a considerable part of the time between 55 and 58, when war broke out again, was certainly employed by Corbulo in bringing the army up to scratch. He did this by discharging a large number of men, by enrolling fresh troops in Cappadocia and Galatia, by transferring one legion and its auxiliary troops from Moesia, and above all by enforcing strict discipline. In the winter of 57–8, when the war was resumed, Corbulo went straight into Armenia and in spite of the severity of the climate kept his troops under canvas, probably on the highest part of the Armenian plateau, in a favourable position to watch the moves of Tiridates who, sustained by his brother and the faction faithful to him, once again overran the country, attacking the supporters of the Romans but always avoiding pitched battles. Corbulo then divided his forces, so as to attack in his

---

[1] TAC., *Ann.*, XIII, 9, 3.

turn from various directions. He ordered Antiochus to invade Armenia from Commagene, and Pharasmanes – who in order to demonstrate his loyalty to the Romans had even killed his son Radamistus – to invade it from the other side. Tiridates, finding himself in an awkward situation, tried to open negotiations but used a threateningly superior tone which did not deceive the Roman general: evidently Vologaeses had once again been forced to look after his own affairs. In fact, the great revolt of the Hyrcanians had broken out. Corbulo's reply, that Tiridates should send a petition to Nero and, abandoning large ambitions, be content to obtain from the emperor's hand a 'regnum stabile'[1] – a reply that amounted in practice to the offer of the solution finally achieved, the recognition of formal Roman sovereignty over Armenia in the person of a Parthian prince – did not seem for the moment satisfactory and Tiridates, after an attempt at a parley frustrated on the Roman side through justified mistrust, started guerilla warfare again, trying to cut off the supplies coming from Trapezus. But this move also failed; Corbulo conducted a vigorous offensive campaign, taking one city and fortress after another, including the one called by Tacitus (*Ann.*, XIII, 38, 2–5) 'Volandum', probably not far from the capital, Artaxata. To protect his capital Tiridates finally appeared on the scene with substantial forces, hoping to lure the enemy into an ambush by the tactic of unexpected flight. When this last manœuvre also failed he withdrew, and Artaxata opened its gates to the Romans. The city was destroyed because it was too big to garrison, but probably not before the army had spent the winter of 58–9 there. The capture of the most ancient Armenian capital, announced in Rome at the end of 58, was the occasion for hailing Nero as *imperator* (probably for the sixth time) and voting him special honours.

In 59 and 60 Corbulo remained in Armenia completing the conquest. Moving away from Artaxata in the spring of 59, he marched south towards Tigranocerta, possibly traversing in reverse the route of Xenophon's Ten Thousand. He met little resistance and eliminated without mercy any that he did meet, but his troops suffered from the heat and the difficulty of obtaining supplies. After also experiencing an attempt at assassination, he reached the second capital, which surrendered, while the neighbouring fortress of Legerda was taken by assault. During the course of the year a request for a treaty of alliance was made at Rome by the Hyrcanians, who were keeping the Parthians occupied. We do not know the outcome of the request, but Corbulo arranged the journey of

---

[1] *Ibid.*, 37, 5.

the ambassadors in such a way that they avoided territory controlled by their common enemies. The winter of 59–60 was probably spent at Tigranocerta, for it was from there that in the spring of 60 Corbulo, sending Verulanus Severus on ahead with the auxiliaries, then moving personally with the legions, repelled Tiridates, who had re-entered Armenia from Media Atropatene. He drove Tiridates out of the country, finally robbing him of any inclination to reconquer the kingdom by force, and proceeded to carry out punitive expeditions against disloyal regions, enforcing in practice a direct occupation[1] which, although it did not represent the policy originally envisaged, had come into effect almost of its own accord after Tiridates's refusal to listen to his advice. Then suddenly, like a sort of *coup de théâtre*, possibly due to the direct intervention of Nero, in whom it is legitimate to assume some feelings of sympathy for the scions of eastern royal families who were guests of the imperial palace, the new king of Armenia arrived upon the scene, appointed by the Princeps in an unexpected return to the most orthodox Augustan practice. This new king was Tigranes (V), grandson of the Tigranes IV placed on the throne of Armenia by Augustus in A.D. 6 (that particular Tigranes had not stayed long in Armenia and had been put to death in Rome in 36), great-grandson of Herod the Great and also, on his mother's side, of Archelaus, the last king of Cappadocia, who had died in 17. Having spent a long time as a hostage in Rome, he received a mixed welcome in the kingdom assigned to him, but certainly not an enthusiastic one. His throne was buttressed by a Roman force of a thousand legionaries, three auxiliary cohorts and two auxiliary *alae*. The frontier regions of Armenia were assigned to the neighbouring kings – Pharasmanes of Iberia, Polemo of Pontus, Aristobulus of Lesser Armenia and Antiochus of Commagene – as a reward for their intervention. Corbulo, his task completed, withdrew into Syria, of which he was now governor, since Quadratus had died.

Thus in 60 the Armenian question was solved by a settlement very similar to the previous ones of Zeno Artaxias and Mithridates, except that it did not in fact take account, with this king fallen from the heavens, of local circumstances and tempers. For this reason it could not last. As well as internal opposition there was the threat from outside. Vologaeses, still involved in the fighting in Hyrcania, would have been glad for the moment not to intervene, but the refugee Tiridates insisted on his intervention to erase the shame of his own expulsion, especially as Tigranes had also dared to start attacking the neighbouring countries. He

---

[1] TAC., *Ann.*, XIV, 26, 1: 'possessionem Armeniae usurpabat'.

had invaded Adiabene, whose king, Monobazus, called on Vologaeses for help and threatened to go over to the Romans if he was left in the lurch. Vologaeses then decided on war; he solemnly bestowed on his brother the throne of Armenia and, giving him a force of cavalry led by Moneses, a Parthian grandee, and an Adiabenian force under Monobazus, he sent him into Armenia to drive out Tigranes. Vologaeses himself, after concluding the war with the Hyrcanians and probably leaving them independent, turned against Syria. Confronted with a complex situation, Corbulo decided for the moment to send two legions under Verulanus Severus and Vettius Bolanus as a garrison to Tigranes, with orders not to become involved too precipitately; and he wrote to Nero that Armenia needed a general of its own, since he himself had enough to do defending Syria, against which the main Parthian offensive in the now general war seemed to be aimed. He also reinforced the defences of the Euphrates. Meanwhile Tigranes, with the help of the Romans, was making a good job of defending himself against Moneses at Tigranocerta. Corbulo, from the Euphrates, despatched to Vologaeses, who was at Nisibis, halfway between Armenia and Mesopotamia, the centurion Casperius to remonstrate about the attack on a prince under Roman protection and to request him to stop the siege. Vologaeses, who even then did not want a direct confrontation with the Roman forces and was badly off for supplies, replied that he would apply to Nero to obtain for his brother what he had been offered and refused in 58, that is, peaceful possession of Armenia. Meanwhile he ordered Moneses to raise the siege of Tigranocerta and himself retired to his dominions. Naturally the Romans also retired, going off to spend the winter of 61–2 in Cappadocia and taking with them Tigranes, who now disappears without trace from the story.

Vologaeses and Armenia waited for Nero's reply to the embassy which had been sent to him. But the reply was evasive, and in an already curious situation, which betrayed a characteristic oscillation in policy (in fact, Tigranes and the solution of an anti-Parthian protectorate having been dropped, there was no obstacle to returning to the previous solution, always favoured by Corbulo, of recognizing a Parthian prince), there was now interposed the attempt at a third solution, that of direct occupation. An unfortunate plan, not in principle but through its incautious execution, it nevertheless prepared the way for the definitive solution. But it is characteristic that the decisions of the central government always followed, with some delay and in a clumsy fashion, the aims and forecasts of Corbulo, except for the experiment with Tigranes, a scheme never foreseen or desired by Corbulo. Even the starting-point of the decision to send another general with the task of direct conquest had been provided, in the last analysis, by Corbulo's request – recorded above, and naturally made with a different intention – to be relieved of responsibility for the Armenian theatre of operations.

The new commander, L. Caesennius Paetus, who had just been consul in 61, arrived in Cappadocia early in 62 and began his activities by belittling those of Corbulo and proclaiming to all and sundry that Armenia would very soon be brought under direct Roman administration. He had at his disposal two legions with numerous auxiliary forces, and a third legion was on the point of arriving from Moesia. However, he did not think it necessary to wait for it and, in spite of bad omens at the crossing of the Euphrates, invaded Armenia, marching in the direction of Tigranocerta. At Randeia, a spot on the right bank of the Arsanias, near the town of Arsamosata, he began to build his main camp and from there he did no more than raid and loot a land devoid of Parthian troops. He then withdrew, after sending to the Princeps letters 'qusai confecto bello, verbis magnificis, rerum vacuas'.[1] Vologaeses had for some time been watching the Syrian front, but seeing that there was nothing to be done there thanks to the formidable defences erected by Corbulo on the line of the Euphrates he turned with all his forces towards Armenia, soon putting in an awkward position the inept Paetus who, after a series of errors and unfortunate moves, decided to inform Corbulo of the situation. However, pride induced him to minimize his difficulties and consequently Corbulo, while preparing the requested reinforcements, did not attempt to hurry. After a more serious defeat, which led to the Parthians' closely besieging the camp at Randeia, Paetus was overcome by panic and sent his rival a message begging for help. Corbulo then set out in person, with substantial forces and a long caravan of camels carrying supplies, and proceeded by forced marches through Commagene and Cappadocia, where he began to meet stragglers from Paetus's army. Meanwhile Paetus had surrendered to Vologaeses. The conditions of the capitulation were that while the Parthians raised the siege of Randeia and left the area, reserving the right to send to Nero another embassy to repeat the request they had made before, the Romans were to evacuate Armenia, leave their supplies where they were, and build a bridge over the Arsanias to facilitate the departure of the Parthian forces. The news that Corbulo was only three days' march away may well have induced Vologaeses to end hastily and on relatively mild terms what was really the only direct clash between the Parthian king and the Romans in the whole war, but the fact remains that this clash

[1] TAC., *Ann.*, XV, 8, 2.

was resolved by the discomfiture of the Romans. It is thus not surprising that there was a widespread rumour that they had been forced to pass under the yoke, particularly as Paetus's retreat from Randeia was a precipitate flight. The two Roman armies met near the upper reaches of the Euphrates. When he had recovered his breath the cowardly fugitive suggested that they returned together into Armenia, but Corbulo replied drily that those were not the orders of the Princeps and turned back into Syria, while Paetus moved into Cappadocia, where he spent the winter of 62–3. On the Euphrates, instead of the expected attack from the Parthians came a proposal for negotiations. Vologaeses demanded the demolition of the forts built by Corbulo on the far side of the Euphrates and Corbulo demanded the complete evacuation of Armenia. The two sides agreed on these terms and at the beginning of 63 Armenia was once again independent.

But this could only be a transitory solution. Early in the spring of 63 ambassadors from Parthia arrived in Rome with a letter from Vologaeses saying that in spite of the victory gained by the Parthians Tiridates intended to accept the crown of Armenia from the Roman emperor and were it not for religious scruples he would come personally to Rome to receive it; however, he would assume it before the insignia and effigy of the Princeps, in the presence of the legions. Meanwhile Paetus had sent a false report implying that everything was going splendidly; he was given the lie by a centurion accompanying the Parthian delegation, but it was not thought prudent to accept the proposals of a victorious enemy and the ambassadors were sent away without any concession, though with gifts and the clear hint that if Tiridates had presented himself to the Princeps in person he would have got what he wanted. From now onwards the solution foreseen from the start, and then replaced by others through force of circumstances or less justifiable reasons, was inevitable. However, the compensation for the new situation, which might give the impression of weakness on the part of the Romans, was to be a demonstration of force and a permanent strengthening of the forces in Syria. So another legion came from Pannonia and the army of the East rose to the strength, never reached before, of seven legions. Corbulo, still simply *legatus Augusti pro praetore*, nevertheless received the *imperium maius* over all the governors and procurators of the neighbouring provinces, and also authority over the kings and tetrarchs. The new governor of Syria was C. Cestius Gallus. Caesennius Paetus, recalled to Rome, escaped with some banter from Nero and survived him to be sent back to Syria in 70 by Vespasian, who was a relative and friend of his and evidently offered him the chance to retrieve his reputation. The war was now resumed. Corbulo entered Armenia from Melitene with four legions, the *auxilia* and contingents from the allied kings, but he had not advanced far along the route once traversed by Lucullus when he was met by messengers from Tiridates and Vologaeses. They were well received, just as if everything had been arranged in advance, and a time and place for the conference were agreed upon. Tiridates suggested Randeia as the site and Corbulo did not reject this. There, Tiridates, in a solemn ceremony, laid down his crown before the statue of Nero, swearing that he would take it back only from Nero's hand, in Rome. He then handed over his daughter as a hostage and a 'supplicatory' letter to the Princeps, and went back to his brothers, Vologaeses, who had retired to Ecbatana, and Pacorus, king of the Medes. Vologaeses for his part wanted from Corbulo only a guarantee that his brother would not be subjected to any humiliation. The journey to Rome was undertaken in 66, as we have seen. Armenia thus became the preserve of Parthian younger sons, under the aegis of Rome, and for many years there were no more conflicts to lament.

The other important external event of Nero's reign was the revolt of 61 in Britain. A. Didius Gallus, sent to Britain by Claudius in 52, had continued, via his subordinate commanders, the guerilla war against the Silures of Wales. Q. Veranius, the former governor of Lycia, who succeeded Didius Gallus in 58 and died the same year or in 59, was more heavily engaged with the same tribe, probably in the execution of fresh instructions from the central government. Veranius was succeeded by the able general C. Suetonius Paulinus, who was operating in the island of Mona (Anglesey), centre of the Druidic cult and of nationalist resistance, in continuation of the large-scale action initiated by his predecessor to finish off once and for all the struggle against the Silures, when an unexpected and terrible revolt broke out in the part of the province already pacified. The Roman administration, somewhat harsh in countries recently occupied, had already provoked serious discontent by its greed, but what caused the gravest trouble were the speculations of Roman money-lenders (Cassius Dio even mentions Seneca's name: LXII, 2, 1). On top of this came the disillusionment of the Iceni, who had hoped to preserve their independence under the protection of the Romans and were infuriated when, on the death of their king Prasutagus in 61, his wife Boudicca was impeded in her attempts to govern and subjected to every kind of harassment. Putting herself at the head of the revolt, she persuaded the Trinobantes and other peoples to join her and fell on Camulodunum, where the native population, tired of the insolence of the officials and veterans, sided with the insurgents. There was a terrible massacre of the colonists; the procurator, Catus Decianus, who, through his acts of violence, bore the main responsibility for the rebellion, was overwhelmed, thanks to the inadequacy of his forces and his own military ineptitude. However, he succeeded in escaping to Gaul. The same fate overtook Petilius Cerialis who, in command of a whole legion, just managed to take refuge in his camp with the cavalry, after losing all his infantry. The avalanche then turned on London and Suetonius Paulinus, although he arrived in time to defend it, sacrificed it because he saw that his forces were not big enough to save the town. However, he took away with him all those who wished to follow him. Verulamium was also captured by the rebels, and altogether seventy thousand Roman citizens and Britons friendly to the Romans were massacred. Paulinus, still short of troops (he had only one legion and part of another, with a few auxiliary detachments) and also embarrassed by the refusal of one of his own subordinates, the *praefectus castrorum* Paenius Postumus, to obey his orders, did not lose heart but waited for an opportune moment and place to attack. He found them when he succeeded in luring the Britons, emboldened by success, into a gorge in the hills where, with his rear secure, he was able to rout the disorganized horde with a well-calculated attack. Boudicca killed herself and the disobedient Roman officer did the same. The suppression of the revolt continued inexorably, with the help of reinforcements which had arrived in the meantime from Gaul. However, with them came the new procurator, Julius Classicianus, an intriguer who did nothing but create difficulties for the governor and incite the Britons. He even went so far as to write to Nero that Paulinus would have to be replaced if military operations were to be ended. Nero sent the freedman Polyclitus to carry out an enquiry and for the moment Paulinus retained his command; but after losing some ships in an accident a little later he had to hand over to P. Petronius Turpilius. Turpilius and his successor, M. Trebellius Maximus, who replaced him after a year and governed Britain for eight years, not only refrained from any further military operations, probably in accordance with the directives resulting from a new policy towards Britain, but also took good care not to hamper the activities of the imperial procurators.

As for the other provinces and frontiers of the empire, apart from the provisions made for Greece and the plans discussed in his last few years for expansion in the East, Nero's reign does not present any exceptional events or any signs of detailed interventions differing from those of his predecessors in the matter of roads, the construction of buildings

and monuments, measures to help communities and small border actions.[1]
On the Rhine the only year in which there was any activity was 58, when
the long peace – utilized for peaceful works like the excavation of a canal
between the Saône and the Moselle – caused the false rumour to spread
among the Germans that the governors had been instructed not to take
any action on their own initiative against the enemy, and the Frisii tried to
seize some territory belonging to the Romans but left unoccupied. They
were promptly driven out again, and when the Ampsivarii tried to occupy
the same land, with assistance from the Bructeri, the Tencteri and other
tribes, they met an energetic response from the whole army of Lower
Germany, and everything grew quiet again. For the rest, the disputes
among the Germans themselves, such as the conflict that broke out at
that time between the Hermunduri and the Chatti, ending in the discomfiture of the latter, ensured the security of this sector of the frontier.
On the Lower Danube, in spite of the reductions in the garrisons resulting
from the despatch of legions to Syria, there are records of noteworthy
operations, especially in the funerary inscription of Ti. Plautius Silvanus
Aelianus,[2] who was governor of Moesia roughly from 57 to 67. Silvanus,
facing the threatening movements of the Sarmatians (Iazyges and Roxolani) who arrived on the Danube about 62, defeated them, together with
the Dacians and Bastarnae (non-Sarmatian peoples), on the far side of
the Danube and settled many of them to the south of the river as colonists,
while in their territories to the north of the river he founded vassal states.
He then intervened on the coast of the Black Sea, to free the Greek city
of Chersonese from a siege by the Scythians. About the same time, to
judge from the disappearance between 62 and 68–9 of coins of the kingdom of Bosporus bearing the heads of native rulers, it may be supposed
that, on the death or deposition of King Cotys, direct rule was introduced
there, as a prelude to the conquest of all the Black Sea coastline. Another
aspect of this plan was the annexation in 64 of the kingdom of Pontus,
now taken from King Polemo, who had received it from Gaius in 38, and
added to the province of Galatia. Polemo had to content himself with that
part of Cilicia which he had been given in return for Bosporus when this

[1] However, evidence of such interventions is somewhat less frequent than it is for the
reigns of Tiberius and Claudius. There are interesting 'epistulae' on fishing rights on the
lower Danube written by various governors of Moesia (*Suppl. Epigr. Gr.*, I, 1923,
No. 329). There is also an inscription about a delimitation of frontiers by a governor
between the Sagalassi and the village of Timbrianasso in Phrygia, 'ex epistula' of Nero
(*Or. Gr. Inscr. Sel.*, 538). Also the *S.C. Volusianum* of 56, about the prohibition on the
purchase of houses for demolition; it repeats the similar decision taken under Claudius
(see above, p. 138).
[2] *CIL*, XIV, 3608 = *ILS*, 986.

was taken from him by Claudius in 41. The policy employed thus followed the traditional one, just as the instruments of its implementation
remained the same. The legions, with slight changes, were stationed
where they had been under Augustus; the commanders were still members
of the senatorial aristocracy; and the administrative apparatus was born
and perfected out of the Augustan settlement. But after 66 it was not
only the internal situation that deteriorated rapidly. For the first time in
the history of the principate Nero succeeded in spreading the revolution
to the armies and the provinces, and for the first time the loyalty of the
troops to the family of Caesar and Augustus failed.

THE COLLAPSE

After the reception of Tiridates, Nero lived in a permanent state of
exaltation and of longing to give fresh proofs of his talent and greatness.
He now decided on the tour of the East which was to be at the same time
both a demonstration of homage to art and culture, with the liberation
of Greece and participation in its glorious old contests, and a demonstration of conquering power, with a resumption of the plans for expansion
in the footsteps of Alexander and Caesar. The warning provided by the
discovery at Beneventum of a new conspiracy, known as the Vinician
conspiracy after Annius Vinicianus, Corbulo's son-in-law, was of no
avail. Just after marrying Statilia Messina, widow of the consul M. Atticus
Vestinus, who had died as a result of the Pisonian conspiracy (though it
is not certain that Statilia accompanied him on the journey), and after
ordering a concentration of legions in Egypt, he set out towards the
end of September 66, with his *Augustiani*, a contingent of praetorian
guards under the command of Tigellinus and also the big troop of
senators, knights, freedmen and slaves forming his court. He left Rome
under the control of other palace freedmen, headed by Aelius. However,
in the end the tour was confined to Greece, for the ambitious eastern
plans – quite apart from the question of their practicability and usefulness
to the empire – were brought to an end by the outbreak of the Jewish
revolt. As far as can be judged from the tendency to direct annexation
already apparent many years earlier in the Pontic states and from the
activities on the Black Sea of the governors of Moesia – activities intended
to convert this sea into a completely Roman lake (the *classis Pontica* was
created at this time) – these eastern plans consisted principally in the
development of this policy by means of a powerful offensive against the
Sarmatians and the conquest of the whole Caucasian region. An advance

TA—G

through Egypt towards Ethiopia may possibly also have been contemplated. In 66 Nero ordered the enrolment of a legion, the *Italica*, consisting entirely of young men at least five feet ten inches tall; with this legion, which he called 'the phalanx of Alexander the Great', and with those free after the Armenian wars, he probably meant to make an expedition to the 'Gates of the Caucasus',[1] subduing the peoples between the Black Sea and the Caspian and the Sarmatians of south Russia. In reality it is dubious whether even a victorious campaign would have succeeded in putting an end to the pressure of the tribes, in lively movement at that time, and whether the frontier line of the Roman state could have been extended for several hundreds of miles across the steppes, without the usual natural support of rivers, simply to protect a coastal strip, just when a compromise was being accepted for Armenia which in practice abandoned it to the Parthians. The empire was quite vast enough for the capacity of its administrative machinery, and the limits of the equilibrium achieved, limits understood intuitively by Augustus, could not with impunity be exceeded by wild plans of pure conquest. The same absence of an urgent, justified need is also perceptible in the plan to attack Ethiopia, a plan overvalued by modern historians as a basically economic and commercial enterprise, if in fact this idea ever lodged in Nero's mind, seeing that only Pliny (*Nat. Hist.*, VI, 181), who was extremely hostile to Nero, mentions it. However, the concentration of forces in Egypt in 66 is a fact, and it is not impossible that the exploratory journeys made earlier in the kingdom of Meroe inspired a desire in the Princeps to undertake some enterprise in this area. However that may be, everything was put off when, in the autumn of 66, the state of tension and disorder that had been dragging on in Palestine for some years erupted into open warfare.

The situation in this difficult country up to the time of Claudius has already been described. Antonius Felix, Pallas's brother, had ruled as procurator until about 60, succeeding, in spite of the rascalities of every sort which he committed, in holding in check the population, among whom brigandage had developed and sects of fanatics flourished. His successors, Porcius Festus and Lucceius Albinus (up to 64) had done nothing, but the procurator sent in 64, the easterner Gessius Florus, began once again to harass the Jews persistently and gave the final stimulus to

[1] That is, to one of the Caucasian passes, probably the Krestovvj pass (2388 metres), between the valleys of the Terek and the Ksanka. But the sources (TAC., *Hist.*, I, 6; SUET., *Ner.*, 19, 2; CASS. D., LXIII, 8, 1), by an error frequent in the ancient writers, say the 'Caspian Gates', which lie between Media and Hyrcania, to the south of the Caspian Sea.

rebellion when in May 66, after confiscating part of the temple treasure, he used violence to suppress the people's remonstrations. Even King Julius Agrippa II, who in 61 had received parts of Galilee and Peraea and certain rights with regard to the high priest already possessed by Agrippa I, was quickly eliminated from the scene by the infuriated population of Jerusalem when he tried to intervene with his little army to make counsels of peace prevail. By September the revolt had spread to the whole of Judaea and even to the Jews outside Palestine, for conflicts between Jews and Greeks, and mutual massacres, occurred for example in Tyre and Alexandria, where the rebellion was only just held in check by the prefect, Ti. Julius Alexander. The governor of Syria, Cestius Gallus, arriving at Jerusalem with a whole legion, several detachments from others and many auxiliaries, had to retire hastily, losing his baggage. There were various different tendencies among the Jews, but this encouraged the party that favoured war *à outrance*, and in February 67 T. Flavius Vespasianus arrived, appointed by Nero, to face the confused and dangerous situation. The war which he waged will be described in due course, but the forces which he brought with him, taken as they were from Syria and Egypt, indicated that the plan for eastern conquest had been buried once for all.

The shameful doings of the Princeps in Greece, and the crimes perpetrated at the same time by his representatives in Rome, are recorded only in the anecdotal and therefore fragmentary narrative of Suetonius and in the epitome of Cassius Dio; there is thus no certainty about their chronological order, nor is it possible to distinguish from the truth what may be invention and exaggeration inspired by the growing hostility which was continually gathering weight. The senator who acted as Nero's herald in the arena during the stay in Greece, the historian Cluvius Rufus, became after the tyrant's death one of the principal sources of the tradition hostile to him. If he was forced to undertake the duty of herald he must have certainly wanted to pay Nero back for the humiliation; if on the other hand he assumed the post in all seriousness and of his own free will, he was bound to attack the fallen emperor all the more bitterly to hide his own complicity. Hardly had Nero completed the crossing to Greece when he performed as a singer in Corcyra. He then took part in the games at Actium, and at the end of November he was in Corinth, where at the Isthmian games, in a turgid speech preserved in an inscription from Acraephiae,[1] he proclaimed the freedom of Greece from the very spot whence it had been proclaimed two and a half centuries

[1] DITTENBERGER, *Syll.*[3], 814; *ILS*, 8749.

earlier by T. Quinctius Flamininus. This freedom consisted in practice in the cessation of the provincial régime and hence in immunity from tribute for those communities which had not already attained the status of *civitates liberae et immunes*; it certainly did not signify independence in home and foreign policy. However, the measure was welcomed with enthusiasm by the Greeks, certainly for the material advantages which it conferred, and the testimony of Plutarch, for example, then a young man,[1] shows us that it was taken seriously. The Senate was compensated for the loss of the province by having Sardinia allotted to it. In 67 Nero ordered the celebration, at the wrong time, of all four national games of Hellas, so that he could take part in all of them, as he in fact did, competing with great seriousness in the chariot races, the recitation and the lyre-playing, although he knew that victory was secure, particularly as it was awarded to him on one occasion when he fell from the chariot and did not arrive at the finishing line, and even in contests in which he was not competing. The other great public occasion of the year was the solemn inauguration, in September, of work on the canal through the isthmus of Corinth, an enterprise of relative utility, but calculated to excite admiration for the power of a Princeps victorious over nature herself. He visited the whole of Greece, though characteristically avoiding Sparta and Athens, and, in spite of the immunity he had granted, began to squeeze the rich for the expenses involved in having the honour of his divine presence on the soil of Hellas. At the same time, not forgetting the government of the empire, he exercised it through executions and confiscations, while his representatives did the same in Rome. Among those who died, victims of the suspicions left in Nero by earlier conspiracies or inspired by the fear of new ones, were the two commanders of the armies of the Upper and Lower Rhine, the brothers Scribonius Rufus and Scribonius Proculus, who were summoned to Greece by the Princeps and welcomed on their arrival with the order to kill themselves. The fate of the great Corbulo was particularly miserable: he had scarcely landed at the port of Cenchreae on the Saronic Gulf when he received the fateful order and killed himself, simply exclaiming, 'It serves me right'.[2] The alarm aroused among the commanders of the armies by these incidents came simply as an addition to the malaise already widespread, especially in the West. Nero, far removed in descent from the military heads of the dynasty, who had been loved blindly by the soldiers, ought to have renewed the weakened attachment by serving personally with the armies. Instead, he had never put in an appearance either in Britain or in the East;

[1] *De sera numinum vindicta*, 22 (*Mor.*, 567 f.).   [2] CASS. D., LXIII, 17, 6.

and now that he had outlined a plan for expansion he let it be understood only too clearly that his share in the proceedings would be confined to parades and spectacles. In any case, the Jewish revolt had suddenly induced him to drop the whole project. Moreover, the generals who had fought on his behalf had now reached the point of having to fear for their own lives; and the legions that were heavily engaged in suppressing the rebellion in Judaea knew that meanwhile the Princeps was enjoying himself in Greece. It is therefore not surprising if the armies resurrected the principle which had led to the empire, that of attachment to the general in immediate command rather than to a higher and semi-abstract authority, which had once been the Republic and was now a distant and indifferent emperor. The feeling of loyalty to the house of Caesar, a feeling which had emerged from the conclusion of the civil wars and been preserved under Caesar's successors, superseding ancient republican patriotism and fulfilling the same function, now tended to be replaced by a feeling of loyalty only to the troops' own commander, once again seen as arbiter in the concession of immediate and future material advantages. Nor is it surprising that as respect for the central authority declined in the instruments best qualified to represent it in the provincial world – the armies and their generals – this provincial world itself began to display the same slowness to obey the central authority, and separatist movements were born, encouraged in the provinces of the West by jealousy of the privileges granted to the Greeks.

All this was provoked by Nero's thoughtless attitude before and during his tour, while at Rome the government of freedmen had now to struggle every day with more and more threatening situations, for even the urban proletariat was irritated by the irregular arrival of corn, due probably to the re-routing of ships from Egypt to Palestine to supply the army engaged there, but easily attributed by popular rumour to the need to victual Nero and his retinue in Greece. At the end of 67 Aelius, besieged by difficulties, warned the Princeps that it was advisable for him to return; he did not succeed in convincing him and therefore went in person to Corinth to beg him to come back. Nero now returned, but only to celebrate triumphs for the victories he had won. This he did in 68 at Naples, entering the city on a chariot drawn by white horses through a breach made for the purpose in the walls; and then at Rome, where with the same ceremonial and amid the delirious acclaim of the fickle mob he went up to the Capitol like triumphing generals of old, and then to the Palatine, to dedicate to Apollo the eighteen hundred and eight crowns won in Greece. In March he was back in Naples, where he received the news that C. Julius Vindex, governor of one of the Gallic provinces, probably Gallia Lugdunensis, had rebelled.

However, the situation was not desperate. This and other provincial uprisings could still have been mastered if they had not finally offered the city of Rome itself the chance to shake off the tyrant and if Nero himself had acted with decision and seriousness. The reports of our sources[1] on the subject, even though the anecdotes they include may be exaggerated, are certainly true and correspond with Nero's whole attitude and character. The man who had seen the position of Princeps as that of some one possessing unique personal power which allowed him to do anything he fancied was to pass from fury to panic and to live in a state alternating between anguish and exaltation when he felt his position begin to totter. It is hardly surprising that, abandoned by Tigellinus, whose eclipse at this particular moment is one of the mysteries of these tumultuous events, he should have lost his head and after a period of incredulity and indifference taken to precipitate action: he went to Rome and tried demonstrations of force, deposing the consuls and making himself sole consul. He also considered appearing before the armies to recall them to loyalty by his mere presence. On the other hand, he did not give up the usual shows and exhibitions of artistry; none of the insults hurled at him by Vindex hurt him as much as the charge that he was a poor lyre-player. When he was preparing to set out for the armies he planned that his women should accompany him dressed as Amazons; and when the scarcity of food in the city gave fresh cause for discontent there was a rumour that a ship had come all the way from Alexandria with a cargo of special sand for the arena.

Vindex, an Aquitanian of a royal stock which had received citizenship from Caesar (his father before him had been a senator), rose to the cry of 'freedom from the tyrant', and his revolt was nourished by the upsurge of a desire for autonomy among the Gauls, who were no longer disposed to obey like slaves a distant despot regarded as mad by all right-thinking people. This revolt was followed, thanks to the manœuvres of this same Vindex, by that of the elderly and experienced general Ser. Sulpicius Galba, governor of Hispania Tarraconensis for the last eight years, who on 2 April proclaimed himself the representative of the Roman Senate and people. He gained the support of M. Salvius Otho, the governor of Lusitania, and of A. Caecina Alienus, quaestor of Baetica, and at once began recruiting a legion of provincials, the VII, and a large number of auxiliary troops. However, Vindex was defeated by the army of Upper

[1] SUET., *Ner.*, 40-9; CASS. D., LXIII, 26-7.

Germany, under the command of Verginius Rufus, who, in spite of his soldiers' offer to make him emperor, remained for the moment loyal to Nero. Galba on the other hand was declared *hostis publicus* by the Senate. But Nero did not put into effect his plan to join the armies; he confined himself to forming a legion, the I *Adiutrix*, out of the sailors from the fleet at Misenum, and probably sent one of his lady friends, Calvia Crispinilla, to persuade the commander of the legion in Africa, Clodius Macer, to come to Italy to help him. However, the result was that he too rebelled against Nero, though without joining Galba, while the legion of *classiarii* was enrolled so slowly that it could not be employed. The generals to whom Nero entrusted the armies, Rubrius Gallus and Petronius Turpilianus, though loyal to him, in practice did nothing. Verginius Rufus, although he had stifled the rebellion in Gaul, declared himself at the disposal of the Senate, that is, he refused obedience to the Princeps. The Senate in its turn had already been negotiating for some time with emissaries from Galba. The situation came to a climax when the praetorian prefect, Nymphidius Sabinus, who had been placed alongside Tigellinus after the fall of Faenius Rufus, made common cause with the Senate.

The end came in the course of the flight which Nero began down the Via Ostiensis, probably trying to embark for the East, which he believed to be loyal to him. Taking refuge in the Horti Serviliani until the fleet was ready to sail, he was finally abandoned by the praetorian cohort which had still been accompanying him. Meanwhile in the praetorian camp Nymphidius with members of the Senate announced Nero's flight and promised a donative of 30,000 sesterces per man in return for the proclamation of Galba as the new emperor. The praetorian guards agreed and the Senate declared Nero *hostis publicus*. In the villa of the freedman Phaon, between the Via Nomentana and the Via Salaria, whither he had meanwhile fled, amid the humiliating ups and downs picturesquely described and exaggerated by the tradition, the fugitive, crushed by the latest news and feeling his pursuers on his heels, finally killed himself with the famous words 'qualis artifex pereo', 'what an artist perishes in me!'. A little over thirty, he had reigned for rather less than fourteen years. His nurses and the faithful Acte buried him in the tomb of the Domitii, not in the mausoleum of Augustus.

The death of 'the last of the sons of Aeneas'[1] also put an end to the Julio-Claudian dynasty. This, together with the recollection of an experiment in reigning by no means unwelcome to everyone, may explain

[1] CASS. D., LXIII, 29, 3.

the aura of worship and legitimist nostalgia that gathered round Nero's memory. For a long time his tomb was covered with flowers; Otho did not know whether to gratify or oppose the people's wish to keep his memory alive and in the end agreed to be hailed 'Nero Otho';[1] Vitelliui celebrated public sacrifices in his honour; and even twenty-eight years later, in the choice of Nerva after the fall of the Flavians, some weight was attached in certain circles to Nerva's distant kinship with the Julio-Claudians and his friendship with Nero. In addition, the report that Nero was not dead but had succeeded in escaping ensured success for the impostors who sprang up in profusion, especially in the East, claiming to be the emperor returned to life. His concept of the imperial authority as a principle of sovereign splendour, the omnipotent source of all good and evil, had been quite understood and accepted by his subjects in the East and by the lower classes even in the West, who long preserved his fame. It was only the Jews and Christians, with their superior moral conscience, who execrated his memory and – independently of the official opinion hostile to him deliberately created in the Flavian era – passed down to the Middle Ages the demoniacal figure round whom crystallized the most fantastic collection of legends attracted by any of the Roman emperors, with the result that even today Nero is the best known of them.

Leaving aside consideration of Nero's person, about which there will always be an element of mystery, if we want to understand the real significance of his reign, we must see in it the extreme manifestation of a concept of autocracy nurtured in one particular family, the first to rise from the heart of the Roman aristocracy – and always in intimate contact with it, even though at times opposing and oppressing it – to the position of personal dominion rendered inevitable for the solution of the technical problem of empire. But while some members of the family – Augustus, Tiberius, Claudius – were aware of the real nature of the problem and took pains to keep their autocratic position within the limits in which it functioned to the advantage of the state, thus justifying the immense power of that position by paying formal homage to tradition, others – Gaius and Nero – took the autocratic position both in form and practice as an end in itself. They conceived it as a chance to exercise absolute personal power under the religious aspect of assimilation to divinity itself, either in the crude, simplistic form adopted by Gaius or in the finer and more elaborate form peculiar to Nero. The Roman tradition, henceforth accepting the principate, could not accept these forms of it, for which the aristocratic society which still feebly represented it was not

---

[1] TAC., *Hist.*, I, 78, 2.

ripe. Thus Gaius and Nero fell. The effects of Gaius's fall remained confined, partly thanks to the shortness of his reign, to the urban circle; but the opposition provoked by Nero was so wide that for the first time it extended to the armies and the provinces, and affected the legacy of military loyalty, so that his fall involved the empire too.

The Julio-Claudian dynasty had run its course, but the principate did not come to an end. The Civil War was fought precisely to create a new Princeps. In the matter of which person and family should head the empire, the situation returned more or less to the beginning again: the legions had to decide, just as in the time of Octavian and Antony. But as for the survival of the imperial régime as one of the facts of life, there was no doubt at all about that; the administration founded by Augustus and consolidated by Tiberius and Claudius continued to function, and the settlement it guaranteed had shown that it could run on its own, even with a lyre-playing charioteer at the summit.

II

CRISIS AND RENEWAL: FROM GALBA TO TRAJAN

V

THE PRINCIPATE'S
FIRST CRISIS
OR THE YEAR OF THE
FOUR EMPERORS

THE REIGN OF GALBA

The acclamation of Galba as Nero's successor, endorsed as it was by the Senate, might have made it seem as if the ideal of a Princeps chosen by the aristocracy had been achieved. In reality the approval of the Senate only confirmed the *fait accompli* of acclamation by an army, and in the special circumstances created by the absence of any heirs to the emperor who had been overthrown. Thus what seemed to Tacitus, who looks on it sympathetically from the theoretical angle, like an experiment in a legalized senatorial principate after the reign of a family dynasty – 'sub Tiberio et Gaio et Claudio unius familiae quasi hereditas fuimus' (*Hist.*, I, 16, 1) – was in fact only an episode, an uncertain one full of mistakes, in the general political crisis. Theoretically, Galba could have been the most suitable candidate for an immediate renewal of the principate according to a new formula. Not related to the Julio-Claudian families, although he had enjoyed the favour of Livia and had been highly regarded by Augustus, Tiberius, and, in particular, Claudius, a member of a family belonging to the old republican urban nobility, but at the same time a typical example, in his long career, of the senatorial magistrate in the service of the empire according to the Augustan scheme, Servius Sulpicius Galba was for these reasons equally acceptable to the supporters of an aristocratic revival pure and simple and to those who wanted a man of experience at the head of the empire. His age – seventy-two – and the fact that he had been left rather to one side by the last of the Julio-Claudians were further factors in his favour. However, in practice, the old aristocrat did not know how to control the many elements in the complex situation, especially the praetorian guard, the armies and, within the confines of the nobility itself, the rival army commanders. Consequently, although he was the most distinguished representative of that section of his own class least compromised by association with the fallen dynasty and thus almost naturally marked out to succeed it, he was only able to put into effect the mere outline of a theoretical programme, that of a senatorial principate, and to show at the same time that there was no substance or staying power in this programme. The struggle started again, the struggle to find a new kind of aristocrat, nearer to the Julio-Claudians and nearer to practical reality. After Otho's attempt, still in some measure an urban and palace affair, Vitellius and Vespasian, at the head of legions whose independence of one another and of the central authority had been accentuated by their progressive provincialization, and whose brute force – as in the days of the civil wars – was the decisive element, took possession of the empire by conquest. Vespasian, not very different morally from the others, no different from the average type of senatorial man of affairs produced by the Italian – no longer just the urban – nobility, and matured in the service of the empire, knew how to give permanence to the effects of the assertion of military power and ended the crisis. It was a swift crisis, for scarcely a year and a half passed between the disappearance of Nero and the Flavian victory, but one comparable in intensity only with the hardest moments of the civil strife that had ended a hundred years earlier with the victory of Actium.

The news of Nero's death, brought by the freedman Icelus along with the announcement of Galba's proclamation as emperor by the praetorian guard and the Senate, reached Galba while he was still in Spain, at Clunia, and extricated him from the difficult situation created by the defeat and death of Vindex. At Vindex's instigation, Galba had in fact begun the revolt and, proclaiming himself the representative of the Senate and Roman people, had extended it to the whole of Spain, gaining the support of Otho in Lusitania and Caecina in Baetica. He had enlisted soldiers to form a new legion to add to the one he commanded already, had sent letters and invitations to other provinces as well, and had negotiated with the Senate about the size of the donative to be offered to the praetorian guards – the 30,000 sesterces per man which, though only promised, decided the fate of Nero. One of his first followers, T. Vinius, the commander of the legion stationed in Hispania Tarraconensis, was already in Rome looking after these manœuvres. Towards the beginning of July Galba himself, having received confirmation of what had happened so far from T. Vinius, now back in Spain, and having finally assumed the title of Caesar, set out on the march to Rome with Otho and all the others. Full of illusions and good intentions, but lacking any clear vision of things and perhaps weary from old age, he thus inaugurated the series of errors (well and truly noted by Tacitus, who seems to regret them) which after seven months were to bring about his downfall. This series of errors can be reconstructed fairly clearly, although it is impossible to determine the chronological sequence of events in the second half of the year 68. The *Histories* of Tacitus begin in fact with 69, and for the previous year they give only a general picture of the situation at Rome and in the provinces.

Galba's first and fundamental mistake was probably to believe that his position was solid and beyond question after the Senate had given its approval and that he could act with despotic rigour against anyone who threatened him in any way. For example, he began by severely punishing the Spanish cities which had not followed his lead in the revolt against Nero. But the troops of the various groups of legions, having just discovered the famous 'arcanum imperii' – the ability to proclaim an emperor on their own account – were not at first prepared to give unconditional obedience to a Princeps not chosen by themselves. The German legions, who had already wanted to make Verginius Rufus emperor, renewed the offer on the death of Nero and when it was declined they swore allegiance to Galba only with reluctance, persuaded to do so by Verginius himself. Galba rewarded him for this by taking away his command and by treating him coldly when he met him, probably on the way through Gaul. The Rhine troops, whose interests must by now have been fairly closely linked – through long residence and the size of the native auxiliary units attached to them – with those of the Gallic population, were angered not only by the appointment to Verginius's post of a commander incapable of winning their esteem, the old and inept Hordeonius Flaccus, but also by the granting of citizenship and exemption from taxes to tribes which had assisted Vindex, while the Treviri, the Lingones and the city of Lyon, which in point of fact had fought with the legions under Vindex for the unity of the empire, were punished by the new emperor with loss of territory and revenues. On the other hand, even those who favoured Galba, worried by the knowledge that they had not sided with him at once and pondering on the fate of Verginius, feared his ill-advised severity. It was in vain that Fabius Valens, the commander of a legion, showed his zeal by killing, with his colleague Cornelius Aquinus, his own superior officer, Fonteius Capito, governor of the Lower Rhine, who was suspected of plotting against Galba, for the latter showed no sign of gratitude. Capito's fate was suffered in Africa by Clodius Macer, commander of the III *Augusta* legion in Numidia, who, striking a characteristic attitude as a champion of the Republic and a liberator, had enrolled another legion and was intercepting the corn supply to Italy until the procurator Trebonius Carutianus dealt with him on Galba's orders. Others in Spain and Gaul met the same end.

Discontent was increased by the view that the new emperor was dominated by advisers of the worst sort: the freedman Icelus, raised by Galba to equestrian rank, the discredited senator T. Vinius, nominated to be consul with Galba in 69, and Cornelius Laco, an arrogant and stupid man who was appointed prefect of the praetorian guard as soon as Galba was acclaimed emperor. In reality Galba must have found it natural to make use of men already in his household, like the freedman, or on his staff, like the commander of his legion and a member of his provincial governor's council, and the worst judgements on these men look rather like excuses produced by the tradition sympathetic to the old senatorial Princeps. But in the case of the appointment of Cornelius Laco at any rate, the error is manifest, not so much because of the questionable wisdom of putting a financial official at the head of the praetorian guard in those hard days as because of the reaction immediately provoked at Rome, where the praetorian cohorts were restless and ready for further changes. They had abandoned Nero more through external pressure than from their own conviction, they were jealous of the legionary troops and above all they had seen no sign of the arrival of the donative promised 'sub nomine Galbae'. Their commander, Nymphidius Sabinus, who had entertained hopes of a very high reward for the part he had played in tipping the situation in Galba's favour and then found himself pushed brusquely aside, rebelled and tried to seize the principate. The attempt, a tremendously bold one for the son of a freedman, was nipped in the bud by the praetorian guards themselves. This was the moment for Galba to reward their loyalty to the concept of an aristocratic principate and in particular to bind them to his own person by paying the donative. Instead, when requested to do so, he replied in old-fashioned Roman terms that 'he levied soldiers, he did not buy them'![1] And he was implacable in pursuing the real or alleged accomplices of Nymphidius such as King Mithridates of Pontus and the consul designate, Cingonius Varro, who was put to death without trial. He also made an early start on the task, continued after his arrival in Rome, of eliminating those associated with Nero; the first to fall in this purge was the ex-consul Petronius Turpilianus, whose only fault

[1] TAC., *Hist.*, I, 5, 2.

was that of being appointed to command, with Rubrius Gallus, the army of repression which had done nothing. Other minor figures also fell, but for some mysterious reason the vile Tigellinus escaped; he reappears on the scene in comfortable exile at the seaside resort of Sinuessa.

By the time Galba reached Rome, not before the autumn of 68 although the senatorial delegation which had gone to meet him at Narbonne had pressed him to come quickly, his initial popularity, if it had ever been great, must have almost vanished; nor had the senators themselves much to hope for by way of effective implementation of a senatorial principate, notwithstanding the principles of policy already widely diffused by the propaganda of coins bearing such legends as 'Libertas restituta', 'Roma renascens', 'Felicitas publica', and the dedication on 15 October of a statue 'Libertatis restitutae Ser. Galbae imperatoris Augusti'.[1] In any case, it was implicit in the intention expressed by Galba in numerous coins commemorating Augustus that the liberty proclaimed would not exceed at the maximum the bounds of the Augustan principate, once again put forward as a model, and the Senate would have certainly been content with this. Rome was full of soldiers, for the legion enrolled in Spain had arrived with the emperor; in the outskirts there was already the legion formed by Nero out of the sailors of Misenum, the I *Adiutrix*, and there were also detachments of troops summoned by Nero from Germany, Britain and Illyricum for the projected eastern campaign and then recalled for the rebellion of Vindex. Unfortunately one episode confirmed people's fears even before Galba entered the city. The *classiarii* of the legion only just formed went to meet him, requesting him insistently to recognize them as a 'iusta legio'; Galba launched his cavalry against them and then put to death one in ten of those who had escaped the massacre. After entering Rome he persisted in employing his own kind of policy, which was not wrong in itself but politically counter-productive. In the matter of granting citizenship and distinctions he was sparing, and this need not surprise us; the only trouble was that when he did indulge in this, with the Gauls who had supported Vindex, for example, or when he gave the gold ring to Icelus, his preferences were not well judged. Thus the measures in favour of those persecuted by Nero, although permitting return from exile and the rehabilitation of people of merit, also opened the way to trials of informers, in which, in spite of the good intentions proclaimed by edict, justice was subjected to the tortuous course of the circumstances of the moment.

As for public works, Galba's name is linked to the 'horrea Galbiana',

[1] *CIL*, VI, 471 = *ILS*, 238.

which he probably only restored.[1] The policy of economy, possibly necessary at the centre after Nero's prodigality but nevertheless limited to the court, for Galba did not apply any harsher fiscal measures to the finances of the state – he granted exemptions straightaway, as we have seen, and even left Greece with the immunity bestowed on it by Nero – was naturally interpreted as a sign of personal meanness. The appointment of a commission of fifteen or thirty knights to recover a proportion (nine-tenths) of the sums distributed by Nero to his favourites corresponded with the demands of justice but did not accomplish anything concrete, since the money had already been spent, and if anything created some new enemies. The transference to the praetors of the management of the treasury of Saturn, entrusted since 56 to the 'praefecti aerarii Saturni', if it is to be placed at this moment, would indicate a concession to the normal functions of the senatorial magistracy as compared with the tendency to use 'commissars', so to speak, but this move was more of a formality than anything else. The plan to fix the duration of posts entrusted to senators and knights at a maximum of two years and to assign such posts to men who did not want them, though good in itself, was obviously easier to enunciate than to apply. The energetic action taken about the armies also corresponded to the need for a complete restoration of order and to a principle of geographical rotation not inopportune in itself. Thus the legion recruited in Africa by Clodius Macer was disbanded; but Galba must have soon repented of the unreasonable haste with which he sent to Pannonia the VII legion, which he had enrolled himself and which had accompanied him to Rome. In general, the policy of austerity, imposed after years of liberality, was badly received by the urban populace, which made no secret of its ill humour, all the more since so far as the venality, insolence and greed of freedmen were concerned nothing was changed. And the people, who paid attention to such things as well, did not like Galba's advanced age and unattractiveness, compared with Nero's youth. Thus on one occasion when the actor in a well-known Atellan farce intoned the line 'here comes the rustic from the country',[2] the spectators all recited the chorus together, amid roars of applause.

The praetorian guards still awaited the payment of the donative and were champing at the bit. The disbandment of the imperial bodyguard, the German 'corporis custodes', who were discharged without any bounty, increased the ill-feeling. Fortunately through all these months, perhaps because of the hard war being waged against the Jews, perhaps because of

---

[1] *CIL*, VI, 8680 = *ILS*, 239.   [2] SUET., *Galb.*, 13.

the natural delay in the repercussion of western events on the East, the eastern legions had remained quiet and sworn formal allegiance to Galba; only the troops summoned by Nero from Illyricum had shown a preference for Verginius Rufus, and even they had finally declared, like all the rest, for Galba. In Egypt the prefect, Ti. Julius Alexander, had obtained oaths of loyalty to Galba – before he was even requested to do so – as soon as he heard of Galba's proclamation as emperor by the Senate and the praetorian guards; and a number of inscriptions in honour of Galba are extant in various parts of the empire, in spite of the brevity of his reign.[1] But the storm clouds were gathering, both at home and, in the shape of discontent in the armies, abroad.

The almost simultaneous but quite separate action taken by both opposition movements not only sealed the fate of the old emperor but also complicated subsequent events horribly. On 1 January 69 Galba, for the second time, and Titus Vinius, his right-hand man, took office as *consules ordinarii*. On the same day, while at Colonia on the Lower Rhine the legions were swearing allegiance to Galba, at Mainz two of the three legions of Upper Germany, the IV and XXII, overturned the images and refused to take the oath of allegiance to the emperor, pronouncing it instead in the name of the Senate. The governor, Hordeonius Flaccus, did nothing to stop them. They left the choice of a successor to the Senate and people, thus masking sedition with deference, as Tacitus puts it (*Hist.*, I, 12, 1). Suetonius (*Galb.*, 16, 2) says their request for a successor was directed to the praetorian guards, and this sounds more probable. It may be that the army of Upper Germany made this request not out of deference to the decisions of the Roman Senate and people but simply because there was no one else at hand who could be hailed as emperor except the detested Hordeonius Flaccus. Yet if things had turned out that way many misfortunes would have been averted. Instead, during the same night of 1–2 January a standard-bearer of the IV legion had run to Colonia to announce the refusal of the oath to Aulus Vitellius, the son of Lucius Vitellius, who had been sent by Galba to take up the post of governor of the Lower Rhine, vacant since the elimination of Fonteius Capito. Vitellius had arrived about a fortnight earlier. The messenger found him dining and it soon became apparent that the new emperor was not to be awaited from Rome but was to be created on the spot. Vitellius passed on the news of the revolt to his officers and the legions: they could either crush the rebels or make common cause with

[1] *CIL*, II, 2779, from Clunia, in Spain; *CIL*, III, 8702 = *ILS*, 237, from Salonae (Split).

them and accept the new emperor, to be created immediately. Fabius Valens, who hated Galba for the reason mentioned earlier, and Caecina Alienus, the ex-praetor of Baetica, who had been punished by Galba for certain frauds committed while he was still in Spain, had already won over the new governor. Valens, who had his camp not far from Colonia, now hastened there and his legion (the I) was the first to acclaim Vitellius emperor; the others and the auxiliary units followed suit and the local population gave enthusiastic support to the troops' revolt. On 3 January the army of Upper Germany, which had left the choice to the Senate and people, also swore allegiance to Vitellius.

The first news arrived in Rome some days after 1 January; it had been despatched by the procurator of Gallia Belgica, Pompeius Propinquus, evidently before the developments which led to the acclamation of Vitellius, and Galba decided to put into effect a plan which he had already contemplated, that of associating with himself by adoption a colleague and successor. Such a move, in itself excellent and capable of resolving a crisis of this sort if made at the right time, as it did twenty-nine years later when Nerva adopted Trajan in similar circumstances, was instead simply the last, irremediable error. What is inexplicable – unless one remembers the abstract attitude and utopianism from which the old Princeps suffered – is that he left aside candidates who were much more natural ones in the circumstances and, 'seeking not what was most pleasing to himself but what was most useful to the Romans',[1] put forward with great solemnity in certain 'comitia imperii'[2] a model gentleman, the thirty-year-old L. Calpurnius Piso Frugi Licinianus, a descendant of Pompey the Great and Crassus the triumvir, a relative of people per-secuted by the Julio-Claudians and himself recently returned from exile. On 10 January, a day of ill-augury through the bad weather that raged, Galba went to the praetorian camp and in a brief speech, which among other things minimized the scope of the German rebellion, communicated the choice and the adoption to the cohorts, which out of respect for their prefect, Cornelius Laco, who favoured Piso – while Titus Vinius, more rationally, supported Otho – gave their approval, though grumbling about the old man's 'antiquus rigor' and 'nimia severitas',[3] which were presumably paralleled by similar qualities in the young man. There was no word even now of the donative. The choice was naturally given a better welcome in the Senate, since it corresponded, both in the requisites possessed by the person concerned and in the manner in which it had been made, with the theory of the principate most acceptable to the

[1] PLUT., *Galb.*, 21, 2.   [2] TAC., *Hist.*, I, 14, 1.   [3] *Ibid.*, 18, 3.

urban aristocracy. The joint rule lasted five days. The nomination of Piso had particularly offended Otho who, because of his past and present services and of the favour he still enjoyed with Galba, had taken it for granted that he would be the man selected, especially as his hopes and plans were encouraged by the troop of freedmen and astrologers he kept in his household. He also enjoyed popularity with the praetorian guards, who had received benefits from him; at the court, which appreciated him 'Neronis ut similem';[1] and with the people, who were counting on a change from the present stinginess. In his legitimate expectation of the succession Otho had probably already initiated negotiations with the praetorian guard, in which an agent of his, Maevius Pudens, one of the loyal followers of Tigellinus, was in the process of securing concrete support for him, thanks partly to the negligence of the prefect. He was also negotiating with Titus Vinius to marry his daughter and thus to procure himself further adherents. When Piso was adopted in his place, Otho, up to his neck in debts, compromised by his own manœuvres and blinded by shame, decided to act with open violence. Because of the general discontent the enterprise succeeded with incredible ease. At that particular moment, while the activities of the commission set up to recover the sums of money given away by Nero were creating a hubbub, some of the tribunes of the praetorian and urban cohorts and of the fire brigade were summarily dismissed. Meanwhile something must have leaked out; the praetorian guards were restless and the restlessness spread to the legionaries and auxiliary troops present in Rome. But Galba did not become aware of this, mainly through the ineptitude of Laco. Worse and worse news was still arriving from Germany. By now the acclamation of Vitellius must have been known, although it was officially kept secret, and it was decided to send a commission with Piso and Laco. But the latter refused to go and others, though appointed by the Princeps, sought to make excuses and have themselves replaced.

On the morning of 15 January, Galba, amid unfavourable auguries, was making a sacrifice before the temple of Apollo. Those present included Otho, who made some pretext to leave and met by arrangement, at the golden milestone in the Forum, the praetorian guards waiting for him there, twenty-three in number. With somewhat mixed feelings he climbed into a litter and was carried hurriedly to the 'castra praetoria', with a few other people tagging on behind. In the camp he was hailed as emperor by the troops, and the officers, more astonished than convinced, accepted the *fait accompli*. A day of horror followed. When the news became known

[1] TAC., *Hist.*, 13, 4.

there was an attempt to take defensive measures. Piso tried, with some success at first, to secure the loyalty of the praetorian cohort on guard at the palace, giving his word – it was high time – that there would be a donative. Other people were sent to the various units quartered in the city, that is, to the detachments of the Illyrian and German armies and to the legion of sailors, and even to the 'castra praetoria', to see if there was any chance of inducing the praetorian guards to change their minds. Among all these only the soldiers from Germany, who had not been maltreated by Galba, seemed disposed to fight for him, but in the event they did nothing. The rest repelled the ambassadors by force of arms. No one dared even to ask for any support from the *classiarii*, fresh as they were from decimation, and they at once made common cause with the praetorian guard. Galba's own legion would have now been valuable, but it was already far from Rome. The situation was thus desperate. Not knowing whose advice to follow – some people exhorted him to shut the palace gates and defend himself there, others to show himself in the Forum – and encouraged by a crowd calling for the punishment of Otho, Galba did have a moment's respite when the false news spread that the usurper had been killed in the barracks. In this brief interval of illusion and exaltation, which induced him – against the advice of Titus Vinius – to leave the palace and go up to the Forum, while Piso must presumably have gone to the praetorian barracks, he still had time to utter one of his characteristic phrases, 'commilito, quis iussit?',[1] to a soldier who, in pretence, showed him the sword with which he asserted that he had killed Otho. In reality the latter had already received the oath of the praetorians and the legionaries, amid growing enthusiasm excited by speeches and promises, so that while Galba was nearing the Forum the soldiers with their weapons in their hands were on the point of arriving there. This bad news was brought by Marius Celsus. In the panic that followed some people advised Galba to turn back and others counselled him to go up to the Capitol or else to mount the 'rostra'. The people watched as if at a show. Galba was being tossed this way and that when the praetorians and legionaries burst into the Forum. The cohort still escorting the old emperor abandoned him, and he, thrown out of the litter near the 'lacus Curtius', was riddled with sword-thrusts. Titus Vinius was killed near him although he protested his friendliness and his connivance with Otho – truthfully, as many people were inclined to think. Not much further away, at the entrance to the temple of Vesta, whither he had succeeded in escaping thanks to the heroism of a loyal

[1] TAC., *Hist.*, 35, 2.

centurion, Piso fell. Before the bloody day was over, the Senate and people hastened to pay homage to the new Princeps.

Such was the tragic end of the life and reign of Galba, a victim of his own mistakes and of events too big for him. He was overwhelmed by the results of his own action, which did not match the conditions prevailing. Tacitus, the kindliest of his judges, regarded him as a theorist who should never have moved over to action: 'omnium consensu capax imperii, nisi imperasset'.[1]

THE REIGN OF OTHO

The arrival on the throne of Otho, to whom the Senate hastened to vote tribunician power, the title of Augustus and the other customary honours, might have raised hopes that a solution to the crisis had been reached, if only the legions of Germany, which had refused to swear allegiance to Galba and had at first left the creation of a new emperor to the Senate and the praetorian guards, had waited for the choice now made by the praetorians and approved by the Senate. Unfortunately, they had already hailed Vitellius as emperor. It was in vain that Otho sent a senatorial commission to tell the armies of the Rhine that Galba was dead, that the Princeps had already been elected and that they should be obedient to him. It was in vain that Otho offered personally, as a compromise solution, to associate Vitellius with him in office and to become his son-in-law. His rival – already proclaimed emperor – and the armies of Germany would not be moved, and from the start, the sad expectation of civil war clouded the good prospects of a moderate reign offered by the new Princeps.

Marcus Salvius Otho came from the urban, not the ancient aristocracy, for his grandfather had been the first member of the family to enter the Senate, in the time of Augustus, and Claudius had made his father a patrician; nevertheless the family was one worthy of respect. A sister of Otho's had been betrothed to Drusus, the son of Germanicus. When his friendship with Nero broke up in 58 Otho was sent, although only of quaestorian rank, to govern distant Lusitania, and in ten years the young aristocrat's soft and fickle character, a typical product of Nero's circle, must have matured to some extent. Now thirty-seven and also endowed with positive qualities, although to some he still appeared too similar to Nero, he might have turned out to be not unworthy of the principate and

[1] *Ibid.*, 49, 3.

with time might have made people forget the brutal fashion in which he had acquired it. In fact, on the very day following the revolt, after the inevitable execution of Laco and Icelus, steps were taken to ensure that all the dead were buried. Marius Celsus, friend of Galba and consul-designate, was saved by Otho himself from the wrath of the praetorian guards, who were already fairly satisfied to have chosen on their own authority the two prefects, Plotius Firmus and Licinius Proculus, and also the *praefectus urbi*, Flavius Sabinus, Vespasian's brother, who had already held the post under Nero.

On the whole, what we know of the brief period that elapsed in Rome before Otho set out for the fighting demonstrates the concern of the new Princeps to make himself universally acceptable, a task which he knew how to perform with considerable tact, especially the difficult part of balancing the various factors in the situation. The praetorian guards were in fact devoted to him, so much so that, strange though it seems after what had happened, not even he, as far as we know, spoke of a donative, and this does not seem to have upset them. When he wanted to abolish the custom of buying from the centurions exemptions from heavy duties, an abuse which turned the soldiers into plunderers through the need to acquire the necessary money and put them into continual conflict with prosperous citizens, he had to indemnify the centurions out of his own pocket. The warmth of the praetorians' attachment to him was proved by an obscure episode in the early days of March. When a false alarm was raised by the nocturnal transference of a cohort from Ostia to Rome, some soldiers rushed to the palace, where Otho was dining with the most illustrious senators, and telling him that they feared that the senators were in the act of betraying him made ready to massacre them on the spot. They were only restrained by the Emperor with some difficulty. However, a troubled twenty-four hours followed. Otho appeared at the camp; he pleased the soldiers with speeches and a donative of 5,000 sesterces; but he also punished those most involved. The people had a liking for the young Princeps, who in turn calculated rightly on the sentimental reactions in the lowest classes to a rehabilitation of Poppaea Sabina and of Nero himself, but in this activity he respected the limit set by the disapproval of the upper classes, especially the nobility. He there-fore sacrificed Tigellinus, equally detested by both Nero's friends and his enemies, but others, like Calvia Crispinilla, soon to make a very good marriage, were saved. As for relations with the Senate, after assuming the consulship with his brother Titianus, as early as 1 March he relinquished the office in favour of Verginius Rufus, 'ut aliquod exercitui Germanico delenimentum',[1] and Pompeius Vospiscus, leaving unchanged the nominations already made by Nero and Galba for the succeeding consulships. In addition, he recalled exiles and restored their honours.

So far as his own position was concerned, the ceremonies connected with his various civil and priestly investitures are known to us from the *Acta* of the *Fratres Arvales*; they extended from January to March 69. With these ceremonies Otho grafted himself on to the tradition of the Augustan principate in what seemed the most legitimate way; and this gave him a great advantage over Vitellius. In fact the provinces, especially the eastern ones, swore allegiance at once to the Princeps created – it did not matter how – in Rome. The concept of the Augustan principate, aristocratic and urban in nature, was on the whole still unquestioned, and the crisis now shaking it did not concern its nature but was simply the struggle for the conquest, at Rome and by the armies, of a principate so conceived. Vitellius and Vespasian also belonged to the Italo-urban nobility of Julio-Claudian times. Otho then sought the favour of the provinces directly, giving citizenship to the Lingoni, who had been badly treated by Galba, and granting privileges to Spain, Africa and Cappadocia. His 'clementia' in regard to the provincials, or at least his care for them, is explicitly referred to in a document dealing with a territorial dispute in Sardinia;[2] and the promptness with which Othonian coins were struck at Antioch and an inscription like the one from Tafas in Syria, 'pro salute' of Otho,[3] confirm a rapidly acquired prestige. Nor did this prestige lack the lustre of military success against outsiders, for on the Lower Danube an eruption of the Roxolani into Moesia was repelled. Otho skilfully made the most of this victory by rewarding the commanders and commemorating it on coins: 'Victoria Othonis, Pax orbis terrarum'.

But it soon becomes apparent when one looks at the facts of the situation that this universal peace was only a figment of wishful propaganda. War was inevitable. The whole of the East and Africa were for Otho; and at first Spain too, where the historian Cluvius Rufus was governor, sent there by Galba, seemed favourable to him; but soon afterwards it declared for Vitellius, like Narbonese Gaul, which was too close to the armies of the Rhine not to think as they did. Aquitania, which at first had been forced by its governor, Julius Cordus, to declare in favour of

---

[1] TAC., *Hist.*, I, 77, 2.
[2] The decree of L. Helvius Agrippa, proconsul of Sardinia, dated 18 March 69, *CIL*, X, 7852 = *ILS*, 5947.
[3] *Inscr. Gr. ad res. Rom. pert.*, III, 1164.

Otho, had later changed over to Vitellius, who also enjoyed the support of the governors of Belgica, Lugdunese Gaul and Raetia. Britain backed him too, but only detachments of its legions took part in the struggle. The conflict thus characteristically also took the shape of a clash between the eastern and western parts of the empire. The situation was confused at Rome, where rightly or wrongly people thought they saw emissaries of Vitellius everywhere, and all kinds of threats hung over the lives of the two rivals' families, which were both in the city, while the Senate tried to please the present Princeps without compromising itself in the eyes of the future one. There seems to be a curious reflection of this in the absence of any senatorial coins dating from this period. However, the praetorian guards rejected Fabius Valens's invitation to go over to Vitellius. The negotiations, conducted through an exchange of letters which became continually harsher in tone, had to be regarded as having failed when the envoys sent by Otho to Lyon and to the armies of the Rhine did not return. In any case, Valens and Caecina had started to march even before the fall and replacement of Galba were known and it was very difficult to halt them. The Tiber overflowed its banks, causing a famine, and this, interpreted as an unfavourable omen, increased the expectation of sad events, in which Italy was bound to be involved, for the principate was always won in Rome.

The first few days after his acclamation were employed by Vitellius in settling the aftermath of the revolt of the legions. While pleasing the legions by putting to death those whom they disliked, he nevertheless saved from the soldiers' fury some whose death would have been a loss, such as Julius Civilis, who had great influence among the eight cohorts of Batavians, 'auxilia' of the XIV legion, which were stationed among the Lingoni and were turbulent and independent in their behaviour. By means of other expedient measures, such as the transference from freedmen to Roman knights of the posts closest to the Princeps and the payment of compensation to the centurions for the loss of the fees for exemptions, now prohibited, just as Otho was in the process of prohibiting them in Rome for the praetorians, he brought back a certain amount of order into the army with which he prepared to follow Valens and Caecina. Valens led part of the army of Lower Germany, with the eagle of Legion V *Alaudae* and auxiliaries – in all, 40,000 men; Caecina had 30,000 men from the army of Upper Germany, the core of which was formed by the legion from Vindonissa, the XXI *Rapax*. He also had a good number of auxiliary troops. Both commanders had already covered a considerable distance, disregarding the fact that it was winter and sowing terror wherever they passed. Valens had marched across Gaul, picking up another legion, the I *Italica* and the *ala Tauriana* of cavalry at Lyon, threatening and blackmailing the local populations, and also providing the spectacle of furious quarrels in his own ranks between the legionaries and the Batavian auxiliaries. He was now approaching the western Alps. Caecina's march, though not so long, was even more damaging in its effects. Some units of Helvetian auxiliaries did not favour Vitellius and had intercepted the messengers carrying the invitation to rebel to the legions of Pannonia. The XXI legion started the war soon after leaving their camp at Vindonissa, storming and destroying the neighbouring township noted for its thermal springs (Baden). The capital itself, Aventicum (Avenches), only just escaped the fury of the legionaries and auxiliaries, mostly Raetians. With their tempers roused by this start and elated by the news that south of the Alps the situation was turning in their favour, Caecina's soldiers did not hesitate to tackle the 'Alpis Poenina' (Great St Bernard pass) in the middle of winter. Near the River Po a cavalry formation, the *ala Siliana*, remembering its service in Africa under Vitellius when he was proconsul there, declared for him, and so did the bigger towns in Gallia Transpadana. Caecina at once sent some auxiliary detachments into Italy, with the intention of himself moving into Noricum to combat the procurator, Petronius Urbicus, regarded as a supporter of Otho, and of then entering Italy with the main body of his army from the eastern Alps. But changing his mind, almost certainly to take advantage of the exceptionally favourable situation and to forestall any counter-move by Otho, he himself swiftly followed the auxiliary units and, crossing the snows of the high Alpine pass, dropped down into the valley of the Po. Towards the middle of March he must have reached Cremona with the whole of his army.

Otho had not yet moved from Rome, although the strategy devised by his generals – who were neither few in number nor unskilful: Marius Celsus, who had served with Corbulo, Suetonius Paulinus, the conqueror of Boudicca, Annius Gallus, a man of good sense, and Vestricius Spurinna, who was to show himself one of the best men in the field and was also to distinguish himself later on – was based on the principle of preventing the union of Valens's troops with those of Caecina and demanded rapid action. However, the necessary forces were lacking. Soon it was no longer possible to count on the army of Dalmatia and Pannonia arriving in time, although the four legions, Galba's VII, the XI *Claudia*, the XIII *Gemina* and the XIV *Gemina* were already on the move, preceded by the *alae* and auxiliary cohorts, and swift-moving bodies, with two thousand men in each, were advancing by forced marches. So far as these troops were concerned, it was therefore necessary to rest content with keeping open for them the road into Italy from the direction of Aquileia. Thus the only men at Otho's disposal were the praetorian cohorts, not used to campaigning, the legion I *Adiutrix* and some detachments of legionaries; in all possibly 25,000 men, plus 2,000 gladiators commanded by Marcius Macro. When these forces began to move, Valens on one side and Caecina on the other were already arriving at the Alps. Otho himself set out even later, not before 15 March, when the news reached Rome that Caecina had crossed the Alps. One part of the troops sent on ahead by sea, mainly ex-*classiarii*, had made for the coast of Narbonese Gaul. The rest, that is, five praetorian cohorts, Legion I *Adiutrix*, some detachments of cavalry and the gladiators, not more altogether than 12–15,000 men, were defending the line of the Po – the only reasonable strategic deployment, given that the enemy was already in Italy – with their principal strong point at Piacenza, occupied by Vestricius Spurinna. They were also protecting the approaches from the east, through the efforts of Annius Gallus, who had crossed the Po at Ostiglia and pitched camp between this town and Verona. However, the expedition sent to Narbonese Gaul did not succeed in delaying Valens's march very much, in spite of gaining some victories over the procurator of the Maritime Alps and over a detachment of Vitellius's auxiliaries, under the command of Julius Classicus from Trier, which had been sent by Valens to Forum Julii (Fréjus). Undisciplined men commanded by leaders of lowly origin and little authority, these troops of Otho's were incapable of exploiting their success and preferred to pillage the coast from Albintimilium (Ventimiglia) to Albingaunum (Albenga) and then to rest on their positions, which were not bad ones thanks to their control of the sea and to the support of the province of Sardinia and Corsica, loyal to Otho. On the Po the situation was by no means unfavourable. If Otho's troops had not succeeded in occupying Ticinum (Pavia) and an attack on Cremona had failed, Caecina for his part had not succeeded, in spite of his numerical superiority, in opening the road towards central Italy. As a result, the two sides' positions had become stabilized, after a series of reciprocal long-range blows along the river. In particular, the failure of Caecina's attack on Piacenza, where he had arrived towards the middle of March by the road leading from Ticinum, had forced him to cross to the north side of the river again and block the way to Cremona. His propaganda, accompanied by a show of mildness, was having no better success. The morale of Otho's troops on the other hand was raised by their victory at Piacenza, won without even involving Legion I *Adiutrix*, which Annius Gallus was bringing back by request to help them and which had been halted with difficulty at Bedriacum, to the north of the Po, in a threatening position for Caecina; moreover, the bold raids across the river by the unit of gladiators kept Vitellius's supporters in check. The soldiers' enthusiasm had to be positively damped down by their leaders, and this provoked suspicions which resulted in serious damage to Otho's cause.

Otho himself first gave a display of generosity, granting recalled exiles the remains of the property confiscated to recover the sums given away by Nero, and took measures to ensure security, inviting the Senate to accompany him in the field (this was obligatory for some, including L. Vitellius, his adversary's brother) and entrusting Rome and the empire to his brother Titianus; then he set out for the north, probably with Suetonius Paulinus, Marius Celsus, the praetorian prefect Licinius Proculus and the consul designate Flavius Sabinus. He made the march on foot at the head of his troops – the remaining praetorian cohorts and the last detachments of veterans and *classiarii* which he had succeeded in putting together – and, leaving the senators at Modena, he joined his army on the Po, establishing his headquarters at Brixellum (Brescello). The decisive phase was beginning to take shape. Caecina's forces, which had not been reinforced but had rather tended to shrink through their lack of success, were concentrated round Cremona and now faced, in the region of Bedriacum (Calvatone), about nineteen miles to the east of the town, where the Via Postumia runs close to the Oglio, the main body of Otho's troops, which must by now have been almost equal in number, for some detachments at least of the Dalmatian and Pannonian legions had already arrived and the main body was not far off; even the legions of Moesia were on the move, sending on ahead more quickly, as usual, the auxiliary troops. Caecina saw the need to act quickly if he wanted, by gaining some success, to combat the moral effect of the reverses before the arrival of Valens, now not far away. In the locality known as *ad Castores*, a dozen miles to the east of Cremona on the Via Postumia, he set up an ambush. But Otho's troops were informed of it; they pretended to run into it by pursuing Vitellius's cavalry, which had the task of drawing them into the trap, and then when they reached the spot they came to a sudden halt, forcing the enemy lying in wait to reveal themselves too early. Encirclement followed and no one would have escaped had more decisiveness been shown by the generals, Suetonius Paulinus and Marius Celsus, whose manœuvres had nevertheless been excellent. As it was, part of the Vitellian troops succeeded in withdrawing. However, Suetonius Paulinus did not want to go on further towards Cremona. He must have had his own good tactical reasons for the decision, but this and his earlier cautiousness aroused anger and suspicion. The lesson of the defeat helped Caecina's soldiers and also those of Valens, who had arrived at Pavia after all kinds of vicissitudes. His greatest worry had been the cohorts of Batavians, who were quarrelsome and disloyal; he had even tried to split them up on the way by sending some of them to help the cohorts of Treviri, hard pressed by Otho's men on the coast of Narbonese Gaul, but this had only caused the outbreak of a mutiny in which Valens himself had been in some danger. At Pavia, when the news of Caecina's discomfiture arrived, there was a fresh mutiny; the soldiers blamed Valens's delays for Caecina's lack of success and without waiting for Valens himself all rushed to join the other general. That was how the two armies joined forces. Vitellius's generals had at their disposal at least 70,000 men with whom to finish off the war quickly, and were only waiting for a good opportunity to be offered by some error on the part of their opponents. Meanwhile, as a diversion, they began to build a bridge across the Po, near Cremona, facing the gladiators. The latter tried to stop the work, but had the worst of the fighting, making it necessary for Vestricius Spurinna to intervene from Piacenza to help them. Their commander, Marcius Macro, blamed as usual for his men's failure, was replaced by the high-ranking Flavius Sabinus, the consul designate.

Fortune was beginning to change for Otho's troops, who were in fact somewhat baffled. The union of the two enemy armies had not been prevented. That there would have to be a battle was certain, but opinions were divided on the question whether to face the struggle now or wait. Suetonius Paulinus, Marius Celsus and Annius Gallus, the strategists, were in favour of waiting until, with the arrival of the rest of the XIV legion (the XIII certainly, the VII and the XI probably, and part of the XIV had already arrived) and the nearer approach of the Moesian legions, some auxiliary detachments of which may have already arrived, the army, which must already have numbered at least 50,000 men of excellent morale, could count on a still more favourable relation to the enemy army. This had more than doubled with the arrival of Valens but could not be reinforced any further. Otho, his brother Titianus – summoned from Rome to take supreme command of the army – and the stupid, interfering Licinius Proculus, the praetorian prefect, were in favour of attacking at once. They too had good reasons for their view, the main one being the advisability of taking advantage of the good fighting spirit of the troops. This in fact was the decision taken, but Otho himself ruined by a fatal mistake what was possibly on the whole the best plan in view of the swiftly changing fortunes of civil wars. Exhorted to do so by his worst advisers, with Paulinus and Celsus offering no opposition so as not to look as if they wanted to expose the Princeps to danger, Otho left the camp at Bedriacum and returned south of the Po to Brixellum, taking a strong detachment with him. The army was thus left under the command of Titianus, who had to be obeyed – a fresh source of confusion – by the other generals, still suspect after the encounter with Caecina; and it did not help the soldiers' morale to see the Princeps taking shelter behind the Po instead of leading them personally into the decisive battle.

The initiative in this encounter, the so-called 'first battle of Bedriacum', seems to have been taken, so far as the course of events can be reconstructed from the not very clear account of Tacitus (*Hist.* II, 40–5), by Otho's troops who, leaving a certain number of men at Bedriacum with the baggage, began to march westward, with the intention of reaching the spot, beyond Cremona, where the Adda flows into the Po. They may have wished to choose a field of battle which would cut the enemy's communications with Pavia and Milan and leave him instead, having been drawn to some spot west of Cremona, with his rear threatened by the gladiators and the three praetorian cohorts that had joined them from Piacenza, in all a strong body of at least 5,000 men. And in fact to confront these troops Vitellius's generals had to deploy near the Po, downstream from Cremona, the eight cohorts of Batavians that had arrived with Valens. The Othonians' plan was a reasonable one, but it presupposed that the Vitellians would not try to wreck it in the preparatory phase, that is, during the march to the new position, and this was clearly expecting too much, as Paulinus and Celsus vainly pointed out during the first halt in the march, only four miles from Bedriacum. It was in fact almost impossible for the big army – which because of the ditches and vegetation in the open country necessarily had to channel itself along the Via Postumia and then, to get round Cremona, use some still fairly important road – to avoid passing too close to the enemy; who, waiting for nothing else than to get it within range, would no doubt attack it while it was on the march, and thus in the worst conditions, without even letting it approach Cremona. But Titianus and Proculus, executing Otho's orders, resumed the march, confident – incredibly – of passing undisturbed under the eyes of the enemy, and everything turned out exactly as was to be expected. When the advancing army, tired by the miles it had covered during the day, was a short distance from the Vitellian camp, which lay to the east of Cremona, two *alae* of cavalry met the Vitellian cavalry. The latter, pushed back to their lines, were welcomed by the I *Italica* legion with drawn swords and forced to take up their position again in the battle array, to which Valens and Caecina, perfectly informed of the adversary's moves, were just putting the final touches in an orderly fashion. A short distance away, behind the trees and bushes, Otho's troops were taking up their positions in the natural confusion of a swift deployment from marching order to battle order, a confusion heightened by the false rumour that the enemy troops had abandoned Vitellius and begun to fraternize. When the deployment had been completed somehow or other, with the centre on the Via Postumia and the wings to each side of it, Otho's troops attacked first and the battle raged bitterly, on the raised road and in the fields amid the vines and thickets. Legion I *Adiutrix* captured the eagle of the XXI *Rapax*, but its commander subsequently fell dead on the field of battle; the Vitellian V *Alaudae* repelled the XIII, and the standard party of the XIV was surrounded. It became clear that Otho's troops were going to be defeated. Of the generals, Paulinus and Proculus were the first to fade away. Valens and Caecina threw fresh forces into the battle; the eight cohorts of Batavians, under Alfenus Varus, also arrived from the Po, where they had beaten the gladiators, and made the Othonian left wing crack. Then the centre also cracked and the survivors, who fled back along the road they had just traversed, were massacred by the victors. During the night those who escaped reached the camp at Bedriacum, which was full of lamentations and recriminations against the generals. The Vitellians did not need to take it by assault; its occupants offered to surrender, and the next morning the two armies were fraternizing with each other. The praetorian cohorts alone, with their prefect Plotius Firmus, and the detachments sent on ahead from Moesia, begged the emperor not to give up the struggle, since all was not lost and the legions from Moesia were already at Aquileia. But Otho decided not to try again; he advised everyone to throw himself on the mercy of the victor, destroyed all compromising documents and during the night committed suicide. It was about the middle of April 69, and the very troops who had rebelled against Galba had avenged him after only three months, by defeating the usurper and forcing him to kill himself.

THE REIGN OF VITELLIUS

However, the disappearance of Otho did not resolve the crisis, which was still in full swing. The political equilibrium of the empire had been too profoundly disturbed and the process initiated by force of arms was to continue, with the armies themselves as the protagonists, until a new equilibrium had been attained in which the strength of an emperor definitively victorious, the unanimity of the armies and the restoration of the Senate's prestige coalesced to re-establish in its essential elements the settlement achieved by the Augustan principate. This could not happen until the armies of the East, which were certainly not disposed to bow to Vitellius for his partial victory, had had their say. And so the civil war continued. The day after Otho's death the troops at Brixellum surrendered. The senators who had remained at Modena found themselves in a critical situation. The news being uncertain, they were divided between fear of prematurely abandoning the loser and fear of being too late in paying homage to the victor, especially as they had his brother, L. Vitellius, with them; returning to Bologna and feeling safe at last, they voted the usual honours. In Rome, where Flavius Sabinus had accepted in his capacity as *praefectus urbi* the oath of allegiance to Vitellius from the few soldiers who can have remained there, the change of Princeps was taken calmly. Galba's memory was rehabilitated, a message from Valens was read and a delegation was sent to express thanks to Vitellius's army, which in the meanwhile, dispersed among the municipalities and colonies of Italy, was reviving after a century of peace the memory of the horrors of the civil wars. Vitellius, unaware of his partisans' victory, was preparing to move into Italy with an army consisting of all the remaining forces of the Rhine and eight thousand men summoned from the army of Britain. He had left Hordeonius Flaccus to guard the frontier with a few veterans, but had ordered massive levies in Gaul to bring the garrisons up to normal active strength again.

Receiving news of the victory and also the report that Mauretania had gone over to him, he held court at Lyon, where victors and vanquished met to pay homage to him: Valens and Caecina were granted special honours, Marius Celsus was confirmed in his designation as consul and Titianus was soon pardoned. Paulinus and Proculus had to exert themselves rather more but were not forced to demean themselves by admitting that they were traitors. On the other hand, the bravest of Otho's centurions were put to death and this probably cost Vitellius, right at the start, the tepid loyalty of the Illyrian legions. Even at Lyon the innate weakness of the new emperor, deprived as he was even of the stimulus of wondering whether the war would end successfully, and puffed up with pride, made itself visible in that habit of capriciousness and wasteful ostentation, of base, unrestrained indulgence in food and pleasure, that

T A—H

passed into tradition as his principal characteristic and must have corresponded, from what we know of his acts, to a gross and vulgar conception of the principate. Of the varied types that emerged from the Roman aristocracy in the whirligig of the year of the four emperors, Vitellius was certainly the worst; yet the tradition speaks with respect of his wife Galeria and his mother Servilia, who seem to have been superior women. He began to show his true colours straightaway at Lyon by giving, against his original inclination, the knight's ring to the freedman Asiaticus, a typically servile courtier, and by the grotesque pomp with which he had his still infant son honoured; the child was christened Germanicus and adorned with the imperial insignia. Then, badly advised by his brother Lucius, who had joined him, and other counsellors of tyranny, he also committed a number of acts of cruelty, thus putting a blot on the better side of his character, a certain indolent good nature. This alienated many people's sympathies, although some of his preceding acts, such as his rejection of the titles of Caesar and Augustus, must have been well received.

As for the most urgent problem, the settlement of the defeated army, this was done not without difficulty and some rumblings of discontent, especially in the XIV legion. This legion, which had arrived shortly after the battle, was sent back to Britain, whence it had been recalled by Nero, but the journey was full of vicissitudes: in a quarrel with its own old auxiliaries, the Batavians, Turin was half burnt down. The I *Adiutrix* was despatched to Spain. The VII and XI were sent back to their provinces and the XIII was kept for a little while in Italy to help with the work on the amphitheatres being built at Cremona and Bologna. The troops from Moesia who had arrived at Aquileia were obliged to turn back. The praetorian cohorts were discharged and replaced by sixteen new ones, drawn entirely from the army of Germany – a move which created further discontent. The Batavian cohorts were sent back to the Rhine and many Gallic cohorts were sent home, as were the soldiers hastily enrolled to bring up to strength the cadres of the army of Germany. With strange inconstancy and somewhat misplaced confidence, Vitellius then began to discharge a large number of soldiers, justifying his action on financial grounds. Meanwhile he had crossed over into Italy, but his slow progress towards Rome, at the head of an army of 60,000 men which regarded itself as in conquered territory and behaved accordingly, increased the general ill-will. At Pavia the underlying disquiet broke out in the suspicions of the soldiers against Verginius Rufus, who, after a fleeting appearance at Otho's camp at Brixellum after the defeat, was now with the victors. Forty days after the battle, that is, towards the end of May, Vitellius visited the site of the victory that had secured the principate for him. At Bologna he was present at the games given by Valens, just as at Cremona he had watched those organized by Caecina. Then he continued on his way, stopping in all the cities and continually flattered by the spongers who came to meet him from Rome, especially erstwhile supporters of Nero. Vitellius had in fact been an admirer of Nero. Then came the news that the East had sworn allegiance to him, and the arrogance of his men knew no further bounds. Seven miles from Rome they massacred a number of civilians and soon afterwards the soldiers of four legions, detachments of four others, twelve *alae* of cavalry and thirty-four auxiliary cohorts poured into the city.

The story of their sojourn there and of the conduct of Vitellius as Princeps is in fact a repetition of that of Galba a few months earlier, made worse by the much larger forces involved. While the troops, scattered all over the city, were no longer held together by any semblance of discipline and the diseases caused by the hot southern summer claimed many victims among the soldiers, who were not used to the climate, the emperor, who on entering the city had gone up to the Capitol and greeted his mother as 'Augusta', though still refusing this title for himself, pursued between one banquet and the next a policy that was not devoid of basic good will but was extravagant, disorganized and above all rendered sterile even in its good intentions by the general lack of esteem for his own degraded person. He posed as a modest man of the people, recommending his candidates for the consulship like a private citizen, watching shows without undue ceremony and going assiduously to the Senate, in which he even allowed himself to be contradicted. Galba's phrase, 'Libertas restituta', reappeared on coins. To procure the consulship for Caecina and Valens, who held the office in September and October, he had disregarded other earlier designations. All he could do with the two generals who had given him the throne and hated each other was to strike a balance between them by favouring both; and this only increased the confusion. Command of the praetorian guards was given to Publilius Sabinus and Julius Priscus, one Caecina's creature, the other that of Valens, while coins expressed more of a wish than a reality in the inscription 'Concordia praetorianorum'. Valens and Caecina, instead of employing their undeniable virtue of energy in the service of the Princeps, plundered other people's property to their own advantage, while the nobles reinstated by Galba obtained nothing. There was also confusion among the soldiers, with indiscriminate recruitment to the praetorian and urban cohorts and gratification of their every wish. Even here the facts were soon to show that the legends on the coins, 'Consensus' and 'Fides exercituum', expressed only what it was desired that people should believe. Confusion was also caused by the ostentatious rehabilitation of Nero's supporters, by the atmosphere of continual holiday and by the wild expenditure. In four months the freedman Asiaticus had already surpassed in wealth and power Nero's freedmen, while the Princeps, thinking to enjoy the present, squandered nine hundred million sesterces. It may be that the feeling in the air that the situation was provisional, that fresh developments could be expected – a feeling only too natural after the events of the year – together with the reality, of which he was already aware, of the rebellion in the East, induced Vitellius cynically to make 'carpe diem' his normal rule of conduct, and this inference seems to be confirmed by his public reaction to the storm when it broke. It came this time from the East. That presages and anticipations of what was to happen abound in the tradition, that in Tacitus's narrative and elsewhere the figure of Vespasian looms up as early as the time of Galba's arrival in Italy (*Hist.*, I, 10), and that details such as Galba's alleged intention to adopt Titus and the mystical prophecies of the flattering priests of eastern sanctuaries are carefully noted – all these things are naturally to be explained *ex eventu*. Nevertheless, it must have been a fact that the East, having learnt the lesson provided by the West, would want to make its own weight felt and that its own candidate would finally succeed in imposing himself on the empire, reaping the fruits of everyone's errors.

At the time of Nero's death Syria was being governed, with the aid of three legions, by one of the many by no means contemptible generals and statesmen produced by the Julio-Claudian age, namely Licinius Mucianus, the cultivated writer and cheerful pleasure-seeker described by Tacitus (*Hist.*, I, 10; II, 5, 1). In charge of the war in Judaea, now reduced to the siege of Jerusalem, was the ex-consul Flavius Vespasianus, another general of the same stamp but one also endowed with the tenacity and realism of the old Italian country people, from the ranks of whom he had only recently emerged; he and his brother Sabinus, sons of a modest knight from the Sabine region, had been the first members of their family to enter the Senate. They had then gone through the normal career with credit but without achieving exceptional distinctions. Vespasian had declared at once for Galba and sent his son Titus to pay homage to him. But the latter, hearing at Corinth of Galba's death and at the same time of Vitellius's rebellion, had returned after a good deal of hesitation to his father, whose three legions, together with those of Mucianus, had already sworn allegiance to Otho. However, no one made any move during the conflict in Italy and when the news of Vitellius's victory arrived allegiance was sworn to him as well. But the strong block of eastern legions, which during the intervening period of waiting must have been measuring its own strength, now increased by the harmony restored between Mucianus and Vespasian, who had been divided earlier and then reconciled by Titus, was ready to enter upon the scene. The initiative came from a point on the periphery, and we are not at all clear about the web of influences that set it in motion. The story that Otho nominated Vespasian in a letter as his avenger[1] is obviously a fabrication, and it is dubious whether the start of the whole affair was concentrated in one single episode recorded by Suetonius (*Vesp.* 6), according to whom a detachment of troops from Moesia, surprised at Aquileia by the news of the death of Otho, proclaimed Vespasian emperor at the suggestion of elements of Legion III *Gallica*, just transferred from Syria – a proposal which was adopted by the prefect of Egypt, Ti. Julius Alexander. Nevertheless, it must certainly be accepted that there was a chain of contacts right across the whole of the East. The army of the Danube in particular, still upset by the result of the Othonian war and badly treated by Vitellius, must have counted, for a prompt revenge, on the support of the Syrian army, with which it was bound by ties of friendship through the frequent exchanges of legions that had occurred in the time of Corbulo. Thus from the XIII legion, which had finally returned from Italy savagely offended by being assigned at Cremona to work, amid the jeers of the local populace, on the construction of the amphitheatre, right to the East and Egypt, where those of Vitellius's supporters who had joined the army there had annoyed everyone, there stretched an array of forces comprising more than half the legions of the empire.

Since no one among the governors of Dalmatia, Pannonia and Moesia was the sort of person to put himself at the head of the revolt (Antonius Primus, destined to come to the fore in subsequent events, was only the commander of a legion), all eyes were turned towards Mucianus and Vespasian, neither of whom, however, wanted the glory and responsibility of such an enterprise, the former through lack of ambition, the latter through prudence; so much so that they had sworn allegiance in swift succession to Galba, Otho and Vitellius, though they could easily have refrained from doing so. The sixty-year-old Vespasian, a man accustomed in his career to take things as they were and not as he would like them, hesitated before accepting, probably thinking of the strategic difficulty

---

[1] SUET., *Vesp.*, 6, 4.

of an expedition against Italy. Eventually, however, under pressure from many sides, egged on by Mucianus in particular, and encouraged by the favourable prophecies current – which he made a show of believing, for he was certainly aware of their propaganda value, especially in the East – he gave way to the now unanimous feeling. On 1 July 69 Ti. Julius Alexander, the nephew of Philo, made the legions of Egypt swear allegiance to Vespasian, and that day was regarded as his *dies imperii*. On 3 (or 11) July the legions of Judaea swore the oath to him with enthusiasm, hailing as emperor the general who had been with them for two years, sharing their fortunes and their hardships. At Antioch Mucianus easily gained support for Vespasian by saying that Vitellius intended to change round the legions of Syria and those of the Rhine. In a few days all the eastern provinces were with him, and these were joined by the main client princes – Sohaemus of Sophene, Antiochus of Commagene, Julius Agrippa II, who had come swiftly from Rome, and his sister Berenice. While preparations went ahead fast and furiously, a general council was held at Berytus (Beirut), at which it was decided to conclude agreements with the Parthians and the Armenians to secure the rear, to hand over the command in the Jewish war to Titus, to occupy Egypt so as to control the food supply to Rome and to start on the march against Italy. All this was done, with the shrewd addition of a promise of re-engagement and compensation for all praetorians and ex-praetorians hostile to Vitellius.

Rather surprisingly, the expedition to Italy was led by Mucianus, while Vespasian himself took control of Egypt. So Mucianus set out with Legion VI *Ferrata*, and 13,000 men drawn from the other legions, at a rate not too fast to prevent him duly plundering the rich cities of Asia on the grounds of levying a contribution to the expenses of the war. As yet he had no precise goal, for the legions of Moesia and Pannonia had not yet officially declared for Vespasian and a seaborne invasion of Italy from Dyrrhachium (Durazzo, now Durrës) was still a possibility. This was after all the shorter route and the order given to the *classis Pontica* to mass at Byzantium may have lent colour to the probability of this plan. But doubts were resolved by the behaviour of the armies of the Danube, which went over to Vespasian almost as soon as they heard of his acclamation as emperor, the first of them to make the decision being the III, which had recently been transferred from Syria. Aponius Saturninus, the governor of Moesia, did not follow this line at once but on the contrary gave immediate advice of the defection to Vitellius and tried to secure the assassination of the commanding officer of the VII *Claudia* legion, which together with the VIII *Augusta*, also back from Aquileia, had been forced to rebel but later fell in with the idea. All three legions then invited the legions of Pannonia to unite with them and these (the VII, Galba's, and the XIII) agreed immediately, remembering the battle of Bedriacum. The commander of the VII, Antonius Primus, and the procurator, Cornelius Fuscus, a senator by birth who had preferred to enter the equestrian order and to stay in it, were the guiding spirits of the revolt, supplanting the provincial governors, Tampius Flavianus of Pannonia and Pompeius Silvanus of Dalmatia, 'divites senes'.[1] After a careful survey of all the resources available had been made, messages were despatched to the other legions which had fought for Otho, the I *Adiutrix* in Spain and the XIV in Britain, and letters were sent all over Gaul. It was in fact possible to count on favourable circumstances even in the West. Hordeonius Flaccus on the Rhine and Vettius Bolanus, recently sent to Britain to replace Trebonius Maximus, were tired of facing the local dangers and were unfaithful to Vitellius; in Spain the recent allegiance of the troops to the new Princeps could be tested; and in Africa, where Vitellius's orders to enrol fresh troops had found favour because – one of the mysteries of human affairs – his own governorship was recalled with enthusiasm while Vespasian's had left a very bad memory, the double game played by the commander of the III *Augusta* legion, Valerius Festus, ensured a good position for the Flavians.

Vitellius cannot have been in Rome very long (he entered the city on 17 July) when he received the letter from Aponius Saturninus; in any case, it is difficult to believe that the news of Vespasian's acclamation in the East in the early days of July had not arrived even earlier. Thus Vitellius's inertia was all the more reprehensible and his attempt to escape from reality by trying to disregard it was ignoble. Finally, when he could no longer hide from himself or from others the gravity of the situation, he ordered Valens and Caecina to prepare for war. But since Britain, Germany and Spain had not responded to the request for reinforcements, the army was simply the one, numerous and loyal but in a fairly sorry state, that he had brought with him to Rome; Valens was ill and when Caecina set off he was already meditating betrayal. This time, too, the strategic line of defence was bound to be the Po, but with the main strong-point at Hostilia (Ostiglia) rather than Piacenza, since the enemy was expected to come from the north-east. The forces were in fact distributed along the Po from Hostilia to Cremona, which was reached first and occupied by the cavalry on the orders of Caecina, who meanwhile, on

---

[1] TAC., *Hist.*, II, 86, 3.

the pretext of making contact with the fleet, had gone off towards Ravenna and then proceeded to Patavium (Padua), where he came to an agreement with the prefect, Lucilius Bassus, to go over to the enemy. In the interval, and while Mucianus was still far away at Poetovio (Ptuj, on the Drava), a council of war was held by the Flavians near the head-quarters of the XIII legion and possible plans were discussed: was it better to occupy the Alps and wait for Mucianus and the other legions to arrive, or go straight on into Italy and fight? The bolder alternative pre-vailed, thanks to the enthusiasm of Antonius Primus, who was supported by Cornelius Fuscus.

An appeal was immediately despatched to the legions of Moesia; the chiefs of the Iazyges over the frontier were summoned to the army with the object of securing the rear from surprise, as had been done in the East; certain allied princes, in particular two kings of the Suebi, Sido, Vannius's successor, and Italicus, were drawn into the rebellion; and forces were sent to the Inn to keep an eye on the procurator of Raetia, Porcius Septimius, who was extremely loyal to Vitellius. Antonius Primus, assisted by Arrius Varus, who had commanded a cohort under Corbulo, then hastened to occupy Aquileia with detachments of infantry and cavalry, pushing on as far as Opitergium (Oderzo) and Altinum (Altino), where a garrison was left against possible attacks from the fleet at Ravenna, whose intentions were not yet known. Padua and Este went over at once to the Flavians, who were particularly favourably received by the inhabitants because of Antonius's strict order to abstain for the moment from any kind of looting; in his risky advance he did not want any hostility in his rear. Near a spot called Forum Alieni, of uncertain location, at a crossing over a river (the Adige?), a Vitellian detachment, the first one encountered, was put to flight. Nevertheless, the balance of forces was still favourable to the Vitellians, who, with their main body occupying an excellent position between Hostilia and the River Tartarus, where the roads to the south had to cross it, could easily make a short advance to meet the enemy and destroy him. But with Caecina's treacherous inertia compensating for Antonius's imprudence the Flavian army could perfectly easily be reinforced. The first legions to arrive at Padua were the VII (Galba's) and the XIII *Gemina*; then came the VII *Claudia* with Aponius Saturninus, and after that the III *Gallica* and the VIII *Augusta*. The only one of the legions from Illyricum and the Danube still missing was the XI *Claudia* from Dalmatia. There were in addition, as usual, the auxiliaries and also the re-engaged praetorian guards. Setting up his headquarters at Verona, Antonius busied himself tirelessly with preparations for the imminent operations. Cleverly getting rid of the not very loyal Aponius Saturninus and Tampius Flavianus, forced by a timely mutiny to leave the army, and with the command thus unified, he did his best not to worry about the orders to wait which came from Vespasian and Mucianus; in effect, he had already disobeyed orders by going beyond Aquileia and all he could now do was press on. Just at that moment the Ravenna fleet, manned largely by Dalmatians and Pannonians, declared for Vespasian; the instigator of the movement, the prefect Lucilius Bassus, taken to Hadria, arrested as a matter of form and soon afterwards released, was replaced by Cornelius Fuscus.

Caecina's move was not so successful. After winning over some of the officers of that part of the army encamped near the river Tartaro, he was unable to bend the loyalty of the ordinary soldiers, who were furious at the proposed betrayal, put the general in chains and chose other leaders. However, Caecina's action did not entirely fail to produce the desired effect, for the new, inexperienced leaders at once committed a grave strategic error. Probably with the aim of not remaining divided in face of the now powerful enemy, the army at Hostilia, instead of summoning all the forces available to join it in a position of great strategic value, itself decided, although it was bigger, to join the troops at Cremona. So destroying the bridge over the Tartaro, leaving Hostilia and crossing the Po, it made for Cremona along the south side of the river. When Antonius was informed of their departure, thinking perhaps that the march would be made by the shortest and most natural way, that is, along the north side of the river, he decided to hurry at once himself from Verona to Cremona, so as to arrive possibly before the two armies joined forces or at any rate before they got their second wind and re-grouped, encouraged by the increase in numbers and under new command, especially as the arrival of Fabius Valens was expected, for whose strategy Antonius showed considerable respect. But his worries on this score turned out to be unfounded, for Valens, after recovering and leaving Rome – reluctantly – only a few days after Caecina, had slowly traversed an Italy probably already in ferment and had not hurried in the slightest at the grave news brought to him. When he heard about the defection of the fleet, he confined himself to sending to Rimini, as reinforcements, some cohorts which had arrived from Rome, and himself remained in Etruria, where he was still lingering even when the decisive battle had already been fought near Cremona. This was what is known as the second battle of Bedriacum.

Antonius had in fact arrived in this locality from Verona in two days of swift, forced marches along the Via Postumia, and here he had halted. The next day, leaving the legions to fortify the camp, he pushed on towards Cremona with some auxiliary detachments, on the pretext of making a reconnaissance, but in reality to stoke up the soldiers' hatred and greed for the final struggle, now within sight, by at last allowing them to pillage. On the Via Postumia, eight miles to the west of Bedriacum, Antonius had halted with 4,000 cavalry and was shielding the auxiliaries who were scattered over the countryside looting when suddenly – it was just before midday – the Vitellians appeared. Arrius Varus launched himself into the attack with part of the cavalry and drove the Vitellians back, then, repulsed in his turn, he had to withdraw and this caused confusion among the Flavians, assembled in the meantime by Antonius, who had also sent orders to the legions to leave the camp and join him, no doubt hoping, since it was the Vitellian troops from Cremona who were offering battle, to crush them with superior numbers. In reality he was running a very serious risk, and he only just managed by his own coolness to reform his cohorts and *alae* which then made a counter-attack and pushed the Vitellians back towards Cremona. The two Vitellian legions, the I and the XXI, which had issued from their camp near the city at the news of the success of their cavalry and then advanced, in an incautious move, along the road, just had time to retreat, driven back by the fugitives and closely pursued by the victorious Flavian cavalry. However, Antonius, knowing how tired his men were (they had covered at least sixteen miles from Bedriacum, fighting on the way), did not press the pursuit very far. But at nightfall the main body of the legions called up by Antonius arrived; elated by the victory, they demanded with threatening insistence to go straight on to Cremona, not more than four miles away, to receive the surrender of the vanquished or to take the city by assault. A mutiny was on the point of breaking out when the situation was once again saved by the folly of their adversaries. The lack of a leader in an army full of fighting spirit was now revealed.

The army from Hostilia had arrived that very evening at Cremona, after covering thirty miles during the course of the day, and the wisest plan would have been to billet it in the city for the night, so that next morning the six legions, reunited, could give battle, fresh and rested, to the Flavians, who were numb after a night in the open, without provisions, far from their base. Instead the Vitellians preferred to fight at once. There was nothing left for Antonius to do but deploy his army: in the centre, on the high embankment of the Via Postumia, the XIII legion; to the left the VII, Galba's, and the VII *Claudia*; to the right the VIII *Augusta*, the III *Gallica* and the praetorian guards; on the extreme wings the auxiliary cohorts; the cavalry towards the wings and a bit to the rear; and in front Sido and Italicus with the Suebi. The darkness which had already fallen interfered somewhat, but not seriously, with the deployment against which now advanced, from the direction of Cremona, four whole Vitellian legions and elements of another seven, already thrown into rather more disorder by the mere march up to the battlefield. The great battle began at nine o'clock in the evening and lasted the whole night, with alternating fortunes. When the VII *Galbiana* was hard pressed, Antonius sent up the praetorians as reinforcements, but they were driven back; on the road the Vitellians hammered the enemy with artillery and Legion XIII had a testing time. The Flavians gained an advantage when the moon rose and shone in the faces of the Vitellians; and their morale rose when, after the sun had risen and been hailed, in accordance with their custom, by the Syrians of Legion III, the Vitellians, hearing a rumour that Mucianus had arrived and that the salute was for him, lost heart and began to give ground, hampered by their own machines; one last attack in the centre overwhelmed them, and the fugitives sought shelter in the camp in front of Cremona. This was immediately besieged by the Flavian troops, who were exhausted but had to carry the enterprise through to the end for fear of losing the fruits of victory and finding themselves once again in a dangerous position. When their assault was losing its impetus someone's finger – perhaps that of Antonius himself – pointed to the prize: Cremona. One last assault and the camp was taken by storm. Cremona was now before them, but encircled by old and solid walls and by towers, full of armed men, of citizens determined to defend themselves and of visitors, for it was the time of the fair. Nevertheless, the Flavians began the siege, but they did not have to labour long; the leaders of the Vitellians, trying to use Caecina as an intermediary, surrendered. The people of Cremona had to foot the bill. After four days of the most savage pillaging the prosperous old colony was reduced to a heap of smoking ruins: 'bellis externis intacta, civilibus infelix'.[1]

Antonius's successful audacity had in effect ensured the victory of the Flavian cause – and with the army of the Danube alone, which thus in the autumn enjoyed its revenge. The road to Rome was open. Mucianus and Vespasian, although concerned, especially the former, that the initiative continued to lie outside their control, could certainly not forbid any further advance. So Antonius, after reorganizing the beaten legions and sending them off to the Danube to replace his own, and after garrisoning

---

[1] TAC., *Hist.*, III, 34, 1.

the Alps and taking measures to ensure that news of the victory was disseminated in the West, left the main body of his troops at Verona and set off again with the rest at the beginning of winter. Leaving a trail of robberies and atrocities he arrived with his army, which victory had spoilt, at Fanum Fortunae (Fano) and, calling up the rest of his forces from Verona, resolutely crossed the snow-covered Appennines. Vitellius's situation was a difficult one. Valens – who would have done better to take command speedily of the army of the Po, now left leaderless – instead of facing the enemy's inevitable advance into Italy after the disaster at Cremona, had gone to Narbonese Gaul to rekindle the war there and soon been taken prisoner; a mad project had failed miserably. This had decided the troops in Spain and Britain to join Vespasian; and on the Rhine the rebellion of Julius Civilis had broken out. Yet in his stolid inertia the Princeps was not even capable of making the best use of the forces still at his disposal and, preferring to display energy in getting rid of alleged rivals rather than in taking some sort of strategic decision, he compromised his own cause completely.

When he at last took action, sending the praetorian prefects Julius Priscus and Alfenus Varus with fourteen praetorian cohorts, all the *alae* of cavalry available and also a new legion of *classiarii*, the II *Adiutrix*, to occupy the Appennine passes, and putting the city of Rome itself in a state of siege under his brother Lucius, it was too late. These forces were unable to advance beyond Mevania, in the south of Umbria. It was even worse when Vitellius in person, after bringing forward the *comitia*, designated the consuls for many years and nominated himself consul for life. He proceeded with a big retinue of senators to the camp, only to turn back hurriedly when he heard of the defection of the fleet at Misenum. Withdrawing his forces to Narnia (Narni) and dispersing them further by sending part of them into Campania under the command of Lucius, he had no option but to await the end. Antonius had advanced without meeting any resistance as far as Carsulae, a little to the north of Narnia, and his auxiliaries were burning to throw themselves on Rome before the legions caught up with them. The Campanians, Samnites, Paeligni and Marsi were all against Vitellius, and more and more Vitellian tribunes and centurions went over to their opponents' camp. The praetorian prefects returned to the city. However, the soldiers remained loyal and only when they were shown the head of Valens, executed in prison at Urbinum, did they all surrender, but with dignity, to Antonius who, welcoming them with kindness, left them as a garrison where they were.

The war was virtually over, but the situation dragged on uncertainly thanks to the underground manœuvres which, originating no doubt in the Flavian leaders' own jealousy of Antonius, led to a number of obscure and somewhat surprising episodes. Apart from the fact that Flavius Sabinus, Vespasian's brother, still belonged officially to the Vitellian party, exercising the functions of *praefectus urbi*, what Tacitus tells us about Petilius Cerialis, a close relative of Vespasian, who left Rome and joined the Flavians in their camp at Carsulae only at the last moment; about Sabinus himself and Domitian, who although able to escape preferred to stay in the city; also about the secret offers of an honourable retirement made to Vitellius independently by Antonius and Mucianus; about the advice given by the Roman nobility to Sabinus – who declined it – to forestall the generals and win Rome for his brother; and finally about the talks between Sabinus and Vitellius, to which Cluvius Rufus and Silius Italicus testify, all seems to suggest a wide-ranging attempt, dictated by confessed or unconfessed motives, to end the war otherwise than through the pure and simple conquest of Rome by Antonius Primus's army. But this was not in the end avoided and all that happened was simply an increase in the number of misfortunes.

Antonius, not devoid of suspicions, persuaded himself to await the result of the negotiations at Ocriculum (Otricoli), while the soldiers celebrated the Saturnalia, now convinced themselves that it would be necessary to wait there for Mucianus. Meanwhile in Rome, on 18 November, Vitellius, after receiving news of the defection of the cohorts at Narnia and evidently not moved by the fact that in the south his brother Lucius had scored a success by taking Terracina by surprise, abandoned the palace and offered his abdication. But the people and the soldiers – some of whom did not know about the manœuvres going on – would have none of it and decisively forced his hand with an uncontrollable outbreak of fury. While Vitellius was constrained to return to the palace, where he continued to be as submissive as ever, his old German soldiers and the rabble drove away the Flavians who had come in rather too much of a hurry to congratulate Sabinus and could no longer turn back. A scuffle broke out between the supporters of Vitellius and a group accompanying Sabinus. Sabinus took refuge on the Capitol with a large troop of people and sent a message to the army to resume the march on Rome. During the night he did not attempt to escape, although the siege of the Capitol was a fairly lax one, but instead summoned his children and his nephew Domitian to join him and sent a protest to Vitellius, who replied with excuses. Perhaps he did not expect Vitellius's supporters to do what they in fact did: the next day they took the Capitol by assault and set fire to the temple; Sabinus was captured and killed, against the wishes of Vitellius, while almost all the rest, including Domitian, succeeded in escaping. When he received Sabinus's message Antonius promptly approached the city by the Via Flaminia and by the night of 18/19 December he was at Saxa Rubra, opposite the Milvian bridge. Here he learnt what had happened during the day and that the populace and the slaves were in the process of arming themselves, amid the enthusiasm roused by their success; in fact, besides the episode on the Capitol, the Vitellians had also had the better of a clash with Petilius Cerialis's cavalry, which had arrived by the Via Salaria. Vitellius for his part made yet another attempt at negotiations, but the Flavians gave a cool reception to the senators and Vestals sent to meet them and an even less encouraging one to Musonius Rufus, who conceived the notion of confronting them with a philosophical discourse. On the 20th they entered the city in three columns, meeting bitter resistance; the last defenders, concentrated in the 'castra praetoria', all fell with wounds in the breast; they were worthy of a better cause. Vitellius, after emerging from the palace and then hiding again, was dragged out, pulled ignominiously across the Forum, rolled down the Gemonian steps, killed there and then thrown into the Tiber. With the emperor dead, the Senate keeping out of the way, and the elimination, thanks to the disappearance of the ambitious and devious Sabinus, of an undeniable difficulty for the Flavian cause, Domitian, son of the new but distant Augustus, was hailed as Caesar by the soldiers.

Three times in fourteen months Rome had seen the arrival of armies belonging to men out to acquire the principate by conquest. Now no one could say for certain that the violence and looting carried out in the captured city by the Flavians would form the inhabitants' last experience of this kind. But the confident belief that such was the case was induced not only by the hope that the civil war, which had started in Spain and Gaul, spread to Germany and Illyricum, and traversed Syria, Egypt and all the provinces, had finally completed its destructive cycle, but also by the weariness of Italy and the words of wisdom and peace which came from the new Princeps. The reality did not belie the expectations.

VI

VESPASIAN AND TITUS

The fusion of old and new once again took place in accordance with the principle of empiricism which had always guided the development of the Roman state. The victory had been won much as it had been in other civil wars for the position of Princeps: Antonius Primus had really completed his task only in Rome, Mucianus was making for Rome and Vespasian had to come to Rome and to govern the empire from there. A purely military victory, it repeated that on which the *de facto* legitimacy of the Augustan principate had once been founded, and it was precisely the Augustan principate, now established by the tradition of a century, that this victory aimed at restoring. But the very severe crisis had not shaken the Roman political world in vain. With the fading of the bloom of the urban emperors – all of them destroyed by the emptiness of their aims, inspired by utopian policies or by no policy at all, and the toys of those wild elements which they imagined they dominated but in fact did not dominate at all – the Princeps who now followed brought with him, finally matured by the strain of the crisis – though probably he was no more aware of it than his predecessors had been of their own still immature standing – the new element which, grafted on to the old, still-standing trunk, was to ensure the exuberant continuation of the empire at its political summit. This new element came from the acceleration given by the year of conflict to the existing tendency to a political levelling-up of the empire caused by the already well-established uniformity of the administrative system. The administration was once again the saving element, the robust platform on which political order, disturbed by an eminently political crisis, was re-established. Under the Julio-Claudians the two spheres, politics and administration, had been in all essentials separated at the top, and this had been beneficial, for if notable advantages flowed from those emperors who glimpsed their interdependence and, out of a personal sense of duty, made themselves useful to the empire, not much damage could be caused by those who failed to perceive it. As we have seen, the empire functioned excellently under Gaius and Nero, whose metropolitan extravagances did not much affect the running of the general administration. But from now onwards, after the universal storm that had shaken every part of the Roman dominions, after the demonstration of the unhappy results of the efforts of emperors in the purely urban tradition, whether well-intentioned or simply bent on enjoying power as a sort of prize, there would be no room at the top of the organization for any Princeps who was not aware both of his political and administrative functions, who was not the Princeps of the *whole* empire as a totality, instead of just the more or less capricious lord of the urban aristocracy.

It was certainly circumstance that made Vespasian into such a Princeps rather than his upbringing, which was still that of the Julio-Claudian nobility. An Italian, from a family that had only recently emerged from the lower orders, with personal qualities of solid practicality admirably suited to carrying out the necessary fusion of political power and administrative needs, first acclaimed in the East and therefore closer to the feeling of imperial community in this region, which differed in so many ways from the others, he was made Princeps in Rome and it was in Rome that he received the approval of the Senate in accordance with the old rituals; but it was in the provinces that he began to exercise his functions and continued to exercise them for a considerable time – not like Galba or Vitellius, just while waiting to reach the capital, or like Nero in Greece. This was a valuable experience mutually shared by both Princeps and provinces and one destined not to be forgotten when Vespasian, having arrived in Rome and moved aside his son Domitian, who was already 'playing the emperor's son'[1] in the old way, made it the foundation of the new principate. Thus it is right to equate the reign of Vespasian with the first decisive change of direction in the empire. Now that the concept of the functional nature of the Princeps had been developed and made consciously operative, now that the Princeps formed an apex equidistant in all respects (not, as before, just in some areas) from the base – now levelled up – of the empire as a reality, the Roman imperial state resumed, after this first crisis, its still prosperous progress along the road leading eventually to the paternalism of the Antonines.

While the new Princeps was still far away, the last hotbeds of civil war were in the process of being eradicated. Lucius Vitellius, who held Terracina, surrendered and was put to death; his men were subsequently incorporated in the Flavian praetorian cohorts. The Campanian towns still in turmoil were pacified by the stationing of garrisons in them. Capua enjoyed the expensive privilege of giving hospitality to Legion III *Gallica*

---

[1] TAC., *Hist.*, IV, 2, 1: 'filium principis agebat'.

for the winter. The Senate voted the usual honours to Vespasian; and after one of his messages, moderate and auspicious in tone, had been read out, made him consul, with his son Titus, from 1 January of the coming year. Mucianus, whose imminent arrival was announced, was granted the triumphal regalia for his victory over the Sarmatians; for during his march he had been heavily engaged in Moesia – shorn of its legions, which had gone to Italy – in repelling a strong attack by the tribes from the far side of the Danube. Antonius Primus was given only the consular insignia, and Cornelius Fuscus and Arrius Varus the praetorian insignia; this moderation must have been the result of special instructions. The emperor's nineteen-year-old son, present in Rome, was given the praetorship with the consular imperium, but for the moment he did not take much interest in public affairs, which were still all in the hands of Antonius. Arrius Varus commanded the praetorian guard and in fact the city was at the mercy of the soldiers; in the Curia the senators, who had got their breath and courage back at the prospect of stability offered by the new situation, were already immersed in the innocuous diatribes which did duty for freedom, either studying modes of flattery, as in the discussion on the mode of choosing the honorary ambassadors to be sent to Vespasian, or else publicly recalling, so as to rehabilitate it without danger, the memory of those suppressed by the preceding régimes. The arrival of Mucianus put an end to this phase of uncertainty. But metropolitan events in the year 70, which was one of reorganization, were complicated by the serious events abroad: the Germano–Gallic revolt on the Rhine, which may be regarded as a direct sequel of the civil war, and the Jewish war, which must have been prolonged by the civil war.

When Antonius Primus, in the summer of 69, had sought to prevent reinforcements coming to Vitellius from the other side of the Alps, Julius Civilis, a Batavian chief who had served for a long time in the 'auxilia' and now possessed citizenship, had willingly agreed to foment trouble on the Rhine so as to prevent the few troops left there from moving into Italy. Giving out that he was upholding the Flavian cause and only lukewarmly opposed by the governors themselves, Hordeonius Flaccus and Dillius Vocula, who, unlike their own soldiers, had little liking for Vitellius and were awaiting the outcome of events, Civilis had succeeded, in the short space of time before news of the battle of Cremona arrived, not only in raising in revolt his own Batavians and the neighbouring Canninefates and Frisii but also in rallying to his standard other tribes from the left and right banks of the Lower Rhine, such as the Tungri and Nervii of Belgica and the Bructeri and Tencteri from Germany. The 'auxilia' from these same tribes were also with him, having abandoned the legions, and a particularly substantial addition to his strength came with the adhesion of the eight Batavian cohorts back from Italy after the Vitellian victory in April. With these forces, fighting officially in the name of Vespasian against the Vitellians, he defeated the legionaries and besieged the camp at Vetera, which however it was possible to relieve thanks to victories won by detachments from Mainz.

Until now the fighting had been disguised as factional strife, but after the defeat of the Vitellians at Cremona the situation was clarified; the soldiers swore allegiance, if without enthusiasm, to Vespasian and Julius Civilis became a rebel who had to be crushed. But the wretched state of the legions, now a mere shadow of the once powerful Rhine army, favoured the Batavian's ambitious plan to continue the war openly at the head of a general rebellion by the Germans and Gauls against Rome. Fortune smiled on him at first. While the Roman soldiers, in a continual state of mutiny (at Novaesium [Neuss] they killed Hordeonius Flaccus), were reduced to defending a number of bases – Vetera, Novaesium, Bonna, Moguntiacum, where the camp was only saved by a rapid thrust on the part of Vocula – Civilis succeeded in gaining the support of some Gallic leaders who, like him, had spent their lives in the Roman armies: namely Julius Classicus, Julius Tutor and Julius Valentinus of the Treviri, and Julius Sabinus of the Lingones. Elated by omens which – like the intervening fire on the Capitol – were made to indicate by the fanatical interpretations of their priestesses that the moment had come to turn into a reality the ever recurrent dream of the 'imperium Galliarum', and in spite of the fact that they were not followed by the whole of Gaul, for the Sequani were soon at odds with the neighbouring Lingones and even the Mediomatrici (of Metz) with the Treviri on their borders, they quickly reduced the Romans, who were also left leaderless, to dire straits. Vocula was killed at Novaesium by his own men, who included many of the Gauls hastily enrolled by Vitellius, and other commanders of legions also fell in the fighting; one, Munius Lupercus, was actually sent as a gift to Veleda, the greatest prophetess of the Germans, and killed on the way. In the end all the Roman camps from Mainz to the sea were destroyed. Colonia, the great city that radiated Roman influence, surrendered, and the remains of the army, concentrated at Novaesium, lowered themselves to the ignominy of swearing allegiance to the Gallic empire. But that this stage of affairs could last for long was pure illusion, if only because of the incomplete support of the Gauls and the somewhat unnatural Gallo-Germanic alliance, already cooling as a result of the victory itself. On top of this a swift reaction by the Romans was inevitable. A defeat suffered by the Lingones, who were beaten by the Sequani, was enough to make most of the Gauls see reason; in a conference held in the territory of the Remi the majority declared themselves hostile to the movement.

Meanwhile the powerful army sent by Mucianus to restore the situation had already crossed the Alps. It was formed of troops collected from the large numbers available in Italy after the victory, and consisted of the XI *Claudia*, the VIII *Augusta* and the VII *Claudia*, all Flavian legions, and in addition the XXI *Rapax* and the II *Adiutrix*, ex-Vitellian legions but ones that had had no contact with Lower Germany. Moreover, Petilius Cerialis and Annius Gallus, the experienced generals chosen for the campaign, were also authorized to call on the army of Spain and one British legion. A total force of seven or eight legions and their auxiliaries was bound to be able to deal quickly with the revolt and to re-establish the formidable Rhine defences. Annius Gallus probably looked after Upper Germany and Petilius the rest. The valleys of the Rhine and Moselle were swiftly reoccupied; repeatedly defeated, the Lingones and the Treviri had to submit and the 'imperium Galliarum' was destroyed. The XIV legion, arriving from Britain, also forced the rebellious Belgi to return to their allegiance. Classicus and Tutor took refuge in the north with Civilis, who was now reduced to defending himself just with the tribes which had started the revolt. After the successes gained by his good strategic direction of the operations and by the tact with which he had restored the fighting spirit of the legions and fear of the Roman name among the local peoples, Petilius Cerialis reoccupied Colonia and then had to confront the most difficult part of his task. Civilis, although beaten in a big battle at Vetera, still gave his adversary a good deal of food for thought, ensconced as he was in the difficult terrain between the rivers. However, Cerialis succeeded in occupying the heart of the Batavian territory, the 'insula Batavorum', and although we do not know the end of the story, since the *Histories* of Tacitus break off just at the point where Cerialis and Civilis are meeting to discuss negotiations for peace, we can assume that this means that the rebellion was now completely spent.

So ended, before the winter of 70, this peripheral reflection of the great crisis, after bringing to the surface various interesting factors which would have to be taken into account in the local and general politico-administrative reorganization. In the event, while Cerialis personally did not indulge in any fierce repression or reprisals but simply re-established the authority of Rome, the central government, though restoring to the local peoples their previous status – the Batavians themselves still paid only the tribute paid by the 'auxilia' – nevertheless completely changed the system of using auxiliary troops in the area where they had been recruited. This change broke the bond with the local population which had caused the 'auxilia' to live in continual friction with the legions and finally to rise against them and against the Roman name, impelled by the nationalist aspirations fostered by continual contact with their tribes. Gallic and German auxiliaries were no longer commanded by chiefs from their own peoples and had to serve elsewhere. Finally, with the suppression of the numbers and names of the legions which had most disgraced themselves and the transfer of others, the powerful defensive apparatus along the Rhine was completely restored and security against external threats, a factor pushed into second place by the blind necessities of the civil war, was re-established.

Meanwhile at the other end of the empire the Jewish war was drawing to a close. This was not the only other theatre of war in the year 70. In Britain the intervention in 69 on behalf of Queen Cartimandua, queen of the Brigantes, had been only the start of operations which were to occupy such a large part of the Flavian period. In Africa Valerius Festus, commander of Legion III *Augusta*, after being involved in the obscure assassination of the proconsul L. Calpurnius Piso (towards June 70), had then carried out some operations against the Garamantes, who had been called in by the people of Oea (Tripoli) to help them against the town of Leptis in the course of the municipal conflicts encouraged by the confused general situation. In the East itself, the pro-Vitellian revolt of one Anicetus, a freedman of that King Polemo installed in Pontus by Nero, had been suppressed by detachments sent direct by Vespasian himself during Mucianus's march, and after the above-mentioned action of Mucianus against the Dacians and Sarmatians who, probably in November 70, had invaded Moesia, there were further serious attacks in 70 along the Lower Danube by these peoples, in which the governor of Moesia, Fonteius Agrippa, fell on the field of battle; however, he was soon avenged by his successor, Rubrius Gallus, who restored the situation.

But the Jewish war remained the biggest open conflict. Vespasian had conducted the war with varying fortunes since 67, and in 69, when he was acclaimed emperor, it only remained to capture Jerusalem and eliminate the resistance of some other fortresses. He had in fact just resumed operations more energetically, but when the command passed to Titus the Jews were able to profit by a further delay, for it was only in the spring of 70 that Titus reopened the campaign, accompanied by Ti. Julius Alexander, whom a recently published papyrus has shown to have participated in the war in the capacity of *praefectus praetorio*.[1] Titus had at his disposal all that was left of his father's three legions – after Mucianus had taken detachments from each – and also Legion XII *Fulminata* and large detachments from the Egyptian legions. With these forces he invested the city, inside which, although discords had not ceased, the party for war *à outrance* had gained the upper hand over the peace party almost completely and a fanatical throng from all over Judaea had gathered, determined to resist to the end. The first and second rings of walls were stormed towards the end of May, but the defenders did not surrender, vigorously repulsing both the attacks of the besiegers and the advice to surrender given to them by their fellow-countryman Flavius Josephus, who was now with the Romans. In June the tower of Antonia also fell and only the temple was left; this was taken in August and destroyed by the express orders of Titus, if we are to accept the testimony of Tacitus, which is more acceptable than the adulatory account of Josephus. Resistance continued in the upper part of the city until September, and for years after that in Herod's fortresses of Macherus and Masada; the latter was only taken in 72 and its defenders, known as the 'Sicarii', all killed themselves. But these operations were conducted by two subsequent field commanders, Lucilius and Flavius Silva; for one of the results of the Jewish war was that the commanding officer of Legion X *Fretensis*, which was left as a permanent garrison in the country, became to all intents and purposes the governor of the province, taking precedence over the procurator. Meanwhile at Rome in 71 Titus, with his father and brother, celebrated a triumph by hauling up to the Capitol all the spoils of war, which included the seven-branched candlestick taken from the temple and the captured Jewish leaders, who were subsequently put to death or imprisoned for life. The people of Rome were thus given clearly to understand, by means of a spectacle not seen for a long time in commemoration of an authentic victory, that the authority of the principate had been reinforced and also that the new dynasty was asserting its position.

This assertion of power was by now real and unquestioned, but the year of Vespasian's 'adventus' had still been a rather unsettled one even at home. In the absence of the Princeps, an absence evidently foreseen in the plans for the immediate reorganization of Rome and Italy after the war, operations were directed energetically by Mucianus. Almost as soon as he had arrived in the city towards the end of December 69 he had injected

[1] *Hibeh Papyri*, II, London 1955, No. 215, pp. 135–7 (TURNER); cf. E.G. TURNER in *Journ. of Rom. St.*, XLIV, 1954, p. 54 ff. He was already known from a Syriac inscription as 'prefect of the Jewish army', *Or. Gr. Inscr. Sel.*, 586.

an element of order into the situation by demonstrating his authority as the emperor's sole lieutenant; Antonius had sunk almost naturally into the background, for the people, intuitively appreciating the essence of the situation, had been pretty quick in transferring their loyalty and respect. Mucianus's authority had subsequently increased when, with the admixture of the fear roused by some inevitable reprisals, such as the execution of the freedman Asiaticus, the elimination of a suspected rival, one Calpurnius Piso Galerianus, adoptive son of the protagonist in the Pisonian conspiracy under Nero, the mysterious assassination of another Piso, proconsul of Africa (see above, p. 232), and finally the cruel execution of Vitellius's little son, he proved that he had firmly in his grasp all the different elements in the situation – the remains of the Vitellian opposition, the generals and soldiers, the Senate and Domitian. Antonius, who was responsible for the victory, gave him rather more food for thought, and so did Arrius Varus; but, tricking Antonius's impetuous spirit with the promise of the governorship of Spain, he took the military forces away from him, sending back to Pannonia the very legion, the VII, which had been his own and to Syria the III *Gallica*, which had particular ties with Arrius. All the rest were despatched to the Rhine under other generals. It was in vain that the two men champed at the bit; Mucianus actually succeeded in removing Arrius from the command of the praetorian cohorts and in transferring him to the corn supply. At the head of the praetorian guard, in which he had already appeased one mutiny, he placed Arrecinus Clemens, a friend of Domitian and son of the man of the same name who had been prefect under Gaius. He did this only after carefully weighing the need to secure the best balance of all elements against the danger of making a serious exception to the usual rule, for Clemens was a senator. When Antonius, now stripped of his authority, made up his mind to go and complain personally to Vespasian his ephemeral glory finally faded away amid indifference.

The Senate was soon put under the same sort of control. It was convoked on 1 January by the urban praetor, Julius Frontinus, in the absence of the consuls Vespasian and Titus, and subsequently met frequently; its decisions could now at last be made in safety, if not in freedom, which remained restricted, as usual. It voted thanksgivings to those who had contributed to the victory; dismissed from his post anyone who had opposed it, like Tettius Julianus, who had not followed his legion in its new allegiance, though he was later reinstated 'postquam cognitum est ad Vespasianum confugisse';[1] and resolved – at Domitian's suggestion – on

[1] TAC., *Hist.*, IV, 40, 2.

the rehabilitation of Galba's memory, though Piso's was left as it was. It also set up commissions for the compensation of losses due to the war, for the restoration of the bronze tablets on which the laws were inscribed, for the rectification of the records 'adulatione temporum foedatos'[1] and finally for the control of expenditure, proposing the raising of a loan of sixty million sesterces from private individuals (a project never actually carried out) and also granting equestrian rank to one Ormus, a freedman of the Princeps. It then proceeded to tear itself apart with accusations and trials; and when with mutual concealments and unmaskings it reached the painful decision that all the senators should swear a solemn oath that they had never done any harm to anyone or profited from the communal misfortunes and thought it had fully recovered its freedom, an intervention by Domitian and Mucianus suddenly cooled its enthusiasm: 'patres coeptatam libertatem, postquam obviam itum, omisere'.[2]

On top of everything else, a novel element was provided by the position of Domitian. His name, 'Caesar Domitianus', was put down first in the official acts, but it was Mucianus who in practice acted as Princeps, not without exciting some disquiet in the boy, whose hard and jealous temperament must have already revealed itself. In fact, after a carefree start, after his first embarrassed interventions in the Senate and the purely formal motions which he proposed in his capacity as praetor, he began, as far as we can see, to make one or two moves of his own in the dangerous area of the effective power of the Princeps; and it looks as if the annoying reports about Domitian that reached Vespasian, and Titus's intercession with his angry father, must refer to something other than his lazy behaviour as a private citizen. There is the fact that Mucianus did not consider it possible to take personal command of the army sent off to the Rhine because he was worried about leaving Domitian in Rome. Among other things, the youth's friendship with Arrius Varus was suspicious, and what happened when the two of them wanted to go to the theatre of war and Domitian, on the advice of Mucianus, stopped at Lyon, where he sounded out Petilius Cerialis himself, offers material for speculation, even though the affair is presented by Tacitus (*Hist.*, IV, 85–6) as rumour. However, nothing came of this either. Rome, rescued from the danger of famine, too, by the supplies flowing again from Egypt and symbolically confirmed, so to speak, in its feeling of peace by the start made on rebuilding the Capitoline temple, now saw the arrival in the month of October, together with news of the victorious conclusion to the foreign wars, of Vespasian.

---

[1] *Ibid.*   [2] *Ibid.*, 44, 1.

THE REORGANIZATION OF THE EMPIRE

The Princeps had spent about a year in Egypt, for military reasons so long as the war continued, and after that for reasons that are not very clear. However, it was certainly not because he did not yet consider his own position sufficiently secure. Indeed, the very opposite seems more likely: he began to govern the empire from the periphery with every confidence, waiting only for the summer and favourable winds to reach Rome and normalize the situation in his imperial capital as well. His first message to the Senate has already been mentioned. He sent others from Alexandria: one ordering the reconstruction of the Capitol, another can-celling the *atimía* inflicted on those executed for treason by Nero and his successors and forbidding such prosecutions in future; and also one giving instructions for a first expulsion of astrologers. This last measure is a rather surprising one, for accounts of Vespasian's stay in Egypt are largely concerned with his relations with magi and wonder-workers, even attributing to the emperor himself the miraculous ability to make the blind see and cripples walk again. But apart from these practices, in which he almost certainly acquiesced out of consideration for their local politi-cal value, and apart from the episodes recorded in connection with his not very cordial relations with the Alexandrians, irritated by his fiscal measures in spite of the enthusiastic welcome which they had originally given him, he showed right from the start the essential seriousness of his approach by maintaining close contact with Rome, by increasing the grain supply and by immediately setting about financial reform. It was an interesting experiment, especially after what had happened, to grasp the threads of the situation from a distance, and that it was successful speaks equally well for the man and the solidity of the system. He had also taken advantage of the slow journey to Rome, a journey which probably began in the early days of August 70, to make himself familiar – as is clear from successive decrees issued – with local situations – in Rhodes, in the cities of Asia, in Greece. At Brundisium, where he landed after the voyage from Corcyra, Mucianus was there to meet him; and Domitian came to meet him at Beneventum. As for the welcome by the Senate and Italy, the procession usual at such arrivals took place along the Via Appia. Inscriptions, coins and – if the second frieze of the Cancel-laria[1] represents Vespasian's *adventus*, commemorated later, in the reign of Domitian – sculptured monuments preserve the memory of the arrival, particularly in the symbolic transfiguration of 'Fortuna Redux'.

[1] F. MAGI, *I rilievi Flavi del palazzo della Cancellaria* Rome 1945, p. 106 ff.

There is little information about Vespasian's first acts in Rome, and in general, with the disappearance of Tacitus's narrative, there is no adequate basis for a strictly chronological reconstruction of the rest of his activity. It will therefore be necessary to consider this activity as an organic whole, though we shall also try as far as possible to give some idea of its chronology. It was noteworthy not so much for grandeur of aim as for realistic conformity with necessity. Vespasian soon showed his gifts of wisdom and good sense by inaugurating in the palace a mode of life devoid of excessive outward pomp, which could have provoked comparisons with the modesty of his previous status. The *civilitas* of the Augustan programme, according to which, in the legal and formal fiction intended to form the official reality, the Princeps was to seem a citizen among citizens and not the monarch, was reinstated again, if rather as a personal attitude dictated by the wish to be a good father: that the Princeps was henceforth openly an autocrat could certainly no longer escape anyone and the republican façade restored by Vespasian was no longer intended to be the expression of a political programme seriously and anxiously pursued (as it was with Tiberius, as we have seen) but simply a homage to the tenacious Roman tradition. The principate henceforth revolved more openly around the power that formed its real essence and ran in point of fact on more simplified lines.

The position of Vespasian, apart from the controversial evidence of the so-called *lex de imperio*, partially preserved on the famous bronze tablet found by Cola di Rienzi, is clear. The purely military origin of his power was in the tradition of the principate. But he affirmed the principle of dynastic succession even verbally with an unprecedented energy. The words 'either my sons will succeed me or no one will'[1] were certainly not intended to convey merely the fatalistic acceptance of two alternatives – the continuation of the empire in his own family or a return to the republic. From the start, Vespasian and his sons formed a dynastic unity. Titus, *Caesar* and *princeps iuventutis* since 69, his father's colleague in seven of the eight consulships held by Vespasian after coming to the throne, colleague in the *tribunicia potestas* from 1 July 70, colleague in the censorship in 73 (but *designatus* from 71), *imperator*, though not usually employing the title as a forename like his father and also distinguished in outward regalia, was a genuine co-ruler. In any case, right from the time of the acclamation his position was such (Tacitus [*Hist.*, II, 77] makes Mucianus call him 'capax imperii' and according to Josephus [*Bell. Iud.*, IV, 597 (10, 3)], the soldiers hesitated between the father and the son) as to cause him to be

[1] SUET., *Vesp.*, 25; CASS. D., LXVI, 12.

regarded in fact as pretty close to the emperor. The position of the youth Domitian was built up in accordance with a very precise scheme: officially known in the East as *Caesar* and *princeps iuventutis* at the same time as Titus and even before the arrival of the Flavian party in Rome, invested during his father's lifetime with six consulships, only one of which however was an ordinary one, endowed as well as his brother with the right to coin money bearing his own likeness, he too was clearly marked out, though on a lower level, for the imperial succession and shared meanwhile in a family dominion more closely knit than anything seen before. But for all that there is no trace of a collective direction of affairs. Vespasian exercised power in person. The discreet collaboration of Mucianus so long as he lived (he died not earlier than 75 and not later than 77) and that of the sons do not prevent us from recognizing in his rule the imprint of his own characteristic mentality and his own personal energy, and above all the application of his concept of the functional duty of the position of Princeps. Thus after formally restoring the original appearance of the principate by the immediate assumption of a name – *Imperator Caesar Vespasianus Augustus* – which exactly reproduced that of Augustus, he modelled himself rather on Claudius in his deeds, though substituting for the latter's disorderly pile of good intentions a persevering and balanced course of action. This was not only revealed in his initial promises and first acts (restraining of Domitian, moderation in rewards to the troops, mildness towards the Vitellian party), but also lasted as the normal state of affairs throughout a reign in which for the first time the spontaneous process of consolidation going on in the multiform life of the empire was encouraged and sometimes guided systematically and coherently from the top: 'per totum imperii tempus nihil habuit antiquius quam prope afflictam nutantemque rem publicam stabilire primo, deinde et ornare'.[1]

There was thus a state of equilibrium, the foundations of which were formed by the emperor's relations with the various elements in Roman society, especially the Senate. The nobility was still after all what counted for most above the anonymity of the life that swarmed, but politically had as yet almost no voice of its own, throughout the empire. We have already spoken of the Senate's attitude immediately after the Flavian victory. With what sort of prestige it could confront the new emperor after hailing three others in the space of a year can be imagined. Even if we do not see it as a unanimous body which changed sides at the same moment – this would be unreal – but take account of the successive prevalence of

[1] SUET., *Vesp.*, 8, 1.

different currents of opinion, and in particular of the more or less active presence of separate individuals, it cannot be said that it did not continue to be what it had always been under the principate and did not demonstrate this with the usual flattery. The tone of the relations between the Princeps and the Senate must therefore have been set, as always, by the Princeps. Vespasian knew how to strike the right note. A number of circumstances made this easier for him. The newness of his own family, its relative isolation and lack of bonds with the urban aristocracy, and even – a by no means negligible detail after the experience of women like Messalina and Agrippina – the absence of an empress and of imperial ladies in general (Vespasian's wife Flavia Domitilla had been dead some time and in her place he had privately resumed relations with a friend of his youth, Antonia Caenis, one of Antonia's freedwomen; his daughter Flavia Domitilla was also dead and Caenis's child, Flavia Domitilla, must have still been very young, like little Julia, Titus's daughter), while on the one hand causing a latent antipathy never overcome in spite of the modesty of the court, on the other eliminated the possibility of intrigues. In any case, as we can gather from the names themselves – for those of the old republican and Latin families grow scarcer and scarcer – the aristocracy itself had been largely renewed and changed in composition by natural causes, even before the measures of the beginning of the reign and the *lectio* of Vespasian's censorship brought the number of families in the senatorial nobility up from two hundred (this was the number that remained) to a thousand. For some time now the aristocracy had no longer questioned, from a practical point of view, the principate itself but only the person of the Princeps; and this new, more broadly based aristocracy, chosen naturally to a large extent from the ranks of Flavian supporters, a more bureaucratized aristocracy, with its own business affairs to look after, to which the imperial adminstration did not give offence by rousing suspicions of political oppression but offered opportunities for the satisfaction of pride and the gaining of profits, was all the more disposed to live in harmony with a Princeps who embodied the ideals of its own Italian and provincial origins.

For the rest, in Vespasian we also meet the attitude and behaviour traditionally attributed to the good Princeps in the field of relations with the Senate: assiduous attendance at its sessions, requests for advice, affability and easy accessibility, granting of free speech, tolerance of jokes and gibes, forgetfulness of insults, no reprisals or trials for treason, and generous subventions to individuals lacking the property qualification for their rank. In the more crucial matter, too, of employing the senatorial aristocracy to govern the empire, and in spite of the increasing number of knights and freedmen in administrative posts and his advocacy of a certain *de facto* parity between the two orders (a parity proving in any case to be natural and inevitable in the development of the administrative system created by Augustus), Vespasian managed to secure the allegiance of a strong group of excellent collaborators. The trust he reposed in the senatorial class and in the old system of magistracies was revealed not so much in his own frequent assumption of the consulship – for the fact that he always held it with his son Titus (except for the third, in 71, in which his colleague was M. Cocceius Nerva, the future emperor) indicated rather that he did not intend to share the supreme post with strangers outside the family and thus confer on them an excessive honour to the detriment of the compactness of his dynastic plan – as in the reduction of the duration of the supplementary (*suffecti*) consulships, a means of creating a greater number of consular colleagues for the practical needs of administration. Similarly, a conservative wish to make the most of the old governing class was displayed not so much by the transference to senators of the praetorian prefecture and the supposed and possibly only temporary return of the treasury to the praetors – this cannot be interpreted as a retreat from the tendency to 'comissarial' rule – as by the fact that the new Princeps was generous with honours to individual senators. The highest distinctions were granted in 73 to the great governor of Moesia, Plautius Aelianus, then just back from governing Spain and destined for the prefecture of the city. Even men like Tampius Flavius, Pompeius Silvanus and Aponius Saturninus, who had had no sympathy for him in the course of the struggle, were honoured with fresh consulships and the proconsulships of Africa and Asia, the very highest posts in the career of provincial government.

Yet in this policy of deference to the Senate, extolled on coins in particular by the motif of 'Libertas' and recognized by tradition, Vespasian had to cope with an opposition inspired for the first time by theoretical principles. The opposition of philosophers like Helvidius Priscus, son-in-law of Thrasea Paetus, must have worried Vespasian seriously, if when it was transferred by Priscus to the field of practical decision-making, in the form of sterile but obstinate obstruction, it could provoke the Princeps to one of the severest acts of repression in his reign. The fact was that as the shape of the principate became better defined, so also a doctrinaire opposition became better defined; by now even Romans must have been capable of developing a consciously thought-out political theory. But the conversion into practice of political utopias was not in the Roman character, and even less in Vespasian's; hence his harsh reaction. The tradition of the *continuous* conspiracies of which Suetonius speaks (*Vesp.*, 25) is more obscure. It would seem to indicate a more realistic kind of opposition; but so far as actual names are concerned the only conspiracy we know of is that of T. Clodius Eprius Marcellus and A. Caecina Alienus, the betrayer of Galba and Vitellius, which was discovered in 79. Even in this case we have no details at all.

On this basis of cordial agreement with the aristocracy Vespasian developed his lasting work of reorganization, though with the independence which he enjoyed thanks to his real position as an autocrat. He began with the finances, the most devastated area. Not that the fiscal resources of the empire were exhausted, but the mad enterprises of Nero, the exemptions granted and the difficulties which the civil war had imposed here and there on the apparatus of assessment and collection, though this now functioned on its own like the whole administrative system, must have created some imbalances. That the *aerarium* and the *fiscus* in Rome, that is, the old official treasury and the imperial treasury, now well organized as the financial centre of the state controlled by the Princeps, should have been found empty by Vespasian is hardly surprising when one thinks that in the previous year, with the war in Italy and so many armies quartered in Rome, three emperors must have plunged their hands into these treasuries, without any regular influx of revenue to fill the gaps as they were made. So once peace and confidence had been re-established the new emperor's task was simply that of restoring the normal balance between income and expenditure. And since his own matter-of-fact and calculating nature (rather too calculating personally, to judge from the many anecdotes that flourished round his reputation for avarice, unanimously regarded by tradition as his only defect) inclined him to take a special interest in this department of affairs, in the end it was financial activity that more or less gave Vespasian's reign its characteristic stamp, although we are better aquainted with the results than with the individual measures.

In the matter of the reorganization of the collection of taxes, it is in fact only conjecture that the census of 73–4 was made the basis of the system; and as for the abolition of the exemptions granted by Nero and Galba, we know that Greece's immunity was cancelled (but we do not know when; probably in 73 or 74) and that the taxes abolished by Galba were reimposed, certainly in Spain and Gaul in particular, but we also know that some privileges were confirmed. This is clear from the letter (dating possibly from 72) to the Vanacini, a Corsican people, and from the edict found at Pergamum on the immunity of doctors and teachers

(A.D. 74). As for new taxes, apart from the notorious *vectigal urinae* we do not know for certain of any. The tax flowing from 71 onwards into the so-called *fiscus Iudaicus* only represented the transference to Capitoline Jupiter of the didrachm previously paid by the Hebrews to the temple at Jerusalem; and the institution of the *fiscus Alexandrinus*, and possibly that of the *fiscus Asiaticus*, cannot have been intended, from the little we know about them, as the creation of central treasuries for new taxes; it must have derived from the tendency to ever more specialized organization of the system of collecting and accounting for the old taxes, particularly for those parts of the empire which were most lucrative from the point of view of tribute. Probably the re-injection of order into the incomings and of a degree of moderation into the expenditure was sufficient to restore a healthy situation and even to secure a large increase in income; the revenue from some provinces doubled – a natural phenomenon in view of the general economic development.

Vespasian does not seem to us to have pursued an oppressive fiscal policy, but simply to have been attentive to securing profit for the state – for example, from the sale of the *subseciva*, that is, pieces of ground left over from previous sales or allotments of public land and occupied illegally – and in general to recovering possession of land wrongfully held, as is recorded by the writers on land-surveying and confirmed by numerous inscriptions (from the *vinea publica* in Rome and many localities in Italy – Pompeii, Puteoli, Capua, Salernum, Cannae – and abroad – Cyrenaica, Africa and Gaul). He was also keen on systematizing the sources of income in the provinces, as for example in the order given in 71 to Lucilius Bassus, then governor of Judaea, and L. Laberius Maximus, the procurator, to draw up a general contract for the revenue from Palestine. He was careful to limit the expenses of provincial communities, moderating the prodigality of certain cities in Asia in particular and laying down among other things that no delegation sent to the Princeps should be composed of more than three members. He was careful to fix censuses and land registrations with accuracy, sending to Africa, for example, in 75 a consular official, Rutilius Gallus, and a praetorian official, Sentius Caecilianus, to demarcate *Africa Vetus* and *Africa Nova*. He took pains to organize the vast imperial domains with a view to securing a larger and more constant income from them; and to draw profit, so it seems, from the trade in goods such as spices which constituted tribute in kind from the East, if the foundation of the *horrea piperataria*, for example, on the Via Sacra is in fact due to him. As for the charges of meanness and of low deals transacted through Caenis out of greed for profit, they can easily be explained by the discontent of people not accustomed to a justly severe administration; the Alexandrians, for example, never forgave him for this. On the contrary, it should be borne in mind that the tradition does not record any acts of violence or confiscations by Vespasian and speaks of no governor accused of extortion at any time in his reign except for C. Julius Bassus, probably quaestor of Bithynia, who was acquitted; thus the provinces testify in his favour. In this connection a document discovered recently[1] has shown us that the concern, subsequently characteristic of Nerva and Trajan, not to burden the provinces with the postal service (*cursus publicus*) was already felt by Vespasian. And in the matter of expenditure we can criticize neither the moderation in the *congiaria* to the people (only one, of 75 denarii, in 71, and in Titus's name) and in the *donativa* to the troops (not more than 25 denarii per head), that is, in the distributions from the private purse, nor the regularity imposed on the use of public money; for example, the debate about competence in connection with financing the restoration of the Capitoline temple, a debate which took place in 70 when Vespasian was still absent but Mucianus was present, and which is reported by Tacitus (*Hist.*, IV, 9), may not have been due simply to the caprice of the quibbling Helvidius Priscus. The expenses of Vespasian's reign were the usual ones: the army, public works, corn supply, shows. The novelty lay if anywhere in the fact that they were controlled. As a global figure they will have been even higher than before, in proportion to the increase in economic volume of the whole life of the empire and to social evolution, in which the state took on expenses previously not considered its concern. The best known one is the salary paid to teachers of rhetoric, but institutions such as the *alimentationes* were not far away now. Personally Vespasian was wisely generous, encouraging the arts and giving assistance when disaster struck. The monuments built in his reign testify not only to the restoration of financial equilibrium but also to the large scope of his plans for works of public utility or simply munificence.

This building activity can also be dated with passable accuracy by means of coins and inscriptions, and it turns out to be pretty imposing. Having from the beginning encouraged by legislation private operations at Rome, where the damage caused by the fire in Nero's reign had not all been made good, Vespasian then set to work with a will on his own account. Very soon after his arrival from the East he hastened the actual start of work on the reconstruction of the Capitoline temple (already

---

[1] R. MOUTERDE and C. MONDÉSERT, in *Syria*, XXXIV, 1957, pp. 278-84 = *Inscriptions grecques et latines de la Syrie*, V, No. 1999.

inaugurated officially on 21 June by the praetor Helvidius Priscus) by carrying up some stones on his own back; and the appointment as clerk of the works of a knight, L. Julius Vestinus – not as was usual, of a senator – was significant. By 71 the temple was finished. The neighbouring *tabularium*, also destroyed in the fire of 69, was rebuilt as well, and in it were deposited, 'undique investigatis exemplaribus',[1] the principal documents: three thousand bronze tablets. Naturally the temple of Vesta, too, had to be rebuilt quickly, and it was not long before that of *Honos* and *Virtus* at the porta Capena was restored, as part of the new principate's policy of moral reconstruction. In 71 the motif of peace, which also dominates the coinage, was officially blessed by the start of work on the *templum Pacis*, dedicated in 75. In 71, too, the decision was taken to build the arch on the Velian, the so-called Arch of Titus, and in the same year work was also proceeding fast and furiously on more prosaic tasks: those of re-paving all the streets of the city, consolidating the banks of the Tiber, increasing the number of granaries (there are records of *horrea Vespasiani*) and carrying out special maintenance work on the aqueducts – the course of the *aqua Claudia* and its sources, the *Curtia* and the *Caerulea*, was regulated and in the urban distribution network, too, the numerous *fistulae aquariae* bearing the name, or dating from the time, of Vespasian indicate intense activity. Rome must have put on a new face, as in the time of Augustus, so that in 73, when Vespasian and Titus as censors proclaimed the re-foundation of the city, and also in 75 when, extending the *pomerium* again, for the first time since Claudius, they set up the new boundary posts of the sacred perimeter, the symbolism of these acts must have been paralleled by the solid reality of the work accomplished. In the last few years of the reign representational building gained the upper hand. When the temples of Peace and Divus Claudius had been finished, and the colossal statue of Nero had been altered and dedicated to the Sun, the grandiose Flavian amphitheatre, constructed on marvellously rational lines from both the architectural and the functional point of view, rose for the entertainment of the public in the hollow between the Palatine, the Caelian and the Esquiline, an area which had been included in the gardens of Nero's *domus aurea* and had been occupied by a lake. The part of the amphitheatre erected by Vespasian was inaugurated in 79. Titus and Domitian completed it.

Evidence of building activity in Italy and the provinces is also plentiful. Not only did the Emperor – solemnly proclaimed 'conservator caerimoniarum publicarum et restitutor aedium sacrarum'[2] in 78 by the *sodales*

---

[1] SUET., *Vesp.*, 8, 5.   [2] *ILS*, 252.

Titii – restore the rites and temples of the city of Rome; there are also records of interventions at Herculaneaum (in 76, in connection with the temple of the *Mater Deum*, destroyed in the earthquake of 62); in the Sabine district (in connection with an *aedes Victoriae*); and also in other places. Numerous, too, are the records of baths, theatres, amphitheatres (the one at Puteoli in particular) and of secular buildings in general. But it is particularly milestones and inscriptions on bridges that bear witness to Vespasian's assiduous concern for a radical reorganization of communications throughout the empire. Such evidence occurs as early as 70 and again in 74 in Sardinia; in 74 between Upper Germany and Raetia; in 75 and 76 in Africa, Asia and Lesser Armenia; between 76 and 78 in Italy (Via Appia, Via Latina, Via Cassia, Via Flavia from Trieste to Pola); and also in Spain (77, Via Bracara-Asturica; 79, in Baetica and Callaecia), in Cilicia (77, bridge at Seleucia over the Calicadnus) and in Bithynia (78). It was normal for soldiers to be assigned to work on military roads near the frontiers, but under Vespasian the troops also constructed some of the big legionary camps in stone; there are particular mentions of those at Vindobona and Carnuntum on the Danube, which were completely rebuilt, but all of them, especially those on the Rhine, must have been in a sorry state after recent events.

Besides these works of physical repair, meritorious though they were, there was the restoration of military morale and the reorganization of the army and of the machinery of government. It was the army that had decided the fate of the principate and it was now a question of seeing whether a Princeps to whom the army had given power could succeed in resuming complete control of this dangerous instrument. Vespasian did succeed in doing this, and, as far as can be seen, with ease. The general equilibrium between the various elements in the state had not been disturbed as they were to be a hundred and fifty years later, and the military anarchy of the year of the four emperors was quite different from that of the third century. The renewal of the aristocracy brought in itself the advantage of placing at the head of the military formations 'new men', matured by long service without favours or privileges: Trajan, the future emperor, did ten years' regular service as a military tribune. The old urban nobility could also follow a career that kept them right away from the army, as Nerva did, and young scholars like Pliny who held the office of military tribune as a formality would never again be called upon to command a legion. Circumstances certainly imposed specialization in the military field, but Vespasian encouraged the tendency, which was fertile in political consequences. As for individual problems, the armed forces were

TA--I

soon restored to normality with the help of a few measures dictated by events, such as the disbandment of the legions that had mutinied on the Rhine and the modifications in the recruitment and employment of auxiliaries. The disbanded legions were replaced by three new ones, the IV *Flavia Felix*, which was posted to Dalmatia, the XVI *Flavia Firma*, possibly destined for Cappadocia, and the II *Adiutrix*, already formed by Vitellius, as the I *Adiutrix* had been by Nero and Galba, out of sailors from Misenum, and now regularized by Vespasian and sent to Britain. The VII legion, which had been enrolled by Galba, was now christened VII *Gemina*, and from Pannonia, whither Mucianus had despatched it, it now returned – if it had ever arrived – to stay for a while on the Upper Rhine. Finally, about 74, it went back to Spain, where it had been re-cruited in the beginning and where it remained ever afterwards, becoming simply the 'legion', a name that stuck to the camp and to the city that rose round it, Leon. As for the settlement of the Vitellians, which might have appeared the most difficult task, it did not present any difficulties so far as the legionaries were concerned. In fact, of the legions whose eagles were present at the Battle of Bedriacum on Vitellius's side – the I *Italica*, the V *Alaudae*, the XXI *Rapax* and the XX *Primigenia* – none, it seems, was disbanded; they were only transferred, the last two simply from the Upper to the Lower Rhine.

Other modifications in the distribution of the defence forces were im-posed by the situation on the frontiers. Thus in quiet Spain the garrison, already reduced earlier from time to time, fell finally to one single legion (or exceptionally two) from the three of the Augustan dispensation; on the other hand, the army of Britain was brought up to its full strength of four legions. The Rhine once again had eight legions, and six (or seven, if the survival of the V *Alaudae* after 70 is accepted) guarded the Danube region from Dalmatia to Moesia, while on the river itself the Pannonian and Moesian fleets, evidently strengthened, acquired the title *Flaviae*. The East witnessed a more extended deployment of its forces, usually con-centrated before in Syria, for one or two legions were permanently stationed from 70 onwards in Cappadocia, which consequently ceased to be administered by a procurator and came under a governor (possibly the governor of consular rank who also looked after Galatia, or else a praetorian dependent on him). Thus in his attitude to the Armenian problem Ves-pasian resumed the strategic position of Caesennius Paetus, which was destined to prepare the base for Trajan's campaign and to remain funda-mental for centuries. One legion never moved out of Judaea again. There was no change in Egypt or Africa, except for the transference of the III legion from Ammaedara to Theveste, further inland. So with Vespasian began the tendency, imposed by the growing aggressiveness of the tribes outside the frontiers and by the desire to avoid too massive concentrations of legionary troops, to thin out into a more continuous line the bulwark of armed forces still stationed by Augustus in a few powerful bases, where they were quartered in concentrations of up to three or four legions.

It is characteristic, for example, that, as is attested by a recently discovered inscription,[1] as early as 81, in the last few months of Titus's reign, the commander of Legion III *Augusta* built at Lambaesis, though on a site subsequently discarded, a stone camp (the oldest in a locality that later became important) for a permanent detachment of the legion itself. Another phenomenon, from which historians have wrongly deduced the existence of some positive measure on these lines by Vespasian, was the almost total disappearance, even from the western legions, of the Italian element, evidently no longer attracted, for economic and social reasons, to service in the legions when the more lucrative enrolment in the praetorian and urban cohorts sufficed to satisfy the few in Italy who still aspired to a military career. These cohorts on the other hand were a little more difficult to reorganize, for in contrast to the proposal to reduce the cadre of sixteen cohorts instituted by Vitellius there was the re-engagement, for obvious political reasons, of the praetorians discharged by Vitellius who had already fought on the Flavian side, and the need to keep the promise that the soldiers who had most distinguished themselves could transfer from the legions to the praetorian guard. On top of this, many of those enrolled by Vitellius refused to leave the service: 'preces erant, sed quibus contra dici non posset'.[2] We do not know exactly how the problem was solved. All the men were retained in 70, even Vitellius's praetorians, possibly by dint of even sending some units outside Italy (where some of the urban cohorts were also sent; the newly created I *Flavia* to Lyon, for example, and the XIII to Carthage), and men were discharged little by little, so that there must have been some tendency to a reduction in manpower. As for the number of cohorts, only towards the end of the century can we be sure that it was then ten, a figure that remained unchanged for two centuries. The reduction to nine attributed to Vespasian is not absolutely certain, and the fact that the praetorian guard stayed throughout the reign in the hands of the Emperor's own son and co-ruler shows that it was regarded as one of the instruments that required the most delicate handling. The urban cohorts were also

[1] *Ann. Ep.*, 1954, 137.　　　　　　[2] TAC., *Hist.*, IV, 46.

reorganized. Command of the fleets of Ravenna and Misenum (now probably a praetorian appointment), which in 71 was still, exceptionally, united in the hands of one single prefect (still Lucilius Bassus, the Vitellian prefect), was also divided again. In general, Vespasian's not very ostentatious measures restored order, and the army, relatively more disciplined and well commanded, a formidable force in its new camps, reached a high standard of efficiency, subsequently protecting almost unchanged for another century the fortunes of the empire and also those of the men at its head.

The reorganization of the actual machinery of government in Rome, Italy and the provinces was equally unspectacular but just as realistic and detailed. So far as the organs of government were concerned, we have already seen that the senatorial nobility continued to furnish the emperor's most highly placed collaborators. The shrewd use of qualifications and bents is demonstrated by, among other things, the commands held in Britain by Petilius Cerialis and Julius Agricola, both already familiar with the province through having been there before, and the employment in problems concerning the restoration of boundaries in Cyrenaica of a certain Q. Paconius Agrippinus, who as quaestor in this very province of Crete and Cyrene, under Claudius, had carried out a similar operation in Crete. Thus Vespasian did not hesitate to introduce into the Senate and so place on the highest plane of service to the empire men of eastern and African origin such as C. Caristanius Fronto, a member of a family from Antiochia in Pisidia which since the Augustan age had furnished loyal administrators at the equestrian level. Other examples of the same process were C. Antius A. Julius Quadratus from Pergamum and Ti. Julius Celsus Polemeanus of Ephesus, both destined to have splendid careers as governors of eastern provinces, and the two Numidians from Cirta, Q. Aurelius Pactumeius Clemens and Q. Aurelius Pactumeius Fronto, the latter of whom, *adlectus* among the praetorians, subsequently became the first consul of African birth (A.D. 80). But the equestrian officials also increased in number and importance, particularly in connection with the above-mentioned improvements in the financial organization. The palace freedmen, on the other hand, wielded considerably less influence than they had done earlier; the official hierarchy had now supplanted what had in fact been that of the emperor's private servants, who were also pushed to one side by the intense personal activity of Vespasian and of his closest colleague, Titus, who himself attended to the drafting of edicts and letters.

As for the object of the business of government, that is, the population of the empire, Vespasian, combining the strictness of Augustus with the generosity of Claudius, gave a great deal of attention to the social order, extending his concern even to the lowlier ranks of the citizen body. Through the censorship of 73–4, almost certainly modelled on Claudius's example, he exercised an effective official control, having lists made which for Italy were arranged in regions, and within the regions by municipalities, with exemplary precision; but many other pieces of information indicate the pains he took to increase and watch over the citizen body. The numerous 'Flavian' foundations and re-foundations in Italy (Reate in 71, Paestum, Sinuessa, Bovianum Undecimanorum) and abroad, even if they are sometimes attributable to the sons, demonstrate intense activity in the foundation of colonies in the traditional way, and the widespread diffusion, especially in Sardinia and Spain, of the Quirinal tribe, the personal tribe of the Princeps, reflects large grants of citizenship both to individuals and to communities. Moreover, among the provisions of the censorship was the granting in 74 of the Latin right to the whole of Spain, as a preparatory step to full citizenship. It also started to become the practice to grant Latin rights on a large scale to soldiers who were not citizens (especially to the *classiarii*). No less generous was the concern for communal welfare, from the attention devoted to the corn supply at Rome, to helpful interventions in Italian cities to assign or restore lands, or to arrange other benefits. The many dedications preserved all over the empire bear ample testimony to these activities. For the first time since Augustus and Tiberius the provincial world had an emperor who was personally acquainted with almost all of it; Vespasian had been in Thrace, Crete, Cyrene, Gaul and Germany, Britain, Africa, Syria, Judaea, Egypt, the coast of Asia, Greece and even the Aegean islands, either at some stage in his career or in the course of his return to Rome from the East. He certainly made use of this experience in his reforms, although not all of them are clearly known, since our information is based mainly on a few lines of Suetonius (*Vesp.*, 8, 4) and the epigraphical material.

To begin with Spain, the long list of *municipia Flavia* indicates one of his favourite activities, which was continued by his sons. However, it looks as if he did not introduce any administrative changes there, and this is also true of the other western provinces. His interventions were concerned with individual communities and particularly with the foundation of colonies, which were intended to form new centres of Romanization. It was he who granted the title of colony to Aventicum (Avenches) in the territory of the Helvetii and apparently also (though it may have been his sons) to Forum Segusiavorum, near Lyon. The boundaries between the

Alpes Poeninae and the territory of Vienna were fixed by an imperial commission. It was under Vespasian (or his sons) that the big centres of Pannonia – Sirmium and Siscia – began their career as cities; they were largely populated by men discharged from the Ravenna fleet who went as colonists. Scardona in Dalmatia, Scupi in Moesia, Deultum and Flaviopolis in Thrace and many other towns received the epithetic 'Flavian', thanks probably also to Vespasian's sons, who in this field continued their father's policy.

In the East, however, there were also some administrative changes, and important ones. Achaea (possibly in 73) became a senatorial province again under a proconsul of praetorian rank (and it now seems certain that Sardinia, handed over by Nero to the Senate, now became imperial territory again), but Thessaly was detached from it and united with Macedonia. Epirus and Acarnania were probably also separated from the province of Achaea, just as the Hellespont area, so it seems, was administered by a procurator independently of the neighbouring provinces of Asia, Thrace and Bithynia; unless, as was probably the case with the mysterious 'provincia insularum', the institution of which was also attributed to Vespasian, it is a question of the fragmentary or misinterpreted record of a special financial organization. The actual province of Bithynia and Pontus seems to have become for a brief period, in 78, an imperial province; and some free cities such as Rhodes, Samos and Byzantium were incorporated in the adjoining provinces. Lycia and Pamphylia were given their definitive organization. Further to the east a special grouping of regions was created. We have already mentioned the stationing of troops in Cappadocia, under an officer who reported to the consular governor of Galatia. In 75 Lesser Armenia, too – taken in 71, in exchange for Chalcis, from Aristobulus, who had received it from Nero in 57 – was made part of this grouping, which operated principally in the field of relations with Armenia and Parthia, as is clear from the traces of activity encountered up to the Caucasus area. Pontus, Phrygia, Pisidia, Lycaonia and Paphlagonia are also mentioned as forming parts of this characteristic system. Other alterations, such as the incorporation in Syria of Cilicia Aspera and Commagene, taken from Antiochus IV (in 72), will be considered in connection with the latter's relations with the empire. 'Flavian' cities flourished in these territories: Flaviopolis, for example, in Cilicia, which dated its history from 73–4, and Samosata Flavia, Antiochus's old capital. Emesa, whose king, Julius Sohaemus, seems to have been honourably retired, may also have been united to Syria at this time. Palmyra, the caravan city on the road from Damascus to the Euphrates, which had hitherto maintained complete autonomy, must have been sub-

jected to some kind of greater control by an emperor particularly interested in the fiscal profits to be drawn from trade. In Palestine, where
fighting did not end completely until 72 and where the government remained for practical purposes in the hands of the military commander,
the astute Julius Agrippa II not only managed to keep his throne until his
death (probably in 93) but also received further territory from Vespasian,
on top of all the gifts from the Julio-Claudian dynasty. Caesarea also
became a 'colonia Flavia' and in 71 eight hundred veterans were settled
at Emmaus. In Egypt, as well as the work of religious pacification between the Jewish and pagan elements, there was also building activity; a
dyke at Oxyrhynchus was still connected more than a hundred years later
(in 188, *Pap. Oxy.* 1112) with the name of Vespasian. In Africa, as well
as the concern shown, here as everywhere else, for the material improvement and embellishment of the towns, as testified, to take one example
alone, by the numerous inscriptions from Leptis which have recently
come to light, the big centre of Ammaedara, in the interior, acquired the
title of 'colonia Flavia' and the above-mentioned[1] Sentius Caecilianus
exercised in 75, with the title of *legatus Augusti pro praetore ordinandae
utriusque Mauretaniae*, some sort of exceptional administrative control in
the two normally procuratorial provinces.

Thus there were extensive and detailed interventions, characteristic of a
period of reorganization and experimentation. But the legislative documents preserved concerning this activity, and indeed all Vespasian's
governmental activity in general, are not very numerous. There are the
military diplomas, the already cited rescript to the Vanacini of Corsica
(A.D. 72), a similar one to the Saborenses of Spain (A.D. 77) and the
mention in Pliny (*Epist.*, X, 65, 3) of 'epistulae divi Vespasiani ad
Lacedaemonios'; to these we can possibly add, if the *lex Manciana* referred to in a famous inscription of the early second century does really
bear the name of T. Curtilius Mancia who was consul in 55 and could
have been proconsul of Africa under Vespasian or simply possessed extensive estates there, one more typical testimony to the period's attention to the smallest administrative details.

We also have records of a few other measures in the field of civil law.
There was the *senatusconsultum Pegasianum* (72) dealing with certain conditions for the acquisition of citizenship by the *Latini Iuniani*; a second
decree of the same name, perhaps dating from 73, dealing with testamentary bequests; a *senatusconsultum Plancianum* on the admission of
paternity (though it is not certain that this belongs to the reign of

[1] p. 242

Vespasian); and a *senatusconsultum Macedonianum* re-enacting a measure of Claudius's dating from 47 on loans to sons of the family, with the stiffer provision – probably provoked by the case of a cruel son, a certain Macedo, who killed his father – that such loans should not be recoverable even after the death of the parent (another measure of Claudius's that was re-enacted by *senatusconsultum* was the law of 52 on the slave status affecting a free woman who married a slave). In addition there were the measures already mentioned dealing with *subseciva*, those designed to encourage building, and the arrogation to the Princeps of the right to confer the *ius trium liberorum* independently of the condition required to obtain it. But precisely in the field of the administration of justice we have ample general information on the honour in which jurists were held under Vespasian (Pegasus, head of the Proculeiani and *praefectus urbi*; Arulenus Caelius Sabinus, head of the Sabiniani, of consular rank), on the scrupulousness with which Vespasian himself took part in the arguments, and above all on the abolition of trials for treason. Clemency, which before might have been part of an emperor's personal disposition, was for Vespasian among the requirements of a functional, rational dispensation of justice. Perhaps this was why he did not feel able to show it to the Lingonian Julius Sabinus, one of the leaders of the Gallo-Batavian rebellion of 70, who was kept hidden in a cellar by his wife Epponina for a good nine years, until 79, and inexorably executed with her almost as soon as he was discovered.

Thus Vespasian's attitudes, sometimes apparently contradictory in regard to religion, worship and the mystical and magical elements already widely diffused in the life of the empire, all derive in the last analysis from his realism. Although he may have been secretly very amused at Alexandria to see certain cripples straighten up at his touch, he took good care not to enquire into the fabrication of the thaumaturgic qualities which people wanted to attribute to him; nor did he ever reject the prophecies which assisted his extraordinary ascent to power, from the one made at Paphos, in the temple of Aphrodite, to his son Titus returning from his interrupted journey to pay homage to Galba, to the prophecy of Basilis at Mount Carmel, the spells of this or another Basilis in the Serpaeum at Alexandria and the divinations of Apollonius of Tyana, whom the tradition also says he met in the very same temple. But when, even during his stay in the Egyptian city and later, more seriously, at the end of 74, astrologers and philosophers showed themselves to be dangerous to the security of the state, he did not hesitate to expel them from Rome. In any case, in his position he could not afford to show no interest in the ferment of mysticism which in various forms, in both East and West, agitated the lower strata of the empire and the border-lands of the empire, as we can see for example in indications preserved in writings particularly characteristic of these feelings, such as the life of Apollonius of Tyana by the deutero-Philostratus. Although a restorer of traditional worship, he did not oppose foreign religions; in any case, tolerance towards Christianity was natural after the Neronian persecution. So little moved by the cult of his own person that he made a joke about it as he was dying, and strict in excluding his family, closely bound to him as it was in the dynastic concept, from excessive religious honours, he was nevertheless very well aware of the imperial cult's political value. He not only revived in Rome the worship of the last of the deified Caesars – Divus Claudius – but also encouraged the spread all over the empire of *concilia* and *flamines* for the cult of the emperor. It was he who introduced the cult for the first time into Africa, and possibly into Baetica and Narbonese Gaul. It was the same with games: personally an enthusiast for stage shows, but not for gladiators, he did not grudge them to the people; in a more restricted circle, by reviving public recitations and giv-ing generous aid to poets and artists, he furthered his own preferences as a man of taste without harming general political interests.

It is in this combination of attitudes and achievements that Vespasian's contribution to the reorganization and development of the empire lies.

FOREIGN AFFAIRS: WARS AND CONQUESTS

For many long years after the Batavian and Jewish wars the Roman forces did not have to face comparably serious situations, but the reports in our sources, though sporadic, and the large number of imperial salutations (twenty, fourteen of them occurring from 71 onwards), which Vespasian certainly did not permit himself without good reason, warn us that these forces were not completely inactive either, confronted as they were with the awakening Germano-Sarmatian world and the ever-recurring problems of the eastern frontier. The armies, more widely deployed than before, as we have said, in their defence of the frontiers, were employed by Vespasian and his sons, who were faithful to the Augustan concept of not extending the process of conquest, in strengthening the existing line and making it an almost visible and physical bulwark against the tribes pressing in against it. The fighting that took place was all linked to this aim. One of the principal theatres of war was still Britain. After the revolt of Boudicca some years of relative calm had elapsed in the province, from which some of the Roman forces had actually been withdrawn, first through Nero's preparations for his great eastern enterprise and then through the Civil War. But once the Batavian war was over, possibly even before the end of 70, Vettius Bolanus, who had been sent to Britain by Vitellius, was replaced by Petilius Cerialis, the vanquisher of Civilis, with the II *Adiutrix*, which brought the army of Britain up to a strength of four legions. Cerialis was soon engaged with the Brigantes, a group of tribes in what is now the north of England, whose queen, Cartimandua, expelled by her own people and given assistance by the Romans, had nevertheless not succeeded in regaining her throne. All we know of Cerialis's campaigns, which lasted from 71 to 73, since in 74 he was back in Rome as *consul suffectus* for the second time, is that as a result Roman influence, if not occupation, extended more or less to the line on which Hadrian's wall later rose, and possibly even further north; it is certainly from these campaigns that the first fortifications of the legionary camp of Eburacum (York) date, and the traces of contemporary roads and small forts point to the waging of a difficult war amid thick forests. Such, too, was the campaign against the Silures of south Wales, who were finally subdued by Cerialis's successor, Julius Frontinus, the writer and future *curator aquarum* in Rome, between 74 and the end of 76. Better known in detail are Julius Agricola's campaigns, recounted with filial admiration, if not chronological and geographical precision, by his son-in-law Tacitus. Sent by Vespasian in 77 or more probably 78 to a province of which he had already had experience as a tribune under Suetonius Paulinus and more recently, between 70 and 73, as commander of a legion, he put the Roman administration in the areas already occupied on a fairly firm basis, mainly by giving up plundering methods and hastening the establishment of a normal provincial administration. He then made the whole island of Britain feel the effects of a number of well-planned expeditions. The conquest of north Wales was completed soon after his arrival by the victory over the Ordovices; and the island of Mona opposite was also now subdued. Agricola then turned his attention to the north of Britain. After a mopping-up operation in the territory already occupied, in 80 he launched a strong attack across the Tyne–Solway line into new country; then, withdrawing the main body of his troops at the onset of winter, he left behind a series of strong points with well-provisioned garrisons whose job it was to maintain the forward bases for the next stage of the conquest, which according to his plans was to be complete and definitive. And in fact in 81 he reached Clota and Bodotria, the two estuaries (Firth of Clyde and Firth of Forth) between which the wall of Antoninus subsequently ran. In 82 he crossed this line, fighting tribes near the west coast and possibly preparing a concentration of forces for a crossing to Ireland, a project which he never carried out. In 83 he continued the invasion with a wider strategic design, splitting the land forces up into more columns and combining their operations with the advance of the fleet along the coast. This manœuvre led in 84 to one decisive battle against all the Caledonians united under one leader, Calgacus, near a certain Mons Graupius. The result was a complete victory in which the auxiliary troops almost alone were engaged, while the fleet, sailing round the northern tip of Scotland, completed the circumnavigation of Britain. It was also Agricola's last victory, for he was now recalled to Rome. The reasons why these operations were not followed by others and by the permanent occupation of the territory involved will be discussed in connection with the general policy of Domitian.

There are brief mentions of two campaigns on the Rhine, one conducted between 73 and 74 by the governor Cn. Pinarius Cornelius Clemens with the army of Upper Germany, the other waged in one of the years between 75 and 78 against the Bructeri by the army of Lower Germany under the leadership of C. Rutilius Gallicus. The latter campaign led to the capture of Veleda, the German prophetess, who finished up giving oracles in return for payment at Ardea in Latium. We do not know whether the action against these same Bructeri attributed to T. Vestricius Spurinna in an allusion in one of Pliny's letters (II, 7, 1–2) and the episode recounted by Tacitus (*Germ.*, 33) of a battle in which 60,000 Bructeri were massacred by other Germans before the eyes of the Romans belong to this same campaign or to a later one. But what is more interesting than the actual military operations, few details of which are known to us, is the systematic work carried out on the creation of an effective frontier in the delicate angle between the Rhine and the Danube. For a start, Vespasian transferred the bases of the auxiliary troops to the right bank of the Rhine, stringing out an artificial line of forts at a certain distance from the river from the latitude of Mainz down to that of Strasbourg and from here south-east to Lake Constance, roughly skirting the eastern edge of the Black Forest; inside this line ran a new road. This was the first outline of the formidable defences that Domitian was to construct much further inside German territory and that the Antonines were subsequently to reinforce; but above all it was the first appearance of the concept of the *limes*. The lands thus acquired, occupied by colonists mainly from Gaul, were called according to Tacitus (*Germ.*, 29) the 'Agri Decumates'; but he is the only authority for this name, and it may not have lasted long. On the Upper Danube Vespasian probably confined himself to consolidating the bases already established along the river by Claudius, and it is not certain that he ever crossed the river. The fortified camps built on the Lower Danube and the reinforcement of the garrisons there have already been mentioned. The operations conducted against the Dacians by the governor of Moesia, Rubrius Gallus, the avenger of Fonteius Agrippa, sufficed to keep them at a respectful distance for some years.

   The situation in the East must have been similar to the one which faced previous emperors, but far fewer details of it are known. The principal event was the war against Antiochus IV of Commagene, the king favoured by Gaius and Claudius and one who had also been among the first to do homage to Vespasian. The notice of plots between Antiochus and Vologaeses, the king of Parthia, was given to the emperor at the beginning of 72 by the governor of Syria, Caesennius Paetus. Whether the accusation was true or false, or perhaps a deliberate exaggeration of tenuous hints, as seems probable, since the governor, just appointed by Vespasian – a relative – to the province in which he had disgraced himself in the time of Corbulo, was probably trying to repair his reputation in this same province, the fact remains that he was given *carte blanche* to proceed against the real or alleged rebel. Commagene was invaded by the VI *Ferrata*, together with auxiliary units and contingents from local kingdoms, and the only strong resistance encountered was offered by Antiochus's sons, Epiphanes and Callinicus, who valiantly opposed the assault on the capital, Samosata. After the flight of Antiochus to Tarsus in Cilicia they withdrew and took refuge with Vologaeses. Handed over by the latter to the Romans, they joined their father in a comfortable exile in Sparta; they too were granted citizenship. Commagene was joined to Syria and Samosata became *Flavia*. In 72, as we have seen, the Jewish war finally came to an end, with the frightful episode of the fall of Masada, but disturbances continued and were extended to Egypt in particular by the fanatical sect of the Sicarii. The prefect, Ti. Julius Lupus, on the instructions of Vespasian, took steps to close the ancient Jewish temple of Leontopolis in the district of Heliopolis and at the end of 72 Cannius Paulinus, the vice-prefect who had succeeded Lupus when the latter died in the intervening period, actually demolished it. However, the proconsul of Crete and Cyrene had to deal a little later with the last outcrops of the movement. The Parthians were active again in 75 and 76, but as usual our information is fairly vague. It seems that Vologaeses requested help against the Alans, who are certainly known to have invaded

Media and Armenia in 71, and Vespasian replied that he did not wish to become involved in other people's affairs, notwithstanding Domitian's insistence that the command in question should be entrusted to him. When his request was refused Vologaeses is supposed to have started hostilities against the Romans. There seems to have been some kind of intervention by the Roman army, for an inscription tells us that in 75 legionaries were engaged at Harmozica (Tiflis), on the invasion route of the Alans, in building a wall for Mithridates, king of the Iberians. Moreover, the military importance assigned to Cappadocia, an importance demonstrated not only by the permanent stationing of troops there, as mentioned above, but also by intense activity in building fortifications and roads, was clearly related to the Partho-Armenian problem, even if Vespasian made no change in his predecessor's policy towards it. As for the war against Vologaeses, the contradictory reports in the historico-narrative sources[1] would incline us to have strong doubts about it, were it not that Pliny, in his *Panegyric* (14, 1), alludes to the glory won by the young Trajan fighting against the Parthians with his father, who was governor of Syria just at this time, between 75 and 79, and were it not for the need to find a reason for the three, and perhaps four, salutations as 'imperator' which Vespasian received in 76. However, no big campaigns can have been involved. By the last few years of the reign, abroad as well as at home, the most stable and well-ordered security system ever enjoyed by the empire had been organized.

THE REIGN OF TITUS

Vespasian's end came unexpectedly, for he was still hale and hearty. Falling ill with fever in Campania and going to Aquae Cutiliae in the Sabine region to take medicinal baths, he died there on 23 June 79, at the age of sixty-nine. Laid at first in the mausoleum of the Julio-Claudian emperors, he was later interred in the *templum gentis Flaviae* and deified, and for the first time since the death of Augustus the memory of the late Princeps aroused universal approval and esteem. For the upper classes this may have been simply a recognition that his principate had not been as bad as they had expected,[2] but the widespread diffusion of the anecdote about the moment of his death – Vespasian had had himself raised out of the bed, saying that the emperor died on his feet – expressed the popular

---

[1] AUR. VICT., *De Caes.*, 9, 10 (affirmative); *Epit. de Caes.* 9, 12 (negative).
[2] TAC., *Hist.*, 1, 50, 4: 'et ambigua de Vespasiano fama, solusque omnium ante se principum in melius mutatus est'.

recognition of the concept of the Princeps's function which he preached and practised. The succession presented no problems. Titus, already co-ruler, assumed the titles of Augustus and *pater patriae*, and became *pontifex maximus*. There was no acclamation of *imperator* for his accession to the throne; and he continued to number his consulships, *tribunicia potestas* and imperial salutations (from XV to XVII, for Agricola's victories) in the series initiated when his father was alive. On 24 June, at the age of thirty-nine, Titus was sole Princeps, *Imperator Titus Caesar divi Vespasiani filius Vespasianus Augustus*. There is no record of a formal conferment of powers by the Senate, but there almost certainly must have been one. With a restrictiveness characteristic of the father's dynastic concept and justified in any case by the difference in the two brothers' positions – for Titus, the victor of the Jewish War, was from a political point of view a good deal closer to his father than his young brother was to him – Domitian was nominated from the first day of the reign *consors* and *successor* of the Princeps but not *particeps imperii*, as Titus had been in relation to his father. Thus Domitian did not receive the *tribunicia potestas*, nor had he any title at all to the name of *imperator*; he remained Caesar and *princeps iuventutis* and was given only the designation for the ordinary consulship in 80, with Titus. His proposal to win over the soldiers by offering them double the donative disbursed by Titus and his accusations that his brother had altered the father's will to change his own position availed him nothing. Thus a secret hostility smouldered between the two brothers throughout the reign.

With the advent of Titus, Vespasian's mode of government went on almost unchanged in spite of expectations to the contrary. The figure of the new emperor must indeed have posed a few problems. Physically he was very like his father, but his very different temperament and educa-tion – he had grown up with Britannicus at the court of Claudius, and under Nero had lived the life of the gilded youths close to the emperor – certainly made him more like an Otho or a Vitellius; in his culture and tastes he was a typical product of the Neronian age. In the crisis of 69, as quaestor and commander of a legion, being more popular than his father, he might well have added one more to the series of emperors like Otho and Vitellius if the acclamation of the father instead of the son had not turned the fortunes of the empire in a better direction. And after ten years of Vespasian there was no longer room for anyone who meant to behave like Nero. Titus came to the throne with a bad reputation. Dissolute in his private life, violent in the exercise of his official functions, as he showed when he was prefect of the praetorian guard by his brutal elimination of Caecina Alienus, suspected in 79 of conspiring against Vespasian, target of the persistent accusation (which the Emperor Hadrian believed) that he had poisoned his father as the crowning touch to behaviour that had long been disloyal, he must have hurt traditional Roman sensibilities when, already divorced from his second wife, Marcia Furnilla, mother of Julia (his first wife, Arrecina Tertulla, had died), he showed every intention of marrying Berenice, the Jewish princess who had come to Rome in 75 with her brother, Julius Agrippa II. It is true that he sent her away when his father was still alive; and it is certainly rash to speak of a constitutional conflict with Vespasian, or even of a rebellious attitude on the part of Titus, simply on the basis of the evidence of the presence and different placing of the title *imperator* on coins and in inscriptions during the ten years of co-rulership. There is much ampler and more explicit testimony to Titus's complete loyalty; nevertheless, contemporaries' fears of the worst and the surprising change he displayed are also undeniable facts. It may be that he laid aside one mask to assume another – a move that could well be attributed to the cynical refinement and poetic versatility of a graduate of Nero's court – but this remains a secret of his complicated nature. It is better not to construct ingenious hypotheses on the interplay between strength and nobility and on the eclipses and reappearances of Berenice, but to remember instead that alongside his father he had learned to govern; left alone and endowed with sufficient mental balance to value the best in his own interests, he was evidently led by the excellent state of the empire to continue along his father's path and to follow his example, granting himself personally only the pleasure of exempting himself from the odious roles which, in a subordinate position, he had not hesitated to assume. This attitude, and a generosity all the more marked in comparison with Vespasian's parsimony, characterized all the reign's activities, which unfortunately are not very well known to us in detail.

Titus began with a donative to the soldiers and the confirmation – unsolicited and combined in one single edict – of all the gifts and privileges granted by his predecessors. In the palace his father's frugality continued to prevail and persons of good sense and authority gained the upper hand decisively as advisers over the leisure companions of the court. Berenice, who had again appeared in Rome, he sent away once and for all, *invitus invitam*.[1] On the other hand he recalled Musonius Rufus from exile and made peace with the philosophers, as with everyone else. The intention to be moderate, explicitly asserted on various occasions – when

---

[1] SUET., *Tit.*, 7, 2.

he took office as *pontifex maximus*, for example – was scrupulously fulfilled. Tradition has only preserved episodes, but enough of them to prove a systematic and coherent line of conduct which can be reduced to radical paternalism, for according to his declared aims not only the *sollicitudo principis* but also the *parentis affectus*[1] were to justify the office of the man who had the power in his hands – a power further strengthened by Titus, as is clear from his own behaviour to Domitian, in the form of a despotic personal régime. This reality being now accepted, the Senate naturally saw the ideal Princeps in this despot who sent no senator to his death – not even confessed conspirators tried and condemned by the Senate itself – who discouraged informers with punishments and laws limiting the possibility of making accusations, who in 81 out of homage to the Senate renounced the ordinary consulship after holding it almost uninterruptedly for ten years and in the same year shortened the terms of supplementary consulships so as to be able to grant the honour to a larger number of senators, and finally who missed no opportunity to help people with his own money, actually forestalling requests, and making promises without worrying about whether he could keep them because, he said, 'it was not right that anyone should go away disappointed from a conversation with the Princeps'.[2]

The numerous calamities of Titus's reign certainly offered plenty of scope for his desire to do good. On 24 August Pompeii, Herculaneum and Stabia were destroyed by the famous eruption of Vesuvius which also killed Pliny the Elder, who as prefect of the fleet based at Misenum had sailed up to the scene of the disaster. Titus hastened to Campania and also returned there the following year. So that the aid and work of reconstruction should be properly organized, he expressed the wish that two *curatores restituendae Campaniae* should be appointed, drawn by lot from those of consular rank. He provided the necessary money largely from his own resources, but he also rightly employed – thereby causing a revision of the common judgement on his financial light-heartedness – the property, which must have been considerable in view of the unforeseen catastrophe, of people who had died without heirs. Such property, becoming *caduca* again, belonged by right to the *aerarium populi Romani*. Traces of the part played by the emperor in the reconstruction have been preserved in inscriptions at Sorrento and Naples, where the damage caused by the earthquake accompanying the eruption was repaired.[3] In Rome, while Titus was once again in Campania, a fire devastated part of the Campus Martius, from the Pantheon southward, and then raged in

[1] SUET., *Tit.*, 8, 3.   [2] *Ibid.*, 8, 1.   [3] *Not. d. Sc.*, 1901, p. 363 f., *CIL*, X, 1481.

the area of the Circus Flaminius and right up to the top of the Capitol. Cities, private citizens and foreign princes competed to offer the means for reconstruction, but Titus shouldered all the expenses himself, appointing a large commission of knights to supervise the work. On 7 December of the same year, a little less than ten years after Vespasian's reconstruction, the Fratres Arvales pronounced the prayers 'ad restitutionem et dedicationem Capitoli'[1], but it was Domitian who dedicated the completed temple. Meanwhile an epidemic also sowed sorrow in Rome and the Princeps did all he could in the way of providing human assistance and of carrying out expiatory and propitiatory rites. Nevertheless, this year of calamities also witnessed the hundred days of feasts and shows to inaugurate the Flavian amphitheatre and the baths built not far from it, in part of Nero's *domus aurea*. Pomp and munificence were accompanied by administrative zeal; the *praefectus annonae* himself was given the task of allocating the seats, as was accurately recorded, in so far as it concerned them, by the Fratres Arvales in their acts. After this festival, in which – through some peculiarity of a morbid temperament, or a presentiment, or awareness of an incurable disease – Titus is supposed to have wept in public, 'he did nothing more of importance', according to Cassius Dio (LXVI, 26, 1), until the moment of his death, on 13 September 81. We thus come to lack, as for so much of his father's activity, the already tenuous chronological thread stretching between his works and best preserved by Dio alone, whose narrative at this point is itself, of course, a patchwork put together by his epitomizers.

However, evidence of interventions, sometimes even datable ones, is preserved in a good number of inscriptions, especially in the field of public works. In Rome, for example, inscriptions record the restoration of the *aqua Marcia* in the second half of 79 and that (in 81) of the *Curtia* and *Caerulea* springs, already repaired once by his father. In both Italy and the provinces assiduous attention was paid, given the brevity of the reign, to the care of the roads: to the Via Aurelia, the Via Flavia from Trieste to Pola (79) and the Via Flaminia in Italy; to the *via nova* in Spain from Bracara Augusta to Asturica (80), on which Vespasian had already worked; and to the roads of Numidia (79), Cyprus (81) and those of a good part of Asia, all completely remade in the year 80, as is recorded by a milestone from the road between Ancyra and Dorylaeum. In Egypt there is testimony to the care he gave to the maintenance of the canals.[2] And the character of the epigraphical evidence makes it legitimate to think that Titus's interventions may have been even more extensive and the chorus of

[1] *CIL*, VI, 2059.   [2] *Or. Gr. Inscr. Sel.* 672–3.

recognition even louder than the imposing one which rises from such evidence as we possess already: in Rome, the dedications on the arch in the Circus Maximus (81) and on the famous arch *in summa sacra via*, the latter erected after his death; in Italy, the honorary municipal offices conferred on him (agonotheta, gymnasiarch, possibly demarch at Naples); in the provinces, besides similar honours (archon at Delphi), the dedications to him of public works such as an amphitheatre at Laodicea in Phrygia, a *témenos* consecrated to Aphrodite Cypria and himself as a god in Cyprus, baths and a porch at Aperle in Lycia, the restoration of the Augusteum at Ephesus, and ordinary dedications at Smyrna, at Ephesus, in Cyprus, in Moesia (Varna), in Egypt (Karnak) and in Africa (Hippo).

Similarly, only a general judgement about standards of government can be formed from the scanty evidence available. Concern to reinforce the social security already guaranteed by Vespasian in a rigidly conservative sense is evident from the respect for other people's property; Titus too abstained completely from confiscations and the imposition of contributions. The same attitude is reflected in his legislative activity, for example on the subject of trusts (testamentary bequests), a matter which, by passing in the age of the principate from the field of moral obligation to that of legal obligation, showed in itself a hardening of the codified law of property. In reducing to one, from Claudius's two, the praetors concerned with trusts Titus probably took cognizance of the adjustment of society to a principle that had become normal and therefore required less juridical intervention. For the rest, Vespasian's liberality in the matter of citizenship was continued by Titus: *leges de civitate et conubio* applying to the auxiliary troops are known from a good five military diplomas preserved from his brief reign, which also provide testimony to his partiality for the soldiers, who were granted for the first time, after a temporary experiment by Caesar, the right to make wills freely. Aventicum, the Helvetian town, received benefits from him; Caesarea in Palestine, a colony of Vespasian's, received immunity; and an *epistula* to the Lacedaemonians on the status of boys born free, exposed and then brought up as slaves, if authentic (at Pliny's request to look it up in the archives, Trajan replied that he could only find a letter from Domitian on the subject, PLIN., *Ep. ad Trai*, 65 & 66), also shows the humanitarian considerations which were part of the climate of the age and which offered the most fruitful opportunities for the now confirmed paternalism of the principate. Thus the nature of Titus's political activity is fairly clear: it followed the lines laid down by Vespasian, with the modifications suggested by a nature that was more sensitive and more eager for applause.

The greatest reservation touches the financial administration, but it may have been the subject more of a pose of nonchalance than of real and culpable negligence if, besides the sensible financing of the reconstruction in Campania already mentioned, the fact that Titus enjoyed the fruits of the so-called *subseciva* just as much as his father may be regarded as a reliable indication. Moreover, the recently discovered letter from Titus *ad Muniguenses*[1] testifies to a generosity that was also shrewd.

So far as external events are concerned, Titus's reign lacks any that would enable us to evaluate his foreign policy, for they amount simply to the continuation of Agricola's campaigns in Britain and to some activity in the East against a false Nero who was driven over the Euphrates and took refuge with Artabanus IV, the new king of Parthia. Nevertheless, the Emperor must naturally be allowed the glory of having been the courageous fighter and skilful victor of the Jewish War.

The last record of Titus's participation in official events dates from 19 May 81, when he attended the rites of the Fratres Arvales.[2] In the summer, already ill, he went to the Sabine district, taking Domitian with him. He caught a fever, and over-indulgence in the cold baths at Aquae Cutiliae, a habit which had already been fatal to his father, provoked or hastened his death, when he was only forty-two, on 13 September, in the house in which Vespasian had died. The poor relations existing between Titus and Domitian and the latter's suspicious behaviour (he is supposed to have hurried to Rome without waiting for his brother's death) gave rise to the facile rumour, which received a varying reception in the tradition, that Domitian had either poisoned Titus or at any rate hastened his death. It is certainly a fact that amid the universal spontaneity of the tribute to Titus in Rome and in the empire no honour was paid by Domitian to his brother's memory except deification, which, it seems, had still not taken place on 1 October. Nevertheless, in view of the recorded information about Titus's previous state of health, it would seem that we can exclude the hypothesis that a crime was committed – a crime moreover already attributed to Titus himself with regard to his father. So ended an attempt at ruling that was too short to produce results of any great scope. But apart from exaggerations about the happiness of an administration too easily contrasted in the tradition with the one that followed it, and certainly to be regarded as more normal and closer, as we have seen, to the one that preceded it, there remains the doubt whether the kindly god-on-earth that Titus set out to be – on the basis of near-Neronian schemes and a liberality that was made into the greatest virtue

[1] *Ann. Epigr.*, 1962, 288.   [2] *CIL*, VI, 2060.

of the reign – would not in the long run have brought harmful consequences for the empire. So it seems as if we should conclude, with one of
the ancients, that the swift passing of the Princeps, 'amor et deliciae
generis humani',[1] was not the smallest factor in producing the verdict on
the man himself: 'imperii felix brevitate'.[2]

[1] SUET., *Tit.*, I.   [2] AUSON., *Opusc.*, XIIII, 2, II (p. 184 PEIPER).

VII

DOMITIAN

DECLARED AUTOCRACY

That on the death of Titus there can have been any doubts about the succession of Domitian does not seem likely. Even if his father and his brother had kept him away from the effective exercise of power and had been privately cool with him, they had certainly not thought of excluding him from the dynastic rights strongly affirmed by Vespasian in founding the position of his family. The Senate, which had certainly taken note some time before of these intentions, and more recently of the clear designation of the *consors et successor* made by Titus, could hardly delude itself into thinking that it could change the prearranged course of events. In fact, on the very day of his brother's death Domitian presented himself to the praetorian guards in Rome and after the usual negotiations about the donative, which was equal to the one granted two years earlier by Titus, was hailed as emperor by them. On the following day the Senate carried out the usual formal conferment of powers and there is no evidence to suggest that it had ever considered for a moment, as it had at the death of Gaius, the possibility of doing otherwise. On the same day the Fratres Arvales offered a sacrifice for the new Augustus – *Imperator Caesar Domitianus Augustus* – who was now solidly confirmed in his position, even if the assumption of the other titles, like *pater patriae* and *pontifex maximus*, and the remaining formalities, such as acclamation by the comitia, came somewhat later, together with the nomination to a new consulship, his eighth; but all these formalities took place during the course of the autumn of the same year, 81.

Thus at the age of thirty Domitian occupied the position he had long desired; and it is understandable that he should have occupied it with a feeling of revenge for the past and a polemical wish to make changes in the policies pursued by those by whom he had been kept – and rightly – in the background. His arrogant behaviour after the Flavian victory has already been described. Checked first by Mucianus and then by his father, he had been unable to do any harm, and for a time he had affected an attitude of humility, giving himself as his official occupation the study of poetry. Subsequently, sharing as he did in the outward honours but not in the substance of power, which he nevertheless felt capable of exercising, and with certain original ideas of his own, he must have gradually become embittered. There is explicit evidence that he was champing at the bit, especially during his brother's reign. On the other hand, the proofs of obstinacy and wilfulness provided by episodes in his private life such as his marriage to Domitia Longina, daughter of the great Corbulo, who was snatched in 70 from her husband L. Aelius Lamia Plautius Aelianus, and his refusal of Titus's offer of his daughter Julia, whom he nevertheless appropriated after she had been married to her cousin Flavius Sabinus, while Titus was still alive, were not good auguries for the future. Having reached the throne, and being opposed in particular to his brother's easy-going attitude, which he criticized openly, he soon showed the tendency to rigid systematization, to a pedantic, formal display of the emperor's superiority. He continued in substance the autocratic reality of his father's and brother's reigns, but without the balance and good sense of Vespasian and without the detachment – whatever one my think of it – of Titus; and above all without the formal respect for the Augustan scheme. Once again, as in the days of Gaius and Nero, a Princeps was showing without any disguise what he really was, the declared despot. And since Domitian did not exercise his own will simply in the sphere of personal caprice, like the two Julio-Claudian emperors, but, with more resemblance to Tiberius (the comparison was made by the ancients themselves) and drawing on the experience of Vespasian, had a quite different conception of the nature and function of the principate as the motive power of the ad-ministrative machine, his deliberate stubbornness resulted on the one hand in a beneficial attention to the practical government of the empire but on the other in the uncompromising imposition of his own wishes, no matter with whom he was dealing. And this, as usual, was the high road to a disastrous collision with the senatorial aristocracy.

Expectations aside, Domitian soon showed quite clearly what his intentions were, by the deliberate accentuation, right from the moment of his succession, of the concept of personal monarchy. The coincidence of the imperial salutation – something neglected by Titus – with the accession to the throne, the immediate conferment on Domitia of the title of Augusta, which meant a return to the Emperor's side, for the first time since Agrippina and Poppaea, of the official figure of an empress, and the importance assigned to the deification of the little Flavius Caesar, born in 73 and removed by death when he was still a child, whether it occurred before or soon after Domitian's accession, are all significant pointers. The fact that he assumed the consulship another ten times, reaching the number, unprecedented for the eponymous magistrature, of seventeen, and from 84 onwards – after the enunciation of the plan, never put into effect, for a decennial consulate – without even the formality of nomination; the fact that he held perpetual powers as censor, first in the form of the *censoria potestas* (possibly from 84), then with the title, also unprecedented, of *censor perpetuus* (from the end of 85); and the fact that he adopted at the first opportunity the cognomen of Germanicus, as an epithet of victory, and changed the names of the months, calling September Germanicus and October Domitianus, all confirm on the formal plane as well the existence of a characteristic design. This design was also reflected in the religious field: by the special arrangements made at Rome for the cult of his father and brother, a cult which he brought into an original relationship with the cult of Jupiter, his own highest guardian divinity; by the transformation of the house where he was born into the *templum gentis Flaviae*, the sanctuary and mausoleum of his deified relations; and finally by the claim, assiduously satisfied by the choruses of flatterers, to the mode of address *dominus et deus*, while the outward displays of pomp must have aroused lasting impressions about the supreme majesty of his own exclusive pre-eminence.

The same intentions also stood out from the beginning in the field of the practical activity of governing, for after the indispensable homage to the past (deification of his brother and commemorative speech in October; inauguration, possibly on the same occasion, of the arch on the Velian; edict confirming the concessions granted by Vespasian, Titus and their predecessors), Domitian would not let himself be persuaded to give legal form to the custom prevailing with Titus that the Princeps should abstain from pronouncing capital sentences on senators. He was certainly aware that he was thus retaining power, even regarded as a theoretical duty, intact, though unfortunately with the risk – aggravated rather than avoided by his despotic attitude – of a malevolent interpretation. Thus although he sought the collaboration of the upper classes, and although the emperor's 'consilium' saw its official position among the organs of the state actually strengthened in his reign, by starting out with harsh treatment of the friends of his father and brother he alarmed an aristocracy which, after being thoroughly renewed by the very advent of the Flavians, demanded only a minimum of tact to appease its sensibilities. At the same time he proceeded to govern in a manner conflicting more in appearance than in reality with that of his predecessors, for the abolition of the *ludi*

circenses in honour of Titus's birthday and the custom of putting his own
name alone on monuments begun by his father or brother and finished by
him are details of no importance; and it is hardly permissible to see the
most characteristic side of a policy opposed to the previous one in, for
example, the solution on different bases of the problem of the *subseciva*, a
solution applied in 82, or the prohibition of castration, a measure attributed to the early years of the reign and introduced with the precise
intention of reacting against a predilection of Titus's. In the last analysis
these measures testify in Domitian's favour. For the rest, in matters of
real concern to the empire he showed that he meant to follow his father's
path; for example, the care applied to the local implementation in Spain
of the general grant of Latin rights is demonstrated by the famous municipal statutes of Malaca and Salpensa, both promulgated not later than 84;
and the inscriptions, also recently discovered, regarding delimitations or
restitutions of boundaries indicate the prosecution of another characteristic
interest of Vespasian's. It was much rather the rigorous systematism that
he demanded in the functioning of the state, his obstinate determination
to take an interest in everything, and the inflexible severity with which he
kept watch even on the field of private morality and controlled the
administration of justice (as usual, the element most likely to arouse
sinister impressions) that soon brought home most clearly the change in
approach at the summit of the principate. Less than two years after his
succession, while privately Domitian was behaving at variance with his
own moralistic zeal (he repudiated his adulterous wife and executed her
accomplice, the dancer Paris, then summoned her back to him and at the
same time kept with him his niece Julia, with whom he had begun to live
openly during Domitia's absence), publicly he was in open conflict with
the Senate, many members of which, if we are to accept the combined
and by no means incredible evidence of Eusebius and Cassius Dio,[1] were
put to death, exiled or forced to commit suicide. It is understandable how
the tradition formed by the subsequent hatred, a tradition unanimous in
affirming a gradual decline in relations between Emperor and Senate,
dated from this time the irreparable collapse of the previous tolerable
balance of virtues and vices and the clear beginning of the tyranny which
turned even Domitian's virtues into defects.[2]

---

[1] EUSEB.–JEROME., *Chron.*, *ab. Abr.* 2099 (Oct. 82–Sept. 83); CASS. D., LXVII, 3,
3–4.
[2] SUET., *Dom.*, 3, 2.

THE CONFLICT WITH THE ARISTOCRACY

We cannot tell to what extent the tradition altered the facts of Domitian's activity against the Senate, especially as strands of another more general movement of opposition are entwined in it, that of the philosophers. But since precisely on the subject of this anti-senatorial activity the tradition, as was to be expected, is relatively more abundant, as it is for Tiberius and the other emperors who had found themselves at daggers drawn with the Senate, it is possible to reconstruct the main lines of the struggle tenaciously waged by the Princeps. In the end he became the victim of his own efforts, but nevertheless the experience of full, declared autocracy and the further thrust he gave to administrative centralization remained permanent advances in the Augustan principate's progress towards complete domination.

Domitian did not nourish Tiberius's illusions on the subject of the collaboration of the Senate as a collective organ, nor was he disposed to continue, even formally, the deference with which his father and brother, faithful to the Augustan model, had softened for the highest class in the state the real relationship of absolute lordship. We have already mentioned his hard treatment of his predecessors' friends and of the other signs of frank but crude behaviour. Not that he undervalued what was still the only distinguished class in Roman society, for he too worked to guard its dignity. He forbade libels on members of the nobility, deprived courtesans of the privilege of riding in a litter, which made them look offensively like matrons, and expelled from the Senate a man of quaestorian rank because of his passion for dancing and pantomime. These are particular instances of the strict control of manners which he undertook with zeal amid his other governmental tasks. He did not even act, at any rate at the start, in a mean or illiberal way: he refused to accept legacies from those who had children, and he made generous gifts, on the occasion of public festivals, even to senators and knights, though the mode of dispensing these gifts (baskets of foodstuffs to carry home and handfuls of 'tesserae' thrown in the air among the senatorial and equestrian seats in the theatre) was not the most dignified, at least to our taste. But when any aspect of his own superiority was in question he showed no regard for anyone. This was particularly so where any suspicion of possible rivals was concerned, as in the case of his cousin, T. Flavius Sabinus, Julia's husband. Even before he came to the throne Domitian disliked Sabinus; the *lapsus* of a herald, who had proclaimed him 'imperator' instead of 'consul' at the consular elections, though not noticed at the time (Sabinus was consul with

Domitian in 82), caused his downfall at the first opportunity, probably in conjunction with the already mentioned hecatomb of 82–83, since it was from that time that the downfall of his friend Dio of Prusa dated.

The first military campaign under the Emperor's direct command, the one against the Chatti in 83, with the monumental celebration of his victorious return – if it is indeed this which is commemorated by the first frieze of the Cancellaria[1] – subsequent triumph and the grant of the permanent right to use twenty-four lictors and to wear triumphal dress in the Curia, increased the autocrat's detachment still further. He became more and more isolated in splendour and hatred. We certainly cannot blame the tradition for regarding the cold welcome given to Agricola, who returned at this time (the end of 84) from Britain, as due to envy and jealousy. On the other hand, the bond between the emperor and the army, an essential factor in the practical reality of the principate, was reinforced by the concession of something that the troops had long been demanding – an increase in pay; even now they did not get the denarius per day which they had requested and had not obtained from Tiberius after the death of Augustus, but their pay did rise from 225 to 300 denarii per year. In 86 the initial success against the Dacians and the one against the Nasamones in Africa, which Domitius reported to the Senate in terms suggesting that this tribe had ceased to exist in response to his own wishes and merits, produced fresh exaltation. In the summer of the same year Domitian instituted quadrennial games in honour of Jupiter Capitolinus, with athletic contests, chariot races and literary competitions which last he had already also added to the old *Quinquatria*, which he celebrated at the Alban villa in honour of Minerva, another of his particular guardian deities. These Greek games, although they now offended aristocratic traditionalism less than they had in the time of Nero (so little, indeed, that they were retained even after their founder's death, for centuries), with the religious ceremonial surrounding them – intended to create round the Princeps, who presided over them, an atmosphere of mystical superiority – made officially clear, and hence more irritating, the project of self-deification, inseparable in any case from the notion of autocracy as conceived by Domitian. In 87 there was some sort of move against the new Nero, for a sacrifice by the Fratres Arvales on 22 September is recorded with the formula usual for the discovery of a conspiracy, 'ob detecta scelera nefariorum'.[2] This was probably followed by trials, of which, however, we know nothing. Whether we should place then or later the condemnation in his absence of C. Vettulenus Civica

---

[1] F. MAGI, *op. cit.*, p. 98 ff.   [2] *CIL*, VI, 2065.

Cerialis, proconsul of Asia, who was executed in office shortly before the possibility of obtaining the same province arose for Agricola,[1] depends on the calculation of the usual gap between the consulship and this proconsulship, at that time 13–15 years, so that Agricola, consul in 77, saw his turn for possible selection arrive about 89–91. But clearly it cannot be proved that the item in the Acts of the Fratres Arvales refers to the downfall of Cerialis.

The atmosphere of pomp and ceremony was renewed in the autumn of 88 with the *ludi saeculares,* celebrated for the first time since those of Augustus and Claudius, but five years before the completion of the 110 years of the Augustan computation, with the aim, expressed particularly in the coins, of extolling the advent of the new Flavian century, just as in 83–84 the coinage had carefully commemorated the exact centenary of the games of 17 B.C., the beginning of the Augustan 'saeculum novum aureum'. Tacitus took part officially as quindecemvir and praetor (*Ann.*, XI, 11, 1). But the effect on the aristocracy cannot have lasted long, for very soon afterwards open revolt broke out. It was only through the changed conditions in the empire, which were different and better, thanks partly to Domitian, that the situation of 68 did not repeat itself. But the feelings which inspired the move were similar. At the beginning of January 89 L. Antonius Saturninus, the commander of the legions of the Upper Rhine, a senator as a result of Vespasian's *adlectio* and also an ex-consul, had had himself hailed 'imperator' at Mainz by the legions stationed there, the XIV *Gemina* and the XXI *Rapax*, which put at his disposal as a fighting fund the savings of the legionaries, kept in accordance with custom with the eagles. We are not told whether the other two legions of Upper Germany, the VIII *Augusta* at Strasbourg and the XI *Claudia Pia Fidelis* at Vindonissa, also joined the revolt, but it is probable. The declaration was not made on the spur of the moment. Saturninus, recently offended by the Princeps, must have established his contacts in Rome, and the moment chosen, while the Dacians were active on the Danube and in the East the Parthians had also moved in conjunction with the appearance of the umpteenth false Nero, seemed the most favourable to success. He had not omitted to seek support even from the Germans, and he must doubtless have had some sort of informal agreement with other army commanders; for example, if the downfall of Sallustius Lucullus, Agricola's successor as governor of Britain, is to be placed round about 89–90, he was certainly not ruined merely by the banal charge of having invented a new kind of javelin and called it by his own name. But the rebellion failed

[1] TAC., *Agr.*, 42.

within the space of a few days as a result of various hitches and not least through the determination of Domitian. The records of the Fratres Arvales for January 89,[1] which can hardly refer, it would seem, to any other campaign, give us a vivid account of the rapid sequence of events. Whether on 1 January the Princeps was already on the road to the north with the praetorian cohorts, *en route* for the Danube (as one would be inclined to think from his failure to assume the consulship for the first time after eight consecutive years), and, receiving the news on the road, rapidly changed his destination and plans, or whether he left Rome after receiving the news there, the fact remains that on 12 January he must have been marching against the rebel, while from Spain Ulpius Traianus, on his orders, was leading towards Germany by forced marches the VII *Gemina* legion, summoned in preparation for a long, hard struggle. Instead, on 25 January the Fratres Arvales were already making sacrifices in Rome 'ob laetitiam publicam', that is, for the victory. The war was over. Saturninus had been overcome on the Rhine by the army of Lower Germany under the command of A. Lappius Maximus Norbanus, who in all probability was the governor of the province, while owing to an unexpected thaw the Germans, who were certainly Chatti, did not succeed in crossing the river and from the far bank could only watch the spectacle of two Roman armies locked in combat. The situation had thus been resolved in the same way as in 68, when Verginius Rufus had defeated Vindex, except that on this occasion the whole episode finished there.

To be on the safe side, Lappius Maximus, whose loyalty, like that of Verginius once before, was not free of all suspicion in spite of his decisive stand for Domitian, destroyed the correspondence of the defeated governor, who had been wounded on the field of battle and killed soon afterwards. Domitian went on just the same to Mainz and there began reprisals against the most direct accomplices with savage enquiries and punishments. He refrained from taking action in Rome until later. For the moment he sent the rebel's head to be exhibited on the Rostra. It appears in fact that his return occurred very quickly. His certain presence in Rome is not attested until the end of 89, on the occasion of the Dacian and German triumph (over Saturninus's allies the Chatti, whom he must have reduced to some kind of order); and it is impossible to know whether during the course of the year he went straight from the Rhine to the Danube, without returning to Rome. What is certain, however, is that the whole episode, though it had ended without any serious consequences, increased in the emperor's suspicious mind the concern for his own safety.

[1] *CIL*, VI, 2066.

Thus while on the one hand he put on ever more grandiose and extravagant displays of pomp to celebrate his own person, on the other he took subtler and crueller measures to protect himself from the enemies and conspirators he saw everywhere. Amid the splendour of the triumphal games, while Domitian was assuming, even if not officially, the title of *Dacicus*, while throughout the empire the year's victories were celebrated with honours out of proportion to the significance of the successes, and while the Senate was voting the erection of a big equestrian monument in the Forum – the *equus magnus Domitiani* subsequently inaugurated in 91 – the nightmarish atmosphere did not disperse. Before the end of the year came the expulsion from Rome of the mathematicians and philosophers, particularly the Stoics, who were suspected of feeding the opposition. Even if we discount the macabre stories in which the tradition crystallized its hatred – stories like the one recounted by Cassius Dio (LXVII, 9) of the invitation to a chilling ceremony at which, in surroundings draped for mourning, the senators were forced to contemplate their own tombstones, amid even clearer signs of imminent slaughter – the remainder of that year did in reality witness the start of the henceforth uninterrupted series of condemnations for treason which soon led to the terror.

The informers, hitherto kept at a distance, returned to become, together with a retinue of *agents provocateurs*, much-heeded instruments for the persecution of the emperor's opponents. Senators such as Aquilius Regulus, who had already disgraced himself under Nero, Fabricius Veiento, Valerius Catullus Messallinus, Mettius Carus, Arrecinus Clemens, Baebius Massa and Publicius Certus, and persons of low extraction collaborated with equal zeal. That senators should lend themselves to this sad work is not particularly surprising (cases against senators were normally conducted in the Senate, though in the intimidating presence of the Princeps and his guards), but it helps us to understand the real situation, which was composed, as in every age, of differing personal attitudes, for otherwise it would be impossible to explain how under this same Domitian some of the most notable figures of the following period passed undisturbed through the first stages of an unblemished career in the field of administration. But the realities of a struggle that was always being renewed – its only fixed point being the emperor's claim to the recognition of his sovereign majesty, together with his now pathological preoccupation with his own safety – were such that his enemies were continually changing in face of his suspicion and of the terrible and solitary punitive power which in this field absorbed the energy otherwise employed beneficently in the government of the empire. Not even erstwhile friends were safe, as we can see from the ambiguous figure of M. Cocceius Nerva, his future successor, consul with Domitian in 90 and three years later in disgrace; his friend Julius Bassus, dismissed for some unknown reason; Arrecinus Clemens, a friend and informer who was subsequently put to death in 93; and Baebius Massa, another informer, abandoned in the same year and left to be condemned in a senatorial trial for embezzlement, the prosecutors being Pliny and Herennius Senecio, persons whom we should be loath to regard as agreeable to Domitian. But others preferred to stand aside. Agricola did not receive either the promised governorship of Syria or the proconsulship of Asia. Cornutus Tertullus remained a complete stranger to public life throughout the reign. There were even men like Corellius Rufus, who put up with the pain of a serious illness just for the pleasure of surviving the tyrant's death by one day.

We do not know much about particular episodes or individual victims in the years 90–93, and there is the usual uncertainty about chronology; some events can equally well be placed at a different moment, as we saw in the case of the deaths of Flavius Sabinus, Civica Cerialis and Sallustius Lucullus. We can hardly even form any opinion about the charges preserved by the tradition; most of them sound futile – the sort of thing which infuriated Tiberius and which he dismissed. Salvidienus Orfitus was exiled on a charge of conspiracy and later put to death. Manius Acilius Glabrio, consul in 91, was forced to fight wild animals at the Alban villa, then exiled and in 95 put to death. Salvius Otho Cocceianus was killed for celebrating the birthday of the emperor Otho, his uncle, and Aelius Lamia Plautius Aelianus, the ex-husband of Domitia, for certain witty remarks uttered twenty years previously. Mettius Pompusianus was banished to Corsica and then put to death in 91 on the grounds that astrologers had foretold an imperial destiny for him, that he possessed a map of the Roman dominions, was continually quoting speeches by kings and generals from Livy and had given two slaves the names Mago and Hannibal. Mettius Rufus, prefect of Egypt from 89 to 91, and Mettius Modestus, an enemy of Regulus, were probably caught up in the ruin of their relative. And now the blows also began to fall, both in Rome and elsewhere, on people who did not belong to the urban aristocracy but were suspected of opposition: on the rhetorician Hermogenes of Tarsus, executed with his copyists for inserting certain allusions in one of his tales; on another teacher of oratory, Maternus, possibly the interlocutor in the *Dialogus de Oratoribus*, also killed for a dissertation on tyranny; and on the rich Athenian Hipparchus, grandfather of Herodes Atticus, whose property was confiscated after he had been condemned to death on some unknown charge. Even some quite humble people had to suffer; for example, the spectator who imprudently shouted something in favour of a gladiator whom the despot did not like and was thrown to the dogs then and there.

All this must doubtless be just one somewhat limited aspect of an activity that was much more complex and had its positive sides, and we know that in no field is it more necessary to carry out the task of re-assessing the evidence and reducing it to its true proportions than in that of personal acts of this sort, amplified and emphasized as they were by the tradition about the emperors. Nevertheless, even when these actions are cut down to size and placed in their limited context they remain an unquestionable reality; the now swiftly approaching end cannot be explained in any other way. A further embittering of the Emperor's character can also be detected in the capricious oscillations apparent in his public behaviour. After the death of Julia, between 87 and 89, in sus-picious circumstances, her deification, and the disappointment of his hopes for fresh offspring, for which flattering poets had sounded the trumpets in 90,[1] for some unknown reason in 91 he would not assume the consulship; and he showed the same unwillingness in the years 93, 94 and 96. And after the dedication of the *equus* in the Forum had been celebrated and the homage of the gold and silver statue on the Capitol accepted, he was nevertheless unwilling to celebrate a triumph for the Sarmatian war, the last of the campaigns he led, and on his return, on 1 or 2 January 93, he contented himself with carrying a crown of bay leaves up to Jupiter Capitolinus. There were sacrifices for him, a triumphal arch and the title, though this was not official either, of *Sarmaticus*. The people received a *congiarium*, the third distributed by Domitian (the first probably took place in 84 and the second in 89), not that he needed to solicit the favour of an element with which he had never been in conflict, for the urban proletariat, always punctually provided with bread and circuses, did not find this emperor any worse than the others. The conflict, henceforth irreconcilable, was with the aristocracy, which embraced the majority of his opponents. Discontent grew in the circles nearest to the Princeps and now entered the palace. By August 93, when the death, itself suspicious, of Agricola spared him the pain of seeing a tyranny until then intermittent become continuous, the terror had begun.[2]

[1] MARTIAL, VI, 3; STAT., *Silv.*, I, 1, 74.
[2] TAC., *Agr.*, 44, 5; PLIN., *Pan.*, 95, 3; *Epist.*, III, 11, 2–3.

THE GOVERNMENT OF THE EMPIRE

The 'administrative' acts of Domitian's reign have been illuminated, as far as they can be, by recent criticism which, recognizing the defects in Domitian's character – his arrogant theoretical rigidity and lack of practical flexibility – has tried to evaluate his actual achievement, which was distorted and obliterated by a hostile tradition. From this point of view the facts speak decisively in his favour. Domitian's autocratic conscience and energy made their mark not only on the aristocracy but also on the palace. The imperial cabinet naturally assumed great importance in a still more centralized system, but the continual control of the Princeps, who not only dictated the letters to his officials and took an interest in every administrative detail but kept watch on them through the very need to ensure his own safety at every moment, did not allow it to become omnipotent. He also gave firm direction to the 'consilium', which certainly did not only discuss such questions as the one immortalized in Juvenal's fourth satire. For the first time some of its members were knights, whose career took a further step under Domitian towards definitive official status. A knight, Gnaeus Octavius Titinius Capito, was *procurator ab epistulis et patrimonio*, that is, chief political secretary and administrator of the imperial fortune, and another man who became a knight in the course of his career after starting as a freedman, Claudius Etruscus, was the *a rationibus*, or director general of the finances. Central control of the collection of the *vicesima hereditatium* was also handed over to a procurator who was a knight. And these posts henceforward remained the preserve of the equestrian class; this was a natural result of the irresistible tendency for the emperor's private officials to be transformed into state officials. But even though there were also, exceptionally, posts of unprecedented importance for knights – there was the case of a procurator of Asia who temporarily exercised the functions of the deceased proconsul – while during the same period the duties and posts of the senatorial class, understandably enough, did not increase – the knights too, like the senators, were kept in the usual meticulously defined social compartments. In this connection it would be interesting to know the criteria applied by Domitian in the *adlectio* of senators, but on this subject we are almost completely in the dark. Perhaps we can derive some clue from his refusal to re-admit to the Senate a person expelled from it by Vespasian, one Palfurius Sura, even thought he was dear to Domitian's heart as an informer. The same fondness for system entered into the concept of order rigidly defended by the Princeps in his actual legislation on manners. To the measures already described we must add, especially for the knights, a more precise regulation of seats in the theatre and the deletion of a knight from the register of judges for taking back his wife after accusing her of adultery. In general, in the field of public morality Domitian unearthed archaic laws and applied them without distinction to both classes. For example, he condemned both senators and knights on the basis of the *Lex Scantinia*, which dealt only with offences by senators, and he punished unfaithful Vestal virgins mercilessly: on the first occasion, in 83, the only favour he granted three of them was the choice of mode of death, a piece of severity which caused the pontifex Helvius Agrippa to have an apoplectic seizure; on a second occasion, in 91, he inflicted on the chief Vestal, Cornelia, the archaic punishment of being buried alive, while her accomplice, Celer, was beaten to death by rods in the Comitium. Another accomplice, the ex-praetor and orator Valerius Licinianus, whose guilt could not be proved, was banished.

This severe and systematic attitude applied, however, not only in these terribly exemplary cases, but also to the practical business of day-to-day administration. In conformity with the tendency of the times, the urban offices were made more functional (for example, by the further restriction of the consuls' and praetors' powers and the increase of those of the *praefectus urbi*); magistrates and their subordinates were strictly controlled; and provincial governors were supervised and treated impartially, so that, according to the significant testimony of Suetonius (*Dom.*, 8, 2), 'they were never more moderate or more just'; and it is worth noting that the men in question here subsequently behaved in a far from exemplary fashion. The praise reluctantly bestowed by the tradition receives confirmation from the little we know from other quarters of Domitian's provincial administration – the little which we must suppose to have survived the larger amount erased by the 'damnatio memoriae' and which can be distinguished from the work of his father and brother, frequently lumped together under the heading 'Flavian'. As far as we can see, the empire did not feel the struggle going on at the top; in practice, the state of affairs established by Vespasian continued, as we saw, for example, in the matter of Romanization in connection with the Spanish municipal statutes. As for legislative measures, the already mentioned solution of the problem of the *subseciva* – a solution which favoured the sitting tenants (judgement between Firmum and Faleria in Picenum, dated 19 July 82) and was also extended to the provinces – indicates indeed greater liberality. It used to be thought that the local burden inherent in the 'cursus publicus', that is, services to the official post, had been exacerbated under

TA—K

Domitian, since an alleviation of it in Italy was celebrated as one of his successor's merits. But this view, which could also be a tribute to Domitian's precision in demanding contributions, has been proved false by the letter, now published,[1] from Domitian to Claudius Athenodorus, a procurator (probably of the patrimonium) in Syria; in this letter the Princeps prohibits, with clarity and energy, abuses in the requisitioning of beasts of burden, for he was concerned to respect the property of the provincials and to guarantee the smooth functioning of agriculture – conditions necessary to ensure, from the fiscal aspect too, the regularity of the administration. The edict of 92, which limited the cultivation of the vine in favour of wheat in both Italy and the provinces (in the latter it involved the destruction of some of the existing vineyards), though the circumstances surrounding it are not entirely clear and it was not rigorously applied everywhere, is characteristic as evidence of a rudimentary economic *dirigisme*. As for public works in Italy and the provinces, the only sufficiently definite records speak of work on an aqueduct at Tivoli (88) and on others at Ostia, Rimini and Lilybaeum; of the excavation of a canal in Egypt; of a restoration of the temple of Apollo Delphicus, of the construction of the Via Domitiana between Sinuessa and Puteoli, completed in 95; and of repairs to the Via Latina, to the roads of Asia (82), Sardinia (83), Baetica (Via Augusta, 90) and Africa (Carthage–Theveste), and to the big military road on the right bank of the Danube between Viminacium and Ratiaria (92). It has also been ascertained that T. Pomponius Bassus, the governor of Cappadocia and Galatia whose name figures on a large number of milestones from the eastern parts of Asia Minor, was appointed by Domitian and may have already begun in his reign the big reorganization of roads which continued under Nerva and Trajan up to the year 100. Finally, there are reports of the construction of various monumental buildings here and there in Domitian's honour; clear traces of these have been restored to us by, for example, the excavation of the cities of Tripolitania. But all these things are only scattered fragments from the great shipwreck of information. Moreover there is often the added difficulty, particularly where the remains of monuments are concerned, of distinguishing work of Domitian's reign from that of the succeeding reigns, the age of Trajan and Hadrian.

As for the organization of the provinces, Domitian, like his father, acted with equal feeling for their specific, current needs and for the now crystallized needs of the organic system which was superimposing itself more and more with a force of its own – the force of the administrative

[1] *Syria*, XXXIV, 1957, p. 278 ff. (see above, p. 243, n. 1).

apparatus – on the age-old empirical creation embodied in the Roman state. Thus the increased military importance of the Danube frontier led in 86 to the division of Moesia into two provinces, Upper and Lower Moesia, both under governors of consular rank. The military districts of the Upper and Lower Rhine, which belonged to Belgica, assumed the shape – probably in 90, after the rebellion of Saturninus – of regular provinces, Upper and Lower Germany. Elsewhere the peaceful conditions caused an increase in the civil administration as compared with the military authorities, as in Britain, where the pacification completed by Agricola in 84 and the renunciation of further offensives against Caledonia, with the consequent recall to the continent of one legion (the II *Adiutrix*), may have led to the creation of the *iuridicus provinciae Britanniae* alongside the governor to administer part of the territory. The same thing seems to have happened in Tarraconese Spain, where it looks as if the institution of the *iuridicus per Asturiam et Callaeciam* goes back to 89, when the legion was called away to help in suppressing the revolt of Saturninus. As for the financial administration of the provinces, one single procurator was put in charge of the provinces of Pannonia and Dalmatia; the reason for this step is unknown, but it certainly resulted in a further centralization of control. Arrangements tried experimentally by Vespasian on a provisional basis, such as the special union of Cappadocia with Galatia, became permanent. In the East there was also a continuation of the tendency to direct annexation, that is, to the standardization of conditions in Rome's dominions. Domitian's reign saw the disappearance of the last important client kingdoms still existing, almost anachronistically, within the confines of the empire. Such was the fate in 92 of the kingdom of Chalcis, probably on the death of Aristobulus, a member of the Herod family, who had received it in 71 in exchange for Lesser Armenia. The same thing happened, probably in 93, to the kingdom of Julius Agrippa II, who had thus reigned for another twenty years after the fall of Jerusalem, always remaining with his Ituraeans on friendly terms with the Princeps and reading in peace and tranquillity the volumes of the Jewish History submitted one by one to his judgement by Flavius Josephus who, enjoying Domitian's favour as he had that of his predecessors, had obtained from the former immunity from taxation for the estates already restored by the latter. These are specific cases of the acceleration given under the Flavians to the process of universal standardization, which was to produce the new society of the second century. Not long afterwards in fact another member of the Herod clan, Julius Alexander, to whom Vespasian had given in 72 a part of Cilicia taken away from Antiochus of Commagene, held the consulship. His son Julius Agrippa was quaestor of Asia, and one Julius Alexander Berenicianus, almost certainly a member of the same family, was also consul and in 132 proconsul of Asia, thus marking the complete fusion of the house of Herod the Great with the Roman aristocracy.

Not much is known about Domitian's relations with individual communities. The provisions for the Spanish municipalities have already been mentioned. His name occurs at Delphi, in a fragment of a letter concerning the Pythian games; in Achaea in connection with letters sent successively to the proconsuls Avidius Nigrinus and Armenius Broccus on the problem of children exposed to die; at Corinth, which obtained once more from him the right to strike coins and assumed the title of Colonia Flavia (though the title disappeared again after his death); at Pergamum through the decree of 93–94 restricting the immunity granted by his father to rhetoricians; and at Athens, where he was eponymous archon after 85. We can imagine that, granted the sort of character he possessed, the usual honorific relations were attended by a particularly attentive paternalism. More noteworthy were his provisions for the defence of the provincial world, a defence organized with a lively sense of expediency.

That Domitian, with his policy of absolutism, should seek the support of the army was natural, and he did not repeat Nero's mistake of not assuming personal command in its campaigns. But in the general organization of the forces, too, he displayed his gifts of clarity and order, and the capacity to learn from the lessons taught by the facts. He returned, for instance, to the principle of collegiality in the command of the praetorian guard. He was less inclined to increase the number of soldiers than to reduce it, possibly because of the greater expense involved through the increase in pay, and it is probable that in his reign the discharge of the Vitellian praetorians was completed and the number of praetorian cohorts fixed at ten. Generous but not weak with the troops, he was liberal about granting citizenship to the auxiliaries, as is shown by the numerous military diplomas dating from his reign. He also made personal gifts and after the revolt of Saturninus rewarded the loyal legions with bounties and the title *Pia Fidelis Domitiana*, which was also extended to the auxiliary units and the Rhine fleet. But he also took precautions, forbidding the permanent stationing of more than one legion in any one camp and the depositing of more than a thousand sesterces per soldier with the eagles. Of the old legions, the V *Alaudae* did not survive his reign (if indeed it did not disappear in 70), nor did the XXI *Rapax*; but he created, probably in 83 for the war against the Chatti, the I *Flavia Minervia*. Movements of forces for the various campaigns were frequent, but their final deployment in Domitian's last years, which were relatively peaceful, is significant for the continuation of Vespasian's frontier policy, and for the evaluation of the situation outside the frontiers and the new points of pressure. The use of legionary detachments (*vexillationes*) in theatres of war far from the legion's base had become general and the garrison system was firmly established. The most interesting proving ground was that *limes Germaniae Superioris et Raetiae* which had been strung out between the Rhine and the Danube as a result of the German wars and which was garrisoned in the front-line forts by auxiliary units linked to legionary detachments lying further back in an exemplary system of defence. The Germano-Sarmatian world henceforth kept almost two-thirds of the Roman forces occupied, not so much on the Rhine as on the Danube. It was under Domitian in fact that the army of the Rhine lost its primacy, declining from eight to seven legions, while the Danube army, including the Dalmatian legion – this one too being close to the river – amounted now to ten legions, with proportionate auxiliary forces. Spain still had its single legion, Britain three, Cappadocia two, Syria three, Judaea one, Egypt two and Africa one; auxiliary cohorts and wings were scattered almost everywhere, but on the whole there were no innovations in these sectors. They were deliberately left in peace by the Emperor, who was wisely concerned not to multiply dangerous frontiers. Those which were already dangerous sufficed to satisfy his ambitions in the field of military glory. In short, Domitian succeeded in defending the empire effectively; and the troops as well as the provincials showed a sincere attachment to him.

Under a Princeps so attentive and precise we must assume that the finances were carefully managed; and in fact we have no reason to suppose that Domitian did anything but follow in his father's footsteps and continue to run the empire on the same austere lines; the only difference was that his methods aroused greater dislike because of the existence of other motives for hatred. This is probably what we should read between the lines of the exaggerations and distortions of the tradition, which, recognizing in Domitian a certain initial generosity (an example was the cancellation of cases between citizens and the treasury about sums of money outstanding for more than five years) and then accusing him of bad government, put down his greed to lack of money, just as it ascribed his cruelty to fear: 'super ingenii naturam inopia rapax, metu saevus'.[1] But there has been much discussion about a financial crisis in which it is difficult to believe; except within the limits, understandably exaggerated

---

[1] SUET., *Dom.*, 3, 2.

by the stinging memories of confiscations left in the senatorial class –
memories more apt in themselves to leave an impression on the tradition –
of an increase in urban and court expenditure. After Vespasian's reorganization the revenue produced by the empire, with its growing
prosperity, cannot but have increased, and the fiscal severity which is
ascribed to Domitian as a defect – it is alleged to have taken positively
odious forms, such as those which Suetonius says he witnessed with his
own eyes[1] (*Dom.*, 12, 3) – and which, reduced to its true proportions, may
have been no more than administrative meticulousness, is our guarantee
that little can have escaped taxation and that the inflow of tribute must
have been regular and imposing. The army was certainly a heavy expense,
particularly with the increase in pay and the active service involved in the
numerous campaigns, but, as always in the past, not so heavy as to endanger
the balancing of the ordinary account, in which it formed by far the
largest single item. Building work in Rome may have weighed down the
extraordinary account, since expenses of this sort, which had always been
to a certain extent private in character, were no longer assisted by extraordinary incomings such as the booty from lucrative wars. But even this
activity, which consisted mainly of completing his father's and brother's
projects, cannot have exceeded the bounds of the possible. Numerous
buildings were indeed involved, not all of them for display and many of
them made necessary by the state in which Rome had been left after the
recent disasters, the last being the fire of A.D. 80. Thus Domitian restored
the Capitoline temple (82), the temple of Castor and Pollux, the temple
of Divus Augustus and the house of the Vestal Virgins in the Forum, and
on the Palatine the temple of Apollo with its libraries and the palace of
Tiberius, in which he must have rebuilt the façades looking on to the
Forum. Behind the Capitol and in the Campus Martius he had work
carried out on the portico of Octavia and on Agrippa's Pantheon, and he
rebuilt from the foundations the temple of Isis and Serapis, all buildings
affected by the fire. He naturally took the opportunity to clean up and
embellish the neighbouring areas, for example by constructing in the
Campus Martius, in honour of Vespasian and Titus, the *templum* or *porticus
Divorum*; by renovating the Curia and the *Chalcidicum* or *atrium Minervae*,
a portico that flanked it; by the transformation, begun by him and completed by Nerva, of the old passage of the *Argiletum* into an elegant forum
dominated by a temple of Minerva; and by beginning on the excavation –
a task continued by Trajan – of the slope of the Quirinal to enlarge eastward the space at the foot of the Capitol. He also completed other build-

[1] In connection with the *fiscus Iudaicus*.

ings, such as the Flavian amphitheatre – which was endowed with the last rows of seats and the building for a school of gladiators – and the baths of Titus. The temple of Vespasian in the Forum, built by the Senate, the *equus* dedicated to Domitian, also by the Senate, and the conversion of the house where he was born into a temple-cum-mausoleum, like the commemorative arches, formed part of the obligation to celebrate the state.

Other buildings and monuments were clearly inspired by personal motives: for example, by the wish to celebrate military glory in the trophies of the Capitol square, which must be attributed, it seems, to Domitian, even if they were utilized again later by Alexander Severus; by the desire for superhuman splendour in his residence – the *domus Augustana* – built by the architect Rabirius on the Palatine, with its public and private palaces, libraries, hippodrome, baths (only started) and various dependent buildings; by traditional religious feeling in the temples, such as the one raised on the Capitol to Jupiter Custos, in place of the shrine dedicated to Jupiter Conservator where he had found refuge as a young man in 69; by his liking for Greek civilization in the Odeum and the big stadium for gymnastics built on the Campus Martius (Piazza Navona), and at the same time by his deference to the populace's fondness for shows of the Roman sort in the basin for sea-battles made on the right bank of the Tiber. But other works, such as the restoration of the temple of Venus Genitrix, were a matter of ordinary maintenance, or of a utilitarian character, like the fountain on the Esquiline known as the 'Trofei di Mario', the 'horrea' connected with his name and the improvements in the water supply (it was probably Domitian who first brought the *aqua Claudia* up to the Palatine) abundantly attested by the *fistulae aquariae*, which fortunately escaped the effects of the 'damnatio memoriae'. As for villas, he was responsible for the construction of the splendid Alban villa, but the others at Tusculum, Antium, Circeii, Gaeta and Baiae had already been built by his predecessors and at the most underwent some restoration at his hands. On the whole, therefore, it was a question of embellishing Rome, a work spontaneously induced by the prosperous conditions of the 'pax Flavia' inaugurated by Vespasian, just as once the 'pax Augusta' had stimulated the great rebuilding programme carried out by Augustus. What was done might be described as a sort of preparation for the splendours of Trajan's age. Certainly this concentrated expenditure, all by its nature falling on the funds of the Princeps, must have made a considerable impression, and it is not surprising that the tradition should make the confiscations and enforced legacies look to a certain extent welcome and sought after, while the basically always delicate balance of the

Roman budget gave the idea of constantly imminent bankruptcy every appearance of credibility. Domitian spent a great deal because, with his attention to the collection of taxes, he could afford to do so; and it is no more imputable to his absolutism than to the spontaneous development of the relations between the state administration – the *aerarium Saturni* – and the public and private administration of the Princeps – the fiscus and the patrimonium – if the tradition notes, naturally to his discredit, that he incorporated in his own income the revenues from the aqueducts, which were the concern of the treasury.

With strictness of control over the administrative organs Domitian combined, as his principal positive gift – at any rate in the early years of the reign – strictness and fairness in the administration of justice. We are told in fact of the care he took to look at cases personally and to remind centumviri and judges of the need for incorruptibility, of his carefulness and impartiality even in cases where one of the parties was the state treasury or his own personal one, of the zeal with which he demanded a verdict of guilty, and of the inexorability with which he applied the penalty, especially in instances of contraventions of his laws and censorial directives on questions of morality. Some cases of this sort have already been mentioned – the terrible one of the Vestal Cornelia, for example – and in fact a considerable proportion of his known legislation refers to this subject, from the revival, in 89, of the *Lex Iulia* on adultery to the ban on the acceptance of legacies by courtesans, and from the obligation to wear the toga in the theatre to the relegation to private stages of the immoral shows of the pantomime actors. This was in addition to the regulations – to which we have already referred – for the rigorous defence of the social order, a field in which, significantly, the recurrent problem of slaves appears once again: an edict excluded them from the suspension of charges and provisional freedom granted by the Senate on the occasion of public holidays to accused persons in prison, and a *senatusconsultum* laid down that anyone who reported fraudulence in the freeing of a slave should become that slave's master. These were severe regulations and as a rule they were enforced: a centurion who was shown to be a slave was restored to his master. But the scrupulous administration of justice degenerated only too easily into judicial persecution when trials for treason began to multiply. Then the wider use of these very procedures of prosecution and enquiry, of informers and torture, together with some arbitrary executions resulting from sudden feelings of injured despotism, obscured Domitian's previous reputation for equity and implanted in the tradition the lasting memory of infamy.

As for Domitian's passion for shows, and his religious and cultural arrangements, both personal and public, they reveal the fundamental realism of his autocratic policy. Aiming in the last analysis and with more likelihood of success at the same goal, he was neither a fanatic like Gaius nor an incautious exponent of exotic innovations like Nero. That while himself preferring Greek games he should preserve and encourage Roman ones, with buildings for them, the foundation of four official schools of gladiators, assiduous attendance at shows, and loud support for certain fighters and certain factions in the circus (he added two new ones to the four traditional factions) is certainly explained by his need to retain the favour of the populace. And that he should go back to obliging the quaestors designate to give gladiatorial shows at their own expense may indicate that his archaism was, from certain points of view, not disinterested. But his traditionalism in religion was the result of a political choice: lord and god, but a god amid Roman gods. Jupiter and Minerva first of all, then Mars and Venus, Neptune and Vesta, Ceres and Rome were the divinities that received most worship; among foreign deities, Isis alone, now acclimatized and the object of Domitian's gratitude for his escape in 69, which he made dressed as an acolyte of the Egyptian goddess, received equal attention. But eastern religions in general were viewed with mistrust, and Judaism and Christianity may have been persecuted. The Princeps – who consulted the Praenestine oracles at the beginning of each year; ordered that a tomb built of stones intended for the Capitoline temple should be destroyed and that the bones it contained should be thrown into the sea; and fulfilled a vow made under Nero but forgotten until his own time – regulated even religion systematically to a political end; but he shrewdly chose the ancient Roman religion, not the hybrid fantasies of his predecessors, in the enterprise of claiming equality with the gods. However, he asserted this claim quite openly, with serious consequences in the political field as well; for it was now that the crime of treason became for the first time a crime of impiety, and adoration of the Emperor as a test of homage – a procedure which played such a big part in the long struggle between Christianity and the empire – had its roots here.

It remains to say something of Domitian's cultural interests. His attempt to control opinion, which led him into the conflict with the philosophers, was purely political in inspiration and forms a part of that side of his activity which we have already described; it was a particular aspect of his struggle against the senatorial opposition. This apart, he paid honour to Quintilian; he gave him an official salary as a public teacher of rhetoric, put him in charge of the education of his two nephews, the sons of Flavius Clemens, who were called Vespasian and Domitian and marked out for the succession, and rewarded him with the consular insignia. He devoted considerable care to rebuilding the stocks of books in the public libraries, which had suffered losses in the fires, securing copies of books from as far afield as the library at Alexandria. He reserved an important position in the games, especially the *Ludi Capitolini*, for poetic contests, and they became solemn courts of poetry (fifty-two poets competed in 94 in Greek poetry alone), even in the atmosphere of literary dilettantism, not to mention humiliating flattery, characteristic of the age. Finally, he set an example to private citizens and local communities which bore fruit in the initiatives recorded – as are the public assistance institutions – even for Domitian's age in Pliny's letters. All these things are not the smallest claims to merit of a practical activity that was on the whole broadly positive.

THE WARS WAGED BY DOMITIAN

The way in which tradition reports Domitian's activity on the frontiers is the best measure of the distortion imported into this tradition by its denigratory aim. Rash and unnecessary campaigns, exaggerated or false victories, treaties concluded on shameful terms – such are the principal themes. The reality was different: the limitation of the theatres of operations, in order to concentrate attention on the points of real danger, is sufficient to reveal a responsible policy.

The first war was in 83, against the Chatti. It has been reconstructed by modern scholars mainly in connection with the archaeological research on the German *limes*, and its broad lines can now be glimpsed. There can be little doubt that on the right bank of the Rhine Domitian meant to pursue his father's policy of consolidating the territory, the organization and the protection of those Germans who were already Romanized. It was the opposition of the Chatti, the big tribe residing in the interior between the Cherusci and the Hermunduri, in the rear of the Romanized tribes nearer the Rhine, that provoked the campaign. Probably in the spring of 83 Domitian, accompanied by a headquarters staff that included Julius Frontinus, went to Gaul on the pretext of holding the *census* and began the war with the four legions of Upper Germany (the I *Adiutrix* and the XIV *Gemina* from Mainz, the VIII *Augusta* from Strasbourg and the IX *Claudia Pia Fidelis* from Vindonissa), to which he added the XXI *Rapax*, summoned from Bonn on the Lower Rhine (where it was replaced by the newly formed I *Minervia*), detachments from the forces in Britain (at least one *vexillatio* from Legion IX *Hispana*) and also the auxiliary units. This campaign probably ended without any big pitched battles, but the Chatti were discomfited and in the autumn Domitian almost certainly returned to Rome, leaving the commanding officers of the legions to continue the work of occupation, which lasted some time; the coins bearing the inscription 'Germania capta' date from 85. Domitian's desire, by means of the triumph and all the honours possibly assumed even before the end of 83, to take advantage of the success to throw his own person into particular relief belongs to another chapter of his activity, that of the affirmation of his autocratic position vis-à-vis the aristocracy. The campaign in itself was useful, even if the lack of sensational victories and the particular strategy employed – the use of multiple columns directed from a headquarters in the rear – soon provoked malicious comments in Rome. But the facts known – the construction of *limites*, that is, of transverse roads, the flexible use of the cavalry, which was also accustomed to fighting on foot in forests, the compensation of the local inhabitants for land taken over for the construction of fortifications, and finally the merciful peace terms granted to the enemy – suggest that the campaign merits a favourable verdict, both from the military and the political points of view. The same verdict is indicated by the traces on the terrain of the system that Domitian created in the regions that are now Hesse, Württemberg and Franconia, with its network of palisades, forts and roads, a sort of huge outfield in front of the legionary bases, occupied, as if by advanced sentinels, by garrisons of auxiliary troops, the garrisons that subsequently moved up to the periphery and merged under Hadrian and Antoninus Pius into the definitive linear *limes*. The systematic design behind this work is also demonstrated by the above-mentioned creation, not later than 90, of the regular provinces of Upper and Lower Germany, while the resulting possibility of reducing the Rhine forces to six legions (in 92, when the XIV *Gemina* followed the XXI *Rapax* to the Danube), to the benefit of the more seriously threatened Danube frontier, can also figure on the credit side of Domitian's policy: 'provinciis consuluit'.[1]

The second war was against the Dacians. For some time the greatest pressure from tribes outside the empire had been exerted on the Lower Danube, and if this was the principal reason for halting the war in Caledonia, which may have been regarded as a needless expense once the aim of protecting the province had been achieved, it is not one that

[1] FRONTIN., *Strat.*, I, 1, 8.

reflects any discredit on Domitian, apart from his coolness to Agricola. On the left bank of the Danube Roman influence had been spreading for some years in the form of client relationships. Since the time of Tiberius the Quadi and the Marcomanni, tribes of German stock (Suebi), had been unswervingly loyal; their princes Sido and Italicus had recently fought in Italy for Vespasian. The Iazyges, a Sarmatian people dwelling between the Danube and the Tisia (Tuza), were more restless, but they too were clients of the Romans, like many of the trans-Danubian tribes facing Moesia. The Dacians, however, the main body of whom occupied the uplands of Transylvania, had been threatening the empire for years, and to their pressure was added, on the lowest part of the river, that of the Roxolani of Bessarabia. The tension became dangerous when the Dacians succeeded in forming an extensive unified state. But it is also difficult to reconstruct the course of this first Dacian war of Domitian's; provoked by one of the many incursions of the Dacians into Moesia, probably in the winter of 85, it developed in 86 with two expeditions. The first, in which the emperor took part, was in fact the sequel to the discomfiture of the governor Oppius Sabinus, who was defeated and killed in the province by the Dacians. Under the leadership of their king, Diurpaneus, they had crossed the Danube in winter on the pretext of fearing a Roman invasion and of therefore wishing to forestall it. This first operation, carried out with large forces (five, possibly even six or seven legions, with the appropriate auxiliary troops and the praetorian cohorts) and commanded in the field by the praetorian prefect Cornelius Fuscus in person, while Domitian exercised strategic control from a town in Moesia, ended, though after a hard struggle, in the Romans' favour. The Dacians were driven back across the Danube. Peace proposals put forward by Decebalus, who had emerged as new king of the Dacians during the course of the war, were rejected, but a second Roman thrust into enemy territory ended in a disaster, in which Cornelius Fuscus himself perished, the Roman camp was taken and a standard was also captured, either that of a praetorian cohort or possibly the eagle of the V *Alaudae* legion, which would thus have ended its career on this occasion. It is uncertain whether Domitian was still in Moesia during these events or whether he had already returned to Rome. He was certainly in Rome in the summer of 86 for the inauguration of the Capitoline games. Although it is almost certain that the monument near the Tropaeum Traiani at Adamklissi in the Dobruja commemorates those who fell with Fuscus, it is difficult to believe that it marks the site of the battle, for Fuscus crossed the Danube. But the fact that the division of the province of Moesia into two parts, *Superior* and *Inferior*, belongs to this period is a significant confirmation of the attention demanded by this sector of the frontier.

The defeat of Fuscus did not remain unavenged for long. But to continue to deal with this military activity so far as possible chronologically, the year 84–85, or possibly 85–86, witnessed the operations in Africa against the Nasamones, who rebelled and were defeated by the commander of the III *Augusta* legion, Flaccus, and also a war, perhaps in 84–85, in Mauretania. These were probably only episodes – fragments that have survived – in the long struggle to defend the territory colonized by the Romans and to find a line that could be organized as a *limes*. Other indications of this struggle are the movement of the garrisons towards the south and the west – as described earlier – and the temporary placing of Mauretania under the administration of a governor. This is almost all we know by way of facts – so poor is our information – about the vast region which moved into the foreground of the empire's life only under Hadrian, though certainly not suddenly.

In 88, we are told, operations on the Danube were resumed. And in fact no fresh salutes as *imperator* are recorded for 87, while a good seven (XV to XXI) follow in 88 and 89, two of them between 14 September and 7 November 88. This time, too, it seems difficult to determine the chronological sequence of events in the campaign and Domitian's part in them, complicated as the picture is by the simultaneous occurrence in Germany of the activity connected with the revolt of Saturninus. The new campaign was mounted with care. Legion IV *Flavia Felix*, already employed in 86, now moved finally from Dalmatia to Moesia and if, as is probable, the I and II *Adiutrix* were already in that theatre of war, there was certainly no further thought of sending them back to the bases in Germany and Britain whence they came. In any case, the auxiliary units despatched to the Danube had not been back for years to their original stations. There is even evidence that an urban cohort, the XIII, from Carthage, was present in these operations. Domitian also chose the most suitable commander. The ex-consul Tettius Julianus who was now sent to the Danube had already commanded the VII *Claudia* in Moesia and in 69 had been among those rewarded by Otho for the success against the Roxolani. Having, among other things, restored discipline, he marched against the Dacians and advanced into their territory, almost reaching Decebalus's capital, Sarmizegetusa, though we do not know from what base or by what road. We only know that almost certainly in the autumn of 88, while Domitian was still engaged at Rome in the celebration of the *Ludi Saeculares*, Tettius gained at Tapae, possibly near the Iron Gate pass (not to be confused with the well known Iron Gates on the Danube), a great victory. It seems, however, that either deceived by Decebalus about the real strength of his forces or else, more probably, because of the onset of winter, he did not advance any further. Nevertheless, the Dacians sued for peace. At this point, it appears, we should place the personal intervention of the Emperor, who came from the Rhine, possibly bringing with him Legion XXI *Rapax*, one of those that had revolted. But meanwhile the situation on the whole Danube frontier had become more complicated. The client peoples bordering on Pannonia, the Marcomanni, and the Quadi, and also the Iazyges, probably encouraged by the defeat of Fuscus and the enterprise of Decebalus, and possibly also under pressure in the rear from the general restlessness of the Germanic and Sarmatian tribes, were refusing to honour their obligations as clients of the Romans and had already refused to send reinforcements for the Dacian war. Ostensibly on the pretext of punishing them for defaulting in this way, Domitian was forced to confront them, especially since they had been further irritated by the massacre of one of their delegations, which probably included some deserters. This was the salvation of Decebalus, who got his peace, on terms that seemed shameful to the anti-Domitian tradition but in fact were no different from those normally granted to client kingdoms, even down to the clause, which seemed scandalous, granting financial and technical aid to build fortifications and works of public utility. However, Roman forces were able to make use of Dacian territory for the war against the Iazyges, Marcomanni and Quadi, so that they could be attacked from Dacia as well as frontally from Pannonia. Almost nothing is known of the operations, which were directed by the Emperor from a headquarters, as usual, but it does not look as if they were particularly successful. There must have been some reverse, and in any case the war was not concluded in 89, which was only the first of a long series of restless years in this area. When Domitian returned to Rome towards the autumn he celebrated a triumph over the Chatti (that is, for victory over Saturninus) and the Dacians; but there was no allusion to the Danubian Germans or the Sarmatians.

The war was resumed in 92 in grand style, with the Emperor taking part in person. He had already tried to use the weapons of diplomacy. If certain fragments of information in Cassius Dio (LXVII, 5, 1–3) are to be referred to this moment, Domitian had devoted some attention to creating friendships among the Germans, particularly those in the rear of the Suebi. Besides granting financial assistance in 89 or 90 to Cariomerus, king of the Cherusci, to help him recover the kingdom from which he had

been expelled by the Chatti, about the same time he gave a splendid welcome to Masua, king of the Semnones – a Suebian tribe residing in
Upper Saxony to the north of the Marcomanni – who had come to Rome
with the priestess Ganna to pay homage to the Emperor. But the despatch
into the heart of free Germany of a contingent, though a small one, of
cavalry to help the Lugii of Silesia, who were engaged in a war with the
Suebi, in other words with the Marcomanni and Quadi, provoked an unexpected irruption of the latter, in combination with the Iazyges, into
Roman Pannonia. The bill for this was footed by one whole legion,
probably the XXI *Rapax*, which was annihilated with its commander. As
usual, little is known of the campaign that followed. The absence of
Domitian in Rome lasted eight months, from May 92 to 1 or 2 January
93. It must be assumed that, employing the powerful forces available on
the Danube (from this time onwards the garrison of Pannonia alone consisted of four legions and five were permanently stationed in the two
Moesias) and also summoning some detachments (*vexillationes*) from the
Rhine, he not only expelled the invaders from the province but also
advanced into their territory, defeating the Iazyges in particular. In fact
the war was known as the Sarmatian war and it was for the victory over
the Sarmatians that Domitian offered the crown to Jupiter and assumed
the unofficial title of *Sarmaticus*. The contest with the Marcomanni and
Quadi remained unfinished. However, no campaigns are recorded for the
last few years of the reign, and in the troubled peace guarded by the
formidable legionary camps, now all abutting on the great river (there is
reason to think that Brigetio and Aquincum also date from Domitian's
time), the exile Dio of Prusa carried out his trips among the Sarmatians and
Dacians and by his study of the 'primitive peoples' helped from this
frontier of the empire to feed the same politico-moral debate to which a
little later Tacitus was to bring the material concerning the Germans:
an interesting back-drop to the moral relationship between the empire and
the tribes outside it, a relationship that became more and more conscious
as the wall of physical defence rose and became permanent.

As for the East, throughout the reign we hear no report of any warlike
activity apart from the above-mentioned episode of the false Nero, and if
one can speak of an eastern policy in connection with Domitian it consisted entirely in preserving his father's system of keeping watch on
Armenia and the Parthians from Cappadocia and, in the rear, from the
client princedoms of the Caucasus, where the inscription of a centurion of
Legion XII *Fulminata*, recently found in the area of Baku,[1] indicates the

[1] *Ann. Ép.*, 1951, No. 263.

presence, as under Vespasian, of Roman soldiers occupied on garrison duties and in building fortifications.

THE TERROR AND THE END

After the campaign of 92 Domitian never left Rome again and urban events alone came to occupy the foreground. After Agricola's death the trials became more frequent; the special target was the circle which, adhering to republican ideals and cultivating the memory of the Stoic martyrs Thrasea Paetus and Helvidius Priscus, was destined, by the very attractiveness of the noble motives for its aversion to the despot, to leave the broadest impression on a tradition predominantly coloured by philosophy. And certainly, even if the opposition was not only of this kind and was inspired, especially in circles closer to the Princeps, by the somewhat more realistic motives of fear and self-defence, the philosophical sources and the Jewish and Christian tradition do provide a glimpse, in this last phase of the struggle, of the intervention to some extent of ideological and religious factors. The condemnation of Helvidius Priscus – son of Vespasian's opponent of the same name, an ex-consul living in dignified retirement – like the condemnations of Junius Arulenus Rusticus and of Herennius Senecio, certainly came about as a reaction to anti-imperial Stoicism, possibly not only on the part of Domitian but also on the part of a Senate irritated by utopian extremism, which only succeeded in exasperating the Emperor's vicious inclinations with consequent danger to everyone. It was in the Senate that the trials were conducted and senators upheld the charge, even if tradition speaks of a senate-house encircled by soldiers and of the grim presence of Domitian. All three were found guilty and executed, apparently because of their writings, that is, for expressing their opinion. The first had written a mythological farce in which Domitian claimed to recognize himself and the two others had composed the panegyrics of Thrasea Paetus and Helvidius the elder. Their relations and friends were also persecuted: Arria and Fannia, the widows of Thrasea and Helvidius respectively, were banished and their property confiscated, a fate that also overtook Arulenus Rusticus's wife, Verulana Gratilla, and his brother, Junius Mauricus.

These incidents probably took place in 93 and 94, but it subsequently becomes difficult to trace the chronological sequence of events either in the tradition of continuous political terror or in the still more confused tradition of the relations with philosophers, thaumaturges and religious sects. Uncertainty surrounds in particular the date of the *senatusconsultum* expelling all philosophers from Rome and Italy, a measure affecting, among others, Epictetus. However, the death of T. Flavius Clemens in 95 marked a definite turning-point: the beginning of the end. A mild man, cousin to Domitian, father of the two boys designated for the succession and the Emperor's colleague in the ordinary consulship assumed by Domitian in 95 only at the insistent request of the Senate, he had hardly laid down his office after four months when he was implicated with his wife Domitilla and others in a trial which cost him his life, while Domitilla was banished to Pandataria. The death of Acilius Glabrio, already in exile since 91, is probably also to be connected with this episode. The accusation made against them of *atheótes*, that is, of impiety vis-à-vis the state religion, fits in perfectly with the views of Domitian and thus gave rise even in antiquity to the supposition that Clemens and his family had embraced Christianity and that their fall formed part of a persecution expressly directed by the Emperor against the Christians. But the late writers who actually speak of formal edicts of persecution can hardly be regarded as reliable sources of information. Certainly something of what has come down to us concerning the inquisitive and morbid attitude of Domitian to men and ideas belonging to the philosophical sects and to foreign religions may be true. Nevertheless, the stories are clearly tendentious and rhetorically elaborated, whether they deal with the interrogations and lectures of Apollonius of Tyana[1] or with the conversation with the two Jews,[2] which is supposed to have induced the despot to revoke the order, already given, for the execution of all the descendants of David in the fear that this stock would produce a rival (an obvious repetition and application to the supreme emperor of the famous Herod episode). The greatest value we can give to such anecdotes is that of confirming an acute and open conflict with an opposition furnished, for the first time to such a significant degree, with spiritual nourishment by philosophy and foreign religious beliefs. It is natural that many blows should have fallen on the Jewish element, which had been exposed since the time of Gaius to suspicion and recurrent police measures on the part of the state; and it is also natural that Christians as well should have felt the effects of the full enforcement of such measures encouraged by Domitian: St John the Apostle's exile in Patmos (93–96) was a specific case of this.

Apart from this side of the situation – certainly an interesting one since it involved much wider strata of society in the anti-imperial

[1] PHILOSTR., *Vit. Apoll.*, VII, 4. 9–10, 29–34.
[2] HEGESIPP., in EUSEB., *Hist. Eccles.* III, 19. 20, 1–6; cf. OROS., VII, 10, 6.

polemic – the struggle went on and was resolved in the more restricted circle that may be described as politically qualified in the traditional sense. The death of Flavius Clemens alarmed even Domitian's closest collaborators, especially as it was followed, amid the usual steady series of condemnations of senators, by the prosecution of the praetorian prefects (their names are unknown) and by the execution of the secretary *a libellis*, Epaphroditus, for being the person who almost thirty years before had helped Nero to commit suicide. The last days of the reign passed in a desperate duel. The Emperor felt more and more threatened and sought to protect himself by all kinds of cruel tricks: 'callida et inopinata saevitia'.[1] Those under suspicion, having exhausted the resources of flattery to no avail, now turned their thoughts to assassination. The new praetorian prefects, Petronius Secundus and Norbanus, the chamberlain, Parthenius, whose privilege of wearing a sword placed him on a par with the praetorian prefects, Epaphroditus's successor as *a libellis*, Entellus, and a number of senators took decisive action, after agreeing on the choice of a successor in the person of the former consul, M. Cocceius Nerva, and quite probably with the connivance of the empress herself. The actual executor of the plan, which was designed with the shrewdness necessary to overcome all the precautions of the extremely suspicious Emperor, was the freedman Stephanus, a steward of the exiled Domitilla. Obtaining access to the Emperor on the pretext of presenting a petition, he attacked him and stabbed him to death after a fierce struggle. Stephanus was killed immediately by the first people to reach the scene, but the plot had succeeded. On the same day, 18 September 96, Nerva was hailed as Princeps.

So ended, in the prime of life (Domitian was then forty-five), the career of the third Flavian emperor; the long struggle which he had tenaciously waged with the aristocracy to carry through his policy of absolutism had resulted in failure. His death meant the disappearance of a Princeps possibly even more detested than Nero, if it was to denigrate him even further that the physical characteristic which distinguished him from his predecessor along the path of despotism was added by Juvenal to his description of Domitian: 'calvus Nero'.[2] Reserved and bad-tempered, tall but not well proportioned, with a face that always looked flushed and large weak eyes,[3] Domitian was certainly not a man who inspired affection; and the harshness with which he pursued a well-defined aim confirmed in the view of those who suffered it the sinister promise of his character and appearance; hence the tragic end to the long conflict and his

---

[1] SUET., *Dom.*, 11, 1.   [2] JUVEN., *Sat.*, IV, 38; cf. SUET., *Dom.*, 18, 2.
[3] SUET., *Dom.*, 18, 1; cf. TAC., *Agr.*, 45.

total condemnation by the tradition. But that conflict and the final defeat formed only one aspect and certainly a negative one of a career not without great merits: the characteristic merits of that Flavian dynasty which, occupying the throne for the space of a single generation, succeeded in consolidating the Roman state in its concrete governmental structure, which counted more than anything else for the prosperity of the empire.

VIII

NERVA

SUCCESSION AND WORK

The emergence of Nerva looks at first sight like an experiment so surprising in the history of the principate as to call for a brief examination of the causes and circumstances of the succession and of the real nature of the régime that followed it. Apparently the Senate had achieved its old aim of putting one of its own members on the throne and keeping him there. In reality the fact that the principate was what it had always been, that is, government by an autocrat, was clearly demonstrated by Nerva himself in his adoption of Trajan and nomination of him as successor. In any case, the Senate had only participated in the replacement of the Princeps and it had certainly not been in the forefront of events. The praetorian prefects and the palace had taken the initiative and played the chief part in the plan's execution. That senators should have taken part in the conspiracy was natural, their class being still the best qualified in public life as well as the one most exposed to Domitian's blows; and that a senator should have been nominated as Princeps was just as natural, not only for the same reasons but also because in the atmosphere of 'libertas' which was bound to follow the elimination of the aristocracy's tyrannical oppressor the utilization of the Senate, at any rate formally, was bound to be an essential element. But Nerva was not elected by the Senate, which confined itself to approving with applause and congratulations the choice made by the praetorian prefects, the palace ministers and the group of senators in contact with the conspirators.

Why Nerva was chosen and why he accepted, abandoning a life which until then had been a masterpiece in the art of balancing, to expose himself to the risks of a situation full of unknown factors is another problem. Cassius Dio's explanation (LXVII, 15, 5), 'because he was extremely noble and amiable and had been exposed to danger under Domitian', contains only part of the truth. Nerva was in fact one of the few senators belonging to the old republican nobility and was among the most senior in rank; in 93, together with others, he had run into some kind of trouble and had endured, it seems, a brief exile, either enforced or simply self-imposed for reasons of prudence. This sufficed nevertheless to place him, though not too decisively, in the anti-Domitian camp, even though he had been *consul ordinarius* in 90 with the Princeps. But other considerations may have made him unanimously acceptable. His mildness guaranteed the Senate deference for the future and removed the worry of investigations into the past. Moreover, his own previous life, so wonderfully well balanced, ensured that he was still on friendly terms with all those who, after less than thirty years, may have retained their fondness for the Julio-Claudian family and who remembered that, apart from being related to that family, he had been dear to Nero. With the Flavian senators, he had gone through the traditional career – right from the start he had been in such favour with the new dynasty that he was the only person taken by Vespasian as his colleague in the consulship outside Titus (in 71) – and with them he had lately shared the dangers, though not to such an extent as to be the declared enemy of those who presumably still felt some affection for Domitian: primarily the praetorian guards and possibly the armies, whose possible reactions had also to be taken into account. Cause for calm on that side may have been seen in the fact that Nerva, as far as we know, had never held any military commands and was therefore in a position of neutrality with regard to the big army commanders. Finally he had neither children nor close relatives; with him the family would come to an end. This consideration must have been decisive, for the Senate probably thought that at his death, possibly in the not far distant future, it would be in a position to control the choice of a successor, thus re-inforcing the vague and in practice illusory principle that the emperor should emerge from the Senate. As for the reasons that can have induced Nerva to embark on what looked from every angle like an adventure, those are more difficult to specify. That he was totally unaware of the risks and accepted out of sheer naïvety is not suggested for a moment by our sources and is unthinkable in such a shrewd man. On the other hand, his very temperament and his, so to speak, characteristically neutral position, exclude the possibility that he meant to avenge the wrongs possibly done to him by Domitian. Ambition may have helped to make the idea of the position of eminence to which he was called look attractive to him and to make the burden of responsibility look less heavy, but it seems unlikely that this was his principal motive. Nor was Nerva the man to make up his mind suddenly to sacrifice himself to the common good. He really accepted because he felt what everyone felt: that with the disappearance from the scene of the Flavian dynasty, at a moment of uncertainty and suspense, only a man who represented an equilibrium between parties waiting, but ready to clash, could offer any real hope of a relaxation of tension. This man with a widespread reputation for moderation and liberality, who was cultured, eloquent, expert in law, and certainly bound by personal acquaintance and influential relationships to a vast circle of people, seemed to be the person best fitted to achieve the common hope.

In actual fact the situation was calm but extremely delicate. Amid the indifference of the populace and the suppressed restlessness of the praetorian guards, and while the reaction of the legions still hung in the balance, the Senate, forgetting its dignity and also its habitual prudence, gave vent to its hatred of the fallen tyrant, destroying statues, voting the revocation of his decrees and a 'damnatio memoriae' which was executed in Rome and Italy, as the inscriptions show, with savage pedantry, and finally passing on to personal vendettas with an impetuosity successfully bridled in fact by Nerva. It was his first successful act of government and one that redounds to his credit, if indeed the end of the jubilation is not to be connected with the subsequent attitude of the praetorian cohorts which, although recalcitrant, were at first kept in check by their prefects until for reasons that are obscure they regained the upper hand. The armies and the provincial governors were the real unknown factor; however, apart from some slight indications of restlessness, they made no move, possibly because they too were waiting to see how the situation developed. The foreseeable and much-feared tragedy which could have brought back the horrors of 68–69 did not break out. If this was due simply to the happy choice of Nerva on the part of a few senators in conjunction with the commanders of the praetorian guard and the palace officials, this fact is in itself very interesting; but it may be supposed that other, deeper causes operating at the time exerted their inflence to produce a better end to a situation so similar to the one that followed the disappearance of Nero. Since then a profound change had taken place in the balance of the empire's forces, in its social structure and possibly in its civil customs, a change there is no reason not to attribute largely to the efforts of the Flavian emperors, Domitian included. Order having been restored and the idea of the Princeps as the exclusive physical apex of this order having henceforth become something that was no longer questioned, the effectiveness of an enlightened but inflexible central power was felt for the first time in all sections of the imperial organization and was regarded as the guarantee of the now definitive and immutable state of human life under Roman sway. Italy and the provinces had drawn the greatest benefit from the 'pax Flavia' and the municipal bourgeoisie which was flourishing just at that time gained from the conditions of general security an increase in prosperity and a good reason for not wanting any change. It was natural that such feelings should be shared to some extent by the armies, closely linked as they were to the populations of the provincial municipalities from which the legionaries were recruited and which on the whole also provided the officers, themselves connected, in the senior grades, with the Senate. The new reality was the provincial world, with its conservative interests, its demand for order and its whole complex of sane forces and honest principles. The Flavian emperors, seeking to enforce despotism, created order and made it possible for the apparent bankruptcy of their policy to give rise to the so-called 'liberal empire'. That is why, when an emperor was eliminated on the initiative of a small number of men, the consequences did not go beyond the ill-humour of the most pampered of the military units; and the provincial commanders, no longer for the most part ambitious, unpredictable nobles from the capital, friends and rivals of the Princeps, but solid functionaries, preferred the interests of the empire, or at any rate prudent delay, to a struggle for the succession masquerading under the pious pretext of avenging the dead emperor.

The senator chosen to succeed the dead man, M. Cocceius Nerva, began to rule under the name of Imperator Nerva Caesar Augustus and with all the powers and prerogatives of his predecessors. His first enactments concerned the Senate alone. We know nothing about the donative to the soldiers, though coins of 96 record a *congiarium* to the people. But granted the uncertainty of the situation, an uncertainty due precisely to the military element, and seeing that the praetorians were appeased in the early days of the reign, it is reasonable to assume that the donative was in fact paid, especially as the instructive memory of the fatal consequences of Galba's refusal on a similar occasion certainly remained alive. A whole series of measures – tangible expression of the recovery of 'libertas' as it was understood by the senatorial class – was immediately taken to dispel the atmosphere of fear and suspicion generated by Domitian's hatred of the aristocracy. This aristocracy had no aspirations beyond the attainment of personal security, and the measures all seem to be inspired by this pre-occupation. Nerva made these concessions with a good grace and perhaps even gave too much trust to the Senate, which did not know how to repay him with its support at the critical moment when the praetorians revolted.

First in order of time must have come the undertaking not to sentence to death any senator; thus was affirmed the principle of the Senate's independence of the emperor's criminal jurisdiction. This, if it was a safeguard against caprice – though rather a theoretical one, since the extent of its practical application seems to have depended for almost a century on the personal attitude of the emperor concerned – led on the other hand under Nerva, and also under Trajan, to those theatrically arranged and scandalously prejudiced senatorial trials recorded so vividly by Pliny. Naturally those who had been accused under Domitian of impiety were immediately released; such accusations, and that of Judaism, were forbidden for the future, and people who had already been condemned on this and similar charges hastened to return from exile. However, to judge from the case of Valerius Licinianus, who had been banished for the scandal with the Vestal Cornelia and was allowed only a change in his place of exile by Nerva, all this was done with some discernment. Persons of merit – Junius Mauricus, Arria and Fannia, Dio Chrysostom – were enabled to resume their normal lives. Another act of justice was the restoration of goods confiscated. It is also understandable that while it was being decided to melt down the statues of Domitian, not just out of hatred but also in the context of the programme of economic austerity, Nerva had to prohibit the making of any likenesses of himself in gold or silver. But the most welcome measures were certainly those which, modelled on similar ones of Titus's, authorized the Senate to take vengeance on informers. However, Dio's account (LXVIII, 1, 2) of the punishments inflicted on slaves and freedmen who had denounced their masters, and of the prohibition on the acceptance in future of accusations by such persons, together with what Pliny says (*Epist.*, IX, 13, 4) about the reprisals taken by everyone against his own enemies, 'dumtaxat minores', indicates that only people in low positions felt the full fury of the on-slaught. There were no proceedings against senators; thanks to Nerva's oath the trials would have had to be mounted by the Senate itself, and it is hardly likely that the Senate was in favour of opening enquiries that would have disquieted almost everyone. Even those senators who had been the most shameless in making accusations under Domitian, men like M. Aquilius Regulus – the only person of whom the mild Pliny speaks with disdain – and Fabricius Veiento, did not suffer serious harm; the former was not even expelled from the Senate and the latter not only dared later to speak on behalf of Publicius Certus, another man of the same stamp, when he was accused by Pliny of being responsible for the condemnation of Helvidius Priscus, but was even able to sit at table with the Emperor. When the conversation turned on one occasion at that table to Catullus Messalinus, the fierce blind informer who had died before Domitian, and

Nerva asked what his fate would have been if he were still alive, Junius
Mauricus replied, 'He would be here at dinner with us'. And we know
how this charge of Pliny's was to end – a charge made out of vanity and the
desire to show off, at a time when it was now certain that, apart from
causing a little gossip, it would fall on the empty air, without harming
anyone. The exclusion of benefits and privileges from the general revocation
of Domitian's acts must also be regarded as belonging to the same order
of ideas.

Nerva's concern to support the Senate is thus evident. But it does not
look as if one can speak of a 'senatorial principate'. Apart from the advice
of individual senators, his friendly contacts with all of them, and an
ostentatious parity in public relations (he caused 'aedes publicae' to be
written on the façade of the palace, and this was certainly not just to
indicate officially the residence of the pontifex maximus), he received
nothing more from the Senate as a whole than acclamations and the usual
congratulations. For his own part, following in the wake of the Augustan
tradition, like the 'bad' Princeps who preceded him and the 'good' ones
who followed him, he was 'lord' in fact and by right. If any significance
is to be assigned to the account of the conspiracy of C. Calpurnius Piso
Crassus Frugi Licinianus, a fanatic who repeated his attempt against
Trajan and came to a bad end under Hadrian, but who on this occasion,
according to Cassius Dio (LXVIII, 3, 2), also enjoyed the support of
other senators, we must assume a certain amount of senatorial ill-will
towards Nerva for being much less submissive to the Senate than had been
expected.

We know very little about the rest of his political activity, up to the
stormy events that led to the adoption of Trajan, and that little is too
colourless to indicate the lines of a definite policy. Among legislative
measures we are told of the veto on castration – a re-enactment of a
decree of Domitian's, of the prohibition of marriages between uncles and
nieces, of a less repressive attitude to the Jews and anyone who professed
their religion (and certainly to philosophical and religious sects in general),
and of the restoration to the public stage of pantomime, banished by
Domitian to private stages. We have clear evidence of innovations in
court customs and in the Princeps's relations with society in Pliny's
Panegyric on Trajan (47, 4; 51, 2); and we can be sure that Nerva continued his own habits of simplicity, generosity and good fellowship with
all. The appointments and nominations he made, such as those of Frontinus
as *curator aquarum*, Pliny as *praefectus aerarii Saturni* and Trajan as governor
of Upper Germany, cannot but testify to his discernment. Similarly, his

assumption of a third consulship, on 1 January 97, with the venerable senator L. Verginius Rufus – also consul for the third time – as his colleague, was a significant event, both for its recall to the political scene after a long absence of some one who had played an important part in Nero's last days and the subsequent crisis but had later stood apart during the whole Flavian period, and also because the concession of such an honour was not only a general homage to the Senate but also seems to have corresponded with a definite intention of Nerva's in his choice of senatorial colleagues – a choice that was more personal and freer than people think. For the rest, the annals show, in the now habitual assumption of the ordinary consulship by the Princeps (in 98 Nerva was still consul, naturally with Trajan) and in the large number of pairs of supplementary consuls, the continuation of Flavian criteria with regard to the qualification of men destined to be the empire's officials.

As for public works in Rome, the main one was the completion of the forum known in fact as Nerva's forum or the Forum Transitorium, which was dedicated towards the end of 97 or early in 98. An inscription to 'Libertas' put up by the Senate and people[1] does not indicate the construction of a temple but simply constituted a homage to the restorer of freedom. Another inscription[2] refers to repairs to the Colosseum (or Flavian amphitheatre), and some *horrea Nervae* are also recorded. We know from Frontinus of the care devoted to the more systematic organization of the aqueducts, and we also hear of work to repair damage resulting from Tiber floods. On the whole it is a question of normal activity, from which it is impossible to conclude either that Nerva spent a great deal of money on building or that he had any intention – which would be difficult to establish, granted the shortness of his reign – of effecting economies. This is a point that has provoked discussion between those who, accepting a bankruptcy caused by Domitian, are led to attach too much value to the reports of certain measures taken by Nerva to restore the balance and, vice versa, those who, not accepting such a bankruptcy, minimize the importance of these measures so as to arrive at a completely negative verdict on Nerva's financial policy, and not on this side of his activity alone.[3] In reality, under the new Princeps the general administration of the empire continued on its regular course and any economies that may have been made were confined to the limited field

---

[1] CIL, VI, 472 = ILS, 274.   [2] CIL, VI, 37137.

[3] For the two positions see in particular A. STEIN, in P.W., IV, 1900, cc. 143–6 and R. SYME in Journ. of Rom. St., XX, 1930, pp. 55–70 and Philologus, XCI, 1936, pp. 238–245.

of court and city expenses. These economies subsequently assumed, in a tradition that is eminently laudatory and concerned to underline the contrast with the previous régime, a wider significance than they actually possessed.

Nerva's financial measures were in fact of only modest practical importance. They were not intended to deal with a non-existent situation of general disaster but simply to inaugurate, possibly more for moral and propagandist reasons than through financial necessity, a habit of austerity. In tune with this aim was the search for ways of raising money, ways which were certainly not sufficient to restore to health the ailing finances of a ruined state but were obvious enough to serve as an edifying example: the personal economies of the 'frugalissimus princeps', the sale of private and imperial property, the reduction in the number of shows and sacrifices. Even the senatorial commission created 'minuendis publicis sumptibus' had a somewhat ornamental function belonging to the same order of ideas. Moreover, the measures taken on the fiscal side correspond to the demand for universal justice which was becoming a more and more accepted part of the empire's now declared paternalism; this is true, for example, of the abolition of certain additional taxes which had been imposed on cities by way of punishment, of the more equitable application of taxes to the Jews, of the relief granted to the Italians from the burden of the 'vehiculatio', and of the creation of a praetor (who took the place of the *fideicommissarius* suppressed by Titus) to deal with disputes between the fisc and private individuals. Nor could Nerva fail to continue, according to the same criteria, the work of social levelling initiated by the Flavians in Italy and the provinces, either with measures of the sort in the air at the time, such as – it seems – institutes for the provision of food and encouragements to public benefaction, or with more traditional measures like the distribution of land on an individual basis (decreed by a law which was the last comitial one of the empire), colonizing activity and the infinite variety of interventions documented, as usual, by inscriptions and proving, by the very extensiveness of the finds and their relative abundance for the shortness of the reign, the wide interest taken by the Princeps in such matters. In Italy and in every part of the empire there is evidence of Nerva's active presence. What is particularly noteworthy is the attention given to the roads; there were substantial repairs to the Via Appia and other important ones in Spain, Gaul and Asia Minor.

So far as defence is concerned, the epithet 'Nervia' or 'Nerviana' assumed by some auxiliary formations and the two military diplomas known, one dating from the early days of the reign (10 October 96) and referring to cohorts stationed in Sardinia, the other dating from 97 and dealing with units from Moesia, bear witness to the continuation under this most civilian of emperors of all the normal military privileges. There are only a few uncertain reports of military operations. Vestricius Spurinna's march through the territory of the Bructeri, the chronology of which is uncertain, is even less likely to belong to this period than to others that have been suggested (see above, p. 255). The title of *Germanicus*, assumed by Nerva towards the end of 97 and extended to Trajan, the arrival of the news of a Pannonian victory right in the middle of the ceremony of adoption and the reference in an inscription to a 'bellum Suebicum' of Nerva's[1] are to be linked and taken to indicate some episode or other – possibly of no great importance but opportunely incorporated in the imperial propaganda – in the series of conflicts, left unfinished under Domitian, with the Germanic peoples on the other side of the Danube, in other words with the Quadi and Marcomanni.

THE ADOPTION OF TRAJAN AND THE END

Nerva's surprise move of adopting M. Ulpius Traianus, the governor of Upper Germany whom he had himself appointed some months before, and of taking him as co-ruler, are usually, and rightly, placed in close and immediate connection, in accordance with the evidence of Pliny (*Panegyric*, 6–7), with the action taken by the praetorian guards under the leadership of the new prefect, Casperius Aelianus, presumably in the summer of 97. The praetorians are supposed to have called on Nerva to punish the men who had killed Domitian. His resistance, and the offer of his own life instead, were of no avail; he was brushed aside, and he not only had to suffer impotently the execution of Petronius and Parthenius but even to thank the avengers in a public speech. No one else, not even the Senate, moved a finger to help him. The affair was a serious impairment of the imperial authority itself and, although limited to the field of the already rather stormy relations between Nerva and the praetorian guard, unquestionably damaged the old emperor's prestige. In fact something rather mysterious had occurred. Casperius Aelianus, even if we discount a later tradition that made him a friend of Apollonius of Tyana, and hence presumably of Nerva, was among the men set aside by Domitian, who replaced him, possibly in 94, with Petronius. Granted that he was still popular with the praetorians, his reinstatement in office might have served for the complete pacification of the guard. But if this was the

[1] *CIL*, V, 7425 = *ILS*, 2720; cf. *Ann. Ép.*, 1923, 28.

calculation that induced Nerva to substitute Casperius for Norbanus, one of the two prefects in office, both of them loyal, it turned out to be false. The whole matter came to an end – so it seems – once satisfaction had been obtained, and Casperius continued to be simply praetorian prefect, but Nerva turned the lesson to unexpected account and, thinking above all of his own age and of the need for security, decided personally on the act which was to have such happy and long-lasting consequences.

Towards the end of October 97 he went up to the Capitol to lay on Jupiter's knees the laurel from the 'litterae laureatae' that had arrived with the news of a victory in Pannonia, and to celebrate a sacrifice. By the altar, in the presence of a large crowd, he spoke aloud the formula of adoption, which was certainly heard with amazement, and at once also proclaimed Trajan – as his son – Caesar. On a second occasion, in the Senate, he had him acclaimed *imperator* and arranged for the *tribunicia potestas* to be conferred on him. When Nerva assumed the victorious epithet 'Germanicus' he gave it to Trajan as well; and in addition he nominated him as his colleague in the consulship due to begin on 1 January 98. Trajan was thus co-ruler and successor designate. His agreement was certainly secured in advance, and there is no occasion to discuss the form of this adoption from the legal point of view and in comparison with that of Piso by Galba. Probably Nerva worried little more about the legal forms than Galba had. The only difference was that he was more astute and was able to take advantage of more favourable circumstances. The unexpected and also extremely public and sensational proclamation, more or less consecrated as it was by religion, confronted everyone with a *fait accompli* while at the same time the general situation revealed no serious reasons for conflict. The armies were quiet; the violent attitude of the praetorian guards had abated once they had extorted satisfaction; and the unexpected decision had left no time for the emergence of anyone inclined to oppose Trajan, who in any case enjoyed the favour of almost all the armies. The situation had been very different in Galba's time: the adoption of Piso, a man who among other things was not acceptable to the soldiers, came as no surprise to parties already in conflict and, presented indecisively, merely provided a fresh element of discord.

As for the advice that Nerva may have listened to, what the sources say about the Spaniard L. Licinius Sura as the principal author of Trajan's nomination is rendered extremely plausible by the fact that Sura, who had himself long been operating on the Rhine, may in practice, through the contiguity of his command and the friendship which always bound him to his fellow-countryman, have exerted considerable influence during the preparatory phase of Nerva's decision. Nerva for his part must already have cast his eye on the energetic and upright general in the moment of crisis that followed the death of Domitian, and he had given him the most important military command. It is not possible to discern other influences. In particular there is no sign at all of any initiative by the Senate; and it is by no means unlikely that Nerva's action came as a bigger surprise to the Senate than to anyone else, for it now had to abandon once for all – thanks precisely to the efforts of the frail old man who had emerged shortly before from its own ranks – the illusion that it could dispose of the throne as it pleased. Cassius Dio (LXVIII, 4) says explicitly that Nerva took account only of Trajan's personal merit in adopting him and paid little attention to the fact that he had relations of his own, though not close ones, and above all to the fact that the man adopted was not an Italian – something so unusual as to guarantee, since it was accepted without a whisper, the validity of the reason adduced by the historian. And finally that Nerva's choice was a free one also emerges from Pliny. It is clear, among the panegyrist's pompous circumlocutions, that where he speaks (Ch. 5; cf. 23, 4; 94, 4) of the *omen* which all understood and only Trajan persisted in not wishing to understand (when, appointed governor of Upper Germany, he went up to the Capitol, the people's cry of 'salve Imperator' on the opening of the doors of the temple and the appearance of the image of *Iuppiter Imperator* was taken by everyone as an augury for Trajan and not referred to the god), we should discern no more than the universal affection surrounding Trajan before as well as after his adoption and not a genuine popular acclamation or, worse, the disguised outline of a military manifesto. Of course, Nerva wisely calculated – and *in primis* – on this circumstance. Thus even if we take into account all the external reasons which determined the decision, it is impossible not to recognize in its author that exclusively personal merit which all the ancients agree in attributing to him, even sometimes going so far as to assert, unjustly and with little regard for the facts, that in the last analysis it was the only good thing he ever did.[1]

Trajan did not come to Rome at once; he did not even come to assume the consulship on 1 January, nor did he move at the end of January when his cousin Hadrian brought to Cologne, where he happened to be at the time, the news of the death of Nerva, which had occurred on the 27th or 28th of that month. Of the activity of the two emperors in their three months of co-rulership we know nothing. But Trajan's delay indicates that the situation was quiet and that the old Princeps, dying after wisely providing for the future of the state, had opened the way to the best

[1] JORDANES, *Rom.*, 266.

hopes. After the funeral Nerva's ashes were laid in the mausoleum of Augustus and at the instance of Trajan, who took part from a distance in all the honours with an outward show at any rate of filial piety, his apotheosis was voted at once by the Senate. Trajan, sole and unopposed emperor, did not arrive in Rome until the spring or summer of 99. The empire, both at its centre and in the provinces, continued to enjoy the effects of the vigorous and ordered administration which it had acquired under the Flavians and which Nerva had known how to preserve.

IX

TRAJAN

OPTIMUS PRINCEPS

Although the new Princeps was absent from Rome, his position was so secure that Casperius Aelianus, the turbulent praetorian prefect, could not fail to obey the order to report to his headquarters where, together with his accomplices, he paid with his life for the outrage inflicted on Nerva. The peacefulness of the situation also made it possible to complete without haste the new arrangements on the Rhine frontier. These arrangements continued Domitian's policy, which had already been adopted by Trajan himself as Caesar and was intended to make troops available for a resumption of the campaigns on the Danube. The arrangements are not known in detail; that at the moment of succession Trajan was at Cologne, in Lower Germany, may signify that after his adoption he exercised his *imperium maius* over both the Germanies and attended personally to their reorganization, which may even have included some military operations. The importance attached to this sector of the frontier is indicated by the names of the governors left in command of Upper and Lower Germany respectively, L. Julius Ursus Servianus and L. Licinius Sura, men even then in the very first rank of the aristocracy of Trajan's reign. Both were of Spanish origin; the former was a relation of the emperor's, the latter his intimate friend. In the winter of 98–99 Trajan made a raid across the Danube to carry out the operations which Pliny mentions (*Pan.* 12) simply so that he can describe the terror inspired in the barbarians, finally induced once more to respect the name of Rome. In reality these operations were forerunners of the big campaign of which the Emperor was certainly already thinking, as is clear from the orders given for the construction of roads and forts in the sector of attack. After all this, in the spring or at the beginning of the summer of 99, Trajan finally listened to the people's wishes and prayers and started out on his triumphal progress towards Rome. With his entry into the city the new, celebrated régime really started.

What the essential novelty of this régime, which perfected the brief experiment of Nerva, actually was, cannot easily be defined by the production of facts and measures preserved in reliable and uninterrupted chronological order. Even now there is no trace of abstract definitions dealing with the constitutional position of the Princeps and his functions or with the relationship between the Princeps and the Senate. Trajan was an autocrat like his predecessors, once again with universally acknowledged faithfulness to the Augustan model. The guarantees given to the senatorial class, like those already given first by Titus and then by Nerva, were gracious concessions. Apart from the collaboration, ever more committed – let us recognize the fact – and professional, of individual members of the senatorial aristocracy in the practical government of the empire, the Senate continued to be simply the assembly of *grands seigneurs* (the new *grands seigneurs* of the Flavian aristocracy), whose full-dress sittings, halfway between the meetings of a consultative assembly and those of an academy, certainly did not reveal the solid and exclusive collective care of part at least of the work of government. Yet the atmosphere which imperial society breathed had become quite different. A clear indication of this is the mental attitude of Tacitus in his judgement of previous emperors. The principle of reconciliation between freedom and principate put into practice by Trajan must have been a reality. Obviously one would need to discuss the meaning assigned at that moment and by different individuals to the always relative concept of freedom; but that such a reconciliation was in operation and distinguished the happy reality of the time is too clearly attested by contemporary opinion, which was pleased with it or content with it. It was, if only through the personal qualities of an emperor particularly sensitive to the demands of contemporary opinion, the basic reality of the age of Trajan. The state of equilibrium that had developed from the Augustan seed principally through the efforts of Claudius and Vespasian, and had matured with the formation of the new aristocracy, the new bureaucracy, the new manners and the new imperial awareness in the provinces, had now reached the fullness of perfection dynamically maintained by Trajan throughout the course of his reign. Right from the start of the reign, thanks to the conjunction of a man who was in many respects exceptional with a series of favourable circumstances, a *felicitas temporum* never before attained seemed to come into being. The contrast with the 'tyranny' and the 'tyrant' eliminated shortly before naturally increased in the eyes of those involved the difference between the two régimes and the merit of the man concerned: *optimus princeps*.

The basic testimony to the state of mind of educated Roman society,

TA—L

a mirror reflecting the state of affairs established in public relations by the advent of Trajan, is the 'thanksgiving' pronounced by Pliny when he took office as consul on 1 September of the year 100. The actions of another two years had finally confirmed the promise of the reign and bore out the universal conviction that internal security had now been attained under the liberal and enlightened rule of an ideal Princeps; for clearly the consul, in the simulated boldness of his words of exhortation, would have recommended the Emperor to do nothing that he was not already doing. Indeed, Pliny says explicitly that these speeches served precisely 'to make good emperors realize what they were doing and bad ones realize what they ought to do' (*Pan.*, 4, 1). The substantial validity of Pliny's evidence is thus indubitable, and in spite of the difficulty of the rhetorical and allusive style and the eulogistic amplifications, though these are kept within some kind of limits by independence and dignity (a completely shameless flatterer would have avoided touching, in the presence of the reigning emperor, on the theme of the succession [ch. 44]), it provides us with a precious balance-sheet of the opening period of Trajan's reign. Even the chronology is fairly precise, for as far as we can see it was not adulterated with dates known *post eventum* during the recognizable later re-working. What come out particularly clearly are the main lines of political life, even though elaborated and fixed in the subsequent literary version which we read. They almost constitute a programmatic manifesto, the senatorial manifesto of the theory of the good princeps, but not so much so as to look idealized in comparison with a reality which contemporary readers could note for themselves.

This reality remained that of the autocracy. Pliny had no illusions on the subject, and the tone of his speech does not allow us to take any other view in our general interpretation of this moment in history. But within this essential limit Pliny the senator expresses with eloquence the satisfaction of his class at the guarantees of security and dignity finally obtained in a way that seemed likely to last. The very form of the choice of Princeps, by adoption, with the probability of its being repeated, thus becoming custom if not law, promised the continuation of a system calculated to give a permanent assurance about the quality and attitude of the Princeps selected and at the same time to lessen the distance between the Princeps and the aristocracy, every member of which had the theoretical possibility of rising to the summit of the empire. This blueprint of the emperor's position, a blueprint which had been arrived at gradually by dint of various experiments beginning with that of Augustus and above all with the ever clearer development of the concept of the emperor's administrative functionality as opposed to that of mere despotic power, was followed rigorously by Trajan. His somewhat unexpected elevation to the principate had crowned a normal senatorial career, one particularly devoted, from personal taste, to military tasks.

Trajan's father had been the first man in his family to enter – in Spain – the Roman aristocracy, in fact the patriciate of the municipal aristocracy of his native Italica, and he had particularly distinguished himself under Vespasian, reaching the consulship, probably in 70, and holding successively the most important provincial commands, such as the governorship of Syria (75–79) and the proconsulship of Asia (79–80). The new Princeps thus already represented the second generation of the new Flavian nobility. Prepared for the duties of government by a practical and severe professional career which, as for many others, nullified the political effects of serving under Domitian (he was *tribunus militum* for ten years from 71, praetor towards 87, commander of a legion at the beginning of 89, when he hastened from Spain on the Emperor's orders for the war against Antonius Saturninus, and finally *consul ordinarius* in 91), with his military and civil experience, with a sense of moderation derived from familiarity with practical administration and at the same time from the solidarity which he always preserved with the class from which he sprang, object of a deference which he regarded as not only harmless but also useful, he soon gave excellent proof of his quality in the application of the new happy imperial theory, sticking nevertheless in substance to the tradition, basically unchanged, of the principate.

Thus the letter sent to the Senate after his succession to confirm the guarantee already given by Nerva not to send any senator to his death (in practice this meant the abolition of trials for treason) was promptly followed by the refusal, customary in any case, of the title of *pater patriae*, which was however accepted a little later on – this is also clear from inscriptions and coins – from the time of the consular elections of 98 for 99. His modest demeanour – he behaved almost as if he were on a par with the commanders of the legions – did not prevent him from restoring discipline in the armies, including, of course, their officers. The journey back to Rome, famous for the respect paid to the places traversed and for the care with which the relative expenses were recorded – a detail certainly belonging to the same order of ideas as the reorganization of the *cursus publicus* already promised by the Flavian emperors and Nerva – more or less symbolized for Italy and the provinces the supreme advantage of the imperial régime, that of the unity and homogeneity of the authority, with one single master to serve, so long as this master was not, in the eyes of the senators of course, a Domitian. The same feelings were inspired in the population of Rome and the upper classes of the capital by Trajan's entry into the city on foot – certainly more welcome to the Senate than to the people, which also appreciated pomp – by the continuation of his modest behaviour (easy accessibility, abolition of ceremonial, a house open to everybody, frugal meals, simplicity and virility in his personal recreations – hunting, swimming, tiring voyages), by his constant kindness and practical generosity, by his cordial and respectful attitude to his friends and his firm but not harsh treatment of dependants, by his restrained punishment of informers – all, of course, 'minores' – and by his moderation in the matter of honours. He accepted only two statues – bronze ones at that – in the hall of the temple of Capitoline Jove, thus showing in fact a curious restraint in the matter of the imperial cult, and did not wish for acclamations in the theatre or tributes of homage in the Senate. His family, especially his sister Marciana and his wife Pompeia Plotina, neither of them yet an Augusta, rivalled the Princeps, at any rate at the start, in the moderation of their mode of life. The empress who, on entering the palace for the first time, expressed the wish that she could leave it at any time unchanged,[1] reinforced the tacit agreement that there should be formal parity between the house of the Princeps and the highest families of society, in a relationship marked by consideration and discretion on both sides. As for the other members of the family, Trajan's father was certainly already dead; Salonia Matidia, the daughter of Marciana (left a widow when she was still young by C. Salonius Patruinus), had two daughters by one L. Vibius, Vibia Sabina and Vibia Matidia, the first of whom, in the year 100, was on the eve of her marriage to Hadrian, another member of the Spanish branch of the family. Thus the family was an ideal one judged by the aristocratic ideal of the age; yet for all that there were signs again of the family dynasty, a natural consequence of the principate, which always remained a despotism.

The indispensable corollaries of this reality were the object of the most careful attention right at the beginning of the reign. While the donative to the soldiers was paid in instalments – another sign of the stability of the situation – the *congiarium* to the people, at the customary rate of 75 denarii per head, was distributed at one blow – possibly on the anniversary of Trajan's succession and in any case before the consular elections of October 99 – with scrupulous care and every effort to ensure that everyone received it, even those absent through illness or business. The corn supply attained such organizational perfection that it was even found

[1] CASS. D., LXVIII, 5,5.

possible to furnish Egypt with grain when the country that usually fed Rome was smitten by famine as a result of an exceptional drought. The service of *frumentationes*, that is, the permanent distribution of free grain to those among the urban proletariat entitled to it, was perfected by the prompt addition to the lists of new names as vacancies gradually became available and by the inscription of 5,000 boys. All these measures are deliberately confused with one another and particularly with the outstanding innovation due to Trajan's humanitarianism, the *alimenta*, in the picturesque but in this field somewhat general eloquence of Pliny, who was concerned when he rewrote his speech of praise not to insert anachronisms. In fact, at the time of the *Panegyric* the *alimenta* had not yet been organized.

The important thing is that even in his initial programme Trajan was giving more attention than we should have expected from his reputation as an enlightened emperor to these and other aspects – even more demagogic ones, in our eyes – of public life. Even though we must certainly take care not to make judgements without taking into consideration the tastes and customs of the period, the unprecedented abundance of shows, and in particular of the bloodthirsty performances of the amphitheatre, betrayed too clearly somewhat crude personal inclinations and a condescension to the worst instincts of the urban throng, as well as the germ of that love of the grandiose and marvellous which subsequently grew stronger after the Emperor's victorious wars and finally carried the atmosphere of baroque and weary pomp at Rome to a zenith of splendour that was also a prelude to the decline. The humane Pliny uses the reasons already advanced by Cicero (*Tuscul.*, II, 41) in an attempt to defend the horrible combats between gladiators, whose 'pulchra vulnera' (*Pan.*, 33, 1), he says, are part of a masculine education; he could hardly fail to take this attitude in a eulogistic review in which everything was laudatory, down to the dialectic acrobatics employed to approve a step taken by Trajan – again in the field of shows – which had also been taken by Domitian but revoked by Nerva, namely the suppression of pantomimes: 'both measures were just,' says Pliny, 'for it was opportune both to restore the shows that a bad Princeps had suppressed, and to suppress them again once they had been restored'! (*Pan.*, 46, 3). Certainly as well as displaying these attitudes, which testify in any case – even if we discount Pliny's exaggerated personal loyalty – to his positive and realistic approach to things, as was already noted by men of the following generation,[1] Trajan was open to all cultural currents, even if personally he was not a refined

[1] FRONTO, *Princ. Hist.*, 18.

orator or writer. After only two years of his reign he received merited praise as an incomparable protector of literature and the arts, while Rome was embellished by his restorations and new buildings, which were not intended for his own use, but devoted to the public welfare. A good example is the enlargement, possibly already complete by the year 100 and recorded on coins and in inscriptions, of the Circus Maximus, a task achieved by knocking down Domitian's private box and using stones from his basin for naval battles, so as to provide (again!) five thousand extra seats.

We are also informed by Pliny about Trajan's administrative activity proper, and we receive the impression that the difference from Domitian's régime resided more in the way in which the organization functioned than in its substance. Pliny admires the good order of the aerarium, clearly distinguished from the fiscus, as it had been under the Flavian emperors, and reduced in function; he praises the moderation of the fiscus, the now dominant state treasury, and appreciates the frequent likelihood of private citizens' emerging victorious from lawsuits with it; the *praetor fiscalis* instituted by Nerva was retained and appointed by lot; Trajan's procurators, says Pliny, were exemplary, and the tribute paid to them by the consul in the name of the senatorial class, like that paid later on in the speech to the palace freedmen, is certainly full of significance. The security of wills and the freedom from the obligation to make bequests to the Emperor were, as usual, consequences of the Emperor's own character. The custom of giving a public account of expenditure continued the controversial opposition initiated by Nerva to the alleged financial absolutism of Domitian; and the pursuit of a more liberal policy, also initiated by his predecessor, was exemplified by the exemptions from payment of the *vicesima hereditatium*, the estate duty of 5 per cent instituted by Augustus to support the *aerarium militare* and falling exclusively on Roman citizens. Trajan now eliminated the last inconveniences deriving from this very condition, which sometimes led people to regard the acquisition of citizenship as a hardship. In fact, legacies going to close relations and legacies of small value had been exempt from the start, but since a foreigner who acquired Roman citizenship broke all legal ties with relatives, even his father or his sons, who remained without it, he lost the right to exemption. The most frequent case was that of the relationship between a father and sons born before the father had acquired citizenship: unless the special favour of the Princeps conferred on the person concerned the *patria potestas* on the *ius cognationis* with, so to speak, retrospective effect, the relationship for the purposes of inheritance was the same as that between strangers. This special favour became a right through the arrangements of Nerva and Trajan, by whom the benefits were extended liberally to new citizens as well.

Nor did it seem that the finances had necessarily suffered through this fiscal mildness: Trajan had even renounced the *aurum coronarium*, the collection made in the provinces on the occasion of an emperor's accession to the throne. In posing the problem, Pliny also indicated the right solution: parsimony on the part of the Princeps, in other words the precise and ordered functioning of the administration from top to bottom, was sufficient to keep the budget balanced. In the last analysis that was how the empire had functioned under the Flavians. So it was not surprising that Trajan should have started on the civil side of his principate by the most assiduous and active participation in the sittings of the Senate and in the administration of justice: he was equally endowed with formal deference and a real sense of administrative duty.

The consular elections of 99 for the year 100 bulk particularly large in Pliny's speech, together with the elections of praetors, aediles and tribunes held on 9 January 100 under the presidency of Trajan and also the assemblies for the proclamation of supplementary consuls (who included Pliny himself). Although everything proceeded in accordance with a prearranged plan, in conformity with the autocratic reality, the figure of the Princeps, a consul in the ancient mould, a senator among senators, certainly caused sincere emotion in the panegyrist, who otherwise would not have permitted himself to hint politely but firmly that this conduct of Trajan's should set the definitive pattern for the relations between the emperor and the Senate, at any rate when the emperor held the office of consul. In fact Pliny, placing beyond discussion the immense real superiority of the autocrat ('. . . in you alone the state exists, in you alone we all exist . . .', 'by you we are saved and to you we are subject, but in such a way as to be subject to the laws . . .'), was only exalting, if we read the final chapters of his speech aright, Trajan as consul, wishing to test (and in reality already granting as proved) the thesis that 'a good consul and a good Princeps were one and the same thing'; he was thinking, of course, of a personal union, not a constitutional one. In this way the orator expressed the pleasure of the Senate at seeing the elections being conducted in the traditional style without any special privileges for the Princeps, and at visualizing and admiring Trajan in the eyes of the barbarians as consul rather than emperor. While this may have been a rhetorical image, even in the elections we find no departure from the usages of the principate (*commendatio* by the emperor, election by the Senate, *renuntiatio* before the people) except in the personal attitude of

more emphatic respect on the part of the Princeps; and in a more decidedly constitutional field Trajan's oaths after his election as consul and
on laying down office, oaths taken before him only, it seems, by Augustus
as consul in 28 B.C.,[1] obviously concerned only the office of consul, and
their validity was thus limited in time and application, even if they
acquired from the person elected, who was the Princeps, a heightened
significance, though never such as to introduce the form of a constitutional
principate. 'You have submitted yourself to the laws' (*Pan.*, 65, 1); yes,
but always in relation to the consulate, even if the praise could be extended, in the individual case of Trajan, and as a *de facto* not a *de jure*
reality, to the Princeps. 'No longer the Princeps above the laws, but the
laws above the Princeps' (*ibid.*); this would be a surprising assertion, were
it not soon clarified and qualified: 'the things which are not lawful for
others are not lawful even for Caesar *as consul*'. This was Trajan's formal
homage – and not for that reason of small importance in the oft-illustrated
concept of the principate – to the Republic; and it was entirely his own
achievement that the words of exhortation addressed to the Senate on
1 January 100, when he took office, calling on it 'to take up freedom
again, to assume with him the care of the common empire, to watch with
him over the common good and to be zealous' (*Pan.*, 66, 2), now an empty
formula, were finally believed. As for the real facts of the situation, that
is, whether in practice the consuls and other magistrates were nominated
entirely or only in part by the Princeps, Pliny's circumlocutions are not
the sort of language ever to yield a clear answer; the consuls were certainly
all nominated by the emperor, but the other magistrates, it seems, only
in part.

Trajan, consul for the second time with Nerva on 1 January 98, had
refused the consulship for 99 but accepted it for 100, always of course,
according to Pliny, for the best of reasons. In 100, consul for the third
time (we do not know for how long), following the example of Nerva, who
in 97 had been *consul* III with Verginius Rufus, also *consul* III, he had
distinguished with the honour of a third consulship two men of great
merit, Julius Frontinus and Vestricius Spurinna, and possibly a third,
whose identity is unknown. And certainly the desire that his colleagues
should be completely equal to him in consular dignity was a demonstration calculated to mark a new era, even if his subsequent acceptance of
a fourth consulship for 101, as ardently requested by Pliny (*Pan.*, 78–9),
was soon to make it a rare occurrence in the history of the imperial
consulships.

[1] CASS. D., LIII, 2, 7; cf. CASSIOD., *Var.*, 8, 3.

Thus in the idyll produced by the restoration of equilibrium between irreconcilables it was admiration for the Princeps in the garb of consul that provided the chief focus for senatorial feelings. 'Non est hic dominus, sed imperator, sed iustissimus omnium senator' (MARTIAL, X, 72, 8-9). Appreciated for his modesty, not only through opportunism but also, at any rate according to Pliny (*Pan.*, 76, 8-9; 85, 7), through the effect of a greater maturity in general feelings and manners, liked by everyone for living on common terms with the senators, with whom he had shared – people said with some deliberate exaggeration – the dangers under the tyranny, he was not even feared in the matter of social innovations, for, since the populace had been stuffed with bread and circuses and philanthropic measures taken to remove the threat of a decrease in the size of the citizen body (the concept of *occasus imperii, occasus reipublicae* makes its explicit and significant appearance precisely in Pliny's *Panegyric*, Ch. 26), his conservatism was well tried. His complete solidarity with the aristocracy in the ever-recurrent problem of the slaves, whom he deprived of the right, utilized by the tyrants, to be heard in accusations against their masters in connection with the crime of treason, thus eliminating at the root what Pliny called a 'servile bellum' of a new kind, had already produced the greatest tranquillity on the subject,[1] and other measures were to follow in the course of the years favouring concrete aristocratic privilege, equitably allowed and guaranteed for both the descendants of the old republican nobility and the new nobles. It would have been difficult in any case to imagine any social order without this privilege. Feeling safe and grateful, nobles both of ancient lineage and of recent ascent competed for the 'iudicium principis, suffragium principis' – rewards and requisites for advancement in their careers – and restored, enlarged and embellished their houses – a sign of confidence in the future.

The Princeps, who had finally marked out the boundary between 'dominatio' and 'principatus', between despotic will and the authority of an enlightened leader, and had not assumed as official posts either the censorship (unlike Domitian) or a *praefectura morum*, because he thought that his own whole life should be a censorship by example and a perpetual censorship, thereby expressed not only a moral proposition which he put into practice by his own virtue and merit but also the political concept

---

[1] The more extensive application of torture to slaves provided for by Trajan (*Digest.*, XLVIII, 18, 1, 11 and 12), as a result of which masters came in some ways to be more seriously affected by their possible confessions, did not concern trials for treason; and the measure did not remain in force very long (*ibid.*, 19).

of the functional position of the autocrat, bound henceforth to an 'officium' which could not be evaded in any way by whoever rose to the summit of the empire. The first of the speeches 'On Ruling', delivered in the same year as Pliny's thanksgiving and also in the presence of the Emperor, by Dio Chrysostom (Or., I, 15–29), expounds in a theoretical style and with a theoretical aim the Stoic–Cynic ideal of the monarch, a man invested by divine providence with a power that is not a privilege but a duty, tied to a life that must be hard work not pleasure, the benefactor and father, not the master of his subjects; and the speech looks like a portrait of Trajan. The 'optimus princeps', physically attractive with his tall and well-built figure, in the prime of life (he was not far from fifty) but appearing more serious and dignified through early greyness, looked among his fellow citizens in every way like a father among his children. That is how he is presented in the encomiastic portrait, which is an embellished but not distorted picture of the reality: paternalism.

THE DACIAN WARS

When Pliny delivered his speech everyone knew from the preparations already made that war against the Dacians was imminent. The consul's words on the subject, all aimed at exalting the moderation of Trajan, who 'did not fear, but did not seek wars', are rather elusive, it is true, and the military aspect of the Emperor's glory is not given, at any rate in amount of space, the recognition granted to his civil virtues, so much so that one might be tempted to think that there was a secret senatorial hostility to the campaign in Dacia, had not Pliny himself, in rewriting the speech, deliberately sought and found a way of positively inserting, in the guise of prophecy, eloquent allusions to the victorious end of the war and to the triumph; and, above all, had his own ideas not corresponded, as they do correspond, with the facts revealed by the structure of Trajan's foreign policy as a whole. In spite of the thirst for glory attributed to him by the ancients and the reputation for being the warrior emperor *par excellence* conferred on him by modern historians, it emerges fairly clearly that Trajan did not seek war for war's sake. The peaceful situation on the Rhine, in Africa, where all that happened under Trajan was the execution of the important but not very conspicuous work of reinforcing the southern *limes* (the line of forts to the south of the Aurès was built in the early years of the reign), and in Britain, where almost nothing of any importance is recorded under Trajan, indicates the continuation of the

normal frontier policy laid down by Augustus. As for the Danube, operations had in practice never ceased; the war was an unsought legacy and
even the settlement imposed after the success of the first campaign, that
of 101–102, showed that the new emperor, apart from contributing
greater military experience and taking part personally in the fighting,
was not going beyond, for the moment, Domitian's policy of conciliation.

The revolt of Decebalus, the Dacian king reduced by Domitian to the
status of client prince, had been long prepared. Saved in 89, as we have
seen, by the outbreak of the war against the Suebi and Iazyges, and
guaranteed by its prolongation against possible interventions in his
kingdom by the Romans, who were engaged on the middle Danube and
of whose weakness he was moreover assured, he had conceived an ambitious plan which may even have aimed at reconstituting the domain of
Burebista, the king who had unified the Dacian tribes in the time of
Caesar and had made them the nucleus of a large if ephemeral Danubian
empire. His plan was put into effect with a surprisingly wide consideration
of all the factors required for success. Having unified the Dacians under
his own authority and overcome all internal opposition, he coolly built
fortifications right up to the vicinity of his capital, so as to be prepared
for anything, even resistance to the death in the heart of his kingdom,
and then sought to construct a system of foreign alliances. He easily
secured the adhesion of the Bastarni and Roxolani to the east, thanks to
their old aspirations to Lower Moesia, but he did not succeed in gaining
the support, which was essential to him, of the Quadi and Marcomanni,
quiet since 97, or even of the Iazyges, now faithful to Rome. However,
he organized a threatening chain in their rear, winning over the Buri,
who lived between the upper Oder and the Upper Vah, in the Beskid
mountains (southern Poland), and other tribes – the Cotini, the Osii,
the Anartii – placed so as to form a continuous network between his own
kingdom and Rome's German ally. It is probable that he had also sought
support among the Black Sea peoples; but what is interesting is his conduct
of intrigues on the southern side of the Danube, across which ran lines
of communication which he cleverly exploited. Detaining the technicians
sent to him by Domitian, welcoming deserters, possibly favoured un-
consciously by the literary opposition working on the theme of sympathy
for primitive peoples and by the research journeys of men like Dio
Chrysostom, he had made himself ever stronger and more independent
with his tactics of infiltration rather than massive offensive pressure, aided
by the inertia of the legions, who had their eyes more on the Suebi
(Quadi and Marcomanni). The ruthlessness of the legions in 96, at the

succession of Nerva (one episode, in which the protagonist was Dio returning from Dacia, is recorded precisely in connection with the army of Moesia), could not but help him, and thus when Trajan intervened Decebalus's insolence had been openly challenging the forces of the empire for some time. Hadrian, who in the last period of Domitian's reign had served as a tribune in both Upper and Lower Moesia, went in 97 to Trajan on the Rhine and must have taken precise information with him. Hence the measures already mentioned; to these must be added the construction of the road on the right bank along the Danube gorge, opposite the sector between Orsova and Turnu-Severin, finished in the year 100; the work on the road further upstream built by Tiberius and repaired by Vespasian, Titus and Domitian; the erection (in 99) of forts, like those of which remains have been found at Prahovo, on the eastern boundary of Upper Moesia, and possibly at Pontes (Kladovo). All these works were intended to counter the attacks of Decebalus and to form bases for the advance against him.

This began – we do not know on what immediate pretext – in the early summer of 101, after careful logistic preparations and a concentration of forces the like of which had never been seen before for an expedition of this kind. Even if Trajan's two new legions, the II *Traiana* and the XXX *Ulpia*, had not yet been formed at this point, the nine legions already proved to have been on the Danube under Domitian were employed, and soon after the start of the war XI *Claudia* came from Vindonissa, followed, in the winter it seems, by I *Minervia* from Bonna. The latter had already taken part, perhaps only in *vexillationes*, in the Sarmatian war, but it was now transferred complete. *Vexillationes* of other legions came from the Rhine and possibly from the East. Altogether Decebalus was faced by a powerful force of about 80,000 legionaries; to these must be added the regular *auxilia*, usually equal in number to the legionary troops, besides the irregular auxiliaries contributed by various peoples – Germanic (Quadi and Marcomanni), Sarmatian (Iazyges) and even Mauretanian (it is now that we meet for the first time, at their head, the curious figure of Lusius Quietus). The *classis* of the Danube was naturally employed, and with the Emperor, who had left Rome on 25 March 101, came the praetorians. Their leader, Tiberius Claudius Livianus, who stayed in the post for more or less the whole of Trajan's principate, the first in the series of prefects-cum-officials, of high professional skill and unquestioned loyalty, who characterized the age of the Antonines, was on the staff, together with other men of proven capacity like Licinius Sura. Hadrian also came as *comes*, without any specific operational command. The com-

manders of the legions, as far as we know, were well chosen, like the
governors of the Danubian provinces, replaced shortly before the war:
in Pannonia there was the Turinese Q. Glitius Atilius Agricola, who had
been consul in 97, was to be consul again in 103 in reward for his services,
and was later to crown a brilliant career, begun under Vespasian, by
becoming prefect of the city; in Upper Moesia there was C. Cilnius
Proculus, a former consul (he had been consul in 87) who had already
been governor of Dalmatia and was also appointed to the staff later on
by both Trajan and Hadrian for operations in Dacia and Moesia – in
short, an expert on Danubian problems; and in Lower Moesia there was
the able Manius Laberius Maximus.

At which points the Danube was crossed and what the directions of the
advance into enemy territory were is not precisely known, nor can we claim
to be able to settle these details from the most complete but also the least
explicit source of information about the Dacian wars – Trajan's column.
However, it is certain that the crossing was made from two points in
Upper Moesia. That one of them was opposite Lederata, at the start of
the road leading through Tibiscum towards the interior of Dacia, is
possibly indicated by the names cited in the only fragment preserved of
Trajan's own journal of operations, which may have been the narrative
translated into visual terms by the sculptor of the column: 'inde Berzobim,
deinde Aizi processimus'.[1] Both are places in the Banat, along this road.
That Tsierna was the point of departure of the other column is only a
likely hypothesis. But it is certain that the advance of the combined army
continued from Tibiscum up the valley of the Bistra towards the Iron
Gate – probably the road followed by Tettius Julianus in 88. The
Dacians retreated, apparently without offering any resistance, but this
did not make Trajan hurry, since he wished to secure the conquest
systematically. To this end he established garrisons, strongholds and
supply bases, also extending to the north and east the occupied area in
the Banat to ensure further supplies of corn and livestock. The value of
this procedure was revealed when, with the summer now over and the
failure of the attempt to reach and break through the Iron Gate, after
an engagement at Tapae in which the Romans suffered such losses that
they even lacked the material to bandage the wounded, not an inch of
the occupied territory was yielded. But the campaign of 101, as is also
clear from the scanty references to it on coins, could not be regarded as a
success. Even the counter-offensive mounted from Lower Moesia to repel

---

[1] In PRISCIAN, *Inst. Gramm.*, VI, 13 = PETER, *Hist. Rom. Reliquiae*, II, 117.

the diversionary attack conceived by Decebalus's fertile strategic imagination – an action contemporaneous with the operations in the Banat –
though later inevitably depicted on the column thanks to the nature
of the sculptured narrative, had succeeded only in closing a gap. Dacians,
Bastarni and Roxolani had crossed the Danube and possibly even endangered the very headquarters of the governor of Lower Moesia, seeing
that it was possible for them to capture one of his slaves, the Callidromus
sent by Decebalus – obviously at the zenith of his ambitious elation –
to Pacorus II, king of the Parthians, with an offer of alliance and as a
proof of his successes. Trajan himself, probably leaving to others the
conduct of the slow and systematic operations in the Banat, had moved
swiftly with the praetorians and the Danube sailors, going down the river
with a flotilla and disembarking at a spot which naturally cannot be
specified but may actually have been Novae. The Roxolani and the
Dacians were defeated separately; we do not know where, but probably
on the south side of the Danube (the Dacians at the spot where Nicopolis
rose?). They were chased back over the river and subsequently pursued
further, but not by Trajan, who went back to resume command of the
main army. He led it in the not very favourable encounter already
mentioned and then settled it in winter quarters.

In 102 the war was resumed; all we know about its course is that the
struggle was a hard one, notwithstanding the progressive internal collapse
and break-up of the system of alliances created by Decebalus. A conjectural chronological thread can be obtained from the reciprocal illumination furnished by the fragments of Cassius Dio and the scenes represented
on the column. Thus the confused reports of Dio-Xiphilinus (LXVIII, 8, 3)
about the somewhat irregular activity of Lusius Quietus seem to be
explicable in the following way. While Trajan, with the bulk of the
army, was assaulting the Iron Gate frontally and proceeding securely
but slowly towards Sarmizegetusa (the column shows in this connection fearful hand-to-hand fights, submissions of local chiefs, an
'adlocutio' by Trajan to the troops and possibly his salutation as imperator), the Moorish leader, probably starting from the places in Wallachia where the army of Lower Moesia had spent the winter, had
made an incursion with his light-armed troops, emerging from the south-
east, through the pass of Surduk, into the plain where the capital lay,
and threatening Decebalus in the rear. The latter was thereby induced to
make a first and insincere request for peace. Licinius Sura and Claudius
Livianus – the highest-ranking men after the Princeps – who were sent
to negotiate, recognized that Decebalus's request was insincere and

returned without concluding any treaty, while Decebalus had achieved his aim of gaining time and neutralizing the threat posed by Quietus.

But in the last analysis time was working more in favour of the powerful Roman organization. The conversion of the whole of the Banat into a fortified area and supply region firmly connected by a network of roads to the bases on the Danube (and to Viminacium in particular) made it possible to take considerable forces from this front for a big outflanking manœuvre. Under the command of the Emperor himself a body of troops moved by water down to Oescus (which seems to be recognizable on the column) and from there pushed into Dacia, going up the valley of the Aluta (Olt), without encountering any resistance, towards the Red Tower gorge. Probably Laberius Maximus's men, remaining on the far side of the river after pursuing the retreating Dacians the year before, had prepared the terrain for the advance. Even now, though advancing rapidly, Trajan did not omit to build roads and fortifications. Requests for peace now began to pour in again from Decebalus, who was assailed on two fronts by forces a good deal more imposing than Lusius Quietus's handful of cavalry and was henceforth deprived of resources. What happened in the interior of Transylvania is not known precisely, our information being based exclusively on the scenes on the column: a battle won by the Romans, the capture of a fortress, another big battle, the submission of Decebalus. The attempt to pin-point the line of the Roman advance is a risky business, but of the various reconstructions the suggestion that Trajan, after reaching Cedoniae (Sibiu), chose the harder but safer plan of attacking directly the line of fortifications running along the spurs of the Transylvanian Alps up to Sarmizegetusa does not seem to suit the topographical conditions so well as the rather more natural idea that from Sibiu he reached the Mureş at Apulum (Alba Julia) – which would be the fortress taken by assault in the scene on the column – marched from there along the Mureş up to its confluence with the Strei, and going up the valley of the Strei – and now in sight of Sarmizegetusa – fought and won the last battle. If this route, which from Cedoniae onwards left his left flank open to attack from the above-mentioned line of fortifications, had been the trap into which Cornelius Fuscus had fallen in 86 (but how much is known for certain about the route he followed?), the superiority of Trajan's forces and his cautious manner of waging war may well have neutralized the risk. In fact the success must have been complete; Decebalus, abandoned by some of his own people (in the representation of the final battle Dacians are to be seen fighting against Dacians), threatened with encirclement, surrendered in that same autumn of 102.

He laid down his arms, bowed his knee in the presence of Trajan and was granted peace. A delegation left at once for Rome to ask the Senate to ratify the terms. The conditions were as follows: surrender of weapons and engines of war, demolition of fortifications, evacuation of the lands occupied by Decebalus, particularly at the expense of the Iazyges, the promise to have the same friends and enemies as the Roman people, and an undertaking not to welcome Roman deserters; in short, the conditions of a client kingdom. Thus in spite of the hard war Decebalus remained king of the Dacians, as he had in 89, and he was resolved to make use of the respite obtained to mount yet another revolt.

The enterprise was now certainly more difficult, for even if Trajan had not judged it expedient to annex directly this wedge of territory sticking out from the Danube into the midst of restless tribes, but like Augustus, whose generals had penetrated as far as Apulum in 10 B.C., and like Domitian more recently, had remained content to leave a client state in existence, nevertheless more ample precautions were taken. The network of roads guarded by garrisons enveloped Decebalus's kingdom, in which tribal particularism was encouraged as opposed to the tendency to centralization. For some time an army of occupation also remained in Dacia, stationed at Sarmizegetusa and other strategic points. It was subsequently withdrawn to Drobeta (Turnu-Severin) when the bridge across the Danube there was completed by the auxiliaries of the Moesian army, the sailors of the Danube fleet and detachments of legionaries. More than a kilometre long, with stone piers and a wooden superstructure, built at the best spot to serve the various roads leading into Dacia, this splendid piece of engineering, always admired for its technical daring and happily chosen site, was the masterpiece of Apollodorus of Damascus, who actually wrote a book about it. This fixed crossing naturally facilitated access to and control of the client kingdom. Yet Decebalus succeeded yet again in raising a formidable revolt, and for that we must admire his indomitable spirit of independence. But his behaviour was disgracefully disloyal. Calmly violating the treaties, he punished supporters of the Romans as soon as he could and began once again to welcome deserters, seek allies, prepare arms and raise fortifications. The return to normal administration on the Danube, with the arrival of new governors (as many as three followed each other between 102 and 105 in Lower Moesia) and the return of the troops to the big legionary camps, may have fed his illusions.

In 105 the situation was alarming. Since he was then attacking the Iazyges, Decebalus must without doubt have been in possession of the Banat, already controlled once by the Romans. Trajan, who in December

102 had celebrated a triumph in Rome, assuming the title of *Dacicus*, and had fêted the victory at some length with games and a *congiarium* distributed in January or February 103, now saw that hostilities were again inevitable and caused the Senate to declare war. Leaving Rome on 4 June 105 – a date learnt recently from the *Fasti Ostienses* – and travelling, as in 102, with the praetorian guards and their prefect Tiberius Claudius Livianus, as well as, once again, Licinius Sura and other expert colleagues, he arrived by land and sea at the Danube, probably at Pontes, opposite Drobeta. The route he followed is still a matter of controversy, but while the critical nature of the situation, and hence the need for rapid intervention, rule out too long a detour (a journey via Egypt up to Thrace has even been suggested!), the crossing from Ancona to Iader, with direct continuation towards the Danube, or better still – because it corresponds with the most natural and convenient route – from Brindisi to Durazzo, and thence via Lissus and Naissus to Pontes, is indubitably more likely. But everything depends on interpretation of the scenes on the column, which, together with a few remarks of Cassius Dio (LXVIII, 12, 1 ff.), are also the principal source for what happened after the declaration of war and during the emperor's journey to the front. Dacian pressure on the Danube must have made itself felt in various not unsuccessful operations, particularly in attacks on detachments working on roads on the left bank of the river (from Drobeta towards Tsierna?). An ex-consul, Longinus, possibly commander of the VII *Claudia* which had its camp at Viminacium and had hastened to help, was captured; the bridgehead of Drobeta must have been in serious danger; and a big invasion of Moesia may have been imminent. That the situation was grave is clear from the slowness and extreme caution of Trajan's action. After reaching the theatre of operations and reassuring people by his mere presence, he spent the rest of 105 and the early months of 106 restoring security and assembling sufficient forces to pass over to the counter-attack. The great bridge was undoubtedly the spot where not only the military but also the diplomatic preparations were concentrated. Even by the winter this energetic and systematic activity seemed to be bearing fruit. Ambassadors from the Bastarni, the Iazyges and other peoples whom Decebalus had not succeeded this time in enticing on to his bandwagon all came to Trajan's headquarters at Drobeta. Defections began even among the Dacians. As early as this, if Cassius Dio's chronology (LXVIII, II, 1) is to be reconstructed in this way, Decebalus asked for peace. Trajan proposed unconditional surrender. The Dacian king's response was an attempt to have Trajan assassinated by deserters.

The Roman offensive, launched in the early summer of 106, was aimed straight at Sarmizegetusa, in two columns. As usual, the routes taken cannot be specified, since the column shows us only a mountainous landscape and fields of ripe corn. But if we assume as the point of departure, and this seems fairly probable, the bridge at Dobreta, one column, going up the river as far as Tsierna (Orsova) and then advancing up the valley of the Cerna, probably followed the Iron Gate route, and the other, reaching the valley of the Iui, will have debouched, via the Surduk pass, into the plain of Sarmizegetusa from the east. There is no hint of any resistance during the march and even the fortified camp into which Decebalus had transformed his capital did not present any particular obstacles to assault by the legions. Before a regular siege had been organized many of the Dacian notabilities surrendered. Decebalus fled. The town was burnt down, the troops hailed Trajan as *imperator* (the V salutation) and soon afterwards the fighting moved to the north, on the tracks of the fugitive, for whom there was naturally no longer any hope of pardon. We do not know what battles followed or where they took place; the column shows us further fighting and more fortresses being taken, and Cassius Dio confirms these events, speaking of a hard struggle. Probably the pursuit took place along the valley of the Strei in the opposite direction to that taken in 102 and reached Apulum via the valley of the Mures. At Apulum the Mures was probably crossed and followed upstream to a point where, after capturing a fortress and receiving the submission of the Dacians, Trajan set up his headquarters for the last mopping-up operations before direct annexation, now firmly decided upon.

It was now early September and the Emperor, already back in Sarmizegetusa (he does not appear on the column again), was hailed as *imperator* for the second time that year (the sixth salutation of his principate). The operations entrusted to detached units extended right to the borders of Dacia and the most remote parts of the eastern Carpathians, as we can see from the picturesque details of the scenes on the column, which show wild boars and deer in an Alpine landscape. Decebalus forestalled capture by committing suicide. The story that his head was sent to Rome, a story quoted by Cassius Dio, has been confirmed recently from the *Fasti Ostienses* which have also finally fixed the time when the war ended: autumn 106. Two sons of Decebalus were taken prisoner and the Dacians had much to suffer from their defeat, even if there is no need to think that they were annihilated as a people. No doubt many fled to the Bastarni and other neighbouring peoples, and some thousands were taken to Italy as slaves and gladiators; but the long lines of marching Dacians on the column are more probably the men returning to their homes after the war. What is certain is that in the province of Dacia, perhaps set up personally by Trajan who stayed there for the last few months of 106, there were Dacians left, particularly in the northern regions, as is clear from the titles of auxiliary units and from the names of people and places, even if considerable immigration was encouraged from the Balkans, especially Pannonia.

A dangerous enemy had been eliminated and circumstances – in this case the incorrigible arrogance of a client prince more than a theoretical plan – had led to the creation of a new province in a sector of the frontier of exceptional importance. That as a result Trajan should see his own military glory increased – deservedly – and excessively exalted was natural. A new era was marked by the second Dacian triumph, celebrated in the early months of 107 in a setting of festivals organized by Hadrian, praetor in 106, accompanied by a generous distribution of rewards to colleagues and by the third *congiarium*, bigger than the previous ones, to the people (26 May or 25 June 107), and followed in practice by three years of festivals, what with the preparatory games (*lusiones*) and the great games (*munera*), the exact figures of which, including the number of pairs of gladiators employed, have been preserved in some fragments, recently discovered, of the *Fasti Ostienses*.[1] The 'Victoria Dacica' was amply commemorated by the coinage with a large-scale issue; the designs are quite varied but they all come back to the concepts of the majesty of the empire, of the force of its arms, and of the peace and security won by the Emperor and approved by the Senate. The Senate voted the erection of the storied column and also of an arch with scenes from the war, entrusting the execution to the greatest artist of the age, Apollodorus of Damascus, who was to make use of the resources made available by the Dacian booty – the striking booty in gold and slaves that recalled days of glory long forgotten. Thus what might have appeared a resumption of the policy of conquest aroused enthusiasms and opened prospects at home and was noted with attention abroad – if it was at this time that ambassadors arrived from as far away as India to pay homage to the conquering Princeps.

In fact, in accordance with the usual Roman empiricism, the organization of Dacia did not go beyond the limits of immediate requirements. Dacia was not conquered for the sake of conquest or as the beginning of a vast settlement. The defensive situation on the Danube was indeed considerably improved by the creation of this powerful bastion on the far

[1] DEGRASSI, *Inscr. It.*, XIII, 1, p. 199, 227 ff.

side of the river, in the mountainous area of Transylvania. But a rational and comprehensive plan would have considered the elimination, by direct annexation, of the salient occupied by the Iazyges, who just at the end of 106 had rebelled in protest against the Romans' failure to restore to them the lands taken from them by Decebalus; they may have made a deep incursion into Pannonia and been promptly defeated by Hadrian, governor of Lower Pannonia, which had been separated just at that time from Upper Pannonia. Instead, they were left, in spite of the restlessness they displayed later on as well, with the status of clients; similarly, to the east of the Dacian territory organized into a province, tribes just as restless, the Roxolani in particular, were left in the same position as before. It is true that the Romans succeeded in securing, partly in territory directly controlled and partly in the territory of clients, the great road leading from Aquincum through the lands of the Iazyges, northern Dacia, Moldavia and Bessarabia straight to the Black Sea. But this was not a road running along behind a grand, new *limes*, for neither Trajan nor anyone after him, except perhaps Marcus Aurelius, ever thought of pushing so far to the north. The defence system remained anchored to the Danube. Into Dacia went certainly two and possibly three legions (certainly the XIII *Gemina* and possibly the IV *Flavia* and I *Adiutrix*); but these were soon reduced to one, the XIII *Gemina*, stationed at Apulum. The camps of Oescus and Ratiaria on the Danube, once emptied of soldiers, became civilian towns with the title of colonies, though the settlement of veterans in these places continued to lend them a certain defensive character. But the other legionary camps on the right bank of the river, with their powerful force of at least nine legions, remained unchanged: Vindobona, Carnuntum and Brigetio in Upper Pannonia, Aquincum in Lower Pannonia; Singidunum and Viminacium in Upper Moesia; and Novae, Durostorum and Troesmis in Lower Moesia. The directly annexed regions of the Banat and Moldavia were not incorporated in Dacia but 'assigned' to Upper and Lower Moesia respectively, as special administrative appendages, outside the defensive system of the legionary camps.

The settlement was thus a practical, contingent one, but the work of Romanization in Dacia, conducted with vigour right from the time of the first governor, the ex-consul Decimus Terentius Scaurianus, who had also taken part in the war as a member of Trajan's staff, did not differ from the work normally carried out in provincial territory. The attention given to communications is perfectly comprehensible, especially when the gold mines – to which Dalmatian workmen were transferred *en masse* –

were re-opened and the road from the Iron Gate through Tibiscum and Tsierna to Drobeta became the 'gold road'. Very few colonies were founded; really only Colonia Ulpia Traiana Augusta Dacica Sarmizegetusa, founded in 110 with veterans and thus with a military aim in view as well, for Tsierna and Drobeta, on the river, did not yet possess regular urban status. But though limited, and precisely because within these limits it corresponded with the demands of the real situation, Trajan's activity was fruitful in results. The Balkans, long tried not only by invasions but also by the preparations for war and by concentrations of armies, had half a century of peace and enjoyed their most prosperous period. Not only did Dalmatia find an outlet for its superfluous population but the neighbouring provinces in particular – Pannonia and Moesia – benefited by the security that had been achieved; the old Greek cities of the coast, Tomis, Histria, Olbia and others, flourished again through the intensified commercial relations with the East and the greater security of communications rendered possible in the hinterland, right to the distant West; and urban life developed even inland, either in completely new foundations like Tropaeum Traiani, Nicopolis and Marcianopolis or in ones based on existing inhabited or military centres such as Colonia Ulpia Traiana Poetovio in Pannonia, where veterans of the II *Adiutrix* were settled, Colonia Ulpia Oescus, the ancient capital of the Thracian Triballi and later a legionary camp, and in Upper Moesia Colonia Ulpia Traiana Ratiaria and the Municipium Ulpianum (Kossowo) in Dardania. Indirect advantages were also felt by Thrace, raised to the status of a province after 107 with a governor of praetorian rank and studded with colonial foundations (Nicopolis by Mestum, Anchialos, Augusta Traiana Serdica, Pantalia, Topiros, Traianopolis, Plotinopolis), which rapidly increased the degree of urbanization, here completely Greek in character, as also in part of Moesia. Thus last but not least among the concrete results of a campaign judiciously conducted to resolve a situation that had dragged on for nearly half a century was an acceleration in the process of raising the empire's general level of civilization.

PUBLIC WORKS

After the second Dacian war Trajan made his longest stay in Rome, from early in 107 to the autumn of 113, almost seven years in which are naturally to be placed, so far as we can tell from the scanty chronological information, most of what is known of his activity at home. Examination of the facts and of the measures taken shows that, even in the outward climate of magnificence (festivals and games) in which the 'felicitas temporum' crystallized after the victory and in which the concept of the peak finally attained in the development of the imperial commonwealth was made manifest to men in the form easiest for them to understand, Trajan's mode of government did not exceed in essence the principles adopted of moderation and administrative 'functionality'. The games were in fact the greatest expression of public urban life. We must therefore seek to base our judgement not on the spectacular grandeur of these games and on their protraction *ad nauseam* (between 107 and 113 the only years without extraordinary games, though certainly not without ordinary ones, were 110 and 111), but rather, while taking account of the dangerous tendency revealed by this love for the big and strange, on as much as can be discovered of the practical work of government.

From this point of view, actual building activity in Rome never exceeded the limits of necessity, or at most of a munificence guided by good sense. The list of works carried out by Trajan in Rome is not long, and it is a question for the most part of restoration, or of the continuation or execution of enterprises initiated or planned by Domitian; even the most grandiose piece of building, the forum and basilica named after Trajan, were part of Domitian's plan for the reorganization and enlargement of the imperial fora. Naturally special care was devoted to works of public utility. Pillars dating from 101 to 103 show that there was a boundary line between public and private land along the banks of the Tiber, probably for the whole course of the river through the city, since the boundaries drawn by subsequent emperors always refer to that of Trajan. The drawing of this boundary coincides with the appearance of the post, entrusted to a single individual of consular rank, of *curator alvei et riparum Tiberis et cloacarum urbis*. This official replaced what had originally been an old senatorial college and then (since Vespasian) a *curator*, both concerned with the Tiber alone. In accordance with the tendency of the times there was thus for this important task, parallel to that of the *curator aquarum*, another ordinary administrative official, even if he belonged to the senatorial aristocracy, at the head of a technical service and no longer of a commission. Trajan had other works carried out on the lower course of the river, near its mouth, as part of the replanning of the Portus Augusti, the artificial sea port adjoining the river port of Ostia, but also with the aim, pursued by Claudius as well and destined to remain once again unachieved, of reducing damage from floods in Rome. The *fossa Traiana*, which replaced the *fossae Claudianae* and corresponded more or less to the present-day Fiumicino canal, the hexagonal port excavated before 113 further inland than Claudius's harbour, which was also restored and cleared of sand, and the residences and warehouses built were magnificent works of public utility, part of the programme for the improvement of Italian ports made necessary by the growing commercial prosperity and the needs of the corn supply. Not even old Ostia, with its port on a natural branch of the Tiber, was neglected, as is shown by the ample traces of rebuilding in Trajan's period and by the discovery of one of the best statues known of the 'optimus princeps'. Literary and monumental evidence such as Pliny's description[1] of the work on the port of Centum-cellae (Civita Vecchia) and the arch of Ancona, erected in 115, speak of the same care for these important ports of call, while there are other less reliable references to similar work at Terracina, Puteoli, Rimini and the Sicilian ports.

The attention paid in general to the system of aqueducts in Rome, a system which must by now have been a technical marvel, is attested by Frontinus's *De Aquis*, the work of a new kind of senatorial official who, in deferring to the Emperor's arrangements, was also pleased with the department assigned to him and, feeling the responsibility involved, expressed his pride in the benefit to the public arising out of the scrupulous administration of a sector so important for the material side of life. But besides Frontinus's testimony, which is valid for the early years of the reign (the author died not later than 104), and the detailed evidence of the numerous *fistulae aquariae* – the lead pipes for the distribution of water to private citizens, a service which Trajan wanted to be a generous one – there is evidence of exceptional work: the extension of the *aqua Marcia* to the Aventine, by Trajan, it seems, rather than by Nerva;[2] the shifting, already planned by Nerva and carried out by his successor, of the source of the *Anio Novus* near Subiaco, so that the water flowed fresher and purer into the canal already built by Claudius; and finally the construction of a completely new aqueduct, the *aqua Traiana*, which was fed by springs in the region of Bracciano, arrived at the Janiculum and was distributed in Trastevere, passing then, however, as is clear from recent finds, also to the left bank of the river and ending on the Oppian hill. This great piece of engineering, commemorated on coins and in an inscription of 109,[3] was inaugurated, as has recently been learnt from the *Fasti Ostienses*,[4] on 24 June 109, two days after the baths.

These baths, apart from the forum, were the most important work from either a utilitarian or a monumental point of view. Possibly planned

---

[1] PLIN., *Epist.*, VI, 31, dating possibly from 106.   [2] FRONTIN., *De Aq.*, 87.
[3] *ILS*, 290.   [4] DEGRASSI, *Inscr. It.*, XIII, 1, pp. 199, 229.

by Domitian and probably under construction from 104 onwards to the designs of Apollodorus, who superimposed them on part of Nero's *domus aurea*, now burnt out and filled with rubble, they completed the recovery for public use, already furthered by the Flavians with the construction of the amphitheatre and the baths of Titus, of the huge area occupied by Nero between the Palatine, Caelian and Esquiline hills. Adorned with splendid works of art, they became, with their grand and richly articulated plan, the model for buildings subsequently erected for the same purpose. Meanwhile (in 107 the Senate voted the erection of the column for the Dacian wars, to adorn a series of monumental buildings certainly already in course of construction), work was going forward to increase the area devoted to fora and to connect it with the Campus Martius, in accordance with Caesar's old plan, which Domitian, it seems, had just started to put into effect. The plan was now carried out, according to the simplest interpretation of the cryptic inscription on the base of the column,[1] by excavating to a height equal to that of the column the slope of the Quirinal, at the spot where subsequently the brilliant solution was adopted of siting the *tabernae* sheltering behind the right-hand semi-arch of the forum, the so-called 'Trajan's Market'. The level space thus obtained was laid out, again probably to the design of Apollodorus, as a huge square, the actual 'forum' of Trajan, surrounded by a wall of tufa clad with marble and flanked by colonnades, with two apses, one towards the Capitol and the other towards the Quirinal. In 117 the entrance was adorned with an arch in honour of Trajan, an equestrian statue of whom stood in the middle of the forum; statues of famous men were placed all round and decorations and reliefs must have abounded, as is clear from various fragments now scattered but coming in all probability from here. In the background, three feet above the level of the square, at the top of a broad flight of steps of deep yellow marble, there rose in splendour with its forest of columns, covered by a roof of bronze, the Basilica Ulpia, through which one passed to the more confined space behind, which sheltered – between the two libraries, one Greek, one Latin – the hundred-foot-high storied column, bearing on its summit the gilded bronze statue of the Emperor. Its base was destined to receive his ashes and thus act as his mausoleum. The forum and basilica were inaugurated on 12 May 113, the day also of the dedication of a restoration of the neighbouring temple of Venus Genitrix in the forum of Caesar. All these pieces of information have been freshly acquired from the *Fasti Ostienses*.[2] With this work, accompanied by the new arrangement of the commercial buildings, a

---

[1] *ILS*, 294.   [2] DEGRASSI, *Inscr. It.*, XIII, 1, pp. 201, 203, 230 ff.

decisive step forward had been taken in laying out the representational centre of the capital of the world. In order to eliminate the peculiarity of this last imperial forum, that of being the only one without a temple, possibly because of the practical, utilitarian, and hence profane, concept on which it was always based, Hadrian subsequently erected, beyond the libraries and on the axis of the whole complex of buildings, the temple of Trajan and Plotina.

As for other works in Rome, the records are not so clear. The period in which the last traces of the Neronian fire and subsequent ones were erased and the city assumed its final splendid appearance must certainly have witnessed innumerable contributions by the Princeps, but to some extent on obligatory lines. The re-opening in 101[1] of the library attached to the *templum Divi Augusti* was probably the final stage in the restoration undertaken by Domitian after the fire of 80 and continued by Trajan. A restoration of the temple of the Dioscuri, assumed recently simply on the basis of stylistic considerations, might still be regarded as dubious, had the epigraphical evidence (*Fasti Ostienses*) not confirmed in a surprising way the similar conjecture already made concerning the temple of Venus Genitrix.[2] A temple of Divus Nerva, which seems to have been in course of construction between 100 and 104, was an obligatory work; the 'naumachia vaticana', completed by Trajan and inaugurated on 11 November 109,[3] had quite probably been begun by Domitian; the Pantheon, struck by lightning and burnt down, must have been restored, together with the adjoining Baths of Agrippa, though only essential repairs can have been carried out if a little later Hadrian rebuilt the whole edifice from the foundations; the Flavian amphitheatre naturally needed maintenance work; only Domitian's Odeum, in the restoration of which Apollodorus had a hand, was so finely embellished that for centuries it remained one of the most admired buildings in Rome. Reports of other new buildings are uncertain. The military amphitheatre is now un-animously attributed to Septimus Severus. As for the *Thermae Suranae* on the Aventine, once the plebeian hill but now the most aristocratic one, with the rich houses of Licinius Sura, Ummidius Quadratus Bassus and possibly Trajan and Hadrian themselves, it is not known whether they were built by Sura himself or by the Princeps in memory of his friend, who died in 110, and whether they were a new building or Sura's own

---

[1] MARTIAL, XII, 3, 8.

[2] A. VON GERKAN, 'Einiges zur Aedes Castoris in Rom.', in *Röm. Mitt.*, LX–LXI 1953–4, pp. 200–6. For the temple in the forum of Caesar, cf. R. PARIBENI, *Optimus, Princeps*, II, Messina 1927, p. 32.

[3] DEGRASSI, *Inscr. It.*, XIII, 1, pp. 199, 229.

mansion converted into baths. The allusions to a temple of Fortuna and to an Ara Pudicitiae Augustae, in honour of Plotina, are vague; nor can we infer from the famous 'plutei' of the forum, even if they are to be ascribed to the age of Trajan, that he made modifications to the *Rostra*. There remains the report, an isolated and not too reliable one,[1] of the construction of a theatre in the Campus Martius, subsequently demolished by Hadrian, allegedly on the instructions of his predecessor himself. Uncertain, too, are the references to arches which were dedicated to him, apart from the one in the forum; the so-called arch of Drusus (probably part of an aqueduct) near the gate to the Appian Way may have been, and the same is true of another one in the Campus Martius, opposite the Partheon, built in his honour by Hadrian, and recorded only in medieval documents under the name of *arcus Pietatis*.

The building activity in Italy and the provinces, so far as it can be distinguished and dated amid the spate of works which renewed and unified the physical appearance of cities and regions in the second century, is also characterized by grandeur, but not a grandeur divorced from a consideration of what was necessary or from the realistic assessment of means proper to a responsible administration. This is true particularly of the roads. Trajan's work in this field continues a firm tradition and it is almost all connected, through Nerva's activity, intense for his short reign, with projects initiated by the Flavians. One cannot speak of a revolution in communications comparable with that marked by the Napoleonic carriage road, the railways or the motorways of today; such a change was not demanded by any corresponding technical development. Nevertheless, there is a good deal of evidence of activity. Two new Italian roads bear Trajan's name: the *Traiana Nova*, laid in 108 from Volsinii to the territory of Clusium, later known by the muddled name of *Tres Traianae*, probably in allusion to branch roads, and entrusted to the *curator* of the Clodia, the Cassia, the Ciminia and other minor roads, in short of the whole road network of southern Etruria; and the *Via Traiana*, an alternative to the Via Appia, from Benevento to Brindisi via Canusium and Celia instead of Venosa and Tarentum, finished in 109 and regarded, to judge by references on coins, inscriptions and monuments (the great arch of Beneventum at the start of it, dating from 113–114) and from the fact that it had its own *curator*, among the Emperor's most important works. The Via Appia was almost completely remade, particularly along the difficult stretch through the Pontine marshes, and by cutting through the Pisco Montano the ups and downs of the cliff of Terracina were eliminated. The work,

---

[1] SCRIPT. HIST. AUG., *Hadr.*, 9, 1–2.

initiated by Nerva, continued at least until 112. Also in Campania the road
from Naples to Puteoli, begun by Nerva, was completed in 102 and at
the end of it an arch was erected. As for the other roads leading to Rome,
work on the Via Latina is commemorated by milestones dating from 105
and 115, there was work on the Via Salaria a little beyond Rieti in 111,
and the Via Sublacensis, a branch of the Valeria, has yielded a milestone
dating from 103–105. On the Via Flaminia a bridge built in Trajan's
time is still in use near Fossombrone; a bridge on the Via Aemilia is
recorded by an inscription from the year 100; and in fact traces of road
works that can probably be assigned to Trajan's reign appear almost
everywhere.

So far as the empire is concerned, it will suffice to cite some of the more
significant evidence, if we bear in mind that there are very few provinces
in which Trajan's milestones have not been found. These milestones not
only bear witness to the maintenance work, both normal and exceptional,
which was now among the regular tasks of the administration, but also
draw attention to improvements and even new undertakings. There are
records of radical restorations in Sardinia, where the bridge over the Tirso
near Forum Traiani (Fordongianus) may also date from Trajan's reign;
in Spain almost all the roads provide reminders of Trajan, as do the remains
of bridges. Some of these bridges, like the one at Alcantara over the
Tagus, built – a significant detail – with the help of financial contributions
from the local municipalities, certainly belong to Trajan's time, while
others can probably be assigned to it; for example, the two near Emerita
(Merida) in Lusitania or the two splendid ones which can be admired near
Salamanca. On the other hand, there is little evidence of work on the roads
in Gaul; their firm and ideal lines, and probably the greater care they
had received in every period, may account for this fact. The reorganization of the Germanies at the beginning of the reign naturally included
road works, amply indicated by the milestones found on both the
Upper and the Lower Rhine and belonging for the most part to the
years 98–100. However, there is no trace of a permanent bridge over
the big river like the one built after 102 over the Danube – in a section
of the frontier that had become by far the most important and was
provided just at that time with a magnificent road system. The roads of
Pannonia and Moesia led to the road along the Danube, completed by
means of the large-scale works already mentioned, and into this road, at
the bridge of Dobreta, ran the already extensive network in the new province of Dacia. There is little evidence of work, which was certainly not
lacking, in the other Balkan provinces – Dalmatia, Macedonia and

Thrace – or in Achaea, but the evidence is relatively abundant for the provinces of Asia Minor. Apart from the restoration (100–102) of the ten miles of the *Via Sacra* from Miletus to the sanctuary of Didyma, a piece of work that gained Trajan the honour of two arches and six statues, intensive care was given to the great roads of communication leading to the Euphrates; this care was inspired by the strategic reasons governing the policy of the Flavians in this sector, and was thus not dictated by forward planning for the Parthian campaign. In fact the restorations, continuing those of Nerva, date from the early years of Trajan, and we have already seen that the work carried out by T. Pomponius Bassus, governor of Galatia and Cappadocia, on the roads of the east-central part of the Anatolian peninsula, may have started under Domitian. However, the accounts lead us to believe that the general plan was on a grand scale; the north to west road from Mazaca in Cappadocia to Tyana and Cilicia, across the Cilician gates, was renewed, and so was the road linking Ancyra to Amasia, the most important centre in Galatian Pontus, which was at that time in the Galatian-Cappadocian provincial system, still undivided in the early years of Trajan's reign. From Amasia, which was also at the end of the great north Anatolian road which ran across Paphlagonia from Bithynia (this road too shows traces of repairs probably carried out in Trajan's time), two roads on which important work was done ran towards Armenia, one south-eastward across Pontus Polemoniacus, the other eastward along the valley of the Licus. Other evidence (at Cyzicus, and possibly near Smyrna) indicates that the roads in the west were not neglected either, though they were of more commercial than strategic interest. In the Middle East area the road built after the annexation of the kingdom of the Nabataeans and finished towards 111, 'a finibus Syriae usque ad mare Rubrum', that is, from Damascus to Akaba, with a branch running through Philadelphia, Gerasa and Pella (milestones dating from 112) was the most important enterprise; but intensive work was certainly carried out in Syria and on the whole Euphrates front for the Parthian war, and also well inside the territory conquered, as is attested by a milestone of 116 found recently at Singara, near the Tigris, and by the triumphal arch, also dating from 115 or 116, erected at Dura, on the middle Euphrates. In Egypt both land and water communications were looked after; the old canal from Memphis to the lake of Ismailia was brought back into commission by dint of so much labour that it subsequently bore Trajan's name; as for the roads, milestones recording Trajan's work have been found as far south as Nubia. In Cyrenaica the road running up from Apollonia, on the coast, to Cyrene was rebuilt, and the harvest of milestones from Africa and Mauretania (dating particularly from between 100 and 105), on the roads linking the old centres of civil life and the new ones that had risen round the advanced garrisons, and the inscription preserved from a bridge of 112, show the constant care given to the roads throughout the duration of the reign. Such was Trajan's work on communications: assiduous and impartial in every part of the empire, on a grand scale but always justified by the concrete requirements, like the rest of the activity he promoted or permitted local communities to carry out, as is well known from the tone of some authorizations for public works granted to Pliny for towns in Bithynia.

It would take too long to survey the public works of every kind, to which there is an imposing amount of testimony, even when one bears in mind the relatively greater abundance of epigraphical evidence characteristic of the second century. However, a brief note on the principal ones may be of interest and serve to illustrate the criteria mentioned. Utilitarian enterprises prevail everywhere. There are traces at Ephesus of work on the harbour, in addition to the work on Italian harbours already mentioned. Numerous aqueducts were built: in Italy in the region of Centumcellae, at Forum Clodii (Bracciano), at Subiacum, at Talamon and possibly at Ravenna; in the provinces at Segovia (Spain), together with the imposing bridge still preserved; at Iader (Zara) in Dalmatia, at Nicomedia, Sinope, Miletus (this one was started by Trajan's father when he was in Asia as proconsul), at Smyrna (also begun, and possibly completed, by the Emperor's father), at Antioch in Syria (where the canal to regulate the flow of the Orontes was probably also excavated at this time), in two places in Arabia, and finally in Egypt, to provide water again for the porphyry quarries of the Mons Claudianus in the desert area along the coast of the Red Sea. The record of work to regulate Lake Fucinus (117) may indicate the improvement of the outlet constructed by Claudius. Research, now very active, on legionary camps and fortifications has revealed almost everywhere clear signs of important works and modifications during Trajan's reign in Britain, on the Rhine, on the Danube and in the East.

As for urban buildings like theatres and baths serving for both use and display, the records of new constructions and restorations are modest in number, especially when one bears in mind the increasing urbanization (evidence in Narbonese and Lugdunese Gaul, Moesia, the cities of Bithynia, Pontus and Asia, at Antioch, in Crete and in Africa). It is interesting if, as seems likely, we should regard as general the criterion recommended by Trajan to Pliny in connection with the baths which the citizens of Prusa wished to build: 'Let them build them, provided that they do not load themselves down with an excessive financial burden and then cannot meet ordinary expenses' (*Epist*. X, 23–4). Interesting, too, is the Emperor's response to the news of work lightly undertaken and negligently executed by the people of Nicaea on a theatre and gymnasium, which, though not even finished, were already on the point of collapsing: 'These Greeks have a passion for gymnasiums, and for that reason their original plans were perhaps a little grandiose; but they will have to be content with one sufficient for their needs' (*Epist*. X, 40, 2). This prudence and parsimony proved no hindrance, especially where Asian magniloquence was involved, to the expression of gratitude, in a host of statues and dedications, to Trajan, 'lord of the earth and sea',[1] 'saviour of the world'.[2] Although these tributes almost certainly originated in bursts of gratitude for benefits and privileges received, they formed part of the imperial cult, like the affirmations of homage to members of the Emperor's family – Plotina, Marciana, Matidia – which are also common, especially in the province of Asia. Temples had now long been accepted in the East by the Princeps while still living. For example, the temple built by the province of Asia about 108 on the highest point in Pergamum – a companion piece to the temple of Rome and Augustus which the citizens of Pergamum already possessed – was dedicated to Trajan and Jupiter Amicalis, and the sanctuaries of Iotape in Cilicia (115–117) and Philae in Egypt were also dedicated to the Emperor. The same is true of the triumphal arches commemorating victories or public works, like those already mentioned, and usually standing at the ends of roads. Many of them have been preserved, in every part of the empire. Notable examples are the arches in Africa at Leptis Magna (109–110), Mactaris and Thamugadi (Timgad).

We find the same enlightened munificence in the works which highly-placed private individuals presented to their own towns. Nerva had already authorized communities to accept legacies from private citizens and Trajan fixed the obligation, transmissible to heirs, to carry out the works promised. Pliny gave a library to Como and a temple of Ceres to Tifernum Tiberinum, where he had a villa; and his father-in-law's father built a portico, also at Como. Servius Cornelius Dolabella Metilianus, doubtless the man who was consul in 113, provided Corfinium with baths and L. Petronius Modestus, a knight, restored the theatre at Trieste. In 113–114 a freedman of Trajan's, M. Ulpius Vesbinus, offered Cere a 'schola' for the Augustales, and fate has preserved the interesting record of the offer and of its acceptance by the citizens of Cere, with the

[1] *IGRR*, IV, 331, at Pergamum.   [2] *IGRR*, IV, 932, at Chios.

granting of the public land required, the whole thing being done with the approval of the *curator* of the town.[1] There are also records of similar donations outside Italy: a senator from Cordova gave a building; Licinius had an arch erected to Trajan *ex testamento* on the road from Tarragona to Barcelona; at Durazzo, in Macedonia, a private citizen gave a library, as Tiberius Celsus Polemeanus did at Ephesus. Celsus was one of the men of Asian origin to whom the Flavians had opened the way into the Senate; others were the two famous citizens of Pergamum, C. Antius A. Julius Quadratus and C. Julius Quadratus Bassus, who were also bene-factors of their native city. There was thus a competition in generosity and pride to collaborate with the Princeps in promoting the common good. Such was the effect of the security guaranteed to the world by the Roman state at the happy moment of its greatest equilibrium.

POLICY AND ADMINISTRATION

The whole series of public works just described represented the material, concretely visible side of the ardent effort to raise the universal standard of civilization to a common level, to attain the sort of life which must have seemed the final and definitive one. Trajan's mode of governing furthered this development, even if it seems difficult to speak of a personal policy and administration in a historical context in which interest moves more and more from the biography of the Princeps to the vast narrative of the history of the world, henceforth proceeding on its own under the direction of institutions now firmly established and perfected. Yet the activity of the autocrat, though itself obeying the laws of 'functionality' and, in the case of Trajan, employed in the conscious fulfilment of a lofty duty, was exercised to powerful effect, forming as it did the control centre and the source of stimuli. It was exercised precisely in the field of administration, in the shape of planning and paternalism, and in this field it fulfilled itself beneficently.

Inspired by the criteria of utility and service which were in the air at the time and had in fact found literary formulation in the speeches of Dio of Prusa, which went as far, it seems, as statements advertising and supporting campaigns, such as that for investment in Italian land, Trajan's administrative policy was liberal and at the same time energetic and controlled. Although he granted what the times and the progres-sive crystallization of the duties of official posts demanded – it was precisely this that constituted the above-mentioned administrative system

[1] *ILS*, 5918a; cf. ARANGIO RUIZ, *Negotia*[2], No. 113.

with the capacity to function on its own – and recognized the abstract and impersonal authority of the 'laws', Trajan did not recline on a bed of bureaucratic automatism, nor did he always renounce, in face of the laws, the right to interpret and correct them. This was well known to Pliny, who expected from the Princeps not only the equitable solution of dubious cases but also the decisive cutting of knots by virtue of his absolute authority, the continual source of fresh legislation: 'since all that is destined to last for ever must be fixed by you, for your deeds and words are entitled to eternity'.[1] Henceforth the strength of a system impressively organized right down to the details produced the result that any fresh intervention by the Emperor did not end with the sporadic case involved, as had largely been the case with the efforts of preceding emperors, from which those of Trajan did not differ in substance, but tended more and more to find its organic place and contribute a subtle improvement to the ordered structure of the imperial régime; so it was, for example, with the planning of public assistance and with the central-ization that had now become normal with the growing diffusion of *curatores rerum publicarum*.

In detail, Trajan's administrative activity was varied and impressive. At the centre, the collaboration of the upper classes developed with him, as with the Flavians, through familiar relations with the 'amici' – who on military campaigns became, as we have seen, the 'comites' – and through the 'consilium', in which, up to his death in 110, L. Licinius Sura must have played the leading rôle. Other counsellors, or 'amici', were the praetorian prefect Claudius Livianus and of course Hadrian, as well as other great names among the provincial commanders – Manius Laberius Maximus and Glitius Agricola, Publilius Celsus and Lusius Quietus, Cornelius Palma and Avidius Nigrinus. There were lawyers, too – Iavolenus Priscus, Titius Aristo and Neratius Priscus, the last of whom, according to one tradition, Trajan looked upon as a possible successor. Nor were men who had been close to Domitian excluded from the council. It was the start of that continuous if unofficial service under successive emperors by a restricted number of people which must have played a part in the continuity of imperial policy. Thus this council was a very important body, in which senatorial collaboration shared to a high degree in the purely political direction of the empire, though to judge by the accounts of meetings which we read in Pliny – who may not have been a regular member of the consilium – and by the relative banality of the questions dealt with, it looks rather as if Trajan

[1] PLIN., *Epist.*, X, 112, 3.

did not always discuss everything with his counsellors but attended to the really important things on his own.

So the administrators of the empire were still, in the highest posts, senators, and in the senatorial class there continued, precisely through this administrative service, the process of renewal of personnel and of the improvement and technical orientation of skills that resulted, in spite of the Emperor's deferential attitude, in the divergence between the functions of the senate as a body and the striking provision of services by individual members of it. In his employment of senators Trajan made considerable use of competent men who came from outside Italy. Easterners like C. Antius A. Julius Quadratus and C. Julius Quadratus Bassus from Pergamum and Tiberius Julius Celsus Polemeanus from Ephesus continued in front-rank positions the careers they had begun under the Flavians; the Moor Lusius Quietus rose rapidly; and among the most active men there were many of Spanish and Gallic origin (particularly from Baetica and Narbonese Gaul), followed by a number of Africans, Dalmatians and Sicilians. The only condition was that these senators had to have at least a third of their property in Italy, so that, at Rome and in Italy, they should feel at home and not like passing strangers in an inn:[1] a provision which certainly also served to express respect for tradition as well as for more concrete economic aims. For the rest, the attitude proposed at the start by Trajan with regard to the Senate was not subsequently belied: after his fourth consulship in 101 he only assumed the chief magistracy twice again (in 103 and 112) and left the honour to the senators. The custom adopted, it seems, by Trajan of renewing the *tribunicia potestas* on 10 December, the ancient date on which the tribunes took up office, and not on the anniversary of accession to the throne, was also a mark of deference. Moreover, the Emperor never failed to take a diligent part in the sittings of the Senate; senators drew up the minutes, it was the Senate's business to make the solemn proclamation of declarations of war and to ratify treaties; new patricians were created; and the favours such as dispensation from age requirements or arrangements to facilitate careers generously granted by Trajan are attested by Pliny's fairly numerous letters of recommendation and by the record, in a more concrete field, of the praises and also of the criticisms and the measures which the Emperor did not spare with regard to individuals. For in reality – it does no harm to repeat it – it was the individuals forming the Senate who counted, because of the functions they exercised in the administration of the empire.

[1] *Ibid.*, VI, 19, 4.

The knights, also increasingly of provincial origin, continued to rise in the social scale, in proportion to the extension and consolidation of their service in the administration. The equestrian career, already the subject of special regulations by the last of the Flavians, was now not far from its final shape, and the equestrian class, as is clear from Pliny's letters and other indications, was in many respects not inferior in prestige to the senatorial class. The posts in the strictly imperial administration, previously held by palace freedmen who emphasized its formally still semi-private character, now passed almost entirely to the knights and, now a regular part of their *cursus*, became completely public. Under Trajan, as far as we can see from the evidence available, twenty new posts were added to the already numerous posts of procurator occupied by knights in the three ranges – henceforth fixed – of *ducenarii*, *centenarii* and *sexagenarii* (paid 200, 100 and 60 thousand sesterces respectively). The *a rationibus* and the *procurator patrimonii*, the highest officials of the imperial finances (public and private respectively) were now regularly knights; and there now appeared – to cite only the principal new posts entrusted to knights – the *praefectura vehiculorum*, a post dealing with the corn supply for Ostia and the directorship of the Ulpian library, besides the procuratorships for provinces newly annexed. The imperial mint was no longer managed by a freedman but by a knight (*procurator monetae*); and an inscription discovered fairly recently[1] has revealed that already under Trajan the historian Suetonius was procurator *a bibliothecis* and *a studiis*, and without first filling the equestrian military posts – a homage by the Emperor to his already accepted literary fame. Another inscription that has come to light recently[2] gives an idea of the rapid advancement of one particular man: eight successive posts were held in ten years by the Dalmatian Q. Marcius Turbo, who in 103 was still a legionary centurion at Aquincum and by 114, at the beginning of the Parthian campaign, had already been prefect of the fleet based at Misenum. He was destined to go swiftly a long way further in special military commands, evidently helped on during his preceding procuratorship of the *ludus magnus* by his services in putting on Trajan's big spectacles and also by the friendship of Hadrian, who later made him his praetorian prefect. The figure of M. Rutilius Lupus, *praefectus annonae* from 103 to 111 and prefect of Egypt from 114 to 117, a knight who owned brick-kilns in Italy, a manu-

---

[1] E. MAREC and H. G. PFLAUM, 'Nouvelle inscription sur la carrière de Suétone, l'historien;, in *Compt. rend. Acad. Inscr.*, 1952, pp. 76–85 (*Ann. Ép.*, 1953, 73).

[2] E. FRÉZOULS, 'Inscription de Cyrrhus relative à Q. Marcius Turbo', in *Syria*, XXX, 1953, pp. 247–78 (*Ann. Ép.*, 1955, 225).

facturer or industrialist – if this description is preferred – utilized in the
public service by Trajan, is also a characteristic one.

The prefectures of the *vigiles*, of the *annona*, of Egypt and of the
praetorian guards, the top posts in the equestrian career, henceforth
fixed in the order indicated, continued to be awe-inspiring positions in
practical government, equal in practical importance and in a certain way
opposed, as in earlier days, though with all the attenuations inspired by
the Emperor's tact, to some of the highest senatorial posts. In particular,
the praetorian prefect, apart from his command of the praetorian cohorts –
always retained – and his participation in military campaigns on the
headquarters staff, acquired also in the civil field, by the very duration
of his office, that increasingly public and semi-magisterial status that
must have made him the Emperor's chief assistant. Sextus Attius Suburanus Aemilianus, the first of Trajan's prefects known to us, whose career
has also been revealed quite recently[1] and is interesting in a different
way from Turbo's, was in office towards 99; tradition admiringly preserved
the words uttered by Trajan as he gave him the sword that was the symbol
of his office: 'I entrust this to you to use for me if I do right, against me
if I do wrong'.[2] A memorable saying in the climate of Pliny's *Panegyric*.
In 101 Attius Suburanus was already consul; he was succeeded as prefect
by the man who from 100 until possibly 117 was the Emperor's shadow,
Claudius Livianus. The last year of the reign saw the appearance, with a
characteristic return to collegiality, of the pair P. Aelius Attianus and
Servius Sulpicius Similis, two men bound to Hadrian, whose succession
they facilitated. Since this is more or less all that is known about Trajan's
prefects it is difficult to say whether by now they already had that criminal
jurisdiction of their own which later was one of their characteristic
powers; probably equipped with the necessary powers of coercion to
exercise their authority, for the rest they must have still acted on the
Emperor's behalf and with his authorization on each occasion, in a relationship of close collaboration (not yet delegation) to which Claudius Livianus's
long and silent service, in a harmonious atmosphere of unchanging friendship and loyalty, bears witness. The existence of an already independent
jurisdiction is not necessarily proved by Trajan's invitation to Pliny to
send a criminal in chains from Bithynia to the prefect, or by his referring
a case to the prefect for supplementary investigation.

When we turn away from the upper classes and look at the citizen body
of Rome and the population of the empire as a whole, we find the process

---

[1] *Ann. Ép.*, 1939, 60 (Heliopolis = Baalbeck, in Syria).
[2] AUR. VICT., *De Caes.*, 13, 9.

of municipalization encouraged by the Flavians, on the foundations laid by Claudius, continuing under Trajan and now becoming spontaneous and irresistible with the extension of Roman civilization; but so far as concerns the Princeps, who was still responsible for the official acts granting citizenship and establishing municipalities and colonies, we see thriving, as the fruit of the most advanced paternalism, quite pronounced humane and cosmopolitan interests. Thus while there is no certain record of colonies founded by Trajan in Italy, apart from the rather dubious references in the *Liber coloniarum* to the planting of veterans at Veii, Lavinium and Ostia, and while in the West – in Spain and Gaul – the municipal settlement in the form of Latin rights and of the ever-wider extension of full citizenship to the principal centres was now a *fait accompli*, in the Danubian regions the colonies already mentioned were still founded with actual colonists and in places useful for defence; these were the last colonies founded before the title became a purely honorary concession. On the Rhine, near the camp of Vetera, rose a Colonia Ulpia Traiana and the camp of Novomagus became the town Ulpia Noviomagus. In Dacia, as we have seen, the Roman system was imposed without delay and immigration was encouraged. An inscription discovered quite recently[1] has disclosed the settlement at Cyrene of veterans from the III *Cyrenaica*, a legion stationed in Egypt. In Africa, where from the ancient cities on the coast to the edges of the desert every shade of civil penetration was to be found, the military camps and forts of the interior protected the vast region occupied not only by the extensive imperial domains, in which the colonists had their own municipal organization, certainly more uniform and egalitarian in view of their common closer dependence on the Emperor, but also by the settlements of the old nomads, who had now become sedentary and were also organized in urban communities after the Roman style. Some of these bear the name of Trajan: Colonia Ulpia Marciana Traiana Thamugadi (dating from 100), Municipium Ulpium Traianum Augustum Thubursicu, possibly Theveste, Thelepte and Diana Veteranorum, and other places, as can be inferred from the wide diffusion of the *tribus Papiria*, Trajan's tribe. Other centres long famous— Hadrumetum, Leptis, possibly Oea – received the title of Colonia. If the so-called *quattuor coloniae Cirtenses* are also to be assigned to Trajan, it was he who regularized the position of Cirta, the only Roman colony founded by a private citizen – by the Catilinarian and Caesarian adventurer P. Sittius, over a century and a half earlier. It had remained ever since in a characteristic state of independence. The

[1] *Rev. Ét. Gr.*, LXI, 1948, pp. 201, 19.

honorific naming of cities after the Emperor also appears elsewhere: there was Traianopolis near Grimenothyrae, between Lydia and Phrygia. The same name is attested in 113–114 as being added to Epiphaneia in Cilicia, while *Heraclea ad Salbacum* in Caria was *Ulpia* for some time, probably as a result of favours gained for his native town by T. Statilius Crito, Trajan's doctor. It is more than probable that Mesopotamian and Armenian towns had the ephemeral status of Roman colonies under Trajan; and the many other spots all over the empire bearing the epithet *Ulpia* commemorate some intervention or other. It is also clear that Trajan must have continued in many places – on the borders of Arabia, for example, and beyond the Jordan (Gerasa) – the work begun by the Flavian emperors.

In this municipal world, in which the practical differences between Italy and the provinces had thus already been notably reduced, there are interventions by the Princeps to be noted, both in the general field of the provincial commands, modified to some extent by Trajan, and in the details of local public life, into which the epigraphical evidence and the tenth book of Pliny's letters give us a better insight than we possess into any other aspect of the history of the empire. In the provincial commands characteristic interventions are indicated not so much by modifications of the structure and by the assignment of territory to one province rather than another (division of Pannonia into Upper and Lower, with two governors, in 106 and 107; Thrace transferred from procuratorial administration to that of a governor; probable shifting further north of the boundary between Asia and Bithynia; return to separate government in Galatia and Cappadocia between 106 and 113; besides, of course, the organization of the new provinces – Dacia, Arabia, Armenia, Mesopotamia, possibly Assyria, all entrusted to governors) as by the appearance of special commissioners, instruments of the emperor's attention to individual situations. The creation of the *legati pro praetore* without any specified task, now attested fairly frequently, was possibly intended to form a corps of officials available precisely for these purposes. An example of a special appointment, though the only one for which there is any evidence and one not easily explicable, may be seen in the *legatus Augusti pro praetore regionis Transpadanae* who appears in an inscription;[1] unusual, too, was the intervention of Gaius Avidius Nigrinus in a dispute between Delphi and Anticyra in 108 or 109 – he was called *legatus Augusti pro praetore* in Achaea, which was governed by a proconsul. And when one Maximus, possibly Sextus Quintilius Valerius Maximus, was sent

---

[1] *ILS*, 1040, from Anzio.

towards 108 to the same Achaea, as we know in more detail from Pliny (*Epist.*, VIII, 24, 2), he too had the exceptional task of 'regulating the status of the free cities'. The case of Pliny, who was sent in 110 or 111 to Bithynia and Pontus as *legatus Augusti pro praetore consulari potestate*, a case actually causing, naturally with the Senate's approval, the transference of the province from senatorial to imperial administration, was the best known and most important one. Moreover, the habit of intervening in this way tended to assume an organic and regular guise. These were the first true *correctores*, as they were to be called explicitly later on; and the very fact that they interested themselves in the 'free cities' indicates a new form of interference in local autonomy by the centre, which overrode, if only through special missions, the normal provincial organs: the very kind of interference practised on a vaster scale in a large number of communities, even those of Roman citizens, all over the empire, including Italy, through the *curatores rerum publicarum* or *civitatium*. True commissioners, chosen in accordance with the importance of the cities, and also not from the upper classes, were given the task by the central government of checking the finances of the communities, whose possible public impoverishment through poor administration would have resulted, for the towns subject to tribute, in a smaller capacity to make contributions, and for all towns in the need for subsidies from the central government, and hence in loss to the state. Their status as representatives of the Emperor naturally conferred on these inspectors, even if the field of their competence was limited, a pre-eminence which acted to the detriment of local autonomy: a state of affairs the mortifying significance of which was reduced when the *curator* became more or less a normal magistrate (in some eastern cities he actually became the eponymous magistrate!), and one which may have been welcome if the first symptoms of reluctance to assume local burdens were already apparent under Trajan. Nevertheless, the system was a powerful incentive to centralization and to an ever lower level of self-government in the towns involved.

On the other hand, local conditions seemed to justify an attention which the very perfecting of the instruments of government made it possible to apply rapidly. The correspondence between Pliny and Trajan reveals interesting details about one region of the empire, details that may be regarded as a sample of what the situation must have been in other areas, especially in the East, which was also in the full, disordered flush of a prosperity unknown before. We know that Pliny was despatched on an exceptional mission, not to repair presumed losses caused by the maladministration of the proconsuls Gaius Julius Bassus and Varenus Rufus, tried ten years earlier, but because there was as a matter of hard fact some local disorder in the towns, whatever their legal status; a disorder which may have continued the parish-pump tradition of the Greeks but was not in conformity with Roman organization, which was now tending to discipline even the base of the society of the empire. The province as a whole was in fact 'respectful and loyal' to the Emperor,[1] but there were disputes between one town and another for reasons of interest and prestige, and also internal quarrels arising out of social envy, the presence of secret societies and possibly, we may think, the religious agitation caused by the spread of Christianity. In some towns the finances were in ruins thanks to expenditure undertaken too lightly; there were age-old problems arising even out of the interpretation of Pompey's old law, which was still the *lex provinciae* for Bithynia and the rest of Asia Minor; and problems caused by later orders issued by the emperors and the subsequent practice of the proconsuls, most of them concerned not to disturb anything. Finally, the adaptation to Trajan's new arrangements was creating another series of problems.

The solutions devised by Pliny in the eighteen months of his command (September 110 or 111 to February 112 or 113), though naturally we know only those which gave him reason to consult the Emperor, bear witness not only to the zeal and quality of service of a member of the new senatorial aristocracy but also to the general criteria of Trajan's administration. The economy observed in public works has already been mentioned. The reorganization of the finances was in any case one of Pliny's chief tasks; the other was the improvement of public order. To quote some examples, very soon after reaching the province he inspected the accounts of Prusa, finding unjustified expenditure, and public money and property held illegally by private citizens. Encouraged by Trajan to eliminate these abuses and to proceed with the inspections and the imposition of economies, he ordered, among other things, the reduction of the huge sum which the people of Byzantium, a free city, spent on sending honorary embassies to the Emperor and the governor of Moesia; but it was inevitable that some cities should protest at the interference, as was the case with Apamea, which boasted of the title of 'colonia Augustea'. The citizens told Pliny that he could make his inspection, but added that he should know that no governor had ever done this before and that the city had the right to administer itself as it pleased. The cautious governor had this put in writing and sent it to the Emperor, who replied that since the people of Apamea had after all accepted the

[1] PLIN., *Epist.*, X, 17b, 1.

inspection he forbore to enquire about the wherefore of their theoretical refusal, 'but they should know that, saving their privileges, it was *by his own wish* that these inspections had been made'.[1] Once the absolute will of the Emperor had been affirmed, the interventions must have been advantageous to the individual community itself, which was thereby led to wonder at the enlightened providence which 'corrected' from the centre, so that all should be in order. Hence the constant preoccupation with ensuring order by demanding a stricter respect for administrative norms, by the elimination of the abuses tolerated by the proconsuls and by the prohibition of association (Nicomedia was not even allowed a corps of firemen, and Trajan shared Pliny's fears about extensive distributions of money and gifts on the occasion of weddings or other feasts given by private citizens). At the same time no exceptional measures were to be taken, such as the employment of soldiers, who were not to be detached from their units for police duties. Above all, there was to be no rigidity in regard to local usages and needs in the exercise of the discretionary action which Trajan several times recommends to his representative and which he practised himself. The most famous case is Trajan's attitude to the problem of the Christians (see p. 354). His humanitarian attitude is also attested in connection with the treatment of boys who had been exposed, taken in and raised in slavery, and whose protectors demanded, on the basis of alleged earlier imperial letters, the reimbursement of the expenses of rearing them before recognizing them as free: 'They must not be denied the right to declare themselves free, nor should they pay for freedom with the price of their food'.[2] Other characteristic traits leap to the eye here and there: 'It is not in conformity with the justice of our times' to oblige people to take as a compulsory loan, as Pliny suggested, public funds that had been recovered and were difficult to place at interest; they ought to be lent obligatorily, though at a reduced rate, to the decurions of the towns.[3] On the subject of an obscure problem in which the restless Dio of Prusa was implicated – he was accused among other things of placing a statue of the Princeps in a burial area, a crime which might have been treason – the clear response was that Trajan paid no attention to such imputations. Strict in demanding respect for the traditional forms and norms (timely renewal of safe conducts, observance of religious prescriptions regarding sacred areas, reminder about the legal requirements for the minimum age of magistrates), the Emperor also granted with good grace what was asked of him (citizenship, *ius trium liberorum*, requested by Pliny for his friend Sueton-

[1] PLIN., *Epist.*, X, 48, 2.   [2] *Ibid.*, 66, 2.   [3] *Ibid.*, 55.

ius), and agreed with lordly condescension when Pliny told him that he had made use, on just the one occasion, of a public safe conduct to arrange travelling facilities for his wife, called to Italy by the death of her grandfather, L. Calpurnius Fabatus.[1] Finally, the letters forwarding the good wishes received by the governor for the solemn anniversaries of the principate, with their corresponding letters of acknowledgement couched in a dry formula, obviously real circulars sent on these occasions to all the governors of the empire, and the certificates of service issued by Pliny to a freedman and procurator of the Emperor, to the prefect 'orae Ponticae' and to another military commander, provide an interesting glimpse of administration in action at the chancellery level.

Not much is added to such copious information about the Emperor's interventions, fragmentary and limited to one point in his dominions though it may be, by the few reports dealing with other regions: delimitations of boundaries between cities, tribes and imperial estates in Africa, and between the colony of Philippi and a private citizen in Macedonia; a settlement of fishing limits in the Danube, at Histria, dictated by Manius Laberius Maximus, the governor of Lower Moesia. All these measures were absolutely in line with Flavian provincial policy. As for Italy, whose inexorable decline in comparison with the advance of the provinces was a clear fact, attempts were made to maintain its preeminence not so much by administrative measures, for precisely in this field its progressive equalization with the rest of the empire was already becoming evident and was to become more evident under Hadrian, as by measures of an economic and social character. The *alimentationes*, a typical product of Trajan's humanitarian paternalism, were exclusive to Italy (outside Italy they are attested in Hadrian's age, and not very reliably, only at Athens). Trajan was in fact responsible for their regular organization, which is fully attested only from his reign onwards, and after 101, in particular by the inscriptions dealing with Veleia and with the Ligures Baebiani (in the region of Beneventum). Sums of money were paid out in instalments by the imperial fisc to individual borrowers as permanent loans. These payments, and the establishment of the institution in general, were looked after at the start by special officials of the new kind chosen from the senators; we know two of them, Gaius Cornelius Gallicanus, an old ex-consul who operated in Aemilia and possibly in other Italian regions, and Titus Pomponius Bassus, another ex-consul, the man who restored the roads of Galatia. It may even have been Trajan who fixed the districts to which the capital sums were assigned, characteristically

[1] *Ibid.*, 120–1.

making them coincide with the road districts, so that the *curatores* of the big roads had this job too; only in areas far from roads, or in special conditions, was the task assigned to *praefecti alimentorum*, chosen from the equestrian order. The farmers who received the money undertook to pay a certain rate of interest (usually five per cent a year) and offered as security one or more of their farms. The inscriptions from Veleia and the Ligures Baebiani contain a list of these 'professiones' of 'obligatio praediorum'. The interest was received by the municipal treasury, but was kept in a separate account, being always regarded as imperial money. A local magistrate administered it, employing it for the monthly distribution of grain or money to the 'pueri' and 'puellae' known as 'alimentarii', the 'legitimi' and 'ingenui' children of the poor families of the community. The boys had to be under eighteen, the girls under fourteen. At Veleia the boys received sixteen sesterces a month, the girls twelve. The charitable aim seems perfectly clear; and it can also be argued that it was helpful to agriculture if farmers could borrow money at five per cent instead of the usual twelve per cent. But it was necessary that they should need it, and this was not inevitable in the non-industrialized agriculture of the time, while the loan, besides being permanent, was possibly in certain cases also compulsory. Moreover, the institution, attested under the humanitarian régime of the Antonines in some forty Italian towns and also, as private foundations, in Spain and Africa, came to an end with the arrival, towards the end of the century, of hard times – a proof of its primarily charitable character.

As for Trajan's financial administration, to judge from the evidence about his general criteria it must have been shrewd and strict, though it seems less so if we judge by the prodigality of the shows. However, if it was possible to face the enormous expenses of running the state and fighting wars, this is to be attributed to the increased resources of the empire (among which may also be included, though not in the first rank, the booty from the wars, soon eaten up by the victory celebrations) and to the further improvement of the tax-collecting apparatus. The contract system more or less disappeared; the various taxes and duties were looked after by the procurators and their subalterns; only the *portoria* – the customs dues – still remained in the hands of contractors, and even these were not the old companies of *publicani* but the *conductores* (called *promagistri* in Asia and Sicily), contractors who personally assumed control of one of the big customs districts and employed their own private slaves. This was the case in every part of the empire except Syria, Judaea and Egypt, where there was a different evolution. Skill in ascertaining and exploiting

every possibility naturally became more refined with the greater flexibility
in the means of assessing and monitoring the sources of revenue, which
were not confined to the tribute of the provincials. There was the impressive yield from imports and customs dues, the organization of which
was improved, it seems, by Trajan through a systematic distribution of
the posts which made possible, on the pattern of what had happened in
Asia Minor, possibly in the early years of the reign, the fusion of the three
Gallic customs districts and the establishment of the *quadragesima Galliarum*,
as well as the unification of the customs duties of the Danube and the
Ripa Thraciae in the one district of the *Publicum Portorii Illyrici*. That
Trajan considered the revenue from customs dues quite important is
also proved by the fact that after the occupation of Mesopotamia he set
up personally the new posts at the crossing points over the Tigris and
Euphrates. Then there were also the products of the mines, now worked
intensively, and of the imperial estates, which were now given an organization very similar to that of the very small provinces. Such was the case
in the Thracian Chersonese, which was put under a procurator, and in the
African estate of the Villa Magna Variana, where both colonists and non-
colonists received from the Emperor's procurators in 117 a statute, modelled
on the already mentioned *Lex Manciana*, fixing their rights and duties.
Thus while preserving at the centre the scrupulous distinction between the
various treasuries – aerarium, fiscus and patrimonium – Trajan was able
to keep all three adequately supplied.   Not only did he abstain from
dipping into the aerarium, the old official state treasury, as was only to be
expected in view of his consistent attitude of deference to the Senate, but
he was also able to follow a policy of exemption, both confirming privileges
(such as the immunity enjoyed by the doctors of the Museum of Ephesus)
and granting others. The slight reduction in the amount of pure silver in
silver coins, an operation also carried out by Nero, and one which might
seem in conflict with the financial soundness indicated, is usually explained
by the supposition that there was an increase in the value of silver as
compared with that of gold, a supposition confirmed in fact by evidence
in Egyptian papyri, which refer to a devaluation of the *aureus*; since gold
coins remained unchanged in weight and purity, as they had under Nero,
the silver ones had to vary. The phenomenon would thus fall within the
sphere of the efforts constantly made by the imperial mint to keep the
bimetallic system in balance. The same aim, and also that of reorganizing
the circulation, probably dictated the withdrawal and melting down,
carried out in 107, of all the worn gold and silver coins, with the characteristic commemorative 'restitution' of some of the most significant

designs of the last century of the republic and the first century of the empire. The propagandist aim here is also quite clear.

There are some traces of measures intended to modify economic situations, one example being the already mentioned investments in Italian land. Here too, however, we possess only fragmentary information about legislative activity, which must certainly have presented, in the *senatus-consulta* and the imperial regulations proper that had now peacefully acquired the value of laws, an organic line no longer discernible except in so far as we may conclude that it was a question of the translation into a varied and detailed set of norms of the Emperor's paternalistic pre-occupations, not only through the protection of public order and the regular administration of justice but also through the wider application of the standards of equity and humanity demanded by the age. Thus alongside the orders restricting associations of people there was extensive legislation in favour of individuals in the field of wills and guardianship; alongside severe regulations on legal procedure there were recommendations on the way to conduct interrogations and the veto on condemning a defendant in his absence or solely on the basis of suspicions, 'for it is better that the crime of a guilty person should go unpunished than that an innocent person should be convicted';[1] and the measures diligently applied to recover for the fisc *bona vacantia* held illegally were tempered by the reward guaranteed to anyone who disclosed the fact of his own free will. To keep commerce honest and to protect the corn supply – a vital field of public interest – forgers of accounts were equated with forgers of wills, and the superintendence of weights and measures was transferred, as we have recently learnt,[2] from the *praefectus urbi* and the aediles to the more solicitous care of the *praefectus annonae*. For reasons of safety the maximum permissible height for private houses, already limited by Augustus, was further reduced (to 60 feet = 17·76 metres). Finally, with the aim of protecting and increasing the dignity of public life at the highest level, candidates were forbidden to distribute more than a limited amount of money and the granting of the *ornamenta triumphalia* was restricted.

The army naturally felt the effect of the universal tendency to regularization and although we do not know of any special innovations that were not a continuation of Flavian policy the Emperor who regarded military operations as his principal field of activity must have given particular attention to military organization. That he laid down regulations and demanded strict order in the units and discipline among the

---

[1] *Digest.*, XLVIII, 19, 5.   [2] *Ann. Ép.*, 1940, 38.

soldiers is well known; it is also proved by the fact that Trajan always had the army firmly in hand, and, as far as we can see, without any difficulty. The praetorian cohorts, now employed on campaigns, as they had been in 69 and under the Flavians, remained ten in number, the strength probably reached under the Flavians; but alongside them appeared a special body of legionaries – in other words, of Roman citizens – the *equites singulares Augusti*, an auxiliary corps of picked men. The *praefectus vigilum* in Rome was also given a *subpraefectus* to help in supervision of the important functions entrusted to this body of city police. As for the legions, recruitment in Italy grew rarer and rarer, although it did not stop altogether – a proof of the spontaneity of the phenomenon, which continued to spread, it should be noted, to Spain, put in an ill humour by the levies, and to Narbonese Gaul, long considered 'Italia verius quam provincia'.[1] Two new legions, the II *Traiana* and the XXX *Ulpia*, were formed in the provinces; we do not know when, nor do we have any details about their recruitment or original destinations; under Hadrian the former was in Egypt and the latter in Lower Germany. Similarly, we do not know for certain whether the formation of these new legions was accompanied by the disbandment of others, nor do we know of any moves by whole legions apart from those provoked by the big campaigns. However, indications are not lacking, in the evidence provided by the origins of the soldiers, of characteristic variations in the areas of recruitment, to the advantage in particular of Africa and the East. Numerous new auxiliary units were created and the difference in legal status between the auxiliary detachments and the legions continued to diminish, particularly because of the growing number of Roman citizens who joined them; the day was not far off when citizenship would be granted, in the form of military diplomas, only to those who did not possess it already. But there was little change in employment even for the auxiliaries, except possibly the continuation of the tendency to more and more flexibility, through the need for internal garrisons as well. This happened in Macedonia, where, under Trajan and without there being any record of special needs, one cohort began to be stationed permanently. However, this tendency was opposed by the Emperor, who several times refused cities' requests for garrisons and also rejected Pliny's proposal to substitute soldiers for public slaves in the guarding of prisons.[2] Naturally the big frontier forts, the fortified camps and the lines of fortifications received the same attentive care throughout the reign, as is shown by the archaeological evidence, in

[1] PLIN., *Nat. Hist.*, III, 4, 31.
[2] PLIN., *Epist.*, X, 19–20, 21–2, 27–8, 77–8.

so far as work carried out under Trajan can be distinguished from that of the Flavians and that of his successors.

Finally, it is interesting to examine the religious policy of a man so happily endowed with a mixture of practicality and idealism. His attitude of personal scepticism combined with a wise understanding of the political value of religion placed him in the blunt Roman tradition followed by Augustus and Vespasian. Accepting the theology of the imperial power, in the shape of the usual personifications extolled on coins – especially 'Felicitas', 'Fortuna', 'Victoria' and 'Pietas', and of the affirmation of a special bond with Jove – with whom he shared the epithet of 'Optimus' – and the exploitation of Hercules in particular (though never to the point of assimilation), he declined, like Augustus, the worship of his person in the West but accepted it in the East, where the main task of the *concilia provinciae* was to attend to the imperial cult – the only task in fact that could be entrusted to such assemblies. But just as Vespasian had deified his daughter Flavia Domitilla, so in 112 Trajan beatified his father as 'divus Traianus pater' just at the moment when Plotina and Marciana, already Augustae, at any rate since 105, were obtaining the right to have their effigies on coins: here we have a clear link between the imperial cult and the dynastic principle. Then, when Marciana died on 29 August of the same year, 112, she was deified at once, contrary to the usual practice, before the burial *funere censorio*, which took place on 3 September; and on the same occasion the title of Augusta was given to Matidia, to whom it had already occasionally been assigned unofficially. All these details have been revealed comparatively recently by the *Fasti Ostienses*.[1] For traditional religion Trajan showed deference but no particular enthusiasm; it is not entirely certain that the *pomerium* was enlarged during his reign. He had no inclination for eastern cults, which, however, he tolerated with good will, just as he was kindly towards the Jews. So far as his attitude in confrontations with the Christians is concerned, our information is based on the famous letters 96 and 97 of the correspondence with Pliny, the authenticity of which is now universally accepted, and on the Christian tradition. In general the latter is favourable to Trajan, under whose régime the Church in Rome was able to enjoy the general atmosphere of tolerance; but apart from the late tradition of persecutions and martyrdoms, of which only those of Simon, Bishop of Jerusalem, and Ignatius of Antioch (which, however, would need to be moved to the reign of Marcus Aurelius) can be regarded as historical, the apologists, starting with Tertullian, did not pardon him for

---

[1] DEGRASSI, *Inscr. It.*, XIII, 1, pp. 201, 230 ff.

the instructions he gave to Pliny (not to accept anonymous accusations, to pardon those who had repented), which, judged by the strict standard of justice, were certainly contradictory. If the Christians were guilty, why not seek them out? If they were innocent, why should they be punished? But these instructions were not contradictory by the measure of the equity and expediency with which, as we have seen, the central government sought to take account, in practice, of local customs and needs. All the more so since there was no law on the subject and Christianity could be regarded sometimes as a danger to public order to be controlled by police measures, at others as a criminal movement classifiable under various common offences, or even simply, as in Nero's reign, as a scapegoat. In reality the official world knew little about the Christians; Tacitus showed that he had a very curious idea of them in the famous chapter he devoted to them in the *Annals* (XV, 44); and Pliny reveals his knowledge to be slight. The miracle of the Church certainly does not go down in our estimation when we realize that it was then still small and unknown, with Christian society advancing laboriously in the world, faithful to the exhortations of St Paul: 'Do all that lies in you, never complaining, never hesitating, to show yourselves innocent and singleminded, God's children, bringing no reproach on his name. You live in an age that is twisted out of its true pattern, and among such people you shine out, beacons to the world, upholding the message of life'.[1] Trajan's attitude is explained on the one hand by scornful hostility to what was believed to be a superstition, despised as just another of the many religious faiths then multiplying, rejected by philosophy (St Paul's lack of success with the Athenian Areopagus will be recalled), and also considered dangerous to public order through its refusal of religious homage to the emperor; and on the other hand by traditional tolerance and the ideals of justice and humanity characteristic of the age. It is another testimony to Roman good sense in normalizing situations by treating them realistically.

THE ZENITH OF THE EMPIRE

In the time of Trajan the empire's life seems to have brought to a conclusion not only the cycle initiated by the Flavians but also one of the great epochs in the civilization of the ancient world. Pliny's letters enable us to reconstruct political, social, cultural and even economic life at the level of the aristocracy, and moreover only in relation to Italy;

[1] PAUL, *Philipp.*, II, 14–16 (Knox translation – Trans.).

but innumerable other pieces of evidence bring light and shade to the general picture.

Through Pliny, whose letters cover, with their first nine books, roughly the period 97–109, we know what senators really did when they were not employed in provincial commands and what relations were like (formal relations, at any rate) between themselves and with the Princeps. Usually everything went on in an atmosphere of dignified deference, of ostentatious awareness of duties, and at the same time of respect for the conventional norms observed by those who knew how to live an elegant and civilized life. A life dedicated to one's country and an old age devoted to oneself and to studies: this was Pliny's ideal and that of many others. The Princeps was naturally the recipient of a good proportion of the obligatory deference. Congratulations, thanks, recommendations and requests were directed to him in the style of devotion and impeccable etiquette exemplified in the first fourteen letters of Pliny's correspondence with Trajan. But we learn of one undignified uproar during the elections in the Senate, notwithstanding the secrecy of the ballot; and on another occasion, again on the occasion of a vote, obscenities were written on the ballot papers. Pliny appealed to the Emperor, 'who every day was caused much worry and hard work by this impotent and yet unbridled arrogance of ours'. But it would be quite out of place to imagine that there was any resistance or even actual underground opposition. The only conspirator of whom we know under Trajan is that Calpurnius Piso Crassus Licinianus already described as a fanatic in connection with his similar behaviour under Nerva; the Senate itself judged him on this occasion, too, probably banishing him to an island.[1] Another man who was living on an island at the beginning of Hadrian's reign, if we are to accept the truth of a report in the *Historia Augusta* (*Hadr.* 5.5), was Manius Laberius Maximus, the capable governor of Lower Moesia during the first Dacian war; and it is certainly true that we do not hear any more of him during the whole of Trajan's reign. But whatever view we should take of these dubious episodes, official and real public life, the republican façade and the practical autocracy, were now all of one piece. 'Everything is subject to the will of one man, who has assumed on his own, for the common good, the cares and labours of all.' Thus if one or two critical voices can be heard, the régime in itself was beyond discussion.

In Pliny especially, praise of days gone by and a certain pessimism of manner were partly a literary pose, partly dictated by concern that the 'felicitas temporum' should not be clouded by any vulgarity in practical

---

[1] CASS. D., LXVIII, 16, 2; EUTROP., VIII, 4.

life. Herein lies the significance of his scruples about the compatibility of the post of tribune of the people with the exercise of advocacy, and of his jeremiads on the intrusiveness and lack of dignity of the young orators, supported by organized *claques*, particularly in the courts presided over by the centumviri, or else on the haste and carelessness which were becoming more and more widespread in the hearing of cases. Decorum is what Pliny demanded and never tired of recommending as the greatest public virtue, in the succession – the rapidity of which he also emphasized – of persons and circumstances; decorum in defending people in the courts, a service which ought to be, in conformity with the best tradition, free; decorum in readers and listeners at literary recitations; decorum even in wills – a posthumous reason for public approval of anyone who had lived a good life. The comparison with Cicero's environment, which a man like Pliny could not fail to make, and the observation that there was now less room to breathe, was also confined purely to this oratorical field, as it is in the *Dialogus de Oratoribus*; for in the real political situation the splendid works of the 'greatest' Princeps offered instead the opportunity to insert in speeches, 'great, new, true things' – as for example in the advice to a consul elect, who had asked him for it, on the way to behave with the Princeps.

Such, then, was the ideal of aristocratic life: a hedonism composed of the satisfaction of cultivating the old Roman virtues, that is, the love of glory, and the duty, sometimes keenly felt, of public service, yet embracing at the same time material interests and the pleasures of a quiet life, of elegance and culture. It was impossible to speak of servility in men who, for both subjective and objective reasons, were not aware of serving. The memories of the past were in fact once again incorporated, as in the time of Augustus, in official state patriotism. Titinius Capito, a private worshipper of those memories, could with impunity keep at home statues of Cato, Brutus and Cassius and obtain permission from the Emperor to put up a statue of L. Silanus, Nero's victim, in the forum; and Pliny was exploiting a theme now become legendary when he told the story of Arria, showed himself apprehensive for the safety of Fannia and recalled his own efforts against the persecutors of Helvidius Priscus. These sentiments also marked the reconciliation of the principate with philosophy, a fact of capital political importance, and one not due only to the philosophical sympathies of Plotina. It was in the philosophico-literary climate guaranteed by the political peace that the educated society of the century was to live. Pliny's numerous correspondents must naturally have been in a position to appreciate his stylistic felicities and to return them; many of

358 CRISIS AND RENEWAL: FROM GALBA TO TRAJAN

these correspondents were men of letters and poets. Literary and academic themes are moreover predominant in Pliny's letters, so much so as sometimes to give the justified impression of emptiness and futility. But, seen in the context of their period, these literary occupations, of which Pliny was a leading exponent, formed the highest employment of the mind, especially as they were not simply an end in themselves, but, in the case of Pliny, also justified themselves as a theoretical and practical encouragement to studies. Pliny revealed very clearly the conviction that they were still also a preparation for forensic practice in the satisfaction he obtained, for example, from the oratorical success gained in a case by two young men whom he regarded as his pupils. Nor was some of his advice devoid of wit: for example, his friend Caninius Rufus had disclosed his intention of writing a poem on the Dacian wars; after previously reminding him of the difficulties of the subject without dissuading him from attempting it, he wrote a little later proposing that Caninius should enshrine in his verses the strange story of a dolphin that had attracted much attention at Hippo. This story reveals, among other things, the passion for the marvellous which was characteristic of the age, a passion present even in highly educated circles (and in men in whom we should not expect to find it, if letter VII, 27, which deals with ghosts, was addressed to Licinius Sura, the statesman closest to the Princeps, as would appear from the fact that the same man was the recipient of another letter dealing with a question of physics – the unusual properties of a spring near Como).

Dedicated to these and similar occupations in the splendid country villas where they usually resided, the members of the aristocracy lived lives of refined superiority and died refined deaths; often, when they were smitten by incurable disease, they would decide on a voluntary end, as did Corellius Rufus, Silius Italicus and others. We possess an interesting portrait of the ideal gentleman of the senatorial order (though similar portraits are not lacking for the equestrian order), namely that of Minicius Aelianus, who on Pliny's advice was to enter Arulenus Rusticus's family – a family rich in the noblest memories – as a son-in-law. 'A native of Brescia, a city of this Italy of ours that still retains and preserves much of the old modesty, frugality and – let us be honest – rusticity'; son of a knight because his father, though called to the Senate by Vespasian, had preferred to stay in the equestrian order (a characteristic case, but one not unique in that age); strictly brought up by his parents, who came originally from Padua, another bastion of the good old ways; active but not a busybody, he has honourably completed the (senatorial) career up to the praetorship; of handsome appearance, he is distinguished by a 'senatorius decor'; and finally he is quite rich, a detail of the greatest importance, since a fixed amount of wealth was the indispensable requisite for membership of either the senatorial or the equestrian class and not just a casually welcome reason for interest to the practical and realistic Roman mentality. Moreover, that material interests enjoyed no less honour than intellectual ones may be indicated by the lively *esprit de corps* which was evident in the famous cases against senators, notorious without being damaging, with their mild sentences; they were among the anxieties confessed by Pliny every time that a 'periculum senatoris' appeared. Attention to private interests was just as close, even though tempered in the best families by nobility and humanity.

The wealth of the aristocracy in Italy lay entirely in land. In his frequent allusions to the administration of his affairs, Pliny always presupposes that the largest part of his income comes from farming, although he also lent money at interest. His laments are characteristic of an agricultural economy, with its ups and downs: farms ruined by hail in Etruria, a very good yield on the other side of the Po, but low prices; uncertainty whether to enlarge one of his farms by buying land contiguous with it, 'with the dearth of tenants and the bad times prevalent, so that the fields produce – and are worth – nothing any more'. There was a rise in prices and values when Trajan obliged senators to invest a third of their fortunes in Italian land. This must have produced some changes in the ownership of property, although we do not know how important they were or what consequences they produced. Another interesting detail revealed by Pliny concerns the difficulty of leasing farms, that is, of finding free-born tenants, in spite of his own generosity in giving discounts on debts. In the end, seeing that tenants were no longer succeeding in raising sufficient money out of their produce to pay their rents and were getting further and further into debt, he decided to collect produce instead of money. He introduced 'colonia partiaria' and put in his own *vilici* as supervisors, so that the free-born tenants found themselves under the control of the landlord's slaves. Intent on organizing this scheme, Pliny was unable to be present when his friend C. Valerius Paulinus took up office as consul on 1 September 107. Pliny's letter of apology to Paulinus provides us with a firm date for his innovations as well as giving us a glimpse of general social conditions.

In fact, the security guaranteed by the state and the humanitarianism of the age helped to keep things in balance. Such was the case, for example, with the problem, always a burning one, of freedmen and slaves. Twice we find Pliny taking up a position in cases of the application of the severe law which said that the whole *familia* of slaves had to be questioned under torture and possibly pay with their lives when a slave had used violence against his master. On the first occasion the procedure was rigorously enforced, but Pliny firmly branded the master, the son of a freedman, 'proud and cruel, a man who did not remember, or rather remembered only too well, that his father had been a slave'; on the second occasion, in the obscure affair of the consul Afranius (A.D. 105), where it was suspected that Afranius had been killed by his own freedmen, Pliny defended those accused and obtained their acquittal. No doubt Pliny and all his friends could not have any other attitude to slaves and to the organization of society than that of their age, an attitude that even the revolutionary force of Christianity could only modify slowly so far as the concrete social reality was concerned. But just as St Paul, while regarding slavery as an existing and for the moment ineradicable fact and even exhorting slaves to obey their masters as they would Christ, did not fail also to remind masters to treat their slaves without harshness, in the name of their common Lord in heaven, so the pagans continued to act in practice for humanitarian reasons. Nor must we forget, in Roman society in particular, the private manufactory of citizens always constituted by the 'manumissio' of slaves. The position of freedmen could even become excellent. It is difficult to forget the care that Pliny took of the freedman Zosimus and of Encolpius, who may still have been a slave. When both fell sick, the former was sent as far as Egypt and then to Forum Iulii (Fréjus) in search of healthy, restorative air, and the latter was affectionately nursed. Here we see a humanity and generosity that also coloured the munificence, both private and public, which found expression in buildings meant not only for display but also for use, and in charitable foundations.

The other contemporary literary voices confirm what can be extracted from Pliny at the level which he portrays, that is, the highest level of society. These voices range from the many discourses of Dio Chrysostom on the ideal monarchy, inspired by Stoic–Cynic theories but deliberately studded with allusions to Trajan's embodiment of it in practice, to the acknowledgements of Tacitus in the implicit contrast – a contrast underlying all his work – between past and present.

But we can also gain some idea of the general life of the empire, and particularly of economic conditions, from humbler and more scattered evidence. The spirit of order and duty, the sense of peace and security guaranteed by the state, must have permeated to some extent every social stratum of the empire; it was not long before the *Disciplina Augusta* was to appear among the symbolic personifications figuring on coins – under

Hadrian, to be precise. We have already spoken about the tendency to urbanization, a spontaneous phenomenon, but one guided by the central government. Thus apart from a few rugged and remote regions where the primitive shepherd's life still existed (during the Dacian wars, some of the Asturians, though belonging to Romanized Spain, were not even incorporated in the auxiliary troops; in other words, they were treated as barbarians), the great majority of people lived in the urban, municipal system now in process of reaching completion; after Hadrian, in fact, very few new towns were founded. What life was like in the towns and the respective districts can be deduced from various pieces of evidence that serve for the reconstruction of an average picture, which we shall be content here to summarize, since there is no point in taking account of the naturally differing conditions in the various parts of the empire. Except in the regions subject to special conditions (Egypt, certain parts of the East, big imperial domains), society now reflected, in its ever more emphatic standardization, Roman and Italian society, apart from the possession or otherwise of citizenship. Here, too, there were wealthy personages, often unselfishly engaged at some personal sacrifice in local government; free men occupied in the towns as craftsmen, in the countryside in agriculture, more often as tenants than as smallholders; and finally slaves. As for the ethnic composition of the people, the mixture of native provincials with the descendants of the vigorous Italian emigration to the provinces even in the republican era, with freedmen liberated in Italy, who for the most part bought land in the provinces, until Trajan prohibited emigration from the peninsula, accentuated the standardization and assimilation to Rome and Italy, where the age-long importation of provincial blood, especially through the freeing of slaves, had in its turn changed the original characteristics and made them approximate to those common to the whole Romanized world. As for cultural conditions, the standardization was a consequence of these same intensive ethnic exchanges, while the greater ease of communications, the multiplication of the opportunities for trade and finally that potent instrument of unification, the army, now completely provincial in composition but always under the firm control of officers from Italy or the most Romanized provinces, accelerated still further a process now far advanced. The East spoke Greek and the Hellenistic tradition flowered again – encouraged by the unity and peace prevailing – but western Europe, the Danubian regions and Africa were completely Latinized in language and literary tradition. Everywhere the gods were assimilated to those of Rome; the consciousness of a unity of spirit and also of interests was widespread, and even explicitly celebrated in the concept of the 'pax Romana'.

This happy political situation favoured economic development, which in its turn generated relative prosperity and wealth; that its distribution was defective is natural, given the social structure of the ancient world, and it would be unhistorical to be surprised at this. The burden of taxation on the provinces was not heavy at this period and did not really interfere with the development of local resources, except perhaps when there were requisitions for armies passing through or engaged in campaigns. The principal source of wealth was commerce, which developed on an inter-provincial and even an international scale (with India, equatorial Africa, etc.). Numerous pieces of evidence situate in Trajan's age the biggest increase in the traffic of the so-called caravan cities, especially Palmyra and Petra. The attention given by the emperor to harbours and roads is an indication of the lively development of commerce in general, while buildings like Trajan's market in Rome or the warehouses of Ostia testify to its imposing volume and the modernity of its methods. The Syrian merchants established in Dacia and the offices of Palmyran merchants in the Aegean bear witness to its widespread nature and sophisticated organization. Bound up with commerce was the transport industry, of primary importance for the corn supply in particular and favoured by the total suppression of piracy and brigandage. But it is improper to speak of industry, except in the sense of the crafts characteristic of the various regions – the textile work of Asia, for example, known to us from the letters of thanks sent by the Princeps to one Claudius, of Pessinus in Phrygia, for his gift of woollen clothing.[1] Money acquired in commerce was lent out or invested in land.

Thus with the diffusion of prosperity and the awareness of the achievement of an order which it would have been folly to change, and to preserve which many men were prepared to pay a heavy personal price, like some well-known benefactors of their own cities, especially in the East, the empire (if it is legitimate to employ obviously relative concepts) had arrived at the zenith of its long evolution, at the most harmonious balance of all the great elements of which it was composed: the authority of the Princeps and the collaboration of the aristocratic classes, imperial society and administration, culture and economic life.

Beyond this point, in spite of the intense and masterly activity of the jurists, which was directed to making empirical advances permanent juridical conquests, and in spite of the further crystallization of the

[1] *Inscr. Gr. ad. res Rom. pert.*, III, 228 D.

structure effected by Hadrian precisely to buttress and preserve this state of equilibrium, the general decline was to set in inexorably. The seeds of it were already present in Trajan's age, not so much in the negative aspects of the situation – local disputes, social and nationalistic intolerance (Judaea, Alexandria, etc.), famines, particular economic difficulties – that occur in every age, even prosperous ones, for golden ages are unknown to history, as in mental attitudes and the material organization itself, which was splendid but not entirely healthy. Juvenal's satires, aimed at the dead, speak to us clearly of the corruption of the living, a corruption no longer even checked by the efforts, moral in their way, of Domitian. We have seen in Pliny and his correspondents noble examples of political dedication, but we can also already glimpse the egoistic enjoyment of riches, the static defence of privilege, the abandonment to the attractions of an *otium* not always devoted to study – in short, all the things that were to lead to a dangerous stagnation of ideas. The convenient system of leasing farms to tenants prepared the way for a new kind of slavery; paternalism dulled initiative and responsibility; wealth was only an end in itself for men who often spent it unproductively on pomp and luxury. 'It pleased their vanity when they could walk through the towns and see handsome buildings inscribed in large letters with their names, but those very buildings were soon to crash in a ruin which the builders did nothing to stem. The prosperous men were wasters of nature's resources; they created nothing. Not one penetrating discovery in any science, not one principle of art, not one lasting book, not one constructive idea in government came for the benefit of later generations from all those successful men of the magnificent second century.'[1]

THE CONQUEST OF THE EAST AND THE END

The first shock to this equilibrium was administered by Trajan himself with the Parthian campaign. The reasons for this resumption of the policy of conquest in the eastern sector have been much discussed, since the only explanation left us by the ancients – love of glory[2] – did not seem adequate. In reality, this motive may well have played its part, possibly not so much in the shape of a personal impulse of Trajan's as in the form of a feeling dominating the opinion of the age, excited by the recent conquest of Dacia and the endless magnificent festivals with which it had been celebrated and desirous of fresh glorious enterprises, but the underlying

[1] TENNEY FRANK, *A History of Rome*, London 1923, p. 526.
[2] CASS. D., LXVIII, 17, 1.

causes must have been different and connected with objective circumstances of considerable weight. The attempt to determine these causes, as well as to reconstruct the chronology of events, has led scholars in recent years to look again at the tradition, which is reduced to a miserable state at this point. While the chronological thread of the campaign has been put together again in a satisfactory way, the problem of the causes, as is natural, has not emerged – nor will it ever emerge – from the realm of hypotheses, two of which now hold the field: either Trajan wanted to secure for Rome control of the roads used by the caravan trade, or else he wanted to give the empire a definitive frontier in the East as well. In fact, the annexation of Arabia Petrea, that is, of the old kingdom of the Nabataeans, carried out by the governor of Syria, Cornelius Palma, round about the end of the Dacian war in 105–106, would lend colour and support, by way of analogy, to both hypotheses, since the big new road running from Akaba, on the Red Sea, via Petra to Damascus and the line of forts protecting it to the east reveal the design of a stable system of security, useful both to merchants and for strategic purposes, a design possibly to be carried right up to the Black Sea. Nor need we make difficulties about attributing to Trajan, who had solved the Dacian problem by conquest and annexation, the general idea of applying the same methods beyond the Euphrates as well. But any attempt to trace a precise, premeditated plan is always confounded by the impossibility of finding full evidence for it in the accounts provided by the sources. For this reason we shall refrain here from pointing to motives that are too remote and general, for in any case they were evidently distorted very soon after the enterprise by Hadrianic propaganda and further altered in the course of the century by the political evaluations suggested by the repetition of similar situations, as is clear in Fronto in connection with the enterprise of Lucius Verus.[1] Instead, we shall simply reconstruct the course of the campaign on the chronological lines which are now – as we have indicated – fairly certain.

It cannot be said with any confidence that preparations for the campaign were made a long way ahead with a view to the final objective. The road works in Galatia and Cappadocia were already begun, as we have said, under Domitian; they were continued under Nerva and were completed in the early years of Trajan's reign. The strategic importance assigned to these eastern provinces, with the consequent stationing of troops there and the development and elevation in status of a number of towns (Amisus became a *civitas foederata*, possibly in 112; Melitene became the

---

[1] FRONTO., *Princ. Hist.*, pp. 192–214, VAN DEN HOUT (= 204–26 Naber).

metropolis of the region, though at what date is not known) is perfectly in line with the Flavian policy continued by Trajan. The task entrusted to Pliny in 110 or 111 can hardly be seriously interpreted as a preparation for war simply on the basis of an allusion to an exceptional procurement of corn and of the appearance of some foreign personages, among them the Callidromus whom we have already met in the first Dacian war, Decebalus's ambassador to Pacorus II, King of Parthia. These references occur, with a strangeness that is indeed a little perplexing, in some of the letters present in the collection without the corresponding replies from the Emperor. Trajan certainly devoted particular attention to the problem of the eastern frontier, like all his predecessors, whose policy varied only in methods according to the prevailing circumstances; and in this connection it should not be forgotten that the passing of the whole East under direct rule and the disappearance of the last client kingdoms inside the frontiers of the empire (Julius Agrippa's princedom came to an end towards 93, the Nabataean kingdom in 106) made the pressure on the Roman defence system more homogeneous in every way and recourse to an aggressive solution of any problems that arose more natural. Trajan had had personal experience of the situation on the Euphrates when he was a military tribune and certainly remembered the work put in by his father under the Flavians to set up an efficient line of defence for Syria. Thus when a new Armenian crisis arose, the Roman war machine, already formidable in the Cappadocian sector – strengthened by the Flavians – and reinforced by transfers of troops from other sectors, transfers not ordered, so far as we know, before the emergence of the crisis, it sought the solution, possibly the definitive one, in recourse to arms.

The situation on the far side of the Euphrates had been confused for some years. The king of Parthia, Pacorus II, who had succeeded Vologaeses I towards the year 80, had died in 109 or 110; and since then the country had been ruled, amid the turbulence of feudal struggles, not by one of his sons but by his brother Chosroes. As for Pacorus's sons, Parthamasiris and Axidares, the latter, being the younger, had received from his father the throne of Armenia, with Roman approval; but Chosroes supported his other nephew, Parthamasiris, who made himself king of Armenia on his own account, thus disregarding the Neronian compromise. This was the occasion of the war, which was apparently initiated to support Axidares. Trajan, now sixty years old, left Rome, amid scenes of great enthusiasm, towards the end of October 113, possibly on the anniversary of his adoption. Coins record the *profectio*. Embarking at Brindisi he sailed over to Greece. In Athens an embassy from Chosroes proposed in vain the recognition of Parthamasiris. Crossing over to Ephesus, he went by land to one of the ports in Lycia or Pamphylia (Patara or Attalia?), then on by sea to Seleucia Pieria and from there to Antioch, which he entered in the early days of January 114 (perhaps on 7 January). That the war had already begun with an invasion of Syria by the Parthians, who had actually occupied Antioch, now liberated by Trajan, is an idea derived by the late chronicler John Malalas (sixth century) from his confusion of the names and later events in this same war and subsequent ones, particularly the one waged by Valerian.

Trajan stayed in Antioch for the first three or four months of 114, certainly not just making sacrifices and consulting oracles, as the sources would have us believe, but also supervising the preparations for the attack, in which the Romans were to take the initiative. It was certainly Antioch that witnessed the concentration under the Emperor's direct command of the legions already present in Syria and those summoned from Judaea, Arabia and Egypt: the IV *Scythica* and the VI *Ferrata*, the X *Fretensis* from Jerusalem, the III *Cyrenaica* from Egypt and the III *Gallica*, though possibly not the whole of it. Another concentration was in process of taking place in Cappadocia, at Melitene or Satala, where the legions of Cappadocia (the XVI *Flavia Firma*, the XII *Fulminata*) were being joined by troops from the Danube, who had wintered on the way in Galatia: the whole of the XV *Apollinaris* and possibly the VII *Claudia* and the I *Adiutrix*, together with *vexillationes* from various others. The XI *Claudia*, the XIII *Gemina*, the II *Traiana*, the XXX *Ulpia*, the I *Italica* and the V *Macedonica* are all mentioned, with varying degrees of probability, as having sent detachments. The exact list of forces is difficult to reconstruct, since we do not possess any proof of participation in the war even for those legions which certainly belonged – and had done for some time – to the garrison of Syria and were undoubted employed. It is thus difficult to know whether the evidence, usually consisting of the mention of military awards, refers to the participation of whole legions or simply of detachments. But it may be regarded as very probable that the legionary forces involved amounted to at least eleven legions, and to these must be added the *auxilia*.

Trajan set out from Antioch in the spring of 114, marching towards the north-east, and after going up the valley of the Murad Su and making a thrust as far as Arsamosata, which gained him the submission of southern Armenia, he crossed the Euphrates again and at Melitene or Satala met the rest of his forces. He now advanced with the whole army, without encountering any resistance, into the heart of Armenia, going up the valley of the Kara Su as far as Elegeia (Ilica), astride the basins of the Euphrates and the Araxes, in the neighbourhood of Erzerum. Here Parthamasiris laid his crown at Trajan's feet. Trajan did not replace it on his head, as Parthamasiris had hoped, nor did he restore it to Axidares; instead he unexpectedly proclaimed the annexation of Armenia to the empire. Thus the Dacian precedent was operative and the political plan of the whole war was at last revealed. Parthamasiris, sent away with an escort, was killed on the road, not without some shadow of suspicion attaching to Trajan. No more is heard of Axidares either. The campaign must have been a fairly swift one, so that the whole of the summer of 114 was available for imposing on the conquered territory that first organization which scholars have thought they could discern by combining a few scattered references in the sources. Probably, as had also happened in the trans-Danubian region, only part of Armenia was annexed, coming in to form part of the system comprised by Cappadocia – Pontus Polemoniacus – Lesser Armenia. Its first and only governor was L. Catilius Severus, an illustrious ex-consul who was subsequently to become even more illustrious. The eastern part of Armenia remained free, possibly under the same Axidares. Meanwhile delegations arrived from all sides to do homage to Trajan, who as well as posting garrisons and launching offensive thrusts (Lusius Quietus operated against the Mardi, to the east of Lake Van) looked after the diplomatic negotiations. In the Caucasian area, which had been the object of attention from the Flavians, a system of client princedoms was now organized: the Iberi, Colchi, Eniochi and Macheloni are all mentioned in this connection. The Albani and Apsili were given a king. The *Portae Caspiae* in the Caucasus were probably reached and garrisoned, and garrisons were also posted in the coastal towns from Trapezus to Dioscurias, as part of a settlement that here remained lasting. Everything leads us to believe that this rapid success, which, when the news reached Rome, renewed the enthusiasm already expressed at the end of the Dacian wars for the extension of the empire, was the occasion of the bestowal on the Emperor of the title of 'Optimus' (end of August – early September 114) and of his seventh salutation as *imperator*.

At the beginning of autumn 114 Trajan turned south, debouching from the pass of Bitlis into the basin of the Tigris. We know very little about the operations in Mesopotamia, which in any case seem to have been few in number and not very complex; but since Trajan spent more than a year there, in contrast to the lightning war in Armenia, scholars have found themselves faced with the difficulty of accounting for the so-called 'empty year', 115. Some people have sought to overcome the difficulty by putting back by a year Trajan's departure from Rome, or else by putting forward by a year the campaign in Babylonia and, after the recent more reliable acquisition of some fixed chronological points (departure of Trajan from Rome in October 113, earthquake at Antioch in December 115), by supposing that the year was occupied in the organization of a definitive frontier line between the Euphrates and the Tigris, in the south of Mesopotamia. In reality, the information at our disposal does not allow us to do any more than formulate hypotheses about a systematic plan of operations; and the known facts, which hang together plausibly enough, tell us only that, still in the autumn of 114, Trajan was dealing with the Mesopotamian princes: one Mannos, leader of the Arabs who had their centre at Singara; a certain Manisaros of Gordiene, and finally Mebarsapes, king of Adiabene (or else of Assyria). After Nisibis (probably controlled by Mebarsapes) had been captured and his adversaries had taken refuge on the other side of the Tigris, Trajan accepted the offer of peace and alliance made by Abgar, prince of Osrhoene, and spent the winter of 114–115 as his guest at Edessa, while Lusius Quietus, pushing south-east from Nisibis, occupied Singara, an important strategic position, and possibly advanced even now as far as Hatra, and Libbana on the Tigris. The capture of Nisibis and Singara could have been the occasions of Trajan's eighth and ninth salutations as *imperator*.

The only events that can be placed in 115 are the submission of the Cardueni (Gordiene) and the Marcomedi (in Media Atropatene), the annexation of Antemusia and a thrust along the Euphrates to Dura-Europos. The war was thus carried beyond the Tigris and it is probable that Adiabene was also attacked, but there is no trace of this in the sources. As for Antemusia, at Abgar's instigation Trajan occupied its capital, Batnae, not far from Edessa, taking it from Sporaces. This would have taken place on the way back to Antioch, towards the end of 115. In the course of the year an arch, with an inscription in which the dating elements are unfortunately not all legible, was erected by the soldiers of the III *Cyrenaica* at Dura-Europos, the important caravan centre; this is a sign that advanced posts had been pushed out quite a long way south along the Euphrates, as they had been, down to Libbana, on the Tigris. The unknown victories of this year must have been the occasions of the tenth and eleventh salutations as *imperator*. In December, after almost two years, Trajan returned to Antioch. On 13 December the city was half destroyed by an earthquake, which claimed victims in the Emperor's own retinue. This is all that is known about the facts and the military operations, but a new province,

Mesopotamia, had been added to the empire, and this must have demanded struggles – which our information, scanty though it is, shows to have been stiffer than those in Armenia – and a great deal of hard work. This remains true even if we do not accept the hypothesis of a laborious organization of a powerful definitive *limes*, which, with the Arabian one and the one already established on the eastern border of Armenia, would have consolidated between the Euphrates and the Tigris, along the Chaboras and the hills of Singara, the great new frontier from the Red Sea to the Caucasus, the object of the whole war. This hypothesis does not stand up to the fact that this very line was crossed immediately afterwards by Trajan himself – a move already heralded in 115 by the advanced posts set up at Libbana and Dura. But in any case the report to the Senate and the consequent conferment of the title 'Parthicus', the date of which, 20 February 116, has been revealed by the *Fasti Ostienses*,[1] set the seal on an important series of events, also alluded to in coins of winter 115–116: 'Armenia et Mesopotamia in potestatem populi Romani redactae'.

The campaign for the annexation of Assyria (Adiabene) and Babylonia began in the spring of 116. The account in the sources – a confused one, as usual – gives us to understand that two different columns marched towards Ctesiphon, one by the 'road of Alexander', on the far side of the Tigris, through Gaugamela and Arbela, the other by the 'road of the Ten Thousand', along the valley of the Euphrates. With which of the two Trajan travelled is clear at the beginning, but obscure at the end. It is certain that the Emperor was with the first column at Nisibis, where the boats carried to the Tigris on carts were built, and also that he was present at the crossing of the river, when resistance was encountered, but his whereabouts then becomes uncertain. Cassius Dio's allusion (LXVIII, 27, 1) to certain bitumen wells visited by Trajan does not really clear the matter up, since there are wells of this sort both on the other side of the Tigris (at Kerkuk) and near the Euphrates (at Hit). It is certainly probable that at some time or other Trajan moved across from one army to the other and after breaking the resistance of Mebarsapes in Adiabene proceeded by water, along the Euphrates and the canals of Babylonia, towards the winter capital of the Parthian kingdom. When Seleucia and Ctesiphon had been occupied Chosroes fled.

Of the two salutations of this year, the twelfth and the thirteenth and last, the first was probably for the passage of the Tigris or the victory in Adiabene and the second must have celebrated the event which virtually brought the war to a close. It was the summer of 116 and Trajan thought

---

[1] DEGRASSI, *Inscr. It.*, XIII, 1, pp. 203, 232 ff.

that he would complete the task by pushing on by water as far as the Persian Gulf and receiving the submission of Mesene, where he left King Attambelos as his vassal, and of Caracene. It was this maximum extension of the conquest which, when news of it reached Rome, aroused senatorial enthusiasm, the authorization for all the triumphs which the Emperor wished to celebrate over so many peoples whose names were positively unknown, and the decree ordering the erection of the triumphal arch in Trajan's forum. That Trajan had thought of an expedition to India was too picturesque an idea to be neglected by the ancient historians, who evoked with emotion the figure of the Roman emperor standing on the shore of the ocean and gazing beyond a ship sailing towards India, with sorrow in his heart that he was now too old to undertake the enterprise.[1] Whether or not he ever did have such an idea, Trajan now turned back this same autumn (116) towards the north and stopped for the winter in old Babylon, now in a state of decay but full of historical memories, duly honoured by the Emperor, among other things with a sacrifice in the house where Alexander had died.

But meanwhile the situation had undergone a profound change. Shocked by the loss of Ctesiphon, the Parthians had recovered a momentary unity and, profiting also by the discontent inevitably caused by the upheaval of the conquest and the new administrative system (especially the fiscal part of it) among non-Parthian elements such as the merchants who monopolized the traffic on the caravan routes and the numerous Jews, had raised a general and formidable revolt, which, favoured by the Emperor's absence and by the dispersion of his forces, had extended by the autumn of 116 to almost all the regions freshly occupied. But a popular movement could certainly not have overcome the Roman forces had it not been joined, from Media, by an attack in the grand style by Parthian armies. The confused accounts of Cassius Dio and Malalas seem in fact to allude to an invasion of Armenia and Mesopotamia led by Arsacid princes, one Meerdotes and one Sanatruces, whose relationship to Chosroes is not very clear (brother and nephew?). Even Abgar of Osrhoene, abandoning his cautious policy, joined the revolt, and among the cities induced to rebel was Seleucia, not far from Trajan's headquarters; these facts are indications of the gravity of the situation. However, it was faced with decision, in both the military and diplomatic fields, and in the end peace was successfully restored. Erucius Clarus and Julius Alexander, probably commanding officers of legions, looked after the reduction of Seleucia, that is, they were in charge of the southernmost sector and operated with success. One

[1] CASS. D., LXVIII, 29, 1.

Maximus, possibly Appius Maximus Santra, was defeated and killed, perhaps not far from the borders of Armenia, but Lusius Quietus once again performed one of his memorable services, defeating and killing Sanatruces, who had come down with his Parthians from Media Atropatene, and quelling the revolt in Mesopotamia by the capture and destruction of Nisibis and Edessa. At the same time he also ended the Jewish rising if, as would appear, it was simultaneous in that region with the Parthian action. Almost everything had been recovered, even if Assyria, never mentioned in connection with the revolt, was lost and fighting continued in Armenia, for it seems that we should place well into 117 the agreements made between the governor, L. Catilius Severus, and Vologaeses, Sana-truces's son, who remained king of Armenia for a long time into Hadrian's reign. These agreements must certainly have included cessions that left less territory under direct Roman rule.

Trajan's policy now took a fresh turn, granted that it is possible to establish any kind of reliable order in a series of events totally deprived of any chronological thread. At Ctesiphon, with great solemnity, he crowned as king an Arsacid prince whom he had probably succeeded in detaching from the coalition by promising him this recognition: this prince was Parthamaspates, possibly the son of Chosroes himself. Babylonia and all the lands to the south of Mesopotamia proper, including the region of Dura-Europos (as seems to be confirmed by a recently discovered inscription[1]), were left to the new king, on whom coronation by the Romans – 'rex Parthis datus'[2] – conferred the appearance of a vassal sufficiently to compensate for and cover up on one hand the renunciation of the original policy of direct annexation and to nourish on the other, among the Arsacid princes, sound reasons for suspicion and discord. In fact Parthamaspates was never recognized by the Parthians as their king. From Ctesiphon (it was now probably the spring of 117) Trajan resumed his journey northward, taking with him a daughter of Chosroes and also his throne. He invested the town of Hatra, near the Tigris, which was evidently still in revolt, but did not succeed in taking it and did not think it worth while settling down to a long siege. To this setback, not so important in itself but a factor contributing to a state of mind conducive to hasty liquidation, was added in this same spring the rising of the Jews in Cyprus, Cyrene and Judaea itself.

In Egypt, the riots, nourished by social problems as well, had assumed alarming proportions since 115. Troops to quell them could only be

[1] *Ann. Ép.*, 1936, 68–9; cf. 1940, 234–5.
[2] MATTINGLY, *Coins of the Rom. Emp. in the Br. Mus.*, III, p. 223.

detached from the army concentrated for the Parthian campaign and now scarcely sufficient to hold its positions. Force of circumstances had indicated the limits of possibility for the expansion of the empire in the East. Trajan learned the lesson. He did not give up those parts of his conquests which he regarded as defensible and permanent improvements to the eastern frontier, but, perhaps already ill and preoccupied with the problem of the succession, he entrusted the supreme command to Hadrian, with the task of completing the pacification, and at the end of July set out for Italy. Plotina, who had accompanied him on the expedition, was with him. At Selinus in Cilicia, not later than 9 August, he suffered probably a cerebral haemorrhage or thrombosis, if Cassius Dio's remarks on the Emperor's state of health towards the end of his life can be interpreted as giving a typical clinical picture of hypertension, and soon afterwards died, though not without first adopting Hadrian as his son and thereby marking him out as successor. This was done in circumstances that were really too obscure and precipitate not to give rise and lasting currency to the rumour that the throne had been secured for Hadrian only by the intrigues of the imperial ladies, Plotina and Matidia, and of the praetorian prefect P. Aelius Attianus.

The responsibility for bringing the war in the East to an end thus passed to others. Trajan for his part had not intended to renounce the new arrangement of the frontier, now advanced well beyond the Euphrates; he wanted the security problems of Syria to receive, like those of Moesia, a definitive solution. This was typical of Trajan's character and of his political and strategic thinking; it was with this plan in mind that he had begun the campaign and with this same aim that he had left it in the hands of others after the facts themselves had indicated the limit between the possible and the impossible. With the same realistic spirit reflected in the Dacian wars and in all his governmental activity, Trajan had adapted means to needs and solutions to circumstances. The client kingdom on the shores of the Persian Gulf was not alien to the Augustan canons; the treatment of the kingdom of Osrhoene, which was not annexed but left autonomous in the triumphal moment of conquest, and in the heart of the occupied territories, exemplified the usual criterion of elastic adaptation to circumstances. Thus there is nothing, even in this last enterprise, that could induce us to deplore the fatal decay of a rule at first meritorious, then spoilt by the obstinate pursuit of a dream of pure ambition, even (this too has been postulated) under the effect of a mental transformation in the direction of megalomania. It is not stated that the exaggerated honours paid him at Rome and the enthusiasm displayed at the news of the new victories were sought by him; nor was the love of glory incompatible with the sensible conduct of the war. Right to the end Trajan was the responsible statesman and general, determined to execute the plans justified by previous experience, but at the same time ready to correct them in the light of current requirements. And, even if the general equilibrium of the empire was to some extent shaken by Trajan's eastern campaign, this acquits him of the charge of squandering forces uselessly in a vain enterprise.

III

HADRIAN
AND THE
ANTONINES

X

HADRIAN

PAX ROMANA AND AETERNITAS IMPERII

Hadrian's succession was the most natural one, even if the tradition, wondering why Trajan could not bring himself to nominate an heir until the last moment (and perhaps not even then), thought it discerned in him signs of an invincible distrust of the qualities of the man who was nevertheless his nearest relative and had been for years his closest collaborator. The same uncertain tradition even attributes to Trajan on one occasion the intention of designating someone else – the eminent lawyer Neratius Priscus. But it is difficult to imagine that such a shrewd statesman could have seriously thought of setting aside the man who had modelled himself completely on Trajan, had assisted him throughout the course of his reign, was popular with the armies and, now fully mature (he was forty-one), gave more promise than anyone else of being able to go forward on his own with the necessary experience and by the road so far pursued in the government of the empire. It is also just as difficult to believe that Trajan the aristocrat should take his own republican legalism so literally as to pass over his own kinsman, particularly when this kinsman was also a man so worthy of succeeding him. When Trajan set out for Italy, the general view was certainly that Hadrian had not been left at Antioch simply as governor of Syria, and his prompt acclamation by the army almost as soon as the news of Trajan's death reached Antioch, on 11 August 117, confirmed this view in a perfectly natural way. This is the simpler reality at the heart of the spate of conflicting rumours current; such rumours inevitably sprang up round every succession to the principate, in a system that theoretically came to an end every time an emperor died and began again every time a new one came to the throne.

It was fortunate for the empire that Trajan's activity was continued and developed by his successor on just the same basic lines and crowned in a manner that was in complete conformity with its premises. Hadrian came at the right moment. He was the man best fitted at that particular point to consolidate into a system the innumerable impulses received from

Trajan's dynamism; everything that the young man had learnt from an experience extending over the whole length of his predecessor's reign and gained in a position quite close to him, the mature man, an organizing genius in the tradition of Augustus and Vespasian, wished to see fixed in theory and translated precisely into practice as the universal, constant rule in the administrative life of the empire. To put this programme into effect, Hadrian not only used his awareness of the emperor's formal duties, an idea by now a traditional part of the concept of the principate, but also carried the sense of personal duty to the point of considering his own physical presence necessary in the greatest possible number of places, with the object of ascertaining needs and adapting measures to suit them. Thus paternalism made itself evident in an extreme form. When no military expedition was involved, Trajan sent his trusted officials: Hadrian both sent his officials and went himself, thus taking on an immense burden of work. By doing this he may also have been satisfying the aspirations of his inquisitive and adventurous nature, but the administrative interest was always predominant; and this may be a better key than any mystical theory to the whole activity of Hadrian, whose principate represents the complete achievement of organizational perfection, in other words the natural conclusion to the process initiated by Augustus. In fact the reconstruction carried on up to this point, with its concern for administrative progress as the concrete basis for the development of the empire, reaches its natural culmination in the activity of the emperor who was the systematizer *par excellence*.

Hadrian – P. Aelius Hadrianus – was born on 24 January 76 at Italica of a family that had belonged to the senatorial order for at least three generations. Hadrian himself in his autobiography boasted of its remote ancestry, which could be traced back to farmers from Hadria in Picenum who had moved to Spain in the time of the Scipios. His father, P. Aelius Hadrianus Afer, was an ex-praetor when he died in 86. All that is known about his mother is her name, Domitia Paulina, and her place of origin, Gades; but she too must have been of high birth. The ten-year-old boy, left with a sister possibly older than himself and also called Domitia Paulina, who subsequently married the illustrious senator L. Julius Ursus Servianus, had as guardians the future emperor Trajan, then of praetorian rank, and the knight P. Acilius Attianus, the future praetorian prefect. Hadrian was related to the Ulpii, since his grandmother, either on his father's or his mother's side (we do not know which) was Trajan's aunt; the tie was later strengthened when, in the year 100, Hadrian married Vibia Sabina, the twelve-year-old daughter of Matidia. This clearly dynastic bond lent further distinction to the young man, already in the front rank of the society typical of the new aristocracy and prominent in the career of service to the empire. Trajan had in fact brought him to Rome in the very year of his father's death and had looked after his literary education. It was then that Hadrian's enthusiastic admiration for Greek culture had begun. Three more years at Italica, from 90 to 93, devoted to physical exercise, particularly hunting, had completed the formation of his character. In 93 he had started on the official career as *decemvir stlitibus iudicandis* and had also held the offices, confined to the richest young nobles, of *praefectus feriarum Latinarum* and in particular of *sevir turmae equitum Romanorum*. His military service, from 94 to 97, just at the time of Domitian's reign of terror, had kept him far from Rome, whither he had returned in 99 with Trajan, close to whose side he was subsequently to remain. Continuing his career with some acceleration, thanks to the Emperor's favour, in 101 he was *quaestor Augusti* and custodian of the senatorial records; then he took part in the first Dacian war, on Trajan's staff. The tradition, in its crass hostility, simply says that at that time he was a welcome companion of the Emperor in his drinking bouts. In 105 he was tribune of the people, just at the time when the second Dacian war broke out, and although not yet of praetorian rank commanded Legion I *Minervia*. However, the praetorship followed promptly, in 106; in 107 he was governor of Lower Pannonia and in 108 reached the consulship. Priestly appointments accompanied his ascent; before 112 he was *sodalis Augustalis* and *septemvir epulonum*. The Athenians, 'subtils courtisans de l'avenir',[1] asked him in 112 to be their archon.

We do not know much about his collaboration with Trajan in the latter's last few years, but the lack of information does not prove that it was not intimate; rather the reverse. Trajan had always singled him out for special marks of distinction, less by the award of military honours, which were shared with others, than by assigning to him personally part of the booty in the first Dacian war and by giving him during the second the ring which Trajan had received from Nerva. The Emperor also disregarded the inevitable slanders fabricated, according to the tradition, particularly by Hadrian's relation Ursus Servianus – if the whole story is not mere invention based on the subsequent sad fate of Servianus. The fact is that, when Trajan died, Hadrian was at the head of the only large group of legions on active service at that moment and this may well have been equivalent to a clear designation. Hadrian thus found himself

[1] J. CARCOPINO, 'L'hérédité dynastique chez les Antonins', in *Rev. Ét. Anc.*, LI, 1949, p. 281.

emperor, and it is of no significance that, returning to the most genuine tradition of the principate – acclamation by the soldiers – he interrupted the new custom, which could really boast of only one previous success – Nerva's nomination of Trajan. Action was taken to legitimize the formally risky succession in accordance with the new practice inaugurated by Nerva, and to bring it into line with the tradition of a principate definitively at peace with the aristocracy. This was done by Plotina and Attianus, who made known the adoption *in extremis* or forged the official documents; by the zealous coiners of the solitary *aureus* with the legend 'Hadriano Traiano Caesari'; by those who issued not much later from the imperial mint in Rome coins deliberately recording the *adoptio*; and finally by Hadrian himself. Immediately after his salutation as *imperator* he sent letters from Antioch to the Senate asking for the apotheosis of Trajan, making his excuses for not awaiting senatorial ratification, which he now requested, and renewing the promise to govern for the good of the state and not to put to death any senator.

The 11th of August 117 remained Hadrian's *dies imperii*. A double donative was paid to the soldiers. The Senate could do nothing but take cognizance of the facts. It replied to the distant Emperor, granting apotheosis to Trajan, recognizing Hadrian's accession and loading him with honours: a triumph, the title of *pater patriae* and probably the extension to him of the epithets owned by Trajan, *Optimus Germanicus Dacicus Parthicus*, which appear, certainly not by chance, on the first coins issued for the new Princeps by the mint at Rome. A fresh message from Hadrian evidently put things in their proper place: no triumph, which was to be kept for his father, now a god; no title of father of his country until he had earned it by his own personal actions, just as Augustus had only accepted it late in the day (in fact Hadrian declined it a second time and assumed it only in 128); and Trajan's epithets also disappeared from the official name: *Imp. Caesar Traianus Hadrianus Augustus*. For the last time – and it is not the only detail that puts Hadrian nearer to his predecessor than to his successors – the forename *imperator* replaced the personal forename, in full accordance with the tradition established by Augustus and the Flavians. The family name, too, another detail regarded by the Flavians – who were followed in this by Nerva and Trajan – as incompatible with the principate, was absent – also for the last time – from the imperial name. Like all his predecessors, Hadrian was soon *pontifex maximus* and became a member of all the priestly colleges. Like Trajan, he reckoned his first *tribunicia potestas* from the *dies imperii* to the next 9 December and began the second on 10 December 117, though subsequently always omitting any numerical indications on coins and frequently in official inscriptions as well. He thereby denied us precious chronological assistance, especially since the consulships he took up as emperor, only two in number, were held in 118 and 119, after which year the title *cos III* is repeated, with very little value for dating purposes, for nearly twenty years; the only dividing line is the one provided in 128 by the appearance of the title *pater patriae*. Here too Hadrian followed Trajanic usage in both form and substance: his few consulships, and these actually held for a good many months with several successive colleagues, indicated the Emperor's deference to the career and personages of the aristocracy which he thus aimed to honour.

Hadrian practised the same substantial continuity in his governmental activity right from the start, notwithstanding the appearances to the contrary put in excessive if understandable relief by the tradition. The liquidation of the eastern campaign had already been begun by Trajan. Chosroes returned, it is true, to Ctesiphon, and a king, probably one Vologaeses, was recognized in Armenia. But if Parthamaspates could be compensated with Osrhoene, Roman influence, even without direct occupation, must certainly have been stronger than it had been earlier beyond the Euphrates and the old frontier; moreover, the ties between Palmyra and the empire became closer and the commercial routes could consequently be exploited with more security. To be on the safe side, Hadrian never returned the throne taken away by Trajan; all he did was to send back Chosroes's daughter, and this only some years later. When, about a dozen years later, he called together the principal client princes in Cappadocia and almost all of them accepted the invitation, the new settlement, firmly consolidated, must have seemed like anything but the result of a capitulation. In point of fact, Hadrian adopted as a system all the limits suggested to Trajan at various times by experience and by the calculation of immediate possibilities and local situations. The resulting policy may seem renunciatory and pacifist in comparison with Trajan's, which was certainly brilliant, though wrongly regarded as bellicose and imperialistic. By analogy with the 'renunciations' in the East, and as part of the development by the tradition of an alleged 'Hadrianic' policy as opposed to that of Trajan, the notion was even conceived of a projected withdrawal from Dacia, which Hadrian was supposed to have subsequently postponed. In this connection there is, it is true, the somewhat mysterious report of Cassius Dio (LXVIII, 13, 6) about the demolition of the paving of the bridge at Dobreta, but apart from the fact that the bridge had been technically designed for this possibility by Trajan, the action taken in reality by Hadrian precisely in the Danubian sector at the beginning of his reign bears witness to an attitude quite other than renunciatory. Moreover, just at that time Hadrian found himself engaged in military operations on various fronts and the task of pacification was pursued everywhere by force of arms, as it always was subsequently whenever the necessity arose – in practice only once on a large scale, at the time of the big Jewish revolt of 132–5. And it is well known that on that occasion Hadrian did not use kid gloves and afterwards did not decline the characteristic recognition of military success, salutation as *imperator* (imp. II appears from 135 onwards). Thus while not forgetting that the idea of enlarging the empire, which Trajan himself had renounced, could certainly not be entertained by Hadrian, who was still more faithful to the Augustan canons, we should consider whether the peacefulness of his reign – once the initial disturbances had been quelled – was not largely determined by an objective absence of reasons for war, in a period, unfortunately of short duration, of singular peacefulness among the peoples bordering on the empire. To all this must be added the fact that Hadrian did not even abandon the Arabia annexed by his predecessor. The famous renunciations are thus reduced to the execution of what Trajan had already decided for the East.

Moreover, current problems were tackled with decision. The Jewish revolt was nearing its end and Q. Marcius Turbo, who had stifled it in Egypt and Cyrene, was free to be sent, at the earliest in the spring of 118, to suppress the disturbances that had broken out in Mauretania. In another peripheral area of the empire – Britain – the rebellion of the Brigantes was quelled energetically and by 119 peace had returned. As for the Sarmatian threat on the Danube, Hadrian looked after this personally on his way to Italy. Like Trajan after Nerva's death, he did not hurry back to Rome. Having done homage to the mortal remains of his predecessor, which were then taken by ship to Italy by Plotina, Matidia and Attianus, he had then returned to Antioch. There he had opened relations with the Senate from a distance. From this point of view too he meant to continue Trajan's policy, but he had to overcome some distrust. Some difficulties must have been caused by Trajan's 'marshals'. As far as we know, Lusius Quietus was not employed by Hadrian, who preferred the knight Q. Marcius Turbo both for the operations against the Jews and then as commander in Mauretania. And there are signs of serious events, in which however Hadrian seems to have played the part of conciliator. When Attianus, having installed himself at Rome in his post of praetorian prefect, in an excess of zeal marked out a number of senators – Baebius

Macer, then *praefectus urbi*, Manius Laberius Maximus and the notorious
Calpurnius Piso Crassus Licinianus, already known under Nerva and
Trajan for his mania for conspiracy – as dangerous, Hadrian paid no
attention to the accusation; Piso was later killed accidentally in an attempt
at escape from the island to which he had been banished. More sensational
was the case of the 'four ex-consuls' condemned and executed, whether by
the Senate or by the *consilium* chaired by Attianus in Hadrian's absence is
uncertain, shortly before the latter's arrival towards the middle of 118.
Among the charges against them was that of making an attempt on the
Emperor's life. The disagreement about the facts is obviously very
important, but unfortunately impossible to resolve; the circumstances and
responsibility remain so obscure as to permit no conclusion, either about
the reality of the attempt itself or the part played in the whole affair by
Hadrian.

   In the early days of November 117, after completing the settlement in
the East and leaving as governor of Syria L. Catilius Severus, the ex-
administrator of Armenia, Hadrian himself had left Antioch and, accompanied by the troops returning to their stations on the Danube, had
arrived, via Asia Minor – where there are records of this prelude to the
grand tours to come – in Moesia, to confront the double threat posed by
the Iazyges and Roxolani. With the latter he had come to an agreement
personally. If this agreement was made with King Rasparaganus, who
appears later on at Pola, with his son, as a Roman citizen – *P. Aelius
Rasparaganus, rex Roxolanorum*[1] – we must conclude that the latter was
either ejected by his own people or removed by the Romans; and in
either case Hadrian cannot be blamed for a weak policy. With the
Sarmatians to the west of Dacia there had remained no alternative but war,
and Hadrian had at first entrusted operations to the illustrious Pergamene
ex-consul C. Julius Quadratus Bassus, in the capacity of governor of
Dacia. When Bassus died in combat, Hadrian handed over the task to his
trusted subordinate Q. Marcius Turbo, only just free from his mission in
Mauretania, giving him an extrordinary command over Lower Pannonia
and Dacia. This command was subsequently confined to Dacia, with the
insignia and prerogatives of prefect of Egypt. It may well be that in this
series of events and in the climate of animosity on the part of illustrious
members of the senatorial order who had been Trajan's principal colleagues,
and possibly rivals of Hadrian, and now found themselves set aside, an
opposition developed which was disposed even to get rid of Hadrian.
Certainly if it could be demonstrated with certainty that C. Avidius

[1] *CIL.*, V, 32 and 33 = *ILS*, 852 and 853.

Nigrinus, named as leader of the conspiracy, was actually in command in Upper Moesia (and Dacia) in 117 and just at that time was dismissed by Hadrian, his fate, which would turn out to be so similar to that just suffered by Lusius Quietus, might confirm that Hadrian was striking deliberately in a certain direction. But this is anything but certain, and we have no option but to be content with the meagre indications of the tradition, with all their inconsistencies.

The facts can be reduced to these: that four ex-consuls, C. Avidius Nigrinus, the great Lusius Quietus, A. Cornelius Palma Frontonianus, twice *consul ordinarius* and conqueror of Arabia, and L. Publilius Celsus, also twice consul, were tried at Rome *in absentia* and executed at Faventia, 'in itinere',[1] Terracina and Baiae respectively. Where and how the attempt on Hadrian's life could have taken place (during a sacrifice or a hunt, say the sources) is difficult to imagine. As for the question of responsibility, Hadrian's own explanation[2] is 'senatu iubente, invito Hadriano'. Without entering into a discussion of the sincerity of this explanation and considering only the 'cui prodest?', we may wonder whether, comparing the two advantages, that of eliminating (and was physical elimination really necessary?) adversaries and that of preserving the Princeps–Senate idyll, that is, the most important prerequisite for equilibrium in the imperial life of the age, Hadrian the shrewd politician would have hesitated in his choice. In fact for him the episode was a misfortune, and consequently we can accept as sincere his recriminations against the precipitate action of the man really responsible for the operation, the praetorian prefect Acilius Attianus, whom not long afterwards (not later than 120) he pensioned off, together with his colleague Servius Sulpicius Similis, granting them the consular insignia. We know the hard work which Hadrian put in when he arrived in Rome, round about the beginning of July 118, to dissipate the impression left by the event. Yet the protestations and oaths in the Senate, the repetition of the guarantee not to put any senator to death without senatorial authorization, the double *congiarium* and the shows presented to the people, the scrupulous deference for republican structures and above all twenty years of clemency never availed to reconcile him completely with the aristocracy.

Hadrian had now reached the seat of empire. On 1 January 118 he had entered, *in absentia*, on his second consulship, for which he may have been nominated when Trajan was still alive. His first colleague was his sister's son-in-law, Cn. Pedanius Fuscus Salinator, who was followed by at least three others, the last of them being the distinguished orator

---

[1] *V. Hadr.*, 7, 2.   [2] *Ibid.*: 'ut ipse in vita sua dicit'.

C. Ummidius Quadratus, a friend of both Hadrian and Pliny. Hadrian may have still been consul when he made his entry into Rome, for there is no record of any successor, at any rate up to 9 July. He was soon designated *consul III* for 119, and in that year he actually exercised the office in the city for four months, with P. Dasumius Rusticus, who may have been another relative, and his friend A. Platorius Nepos. He wished to make his return resemble Trajan's in every way. And, going further than Trajan, he never assumed a fourth consulship. He thus remained equal, so far as this honour was concerned, to the only two private citizens known, of the *plurimi* mentioned by his biographer,[1] who for the last time in the history of the empire were consuls three times – his relation Ursus Servianus and M. Annius Verus, grandfather of the Emperor Marcus Aurelius, and was hardly superior to the numerous men who were consul twice. Thus the new reign grafted itself on to the tradition, and the honours paid to Trajan's memory – posthumous triumph, institution of the *ludi Parthici*, which were celebrated at some length, the cult of *Victoria Parthica Augusta*, the issue of coins in 117 and 118 in honour of *Divus Traianus* and of the living Plotina and Matidia, and the revival of the figure of *Hercules Gaditanus*, the Spanish divinity dear to Hadrian's predecessor – all gave outward emphasis as well to the sense and aim of continuity. Similarly, in a more practical field, the generosity and policy of liberality with which Hadrian remitted, in the first few days after his arrival, debts of nine hundred million sesterces to the fisc for arrears of taxes, causing the registers to be burnt in Trajan's Forum; the renunciation of the *aurum coronarium* for Italy and its reduction for the rest of the empire; and the transference of confiscated goods to the *aerarium Saturni*, were not acts for which there was no precedent. The same is also true of the theoretical speech made by Hadrian in the Senate, naturally in a tone of deference to that body, on the *aerarium* itself; of the aim of administering the *fiscus* accurately and strictly, without creating fresh taxes; and of the maintenance of the best standards in the coinage. All this was due to the continued good management of revenue and expenditure, as a result of which Hadrian's open-handedness achieved the prearranged political goals without detriment to financial equilibrium.

The originality of the new reign must have lain elsewhere. The plan, attributed to Hadrian in connection with the remission of debts, of examining every fifteen years the whole fiscal structure, if authentic, must have improved still further the existing system of censuses and land registers. This was an aspect of that precise regulation of everything to

[1] *Ibid.*, 8, 4.

which Hadrian soon turned his hand, finally establishing order as the fundamental aspect of public life. New concepts also appeared right from the start in the imperial symbolism. *Pietas, Concordia, Iustitia, Pax* were the motifs predominant in the coinage at the end of 117, in 118 and in the early part of 119. Justified as these motifs were by the facts, since after less than three years of the new principate no war was being waged on any frontier and peace and concord reigned – at any rate on the surface – in every corner of the empire, they received a new and special significance from the idea of permanence, of 'aeternitas', deliberately associated with them. There appeared on coins the legend 'saeculum aureum' and the sign of the phoenix to symbolize the renewed prosperity and perennial vitality of the Roman state. The interest shown by Tacitus in the details of the mythical bird which is always born again from its own ashes – an interest illustrated in a whole chapter of the *Annals* (VI, 28) – may incline us to think that he lived long enough to see this coin and to hear the talk it aroused.[1] Public opinion must certainly have been guided by this and other means to support the work of the Emperor who for the first time in the history of Rome made everything the subject of a precise and theoretical programme, and out of the concrete, empirical existence of all that had been produced by the slow, centuries-long growth of the civil structure now formulated the abstract concept of the perpetuity of the empire, to be defended in peace.

HADRIAN'S JOURNEYS

In the first three years of his sojourn in Rome only one excursion by Hadrian is recorded – a trip into Campania in 119 or 120. He was busy reorganizing the central administration and did not yet have time to travel. But even this brief foray had been different from the usual pleasure trip to the pleasant imperial villas. 'Omnia oppida beneficiis et largitionibus sublevavit',[2] which was what he was to do on a vast scale throughout the empire. We do not know precisely when the first big cycle of visits to the provinces began. Except for the fact that Hadrian was employed establishing the order which his systematic mind desired, little is known about the first years of the reign. On 24 January 119, his birthday, he once again gave the populace big shows, accompanied, as we know from coins, by the third *congiarium*, unless this was distributed a few days earlier, on 1 January, on the occasion of his assumption of the

[1] H. MATTINGLY, *Coins of the Rom. Emp. in the Br. Mus.*, III, London 1936, p. CXXVII.
[2] *V. Hadr.*, 9, 6.

consulship, and thus initiated the displays of liberality linked with imperial consulships. Then followed the downfall of Attianus and Sulpicius Similis, who were replaced as praetorian prefects by Q. Marcius Turbo and C. Septicius Clarus, Pliny's friend and the dedicatee of Suetonius's *Lives of the Caesars.* Since Turbo must first have completed his task in Pannonia and Dacia, the event should probably be placed in the year 120 and in any case before the journey to Campania. Hadrian's biographer, who gives this chronological order, says that the journey came after the liquidation of the prefects 'quibus debebat imperium' and thus lets it be understood that in these first years Hadrian must have been developing full independence of action, not only in the administrative field and not only vis-à-vis Attianus. At the end of 119 Matidia died and was splendidly honoured with funeral games, a speech by the Emperor – a fragment of which had been preserved – and deification, voted on 23 December 119. Of Hadrian's relations with Plotina, who died a couple of years later in 122, we know no more than we can glean from the fragments – authentic, it would seem – of an exchange of letters that probably took place in 121, namely news of an intervention, at Plotina's request, in favour of a philosophical sect in Athens – nothing therefore of any general political significance.

By 120 or 121 Hadrian's position in Rome must have been so firmly based, the functioning of the central administration so secure and well ordered, and the idea of the Emperor's majesty so firmly rooted throughout the empire, that it was possible for him to contemplate the execution of the most original part of his programme, the part that remained the best-known aspect of his reign, and of his reign alone, namely the personal inspection of the provinces and the armies. Unfortunately only the most miserable scraps of information have been preserved about this interesting activity, which was certainly recorded in Hadrian's own autobiography. It is only with difficulty that we can succeed in inserting in the brief and general accounts furnished by the literary sources the dates of the in-scriptions – in themselves sometimes weak enough evidence of the presence of the Emperor in this or that spot – and those on coins. Thus Hadrian's itineraries can only be reconstructed on largely hypothetical lines, and the uncertainty begins with the date of his first departure; we cannot even be sure whether it took place in 120 or 121. The prominence given on coins[1] to the birthday of Rome in 121, an event which people have tried to connect with the start of work on the temple of Venus and

---

[1] COHEN, II, p. 117 ff., Nos. 162–4; cf. MATTINGLY, *Coins of the Rom. Emp. in the Br. Mus.,* III, p. CXVI.

Rome, the *templum Urbis* on the Velia, has suggested the idea that Hadrian was present at the important ceremony of initial dedication, which according to this theory would have taken place on 21 April 121. But the connection is arbitrary, notwithstanding what we know of his deliberate exploitation of the 'natalis Urbis'. On the other hand, an inscription of 121 which gives Hadrian the title of *proconsul*, already used occasionally by Trajan and always by his successor when he was outside Italy, proves that he was already away from Rome in 121; though not necessarily before 21 April.[1]

The Emperor's immediate destination was Gaul, but it is useless to look for traces of his itinerary in his biographer's general outline: 'he helped all the towns with various kinds of liberality'. Nor is there any ordered list of places and events for Germany, where Hadrian proceeded next; instead we find, occasioned by the visit to the legions of the Rhine, the rhetorically embroidered *topos* of the good general, the restorer – like Scipio Aemilianus, Metellus and his 'father' Trajan – of military discipline. Discipline, which was among his principal concerns throughout the reign – so much so that his military regulations were still in force in the time of Cassius Dio (LXIX, 9, 4) – must indeed have been tested during the inspection of the army of Germany, but Hadrian certainly also interested himself in the further organization of the *limes*, and traces have been preserved of road works in the valley of the Rhine, works that can be referred to these very years 121–122. Then there are records in the coinage of a visit to Raetia, Noricum and probably even Pannonia; but there is no proof that this visit took place by way of a detour from the visit to the Rhine except the likely hypothesis that he wanted to look at the whole Rhine–Danube defensive system, not just a part of it. Perhaps early in the spring of 122 Hadrian sailed to Britain from the *Insula Batavorum*, where he had arrived by descending the Rhine, near the mouth of which he founded a *Forum Hadriani* (Voorburg, between Rotterdam and Leyden). It is probable that he took with him at that time from the camp at Vetera, or ordered to follow shortly afterwards, the VI *Victrix* legion to reinforce the garrison of the province in which the revolt of the Brigantes had recently been quelled; and this even if, as it would seem, the IX *Hispana* legion, once thought to have been destroyed by the rebels before 117, was still in existence. Hadrian's plans for the defence of Romanized Britain demanded in fact a large labour force, and when, as an immediate consequence of his visit, work began on the great fortified line from the Solway to the Tyne, with its attendant roads, legionaries and auxiliaries

[1] *CIL*, VI, 1233.

were heavily engaged, under the direction of A. Platorius Nepos, one of the Emperor's close associates, transferred at that time from the command of Lower Germany to that of Britain, where he had certainly arrived by the middle of 122.

Meanwhile Hadrian had returned to Gaul and reached Gallia Narbonensis. That the cause of this swift journey was the news of riots in Egypt caused by the frantic enthusiasm that greeted the much heralded appearance of a bull Apis is stated by the biographer (12, 1); that a vigorous letter from the Princeps was sufficient to pacify the rioters derives from the place where the ingenious editor has placed, rightly in all probability, a fragment of Cassius Dio, whose text is in poor shape at this point.[1] The visit to the cities of Narbonese Gaul must have lasted until near the end of 122, for the winter which the biographer (12, 3) describes as spent at Tarragona in Spain can only be that of 122–123. In 122 Plotina died and Hadrian, either because he received the news at Nemausus (Nîmes) or because he wanted to honour this splendid city above others, had a temple in honour of the deceased empress built there and consecrated it himself. The stay at Nemausus is also recorded in inscriptions. Probably on the occasion of the Emperor's visit, Avignon received the title of *Colonia Iulia Hadriana Avennio*. *Colonia Iulia Apta* (Apt) became the burial place of Borysthenes, the horse used for hunting by Hadrian, who composed for the occasion a poetic epitaph, preserved in an inscription. As can be seen, the evidence is disparate and fragmentary, but it is sufficient to illustrate the varied interests of the imperial traveller, who divided his time between official festivities, the pleasures of the chase and administrative inspections.

At Tarragona the number of statues dedicated to him was so great that later on a special magistracy had to be created to look after them.[2] But he also took advantage of the winter pause to call together the representatives of the province to discuss a scheme to levy troops. We do not know in detail how Hadrian responded to the lively opposition of the provincials to this plan; his biographer's 'prudenter et caute consuluit' (12, 4) leaves our curiosity totally unsatisfied. At Tarragona he also restored the temple of Augustus, at his own expense. We are also informed of an attempt on his life by a slave, who was found to be mad and instead of being punished was entrusted to the care of a doctor. Hadrian then continued his journey southward, going as far as Gades. On this occasion he did not stop at his native town of Italica. He may have done it a favour by now granting it the longed-for title of *colonia*, requested for some time and refused for the

[1] CASS. D., LXIX, 8, 1a; BOISSEVAIN, III, p. 229.   [2] *ILS*, 6930.

historical reasons explained by Hadrian in the Senate and mentioned by Aulus Gellius (*Noct. Att.*, XVI, 13) – namely, that the title of *municipium*, obtained by the little town, originally a Roman colony, a century earlier as a mark of honour, was a greater not a lesser dignity – but the sources show a noteworthy concern to underline the Emperor's impartiality. The western part of the great journey ended with an excursion into Mauretania and some kind of military operation there, for which the Senate voted *supplicationes*. Before the end of 123 Hadrian sailed either from Mauretania or Spain straight to the East. He did not return again to the European West.

A reference by the biographer – just at the very point in his confused narrative where he moves to the eastern part of the peregrinations (12, 8) – to strained relations with the Parthians might suggest that it was fear of surprises in the Syrian sector that induced Hadrian to make his swift journey and to skip the whole coast of Africa. In fact in 123 the Parthamaspates set up in Osrhoene in 117 did cease to reign there, and this could have been a factor in the tension supposed to have been resolved by the Emperor through a parley – the biographer does not say with whom, but evidently with the king of the Parthians. If the report occurs at the right chronological point, Hadrian must have gone first to Syria and from there across Asia Minor to Greece. But it is difficult to speak of a voyage straight to Syria, especially as all the reliable pieces of information about the first journey are confined to the provinces of Asia and Bithynia. The famous parley remains suspended completely in the air. Moreover, the attempt to trace any kind of itinerary is an almost hopeless enterprise when the only known facts about this first eastern journey are that Hadrian was certainly at Stratonicea and some other spots in Phrygia, in the Troas, at Cyzicus, at Nicomedia and Nicaea, that at one point he set sail from Ephesus for Rhodes and finally crossed from Asia to Achaea 'per insulas' (*V. Hadr.*, 13, 1) – how, when and by what route is unknown. Thus all we can do is assemble the scattered pieces of testimony to Hadrian's presence – which are more abundant in the magniloquent East than in the West – in so far as they can be distinguished from those referring to the second journey of some years later.

The visit to the Greek-speaking East, made now without any military preoccupations, must have been very agreeable for the philhellene Emperor, who for three or four years, probably (though not certainly) accompanied by Sabina, passed from one city of Asia and Greece to another, amid scenes – to judge from the superlatives enshrined in stone – of indescribable enthusiasm. Hadrian had already intervened with the sort of measures and works which the Flavians, Nerva and Trajan had all bestowed liberally on the eastern provinces: there are records of benefits conferred at Traianopolis in Mysia in 119, at Pergamum and Magnesia between 119 and 121 and at Ephesus in 120, here in the shape of an intervention exactly in the spirit of Trajan's instructions to Pliny, while in 122 a general improvement of the roads of Galatia, possibly with a view to the coming of the Emperor, had been effected by the governor, A. Lartius Macedo. However, it does not seem as if Hadrian actually visited Galatia on this first journey. The cities of Bithynia, particularly Nicomedia and Nicea, only just recovering from the damage caused by the earthquake of 120, were certainly visited, but probably later on in the tour, for Hadrian, coming from the distant West (the idea that he went as far as Syria can almost certainly be excluded), will have more probably disembarked at some port in southern Asia Minor (Ephesus ?) and then proceeded north by land. On the other hand, it is not even certain that he went first to the cities of Ionia and Phrygia, but in the space of a further year (summer or autumn 123–autumn 124) various comings and goings are conveniently recorded for us. Naturally an honorific inscription like the innumerable ones already dedicated to his predecessors, or the granting of his name to a city, is not enough to prove that the Emperor passed that way; but his minute interest in everything and the jealous competition of the cities to secure his divine presence are our guarantee that few places will have been neglected.

However, the principal records are confined to a fairly small number of areas. In Bithynia, Nicomedia, generously favoured, and Cios assumed the epithet *Hadriana*; in eastern Bithynia Prusa on the Ipius gave two of the local tribes the names of Hadrian and Sabina; and neighbouring Claudiopolis, which assumed the epithet *Hadriana* as well as the ancient name of Bithynium, was certainly particularly favoured right from this first journey, even with the institution of festivals, since it was the native city of Antinous, the Emperor's favourite young page. In the part of Asia looking out over the Propontis Hadrian left an imposing memorial at Cyzicus, also recently damaged by the earthquake, in the form of the assistance he provided for the construction of a temple dedicated to him which was among the biggest in the world. On the occasion of his visit the agora was probably paved, the city received the titles of *Hadriana* and *neocorus* (that is, custodian of a temple to the emperor), and instituted festivals in Hadrian's honour. In this region Hadrian is also recorded as having visited, in all probability at the same time, Parium, which hailed him as its founder, Apollonia in Mysia and Miletopolis, which added to his title of founder that of benefactor as well. He certainly went to the neighbouring Troad – where he restored the so-called tomb of Ajax at Ilium and bestowed benefits on the by then more important town of Alexandria Troas – if only to pay homage to its historical and literary memories; and that the visit probably took place in 124 can be proved by the repairs to the coastal road, which are datable to that year. In the interior of the province he undoubtedly stayed at Pergamum, the capital, and conferred honours on it, without forgetting its rival Smyrna, whose ambitions he flattered by allowing it to embellish itself, like Pergamum, with two temples to the Emperor and to institute, again like Pergamum, the association of the dancers of Dionysus. The Ionian city, which received other favours, instituted festivals and assumed the title of Hadriana, commemorated the happy moment in a high-sounding inscription of the year 124.[1] In fact, Antonius Polemo, one of the sophists of the Smyrna Museum, succeeded in touching the Emperor, an admirer of his teaching, for the substantial sum of ten million drachmas for the city's buildings.

Hadrian's interest in urban organization, which in his view had everywhere to form the basis of ordered, civilized life, also found expression in the foundation of new towns and the rehabilitation of decaying old ones. The form used here was generally that of the Greek *polis*, with the local organization still formally modelled on Athenian democracy. Three new towns – Hadrianeia, Hadriane and Hadrianotherae – were founded in the interior of Mysia, the last of them – so the story goes – to commemorate a particularly noteworthy bear hunt. All three were situated in fairly favourable commercial and strategic positions, on the roads between Bithynia and Galatia, and in fact prospered; but their presence as organized *poleis* in an area only superficially Hellenized was a complete novelty. Another Hadrianopolis resulted from the reorganization of the *Caesareis Proseilemmenitae* ('the collected Caesareas') on the border between Bithynia and Paphlagonia; but it was especially Stratonicea, not far from Pergamum, that blossomed again after becoming Hadrianopolis, assisted as it was by the Emperor both when he was there and later (Hadrian's letter of 127). There are other records, almost certainly of this first journey, in Lydia, at Thyatira and Nacrasa, and a certain amount of time must have been devoted to the cities of the coast and the nearby islands: Erythrae, where Hadrian probably arrived by sea from Smyrna, since festivals were established to celebrate his landing, Miletus, Ephesus and finally Rhodes, possibly the goal of an excursion.

From one or other of these cities the 'New Dionysus', as Hadrian was

[1] *IGR*, IV, 1398.

called by spontaneous identification and association in worship with the travelling god who dispensed happiness, crossed over to Athens, which he had reached by the end of September 124. Arriving just in time for the Great Eleusinia, celebrated from 15 to 30 Boedromion (first fortnight of October), he had himself initiated in the mysteries, attaining the grade of *mystes*, an honour which the initiating priestess recorded in verses.[1] She boasted of having initiated the master of the world who, in exchange, provided Eleusis with good dykes against the floods of the River Cephisus and with a bridge. He also exempted the people of Eleusis from the tax on fish and possibly restored the ten per cent tax to the temple. The inscriptions, the statues and all the various signs of gratitude to the Princeps and his consort, 'Nea Demeter', may naturally also refer to the second visit, but from this time onwards the greatest mystery centre of the Greek world played an influential part in Hadrian's religious interests. During his stay in Athens, which must have lasted the whole winter, for in March 125 he presided over the contests of the Great Dionysia, he was certainly able to satisfy his taste for Greek culture; but he did not forget the practical side of life, if the reform of the law and the measures to encourage trade date from this first sojourn. It was certainly now that he initiated the building activity that was to give back to the city its ancient splendour. He also travelled through the rest of Greece and the most substantial evidence of the lasting memory of his presence in almost every place is to be found in Pausanias's guide book, itself probably the result of the stimulus given by the travelling Emperor's memorable visits to the tourist and antiquarian exploitation of the Greek monuments. But the attempt to distinguish the spots visited on the first and second trips, or to trace any kind of itinerary, is once again a hopeless enterprise; our only clue, though not a decisive one, is the question of time: the apparently shorter duration of the second stay of 128–129 leads us to think that Hadrian had satisfied during the first stay his desire to see all the famous places of Greece and that on his second visit he concentrated his attention on Athens.

There are records of two visits to Sparta, one of which no doubt took place during the first journey. His presence in the Peloponnese is also attested at Mantinea, which on Hadrian's orders adopted its old name again, after bearing for over three hundred years that of Antigoneia: here the Emperor composed an epitaph for the tomb, which was restored, of Epaminondas and repaired the sacred enclosure of the temple of Poseidon. At Mycenae he gave a peacock made of silver studded with jewels to the

[1] *IG*, II–III², 3575.

temple of Hera, and at Argos, whither he transferred the ancient games from Nemea, he revived certain competitions that had for some time been abandoned. He presented Corinth with an aqueduct and baths, repaired the coast road to Megara, and there restored the temple of Apollo, instituting a sacerdotal college of Hadrianides. Naturally he did not fail to visit Delphi, where he interrogated the oracle on the fundamental literary question, the birthplace of Homer. The Amphictyonic Council, grateful for the decrease he had ordered in the number of Thessalian votes on the council itself, to the advantage of Athens, Sparta and other more illustrious cities, dedicated a statue to him in addition to the two already erected in the first years of the reign by Delphi and the Amphicty-onic Council, the second of them on a motion drawn up by an exceptional councillor, the aged Plutarch. At Delphi the news now also reached him of the honour of another statue voted by the representatives of the Greeks meeting at Plataea, as they did every year, to commemorate the victory. There are also other records of his visit to central Greece. From there he sailed over to Sicily in the summer of 125, or 126 if his travels round Greece lasted that long. His arrival and beneficent stay in the island were commemorated, as always elsewhere, by coins marking the *Adventus* and *Restitutio*: we also have the report, significant only for his personal bio-graphy, of his ascent to the summit of Etna to contemplate the rising of the sun. His first big tour now completed, Hadrian returned to Rome, where he certainly was in 126, for the *Fasti Ostienses* mention under this year his dedication of a restoration of the *templum* or *porticus Divorum* in the Campus Martius, on which occasion he gave splendid shows, with 1835 pairs of gladiators.[1]

The same *Fasti Ostienses* have also revealed a hitherto unknown journey in 127 – a tour of Italy that began on 3 March. All we had before was numerous records of acts of liberality, dating from this year, in towns in the Sabine region, in Picenum and in Campania; the new document con-firms that they were performed by the Emperor in person.

From 20 to 30 October 127 the votive games for the tenth anniversary of Hadrian's accession certainly represented, in the profound peace that reigned everywhere, the greatest celebration of a state of affairs established on a durable basis. The coins, which had already borne for some years, in imitation of those of Augustus, the simple inscription *Hadrianus Augustus* and had tended to idealize the portrait of the Princeps, repeated the motif of the *Aeternitas* of Rome and the empire, celebrated the guardian deities, especially Venus and Rome, represented insistently the gallery of imperial

---

[1] DEGRASSI, *Inscr. It.*, XIII, 1, pp. 203, 233.

virtues and alluded to the old Roman legends and the age of gold. The Emperor himself must have thought that he had fulfilled his duties to the state and made his own programme a reality; in 128, possibly on 21 April and possibly in connection with some important moment in the construction of the *Templum Urbis*, he finally accepted the title of *pater patriae*, and in the same year his consort became *Sabina Augusta*. The first coins with the new title, which lay particular stress on the motif of *Concordia*, display the aim, largely achieved, of perfect harmony between all the elements of public life, especially between the Senate and the Princeps, who could now resume his travels in perfect peace.

He started again with Africa, where he certainly was in the summer of 128. He landed at Carthage, and the rain that fell just as he arrived after five years of drought made it seem as if he had been sent by heaven. The city temporarily assumed the name of Hadrianopolis, while Utica and Zama now received the coveted title of colony. From here Hadrian made his way inland to inspect the apparatus of defence, Legion III *Augusta*, now permanently stationed at Lambaesis, and the numerous auxiliary detachments. The names of the places that offer certain or almost certain proof of the Emperor's presence allow us to construct a rough itinerary through Avitta Bibba, Lares, Theveste and Thamugadi to Lambaesis. Here a curious monument provides rather interesting testimony to the nature of Hadrian's inspection of the armies. Fragments from the base of a commemorative column give us extracts – naturally only from the laudatory passages – from five *adlocutiones* that Hadrian gave, on different days during the manoeuvres, to the legionary infantry and cavalry and to the auxiliaries. Early in July 128 the Emperor reviewed, after the manoeuvres on the plain near the camp of Lambaesis, the whole III *Augusta* and an auxiliary cohort, the II *Hispanorum equitata*. He praised the soldiers' standard of tactical training, which was high in spite of constant guard duties and construction work on the camp – work rendered heavier by the reduction in the number of men available owing to their continued employment in detached units – and congratulated the commanding officer, Q. Fabius Catullinus, who two years later, in 130, attained the consulship. Turning then to the cavalry, he declared that he appreciated the simple but laborious and useful exercise which they had demonstrated – a sweeping charge in full heavy armour. Finally the auxiliaries, with their commander Cornelianus, received much praise for their construction of defences and for the demonstration of an attack in support of the legionary cavalry. These are fragments of the big speech in which the Emperor, who far from forgetting the strategy learnt from Trajan tended by his nature to theorize about it, summed up, after a day spent with the troops on manœuvres under the blazing African sun, the results of the exercises and imparted instruction, praise and encouragement. On 7 July he visited an auxiliary cohort at Zarai, in the neighbourhood of Lambaesis, and five or six days later inspected *ala* I *Pannoniorum*, assembled for the occasion in the camp of cohort VI *Commagenorum equitata* – we do not know precisely where. However, his stay in Africa was not devoted exclusively to the army; records of Hadrian are preserved in many cities, which no doubt received benefits from him; but it is always uncertain whether the benefits were conferred by the Emperor in person and on this particular occasion. He also probably had a look at the imperial estates.

It may be that the return journey was made by the most direct route to the sea, from Lambaesis to Rusicade via Cirta, the road restored by Sex. Julius Maior, who had been commander of the III *Augusta* in 126, before Catullinus. By August Hadrian was already in Italy; the praetor P. Cluvius Maximus Paullinus was sent to meet him, probably in Campania, in the capacity of ambassador of the Senate, as we know from a recently discovered inscription which is worth mentioning, not only because it has restored to the light of day the name of one of the men who traversed the famous *cursus* under Hadrian and his successor, but also because there is no other evidence of similar embassies at the return of the Emperor.[1] Hadrian then went on to Rome, but not with the intention of staying there. A few weeks later he set off, this time certainly with Sabina, for the second grand tour of the East, in time to be in Athens in the early days of October 128 for his second initiation into the mysteries of Demeter during the Great Eleusinia. He now attained the higher rank of *epoptes*, another factor calculated to add to the aura of divinity which accompanied him, an aura spontaneously accepted and almost created in advance by the eastern mentality. In fact, even if the construction of the Olympieum, the biggest of the splendid buildings whose foundations he had laid, or whose completion or restoration he had promised, during his previous stay in Athens, was not yet finished and only the *cella* of the god was completed and inaugurated, Hadrian, whose statue already stood in the agora on an equal footing with that of the father of the gods, was now assimilated to him in worship and assumed the name of Olympius, which in the East formed part of his official title. Many cities of Greece and Asia were subsequently anxious to place their own statues of Hadrian in the Athenian temple. Other buildings in Athens – the Pantheon, a porch, a

[1] A. DEGRASSI, in *Epigraphica*, I, 1939, pp. 307–21.

gymnasium, a temple of Hera – were either inaugurated at this time or are connected in some way with the visit; a new aqueduct, carrying water from Mt Lycabettus, was started, and completed under Hadrian's successor; but, above all, the eastern part of old Athens, along the Ilissus, was replanned and called Hadrianopolis. A new tribe, the Hadrianides, was formed to embrace its inhabitants. An arch that still exists bears on each side sonorous inscriptions: 'On this side the Athens of Theseus, the earlier city, on this the city of Hadrian, not of Theseus' (*IG*, 11–111², 5185).

From Greece the Emperor crossed over to Asia – and this detail is known for certain – from Eleusis to Ephesus, probably in the spring of 129, after a winter in Athens that ended with his presence at Eleusis on the occasion of the Little Eleusinia (1 March). The title 'Olympius', which appears in inscriptions, helps to distinguish records of this tour from those of the preceding one, but there is still just the same uncertainty about the itinerary. It seems that he stopped for some time at Ephesus, treating the city to a distribution of corn imported from Egypt, organizing work on the River Cayster so as to improve the port, which was silting up, and starting work on an Olympieum, so that Ephesus could achieve its ambition of being, like Pergamum and Smyrna, doubly *neocorus*: things for which the Ephesians subsequently showed ample gratitude through statutes and dedications to Hadrian Olympius, Panhellenius and Panionius and by adding the title of Olympian to the Hadrianic festivals established on the occasion of the first visit. From Ephesus he must have made excursions with Sabina, the 'Nea Hera', to the neighbouring cities and to those of Caria. There are records at Miletus, at Tralles, at Nyssa, at Laodicea and in other places, as well as at Cibyra. But here he must have already been on the way to Syria, which he intended to reach this time via the southern provinces of Anatolia. From Cibyra in fact he must have entered neighbouring Lycia, where there are numerous pieces of testimony to his visit: at Patara and Andriace (the port of Myra), where he had big *horrea* built, at Olympus and at Phaselis, where he built a temple that was completed in 131; there are also records of his presence in two other localities in the interior, Acalissus and Corydalla. In Pamphylia he certainly visited Attalia, at that time the principal town, and from there he pushed inland to Termessus, Cremna (which was already a Roman colony), Pogla and Sagalassus. From Pamphylia he probably continued his journey by sea, sailing along the coast and landing to visit the cities of Cilicia, many of which added Hadrian's name to their own (like Tarsus and Mopsuestia, the principal ones) or else simply changed their name to Hadrianopolis. He reached Antioch – if we are to believe a late and questionable chronicler[1] – on 23 June 129, and there celebrated great festivals, though in the end the arrogance of the citizens of Antioch began to annoy him, so much so as to make him think of dividing the province of Syria into two parts to mortify the city's pride – a plan never carried out, if it ever really did pass through his mind. The ascent of Mount Casius, sacred to Zeus, an ascent completed dramatically in a raging storm, seems on the other hand quite credible when we think of his ascent of Etna three years earlier.

Now came the most romantic part of the tour, the journey to Arabia and Egypt. Whether we should place before this – and possibly even before the entry into Antioch – a visit to the legions of Cappadocia, with re-cruitment in the area and a meeting with the client princes, as the really rather vague narrative order adopted by his biographer[2] seems to indicate, is impossible to decide. All we can say is that a thrust into Cappadocia before the arrival at Antioch, if this took place as early as June – Hadrian had left Athens possibly in March and had not come, as we have seen, by the most direct route – does not seem very probable. It is thus probably better to assume that from Antioch the Emperor made tours of inspection and that among these was the trip up to some point on the Armenian frontier, possibly Samosata or Melitene. The biographer speaks on the same occasion of terrible severity in the punishment of high provincial officials, probably colouring his narrative to fit in with the usual minute-ness of Hadrian's inspection. And this activity may well have radiated from Antioch, in 129. The recruiting drive will have helped to make the eastern defence apparatus more efficient, and strengthening the defences was certainly one of the aims of Hadrian's tours; the meeting of princes, following an invitation that only Pharasmanes of Iberia took it upon him-self to decline (that Chosroes did not come was natural; however, it was on this occasion that his daughter was restored to him), was part of the same programme. The southern excursion in 129, to Palmyra, Damascus and possibly even Petra (which became either now or in the following year Petra Hadriana), with the return trip through Gaza and probably along the coast through Tyre and Berytus, was also based on Antioch, if, as seems likely, the winter of 129–130 was spent there. However, it cannot be ruled out that Hadrian did not return to Antioch but spent the winter at some other city (Gerasa ?).

What is certain is that in the spring of 129 he started out southward again; it was probably now rather than in the previous year – though as usual we cannot be sure – that he visited Jerusalem, still largely in

[1] MALAL., XI, 278.   [2] V. Hadr., 13, 7–14, 3.

ruins, and gave the fatal order to rebuild it as Aelia Capitolina, that is, with the deliberate intention of setting up the supreme Roman god against the Jewish Yahweh. Since Vespasian's time the Jews had been paying the didrachm to Jupiter Capitolinus, but they could not tolerate the substitution of this god for their own – an operation attempted in vain by Gaius – in his most sacred abode. At Pelusium, the gateway to Egypt, Hadrian paid honour to and restored the tomb of Pompey. In the summer he was in Alexandria and spent at least two months there, among other things in learned conversation with the scholars of the Museum, in whom however he aroused a certain amount of ill humour by adding to them as supernumeraries, really at his own expense, scholars and poets from all over the Roman world, among them the panegyrist who accompanied him everywhere, Antonius Polemo of Laodicea. Hadrian then sailed up the Nile into Upper Egypt, taking Sabina and his retinue with him.

On 30 October, opposite Hermopolis, halfway between Memphis and Thebes, his favourite, Antinous, was drowned in the Nile, accidentally according to Hadrian's own written statement, which there is no reason to doubt, in spite of the gossip preserved by the tradition. The Emperor's reaction was certainly disconcerting: unconsolable grief, the foundation of a city – Antinoopolis or Antinoe – at the scene of the accident, the dedication of statues to the boy all over the world and even deification. That a real cult was instituted is shown by the creation of an oracle – at Mantinea, the supposed mother-city of Bithynium – and the diffusion everywhere of games in honour of Antinous. And the cult lasted quite a long time. A willing astronomer discovered a new star in the heavens, the spirit of Antinous, and a poet, Pancrates, who gained free board and lodging at the Museum of Alexandria by his efforts, sang in verses that are by no means contemptible, as we can judge from the fragment preserved in a papyrus,[1] of the flower that sprang from Antinous's blood when he was wounded in a hunt – a lion hunt – in Egypt. Perhaps it is in the sphere of hunting and of the sort of mysticism with which Hadrian endowed this, his greatest and almost morbid passion, a mysticism which may have found an echo in the feelings of an age dominated by the leisured pursuits of peace, that we should look for the key to this apparently disproportionate exaltation; the temple dedicated at Lanuvium in 133 to Antinous and Diana the huntress may possibly confirm the connection.

By 21 November 130 the imperial party had reached Thebes and there

[1] P. Oxy., VIII (1911), 1085; already alluded to by ATHEN., XV, 677 d–f.

heard the colossal statue of Memnon produce its echo. What Hadrian did during the further year spent in Egypt, which he left only in the late summer of 131, we simply do not know. The return journey was made through Judaea and Syria. From northern Syria – if this is the right spot to place a report by Flavius Arrianus, governor of Cappadocia from 134 to 137 and author of the *Voyage round the Euxine* – Hadrian went to Trapezus on the Black Sea, evidently travelling along the Armenian frontier in a journey which the historian compares with that of Xenophon and which was certainly distinct from the tour of inspection in Cappadocia two years earlier. The visit to Trapezus, which some scholars, for not particularly convincing reasons, prefer to place in the first tour of Asia, brought the remote Pontic city the construction of a harbour and a temple of Hermes. It then becomes difficult to follow Hadrian in his return to the West through the northern and central provinces of the Anatolian peninsula. All we can do is mention, from east to west, the towns recording Hadrian in their name or some other title, though the assignment to this period is not always certain. Nicopolis, Neocaesarea and Amasia, all lying along the great northern inland road, added the epithet *Hadriana* to their names; Sebastopolis in Pontus acquired a porch in honour of Hadrian and a priest of Hadrian; and in the course of a detour, which, however, not all authorities are disposed to assign to this journey, he must have reached Lycaonia and granted the status of colony to Iconium: Colonia Aelia Hadriana Augusta Iconensium. He may have visited Bithynium a second time, but this is not at all certain; and what happened after that is completely obscure. All we know is that in 134 Hadrian was once again in Rome, whatever it may be legitimate to infer from two Spanish milestones of that year, four miles apart, one bearing the indication of the proconsulship usual when Hadrian was outside Italy, the other not.[1] In fact many visits attested in various spots cannot be given a date, and it would be unjustifiable to lump them all at random into the years 131 to 134 when some of them could also be inserted in the itineraries of earlier tours. In the absence of any reliable information the mere mention of them will suffice.

On the other hand, the final inauguration of the Olympieum, the worthy dwelling of Olympian Zeus, now finally completed four centuries after its foundation, can be assigned to a third and certain stay in Athens (winter 131–132). But the dedication of the temple of Zeus, celebrated with, among other things, a speech by Antonius Polemo, was not the only ceremony that contributed to the splendour of the visit. The foundations

[1] *CIL*, II, 4821, 4841 (mil. XXXI and XXXV on the Via Bracara – Asturica).

were laid of another great building, the Panhellenion, which, unlike the Olympieum, has not survived; no trace of it remains. It seems that this temple was not completed before 137, but Hadrian created at once the characteristic institution of the 'Panhellenes'. Presenting and exalting in religious form the unity of the Greeks naturally formed part of the programme of spiritual unification, and with these homages to tradition and Greek religious values Hadrian was able to satisfy his antiquarian enthusiasm (rather than a mysticism alien to his typically Roman nature) while at the same time procuring political advantages. In the college of the Panhellenes, which was to meet at Athens and organize the Panhellenic games, all the cities of Greek origin scattered over the Roman world were represented in proportion to their population and importance; and we have records of lively rivalry in the assertion of relative rank. It may be that we should assign to this point of time a trip to the north of Greece, where indications of Hadrian's presence are numerous (valley of Tempe, Dodona, Nicopolis), though they could also belong to an earlier period. Finally, it seems certain that he made a personal inspection, probably in 133–134, of the theatre of the Jewish war. It should also be added that Hadrian must have visited Pannonia, Moesia and Dacia, possibly several times, though it is impossible to say exactly when, for he certainly devoted as much attention to the defence of this frontier, always the most important one, as to that of the others; coins bearing the legends *Adventus*, *Exercitus* and *Restitutio* exist for these provinces as they do for the other provinces visited. Crete and Cyrene must also have been inspected, the former possibly during the first crossing from West to East, the latter from Egypt. Macedonia cannot have escaped attention, nor can Thrace, the site of the most illustrious and lasting of all Hadrian's foundations, Hadrianopolis. But the period and itineraries of these tours are unknown; that Thrace was visited from Bithynia on the very first journey, that is, in 124, is a hypothesis no better or worse than a number of others.

In any case, what is important is not so much the precise chronological reconstruction of these journeys as the fact that they took place at all and were of great political value. Of the sixteen years and more from autumn 117 to spring 134 Hadrian had spent at least twelve visiting the empire. Therein, and in the measures taken as a result of his personal inspections, lay almost the whole of his activity for many long years of his reign and that is how he reckoned to fulfil his duty as Princeps: 'orbem Romanum circumiit'.[1]

---

[1] EUTROP., VIII, 7, 2.

THE ADMINISTRATIVE MACHINE

The minute personal interest Hadrian took in the running of the empire
gave a characteristic look to the administration, which had become in the
natural course of its development and now explicitly and systematically
the principal planned element in the policy of the principate. The greater
attention consequently devoted to it by the tradition has resulted in the
preservation in great abundance of tiny administrative details. The
emphasis on the episodic is also accentuated by the kind of information
predominant: the second century presents us in fact with a very large
number of epigraphical documents, which are by their very nature
fragmentary and limited in the evidence they provide. The general
policy must therefore be deduced as far as this is possible, from the vast
quantity of detailed evidence.

The work of government carried out by Hadrian was truly imposing.
At the vertex of the system, now perfectly organized, he acted, stimulated
and controlled with a degree of adherence to the rhythm of ordinary,
everyday public life never before achieved. He had stated and repeated
that he would govern in such a way as to make it clear that he was the
servant not the master of the state,[1] and in the sense of fulfilling a real
function in the administration his promise was shown to be entirely
sincere. The basis of his activity was naturally still accord with the Senate
and the formal division with it of the direction of public affairs, while
individual senators collaborated in the highest tasks of government.
Hadrian's relations with the senatorial class are in fact described to us by
the tradition as fairly similar to those of Trajan. The titles to public and
private merit attributed to him are a high regard for senatorial dignity
and condemnation of the emperors who had not sufficiently recognized it;
assiduous attendance at the Senate's sittings and continual consultation
of it; subventions to maintain the property qualification of those in low
water through no fault of their own; donations to enable senators to hold
magistracies with due dignity; inclusion of the most illustrious senators
among his *amici*; the exercise of justice in partnership with the Senate; the
extensive use of *senatusconsulta* for legislation; the absence of any appeal
to the Princeps from the senatorial courts; the exclusion of knights from
trials of senators even if the Princeps was present; affability and easy
accessibility; liberality and generosity with advice and gifts; the exchange
of invitations to dinner; visits to sick friends, and in short participation as
an ordinary citizen in every aspect of the common life of the aristocracy.

[1] *V. Hadr.*, 8, 3.

And these claims to honourable fame are all the more credible when we take into account how much less tender the senatorial tradition was to him than to his predecessor. In a word, he made no essential change in the manner or means of collaboration by the senatorial aristocracy in the work of administration.

But alongside the senatorial hierarchy there now stood, regular and complete, different rather than inferior (from the administrative point of view, of course, not from that of social dignity), the equestrian hierarchy. At its head, the two praetorian prefects (or rather just one for most of Hadrian's reign, for we have no clear evidence that Turbo ever had a colleague after the dismissal of Septicius Clarus in 121 or 122) had reached a high position and their purely military competence as commanders of the guard was yielding more and more before the increase in their civil functions: as members of the *consilium* and participants in the imperial courts, they were acquiring a specific judicial competence. Not a long time was to pass before some praetorian prefects were to be at the same time the most famous jurists. The other big prefectures – those of Egypt, the corn supply, the *vigiles* – and command of the fleets continued to remain solidly in the hands of the knights, but the appointment by Hadrian of numerous subordinate commanders such as the *subpraefecti* of the Misenum and Ravenna fleets, in imitation of what Trajan had done with the prefecture of the *vigiles* caused direct imperial control to penetrate to a lower level and accentuated the hierarchical tendency. Not that exceptional appointments were completely eliminated; the dispatch of the mere *primuspilus* Septimius Saturninus to Aezani in Phrygia in 128 to restore boundaries was analogous to Trajan's settlement of three thousand colonists at Cyrene under the leadership of a centurion of Legion III *Cyrenaica*. Similar special appointments naturally continued, but to all intents and purposes the whole transformation and crystallization of the equestrian career meant the establishment of a hierarchical civil service, the embryo of a bureaucracy, and this can be more easily discerned when this service by knights is more and more clearly separated from their military functions and is even exempted from the prerequisite of previous military service, hitherto indispensable. Men of distinction who had not passed through the *tres militiae* characteristic of the equestrian order, and who in many cases were not even knights, were also employed, as *advocatus fisci*, for example, that is, the counsel for the fisc in cases with private individuals, who relieved the procurators of the heavy burden of adjudicating in fiscal affairs and probably rendered unnecessary the *praetor fiscalis*, for whose existence there is in fact no longer any evidence in the age of

Hadrian. These *advocati* or *patroni fisci*, who multiplied and had juris-diction in the provinces as well, were for the most part elderly and authori-tative persons, expert in law, and had a career outside the ordinary *cursus*, which they could join subsequently. Another sign of the formation of the rigid framework of a civil service, one that was to a certain extent more and more impersonal, was the disappearance of the imperial freedmen, already definitively replaced in Trajan's time by the senior palace officials, all knights and members of the imperial *consilium*.

The system of procuratorships was simple and admirable. It had been slowly evolving since the days of Augustus, but Hadrian gave it its final form, making use of the experience gained under Trajan and of his own personal knowledge of all the administrative requirements. The pro-curator's career had a precise promotion ladder, on which the scale of remunerations conferred a surprisingly modern character. Not that re-munerations were lacking for other posts, for even the senatorial governors of provinces had their perquisites; but in the case of the procurators the salary question is particularly significant for its hierarchical effects. Under Hadrian the highest officials were the *ducenarii*, that is, those who received 200,000 sesterces a year; then came the *centenarii* (100,000 sesterces) and the *sexagenarii* (60,000 sesterces). Among the ducenarii were all the top officials of the palace, the *ab epistulis Latinis* and the *ab epistulis Graecis* (posts separated by Hadrian), the *a rationibus*, the *a patrimonio*, the *a libellis et censibus*, the *a studiis* etc., and also, in Rome, to cite only one procuratorship instituted by Hadrian, the *procurator bibliothecae*. Other ducenarii were naturally the procurators governing provinces, that is, those with the *ius gladii*, while the financial procurators in the imperial pro-vinces were usually centenarii, like the highest officials of the fiscal system, whose subordinates were for the most part sexagenarii. Many of these lower posts were in fact created by Hadrian – 17 of them, as opposed to 9 ducenarii and 9 centenarii. The total number of posts in Hadrian's time, according to our present evidence, was 37 ducenarii, 36 centenarii and 35 sexagenarii. Thus the whole administration of a huge empire was run by 108 'directors general'!

Continuing the tradition established since Vespasian's time, Hadrian gave special care to the organization of the revenue. It was the financial administration that absorbed the majority of the new posts of procurator. Little could now escape the customs net except by the kind favour of the Emperor himself, who for example granted exemption from all *portoria* to Antonius Polemo, the orator of Laodicea, and to all his descendants. Such exemptions and exonerations testify moreover to the excellent state of the finances as a whole. The principal duties, that is, the *quadragesima Galliarum*, now unified in one single system, and the *quattuor publica Africae*, were still entrusted to contractors, supervised however in Africa by a procurator centenarius and in Gaul by a sexagenarius. This naturally did not improve the position of the contractor; but these were the closing stages of the century-long transition from contract to direct collection and evidence is not lacking that the figure of the contractor was now in process of disappearing through a natural decline in interest. Hadrian himself had to forbid the use of coercion to make people take on contracts, a practice which had in short the effect of transferring a free contract into a *munus*.[1] There is the case of an individual who, after being a contractor in Hadrian's reign, entered the regular equestrian career and did very well in it under Antoninus Pius; here we have the tendency away from the voluntary provision of services to state employment exemplified in one and the same person.[2] Improvements in organization subsequently made it possible to merge the two customs districts of Illyricum and the *ripa Thraciae*. The periodic census taken in the provinces to ascertain the basis for the collection of tribute, which was still the principal source of revenue, underwent an important modification. It had hitherto been organized by the governor of the province with assistants chosen by himself and at the most approved by the emperor; Hadrian appointed directly – one for each province – procurators (sexagenarii) *ad census accipiendos* and *censitores* for the individual cities or unorganized region, thus going over the governor's head in this important function. This was not a step in a process of depriving the senatorial class of authority but an effect of the tendency to centralization and to the standardization of state structures all over the empire, as also happened with the creation of the *procuratores vicesimae hereditatium*. To collect this tax, which must have remained lucrative in spite of the exemptions granted by Nerva and Trajan, a series of huge districts was organized, which naturally included Italy since the tax touched Roman citizens, and each district was put in the charge of a procurator. It seems unlikely, then, that Hadrian did not duly exploit every possible resource: coins record the mines of Noricum and the *Aeliana Pincensia* in Upper Moesia, near the point where the Pincus (Pek) flows into the Danube. Thus Hadrian had the finances firmly in hand. The coinage, looked after personally by the Emperor when he was in Rome, technically the most handsome in the whole long existence of the Roman state and of

---

[1] *Digest.*, XLIX, 14, 3, 6; XXXIX, 4, 9, 1.
[2] *Ann. Ép.*, 1934, 107; inscription from Capidava, about a *conductor* of the *portorium Illyrici utriusque et ripae Thraciae*.

excellent fineness, formed a worthy reflection of the solidity of the situation.

The other changes made were simply part of the ordinary business of administration. They include the doubling of the procurators in Dacia after the division of the province; the separation of Lycia-Pamphylia and Galatia (made into one financial district by Domitian), with the consequent appointment of two procurators; the promotion to ducenarius of the procurator centenarius of Judaea after the war and the province's increase in importance; the institution of the *procurator Neaspoleos et mausolei* in Egypt, assigned to the granaries for the Roman corn supply, the imperial property in Neapolis (a quarter of Alexandria) and the mausoleum of Alexander; the institution, again in Egypt, of the *antarchiereus*, a subordinate of the *archiereus*, the head of the cult of Alexander; and the separation, in Africa, of the two districts of Hippo and Theveste.

Hadrian's other principal concern in the field of home affairs was to bring order and precision into the administration of justice by dispensing it diligently himself, by reorganizing the courts, by introducing a great deal of legislation and by systematizing the existing juridical heritage. So far as his assiduous participation in trials is concerned, the sources tell us of his jurisdiction as consul and of the public nature of his hearings, which he held not only in the palace but also in the Forum, in the Pantheon and in other places, surrounded by a large troop of senators and ordinary magistrates. Special mention is made of his *cognitiones* with the *consilium*, where he gave the verdict on the basis of the deliberations of the councillors. The information that not only the *amici et comites* of the Princeps (*V. Hadr.*, 18, 1) but also illustrious jurists, approved by the Senate, such as Iuventius Celsus, Salvius Julianus and Neratius Priscus, participated in the proceedings, indicates the scrupulous concern for justice and at the same time the tendency to a more technical approach in this field too. Men of the competence of those named, and also simply legal experts, were soon to form a permanent part of the imperial judicial consilium, as *consiliarii*, but only as such. Among other things, this was to incorporate in the regular institutions the usage, which had originated with the principate, of the *ius respondendi ex auctoritate principis*, confirmed again by Hadrian but not without arousing some uncertainty about the nature and scope of the concession. As for judges and juries, the ever more regular organization facilitated rigid control by the Emperor, who thought that the general level was now high enough to justify setting up in Italy, till then directly dependent on the urban jurisdiction, an organic system of four judicial districts entrusted to the same number of *iudices*, senators of consular rank.

But the measure, although intended to speed up the administration of justice, was not successful, possibly because it was restricted in the scope of its competence and entrusted for its execution to members of the Senate. The real levelling-up between Italy and the provinces was already far advanced, but when Hadrian tried to proclaim it as an official fact, even with a measure that favoured Italy, he thus encountered lively traditional and sentimental resistance. After disappearing under his successor, these officials reappeared in the time of Marcus Aurelius, with the explicit name already used in the provinces of *iuridici* and with their rank significantly reduced to the praetorian level, and this time they stayed. Hadrian had simply been in a hurry; the process was bound to go on eventually. Moreover, the tendency to codify and fix explicitly what had previously been determined by usage and empirical compromise – a tendency already apparent in his predecessors but more marked in Hadrian because of his systematic mind and his clearly and ever more openly autocratic programme – led to the predominance of the swifter imperial legislation over other traditional forms, such as the *senatusconsultum* and the law passed by the comitia, which had remained in use through the usual compromise between deference to the practical monarchy and to the formal republic; it also led to an interest in individual cases, once left to the discretion of the executors and interpreters of the laws and now the subject of precise regulations. For example, in connection with the *ius respondendi*, Hadrian prescribed that when the *responsa* of the experts were discordant the judge should regard himself as free either to accept what seemed to him the best opinion or to accept none of them. This course of action was thus established as the legal norm; but what had been the practice from Augustus to Hadrian?

The same tendency led to the execution of what is regarded as the legal masterpiece of Hadrian's age, the codification of the praetor's *edictum perpetuum*. The date of publication is uncertain, but the emphasis in the coinage on the motif of *Iustitia* and on a whole series of virtues like *Clementia*, *Indulgentia*, *Liberalitas*, *Patientia* and *Tranquillitas*, an emphasis which looks like the systematic illustration of a programme, suggests that publication went hand in hand with the compilation of the great work, which the chronicle of Eusebius – Jerome (p. 200 HELM) – says was finished in 131 and which in any case was more probably completed in the last rather than in the first years of Hadrian's reign. The compiler was a senator possibly of African origin, L. Octavius Cornelius P. Salvius Julianus Aemilianus, at that time, it seems, only of quaestorian rank, but, as the pupil of Iavolenus Priscus and his successor in the direction of the

Sabine School, a famous jurist, a member of the *consilium* and destined to make an honourable senatorial career and to live to see the age of Marcus Aurelius. The text, now lost and known only in part through the allusions of commentators and to the extent that it passed into the *Digest*, must have been the result of the sorting and consolidation in a fixed, definitive form of all that seemed worth preserving of the enormous mass of material accumulated over the centuries by the normative powers of the urban praetor. It probably also embraced the much scantier material deriving from the *praetor peregrinus* and that of the *edictum provinciale*, which for the most part repeated the urban praetor's edict. The same Julianus made a similar compilation of the edicts of the curule aediles. There was thus now an imposing collection of all that part of procedural law, and it was a very ample part in view of Roman usage, which had come into being out of the jurisdiction of the magistrates. It was issued with the permanent validity of law, by means of a *senatusconsultum*, but in practice as a testimony to the final triumph of autocracy in the field of law; from now on the praetor was relieved of the duty of renewing his own edict every year, and it is doubtful whether any magistrate still had any real power or opportunity to make law. Possible future modifications to the edict itself, now fixed once for all, could henceforth only be made on the authority of the emperor; and even this was only a particular case of the now formally recognized equivalence to law of imperial directives in general. The unification of the law, in correspondence with the general unification of civilized life, was a *fait accompli*, and the empire now had its own code of procedure, permanent and equal in every corner of the Roman dominions, though regularly added to by the incessant imperial legislation.

Our information about Hadrian's legislative activity is naturally scattered and fragmentary, as it is for that of his predecessors, but its abundance and variety suggest that this activity was of an unprecedented intensity. Marked by the principles of humanity and paternalistic care already adopted in large measure by Trajan, it was worthy of an age in which, at the conclusion of the age-long movement leading the *ius* from the formal rigidity of the Twelve Tables to a flexible adaptation to life, the jurist P. Iuventius Celsus, twice consul, head of the Proculian School, gave his famous definition of law: 'ars boni et aequi'. After the experience of the last few reigns Hadrian could not do otherwise than reject charges of *lèse-majesté*; this was part of the compromise established between the Princeps and the aristocracy. But in the field of common criminal jurisdiction one of the factors codified as essential was the evaluation of the circumstances and especially of the intention. Hadrian gave precise directives about manslaughter and homicide in legitimate self-defence, even envisaging acquittal, but on the other hand was severe on attempted murder, because 'in maleficiis voluntas spectatur, non exitus.'[1] Thus in a case of removal of boundary stones judgement had to be given 'ex con-dicione personae et mente facientis',[2] for if the transgressors were 'splendidiores personae' they certainly had the intention of stealing other people's property and should be punished with all the rigour of the law, but if they were quite ordinary individuals who had shifted the stone by accident or ignorance a mere beating might suffice. And this consideration of the more distinguished condition of the person as an aggravating circumstance is extremely characteristic, coming as it does just before the incorporation in the law of the privilege of the *honestiores* in the penal code. In other measures it is rather the Emperor's personal generosity that appears. When exile included confiscation of property in his favour, he confirmed the custom, already prevalent in the first century, that part of it should be left for the children of the condemned man. Hadrian, too, like others before him, refused legacies in wills if the testator left children. His liberality in helping children in general is well known; he continued and strengthened the *alimentationes* and also used other means to the same end. The regulation on the ownership and division of treasure trove was pretty favourable to private citizens, for if the discovery was made on the finder's own land he kept the whole treasure; if it was made on someone else's property it was halved between the finder and the landowner; and if it was made on public ground the fisc did not take all but only a share to be determined. There were serious penalties for particularly odious crimes such as the looting of shipwrecks. And the humanity of the times was shown not only, for example, in the suspension of the death penalty for pregnant women but also, as was to be expected in view of previous developments, in the thorny problem of the treatment of slaves.

Any modification of slavery as the social basis of society was less likely to commend itself to Hadrian than to anyone else, for in his austere respect for tradition he had reduced freedmen and slaves to the position appro-priate to them, beginning with those of his own palace. One day, seeing one of them walking proudly between two senators, he had ordered that he should have his ears boxed and be reminded of his status; and on another occasion, in the circus, when he was exhorted by shouts from the people to free a charioteer who did not belong to him, he had pointed out that neither he nor the people was entitled to emancipate someone else's

---

[1] *Digest.*, XLVIII, 8, 14. [2] *Ibid.*, XLVII, 21, 2.

slave or even to coerce his master into emancipating him.[1] On this subject, a good four *senatusconsulta* of Hadrian's reign (*Dasumianum*, 119; *Articuleianum*, 123; *Iuncianum*, 127; *Vitrasianum*, of uncertain date, but belonging in all probability to Hadrian's reign) deal with manumission by will. However, the common law was restricting more and more the master's field of absolute power over the slave. In practice a slave could not be killed by his master with impunity; mutilation and sale for immoral purposes were forbidden; the *ergastula* were closed; and ill treatment was prohibited. Above all, Hadrian limited the use of torture on slaves for the purpose of wringing evidence out of them, and ordered that the severe law prescribing the torture and possible execution *en masse* of all the slaves dwelling in a house in which the master had been killed should apply only to those near the scene of the crime.

In the already rich field of private law a number of interventions by Hadrian are recorded, particularly in the fields of marriage and wills. The legitimization of a child born in the eleventh month after the father's death was declared legally possible, 'requisitius veterum philosophorum et medicorum sententiis';[2] in marriages in which the two partners did not possess equal rights the children had the status of the mother; the position of the mother in cases of intestacy was improved (*s.c. Tertullianum*); and a procedure was established to deal with individuals who retained or sold property when the succession was vacant and the property therefore belonged to the treasury, though a distinction was made between possession of such property in good and bad faith (*s.c. Iuventianum*). The regulation making it impossible for the children of serving soldiers to inherit – a natural consequence of the veto on marriage applying to the soldiers themselves – was mitigated to the extent that such children, fruit of an infringement of military law and hence illegitimate and not susceptible to legitimization, could be considered as relatives and hence enter into possession of propety. The regulations on military wills already issued by Titus were extended and soldiers' wills were regarded as valid even in the case of execution on a capital charge or suicide, provided that the latter was not committed to evade a military punishment; and in these circumstances, if the soldier died intestate and without heirs, what he possessed became the property of the legion.

But the most characteristic side of Hadrian's legislation is displayed in the measures aimed at assuring the order, prosperity and security of civil life. The exemption from taxes of ships assigned to the transport of grain to Rome formed part of his policy on the corn supply; the severe penalties

---

[1] *V. Hadr.*, 21, 3; CASS. D., LXIX, 16, 3.   [2] GELL., *Noct. Att.*, III, 16, 12.

for people who falsified weights and measures guaranteed the honesty of commerce. But decorum and discipline had to reign in every aspect of social life, and to this end Hadrian laid down the most detailed rules: public baths were not to open until two in the afternoon except for reasons of health; there was to be no intermingling of the sexes in them (even in the theatre he distributed gifts to men and women separately); the toga had to be worn in public by senators and knights unless they were returning from banquets; and he himself always received company in a toga and, in Italy, travelled in a toga. This concern about clothes was zealously championed even by the schools, if it is true that T. Castricius, Aulus Gellius's master, pointed out one day to his pupils of senatorial rank that they were not correctly dressed.[1] As for the maintenance of fortunes, the first condition for the preservation of social decorum, he saw to recalling the prodigal to their senses by having people who squandered their patrimony whipped in the amphitheatre, without any further punishment. He frequently appointed guardians, and not only for minors. Everyone had to be at his post, as well-disciplined as a soldier. Local order was further safeguarded, first in Rome, where the *praefectus vigilum* found himself at the head of a hierarchy, never so well organized before, consisting of subordinates with precise responsibilities for policing exactly determined districts. Traces of the public safety regulations have been preserved in the prohibition on taking heavy vehicles through the streets of Rome and on riding on horseback in the narrow lanes of Italian towns, and in the measure obliging people to keep their houses in good condition. In this connection a regulation that is characteristic, because it is only comprehensible in special economic conditions, is the one which, repeating and formulating more precisely the *senatusconsultum Hosidianum* of Claudius's time and the *Volusianum* of Nero's, forbade the demolition of houses for the purpose of utilizing the materials in other localities. The *senatusconsultum Acilianum* (122) prohibited the bequest of artistic furniture, so that the interior decoration of houses should not be impoverished.

The epistulae, rescripts and edicts dealing with the provinces must have been innumerable. We do not possess an integral body of evidence as we do for Bithynia in the time of Pliny's governorship, but Trajan's paternalistic care must have been surpassed by Hadrian's still more detailed attention and by the effects of his presence in person. Modifications to the general organization of the provinces were not numerous, though fairly important: apart from the changes in the financial administration already mentioned, in 119 or the first half of 120, Dacia was divided into two

---

[1] *Ibid.*, XIII, 22, 1.

provinces, Upper Dacia, under a governor of praetorian rank, with the one and only legion that remained permanently on the far side of the Danube, and Lower Dacia, under a procurator, with a garrison of auxiliaries. In addition, a new document[1] attests that by 2 July 133 there already existed, certainly as the result of improvements in the defensive system, *Dacia Porolissensis*, the creation of which had previously been assigned to the age of Antoninus Pius. In 135, after the Jewish war, Judaea was given the name *Syria Palestina* and two legions. Roughly about the same time Bithynia became once again an imperial province and the Senate received Lycia and Pamphylia in exchange. In 136 the border between Moesia and Thrace was marked out and the inscriptions found testify to the substantial extension of the latter to the north – as far as the Danube. The eastern frontier was once again fixed on the Augustan line and marked physically with pillars, at any rate in the sector contiguous with the territory of Palmyra. Hadrian was not the first to keep a close watch on governors in this way. The chief characteristic of his reign lay, rather, in the government of the provinces as well, in the organic and definitive systematization of the bases on which this government was exercised, with a uniform and extremely flexible consideration of all the requirements. We shall speak later of the social order, which was crystallized rather than standardized; but this is the place to give some samples of the material provisions made by Hadrian and of his normative interventions.

Works of public utility were distributed everywhere; some, such as the monumental buildings in Athens and Asia, have already been mentioned in the section on Hadrian's journeys, and the great activity in Rome and its surroundings will be discussed separately. The general statements in the sources – 'in omnibus paene urbibus . . . aliquid aedificavit'[2] – have been confirmed by finds; and certainly the expressions of gratitude for some interventions that have come down to us, numerous though they are, are by no means all those called forth by the Emperor's munificence. In Italy there are records of aqueducts and improvements in the distribution of water in Rome; there is also a record of work on the harbour at Puteoli and of repairs to the outlet from the Fucine Lake. Roads received the careful maintenance usual at this epoch; there are records on the Via Appia, where an interesting milestone of 123[3] testifies to the remaking of precisely $15\frac{3}{4}$ Roman miles in the neighbourhood of Aeclanum, the cost

[1] DAICOVICIU-PROTASE, in *Journ. Rom. St.*, LI, 1961, pp. 63–70 = *Ann. Ép.*, 1962, 255.
[2] *V. Hadr.*, 19, 2; cf. 20, 4–5, and CASS. D., LXIX, 5, 2–3.
[3] *ILS*, 5875.

being shared between the Emperor and the local landowners; on the Via Cassia, from Clusium to Florentia; on the Via Flaminia, near the 'mansio' *ad Martis* (Massa Martana), where in 124 a sustaining wall was repaired; and on the Via Iulia Augusta (milestones of 125, found near the *trofeo della Turbie*). An inscription from Falerium in Picenum records the construction in 119 of a street in the town at the expense of those who owned houses with a frontage on it.[1] The usual Tiber flood led to further work on the bank; we have pillars marking the boundary of the river from Hadrian's time as well. It was also in Hadrian's reign that Ostia experienced the most rapid and exuberant development in its whole history; and at this time the cemetery on the Isola Sacra was in specially full use and was embellished with the monuments recently excavated. Outside Italy – to confine ourselves to official action by the state – there was intense activity on the roads: in Spain; in Africa, on the road from Carthage to Theveste (milestone of 123) and on the road from Cirta to Rusicada, which is known as the *via nova* and was possibly built in the early years of the reign to provide another, shorter outlet to the sea from the interior of Numidia; in Mauretania, on the road from Auzia to Rapidum (milestone of 124); and in Cyrene (118). In Galatia there was the general restoration already mentioned, which between 119 and 122, under the direction of the governor, A. Larcius Macedo, dealt with almost all the roads branching out from Ancyra towards Cilicia, Pontus, Paphlagonia, Bithynia and Phrygia; in Egypt the main road linking the new city of Antinoe with Berenice on the Red Sea was completed in 137. Nor should we forget that the official post, which traversed these roads from one end of the empire to the other (*cursus publicus*), was provided by Hadrian for the first time with fixed stations under imperial supervision in the provinces as well, though the provinces were not relieved of the expense involved, as Italy had been by Nerva. Just as extensive was the attention devoted to aqueducts: a pillar found near Lyon[2] formed part of the limits, established under Hadrian, of the service area of an aqueduct; Dyrrhachium received a new one, as did Carthage after the Emperor's visit in 128; here the structure erected over the springs must have resembled the 'theatre' (so Malalas calls it) built at Daphne, when Hadrian completed the reconstruction, begun by Trajan after the earthquake of 115, of the aqueduct which carried water from there to Antioch.

Temples, baths, theatres, amphitheatres and all the other public works justifying the enthusiastic dedication of arches and statues, and the title on coins of *Restitutor* of various provinces and finally of *Restitutor orbis*

---

[1] *ILS*, 5368. [2] *ILS*, 5749.

terrarum, Locupletator orbis terrarum, can only be mentioned as a whole – and it is an imposing whole. Hadrian, says the biographer (20, 4), did not like to put his name on public works, but the abundance of the pieces of testimony mentioned and the results of excavations assign to his age, and hence to his direct or indirect stimulus, a notable proportion of the stock of Roman monuments, either in the shape of new buildings or of radical restorations. In this way too Hadrian sought to maintain the prestige of ancient cities like Cyrene. But to a greater extent than any other emperor he also founded new cities. Antinoopolis on the Middle Nile rose from nothing, with walls, private houses and public buildings, and the urban organization of the Greek *polis*. Granting the desire for a lasting homage to his favourite (in the event, the town prospered for centuries) and at the same time wishing to extend further in Egypt the Greek style of urban life, confined at that time to the two centres of Alexandria and Ptolemais, he laid out the city on strictly geometrical lines and peopled it only with Greek citizens, induced to come from the Greek communities of Egypt, and with Greek veterans. He attracted these people by granting them privileges; he gave Antinoopolis the constitution of a free city, with the magistrates of the old *polis*, and tribes and demes bearing the glorious names of the gods and heroes of Athens.

The physical layout and civic organization of Antinoopolis, known to us as they are, are interesting because they illustrate not only Hadrian's ideas in connection with the other cities founded in the East but also, in particular, his general policy towards local communities; they enable us to grasp what is, as we have already said, the most characteristic aspect of his reign and to follow the extreme manifestations of his all-embracing paternalism. In general it should be observed that once his antiquarian enthusiasm had been satisfied (and it was in this rather than in any morbid mysticism that his philhellenism consisted), the provisions he made were quite practical and realistic. His beloved Athens not only witnessed festivals and revivals but also received a year's corn supplies, the beautiful meadows of Cephallenia and, for councillors, permanent exemption from tax contracts. Characteristic, too, are his interventions in local legislation, for example at Athens again, where – not as emperor but as Athenian *nomothetes* – he issued a law on the obligatory declaration of the amount of oil produced. Megara was another city that expressed in dedications its gratitude to him as a legislator. His personal presence in itself led him to consider real needs and to grant concrete benefits; it is to these, not to trifles of no consequence, that the expressions of gratitude refer. The fact that these benefits extended to paying the entrance fee – prescribed for supernumerary foreigners – to the *boulê* of Ephesus for the shipowner who had carried him safely in his ship from Eleusis in 129, and on the preceding visit had accompanied him from Ephesus to Rhodes,[1] is as much a proof of the Emperor's liberality as of the minuteness of his attention, here preserved in a rare case among the very many which are forgotten precisely because he so often intervened in person.

Thus the Emperor exerted a direct effect on local life; this was a novelty. But naturally he also made use of the means of intervention created by his predecessor, primarily of *correctores* and *curatores*. L. Aemilius Iuncus, who was consul in 127, was certainly in Achaea before that year, possibly as governor, in which case the province would have been temporarily an imperial one, but it could be as *corrector* of the free cities, like Maxmus, in Trajan's time; and the four people (at least) known to have exercised this highly realistic function (in Syria the jurist P. Pactumeius Clemenis already sent earlier on a special mission to Athens, Thespiae, Plataea and Thessaly, and L. Burbuleius Optatus Ligarianus, previously curator of Narbo, Ancona and Tarracina – thus two experts on the subject; in Asia, about 134–135, the wealthy Athenian orator Ti. Claudius Atticus Herodes; and in Bithynia, towards the end of the reign, the senator from Ancyra, C. Julius Severus, invested, like Pliny, with all the powers of the governor of an imperial province and therefore substituted for the proconsul) demonstrate the continuation of a characteristic attention, exercised through the most appropriate instruments. By no means the last reason for praise here is the utilization, as under the Flavians and Trajan, of Greek and oriental senators; just at this time Flavius Arrianus of Nicomedia, an ex-consul, was appointed governor of Cappadocia. These officials, like the curators sent to individual cities, and sometimes even to bodies inside cities (real commissioners, like the *curator* for the college of elders at Ephesus), carried out their tasks with zeal and even *noblesse* like Herodes Atticus, who assumed responsibility for the deficit of seven million drachmae which he found in the accounts of Alexandria Troas, a debt incurred through the construction, undertaken without the necessary means, of some too grandiose public baths. The only direct evidence preserved of Julius Severus's administration is a delimitation of boundaries between Asian Dorylaeum and Nicaea (which would indicate, among other things, the return to the south, after Trajan's correction, of the boundary between Asia and Bithynia), but its comprehensive benevolence was still remembered in Bithynia in the time of Cassius Dio, who was himself a Bithynian (LXIX, 14, 4). One very concrete measure that brought

[1] *Syll.*[3], 838.

notable advantages was the power to issue one single set of coins for all the provinces of Asia, the so-called *cistophori*, old coins of the Pergamene kings, also struck, but in a small quantity, by Augustus and later by Nerva and Trajan. Many cities now issued them, and the variety of symbols, inspired by local cults and local history, combined with unity of type and weight, contributed to the diffusion of the idea, which certainly figured among the subjects of Hadrian's propaganda, of the mutual collaboration of the individual cities in the great family of the empire.

There are records of other small, concrete interventions: on Hadrian's orders, at an uncertain date, the proconsul of Achaea (rather than of Macedonia), Q. Gellius Sentius Augurinus, settled a border dispute between the cities of Lamia and Hypata in Thessaly. At Beroea, in Macedonia, the fragments of two copies of a letter of Hadrian's dating from some time between 119 and 128 bear witness to the granting of a favour that had been requested; at Thyatira benefits were granted which the citizens decided to commemorate in an inscription to be put up in the Panhellenion at Athens, where the people of Sardis, like others, also left their mark for a similar reason; and, apart from the above-mentioned restoration of borders at Aezani in Phrygia, the inhabitants of Abdera recovered their territory thanks to Hadrian and, adopting the name of Hadrianei, thanked him by placing memorials on the border itself. The hundred or so pillars placed right up on the mountain ridges of the Lebanon to mark out forests and to establish the quality of the trees reserved for public use, perhaps in the application of some law or other, indicate another very practical interest. The three letters sent by Hadrian in 127 to the city of Stratonicea-Hadrianopolis granted the city, which was taking the first steps in its new lease of life, the right to levy taxes for its own benefit on the surrounding territory and laid down criteria for the maintenance of the residence of a local notability who, evidently in financial straits, could not afford to see to it himself; this really was administration *ad personam*. Moreover, the Emperor stated that he had mentioned the matter, for information, to the proconsul and to his procurator – a tribute to the 'usual channels' of the hierarchy paralleled in one or two other examples known to us. As for privileges, there are records of the renewal of the immunity granted by Trajan to the doctors of the Museum at Ephesus, and no doubt doctors in other cities as well enjoyed the same concession. Immunity was also granted to other professions and even to certain magistrates, such as the *agoranomoi*, *sitones* and *elaiones* in the East. This was not a good sign, for as these posts were the most onerous ones, thanks to the victualling obligations attached to them, the privilege granted signified that they were no longer sought after for themselves; and the gap between magistracy and liturgy, between the free exercise of office and compulsory service, went on decreasing inexorably. From 135 to 136 a moratorium on the payment of taxes was granted to the Egyptian peasants, who had suffered losses through the irregularity of the annual Nile flood. More wide-ranging legislative measures were the affirmation that the general law of the empire forbidding burials in towns overrode any municipal statutes allowing it; the exemption from capital punishment of decurions, except for the crime of parricide; the renewal of Nerva's concession to cities allowing them to accept legacies; and a rescript to the people of Nicomedia prohibiting the revocation, except for good reasons, of a decree regularly debated and passed – a really somewhat strange regulation and one certainly not calculated to dam the flow of eastern eloquence.

An important series of measures dealt with the organization of the imperial estates in the area where they were most extensive – Africa. Although these possessions were theoretically private property, their public nature was becoming clearer and clearer. The procurators who were the directors-general of these domains were now no longer distinguished, as we have seen, from the rest in the normal procuratorial career. Under them there might be contractors, *conductores*; the workers were the *coloni*, whose conditions were by no means bad; the only thing was that they were exposed to the danger of abuses in the provision of free labour. Hadrian established precise norms in this very connection in order to protect them, and it is to be presumed that he did this after observing their conditions in 128. A *lex Hadriana*, the existence of which is deduced from a decree of Commodus's, laid it down that they should provide six days' free labour per year, 'binas aratorias, binas sartorias, binas messorias'.[1] Other laws, known from the *ara legis Hadrianae*, erected in the age of Severus and found near the river Bagradas in Tunisia, and also from another inscription of Hadrian's own time, lay down other rules about the occupation 'de agris rudibus aut desertis' – uncultivated lands or lands not cultivated for at least ten years – within the imperial domains and about the division of the produce between the *coloni* and the *conductores*.[2] Thus records of demarcation of territories are more numerous here than elsewhere: at Cirta, in Numidia, the boundary between public and private land, together with certain fields of uncertain ownership, was fixed, and also that between the public land of Cirta and the fields of neighbouring Milev.[3] In the neighbourhood of Thagaste, the boundaries

---

[1] RICCOBONO, *Leges*[2], p. 497.
[2] *Ibid.*, pp. 490–5.   [3] *ILS*, 5978, 5979, 5980; *Ann. Ép.*, 1939, 160.

traced under Domitian or Nerva by a proconsul were brought into force again by a *mensor*, an imperial slave sent for this specific purpose;[1] again in Numidia, but more to the west, the territory of Sigus was defined;[2] in Mauretania Caesariensis, in 128, the boundary between the territory of Igilgili, on the coast, and that of the Zimizes was marked out; in 137 that between the Regienses (the inhabitants of *Ad Regias*, a *statio* on the main inland road of Mauretania) and a *saltus* whose name has not been preserved; and in the same year the procurator of Mauretania Caesariensis defined the territory 'genti Numidarum'.[3]

The Emperor's providence thus reached everywhere, via the quite numerous and efficient organs of the administration, preserving the situation of administrative excellence synonymous with the essential nature of the imperial system. It was only the continuation of a natural development. But with Hadrian the activity of governing, partly through the more direct personal participation of the Princeps and his capacity for theoretical synthesis, was considered reflectively in terms of meritorious service and of spiritual and universal ends. The famous series of coins of the 'provinces', issued both in the gold and silver of the imperial mint and in senatorial bronze in the very last years of the reign, bearing only names and symbols, without any further reference to the concrete circumstances of any particular *adventus* or *restitutio*, signified that Hadrian, with the great experience of his journeys now over, considered and wished that the harmonious structure of the empire should be regarded as complete: unity in variety.

SECURITY AND DEFENCE

Precisely for Hadrian, the peaceful emperor *par excellence*, the sources have left us the relatively most extensive and systematic exposition of personal principles in the field of military theory.[4] No doubt they are partly commonplaces, but it is certain that care of the army was among Hadrian's principal concerns. This was a direct consequence of the defensive policy towards the outside world inaugurated as a systematic development of Trajan's experiences, just when the empire had attained, within the frontiers determined by the insuperable limits of its resources, the appearance of a unitary and sufficiently homogeneous structure, and it now only remained to preserve, to order and to classify. A defensive policy of peace could only be pursued successfully by keeping the army

---

[1] *Ann. Ép.*, 1942–3, 35.   [2] *Ann. Ép.*, 1939, 161.
[3] *ILS*, 5961, 5963, 5960.   [4] *V. Hadr.*, 10, 12, 6; CASS. D., LXIX, 9.

efficient and formidable; discipline and training had to replace the bloody school of war. In any case the concept of the army as a perfect machine always ready for its task was in accord with the universal tendency to organizational precision. This was another of the aims of Hadrian's travels, and he spent much of his time with the armies, which were now so well organized as perfectly consistent and characteristic entities in the areas of their respective defensive tasks that they are mentioned in the currency for the first time in a parallel series of coins, conceived in the same spirit of variety in unity, commemorating the different provinces: *exercitus Germanicus, Raeticus, Norici, Dalmaticus, Moesicus, Dacicus, Britannicus, Hispanicus, Mauretanicus, Cappadocicus, Syriacus.*

However, Hadrian did not carry out any showy reforms in this field either. The novelty of his activity lay, as usual, in a more intensive and detailed participation in everything and in the crystallization of usage in regulations. Attentive to human relations, he put discipline on a firm basis but made it less harsh, applying extensively in the realm of punishment the principle of making it proportionate to the offence, taking an indulgent view, as we saw in connection with the right to bequeath property, of the private feelings of the soldiers, and above all setting an example of justice. No one in the camp was to have a more comfortable life than the private soldier, not even the Emperor himself, who would march on foot, bare-headed and fully-armed, as much as twenty miles, stay with the troops and eat their food, dress plainly, visit the sick, and effectively act as commanding officer in all the most modest duties. Everyone had to be at his post in the ranks, and there were no favours or permits to live outside the camp, in which everything had to be informed by austerity. Account had to be taken of the age of the soldiers, for reasons of efficiency and humanity; praetorian guards had to be of a certain height and to have served for three years in the urban cohorts; the best men had to make a career in the army and the Emperor in person often decided promotions, for which moreover he had issued regulations which took account of merit and length of service. Training exercises, fixed in number and in their main themes, kept the troops in good shape, and if there was any time left over, employment on constructional work, for which corps of technicians were formed, real units of military engineers, removed any possibility of lapsing into inertia. In spite of all this and although he had not commanded them in war and was rather parsimonious with rewards, this Emperor, who knew a large number of soldiers by name, was much loved by them.

Information about fundamental changes in deployment is scarce: we

hear of the return to their bases of the legions employed by Trajan in the
East, of the reduction of the Dacian garrison to one legion, of the probable increase to four of the legions of Britain, of the permanent stationing
of two legions in Judaea after the war of 132–135, of the disappearance of
Legions IX *Hispana* and XXII *Deiotariana*, and of the reduction to one
single legion (the II *Traiana*) of the garrison of Egypt. This is more or less
all we know about changes and moves, which cannot in fact have been
numerous or important if, at the conclusion of the process initiated by the
Flavians, and as indicated in the coins referred to above, the legionary
garrisons were now permanently linked to provinces. As for recruitment,
it used to be thought that Hadrian had given a decisive impetus to the
territorial enrolment of legionaries, a practice which had already been
coming gradually into use, while making no change in the custom introduced by Vespasian of not using auxiliaries in the area in which they had
been recruited. The trouble is that a document recently discovered – a list
of 136 veterans of the II *Traiana* legion, discharged in Egypt in 157 after
being originally enrolled in 132–133[1] – has revealed the surprising
presence of fifteen Italians in one single legion, although only eighteen of
them were known in all the legions from Hadrian's time to Diocletian's;
and of the fifteen three came from Rome, although previously only one
legionary from Rome had been known in the whole of the first three
centuries after Christ! Moreover, the study of military diplomas, for
example of those from Mauretania, has shown that even under Hadrian
the recruitment of auxiliaries on the spot had already assumed considerable proportions. This leads us to be cautious in our conclusions, even if
account is taken in this specific case of exceptional circumstances, of the
fact, for example, that during the Jewish war distant recruitment for the
legions became necessary and there were levies even in Italy – a prelude to
the formation of Marcus Aurelius's Italian legions for the war against the
Marcomanni. Thus, in connection with the auxiliaries, it is dubious
whether Hadrian succeeded in checking the spontaneous tendency to
assimilation with the legionaries, while at a still lower level the demand
for integral organization was already operating with the incorporation of
the irregular units – Trajan's symmachiarii, given lustre by Lusius
Quietus – in the *numeri*, which made their first appearance as regular
formations in the army under Hadrian.

But the impressive remains of the wall in Britain certainly speak in
more eloquent terms of Hadrian's foreign policy, and not only these
remains but those of all the military works, though it is difficult to deter-

---

[1] *Ann. Ép.*, 1955, 238, from Nicopolis.

mine precisely what Hadrian's contribution to them was. It was certainly considerable on the Germano-Raetian *limes*, where he probably built the forts for the cohorts now brought forward to the line of the frontier, which was permanently garrisoned for the whole of its length and further protected – if that is how we should interpret a general remark by the biographer (12, 6), which seems to be confirmed by the archaeological remains – by a palisade. In any case, throughout the reign this bulwark was never attacked, nor are there any reports of restlessness in Germany, unless something is concealed, though it can only be something of little account, under the biographer's remark, 'Germanis regem constituit' (12, 7). For the moment, the last one of complete peace in this sector, the *limes* was more of a customs line crossed by fruitful exchanges – perfectly in harmony with the general principles of Hadrian's foreign policy – with the tribes beyond it, who were becoming more and more Romanized before being overwhelmed themselves by the storm building up in their rear. The camps on the Danube were certainly looked after, like those on all the other frontiers, with the uniformity demanded by the systematic programme applied everywhere. Particularly in Africa, Lambaesis, Gemellae – a camp made permanent in 132, at the edge of the desert – and others preserve a record of the most purely military inspection of all those carried out by Hadrian.

In Britain the plan for a *limes* certainly came from the same desire for permanent stabilization, after the repression of the revolt in 119. The completion of the network of roads, the reduction and concentration of the garrisons in the province and the general regularization of life made it seem indispensable to fix a boundary, which may have been conceived in the first place simply as an administrative line and was then transformed more and more through the chronic restlessness of the tribes into a formidable line of defence. In effect the fortifications were constructed in such a way as to serve against attacks either from the north or the south, and when Antoninus Pius advanced the border further north these fortifications were not abandoned. The problems surrounding the phases of the wall's construction are still not completely resolved in spite of thorough excavations, but the work is sufficiently identifiable in its structure for almost the whole of its length. Built by detachments from the British legions and by auxiliaries, under the command of the governor, A. Platorius Nepos, the powerful barrier ran for eighty miles between the Solway Firth and the estuary of the Tyne. It consisted, looked at in section from south to north, of a triple bank of earth with a ditch (the actual *vallum*) and of a stone wall, also with a wide, deep ditch. Between bank and wall ran a road. Seventeen forts, each capable of holding a cohort, a strongpoint every mile and frequent towers ensured its defence. Three main roads issued from it towards the north, and three big double gates at each fort allowed the cavalry to make sorties in large detachments. It was a question here of a real defensive apparatus in enemy territory and although we lack precise information it was probably put to the test quite a few times. In any case, all Hadrian's military activity was a continuous preparation for war, and every time that the occasion arose the war machine did its duty.

The most striking occasion was the Jewish revolt. The scanty traces left in the tradition of other campaigns under Hadrian, apart from those at the beginning of the reign, underline the routine administrative character of the small repressive actions, normal tasks of an ever-ready machine: 'bella silentio paene transacta' (*V. Hadr.*, 21, 8). Apart from a modest campaign against the Agriophagi of Egypt to protect the road from Thebes to Berenice, the gravest threat was one towards the end of the reign of an invasion of Armenia and Cappadocia by the Alans, who were already overrunning Media and the kingdom of the Albanians, after obscure manœuvres in which a part may have been played by Pharasmanes, king of the Iberians, the man who had refused to attend the conference of 129 but had subsequently exchanged gifts and courtesies with Hadrian. This was a diplomatic development on the lines of traditional eastern politics, which were conducted by Pharasmanes too on the basis of friendship with the foreign princes who maintained relations and sent homages, even from distant Bactriana, and with the peoples who, like the Lazi of Colchis, even received their kings from him. In the case of this movement by the Alans there is a report (CASS. D., LXIX, 15, 1) of an intervention by one Vologaeses, who can only have been the king left by Hadrian in Armenia; equally interested in repelling the invasion, he now turned out to be the natural ally of the Romans. But where military action was concerned, it was the governor of Cappadocia, Flavius Arrianus, who halted the Alans.

The last rebellion of the Hebrews started in 132 and renewed the horrors of the previous ones, even though it remained confined to Jewish territory. The one beginning in 115 had raged from Cyrene to the Tigris and from Egypt to Cyprus. Egypt had suffered particularly, for the Roman troops of Greek origin, few in number because of the Parthian campaign, had been beaten and, withdrawing into Alexandria, had taken revenge on the Jewish population, even destroying the synagogue. Moreover, the leader of the rising in Cyrene, one Andreas or Lukuas, had marched through the Egyptian countryside, laying it waste, until Marcius Turbo had put an end to the open warfare, though not to the riots, which had continued, especially in Alexandria, where they were in any case a long-standing plague. The Roman authorities sought to resolve impartially the problems created by the difficulties Greeks and Jews found in living together, and in the so-called 'Acts of the Pagan Martyrs' we have a record in these very years of cases against Greeks in Alexandria, while the Jewish population there had its rights restored by an edict of the prefect, Q. Rammius Martialis, precisely between 117 and 119. But the Jews' hatred of Roman domination, inflamed as it was by the memory of Titus's war and by mystical expectations, had deep roots and found nourishment above all at Jerusalem, profaned by the impious order to shelter Capitoline Jove in a city which was no longer the old sacred capital of the chosen people but a Roman colony. That this, rather than the ban on circumcision, was the real cause of the rising is more than probable. The ferment continued to grow while the new city was being built and foreigners were taking up residence there. But so long as Hadrian stayed in Egypt and Syria the Jews remained quiet, and even afterwards, certainly saddened by experience, they did not abandon themselves to the usual outburst of furious anger.

Guided by able leaders, Eleazar, the Rabbi Akiba, Simon and particularly Bar Kozebah, who is possibly to be identified with this same Simon, they armed themselves secretly, occupied and fortified certain strategic points in the country and dug refuges and subterranean passages. That the now famous caves of Qumran, near the Dead Sea, played a part during and after this subterranean war is a likely hypothesis. The governor, who, as we have learnt recently from the *Fasti Ostienses*,[1] was Q. Tineius Rufus, an ex-consul, did not at first attribute much importance to the movement and when he began to pay some attention to it the situation was already beyond his control. Jerusalem was captured by the rebels and an insidious guerilla war, spreading all over the country, caused serious losses; this success caused help to flow in from fellow Jews all over the Roman world, and even peoples of other races, either through intimidation or self-interest, favoured the revolt, while the Jewish ecclesiastical authorities tried to arouse the loyalty of the Christian community. The governor of Syria, C. Publicius Marcellus, arriving with detachments from at least six legions and operating near the coast with the *classis Syriaca*, and after him the best general of the time, Sex. Minicius Faustinus Iulius Severus, summoned for the purpose from Britain and appointed governor of Iudaea, gradually broke down resistance slowly but remorselessly. In 134

[1] *Inscr. It.*, XIII, 1, p. 205, 233; *cos. suff.* A.D. 127.

Jerusalem was recaptured. Hadrian himself, who with this event may have concluded his inspection of the theatre of war, let the Senate see the gravity of the losses by omitting in his letter the usual introductory formula, 'If you and your children are well, it is well; I and the armies are well'.[1] But, as in the time of Titus, the capture of Jerusalem did not end the war; it continued with the investment of the various fortresses, until the last of them, Bether, fell in the early part of 135. The Jews could not hope for mercy; prisoners were put to death, all the combatants left alive were sold as slaves, and the population of the capital was finally dispersed and forbidden on pain of death to set foot in Jerusalem again except for one day in the year fixed by the authorities. *Aelia Capitolina* could now rise and start, as the new capital of the province, its age-long life as a Roman city like any other. The name lasted until the age of Constantine. In the context of a general raising of standards, the exceptional harshness displayed by Hadrian – in contrast to his natural tolerance – had been provoked by the exceptional attitude of a people different from all others which, in contrast to the pagan world and the Christian one (in Aelia Capitolina the Christian community prospered undisturbed), sank into ever deeper isolation, even in the universal dispersion, up to our own time, which has seen the Jewish national home refounded, after eighteen centuries, in its own land. To ensure security, two legions, the X *Fretensis*, which was already there, and the VI *Ferrata*, remained permanently in the province, renamed *Syria Palestina*, under an ex-consul. Julius Severus had the *ornamenta triumphalia* conferred on him (for one of the last times in the history of the empire) and Hadrian had his second and last official salutation as *imperator*.

SOCIETY AND CULTURE

Like everything else, the social order achieved under Trajan acquired stability and organization in the time of Hadrian and was to last unchanged under his immediate successors. The problem of social imbalance was certainly noticed and was resolved not by any attempt to level the classes – a policy which would have been alien to the mentality of the age and impossible to put into effect – but by the crystallization of the hierarchy. It was at this time that the concept of *honestiores* and *humiliores* began to take explicit shape and the classes came to be well-defined entities. But we must not forget that the resulting immobility governed the definition of social positions, not the men. The boundaries between

[1] CASS. D., LXIX, 14, 3.

the classes were very real and firmly marked, but they were not impassable. The barrier between slavery and freedom continued to be lowered by the private act of *manumissio*; and the body of Roman citizens received increase not only from this process but also from the frequent granting of citizenship to single individuals, to discharged auxiliary troops and to local communities in the provinces. Moreover, the ordinary citizen, through a career in the army or administrative services, either locally or in the service of the state, could jump the fixed hurdles of the social order and finally fulfil, with the favour of the Emperor, the most ambitious hopes. Men bound to class or trade were only to appear later on, even if the economic roots of the phenomenon were already present in the society of Hadrian's time and the tendency to fix the classes in the abstract was to end by imprisoning men in them in practice.

As for the citizen body, Hadrian looked after its increase as Trajan had done, extending and improving the *alimentationes* (which were still confined to Italy) and paying particular attention to the young. But the principal problem was that of the extension of citizenship. Hadrian could not do otherwise than assist an irresistible tendency, seeking to canalize it even more firmly than his predecessors by a programme of rationally based gradual steps. In any case, the progress of urbanization itself, which amounted to the same thing as the progress of Romanization, marked the stages in the regularization of status. Let us take Africa for example: the process would start with the native *civitas*, autonomous in government and urban in form; the next step would be the *municipium* with Latin rights; then came the *municipium* of Roman citizens; and finally the *municipium* would become a *colonia*, a status which henceforth represented only the honorary crowning of an advance in legal rank recognized by imperial favour but certainly solicited by the community itself, whose sense of being Roman had gradually matured. The establishment of many *municipia* in *Africa proconsularis* is to be attributed to the journey of 128; and that of Choba, revealed by a recently discovered inscription,[1] may date from the earlier excursion into Mauretania. After the disturbances accompanying the Jewish revolt, Cyrene must have not only been rebuilt but also been given a reinforcement of colonists, on top of those already sent by Trajan. The same process is to be observed in the towns of Dacia, not long conquered but rapidly Romanized. The foundadation of colonies by the actual 'deductio' of citizens became rarer and rarer; it had been rendered pointless by the large-scale development of spontaneous Romanization. The towns that had arisen round the big

[1] *Ann. Ép.*, 1949, 55.

camps on the Danube were 'municipalized', although they were still legionary bases. Examples are Carnuntum, Aquincum and Viminacium, which became *municipia Aelia*, naturally with Roman citizenship, like Lambaesis in Numidia; this was an interesting experiment in letting civilians and soldiers live alongside each other, possibly in the context of the general defence plan. A superior grade of Latin right was introduced, the 'Latium maius', as opposed to the ordinary grade ('minus'); it involved conferring full Roman citizenship not only on the magistrates but also on all the councillors of the local senate and hence on all the notable families. In practice all that part of the West organized in towns possessed at least Latin rights. Italy had been Roman for centuries and it was not Hadrian's deliberate intention to lower its prestige; the spontaneous ascent of the provinces reduced the gap of its own accord. The same tendencies were also assisted in the East, where the traditional form of the *polis* was not only respected where it existed but also applied, as we have seen, to the new foundations, with a few exceptions. This was not deference on the part of the 'Graeculus' to personal sympathies, but deliberate policy. Hadrian did not seek out the new; he yielded to natural developments, ordering and systematizing, so that everything became uniform and centralized; but he knew the value of local traditions and himself appreciated the homage paid to him in the invitations to become a city magistrate in Etruria and the Latin cities, and in Greek Naples and Athens. Municipal life continued to be lively in spite of the general standardization, and rivalry was intense, even though now confined to the fields of prestige and commerce. Examples are the revival of Capua as compared with Puteoli, which had been at its zenith under the Flavians, and the interminable disputes of the Asian cities over the title of metropolis and the number of *neocorati*.

The actual life of the empire, in industry and commerce, in relations between places and persons, in economic conditions, must have been substantially the same as it had been in Trajan's age, with a more deliberate emphasis on harmony between the centralized organization and local autonomy, thanks to the now regular and definite functioning of paternalism. The senatorial aristocracy, still at the head of imperial society, was nevertheless becoming more and more widely based, while the importance of the knights continually increased. The prestige of the Roman nobility was extremely high everywhere; to enter this nobility was the supreme ambition of the provincials. In inscriptions in Asia the position of father, brother, grandfather, uncle or cousin to a senator appears as a claim to distinction. As for what these aristocrats did, apart from service in the

administration of the empire, Pliny's picture is naturally still valid, and to
the series of personages portrayed there can be added the figure of Sulpicius Similis, the ex-praetorian prefect, who reckoned that he only really
began to live when he was dismissed, and left the epitaph: 'Here lies
Similis, who in all the years he lived had only seven of *vita*'.[1] Only in the
field of personal relations with the Princeps may Pliny's description need,
it seems, to be modified a little in the direction of the less idyllic. An
attentive and demanding administrator, like Tiberius and Domitian,
Hadrian was respected and feared but not loved by his own class. The
affair of the four ex-consuls was not forgotten and it is not surprising if his
clemency was taken for cruelty checked by fear of coming to the same end
as Domitian; a few episodes, particularly in the last two years of his life,
stained his memory in a tradition already inclined to discredit him. In
fact the matters concerned must have been fairly unimportant and confined to his most intimate circle; altogether he was away from Rome for
at least ten years and no one ever thought seriously of taking advantage of
his absences. He checked up discreetly on his friends, even intimate ones,
and this must have caused irritation; he was also accused of failing to
keep his word; he was not vindictive, but he was suspicious, or perhaps
simply watchful. To judge from the information at our disposal, many
men actually fell into disgrace, but we are not told whether this was
deserved, as seems to have been the case with Attianus and was certainly
the case with Septicius Clarus, who together with Suetonius had failed to
show sufficient respect for Sabina. The death of his relation Ursus
Servianus and his son, and the dismissal of Catilius Severus, the *praefectus
urbi*, are to be linked with the problem of the succession and with the
clouding of Hadrian's mind in his last years. The causes of the cooling of
his relations with Platorius Nepos, Ummidius Quadratus, Terentius
Gentianus and Marcius Turbo are unknown, but they were his close
collaborators and the conflict may have been of a political nature and only
attributed by the tradition to caprice and hatred.

In any case, Hadrian was always rather a curious figure and this increased the gap. His biographer's famous portrait must have reflected
precisely the admiration and fear aroused by a disconcerting personage:
'idem severus comis, gravis lascivus, cunctator festinans, tenax liberalis,
simulator simplex, saevus clemens, et semper in omnibus varius' (14, 11).
The infinite gradations of a character and an activity resulting from a large
and subtle intelligence could only be understood when they were classified
as contrasts. The portrait that can be recovered from the episodes and acts

[1] CASS. D., LXIX, 19, 2.

known to us does not correspond, so far as Hadrian the statesman is concerned, with this precise definition of a double personality; only the variety, not the fickleness or the caprice, was a real trait. He was constantly conscious of his duty and attentive to the business of administration; the variety lay in the boundless extent of the field of interests forming the object of his serious and scrupulous diligence, whether it was a question of the state of the empire's finances, which he knew from memory better than the head of a family knows the household accounts, or of checking the quality of the dishes even in the last courses of an official banquet; there were no contradictions at all in the action he took. Nor was there any conflict between the uniform seriousness of his actions and the gifts and surprises provided by a shrewd generosity on occasions like the Saturnalia or in distributions to the populace, which he treated vigorously and without flattery. Hadrian put his passion for travelling at the service of the state, and no one can reproach him for the time he spent and the risks he ran in hunting, a typical pursuit of royalty in every age as well as his own favourite hobby, one which he cultivated with his usual enthusiasm, even to the point of building tombs for dogs and horses and of enjoying the recipe, described by Aelius Caesar, of a dish of game, the *tetra-* or *pentapharmacum*, a pie filled with pheasant and wild boar. Nor did he lack humour and the capacity to stand back and comment wittily on his own actions – an infallible indication of abiding good sense in important people. If he could not stand those who had grown rich by dubious means and admired and helped instead men of integrity and honour, that was to his credit. Then, in the field of practical expediency, there was the abolition outside Rome of court ceremonial; in the field of sober habits the custom of dining abundantly, but frugally and without wine; and in the field of deference to tradition the respect for the ancient sumptuary laws on banquets, which were enlivened not by wasteful luxury but by plays and readings. The picture is thus one of varied interests and wide-ranging attention, all forming part of the one activity of governing.

But Hadrian was also a man of letters, with noteworthy intellectual interests, and this aspect of his personality contributed in particular to making him seem a curious man – a genuine representative, moreover, of the culture of his time. Ambition, envy and touchiness, as bad sides of his character, are in fact recorded only in the field of his contacts with literature and men of letters and we do not know how much weight should be given to the relevant incidents: intolerance of comparisons, an obsession with fame such as to make him publish his own writings under other people's names, irritation with anyone who contradicted him (Apollodorus, the great artist, is supposed to have lost his life through this), disdain and envy of other poets, even the dead, including Homer. He was certainly a man of refined tastes and vast knowledge; and so long as it was a question of oratorical ability, with which he was naturally gifted and which he diligently cultivated, or of perspicacity in framing legal responses, his culture served the business of governing, just as public life saw the exercise in particular of those gifts which left people agape: he would correct the *nomenclator*, remember whole lists of veterans whom he had heard named some time before, repeat in detail the contents of books read only once, write and dictate at the same time, listen and converse – 'si potest credi', adds the biographer or an interpolator (20, 11).

But Hadrian's participation in the literary and cultural life was wide and enthusiastic. Writers and philosophers had in him a sometimes harsh and biting critic and a tireless interlocutor, who kept them tied down for hours in close discussions, but also a protector. In Rome he founded an academy for recitations, 'ludus ingenuarum astium',[1] which he called the 'Athenaeum'. His was the idea of a pension for old and disabled teachers, and in connection with higher education and the care of cultural tools like libraries, besides making administrative provisions he granted favours and privileges; the correspondence with Plotina already mentioned concerned granting to people who were not citizens the right to direct the Epicurean school at Athens, a school of which the Empress was a patron. However, his favourite philosophers were Epictetus (though he may not have known him personally) and Heliodorus, the same person, it would seem, as the rhetorician of Cyrrhus, C. Avidius Heliodorus, his *ab epistulis* and prefect of Egypt. He knew old Euphrates, the adversary of Apollonius of Tyana, and of the rhetoricians he liked Dionysius of Miletus and especially Favorinus of Arelate, whose study of grammar had not diminished his diplomatic talents, if the stories told about his ready wit are true. On one occasion he politely reminded the Emperor of his own right to immunity in his own city and on another occasion he defended himself to his friends for having ceded victory to Hadrian, although he was wrong, on the correct use of a word by saying: 'You give me bad advice in not allowing me to regard as the most learned of us all the man who is master of thirty legions!'.[2] Witty words to which Hadrian promptly replied in the same vein. His biographer calls him in this connection 'dicaculus' (20, 8), although the only episode he cites – obviously chosen from many – to support the description is not particularly witty: having refused a favour

[1] AUR. VICT., *De Caes.*, 14, 3.
[2] CASS. D., LXIX, 3, 5–6; *V. Hadr.*, 15, 12–13.

requested by a man with white hair, when the latter appeared again with dyed hair and repeated the request, he refused him again, saying, 'I have already said no to your father'. There is more savour to the incident in the baths, which Hadrian visited regularly as a private individual. Seeing a veteran whom he had known in the legions scratching himself against a wall and learning that he was doing this because he did not possess even one slave to do him this service, he made him a present of two, with the means to maintain them. The result was that the next day he found a troop of old men at the baths intent on the same operation, whom he told to scratch each other. Hadrian's participation in the culture of the time must have been on a popular level of this kind. Even his poetry, inspired by concrete occasions and certainly not flying very high, except for the famous apostrophe to the 'animula vagula blandula'[1] written in the twilight of his life, combined in facile harmony the elements of his own common human experience with the tendencies of a school which, obsessed with an essentially romantic exploitation of the simple and primitive, was turning for preference to the ancient poets and launching the fashion of archaism. Thus the Emperor, who was an enthusiastic lover of poetry and literature, an expert on music, medicine, painting and sculpture, and well versed in astrology and arithmetic – in short, a connoisseur of every art – was a typical representative of the civilized spirit of the time.

But another field of intellectual activity, and one more directly relevant to the public interest, was cultivated more than in any other age and actively stimulated by the Princeps, namely, that of jurisprudence, which grafted on to the stem of Roman juridical tradition the impulse to theorize and systematize characteristic of the epoch and created a number of fundamental works. In the early years of Hadrian's reign Iavolenus Priscus, the grand old master of the Sabinians, was still alive. The codification of the praetor's edict in particular provoked a spate of commentaries. Sextus Pomponius and Sextus Puedius inaugurated the series which, continued by Gaius (for the provincial edict) and the writers of the second half of the century, was completed in the third century by the great treatises of Ulpian and Paul. Salvius Julianus himself, the editor of the edict, wrote ninety books of *Digesta*, an ample collection of *responsa* on real and fictitious cases; the work, which is usually regarded as the culmination of Roman jurisprudence, on the basis of what is known of this from Justinian's *Digest*, was continued in the *Quaestiones* of his disciple, Sextus Caecilius Africanus, the last-known head of the Sabinian school.

---

[1] *V. Hadr.*, 25, 9.

The Proculians Neratius Priscus and P. Iuventius Celsus were no less active in producing the same kind of collection, while of the treatises concentrating on civil law one that should be remembered is that of Aburnius Valens on testamentary trusts, a subject evidently of particular interest, as we saw from the *senatusconsulta* quoted in connection with manumission by will. This subject was also treated a little later on by Volusius Maecianus, young Marcus Aurelius's instructor in law. Here too empiricism was yielding to theoretical systematization, and the science, if not yet the philosophy, of law was being born.

Activity in architecture and the figurative arts now also conformed to the canons laid down by educated taste, and considerable influence was exerted by the Emperor himself. From the grandest monuments to coins, there is such a thing as a uniform Hadrianic art, extending moreover with the very same characteristics over an area of unparalleled extent and overflowing with its influence even the boundaries of the empire – something that had never happened before. This is the clearest evidence even for us of the general levelling-up of the standard of life, for art in particular has left tangible remains that we can see with our own eyes. We have already spoken of the number and splendour of the buildings erected in every part of the empire and of the main public works. But it is the monuments of Rome itself that testify above all to the creative activity of Hadrian who, in the universal peace, 'uti solet tranquillis rebus',[1] carried out fully all the projects inspired by his purely Roman technical experience and by his passion for all things Greek. One of the results was a widespread enthusiasm for restoration and renewal, and it may have been more the wish for distinction than modesty that dictated his habit of putting on buildings he restored, even when they were rebuilt from the foundations, the names of the original builders rather than his own. So it was with the Pantheon, and probably with the baths of Agrippa, with the temple and *Atrium Vestae*, the *Saepta*, the *Porticus Argonautorum*, the *Basilica Neptuni*, the forum of Augustus, the *Auguratorium* on the Palatine (restored in 136), the buildings of the Palatine itself, which were extended and completed, and the many temples that were rebuilt. Among these last, apart from that of Divus Julius, and that of the Bona Dea Subsaxana on the lower slopes of the Aventine, was the *templum* or *porticus Divorum* built by Domitian in the Campus Martius, the restoration of which in 126 has been disclosed recently by the *Fasti Ostienses*.[2] Naturally it was in his own name that he dedicated the temple of Trajan and Plotina, that of Matidia, in the Campus Martius, which must have been flanked by the

[1] AUR. VICT., *De Caes.*, 14, 5.   [2] *Inscr. It.*, XIII, 1, pp. 203, 233.

basilicas of Marciana and Matidia, and in addition the mausoleum and the
bridge which gave and still gives access to it. We are not told anything
about the temple of Venus and Rome, but this building, which of all
Hadrian's religious monuments must have been the one most significant
of the concept of Roman universality adopted and propagated by the
Emperor, built as it was with great care over a long period of time (at
least since 121; and in 136–7 the ornamentation was still going on), in one
of the most prominent places in Rome, on a very original plan directly
inspired by the Princeps, must certainly have had its duly acknowledged
place among Hadrian's works. The construction of the temple made it
necessary to move the colossal statue of Nero, already modified by
Vespasian and dedicated to the Sun; and the characteristic order was given
to Apollodorus, though it was probably never carried out, to erect a twin
colossus to the Moon. The villa at Tivoli, being completely private, represented the most untrammelled and complete satisfaction of Hadrian's
enthusiasm for art, and as such it constitutes for us one of the most
curious monuments of antiquity. His journeys over, and ready for a
repose devoted only to acts of government and the intellectual life, the
now sixty-year-old Emperor reserved a good part of his time for art: 'uti
beatis locupletibus mos, palatia exstruere, curare epulas signa tabulas
pictas'.[1] On the slope running down from Tivoli, by extending over a
vast area a villa of the late republican age already intermittently enlarged
in preceding periods of the reign (118–121, 125–128), he reproduced the
most famous places and buildings he had visited on his tours: the Lyceum,
the Academy, the Prytaneum, and the Stoa Poikile of his beloved Athens,
the picturesque Vale of Tempe, and the Serapeum and Canopus in
Egypt. The result was a most curious residence, worthy of the Emperor
with the most original character.

However, these interests did not isolate him, as his literary tastes have
already shown us, from the everyday life of the people. Personal enthusiasm, tradition and political sense all made him a generous promoter
of shows, the most important aspect of social life. Fragments of the *Fasti
Ostienses* have been reconstructed for only three years of Hadrian's reign,[2]
but from them we learn of a good three series of shows which can be
added to those already known from the beginning of the reign and which
confirm the general reports on their abundance. In 126 there was the huge
munus already mentioned with 1,835 pairs of gladiators; in 127, from 20
to 30 October, there were the *ludi votivi decennales*, inaugurated in the
circus with a day of *pyrrhicae*, the military dances of which we know that

---

[1] AUR. VICT., *De Caes.*, 14, 6.   [2] *Inscr. It.* XIII, 1, pp. 203–5, 233.

Hadrian was very fond, as he was, being a great huntsman, of the *venationes*. In Rome he also gave shows of this sort with a hundred lions, and in Athens he presented a show with a thousand wild beasts. He himself practised gladiatorial combat, a habit, it seems, which no longer caused any surprise. He did not neglect the theatre and made his court actors recite for the benefit of the public at large. And among the reports, certainly important in the urban life of the epoch, of the circumstances surrounding the shows, one has come down to us to the effect that Hadrian never sent away from Rome any *venator* or actor. The circus, the amphitheatre, and the theatre, all of which he frequented assiduously, were moreover his principal channel of communication with the populace, at the most easily comprehensible level. In any age the populace always appreciates being taken into the direct confidence of the ruler, particularly when the latter deigns to let it share political judgements expressed in the form of boastfulness and arrogance; such an occasion occurred when Hadrian received in homage from the famous Pharasmanes a number of tunics embroidered in gold, and to mark the gift made three hundred criminals march round the arena all dressed in this fashion. The improved organization of the corn supply was not allowed to stand in the way of special free distributions, which were even more numerous and tended to become larger in size, starting a tradition that could not be broken by his successors; and another four *congiaria* followed the three already recorded at the beginning of the reign: the fourth probably in 125 or 126, on the occasion of Hadrian's return from his first tour, the fifth possibly in 134 on a similar occasion, the sixth in 136 for the adoption of L. Aelius Caesar and the seventh in 138 for that of Antoninus.

An aspect of the greatest interest in a personality so complex and in an epoch so rich in spiritual fermentation is naturally the religious one. However, Hadrian's policy in this field seems to have been more traditionalist than might have been expected from his varied religious experience. Of the three sections of this policy – imperial cult, traditional religion, foreign cults – none was developed to the detriment of the others, and the religious life of the empire continued to maintain a balance between fulfilment of the official ritual duties and toleration of any individual belief which did not endanger public order and safety. Hadrian himself, 'omnium curiositatum explorator',[1] applied to religion his customary thirst for experience and antiquarian enthusiasm. He was not a mystic and the problems of religion aroused much the same kind of interest in him as he felt in those of science, of astrology – a subject which,

[1] TERTULL., *Apolog.*, 5.

it seems, he studied seriously – and of divination. He is said to have given much weight to presages, and astronomical symbols appeared on coins at the time when he was initiated into the mysteries, which he approached with respect but with the sole intention of evoking history and of paying homage to the venerable traditions of the Greek culture that he admired so much. That he was assimilated to Zeus, was regarded as the son of Zeus, and in Egypt appeared on coins as an incarnation of Horus were thus not new elements in the history of the imperial cult in the East; they simply indicated, in accordance with the tendency of the time, the more extensive and uniform organization of these combinations, already familiar to the eastern religious mentality. And the Emperor certainly did not check these manifestations of high political value, except out of politeness, as in 126, when he declined some of the honours offered to him by the Achaean League.

The cult of the Emperor and of his family in the West was marked if anything by parsimony; Hadrian's sister Domitia Paulina, who died in 130 or 131, was not deified, and references to Diva Sabina are few and far between. As for the traditional religion, the sources say that to show his respect for it he effectively performed all the functions of the pontifex maximus. In fact he closely resembled Augustus in his care for the restoration of temples and rituals; moreover, we can imagine the possibilities offered by the antiquities of Rome, both human and divine, which were lovingly investigated for the satisfaction of his antiquarian tastes by disinterment and revival. Then the cult of Rome could not but emphasize and exalt traditional religious feeling, and the symbolism of the coinage was all, so far as it was religious, completely Roman. 'Sacra Romana diligentissime curavit, peregrina contempsit':[1] but perhaps it was not so much a question of contempt for foreign religions as of impartiality, of the essential indifference of the inquisitive, and sometimes of scepticism and irony. Such an attitude was in any case justified if we can accept as authentic (but this is extremely dubious) the amusing description of turbulent Alexandria contained in the form of a letter from Hadrian to his relation Servianus, in the life of the usurper Saturninus in the *Historia Augusta* (Ch. 8), where it is stated that Christians, Jews and Gentiles all worshipped in love and harmony one single god, money.

Hadrian was in practice tolerant, both with the Jews, in spite of the savage war, and with the Christians, who under him lived in peace. There were far too many mystical and fanatical sects for the Emperor to be able to know them and follow their activities, and to all intents and purposes

---

[1] *V. Hadr.*, 22, 10.

he did not bother about them, leaving it to the law and the police bodies to check any dangerous offences they might commit. Trajan had done the same. Thus when we attempt to measure the precise effect created at the time by acts like the presentation to Hadrian in Athens of the *Apologies* of Quadratus and Aristides, we have to see Christianity as the pagans saw it then and to remember the complex variety of the governmental tasks occupying any one of the Emperor's days; it is no good adopting the Christian point of view, which in any case only developed somewhat later. Did Hadrian read these *Apologies*, among the hundreds of petitions and memorials with which he was bombarded during his travels, especially in the loquacious East? His offer of a place in the Pantheon for Christ leaves us somewhat baffled on the subject. The Church was living and developing on its divine foundation and it was in the world, but the world only knew it so far as a foreign movement, sometimes dangerous, and, when it was, to be combated with the rigour of the law. There is no lack of testimony to the continuation of Trajan's attitude, though in a firmer and more coherent way. A much-discussed document quoted in Justin's *Apology* (69), namely an alleged rescript of Hadrian's to the proconsul of Asia, C. Minicius Fundanus, in reply to a query raised by his predecessor, probably in 123, about an investigation similar to the one which had occupied Pliny some ten years earlier, dealt with the acceptance of charges of Christianity and the relevant investigation: firm action was to be taken without worrying about mob hysteria, but only in the case of clear and circumstantial accusations; if the charge was false, the accuser was to be punished. Thus the state's opportunistic concern for local public order emerged as less important, while on the other hand accusers had to think twice before making use of this kind of charge. This turned out to be an indubitable advantage for the Christians, even though the concept of punishability for the mere name (the crimes connected with it – primarily refusal to take part in the imperial cult – being taken for granted) was defined still more clearly. The fact remains that the reports of martyrdoms under Hadrian are not earlier than the fifth century.

Such in broad outline was the activity of Hadrian: 'immensi laboris'.[1]

THE END

The early days of 136 saw the beginning – as a result, so the biographer seems to think, of some over-exertion on his last tour, made when he was

---

[1] *Epit. de Caes.*, 14, 4.

no longer a young man – of the painful malady, perhaps a fever with com-
plications, which led to the sad decline of the Emperor, tortured in mind
and body. He now began to think, with a disconcerting independence of
mind, of the problem of the succession. He had no children and so the
situation prevailing in the last days of Trajan was more or less repeated.
That the suspense attending his decision was great is demonstrated among
other things by the reports of intentions and designations preserved by the
sources and not referring only to the final episodes. If he really did state
that, of ten names suggested to him as those of men worthy of the throne,
Servianus's alone could safely be accepted without examination,[1] he
certainly had no intention of leaving as his successor a man who in the
last years of the reign was over ninety. The report must therefore refer to
a time still distant from the imminent possibility of succession. Even the
name of Avidius Nigrinus, one of the four ex-consuls put to death in 118,
is preserved in the tradition as that of a man marked out for the succession.
It is natural that the names of friends like Platorius Nepos and Terentius
Gentianus should be recorded in the same context. Catilius Severus also
had his hopes and put in more work than the others, it seems, to improve
his own chances. It is characteristic that among those designated, all
senators of high rank, no particular prominence is given to Hadrian's
relations, Servianus and the son of Servianus's daughter Julia, the
eighteen-year-old Cn. Pedanius Fuscus Salinator. In actual fact Hadrian
gave no excessive prominence to his own family. Even if what the tradition
has to say about his poor relations with Sabina, who is supposed to have
been poisoned in 137, is malicious gossip, the fact remains that it was
only in 128 that the Emperor's consort became Augusta and began to
coin her own money; after her death the title *Diva Sabina* appeared regularly on the coinage. But the honour never exceeded the limits of strict
etiquette; Hadrian ensured that the Empress was respected, but it is
doubtful whether she ever exerted alongside her energetic husband, who
liked to keep the reins of power in his own hands, an effective power comparable even with that of Marciana or Plotina. Domitia Paulina, Hadrian's
sister, has already been mentioned. Consequently when, a sick man, he
saw the need for a decision, and the intrigues of a man like Servianus in
favour of his nephew and of friends in their own interests, even though not
amounting to a real conspiracy, gave him the nauseating impression of the
start of a competition over his body, his hand smote the nearest most
severely; old Servianus and the young Fuscus were put to death and the
others forfeited his favour. Probably the 'terror' of the last two years of

---

[1] CASS. D., LXIX, 17, 3.

the reign can be reduced to this episode. This 'terror' is a dark picture painted by the senatorial tradition, which enjoyed describing Hadrian's long physical and moral torment, and his desperate and always un-successful attempts to escape by suicide, as the effect of the solemn curse pronounced by the dying Servianus: 'You, O Gods, know that I am innocent; all I wish for Hadrian is that he may desire to die and be unable to!'[1]

The man adopted and designated for the succession was one of the con-suls of 136, L. Ceionius Commodus, already favoured in his career – as the others had been too – by the Princeps, who had supported his candidature for the praetorship and when it came to the consulship had honoured him with the special subsidy conferred to enable men to sustain the office with splendour. He was the son-in-law of the Avidius Nigrinus already men-tioned as one of the victims of 138 and came from an Etruscan family that had already been illustrious for some generations. We know too little of the circumstances to be surprised at the choice, which on the surface fully realized senatorial aspirations to the designation of a member of the aristocracy, without any dynastic ties, but in fact it was a personal, aristocratic choice, as is shown by the fact that the tradition says that generally it was not well received because of Commodus's moral qualities, which inspired little confidence. It is therefore pointless to seek special reasons to explain a surprise which is our own, not that of the ancients. The modern theory[2] that Commodus was Hadrian's natural son comes up against the insuperable wall of a silence on the part of the tradition so solid as to be amazing when we consider the nature of the suggestion and of the sources for the period, which do not consist just of Pliny's 'pages full of decorum',[3] themselves more or less devoid of news of this kind. Certainly, here too, as in all matters of which nothing is known, it is legitimate to raise possibilities, but one cannot go further than that. Adopted in the second half of 136, L. Ceionius Commodus called himself L. Aelius Caesar, received the *tribunicia potestas* and the *imperium proconsulare* (as *proconsul*, however, not with the title of *imperator*), and struck his own coins. Circus shows, a *congiarium* to the people and a donative to the soldiers accompanied the event. In 137, after entering on his second ordinary consulship, he went as governor, certainly with an *imperium* wider than the normal one, to Pannonia, where he exercised his functions –

[1] CASS. D., LXIX 17, 2.
[2] J. CARCOPINO, 'L'hérédité dynastique chez les Antonins', in *Rev. Ét. Anc.*, LI, 1949, p. 290 ff., see Crit. Notes, p. 699.
[3] R. SYME, 'Antonine Relations: Ceionii and Vettuleni' in *Athen.*, XXXV, 1957, p. 309.

T A—P

with great distinction, it seems; and this fact, in spite of reports asserting that he was already ill before his adoption, suggests that at this stage his health was perfectly sound, so that Hadrian's complaint, mentioned by the biographer, that he had leaned on a falling wall, would have been justly directed against an unexpected blow of fate. The fact remains that in the night before 1 January 138 L. Aelius Caesar died in Rome and on the following day, because of the prayers for the beginning of the year, there was not even any official mourning. Characteristically he was not deified either, although he was given an imperial funeral and his ashes were subsequently deposited in the new mausoleum in Trastevere.

Hadrian's next choice was equally unexpected and independent, to judge from the previous reputation of the man designated. There must have been a good many senators like T. Aurelius Fulvus Boionius Arrius Antoninus, the ex-consul designated for the succession on 24 January 138 and adopted on 25 February. He came from a Narbonese family (from Nemausus) and had been born in a villa at Lanuvium on 19 September 86; thus when he was adopted he was fifty-one, so that an exception had to be made to the law which prescribed for *adoptio*, and *a fortiori* for *adrogatio* (i.e. the adoption of persons *sui iuris*) a difference in age of at least eighteen years.[1] Antoninus's career had been distinguished but not exceptional; *consul ordinarius* in 120, one of the four consular *iudices* in Italy and proconsul of Asia round about 134–135, he had not, as far as we know, held any military commands. He was thus a typical civil servant and had in fact been several times among Hadrian's councillors. The position and relationships of the family were indeed of the first rank: Antoninus was the son of a consul, grandson on his father's side of that T. Aurelius Fulvus who under Nero and the Flavians had held two consulships and been prefect of the city, and grandson on his mother's side of Arrius Antoninus, the man so much admired by Pliny and himself twice consul, besides being the son-in-law – having married his daughter Annia Faustina – of M. Annius Verus, the only senator known to have held three consulships under Hadrian, apart from the Emperor's relation, Servianus. The name *Boionius* came from Boionia Procilla, Arrius Antoninus's wife; there seems to have been no other reason but this lady's exceptional virtue for the commemorative preservation of such a rare family name. Thus Antoninus was certainly a distinguished person but not, at least as far as we know, marked out for the succession by any special reasons evident to all and dictating in themselves the course of events. Thus if Hadrian picked him out entirely on his own initiative and

---

[1] *Digest.*, I, 7, 40, 1.

simply for the qualities he possessed, it is only fair that he should receive the credit for such a happy choice. The new Caesar was placed in a higher position than L. Aelius but not yet in that of co-regent. Having assumed the name *Imperator T. Aelius Caesar Antoninus* and been at once invested with the *tribunicia potestas* and the *imperium proconsulare*, this time with the title of Imperator, he took over a large part of the duties of government and in practice all of them when Hadrian, his health still worse, left the villa at Tivoli for Baiae.

But Hadrian's plans for the succession were not limited to naming his immediate heir. Just as Augustus had done with Tiberius, and as a demonstration that the dynastic tendency of the Roman principate found in the autocrat's will, without any interference from the Senate, the sole surrogate for hereditary succession, so Hadrian obliged Antoninus, who only had one daughter (his two male children and another married daughter being already dead), to adopt in his turn, so that they should be his heirs, the son (not more than eight years old) of the deceased L. Aelius Caesar, L. Ceionius Commodus, who was christened L. Aelius Aurelius Commodus, and the seventeen-year-old youth M. Annius Verus (henceforth known as M. Aelius Aurelius Verus), who was the grandson of M. Annius Verus and thus also the grandson of Antoninus's wife, Annia Galeria Faustina. Hadrian had had his eye on this second young man in particular for some time, partly to do honour to his family, one of the most prominent. He had christened him 'Verissimus' in allusion to his uncommon moral qualities, had granted him at the age of six the honour of the *equus publicus*, and when he was eight had enrolled him in the college of Salian priests, afterwards always taking a favourable interest in his progress. In addition to these arrangements Hadrian now also expressed the wish that L. Aelius should in due course marry the daughter of Antoninus himself, Annia Faustina (Minor). This wish was not in fact respected, for Faustina married her cousin Marcus Aurelius, who himself had been promised in vain, since the time when he had donned the *toga virilis* in 135 or 136, to L. Aelius's own sister, Ceionia Fabia. Nevertheless, the dynastic scheme for the succeeding half-century was fixed, and completely at that, by the will of Hadrian.

The end came soon afterwards. Hadrian breathed his last at Baiae on 10 July 138, in the presence of his successor. The last few months of pain and frenzy, and the fear of explosions of cruelty, must have produced a grim impression, so much so that the Senate tried to refuse deification or at any rate did not take the initiative, which was left to the new Princeps. According to some authorities it was precisely for this display of filial

pietas that Antoninus acquired the nickname of Pius; others ascribed it –
and this is quite credible – to his having saved men marked out as victims
of Hadrian's wrath. Buried at first in the Ciceronian villa at Puteoli,
Hadrian rested later in his own mausoleum. He was honoured at Puteoli by
a temple and the institution of quinquennial games, by another splendid
temple in Rome and also by the creation of a college of *sodales Hadrianales*
and of *flamines* for the new god.

After the death of the emperor who had completed the development of
the administrative machine and used primarily his own talents for the
purpose, the principate lived on, more stable than ever. Henceforth it was
accepted without question as the sole form of rule possible, so much so as to
pass into the hands of a typical senator, though without losing any of its
autocratic content. The man who succeeded Hadrian was conspicuously
different from him, but the imperial organization, guided from the top
with unchanged conservative care, continued its solid life throughout the
reign – the reign of ordinary administration.

XI

ANTONINUS PIUS

TRANQUILLITAS ORDINIS

The Senate's attempt to damn Hadrian's memory and to annul his acts – including the designation of Antoninus Pius as his successor – and the strenuous efforts made according to the tradition by the latter to defend both, should certainly not be understood as a political crisis critical enough to endanger the continuation of the principate, at any rate in the form desired by Hadrian. The episode amounted only to a demonstration against an emperor who from certain points of view only, but ones calculated to offend aristocratic sensibilities in particular, had not left behind a pleasant memory. But the autocrat and the aristocracy were so closely and naturally bound together in a relationship of interdependence, and the principate, the apex of the imperial system, was now such a normal and evident reality, that it was impossible even to think of a change that had not succeeded in other times when the rift between the 'master' of the republic and the republic itself was deep and the veils of the ancient forms shrouded a reality still unwelcome to so many.

Antoninus Pius began his actual reign with harmony completely restored in the Princeps–Senate relationship. And the harmony was not achieved by the sacrifice of the Emperor's power. The retention in the title of the forename and family name (T. Aelius) signified only that a senator could be Princeps, and not that the Princeps wanted to be a senator. Backstage activity, family and party ties can be suspected and in fact glimpsed behind the figure of the new Princeps, but in fact Antoninus governed with absolute independence, with the same unlimited authority as his predecessors and even with the same outward show. He soon received the name *Augustus* and also assumed that of *Hadrianus*; possibly a little later the Senate, to meet the wishes and intentions of a programme already widely publicized, gave him the title of *Pius*, which remained his sole personal title. The designation as consul from the next 1 January – normal accompaniment since the time of the Flavians of appointment and salutation as *imperator* – the subsequently small number of consulships (third in 140, fourth in 145), the usual assumption of the office of Pontifex Maximus and of other major priesthoods, the mere two salutations as *imperator* (on accession and in 142–143), and the postponed acceptance (put off probably until the beginning of 139) of the title of *pater patriae* show that there was no change in the normal practice, except possibly in the direction of both the display and acceptance of a greater and more explicit deference. In fact it was just at this period that the adjectives added to *Princeps* began to herald even in the West the later hyperboles: there were sequences like 'optimus ac sanctissimus omnium saeculorum princeps',[1] and the official use of the expression 'dominus noster' became more frequent. The East, where Antoninus was present only in the endlessly exalted memory of his sojourn as proconsul, found no difficulty in transferring to him the showy titles given to his predecessor and called him the Olympian, the New Dionysus, benefactor and god. Faustina very soon became Augusta – something which had not fallen to the lot of Plotina or Sabina – and statues were put up in honour of the forefathers and all the deceased relations of the new Princeps, whose displays of family *pietas* with political overtones culminated in 139, when, the mausoleum at Trastevere having been completed, the ashes of Hadrian, Sabina and L. Aelius Caesar were finally laid there, together with those of his own three dead children. The tribute paid to public expectations on the occasion of the start of a new reign was also the usual one: a *congiarium* of 75 denarii per head, with a corresponding *donativum* to the troops; and the remission of the whole *aurum coronarium* for Italy and of half of it for the provinces. The discharge of all persons facing prosecution at the moment of Hadrian's death – a continuation of the restraining influence already exerted by Antoninus in the last few months of Hadrian's reign – was a completely autocratic intervention, the Emperor's reparation to the senators who shortly before had felt themselves threatened by the will of another autocrat. As its beginnings promised, the whole programme of the reign was directed towards preserving the existing state of affairs, and this programme was put into effect with a fervour in which the emperor's sense of duty and senatorial loyalty had never been so closely united. Antoninus had witnessed, at an age when he was capable of understanding and judging, the whole reigns of Trajan and Hadrian and belonged to a typically imperial and co-operative aristocracy; when we add to this the personal qualities of the cultivated aristocrat of the period, in their noblest and most humane form, his governmental policy could hardly

[1] *ILS*, 6898.

have been different from what it was, favoured as it was in its execution by the general conditions both at home and abroad.

So began the reign of the *Imperator Caesar T. Aelius Hadrianus Antoninus Augustus Pius*, and his work as supreme arbiter went on for many a year; it took shape in the very large number of acts attested by an imposing body of evidence, especially epigraphical evidence, but it is even less susceptible than the work of other emperors to reconstruction according to any homogeneous chronological scheme which would give some idea of the organic development of definite programmes. The empire lived in the tranquillity of order, or in the peace preserved – the sole policy pursued, and that more by administrative than political means – by a firm hand. How natural this state of affairs seemed to contemporary opinion is clear from the factual presuppositions and the concrete observations made in the famous discourse pronounced, probably on 23 April 143, at Rome, in the Athenaeum built by Hadrian, by Aelius Aristides, the young rhetorician from Hadrianoutherae. This speech, which is tricked out in all the rhetorical phraseology proper to the genre, was purely laudatory in aim; it develops the commonplace of the contrast between past empires and the Roman empire. Once again the Greek mind provided the Romans with a statement in terms of political theory of the empirical reality of their state, certainly not with the limpid profundity of a Polybius, but with indubitable sincerity so far as it was an expression of the judgement which the educated people of a notable part of the Roman dominions passed on their rulers, or rather on the 'ruling power'. This document testifies to the breadth of a consensus co-extensive with the satisfaction at the acheivement of a state of affairs that was probably as good as any that distinguished provincials could conceive, let alone desire. And this provincial voice, paying homage to the empire after five years of a reign which seemed to have consolidated in immutable forms the organization of civilized humanity, completed a cycle. The concept of Rome as an abstract and everlasting entity, the author and centre of the imperial structure, had already been employed by Hadrian. This concept, which combined all the elements of the final imperial reality, now found a response in the empire's gratitude, and the literary tradition initiated the series of hymns to an idealized Rome which was to persist even beyond the well-known paean of Rutilius Namatianus.

In Aelius Aristides's oration we must naturally distinguish between the real basis of facts and the rhetorical exaggerations, between the appreciation of the actually existing structures and the artificial construction of a political ideal out of literary themes. But the speech as a whole is a genuine expression of contemporary mentality and the details it contains are very valuable. The orator was concerned above all to show how the shining reality of the empire had resolved the great problems of liberty, justice and the right relation of human institutions to their divine prototypes. At last the organization of the civilized world was modelled on the order of the universe and in the Emperor's rule a divine Mind was at work; this gave the Princeps, again from a philosophical standpoint (and one that came from Platonic philosophy), a sacred, almost religious character. It was not yet a question of the divine right of kings, but to have progressed so far ideologically along this path, even only in a rhetorical composition, in the middle of the second century and in connection with the Roman principate, was fairly significant. Order resulted in practice from the justice of the governors and the discipline of the governed. With *hubris*, that is, violence and injustice, banished, liberty flourished, corresponding with the rule of justice; the justice of the constitution did in fact give a guarantee against the dangers of arbitrary government, and this was liberty – liberty, of course, in the sense of a personal guarantee for the classes entitled to it, who in any case made no claim to anything else. Rome had achieved the highest perfection in government, 'the definitive art of government', and had organized the world in one single form of civilized life, in a common fatherland; not in common servitude but (and here the Greek is revealed) in a big 'league', under the hegemony of one city, in which liberty was ensured for the individual components. In fact, although the philhellenism of Antoninus was considerably more restrained than Hadrian's, the Panhellenion continued to prosper, thus displaying a vitality that was not simply academic. But the element of greatest and most concrete interest in the speech is the recognition of the advantages of Roman rule. There was particular satisfaction with the administration of justice; this was a long-standing experience of the provinces and the main one that had made them loyal supporters of the principate. The system of military recruitment was also satisfactory, and local conditions of life in the towns, encouraged as they were in commerce and in every peaceful activity, had never been so agreeable. 'Beati' were those who enjoyed the 'pax Romana' and 'miseri' those who were outside the empire or through their own fault were incapable of enjoying this peace; 'beati' therefore were the 'cives', those who possessed the privilege of citizenship, but the rest were 'beati' too, either in the hope of obtaining citizenship, for ascent in the social order through merit was open to all, or in merely remaining citizens of their own towns, which all enjoyed the universal well-being.

The idyllic picture naturally has its limits. Aelius Aristides spoke only in the name of the urban inhabitants of the empire, and moreover of those at the upper or middle level; he disregarded the slaves and took no account, as far as can be seen, of the non-Italian and non-Greek country people. It is not even certain that he expressed the authentic voice of the Italian and Greek country folk, or of the urban proletariat, in associating them, as he does, with the universal chorus of agreement. But we have already spoken several times of the nature of Roman society and of what counted in it. There was certainly much more to the reality than merely what is reflected in the tradition; and we know that all the elements in the shadows of the social structure were also accomplishing their natural development towards the crisis and preparing the ground for future changes. But all this was still far away and certainly could not be foreseen by the men of that age; and no serious presentiment can have disturbed the general equilibrium while everything seemed peaceful and solid. The peace and solidity may well have been superficial and official. But the rhetorician could only refer to what he saw; and since he could not dwell at length on imaginary merits, the reality which he praises must have formed an imposing part of the reality as a whole.

ADMINISTRATION

With Trajan and Hadrian the administration of the empire had attained its final shape. It functioned normally in conditions of internal and external peace which emphasized its regularity and immutability. To examine the rule of Antoninus Pius might therefore seem the pointless rehearsal of a series of acts and measures already noted, were it not that it reveals the continual attention of the Emperor, who was no less active and tireless than his predecessors. Thus 'ordinary administration' seems to have meant only that administrative machinery henceforth existed in a definitive form. This very fact greatly increased the efficacy of any personal intervention and the empire did not notice any diminution of care through the Emperor's never moving from Rome. 'He can stay quietly where he is and govern the whole world by letters, which arrive at their destination almost as soon as they are written, as though borne by winged messengers'.[1] This is a testimony among other things to the perfection of the road and postal system, a fairly conspicuous part of the administration, while the provinces certainly appreciated the Emperor's official reason for giving up tours – the fear that his retinue, if not he himself, might put an excessive

[1] AEL. ARIST., *Or. Rom.*, 33.

burden on them[1]. But this did not make the control from the top any less intense or those at the bottom feel any less sharply the duty of deference to their lord and master, whose position as apex and source of the whole system was perhaps never so openly recognized and exalted. 'If the governors have even the slightest doubt about the validity of legal proceedings or petitions from their subjects, whether in public or private affairs, they at once send to him for instructions and wait until he replies, just as a chorus awaits the signal of the conductor'.[2] Here we see among other things the satisfaction of the provincial, who obeys, but sees that the man who gives him the order also obeys in his turn, in accordance with the rules of a perfect hierarchy of government, at the summit of which the Princeps himself obeyed the consciousness of his own functional duty. This was a fact officially and universally recognized: in Antoninus's coins as well, even in the senatorial ones and at the beginning of the reign (139), when opposition to Hadrian's cosmopolitanism, if there was any, would have been at its sharpest, there appeared a series of 'provinces'.

In the quiet course of a possibly somewhat monotonous life entirely devoted to administration, the Emperor subjected himself personally to a huge mass of work. The normal instruments of administration fulfilled their function and Antoninus made use of them, keeping them under strict control and maintaining, even at the centre, an atmosphere of austerity, under the auspices of the *Disciplina Augusta*. But outside the regular organs of government this Emperor, who aimed at interesting himself in everything, took good care not to encourage the swarms of unofficial intermediaries, who tend to proliferate round a centre of power, the 'swindlers'[3] who make people pay for the real or imaginary employment of their alleged influence. Impartiality and seriousness governed all the Emperor's dealings with others. Everyone was kept at his post by the calm energy of the Princeps, who nevertheless respected rights and privileges. His respect for the Senate, which now consisted to a larger and larger extent of dignitaries from outside Italy – in other words, it was an imperial Senate – was full and sincere but devoid of any weakness. He renewed and kept the promise not to put any senator to death, leaving the Senate to deal with cases of treason, and preserved in his relations with nobles the now traditional simplicity and familiarity and a scrupulous respect for persons and property, receiving and visiting his friends without ceremony, consulting them on everything, refusing legacies from people with children, renouncing confiscations and even restoring to the children the property of men found guilty of embezzlement, provided

---

[1] *V. Pii.*, 7, 11.   [2] AEL. ARIST., *Or. Rom.*, 32.   [3] *V. Pii.*, 6, 4.

only that provincials who had suffered losses were compensated; nevertheless, evidence is not lacking of stern proceedings that also unquestionably
caused a stir, to judge from the traces left in a document like the *Fasti
Ostienses*. The *Fasti* indicate the day (15 September 145) of the trial of
that Cornelius Priscianus who, probably as governor, had made an attempt
at insubordination in Spain; they mention, in 151, the deportation of
three persons for some unknown reason but one serious enough to justify,
perhaps, a large issue of coins bearing the legend *Iustitia*, a legend very rare
in this reign; and finally they record the case of T. Atilius Rufus Titianus,
proscribed after a senatorial trial as 'adfectatae tyrannidis reus.'[1] This case
provoked the only erasure for *abolitio memoriae* in a text in which even the
name of Domitian was preserved.[2] Unfortunately the 'gratiarum actio'
which Fronto pronounced as consul on the Ides of August 143 is known
only from the complimentary allusions to it in the correspondence with
Marcus Caesar, but we may suppose that it would add nothing to what we
know already of Antoninus's relations with the senatorial aristocracy,
except possibly for a discreet comparison, still topical after five years,
with the relations between the aristocracy and Hadrian.[3]

Antoninus adopted the same attitude of cordiality and firmness in his
dealings with the equestrian class, which had become a more and more
imposing and distinguished reinforcement for the aristocracy and the
nursery of fresh forces for the administration, as we can see from the
numerous and detailed *cursus* that appear on inscriptions of the epoch.
His praetorian prefects were kept in post for a long period, were well
rewarded and honoured with promotion to the senatorial class. The two
prefects at the beginning of the reign were M. Petronius Mamertinus and
M. Gavius Maximus; the former was consul in 150 and the latter, 'vir
severissimus',[4] remained in office for twenty years until about 158, thus
repeating the long service of Claudius Livianus and Marcius Turbo and
thereby confirming – if confirmation were needed – the stability of
Antoninus's régime as well. The award of consular insignia was a proof of
the Emperor's high opinion of him, which was not diminished by the
posthumous accusations made against him in the will of Censorius Niger,
another prominent knight and a friend of Fronto, who in fact in some of

[1] *Ibid.*, 7, 3.
[2] *Inscr. It.*, XIII, 1, pp. 205, 207, 233–4, 237.
[3] FRONTO, *Ad M. Caes.*, II, 1, 1, p. 24 VAN DEN HOUT: 'Hadrianum autem ego, quod
bona venia pietatis tuae dictum sit, ut Martem Gradivum, ut Ditem patrem, propitium
et placatum magis volui quam amavi . . . Antoninum vero ut solem, ut diem, ut vitam, ut
spiritum amo diligo, amari me ab eo sentio'.
[4] *V. Pii.*, 8, 7.

his letters gives us a glimpse of this interesting background of the relations of the Emperor's collaborators both with the Emperor and among themselves.[1] Gavius Maximus was succeeded by C. Tattius Maximus, a man who had risen swiftly from modest commands, and his death, towards 160, ushered in the prefects who subsequently remained in post in the following reign, T. Furius Victorinus, transferred from the prefectship of Egypt, and Sextus Cornelius Repentinus, who were both awarded the consular insignia by Pius.

There was certainly nothing new about all this and there was not supposed to be. Hadrian's successor made it more or less clear in the early days of his reign that he wished to be simply the continuator and executor of his adoptive father's designs, and if he was inspired to take this attitude by *pietas* and the desire to vindicate a controversial memory, the noble intent nevertheless coincided with political interest; and the continuation of the system throughout the reign showed the existence of this awareness even at the beginning. Antoninus carried on not only with the buildings started by Hadrian but also with Hadrian's régime. He left in their posts not only those officials, such as the *praefectus urbi*, whom it was now the custom to replace only at their own request, as was the case with Sextus Cornelius Scipio Salvidianus Orfitus,[2] but also the provincial governors and equestrian officials, who were bound more directly and personally to each Princeps. It will suffice to quote the examples of P. Pactumeius Clemens, governor of Cilicia (137–139), C. Iulius Bassus, governor of Dacia (135–139), Q. Lollius Urbicus, governor of Lower Germany probably from 137 to 139, Sextus Iulius Maior, governor of Upper Moesia (136–140), and C. Avidius Heliodorus, appointed prefect of Egypt by Hadrian early in 138 and retained in office until 140. For his own part Antoninus kept men in their commands for long periods of up to six, seven and even nine years; examples are the famous command in Britain of Q. Lollius Urbicus (from 140 to 145) and that of C. Popilius Carus Pedo in Upper Germany (from 152 to 161). We are naturally speaking here of consular commands – praetorians had to continue their careers and rarely spent more than three years in a provincial command – and, of course, of *boni praesides*;[3] for, like Tiberius, one of the emperors most attentive to good administration, who had also left provincial governors in office for long periods, Antoninus did not do this from love of a quiet life but because of the security ensured by con-

---

[1] FRONTO, *Ad Anton. Pium.*, 3. 4. 7, pp. 157, 159, 160 VAN DEN HOUT.

[2] *V. Pii.*, 8, 6.

[3] *Ibid.*, 5, 3.

stant surveillance, apart from the fact that a long command emphasized the character of 'functionary' in the holder.

There were now no longer any innovations to be made. Nine new procurators were created as a result of the division of responsibilities or of various regroupings of provinces for financial purposes, but for the same reasons another seven disappeared, so that in over twenty years the administration acquired only two new high officials – as far as we can tell from evidence such as inscriptions, which can be and often have been given the lie by subsequent discoveries which showed the institution in question to have been already in existence previously. Such is the case, for example, with *Dacia Porolissensis*, which on the basis of previous evidence was thought to have been instituted by Antoninus Pius in 158 or 159 but in fact now turns out to have been already in existence under Hadrian (see above, p. 412). At any rate under Antoninus the names *Dacia Apulensis* and *Porolissensis* become usual, to indicate divisions of the old *Dacia Superior*, and the *Dacia Inferior* of Hadrian's time is known as *Dacia Malvensis*. The governor resided at Apulum, and Dacia Porolissensis and Malvensis were entrusted to procurators. At some point in the reign Bithynia was also placed under a proconsul again, while in Lycia-Pamphylia, which under Hadrian had served as compensation to the Senate for Bithynia, *legati Augusti pro praetore* are attested from the beginning of the reign to the end; the old situation was thus restored. The union with Cilicia of Lycaonia and Isauria – detached from Galatia – as a result of which Cilicia increased considerably in importance, was possibly connected, like their earlier detachment from Cappadocia, with the policy pursued on the eastern frontier. The work of fixing boundaries was also continued, as inscriptions found in recent years in Thrace have shown.[1]

But Antoninus's vigilance, especially in financial matters, is implicitly attested by the biographer's praise for the paternalism with which he looked after everybody and everything 'as if they were his own'. The only instance actually recorded by the biographer of dismissal and reduction of *salarium* in the case of people who received it for sinecures is that of Mesomedes, the Cretan poet and musician who was a friend of Hadrian's and who is known for his hymns, which have come down to us – and this is pretty rare – furnished with musical notation. But the constant revision of this kind of expenditure must have been the rule, together with the rigorous checking – facilitated by the perfect organization – of the provincial accounts. To secure the award of a procuratorship to Appian of Alexandria, the historian, Fronto had to plead for two years with the

[1] *Ann. Ép.*, 1927, 49; 1951, 257; 1957, 279.

Emperor, who was afraid that the precedent might encourage 'the proliferation of a swarm of advocates requesting the same thing'.[1] An example of economy was set in any case by the Princeps himself, who before he came to the throne had lived on the income from his country estates and by lending money out, as everyone did, at interest (the modest rate of interest he asked is recorded – 4 per cent). After becoming emperor he made no changes in the way he kept accounts of his personal fortune; he still lived on the same accurately listed capital assets, imposed frugality on the court, even transferred some of his own property to cope with all the increased expenses, and used for the benefit of the state the income from his own fortune, allocating for his daughter only the capital. The figure of the Emperor who spent the vintage in particular at his villa or at the villas of his friends, though sparing for country pursuits (hunting, fishing, walking) little of his time, which even then was devoted mainly to affairs of state, cannot have existed only in the rhetoric of Fronto's letters.[2]

Once again good administration ensured the availability of sufficient means, and without excessive harshness. They called him 'The man who splits a cumin seed' (CASS. D., LXX, 3, 3), and his precision seemed like stinginess. The same charge had been made against Vespasian as well, and Antoninus suffered the criticism patiently, as being inevitable;[3] but the regularity meant in general fiscal justice and mildness, and in spite of the growing signs of economic exhaustion (for example, the denarius's loss in weight and purity), it was still possible to sustain without obvious difficulties the weight of the ordinary expenses falling on the state treasuries and to keep up as well (and this fell on the *patrimonium* of the Emperor) the splendid munificence inseparable from the majesty of the principate. Here too, however, we can detect the effects of rational calculation. Although the *puellae Faustinianae*, an institution created in 141 in honour of the dead Faustina, continued the use of *alimentationes*, and although the *congiaria* and accompanying donatives to the troops, which were fairly numerous (the distribution made after Antoninus's succession, in 139, was followed by another eight) and of an average amount (90 denarii) larger than usual, furthered an evolution in no way commendable, indeed fatal, in the stagnant life of the city and formed the personal bill paid by the Emperor for his popularity, like the shows, never before so rich in novelties and pomp, precise limits were nevertheless laid down where

---

[1] FRONTO, *Ad Anton. Pium*, 9, 2–3, p. 161 VAN DEN HOUT.
[2] FRONTO, *Ad Marc. Caes.*, II, 6, IV, 6, p. 29, 63 VAN DEN HOUT.
[3] M. AUREL., *Comm.*, I, 16, 3.

expenditure, or loss of income through exemptions and privileges, was less directly justified by some kind of inevitability. This was true above all in the field of public works.

In Rome, once he had fulfilled the demands of *pietas* by finishing the mausoleum and building from scratch the temples of Divus Hadrianus (145) and Diva Faustina, Antoninus carried out only completions and restorations, taking the lead in applying what he had laid down as a general directive, namely that when there was no absolute need for new construction precedence should be given to expenditure on conserving existing buildings.[1] He had work carried out on the Flavian amphitheatre, on the *Graecostadium*, damaged by a fire, and possibly on the Pantheon; reorganized (in 143) the *curia athletarum*, the headquarters of the official athletes on the Esquiline; repaired the bridge of Agrippa (147) and the Sublician and Cestian bridges (152); and rebuilt (158) the temple of Divus Augustus and that of Liber on the Via Sacra. He also had to finish the temple of Venus and Rome. The fire at Rome which destroyed 340 *insulae* and houses, a Tiber flood in 142,[2] and a collapse in the Circus Maximus, with 1112 victims, must have required further interventions. Boundary posts of Antoninus and his two successors dating from the same year, 161, indicate that in the last days of the reign a review of the *termini riporum Tiberis* was in progress.[3]

Outside Rome the continuation or execution of works promised by Hadrian is explicitly attested by the completion of the baths at Ostia, by the construction in 139 of jetties in Puteoli harbour, by the amphitheatre at Capua and by the aqueduct at Athens, completed in 140.[4] Most of the remaining work – on aqueducts (Antium, Scolacium, Odessus, Ipocobulcula in Spain), harbours (Gaeta, Terracina), temples (Lanuvium, Olympia) and various other buildings (amphitheatres at Firmum and Porolissum, baths at Tarquinia, the lighthouse at Alexandria) – consisted of restoration, though this sometimes involved radical reconstruction, as it did with the transformation into a big villa of the Emperor's personal farm at Lorium on the Via Aurelia. The balance was the building activity of a period of intense enthusiasm for the monumental, an enthusiasm which it was possible to satisfy thanks to the still relatively abundant availability of means. The competition in munificence engaged in since the beginning of the century by local notabilities with the aim of beautifying

---

[1] *Digest.*, I, 10, 7.

[2] *Fast. Ost., Inscr. It.*, XIII, 1, pp. 207, 236 ff., where reference to the restoration of the *pons Agrippae* and the *pons Cestii* is also to be found.

[3] *CIL*, VI, 31553-4.

[4] *ILS*, 334 (Ostia), 336 (Puteoli), 6309 (Capua), 337 (Athens).

their cities needed to be nourished by the Emperor's example. Thus there are innumerable references to works carried out in this period in every part of the empire, and the name of Antoninus, who was acknowledged by the Athenians as early as 140 to have increased still further 'the benefits conferred by his divine father',[1] appears everywhere in dedications expressing gratitude, especially in the East, together with those of the great benefactors like Opramoas of Rhodiapolis, Herodes Atticus, the sophist Flavius Damianus of Ephesus, P. Vedius Antoninus, also of Ephesus – to whom the Emperor wrote a letter assuring him of his support in the embellishment of the city and reproaching his fellow citizens for not being willing to help him – and finally, among others, P. Lucilius Gamala of Ostia. The earthquakes and disasters of the reign gave occasions for intervention: in Achaea, in the Aegean islands, in Caria and Lycia after the great earthquake of 142 or 143, in Bithynia, in Lesbos and on the Ionian coast up to Ephesus in 147 or 148, even on the extreme confines of Syria, towards Dura-Europos, in 160, and at Narbonne, Antioch and Carthage after fires.

Assistance to cities, succour in famine and other scourges now formed part of the normal financial aid granted by a paternalistic administration in the general interests of the state. But action to stimulate local resources was never lacking. Antoninus lightened still further the burden of the *cursus publicus* weighing on the provincials. He limited requisitions and forced labour; and especially in connection with the roads, the imposing network of which was maintained with great care and further enlarged, he effected every possible economy. Cuttings through rock, crossings of marshes and large structures (bridge at Narbonne, bridge over the Danube at Dunapentele) were carried out with a zeal and to an extent that make any kind of list pointless, for almost all the empire's roads have yielded milestones of Antoninus Pius; but what are explicitly attested in connection with these works are the contributions of private individuals and communities, with the concession of reimbursement for the latter by means of the collection of tolls.[2] Thus the drainage and repair of an aqueduct tank at Uscosium, in the territory of the Frentani, was carried out in 139 at local expense.[3] The same principles were also applied in the matter of immunities. The exemptions for certain categories of people, particularly in eastern cities (rhetoricians, philosophers, doctors) could not

[1] *IG*, II–III², 3390.
[2] *ILS*, 5878. *CIL*, IX, 670 (private citizens); *ILS*, 2666a. *CIL*, VIII, 10237, 10238 (collective bodies).
[3] *CIL*, IX, 2828.

be suppressed, but they were regulated. Teachers received remunerations paid by the cities, with subsidies from the imperial fisc, and Athens acquired, with the definitive organization by Antoninus of its schools, a real 'university' system. But the number of both teachers and doctors enjoying immunity was firmly fixed: five doctors, three teachers of grammar and three teachers of rhetoric were allowed in small cities, seven, four and four respectively in middle-sized ones and ten, five and five in big ones. Their names were placed in a register by order of the local council and retention of the privilege was made subject to the diligent exercise of their professions.

Thus the alleviation of burdens weighing on the provinces, the control over the justice of exactions, the recommendations to moderation issued to procurators and the sharp lessons given to embezzlers were paralleled by a still greater interference by the centre in local finances: the number of *curatores* was multiplied, accounts were meticulously audited, with the checks going back as far as twenty years, and expenditure, even recurrent expenditure, had more and more to be approved by the Roman authorities. On the subject of the accuracy of the fiscal arrangements, the precision with which they were applied and the process, now far advanced, of assimilating local customs to the legislation of the empire, a document of capital importance is what is known as the *Gnomon of the Idiologus*, which has been known for about half a century. The *Gnomon* is a collection of instructions for the official assigned to the administration of the imperial estates in Egypt; some of the instructions go back to the time of Augustus, but the document as we have it can hardly have been compiled in any age but that of Antoninus. It was an age of apparently definitive organization in all fields, which were firmly controlled by the imperial system, some-times in the form of actual nationalization, as happened with the immunity granted to the corn merchants and the owners of ships intended for the grain supply, who were linked together in a corporation forming, under the control of the state, an essential service. The general tendency to regulate everything includes a first reference to the fixing of a maximum limit for the cost of shows, the prelude to more energetic action by Antoninus's successor. In 147 or 148 the measure providing for the remission of arrears of debt to the fisc, which had been directed by Hadrian to work on fifteen-year periods, crowned with an act of generosity almost certainly involving no serious sacrifice the joyful expectation of the celebrations to mark the ninth century of the foundation of Rome, while at the end of the reign the financial reserves of the state amounted, according to the ancient sources, to 675 million denarii.

All this was only the most obvious aspect of Antoninus's shrewd administration. As for the concrete individual measures taken in the government of the provinces, they followed the same lines of universal and impartial attention. An ostentatious exaltation of Italy at the expense of the provinces cannot be detected in his programme any more than the opposite tendency can be detected in Hadrian's. This is sufficiently demonstrated by the generous criteria for the extension of citizenship, criteria which are not contradicted by the rigorous distinction made between citizens and non-citizens, especially where the laws of inheritance are concerned, in the above-mentioned *Gnomon of the Idiologus*. A further piece of evidence pointing in the same direction is the continuation of the most cordial relations with the Greek element in the empire. Antoninus took no less interest than his predecessors in the local life of the cities, especially those of Greece and Asia, in connection with which evidence abounds. His interest extended to accepting both honorary and practical offices, as is attested by his acceptance of municipal posts (at Sarmizege-tusa, where he was represented by a prefect, and at Delphi, where he was archon between 139 and 142) and by the numerous letters, written at various times throughout his reign, to individuals and to the councils of cities or leagues. He wrote one or more letters to Athens, to Ephesus, to Pergamum, to the Balbureni, to the Tisbenses and the Coronenses, to one Minos of Amorgos, to Sextilius Acutianus of Smyrna (this one, dating from 139, is particularly interesting because its object is to confirm, in response to requests, a measure of Hadrian's), and to the association of Greek athletes at Rome (for religious privileges). He also wrote a whole series of letters to the 'koinà' of Asia and Lycia and finally one to the Panhellenion. The subjects of these letters are, it is true, of no great political interest, but their very modesty testifies to the most detailed interest and enables us to glimpse more clearly than in any other period the real conditions of life in the towns. The style of government was essentially conservative. These towns were continuations of the demo-cratic *polis* only in form; in reality they were timocracies, already worried by social inequalities and by the first signs of general impoverishment, yet more intent than ever on spending for display, on shows and on com-peting in vanity and prestige. Real life, as we have said in connection with Aelius Aristides's oration, was certainly more complex and flowed at a deeper level, not without sending up alarming signs to the surface as well: there were the 'strikes' of masons at Pergamum and Miletus and that of the bakers at Ephesus, the growing indifference about filling magistracies, the accentuation in Egypt of 'anacoresis', and the failures to maintain public order and safety, of which there is evidence almost everywhere. But these were incidents which did not yet shake the general solidity of Antoninus's administration: 'provinciae sub eo cunctae floruerunt'.[1]

LEGISLATION

The striking elaboration of the law initiated under Hadrian continued under Antoninus and the legislation which emerged from this process, even more deliberately inspired by the moral progress made by the human conscience in this epoch, finally came to constitute the most marked characteristic of the whole reign. A very large number of measures became law, either in the form of *senatusconsulta* or in that of the imperial 'constitution', the latter being employed with less and less awareness, even theoretical, of its exceptional character. Even if it was not until the time of Diocletian that the Princeps came to possess a real, formal legislative capacity, and even if the *constitutiones* represented only his interpretative, normative, supplementary activity embodied in *edicta* (ordinances), *decreta* (decisions on particular cases), *rescripta* (replies to queries) and *mandata* (instructions to officials) – whence the theoretical only *ad vitam* validity of the directives of individual emperors – it would indeed be mere sophistry to deny a concrete capacity that produced so much law right from the time of Augustus in the practical circumstances created by the real nature of the principate. Moreover, with Antoninus, and all the more after the codification in Hadrian's time of the praetor's edict, the imperial constitutions served even more clearly for the creation of fresh legislation in every field of law, and not just for normative and interpretative activity in the field of administration. The Emperor's personal participation in the progress of the law also made him tend naturally to prefer the most direct form of legislation, in which it was possible to crystallize at once what was suggested by his own experience (much of it reflecting in fact his own philanthropic spirit) and by that of the superb body of jurists working at this epoch in close contact with the Emperor and equipped moreover with the *ius respondendi*, though this was becoming less and less important since their official positions were more impressive and their influence could thus be incorporated in the general legislation more directly. The *consilium*, to which almost all these lawyers belonged, was thus the principal organ for elaboration of the law as well as for the administration of justice; it was constantly consulted by Antoninus. Of the five legal experts named by the biographer as belonging to the

[1] *V. Pii.*, 7, 2.

consilium, only three are otherwise known: M. Vindius Verus, who was consul in 138 as colleague of another famous jurist, P. Pactumeius Clemens; the above-mentioned knight (and prefect of Egypt towards the end of the reign) L. Volusius Maecianus; and Ulpius Marcellus, who wrote a commentary on Salvius Julianus's *Digesta*. All these are well represented in the quotations in Justinian's *Digest*. But we may suppose that jurists of Hadrian's reign such as Aburnius Valens, Sextus Pomponius and the great Salvius Julianus continued to belong to the *consilium*, not to mention Gaius, whose life remains a mystery, though most of his activity took place under Pius.

To summarize organically all the legislation of Antoninus known to us is a difficult thing owing to the abundance and at the same time the fragmentary nature of the evidence preserved. For this reason, given that almost every book of the *Digest* and of the other juridical texts mentions his name several times, and that a certain number of his provisions have come down to us by way of inscriptions (like the *senatusconsultum de nundinis saltus Beguensis*, of October 138, and the *senatusconsultum de postulatione Cyzicenorum*, of uncertain date) as well as in papyri, we shall confine ourselves here to tracing the main lines of thought inspiring the measures and to grouping them accordingly. The rigorism of formulas had been overcome and in general the predominant influence was that of *aequitas*, as a direct consequence of the importance assigned to 'natural law', of the diffusion of humanitarian ideas and of the establishment of a milder custom in the course of a more moderate application of the actual law, rightly tempered by respect for others and a conciliatory approach. There was no contradiction between this attitude and the appearance now for the first time in the law[1] of the distinction between *honestiores* and *humiliores* for the purposes of punishment, for this was only the passage into law of a juridical practice already followed for some time and operating only in criminal law, not in private law. Nor was it alien to what was *aequum* that the punishment should be commensurate with the individual's own moral sensibility, presumed to be greater in the *honestior*. However, the class that had attained greater moral maturity, toning down the harshness of juridical relations, wanted the conquest to be its own privilege. In criminal law and in criminal trials in general, guarantees for the accused were established – in connection with preventive detention, depositions made to the investigators, the way in which the trial should be conducted, caution in the adduction of proofs, the use of torture, excluded in many cases, and the passing of sentence, which in cases of doubt had to be the

[1] *Digest.*, XLVIII, 5, 39, 8, letter from Antoninus Pius to Apollonius.

one most favourable to the defendant. If judgement had been pronounced in the absence of one of the parties, as the law allowed, Antoninus sought nevertheless to guarantee the party concerned (in a civil case particularly, of course) against possible loss, not always due to his own fault ('he could have failed to appear through not having heard the voice of the town crier very well . . .', *Digest.*, 1, 7) and granted a re-hearing of the case. It is true that conviction continued to involve, for the *servus poenae*, the civil effects fixed by long-standing custom, such as the inability to inherit or to free slaves, but there was the possibility of reduction of the physical punishment and even of pardon – for those condemned to the quarries, for example, if they had become unfit through sickness or old age. Antoninus let proscribed persons keep a twelfth of their property,[1] whereas Hadrian had let only the children have it. We do not possess much information about fresh interventions on the subjects of trials and the penalties for specific crimes: in cases of burglary, the enquiry, which fell to the *praefectus vigilum*, had to take account of the responsibility of the custodians; and the kidnapping of children was to be punished severely, like cattle-stealing, which in some regions (Spain) was a serious threat to public order.

But most of the records of Antoninus's legislative activity refer to the civil law. The new concepts touched upon the moral and juridical relationships of men among themselves and regulated them in more and more detail according to more liberal norms, not of course to the point of turning the established social order upside down, but sufficiently to guarantee the rights of the individual person, including those of slaves. Antoninus was also interested in the problems created by the existence of slavery, that is, in the basic inequality acknowledged at that time *ex iure gentium*, an inequality which introduced into all relationships a complication unknown to our law. Naturally the law of property remained unshaken and absolute, and in conformity with the Roman principle of abstaining from interference in the field of private law, public interventions served only to reinforce it (see for example Pius's interesting confirmation on the subjects of the ownership of sea-coasts, on bird-hunting on other people's property and on the limits of the *ius alluvionis*, that is, the ownership of land taken away from or added to estates by natural alterations in the courses of rivers). Thus Antoninus did not oppose or limit the institution of slavery in itself: 'the power of masters over slaves must remain intact and no man must have his rights diminished'.[2] Indeed, he imposed the obligation to return slaves who had fled without reason,

---

[1] *Gnom. Idiol.*, 36.   [2] *Digest.*, I, 6, 2.

even those who, to escape from slavery, played the final card of choosing to fight in the arena. He even authorized inspections of private property by public officials to see if any 'fugitive' slaves were hiding there. Moreover, so far as the use of torture as a means of investigation was concerned, he did not improve the conditions existing already but rather sought to eliminate subterfuges, such as those of freeing slaves with the sole object of avoiding their being tortured and of holding trials of slaves not in the place nearest the scene of the crime but where the master could defend them and possibly enable them to evade justice. However, the influence of the natural law, which now clearly asserted the illicitness of 'abusing our right',[1] deprived masters once and for all of the power of maltreating slaves, in the same way as spendthrifts had already been prohibited in the Twelve Tables from administering their own estates improperly. To kill a slave without a good reason was a crime; the right of flight to escape serious oppression was recognized, and in this case the master was bound by law to sell the fugitive. In the legislation dealing with freedmen, which abounded in fairly complicated casuistry owing to the various consequences deriving in the fields of family relationships, inheritance of property and legal obligations from the acquisition of freedom and citizenship, a number of favourable arrangements were introduced, but they were hedged about with the most careful safeguards. Attempts at illegal alteration of one's own status were in fact severely repressed; the practice, already used (though still not frequently) in Egypt and Africa because of the particular conditions of citizenship in these two areas, of declaration of birth with the relative certificate, was soon to become obligatory. But masters could not take away the freedom obtained by a slave of theirs. A frequent source of difficulty and dispute was manumission by will, especially if it was done through a trust, that is, if the heirs were given the indirect task of carrying it out. Norms in this field were laid down by Antoninus on the lines of the practice fixed by the four *senatusconsulta* of Hadrian's mentioned, and with the intention of considering the spirit more than the letter of the law in a matter involving a possession of such importance as freedom. For example, he established the validity of the *manumissio* even if it turned out to be written in the will by the hand of the freedman himself but by the clear wish of the master – something that was forbidden by the letter of the law. He entrusted directly to the consuls the required control when freedom through a will was conditional on the rendering of accounts. He resolved cases of uncertainty concerning the children of freedmen created by trust deeds in

[1] GAI., *Inst.*, I, 52.

favour of their right to freedom; he also ensured that they secured the
most favourable interpretation of bequests of maintenance. In short, in
these and similar cases he showed that he wished to protect in every way
the legal path to freedom.

Great progress can also be observed in the field of law dealing with the
family and inheritance. Guarantees were assured for the children, born
and still unborn, in cases of dubious paternity and legitimacy resulting
from divorce, and in cases of uncertainty regarding the free status of the
children of freedwomen. The limits already set to the *patria potestas* were
given very precise legal bases and, *vice versa*, the same treatment was given
to the moral obligation of *pietas* towards one's parents: 'parentum necessi-
tatibus liberos succurrere iustum est'.[1] Greater weight was given to the
wishes of daughters in the matter of marriage. In the matter of adoption
safeguards were erected for the purposes of inheritance. Legislation in this
particular field, in conformity with the needs of the existing social
structure, was concerned above all with the preservation of family estates.
It appointed guardians (including sons as guardians of their fathers –
something previously excluded) for those who did not know how to
administer their own property, concerned itself with guardianship and
dowries in general, set a maximum to gifts from one living person to
another, particularly between husbands and wives (certainly a cause of the
frequent divorces), and laid it down that only persons of clearly defined
status could make wills. Where the succession was open, the bestowal of the
property, especially the dowries assigned to the daughters, was made
obligatory and the whole subject of legacies and trusts was regulated; for
example, the *Lex Falcidia* of 40 B.C. was brought back into full force
again. This dealt with the maximum size of bequests, which were not to
exceed three-quarters of the whole estate, while the heir in any case had a
right to the legitimate share of one quarter (the *quarta Falcidia*). But once
what was possible had been done to prevent the fragmentation of hereditary estates, the rigour of the formulas, the absence of which in wills made
them null and void, was mitigated in this field as well. The conditions
imposed on heirs before they could accept an inheritance were interpreted
with greater liberality and possible obstacles to the physical accomplish-
ment of the acts inherent in the succession were taken into account. The
right to inherit was extended to adoptive daughters and their mother,
which was an improvement on the arrangements laid down by the
senatusconsultum Tertullianum of Hadrian's reign. A period of four years
was established for the prescription of *bona vacantia* and restitution to the

[1] *Cod. Iustin.*, V, 25, 1.

fisc by those who had acquired them in good faith before the declaration of prescription was excluded. As we have already said, moderation on the part of the fisc was one of the policies pursued throughout the reign. There were also further concessions in connection with soldiers' wills, and Greeks who were Roman citizens were allowed to leave their property quite legally to their own children even if the latter remained Greeks: this was a basic exception in favour of *peregrini*, even if those concerned were Greeks, which demonstrates how much personal conditions were being standardized everywhere and moving towards the now not distant goal of complete assimilation. This development can be observed in the law of contracts as well, in connection with commercial transactions, as is clear from the numerous documents that have survived from this very reign recording contracts drawn up according to Roman law, some with *peregrini*, others even between *peregrini* alone, evidently endowed with the *ius commercii*; it is a development that reveals the rapid progress in the empire of that kind of unification which was destined to be the most enduring – that of the law.

'MOENIA MUNDI':
THE DEFENCE OF THE IMPERIAL PEACE

The apparatus of defence established by Hadrian functioned according to the same criteria under Antoninus, who kept the formidable military machine fully efficient, thus retaining the respect of all the external peoples and preserving the peace. He did not attack anyone, but sallies from any direction were promptly dealt with. More frequent and more serious than under Hadrian – preludes to future assaults – they nevertheless broke up, almost unnoticed in the interior of the empire, on the solid peripheral bulwark, the powerful wall of the civilized world. The existing fortifications were maintained and improved and the tremendous vitality of an organism still well able to look after itself also left its mark in the big military camps and the strategic roads. There are traces of important works on the borders of Dacia, where the occupation was further extended; in Mauretania, also in connection with the operations conducted there; and particularly on the Germano-Raetian *limes*. Here Antoninus had forts and towers of stone, with villages to live in, built by – among others – the Britons transported from the island after the war of 139–142 and established as *dediticii Brittones*, organized militarily in *numeri*, along the *limes* of Upper Germany. Later (after 154) the whole central section of the *limes* was advanced beyond the Neckar, and from Miltenberg on the Main to Lorch this section ran in one single straight line for some fifty miles, fortified with big stone forts, a wall and a palisade. There was no further change in the line of the whole Germano-Rhaetian *limes*, which was nearly 250 miles long. But the most imposing new work was the rampart in Britain between the Firth of Clyde and the Firth of Forth, about seventy-five miles to the north of Hadrian's wall. Built of turf, except for a stretch of the eastern section where bricks of clay were used, but resting throughout its length on a stone base sixteen feet wide, the wall ran for about thirty-seven miles, with a wide ditch to the north and a road to the south, more or less along the foot of the hills overlooking to the north the valley now traversed by the Forth–Clyde canal, at the point where Britain is narrowest. Nineteen forts, some in spots occupied by Agricola sixty years earlier, served to quarter the troops of the garrison and in conjunction with those lying to the north of Hadrian's wall and on this wall itself, which was never abandoned, formed a formidable defensive system. It looks as if occupation of this new wall, built by soldiers from all three British legions as an extreme advanced line after the operations of Lollius Urbicus (and so about 142–143), alternated with periods when it was abandoned – the first of these occurring only a few years after its construction. The wall was finally relinquished (except for a brief reoccupation by Septimius Severus) under Marcus Aurelius, or at the latest under Commodus, as finds of coins have shown. The work is to be viewed in close conjunction with Hadrian's wall and the whole defensive apparatus of which the latter remained the essential basis. And the reasons which had induced Domitian to question the expediency of an excessive expenditure of forces in a poor, remote and perennially restless region will have counselled the best way of using these forces, especially now that they were sufficient for defence but no longer superabundant.

The difficulties in recruiting Roman citizens, difficulties of which Hadrian's trouble at Tarragona is only one example, had been growing for some time. Aelius Aristides elegantly turned the phenomenon into praise of Rome, interpreting it as the wish to husband the old communities of citizens and to take advantage of the ambition of those who were not yet citizens by recruiting in those provincial communities with an urban organization (he was thinking particularly of the Greek and eastern *poleis*) which were not yet endowed with Roman citizenship (*Or. Rom.*, 74–5). Those recruited acquired citizenship by the act of enrolment and obviously entered the legions, not the *auxilia;* attracted by this as well as by the opportunity of promotion, by virtue of the long apprenticeship and the discipline they became good soldiers and, forgetting their own origins, regarded themselves simply as Roman soldiers. Although this had been the normal state of affairs for some time, Antoninus must have further extended the entry of non-citizens into the legions. Since there were now many citizens in the auxiliary units as well, and recruitment for these too must have been carried out more and more extensively in the region where they were serving, the difference in composition between legions and *auxilia* was growing still smaller, so much so that to judge from the modification introduced by Antoninus not later than 140 in the terms of military diplomas (except for the sailors of the fleet), limiting the grant of citizenship to those actually discharged and excluding their children and descendants (except for the children of decurions of *alae* and of centurions of cohorts), he must have been worried about eventually finding no more provincials without citizenship to put in the *auxilia*, and wanted the sons of auxiliaries as well to acquire citizenship by serving in the army. For the same reason he maintained, both for legionaries and auxiliaries, the Augustan prohibition on regular marriage. But this was only a piece of formal opposition to an irresistible tendency which developed in step with the standardization of the empire's population and was one of its principal aspects and one of those most pregnant with future consequences.

As for the distribution of the forces and the places where they were stationed, the stable organization of the epoch enables us to know this with some certainty for the legions, and the large number of inscriptions also provides a fairly detailed picture of the distribution of the auxiliary units, the *alae, cohorts* and *numeri*. If we leave aside the auxiliaries, for which too minute a list would be needed, as it would for the fleets and special detachments, the distribution of the legions throughout the reign and beyond (as is clear from a tile found at Rome, *ILS*, 2288) was as follows: three legions in Britain (II *Augusta* at Isca, Caerleon; XX *Valeria Victrix* at Deva, Chester; VI *Victrix Pia Fidelis* at Eburacum, York); two in Lower Germany (I *Minervia* at Bonna, Bonn; XXX *Ulpia* at Castra Vetera, Xanten), two in Upper Germany (VIII *Augusta* at Argentoratum, Strasbourg; XXII *Primigenia Pia Fidelis* at Moguntiacum, Mainz); three in Upper Pannonia (X *Gemina* at Vindobona, Vienna; XIV *Gemina* at Carnuntum, Petronell near Bratislava; I *Adiutrix* at Brigetio, Szöny near Komàrom); one in Lower Pannonia (II *Adiutrix* at Aquincum, Buda); two in Upper Moesia (IV *Flavia* at Singidunum, Belgrade; VII *Claudia* at Viminacium, Kostolak in Yugoslavia); three in Lower Moesia (I *Italica* at Novae, Svistov in Bulgaria; XI *Claudia* at Durostorum, Silistra, also in Bulgaria; V *Macedonica* at Troesmis, Iglitza in Rumania); one in Dacia (XIII *Gemina* at Apulum, Alba Julia); two in Cappadocia (XII *Fulminata* at Melitene, Malatya; X

Apollinaris at Satala, Sadak); three in Syria (XIV *Flavia* at Samosata, Samsat, in Turkey; IV *Scythica* at Zeugma, Bâlkîs, also in Turkey; III *Gallica* at Raphaneae, Chamâ, in the extreme north of the Lebanon); two in Syria Palestina (VI *Ferrata* at Caparcae or Caparcotna, in the north; X *Fretensis* at Aelia Capitolina, Jerusalem); one in Arabia (III *Cyrenaica* at Bostra, Busra in Syria); one in Egypt (II *Traiana* at Nicopolis, near Alexandria); one in Numidia (III *Augusta* at Lambaesis, Lambèse, near Batna in Algeria); one in Spain (VII *Gemina* at Legio, Leon). Altogether there were thus twenty-eight legions – still the Augustan force. Naturally the legions were stationed in the big fixed bases, but movements of troops in the form of legionary detachments, which could be posted quite a long way from their own legion, and the employment of auxiliaries in the most various places in accordance with needs, continued incessantly throughout the reign. Nor should it be forgotten that some provinces, including some of the most restless, like Mauretania, and some of the most exposed, like Raetia and Noricum, never had anything but a garrison of auxiliaries. The total force, which must have amounted to more than 300,000 men, with thousands of ships, wagons and pieces of equipment, was certainly imposing, but not excessive for such a vast defensive task; if employed in time, it could deal with any situation. The Princeps, a civilian by training, did not even take direct command of operations and never left Italy, as a result of which the title of *proconsul* is not found applied to him. The machine must have functioned on its own. People at home subsequently heard of these distant wars 'as if they were myths'.[1]

From 139 to 142 the governor of Britain, Q. Lollius Urbicus, waged and brought to a victorious conclusion the umpteenth war against the Brigantes, deporting some of the beaten enemy to Germany, as we have seen, and starting on the construction of the wall. This was the only military operation of the reign that caused any sizeable stir (salutation as *imperator*, large issue of coins with the motif *Victoria*). It is fairly difficult to fix the dates and elucidate the details of the other campaigns merely mentioned by the biographer (Moors, Germans, Dacians and Alans all figure in the list, besides the general phrase 'multas gentes'; there are also references to revolts in Judaea, Achaea and Egypt). The situation in Mauretania must have been rather serious and the operations of some importance, to judge from a number of pieces of evidence in our hands. Honours were paid in 144 by the decurions of Sala, a particularly exposed city, to the prefect of an ala, 'liberator et patronus', who had helped to keep them safe;[2] the same document bears witness to the presence of a

---

[1] AEL. ARIST., *Or. Rom.*, 70. [2] *Ann. Ép.*, 1931, 36 and 38.

governor in place of the two procurators (who do not reappear until 150); there was work on roads and fortifications over a wide area, even in central and relatively secure regions; and *vexillationes* and cohorts flowed in from Spain, even from Syria and the Danubian provinces, until finally in 149 powerful reinforcements were sent from almost all the legions of the Rhine and Danube and from their respective auxiliaries. The war must have ended soon afterwards with a decisive victory and this victory must have been made effective by the skilful creation of permanent security arrangements, for we do not hear of the region again for another twenty-five years or so. As for Germany, what we know of the struggles maintained by L. Aelius Caesar and his successor in Upper Pannonia, T. Haterius Nepos, who in 138 received the last *ornamenta triumphalia* attested, and the evidence of coins dating from 140 to 141, with the legend 'Rex Quadis datus', suggest the usual thorny relations with the clients on the far side of the Danube – the Quadi, Marcomanni and Iazyges. In Dacia tremendous activity in the way of pacification and defence went on, pursued throughout the reign with operations on the borders, as is clear from the influx of reinforcements and other evidence, and with the construction of forts and *limites*.

The references to alleged revolts are more obscure. In one of these the urban populace of Rome, annoyed by a famine, is supposed to have stoned the Emperor. Nothing is known of rebellions in Judaea, even though Antoninus devoted some attention to the Jews to check their proselytizing activities and took their internal jurisdiction away from them. But it may be that the report conceals the fact that they were once again implicated in the much more certain revolt of Egypt, which broke out between 142 and 144 or in 149 or in 153 (these are the years devoid of known prefects). A victim of this revolt was the prefect himself, Dinarchus, if the man of that name, known from a source that certainly does not enjoy – perhaps undeservedly – much credit[1] is, to be placed in this epoch. Other details, about the causes (economic, religious, political?) and the course of events are unknown; and it cannot be ruled out that it was a question as a whole of operations against banditry, in connection with the spread of *anacoresis*: in 154 the prefect, M. Sempronius Liberalis, published an imperial decree on this subject granting an amnesty to those who returned. Nothing is known either of the disturbances in Achaea – they may have been riots resulting from rivalry in prestige between different cities – and the hypothesis that they were instigated by

---

[1] MALALAS, XI, 280.

the philosopher and adventurer Peregrinus of Parium reposes only on an allusion of Lucian's.[1]

Antoninus's eastern policy continued that of his predecessors. Under him too the Roman name was respected and feared, and Antoninus personally enjoyed great prestige. The distant Bactrians and Hyrcanians, and even the Indians, sought relations with Rome, evidently carried along by the vigorous commercial currents that had existed for some time and had also been encouraged by Antoninus. Our scanty information also indicates extensive and integrated action from the beginning of the reign (the *Scythia* coin dates from 139) in relation to the big semicircle of tribes to the north of the Black Sea, between the mouths of the Danube and the Caucasus, while on the Sarmatian and Scythian steppes there were already signs of the movements which some years later were to have repercussions on the Danubian frontier. Episodes in this activity were the defence of Olbia against the Taurosciti, the mediation between two claimants to the kingdom of Bosporus, the assignation of a king to the Lazi of Colchis and the conflicts with the Alans, now on the Dnieper after being evicted from the Caucasus. There are also traces of special efforts inside the empire, in Lower Moesia and Thrace, to carry on the Romanization and prepare the defences against future threats. Relations with the Parthians were the same as they had been under Hadrian: negotiations over Armenia must have been in progress in the early years of the reign, possibly complicated by the interventions of that Pharasmanes of Iberia who had never been viewed with much favour by Hadrian, but on the accession of the new Princeps had made an ostentatious trip to Rome to pay homage and to try to win him over. As for Abgar, who may have been the son of the king of Osrhoene dethroned by Trajan, the brevity of the biographer's report[2] does not allow us to understand whether he was summoned by Antoninus from his eastern refuge with the Parthians and reinstated in his kingdom – which would be an infallible indication that a fresh wind was blowing – or, already residing in his kingdom, was 'dissuaded' from action against the Parthians. A king was set up in Armenia by the Romans before 144, probably in accordance with the usual compromise solution, after negotiations had almost broken down. King Vologaeses II, who had succeeded Chosroes in 129, had in fact made the most extensive preparations for war and had certainly not been deterred by a mere letter sent to him according to the tradition by Antoninus,[3] but on the contrary by the formidable presence of the army of the East, which had in addition been reinforced.

[1] *De Morte Peregr.*, 19.
[2] *V. Pii.*, 9, 6: 'ex Orientis partibus sola auctoritate deduxit'.   [3] *Ibid.*

However, relations continued to be strained, even, and perhaps still more, after Vologaeses II was succeeded about 148 by Vologaeses III, in whose hands the whole power of the king of kings was once more united, after a long period of division and weakness. The throne seized by Trajan was not restored even now and the army remained on a war footing. But the war was reserved for Antoninus's successors.

For the moment the general equilibrium was maintained, even in the most obvious form of military force, the empire's prop. Yet contemporaries were not unaware, as can be seen from the interesting analysis in the preamble to Appian's *History* (Ch. 7), of the notion that there are limits to aggrandizement and even to the retention of dominion. Appian says that he had seen offers of *deditio* rejected and observes that some provinces were held by the Romans at some sacrifice simply from reluctance to renounce them openly. And the first cracks in the general security, both internal and external, were appearing. Soon, perhaps, a large part of the world's life, reduced to order by centuries of effort, was to escape control, and the Emperor himself, impotent to do anything about the situation, was to appear as just one factor in a total reality that was much more varied and complex; the different elements, no longer covered by the perfect imperial pyramid, were to show themselves openly in conflict.

TRADITION AND CONSERVATION

Meanwhile the idea that the best of all possible states had been achieved, already idealized by Hadrian in the cult of Rome's divine origins and eternal nature, was to give rise to ostentatious forms of traditionalism intended to fix, in a definitive synthesis of past and present, the legacy to be preserved. Religion played a large part in this process. The Senate and people had already paid homage to the Emperor in 143 'ob insignem erga caerimonias publicas curam ac religionem';[1] and his religious zeal was to provoke people to compare him with Numa. Antoninus's 'pietas in sacris' was related above all to the traditional religion, the restoration of which had been promised by other emperors beginning with Augustus, but never in an atmosphere so well adapted to a retrospective survey. But even the imperial cult and the attitude to foreign religions underwent the effects of the spiritual synthesis effected in parallel with the cultural and political unification at this moment of equilibrium and peace, almost of apparent immobility.

[1] *CIL*, VI, 1001 = *ILS*, 341.

The exaltation of Rome and the exploitation of the ancient traditions of her origins were motifs that simply acquired extra solemnity from the recurrence of the anniversary of another hundred years of her existence (celebrated in 148); they had already been given prominence by Hadrian. Certainly their diffusion throughout the empire showed that they were now being publicized on a vast scale; one of the most solemn issues of coins made during the reign, an issue that went on from 139 until 147, precisely in preparation for the centennial celebrations, commemorated all the principal figures and episodes: the landing of Aeneas, Hercules and Cacus, Mars and Rhea Silvia, the she-wolf and the twins, the 'ancilia', the rape of the Sabine women, Attus Navius, Horatius Cocles and the arrival of the serpent of Aesculapius on the island in the Tiber. Official participation went so far as to show the figures of Antoninus and M. Aurelius Caesar, dressed as Aeneas and Ascanius, sacrificing to the Penates. Ancient Latium and the Sabine region, the homeland of Numa, were honoured with restorations, in the first place of the temple at Lanuvium of *Iuno Sospita Mater Regina*, one of the most deeply venerated, and of the main temple of Ceres. Places outside Italy in any way connected with the legends of Rome's origins were also honoured: Ilium had the immunity conferred by Claudius confirmed; Pallantion, a village in the region of Tegea, was raised to the rank of free city immune from taxes, in homage to the Arcadian Evander, and a temple to the hero Pallas was built there. Private Maecenases followed the official example: the temples built or restored at Ostia by P. Lucilius Gamala were dedicated to deities particularly connected with the origins of Rome – Vulcan, the Dioscuri, Venus, Pater Tiberinus, etc. There was a great imaginary return to origins and at the same time to the spirit of the Augustan age as expressed in the *Aeneid*. Yet the equal exaltation of the Greek divinities long absorbed into the classical Pantheon eliminated from the exhumation any suspicion of conservative extremism or boorish exclusivism. Indeed the tendency to religious fusion, without discrimination of origin or nationality, made further progress under Antoninus. There was increasing assimilation of the barbarian deities to the classical ones, as is well known from the innumerable soldiers' inscriptions, and a strikingly widespread extension of the mystery cults, not only the Phrygian ones of Cybele and Attis, already incorporated by long tradition in Roman religion via the cult of the *Magna Mater*, and the Egyptian ones of Isis, which had also been popular for some time, but also the Syrian and Persian ones of *Iuppiter Dolichenus, Sol Invictus* (the great temple of the Sun at Heliopolis, Baalbek, was in fact repaired by Antoninus) and above all, those of Mithras.

The atmosphere of liberal tolerance, not the least proof of which is the validity even in the law courts of the oath sworn by everyone 'propria superstitione',[1] could be enjoyed by the Jews and Christians as well. For the latter Antoninus had no sympathy, but he continued Hadrian's attitude, and his moderating interventions, inspired solely by his sense of justice, ended by protecting them from illegal attacks and fanaticism, especially in the East, where Christians were numerous and unpopular. The problem of the existence of this new religion, universal, organized, and in irreconcilable conflict with a fundamental principle like the cult of the emperor, was in fact now clearly perceived. The Christians were the subject of discussion and they were persecuted in their daily contacts with s ciety. Accused of atheism and wicked deeds, they were sometimes involved in riots and could be victims of the popular fury, like St Polycarp, martyred at Smyrna in 155 (if the date is reliable), on a day when the proconsul obviously allowed himself to be led by the ferocious mob. Antoninus's interventions, like those of his predecessor, were intended to prevent just such instances of summary justice. The now explicit prohibition of the 'nomen' of Christian and of proselytizing remained firmly in force and the principle of the right and proper safeguarding of the security and majesty of the empire and its emperor was thus secured; the traces remaining of Antoninus's measures (rescript to the Ephesians, and possibly similar ones to the Larissans, the Thessalonians, the Athenians and the Greeks in general) demonstrate this concern. In practice, so far as official persecutions were concerned, the Christians were left in peace all through the long period up to the last years of Marcus Aurelius and were able to defend themselves in philosophical and literary circles in apologias. Besides those of Quadratus and Aristides in Hadrian's time, there were the two by the Greco-Palestinian St Justin, probably written between 148 and 161. And the struggle was not confined to combating pagan accusations; there were also apologias aimed at the Jews (the *Dialogue with Trypho* by the same Justin and the lost work by Aristo of Pella, which appeared towards 140), and in the very bosom of Christianity the doctrinal conflicts were already acute with the spread of the Gnostic heresy. The diatribes and fierce conflicts aroused in the Christian community of Rome itself by Marcion of Sinope and the Egyptian Valentinus went on throughout the reign of Pius and left ample traces in Christian literature.

As for the imperial cult, Antoninus made no innovations in it. But the Princeps, long an unquestioned god in the East, was becoming one more and more in the West as well, both in popular feeling, through a process

[1] *Digest.*, XII, 2, 5, 1.

of simplification, and in philosophical theory, which regarded him as the visible manifestation of God or the divine providence. Mere deification after death reflected on the living members of the imperial house a more intense and permanent radiance of divinity when apotheosis, instead of being simply the normal tribute, became, as it did with Faustina, who died in 141, the start of a worship kept fresh and new for a whole reign. There were the biggest issues of coins ever seen for 'divae'; frequent ceremonies attended, on an equal footing with the 'diva', by the Augustus and the members of the family; and the living Princeps was constantly associated with the deified Empress – at Ostia, for example, where, by decree of the decurions, young people about to wed had to pray before the altar of Diva Faustina and the Emperor 'ob insignem eorum concordiam'.[1] In this field, too, the age of Antoninus, for all its apparent immobility, took steps of its own towards an imperial theocracy.

But the age was also rich in spiritual fermentations of one sort and another, often not so much religious as mystical, magic and springing from pure superstition. We have already spoken of the mysteries, so far as religion is concerned. In the particular form of inner spiritual experience, an interesting document is the description in Aelius Aristides's so-called *Orationes Sacrae* of his relations with the god Asclepius, whose advice, received in dreams and ecstasies, he followed throughout the course of a long illness. There is abundant evidence of superstition; among the educated classes in the form of divination of the future and astrology, among all classes in the form of magic and the interpretation of dreams. All the ancient oracles enjoyed fresh popularity, and fortune-tellers and interpreters of dreams multiplied. It is common knowledge what a large part is played by this society, with its need and readiness to believe, in the literature of the age, in Pausanias and Fronto, Lucian and Apuleius. The spiritual mood was basically one of tiredness, reflected in art in the tendency to follow a mannered classicism – the beginning of the 'late antique'.

But for the moment the world seemed bound to continue indefinitely along the traditional lines, and the career of Marcus Aurelius, the successor designate, appeared destined to perpetuate without any problems the existing state of affairs, possibly made even more ideal by the rules of philosophy. Harsh reality was subsequently to belie these expectations, but it should not be forgotten what deep roots Marcus Aurelius's activity had in the reign of Antoninus. Since 138 he had been in the forefront of plans for the succession, taking precedence over the son of Aelius Caesar.

[1] *CIL*, XIV, 5326.

TA—Q

At that time he had been betrothed to Faustina, the daughter of Antoninus and Faustina the Elder. In 139, at the age of eighteen, he had been quaestor and had entered the principal priestly colleges; at the same time he became Caesar and appeared on coins with the Augustus. From 140 onwards when he held the consulate with Antoninus, he even appeared on them alone. His adoptive brother, L. Aelius Aurelius Commodus, was in fact still too young, and at the proper times in his life he received, like Marcus, the appropriate honours (*toga virilis* in 145, quaestorship in 153, consulship in 154 and 161); but he was always kept in the background. Marcus Aurelius Caesar was the Emperor's sole colleague, having also received the *imperium proconsulare extra urbem* and the *ius quintae relationis*, that is, the right to add in the Senate a fifth subject to the four proposed for the day by the Princeps. He was never precisely co-regent, for, quite apart from the decennial vows renewed in 148 and 158 naturally on his own account alone, Antoninus always gave *congiaria* in his own name, even when they celebrated happy events in the lives of his children. Nevertheless, the collaboration must have been effective and the employment of the young Marcus, long educated by the most famous teachers of rhetoric, philosophy and law, cannot have been intended simply to serve as an example to the youth of Rome. Marcus's marriage to Faustina, in the spring of 145, the birth on 30 November 147 of his first-born daughter, Anna Galeria Aurelia Faustina – an event celebrated by the conferment of the title of *Augusta* on Faustina (who began to strike her own coins) and of the *tribunicia potestas* on Marcus, who characteristically remained just Caesar – and then the successive births, up to 160, of a good eight children, some of whom soon died, drew the family bonds even tighter and strengthened the dynastic feeling.

As a result, when on 7 March 161, in the villa at Lorium, Antoninus's life came to a close, after a brief illness, with the first really serene death recorded by the tradition for a Roman emperor, the road lay open to the most peaceful of successions. Quietly prepared for the empire, like an island in a calm lake, itself contained in an island battered by the waves – to use Fronto's baroque simile[1] – Marcus had now to continue on his own, and he sought to do so quite spontaneously, giving due credit to his father's work and above all repaying him for his example by recording with admiration his moral qualities in the portraits contained in his own *Meditations*.[2] Through these portraits in particular Antoninus, wise and constant, serious and industrious, noble and understanding, a man whose

---

[1] *Ad. M. Caes.*, III, 8, p. 41 VAN DEN HOUT.
[2] I, 16; VI, 30.

outward appearance also inspired sympathy, has passed into the tradition, and deservedly, as one of the best emperors, while his principate, though it was not devoid of disquieting signs, has left as its predominant memory the record of the benefits effected by such practical virtue.

XII

MARCUS AURELIUS AND LUCIUS VERUS

THE 'DOUBLE PRINCIPATE'

Marcus Aurelius began his reign with a surprising act. His long regular contact with his predecessor had already indicated in advance that his succession would be a peaceful one and this had been confirmed *in extremis* when Antoninus had recommended Marcus alone to his friends and to the praetorian prefects, and had had the gilded statue of Fortuna moved from his own room to Marcus's. The designation clearly referred to Marcus alone and it was moreover confirmed for him alone by the Senate, which, according to the biographer, went so far as to press him to take up the burden of the empire. Marcus accepted the burden but took as co-regent on an equal footing his adoptive brother, L. Aelius Aurelius Commodus, and inaugurated the unusual system of the two Augusti. For the co-regencies of Galba and Piso, Vespasian and Titus, and Nerva and Trajan had been something different; and the position of *Caesar*, a normal institution since the adoption of Aelius Caesar in 136, occupied by Antoninus in the last sad year of Hadrian and by Marcus (not by Lucius) throughout the whole reign of Antoninus, had emerged more and more clearly as the position of the heir rather than that of the co-regent.

We do not possess sufficient information to be able to understand fully why an heir so clearly indicated and universally accepted, in the prime of life (he was forty) and certainly experienced, even if so far public affairs had not been his pre-eminent occupation, should have called to his side the mediocre Lucius, an indolent and pleasure-seeking youth, neither good nor bad, who would be, at the least, a hindrance in the business of governing, if he really was – and there is no reason to doubt it – the sort of person unanimously portrayed by the sources. Brought up, after his adoption, in the imperial palace with Marcus, educated by the same teachers, though with somewhat less profit even though he always professed respect for them, fond of sport and pleasure and inclined rather to a brilliant outward life, he must have seemed to provide a typical contrast to his adoptive brother, 'a prima infantia gravis'.[1] Antoninus had valued a certain frankness and sincerity in his character, nothing else, and had probably left completely to Marcus the responsibility for deciding whether Hadrian's plans for the succession should be fully implemented. Marcus decided that they should be, but it is difficult to imagine that he acted like this, as the ancients say he did,[2] because he had considered his own frailness of body and desire to devote himself to philosophy and because he found in the young Lucius the things that he himself lacked – physical robustness and the qualities needed for military campaigns; this would have been an error in foresight and judgement which the whole subsequent activity of the two Augusti, reflecting as it does their respective characters, asserts to be impossible. More probably Marcus was giving a sample from the first day of his reign of that devotion to duty which was the constant norm of his life. No doubt he recognized above all the rights of the person whom Hadrian had wanted to be equal to himself, even if this was bound to cause him some repugnance, and therefore resolved in the most open and solemn way, with the solid consequence of easier future control-lability, what was always a problem – the presence of a claimant to the throne.

It is naturally not surprising that Marcus wished this decision, too, to be formally approved by the Senate; his own acceptance of the empire had been signified in accordance with the most traditionally orthodox cere-monial, which demanded a formal refusal first. Thus from the very first day there were two Augusti: *Imperator Caesar M. Aurelius Antoninus Augustus* and *Imperator Caesar L. Aurelius Verus Augustus*. Marcus assumed as cog-nomen that of his adoptive father and characteristically passed on his own to his brother. The office of *pontifex maximus* alone remained naturally undivided and was held only by Marcus. The title of *pater patriae* was adopted officially by both, but not until 166. They both held all the other priestly posts and were also in every other way equal. The two had already begun the year 161 as colleagues in the consulship (Marcus's third and Lucius's second). Together they appeared before the Senate and in the *castra praetoria*, promising the notable donative of 20,000 sesterces a head and receiving the acclamation. The *congiarium* to the people must have followed at once. They then celebrated the solemn obsequies of Antoninus, whose mortal remains were brought from Lorium and probably cremated in the *Ustrinum Antoninorum*, from which soared up the eagle symbolizing

[1] *V. Marc.*, 2, 1.   [2] CASS. D. LXXI, 1.

the apotheosis already granted by the Senate. They both made laudatory speeches, laid the ashes to rest in the mausoleum of Hadrian, looked after the funeral games and inaugurated the worship of the new god, creating a flamen and the *sodales Antoniniani*. Annia Aurelia Galeria Lucilia, Marcus's second daughter, probably born in 149 and thus barely twelve, was promised in marriage to Lucius, and this formed more of a genuine family bond. Coins with the motif and legend 'Concordia Augustorum' celebrated right at the start the union of the two emperors, who from then onwards issued all their official decrees in common, struck coins separately but on an equality, put inscriptions in common on monuments and accepted jointly honorary dedications, including those of books, such as that of the *Strategemata* by the Macedonian rhetorician Polyaenus.

This new kind of co-regency lasted until the death of Verus in the early days of 169; and it was resumed in 177, when Marcus associated his son Commodus with himself in the same way. As for the real business of governing, that fell no doubt principally on the shoulders of Marcus, in the usual fashion of the half-despotic, half-paternalist régime which for some time had ruled the empire, even if the Princeps regarded the principate as a magistracy and the idea of functional duty, already conscious and operative in his predecessors, had now struck much deeper roots in the philosophical view of the world. It was Marcus alone who faced up to the formidable problems that arose with incredible speed after the calm of Pius's reign, the 'Felicitas temporum' still mentioned only in coins dating from the first year of his predecessors. The atmosphere was changed not so much by the natural calamities – a Tiber flood and a famine at Rome, an earthquake in Cilicia – given so much prominence by the tradition precisely to emphasize the damage they inflicted on a reign that had started under the best auspices, as by the threatening aggravation, between 161 and 162, of the crisis that had been hanging over the empire for some time. The disturbances in Britain, the collapse, local though it was, of the Danubian frontier, with the consequent invasion of Raetia by the Chatti, and the outbreak of the Parthian war, long deferred, were only the most glaring outward signs of this crisis.

THE WAR IN THE EAST

Marcus faced the harsh reality. Probably he had no inclination for soldiering and no experience of it, but forced to take up arms and to fight for almost the whole duration of his reign he fulfilled to the best of his ability the emperor's duty, at the head of the great defensive apparatus whose efficiency was now seriously tested in practice for the first time since Hadrian's reorganization, on the whole with happy results. To Britain in 162 he sent Calpurnius Agricola as successor to M. Statius Priscus, destined for the eastern campaign, and in the complete absence of further information we may assume that he succeeded in restoring the situation to normal. Raetia was entrusted to the man most naturally indicated for the task, namely the governor of Upper Germany, C. Aufidius Victorinus, the friend and fellow student of Marcus and son-in-law of Fronto. Here too order was restored, at any rate until the Germans started moving generally again on a vaster scale. But the first few years of the reign were dominated by the war in the East.

We have seen that under Hadrian and Antoninus relations with the Parthians were always tense. If it had never come to a war, that was due simply to the policy of strength constantly pursued by the two emperors, who had taken particular care to maintain and increase the efficiency of the armies of Cappadocia and Syria, in conformity with the general principle of the defence of the empire and in particular with the compromise which had governed relations between the Parthians and the Romans in their clashes over Armenia since the time of Nero. Continuous measures, to which there is interesting testimony for the reign of Antoninus,[1] succeeded for a long time in securing the respect of the Parthians, ruled since 148 by Vologaeses III. In the rapid alternation between strength and weakness characteristic of the Parthian state, the first few years of this prince's long reign (he died towards 193) represented a period of upward ascent, devoted mainly to consolidating the kingdom's newly restored unity. If war played a definite part in his plans, which were kept well in check by the Romans, a good opportunity may have been offered by the change of rulers at Rome. This was always a critical moment; we do not have to attribute to the Parthian king any particularly derogatory view of the qualities of the new Augusti. That events developed on the usual lines, apart from the choice of timing, is shown by the fact that the immediate cause of the war was once again the question of Armenia. However, the sources are in agreement in attributing the initiative to Vologaeses, and his initial successes, which were all the more remarkable in that the Romans, who had been expecting the war for years, were not surprised but overwhelmed by superior forces, indicate the large scale of the strategic plan and the imposing size of the forces employed.

Offensives were in fact launched, certainly before the end of 161, on

[1] *ILS*, 1076; *BGU*, 1564; cf. FR. SCHEHL, in *Hermes*, LXV, 1930, pp. 177-93.

two fronts. An army commanded by one Chosroes invaded Armenia from the south and at Elegeia defeated and induced the suicide of the governor of Cappadocia, M. Sedatus Severianus, who had sought to resist the invader by entering the province with a force of about one legion. A Parthian prince, Pacorus, was placed on the throne of Armenia. Simultaneously, or a little later, another army crossed the Euphrates, entered Syria and severely defeated the governor, L. Attidius Cornelianus. However, the Roman recovery was not long in coming. Seeing the need for one of the Augusti to head the operation, Marcus must have thought that it was better to send Lucius, surrounded by first-class colleagues, than to leave him alone at Rome and take command himself. The departure of both from the city was probably considered inadvisable since the change of régime was still fresh. It is true that the sources are visibly favourable to Marcus and hostile to his colleague, but even when we take account of this and of the efforts deployed by some modern scholars to rehabilitate Lucius, it is difficult to go much further than merely mitigating and explaining the severe ancient judgement on the scanty attention he gave to the enterprise entrusted to him. That he was not in the least offended by the appointment of all the members of his staff by Marcus and that throughout the war he let others do the work while he had a good time and simply took the credit for victory, are facts that are not only undeniable but difficult to explain in any way but by personal laxity and pure and simple enjoyment of the advantages of power. Such an attitude was in any case perfectly in tune, in the eyes of the person concerned and certainly of many others, with a principate conceived as a splendid sinecure; such a view was the opposite of the concept of duty championed by Marcus, but it was by no means incomprehensible to minds far removed from his moral elevation and already prepared, as they would need to be under Commodus, not to marvel at the despot's sublime ease and the appearance of viziers acting on his behalf.

As usual the events of the war, which lasted until 166 and fell, it would seem, into three principal phases – *armeniaca* (161–163), *parthica* proper (163–165) and *medica* (165–166) – cannot be reconstructed with complete certainty. Lucius Verus left Rome not earlier than the end of March 162, accompanied by Marcus as far as Capua. The slow and leisurely nature of the journey by land and sea from there to Antioch – not reached before the end of the year – with long stays at Canusium (where he fell ill and was visited again by Marcus), at Corinth, Athens, Ephesus and in many cities of Asia, Pamphylia and Cilicia, hardly testifies to his zeal, nor is it legitimate to ascribe solely to the malignity of the sources the reproach cast at him of wasting time hunting in Apulia and in musical contests in Greece while the eastern provinces were being devastated by war. Setting up his headquarters, or to be more accurate his court, at Antioch, he did not move again from there except to go to Laodicea, on the coast, in winter, to the neighbouring health resort of Daphne in the summer, to Ephesus in 164 to welcome his wife-to-be and just once in four years to the Euphrates, and it would perhaps be too kind to take the view that he did this in order to gather in his own hands and ensure the unity of strategic and logistic command. At Antioch he held court just as if he were in Rome, and we may suppose that he did it with a certain style, for Lucian speaks with respect of Panthea, the cultured courtesan from Smyrna. But when the sources say that in practice the war was directed by Marcus – even if subsequently, as we know from Fronto, the latter only too naturally sang the official praises of his brother in the Senate – they are substantially speaking the truth. One has only to remember that all the best generals, whose names keep recurring in the course of the war and who include all the most illustrious men of the time and many who were to be even more famous in the very near future (M. Statius Priscus, C. Julius Severus, Cn. Julius Verus, P. Martius Verus, M. Pontius Laelianus, M. Iallius Bassus, M. Claudius Fronto, C. Avidius Cassius, P. Julius Geminius Marcianus, the praetorian prefect T. Furius Victorinus and the young tribune P. Helvius Pertinax), were sent to the frontier by Marcus; that the movement of the legions which brought numbers I *Minervia*, II *Adiutrix* and V *Macedonica* from their camps in Lower Germany, Lower Pannonia and Lower Moesia respectively to reinforce the army of the East was also ordered by Marcus; and that Marcus had already taken the emergency measure of raising troops in Italy. The actual operations were then directed by the generals, with a skill and success reflected not only in the reorganization and strict training of the army, measures for which Fronto (*Princ. Hist.*, 13) naturally assigns the credit to Lucius, but also in its tactical employment, something which the rhetorician is totally unable to illustrate from the activities of his disciple. There is also some talk in Fronto of an offer of peace by Lucius to Vologaeses before the beginning of hostilities, but it is difficult to judge what part is played in the exaggeration or even invention of events by the deliberate parallel – the foundation of this rhetorical thesis – with Trajan's war of 114–117. The praise given by Fronto to Lucius for trying, unlike Trajan, to spare the soldiers' blood was the only euphemistic thing he could find to say in justification of his indolence.

Operations began in the Armenian theatre. Statius Priscus, the new but experienced governor of Cappadocia, concluded the vigorous counter-offensive he conducted there, after his army had been strengthened with some at least of the troops sent from the West, by capturing and destroy-ing the capital, Artaxata. The victory gained the two Augusti their second salutation as *imperator*. Lucius also assumed the title of *Armeniacus*, which Marcus only accepted in 164. Operations were extended to the whole country and beyond it – as far, it would seem, as the northern slopes of the Caucasus – but once again direct annexation was ruled out. After Pacorus had been driven out he was replaced by a prince called Sohaemus, who was possibly an Arsacid and certainly a Roman senator. However, the restored client kingdom was not left to its own devices: twenty years later Kainepolis, the 'new city', regarded after the destruction of Artaxata as the capital, was still occupied by the legionary garrison detached from Satala, a *vexillatio* of Legion XV *Apollinaris*; and no doubt similar garrisons were stationed in other places as well.

The legions of Syria, successfully reorganized by Avidius Cassius, who was probably endowed with a wider command than that of mere governor, and by Pontius Laelianus, *comes* of Lucius, went into action a little later but before the end of 163, when the settlement of Armenia was still going on. In 164, while the war was attaining its amplest dimensions, Lucius returned westward as far as Ephesus to meet his bride-to-be Lucilla, now fifteen years old, who had been accompanied as far as Ephesus with considerable pomp by the bridegroom's sister, Ceionia Fabia, and by her uncle, M. Vettulenus Civica Barbarus, a step-brother of Aelius Caesar. Marcus himself had accompanied his daughter to Brindisi and seems to have intended to go on to Syria, but he had subsequently given up the idea. The wedding must have followed. Meanwhile the offensive was developing in Mesopotamia as well, mainly under the direction of Avidius Cassius. However, it is difficult to reconstruct the course of operations. We possess evidence of two lines of attack, but we cannot distinguish the separate events or arrange them chronologically with any confidence. The province must already have been cleared of invaders at an earlier stage. The Euphrates was crossed, probably on a bridge of boats, in spite of strong opposition from the enemy. The site of the crossing is uncertain, for the sources give us in the somewhat muddled context at least three names of towns on the Euphrates – Zeugma (near Apamea) and, considerably further south, Sura and Nicephorium – thus excluding Europos (a little to the south of Zeugma, near the ancient Carchemish), which is also mentioned and where a big battle is supposed to have taken place; in fact it is now commonly thought that the crossing was made at Dura-Europos. Beyond the Euphrates, operations were conducted in Osrhoene, whose philo-Roman client king had been driven out by Vologaeses, and in Antemusia. Among the places mentioned as occupied are Edessa, the capital of Osrhoene, and Dausara, and there are also references to the siege of Nisibis and to the capture of this important city: evidently the plan of operations demanded that one army, which there is reason to believe was commanded by M. Claudius Fronto and of which the troops already deployed in Armenia probably formed part, should secure the north of Mesopotamia and then advance eastward, as in fact it did in the last phase of the war, beyond the Tigris into Adiabene and Atropatene, the very heart of the Parthian dominions. Another column must have advanced southward along the Euphrates; this will have been the one commanded directly by Avidius Cassius. The above-mentioned big battle at Dura-Europos would have taken place in the course of the advance towards Babylonia, which must have been reached quite swiftly. The Parthians were completely annihilated. Chosroes swam to safety across the Tigris, probably fleeing from one last battle in defence of the capitals. Possibly even before the end of 164 Seleucia, a Greek city, surrendered voluntarily to the Romans, while Ctesiphon, the Parthian capital, was destroyed. But in the following year Seleucia too was sacked and burnt, on the ground that it had not fulfilled the conditions of the surrender. The Parthian expedition was regarded as concluded in 165, the year of the two Emperors' third salutation as *imperator* and of Lucius's assumption of the title *Parthicus Maximus*, which was also assumed by Marcus in 166.

With that, the whole war was virtually over, for the above-mentioned operations on the far side of the northern Tigris, in Media, which went on until the beginning of 166 and gained the Augusti their fourth salutation and the title of *Medicus*, were only the finishing touches to the great success. Peace was concluded in the early months of 166; we do not know if it was hastened by the appearance in the Roman army of the plague, from which Avidius Cassius had already suffered losses at Seleucia and on the way back from Babylonia. None of the clauses of the treaty is known, but the subsequent settlement reveals that, like his predecessors, Marcus did not go beyond the usual principle of security. The territorial gains (Dura-Europos was now within the boundaries of the empire and the important line of the Chaboras was utilized) were determined strictly by this consideration. The client states, beginning with Armenia, were certainly more carefully supervised. Osrhoene became a vassal state again, and the free Greek city of Carrhae was raised, it seems, to the rank of a colony: *Colonia Aurelia Carrhae*. All worries were certainly not over, as will be seen subsequently, and the vast command over the whole East assigned to Avidius Cassius, possibly straight after the war, indicates that reliance was placed on his well-known energy to keep the situation under control. But Roman prestige had been re-established and the empire's superiority over the East had been reaffirmed, a superiority which was not to be questioned again until the weak Irano-Hellenistic state of the Arsacids was succeeded by the Sassanid empire, the genuine heir of ancient Persia. Above all, it had been shown that the empire's iron organization, as consolidated under the last few emperors, was still adequate to deal with crises of this sort.

Just as soon as it was possible, in other words in the spring of 166, Lucius began his homeward journey, fêted in the Asiatic cities through which he passed and in which he left the plague, a disease that was to be carried in the end right to Italy and the West by the troops returning to their stations. The triumph was celebrated in the summer, probably on 23 August, by both Augusti, adorned with the *corona civica*, with all the epithets of victory confirmed by the Senate, and possibly already, though not beyond 12 October, with the title of *pater patriae* (which does not appear any more on Lucius's coins and only after 176 on those of Marcus). Marcus's numerous offspring took part in the triumphal procession. Games and a *congiarium* (the third of the reign; the second had been distributed the year before by Marcus alone) contented the populace, and the celebrations must have been prolonged in an atmosphere of excitement, as was natural for an event that had not occurred for almost fifty years, since the time of Trajan's posthumous triumph in 118. And in this atmosphere – even if we do not believe the certainly exaggerated reports of the colossal orgies of Lucius, who after the victory is supposed to have cast aside every inhibition, including that of his respect for Marcus – we must not fail to note a disconcerting action by the latter. On 12 October he gave the title of Caesar to his sons Commodus and Annius Verus, two children of five and four years respectively – a step which the biographer feels obliged to describe as due to Lucius's suggestion.

THE FIRST SERIES OF WARS ON THE DANUBE – GERMANS AND SARMATIANS

At this point or soon afterwards another serious external crisis erupted, while the plague, soon followed by famine, was already claiming victims all over the empire. It was the start of that series of hard wars on the Danube which was to occupy, with short interruptions, the remaining years of Marcus's reign. Although it was still, seen from inside the empire, a frontier crisis, firmly checked in the end by the defensive machinery and overcome by the still exuberant vitality of the imperial organism, nevertheless its sudden appearance, after sixty years of relative peace in this sector, its gravity and duration and the proximity of the danger to Italy, whose soil was actually trodden again after centuries by the barbarian foot, made a great impression on contemporaries, who were certainly already in a position to understand that this time the struggle was to be explained by deeper and more distant causes. From the tradition that has come down to us concerning these wars, confused and fragmentary though it is, we can gain some idea of the movements of tribes that took place at that time outside the empire in the north and north-east of Europe, and we are led to regard the story of what was still, for these peoples, simply a wave that eventually broke – part of its distant and indirect effects – against the bastions of the Roman *limes*, as the start of the age-long phenomenon of the barbarian invasions.

The arrangement of tribes described in Tacitus's little work on the Germans must have been for a long time relatively stable. A belt of peoples who were in varying degrees clients of the Romans extended beyond the Rhine and Danube from the North Sea to the Black Sea. Beyond these two big rivers, only the *agri decumates*, occupied since the Flavian era, and Dacia, annexed by Trajan, together with the trans-Danubian dependencies of Moesia, formed direct parts of the empire. Chauci, Chatti, Hermunduri, Naristi, Marcomanni and Quadi, all German tribes, succeeded each other from west to east, bordering the empire, up to modern Slovakia. More to the east, north of Dacia, there were the Osii (possibly Illyrians), the Cotini (possibly of Celtic stock) and the Buri (Germans), while the province that stuck out beyond the Danube was flanked, in the direction of the Hungarian plain, by the Iazyges, a tribe of Sarmatian stock, and in the direction of Moldavia and Wallachia by the Roxolani – Sarmatians again – and the Bastarni, who probably had an admixture of German blood. Behind this belt extended other peoples, principally the Semnones and Lombards along the Elbe, the Lugri on the Oder and the Goths round the sources of the Vistula. The Alans, overflowing again from the Caucasus, were also now appearing on the Sarmatian steppes and to the north of the Danube, These 'barbari superiores', however, though not in direct contact with the empire, were not without commercial and even political relations with it. The visit to Rome of Masua, the king of the Semnones, in 89 or 90, Domitian's intervention about the same time in the disputes between the Chatti and the Cherusci, and his great plan to encircle the Marcomanni, Quadi and Iazyges, then at war with the empire, from the north were significant episodes. However, the only tribes who had a permanent link with Rome, in the form of clientage, were the tribes of the belt described, and by their very status they normally formed a cushion against attacks by the peoples of the hinterland, with whom they were frequently at logger-heads through the characteristically Germanic quality of particularism, which was shrewdly turned by Rome to her own advantage.

Thus for decades these peoples, safe on the empire side and interested in maintaining good relations because of all the cultural and commercial benefits and also protection accruing to them as a result, continued to fulfil this function. But they always remained outside the empire; even if they were friends and allies, the legionary camps and the line of fortifications were erected against them and separated them sharply from what was regarded as the civilized world, namely that part of it alone which lay within the Roman dominions. Serious crises, and ones provoked by them, had already arisen at the time of Augustus's settlement; and people had not forgotten the long years of war in Domitian's and Trajan's reigns, wars which had brought permanently to the Danube the main weight of the defence forces. In fact it was precisely these neighbouring peoples, not the distant ones, the repercussions of whose thrusts and movements were scarcely perceptible until this age, who determined the adaptation of the Roman defences to requirements, as has been demonstrated by the interesting results brought to light recently in connection with the varying density of the archaeological finds in the regions inhabited by them. It appears that these peoples, who in any case varied in density, did not press against the *limes* but had their centres more in the interior, except in Lower Austria, Moravia and the Slovakian plain, in short, opposite Upper Pannonia, where contact with the empire was intense and the population thicker. This explains how it is that the forces' deployment – which as a result of earlier experiences slowly changed in accordance with the local conditions actually prevailing in the peaceful decades of the second century, and after Antoninus remained almost definitive – displays on the one hand a further decline in importance of the Rhine garrison and a surprising absence of legionary camps from Strasbourg to Vienna after the abandonment in about 100 of the camp at Vindonissa (Raetia and Noricum were governed by mere procurators); and on the other hand the concentration of three camps and three legions in Upper Pannonia, along a stretch of river not longer (from Vindobona to Brigetio) than sixty-five miles. The relative smallness of the garrison of Lower Pannonia (one single legion at Aquincum) was balanced by the increase in importance of the defences of Dacia. The distribution of the auxiliaries confirms the situation, complementing a powerful apparatus carefully adjusted to correspond with the varying size of the potential threat, which in turn depended on the varying demographic pressure within the tribes, the varying cordiality of existing attitudes to the Romans, the varying strength of the natural defences (the mountains and woods of the frontier with the Hermunduri, or the marshes facing Lower Pannonia), the varying ease and openness of the invasion routes and the varying prospects of success and booty in the lands of the empire.

This state of affairs endured for a long time. It is true that even in the period of most profound peace some hints of danger emerged. From contact with the garrisons, from the sight of the fortifications and from the instructions given to them, these tribes were learning the art of war as practised by the Romans. Peace itself and their now accepted sedentary existence, besides causing their numbers to increase and creating a problem of overpopulation which they could not solve because of their ignorance of intensive cultivation, lessened the differences between them; and since they were no longer fighting among themselves they began to glimpse the prospect of changing fronts and marching together, barbarians of the frontier and barbarians of the hinterland, against the empire. However, the situation was always kept in check and this eventuality only became a reality under the stimulus of distant external events, namely a big migratory movement initiated by the Germans living along the Baltic, who were themselves possibly being pressed by Scandinavian tribes. Another reason why this movement disturbed the position across the Danube was that it came on top of the pressure already exerted for years by the Alans. The sources depict the situation at the tragic moment when the defences had given way and the empire was already being invaded; but the list of some twenty-five tribes named in the course of the war, among which appear both old clients and nations in contact with Rome for the first time, all threateningly hungry for land, and the fact, typical of mass migrations, that women were fighting as well, confirm the long concatenation of causes and the effect, at the moment still external, which precipitated the crisis: the disturbance of the belt of vassal states along the *limes*, with pressure increasing until the front broke at the point already indicated as the most dangerous, in Upper Pannonia.

It may well be that Antoninus Pius's interventions in Dacia, just towards the end of his reign, were dictated by the first big skirmishes arising out of these movements. A first wave of Goths and northern tribes, coming up against the Marcomanni and Quadi, who were still fulfilling their function of protecting the empire, must have 'escalated' at that time along the Carpathians, towards the east, not without causing some restlessness among the sub-Carpathian tribes. The withdrawal of forces for the Parthian war, though done with caution (the three legions were taken from the points least threatened at that moment and replaced by opportune stratagems), certainly weakened the defensive machine, encouraging Rome's barbarian clients, squeezed ever more tightly in the rear, to greater insistence in their demands to be received within the empire and greater boldness when faced with a constant refusal. However, in 163, as is testified by a military diploma found recently and coming from Brigetio,[1] the distribution of the auxiliaries in Upper Pannonia had not yet undergone any changes. Thus, still on the evidence of diplomas,[2] in 164 the situation in Dacia was normal, as it seems that it was in Raetia at the beginning of 166. But we know that this tranquillity was due to the governors, who succeeded in containing the pressure until the end of the Parthian war, while Marcus in Rome was kept fully informed and, according to the biographer, had even spoken of the necessity of a war to a populace already suffering from a famine. When the legions returned to their stations (except for the V *Macedonica*, which did not go back to Troesmis but was sent instead to Potaissa in Dacia) things ought to have improved. Instead came the collapse.

So began the long years of war. The chronological reconstruction of this war is always being attempted, but it is still far from a definitive solution, which is in fact impossible to achieve with the sources at our disposal, however shrewdly all the archaeological, epigraphical and numismatic evidence is utilized. Apart from a few fixed points and a summary classification of the campaigns already indicated by the contemporary official view (*expeditio Germanica prima, expeditio Sarmatica, expeditio Germanica secunda* occur in inscriptions), very little can be recovered from the muddled collection of disconnected reports contained in the *Historia Augusta* and the fragments of Cassius Dio. The Column of Antoninus is not much help either; it seems to be not so much a continuous account in scenes, the chronological beginning and end of which would still have to be established with absolute certainty, as a sort of

---

[1] L. BARKÓCZI, 'A New Military Diploma from Brigetio', in *Act. Arch. Ac. Scient. Hung.*, IX, 1958, pp. 413–21.
[2] *CIL*, XVI, Suppl., 185; *CIL*, XVI, 121.

anthology of episodes, no doubt in chronological sequence, mainly glorifying the army and its courageous leader.

We do not know for certain what the immediate events were which led Marcus, after the return of Lucius in 166, to tell the Senate that it was necessary for both the Augusti to take personal command in the war. We are told in a fragment originating from Cassius Dio[1] of the crossing of the Danube by six thousand Lombards and Osii, who were defeated by the cavalry of one Vindex (M. Macrinius Avitus Catonius Vindex, not the praetorian prefect Macrinius Vindex, who fell in 171) and by the infantry of one Candidus (possibly commander of a legion), of the subsequent despatch to Iallius Bassus, the governor of Upper Pannonia, of a delegation composed of Ballomarius, the king of the Marcomanni, and ten other ambassadors, one for each tribe, and of the conclusion of a peace which re-established the *status quo*. These events indicate the new reality of joint attacks by the frontier tribes and those further back, but they may be regarded as a single episode in the initial situation described in more general terms by the biographer: 'The Victuali and the Marcomanni upset everything, and other tribes who were in flight from the barbarians further back also made war if they were not received into the empire'. In fact it seems that the governorship of Iallius Bassus did not begin before 166, so that his action cannot be regarded as one of the containing actions ascribed to the governors while the Parthian war was still going on. The break-through accomplished, though with only brief success, by the Lombards and their allies, may in fact have been the first sensational act in the series of attacks which followed, and the victory which put paid to it may have been the one which caused the fifth salutation of the Emperors, character-istically already attested in military diplomas of May 167 but only from 168 on coins. This is a surprising discrepancy in documents both emanating from official sources and may indicate, as it has been proved to do in other cases, uncertainty in evaluating a situation that was indeed extremely confused. Another incident that no doubt occurred in the early days was the defeat and death of the praetorian prefect Furius Victorinus, sent to assist the governors in facing the danger as soon as it appeared and while the arrival of the Augusti was being awaited. Their departure from the capital must however have been somewhat delayed, not only by the opposition of Lucius but also by such circumstances as the raging of the plague, which in 167 reached its height at Rome and in the armies. Mean-while the attacks of the barbarians began again and were now concentrated on Dacia, if we accept the evidence, confirmed by hoards of coins, of the

[1] PETR. PATR. in BOISSEVAIN, III, p. 251.

archives concealed by a notary of Alburnus Maior (Verespatak) in northern Dacia, which come to a stop with a document of 29 May 167. In Lower Pannonia discharges were still being given on 5 May – although the province was already under the justly praised command of Claudius Pompeianus, one of Marcus's closest colleagues – and in the same year, 167, work was carried out on the road from Sirmium to Aquincum.

In the absence of other facts and in the complete chronological un-certainty prevailing, it seems nevertheless better to place at this point, and before the departure of the Augusti from Rome, the eruption of the Marcomanni and Quadi into Raetia, Noricum and some parts of Upper Pannonia, and the thrust which reached into Italy, besieging Aquileia and destroying Opitergium (Oderzo). The event, apart from the psycho-logical effect it produced, should probably not be over-estimated. Since the Roman defensive machine consisted essentially of forces covering the frontiers, without any mobile reserve of troops in the rear except the slender praetorian guard, if detachments of barbarians broke the line at isolated points they could push right into Italy (which had no defences at the Alps) or Greece (as the Costoboci succeeded in doing a little later, at a better-guarded spot) – without any hope, it is true, of achieving lasting success or permanent occupation, but nevertheless carrying out brilliant raids almost undisturbed. It is quite possible that on this particular occasion the Romans paid for not giving much attention to the frontiers of Raetia and Noricum. It would seem that we can rule out the idea that it was a question now of a big invasion that broke through the whole Pannonian front and submerged the province: an enterprise of this size would have led to very different developments. As for the precise time, it is certainly difficult to suppose that the barbarians could have penetrated into Italy later on, when operations were going on beyond the Alps under the direction of Marcus, who had provided precisely what was wanting – a mobile force and a system of protection for Italy. Moreover, it would be hard to understand why the Augusti, setting out for a war against the Marcomanni and Quadi which, but for the pre-emptive provocation, would have been an offensive war, should have stopped for a long time at Aquileia, set up their first headquarters there, and not proceeded straight to the Danube, as had always been done in similar cases under Domitian and Trajan.

Thus in the second half of 167 the situation was fairly critical, if not desperate, and Marcus, though still in Rome, took opportune measures – which were certainly not confined to the sacrifices and *lectisternia* recorded by the tradition to exorcize the evils of the plague as well as the threats of war, nor to the distribution of a *congiarium* (the fourth of the reign) – to raise the people's spirits. Although uncertainty reigns here too, by this time the two new Italian legions must have been made fully operational. These two legions were the II *Pia* and the III *Concors* or *Concordia*, later known simply as the II and III *Italica*. Their recruitment from the young men of Italy, who had hardly served at all in the legions for a century, may have begun in the previous year or in 165, when the situation first began to look serious, and had been conducted, as we have learnt recently,[1] by one of the most distinguished generals of the time, Cn. Julius Verus. These forces were not to be assigned at once to a sector of the frontier but were intended to serve as mobile troops, in accordance with the tendency imposed by necessity and demonstrated in the whole subsequent course of the war by the extensive use of *vexillationes* or operational units detached from the legions and put under the direct command of officers of irregular and lower rank, who were known simply as *praepositi*. This practice made up for the now excessive heaviness of the standing army, anchored to its camps like big, immovable army corps; the transfer of the V *Macedonica* from Troesmis to Potaissa remained the only organic change in the deployment of the legions as a whole from Hadrian to Septimius Severus. Obviously further attention will have been given to the various commands, which were entrusted in this interval of waiting, in the provinces threatened, to men of the first rank: besides the above-mentioned Iallius Bassus in Upper Pannonia and Claudius Pompeianus in Lower Pannonia, M. Claudius Fronto now appears in Upper Moesia and Sextus Calpurnius Agricola, soon to be followed by C. Aufidius Victorinus, in Dacia, now united again under one single consular governor with two legions. Not without reason from the angle of his own private conception of the principate, Lucius regarded it as superfluous for the Emperors to move in person. However, Marcus succeeded in imposing the point of view characteristic of his own commitment to the service of the state, and at the beginning of 168, though not before 6 January, for on that day he made a speech in the 'castra praetoria' (doubtless the one at Rome), the solemn departure took place. The date 168 is confirmed by coins.

The concentration of forces must have been marshalled at Aquileia, which had kept the barbarians out by hastily rebuilding its ring of walls. This, having evidently become too small and constrictive, had been knocked down in the first century and not replaced, on the false assumption that it was now no longer required. Repulsed from the city and informed of the preparations being made and of the Emperors' personal participation

[1] *Ann. Ép.*, 1956, 123.

in the war, the possibly thin bands of barbarians who had come down into Italy very soon disappeared over the Alps. This success in itself may have led Marcus to give the wide publicity of the coinage to the fifth salutation as *imperator*. This had been received by the two Augusti in the previous year, but with his well-known scrupulousness Marcus had put off asking the Senate to ratify it until a more decisive victory had been secured. But the goal of the expedition was certainly not Aquileia. Again contrary to Lucius's advice, Marcus crossed into Pannonia. The biographer's sentence, 'composuerunt omnia quae ad munimen Italiae atque Illyrici pertinebant' (14, 6), reflects exactly the plan and the results of the action taken there. Instead of pursuing the Marcomanni and Quadi who had entered Roman territory, and who had already returned home of their own accord, putting to death those who had counselled the unfortunate enterprise (the Quadi even requested the Augusti to confirm their new king), Marcus took note of the proposals for submission and put in train the most urgent measures to re-establish security, at any rate for the moment, particularly the security of Italy. Among these measures was the institution, which there is no reason not to assign to this year, 168, of a characteristic command, the *praetentura Italiae et Alpium*, entrusted to the ex-consul Q. Antistius Adventus. This command comprised a substantial mobile force, possibly including the two new Italian legions with the corresponding auxiliaries, given the high rank of the commanding officer, but certainly supported by a system of fortifications curving round in a semicircle to protect the passes across the central and eastern Alps from Raetia to Dalmatia. Notwithstanding the satisfactory settlement, recorded on coins of the end of 168 in motifs of the return of peace and prosperity, Marcus was nevertheless convinced that the situation remained precarious, that the compromise with the barbarians, with which Lucius was quite content (he pressed again for a return to Rome) could not last long, and that a radical solution could only be imposed by carrying the war into enemy territory and restoring and preserving by force the bond of clientage and the situation existing previously, so far as this was possible, granted the complexity of the causes which had disturbed it. Whether he had already begun to think of the other possible solution, that of direct annexation, it is difficult to say, but Trajan's conquest of Dacia was a precedent that could always be imitated. However, war on such a vast scale, if it was already being considered, had to be postponed to the following year, 169. The Augusti returned to Aquileia where they certainly were from the end of 168 to the early part of 169, while the army continued to be harried by the plague, as we know from Galen, the great scientist and doctor of Pergamum, who had already been in Rome between 162 and 163 and was now invited by the Emperors to come to their headquarters.

During the course of this winter Marcus finally brought himself to accompany his colleague to Rome. Lucius's health had certainly declined, and in fact scarcely had they embarked on the journey when he suffered an apoplectic stroke. At Altinum, towards the end of January 169, he breathed his last, at the age of thirty-eight. Even in connection with this death the tradition cast a shadow of suspicion on Marcus, but it does not deserve any serious consideration. One hindrance had gone with the disappearance of a man whose sole merit according to the tradition was that he was devoid of wickedness, but his death, as well as terminating a period in the reign of Marcus, also marked a pause and concluded one phase of the war on the Danube. The next item on the programme must have been the solemn carriage home of Lucius's mortal remains, accompanied by Marcus, who was not grudging with honours at Rome: he arranged for a splendid funeral, burial in Hadrian's mausoleum, deification with the title of *Divus Verus Parthicus Maximus*, the establishment of *sodales Antoniniani Veriani*, and privileges and gifts for his colleague's relatives and freedmen. Faithful to his constitutional scruples, Marcus then renounced the titles *Armeniacus*, *Medicus* and *Parthicus Maximus*, which he had only accepted for the sake of the principle of co-rulership on an equal footing. But for the moment he did not think of a successor for Lucius, although he made plans to give his widow, his own daughter Lucilla Augusta, in marriage to the valiant Claudius Pompeianus, governor of Lower Pannonia, a senator of recent oriental origin, but already on the way to becoming Marcus's right-hand man; and this despite the facts that the period of mourning was not yet over and that Faustina and Lucilla herself were opposed to the idea.

The stay in Rome lasted for quite a long time; we do not know how far this was due to the plague and how far to other reasons. The projected resumption of operations in the spring of 169 could not take place. Meanwhile on the Danube relative calm prevailed, but neither this nor the enforced delay induced the Emperor to slow down his preparations. Probably in this same year, 169, he further strengthened the legions by extensive recruitment. Naturally, we do not know whether it was at this point that *vexillationes* were summoned from other legions (III *Augusta*, III *Cyrenaica*, X *Fretensis*, XV *Apollinaris*, possibly the XII *Fulminata*, etc.) whose names occur in the rest of the war, but the force available, with twelve whole legions and numerous *vexillationes*, the 34 *alae* and 96 cohorts at least whose presence is attested, and the *numeri* and irregular detachments, must have been the most imposing one ever lined up between Raetia and Dacia. The supply system, which used the waterway of the Danube, was reinforced, 'in procinctu Germanicae expeditionis',[1] with detachments from the fleets of Misenum, Ravenna and Britain. Nevertheless the plague continued to create gaps, which the Emperor sought to fill by ordering the massive recruitment of special auxiliaries, the ones to which the tradition alludes when it says that he enrolled, 'as in the Punic war', slaves, gladiators, and bandits from Dalmatia and Dardania; he also admitted into the army, certainly for the first time in whole detachments, the so-called *diogmitae*, the police of the cities of Asia; and in accordance with a practice already current he engaged German mercenaries – 'Germanorum auxilia contra Germanos'.[2] To this year as well, since an action of this sort presupposes the Emperor's own presence, is to be attributed the sale by auction, with the option of redemption, of precious objects from the palace, with the object of not letting the whole financial weight of the war fall on the provinces. Disturbances in other parts of the empire (Mauretania, the East) must already have been increasing people's anxiety. In the atmosphere of public peril and patriotic enthusiasm which must have surrounded the imminent departure of the Princeps, Marcus forbade the prolongation beyond five days of the mourning for the death of his seven-year-old son, Annius Verus Caesar, and expressed the wish that the games of Jupiter Optimus Maximus (in October) should not be postponed. Immediately afterwards he left Rome; he was to return seven years later.

The reconstruction of the *expeditio Germanica* and of the *Sarmatica*, which immediately followed it, presents the usual difficulties. Only very few fixed chronological points exist round which to hang the information provided by the literary sources, which is relatively abundant but disconnected and difficult to reconcile with the details pictured on the column. It has seemed to some scholars that Marcus's fresh departure, taking place as it did in the autumn, can only be explained by supposing that it was preceded by a big assault on the part of the barbarians; they have therefore placed in 169 the invasion which reached Italy, or else the defeat which cost Macrinius Vindex, the praetorian prefect, his life, or even both events. But if we remove these events, which can be placed better, if without any certainty, at other times, as we have already seen in the case of the thrust into Italy and as we shall see in a moment in the case of the death of Vindex, there is nothing left in the sources (even taking

---

[1] *Ann. Ép.*, 1956, 124.   [2] *V. Marc.*, 21, 7.

account of the evidence of the coinage) with which to fill the year 169, which was thus really the year of preparation for the execution of the plan, already formed in 168, for a return to the Danube to settle the problems once and for all. However, the state of 'relative calm' does not mean that there were no incidents or limited attacks. Within the tribes along the frontier the causes of unrest certainly persisted; and these tribes had time to come to terms with each other and unite. That it was at this time that a band of Costoboci, a tribe living immediately to the north of the Carpathians, succeeded in descending towards Dacia amid the other tribes on the move, in then filtering through the defences and making the famous thrust which took them into Greece, where they damaged the temple of Eleusis, sacked Elatea and were then opposed by Julius Vehilius Gratus Julianus, the future praetorian prefect of Commodus, can be confirmed not only by the likely date of these events, which are recorded in the literary sources,[1] but also by the strengthening of the walls of Salonae in Dalmatia – work which was carried out by *vexillationes* from the Italian legions and can be dated with certainty to 170 – and of those of Philip-popolis in Thrace.

War on a vast front thus began in 170, but we are not in a position to know either where Marcus spent the winter of 169–170 or whether the initiative was taken by him or not. The action may have begun when the whole front had already been overturned by the barbarians and may have had to consist not in an offensive in their territories but in a defensive struggle in the provinces. The latter seems the most plausible hypothesis and may be borne out by the occurrence in the recently discovered *cursus* of M. Valerius Maximianus[2] of a reconnaissance post inside the province of Pannonia immediately after the above-mentioned appointment of super-vising the corn supply along the Danube. The biographer's list of tribes which 'ab Illyrici limite usque in Galliam conspiraverunt', a list apparently meant to allude to this point in time, certainly lumps together names which refer to various different times in the war; but the movement which had either arisen spontaneously or been provoked by Marcus's intervention must have been fairly extensive, though it was headed by the Marcomanni and Quadi, supported by the Iazyges. That the Romans gained some successes in 170 is probable, since specimens of Victoria recur in the coinage; but we must also almost certainly place in this year the death – whether in a victory or a defeat is unknown, but after a series of successes 'adversum Germanos et Iazyges'[3] – of the brave M. Claudius Fronto, now

[1] PAUSAN., X, 34, 5; AEL. ARIST., *Eleusinios.*
[2] *Ann. Ép.*, 1956, 124.   [3] *ILS*, 1098.

in the very high position of governor of Upper Moesia and Dacia combined. And these operations on the Dacian front, which perhaps included the great battle fought and won against the Iazyges on a frozen river (and hence in winter), as well as the massacre of members of the citizen body of Drobeta by native Dacians, another episode that may have formed part of this series of events,[1] will give some idea of the wide extent of the war in this certainly not very easy year. In it Marcus did not receive any salutation; and not only did the victorious epithets shared with Verus disappear from his style, as we have said, but also, even more characteristically, the title *imperator* V.

The new salutation as *imperator*, the sixth, appeared in 171. There were more frequent issues of coins commemorating victory, called explicitly the *Victoria Germanica*. Coins also celebrated the *decennalia* of the reign, in an atmosphere that was certainly more festive than it had been earlier. The year must have brought some big success. What it was we do not know. We do not even know from what base Marcus directed operations. If, as seems to be the case, this is the best time to place a number of disconnected reports, such as those of the death of Macrinius Vindex, the victory of Pompeianus and Pertinax, the prowess of M. Valerius Maximianus – now promoted to the command of an *ala* – who killed in battle the leader of the Naristi, Valaone, and was praised by the Emperor in the presence of the whole army,[2] the events of the year can be reconstructed roughly on the following lines. A powerful incursion of Marcomanni and Quadi (and also of Naristi, neighbours of the Marcomanni and usually associated with them; we hear no more of the Iazyges) took the Romans by surprise at the far western end of the front, towards Noricum and Raetia, when their main attention was perhaps concentrated on another sector. The praetorian prefect Macrinius Vindex was overwhelmed and the two provinces were severely tested. The *praetentura Italiae et Alpium* barred the road to Italy and made a rapid recovery possible. Pompeianus and Pertinax won a big victory near the Danube over the Marcomanni and Quadi, who may already have been on the retreat, and chased them back across the river, after making them restore their booty to the provincials. From now onwards Legions II and III *Italica* were probably stationed permanently in Noricum and Raetia; their presence is recorded, a little later, in the camps of Lauriacum (Lorch) and Castra Regina (Regensburg) respectively. The *praetentura Italiae* may have disappeared. Success in the central sector must have concluded a war that had become,

---

[1] *CIL*, III, 1957, 8009, 8021; inscriptions of victims of 'latrones'.
[2] *Ann. Ép.*, 1956, 124.

perhaps contrary to expectations, defensive, and in the following year, 172, the offensive war proper could at last begin from the now permanent base of Carnuntum. It is from this point, it now appears certain, and not before, that the figures on the column begin.

But the events that followed, up to 175, are very obscure indeed. What seems clear from the allusions in the sources to separate campaigns against various tribes – Marcomanni, Quadi, Sarmati – is the general plan of attack, which aimed at breaking up the unity of the barbarian coalition, fighting the various peoples one by one and possibly setting one against the other. The various reports fit quite well into the framework of this plan, but as for putting them into exact chronological order, this is naturally a different and insoluble problem. However, it seems as if the campaign in the territory of the Quadi, directed personally by Marcus, is to be placed between 172 and 174. The Marcomanni, exhausted by the defeat of 171, must for the moment have taken little part in the proceedings. Some assistance must also have been provided by the Iazyges, until they too, from 174 to 175 (*bellum Sarmaticum*) were in their turn isolated and dealt with. The facts known are few.

Advancing beyond the Danube, Marcus conducted the war with a faith in the divine recorded by the literary sources and attested by the coins, which lay emphasis, particularly in 173 and 174, on religious motifs (mainly Jupiter and Mercury). This attitude not only reflected his own elevated religious feelings but also conformed with the cults and superstitions of the soldiers, if it was now that he agreed to throw two live lions into the Danube for the happy outcome of the expedition, as prescribed by Alexander of Abonoteichos, a man whom Lucian[1] regarded as a false prophet. The episodes that are famous from this point of view and that can certainly be located in this series of events are the lightning from heaven that, following a prayer by Marcus, burnt up an enemy war machine, and the miraculous rain that saved a part of the Roman army commanded by Pertinax when it was reduced to difficult straits by heat and thirst during a big battle, which was thereby transformed from a certain defeat into victory. These miracles were attributed to the intervention of Jupiter and Mercury respectively, the latter being called upon, according to one of the versions of the famous incident— the one which the Emperor's approval made official – as Mercury-Thoth, the personification of the atmosphere, by the Egyptian priest Arnuphis (hence the allusions to the two divinities on coins). Later on, however, the Christian tradition confused the two episodes, that of the lightning and that of the rain,

---

[1] *Alex. vel Pseudomantis,* 48.

because of the name of the XII *Fulminata* (this legion had not in fact moved from its station in Cappadocia, though it may have sent a *vexillatio* to the theatre of war), and attributed the credit for the celestial intervention to the Christians; with some foundation, for there must have been many of them in the army by now and they could certainly have raised their prayers to God at such a difficult moment. This was a story that the polemic against the pagan prejudice about the irreconcilability of Christianity with the empire could certainly not afford to leave unexploited. In any case, the soldier in the scene on the column who is raising his arm in prayer confirms the essential truth of a collective act of religious piety – however it was inspired – in detachments reduced to a critical pass; it was only natural that subsequently everyone should attribute the credit for the salvation to his own prayer. We know that, besides the Christians and the Egyptian thaumaturges, the Chaldean wise men, in the shape of Julian the Theurgist,[1] and even the genuine Roman religious tradition, which represented the 'old man of the rain' on the column as Jupiter, advanced the same claim.

These episodes, which can be placed in 172 or 173, are almost all we know about the operations. Official reflections in the coinage indicate victories: 'Germania subacta' appears in 172, possibly in allusion to the reduction of the Marcomanni and the pacification of a good part of Germany; the motif returns in 173 and is joined by that of 'Victoria Germanica', in evident allusion to more recent successes. Coins of 173 also celebrate the return of 'Securitas' and show the Emperor raising up again a turreted Italia. The epithet *Germanicus*, present in inscriptions from 172 onwards, and also assumed at that time by the eleven-year-old Commodus, appears at the end of 173 on sesterces, though in the dedication on the reverse, not in the official title. It does not appear in the official name until 175.

In the late summer of 173 the bulk of the operations against the Quadi must have been over, for Marcus was then at Sirmium and coins dating from the end of the year allude to the fact that only one wish remained to be fulfilled – the return of the Emperor to Rome. In fact Marcus was visited at Sirmium by a delegation from the Quadi, who asked for and obtained peace, which was still granted on the usual terms of clientage: the Quadi undertook to have no dealings with the Marcomanni or Iazyges, promised to return deserters and prisoners, and furnished horses and cattle; however, they were excluded from Roman markets for fear that Marcomanni and Iazyges might mingle with them to spy and

---

[1] SUD., s.v. *Arnuphis* and *Iulianos* (I, p. 365, II, p. 642, n. 434 ADLER).

make plans. Other tribes also came to ask for peace at the same time. But naturally it was not a definitive peace. These very circumstances throw some light on the strategic and diplomatic plan. It is clear that, although the Quadi and others had been reduced to order, a state of war still existed with the Marcomanni, as it did with the Iazyges – the two wings, now separated, of the grand coalition. Hostilities with the former must have been resumed very soon, and with the latter not much later. The actual details of this resumption of the war from 173 to 174 (which ruled out any possibility of returning to Rome) are not known.

If we recapitulate the interesting diplomatic activities which can be glimpsed at this point and the little that is known of the military operations, the following course of events can be reconstructed for the period between the autumn of 173 and the middle of 174. Counting on divisions among the Germans, Marcus tried to attack the Marcomanni in the rear by sending to the Cotini the able Tarrutenius Paternus, secretary *ab epistulis Latinis* and later praetorian prefect, a jurist who wrote on the art of war and military law. The manœuvre did not succeed, for the Cotini, at first persuaded, later made a swift *volte face* and Tarrutenius only just managed to escape. They were to pay for their perfidy later on, for they were annihilated as a tribe and survived only in the remnants moved inside the empire. The same method was applied simultaneously in other sectors. Battarius, the twelve-year-old chief of some tribe or other, offered his services to the Romans and, furnished by them with the means, helped to keep in check one Tarbus, another chief of an unnamed tribe, who had entered Dacia, likewise demanding help and supplies and threatening war if he did not obtain them. Another tribe that had arrived in Dacia was the Asdingi, a section of the great Vandal nation. They asked the Romans for land in return for alliance; they had their families and animals with them and were thus in the full process of migration. The governor, Cornelius Clemens, set them on the Costoboci, meanwhile protecting their families; but when they grew powerful with success and posed a graver threat to the province he had them attacked by another tribe, the Lacringi. This weakened them and they received money and land from Marcus, on condition that they continued to harry the barbarians with whom he was at war – a task which they carried out faithfully. Complete success against the Marcomanni must have been achieved quite soon, possibly in 173. Peace, which was requested by them, was granted on harsher conditions than those obtained some months earlier by the Quadi: besides being obliged to return prisoners and deserters and being banned from markets, they were required to hand over hostages;

in addition, on the far side of the Danube a strip of land ten miles wide had to be left empty. This strip was probably garrisoned by Roman units and may have represented the first stage in the implementation of a policy of direct annexation.

But now the Quadi rose again. They had not kept faith: during the war they had continued to harbour fugitive Marcomanni; they had not handed back all the prisoners, but only a few sick ones; if they gave back healthy men they kept their relatives, so that the former prisoners returned to them. This, together with the large figures for prisoners given by the sources, is an indication of the extent and gravity of the raids carried out during the big invasions of the provinces. They now drove out their philo-Roman king, Furtius, and chose instead a man called Ariogaesus, demanding that Marcus should recognize him. They also tightened their relations with the Iazyges. Marcus reacted promptly, but the situation in the early part of 174 was once again dangerous, and not only because of the return of the Quadi to the fray. The tribes of the hinterland – if it is to this moment that a number of disconnected reports refer – possibly despairing of finding any outlet in the direction of the Danube, where Marcus's policy had now succeeded in preventing the union of the barbarians, took other paths, towards the west. An incursion by the Chauci into Gallia Belgica was repulsed by the governor, Didius Julianus, the future emperor, and in Raetia Pertinax, now commander of a legion, was operating again, unless the report of this action – which can only be placed here in so far as it is said to have won him the consulship, which he held in 174 or 175 with Didius Julianus, rewarded for the same service – is a muddled re-telling of the operation carried out with Pompeianus in 171. However, the front facing the Quadi was the principal one, and it is typical of the general character of the struggle with the Germans that the Marcomanni, taking advantage of the Romans' difficulties, now sought to make capital out of their loyalty, which was however complete, by obtaining an improvement in the terms of the peace concluded a little earlier. And they did in fact secure the halving of the neutral zone along the frontier and permission to hold markets in stated places on stated days. With the Quadi Marcus was inflexible. When, reduced to difficult straits, they asked for the renewal of the treaty, promising to hand back 50,000 prisoners provided that they were allowed to keep Ariogaesus as their king, he responded, in spite of his usual mildness and generosity, by putting a price on Ariogaesus's head. At this point he also rejected an embassy from the Iazyges led by Banadaspus, one of their two kings. Marcus did not trust them; he had been deceived by the Quadi and henceforth he must have become more and more firmly convinced that only war *à outrance* and possibly, at a later stage, direct annexation, and the completion of the system of which Dacia had for some time been an isolated bastion, could finally resolve the Danubian problem. In the middle of 174 he must have gained the decisive victory over the Quadi for which he received his seventh salutation as *imperator*, and Faustina, who had joined him, possibly the year before, was acclaimed *mater castrorum*. Ariogaesus, who had been captured, was simply banished to Alexandria. The Quadi too had to leave a strip of land along the Danube empty and by way of a start on the policy of annexation they were forced to accept strong garrisons throughout their territory. These garrisons must have remained there permanently, for some years later it was they who stopped the mass departure of the population, which was tired of the strict Roman control.

Marcus now had his hands free to deal with the Iazyges. The details of this *bellum Sarmaticum* are not known either. It lasted from 174 to 175, but had effectively begun with the help given by the Iazyges to the rebellious Quadi. If the battle on the frozen river had belonged to this war, and hence to the winter of 174–175, it would have appeared on the column because of its picturesque aspects, which are also described at length by Cassius Dio (LXXI, 7, 2–5); it is therefore better to assign it, if only hypothetically, as we have done, to Claudius Fronto's operations and the winter of 170–171 – granted, of course, that the episodes on the column are only those of 172 to 175. However, things must have gone well for the Romans. But towards the beginning of May came the news of the rebellion of Avidius Cassius in the East. Marcus must have been worried about its possible repercussions in the army, tested as it was by the interminable war, but we possess no explicit evidence of disloyalty on the part of the commanders and troops of the Danubian army. On the contrary, the whole course of the war demonstrates discipline and attachment to the Princeps who, in spite of his very different tastes and physical frailty, was an example to everyone of military virtue and justice. He had in fact so won the hearts of the soldiers that he was able to refuse the donative after a victory, without provoking any unpleasant consequences, by saying that the money involved was sucked from the life blood of their parents and kinsmen. But the legends 'Fides exercituum' and 'Concordia exercituum' on coins of 171 may allude to some discontent even then, and even though his perseverance in fighting may have been admired and largely shared, there were also, according to the biographers, those who, either because they were dismayed by the losses in the ranks of the aristocracy or simply because they took a different political view, insistently repeated Lucius's demands: end the war and return to Rome. Thus the rhetorical speech which Marcus is made to deliver by Cassius Dio (LXXI, 24–6) may well conceal the fact that there was indeed opposition, now reinforced by the coup in the East.

It is certain that Marcus took energetic measures to deal with this. To make sure of Rome, he not only wrote to the Senate but also sent a force of *vexillationes* under the command of Vettius Sabinianus 'ad tutelam urbis',[1] probably to support the *praefectus urbi*. Egypt's support for the revolt might cut Rome's corn supply and that in itself could be expected to cause disturbances, apart from the possibility of the usurper's having supporters in the city, which was in fact suddenly seized with panic. Marcus summoned Commodus to his side, after having him admitted to all the priestly colleges, and on 7 July 175, in the camp, before the army, gave him the *toga virilis*. He also granted him, in the Augustan tradition, the old title for the heir presumptive, *princeps iuventutis*, with which he began to strike his own coins, and possibly designated him already for the consulship, which he subsequently held in 177. The sixth *congiarium*, distributed at Rome, probably in May by Commodus himself before he left, celebrated all these events. Meanwhile Marcus finished off the war with the Iazyges. The eighth salutation as *imperator* and the title *Sarmaticus*, assumed by him and his son in the summer of 175 – the title *Germanicus* had already reappeared officially in May – celebrated some decisive victory and the end of the war. The Iazyges, who the year before had imprisoned their king Banadaspus for favouring peace with the Romans, were now reduced to despair and begged for the terms granted to the Marcomanni and Quadi. Thanks to the disquieting situation in the East, they received them. They handed over a hundred thousand prisoners, and furnished 8000 cavalry, 5500 of whom Marcus immediately sent to Britain. The only difference was that for them the empty strip along the Danube was ten miles wide.

However, the great plan for direct annexation and the establishment of a Roman Marcomannia and Sarmatia had evaporated. The offensive had been conducted for years with great sagacity, as was demonstrated by the utilization of the discord among the Germans and the successful division of Rome's principal adversaries. Nor had Marcus failed to notice the far-ranging scope and causes of the great problem, namely the migration of the tribes and the hunger for land. This is clear from the attempts he made to settle some groups of barbarians in Dacia, Moesia, Pannonia, the Ger-

---

[1] *Ann. Ép.*, 1920, **45** = *Inscr. Lat. d'Afr.*, 281.

manies and even Italy, at Ravenna, where the experiment nearly ended in tragedy when the rough Marcomanni tried to make themselves masters of the city and were consequently driven out of it – episodes smacking already of another age. But for some time now the resources of the empire had been sufficient only for the task of defence and preservation.

CRISIS IN THE EAST AND THE LAST GERMAN WAR

While battles were being fought on the Danube the other frontiers had not by any means remained quiet. In the West the Moors, as a result of ferments and unrest in their own country – about which however we are not informed – crossed over into Spain, possibly more than once (171–173 and towards 176) and ran riot in Baetica, also pushing into Hispania Tarraconensis and Lusitania. Peace was restored by appropriate measures, including the transference of Baetica to the control of an imperial governor, C. Aufidius Victorinus – in other words, a man of the very first rank. However, the situation must have been serious, even though the scarcity of information does not allow us to form any precise idea of the course of events, particularly of what happened in Mauretania before, during and after the expedition to Spain. There may also have been some kind of disturbance in Britain at this time, to judge from a reference by the biographer, in the context – which can be related to 169/170 – of the start of the campaigns directed by Marcus on his own, and from the above-mentioned despatch to the island of 5500 of the 8000 cavalry furnished by the Iazyges in 175. The mysterious report, also in the biography, of restlessness among the Sequani in Gaul, settled without any military action, is only explicable as the echo of some internal discontent. The old plague of the ancient world, piracy, also raised its head again. It had disappeared for some time from the coasts of Italy and had been controlled in the more remote areas by ordinary measures, including the *praefecturae orae maritimae*, which were very well organized (that of Pontus Polemoniacus rendered indispensable services on the coast of the Black Sea during the Parthian war), but must have been aggravated by the general state of war. It was the same with brigandage. The need to send M. Valerius Maximianus, the courageous prefect decorated in the German war, 'in confinio Macedoniae et Thraciae' in 176 with a strong group of *vexillationes*, 'ad detrahendam Briseorum latronum manum',[1] may indicate the resurgence of old lairs, possibly encouraged by infiltrations from the far side of the Danube and by the remnants of raiding parties; the barbarians who crossed

[1] *Ann. Ép.*, 1956, 124.

the Danube were in fact called *latrones* and *latrunculi* and they carried out robberies in the provinces. And then in Gaul the war already favoured the formation of those groups of deserters of every kind, which in the reign of Commodus were to turn into real and extensive rebellions. All these things, though not of serious concern to the Roman organization's powers of repression, did not augur well.

Restlessness must have been chronic in the East. The special supreme command over all the eastern provinces entrusted to Avidius Cassius, who even before may have been something more than merely governor of Syria, probably came into effect immediately after the Parthian war; no doubt it was demanded by the situation. Operations to restore client conditions in states like Osrhoene, carried out no doubt as a consequence of the humiliation of the Parthians, were probably the cause of the rising by the people of Edessa, who drove out the king, Wael, set up by Vologaeses, and took back their legitimate king, Manu (Mannos) VIII Philoromaios, who was certainly on the throne in 167. However, the proximity of Carrhae, organized as a Roman city and garrisoned, kept the autonomy of Edessa under closer control than before. In Armenia, in spite of the presence of the Roman garrison, Sohaemus, the king established in 167, was actually expelled, and the governor of Cappadocia, Martius Verus, had to put him back on the throne towards 172. In Egypt round about the same time Avidius Cassius took action personally to free the delta from the guerilla warfare being waged by the shepherd-brigands, the people known as the *Bucoli*, who were putting pressure on Alexandria itself. It is quite possible that the big movements of tribes in eastern central Europe and round the Black Sea also threatened the East, even – as some evidence seems to indicate – with attacks by sea to the detriment of Asia Minor; but no specific details are known.

However, the greatest danger came from the most unexpected quarter. In April 175 Avidius Cassius proclaimed himself Augustus, and the provinces from Syria to Egypt, whose favour he had won, rapidly declared their support for him, as we know from the dates of a number of Egyptian documents. In Egypt the fairly efficient administrative machine evidently soon followed the example of the prefect, C. Calvisius Statianus, who was among the first to join the usurper. The latter also appointed a praetorian prefect, but the rebellion halted at the borders of Cappadocia; Martius Verus, who may still have been governor in the early months of 175, sent the official news of the rebellion to Marcus Aurelius on the Danube. What induced the powerful Avidius Cassius, undoubtedly a man of considerable administrative skill and, until the moment of the revolt, loyal and friendly to Marcus, to carry out an act so serious and far-reaching, we do not know for certain. There is no dearth of suggestions, but they are all clearly influenced by various interests: that of making the rebellion seem the result of a series of deplorable misunderstandings; the more general one forming part of the series of anecdotes and moralizations peculiar to the tradition on the philosopher-emperor; and finally the one connected with the gossip that always surrounded Faustina, who is directly implicated on this occasion too. According to this story it was from Faustina that the initiative came: fearing that Marcus would not live much longer and that, once he was dead, Commodus still being very young, the empire would pass into other hands, with a consequent loss of status for herself, she came to an agreement with Avidius Cassius, promising him her own hand and the throne as soon as Marcus disappeared from the scene. False news of this event, so the story goes on, led the hasty governor to take action without waiting for confirmation. The man whom he thought to succeed having been proclaimed *Divus* and the rumour spreading that the legions of Pannonia had proclaimed him, Cassius, emperor, he took appropriate steps to make sure of the succession; when the truth came out he was either unable or unwilling to turn back. We certainly do not need the imaginary correspondence between Marcus and Faustina inserted by the biographer in the life of Avidius Cassius to demonstrate the implausibility of this story. Since 173 Faustina had been on the Danube with her consort, next door to the headquarters frequented by the top-ranking generals, among whom she could easily have found a remedy for her possible worries without seeking one at the other end of the empire. The other version preserved by the biographer, in the section of the *Life* (6,5–9,5) drawn directly from Marius Maximus, sounds more likely: this is that the news of Marcus's death was disseminated deliberately by Cassius himself to eliminate the obstacle of the army's loyalty. Probably it was simply ambition inflamed by a long-lasting and vast command that pushed him into this false step. According to the anecdotal tradition already mentioned,[1] Herodes Atticus wrote him a letter containing one single phrase, 'You are mad'.

Local circumstances that would explain his short-lived success indubitably existed, but we are not informed about them; nor are we aware of any distant support in the way of discontent caused either by the policy of hard work imposed by Marcus or by aspects of his personality. In any case, the measures that Marcus ordered to be taken in Rome blocked any dangerous developments. The fact that the Senate declared Cassius a

[1] PHILOSTR., *Vit. Soph.*, II, 1, 13 (II, p. 70 KAYSER).

public enemy on its own initiative and decreed that his property should be confiscated even before the Emperor moved from the Danube shows quite clearly what the outcome of the coming duel seemed likely to be. When, towards the end of July 175, Marcus set off for the East, accompanied by Faustina and Commodus, he was very soon met by the news of the death of Cassius, killed by his own soldiers, who in repentance now sent the usurper's head to the legitimate Princeps. In the subsequent events, obviously elaborated in the tradition by the dominant motif of clemency, we can only distinguish a number of episodes, in which the part played by Marcus is not always certain. In the East the loyalist revival certainly led to further steps after the suppression of the leader of the rebellion, and these will have included the killing of the unknown praetorian prefect and of Cassius's son, Maecianus. But those who managed to survive the immediate reaction were indubitably treated with generosity. Marcus had in fact continued his journey, as was natural after what had happened, with the object of seeing personally to the pacification, and he had a strong body of troops with him. The barbarians themselves had offered assistance. The literary sources say it was refused because it was not right that they should see fighting between Romans,[1] but the evidence of the inscription of Valerius Maximianus, 'praepositus equitibus gentium Marcomannorum Naristarum Quadorum ad vindictam orientalis motus pergentium',[2] inclines us to the view that it was accepted, in the usual form of contingents levied in the client states. Marcus began by arranging for the burial of Cassius's head, which he did not even want to see. On reaching the rebellious provinces he carried out his investigations with energy and moderation. Burning all the correspondence without reading it (Martius Verus had assumed the responsibility of doing likewise while Cassius was still alive), he simply exiled another of the usurper's sons, Heliodorus, and, more surprisingly, the prefect of Egypt, Calvisius Statianus; other members of the family suffered no harm, except possibly later under Commodus. There were some death sentences in the army. The legal records also tell us, in partial contrast with the reports of extraordinary clemency in the literary sources, that the confiscations stipulated by the law on treason were diligently carried out. But well aware of the dangers involved in cases of this sort when they were abandoned to the course of senatorial justice alone, Marcus, while respecting the competence of the Senate, fixed limits to the enquiries into Cassius's accomplices. By expressing the wish that, just as he had not put any senator to death on his own initiative, so his reign should not have to record the condemnation of any senator by the Senate itself, he

---

[1] CASS. D., LXXI, 27, 1a.   [2] *Ann. Ép.*, 1956, 124.

effectively removed the possibility of any death sentences. On the other hand he must have rewarded the legions that had remained loyal, as is clear from the titles *Certa Constans* which the XII *Fulminata* bore in the last few years of his reign. He was not tender with the seditious cities of Antioch and Alexandria, which had supported the *coup* and which displayed regret even after it had failed, as is proved by the light erasures in the inscriptions; he also laid down that in future no one should govern his own native province (Avidius Cassius, son of Heliodorus, the rhetorician friend of Hadrian and prefect of Egypt, came from Cyrrhus in Syria).

When the situation had been restored and the command of Syria probably entrusted to Martius Verus, who was certainly governing it in 177, Marcus took advantage of his own presence in the East to receive delegations from the Parthians. He was also able to satisfy his own cultural tastes. He left 'vestigia philosophiae' at Alexandria, where he probably spent the winter of 175–176, and also in other places. It is legitimate to suppose that on this occasion the efflorescence, recorded by the sources, of flatterers turned philosophers out of expediency reached record levels. Then in the spring of 176 he proceeded to Antioch, which he had avoided at first, at any rate so far as an official visit was concerned, and from there set out to make the return journey by land across Asia Minor. He entered Cilicia from the Taurus and at the little town of Halala, which subsequently became a colony and was called Faustinopolis, he lost Faustina. Marcus did splendid honour to her memory, already the subject of discussion in contemporary society, which probably took pleasure in exaggerating the contrast between the Augusta's devotion to the sumptuous and – in many respects – free and easy social life of the upper classes (the circles frequented by Verus and Commodus) and the austerity practised by her consort. Many malicious stories were invented; how little truth they probably contained is shown sufficiently clearly by the respectful and affectionate words dedicated by Marcus to a companion who, after presenting him with seven or eight children before the beginning of the reign, had given birth to nearly another half-dozen after his accession to the throne: 'Such a fine woman, so obedient, so loving, so simple!'.[1] The honours requested from the Senate – and granted – were deification, amply commemorated in the coinage with a special mystical emphasis ('sideribus recepta') no doubt suggested by Marcus, and the erection of statues in the Temple of Venus and Rome and in the theatres. On her altars too, as on those of Faustina the Elder, young couples about to marry made offerings. A new alimentary institution, known as the

[1] M. AUR., *Comment.*, I, 17, 18.

puellae novae Faustinianae, was added to the one that already bore her mother's name. A temple was built at the spot where she died. Ceionia Fabia, Verus's sister, the bride once intended by Hadrian for Marcus, now put herself forward, but in vain. Marcus said that he did not want to give his children a stepmother and, imitating Vespasian, lived with the daughter of one of Faustina's procurators.

Some details of the return journey are known, such as the stays at Ephesus, Smyrna, where Marcus met Aelius Aristides, and Athens, where he was initiated into the Eleusinian mysteries. He made the crossing to Brundisium in the late autumn, risking shipwreck. Having left Rome in the autumn of 169 he set eyes on it again in the eighth year after his departure, and the populace, with eight fingers raised, demanded and obtained a *congiarium* in the measure he had promised in a speech: an aureus for every year of his absence. It was the seventh *congiarium*, of 800 sesterces – eight aurei – per head; it was commemorated in the coinage of 177, very probably because it was distributed on the occasion of Commodus's assumption of the consulship. However, before the end of 176, possibly on 27 November, he celebrated with great splendour the triumph *de Germanis* and *de Sarmatis* and gave the title of *imperator* to Commodus, who on 23 December celebrated in his turn the same triumph as his father. On 1 January 177 the fifteen-year-old boy was consul and during the course of that year the titles *Augustus* and *pater patriae* appeared, while his *tribunicia potestas*, even if only conferred in 177, was subsequently reckoned from November 176. Once again there was a co-ruler with equal status, *Imperator Caesar L. Aurelius Commodus Augustus Germanicus Sarmaticus*, and a double principate. On coins issued at the time of the triumph the motif of 'Pax aeterna' underlined the idea of the end of war all over the world; once again, however, the celebration was premature.

The 'eternal peace' was in fact broken in 177, for coins dating from the end of that year commemorate the ninth salutation of Marcus, and Commodus's second, for some victory won by the legions in a campaign the details of which are not known. Since Cassius Dio speaks of Scythians, one would be inclined to think that the new war was caused by the Iazyges; the biographer's reference to Marcomanni, Hermunduri, Sarmati and Quadi may refer to the subsequent general development of the war after the Augusti had intervened. In any case, a victory was won in 177, apparently by the Quintilii, either by the two brothers Condianus and Maximus, who had in a curious fashion traversed the senatorial career together and may now have held some special command in the region newly pacified, or else by their respective sons, Maximus, who had been consul in 172, and Condianus, who was to hold this office in 180. In the latter case there may well be substance in the hypothesis that the former was consular governor of Upper Pannonia and the latter praetorian governor of Lower Pannonia. However, it seemed to Marcus that the situation once more required his own presence. On 3 August 178, after hastening Commodus's marriage to Crispina, daughter of his friend, the illustrious ex-consul C. Bruttius Praesens, after formally asking the Senate, out of constitutional scruples, for funds for the war, and after pushing religious scruples to the point of carrying out, to declare war, the ancient rite of the spear kept in the temple of Bellona – as Cassius Dio says he heard from eye witnesses – he set out with his son.

All we know about the course of the campaign is that a great victory was gained in 179 – we do not know where or against which of the tribes involved in the war – by Tarrutenius Paternus, now prefect of the praetorian guard. This secured Marcus his tenth and last salutation as *imperator* and Commodus his third. In the winter of 179–180 M. Valerius Maximianus, the Pannonian knight raised to senatorial rank on the field of battle by the Augusti and appointed commander of a legion, was already encamped with a group of *vexillationes* at Laugaricium (Trencin, on the course of the Vah), seventy-five miles north of the Danube. Apart from this detail there are only reports of negotiations with various peoples. Even the coins of these years are a good deal poorer in allusions to current events than in the previous wars. However, it seems that Marcus's intention to annex the lands in which he had already left a total of 45,000 men on garrison duty in 175 and to form the provinces of Marcomannia and Sarmatia was now clear and declared; the sources are explicit on this point, denouncing at the same time the fate that prevented the execution of the plan. What we know of the diplomatic activity going on at the time certainly looks like a prelude to this solution, at any rate for Marcomannia. The terms imposed on the Iazyges were made milder, with the object of detaching them from the coalition; they were given permission to come to markets, though the veto on having boats on the river and occupying the islands remained in force, and they were allowed to cross Dacia, on the governor's authorization, to communicate with the Roxolani. The plan was so successful that the Iazyges themselves, and with them the Buri, asked that the war against the Marcomanni and the Quadi, their uncomfortable neighbours, should be continued until they were annihilated. Marcus did in fact prevent an attempt at migration by the Quadi and shut them in an iron vice. Three thousand Naristae extracted themselves from the no doubt oppressive control of the Marcomanni and were received in the empire. With the war going so favourably Marcus found himself in a position to dictate laws on the far side of the Danube and to establish the varying conditions of subjection. Only the last step remained to be taken, but on 17 March 180 he died in the camp at Vindobona, possibly of the plague, though there was also a rumour, heard personally by Cassius Dio, that the end had been hastened by doctors anxious to do Commodus a favour.

Thus once again the fruits of these arduous labours escaped just as they were on the point of being gathered in, for Marcus's successor did not think fit to take the last step. Of the two alternative solutions to the frontier problem, clientage and direct rule, solutions that had been open since the time of Augustus, and even under Marcus had certainly given rise to contrary views and provoked varying and equally well-based preferences (we have only to remember Verus's policy), Commodus chose the first. If subsequent events to a certain extent justified his decision, since for many long years these peoples remained quiet even as clients, the credit for this was due to the tenacious work of Marcus, who had contained the first wave of the great migrations by exhausting its offensive power and by curbing its most perceptible results on the frontier. He had thus made possible a provisional settlement and re-established the security of the empire.

THE WORK OF GOVERNMENT

Marcus Aurelius's rule showed no trace of the abstract approach that vulgar opinion might ascribe to the activity of a devotee of philosophy, and it made no concessions to utopianism. It followed the tradition of the Princeps's task inaugurated by Trajan and, as for principles, it abided by the usual concrete attitude, fitting measures to the needs always indicated in good time and in detail by the organs of a vigilant paternalism. Thus it accorded easily with the practical humanitarianism of Roman Stoicism. The education given to Marcus in his youth was the wide and varied one appropriate to the cultural atmosphere of Hadrian's reign; and in a nature splendidly endowed with intellectual and moral qualities it had flowered in maturity in an exceptionally well-balanced character. His earliest studies had been devoted to rhetoric and philosophy. The sources record the names of the teachers to whom the scion of the Annii, possibly the richest family of the time, and the favourite of Hadrian had been entrusted: first came the *litterator* Euphorion, who taught him the *prima elementa*, the *comoedus* Geminus and the *musicus et geometra* Andro; then came the throng of grammarians – the famous Alexander of Cotieum for Greek, Trosius Aper, Pollio and Eutychius Proculus of Sicca for Latin – and rhetoricians – Aninius Macer, Caninius Celer, Herodes Atticus for Greek eloquence and the great Cornelius Fronto for Latin oratory. The same sources underline the love and reverence felt by the young disciple for these teachers, who were in fact the fine flower of official culture and instruction. Drawn above all to philosophy, Marcus had in the end devoted himself exclusively to this, but had turned, for practical reasons, to the study of rhetoric when collaboration with Antoninus had brought him into contact with public duties. At this time he also sought the assistance in legal studies – just as indispensable for the business of governing – of the jurist Volusius Maecianus, who subsequently remained one of his principal advisers.

But philosophy was his way of life. The Stoic Apollonius of Chalcedon, the Platonist Alexander and the Peripatetic Claudius Severus had introduced him to the various schools, until finally the influence mainly of the Roman Stoic Q. Junius Rusticus, twice consul and later *praefectus urbi*, and probably a descendant of the Stoic martyr of the same name under Domitian, by revealing to him the teaching of Epictetus, converted him decisively to Stoicism, whose exponents he listened to and honoured with special attention, particularly Sextus of Chaeronea, Cinna Catulus and Claudius Maximus. But the completeness of his education (he was also interested in painting, and, like Hadrian, he did not neglect the physical exercises – wrestling, running, hunting), the strength of the genuine Roman tradition and his own personal intelligence not only made him keep a sense of proportion in everything but also gave him the capacity to estimate degrees of usefulness and to distinguish the reality from the utopia; what we have said about the succession of his interests in education and even more what he wrote himself in the first book of the *Meditations* illustrate this point sufficiently well. Thus philosophy, which made him 'serium et gravem' without robbing him of his natural 'comitas' and created privately, in the person of the man who was 'frugi sine contumacia, verecundus sine ignavia, sine tristitia gravis',[1] one of the most admirable human types, did not damage but rather completed the public figure who, though devoted to his favourite study even after he ascended the throne and by no means disdainful of the advice of philosophers, nevertheless avoided an ostentatiously doctrinaire attitude, directing affairs in the most practical manner without letting it be noticed that his activity was all of a piece with his highly tensed nature.

[1] *V. Marc.*, 4, 10.

The core of political life under the principate, namely harmony between the Princeps and the Senate, remained firmly based on the Augustan and Trajanic formula of the despot's formal deference to the republic, cemented even now by the cordiality of his personal relations with the aristocracy and by the loyal collaboration of the latter in the work of the Princeps. The external manifestations of this mutually cordial understanding were the usual ones: assiduous attendance of the Senate's sessions by the Princeps, who would even travel expressly for this purpose from Campania; agreed freedom of discussion in these sittings; participation in the meetings for the election of magistrates, at which even the Princeps awaited the signal of the presiding consul before departing; and personal honours paid on his own initiative, such as that of statues in Trajan's forum to senators who had fallen on the battlefield or died of the plague. Marcus also repeated the guarantee that no senator should be sentenced to death, confirmed that the Senate alone could exercise jurisdiction over senators and supported the failing fortunes of some families with generous subventions. All this was the continuation of an attitude now traditional. Another detail modelled on the example of the best emperors was his habit of affability, of modesty and of tolerance of free speech, a habit that masked the real omnipotence of the despot and made him seem a citizen like the rest in a free city. However, this habit did in fact clash with the tendency, revealed among other things by a resurgence in the power of the palace freedmen, to live a splendid, isolated court life; this was a tendency exemplified by Verus (and probably by the imperial ladies) and it was to triumph with Commodus. In short, Marcus remained faithful to the best traditions of the principate, and the credit for thus resisting current fashion was also due to his personal self-denial.

However, his conduct was not weak: new senators who entered the Curia, even those of provincial origin, were men of proved loyalty, chosen by him, and his own real power was solid enough to enable him even to increase the effective powers of the Senate, particularly in the field of legal jurisdiction, without any risk of misunderstandings. Thus even if other emperors had already welcomed among their *amici* and *comites* the most illustrious members of the aristocracy, constantly consulted the Senate or its most authoritative members, made ample use of legislation through *senatusconsulta* and wished the Senate to declare war and ratify peace, Marcus was the first to give definitive form to its judicial competence, as a sort of court of appeal in comparison with the consular jurisdiction, and he sometimes entrusted to it even *cognitiones* that were his own concern. To individual senators, too, both consulars and prae-

torians, he delegated tasks of jurisdiction and entrusted new departments
of work, notwithstanding the preponderant tendency in the development
of the imperial administration, namely the increase of equestrian posts.
Now that those who followed the senatorial career were predominantly
just as much officials as those who followed the equestrian career, there
was no need to fear dangerous independence. In 163 or 164 the *iudices*
posted by Hadrian in various parts of Italy reappeared; they were now
called *iuridici*, were no longer ex-consuls but ex-praetors, and were
possibly more than four in number. The establishment of a central
praefectus alimentorum of consular rank at the head of the whole system of
alimenta functioning in Italy does not seem to be sufficiently well
proved, but the responsibility of individual senators grew with the
appointment of the *praetor tutelaris* and with the despatch to cities rather
more frequently than before of *curatores* of senatorial rank. The *curatores
viarum* supervised the officials in charge of customs duties and tolls, and
the jurisdiction of the *praefectus urbi*, though not yet defined with the
detailed precision applied by Septimius Severus, must nevertheless have
functioned with some independence if, as would appear from a not very
clear report in the biographer, the Emperor confined himself to regretting
the sentences of exile pronounced by the prefect and took no further
action.

The equestrian hierarchy was not left behind in the general expansion of
the civil service. The famous letter from the praetorian prefects Bassaeus
Rufus and Macrinius Vindex to the magistrates of Saepinium, a letter
dating from 168 or 169,[1] shows that the spheres of competence of these
prefects now included the maintenance of order in Italy, with the
relevant powers of coercion and jurisdiction. The *a rationibus* increased
in importance. He began to call himself the *rationalis* as well and became,
in terms of salary, the first and as yet the only *trecenarius*, as supreme head
of the whole financial administration; directly dependent on him, in the
grade of *ducenarius*, was the *procurator summarum rationum* – a new post –
in charge of the fiscal administration. The same tendency to create
assistants and subalterns is evident in the appearance of a *subpraefectus
annonae* by the side of the prefect, while the tendency to introduce territorial division of posts and fields of competence produced the four
procurators of the *alimenta*, in charge of specified districts of Italy. With
the institution of new procuratorial posts in the *centenarius* and *sexagenarius*
grades both at Rome (a particularly interesting post here is that of secretary
to the praetorian prefecture) and in the provinces, the total number of

[1] *CIL*, IX, 2438.

procurators rose to 124, some twenty more than in the Hadrianic establishment, which had remained unchanged under Antoninus. The very attempt to perfect the administration, with the resultant increase in interference in local affairs, led to an extension of the number of posts and hence to the danger of bureaucratization, but Marcus still managed to keep this danger at bay by his personal supervision of everything.

The social classes were preserved on traditional lines by the strength of his rigorous conservatism. He did not close the Senate to men of merit: the splendid rise of the future emperor Pertinax, a Ligurian of low birth who reached the consulship in 175, caused more surprise to others than to him. Avidius Cassius and Claudius Pompeianus, who became the Emperor's son-in-law, were of Eastern origin; Antistius Burrus, consul in 181 and also married to a daughter of Marcus (Vibia Aurelia Sabina), came from an African family of not very ancient lineage, and of the other three sons-in-law – Cn. Claudius Severus, husband of Anna Galeria Aurelia Faustina and consul for the second time in 173, M. Peducaeus Plautius Quintillus, son of Verus's sister Ceionia Fabia, very probably husband of Fadilla and consul in 177, and M. Petronius Sura Mamertinus, husband of Cornificia and consul in 182 – only the first two belonged to families long illustrious; that of the third had only reached senatorial status in the person of the father, Petronius Mamertinus, Antoninus Pius's praetorian prefect, who had been awarded the consular ornaments by Antoninus and had been *consul suffectus* in 150. Entry to the equestrian class was also easy for men who had served in the army and for the wealthiest and most cultured provincials, and in the equestrian career, too, men of merit could rise to the highest posts. A good example is the characteristic figure of M. Bassaeus Rufus, a poor and rough man of low birth who became praetorian prefect and was honoured after his death in about 177 by three statues erected by Marcus and Commodus. The same honour was paid to the valiant Macrinius Vindex, a man of much the same origins and qualities who fell in battle in 171. To these examples can be added the splendid careers of the African Tib. Claudius Proculus Cornelianus, a man who has come to our notice recently,[1] and particularly of the oft-mentioned M. Valerius Maximianus, a Pannonian who reached senatorial rank.

In this exploitation of all the talent available Marcus continued the enlightened work of his predecessors; if it was a spontaneous phenomenon he did not oppose it. But while recognizing the merits of individual men, he was even more anxious than they to fix and maintain the barriers between

[1] *Ann. Ép.*, 1956, 123.

the classes and to protect their prestige. For example, he was unwilling to appoint senators to the prefecture of the praetorian guard, a post reserved exclusively for knights; senators could not marry or live with a woman who had been convicted; and marriage between ladies of senatorial families and freedmen was absolutely ruled out. Differences in punishments according to class were further elaborated and the use of honorific titles – *clarissimus* for senators and their families, *eminentissimus*, *perfectissimus*, *egregius* for knights, in accordance with a precise scale – now became normal, thus giving an official outward vesture to social differences as well as to the sense of hierarchy. There was also a revival of Trajan's directive, dictated by the traditionalist spirit, that provincial senators should invest part of their wealth in Italian land – a third originally, now only a quarter; the number of non-Italian senators had evidently increased and the availability of land in Italy had decreased. Subsidies and other measures in favour of property were largely directed to the social aim of preserving the census of the aristocracy and with it the existing order. To this and to the general welfare of the society of the empire, even at a low level and in the peripheral areas, Marcus devoted much attention. Grants of citizenship, now set in motion almost automatically, particularly by the machinery of military discharges and municipal offices, went on without any innovation attributable to his individual views. But we must suppose that the phenomenon was now one of such imposing dimensions as partly to escape official control and to create a situation of doubt and confusion, in both good and bad faith, in the checking of the possession of Roman citizenship, with serious consequences in the field of private law. Little more than a generation later the problem was to receive a radical solution by the admission to the *civitas* of all *peregrini* not *dediticii*. Marcus, on the other hand, with his traditional conservatism, sought for the last time to strengthen the dividing wall between citizens and non-citizens by making obligatory throughout the empire the declaration of birth within thirty days already required in Egypt and Africa. At Rome this declaration was made to the *praefecti aerarii Saturni*. And the distinction between the free-born, freedmen and slaves remained clearer than ever. Once he had satisfied – with the scrupulosity which he said he had learnt from his adoptive father – the need to preserve the social order, he could be, like his father, mild and humane in the actual business of government.

The characteristics of Marcus's rule were in fact energy, pertinacity and inflexibility of principle combined with generosity, humanity and understanding in his concrete relations with men. As for the finances, there is no evidence that the system of tribute was relaxed at all; the charge of miserliness levelled at Marcus, as it had been at Vespasian, would rather lead us to think the opposite. Care that unjust exactions should not occur and moderation in cases between the treasury and private individuals had already been recommended by his predecessors, with no detriment to the interests of the state. Indeed, Marcus improved the customs system still further: the five pillars known among the many put up at the gates of Rome between 177 and 180, with the text of a decree[1] establishing the line for the collection of the excise duty – the object being to avoid disputes between merchants and collectors – testify to his concern for the finances as well as to his concern for justice. He also improved the organization of the *vicesima hereditatium*, laid down strict criteria in the matter of collection, exercised tighter control, with the increase in numbers and importance of the *curatores*, of the local finances of cities, and in the field of expenditure was on principle careful and sober, showing particular respect for public money. If his request to the Senate for authorization to use funds from the *aerarium* for the second German war and his declaration about the ownership of the public finances, which ought, he said, to belong to the Senate and people – two details recorded with satisfaction by the senatorial tradition – were the result of his customary concern for formal precision, the restrictions on court ceremonial, the reduction in building activity and the limitation of expenditure on shows were all substantial facts.

The very numerous monuments and buildings of the epoch scattered all over the empire, particularly in Africa, which now attained the greatest prosperity, were almost all expressions of local munificence. In Rome, apart from restorations, new public works were few in number: a column of red granite on a base of sculptured marble and topped by a statue of Antoninus Pius, erected by Marcus and Lucius in the Campus Martius, near the *Ustrinum Antoninorum*, in memory of their deified father; a temple of Jupiter Heliopolitanus dedicated in 176 on the Janiculum; possibly a shrine to *Indulgentia* on the Capitol, which was also the site of the triumphal arch erected by senatorial decree and adorned with reliefs, some of which finished up on the arch of Constantine; and finally the great column commemorating the German and Sarmatian wars, started in 176 and only finished, it seems, in 193. Records of works of public utility (aqueducts, roads) are even less numerous: pillars from the Tiber testify to the continuation in 161 of the new boundary begun by Antoninus and even the milestones only show the attentive execution of ordinary main-

[1] *ILS* 375;, cf. RICCOBONO, *Leges*[2], p. 437.

tenance. Examples of this are the repairs made in 163 to the roads 'per fines Ceutronum vi torrentium eversas'[1] in Narbonese Gaul, and the improvements effected, in connection with the war in the East, to the road network of Syria and Palestine, near Jerusalem (A.D. 162) and in the Anti-Lebanon.[2] The great labours of the preceding reigns and the excellent state of repair prevailing no doubt lightened expenditure in this department. There was intense activity on military installations – attention was given to camps and fortifications, and city walls were either strengthened or built from scratch, especially in the Balkan provinces; but all this was closely connected with the external threat. As for games and shows, although Marcus did not like them he could certainly not think of abolishing them; he himself gave them on a splendid scale – he managed to present a *venatio* with a hundred lions – and during his absence at the wars he ensured that the richest aristocrats kept the urban populace amused. But he tried to restrict expenditure on the theatre and the arena, and one of the most interesting epigraphical documents that have come down to us from his reign, a document which is also important for what it tells us about the procedure in senatorial debates in the imperial age, refers to this praiseworthy aim. This is the 'senatusconsultum de sumptibus ludorum gladiatorum minuendis', which is preserved on a bronze table from Italica in Spain and a marble fragment from Sardis in Asia.[3]

So Marcus did not spend haphazardly but always with the justification of necessity. And until 169 he no doubt had to take account of the somewhat different notions of Lucius. But even the ordinary, essential expenses were big; and they had a fatal tendency to increase and to weigh more and more heavily, by the logic of paternalism, on the centre. Wars, disasters (plagues, famines, earthquakes in the East, floods at Rome at the beginning of the reign) all required action and expenditure. Concern for a good reputation, about which Marcus was very sensitive, like all those who try to be models of virtue, also forced him to be liberal. The populace could no longer be denied *congiaria*, and generous ones at that; and the maintenance of the corn supply, an increase – granted on the occasion of Lucilla's betrothal to Verus – in the numbers of those entitled to free corn, gifts of food and money to Italian cities smitten by misfortunes, subventions and exemptions from tribute for provincial cities (Smyrna, destroyed by an earthquake in 176, Nicomedia, Ephesus, Antioch and Carthage are mentioned in this connection), the greater cost of the regular salaries for the teachers

[1] *ILS*, 5868.   [2] *ILS*, 5841, 5864.
[3] *ILS*, 5163, 9340; cf. J. H. OLIVER and R. E. A. PALMER, in *Hesperia*, XXIV, 1955, pp. 320–49.

at the four big Athenian schools, the innumerable subsidies, and on the other hand the drop in income caused by the remission of taxes (including the *vectigal gladiatorum*, which brought in twenty or thirty million sesterces a year but was rejected as 'blood money'), by the moderation imposed on the fisc, and finally by the big cancellation in 178 of arrears of debt to the fisc and treasury (a practice started by Hadrian), all doubtless helped to make the financial situation worse. This was reflected in the gold and silver coinage, in which the deterioration that had already set in became more marked, and even in the bronze coinage, for the orichalc of the sestertii and dupondii could scarcely be distinguished any longer from copper. But to saddle Marcus with the blame for this we should have to be able to demonstrate quite clearly that the above-mentioned displays of generosity could have been avoided and that he could have controlled and guided differently the economic development of his age. He must rather be given the credit for shouldering part of the expenses himself and relieving the state finances when, in 169, convinced of the duty incumbent on the Princeps to pay in person, he auctioned the precious objects in the palace to meet the cost of the war.

He showed the same care for both theoretical order and the concrete needs of individuals in his administration of the provinces and in the command of the armies, which last, though not desired, was the preponderant occupation of his life as emperor. Modifications in the organization of the provinces were made in accordance with the needs already mentioned in the account of the wars. Lower Pannonia was given a consular governor; Dacia was re-united, also under an ex-consul; and Noricum and Raetia, having acquired a permanent legionary garrison, were given praetorian governors instead of procurators. In the more strictly financial field, at the beginning of the reign – as we have learned recently[1] – the 'sexagenarii' posts of *procurator argentariarum Pannoniarum* and *procurator argentariarum Delmaticarum* were combined under one single *procurator centenarius*. So much for the Danube, where the big combined command of several provinces and *vice versa* the creation of many special commands of small units for tactical purposes displayed swift adaptation to circumstances. The same flexibility is revealed, in other parts of the empire, by the transference of Baetica – Sardinia, at that time under a procurator, being given to the Senate in exchange – from senatorial to imperial rule for the Moorish invasion, by the big command of Avidius Cassius in the East and, after his fall, by the veto on the holding of commands in one's native country. For unknown reasons Bithynia, long used to alternating

[1] *Ann. Ép.*, 1956, 123.

between proconsuls and imperial governors, became at the beginning of the reign an imperial province again and remained such, this time without any compensation for the Senate, since Lycia-Pamphylia too, which under Hadrian had served as a replacement and had become imperial under Antoninus with the return of Bithynia to the Senate, remained an imperial province for the whole reign and possibly for the first few years of Commodus's reign as well.

As for local life, which in some areas was not as flourishing and secure as it had been earlier and was tested everywhere by the plague and by the burden of recruitment (in Spain there is explicit evidence of action to assist the population possessing Italian rights, which was exhausted by levies), Marcus certainly paid no less attention than his predecessors to it. This is attested by the numerous texts that have come down to us of measures dealing with the duties and rights of the people in local communities (immunities, honours) and also, as the expression of gratitude for more tangible benefits, by the very large number of dedications to him and to members of his family and by the monuments raised in his honour, particularly in the cities of Asia and Africa. Less reliable evidence is provided by the titles *Aurelia* and *Aurelium* of colonies and municipalities, titles which are particularly common in Africa (Mactaris, Carthage, Pupput, Thuburbo Maius, Segermes, municipium Furnitanum minus); this is because it is not easy to distinguish Marcus's interventions from those of other emperors with the same name, especially Aurelius Antoninus Caracalla. Accounts of direct contacts with the provincials, such as that of his stay at Ephesus in 176, when, returning from the East, Marcus was detained by the dedication of a monument to him, Diva Faustina and his children, or that of the meeting, at Smyrna in the same year, with the rhetorician Aelius Aristides, who touched his heart two years later when he wrote to the Emperor about the disastrous earthquake, refer only to isolated episodes, but good government and general attention to the raising of standards of civilization must have been a reality in the provinces: 'provincias . . . ingenti moderatione ac benignitate tractavit' (*V. Marc.*, 17, 1).

As a result of this uniform care the gap between Italy and the provinces must have been narrowed still further. In Italy Marcus wore the toga and made the troops wear it; but the very ostentation of the act showed that it was simply a piece of theoretical homage. A new factor in the life of the provinces was the one introduced by the moving of outside tribes into the empire; but the not very detached accounts provided by the sources do not allow us to estimate its extent or importance. Probably it was a sporadic and limited business. For some time past notable foreigners had received personal permission to reside in the empire, and sometimes they had been positively forced to do so to keep them out of mischief. Now large groups of barbarians were admitted to the provinces on the Danube frontier, with the object, say the sources, of providing agricultural labour for the deserted countryside – in other words, as a sort of reparation arranged by a provident Princeps for the sorely-tried provincials. These men will thus have been tenants – free, but tied to the big estates – and they will have provided forces for the army. The phenomenon must have possessed at that moment the significance of a prelude. The walls of the civilized world were beginning to be overtopped and submerged by the first wave of a vaster process of levelling.

It is surprising to note the scanty contribution made to the administration of justice and legislative activity by the specific doctrines privately professed by Marcus. A sense of duty and a scrupulous concern for precision were common to all his activity, and the humanitarian spirit had been informing jurisdiction and legislation as a matter of policy since the time of Trajan. But in practice there was no substantial injection of new ideas: 'ius autem magis vetus restituit quam novum fecit', says the biographer, and this expresses precisely what happened. Here, too, Marcus was a genuine Roman traditionalist and, as in his attitude to religion, revealed that apparent divergence between his own personal spiritual life and his outward conduct which can perhaps only be explained and reconciled by assigning to the Stoicism he practised the exclusive value of a norm for modes of action, not for principles, which remained those of the consciences of people at large.

We have already spoken of the extension of the legal jurisdiction of the senate as a body and of individual senators. The diligence with which Marcus himself personally dispensed justice both in Rome and in the field must have been proverbial, to judge from the traces of it preserved in the sources. In the performance of this duty, too, he showed a characteristic concern for his good name, distrusting informers and rejecting in particular charges liable to raise the suspicion of material advantage to the state through the medium of confiscations. Energetic and understanding, inexorable with serious or odious crimes but inclined to inflict the mildest penalty and to consider the likelihood of reform in other cases, strict and impartial, scrupulously just, even in cases concerning enemy prisoners, meticulous to the point of having cases that had been hurried heard again – particularly those involving the *honestiores*, who in his view were entitled to the consideration of the most deliberate procedure – he left much-admired memories of his criminal justice, clothed by the tradition with all kinds of edifying details, especially in connection with his reaction to the affair of Avidius Cassius. His interest in, and scrupulous treatment of, civil cases must have been just as great, as is clear from the numerous interventions and interpretations attributed to him in the *Digest*. In this field in particular he must have enjoyed the advice, which he asked for freely, of the most competent experts. The praetorian prefects, those loyal men, his colleagues in war and peace, the best in the whole history of these posts, certainly assisted him mainly in the field of criminal justice; but the advice of the original jurist Q. Cervidius Scaevola (the teacher of Paul and possibly of Ulpian), to whom the tradition assigns the position of Marcus's principal counsellor, must have been concerned essentially with the civil law – both its drafting and its application. Civil law must also have been the particular concern of the *consilium*, now quite separate from the Emperor's *amici* and simply an assemblage, more administrative than political, of experts. These experts were not even of the highest rank, for the career structure, so to speak, of the council – whose members were now called explicitly *consiliarii* – consisted of posts for *centenarii* and *sexagenarii*, which were the middle levels of the equestrian hierarchy. This too was a further step towards the fixed and permanent systematization of everything, in the atmosphere of seriousness that must have been the dominant feature of the administration of justice. Marcus also raised the number of days in the year on which cases were heard to the ancient number of 230 again. The number had gradually been reduced by the institution of festivals and holidays. Similarly, to indicate that duty always comes before pleasure, he once postponed the opening of the pantomime performances for nine days, so that the conduct of affairs should not be impeded.

Concern for the precision and clarity of juridical positions as the necessary prerequisite of political and social order, a more and more exactly defined consideration of the intention of acts and, finally, humanity were also the dominant factors in Marcus's abundant legislation, which it is only possible to group, as in the case of his predecessor, under a few main headings – such is the detail revealed in the more than three hundred texts known. These texts are attributed, with a precision that also helps chronology, to the *divi fratres* (161–169), to Marcus alone (169–177) and to Marcus and Commodus (177–178); they almost certainly represent only a small part of the daily labours, which were collected, as far as we know, every six months in *semestria*, for more convenient use in jurisdiction. More circumstantial norms of civil and criminal procedure governed the ordered exercise of justice, taking account among other things of human needs. The notion of 'equal justice for all' naturally continued to remain outside the experience of the age; indeed differences in treatment in the matters of torture and punishment were formulated with still greater precision; an example is the exemption of the *eminentissimi* and *perfectissimi* – the two highest grades in the equestrian class – from plebeian punishments, down to the third generation. But the precise rules established – in the matter of documents required, deadlines and expiry dates – for appearances in court, appeals and adjournments and against the fraudulent extension of cases, certainly brought practical advantages for everyone. Other regulations, such as the veto on calling to court men engaged in the harvest or the vintage or taking part in a funeral, had their roots in a consideration of the interests of individuals as well as of what was fair and expedient. So did the stipulation that in urgent cases (questions of guardianship, for example, or 'alimenta'), the praetor could be approached even on days when he was not hearing cases. Similar considerations also dictated the recommendations not to make witnesses travel for no reason and to be circumspect in accepting evidence, and also the practice – intended to prevent cases going on too long – of regarding them as settled by the confession of the defendant. The same aim was often achieved by the appointment of judges from whose verdict there was no appeal. If we add to all this certain declarations of principle now explicitly included in the legislation – that private rights must be championed not by violence but by legal means, on pain of their lapsing; that consideration of the good faith of acts is fundamental, as is also that of subjective responsibility, so that a lunatic cannot be found guilty (granted all proper checks are made on possible simulation); and that children must not suffer any consequences from the condemnation of the father – we can measure the further progress made in the already extensive humanization of the rights of the person. Here, particularly in the detailed rules about guardianship and custody, wills and succession, families and family estates, social concerns are also revealed. The clearly defined status of the individual had to be the basis of every legal action.

We have already come across the obligation to register birth. But the various gradations of *libertas* and *civitas* posed many problems to be resolved by corrective and interpretative action in which Marcus was tireless. Distinctions in status – it is as well to repeat – were not reduced, but in the problem of slavery the various different cases were constantly resolved in favour of the *libertas* of the interested party. It is true that the masters' property rights over slaves remained complete; not even the imperial estates were excluded from the inspections to track down fugitive slaves. Manumissions *ex acclamatione populi*, which must have been demanded quite frequently for actors and circus champions, the darlings of the populace, but implied an inadmissible coercion of the owner's will, were prohibited, and there was no change in the use of torture in the interrogation of slaves, except indeed for a more generous application of the practice in the case of *servi publici*. But something that had been allowed for some time, namely the purchase of freedom by a slave with the *peculium* which was legally not his own but was regarded as such by a humane extension of the law, was now given legal formulation; the sale of guilty slaves to fight in the arena with wild beasts was forbidden; the faculty of manumission was granted to *collegia* as well; and questions of contested manumission were resolved in favour of the slave. Examples of such contested manumissions were those granted by people in debt to the fisc and those granted to the advantage of slaves under sentence for offences. The former were declared invalid only if intention to defraud the fisc was proved, and the latter were only suspended until the sentence had expired. Enquiries into status were permitted, for example to uncover fraudulent collusion between master and slave in declaring *ingenuitas*, that is, free birth; but if fraud was discovered, the effects of *ingenuitas* did not cease for the period for which it was declared; and any enquiry into status had to stop after the death of the person concerned. An important statute, surrounded by numerous definitions and extensions, laid down that a slave sold with the promise of freedom should become free even if the requisite conditions were not fulfilled by the vendor and the buyer. In the case of a promise not kept by the master, the slave could also seek the help of the law, in Rome from the *praefectus urbi* and in the provinces from the governor. Other measures further guaranteed the rights of slaves in the case of manumission by will or trust deed. The most minute details were covered, even with regard to the time elapsing between the promise and the acquisition, especially for freedmen, who in the meantime could have had children, whose status was determined by that of the mother. An amendment to the *senatusconsultum Silanianum* established, for the period of waiting, the rights of slaves manumitted in the will of a master who had been murdered, granted that the will could not be executed before the murderers had been discovered. The right of freedmen to inherit and own property was also safeguarded, and they were protected from having to make excessive forced loans that went beyond normal obligations to the patron in compensation for liberation. In short, the possibility of cruel and arbitrary treatment was entirely removed, at any rate in law.

For the rest, the more rigorous organization of free society improved the state of public order but not the conditions of the individual. The right of association continued to be regarded with mistrust. It was confined to recognized *collegia* and hedged about with restrictions on aims, frequency of meetings, qualifications of the members and mode of enrolment. The importance assumed by the institutions for guardianship and *cura*, as demonstrated by the creation of the *praetor tutelaris* for Italy and by the large number of regulations on the subject, gives us a vivid picture of the conditions prevailing in a society guided more than before in the private field as well; and the reluctance to assume these tasks of guardian and 'curator' – a reluctance evident from their obligatory nature and from the very carefully defined cases for exemption (*ius trium liberorum*, reasons of domicile, military service, incompatibility with service of the state, 'paupertas, mediocritas, rusticitas et domesticae lites') – proves how heavily and frequently they weighed, like the other *civilia munera*, which were also tending to increase, on the liberty of the individual.

The norms applied in the fields of wills, families, inheritances and obligation improved in some details on the already imposing body of legislation, always in accordance with the criteria of attaching the greatest possible value to intention as compared with the letter and of paying regard to social decorum, for the preservation of family estates and the maintenance of public confidence. Not only was there an improvement, on top of Antoninus Pius's measures, in the conditions of mothers with regard to the succession of children, but the *senatusconsultum Orfitianum* of 178 established that the children, not the collaterals, should rank as the heirs of a mother who died intestate. The military will was the subject of further detailed regulations, and there is evidence of subtle solutions to individual cases in the huge field of legacies and trusts. Action is also recorded to restore inheritances of dubious assignation to the natural heirs. The famous *oratio Marci* of 6 January 168 *in castris praetoriis* established the same juridical privileges in the relations of the children of veterans with the paternal or maternal grandfather. The limitation of the need for paternal agreement to the marriages of children dealt a fresh blow to the *patria potestas*, from which in practice soldiers too had been freed for the purposes of testamentary rights. And all the children had been made exempt, as we have already seen, from the consequences of a father's condemnation by the courts. It was just at this time that the now modest limits of the *patria potestas* were defined; that glorious old basis of Roman society was dissolving into a wider concept of humanity, whence derived, for example, the precise legislation on cases of hindrance to marriage – a matter no longer for family rights but for the laws of the state – the obligations in the matter of *alimenta*, the obligations to help indigent parents, and the equality with that of the father now assigned to the mother's declaration in questions of the recognition of children. Marcus himself had set an example since his youth of giving more consideration to ties of affection in family relations by his generosity to his sister Anna Cornificia Faustina in the division of the family estate and, on her death, by securing for her son, Ummidius Quadratus, a share in the property of her mother and his, Domitia Lucilla, the extremely rich owner of brick works all over Italy and mistress of a huge fortune that had grown in a way characteristic of the beginning of the century by the confluence of a number of different legacies.

To preserve family estates, further rules were added to those already laid down by Antoninus Pius on the subject of gifts between spouses; other regulations governed endowments; and the trustees appointed with liberality must have guaranteed the stability of this important basis of the established order. Numerous, too, were interventions by the state in the field of commercial relations: there were measures to establish a rule of precedence in loans and mortgages; to clarify questions of contract, loss, restitution, division of profits and losses between business partners, and to regulate trade. Characteristic in this connection is the expressly stated freedom of negotiation on prices and quantities of goods, except for grain, and for the need to take local practice into account. Just as numerous were the measures dealing with civic life proper and policing: arrangements for diversions of water and for providing a supply to country estates, regulations on the distance between buildings, on the architecture of baths, on security and morality in the towns, on the proper conduct of religious rites, on graves. The regulations dealing with graves were fairly strict, probably because of the tragic presence of the plague. For the same reason, on general grounds of generosity and also with the interests of public health in mind, Marcus provided for the free burial of poor people carried off by the disease – a humane measure, like the one which made a safety net obligatory for tight-rope walkers. He showed the same humanity in his preference for the use of harmless weapons in shows, so that fierce fights were converted into elegant tournaments – with how much satisfaction to the rough public is not reported; though in this field, where he could not achieve the total abolition of bloodthirsty games, some measures turned out to be positively counter-productive so far as humane objectives were concerned. This was the effect produced, it would seem, by the enforced reduction in the cost of games. Since the low prices laid down by the 'lists of controlled prices' on the table from Italica were those paid by anyone organizing games to the *lanistae* – the managers of the schools of gladiators – for the purchase or hiring of fighters, the measure bene-fited only municipalities or local magnates – who thus came to spend less – and became an encouragement, not an obstacle, to the presentation of shows. The *lanistae*, in fact, now exempted through moral scruples from the *vectigal gladiatorum*, could safely hand over the combatants for even lower sums, especially when those condemned to death passed through their hands at derisory prices. The result must have been the growth of a horrible trade which may have had some bearing on the wretched fate of the Christians of Vienne and Lyon, sacrificed, as we shall see in a moment, in the games connected with the festival of the Ara Galliarum. If it was desired that games should become less frequent, then the cost should have been increased to the point where it was prohibitive, and the tax on the *lanistae* should have been raised, not removed. But it often happens that the best intentions produce the worst results.

Marcus Aurelius's religious policy in particular presents all the problems characteristic of his personality. He – and to a much lesser extent Julian – are the only emperors whose religious feelings, so to speak, are known to us from inside, through their own words. The trouble is that there is a dichotomy between Marcus's words and his concrete acts, which should not surprise us, since we have already noted elsewhere the infrequent translation into systematic practice of the theoretical principles he pro-fessed. His essential consistency lay in always acting to the advantage of the state, and the only element in his Stoic convictions which this action betrayed was the impulse to unconditional fulfilment of duty; there is no sign of doctrinal inspiration. It is this consistency that explains his well-known recourse to foreign rites not devoid of magical practices and his aversion for Christianity, both in themselves attitudes at variance with his personal views on superstition and the solidarity of the human race. Thus his religious policy was mainly dictated by loyalty to tradition and by the anxiety, inspired by the innumerable calamities of the reign, not to leave untried any means of gaining the goodwill of the gods and not to allow any possible danger to spiritual unity in the difficult times prevailing. And he carried out this policy with the inexorable zeal with which, if the public good was at stake, he not only rejected all the attractions of a quiet life but also silenced all the noble feelings of his own private generosity. The traditional religion above all was cultivated and protected. The coin-age, considerably less varied than that of Hadrian and Antoninus, no longer celebrated the glorious legends of the origins of Rome; but the

allusions, lasting throughout the reign, to wars and victories, always referred to the national divinities: Mars in the first place, Minerva the
warrior, Jupiter in his capacities of 'Conservator', 'Propugnator' and
'Victor', all-conquering Rome, and 'Fortuna Redux'.

The religion of Marcus the philosopher was not in conflict with that of
the boy who, appointed at the age of seven by Hadrian to the college of
the Salii, had assumed the office with extreme seriousness and learned the
formulas of the rituals by heart, nor with the veneration preserved for the
whole traditional religion, which he practised with such zeal that he made
sacrifices at home on the days not marked out for public worship and did
not neglect, when the opportunity arose, to be initiated into the Eleusinian
mysteries. In any case, it was fairly easy to reconcile philosophical mono-
theism with the traditional polytheism, especially according to the Stoic
concept of 'Providentia deorum' particularly dear to Marcus and promulgated officially in the coinage as the main element in the mystique, which
he encouraged, of the imperial cult. The idea of the divine investiture of
the Princeps, as the instrument of the gods' providence, was now quite
clear to him and worthy of his restrained attitude. Identification with the
divinity, which was to be effected by his son, was in fact still alien to his
intentions, though he was strict in requiring observance of the cult, which
he regarded as fundamental to the security of the state. In practice the
tendency to identify the emperor under various titles with the godhead
was less marked under Marcus than under his two predecessors, even in
the East, and there was a certain discretion in the honours assigned to living
members of his family and in the worship of dead ones. The instructions
given to the proconsul of Asia in 164 that no special honours were to be
paid to the daughter going out to marry Lucius Verus have been preserved by the tradition;[1] the coins of the two Augustae, Faustina and
Lucilla, specialized in edifying motifs connected with domesticity and
religious piety; and, so far as apotheoses were concerned, the cult of Lucius
Verus was a modest one, of less importance than that of Faustina, which
had the example of the splendid cult of her mother. But few traces have
remained of any special honours for the rest of Marcus's numerous family.

For foreign cults Marcus showed more than customary tolerance. He
took a lively interest in the religion of Egypt, especially during his visit to
that country, and did not disdain to believe astrologers and priests of every
kind, with the aim of placating the angry gods in whatever form they
might be venerated. In the great rites of expiation and propitiation which
took place in Rome in 167 for the plague and the war, exotic ceremonies

---

[1] *V. Marc.*, 9, 6.

were performed, as well as the usual *lectisternia* and *vota publica*, by priests summoned for the occasion. However, this was not without precedent in the Roman tradition: the Sibylline books, when consulted during the war with Hannibal, had caused the introduction at Rome of the Phrygian cult of Cybele.

It was only to the Christians that Marcus was clearly opposed. Philosophical contempt for the allegedly irrational and inhuman behaviour of anyone who offered himself for death with an enthusiasm which seemed against nature, and political concern at the example of disobedience and an obstinacy that in some instances may have been regarded as provocative, here coincided in one of those cases of conscience in which the duty to be inexorable prevailed over the satisfaction of being mild. Not that edicts explicitly ordering persecution were issued; only one legislative text is known that refers in any way to this subject, and it is aimed against 'anyone who does anything by which the fickle minds of men *superstitione numinis terrentur*'.[1] Thus superstition in general was the target and the penalty was banishment to an island, a penalty applied, as we know, in the case of a man who had acted the prophet and terrified people at the time of Avidius Cassius's revolt. But under Marcus the steps taken against the Christians by magistrates and officials, if not positively encouraged, were not curbed, and led to numerous executions. One example was the martyrdom of St Justin and six others, which took place in Rome not later than 167, on information laid by the Stoic philosopher Crescens, and after sentence had been pronounced – for refusal to sacrifice to the gods and disobedience to the Emperor – by the *praefectus urbi*, Q. Junius Rusticus, also a Stoic philosopher and the teacher and friend of the Princeps, who can hardly have remained unaware of the trial. Nor were outbreaks of popular fury repressed with the same efficiency as they had been under his predecessors. The horrible events at Lyon in 177 or 178 certainly did not occur without the knowledge of the Princeps, who may have helped to provide abundant cheap human material in the shape of the Christians through the above-mentioned regulations stipulating a low price for gladiators, and in particular through one which fixed conditions – in Gaul, as it happens – for the sale to the arena of prisoners condemned to death.

Christianity was certainly now widely diffused and motives for hating Christians increased in proportion to the incessant increase in their numbers. The organization of the Church, with its bishops, who in every part of the empire kept in contact with each other and with the bishop of Rome – for whose recognized primacy there is clear evidence precisely

[1] *Digest.*, XLVIII, 19, 30.

at this time – could not but collide, at the very least, with the traditional mistrust of associations. But in fact the conflict was more serious. For some time already the apologists had been engaging in controversy with paganism, and now philosophy replied: in 178 or a little later Celsus's attack on Christianity appeared, and it was in this period that the foundations were laid for that intellectual opposition which, two or three centuries later, was to be the last to yield in the tenacious defence of the pagan tradition. Moreover, the presence of Christianity had provoked a popular resurgence of traditional religious feeling, particularly, as we have seen, in the shape of hatred for, and opposition to, what was called 'atheism' and was regarded as the cause of the gods' anger and of the various disasters. This sentiment came to be shared more and more by the Emperor, with the resultant growth of an atmosphere of persecution, which by the end of the reign had become fairly oppressive and cleared only slowly under the relaxed rule of his successor. The Christian community, now united in a visible society, must have been strongly coloured by humanism, as a result of the varying backgrounds of its members. It was itself torn by controversies and struggles round the two opposing positions which always crystallize in any religion impinging substantially on morality, namely conciliatorism and rigorism (in the shape, at this period, of Gnosticism and Montanism respectively), and it must therefore have come into contact and conflict all the more frequently with a world which now knew it well, in its admirable and disconcerting attitudes. In the reign of Marcus it had a loud say in literature, through the works of the numerous apologists, the Easterners Tatian, Miltiades, Apollinaris of Hierapolis, Theophilus of Antioch, Melito of Sardis and the Athenian Athenagoras; and soon the West was to take a hand with the powerful polemic of Tertullian, an ardent and passionate spirit converted at that time by the sight of the martyrs' heroism – the very thing which put off the cold, rational mind of the philosopher Emperor. Others who were certainly quite on a level with the highest culture of the age, in which they had in any case been educated, were St Irenaeus, the presbyter of Lyon, and the bishops of Rome, Soter, Eleutherus and Victor, whose pontificates succeeded each other through the reigns of Marcus and Commodus and were rich in doctrinal activity and authoritative interventions against heresies.

It was this period that saw the first appearance of the concepts of the Christianization of pagan culture and of the reconciliation of Christianity and the empire for their mutual good. The time was naturally not ripe for such a fusion, though its possibility had already been indicated by the characteristics of pagan culture itself, as reflected in the total scepticism of

Lucian, who dealt with the beliefs and customs of the past as they deserved, and in the mystical aspirations which heralded the future and, present even in the science of Galen, laid the foundations for medieval culture. But for the moment the traditional reaction still had the upper hand both in the cultural field and, even more, in the political field. Thus martyrdoms, few and sporadic in the earlier part of the century, became more frequent, and there is a tendency today to regard the uncertain pages of the *Acta* as more or less authentic when they concentrate in the reign of Marcus even some *martyria* and *passiones* attributed by the tradition to the preceding age (those of St Ignatius of Antioch and St Polycarp of Smyrna, for example) or the succeeding age (St Perpetua and St Felicity). However, the persecution was still not general; the bishops of Rome were not touched and the most serious cases were local ones; those of Carpus, Papilus and Agathonice, killed in the amphitheatre of Pergamum between 161 and 169; and, most striking of all, as described in the passages of the letters from the churches of Vienne and Lyon to the churches of Asia and Phrygia preserved in Eusebius,[1] that of the Christians of Narbonese Gaul, among them the ninety-year-old bishop Fotinus, a boy of fifteen, Ponticus, and the young slave Blandina, exposed to a cruel martyrdom in the arena of Lyon on the occasion of the festival of the altar of the three Gauls, in 177 or 178. The martyrdom of nine Numidian Christians, beheaded on 17 July 180, though it occurred under Commodus, is also to be ascribed to the enduring atmosphere of Marcus's reign.

This hostility was recorded as a blot on the reign by the Christian tradition, which took no account of Tertullian's assertion (probably a tactical move) about a change of attitude after the miracle of the rain.[2] The other blot, the one noted by contemporary opinion preserved in the sources—now, for the last years of Marcus and for the reign of Commodus, primary sources – was his having wanted his unworthy son as his successor. We do not possess sufficient evidence to be able to judge how far the choice was inspired by a reprehensible indulgence in 'benignitas in suos'[3] and how far by motives of political expediency, first among which would be the one already suggested by the experience of ruling in double harness with Lucius, namely the need to conciliate a current of thought, so to speak, that took a wider and less austerely conservative view of the principate. Marcus disapproved of this current, but tried to control and canalize it in official forms. He must also have thought about what would happen after his death; hence the effort to educate his successor, in the hope that Commodus might repeat the apprenticeship which he himself had begun

[1] *Hist. Eccl.*, V, 1–2.   [2] TERTULL., *Apolog.*, 5, 6.   [3] *V. Marc.*, 16, 1.

at the age of seventeen under Antoninus and by which he had been completely moulded. It was an illusion pardonable in a philosopher, who regarded himself so much as the product of education that he thought he could make Commodus his own equal, mastering by means of education a nature about which it was already difficult, it seems, to entertain many illusions. The sources' judgement of Commodus is much the same as their judgement of Lucius Verus: not positively bad, but devoid of the positive qualities of self-control and sense of duty, and already infected with the germs which were to mature into cowardice and lust. For this very reason Marcus arranged for his son to be surrounded by the best advisers – one last illusion preserved as his life approached its melancholy end. On the other hand, the form of succession inaugurated by Nerva and adventurously continued was no longer workable precisely because of the existence of a son of the Emperor. The numerous offspring, particularly female offspring, of Marcus had multiplied the number of relations and caused the ties of the imperial family to extend more widely than they had done since the days of the Julio-Claudians. The succession of the son, the only male remaining to Marcus (even the son born to Verus and Lucilla must have died when he was a baby), was also the most natural one in the context of the problems created by this extension of family ties. The tradition which deplores the choice does not hide the fact that it was regarded as the most natural one and as such was positively acclaimed and celebrated, for it was the first time that the empire had been gained by an emperor born when his father was emperor. This recognition of the dynastic reality was given the clearest official sanction by the posthumous rehabilitation proclaimed by Septimius Severus, who wanted to be known as Commodus's 'brother' and legitimized his own power by linking it to the Antonine line. Thus the tradition that tells of Marcus's sad presentiments, of his tears, of the edifying speech he made on his deathbed, recommending his son to his relations and friends, represents only the rhetorical and moralizing trimming of a simple and inevitable political fact.

Perhaps we can see something else in the noble melancholy of the countenance common to all the portraits of Marcus, in the famous statue on the Capitol, in the reliefs of the Palazzo dei Conservatori, and in all those reliefs in which the decline of the classical renascence that had flourished earlier in the century led, as it did in the whole field of art, to a style technically poorer, but more tortured and pathetic; and perhaps this something was a prevision of the coming transformation of the principate, an awareness of the final uselessness of his struggle to preserve things as they were, and, in short, a retreat into the inward realm of moral ideals.

XIII

COMMODUS

'NATUS IMPERATOR'

The sources on the principate of the last of the Antonines are relatively abundant and to a large extent they are primary sources. Cassius Dio asserts explicitly that from the beginning of the reign of Commodus he is recounting events within his own personal experience; and although the Syrian rhetorician Herodian's reconstruction is based on a pre-accepted thesis and is moralizing in tone he too is close to the events, as is the biography in the *Historia Augusta*, in so far as it derives from Marius Maximus, who was almost certainly the illustrious senator of that name, a contemporary of Cassius Dio's. But the value of the relative immediacy of the testimony is balanced by the marked influence of contemporary opinion, still impassioned and in addition baffled by the official view propagated by Severus, who had posthumously rehabilitated an execrated memory. Thus alongside the mere simplification of moral historiography, which attributed only good to Marcus and only evil to Commodus, whose biography in the *Historia Augusta* is a nauseating rigmarole of baseness of every sort, we find in Herodian an attempt to demonstrate in Commodus a gradual evolution from initial rectitude to subsequent perversion, not through his own fault, but through that of bad officials and advisers and of unfavourable circumstances, while Cassius Dio, though more balanced in his judgement, admits the irreparable ruination of a nature not in itself wicked. All this has obscured one important aspect of the reign in particular, namely the real part played by the officials, whether prefects of the praetorian guard or servants of the bedchamber, who turned out to be wielding the effective power and in the wider tradition were dismissed as criminals. But the real situation can be glimpsed.

The young man who had been 'natus imperator',[1] and had come into possession of the principate with a legitimacy that may well have seemed unprecedented, seized power to enjoy it, not to serve the empire. He made a reality of the régime, already heralded by Verus, of living splen-

[1] HERODIAN, I, 5, 6.

didly on income, a régime based on the still fundamentally good general
conditions, a still formidable administrative organization and the anonymous vitality of the whole imperial structure. This meant completely
repudiating the assiduous efforts of his father, who had maintained, so far
as he had been able, but with total personal commitment, those conditions
of well-being on which the son now counted in order to live his own life
of idle and extravagant regality. The fates wasted little time in demonstrating that Marcus's activity had not been a matter of superfluous zeal,
but quite simply necessary. The effective government of the empire,
assumed by the ministers precisely because the Princeps showed no
interest in it, and carried on, at least by some of them, with a sense of
responsibility, continued Marcus's care just as he had himself arranged by
leaving his son surrounded by the best advisers. Government by the *amici*
of the senatorial class, who included Marcus's valiant comrades-in-arms
and his sons-in-law, was able in fact to function as a council of regency
and guide the empire. But there were too many of them; one single
counsellor, a Seneca or a Mucianus, would have done better. Thus when
his mentors had faded away, when the breach with the aristocracy had
opened up again and when Commodus was on the road followed by
Gaius and Nero, the gap in the machinery of government had to be
filled by whoever, through ambition or cupidity or even simply through
being close to the centre of power, held power in his hands, exercising it
either well or badly, with the close adaptation to circumstances typical of
those with slighter ties with tradition.

Various irresistible tendencies were in fact already at work, shifting, to
the advantage of the provinces and of the power and will of the armies,
that equilibrium which another Marcus would have made great efforts to
preserve, so as to keep the empire a civil rather than a military organization, but which had now to be partly abandoned. Consequently some
scholars have thought they could already see in the reign of Commodus the
beginning of the military monarchy; this view is certainly premature, but
it must be admitted that there are indubitable indications that the road
towards this new and fast approaching reality had been decisively taken.[1]
The only difference was that Commodus was not yet the puppet sovereign
deprived of power by a mayor of the palace who could look forward to
peacefully replacing him; and the senatorial tradition was still sufficiently
strong to initiate within the ranks of its own class, though through the
strength of the armies, any new course of events. Thus this last principate

[1] M. ROSTOVTZEFF, *Social and Economic History of the Roman Empire*, 1926, pp. 450 ff.

on the Augustan formula, now on the threshold of the first important modification, presented in the dozen years or so of a disconcerting reign the most varied mixture of conservatism and signs of revolution.

The abandonment of the policy of conquest was delayed only long enough to give the move a semblance of decency. A few days after Marcus's death Commodus, then nineteen, was presented to the army by his father's *amici* and on this occasion said, willy-nilly, what they made him say, namely that he regarded himself as entrusted to the troops by his father, as their 'princeps natus', that he intended to lead them to fresh victories, and meanwhile was going to distribute a generous donative. It may have been at this point that, in homage to his father, he changed his name, taking more fully that of Marcus: *Imperator Caesar M. Aurelius Commodus Antoninus Augustus*. In these early days he must also have been thinking of Marcus's funeral and of the procession to Rome, where the deification took place, with the addition of *Pius* to the epithet *Divus*, the customary institution of *sodales* and *flamines* and the voting of a temple, while the memory of the best of the emperors soon entered a more spontaneous and sincere area of religion, among the Penates of private houses. However, there is no evidence that the body was accompanied to Rome by Commodus, who meanwhile, at army headquarters, was gradually emancipating himself from his advisers – the chief of whom must have been his brother-in-law, Claudius Pompeianus – and imposing his own views on the conduct of the war. The opposition of the general staff, which had shared in Marcus's plans and collaborated in the hard struggle now nearing a successful conclusion, was of no avail. It is true that support for a peace policy must for some time have been as extensive as that for war *à outrance*, but it would be wrong to give Commodus, who adopted the former policy with relative success, the credit for political clairvoyance when his action was dictated rather by trivial motives – dislike of hard work and sacrifice, and the wish to hasten to Rome to enjoy power without any worries.

On the pretext of fearing some attempt to usurp his authority in Rome, he decided to leave. After changing his commanders, he spent a certain amount of time in warlike activities (receiving in fact his fourth salutation as *imperator*), but even more in negotiations with the barbarians. The Marcomanni and the Quadi were exhausted and could easily have been destroyed; instead they were given peace and client terms, though, to be honest, these were harder than the terms granted earlier. Besides having to hand back prisoners and deserters, they were obliged to pay an annual tribute of corn, though this was soon remitted; they were allowed to hold a market only once a month, in a predetermined spot and in the presence of a Roman centurion; they were not to make war with the neighbouring peoples (Iazyges, Buri, Vandals); and the Quadi had to provide 13,000 men for the Roman army, the Marcomanni rather fewer. Other reports refer to the peace concluded with other peoples, including – mainly – the Buri, who were probably reduced to order by that Sabinianus, doubtless governor of Dacia, who had prevented 12,000 Dacians from the mountains from uniting with the Buri by promising to give them land in Roman Dacia. The demilitarized strip at least five miles wide along all frontiers naturally remained, and the defences of the Danube were further reinforced and linked by *castella*, *turres* and *burgi* to form a powerful system. But a strong impression must have been created by the abandonment of all the garrisons beyond the demilitarized zone, in lands where Marcus had written the last pages of the *Meditations* under the impression that these lands would be for ever Roman. Moreover, the financial assistance granted to the barbarians must have been liable to resurrect the accusation made against Domitian of buying peace; the Germans now regularly incorporated in the army were soon to cause the usual troubles; and finally the admission into the empire's territory of further small groups of colonists started a process that in time was to become uncontrollable.

But the young Emperor could not worry about what still lay in the obscure future. On 22 October 180 he arrived in Rome at the end of a triumphal progress to the capital, bringing peace after twenty years of almost continuous war, and through his very youth, bright with physical beauty and the promise of generosity and indulgence, he may well have seemed a sort of token of happy days to come.

THE EVENTS OF THE REIGN

Hopes of this kind were not disappointed, for the populace which in 175 had seen the boy in a *toga praetexta* grant a *congiarium*, and preside over its distribution in the Basilica Ulpia, now received a quite substantial one (Commodus's third) as part of the victory celebrations also commemorated in the coinage; and the procedure was repeated twice in the two succeeding years. It is with this desire for popularity that the tradition links, very soon after Commodus's return, the start of the extravagances and affronts to the aristocracy. But as for the reports of the triumph of a debauchee, the vulgar speech in the Senate, the orgies in the palace on the Palatine where he went to live, the nocturnal expeditions to taverns and brothels – reports preserved particularly by the biographer and Cassius – they clearly smack of senatorial hatred. Herodian's version of the beginning of the reign may well be more authentic. He says that after visiting the temples and thanking the Senate and the praetorians, Commodus retired to the Palatine, where for two years or so he continued to hold in honour some at any rate of his father's friends, particularly Claudius Pompeianus, C. Aufidius Victorinus and Tarrutenius Paternus, the prefect of the praetorian guard. He had indeed begun to enjoy power in the form he desired. Peace and a plentiful corn supply were to be the external characteristics of the reign, as is clear from the motifs on the coins; amid the splendour of this happiness the Emperor indulged his own tastes and was already having his hunting feats depicted on the coinage. On 1 January 181 he assumed his third consulship in company with one of his brothers-in-law, Antistius Burrus, and the reign would have continued in the relative peace of normal administration on the one hand and the Emperor's caprices – confined to personal debauchery – on the other, had not conspiracies been discovered, as in any case was to be expected.

The first important plot was the one that took its name from Lucilla and in reality it was an obscure domestic intrigue. But from it naturally originated the long series of executions outside the palace of members of the senatorial class, while the Princeps, in whose cowardly heart danger had aroused terror, accentuated still more his own isolation, guarding it now with suspicion and hatred. That Lucilla, the widow of Lucius Verus and wife of Claudius Pompeianus, inspired the plot against her brother and that she did it out of rivalry with Crispina, the Augusta who had robbed her, an Augusta, too, of the first place among the imperial ladies, is quite probable, especially if, as it would seem, Crispina was just at that time on the point of producing an heir for the Emperor. However, Lucilla did not join forces with her husband, whom she hated and who after these events lived in the country without any further bother, but with her cousin Ummidius Quadratus. The only trouble was that the assassin they selected, one Claudius Pompeianus Quintianus, probably a nephew rather than a son of Pompeianus, having confronted Commodus at the entrance to the theatre with every indication of killing him, was unable to refrain from shouting 'the Senate sends you this', and consequently failed in his attempt, giving instead, correctly or incorrectly, an indication about his sponsors which did not go unnoticed. The immediate consequence was the execution of Quintianus, Quadratus, one Norbanus, one Norbana and one Paralius, certainly persons from various classes all directly implicated, among the 'multi participantes',[1] in the enterprise; the mother of the last-

[1] V. Commod., 4, 3.

named was banished, like Lucilla, who was sent to Capri and soon afterwards done away with.

It is more difficult to see the connection with what followed, that is, the downfall of Tarrutenius Paternus and other illustrious people who apparently had nothing to do with the plot. That Paternus was aware of it, as the biographer alone says, may be true, since the collaboration of the praetorian prefects in plots of this kind was traditional and regarded as indispensable for anyone who was to make the attempt with any hope of success. Yet nothing of the sort is said of his colleague Tigidius Perennis, who was certainly in office by this time and would of necessity have been equally privy to the matter; and the elimination by Paternus and Perennis, acting in concert, of Saoterus, Commodus's *a cubiculo*, with the object of freeing the Emperor from a servant who was both hated and causing Commodus to be hated, would seem to testify in favour of Paternus, who – according to Cassius Dio, who defends him – would certainly not have lacked opportunities to get rid of Commodus if he had wished to do so. Thus Paternus was the victim of another plot, one organized by his colleague according to the sources, including Cassius Dio, whose testimony is all the more reliable in that he presents all the rest of Perennis's activity in a favourable light. Whatever the implied charge against him, Paternus, after being removed from his post as prefect and granted the consular insignia, was put to death. With him, or a little later, fell P. Salvius Julianus, consul in 175 and the holder of an important military command, probably on the Rhine; Vitruvius Secundus, the *ab epistulis* and a close friend of Paternus; and the two old and extremely rich Quintilius brothers, with one of their respective sons; the other son, who was in Syria, succeeded in escaping the massacre of his family in the romantic fashion described by Cassius Dio from personal memory.

Other victims of this first onslaught on the aristocracy are also mentioned by name: the noble lady Vitrasia Faustina, the ex-consuls D. Velius Rufus Julianus and Egnatius Capito, both put to death, and Aemilius Iuncus and Atilius Severus, who had been consuls together a little before 183, both banished. It may be that others were involved as early as this, but the general summary, without names, by the most authoritative writer, Cassius Dio, of the innumerable persons eliminated 'on false charges, for unjustified suspicions, conspicuous wealth, illustrious lineage, the excellence of their learning or any other reason for distinction' obviously refers to the whole reign. It should also be noted, if we are to see things roughly in proportion, that neither Commodus's reprisals nor Perennis's politically calculated steps managed to touch the people likely to have disappeared first in a programme of emancipation of the Neronian sort, in other words, the brothers-in-law. It is true that Antistius Burrus and Petronius Sura Mamertinus, the latter with his son, were indeed executed, but a few years later, it seems (not before 187), while the others, at any rate for the moment, and some to the natural end of their lives, were left in peace, like the most important personages surviving from Marcus's reign – Aufidius Victorinus, who disappeared in mysterious circumstances but not until some years later, Helvius Pertinax, and the many talented commanders of the armies. In fact the tradition is basically accurate in depicting Commodus as politically somnolent and inert, only waking up from time to time when danger, real or presumed, seemed close, while a relentless struggle went on at the level of ministers for exclusive influence over Commodus – and hence for effective power – and was the main factor in the production of crashes and victims.

That is what happened after the liquidation of the Lucilla affair. Assuming the title of *Pius* – for what serious reason is not known – and becoming still more isolated in his dissolute life, the Emperor left the reigns of government in the hands of Perennis, who from 182 to 185 was the real ruler of the empire. The verdict of the ancients on this personage is discordant, and since the judgements involved are contemporary ones, it is clear that they reflect the result of seeing from different angles an activity which may have lent itself objectively to various interpretations. According to Herodian and the biographer, he was purely and simply a greedy and ambitious man, and it was he who irremediably spoilt the Emperor, encouraging his tendency to cut himself off from public affairs, so as to have more room to work on his own behalf, with the aim of accumulating wealth and eventually replacing Commodus. With this goal in mind he is supposed to have given the key commands of the Danubian troops to his own young sons (though only one is known to us; he was probably governor of Lower Pannonia), causing them to raise levies to his own advantage. He is also supposed to have made the praetorian guard blindly loyal to himself, taken other suspicious measures in connection with the military commands in the provinces, and finally prepared the way for usurpation in Rome by means of killings and confiscations, the blame and hatred for which fell on Commodus, while he reaped the benefit. It is true that Perennis would not suffer a colleague in his post and was undoubtedly ambitious; but the normal running of the empire in the three years 182–185 was ensured by him, certainly not by Commodus, who was intent on racing, gladiatorial combats and the base conduct which – just in connection with this short period – fills a whole chapter of the biography. Cassius Dio recognizes this fact explicitly and if we consider from what quarter disaster fell on Perennis ('. . . . he was forced to govern the state and therefore when the troops were discontented about something, they blamed him and became exasperated with him'), we must needs suppose that his rule was honest and energetic in its dealings with the very element which, according to the hostile tradition, he is supposed to have sought to win over for his own ends.

The restlessness of the armies, which in the incipient 'general crisis' now looked to the centre with a questioning air,[1] must moreover have been very real, although reports on the subject are confused. After the withdrawal to the near side of the Danube, other operations of a certain importance must have taken place, possibly in Dacia; between the end of 182 and the early days of 183 Commodus received two salutations as *imperator*, the fifth and the sixth; and the skirmishes along the river must have been continuous, even including thrusts across it. The biographer speaks of successes 'in Sarmatia' that are reported by other writers as well and were attributed by Perennis to his son, as well as of operations in Mauretania, which to judge from the evidence of work on fortifications must have taken place between 183 and 185, even after the friendly relations established just at the beginning of the reign – as we know from an inscription discovered fairly recently at Volubilis[2] – with the chief of the powerful tribe of the Baquates. But the scene of the greatest disturbances at this time was Britain, which had already caused worries to Marcus. In 184 an irruption of barbarians across the wall routed a legionary commander with a detachment of troops, and the situation was saved with difficulty – and the imposition of the strictest discipline on the army – by the skilful Ulpius Marcellus; Commodus received his seventh salutation as *imperator* and the title of *Britannicus*. A fresh and more serious danger made its appearance very soon afterwards: in 185 the army of Britain acclaimed as emperor a governor known only by his cognomen of Priscus. Priscus refused the offer, but the disturbances did not end until the despatch to Britain as governor of Helvius Pertinax, who succeeded in restoring the tranquillity referred to, before the end of the year, by the coins normally issued on such occasions: 'Concordia exercituum', 'Fides exercituum'. But the repercussions at Rome were interesting; for according to the tradition Perennis was the victim of them.

---

[1] H. MATTINGLY, *Coins of the Roman Empire in the Br. Mus.*, IV, 1940, p. CLIII.
[2] *Ann. Ép.*, 1953, 79; cf. 1957, 203.

Whether we believe the biographer, who says that the powerful prefect had incurred the hostility of the British legions by putting knights at their head in place of senatorial legates, or accept instead the version of Cassius Dio, who speaks only of a charge of conspiracy brought to Rome by fifteen hundred soldiers and accepted by Commodus, it seems clear that the initiative came from Britain. Certainly it is difficult to believe the absurd number quoted for the members of the curious delegation, as it would also seem sensible to reject the far-fetched details given by Herodian, who among other things attributes the downfall of Perennis to a totally different cause, namely the discovery of the disloyal plans of the son who held the command in Pannonia. However all this may be, the result was that Commodus, at the instigation of the new rising star, the chamberlain M. Aurelius Cleander, believed the accusations and in an unexpected burst of energy stimulated by panic abandoned Perennis to his enemies, who killed him, together with his wife, sister and two sons. On the pretext of having escaped danger he also assumed the title of *Felix*. Inserted in the Emperor's title at this point in the development of the imperial mystique, the epithet subsequently remained there ever after, embedded in a sequence which was the same for all the emperors: *Pius Felix Augustus*. Ambitious, but incorruptible and moderate, a professional concerned only with the security of his master and of the empire – the normality with which it functioned is shown by the complete absence of allusions in the coinage to innovations of any kind – and a good financial administrator (under him no *congiaria* were distributed), Perennis 'deserved a different fate',[1] even though he suffered at the hands of Cleander only what he himself had done to Paternus. His disappearance from the scene marked the end of the least melancholy phase of the reign.

There followed, from 185 to 189, the period of the omnipotence of Cleander, a Phrygian ex-slave. Tigidius Perennis was an Italian, a good soldier, almost certainly appointed praetorian prefect by Marcus, and one of the series of loyal and valuable colleagues of which there was now a long tradition. The new factotum had entered the palace as a youth bought in the slave-market. Growing up on familiar terms with Commodus, he may have been granted his freedom in Marcus's time and had gradually risen higher and higher, until he inherited the influential post of Saoterus – whom he had helped to eliminate – and entered the equestrian class. Hated by Perennis, he had awaited his hour to take Perennis's place in the Emperor's favour. This hour had now arrived, and the disgraceful and unprecedented struggle in which the prize was effective control of the

[1] CASS. D., LXXII, 10, 1.

empire ended this time in the victory of a slave. Cleander's rule, which brought into the foreground elements of the lowest origin, was certainly worse than what had preceded it. The palace freedmen had a free hand to carry out robberies and acts of violence, to commit injustices, to sell privileges, in a word to live riotously, competing in debauchery with the Princeps, who was now abandoning himself more and more to orgies and took no interest in anything but the horses, *venationes* and gladiatorial combats, in which he took part personally, killing wild beasts and men, and displaying as the Emperor's chief pride his murderous aim with a weapon. The principate had in truth never fallen so low and the empire never had at its head such an abject figure as Commodus.

The court was seething with infamy. Up to 187 at any rate, Crispina, the Augusta, must have still been alive; not later than that year she was accused of adultery, banished to Capri and put to death; but the Princeps had innumerable mistresses, among whom Marcia, (who had already belonged to Ummidius Quadratus and was the wife of the latter's bedchamber servant, Eclectus) enjoyed pre-eminence, while Damostratia, another favourite – just to give some idea of the sort of relations existing between the leaders of this high society – was at the same time the wife of Cleander, who in turn shared several mistresses with the Emperor. The political chaos must have grown worse. Even if we allow for the exaggerations of the sources, unanimously hostile after the disappearance of Perennis, the rapid succession of praetorian prefects is an undeniable fact: Niger, one of the two appointed after the death of Perennis, remained in office six hours, and he was followed by T. Longaeus Rufus, Marcius Quartus, who lasted for five days, and P. Atilius Aebutianus, put to death in 187. Aebutianus was succeeded by Cleander – without any difficulty, since he had now been a knight for some time – who was distinguished from the two prefects – his creatures – placed under him by the title *praefectus praetorio a pugione*, that is, equipped with a dagger. The title is not clear, but may have meant that criminal jurisdiction belonged to him alone. Meanwhile the Senate offered his master, as is attested by a coin, the title of *pater senatus*. Public life became totally degraded. The executions of illustrious men began again (L. Antistius Burrus, C. Arrius Antoninus and others were put to death in 187; C. Aufidius Victorinus had already anticipated the end long awaiting him by committing suicide); the Emperor developed still further his own brand of 'mysticism'; and Cleander started selling senatorial positions, patrician honours, military commands and procuratorships even to freedmen, just to make money.

The consuls designated for 189 were twenty-five in number; among them was Septimius Severus. We may assume that the hatred of the aristocracy quickly dismissed as a base commerce the jobbery of a government that also brought men of merit to the fore and must have dealt with some success with problems like the movement of Maternus and his *desertores*, rebels who, heralding the Bagaudi of the third century, stirred up Gaul and Spain and were defeated by Pescennius Niger (the reason for Commodus's eighth and last salutation as *imperator*, in 186), though not before they had put even Italy in danger. The government also had to face threats on the German front and a disastrous resurgence of the plague in 187–188, with two thousand deaths a day in Rome alone. Even so, the few details we possess of individual events certainly do not suggest that the real situation was very different from the one reported and condemned by the sources. Such details include the easy dissuasion of the Emperor from setting out on a German campaign by the prayers of the Senate and people; his taking refuge during the plague in his villa at Laurentum, where he lived in a cloud of perfumes to combat the disease; and the hypocritical employment in the coinage of the motifs of the traditional religion and of 'Roma aeterna' to build up an image of the happy enjoyment of a peace and security guarded by the gods.

However, Cleander's power also came to a swift end, probably in 189. The general dissatisfaction with him, which had spread even to the lower classes because of a famine, was skilfully exploited by a personal enemy of his, one M. Aurelius Papirius Dionysius, who could not forgive him for his own recent transfer, taken as a demotion, from the prefectship of Egypt to that of the corn supply, a lower post. As prefect of the corn supply he deliberately aggravated the shortage of grain until he succeeded in provoking the outbreak of riots. These began in the Circus, during the contests: a troop of children led by a dishevelled woman entered the arena raising cries of protest. The populace joined the demonstrators, rushed to the villa of the Quintilii on the Appian, where Commodus was residing, alternately acclaiming and cursing Cleander, who succeeded, however, in launching some praetorian guards against the mob. The charge left dead and wounded on the ground, but the populace would not yield, and Commodus, who had so far not grasped what was going on, but was now informed by Marcia (or, according to another version, by her sister Fadilla), was seized by panic and in his cowardice gave orders that Cleander should be killed. He handed the body over to the mob, who dragged it through Rome and then vented its fury on the dead man's favourites. His children, including a baby, were also killed, with their respective mothers. This grim episode, which renewed in Rome the long-forgotten experience of civil strife, had a long and bloody aftermath. Unfortunately there was to be no timely awakening on this occasion of the tyrant contentedly insulated in his life of pleasure. No one person ever again wielded the influence of Perennis or Cleander; it was divided between at least three people – Marcia, her husband, the bedchamber servant Eclectus and the praetorian prefect Q. Aemilius Laetus – and this division of power reduced its efficiency, leaving more room for the initiative of the tyrant himself. In fact in his last years Commodus partly overcame the attitude of political indifference and devotion to personal debauchery which had been the one least harmful to the empire. He began to put his own programme into effect by direct action, starting with a massacre of notabilities, including the prefect of the corn supply who had toppled Cleander. But the execution of this programme, a mixture of mysticism and wantonness, ending in practice in the mean reality of the terror which finally destroyed him, will be described a little further on.

THE ACHIEVEMENTS OF THE REIGN

The attempt to find for Commodus too, as in the case of other emperors whose reputation has been tarnished by the literary tradition, grounds for a rehabilitation in evidence of other kinds is a difficult enterprise. The literary tradition is too unanimous and direct to be doubted, at any rate in essentials. Cassius Dio, tired of recounting vulgarities, apologises at one point in his narrative: he reports these things, he says, because they were done by the Emperor and because he himself witnessed them with his own eyes. Marius Maximus read them in the *Acta Urbis*, where Commodus had had them recorded. In short, the reign consists almost entirely of these shameful actions; the rest amounts to very little. It is true that the empire continued to function, but possibly never with so little attention in the field of serious affairs from the man at the head of it. Action taken and works carried out were visibly the product of the ordinary administration and of the governmental activity of the Emperor's ministers – and they were by no means contemptible, especially in the time of Perennis – but as for the direct participation of Commodus, who after his return to Rome in 180 never left the city and the surrounding area, it must have normally amounted simply to indolent and extravagant interventions. The examples cited by the sources are the inappropriate use of circular letters and the despatch to governors of messages containing the one single word 'vale'. The fragments of ceremonial letters, such as the one to the

Athenian *gerousia*, or a document like the *decretum de saltu Burunitano*, do not call for any modification of this basic verdict, which is certainly valid at the very least in comparison with the attitude of the preceding emperors; and in any case such texts belong to the first years of the reign.

This state of affairs must have impinged in the first place on the aristocracy, now at peace with the principate for a century and bound by a tradition of dignified and cordial collaboration; it contained many highly talented men, possessed social cohesion and sanity, and in the near future was to form perhaps the strongest factor in the survival of the Roman state. The natural influx of fresh blood, which had not been opposed by earlier emperors and had finally been generously encouraged by Marcus, now proved – at the start of the big crisis – its worth. Africa in particular, the province soon to assume in its turn the cultural leadership of the western part of the empire, brought the contribution of its fifteen per cent of the Senate – a percentage repeated in the hierarchy of equestrian officials, the nursery of the future Senate as well. These serious-minded men, who after all by their services enabled the Emperor to enjoy his leisure, could be indulgent to him, even laugh at his follies and accord him in public the required applause, but they certainly did not approve of him. The age of carefree Neronian splendour had long passed by. The atmosphere, full of disquiet, must have been one of universal hatred and sufferance, with people simply waiting for the mad despot to disappear from the scene.

Official relations were much the same as usual: the traditional homage was ostensibly expressed by the five consulships (III to VII) held by Commodus in the years 181, 183, 186, 190 and 192. His colleagues were the most illustrious senators, men like Antistius Burrus, Aufidius Victorinus and Helvius Pertinax, whose worth had already been proved by their long friendship with Marcus. Sometimes Commodus also appeared in the Senate, but the memory of Marcus, which might have been a restraining factor, soon disappeared, as is shown by the very brief duration of the issue of coins in honour of 'Divus Marcus'. The first speech he made in the Senate after his return from the Danube – and thus in his first contact with the august assembly – left a painful impression owing to the inanities it contained, and since the account of it in Cassius Dio immediately follows the statement that from this point onwards the historian is writing as an eye-witness, there can be no doubt about the accuracy of the report. The Senate obeyed submissively. The indolent tyranny of Commodus was perhaps not so vexatious as the watchful one of Domitian, and the greater possibilities of self-defence which it ensured were also utilized for a subtle satirical reaction which the stolid tyrant was not even capable, it seems, of perceiving. For example, when the Senate was forced to attend shows it repeated the acclamations until they became ridiculous; when it was requested to give Rome the title *Commodian*, it not only agreed, 'per inrisionem'[1] but also began to have itself called *Commodianus;* and when the titles of the Roman Hercules were put on the reverse of senatorial coins they emerged deliberately separated by Hercules' club in such a way as to form an obscene and savage pun.

So far as practical relations were concerned, the senators were not protected by the traditional guarantee of exemption from normal jurisdiction: in the case of the Christian Apollonius, who was almost certainly a senator, the sentence was pronounced by the praetorian prefect, the knight Perennis. The Emperor's healthy respect for the aristocracy was demonstrated by the fact that he openly kept at Rome as hostages the children of those provincial governors whom he did not trust, while the abundant creation of senators by *adlectio* – possibly much the same thing as the alleged sale of senatorial rank for money – cheapened the whole status of the class. Less respect was also shown for the *praefecti urbi*, illustrious persons normally left in office for many years and replaced only at their own request; now they were changed frequently thanks to the alternation of indolence and impulsiveness characteristic of Commodus's mode of government. We have already spoken of the power wielded by low elements, which was certainly hated even if it was necessary and perhaps not entirely harmful. Through force of circumstances the competence of the praetorian prefects was extended, though they themselves – as we have seen – did not remain immune from precipitate and capricious interference. Thus the functions of the equestrian class increased still further, with ten new posts of procurator as compared with the previous reign, most of them for central offices concerned with the organization of the shows: a *subcurator ludi magni* and five *procuratores familiae gladiatoriae* now made their appearance.

In practice the public games and shows and the private amusements of the Princeps now became a substantial item of expenditure in the general budget. We know little about revenue, but we may assume that the fiscal organization, further improved on the customs side in particular, and no doubt run on strict lines at any rate in the time of Perennis, continued to secure a regular inflow impaired perhaps only by the economic decline which had already set in and which was clearly reflected in the gradual depreciation of the currency. However, the sources speak

[1] *V. Comm.*, 8, 9.

explicitly of a financial crisis as providing the excuse for vexatious measures – for example, the obligation laid on senators to pay every year, 'as first fruits', two aurei per head for every member of their families (five denarii for decurions of provincial towns) on the Emperor's birthday. This crisis is also blamed for the confiscations and for the rapacity and corruption of the administration, while the Emperor's private need for money is said to have actually led him to the miserable subterfuge of asking the Senate for funds on the pretence of making a journey to Africa – a journey never undertaken. A measure of rudimentary economic planning like the list of controlled prices for foodstuffs, which had the natural result of causing them to disappear, and the reorganization of the corn supplies, following a shortage, with the institution of the *classis Africana*, which extended the *munus* of the transport of grain and made it a heavier burden, confirm the existence of economic difficulties in general. But since Commodus's liberality, even in his last years, was not displayed so much in *congiaria* – there were only three of them after the fall of Perennis, the sixth to the eighth, on the now obligatory occasions of the Emperor's assumption of the consulship (in 186, 190 and 192; the ninth, promised, was paid by Pertinax), and they were no more than average in size – we must suppose that the cost of the ephemeral magnificence of the shows was now the biggest item of expenditure, as the sources say.

Not even public works absorbed much money; the depredations of Cleander probably furnished the means for building activities in Rome, but in spite of the statement of Cassius Dio (and it is possibly the only time he speaks less ill of Commodus) that he displayed splendour and love of beauty in Rome, these activities can really almost be reduced to the erection of the *Thermae Commodianae*, though these were certainly grandiose. On another occasion the colossal statue of the Sun was modified to assume the likeness of the new Hercules (Commodus), and the temple of Divus Marcus was built, but this is all we know about public works. Not even those already in progress were completed; it seems that even the execution of the storied column in honour of Commodus's father dragged on through the whole reign. A serious fire at Rome, possibly in 189, must have demanded a good deal of restoration work, and work of considerable importance, if in 190 Commodus refounded the city like a new Romulus, subsequently having himself represented in a group of statuary containing a thousand pounds of gold, with the legendary bull and cow; but we do not possess any details. Epigraphical evidence of work in the empire is also singularly scarce – apart, of course, from work carried out on local initiatives and at local expense; this is particularly abundant in Africa –

and it is all such as not to imply the immediate and constant attention of
the Emperor: a small number of milestones on roads in Gaul, Dalmatia,
Numidia and Mauretania; a few inscriptions on fortifications in Raetia,
Pannonia, Tripolitania and again Numidia and Mauretania, particularly
important perhaps because they demonstrate more the practical efficiency
of Perennis's rule – they almost all date from his period – than the profundity of Commodus's foreign policy;[1] and finally the inscriptions on
two temples at Corinth, paid for by others and dedicated by him. The
last detail seems to confirm what the biographer says about Commodus's
habit of putting his own name on other people's work.

The relative peace on the frontiers also reduced military expenditure.
The modern theory that Commodus granted an increase in pay, a theory not
supported by the evidence of the sources and recently contradicted by a
papyrus,[2] has now been completely abandoned. As for the structure of the
army, the reports of innovations introduced or planned by Perennis are
too uncertain to justify our drawing any firm conclusions, though it is
legitimate to accept the reality of tendencies already at work. It may well
be true that important governors of the calibre of Septimius Severus,
Pescennius Niger and Clodius Albinus, who were to be the protagonists
in the next struggle for power, renewed in its most natural orbit – the
army – displayed intolerance of the decadent central government, even if
their loyalty remained complete throughout the reign. The sources speak
of coins minted, in opposition to the official ones, by Perennis's son,
governor of Lower Pannonia, and by Clodius Albinus; but no specimen
has come down to us. These generals also governed the provinces and they
did it well. The provinces were still living in relative peace, though the
level of life they achieved was now too low, for economic, political and
social reasons, to produce any general prosperity, and organic changes,
thanks to the sluggish functioning of the ordinary administration, were
naturally few. Sardinia may have been finally handed back into the charge
of a procurator, but not even this is certain; the change may belong to the
reign of Septimius Severus. Reports like the one that Commodus gave
the provinces to friends of his own stamp or to those recommended by his
drinking companions, or like the story of the long letters written by
Pescennius Niger first to Marcus, then to his son, proposing a system of
regular provincial commands lasting five years each and entrusted to men
already possessing administrative experience, are scarcely credible outside
the realm of hostile generalizations on the one hand and the lucubrations
dear to the political theorizing characteristic of the third century on the

---

[1] See particularly *ILS*, 395, 396, 5849.   [2] *Pap. Berl.*, 6866.

other. Evidence about the material life of the provinces and of the local communities is also scarce. In the lower strata of the population it can have been neither better nor worse than before, and the custom of attributing personally to the emperor the benefits of the anonymous administration – while the indolence of Commodus did not incur any particular odium – may even have gained him a favourable reputation, especially in Africa, where Severus's rehabilitation was better received than elsewhere, as is shown by the numerous restorations of Commodus's name in inscriptions from which it had been erased. It is to Africa, as a matter of fact, that the most important juridical text of the reign refers, though we do not know how far it is the expression of the Emperor's personal attention and decision. This text, which has been directly preserved, is the decree dating from between 180 and 183 and registering a protest by the farmers of the *saltus Burunitanus*, in the valley of the Bagradas, against the procurator and *conductor* who had been harassing them by transgressing the norms laid down by the *lex Hadriana* on imposts. The decree confirms the validity of these norms.

There is also little to say about the administration of justice and legislation. According to the biographer, who quotes some fairly striking examples, the former was affected by corruption; and the latter was scarce. The sources have preserved in particular the extravagant measures dealing with newly-coined titles, changes in the names of the months, the games and similar futilities. In fact justice and legislation, especially in the field of private law, must have continued along the traditional lines; but some influence must have been exerted by the changed atmosphere, apart from the fact that the tyrant's conflict with the aristocracy must inevitably have been reflected in criminal justice. The trials and condemnations of the last few years of the reign brought back the harshest experiences in this field, arousing fear and hatred in the upper classes. And an intellectual opposition also came into being again. But the knowledge and practice – now professional – of the law in the college of *consiliarii* and in the activity of the great jurists still living, continued the formation of norms at this important moment which formed the link between the jurisprudence of the Antonines and that – no less glorious – of the Severi. The *Digest* has preserved under the name of Commodus, too, measures of the same tone as those of the preceding reigns in the matters of trial procedure, of tax law, of trusts, of manumission and of the status of freedmen, who could actually be sold, to the profit of the patron, if they did not observe their obligations to him. All this makes it clear, among other things, that the traditional social structure was not rocked to its foundations.

As for the spiritual atmosphere of the reign and the attitude of the Emperor in the fields of culture and religion, the programme of isolated and superhuman splendour could have led to the final goal – now inevitable even in the West – of the imperial cult, namely the deification of the Emperor while he was still alive. The ethical progress made in the century of the Antonines, the prevailing mystical tendencies and the influence of philosophy could have conferred a new and decorous form on the creation of full theocracy, as subsequently happened with some of the better emperors of the third century. Instead, memories of the turbid mysticism of Gaius and of the histrionic conduct of Nero paled when confronted with the mixture of the two achieved by Commodus, even though Roman society was now used to the most exotic religious concepts and practices. That the implementation of this programme was gradual and not without a thread of logic has been shown again recently,[1] on the basis of our stock of coins and in particular of so-called medallions, which were fairly plentiful under Commodus – precisely for propaganda reasons – and can be dated exactly.

Animated by a heated mythologizing imagination, Commodus found in what was called 'exuberant piety' a field for the development of his natural tendencies and the full satisfaction of his tastes. The humanitarianism of his father and of the age in general had had some effect on his behaviour: in the first years of his reign, at any rate, he did not go to the point, in public combats, of killing his adversary. With the softening of the gladiatorial games already introduced by Marcus and the accentuation of the 'sporting' element in them, Commodus could have aimed at raising their tone to some extent. But his true instincts were cruel and bloodthirsty and he gave evidence of the sadistic enthusiasm typical of the unbalanced even in the religious field, ordering the devotees of the orgiastic cult of Bellona to really cut off an arm, 'studio crudelitatis',[2] and the priests of Isis to beat their breasts with pine-cones until they were in shreds. He himself succeeded in killing a man in the rites of Mithras, and his participation in ceremonies was in general dangerous for others. Exalted by the desire to imitate the deeds recounted in mythology, he would lay about him with his club of Hercules; on one occasion, shooting arrows at a wretched procession of people afflicted with gout and draped with saddle-cloths to make them look like dragons, he repeated the exploits of the gods' battle with the giants. These may have been fits of madness in his last years or exaggerations on the part of the sources; but

[1] J. BEAUJEU, *La Religion romaine à l'Apogée de l'Empire*, I, Paris 1955, pp. 369–412.
[2] *V. Comm.*, 9, 5.

the personal basis of his mysticism, destitute even of the literary aspirations of Nero, cannot have been very different from the attitude implied by these stories.

The state of peace favoured these developments, and, since it was hardly possible to oppose the Emperor's claim to be himself the fount of peace and of the blessings it brought, they took the form at first of the still traditional exaltation of the 'Felicitas temporum' and 'Securitas publica'. However, they soon turned (the first occasion was in 185), with the concept of the 'Renovatio temporum', into the celebration of the 'Victoria felix' of the Emperor, who himself assumed the title of *Felix*, while the contemporary appearance of the motif of 'Juppiter Exsuperatorius' – 'Supreme Jove' – added to the highest god of tradition, in evident allusion to his identity with the Princeps himself, the attributes of the most abstract supreme god of the astral religions of the East. The fall of Perennis and the advent of inferior persons, who with their adulatory assent certainly encouraged the Emperor's infatuation, rapidly led to bolder innovations. Not that Commodus made any changes in the traditional religion, which still lives on with its customary vigour in the designs of the coins of his early years (Apollo appears with particular frequency); too indolent to carry out a reform of this kind, he simply opened the doors to foreign cults from Egypt and the East, without taking care to preserve for the traditional religion the pre-eminence which was still a condition of political stability. For this reason, for example, he did not worry about the Christians who, enjoying toleration and the changed conditions – the advent of peace had removed the reasons for hating them present under Marcus – spent years in peace. They were perhaps even regarded with benevolence, seeing that the intervention of the many Christians living in the palace itself and in a position, like Marcia, to influence the Princeps all the more when their power was not connected with the aristocratic tradition, protected them from the competition of the oriental cults – though Commodus always had a fanatical preference for these – and especially from the consequences of their refusal to take part in the worship of his person. We have already indicated that the case of the martyrs of Scyllium in Numidia was part of the aftermath of the persecution stimulated by Marcus; the martyrdom of Apollonius between 183 and 185, as the result of a senatorial trial in which the debate was guided by Perennis, was an isolated case. By the last few years of the reign, Commodus's tolerance or negligence had set the example throughout the empire and even personal or local moves against the Christians had almost completely ceased.

The Emperor was interested in something else, namely the extravagant assertion of his own divinity, at first through the disorderly and riotous practice of the most varied cults. Mithras. Isis, Serapis, Bellona and Cybele were all in great favour and the turgid nature of the *vota*, both ordinary and extraordinary, reflected the morbid religiosity of the 'Auctor Pietatis', as he caused himself to be called in coins of 187 and 189. Then he took the final step. In 190 and 191, as a further development of the idea, already asserted in 185, of the beneficent aura emanating from the Princeps, he first abandoned (A.D. 191) the name that linked him to his father's tradition and resumed his own forename and the family name of Hadrian – *L. Aelius Aurelius Commodus Augustus Pius Felix* – which brought him closer to L. Verus; then everything had to be 'Commodianus' – the months, the names of which were changed, all twelve of them; Rome itself, which became 'Colonia Lucia Aurelia Nova Commodiana'; the Senate, the Roman people and the legions, the local decurions, as is testified by inscriptions;[1] the new fleet established for the import of grain from Africa and its port, Carthage, which was called 'Alexandria Commodiana togata'; and the very day on which these decisions were taken, 'dies Commodianus'. It goes without saying that the golden age brought back to the world was called the 'Saeculum aureum Commodianum'; it had to be mentioned in the heading of every official letter.

The appearance of the formulas 'Hercules Commodianus', 'Liber Pater Commodianus', represented the last stage before complete identification with the deity. This took place in 192, when Commodus became Hercules, 'Hercules Romanus'. He made the Senate recognize him officially as a god, had sacrifices made to himself and created the *flamen Herculaneus Commodianus*. Hercules, preferred as the symbol of physical strength, of which the god-emperor gave liberal displays during the course of his exploits in the arena, now headed the empire. In Rome statues of Commodus-Hercules multiplied. The head of the Colossus was changed yet again and replaced by that of Commodus, with the attributes of Hercules and an inscription immortalizing his new kind of glory: '*Primus palus secutorum*: the only man who fighting left-handed defeated twelve times a thousand men'.[2] But he was not content with this and, developing other themes from myth and the field of self-exaltation, also wanted the titles of *Pacator orbis, Conditor, Invictus, Amazonius, Exsuperatorius*, the last of these being intended to indicate his superlative excellence, surpassing that of all mankind: 'so superlative was his insanity, the

[1] *ILS*, 400: 'decuriones Commodiani' of Trevi on the Anio (A.D. 192).
[2] CASS. D., LXXII, 22, 3.

scoundrel', in the words of a posthumous comment by a contemporary.[1] In fact all that had happened was that the principate had reached the goal heralded at least since Trajan's time by the linking – always underlined as particularly significant – of the cult of Jove and Hercules with the figure and power of the emperor. But the personal embodiment given to this concept by Commodus, with all the originality of wild eccentricity and contrary to all the rules of common sense, could not be the definitive one.

THE END OF COMMODUS AND THE TWILIGHT OF THE PRINCIPATE

However, it was not the reaction of traditional feelings and surviving propriety that put an end to this ignoble experiment. The Senate would certainly never have taken any collective initiative, in spite of the threat hanging over it. The offences against tradition could even be accepted, as we have seen, with ironic forbearance and with the applause which the fallen despot subsequently paid for with the ferocious *adclamationes* uttered against his abhorred memory. But the physical danger to life and property must also have seemed intolerable. It became more intense after 190 and did not weigh solely on the aristocracy, while at the periphery of the empire the perplexity of the armies and their leaders when confronted with the growing inanity and laxity of the centre must have roused the sort of expectations current in the last year of Nero. However, the liberating revolt did not come from this direction either. Once again it developed out of the danger constantly threatening the emperor's intimates.

These last few years must have been painful for everyone. The whirl of praetorian prefects appointed and then soon disappearing, victims of the Emperor's whim or of the intrigues surrounding power, went on unabated. The year 190, at the latest, saw the fall of L. Julius Vehilius Gratus Julianus, a man who had had a long and distinguished career and may have been in post when Cleander was still alive, and of one Regillus, of whom nothing more is known. Possibly in 191 a certain Motilenus was put to death; we do not know anything else about him either, except that he must have preceded Q. Aemilius Laetus, who was in post in 192. Suspiciousness was beginning to get the upper hand over the tyrant's habitual indolence. Biting references by actors to the Emperor, like those preserved, according to the biographer, by Marius Maximus, were not tolerated, and the aristocracy was smitten by a wild bout of persecution, dictated as

---

[1] CASS. D., LXXII, 15, 4.

much by the prospect of profitable confiscations as by a cordial return of hatred. After the repression – already mentioned – that followed the fall of Cleander and after the elimination of Gratus Julianus and his colleague, Commodus ordered the killing between 190 and 191 of the two Silani, probably D. Julius and Q. Servilius, consuls in 189, with their families, and in addition of the illustrious senator M. Antonius Antius Lupus and his own brother-in-law M. Petronius Sura Mamertinus, together with the latter's brother, M. Petronius Sura Septimianus, and his son, Petronius Antoninus. Then, on one single occasion, he eliminated – again with their families – six ex-consuls, known to us almost solely from the account of them given by the biographer in this connection. These six were Allius Fuscus, Caelius Felix, Lucceius Torquatus, Lartius Eurupianus, Valerius Bassianus and the better-known Pactumeius Magnus. In the provinces the Emperor's assassins accounted for a proconsul of Asia, Sulpicius Crassus; one Julius Proculus and the ex-consul Claudius Lucanus, also in Asia; in Syria, after an adventurous attempt at flight, Julius Alexander of Emesa, whose skill in hunting was intolerable to Commodus; and finally in Achaea Annia Fundania Faustina, his father's cousin, 'et alios infinitos' as the biographer sums it up, content to enumerate only the most famous victims. He confines himself for the rest to referring to plans – plans with financial overtones – for further massacres: of fourteen rich men for the exclusive purpose of gain; of others on the pretext of a fictitious conspiracy; and of many more without any further pretence of justification. Even if these were only intentions, subsequently debited to the hated despot's account as if they were facts by the hostility of the sources, the fact remains that the atmosphere, already rendered heavy and turbid by Commodus's claims to religious pre-eminence and by his demands for applause for his mad gladiatorial exhibitions, must have been anything but relaxed. The statue of the Roman Hercules, erected in front of the Curia in the pose of drawing a bow against the Senate, was in itself a whole programme of action.

In 192 one particular series of exploits in the Flavian amphitheatre must have created a profound impression, to judge from the position it occupies in the sources as a typical example of Commodus's activities in this field. It is especially interesting that the versions of Cassius Dio and Herodian should be in substantial agreement; the former was an eyewitness of the events, and in all probability the latter was too. Commodus's speciality was the *venatio*; he was also passionately fond of horses and took part in races, wearing the colours of the *prasini*, the faction he favoured in the circus. However, he only did this in private.

On one occasion he wanted to drive a chariot in the circus, but in the end confined himself to acting as starter, wearing a dalmatic. Combats with men and beasts were the greatest public manifestation of his divine strength. He had already killed exotic animals – elephants, hippopotamuses, rhinoceroses and giraffes – in the arena on other occasions; and if we add the gladiatorial combats in which he took part while his father was still alive to the numerous ones belonging to his shameless reign – as a crowning disgrace, they were recorded in the official annals – they amount to more than a thousand. He now assembled the Senate and people, both of them cowed by the massacres threatened on other occasions and also because anything could be expected from an individual who was cruel and malicious even in his jokes. As usual, he received the senators before the show in a long silk robe, subsequently exchanged for the purple cloak with a Greek chlamys and the diadem; he had the lionskin and club of Hercules carried on the imperial throne. Entering the arena himself in the guise of Mercury, dressed only in a tunic and barefooted, he inaugurated the games. On the first day, shooting arrows from a hunting-tower that protected him against any kind of danger, he slew a hundred bears. Then, tired, he drank a long draught from a cup shaped like a club, while the whole populace – 'and we too', says Cassius Dio – shouted 'Good health'. And so he went on for fourteen days, killing both fierce and harmless animals and then passing on, as his enthusiasm and cruelty mounted, to combats with men, amid the forced acclamations of the senators, who had to smile even at threats. One spectacular kind of hunt was the ostrich hunt: the ostriches were killed with arrows equipped not with pointed heads but with blades shaped like a half-moon, which cut straight through the neck so that the unfortunate birds went on running without heads. This kind of hunt is confirmed by a figure on the so-called Sarcophagus of Meleager, in the Museo Capitolino in Rome. Commodus then walked towards the senatorial boxes, holding in his hand an ostrich's head and signifying with an eloquent gesture that he would do the same to the senators, who, following the example of Cassius Dio, bit firmly into the leaves of their laurel crowns to prevent themselves from giving vent to a dangerous burst of laughter.

The end of madness like this could not be far distant, and hindsight subsequently also discovered the prodigies heralding it: besides the usual signs and wonders – comets, inexplicable periods of darkness, unfavourable flights of birds, statues walking or sweating, mourning garments put on at the wrong moment – on the last day of the games the Emperor's helmet was accidentally carried out of the amphitheatre through the *porta Libitinaria,* and a fire, later miraculously extinguished, destroyed the temple of Peace and, attacking the temple of Vesta, endangered the alleged Trojan Palladium kept there, which was removed for safety to the imperial palace. What finally precipitated the end was Commodus's plan to kill the consuls designate for 193, Erucius Clarus and Sosius Falco, and to make a theatrical entry in their place upon an unexpected eighth consulship, starting out from the gladiatorial barracks on the Caelian, with the title – inherited from a famous dead gladiator – of *palus primus secutorum* and accompanied by a troop of champions of the arena. The chamberlain Eclectus and the praetorian prefect Aemilius Laetus, who had already been forced to fight by their master's side in the games and were clearly in danger, took the initiative according to Cassius Dio, who leaves somewhat obscure the part played by Marcia. She is in the foreground in Herodian's dramatic narrative. But on the details of the decisive action the two versions coincide. Having failed to persuade the Emperor to abandon his mad plan, and being directly exposed to his anger, the three decided to do away with him. On the night of 31 December 192, when everything was ready for the next day's festivities, including the host of medallions in honour of the Roman Hercules struck for distribution with the gifts, they administered poison to him. When this did not take effect, the athlete Narcissus, the Emperor's instructor, was bribed to strangle him in his bath. Such was the wretched end, at the age of thirty-one, of Commodus, who was noble, handsome and strong, but a scoundrel.

What followed – the dumping of the body outside the city (it was subsequently buried in the mausoleum of Hadrian by Commodus's successor, who placed on the tomb the sober inscription which has been preserved[1]); the hailing of Pertinax, accepted without enthusiasm by the praetorians; the *damnatio memoriae* voted by the Senate, together with annulment of Commodus's laws, suppression of his titles and furious destruction of his statues; the revival of illusions (the statue in front of the Curia was replaced by a statue of *Libertas*); and then, after only four years, when two successors had suffered the same sad fate and the third had emerged from the struggle in an atmosphere now profoundly changed, the senatorial rehabilitation and deification, with the priest already instituted in his lifetime, the *flamen Herculanius Commodianus* – all this was the swift and tragic development of a political crisis long latent, the motive that inspired Cassius Dio to write his whole history of the Roman state.[2]

In fact not only had an emperor fallen, one of those 'youthful emperors'

[1] *ILS*, 401. [2] CASS. D., LXXII, 23, 2–5.

intent on enjoying power just as they pleased, whom the tradition contrasted – not so ingenuously, having had this view confirmed by events – with the old ones, expert administrators and moderate masters;[1] the principate itself – the one modelled on the genuine Augustan pattern, preserved until then in all essentials – had entered the twilight of its existence. Established by Augustus on the solid lines of practical administration, which had afterwards formed its leading characteristic, it was still working splendidly from this point of view and could still overcome, as in fact it did, the most severe difficulties. But many things had changed, even though this process of evolution had been curbed, as usual, by the instinctive conservatism of the Romans. The principate, seen as the real 'primacy' of one man based on the concrete strength given him by victory and on the universal consensus, and the legal fiction which had first reconciled in a happy formula the monarchy with the republic and then, when – with the disappearance of the urban aristocracy – the original reasons for this formula lost their validity, had crystallized in the harmony of the more open but always cordial Princeps–Senate relationship characteristic of the Antonines, had certainly served their time. There were indubitably no traces of this definition and of this fiction – which had already been suspended during the immature experiments of Gaius, Nero and Domitian – in the theocratic apotheosis of Commodus, which was the extravagant and eccentric climax of a process which had nevertheless been furthered even by emperors with the best reputations. Subsequently, even in the experiments with a senatorial principate which the deliberate political theory of the third century sought to insert into the practical chaos, there was never any further doubt of the emperor's open right to be fully, in name and in fact, the autocrat; and he eventually became the lord god of Diocletian's theocracy. On the other side the army, the fundamental basis of the principate as a real power, had undergone the most profound transformation, being the body most closely linked to the conditions prevailing in the vaster society of the empire. Now that the Augustan fiction, which among other things had kept a military monarchy looking like a civilian empire, was threadbare, the armies were once again to get the upper hand, not just for the transitory purpose of replacing an emperor, but – now that the ingenious and laborious equilibrium had been shattered – for the permanent affirmation of a claim sustained by force alone. Aelius Aristides's 'Soldiers of the empire' were now to have a much more direct and exclusive say in the appointment of the Princeps and to transform the very concept of the principate.

[1] HEROD., I, pr.

Behind them stood imperial society, the real agent of the transformation, however heedless and unthinking; a society which, as it stabilised and grew, was now close to reaching but not to sweeping away the barriers of Roman tradition.

APPENDICES

PART I

CRITICAL NOTES*

ON THE SUCCESSION OF TIBERIUS

The first succession is naturally a crucial point for examination and comparison in the debate that has revolved for some time round the origin and nature of the principate. For the vast literature anterior to 1934 on this general problem the reader is directed to the summaries and bibliographical lists of the *Cambridge Ancient History*, Vol. X, but special mention must be made, because of the important part it plays in the discussion of the position of Tiberius in relation to Augustus in the years 4–14, of KORNEMANN's study, *Doppelprinzipat und Reichsteilung im Imperium Romanum*, Leipzig 1930. For later works still dealing with the general problem of the nature of the principate, and hence containing indispensable references to Tiberius during the preparation for and moment of succession, see the reviews by G. I. LUZZATTO, 'Epigrafia giuridica greca e romana', III (1939–49), XVII Suppl. to *Studia et documenta historiae et iuris*, 1951, pp. 166 ff., 'Rassegna epigrafica greco-romana', in *Iura*, VIII, 1957, pp. 245–62, particularly pp. 253 ff., and also the critical bibliography of M. A. LEVI, *Il tempo di Augusto*, Florence 1951, pp. 451–82. Other works that deserve mention among the vast output on the same subject are the fundamental study of A. VON PREMERSTEIN, 'Vom Werden und Wesen des Prinzipats', in *Abhandl. d. Bay. Ak. d. Wiss*, Phil-hist. Abt., NF, Heft 15, Munich 1937; a book that also raises problems, though it is less rigorously juridical and based rather on prosopographical analysis, namely R. SYME, *The Roman Revolution*, Oxford 1939 (repr. 1952); and the recent study by A. MAGDELAIN, *Auctoritas Principis*, Paris 1947, which carries further the convincing conclusions on *auctoritas* as the real extra-juridical basis of the Princeps's

---

* The reader will find here, besides the arguments for the hypotheses accepted in the main text, details of the principal documents discovered recently and of the monographs useful for acquiring an up-to-date knowledge of the state of the problems. Since it was necessary to establish a chronological point of departure, this has been fixed at the publication of Volumes X and XI (1934 and 1936 respectively) of the *Cambridge Ancient History*.

power already asserted by Syme and clarified and confirmed by numismatic investigations (among others M. GRANT, *From Imperium to Auctoritas. A Historical Study of Aes Coinage in the Roman Empire 48 B.C.–A.D. 14*, Cambridge 1946, and C. H. V. SUTHERLAND, *Coinage in Roman Imperial Policy, 31 B.C.–A.D. 68*, London 1951), as well as the work cited of M. A. LEVI. See also L. WICKERT, 'Princeps', in *P.W.*, XXII, 2, 1954, pp. 2057 ff.

We must also mention some studies which are still general in respect of the specific event of the succession of Tiberius but particular in respect of the problem of the imperial succession: in itself a formidable problem and an almost insoluble one so far as finding a statutory principle of succession is concerned. In reality this never existed, since it would have been juridically in contradiction with the very concept of the principate, which was a personal and not an institutional régime. It is thus a question of seeking the factors which from time to time actually determined the succession. J. BÉRANGER, 'L'hérédité du principat. Note sur la transmission du pouvoir impérial aux deux premiers siècles', in *Rev. Ét. Lat.*, XVII, 1939, pp. 171–87, sees the principle of a victorious *clientela* that eliminated all the others as conditioning adoption and the transmission of power; this view was adopted and fully worked out by M. H. PRÉVOST, *Les Adoptions politiques à Rome sous la République et le Principat*, Paris 1949 (Publ. Inst. de Droit rom. de l'Univ. de Paris, V), with examination of the precedents on adoptions in the republican *nobilitas* and the adoption of Octavian by Caesar, traced back to the principles of *clientela* and *fides*, which is the moral bond involved; through the bonds of clientship, Prévost thinks, the choice of the successor exerted an influence capable of forestalling the decisions of the Senate and the army. This thesis, which seeks to explain with greater juridical precision, in the realm of custom and private institutions, what may be regarded in general, and looking more at men than schemes, as the inevitable secret work of persons and parties in the preparation of successions (work also mentioned in the text in connection with the succession of Tiberius), is certainly ingenious and has much truth in it, but possibly does not take account of all the elements in the actual historical development, which seldom conforms to schemes. This was noted by R. VILLERS, 'La dévolution du principat dans la famille d'Auguste', in *Rev. Ét. Lat.*, XXVIII, 1950, pp. 235–51, where much space is given to consideration of the contingent motives which, determining the succession in the Julio-Claudian house more or less empirically on each occasion (Tiberius succeeded, Villers suggests, through 'la politique active et prévoyante' of Augustus, Caligula through the 'hésitations' and 'passivité' of Tiberius, who found himself becoming 'l'inventeur du principat'), led people to regard heredity as in practice conferring a right. Adoption as a means of arranging the succession is dealt with by H. SIBER, 'Zur Prinzipatsverfassung', in *Zeitschr. Sav. Stift.*, Rom. section, LXIV, 1944, p. 266 ff. (cf. the same writer's *Römisches Verfassungsrecht in geschichtlicher Entwicklung*, Lahr 1952, pp. 315–19) and by J. CARCOPINO, 'L' hérédité dynastique chez les Antonins', in *Rev. Ét. Anc.*, LI, 1949, pp. 262–321, the latter paying particular attention to the adoptions after Nerva. The question of education with a view to succession, in particular for the Julio-Claudian emperors gradually designated for it (beginning with Octavian and going on to Tiberius, Gaius and Lucius Caesar, Germanicus, Claudius, Caligula, Nero and Britannicus) is discussed in E. R. PARKER's study, 'The Education of Heirs in the Julio-Claudian family', in *Amer. Journ. of Phil.*, LXVII, 1946, pp. 29–50. On the whole problem of the transmission of power in the principate one should read the five pages of P. DE FRANCISCI, *Arcana Imperii*, III, I, Milan 1948, pp. 321–38, as well as Chap. I (pp. 1–24) of M. HAMMOND, *The Antonine Monarchy*, Rome 1959 (Papers and Monographs of the Amer. Ac. in Rome, XIX); and on the juridical and administrative aspects proper F. M. DE ROBERTIS, *Dal potere personale alla competenza dell' ufficio*, in *St. et. doc. hist. et iuris*, VIII, 1942, pp. 255–307. See also the clear summary of V. ARANGIO RUIZ, *St. del dir. rom.*, Naples 1957, pp. 226 f.

But what interests us here in particular is the fact in itself of Tiberius's succession, which has also been the subject of much recent study. Research into the manner and time of Tiberius's succession, and into the essence of his powers as Princeps, has always centred on the chapters in Tacitus, *Ann.*, I, 11–13, on the sittings of the Senate after the death of Augustus, in particular on the second, of 17 September (a date recorded in the *Fasti Amiternini*, *CIL*, I², p. 244, the *Fasti Oppiani*, *CIL*, VI, p. 3315, and the 'Antiates ministrorum domus Augustae', *CIL*, I², p. 248 = I. *It.*, XIII, I, p. 32). At the same time the position of Tiberius in the last few years of Augustus's principate has also been subjected to systematic examination. Among less recent studies of this crucial double question, ones still valid are those of PH. FABIA, 'L'avènement officiel de Tibère. Examen du récit de Tacite (*Ann.*, I, 11–13)', in *Rev. de Phil.*, XXXIII, 1909, pp. 28–58, and H. DIECKMANN, 'Die effektive Mitregentschaft des Tiberius', in *Klio*, XV, 1919, pp. 339–75. In recent years the question has been re-opened in two important studies, that of J. SCHWARTZ, 'Recherches sur les dernières années du règne d'Auguste (4–14)', in *Rev. de Phil.*, 3ᵐᵉ série, XIX, 1945, pp. 21–90,

and that of A. PASSERINI, 'Per la storia dell' imperatore Tiberio',
in *Studi giuridici in memoria di P. Ciapessoni*, Pavia 1947, pp. 196–218.
Schwartz examines the gradual conferment on Tiberius of the powers
which little by little brought him close to the position of effective ruler
alongside Augustus, paying particular attention to the chronological
problems but also examining the nature of these powers themselves,
especially those conferred in A.D. 13 (see particularly pp. 39–47). Passerini
re-examines in the first part of his essay (the second part, pp. 219–33, is
devoted to the trial of Libo Drusus) the text of Tacitus, comparing it with
Cassius Dio and clarifying in all probability the true nature and extent
of the powers conferred and of those assumed for the first time at the
sitting of 17 September 14. He also gives an exhaustive explanation of
Tiberius's attitude of reluctance. This attitude is also the subject of a
study by the above-mentioned Béranger, 'Le refus du pouvoir', in *Mus.
Helv.*, V, 1949, pp. 178–96, according to which the refusal of power
became a sort of official formula used by the Princeps to avoid the appearance of tyranny (for Tiberius in particular, see p. 183). On the moment of
Tiberius's succession, we must mention because of its importance, though
it is not recent, E. HOHL, 'Wann hat Tiberius das Prinzipat über-
nommen?' in *Hermes*, LXVIII, 1933, pp. 106–15, and also D. M.
PIPPIDI, 'L'avènement officiel de Tibère en Egypte,' in *Rev. hist. du
Sud-Est européen*, XVIII, 1941, pp. 87–94 (= *Autour de Tibère*, pp. 123–32).

For the aspect of conspiracy – not sufficiently proved by the sources –
in the succession of Tiberius, see the summary of a communication by
F. M. WOOD, JR., 'Tiberius' Accession. The Plot and the Leading
Character', in *Trans. and Proc. of the Amer. Phil. Ass.*, LXXI, 1940, p. LII,
and for an alleged initial deviation by Tiberius from the political line
marked out by Augustus, in so far as he let the Senate participate in
matters concerning the army, see R. S. ROGERS, 'Tiberius' Reversal of
an Augustan Policy', *ibid.*, pp. 532–6. But this forms part of the policy
of deference to the Senate bound up with the legal fiction – strictly
observed by Tiberius – of the principate, and in any case is entirely a
matter of formalities; on the relations between army and Senate see in
particular p. 22 in the text – the episode of the attempted lynching of the
senatorial emissaries.

As for the sentiments of the provinces about the first imperial succession,
the formation in them, especially the eastern ones, of a dynastic feeling
in regard to the family of Augustus is sufficiently demonstrated by the
numerous altars and monuments dedicated in common to various
members of the family. To quote only a few examples discovered in

recent years, there are the bases from Lindos, one of them dedicated as early as 9–6 B.C., with the statues of Tiberius, Drusus and Julia (BLINKEN-BERG–KINCH, *Lindos*, II, 1941, cc. 736–8, no. 385 = *AE*, 1948, 183) and the other with Drusus II, Divus Augustus, Germanicus and probably Agrippina and Livilla (*ibid.*, cc. 765–70, no. 414 = *AE*, 1948, 184); the dedication of a portico at Aphrodisias, to Aphrodite, Divus Augustus, Tiberius, Julia Augusta and the Demos (IACOPI, in *Mon. Ant. Lincei*, XXXVIII, 1939, cc. 86–96 = *AE*, 1947, 147; there is also something similar at Apollonia in Pisidia, above the base containing the *Res gestae divi Augusti*: see BUCKLER, CALDER and GUTHRIE, *M.A.M.A.*, IV, 1933, p. 50); the group in the *cella* of the temple of Bel at Palmyra, consisting of Tiberius with Drusus on his right and Germanicus on his left (SEYRIG, in *Syria*, XIII, 1932, p. 275 = *AE*, 1933, 204); the neo-Punic inscription from Leptis Magna (*Afr. Ital.*, VI, pp. 15–27; cf. *Inscr. of Roman Tripolitania*, p. 12, no. 28) dating from 14–19 and mentioning Divus Augustus, Livia, Agrippina the elder and Agrippina the younger, Germanicus and Drusus, Antonia the younger and Livilla; the altar discovered in 1931 at Liubuškoga, in Herzegovina, with a joint dedication to Tiberius and Divus Augustus (*Bull. Ist. Arch. Bulgare*, XVI, 1950, p. 235 = *AE*, 1950, 44; cf. DEGRASSI, *Mem. Lincei*, ser. VIII, vol. II, fasc. 6, 1950, p. 318, n. 6); the curious complex from the forum at *Colonia Iulia Ruscino* (Castel Roussillon), where the numerous dedications found (*Inscr. Lat. de Gaule*, 616–29) indicate the successive addition, between A.D. 8 and 39, of the statues of various members of the Julio-Claudian family, with a typical enlargement of the dynastic-cum-religious concept; and finally the inscription from the amphitheatre of the Three Gauls, at Lyon (in *Compt. rend. Ac. Inscr.*, 1958, pp. 106–10, = *AE*, 1959, 78 and 81). Other significant dedications are the one to Tiberius, soon after his accession, at Antiochia in Pisidia (*AE*, 1941, 145) and the one, recently discovered, by tribes in Noricum, to Julia, the wife of Tiberius (*AE*, 1954, 241, cf. 1952, 212–13).

For other questions touched on in the paragraph on the succession, see: on the concept of *libertas* as an element in the policy of the principate, CH. WIRSZUBSKI, *Libertas as a Political Idea at Rome during the Late Republic and Early Principate*, Cambridge 1950, particularly p. 97 onwards, and in general on the ideological aspects of the principate the already-mentioned BÉRANGER, *Recherches sur l'aspect idéologique du principat* (Schweizerische Beiträge zur Altertumswissenschaft, Heft 6), Basle 1953. On the date of Augustus's marriage to Livia (17 Jan. 38), learnt recently from the *Fasti Verulani* (*Not. d. Sc.*, 1923, p. 196) together with the date of

M. Antony's birthday (14 Jan.), which according to SUET., *Claud.*, 11, 3 and CASS. D., LX, 5, 1 was the same as that of Drusus's birthday and has therefore created the so far unsolved problem of reconciling the latter with the literary tradition, which is unanimous in saying that Drusus was born after Livia's marriage to Octavian, see CARCOPINO in *Rev. Hist.*, CLXI, pp. 225–36; GROAG, *Prosop. Imp. Rom.*[2], II, p. 196. For the chronology of the military operations and triumphs of Tiberius before 14, see G. M. BERSANETTI, 'Tiberiana', in *Athen.*, XXXV, 1947, pp. 3–16, and the bibliography assembled there; also J. SCHWARTZ, *art. cit.*, pp. 71–6, whose dating of the *clades Variana* in 10 and the Illyrian triumph of Tiberius in 13 does not, however, seem probable. On this see latterly E. HOHL, 'Die Siegesfeiern des Tiberius und das Datum der Schlacht im Teutoburger Wald', in *Sitz.-ber. d. deutsch Ak. d. Wiss. zu Berlin*, Kl. für Gesellschaftswissenschaften, 1952, no. 1, pp. 24, especially pp. 17, 24, who adduces good arguments for putting the *ovatio ex Pannonia* in 9 B.C., the first triumph on 1 January 7 B.C. and the second (*ex Ilurico*) on 23 October A.D. 12, while the *terminus ante quem* for the battle of the Teuto-berg Forest would be 16 January A.D. 10; see also L. POLACCO, 'Il Triumfo di Tiberio nella tazza Rothschild da Boscoreale', in *Mem. Acc. Patav. Sc. Lett. e Arte*, LXVII, 1954–5, pp. 3–20. On the assassination of Agrippa Postumus, see A. E. PAPPANO, 'Agrippa Postumus', in *Class. Phil.*, XXXVI, 1941, pp. 30–45, whose hypothesis that Agrippa was the organizer of a plot against Tiberius frustrated just in time has been followed by the somewhat bold theory of W. ALLEN, JR., 'The Death of Agrippa Postumus', in *Trans. and Proc. of the Am. Phil. Ass.*, LXXVIII, 1947, pp. 131–9, suggesting that the youth died a natural death trans-formed into a violent one by the anti-Tiberian tradition in connection with the trial of Clemens in A.D. 16 (on which see J. MOGENET, 'La conjuration de Clemens', in *Ant. Class.*, XXIII, 1954, pp. 321–30). A balanced survey of the evidence, accepted in the main text, is that of E. HOHL, 'Primum facinus novi principatus', in *Hermes*, LXX, 1935, pp. 350–5. See also M. L. PALADINI, 'La morte di Agrippa Postumo e la congiura di Clemente', in *Acme*, VII, 1954, pp. 313–29; in Paladini's view both the death of Postumus and that of Clemens were ordered by Tiberius. For the coins referring to the succession, see M. GRANT, *Aspects of the Principate of Augustus*, p. 24 etc., C. H. V. SUTHERLAND, 'The Symbolism of a Unique Aes Coin of Tiberius' in *Numism. Chron.*, 6th Ser., X, 1950, pp. 290–7, on a coin of A.D. 15 which bears the typic-ally Roman symbol of the civic crown on a ceremonial chair peculiar to the Princeps and confirms the deliberately civil character of Tiberius's principate.

ON THE RULE OF TIBERIUS

The difficulty of describing the governmental acts of Tiberius in continuous chronological succession derives not only from the real complexity
of his activities but also from the way in which they are presented in the
sources. Not only is the narration of the facts constantly accompanied by
judgements on them, but sometimes the relation of the individual acts is
also replaced by a generalized account of a whole series of acts, without
any precise chronological indications. This is particularly the case with
SUETONIUS (cf. Ch. 26–38), and even more so with the general enthusiasm of VELL., II, 126. The situation is not so bad with TACITUS
and CASSIUS DIO, where the chronological thread is better preserved, in
spite of the prevalently anecdotal – and hence fragmentary – nature of
their accounts. This partly corresponds to the known position of ancient
historiography, confronted as it was with a stretch of activity divided into
two clearly contrasted periods, that of the *mitia* or *prima tempora*, which can
easily assume the general look of a time of excellent intentions, though
ones not carried through, and that of the horrors of the tyranny, chopped
up into the disgraceful deeds of the last few years. Modern historiography
does not escape the difficulty, especially if it is rightly concerned to
eliminate or at any rate soften the antithesis between the two periods
which was never questioned by the ancients. Thus – to mention only the
chief attempts at a reconstruction – we see DESSAU, *Gesch. d. röm.
Kaiser*, II, 1, Berlin 1926, pp. 1–103, following, with interruptions and
various retracings of his own steps, the chronological line, keeping fairly
close to Tacitus and consequently reaching an unfavourable verdict on the
second period; on the other hand, we see others like MARSH, *The Reign of
Tiberius*, London 1931, L. HOMO, *Le Haut-Empire*, Paris 1933, pp.
189–235, CHARLESWORTH, in *Cambr. Anc. Hist.*, X, 1934 (repr. 1952),
pp. 607–52, organizing their exposition in accordance with a logico-
chronological criterion which makes a *vue d'ensemble* and the consequent
comprehensive judgement easier and clearer. This is the criterion followed
in the text. What follows is a brief survey of recent discussions of the
numerous problems that arise in connection with the subject.

On *the rebellions on the Rhine and the Danube* TACITUS's account is
generally accepted, although a comparison of it with CASS. D., LVII,
3–6, shows that there are certain inconsistencies in it owing to the insertion
of materials from various different sources (see bibl. in G. WALSER,
*Rom, das Reich u. die fremden Völker in der Geschichtsschreibung der frühen
Kaiserzeit*, Baden-Baden 1951, p. 55), and varying degrees of relative

importance are attributed to the two events. MARSH, pp. 52–5, returns to
the Pannonian revolt, minimized by DESSAU, II, 1 with a fairer estimate
of the work of Drusus. The kinship between Sejanus, who accompanied
Drusus, and the governor Junius Blaesus are underlined, in regard to
subsequent events as well, by SYME, *Rom. Rev.*, p. 437. The revolt on the
Rhine and Tacitus's conclusions about the behaviour of Germanicus are
mentioned in all the recent studies of Tacitus; see in particular WALSER,
op. cit., pp. 55–9.

The relations between Tiberius and the nobility have been clarified not only
by studies of the formation of the literary tradition hostile to Tiberius but
also by prosopographical research and research into the *fasti* like that
embodied in the senatorial registers of S. J. DE LAET, *De Samenstelling van
den romeinschen Senaat gedurende de eerste Eeuw van het Principaat* (28 voor
Chr. – 68 na Chr.), 1941, and in that of K. TH. SCHEIDER, *Zusammensetzung des Römischen Senates von Tiberius bis Nero*, Diss., Zürich 1942, and
also by the researches of A. DEGRASSI, 'Osservazioni su alcuni consoli
suffetti dell'età di Augusto e di Tiberio', in *Epigraphica*, VIII, 1946
(pub. 1948), subsumed in *I fasti consolari dell' impero romano*, Rome 1952,
pp. 3–10. Nothing new is added to our previous knowledge of Tiberius's
attitude to the Senate in general by the article of E. KORNEMANN, 'Das
Prinzipat des Tiberius und der "Genius Senatus",' ed. A. REHM, in
Sitz.-ber. d. Bay. Ak. d. Wiss., Phil.-hist. Kl. 1947, Heft 1, but it does have
the merit of providing a clear picture of the deliberately civil nature of the
principate accentuated by Tiberius – as compared with Augustus –
precisely by the use he made of the Senate. What is new and characteristic,
on the other hand, is the idea that it was precisely the consequences of this
'infelice amore' (p. 26) of Tiberius's that had repercussions on the subsequent history of the principate by way of the awareness acquired by the
Senate of its own autonomy, which was felt particularly sharply at certain
moments (cf. the GENIUS SENATUS of Galba's coins and the resurgence
of regard for the Senate as an entity under Nerva and Trajan). As for
episodes of alleged organized resistance, see W. ALLEN, JR., 'A Minor
Type of the Opposition to Tiberius', in *Class. Journ.*, XLIV, 1948,
pp. 203–6, and R. S. ROGERS, 'An Incident of the Opposition to
Tiberius', *ibid.*, XLVII, 1951, pp. 114 f. In the same field – Tiberius's
relations with the *ordines* of Roman society and the composition of these –
special interest resides, after the weighty general investigation of A. STEIN,
Der römische Ritterstand, Munich 1927 (for Tiberius in particular, see
pp. 277 f., 429 f. and 434), in the two studies of S. J. DE LAET, 'Le rang
social du primipile a l'époque d'Auguste et de Tibère', in *Ant. Class.*, IX,

1940, pp. 13–23, in which the hypothesis is put forward that under Augustus and Tiberius *all* the *centuriones primipili* were knights (a hypothesis which really leaves us somewhat puzzled: the passage in OVID, *Amor.*, III, 8, 9 ff. seems clearly to refer to a knight who *had been*, not who *was* a *primus pilus*) and 'La composition de l'ordre équestre sous Auguste et Tibère', in *Rev. Belg. Phil. et. Hist.*, 1941, pp. 509–31, which expounds the view, largely confirmed by the facts, that the first two emperors introduced into the equestrian order the military, municipal, provincial and intellectual élites. On individual members of the aristocracy, see R. SYME, 'Marcus Lepidus, *capax imperii*', in *Journ. Rom. St.*, XLV, 1955, pp. 22–38; cf. R. SYME, *Tacitus*, Oxford 1958, pp. 751 f.

On the transference of the elections from the comitia to the Senate, the already considerable bibliography (see also MARSH's appendix in his book on Tiberius, pp. 296–303, and an important study by SIBER, 'Die Wahlreform des Tiberius', in *Festschrift Koschaker*, I, Weimar 1939, pp. 171–217) has been unexpectedly enlarged by the discovery of the bronze tablet of Magliano, the *'tabula Hebana'*, which contains a *rogatio* on the honours to be paid to the memory of the deceased Germanicus, which were to include the assignment of his name to five new voting centuries, as had already been done for Gaius and Lucius Caesar. The penetrating studies provoked by this discovery after its publication (*Not. d. Sc.*, 1947, pp. 49–68 and 339, ed. P. RAVEGGI, A. MINTO, U. COLI = *AE*, 1949, no. 215; new fragments were later published by COLI, 'Due nuovi frammenti della Tabula Hebana', in *Parola del Passato*, 1951, pp. 433–8 = *AE*, 1952, no. 164), to establish the text, to define its content and to integrate it accurately in the existing body of knowledge about electoral institutions, have been listed by G. TIBILETTI, *Principe e magistrati repubblicani*, Rome 1953, pp. 238–89, to which the reader is directed, with a reminder of the historical conclusions which Tibiletti has drawn from these studies, namely that Tiberius continued Augustus's policy of trying to use the nobility in the service of the new political reality – the monarchy. To Tibiletti's bibliography must now be added C. GATTI, 'Gli "equites" e le riforme di Tiberio', in *Par. Pass.*, 1953, pp. 126–31 (on an integration suggested by SESTON); H. LAST, 'The Tabula Hebana and Propertius II, 31', in *Journ. of Rom. St.*, XLIII, 1953, pp. 27–9 (on the placing of a statue of Apollo); J. H. OLIVER and R. E. A. PALMER, 'Text of the Tabula Hebana', in *Am. Journ. of Phil*, LXXV, 1954, pp. 225–49 (the first complete edition, with the new fragments, apparatus criticus, indices, commentary and also a comparison with the *tab. Ilicitana*); A. H. M. JONES, 'The Elections under Augustus', in *Journ. of Rom. St.*,

LXV, 1955, pp. 9–21; J. BÉRANGER, 'La démocratie sous l'Empire Romain: les opérations électorales de la Tabula Hebana et la "destinatio" ', in *Mus. Helv.*, XIV, 1957, pp. 216–40; S. WEINSTOCK, 'The Image and the Chair of Germanicus', in *Journ. of Rom. St.*, XLVII, 1957, pp. 144–54 (on the honours of the image and the seat in the theatre); R. SYME *Tacitus, cit.*, pp. 756–60.

On the outward and formal manifestations of the civil nature of Tiberius's principate, the article by K. SCOTT, 'Tiberius's Refusal of the Title "Augustus" ', in *Class. Phil.*, XXVII, 1932, pp. 43–50, arguing against the too resolute disbelief of DESSAU (II, 1), is well known; in defence of the passages in CASS. D. (LVII, 8, 2) and SUET. (*Tib.*, 26, 2), it shows that, as in the field of emperor-worship, so with regard to the title of 'Augustus' Tiberius was probably driven to accept it reluctantly. But the situation is illuminated above all by A. ALFÖLDI's splendid researches into ceremonial and dress, 'Die Ausgestaltung des monarchischen Zeremoniells am römischen Kaiserhofe', in *Röm. Mitt.*, XLIX, 1934, pp. 1–118 (for Tiberius and the simplicity of his relations with the senators, see particularly p. 25 f.) and 'Insignien und Tracht der römischen Kaiser', *ibid.*, L, 1935, pp. 1–171 (especially the chapter on the dress of the Princeps as senator and magistrate, in which Tiberius figures prominently, pp. 9–25). A new inscription from Leptis Magna (*Inscr. of Roman Tripolitania*, 329), which calls Tiberius *imperator* and *pater patriae* (cf. *ILS*, 151), confirms provincial usage in the early days of the reign, when his repeated refusal of these titles was still not known. For what can be deduced on the same subject from coins, see the works cited at the end of this section.

The various branches of *Tiberius's administration* have also been the subject of study in recent years. So far as the financial situation in general is concerned, most scholars now accept the view expounded particularly by FRANK, 'The Financial Crisis of 33 A.D.' in *Am. Journ. of Phil.*, LVI, 1935, pp. 336–41, and adopted again in *An Economic Survey of Ancient Rome*, V, Baltimore 1940, pp. 32–5. The subject has also been discussed by SCOTT and ROGERS, 'The Crisis of A.D. 33', in *The Clevelander*, VI, 1931–2, pp. 7–18, and S. J. DE LAET, 'La crise monétaire de l'année 33 ap. J.-C.', in *Revue Belge de la Banque*, V, 1941, pp. 245–52 and 297–304 (studies not accessible to me). Cf. also A. GRENIER, 'Tibère et la Gaule', in *Rev. Ét. Lat.*, XIV, 1936, pp. 373–88, on certain aspects of the crisis in Gaul advanced as the principal cause of the revolt of 21. According to this view, based mainly on TAC., *Ann.*, VI, 16–17, where there is a reference to measures taken in 33 by Tiberius to obviate the scarcity, and hence the

high cost, of money, the crisis was the consequence of the policy of
monetary contraction initiated by Augustus himself in A.D. 10 after
a period of abundant issues and continued by Tiberius, who in this field
too acquired the prosaic task of establishing normality after the easy ways
of the early part of Augustus's reign in particular (see especially GRENIER,
p. 388). As a whole, however, the finances, run strictly, must have been
healthy. On the central organs of the financial administration and the
development under Tiberius of the embryonic imperial state treasury
which was to emerge quite clearly, not before the age of Claudius, as the
fiscus, as opposed to the *aerarium*, see GARZETTI, 'Aerarium e fiscus sotto
Augusto: storia di una questione in parte di nomi', in *Athen.*, XLI, 1953,
pp. 298–327, and the studies cited there. As for the bureaucracy, the
general studies of the officials and of the system of taxes in the early
empire naturally deal fully with the period of Tiberius. On the development of the bureaucracy out of the private staff of the Princeps,
a development which, beginning under Augustus, becomes clearer and
clearer under Tiberius (we know of 29 procuratorships that existed in his
reign) and assumes its definitive shape under Claudius, see H. G. PFLAUM,
Essai sur les procurateurs équestres sous le haut-empire romain, Thèse, Paris 1950,
particularly pp. 8 f. and pp. 34 f. (cf. *P.W.*, XXIII, 1, 1957, c. 1240 ff.),
and on the administration of the customs dues, some of them organized
under Tiberius (the *quadragesima Galliarum*, for example, and the *publicum
portorii Illyrici*), see J. S. DE LAET, *Portorium*, Bruges 1949, espec. pp.
170 ff., 235. An interesting figure in the story of this development is that
of C. Herennius Capito, a procurator of the patrimonium, who administered in Palestine the property left by Salome to Livia and subsequently inherited by Tiberius and Gaius (P. FRACCARO, 'C. Herennius
Capito di Teate, procurator di Livia, di Tiberio e di Gaio', in *Athen.*,
XXVIII, 1940, pp. 136–44).

The principate of Tiberius is also an important moment for the
consolidation of the *municipal policy* and the *organization of the provinces*. The
local coins show – contrary to the views of DESSAU, II, 1, p. 90, and
SCRAMUZZA, *The Emperor Claudius*, Cambridge, Mass. 1940, p. 279,
n. 26 – that the foundation of colonies was not suspended under Tiberius
but on the contrary was possibly more intense than in the last years of
Augustus (Emona, Tifernum, perhaps Panormus, and also in Illyricum
and Pannonia). Some municipia were also founded – Cambodunum
(Kempten), for example. On the other hand, the veto on inscribing coins
with the name of *praefecti* taking the place of the Princeps as municipal
magistrates, while indicating Tiberius's wish not to give emphasis to the

imperial family, is also an interference in the local coinage, one which continues and confirms the various kinds of interference in municipal life already initiated with Augustus. For Tiberius's direct interventions in the provinces, see the article by A. GRENIER already cited, particularly on the problems of administration. Tripolitania is dealt with S. AURIGEMMA, 'Augusto, Tiberio e la Tripolitania', in *Libia*, III, 1939, fasc. 3, pp. 24–9. On the provinces newly instituted under Tiberius, see, for the controversial origins of Moesia, A. STEIN, *Die Legaten von Moesien*, Budapest 1940, pp. 15–17, and for Raetia R. HEUBERGER, 'Wann wurde Rätien Provinz?', in *Klio*, XXXIV (NF XVI), 1941, pp. 290–2, which brings down to the period of Claudius the constitution of the regular procuratorial province. K. CHRIST, 'Zur römischen Okkupation der Zentralalpen und des nördlichen Alpenverlandes', in *Historia*, VI, 1957, pp. 416–28, deals mainly with the conquest. A new list of the prefects of Egypt under Tiberius, modifying REINMUTH's, also recent, in *Klio*, Beih. XXXIV, 1935 (cf. recently, by the same writer, the heading *praef. Aeg.*, in *P.W.*, XXII, 2, 1954, *c.* 2369 and Suppl. VIII, 1956, *c.* 525 ff.) is to be found in R. S. ROGERS, 'The Prefects of Egypt under Tiberius', in *Trans. and Proc. of Am. Phil. Ass.*, 1941, pp. 365–71, now slightly modified in its turn by that of A. STEIN, *Die Präfekten von Aegypten in der römischen Kaiserzeit*, Berne 1950, pp. 23–7. Tiberius's *policy towards foreign peoples* has been illustrated, with ample references to his programme of halting conquest and of diplomatic action, together with a useful picture of the actual standard of civilization and of the concrete relations with Rome of the peoples immediately beyond the frontier, by the abovementioned WALSER, *Rom, das Reich*, etc., if from the angle of literary research. See also the summary by A. ALFÖLDI, 'Die ethische Grenzscheide am römischen Limes', in *Schweizer Beiträge zur allgemeinen Gesschichte*, VIII, 1950, pp. 37–50, for the elements drawn mainly from Tacitus, and the art already cited of K. CHRIST, particularly p. 427 f. The most exhaustive survey of the Germans' relations with Tiberius is the one by L. SCHMIDT, *Geschichte der deutschen Stämme bis zum Ausgang der Völkerwanderung, Die Westgermanen*, I², Munich 1938, pp. 91–127 (Angrivari and Cherusci), 153–8 (Marcomanni and Quadi, Maroboduus). On the other individual external events in Tiberius's reign, see latterly R. SYME, 'Tacfarinas, the Musulami and Thubursicu', in *Studies in Roman Economic and Social History in Honor of A. Ch. Johnson*, Princeton, N.J., 1951, pp. 113 f.; P. ROMANELLI, *Storia delle provincie romane dell'Africa*, Rome 1959, pp. 227–45 (for the war with Tacfarinas); R. BARTOCCINI, 'Dolabella e Tacfarinas in una iscrizione di Leptis

Magna', in *Epigraphica*, XX, 1958 (1960), pp. 3–13 (publication of a dedication, found in 1937, to *Victoria Aug.* put up by Dolabella *occiso Ta(cfa)rinate*; cf. ROMANELLI, *Prov. Afr.*, p. 670 f.). For the presence of Drusus on the Danube at the time of the war between Maroboduus and Arminius, see the inscription found recently at *Aquincum* in *Diss. Pann.*, ser. II, 10, pp. 287–311, while the one also found recently at Lissa, from A.D. 20 (*Fasti Archaeologici*, IX, 1954, p. 473 f.= *AE*, 1957, 152), confirms the stay of Drusus in Dalmatia already known from TAC., *Ann.*, II, 44, 53; III, 7.

As for the *frumentationes* and *congiaria*, the old treatments of these subjects (especially Marquardt's lists) are now completely replaced by D. VAN BERCHEM, *Les distributions de blé et d'argent à la plèbe romaine sous l'empire*, Geneva 1939 (for Tiberius, pp. 80 ff., 144–6) and G. BARBIERI, in *Diz. Epigr.*, IV, p. 838 f. For the financing of the *frumentationers*, where the Augustan system continues unchanged (until Claudius), see G. E. F. CHILVER, 'Princeps and Frumentationes', in *Am. Journ. of Phil.*, LXX, 1949, pp. 7–21 (for Tiberius, pp. 14–16).

So far as innovations in the *administration of justice* are concerned, special attention has been given recently to the question whether the official origin of the *ius respondendi* should be placed under Tiberius. H. SIBER, 'Der Ausgangspunkt des ius respondendi', in *Zeitschr. d. Sav. Stift.*, Rom. Abt., 1941, pp. 397–402, explaining the passage of Pomponius in the *Digest*, 1, 2, 2, 48–50, already maintained that Tiberius, fascinated by the interpretative activity of the great jurist Masurius Sabinus, probably authorized him to give his opinions 'ex auctoritate principis'. The same opinion on the problem, which concerns one of the most characteristic aspects of the juridical conception modified by the general tendency of the principate, is shared by A. GUARINO, 'Il ius publice respondendi', in *Rev. Intern. de Droit de l'Antiquité*, II, 1949 (Mél. de Visscher, I), pp. 401–19, who, after discussing and summarizing the debate (the other principal participants in it are DE VISSCHER, SCHULZ, ARANGIO RUIZ, and the above-mentioned SIBER; see the quotations in Guarino himself), ends by attributing definitely to Tiberius the start of the usage still in full force under Hadrian.

On Tiberius's attitude and measures in the field of religion and worship, new pieces of evidence have come to light recently: for his scrupulousness in the practice of the traditional religion there is the fragment of the *Acta Arvalium* published by E. GHISLANZONI, 'Nuovo frammento degli Atti dei fratelli Arvali', in *Athen.*, XXXIV, 1946, pp. 188–212; and for his severity in the repression of abuses in foreign rites, there is the confirmation of the passage in JOSEPH., *Ant. Iud.*, XVIII, 65–84 (3,4) by the discovery in the Tiber of a remarkable collection of rattles of an unusual type, and of Italian manufacture, a discovery which sheds a particular light on Tiberius's measure (F. W. VON BISSING, 'Sul tipo dei sistri trovati nel Tevere', in *Bull. Soc. Arch. Alex.*, NS IX, 1936–7, pp. 211–24). But it is particularly Tiberius's attitude to emperor-worship that has become the centre of interest and provoked a large number of studies as a consequence of the discovery of the inscriptions from Gythium in Laconia, published for the first time by S. B. KONYEAS in *Ellenicá*, I, 1928, pp. 16 and 38 (= *AE*, 1929, 99 and 100; cf. O. MONTEVECCHI, 'Osservazioni sulla lettera di Tiberio ai Giteati', in *Epigraphica*, VII, 1945, pp. 104–8) and containing among other things a decree of the city, which, probably in the last few months of 14 or at the beginning of 15, instituted a musical and theatrical competition in honour of Augustus and his family, and a letter of Tiberius's, dating from the same time, in which he thanks the people of Gythium but decisively refuses any kind of divine honour for himself. This attitude was already known in general terms from TAC., *Ann.*, IV, 38 and CASS. D., LVI, 35–42 (see in this connection K. SCOTT, 'Tacitus and the Speculum Principis', in *Am. Journ. of Phil.*, LIII, 1932, pp. 70–2, and D. M. PIPPIDI, 'En marge d'un éloge tibérien d'Auguste: Dion Cassius et la religion des empereurs', in *Rev. Hist. du Sud-Est européen*, XIX, 1942, pp. 407–18 = *Autour de Tibère*, Bucharest 1944, pp. 133–45). Complete bibliography on the subject (up to 1947) in J. TONDRIAU, 'Bibliographie du culte des souverains hellénistiques et romains', in *Bull. Ass. Budé*, 1948, pp. 106–25; for Tiberius in particular see L. R. TAYLOR, *The Divinity of the Roman Emperor*, Middletown, Conn. 1931, p. 239 f. and D. M. PIPPIDI, *Recherches sur le culte impérial*, Paris-Bucharest n.d. (but about 1940), pp. 47–73 and 193–201, where, in connection with the consecration of the *ara numinis Augusti* at Rome by Tiberius (*Fasti Praenestini*, *CIL*, 1², 1, p. 231), the question of the chronology of Tiberius's triumphs is also touched on in discussion with Taylor (see above). It becomes clear from all this that Tiberius's attitude was the same as Augustus's had been, though usually overlaid with greater tact, namely one of reluctant acceptance of an irresistible tendency, with expedient gradations to accord with local usage. It is even clearer that Tiberius, a Roman after the old style, found the deification of a living man repugnant; but the tendency made itself apparent on its own account, even in Italy and the West, from the altar dedicated in A.D. 4 to his *adventus* – when he was still only the adoptive son of Augustus – by the *Licinius* of *CIL*, XIII, 1370, a *negotiator* from Narbonese Gaul who had settled among the Nervii of Belgica (J. HEURGON, 'L'inscription de Tibère à Bavai', in *Ant. Class.*, XVII, 1948, Mél. Van de Weerd, pp. 323–30), to the inscriptions of Tusculum, *CIL*, XIV, 2591, 2592, which link the cult of Tiberius with that of the Dioscuri, in memory of the fraternal couple Tiberius and Drusus, just where Tiberius repeatedly stayed, in his villa, between 29 and 34, that is, after the final withdrawal from Rome (G. MCCRACKEN, 'Tiberius and the Cult of the Dioscuri at Tusculum', in *Class. Journ.*, XXV, 1940, pp. 486–8). Something which is constantly confirmed by the official testimony of the coinage (see GRANT, *Aspects*, etc., espec. pp. 104 ff.). Moreover, the terms in which Tiberius, Germanicus and Claudius refuse divine honours offered by the Greeks have caused people to think that Augustus himself had already devised a formula which, while signifying refusal, expressed thanks for the intention (M. P. CHARLESWORTH, 'The Refusal of Divine Honours, an Augustan Formula', in *Papers of the Brit. Sch. at Rome*, XV, 1939, pp. 1–10, based also on the precedent of *L. Vaccius Labeo* of IGR, IV, 1302). So far as nascent Christianity is concerned, the only thing that needs to be mentioned is the much-discussed passage in TERTULL. (*Apolog.*, V2e XXI 24), according to which Tiberius intended to recognize the divinity of Christ and prohibited the persecution of the Christians (cf. EUSEB., *Chronicle*, pp. 176 f. HELM). The evidence of this passage is generally rejected (see CIACERI, *Tiberio successore di Augusto*, Rome 1944, pp. 339–46); but see now C. CECCHELLI, 'Un tentato riconoscimento imperiale del Cristo', in *St. Calderini-Paribeni*, I, Milan 1956, pp. 351–62; M. SORDI, 'I primi rapporti fra lo stato romano e il Cristianesimo, e l'origine delle persecuzioni', in *Rend. Acc. Lincei*, ser. VIII, XII, 1957, pp. 58–93. As for relations with the Jews, the expulsion from Rome in 19 seems to have been provoked by incidental reasons of security; on the whole Tiberius continued Augustus's sympathetic attitude to them (E. M. SMALLWOOD, 'Some Notes on the Jews under Tiberius', in *Latomus*, XV, 1956, pp. 314–29).

Finally, the manifold aspects of Tiberius's activity considered above receive further illumination and co-ordination from our knowledge, furnished primarily by numismatic research, of the slant deliberately given to official propaganda. CLEMENTIA and MODERATIO are the 'virtues' most frequently proclaimed for Tiberius (the second is exclusive to him). With some reservations, research in this direction in the last few years has proved very fruitful for the history of Tiberius's reign, from the first studies of CHARLESWORTH, *The Virtues of a Roman Emperor:*

Propaganda and the Creation of Belief, London 1937, and SUTHERLAND, 'Two "Virtues" of Tiberius, a Numismatic Contribution to the History of his Reign', in *Journ. of Rom. St.*, XXVIII, 1938, pp. 129–40, to more recent ones such as the first part ('Some Imperial Virtues of Tiberius') of ROGERS, *Studies in the Reign of Tiberius*, Baltimore 1943 (cf. the same scholar's 'Roman Emperors as Heirs and Legatees', in *Trans. and Proc. Am. Phil. Ass.*, LXXVIII, 1947, pp. 141–6, on the *moderatio* of Tiberius in the field of inheritance as well) and the studies of GRANT, among which the oft-cited *Aspects of the Reign of Tiberius* is fundamental. In short, through all the pieces of evidence emerging from research, the governing principles of Tiberius's policy may now be regarded as known with some certainty.

GERMANICUS

Faced with the unanimous exaltation of Germanicus by the ancient sources, modern criticism has taken various different lines, seeking to deduce the real traits of his character and the true nature of his achievements, particularly from Tacitus, who turned him into an idealized hero, like Corbulo and Agricola, in accordance with the concept of 'virtues' (WALSER, *op. cit.* (1951), pp. 53–65), to embody the opposite principle to the one symbolized by Tiberius (cf. CH. CHR. MIEROW, 'Germanicus Caesar Imperator', in *Class. Journ.*, XXXIX, 1943–4, pp. 137–55). After the balanced judgement of M. GELZER in *P.W.*, X, 1918, c. 456 f., the general estimate has remained roughly the one adopted in the text of the present book – slightly more favourable in DESSAU, II, 1, pp. 12 ff., slightly more severe in MARSH, *op. cit.*, pp. 53 ff.; in other words, it is agreed, with some reservations, that Germanicus possessed humane qualities and his loyalty to Tiberius seems to be indisputable, but the verdict on him as a statesman and a general is basically a negative one. In any case, the question forms part of the general one of the formation of the whole tradition on the age of Tiberius. In this line of enquiry, after the important dissertation by G. KESSLER, *Die Tradition über Germanicus*, Berlin 1905, on the source of Tacitus's information about the young prince, which is supposed to have been a biography written by a friend and seen both by Tacitus and Cassius Dio – a thesis demolished by MARSH in his examination of Tacitus's account of the meeting of the Rhine legions (*op. cit.* (1931), pp. 267–71) – it is necessary to go back for Germanicus as well to the results of the most recent research on the sources and technique of composition employed by Tacitus. As for particular questions, the greatest attention has been paid to the German campaigns, not without incidental political colouring, beginning with the second edition, revised after the First World War, of F. KNOKE, *Die Kriegszüge des Germanicus in Deutschland*, Berlin 1922, who ends significantly by quoting an inflamed passage of Fichte. The narrative of L. SCHMIDT, *Die Westgermanen*, I, pp. 111–22 (see espec. p. 120 f.) is equally infected by ultra-nationalism, and there have been various recent controversies centring round the figure of Arminius (E. HOHL, 'Um Arminius, Biographie oder Legende?' in *Sitz.-ber. d. deutsch. Ak. d. Wiss. zu Berlin*, Kl. für Gesellschaftswissenschaften, 1951, no. 1, with up-to-date German bibliography on Arminius, pp. 21–7), whom the author, interpreting VELLEIUS, II, 118, 2 differently from usual, considers, because of long service in the Roman army, to have been much more thoroughly Romanized than people have been accustomed to think; he actually makes him take part in Gaius Caesar's Armenian campaign – hence his name. See also H. GLAESENER, 'Arminius, Ségeste et Thusnelda', in *Les Ét. Class.*, XXII, 1954, pp. 31–48 (on the political and domestic motives of Arminius's action) and the discussions of individual questions such as the supposed recovery of the eagles lost in the *clades Variana* (E. BICKEL, 'Der Mythus um die Adler der Varusschlacht', in *Rh. Mus.*, XCII, 1943–4, pp. 302–18; references to the expeditions of Germanicus, p. 302 f.) and the route followed by Germanicus in his thrusts (on that of 15, there is a discussion of the contradiction in TAC., *Ann.*, I, 63, 11–I, 70, 20 by C. O. BRINK, 'Tacitus and the Visurgis', in *Journ. of Rom. St.*, XLII, 1952, pp. 39–42). The whole problem of the campaigns in Germany and of reactions in Rome has been recently discussed afresh by E. KÖSTERMANN, 'Die Feldzüge des Germanicus 14–16 n. Chr.', in *Historia*, VI, 1957, pp. 429–79, who allows diffidence and fear in Tiberius in his dealings with Germanicus. On the behaviour of Germanicus in the East, F. DE VISSCHER, 'Un incident du séjour de Germanicus en Égypte', in *Muséon*, 1946, pp. 259–66, goes back to the edicts issued in Egypt (published by WILAMOWITZ and ZUCKER in *Sitz.-ber d. Preuss. Ak. d. Wiss.*, 1911, pp. 794–821, on which see particularly WILCKEN, in *Hermes*, LXIII, 1928, p. 48), while the striking of silver drachmas with Germanicus's own effigy at Caesarea, when he only had the right to put his likeness on bronze coins, would prove that he exceeded his powers (W. WRUCK, *Die Syrische Provinzialprägung von Augustus bis Traian*, Stuttgart 1931, p. 51). See also the fresh discussions of the whole eastern mission: C. QUESTA, 'Il viaggio di Germanico in Oriente e Tacito', in *Maia*, IX, 1957, pp. 291–321, which takes the view that Germanicus represented the easternizing tradition of Mark Antony; E. KÖSTERMANN, 'Die Mission des Germanicus im Orient', in *Historia*, VII, 1958, pp. 331–75.

The opposition between partisans of Germanicus and partisans of Drusus, which passed from idealistic attitudes (admiration for Cato, etc.) into practical indulgence in real plots and thus became a dangerous political factor is dealt with by W. ALLEN JR. in his article 'The Political Atmosphere of the Reign of Tiberius', in *Trans. Proc. Am. Phil. Ass.*, LXXII, 1941, pp. 1–25. The good relations actually existing between Germanicus and Drusus and their positions of official parity in regard to the succession are reflected in the coinage and in many eastern inscriptions (*philadelphoi*), as in those of Forum Novum in the Sabine district (Vescovio), discovered recently (*AE*, 1945, 41–2, cf. 47–8). An indication of open adhesion to Germanicus after his death is to be found in the dedication from Sua, in Proconsular Africa, if *Inscr. Lat. Tun.* 682 does in fact refer to him (this is contested by DEGRASSI, in *Bull. Mus. Imp. Rom.*, 1938, p. 136).

A curious relic appertaining to the whole family of Tiberius and Germanicus and one round which debate has gone on for three centuries, with a notable increase in intensity in recent years, is the so-called Grand Cameo of Paris. Even though the contribution of this gem to history is certainly reduced precisely because history, to the extent that it is known from other sources, brings its own arguments for the identification of the figures of the composition as a whole and therefore gives more than it receives (as is usual with works of art of this kind; it is the same with the simpler cameo of Vienna, representing Augustus and Tiberius and referring almost certainly to Tiberius's triumph of A.D. 12), the discussion itself has thrown into relief interesting aspects of the internal relations in Tiberius's family and of the dynastic question – one of the crucial problems of Tiberius's reign, as it had been of Augustus's. After R. BIANCHI BANDINELLI, 'Per l'iconografia di Germanico', in *Röm. Mitt.*, LXVII, 1932, pp. 153–69, had called attention to the still very uncertain iconography of the young prince, and after L. CURTIUS, 'Ikonographische Beiträge zum Porträt der römischen Republik und der Iulisch – Claudischen Familie, VI, Neue Erklärung des grossen Pariser Cameo mit der Familie des Tiberius', in *Röm. Mitt.*, XLIX, 1934, pp. 119–56, had re-opened with a new interpretation (work executed, says Curtius, at the beginning of Caligula's reign, in 37, to commemorate the moment at which, after the death of the younger Drusus in 23, and before that of Julia Augusta in 29, the young Gaius was presented as *princeps iuventutis* in place of Drusus) a question which had now gradually come to rest, from BERNOULLI, *Röm Ikonogr.* II, 1, 1886, p. 282, up to

GAGÉ, 'La Victoria Augusti et les auspices de Tibère', in *Rev. Arch.*, XXXII, 1930, 2, pp. 1–35, especially p. 20 ff. (bibliography in Curtius, p. 120), in the conclusion that the Paris cameo was concerned with the despatch of Germanicus to the East by Tiberius, hardly a year has passed by without interventions on the subject. These contributions were at first fairly cautious and lukewarmly favourable to the interpretation of CURTIUS (e.g. GAGÉ, 'Un manifeste dynastique de Caligula', in *Rev. Ét. Anc.*, XXXVII, 1935, pp. 165–84, who accepts Curtius's dating but not his identification of all the figures, not even that of Caligula himself; F. POULSEN, 'Probleme der röm. Ikonographie', in *Kgl. Danske Videnskabernes Selskab, Archaologisk–kunsthistoriske Meddelelser*, II, 1, 1937, pp. 32–45, and 'Röm. Privatporträts und Prinzenbildnisse', *ibid.*, II, 5, 1939, p. 15 f., who accepts the dating and identification of the figure of Alexander, but not that of Caligula and of the alleged allegorical figures of divinities), then, starting with the stand taken by E. HOHL, 'Der Cupido der Augustusstatue von Primaporta und der grosse Pariser Cameo', in *Klio*, XXXI, 1938, pp. 269–84, and considering the impossibility of a definitive identification of the figures, the contributions turned more and more decisively to the most ancient interpretation, partly for the reason mentioned above and already given due weight by J. P. V. D. BALSDON, 'Gaius and the Grand Cameo', in *Journ. of Rom. Stud.*, XXVI, 1936, pp. 152–60, namely that little can be expected for history from the interpretation, already based solely on history, of works of art of this sort. For a complete bibliography on the history of the question, see particularly B. SCHWEITZER, 'Entstehungszeit u. Bedeutung des grossen Pariser Kameo', in *Klio*, XXXIV, 1942, p. 328 ff., and A. W. BYVANCK, 'Notes archéologiques, IV: L'interprétation du Grand Camée de France', in *Mnem.*, III, 13, 1947, pp. 238–40. More recently E. HOHL has returned to the theme again in 'Der grosse Pariser Cameo als geschichtliches Zeugnis', in *Arch. Anzeiger*, 1948–9, cc. 255–60, where he adduces further reasons for assigning the work to the occasion of the death of Germanicus. In the view of J. CHARBONNEAUX, 'Le Grand Camée de France', in *Rev. Arch.*, XXIX–XXX, 1948 (Mél. Picard, I), pp. 170–86, the work was commissioned by Agrippina and the dominant figures in it are Tiberius and Germanicus (cf. 'Un camée antique du Musée du Louvre', in *Bull. van de Vereniging tot Bevordering der Kennis van de Antieke Beschaving*, Leiden, XXIV–XXVI, 1949–51, pp. 63–9). GRANT too, *Aspects* etc. p. 109, n. 131, favours HOHL's interpretation and underlines the scanty value of works such as this as historical sources because of the uncertainty of their dating. See also latterly GERDA BRUNS, 'Der grosse

Kameo von Frankreich', in *Mitt. d. deutsch. arch. Instituts*, VI, 1953, pp. 71–115, with further bibliography and the revolutionary suggestion that the gem belongs to the age of Hadrian (adoption of Aelius Caesar) and was later modified and given its present appearance by Catherine de' Medici, with reference to the court of France in 1573–4. Whatever the intrinsic worth of this hypothesis, the mere fact that it can be advanced shows once and for all what the historical value of this kind of evidence is. Against BRUNS, see J. BABELON, 'Observations sur le camée de la Sainte-Chapelle', in *Jahrb d. deutsch. arch. Inst.*, LXIX, 1954, Arch. Anz. C. 251 f.; A. RUMPF, 'Römische historische Reliefs, 2, Der cameo von der Ste Chapelle', in *Bonn. Jahrb.*, 155/156, 1955–6, pp. 120–7. See also now *Encicl. Arte Antica*, II, 1959, pp. 295–8 (L. ROCCHETTI).

THE TRIALS

After the studies of E. CIACERI, from that of 1898 (*Le vittime del despotismo in Roma nel I secolo dell'impero*, Catania) to that of 1909–10 ('La responsibilità di Tiberio nell'applicazione della "Lex Iulia maiestatis",' in *Studi storici per l'antichità classica*, II, pp. 377–415, III, pp. 1–30, reprinted under the title 'L'imperatore Tiberio e i processi di lesa maestà' in the volume *Processi politici e relazioni internazionali*, Rome 1918, pp. 249–308), mapping out the stages of a move from a position of hostility to one decidedly favourable to Tiberius, and after the detailed and penetrating analysis of F. B. MARSH (*The Reign of Tiberius*, espec. pp. 105–21, 289–95), which is still the best summary of the subject, the question, which continues to remain essential to any rehabilitation of Tiberius, has continued to attract attention, always with results favourable to the Emperor. The method used is that of the objective interpretation of the facts preserved by Tacitus and of those preserved by other sources when they are confirmed by Tacitus (MARSH). Earlier studies of details of the trials by R. S. ROGERS ('Lucius Arruntius', in *Class. Phil.*, XXVI, 1931, pp. 31–45; 'The Date of the Banishment of the Astrologers', *ibid.*, pp. 203 ff.; 'The Conspiracy of Agrippina', in *Trans. Proc. Am. Phil. Ass.*, LXII, 1931, pp. 141–68; 'Ignorance of the Law in Tacitus and Dio: Two Instances from the History of Tiberius', *ibid.*, LXIV, 1933, pp. 18–27; and 'Der Prozess des Cotta Messalinus', in *Hermes*, LXVIII, 1933, pp. 121–3) were followed by his important book *Criminal Trials and Criminal Legislation under Tiberius* (Phil. Monogr. publ. by the Amer. Phil. Ass., VI), Middletown, Conn., 1935, in which for the first time the material is presented in an organic and comprehensive way in accordance with the chronological order of the trials, with a statistical conclusion (pp. 190–205) and systematic lists of the defendants (pp. 206–11), of the accusers (pp. 212–14), of the defending lawyers and witnesses (215) and of the laws connected with the trials (216). Among other reviews of this book the important one by B. KUEBLER, in *Phil. Wochenschrift*, LVII, 1937, cc. 380–9, should also be seen. But see the criticisms of C. W. CHILTON, 'The Roman Law of Treason under the Early Principate', in *Journ. Rom. St.*, XLV, 1955, pp. 73–81. E. KÖSTERMANN, 'Die Majestätsprozesse unter Tiberius', in *Historia*, VI, 1955, pp. 72–106, confirms Tacitus's objectivity. On individual trials see E. BIGNONE, 'La veridicità storica di Tacito a proposito del processo di Cremuzio Cordo', in *Rend. Acc. Italia*, II, 1941, pp. 430–2, an analysis of TAC. *Ann.*, IV, 34–6, resuming that of G. M. COLUMBA, 'Il processo di Cremuzio Cordo', in *At. e Roma*, IV, 1901, cc. 361–82; and A. PASSERINI's study, 'Per la storia dell' imperatore Tiberio, II, Il processo di Libone Druso', in *Studi giuridici in memoria di P. Ciapessoni*, Pavia 1947, pp. 219–33, whose conclusions about the real attitude of Tiberius, as it emerges from Tacitus's narrative when this is read without accepting the writer's implications, have been adopted in the text of the present book. Mystical motives of an oriental type are discerned in Libo Drusus's conspiracy by E. F. LEON, 'Notes on the Background and Character of Libo Drusus', in *Class. Journ.*, LIII, 1957, pp. 77–80.

SEJANUS. THE LAST YEARS OF TIBERIUS

The most complete account of Sejanus's activity and the most balanced general appraisal of it is that of F. B. MARSH, *op. cit.*, pp. 160–99 and 304–10, whose conclusions are generally accepted so far as the reconstruction of events is concerned. Subsequent studies aim for the most part at going more deeply into collateral questions or at rectifying details as a result of the discovery of further evidence. It is probable that there was no actual conspiracy by Sejanus against the life of Tiberius (but see L. PARETI, *St. di Roma*, IV, Turin 1955, p. 752). The tendency to minimize the political aspect of the Sejanus affair has become evident in recent years in the studies by M. DURRY, *Les cohortes prétoriennes*, Paris 1938, pp. 151–7, espec. 154, and A. PASSERINI, *Le coorti pretorie*, Rome 1939, pp. 276 f., with its allusion to the relatively still small importance of the praetorian prefecture under Tiberius ('this small consideration [of Augustus] for the new official was shared by Tiberius; indeed it was the reason why he allowed Sejanus to pursue his mad dream so long undisturbed', PASSERINI, p. 272). See also latterly G. TIBILETTI, *Principe e magistrati repubblicani*, *op. cit.*, pp. 249 ff., who suggests that Sejanus's action was really just an episode; it may have represented the first failure of the Augustan system, but its significance was limited and Sejanus himself did not exceed the bounds of the aristocratic state; he eagerly sought nobility for himself. There is no trace under Tiberius of any attempt to adopt an anti-aristocratic position in order to put absolutism above, and make it independent of, the traditional framework of the aristocratic state, and there is thus even less reason to descry anything of the sort in the entirely personal action of the ambitious praetorian prefect. See also the monograph by M. FRIEDENTHAL, *Seian*, Diss., Heidelberg 1957.

The dedication to *Concordia* of the acephalous inscription *CIL*, VI, 93, would assume a quite special significance if it should in fact be completed, as seems almost certain, by the name L. *Fulcinius Tiro*, *cos. suff.* 1 July 31, on the basis of the Lusitanian inscription (dated 1 January 31) recently published by M. HELENO and S. LAMBRINO, 'L. Fulcinius Tiro, premier gouverneur de la Lusitanie, sur une tabula patronatus', in *Compt. rend. Acad. Inscr.*, 1952, pp. 472–6 (= *AE*, 1953, 88–9); cf. S. LAMBRINO, 'L. Fulcinius Tiro, gouverneur de Lusitanie, sur une tabula patronatus de Juromenha', in *Arquéologo Português*, NS, 1, 1953, pp. 1–24. This governorship of Fulcinius Tiro was unknown; he is now the most ancient governor of Lusitania known. Cf. G. HEUTEN, 'Les gouverneurs de la Lusitanie et leur administration', in *Latomus*, II, 1938, pp. 256–78.

Considerable attention has been paid to the figure of Tiberius's son Drusus, the very serious consequences of whose death on the rest of his father's reign had already been rightly indicated by DESSAU, *Gesch. d. röm. Kaiserz.*, II, 1, p. 33. In the view of R. S. ROGERS (see also his 'Drusus Caesar's Tribunician Power', in *Amer. Journ. of Phil.*, LXI, 1940, pp. 457–9, on the counting of the *trib. pot.*, the II from the spring of 23, without any connection with those of Tiberius), the relations between Sejanus and Drusus, the beginning of which is put back as far as possible (the episode of the slap should be placed in 20 and the mutual antipathy might have begun even earlier), were indubitably at the bottom of Sejanus's whole design ('Seianus and Drusus Caesar', in *Trans. Proc. Am. Phil. Ass.*, LXXII, 1941, p. XLII ff.), while the problem of the part played in Drusus's death by Sejanus and Livilla is closely intertwined with the same question. The report of the denunciation by Apicata, mentioned by TAC., *Ann.* IV, ii and CASS. DIO, LVIII, 11, 6, and generally accepted, has been questioned again (DESSAU, II, 1, p. 32, n. 1, had already had reservations) by W. EISENHUT, 'Der Tod des Tiberius-Sohnes Drusus', in *Mus. Helv.*, VII, 1950, pp. 123–8, on the basis of the consideration that if, in accordance with the new tendency, Tacitus is read in a sense favourable to Tiberius, he must be read in the same way for all the persons presumably altered by the 'philo-Germanicus' tradition, especially as a discrepancy between the details given by the sources about the massacre of Sejanus's family and those given by the *Fasti Ostienses* (*I. It.*, XIII, 1, pp. 187–217) would be precisely an indication of romantic elaboration on the part of the sources. On this view Livilla and certainly Sejanus would be cleared of the serious accusation. For a different view, see J. P. V. D. BALSDON, 'The "Murder" of Drusus, Son of Tiberius', in *Class. Rev.*, NS, I, 1951, p. 75. However, the *Fasti Ostienses* confirm not only the precise date of the execution of Sejanus's eldest son (24 October) and of Apicata's suicide (26 October) but also that the execution of the other two children took place only in December; thus there is nothing in conflict with TAC., *Ann.*, V, 9, while it serves to correct the amplified and moralizing account of CASS. D., LVIII, 11, 6. From the same *Fasti Ost.* we have also learnt the *cognomina* of the children: the elder son was called *Strabo*, the younger *Capito Aelianus* (possibly adopted by C. *Fonteius Capito, cos* in 12, see DEGRASSI, *I. It.*, XIII, 1, p. 217) and the daughter *Iunilla*. On the *improbae comitiae . . . in Aventino*, that is, the *comitia consularia* of Sejanus, see R. SYME, 'Seianus on the Aventine', in *Hermes*, LXXXIV, 1956, pp. 257–66. The complete name of Macro, Sejanus's successor, is given by the inscription from the amphitheatre at Alba Fucens (*AE*, 1957, 250): Q. *Naevius Cordus Sutorius Macro*.

On Tiberius's movements before his withdrawal to Capri, see R. S. ROGERS, 'Tiberius' Travels A.D. 26–27', in *Class. Weekly*, XXXIX, 1945–6, pp. 26–37 and 42–4, and on the friends of Sejanus in touch with the family circle of the young Seneca, see Z. STEWART, 'Seianus, Gaetulicus and Seneca', in *Am. Journ. of Phil.*, LXXIV, 1953, pp. 70–85, which is also interesting for its fixing of chronological points and for its prosopographical observations on the prefect of Egypt, L. Seius Strabo, Sejanus's father, and his successor C. Galerius, Seneca's uncle (cf. also A. STEIN, *Die Präfekten von Aegypten in der römischen Kaiserzeit*, Berne 1950, p. 24 f.). On Tiberius's eastern policy in his last few years, see A. GARZETTI, 'La data dell' incontro all' Eufrate di Artabano III e L. Vitellio legato di Siria', in *St. in on. di R. Paribeni e A. Calderini*, I, Milan 1956, pp. 211–29.

For criticism of the tradition on the wickednesses of Tiberius's last years, see, after J. CARCOPINO, *Aspects mystiques de la Rome païenne*, Paris

1941, p. 109 f., the above-mentioned D. M. PIPPIDI, *Autour de Tibère* p. 170, n. 2, and, in particular, 'Note sur une épigraphe funéraire grecque, métrique, de Capri', in *Revista Classica*, IV–V, 1932–3, pp. 51–72, repr. in 1944 in *Autour de Tibère*, pp. 89–109, which dismisses once and for all as a fable the tradition that the dead boy of a Greek inscription (*IG*, XIV, 902) from the grotto of Matromania, on the isle of Capri, had been sacrificed by Tiberius, as even GREGOROVIUS had maintained. The inscription probably belongs to the cemetery dating from the end of the second century.

For the tradition on the death of Tiberius, see the observations of MARSH, *op. cit.*, pp. 256–9.

Finally, specific aspects of his character are discussed by K. SCOTT, 'The "diritas" of Tiberius', in *Am. Journ. of Phil.*, LIII, 1932, pp. 139–51, which collects all the episodes illustrating the defect which was the chief cause of Tiberius's unpopularity (see the criticism by D. M. PIPPIDI, *Autour de Tibère*, p. 173, n. 5: not a defect, because Tiberius never sought popularity, but an attitude deriving from Stoic educational doctrine on the exercise of royalty); by J. H. THIEL, 'Kaiser Tiberius. Ein Beitrag zum Verständnis seiner Persönlichkeit', in *Mnem.*, III, 2 (1935), pp. 245–70; II, 3 (1935–6), pp. 177–218; 111, 4 (1936–7), pp. 17–42, to be accepted with caution; by F. PEZZELLA, *L'imperatore Tiberio e la psico-patologia*, S. Maria Capua Vetere 1956; and by A. ESSER, *Cäsar und die julisch-claudischen Kaiser im biologisch-ärztlichen Blickfeld*, Leiden 1958. On the withdrawal to Rhodes, one of the key factors for the understanding of Tiberius's character, see M. L. PALADINI, 'A proposito del ritiro di Tiberio a Rodi e della sua posizione prima dell'accessione all'impero', in *Nuov. Rev. Stor.*, XLI, 1957, pp. 3–34 (the causes are said to be resentment at the insolence of Gaius Caesar, innate pride, and love of solitude); J. A. WELLER, 'Tacitus and Tiberius' Rhodian Exile', in *Phoenix*, XII, 1958, pp. 31–5 (with exaggerated emphasis on the Tacitean 'distortion' of materials dealing with Tiberius).

For the iconography of Tiberius, see L. POLACCO, *Il volto di Tiberio. Saggio di critica iconographica*, Rome 1955; A. ANDRÉN, 'Un portrait de Tibère à la villa San Michele, Anacapri', in *Homm. Deonna*, Brussels 1957, pp. 59–60.

GAIUS AND HIS REIGN

The chief problem is that of the verdict to be pronounced on G.'s mental condition. From this follows the estimate of his personality and his work, in other words the verdict on his principate. The ancients are unanimous in regarding him as mad after the illness which, in the biographies, marks a dividing line, with a scheme partly repeated from the tradition on Tiberius (SUET., *Calig.*, 22, 1: 'hactenus quasi de principe, reliqua ut de monstro narranda sunt'; CASS. D., LIX, 4, 2–6; 6, 3 draws a parallel between contradictory actions). Modern scholars are divided according to the degree of credibility which they attribute to, and the way in which they interpret, the nauseating mass of anecdotes which has made Suetonius's life of G. one of the longest in comparison with the brevity of the reign and which makes us lament, with MOMMSEN (*Röm. Gesch.*, V, p. 4) that for this emperor too, as for such a large part of the history of the empire, 'what merited silence has been told, and what deserved telling has been passed over in silence'; it also makes us lament the loss of Tacitus.

As for modern verdicts, if we leave aside biographies of a defamatory character (such as the notorious one by L. QUIDDE, *Caligula, Eine Studie über römische Casarenwahnsinn*, 3rd. ed., Leipzig 1894, in which people were bound to see, whether they were meant to or not, the figure of the young Kaiser Wilhelm II, hence the numerous editions and translations) and pathologists' reconstructions, and if we refer briefly to the studies that appeared in the period already covered by the ample bibliography in the *Cambr. Anc. Hist.*, X, 1934, pp. 970–2, the only monographs still valid are those of H. WILLRICH and M. GELZER. WILLRICH's 'Caligula' in *Klio*, III, 1903, pp. 85–118, 288–317, 397–470, is an attempt at a complete rehabilitation, to be considered a clear failure as a delineation, based on too slender grounds (one of those advanced is the series of measures taken in Gaul against the soldiers after the conspiracy of Gaetulicus, p. 424), of the figure of a distinguished statesman continuing the programme of Caesar, but useful for its chronological reconstruction and its rectification of many details. M. GELZER's accurate article in the *Real-Encyclopädie*, X, 1918, cc. 381–423, though corrected on some points, still represents the most complete and balanced arrangement of all the material provided by the sources. Naturally neither of these two scholars accepts the theory of pure and simple madness and the series of facts presented coldly and objectively by GELZER is in itself a valid argument for the justice of this position. This position is substantially accepted in the most recent comprehensive monograph, J. P. V. D. BALSDON's *The Emperor Gaius*, Oxford 1934, who retreats from the vindicatory stance of WILLRICH to the *opinio media* which is also adopted in the principal and most recent general histories: by H. DESSAU, *Gesch. d. röm. Kaiserz.*, II, 1, 1926, pp. 133–6 (as it had been already by SCHILLER, *Gesch. d. röm*

Kaiserz., I, Gotha 1883, p. 306), by M. P. CHARLESWORTH, in *Cambr. Anc. Hist.*, X, 1934, pp. 665 ff., by G. M. COLUMBA, *L'impero romano*, Milan 1944, pp. 276–86 (see especially the balanced and penetrating note 6 on pp. 285 f.). DOMASZEWSKI, on the other hand, *Gesch. d. röm. Kaiserz.*, II³, 1921, pp. 1–20, and L. HOMO, *Le Haut-Empire*, 1933, pp. 236–46, are still inclined to put the accent on personal madness. A. MOMIGLIANO's study, 'La personalità de Caligola', in *Ann. Sc. Norm. Pisa*, NS I, 1932, pp. 205 f., denying the personal madness, points to the isolation from tradition and the lack of experience of ruling caused by the particular circumstances of G.'s youth, as a result of which he felt like a despot instead of a Princeps and attempted to achieve the premature aim of an absolute, divine monarchy without taking account of the Senate and of the other elements in the Roman political tradition (cf. *Enc. It.*, under *Caligola*, VIII, 1930, p. 419; 'the policy of inexperience rather than of madness'). A. PASSERINI's little book, *Caligola e Claudio*, Rome 1941, contains no more than a brief profile; it does not attempt a judgement on the central question. On the manner of the succession, see P. GRENADE, *Problèmes que pose l'avènement de Caligula*, summ. in *Rev. Ét. Lat.*, XXXIII, pp. 53–5.

Individual problems of some importance are presented by chrolonogy. On the probable attribution to G.'s reign of Artabanus III's meeting with L. Vitellius, see the art. by A. GARZETTI already cited, *La data dell'incontro all'Eufrate di Artabano III, etc.* J. P. V. D. BALSDON, 'Notes Concerning the Principate of Gaius', in *Journ. of Rom. St.*, XXIV, 1934, pp. 13–24, advances good arguments for placing in G.'s reign the creation of the XV and XXII *Primigeniae* legions (pp. 13–16; cf. also RITTERLING, in *P.W.*, XII, 1924–5, cc. 1244–9, 1758, 1797, and R. SYME, in *Cambr. Anc. Hist.*, X, p. 788 f.; but see A. MOMIGLIANO, *L'op. dell' imp. Claudio*, Florence 1932, p. 112, n. 1). On the other hand I cannot bring myself to accept the chronology Balsdon suggests for Gaius's dealings with the Jews (pp. 19–24), that is, the placing of Philo's ambassadorial journey in the winter of 39–40, with the consequent concentration into the last few months of 40 of all the activity in Judaea of the governor of Syria, P. Petronius. This chronology, already proposed by – among others – SCHUERER, *Gesch. d. jüd. Volkes*, I⁴ Leipzig 1901, p. 500, and CHARLESWORTH, in *Cambr. Anc. Hist.*, X, 662, n. 2., and widely accepted (e.g. by PIGANIOL, *Histoire de Rome*, p. 249; FRACCARO, 'C. Herennius Capito di Teate, procurator di Livia, di Tiberio e di Gaio', in *Athen.*, XXVIII, 1940, pp. 141–4; E. M. SMALLWOOD, 'The Chronology of Gaius' Attempt to Desecrate the Temple', in *Latomus*, XVI, 1957, pp. 3–17; and also all those who place the recall of Vitellius, Petronius's predecessor, in 40), is based mainly on the consideration that the orders given to Petronius by G. for the erection of his statue in the temple of Jerusalem could not be evaded for long, granted the character of G., and on other purely hypothetical circumstances (e.g. that the altar of Iamnia was put up for the German victory, that G. was staying in Campania in the summer of 40, etc.). But the placing of the Alexandrian Jews' embassy in 38–39 and hence the substitution of L. Vitellius for P. Petronius in 39, adopted by MOMMSEN, *Röm. Gesch.*, V, p. 518 f. and by WILLRICH, *art. cit.*, p. 410, and preferred by GELZER in *P.W.*, X, c. 397 ff. (see also MALAL., *Chron.*, X, p. 244, ed. Bonn, which provides independent testimony of P. Petronius in Syria in 39; cf. DE SANCTIS, in *Rev. Fil.*, LIII, 1925, p. 245 f.) seems to accord better with the account of all the Jewish events in Flavius Josephus, *Ant. Iud.*, XVIII, 257–309 (8, 1–9) (particularly the reference to winter in 262, which obviously would not be the case if everything had happened before the end of 40), with the general chronology of G.'s reign preserved by Cassius Dio, and with the particular facts that the Jews of Alexandria will not have waited long to send the embassy, in view of the painful situation created by the incident caused in the summer of 38 by Julius Agrippa as he passed through the city (Gaius on the other hand, having other things on his mind during the German campaign – September 39 to May 40 – may have forgotten, or for the moment considered less important, his order to Petronius) and that the reason for G.'s anger with the recalled governor of Syria, L. Vitellius, was that the latter had allowed Artabanus to be driven out again by his own subjects (CASS. D., LIX, 27, 4), something that had already occurred by the end of 37 (Artabanus probably died in 38). Moreover if Philo, who in the *Leg. ad Gaium* describes so vividly the long period of waiting and all the things that happened before he and his companions were received by G., had arrived in the winter of 39–40, when the Emperor was in Gaul, he would certainly have referred to G.'s absence and might well have gone to see him there as well. There is also the difficulty of putting a stay by G. in Campania (mentioned in Philo) in the summer of 40; this, though not impossible in itself, is pure conjecture, while a stay there in 39 is clearly attested. And finally if the inscription from Teate illustrated by FRACCARO in *art. cit.*, p. 137, was put up personally by C. Herennius Capito, this makes it probable, if not certain, that in 40 he was at Teate and that his report to Gaius on the destruction of the altar referred to 39.

The question of anti-Semitism in general has been treated more recently by I. HEINEMANN, s.v. *Antisemitismus*, in *P.W.*, Suppl. V, 1931, cc. 3–43; and in relation to the writings of Philo particularly by A. MOMIGLIANO, 'Aspetti dell'antisemitismo alessandrino in due opere di Filone', in *Rass. mens. di Israel*, V, 1930, pp. 275 ff.; by S. TRACY, *Philo Judaeus and the Roman Principate*, Columbia Univ., Williamsport, Penn., 1933, partic. pp. 9–21; also in the commentaries on Philo, including H. BOX, *Philonis Alexandrini in Flaccum*, London, New York and Toronto 1939, pp. XXXVIII – LVI. See even more recently H. LEISEGANG, s.v. *Philon*, in *P.W.*, XX, 1941, cc. 42–9. It seems quite probable that in the local Alexandrian question there was a political component, in the sense of a reaction by the Greek population to the privileged status of the large Jewish community, which, as in the whole of the diaspora, enjoyed the advantages both of its own ethnic solidarity and of its local cohabitation (whatever its legal status may have been; see GELZER, in *P.W.*, X. c. 401) and that the religious motive was deliberately employed by the Greeks as an instrument in their struggle in the particular atmosphere of G.'s reign. It is likewise also probable that the embassy to G. aimed not only at justifying the refusal to worship but also at retaining the privileges which the Jewish community enjoyed.

As for G.'s work, on the German and British campaigns it is worth noting, in the art. by BALSDON already cited, besides the discussion of the formation of legions XV and XXII *Primigeniae*, the remarks on the swiftness of G.'s journey to the Rhine (p. 16 f.) and the attempt to explain the story of the order to collect shells as 'spoils of the Ocean' (p. 18). The same scholar, in *The Emperor Gaius*, pp. 58–95, 220 f. summarizing the various verdicts, concludes that these campaigns were more serious than would appear from the tradition. See also E. RITTER-LING, *Fasti d. röm. Deutschland unter dem Prinzipat*, Vienna 1932, p. 13 f.; L. SCHMIDT, *Gesch. der germanischen Frühzeit*, Bonn 1925, p. 118 f. (considers that serious battles took place) and, for the British expedition, R. G. COLLINGWOOD and J. N. L. MYRES, *Roman Britain and the English Settlements*, I², Oxford 1937, p. 75. On the killing of Ptolemy of Maure-tania at Lyon, not at Rome, see J. CARCOPINO, 'Sur la mort de Ptolemée roi de Mauretanie', in *Mél. Ernout*, 1940, p. 39 f. On the important event of the separation of the civil from the military authority in the province of Africa, P. ROMANELLI, *Storia delle prov. rom. dell'Afr.*, Rome 1959, p. 246 ff. On the start of minting gold and silver coins at Rome, MATTINGLY, *Coins of the Roman Empire in the Br. Mus.* I, 1923, pp. CXLII f.: but see M. GRANT, 'The Mints of Roman Gold and Silver in the Early Principate,' in *Num. Chron.*, XV, 1955, pp. 39–54.

On the restoration of the electoral function of the comitia, see the technical observations (according to which it was a question of allowing candidatures outside the recommendation of the Princeps, among which the people, not the Senate, had to choose) of H. SIBER, in *Festschrift Koschaker*, I, 1939, p. 198 f. (cf. *Röm. Verfassungsrecht*, 1952, p. 355). The Spanish milestone with the inscr. *trib. pot. IIII* and *cos. II* (?) from Santiago de Compostela, later than 18 March 40, of recent discovery (*AE*, 1952, 112) forms an addition to the very few known (see the milestone of 39 from Baetica, *CIL*, II, 4716 = *ILS*, 193). The dedication in Narbonese Gaul of A.D. 40, found in 1898 together with a dedication to Tiberius (ESPÉRANDIEU, *Inscr. Lat. de Gaule*, 89) joins the rather less scanty number of inscriptions connected with the sojourn in Gaul, but gives no indication of emperor-worship. The same is true of *AE*, 1935, 91 (= *Bull. Mus. Imp. Rom.*, IV, 1933, p. 49), an ordinary dedication from Crete; on the other hand, in *AE*, 1940, 130 (= *Mem. Ist. Stor. - arch. F.E.R.T.*, III, 1938, p. 50) the dedication on an architrave from Calimnus to G. Caesar Germanicus and Apollo Delius Cresius is more significant in this connection.

On G.'s absolutist and religious concept in particular, the important inscription from Didyma published in 1911 by TH. WIEGAND, which had shed a decisive light on the passage in CASS. D., LIX, 28, 1, where there is a reference to the order given by G. to build a temple at Miletus, has been re-examined, amended and further explained by L. ROBERT, 'Le culte de Caligula à Milet et la province d'Asie', in *Hellenica*, VII, 1949, pp. 206–38. The intervention in connection with the *rex Nemorensis* mentioned by SUET., *Calig.*, 35, 3, as an instance of cruelty and caprice, is put in the context of G.'s religious and political convictions by G. DA A. BERNARDI, 'L'interesse di Caligola per la successione del rex Nemorensis e l'arcaica regalità nel Lazio', in *Athen.*, XLI, 1953, pp. 273–287. On *proskinesis*, forbidden by Tiberius and imposed by G., see G. A. ALFÖLDI, 'Die Ausgestaltung des monarchischen Zeremoniells am römischen Kaiserhofe, II, Die Begrüssung des Kaisers durch Einzelne', in *Röm. Mitt.*, XLIX, 1934, pp. 38–79, partic. p. 39 and p. 63 f.; U. KAHRSTEDT, *Kulturgesch. d. röm. Kaiserz.*, 1944, pp. 16, 282. For the oriental ceremonies at the birth of Julia Drusilla, H. P. L'ORANGE, 'Das Geburstritual der Pharaonen am römischen Kaiserhof', in *Symbolae Osloenses*, XXI, 1941, pp. 105–16, and for G.'s oriental predilections in general, which came to him partly as a spiritual legacy from Germanicus and Antony, P. LAMBRECHTS, 'Caligula dictateur littéraire', in *Bull. Inst. Hist. Belge de Rome*, XXVIII, 1953, pp. 219–32; J. COLIN, 'Les consuls du César-pharaon Caligula et l'héritage de Germanicus', in *Latomus*, XIII, 1954, pp. 394–416.

For propaganda activities as such, see J. GAGÉ, 'Un manifeste dynastique de Caligula', in *Rev. Ét. Anc.*, XXXVII, 1935, pp. 165–84, and the bibliography cited above on the Grand Cameo of Paris.

For particular political relations, on Gaetulicus and other ex-friends of Sejanus who remained undisturbed in the last years of Tiberius and under G. until the conspiracy of 39, see Z. STEWART, 'Seianus, Gaetulicus and Seneca', in *Am. Journ. of Phil.*, LXXIV, 1953, pp. 70–85; on Macro, praetorian prefect at the beginning of the reign and subsequently executed, see F. DE VISSCHER, 'L'amphithéâtre d'Alba Fucens et son fondateur Q. Naevius Macro, préfet du prétoire de Tibère', in *Rend. Acc. Linc.*, ser. VIII, XII, 1957, pp. 39–49.

CLAUDIUS. PERSONALITY, EDUCATION, FAMILY CIRCUMSTANCES

'It is impossible to understand how such a man could ever have been at the same time a puppet in the hands of women and freedmen': thus ROSTOVTZEFF, an admirer of Claudius, in whom he sees the man who in many fields of the life of the Roman empire took the decisive steps and above all created the precedents for the administration of the Flavians and the Antonines (*St. econ. e soc. dell'imp. rom.*, Florence 1933, pp. 88–96; 2nd English edition, Oxford 1957, pp. 79–85; 569–72). The fundamental problem of the conflict between the Claudius of the tradition and the Claudius who emerges from the personal activity of ruling as mirrored in the documents can be reduced once again to the problem of the formation of the tradition itself. The manner of this formation is in part the same for all the Julio-Claudian emperors, but a basic personal feature must be assumed in the reality on which the tradition was built up; otherwise the meaning of satires like the *Apocolocyntosis* would be incomprehensible and we should not have reports preserved like the statement in TAC., *Ann.*, XII, 3, 1, that when Nero, in the funeral *laudatio* composed by Seneca, proceeded to mention the 'providentia' and the 'sapientia' of his predecessor no one could refrain from laughing. This basic feature, which is generally discovered in the misunderstanding, in good or bad faith, of policies repugnant to the aristocratic tradition (generosity in the matter of citizenship, creation of the palace bureaucracy) and in a personal decline in the last years, can also be accounted for logically: anyone who tries zealously to take an interest in everything, as

Claudius did, is bound to depend for his information on intermediaries, confidential assistants and similar persons, who in the case of Claudius must often have been the palace freedmen and the ladies and their family circles, so that, by an easy psychological transposition and generalization, it could be said that he was in the hands of women and freedmen. Today the best balanced reconstructions of Claudius's character and work, based on examination of the literary tradition and guided by the documentary evidence, are to be found in the volumes by A. MOMIGLIANO, *L'opera dell'imperatore Claudio*, Florence 1932 (Eng. trans., with supplements, G. W. D. HOGARTH, *Claudius, the Emperor and his Achievement*, Oxford 1934), and V. M. SCRAMUZZA, *The Emperor Claudius*, Mass. 1940. The latter is useful for its detailed documentation and the completeness of its bibliography up to 1940. The pathologists have also been busy, concluding that Claudius had some abnormality due to premature birth or infantile paralysis. To the bibliography on this subject listed by SCRAMUZZA, p. 238, n.3, should be added ERNESTINE F. LEON, 'The "Imbecillitas" of the Emperor Claudius', in *Trans. Proc. Am. Phil. Ass.*, LXXIX, 1948, pp. 79–86. LEON, having justly noted in Claudius's physical appearance as well those points of resemblance with Tiberius which emerge in the seriousness of intent in both men's work, seems to exaggerate when she sees him, on the basis of 'modern psychological studies in social adjustment', as the victim of 'congenital cerebral palsy', enlarging the remarks in SUET. *Cl.*, 40, 1 into the entirely modern picture of the neglected young prince keeping company with people with whom he liked 'to wander among the *trattorie*, presumably those of the Subura and out in the Campagna', and when she explains his greed for food (SUET., 32, 33) as a result of social isolation. For the pleasant physical appearance of Claudius, and on the portrait drawn by SUET., *Cl.*, 30, confirmed by statues, see, besides the general iconographical publications, M. STUART, *The Portraiture of Claudius. Preliminary Studies*, New York 1938. As for moral qualities, the presence of cruelty in a cultivated and refined man makes us think of personal sadism, but we meet this attitude elsewhere in the literary tendencies of the age, for example in the pleasure taken in dwelling on cruel details in the descriptions of killings by Flavius Josephus. For qualities of mind, see Y. BÉQUIGNON, 'Un trait d'esprit de l'empereur Claude', in *Rev. Arch.*, XXV, 1946, p. 228 f. For a brief profile of the man and his work, besides PASSERINI (cited under *Gaius*), see F. STÄHELIN, *Reden und Vorträge*, Basle 1955, *Kaiser Claudius*, pp. 147–71.

The motives inspiring Claudius's historico-literary activity and its political employment, accurately summarized by MOMIGLIANO, *op. cit.*, pp. 13–41, have received confirmation so far as concerns his Etruscological vocation, as stimulated by practical opportunities and as the reflection of a surviving ancestral Etruscan tradition, from the discovery of the so-called Praises of Tarquinia. These were published by P. ROMANELLI in *Not. d. Sc.*, 1948, pp. 193–270, and discussed afresh by M. PALLOTTINO, 'Uno spiraglio di luce sulla storia etrusca: gli "Elogia Tarquiniensia" ', in *Studi Etr.*, XXI, 1950-1, p. 147 ff., and more recently by J. HEURGON, who had already underlined in a communication to the Acad. des Inscr. et Belles Lettres (*Comptes rendus*, 1950, pp. 212–15, cf. *Mél. d'Arch. et d'Hist.*, LXIII, 1951, p. 119), like the scholars cited, the persistence of historical traditions in the family archives of the great Etruscan families. In another communication to the Acad. des Inscr. (*Compt. rend*, 1953, pp. 92–7, cf. *Ann. Ép.*, 1954, after no. 55) and in the article 'Tarquitius Priscus et l'organisation de l'ordre des haruspices sous l'empereur Claude', in *Latomus*, XII, 1953, pp. 402–17 (cf. *AE*, 1954, no. 126), HEURGON has made further interesting observations; he thinks he can trace, particularly on the basis of inscr. no. 77 ROMANELLI and the probable mention in it of the Urgulanii, who would thus be of Etruscan origin, the direct link between Etruria and Claudius's enthusiasm for Etruscology. In fact, according to HEURGON's ingenious juxtapositions, the person to whom, according to SUET., *Cl.*, 4, 3, Augustus advised that the young Claudius should be entrusted during the banquet of the priests at the *Ludi Martiales*, 'ne quid faciat quod conspici et derideri possit', was his *affinis* the son of Silvanus, the brother of Plautia Urgulanilla, whose husband Claudius was at that time. Claudius would thus have drawn directly on the Etruscan tradition, as represented by the family of the Urgulanii, and the hypothesis is also interesting for forming a picture of his character, although we do not know to what extent this tradition lived on 'derrière les murs sévères des palais toscans' (*Compt. rend. Ac. Inscr.*, 1953, p. 96), nor does it seem that these fragments of praises give us more than general indications.

On other details of Claudius as a scholar and as the friend and correspondent of scholars, FR. CUMONT's hypothesis in 'Ecrits hermétiques, II, Le médecin Thessalus et les plantes astrales d'Hermès Trismégiste' (*Rev. de. Phil.*, XLII, 1918, pp. 85–108), where he identified as Claudius the *Germano Claudio regi* who is the addressee of a letter and of a treatise on medicine discovered by him in a Latin translation contained in a codex from Montpellier – a hypothesis also of interest for the history of the curious literature known as 'hermetic' – has been rejected by H. DILLER, in *P.W.*, VI, 1936, c. 180 f. On the *litterae Claudianae*, see R. P. OLIVER, 'The Claudian Letter Ⱶ', in *Amer. Journ. of Arch.*, LIII, 1949, pp. 249–57.

Another question that belongs to the context of the literary atmosphere of Claudius's reign is the placing of the work of the historian Q. Curtius Rufus, whom some people (K. GLASER, 'Curtius und Claudius', in *Wiener Studien*, LX, 1942, pp. 87–92; I. LANA, 'Dell'epoca in cui visse Q. Curtius Rufus', in *Riv. Fil. Class.*, LXXVII, 1949, pp. 48–70) identify with the rhetorician of the same name, but not with the Curtius Rufus who was governor of Upper Germany under Claudius and proconsul of Africa under Nero (GROAG, in *PIR²*, II, p. 394, no. 1618).

As for members of Claudius's family, a rehabilitation of Messalina by the explanation of her marriage to Silius as an episode in the cult of Dionysus is to be found in J. COLIN, 'Les vendanges dionysiaques et la légende de Messaline (48. ap. J.-C.)', in *Les Ét. Class.*, XXIV, 1956, pp. 25–39, and a literary reconstruction of the figure of Agrippina, whose characteristics are singled out as ambition to rule and, later, rivalry with her son, in E. PARATORE, 'La figura di Agrippina minore in Tacito', in *Maia*, V, 1952, pp. 32–81. There is a defence of Agrippina against the charge of poisoning Claudius in G. BAGNANI, 'The Case of the Poisoned Mushrooms', in *Phoenix*, I², 1946, pp. 15–20. For Britannicus, see P. COLLART, 'Une dédicace à Britannicus trouvée à Avenches', in *Zeitschr. f. schweiz. Arch. u. Kunstgesch.*, II, 1940, pp. 157–9 (cf. *AE*, 1946, 237).

CLAUDIUS'S WORK

The attribution of Claudius's work to the staff of palace freedmen is a possible solution to the problem mentioned above of the conflict between the observable facts – testimony to a public activity of the first rank – and the judgement of the sources on the person of the Princeps. Such a reconciliation was in fact favoured by older reconstructions of the reign (SCHILLER, *Gesch. d. röm. Kaiserz.*, I, pp. 329 f., GROAG, in *P.W.*, III, c. 2778 ff., espec. 2790 and 2835; DOMASZEWSKI, *Gesch. d. röm. Kaiserz.*, II, with the significant division of the chapter on Claudius, pp. 21–46, by the sub-titles 'die Herrschaft Messalinas' and 'die Herrschaft Agrippinas'; HOMO, *Haut-Empire*, pp. 246 ff.). However, the examination of the now numerous documents at our disposal (all collected in M. P. CHARLESWORTH, *Documents Illustrating the Reigns of Claudius and Nero*, Cambridge 1939, repr. 1951, pp. 3–29) – in which it is easy to recognize not only a general unity of style and policy which as such could be the product of a well-organized chancellery but also a characteristic tone which is unmistakable and corresponds too well with what we know of Claudius's cultured and humane character not to be his own personal one

– makes it seem more and more likely that Claudius himself was the sole author of the work achieved in his reign, though no doubt he had a great deal of advice and assistance. This view now forms part of the reconstruction of the figure of Claudius that has become common property (DESSAU, *Gesch d. röm. Kaiserz.*, II, 1, p. 139 ff.; MOMIGLIANO, *op. cit.*, especially pp. 85 f; CHARLESWORTH, in *Cambr. Anc. Hist.*, X, pp. 667–701; SCRAMUZZA, *op. cit.*, espec. pp. 49–50, 86–7; L. PARETI, *St. di Roma*, IV, 1955, pp. 801 ff.). However, there is a vigorous revival of the theory of the freedmen's ascendancy over the Emperor's will in the recent study by H. G. PFLAUM, *Essai sur les procurateurs équestres sous le Haut-Empire romain*, Paris 1950, pp. 36–42 (see also G. M. COLUMBIA, *L'imp. rom.*, p. 307).

However, the public activity that went on under Claudius and on his initiative has in recent years demanded much attention from historians and jurists, and excavations continue to produce fresh documents. To begin with the last, since 1933–4 we have been provided with the inscriptions bearing witness to noteworthy activity at Leptis Magna (*Inscr. of Rom. Trip.*, 337 from A.D. 45–46, 338 from A.D. 53, on a monumental building, 339, 340, the last a dedication to Messalina of 45–46, erased after 48); in Cyrenaica the first milestone of the road from Cyrene to Balagrae, which can be dated to 45–46, has been found (*AE*, 1951, 207); at Hippo Regius a dedication of A.D. 42–43 has been discovered (*AE*, 1935, 32); in Lusitania an interesting dedication from Ammaia of 44–45 (*AE*, 1950, 217); in Hispania Tarraconensis (Leon) five boundary pillars erected 'ex *auctoritate Ti. Claudi Caesaris Aug. Germanici*' between the *prata* of the *cohors IIII Gallorum* and the *civitas Beduniensium* (*AE*, 1935, 13); in Gallia Lugdunensis a fragment of milestone from the road between Lugudunum and Matiscum (Macon), dating from 42–43 (*AE*, 1940, 150); on the Rhine and Danube dedications and inscriptions on objects from legionary camps; a *tabula ansata* of 52–54 from Bonna (Bonn), where the camp was rebuilt in stone at this time (*AE*, 1938, 75); another of A.D. 44, from Gospodin Vir on the Danube (*AE*, 1944, 70): a dedication *divo Claudio* at Savaria (*AE*, 1944, 131), and at Oescus the important inscription, dating from A.D. 42, for the construction of the camp of the V *Macedonica* legion (*AE*, 1957, 286); at Berytus, in Syria, the dedication to Claudius of a big building (*AE*, 1958, 163); in Italy a boundary pillar from Reate which should probably be attributed to Claudius rather than to Vespasian (*AE*, 1940, 56); and at Rome the eleventh pillar known, dating from 44, of the *aqua Virgo*, rebuilt by Claudius (*AE*, 1939, 54).

The principal documents of Claudius's political policy with regard to the empire, that is, the Tablet of Lyon on the concession of the *ius honorum* to the Gauls, and the Letter to the Alexandrians, are still the object of interest, although so far as the former is concerned the interest is mainly concentrated, in the context of the intense research going on at present into the composition of Tacitus's works, on the comparison with the well-known passage, *Ann.*, XI, 23-4, containing a paraphrase of the original speech, set in the atmosphere of opposition (ED. LIECHTENHAN, 'Quelques réflexions sur la Table Claudienne et Tac. Ann., XI, 23 and 24', in *Rev. Ét. Lat.*, XXIV, 1946, pp. 198-209: F. VITTINGHOFF, 'Zur Rede des Kaisers Claudius über die Aufnahme von "Galliern" in den römischen Senat', in *Hermes*, LXXXII, 1954, pp. 348-71; E. SCHOENBAUER, 'Zur Oratio Claudii de iure honorum Gallis dando', in *Iura*, VI, 1955, pp. 160-9; N. P. MILLER, 'The Claudian Tablet and Tacitus: a Reconsideration', in *Rh. Mus.*, XCIX, 1956, pp. 304-15), while so far as the historical interpretation is concerned, the still largely valid commentary of PH. FABIA, *La table Claudienne de Lyon*, Lyon 1929, has now passed, with other contributions (e.g. J. CARCOPINO, 'La table Claudienne de Lyon et l'impérialisme égalitaire', Chap. IV of *Points de vue sur l'impérialisme romain*, Paris 1934, and the review of it by H. LAST in *Journ. Rom. St.*, XXIV, 1934, pp. 58-60), into the monographs on Claudius already cited and into general works on citizenship (A. N. SHERWIN-WHITE, *The Roman Citizenship*, Oxford 1939, pp. 181 ff.). The letter to the Alexandrians forms part of the vast problem of the cohabitation of the Hebrews with the Greeks and the natives in the big Egyptian city and in general with the other peoples of the empire, a problem already alluded to in the notes on Gaius, so that all that need be added here is a reference to the survey by G. I. LUZZATTO, 'Epigr. giuridica gr. e rom', III (1939-40), XVII Suppl. to *St. et doc. hist, et iur.*, 1951, p. 117 f., and to the systematic treatments in MOMIGLIANO, *op. cit.*, pp. 61 ff. and SCRAMUZZA, *op. cit.*, pp. 64 ff. (with the notes to p. 245 ff.). See latterly I. D. AMUSIN, 'Ad. P. Lond. 1812', in *Journ. of Jurist. Papyr.* (Warsaw), IX–X, 1955-6, pp. 169-209.

There are special problems, in the field of external activity, in connection both with resumption of the policy of conquest and with the administrative organization and individual situations in the life of the empire. For the revolt of Furius Camillus Scribonianus in 42 and the immediate reaction of his legions, see A. BETZ, *Untersuchungen zur Militärgeschichte der römischen Provinz Dalmatien*, Baden bei Wien 1938, p. 36 f. So far as conquest is concerned, the most important event, that is, the annexation of Britain, also merits emphasis because of the echo that the subsequent triumph had in literature, as the reflection of a genuine popular enthusiasm (SCRAMUZZA, p. 237, n. 112, as against DESSAU, II, 1, p. 139), which is significant in comparison with the allusions – which might in this case be suspect – in inscriptions and coins (GROAG, in *P.W.*, III, c. 2907). Also in connection with the British campaign, the inscription *AE*, 1947, 76 (= *Hesperia*, X, 1941, p. 239 ff.), completes the *cursus* of the A. Didius Gallus of *CIL*, III, 7247, and makes clear his probable participation with Claudius in the expedition to Britain, where he returned in 52 as governor; C. E. STEVENS, 'Claudius and the Orcades', in *Class. Rev.*, LXV (NS I), 1951, pp. 7–9, tries to defend the passage in EUTROP, VII, 13, 2–3 (but the simplest explanation is still that there is confusion here between the history of Claudius's conquest and Agricola's campaigns). See also A. R. BURN, 'The Battle of the Medway, A.D. 43', in *History*, XXXVIII, 1953, pp. 105–15. On the campaigns of Plautius's successor, the governor Ostorius Scapula, see G. WEBSTER, 'The Roman Military Advance under Ostorius Scapula', *Arch. Journ.*, CXV, 1958, pp. 49–98. As for the fighting in Mauretania and the creation of the two procuratorial provinces, chronology (the war had already begun under Gaius, CASS. D., LX, 8, 6) and details of the successive commands of M. Licinius Crassus Frugi, C. Suetonius Paulinus and Cn. (or C. ?) Hosidius Geta, in 40, 41 and 42 respectively, are not sufficiently certain (MOMIGLIANO, *op. cit.*, p. 107). Hosidius Geta's consulship with L. Vagellius was already known (22 September of an unknown year, *CIL*, X, 1401 = *ILS*, 6043); we now know also that he was consul on 1 August, possibly of A.D. 45, with T. Flavius Sabinus, Vespasian's elder brother (*AE*, 1953, cf. DEGRASSI, *Fasti consolari*, p. 12 f); on the question raised by GROAG, *P.W.*, VII, 1913, c. 2491, whether it is a question of two different men, Gaius (CASS. D., LX, 20, 4), who would be the commander against the Moors, and Gnaeus, the colleague of Flavius Sabinus and of Vagellius (successively, in the same year – which offers no difficulty), see most recently A. E. GORDON, 'Quintus Veranius Consul A.D. 49', in *Univ. of California Publications in Class. Arch.*, II, 5, 1952, p. 317 f; cf. *Amer. Journ. of Arch.*, LVI, 1952, pp. 172–3, and G. Q. GIGLIOLI, in *Rend. Pont. Acc. Rom. Arch.*, XXV–XXVI, 1949–51, p. 67 ff. For the bibliography on the inscription from Volubilis of M. Valerius Severus subsequent to the publication in *Inscr. Lat. d'Afr.* (no. 634, 1923), see L. CHATELAIN, *Inscriptions Latines du Maroc*, Paris 1942, no. 116, and the same scholar's *Le Maroc des Romains*, Paris 1944, p. 294 ff.; also J. TOUTAIN, 'Une inscription de Volubilis', in *Bull. Arch. Comm. Trav. Hist.*, 1943-44-45, pp. 172–6. The dedication to Claudius discovered after the inscription of Valerius Severus and published by L. CHATELAIN (in 1924; see *Inscr. Lat. du Maroc*, no. 56), dates the measure in favour of Volubilis precisely to the year 44. See also *Inscr. Lat. du Maroc*, no. 57. On Ser. Sulpicius Galba's abnormal proconsulship of Africa and the operations he conducted, the inference that these were against the Musulamii, an inference drawn from a comparison with AUR. VICT., *De Caes.*, 4, 2 (CHARLESWORTH, in *Cambr. Anc. Hist.*, X, p. 674; R. SYME, 'Tacfarinas, the Musulamii and Thubursicu', in *Studies Johnson*, Princeton, N. J., 1951, pp. 121 ff.), is quite likely to be correct. Also on events in Africa under Claudius see now P. ROMANELLI, *St. prov. rom. Afr.*, Rome 1951, pp. 259–73. As for legionary dispositions in Spain, see M. MARCHETTI, in DE RUGGIERO, *Diz. Ep.*, III, Rome 1915–16, p. 810 f., which now needs to be modified: in the first years of Augustus the garrison consisted of five legions, two in Hispania Ulterior and three in Hispania Citerior; under Tiberius and Gaius it was still three legions, all in Citerior or Tarraconensis; it was restricted by Claudius to two legions, with the withdrawal of the IV *Macedonica*, which went to the Rhine; and under Nero it was reduced to one (in 63). This was a consequence of the rapid Romanization and led also to modifications in the civil administration. On the importance of Claudius's work for the Romanization of Upper Germany, see FR. SPRATER, 'Obergermanien zur Zeit des Kaisers Claudius', in *Epigraphica*, IX, 1947, pp. 81–9, which deals with the forts and communications of the defence system of the Middle Rhine, between Speyer and Worms. As for the tradition of the last eagle of Varus in German hands, which is supposed to have been recovered by P. Gabinius Secundus in 41–42 (CASS. D., LX, 8, 7, where the names of the tribes conquered need to be corrected to agree with SUET., *Cl.*, 24, 3), see E. BICKEL, 'Der Mythus um die Adler der Varusschlacht', in *Rh. Mus.*, XCII, 1943–4, pp. 302–18, already cited in connection with Tiberius. So far as the Alpine provinces are concerned, we have already seen that it is improbable that the province of Raetia was set up under Claudius, a point of view maintained by R. HEUBERGER, against the accepted view that it was created under Tiberius. The thesis of P. COLLART, 'Quand la vallée Poenine fut-elle détachée de la Rhétie ?', in *Zeitschr. f. schweiz. Gesch.*, 1942, pp. 87–105, who puts the separation of the Valais from Rhaetia in 171, is contested by E. MEYER, 'Zur Geschichte des Wallis in röm. Zeit', in *Basler Zeitschr. f. Gesch.u. Altertumskunde*, XLII, 1943 (Staehelin Festschr.), pp. 59–78, who places the institution of the province of *Alpes Graiae et Poeninae*, to which the Valais, detached from Raetia, was joined at the same time, under Claudius. The localization of the stations of the *Quadragesima Galliarum* made by s. j. DE LAET, *Portorium*, Bruges 1949, p. 158, n. 1, seems to confirm the view of MEYER. See also K. CHRIST, *Zur römischen Okkupation der Zentralalpen und des nördlichen Alpenvorlandes*, in *Historia*, VI, 1957, pp. 416–28. On the reconstruction of Octodurus (Martigny), which became Forum Claudii Vallensium, see L. BLONDEL, 'Les fouilles romaines d'Octodure', in *Annales Valaisannes*, IV, 1940–2, pp. 454–67, to which must be added, for the rapid predominance of the Civitas Vallensium over the pre-existing Celtic centres, a process caused by Claudius's 'nationalization' of the road over the Great St Bernard, D. VAN BERCHEM, 'Du portage au péage. Le rôle des cols transalpins dans l'histoire du Valais celtique', in *Mus.-Helv.*, XIII, 1956, pp. 199–208. On Noricum, see G. CAPOVILLA, 'Studi sul Noricum' in *Misc. Galbiati*, I, Milan 1951, pp. 213–411, partic. pp. 346–66 for Claudius's roads and colonial foundations (on the roads, see now the comprehensive work by T. F. MEYSELS, *Auf Römerstrassen durch Österreich. Von Aguntum nach Carnuntum*, Vienna 1960). On the restless, open theatre of operations on the Lower Danube, see H. NESSELHAUF, 'Die Legionen Moesiens unter Claudius und Nero', in *Laureae Aquincenses Kuzsinkszky dicatae*' II (Dissertationes Pannonicae, II, 11, Budapest 1941); there are the legions which went with Didius Gallus into the kingdom of Bosporus to install Cotys – events that cannot be dated with certainty because of Tacitus's usual departures from the annalistic sequence (*Ann.*, XII, 15–21). On policy in the East, the many pages devoted to Claudius by D. MAGIE, *Roman Rule in Asia Minor*, pp. 540–53, with complete documentation (pp. 1397–1411), summarize and illuminate activity of great interest. MAGIE also refers, in 'A Reform in the Exaction of Grain at Cibyra under Claudius' (*Studies Johnson*, Princeton, N.J. 1951, pp. 152–4), on the basis of inscription *IGRR*, IV, 914, to the work put in on the Princeps by one Q. Veranius Philager – whose name is to be connected with the permanent residence in Lycia as governor, precisely under Claudius, of Q. Veranius (mentioned in a dedication from Cibyra, *IGRR*, IV, 902; cf. A. E. GORDON, *Quintus Veranius Consul* A.D. 49, Berkeley and Los Angeles 1952, p. 240) – to secure the removal of a certain Ti. Nicephorus because of his exaggerated exactions, possibly in the requisitioning of grain and the abuses connected with it. Q. Veranius would have been the first governor of the province of Lycia set up by Claudius (GORDON, *op. cit.*, p. 243; but see E. BIRLEY, 'Britain under Nero: The Significance of Q. Veranius', in *Durham Univ. Journ.*, 1952, p. 89 = *Roman Britain and the Roman Army*, Kendal 1953, p. 2, in whose view he would be the second, although in the postcript to p. 9, accepting the results of the study published in the interim by GORDON and the information that Veranius's governorship of Lycia lasted for at least a *quinquennium*, he implicitly renounces the date of 46 previously proposed for the beginning of the governorship itself; in 49 Q. Veranius was consul), and his sepulchral inscription, recently (1948) identified, has given us details of his career, among others his *adlectio* to the *patricii*, by the efforts of Claudius. On policy towards Parthia and Armenia and in particular on the struggles of Gotarzes and Vardanes, see U. KAHRSTEDT, *Artabanos III und seine Erbe*, Berne 1950, pp. 24–7, and on the fortress of Gorneae (Garni), see the account of the recent Soviet excavations in L. MORETTI, 'Due note epigrafiche, II, Quattro iscrizioni greche dell'Armenia', in *Athenaeum*, XXXIII, 1955, p. 37 f. The problem whether Antonius Felix governed Judaea jointly with Ventidius Cumanus (TAC., *Ann.*, XII, 54) or was his successor in the procuratorship (JOSEPH., *Ant. Iud.*, XX, 137) is probably to be resolved in favour of Tacitus's account (*contra*, E. M. SMALLWOOD, 'Some Comments on Tacitus, *Annals* XII, 54', in *Latomus*, XVIII, 1959, pp. 560–7).

As for the public works carried out in Rome, Italy and the empire, to which the epigraphical discoveries already cited refer, it is only necessary to add here a mention of some recent studies, the results of which have been taken into account in the main text: P. WUILLEUMIER, 'De Lyon à Mâcon', in *Rev. Ét. Anc.*, XLI, 1939, pp. 245–51, espec. 246 f., who, utilizing the discovery of the milestone of Claudius, *AE*, 1940, 156, dating from 42–43, which joins the dozen already known from Gallia Comata and those from Narbonensis already dated to 41, observes that the progressive dates reveal a rational plan of restoration and completion of the road system of Gaul, a plan initiated right at the start of the reign and proceeding from the south-east towards the north and west; cf. H. U. INSTINSKY, 'P. Plautius Pulcher und die Strassenbauten des Kaisers Claudius', in *Phil.*, XLIX, 1943, pp. 245–54; and finally E. SJÖQUIST, 'Studi archeologici e topografici intorno alla Piazza del Collegio Romano', in *Opusc. Arch.*, IV (Acta Instituti Rom. Regni Sueciae, XII), Lund 1946, p. 80 ff., on *horrea* of Claudius rebuilt by Hadrian (and on the subject of activity in connection with the *frumentationes*, see the hypothesis of F. CASTAGNOLI, 'Il Campo Marzio nell'antichità', in *Mem. Lincei*, ser. VIII, Vol. I, fasc. 4, 1947, p. 177 ff., on the Porticus Minucia). In general the beneficent activity of Claudius in the provinces explains his popularity, particularly in the East, where it is expressed in a large number of inscriptions, private as well as public (See V. M. SCRAMUZZA, 'Claudius

Soter Euergetes', in *Harv. St. in Class. Phil.* (St Ferguson), LI, 1940, pp. 261–6.

As for the central principles of government and internal activity, the problem which arises in the case of Claudius as in that of the other emperors, that of the nature of his principate according to the accounts of the Roman tradition, is plausibly resolved by recognizing the impossibility for Augustus's successors of preserving the state of equilibrium which he had achieved. Thus Claudius too, against his conservative instinct and his philo-aristocratic and philo-republican ideas, was forced by the needs of empire to innovate, that is, to destroy the republic more and more (MOMIGLIANO, SCRAMUZZA). In short, it was just a particular case of the inevitable process of the Roman state, which was moving in a violent form from the age of the Gracchi onwards between the poles of innovation, especially through technical needs and in respect of the provincial world, and of tradition, represented particularly by moral, social and constitutional principles and always inward-looking: a process which in the principate of Augustus had achieved a moment of equilibrium soon passed. On Claudius's relations with the aristocracy, see the series of articles by D. MCALINDON, 'Senatorial Opposition to Claudius and Nero', in *Amer. Journ. Phil.*, LXXVII, 1956, pp. 113–32; 'Claudius and the Senators', *ibid.*, LXXVIII, 1957, pp. 279–86; 'Entry to the Senate in the Early Empire', in *Journ. Rom. St.*, XLVII, 1957, pp. 191–5; 'The Senator's Retiring Age, 65 or 60?', in *Class Rev.*, N.S. VII, 1957, p. 108; 'Senatorial Advancement in the Age of Claudius', in *Latomus*, XVI, 1957, pp. 252–62. These articles underline the importance of Claudius's work in the social transformation of the Senate, from the Augustan arrangement to the Flavian one. We have spoken in connection with the Tablet of Lyon of Claudius's interest in the body of citizens and all we need to add here is a reference to his colonial and municipal policy. In this field SHERWIN-WHITE (*op. cit.*, p. 184 f.) tends to minimize the innovatory character of Claudius's activity; in fact his colonies and municipia are not many in number and it is by no means certain which ones belong to him (list in MOMIGLIANO, *op. cit.*, pp. 120 ff., cf. SCRAMUZZA, p. 143 f., with notes 49–58 relating to pp. 281–3, where there is also a complete bibliography). For a municipality perhaps founded by Claudius near Bolzano in the Alto Adige, see A. DEGRASSI, 'Un municipio romano nei pressi di Nalles?', in *Arch. per l'Alto Adige*, XLIX, 1955, pp. 385–9, and for Camulodunum see C.F.C. HAWKES and M. R. HULL, *Camulodunum* (Reports of the Research Committee of the Society of Antiquaries of London XIV), Oxford 1947, pp. 16–21, 34–44, 51–6. For the north-eastern regions of Italy and

Noricum, which received particular attention from Claudius, see A. DEGRASSI, *Il confine nord-orientale dell'Italia romana* (Diss. Bernenses, I, 6), Berne 1954, pp. 39 f. (Iulium Carnicum – doubtful if it was a Claudian colony), 92 f. (on an alleged shifting to the east of the frontier of Italy under Claudius), 98 (on the towns of Noricum); cf. M. PAVAN, 'L'ambiente militare nella provincia del Norico', in *Athen.*, XXXIV, 1956, spec. p. 63. But what is important is the spirit of renewal which makes itself evident on a grand scale for the first time since Augustus. The concession of the honorary title of colony, that is, without the actual settlement of colonists, also begins with Claudius (SHERWIN-WHITE, p. 187 f.). As for the power of creating *patricii*, the examination of the career of Q. Veranius, *in numerum patriciorum adlectus* when he was consul in 49, shows that Claudius made use of it even outside the limits of the censorship (A. E. GORDON, *Q. Veranius, cit.*, pp. 256, 273).

The Claudian bureaucratic organization, which represents a further gain in importance for the equestrian class, deserves the greatest attention. It is now recognized that the initiative in giving a public position to the palace staff came from Claudius and was not a matter of intrusive self-investiture by the freedmen themselves. What remain to be determined precisely are the boundaries and limits of the powers involved, and scholars have been exploring this delicate field of research in recent years. Above all, so far as the effects on the Senate are concerned, indications of the preservation of deference and of a desire to provide compensation whenever any change in competence to its detriment was confirmed are innumerable, and many have been noted in the text. Other pieces of evidence to which MOMIGLIANO points in the same context are of dubious significance; the suggestion, for example (pp. 81 f.), that in his monetary policy Claudius intended to respect fully the rights of the Senate, a notion to be deduced from the introduction of provincial coins with the initials *S.C.* (see C. H. V. SUTHERLAND, 'Claudius and the Senatorial Mint', in *Journ. of Rom. St.*, XXXI, 1941, pp. 70–2; cf. L. LAFFRANCHI, 'La monetazione imperatoria e senatoria di Claudio I durante il quadriennio 41–44 d. Cr.', in *Rev. Ital. Num.*, LI, 1949, pp. 41–51); and the suggestion (*ibid.*) that entrusting to senators Britain and Lycia, 'more important provinces', and to knights Mauretania, Thrace and Judaea, signified greater regard for the Senate; but in Britain, where the conquest was in progress, it was natural that the officer commanding the legions should remain as governor, and as for Lycia, it is questionable whether it was more important than Mauretania or Judaea itself. On the elevation of the equestrian order, the explanation of the passage in SUET., *Cl.*, 25, 1, on the attempt, in the *militiae equestres*, to rank the legionary tribune after the prefect of a cohort or ala, is quite plausible, as an echo of a measure intended to raise the position of the *tribunus angusticlavius* (MOMIGLIANO, pp. 94–6).

The shape of the central financial administration has been clarified in recent years by various studies on the *aerarium* and *fiscus* (H. LAST, 'The Fiscus: a Note', in *Journ. of Rom. St.*, XXXIV, 1944, pp. 51–9; C. H. V. SUTHERLAND, 'Aerarium and Fiscus during the Early Empire', in *Am. Journ. of Phil.*, LXVI, 1945, pp. 151–70; A. H. M. JONES, 'The Aerarium and the Fiscus', in *Journ. of Rom. St.*, XL, 1950, pp. 22–9), so that the institution of the *fiscus Caesaris* at the earliest only under Claudius is now an accepted notion, even though there is no need to exaggerate, as G. E. F. CHILVER reminds us in 'Princeps and Frumentationes' (*Am. Journ. of Phil.*, LXX, 1949, pp. 7–21), and to assign a revolutionary rôle to Claudius, who even in the financial field only fixed and gave definitive recognition to the changes that had slowly come about in the preceding seventy years. Similarly in the field of the *annona*, object of the greatest attention (construction of the harbour at Ostia, granting of privileges in the shape of citizenship to the builders and crews of ships in the grain trade, organization of the distribution at the *Porticus Minucia*), it is natural that the direct interest of the Princeps in the general food supply should take precedence, through the equestrian *praefectus annonae*, over the senatorial interest in the *frumentationes*, an interest represented by the survival, now proved by inscriptions, of the *praefecti frumenti dandi ex S.C.* (G. VITUCCI, 'Note al "cursus honorum" di M. Iulius Romulus, praefectus frumenti dandi ex S.C.', in *Riv. Fil. Class.*, N.S. XXV, 1947, pp. 252–73; cf. the same writer's 'Plebei urbanae frumento constituto', in *Arch. Class.*, X, 1958, pp. 310–14, and H. G. PFLAUM, 'La chronologie de la carrière de L. Caesennius Sospes', in *Historia*, II, 1953–4, partic. pp. 446–50 and also, on the man himself, P. MELONI, 'L'amministrazione della Sardegna nel I sec. d. Cr.', *Ann. Univ. Cagliari*, XXI, 2, 1953, pp. 17–18) and of its probable continued official financing by the *aerarium Saturni*, the very fact of this survival and of the continuation of the same method of financing show that even under Claudius (whose deliberate deference to the Senate – and also Roman spirit of empiricism – we must not forget) there is no need to try to make absolute divisions of authority (it is high time that any idea of a 'dyarchy' was buried once and for all); this field of the corn supply could well be the typical example of the interpenetration and substantial unity of the Emperor's governmental interests.

On the instruments of the Claudian bureaucracy, in other words the procurators and their career, the volume by H. G. PFLAUM already cited, in spite of its too emphatic scepticism about Claudius's personal initiative, is the most complete collection of materials and the best up-dating of HIRSCHFELD. A. N. SHERWIN-WHITE, 'Procurator Augusti', in *Papers of Br. Sch. at Rome*, XV, 1939, pp. 11–26, partic. 20–6, recognizes that Claudius made the greatest contribution between Augustus and Hadrian to the formation of the bureaucracy. His bureaucratic system, especially from the point of view of the links between the procurators on the Palatine and those in the provinces, links symbolized by the relationship between Pallas and Felix – and in general there is no mistaking the correlation between the growing power of the freedmen and the increase in the prerogatives of the provincial procurators – is illustrated by R. BESNIER, first in the summary of a communication ('Observations sur le recrutement et l'accroissement de la compétence des procurateurs provinciaux sous le règne de l'empereur Claude', in *Rev. Hist. Dr. Franç. et Étr.*, IV, 26, 1948, p. 382) and later in the article 'Les procurateurs provinciaux pendant le règne de Claude', in *Rev. Belg. Phil. Hist.*, XXVIII, 1950, pp. 439–59.

Claudius's coinage does not present any special characteristics: his gold and silver coins are the only ones produced and, as under Gaius, were issued at Rome; the senatorial coinage of bronze is also the only one of its kind, but with rough local imitations, which, if favoured by governors and procurators, would indicate not deference but deception with regard to the Senate. However, in this field too a general tendency towards unification is to be observed (C. H. V. SUTHERLAND, *Coinage in Rom. Imp. Policy, cit.*, pp. 123–47; M. GRANT, *Roman Imperial Money*, London 1954, pp. 51 ff.). For types particularly significative of events, see the legends 'IMPER(ator) RECEPT(us)' and 'PRAETOR(iani) RECEPT(i)' of 41 (MATTINGLY and SYDENHAM, *Rom. Imp. Coin.*, I, p. 125 f., H. U. INSTINSKY, 'Kaiser Claudius und die Prätorianer', in *Hamburger Beitr. zur Numismatik*, II, 1952–3, p. 7 f.), which tell us much about the true nature of Claudius's accession.

On Claudius's legislative activity there is a clear and useful comprehensive survey, based on a re-examination of the juridical, literary and documentary evidence, though one conducted with insufficient historical sense, in G. MAY, 'L'activité juridique de l'empereur Claude', in *Rev. Hist. Dr. Franç. et Étr.*, IV, 15, 1936, pp. 55–97, 213–54, which is complemented by discussions of some individual questions in 'Notes complémentaires sur les actes de l'empereur Claude', *ibid.*, IV, 22, 1944, pp. 101–14 (on the adoption of Nero and the elimination of the legal difficulties hindering the *adrogatio* of the young Domitius; on the extension of the *pomerium* for the conquest of Britain; on the *fiscus*, where the observations are not up to date; on the defence of Latinity and on cases of rigour in the punishment of usurpation of citizenship). The question of dating remains open for many measures, e.g. for the *s.c. Vellaeanum* on the *intercessio* of the married woman, which probably belongs to the reign of Nero but was preceded by an edict of Claudius's (R. S. ROGERS, 'Domitius Afer's Defense of Clodilla', in *Trans. Proc. Am. Phil. Ass.*, LXXVI, 1945, pp. 264–70, espec. p. 268, based on *Dig.* 16, 1, 2, par. 1; cf. E. CUQ, *Manuel des Institutions juridiques des Romains*, Paris 1928, p. 658 and note 5; H. VOGT, *Studien zum Senatusconsultum Velleianum*, Bonn 1952), and for the *s.c. Hosidianum*, a renewal under Nero of the *Volusianum* (*ILS*, 6043; the dating of the first is connected with the placing – which is uncertain – of the consulship of Cn. Hosidius Geta and Vagellius, see above, p. 592), etc. In the matter of moderation in the abolition of Gaius's legislation, it appears from DE LAET, *Portorium, cit.*, p. 346 f., that the *vectigal pro edulibus*, for example, instituted by Gaius, was retained by Claudius. For the field of private law, see M. FASCIATO, 'Note sur l'affranchissement des esclaves abandonnés dans l'île d'Esculape', in *Rev. Hist. Dr. Franç Étr.*, IV, 27, 1949, pp. 454–64, who sees in the measure of Claudius's mentioned by SUET., 25, 2 and by CASS. D., LX, 29, 7, not an act of social revolution but, in the veto on the killing of a sick slave by his master, a stage in the limitation of the *dominica potestas*. On the same theme and in the same journal, see A. PHILIPSBORN, 'L'abandon des esclaves malades au temps de l'empereur Claude et au temps de Justinien', IV, 28, 1950, pp. 402–3, who sees here on the other hand a provision intended to strike superstitious beliefs about the temple of Aesculapius on the Tiber island, in the context of Claudius's religious policy. E. VOLTERRA, 'Intorno a un editto dell'imp. Claudio', in *Rend. Acc. Linc.*, ser. VIII, XI, 1956, pp. 205–19, thinks the same edict recognized a form of *manumissio* alien to Roman law, withdrawing the man freed from the *potestas* of the master. In the administration of justice, the impetus given by Claudius to the predominance of the *cognitio* and the fresh step taken down the road of proceedings *extra ordinem*, a fatal move for the principate, are emphasized by MAY, *op. cit.*, pp. 78–83. In fact the ever more centralized administrative system of Claudius is incomprehensible without the correspondingly authoritarian judicial system; the procuratorial bureaucracy necessarily possessed the power to decide matters of dispute in the fiscal field and their decisions had the same validity as those of the Princeps – the first step to the suppression of the *ordo iudiciorum privatorum*. This was a simplification on the same lines as the one by which, in another branch of government, the Senate decreed after the British triumph of 44 that not only the treaties concluded by the Princeps but also those made by his governors should have full legal force – an explicit recognition, in the field of fully delegated authority, of the uniqueness of the source of power and the unification of the system through which this power worked (CASS. D., LX, 23, 6). On Claudius's personal criteria in practical dispensation of justice, the most eloquent document, the fragment of *oratio* on papyrus *BGU*, 611, has now been completely clarified since the edition by J. STROUX, 'Eine Gerichtsreform des Kaisers Claudius (BGU, 611)', in *Sitz.-ber. d. Bay. Ak. d. Wiss.*, 1929, H. 8, with critical text, translation, commentary and subtle deductions about Claudius's personality (cf. SCRAMUZZA, p. 267, n. 27; see also J. H. OLIVER and R. E. A. PALMER, 'Minutes of an Act of the Roman Senate', in *Hesperia*, XXIV, 1955, pp. 321 f.; L. WENGER, *Die Quellen des römischen Rechts*, Vienna 1953, p. 388). On particular cases and Quintilian's references (*Inst. Orat.*, VIII, 5, 16; IX, 2, 20) to the activity of the great advocate Domitius Afer in connection with the suppression of Scribonianus's revolt, see the article by R. S. ROGERS cited above.

Claudius's religious policy, a fairly important aspect of his reign and one well illustrated by various documents, has received much attention from scholars. The principles of this policy, like those of Claudius's legislation, have been summarized by G. MAY, in 'La politique religieuse de l'empereur Claude' (*Rev. Hist. Dr. Franç. Étr.*, IV, 17, 1938, pp. 1–46). So far as emperor-worship is concerned, the situation of Augustus and Tiberius is repeated, particularly in regard to the East, where the personal refusal of divine honours in a more or less fixed polite formula is accompanied by effective practice of the cult on the part of private individuals and communities, with laws sometimes passed for this very purpose (are we to assign to the moment immediately after the creation of the province the institution of the *Koinón* of the Thracians, attested at the beginning of the second century? Cf. BETZ, in *P.W.*, VI A, 1936, c. 462), while we find more frequent use of personification of qualities and glories of the Princeps, e.g. the cult of the *Victoria Britannica*, the first example attested of *Victoriae de gentibus* such as the *Victoria Dacica* and *Parthia* under Trajan (R. O. FINK, 'Victoria Parthica and Kindred Victoriae', in *Yale Class. St.*, VIII, 1942, p. 89 f.). However, even in the East there is evidence of a characteristic attitude on the subject, such as the formula certainly adopted with care by the prefect C. Julius Aquila to interpret the Emperor's concept precisely, 'pro pace Aug. in honorem Ti. Claudi Germanici Aug.', in the inscription from Amastris, *CIL*, III, 6983 = *ILS*, 5883, and the correction of the prefect of Egypt, L. Aemilius Rectus, in the letter to the Alexandrians, in the shape of the insertion of the word '*theòs*' before the name of Claudius. For particular conceptions – used as propaganda by means of coins – of the patriotic religion, see M. P. CHARLESWORTH, ' "Providentia and Aeternitas" ', in *Harv. Theol. Rev.*, XXIX, 1936, pp. 107–32. As for the restoration of the rites and priesthoods of the traditional religion, through Claudius's enthusiasm for history in general and for Etruscan culture in particular, and possibly as a result of specific circumstances, divination was revived; it may be in fact that there is some connection between the measures for the restoration of the 'Etrusca disciplina' in 47 and the Tarquinian praise already cited (J. HEURGON, in *Latomus*, XII, 1953, pp. 402–15), in which the person dedicating it to an ancient M. Tarquitius Priscus, a master in this discipline (cf. also *CIL*, XI, 3370, cf. p. 1337 = *ILS*, 2924 and *CIL*, XI, 7566) is identified, in the climate of Etruscan archaeology of Claudius's reign, with the Tarquitius Priscus who was deputy to the proconsul of Africa, T. Statilius Taurus, in 52–53, whom Priscus accused, as his prosecutor, of 'pauca repetundarum crimina, ceterum magicas superstitiones obiectabat' (TAC., *Ann.*, XII, 59), which suggests that Priscus may have been a sort of religious adviser to Claudius. Claudius cannot be described as being intolerant on principle of foreign religions as virtually all his predecessors and successors can. The case of the closing of the Pythagorean basilica of the Porta Maggiore at the moment of the fall of the above-mentioned T. Statilius Taurus, a case taken up by J. CARCOPINO (*La basilique pythagoricienne de la Porte Majeure*, Paris 1927, pp. 70–5) as proof of intolerance (pp. 62–5), if this closure is indeed to be placed under Claudius, would show by its possible connection with the trial of Taurus that the measure was if anything, as usual, a police one; the same is true of the measure intended to stop the superstitions centred round the temple of Aesculapius, if there is any validity in the already mentioned explanation by A. PHILIPSBORN (see above, p. 600) of the law of 47 on sick slaves. On the other hand we should not exaggerate the scope and form of Claudius's interest in the introduction of the Eleusinian religion and the Phrygian cult of Attis. On the former, see P. GRAINDOR, *Athènes de Tibère à Trajan*, Cairo 1931, pp. 101–5; J. CARCOPINO, *Aspects mystiques de la Rome païenne*, Paris 1941, p. 169; FR. CUMONT, *Lux perpetua*, Paris 1949, p. 243; and most recently CH. PICARD, *L'éleusinisme à Rome au temps de la dynastie julio-claudienne*, in *Rev. Ét. Lat.*, XXVIII, 1950, pp.

77–80. Picard thinks it was a question of Alexandrian Eleusinianism that had already reached Rome in the last days of the republic; he bases his case on the argument that Claudius, who had not been initiated in Attica, could not have tried to introduce the genuine Eleusinian mysteries, and also on the archaeological evidence of a silver patera from Aquileia. As for the cult of Attis, a subject bound up with the problem of the epigraphical evidence of the 'archigalli', the idea of a radical innovation due to Claudius (see partic. J. CARCOPINO, ' "Attideia" ', in *Mél. Arch. Hist.*, XL, 1923, pp. 135–59, 237–324, espec. 241 ff., and *Aspects mystiques* etc. p. 154 ff.), is contested fairly strongly (SCRAMUZZA, pp. 152–5; cf. C. GATTI, 'Per la storia del culto della Magna Mater in Roma', in *Rend. Ist. Lomb.*, LXXXII, 1949, pp. 253–62); in recent years the excavations of the Metroon at Ostia would seem to move the innovation forward pretty certainly to the age of Antoninus Pius (P. LAMBRECHTS, 'Les fêtes "phrygiennes" de Cibèle et d'Attis', in *Bull. Inst. Hist. Belge de Rome*, XXVII, 1953, pp. 141–70), though it was still attributed to Claudius by L. DEROY, 'Que signifie le titre de l'Apocoloquintose?', in *Latomus*, X, 1951, pp. 311–18. Deroy makes it one of the starting points for the satire, alongside generosity in granting citizenship and the mania for bureaucracy, arguing that the 'pumpkinification' symbolizes the union of the initiate with the Great Mother in the cult of Cybele and Attis, a cult introduced precisely by Claudius. As for relations with the Jews and Christians, the chronological problem of reconciling the report of the expulsion from Rome of the Jews, because they were creating a disturbance 'impulsore Chresto' (SUET., *Cl.*, 25, 4), with the report of the measures connected with them recorded by CASS. D., LX, 6, 6 under the year 41, has now been resolved in favour of the date 49–50, on the basis of OROS., VII, 6, 15–16 (cf. SCRAMUZZA, p. 286, n. 20). On the long-debated question whether the phrase in the letter to the Alexandrians, 'a plague now infecting the whole world' (see above, main text, p. 121), referred to Christianity (SCRAMUZZA, p. 285, n. 19) – in which case it would form chronologically the very first reference to Christianity in existence (A.D. 41) – it is naturally difficult to come to a decision, but (apart from the fact that Christianity was certainly not widely enough diffused to justify a concern expressed in such violent terms, for in that case it would have already been universally considered quite distinct from Judaism, something not demonstrated) perhaps Claudius, in spite of his friendship for Julius Agrippa, had sufficient reason to think and write in such terms of the Jewish invasion in itself; the letter is addressed to the Alexandrians, not to the Jews of Alexandria, and for that reason the Princeps was trying to appear impartial. Outbursts of irritation are typical of his style. For the trial of Isidorus and Lampo, the date 53 proposed by WILCKEN (*Grundz. u. Chrest. d. Papyrusk.* I, 2, no. 14, pp. 24–7) is almost universally accepted; see most recently H. A. MUSURILLO, *The Acts of the Pagan Martyrs, Acta Alexandrinorum*, Oxford 1954, pp. 18–26, and, with full survey of the history of the dating problem, pp. 118–24. Finally a lively discussion was started in 1930 by FR. CUMONT, 'Un rescrit impérial sur la violation de sépulture', in *Rev. Hist.*, 55th year, vol. CLXIII, 1930, pp. 241–66, about an inscription said to come from Nazareth and containing a "diatagma" of an emperor not named but quite probably Claudius, on the violation of tombs. This discussion has gone on up to the present time, partly because of the interest of the subject in relation to the allusion of the Gospels themselves to the burial and resurrection of Christ (MATTH. 28: 62–5), in a dialogue which has attracted the participation of students of history, epigraphy and law (ED. CUQ, L. WENGER, A. MOMIGLIANO, J. CARCOPINO, V. ARANGIO RUIZ, G. DE SANCTIS, W. SESTON, M. GUARDUCCI, L. ROBERT, K. LATTE, F. DE VISSCHER, J. H. OLIVER, bibliography complete up to 1936 in *Suppl. Ep. Gr.*, VIII, 1, 1937, no. 13, p. 4, and from 1936 to 1953 in DE VISSCHER, *art. cit.* below, p. 288, n.4; more recently, M. SORDI, 'I primi rapporti fra lo stato romano e il Cristianesimo, e l'origine delle persecuzioni', in *Rend. Acc. Linc.*, ser. VIII, XII, 1957, App. II, *L'editto di Nazareth*, pp. 91–3). The various problems posed by the inscription, the origin and scope of which were still declared in 1937 by SESTON to be enigmas (*Rev. Phil.*, XI, p. 125), are being slowly resolved. Its authenticity is now universally admitted, its provenance from Nazareth is accepted, it is agreed that it dates somewhere in the period from Augustus to Claudius and should probably be assigned to the reign of the latter. The most recent contributions to the subject deal with the form (rescript or edict, or rather a summary extract ?), the character (public or private?), the scope and uniqueness of the document, and above all the question why it contains the threat of capital punishment for a crime (violation of tombs) usually punished in Roman law by a mere fine. For the most recent views, see J. IRMSCHER, 'Zum diátagma Káisaros von Nazareth', in *Zeitschr. f. d. neutestament. Wiss.*, XLII, 1949, pp. 172–84, who adduces JOSEPH., *Ant. Iud.*, XVIII, 29 ff., and particularly F. DE VISSCHER, in the communication 'L'inscription funéraire dite de Nazareth', in *Compt. rend. Ac. Inscr.*, 1953, pp. 83–92, in the article 'Le "Diatagma" dit de Nazareth sur les violations de sépultures', in *La Nouv. Clio*, 1953 (Mél A. Canoy), pp.

18–30, and at greater length in *Arch. d'Hist. du Dr. Orient. – Rev. Intern. des. Dr. de l'Antiq.*, II, 1953, pp. 285–321, who attempts a fresh interpretation of the text, concluding in favour of its private and individual character, from which it follows that the final threat of the death penalty would have the force of a sepulchral imprecation and the importance of the inscription is minimized, though it remains useful as a source of knowledge of the law and of Roman funerary customs. This is a conclusion that eliminates imaginative theories and probably reduces things to their true proportions, and it has been promptly accepted by J. H. OLIVER, 'A Roman Interdict from Palestine', in *Class. Phil.*, XLIX, 1954, pp. 180–2, with the proviso that the addition to the emperor's actual 'diatagma' would not have been the work of a private individual but that of a magistrate, as an *interdictum* based on the request of Jews concerned with the observance of their local laws; which eliminates the difficulty, noted by ROBERT in *Rev. Ét. Gr.*, LXVII, 1954, p. 176 f., of such a threat emanating from a private citizen.

NERO, PERSONALITY AND MILIEU

The epigraphical and papyrological evidence that has come to light with some, if less, abundance on Nero too has not produced, as it has for Claudius, any profound modifications in the figure delineated by the literary tradition, which seems on the contrary to be confirmed by the inscriptions (SUETONIUS in particular: see N. NELSON, 'The Value of Epigraphic Evidence in the Interpretation of Latin Historical Literature', in *Class. Journ.*, XXXVII, 1942, pp. 281–90). The substantial unanimity of the sources (A. MOMIGLIANO, *Osservazioni* [cited in the main text, p. 104], pp. 323–36) makes only one reconstruction possible, in which the contradictions and obscure sides still remain. It is in fact a vain enterprise to estimate every report in Tacitus, Suetonius and Cassius Dio as hostile or favourable and to try to determine by inference the source of the sources, and hence the value to be assigned to the report itself. In all the authors cited the tendency is the same, and it is hostile. It may be that there were sources favourable to Nero (cf. JOSEPH., *Ant. Iud.*, XX, 154 [8, 3]), but we cannot discern them behind our authorities. Naturally any report that does not produce the usual negative effect will also be in Nero's favour, just as not everything in his actual principate will have been bad. But a statement like that of SUETONIUS's (19, 3), 'haec partim nulla reprehensione, partim etiam non mediocri laude digna in unum contuli, ut secernerem a probris ac sceleribus eius, de quibus dehinc dicam', that is, 'note that I have hurried through the little good so as to be free to describe the much that was bad', removes any possibility of estimating the value of the sources by this method. Everything comes back to the internal standards of the book, to the author's personal plan of composition. Internal research of this kind, with a comparison of the subjective attitudes of the individual authors to their common material, has been undertaken by K. HEINZ, *Das Bild Kaiser Neros bei Seneca, Tacitus, Sueton und Cassius Dio*, Diss., Berne 1946 (pub. 1948), who comes down in favour of the substantial truth of the picture of Nero presented by the tradition. Concrete results can be obtained by directing one's attention to the cultural climate and examining the numerous literary works which bring to life the society of the time – investigating in particular the allusions in contemporary poetry.

The assessments suggested by investigation of this sort, together with the more searching re-examination of the historico-narrative sources for concrete facts, have led to the present reconstruction of Nero's biography, while research into the administrative, economic and social conditions of the empire, and the contributions made to prosopography by epigraphy, have in recent times cleared up some points which are also useful for the reconstruction of the general history of the reign. A biography of Nero along these lines has indeed already been attempted in the works of SCHILLER, *Gesch. d. röm. Kaiserz.*, Gotha 1883, pp. 344–62, and B. W. HENDERSON, *The Life and Principate of the Emperor Nero*, London 1903–5, and in the art. by HOHL for *P.W.* (Suppl. III, 1918, cc. 349–94), who follows in all essentials the two previous writers. This picture was accepted in the cited histories of DOMASZEWSKI (II[3], pp. 47–78), DESSAU (II, 1, pp. 174–299), HOMO (pp. 282–321), COLUMBA (pp. 317–45) and finally in the chapter of the *Cambr. Anc. Hist.* (X, pp. 702–42) by A. MOMIGLIANO. It is only more recently that treatments like that of M. A. LEVI, *Nerone e i suoi tempi*, Milan 1949, have taken account of the life of the age as a whole and given more scope to the depiction of the milieu in which Nero's activity took place. His figure becomes a little more lifelike when seen thus in deeper perspective, but the fundamental problems are not really clarified. Nero, too, has attracted the psychologists (e.g. G. WALTER, *Néron*, Paris 1955, to quote only a recent example), and biographies appear frequently (C. M. FRANZERO, *The Life and Time of Nero*, London 1954, has not been accessible to me). But research into the literary scene is particularly active. It is a matter mainly of studying the problem of Nero and Seneca (E. LEPORE, 'Per la storia del principato neroniano', in *Par. Pass.*, III, 1948, pp. 81–100; H.

BARDON, *Les empereurs et les lettres latines, d'Auguste à Hadrien*, Paris 1940, pp. 221–56; F. MARTINAZZOLI, *Seneca. Studio sulla morale ellenica nell'esperienza romana*, Florence 1945; F. GIANCOTTI, 'Il posto della biografia nella problematica senechiana', I. II. III. IV, in *Rend. Acc. Lincei*, ser. VIII, vol. VIII, 1953, pp. 52–68; 102–18; 238–62; vol. IX, 1954, pp. 329–44). The chronology of the writers' works is of fundamental importance for establishing the correspondence between the allusions and the events of political life, though research on the subject always revolves within the limits of a combinatory procedure not exempt from the risk of becoming a vicious circle when attemps are made to attain too detailed results. Thus in the eclogues of Calpurnius Siculus, in Book I of Lucan's *Pharsalia* and in the *Carmina Einsiedlensia*, it is not difficult to see reflected hope and enthusiasm for the dawn of a happy age to come with the new Princeps (A. MOMIGLIANO, 'Literary Chronology of the Neronian Age', *Class. Quart.*, 1944, pp. 96–100; on the theme of the 'felicitas temporum', see E. MANNI, 'La leggenda dell'età dell'oro nella politica dei Cesari', in *At. e Roma*, XL, 1938, pp. 108–20, espec. 113 ff.; W. SCHMID, 'Panegyrik und Bukolik in der neronischen Epoche', in *Bonn. Jahrb.*, CLIII, 1953, pp. 63–96), and the gradually growing disillusionment is clearly discernible as Lucan's poem proceeds (A. PUNTONI, 'La composiz. del poema lucaneo', in *Rend. Acc. Lincei*, ser. VIII, vol. II, 1947, pp. 101–126, espec. 102 f., 126; M. PAVAN, 'L'ideale politico di Lucano', in *Atti Ist. Ven.*, CXIII, 1954–5, pp. 209–22, G. DE PLINVAL, 'Une insolence de Lucain', in *Latomus*, XV, 1956, pp. 512–20; G. K. GRESSETH, 'The Quarrel between Lucan and Nero', in *Class. Phil.*, LII, 1957, pp. 24–7). With the works of Seneca, Petronius and Persius the problem is more complex. Take the *Apocolocyntosis*, for example. This is now generally placed between A.D. 54–55 – when it would have represented most logically the spontaneous anti-Claudian reaction (MOMIGLIANO, *art. cit.*, p. 96 f.; and if the pumpkin recalls the *fritillus*, that is, the box for throwing dice, of which Claudius was passionately fond [F. A. TODD, 'Some Cucurbitaceae in Latin Literature', in *Class. Quart.*, XXXVII, 1943, pp. 101–11, espec. 103–7], this detail demands all the more that Claudius should have not long been dead) – and A.D. 60, when it would have been written most probably on the occasion of the *Neronia*, to indicate the abandonment of the cult of the divine Claudius and the inauguration of the 'new development' of theatrical and literary splendour (J. M. C. TOYNBEE, 'Nero Artifex. The *Apocolocyntosis* Reconsidered', in *Class. Quart.*, XXXVI, 1942, pp. 83–93), as if Nero had not displayed a passion for these things right from the start of the reign, and in any case long before 60, supported by Seneca. The intermediate solution (K. BARWICK, 'Senecas Apoc. eine zweite Ausgabe des Verfassers', in *Rh. Mus.*, XCII, 1943, pp. 159–73) postulates a first anonymous edition, without the praises of Nero, and a second with the addition of these, published by Seneca in support of Nero against Agrippina, while the identification of the unknown god of Ch. 8 with Julius Caesar, proposed by L. HERMANN, 'Le dieu inconnu du chapitre VIII de la satire sur l'apothéose de Claude', in *Latomus*, X, 1951, pp. 25–6, seems tinged with the interpretation of the tyrannies of Gaius and Nero in a more Caesarean than Augustan sense. As for the other works of Seneca, the one with the greatest programmatic significance, the *De Clementia*, was probably finished before the end of 55 (S. PANTZERHIELM-THOMAS, 'Adnotatiunculae ad Senecae libros de clementia', in *Serta Eitremiana* [Symbolae Osloenses, XI], Oslo 1943, pp. 165–8; F. GIANCOTTI, *Il posto* etc. IV, 1: *Sfondo storico e data del De clementia*, pp. 329–44 (beginning of 56), taken up again by the same writer in 'Replica a un nuovo tentativo di porre il "De clementia" avanti la morte di Britannico', in *Rend. Acc. Linc.*, ser. VIII, XI, 1956, pp. 3–13, as against V. CAPOCCI, 'La cronologia del "De clementia"', in *Ann. Fac. Lett. Nap.*, IV, 1954, pp. 61–73); and that the work of Seneca the writer was closely bound up, at any rate on this occasion, with the work of the statesman is apparent from the different tone of the works composed under Claudius (W. H. ALEXANDER, 'Seneca's "ad Polybium de consolatione", a Reappraisal', in *Trans. Roy. Soc. of Canada*, ser. III, sect. II, XXXVII, 1943, pp. 33–55; P. GRIMAL, 'La date du De brevitate vitae', in *Rev. Ét. Lat.*, XXV, 1947, pp. 164–77 (A.D. 49)). Closely connected with this is the question, already vividly posed in CASS. D., LXI, 10, 1–6 (cf. TAC., *Ann.*, XIII, 42), of Seneca's intellectual integrity and of his participation and responsibility in certain of Nero's crimes (M. N. DURIÉ, 'Vereinigung der Politik und der Philosophie bei den Römern', in *Ziva Antika*, X, 1960, pp. 103–24). While E. CIACERI, 'Nerone matricida', in *Rend. Acc. It.*, ser. VII, vol. III, 1941–2, pp. 289–98, espec. p. 294 ff., attributes the responsibility for the matricide to Seneca and Burrus, who wanted to eliminate the interference of Agrippina in affairs of state, and reduced the part of Nero to mere compliance, then emphasizing his grounds for remorse, nowadays the defenders of Seneca are in the ascendant: W. H. ALEXANDER, 'The Enquête on Seneca's Treason', in *Class. Phil.*, XLVII, 1952, pp. 1–6 (the argument is that Seneca's unswerving loyalty to Nero is certain; he was regarded by public opinion as privy to the Pisonian conspiracy simply because of his friendly relations with Piso); F. GIANCOTTI, 'Seneca amante d'Agrippina?', in *Par. Pass.*, VIII, 1953, pp. 52–62 (cf. *Il posto etc.*, III: *Seneca antagonista d'Agrippina*, pp. 238–62); W. H. ALEXANDER, 'The Communiqué to the Senate on Agrippina's Death', in *Class. Phil.*, XLIX, 1954, pp. 94–7 (where a reason already advanced by C. PASCAL, *Seneca*, Catania 1906, p. 43, is called into play again and it is asserted that the silence of Cassius Dio, who was hostile to Seneca, is decisive in indicating that Nero's report to the Senate on the death of his mother was not written by Seneca). But many points certainly remain obscure (A. PITTET, 'Le mot consensus chez Sénèque. Ses acceptions philosophiques et politiques', in *Mus. Helv.*, XII, 1955, pp. 35–46, espec. 45 f.: R. S. ROGERS, 'Seneca on Lentulus Augur's Wealth. A Note', in *Class. Weekly*, XLII, 1948–9, pp. 91–2; H. E. WEDECK, 'The Question of Seneca's Wealth', in *Latomus*, XIV, 1955, pp. 540–4; F. GIANCOTTI, *Il posto etc.*, 'Sopra il retiro et la ricchezza di Seneca', in *Rend. Acc. Linc.*, ser. VIII, XI, 1956, pp. 105–19; E. BICKEL, 'Seneca und Seneca-mythus', in *Altertum*, V, 1959, pp. 90–100.) On the *Octavia*, which is supposed to resume the tone of the *Apocolocyntosis* in order to register the disappointment of a hope and would thus be a genuine work of Seneca, see B. M. MARTI, 'Seneca's "Apocolocyntosis" and Octavia, a Diptych', in *Amer. Journ. Phil.*, LXXIII, 1952, pp. 24–36; cf. F. GIANCOTTI, *L'Octavia attribuita a Seneca*, Turin 1954. Allusions to contemporary life can be traced in the little poem on the civil war inserted in Petronius's *Satyricon*, in place of LUCAN, *Phars*, II, 667 f. (on the excavation of the canal Ostia-Lake Avernus: P. GRENADE, 'Un exploit de Néron', in *Rev. Ét. Anc.*, L, 1948, pp. 272–87; see also on this project A. MAIURI, 'Fossa Neronis', in *Bull. Vereiniging Antieke Beschaving*, Leiden, XXIX, 1954, pp. 57–61), but more interesting are the satirical allusions, hostile to the Princeps, which people think they can discern in Petronius (R. H. CRUM, 'Petronius and the Emperors, I: Allusions in the "Satyricon". II: "Pax Palamedes"'!, in *Class. Weekly*, XLV, 1952, pp. 161–7, 197–201) and Persius (W. C. KORFMACHER, *A Résumé of the Persius-Nero Question*, summ. in *Trans. Proc. Am. Phil. Ass.*, LXIX, 1938, p. XLII; L. HERMANN, 'Les premiers oeuvres de Perse', in *Latomus*, XI, 1952, pp. 199–201), and the various aspects of the conflict between the principate and philosophy, set alight under Nero by the fires of martyrdom (J. KORVER, 'Néron et Musonius. A propos du dialogue du Pseudo-Lucian "Néron, ou sur le percement de l'isthme de Corinth"', in *Mnem.*, IV, 3, 1950, pp. 319–29). In the context of these literary allusions it is also worth mentioning the theories of L. HERRMANN, 'La date du roman de Ninus', in *Chron. d'Egypte*, XIV, 1939, pp. 373–5, who makes the 'Romance of Ninus' a *roman à clé* written in the Neronian age, with the ancient Assyrian king representing Nero, and A. H. KRAPPE, 'La fin d'Agrippine', in *Rev. Ét. Anc.*, XLII, 1940 (Mél. Raidet), pp. 466–72, who sees on the contrary in the account of the end of Agrippina the literary re-working of mythological and eastern stories, in particular the story of Semiramis. And finally we must mention the most recent attempts at explaining, generally with a view to rehabilitation, the cultural enthusiasm and the exhibitionism attributed to Nero (A. LESKY, 'Neroniana', in *Annuaire Inst. Phil. Hist. Orient.*, IX, 1949 [Mél. Grégoire], pp. 385–407, for the recitations of tragedy; M. P. CHARLESWORTH, 'Nero. Some Aspects', in *Journ. Rom. St.*, XL, 1950, pp. 69–76, who tries to reduce Nero's histrionic displays to more sober proportions, observing that the habit of singing *habitu tragico* was common, that the admiration for everything Greek was sincere, and that Nero did not have a true policy of self-deification like Gaius, but simply one of the manifestation of power in an extravagant form). The revaluation of Philostratus carried out by F. GROSSO, 'La "Vita di Apollonio di Tiana" come fonte storica', in *Acme*, VII, 1954, pp. 333–532, helps us to understand more clearly the cultural background, especially that of the philosophical opposition and of eastern currents of thought, of men like the Cynic Demetrius and the Pythagorean Apollonius of Tyana (espec. pp. 379–88), while evidence of the atmosphere of approaching tragedy is provided by the memory, which remained vivid, of the numerous comets that appeared during the reign (R. S. ROGERS, 'The Neronian Comets', in *Trans. Proc. Am. Phil. Ass.*, LXXXIV, 1953, pp. 237–49).

An attempt to divide Nero's reign into periods (54–64 constitutional period, 64–68 period of despotism and deification after the style of Hellenistic monarchs) on the basis of the iconographical evidence is made by H. P. L'ORANGE, 'Le Néron constitutionnel et le Néron apothéosé', in *From the Coll. of the Ny Carlsberg Glyptothek*, III, Copenhagen 1942; but one should remember what was said above (p. 574 f.) about this kind of source. On the ancient expression 'quinquennium aureum' attributed by Aurelius Victor to Trajan, see F. A. LEPPER, 'Some Reflections on the "Quinquennium Neronis" ', in *Journ. Rom. St.*, XLVII, 1957, pp. 95–103. On the survival of Nero's memory, see most recently A. E. PAPPANO, 'The False Neros', in *Class. Journ.*, XXXII, 1937, p. 385 ff. As for the atmosphere in general and as it affected aristocratic society, the idea that the nobility of the Neronian epoch was impoverished and fearful of losing everything, and was therefore pessimistic and took refuge in philosophy, with a purely academic regret for the republic – the principate being in fact what preserved their surviving positions – has been put forward by IZA BIEZUNSKA-MALOWIST, *Les opinions de la nobilitas romaine à l'époque de Néron et leur fondement économique et social* (Travaux de l'Institut d'Histoire de l'Université de Varsovie, V), Warsaw 1952 (in Polish, with a French summary); even the premises of this thesis are questionable. For Nero's relations with the aristocratic circles closest to him, see R. S. ROGERS, 'Heirs and Rivals to Nero', in *Trans. Proc. Am. Phil. Ass.*, LXXXVI, 1955, pp. 190–212; A. DEGRASSI, 'Un nuovo frammento dei Fasti dei sodales Augustales Claudiales', in *Epigr.*, IV, IV, 1942, pp. 17–22, from which it appears that in 64–65 the highest society was all engaged in the imperial cult. As for individual persons of the age besides Seneca, there is a fresh examination of the Tacitean tradition on Agrippina in the *art cit.* by E. PARATORE, in *Maia*, 1952, p. 32 ff. (see also the same writer's 'Un evento clamoroso nella Roma di millenovecento anni fa', in *Stud. Rom.*, VII, 1959, pp. 497–510). A new inscription from Amisus (Pontus), mentioning in curious proximity Nero, Poppaea and Britannicus and dating from between 63 and 65, probably indicates that people believed, or pretended to believe, the version of the death of Britannicus given by Nero (*SEG.*, XVI, 1959, no. 748 = *AE*, 1959, 224; cf. ROBERT, in *Rev. Ét. Gr.*, LXXI, 1958, p. 329, no. 48-). The sojourn at Marseilles, or more precisely at Glanum (St Rémy), of Faustus Cornelius Sulla, sent to live there compulsorily by Nero in 58, is confirmed according to J. CARCOPINO, 'Note sur une inscription de mosaique trouvée à Glanum', in *Compt. rend. Acad. Inscr.*, 1949, pp. 264–70 and 340–1, by the inscription on a mosaic (on the *graffito* date which accompanies it and is on the other hand a modern forgery, see the same scholar's 'Note sur un graffito latin découvert dans les ruines de Glanum', in *Studies Robinson*, II, 1953, pp. 398–411). The career of Afranius Burrus is studied, with a view to determining precisely his relations with Seneca, by W. C. MCDERMOTT, 'Sextus Afranius Burrus', in *Latomus*, VIII, 1949, pp. 229–54. Still on the subject of Burrus, there is a discrepancy between Tacitus and Cassius Dio (one of the few) on the time of his death. CASS. D., LXII, 13, 1–2, says that Burrus opposed the killing of Octavia. Octavia was killed on 9 June 62. From Tacitus, whose chronology seems preferable, it would appear that Burrus died first, probably at the beginning of the year. It is probable that Burrus's opposition referred to previous intentions expressed by Nero and was erroneously transferred by Dio to the final episode. It is worth noting that after the divorce Octavia had Burrus's house and the estates of Rubellius Plautus (TAC., *Ann.*, XIV, 60, 4); evidently Burrus was already dead (but according to Cassius D. he was eliminated precisely because of his opposition). Finally, on the personal relations of Nero with the holders of the imperial *curae* and with the equestrian class, see GORDON, *Q. Veranius* etc. (see above, p. 594), pp. 256–62, 273.

THE REIGN OF NERO. INTERNAL PROBLEMS

The problem of separating from the political activity as a whole of Nero's reign what was due to Nero's personal initiative is not easy to resolve. The documents do not enable us, as they do for Claudius, to pin-point distinctly original characteristics, for the letters to the people of Rhodes (*Syll.*³, 810; see the edition by G. PUGLIESE CARRATELLI, 'Note su epigrafi rodie dell'età imperiale. II: L'intestazione dell'epistola di Nerone ai Rodii', in *St. di Ant. class. offerti a E. Ciaceri*, 1940, p. 255 f.) and to Meophilus (*O.G.I.S.* 475), and the Corinth speech granting freedom to the Greeks (*Syll.*³, 814 = *ILS*, 8794), which form the most extensive pieces of testimony to direct interventions, do not contain any elements in conflict with the personality described by the tradition and the honorific inscriptions or inscriptions referring to public works, a few more of which (they are less numerous than for Claudius, but this may be a result of the *damnatio*) have come to light recently, do not show anything more – the custom now being established – than the ordinary processes of administration or else, in so far as they reflect the gratitude of the East for the benefits from the philhellene Princeps, do no more than confirm an aspect of Nero already well known. But so far as participation in the central government is concerned, the development outlined in the main text of an attempt at emancipation from his advisers, and of a progressive, capricious intrusiveness, with a few moments of zeal for serious matters but on the whole more enthusiasm for the execution of his programme for the assertion of power in the extravagant form of a pseudo-cultural superiority, seems the least arbitrary interpretation of the tradition and the one that best reflects the disappointment people felt (there must be doubt about the alleged 'politica augustea' to be inferred, at any rate for the programme of the early days of the reign, from the numerous references to Augustus in the works of Seneca; see P. JAL, 'Images d'Auguste chez Sénèque', in *Rev. Ét. Lat.*, XXXV, 1957, pp. 242–64).

   Here therefore we shall sum up the present position on the traditional questions (internal reforms and external events, fire and persecution of the Christians, public works) in themselves, beginning with a mention of the most recent epigraphical discoveries: five inscriptions of *corporis custodes* of

Nero, at Rome (*Not. d. Sc.*, 1950, pp. 86–90) and, in the provinces, a pillar from Cyrenaica, with an inscription in Latin and Greek, for a restitution of public land occupied by private individuals, possibly in connection with the judgement mentioned by TAC., *Ann.*, XIV, 18 (*AE*, 1934, 260 = *SEG*, IX, 352); four pillars in Syria (at Nebi Sit) to indicate the boundaries of an imperial domain or the frontiers of the province (*AE*, 1953, 151); the inscription from an acqueduct in Cyprus (*AE*, 1953, 166); a monumental inscription from Leptis Magna (*Inscr. of Rom. Trip.*, 341), the only one compared with the numerous ones of Tiberius and Claudius, an inscription from the end of 57 in the forum of Volubilis, built in the Neronian age (*Inscr. Lat. du Maroc*, 58), and the dedications from Lycopolis in Egypt (*Journ. Hell. St.*, LXII, 1942, p. 17), from the *colonia Ptolemais veteranorum vici Nea Come et Gedru* in connection with the construction of the road from Antiochia to Ptolemais (A.D. 56. *AE*, 1948, 142), from Palmyra of A.D. 63 (*Syria*, XXII, 1941, p. 175) and finally the one, already noted (*IG²*, II–III, 3182) and reconstructed by A. V. GERKAN with the collaboration of W. KOLBE as a dedication to Dionysus Eleutherius and Nero, from the stage of the theatre of Dionysus at Athens (A. v. GERKAN, 'Die Neronische Scaenae Frons des Dionysos-theaters in Athen', in *Jahrb. d. deutsch. arch. Inst.*, LVI, 1941, pp. 163–77, espec. 174 ff.). As for internal events, the coinage, already exploited to promulgate the young Nero as heir (J. BABELON, 'L'enfance de Néron', in *Rev. Num.*, XVII, 1955, pp. 129–52) reflects in the early days the gradual diminution of Agrippina's power (SUTHERLAND: *Coinage in Roman Imperial Policy*, p. 152 f.); but the most interesting event is the reform of 64, followed by the abundance of issues in the years 64–68 (SUTHERLAND, pp. 162 ff.; S. J. DE LAET, 'Une dévaluation dans l'antiquité. La réforme monétaire de l'année 64 ap. J.C. Étude sur les finances publiques sous Néron', in *Rev. de la Banque*, 1943, I and 2; M. RABOSSI, 'La coniazione di Nerone. La riforma dell'oro et dell'argento', in *Acme*, VI, 1953, pp. 479–87), while reflections of the conflicts of the civil war and later of the damning of Nero's memory are to be found in Spanish and also Eastern coins (C. H. V. SUTHERLAND, 'A Coin of Nero Overstruck for Galba', in *Num. Chron.*, XX, 1940, pp. 265–6; TH. O. MABBOTT, 'Epictetus and Nero's Coinage', in *Class. Phil.*, XXXVI, 1941, pp. 398 f.). So far as legislative measures are concerned, the *s.c. Pisonianum* of 57 and the *Neronianum*, possibly of the same year, intended to reinforce the *s.c. Silanianum* of A.D. 10 in the matter of the punishment of slaves and freedmen, probably represent a revival of the senatorial class in comparison with the Emperor's freedmen (L. HERRMANN, 'La genèse du s.c. Silanianum', in *Arch. Hist. Dr. Orient.–Rev. Intern. Dr. Ant.*, I, 1952, pp. 495–505). Too much severity is thought by some to be attributed to Nero by the tradition in the matter of trials for treason (R. S. ROGERS, 'The Tacitean Account of a Neronian Trial', in *St. Robinson*, II, Saint Louis 1953, pp. 711–18, on the trial of Antistius Sosianus in 62, TAC., *Ann.*, XIV, 48, which is supposed to be only the repetition, on a schema going back to Sallust, of the trial of Clutorius Priscus in 21, TAC., *Ann.*, III, 50). On the problem of the *tribunicia potestas* and the imperial salutations of Nero, see T. B. MITFORD, 'Notes on Published Inscriptions from Roman Cyprus', in *Ann. Br. Sch. at Athens*, XLII, 1947, pp. 220 f. On the fire of Rome and the persecution of the Christians, that part of the problem concerning the responsibility of Nero as author of the fire is now resolved in the sense of the fairly clear position of Tacitus: accidental fire, with 'rumor' blaming Nero for it. Consequently recent studies on the subject consider only aspects of it: technical aspects, like the one dealt with by G. LUGLI, 'La vecchia Roma incendiata da Nerone', in *Capitolium*, XXII, 1947, pp. 41–50, or sacral aspects, like the fact that the *dies nefasti* falling round the *dies Alliensis* coincided with the day of the beginning of the fire (G. CRISPO, '17–19 luglio, giorni nefasti per Roma', *ibid.*, XXIV, 1949, pp. 167–74), or else details connected with the interpretation of the sources (M. F. GYLES, 'Nero Fiddled While Rome Burned', in *Class. Journ*, XLII, 1947, pp. 211–17).

As for the blame assigned to the Christians by Nero and the consequent persecution, and the problem of their actual responsibility, the discussion is naturally more sustained, though here too with results pointing to the substantial accuracy of the position adopted by Tacitus: 'ergo abolendo rumori Nero subdidit reos et quaesitissimis poenis affecit, quos per flagitia invisos vulgus Christianos appellabat . . . haud proinde in crimine incendii quam odio humani generis convicti sunt (XV, 44, 4) . . . quamquam adversus sontes et novissima exempla meritos miseratio oriebatur, tamquam non utilitate publica, sed in saevitiam unius absumerentur' (44, 5). It is clear that Tacitus does not believe the Christians *sontes* of anything but the *flagitia* imputed to them in general by public opinion, not of the specific crime of incendiarism. In fact the Christians must have been hated as such because it was believed that they practised a religion which encouraged immorality and crime, if indeed people did not still retain the memory – which had already appeared, it seems, in the reign of Tiberius – of the misapprehension into which the Jews had deliberately led the Roman authorities at the time of the famous trial conducted by Pilate, namely that Christ had opposed the authority of the Roman Caesar (this can be inferred, according to PARETI, *St. di Roma*, IV, p. 736, from the famous passages of TERTULL., *Apolog.*, V, 2, and XXI, 24). Nero took advantage of this attitude (H. LAST, 'The Study of the "Persecutions" ', in *Journ. Rom. St.*, XXVII, 1937, pp. 80–92, espec. 88–92; F. W. CLAYTON, 'Tacitus and Nero's persecution of the Christians', in *Class. Quart.*, XLI, 1947, pp. 81 ff.; K. BÜCHNER, 'Tacitus über die Christen', in *Aegyptus*, XXXIII, 1953 [St Vitelli, IV], pp. 181–92; BR. DOER, 'Neros Menschenfackeln', in *Altertum*, II, 1955, pp. 15–28, who thinks that the ancient penalty for incendiarism was applied to the Christians). That the persecution was regarded as more than a mere political expedient and reverberated through the empire is shown not only by the whole Christian tradition, already naturally hostile to the persecutor, who was seen as the persecutor of the Christian name in itself, but also by the allusions in St Peter's First Epistle and above all in the Apocalypse of St John (XIII, 1–14; XVII, 7–14; cf. H. LAST, *art. cit.*, p. 89; L. HERRMANN, 'Le nombre de la bête dans l'Apocalypse johannique', in *Latomus*, IX, 1950, pp. 287–94; S. GIET, 'La guerre des Juifs de Flavius Josèphe et quelques énigmes de l'Apocalypse', in *Rev. de. Sc. Relig.*, XXVI, 1952, pp. 1–29). Yet the possibility that the persecution was the consequence of a law may be excluded. The discussion centres round the passage in Tertullian, *Ad. Nat.*, I, 7, 9 on the 'institutum Neronianum' (H. LAST, *art. cit.*, and in *Reallex f. Ant. u. Christentum*, II, 1954, cc. 1208–28; L. DIEU, 'La persécution au IIᵉ siècle. Une loi fantôme', in *Rev. d'Hist. Eccles.*, XXXVIII, 1942, pp. 5–19, espec. pp. 10 ff.; J. W. PH. BORLEFFS, 'Institutum Neronianum', in *Vigiliae Christianae*, VI, 1952, pp. 129–45; L. DE REGIBUS, *Politica e religione da Augusto a Constantino*, Genoa 1953, pp. 51–4: all of whom exclude the existence of a law; for the opposite view, see most recently J. ZEILLER, ' "Institutum Neronianum". Loi fantôme ou réalité?', in *Rev. Hist. Eccles.*, L, 1955, pp. 393–9; M. SORDI, *art. cit.*, in *Rend. Acc. Linc.*, ser. VIII, XII, 1957, pp. 58–93; A. OMODEO, *Saggi sul Cristianesimo antico*, Naples 1958, pp. 89 f.). On the problem of the Neronian persecution as a whole, see also M. DIBELIUS, 'Rom u. die Christen im ersten Jahrhundert', in *Sitz.-ber. d. Heidelberger Ak. d. Wiss., Phil-hist. Kl.*, 1941–2, no. 2 (Heidelberg 1942) and, a short note, 'Nero u. die Christen', in *Forsch. u. Fortschr.*, XVIII, 1942, pp. 189–90, who, comparing TACITUS and CLEM., *Epist.*, I, and touching also on the question of the martyrdom of Sts Peter and Paul, says that there was no charge of incendiarism by Nero against the Christians and explains it as arising from a misunderstanding of the passage of Tacitus 'subdidit reos' etc. A. G. ROOS, 'Nero and the Christians', in *Symbolae van Oven*, Leiden 1946, pp. 297–306, attacks Dibelius and returns to the traditional interpretation. For the alleged part played by the Jews in the persecution, J. SCHWARTZ, 'Ti. Claudius Balbillus (préfet d'Egypte et conseiller de Néron)', in *Bull. de l'Inst. Franc. d'Arch. Orient. du Caire*, XLIX, 1950, pp. 45–55, observes (p. 54) that since Balbillus was accused at Ephesus both by the Jews and the Christians of having started the persecution of the Christians, the theory that it was instigated by the Jews through Poppaea falls to the ground. On Poppaea's alleged sympathy for the Jews, see E. M. SMALLWOOD, 'The Alleged Jewish Tendencies of Poppaea Sabina', in *Journ. Theol. St.*, X, 1959, pp. 329–35. On the religious climate in general, see E. BICKEL, 'Pagani, Kaiseranbeter in den Laren-Kapellen der pagi urbani in Rom Neros und des Apostels Petrus', in *Rh. Mus.*, XCVII, 1954, pp. 1–47; 'Politische Sibylleneklogen', *ibid.*, pp. 193–228, espec. 193–209. On the history of the beginnings of the Church in Rome in connection with the presence and martyrdom of St Peter (see L. HERRMANN, 'Le premier séjour de saint Pierre à Rome', in *Latomus*, V, 1946, pp. 303–10, on an alleged first stay under Claudius, and H. GRÉGOIRE, *Les persécutions dans l'empire romain*, Brussels 1951, p. 101 f.), the recent excavations in the Vatican have aroused extraordinary interest. After the official publication of the excavations, by B. M. APOLLONJ GHETTI, A. FERRUA, E. JOSI and E. KIRSCHBAUM, *Esplorazioni sotto la confessione di S. Pietro in Vaticano eseguite negli anni 1940–49*. Vatican City 1951, there have been numerous contributions by scholars holding various different views: to cite only a few (reviews up to 1958 in *Fasti Archaeologici*, VI–XIII), J. CARCOPINO, *Études d'histoire chrétienne. Les fouilles de Saint Pierre et la tradition*, Paris 1953; M. GUARDUCCI, *Cristo e S. Pietro in un documento precostantiniano della necropoli Vatiana*, Rome 1953; H. J. TORP, 'The Vatican Excavations and the Cult of Saint Peter', in *Acta Archaeologica* (Copenhagen), XXIV, 1953, pp. 27–66; J. M. C. TOYNBEE, 'The Shrine of St Peter and its Setting', in *Journ. Rom. St.*, XLIII, 1953, pp. 1–26; H. GRÉGOIRE, 'Le problème de la tombe de Saint Pierre', in *Nouv. Clio*, V, 1953 (Mél. Carnoy), pp. 48–58, J. D. BURGER, 'La tombe de Saint Pierre est-elle identifiée?', in *Cahiers de Foi et Vérité*, XXVII, ser. VII, 3, Geneva 1954; J. RUYSSCHAERT, 'Réflexions sur les fouilles vaticanes, le rapport officiel et la critique. I: Données archéologiques', in *Rev. d'Hist. Eccl.*, XLVIII, 1953, pp. 573–631; 'II: Données épigraphiques et littéraires', *ibid.*, XLIX, 1954, pp. 5–58; H. LAST, 'St Peter, The Excavations under the Basilica in

Rome, and the Beginnings of Western Christendom', coll. in *Proc. Class. Ass.*, London, LI, 1954, pp. 50–1; M. CAGIANO DE AZEVEDO, 'L'origine della necropoli vaticana secondo Tacito', in *Aevum*, XXIX, 1955, pp. 575–7; K. ALAND, 'Petrus in Rom', in *Hist. Zeitschr.*, CLXXXIII, 1957, pp. 497–516; H. CHADWICK, 'Sts Peter and Paul in Rome. The Problem of the Memoria Apostolorum ad Catacumbas', in *Journ. Theolog. St.*, VIII, 1957, pp. 31–52 (on the uncertainty prevalent even among the ancients, since at the time of the Neronian persecution the bodies of the martyrs could hardly have been buried with a great deal of care); etc. The problem of the extent of the Christian conquest in relation to the social classes also demands attention: there is a re-examination in this connection of the authenticity of the correspondence between St Paul and Seneca in A. MOMIGLIANO, 'Note sulla legenda del Cristianesimo di Seneca', in *Riv. Stor. Ital.*, LXII, 1950, pp. 325–44 (= *Contrib. alla storia degli studi class.*, Rome 1955, pp. 13–32); cf. A. BALLANTI, 'Documenti sull'opposizione degli intellettuali a Domiziano', in *Ann. Fac. Lett. Nap.*, IV, 1954, pp. 92–4, who regards the letters as a document of the opposition to Domitian (see below, p. 649); A. KURFEES, 'Zu dem apokryphen Briefwechsel zwischen dem Philosophen Seneca und dem Apostel Paulus', in *Aevum*, XXVI, 1952, pp. 42–8.

Closely bound up with the problems mentioned are those concerning the building activity of Nero for the reconstruction of Rome and of his palace and his religious concepts (rather than policy) in general. The religious character of the *domus aurea*, conceived for the glorification of Nero-Helios, has in fact been noted by H. P. L'ORANGE, 'Domus aurea – der Sonnenpalast', in *Serta Eitremiana* (Symb. Osl., 1942), pp. 68–100, and raised again by A. BOETHIUS, 'Nero's Golden House', in *Eranos*, XLIV, 1946 (*Eranos Rudbergianus*), pp. 442–59, who reduces it to an internal section, the *rotunda*, obviously of oriental antecedents, while the building as a whole simply represented, in conformity with the tradition, an Italian villa inserted by Severus and Celer in the centre of the city. See also A. ALFÖLDI, 'Die Geschichte des Throntabernakels', in *Nouv. Clio*, I–II, 1949–50, pp. 537–66, espec. p. 563; C. C. VAN ESSEN, 'La topographie de la Domus aurea Neronis, in *Mededel. Nederl. Akad. van Wet.*,' Afd. Letterkunde, N.S. XVII, 12 (1954), pp. 371–98; J. W. PERKINS, 'Nero's Golden House', in *Antiquity*, XXX, 1956, pp. 209–19. In the more purely religious field, F. CUMONT's theory, 'L'iniziazione di Nerone da parte di Tiridate d'Armenia', in *Riv. Fil.*, N.S. XI, 1933, pp. 145–54, which suggests that in Rome Tiridates initiated Nero into a particular form of the Mithraic cult, has found neither confirmation nor support; J. SCHWARTZ, 'Dies Augustus', in *Rev. Ét. Anc.*, XLVI, 1944, pp. 266–79, studies the recurrence of the *dies Augustus* as a form of the imperial cult in the dates of the Egyptian documents of the Julio-Claudian era (among other things he refers to the need to move back the date of Nero's birth, on the basis of such documents, to 15 December 35 [pp. 274–277], as against the 37 of Suetonius and the 36–37 of Tacitus. In spite of this slight oscillation, the numerous references in the literary tradition [*PIR²*, III, pp. 32 and 35], which all favour the later date, seem to run counter to the idea of an earlier date.) On the form of the imperial cult of Nero the inscription cited from Lycopolis in Egypt (*Journ. Hell. St.*, LXII, 1942, p. 17), with its allusion to *Tyche*, that is, to the *Fortuna Neronis*, adds fresh details to what was known of the worship and of the honours paid to Nero in the East (A. MOMIGLIANO, in *Cambr. Anc. Hist.*, X, p. 732 ff.; M. A. LEVI, *Nerone*, p. 120 ff.). On one important aspect of the Neronian programme, that of the new types of *ludi*, J. D. P. BOLTON, 'Was the Neronia a Freak Festival?', in *Class. Quart.*, XLII, 1948, pp. 82–90, has pointed to their quadrennial, not quinquennial, nature – a characteristic driving from the Greek model – and A. E. GORDON, *Quintus Veranius, cit.*, makes 57 the *terminus ante quem* for the *ludi maximi* known from SUET., *Ner.*, 11, 2. In connection with the *Augustiani*, which TAC., *Ann.*, XIV, 15, 5, says were instituted for the first time by Nero, it is worth noting the inscription *AE*, 1953, 24, where a 'collegium Augustianorum maius castrense' appears under Claudius, even though the anticipation evidently concerns only the name; and on Nero's performances as an actor, L. DEUBNER, 'Nero als gefesselter Hercules', in *Phil.*, N. F. XLVIII, 1939–40, pp. 232–4, sees him – an interpretation of SUET., *Ner.*, 21, 3 – in the part of Hercules. On the preference for these games as opposed to gladiatorial contests, see A. MAIURI, 'Dell'opposizione ai ludi gladiatori', in *At. e. Rom.*, N.S. II, 1952, pp. 45–8.

THE REIGN OF NERO. WARS AND THE PROVINCES

The main aspect of external affairs under Nero, the Parthian and Armenian question, has received recent treatment (select bibliography in LEVI, *op. cit.*, p. 162, n. 1), for the most part either in support of or against the comprehensive study by W. SCHUR, *Die Orientpolitik des Kaisers Nero*, Leipzig 1923 (Klio, Reih. 15; cf., by the same author, 'Zur Neronischen Orientalpolitik', in *Klio*, XX, 1925, pp. 215 ff. and

'Die orientalische Frage im Römischen Reiche', in *Neue Jahrbücher*, II, 1926, pp. 270–82). SCHUR's theory, that Nero embarked on a policy of expansion again in the name of Hellenism, does not seem proved, since the cession of the throne of Armenia to a Parthian younger son would indicate a policy still more diplomatically conciliating than that of Augustus. Basically the policy is still the Augustan and Tiberian one, tinged with reflections of the sort of interventions characteristic of Nero's extravagance. It is known in any case that even Vologaeses did all he could to avoid war with Rome. Also critical of SCHUR, and dealing particularly with the policy of Corbulo, are A. MOMIGLIANO, 'Corbulone e la politica verso i Parti', in *Atti II Congr. Naz. St. Rom.*, Rome 1931, pp. 368–75, and M. HAMMOND, 'Corbulo and Nero's Eastern Policy', in *Harv. St. in Class. Phil.*, XLV, 1934, pp. 81–104; EVA M. SANFORD, on the other hand, in *Harv. St. in Class. Phil.*, XLVIII, 1937, pp. 75–103, is more favourable to SCHUR and revives the theory that Nero was acting in imitation of the Alexander of legend and that in practice his action was provoked by the actual conditions existing on the frontier. But the projected expedition against the Ethiopians is perhaps not to be taken so seriously as SCHUR takes it (*op. cit.*, pp. 39–61), even if the formation of the *Periplus Maris Erythraei* seems to date from Nero's reign. However it is clear that the attention given by Nero to Egypt was anything but serious and realistic, though the country was labouring at the time under an economic crisis (H. I. BELL, 'The Economic Crisis in Egypt under Nero', in *Journ. Rom. St.*, XXVIII, 1938, pp. 1–8; for Nero's interest in African grain, G. PICARD, 'Néron et le blé d'Afrique', in *Compt. Rend. Ac. Inscr.*, 1956, pp. 68–7;) and shaken by the usual social ferments. This is shown by documents like the edict of Ti. Julius Alexander (*O.G.I.S.*, 669, cf. MITTEIS, *Chrest.*, 112, p. 102), which is a month later in date than Nero's death but deals with the situation existing previously, and the *pap. Yale* inv. no. 1528, which came to light in 1933 and is an extract from a report dealing with the relations of the prefect C. Caecina Tuscus with the troops in the year 63; it testifies to the discontent of the army itself (C. B. WELLES, 'The Immunity of the Roman Legionaries in Egypt', in *Journ. Rom. St.*, XXVIII, 1938, pp. 41–9). On individual points in the Armenian campaigns, the chronology which puts the capture of Artaxata at the end of 58 (ANDERSON, in *Cambr. Anc. Hist.*, X, p. 762; SCHUR, *op. cit.*, p. 11, etc.) is preferable, because the harsh winter mentioned by TAC., *Ann.*, XIII, 35, 3, can only be that of 57–58, and in addition the arrival of the news at Rome and the honours connected with it fit better at the end of 58 (see also T. B. MITFORD, 'Notes on

Published Inscriptions from Roman Cyprus', in *Ann. Br. Sch. Athens*, XLII, 1947, p. 219 f.). On the problem of Tacitus's silence about where the winter of 58–59 was spent, which has led some scholars to move the capture of Artaxata to 59, see ANDERSON, *ibid.*, p. 880, n.4. Our knowledge of the history of the peoples to the north and south of the Caucasus and of Armenia in particular has recently been increased by contributions from Russian scholars (B. B. PIOTROVSKY, *New Contribution to the Study of Ancient Civilizations in the USSR*, Moscow 1955, espec. pp. 39–56 of the Eng. transl. [Reports of the Soviet Delegations at the X International Congress of Historical Sciences in Rome]; K. V. TREVER, *Ocerki po historii kultury drevnej Armenii = Contribution to the History of the Civilization of Ancient Armenia*, Accad. delle Sc. dell'URSS, Moscow and Leningrad 1953, with inscriptions which could date from the Neronian age, cf. L. MORETTI, *art. cit.* [see above, p. 595], pp. 37 ff.). The inscription of Ti. Plautius Silvanus Aelianus (*CIL*, XIV, 3608= *ILS*, 986), with its references to movements of the tribes beyond the Danube and to operations beyond the *Borysthenes* (Dnieper) is also an interesting source for eastern events: D. M. PIPPIDI, 'Tiberius Plautius Aelianus et la frontière du Bas-Danube au Ier siècle de notre ère', in *Studii si cercetări de istorie veche*, VI, 1955, pp. 355–83 (Rumanian, with French summary; cf. *Contributii la istoria veche a Romîniei*, Bucharest 1958, VII, pp. 137–70), shifting the dates of Plautius Aelianus's governorship to 57–67, has seen his operations as aimed at obtaining security for Moesia without conquering and annexing land on the far side of the Danube; he thinks the expedition against the Sarmatians took place in 62, and the action in the Tauric Chersonese would have been diplomatic, with a naval demonstration, in the framework of Nero's eastern projects (E. CONDURACHI dissents; see his 'Tiberius Plautius Aelianus e il trasferimento dei 100,000 Transdanubiani nella Mesia', in *Epigraphica*, XIX, 1957, pp. 49–65). Interesting, too, are the inscriptions which mention the presence in Armenia of Corbulo (*ILS*, 232 and 9108). On the big inscription from Histria (*SEG.*, I, 1923, no. 329= CHARLESWORTH, *Documents*, etc., pp. 35 ff., no. 9), containing the five letters from various governors of Moesia on fishing rights in the Lower Danube – an inscription of Trajan's time (see below, p. 672) but one that concerns various previous governors of Moesia – see A. STEIN, *Die Legaten von Moesien*, Budapest 1940, pp. 326–32, who revives the discussion by H. DESSAU ('Zur Reihenfolge der Statthalter Moesiens', in *Oesterr. Jahresh.*, XXIII, 1926, Beibl., col. 345–358) and establishes a plausible chronological list of governors of the province under Nero and, most recently, D. M. PIPPIDI, 'I' "Horothesia

Laberii Maximi" (Quarante ans après sa découverte)', in *Studii si cercetări de istorie veche*, VII, 1956, pp. 137–58 (Rumanian, with French summary; cf. *Contributii, cit.*, VIII, pp. 171–96).

With regard to Nero's policy towards Britain, the arguments of C. E. STEVENS, 'The Will of Q. Veranius', in *Class. Rev.*, LXV (N.S.I.), 1951, pp. 4–7, who, taking as his starting point the remarks of SUET, *Ner.*, 18, according to which Nero intended to abandon Britain – a view subsequently changed as a result of the boastful reports sent to him by Q. Veranius (TAC., *Ann.*, XIV, 29, 1; *Agr.*, 14, 2–3) – judges the latter severely, blaming him for having caused from afar the revolt of 61, have been opposed by E. BIRLEY, 'Britain under Nero: The Significance of Q. Veranius', in *Durham Univ. Journ.*, 1952, pp. 88–92 (= *Roman Britain and the Roman Army*, Kendal 1953, pp. 1–9), whose observations on the front-rank position of Q. Veranius have been confirmed by the inscription published by A. E. GORDON, *Quintus Veranius cit.*, p. 241 f., 262–5, 273. The general reconstruction of Nero's policy in Britain outlined by BIRLEY, pp. 7 f. – discussion on the attitude to be adopted to Britain and prospect of a possible renunciation of direct occupation (that is, adoption of the 'client state' régime), decision in favour of an energetic policy with the dispatch of Q. Veranius, then of C. Suetonius Paulinus, return after the revolt of Boudicca to a more conciliatory mode of government with Petronius Turpilianus and Trebellius Maximus – can also be accepted. On the date of the death of Q. Veranius, who was sent to Britain in 58 and died 'intra annum' (TAC., *Agr.*, 14, 2) and thus either in the same year 58 or in 59, according to whether the phrase is taken to mean 'within the calendar year' or 'within a year of his arrival', GORDON, *op. cit.*, p. 266, prefers the first interpretation, which seems the most natural, although the *biennio* used immediately afterwards by Tacitus (*ibid.*) for Paulinus's operations preceding the outbreak of the revolt in 61 would suggest that Tacitus had 59 in mind. See also, for the degree of civilization attained, the book by HAWKES-HULL cited earlier, *Camulodunum*, espec. pp. 38 f., 56.

The chronology of Nero's tour of Greece is also uncertain, particularly the date of the Corinth proclamation contained in the inscription from *Acraephiae* (*ILS*, 8794). However, the date 28 November 66 (not 67) seems preferable, if only because of the concrete fact that on 1 July Sardinia, the province transferred to senatorial administration in exchange for Greece, was governed by a proconsul (MOMIGLIANO, in *Cambr. Anc. Hist.*, X, p. 735, n. 2; P. MELONI, 'L'amministraz. della Sard. nel I sec. d. Cr.', in *Ann. Fac. Lett. Cagliari*, XXI, 1953, p. 128; cf. the same writer's *L'amm. della Sard. da Augusto all'invasione vandalica*, Rome 1958, pp. 22 ff., 188 f.). None of the sources says that his wife Statilia Messalina was with Nero in Greece, and her presence seems to be excluded if we can accept as true the accounts of certain mad acts like Nero's marriage in Greece to Sporo-Sabina (CASS. D., LXIII, 13; cf. SUET., *Ner.*, 28, 1); but we are left with the difficulty not only of explaining the presence of Statilia's name on a Boeotian inscription of the end of 67 (*Inscr. Gr.*, VII, 2173) and the fact that at Acraephiae (*ILS*, 8794) a statue was dedicated to her too – something that could have been done even in her absence – but also of justifying the official phrase (which is, however, an addition) '[pro salute] et reditu impera [toris Neronis Claudi Caes(aris) Aug(usti) Germ(anici) et Messalinae Coniugis eius]' in the Acts of the Arvales (*CIL*, VI, 2044, minutes of the day 25 September 66).

As for the events that led to the fall of Nero (H. MATTINGLY, 'The Events of the Last Months of Nero, from the Revolt of Vindex to the Accession of Galba', summ. in *Num. Chron.*, ser. VI, XIII, 1953, p. III), it is worth noting in CASSIUS DIO (and it would be interesting to establish how far it is a question of the influence of his own age, naturally trying to trace back to Vindex the origin of the concept of an *imperium Galliarum*) the insistence on emphasizing the alienation of the provinces caused by the recognition of the Emperor's unfitness to hold the position of head of the empire, and in general the historians' attention to separatist ferments (see the speeches of Boudicca and Vindex, LXII, 3–6 and LXIII, 22, 2–6, the amazement of Tiridates at the general's forbearance, LXIII, 6, 4, and the sympathy of the provincials in the theatre, LXI, 17, 4–5), while the moral reasons for the provincial world's opposition to Nero vividly enunciated by Dio recur by a characteristic coincidence in the life of Apollonius of Tyana – the first-century wonder-worker persecuted by Tigellinus and Nero – by Philostratus (*Vit. Ap.*, V, 10), cf. E. PARATORE, *Tacito*, p. 540; F. GROSSO, *art. cit.*, pp. 388–90. However, the coinage of the civil war lends no support even in the case of Vindex for the idea of a separatist movement (MATTINGLY and SYDENHAM, *Rom. Imp. Coin.*, I, pp. 178 ff.). More recently, the character of revolt against Nero, not against Rome, has also been pointed out by P. A. BRUNT, 'The Revolt of Vindex and the Fall of Nero', in *Latomus*, XVIII, 1959, pp. 531–59.

THE YEAR OF THE FOUR EMPERORS

After the old exhaustive treatments of the various problems relating to the political and military realities of this series of events so abundantly and minutely preserved in the tradition (besides the reconstructions in the general histories, the various studies of PH. FABIA in relation to the *Historiae* of Tacitus [see citat. in *Cambr. Anc. Hist*, X, p. 990] and, for the military side, the monographs by MOMMSEN, 'Der letzte Kampf der Römischen Republik' and 'Die zwei Schlachten von Betriacum im Jahre 69 n. Chr.', in *Ges. Schr.*, IV, p. 333–47 and 354–65 are still basic; useful, too, are B. W. HENDERSON, *Civil War and Rebellion in the Roman Empire*, London 1908; E. G. HARDY, *Studies in Roman History, Second Series*, London 1909, pp. 130–268), interest has been concentrated more recently on examining the verdict in literature and culture on the crisis of 68–69 or else on seeking the key to a deeper explanation, on the political plane and in the general context of the development of the empire, of the history of the period. Thus, in P. ZANCAN, *La crisi del principato nell'anno 69 d. C.*, Padua 1939, we find an investigation in which the most interesting part is precisely the comparison between the interpretations of the various authors – Tacitus, Plutarch, Suetonius, Cassius Dio (espec. pp. 83 ff.). Through this examination and spotlighting of individual characteristics, personal reactions to events, which differ in the various authors, the familiar factual unanimity of the sources is overcome. But with this the problem of historical reconstruction naturally shifts from the objective plane to the subjective plane, from that of facts to that of interpretation, and the boundary between the two spheres is not always grasped; what always prevails, as the author says she has seen in the work of Tacitus, is the 'resolviersi della storia nel pensiero' (p. 126, n.1). The author herself is aware of this in her last few pages, which, in the form of a critique of modern opinions, justify the adherence to 'Kulturgeschichte'. In fact the detailed and sensitive examination of the sources leads in itself to a tendency to take account of the subjective elements. Thus we notice that Tacitus has little sympathy for the Flavians (see espec. *Hist.*, IV, 1), that in the *Histories* we meet again the philosophical sympathies of the *Annales* (Helvidius Priscus, the new Thrasea Paetus, IV, 4, 3) and the political sympathies that certainly reflect personal relations between aristocrats (no sympathy, for example, for Hordeonius Flaccus or Dillius Vocula, while Petilius Cerealis is put in a decent light *Hist.*, IV, 77, 2–3, and criticized, but with restraint, in V, 21–2), and that the cross-section of characters, types and aspirations of the ruling class of the age personified by Galba, Otho (for Otho, see the analysis by F. KLINGNER, 'Die Gesch. Kaiser Othos bei Tacitus', in *Ber. über die Verhandl. d. Sachs. Ak. d. Wiss. zu Leipzig*, Ph.-Hist. Kl., XCII, 1940, Heft 1, espec. pp. 26 f.) and Vitellius is certainly constructed with a view to artistic and moral symmetry. But

624 APPENDICES

we note this precisely in order to disinter the lines of the objective reality, which in the last analysis is the only thing that counts in the historical reconstruction.

It is on the concrete reality that E. MANNI, 'Lotta politica e guerra civile nel 68–69 d. C.', in *Riv. Fil.*, XXIV, 1946, pp. 122–56, tries to base the political judgement of the crisis, while G. MANFRÉ, *La crisi politica dell'anno 68–69 d.C.*, Bologna 1947, turns to the search for an ideal that would provide a unified explanation of the history of the period and finds it in the 'spirit of liberty in the provinces asserting their rights against the Senate via the legions'. Spirit of liberty, but not separatism. 'The crisis was a phase in the political evolution of the Roman empire, that is, of the universal process of unification of the provinces.' And also the completion of the revolution carried out by Caesar and Augustus, with the choice of the emperor now made outside the urban circle. However, in spite of the confirmation that this view seems to receive from the proven continually-growing provincialization of the legions (G. FORNI, *Il reclutamento delle legioni da Augusto a Diocleziano*, Milan and Rome 1953, p. 65 ff.), the latent rivalry between the armies already inherent in the Augustan system is probably enough to explain a considerable part of the struggle (G. E. F. CHILVER, 'The Army in Politics, A.D. 69–70', in *Journ. Rom. St.*, XLVII, 1957, pp. 29–35), and the reconstruction presented in the main text clearly reveals the permanence of the fundamental concepts of the Augustan principate, including the concern for harmony with the Senate. What is particularly significant is Otho's attempt to regularize his position by assuming the specifically priestly offices, as attested by the *Acta Arvalium* (see above, main text, p. 205); this should be compared with the assumption of all these offices together by Nero through the act of putting on the *toga virilis* (M. W. HOFFMAN LEWIS, *The Official Priests of Rome under the Julio-Claudians*, Rome 1955, pp. 100 f.) and the same privilege enjoyed immediately afterwards by Titus (who in 71 was *collegiorum omnium sacerdos*, CIL, VI, 31294 = ILS, 258) and Domitian. Moreover, the instructive motifs of the coinage of the period offer further evidence, from that of Vindex and Galba (C. H. V. SUTHERLAND, 'A Coin of Nero Overstruck for Galba', in *Num. Chron.*, XX, 1940, pp. 265–6; COLIN M. KRAAY, 'The Coinage of Vindex and Galba, A.D. 68, and the Continuity of the Augustan Principate', *ibid.*, ser. VI, vol. IX, 1949, pp. 129–49, and the same scholar's *The Aes Coinage of Galba*, New York 1956 (Num. Notes and Monogr., 133); see also the inscriptions quoted in the main text, and E. MANNI, 'Genius populi Romani e Genius aetatis aureae', in *Rend. Acc. Bologna*,

Cl. Sc. Mor., IV, 2, 1938-9, pp. 40-66, espec. 44 ff.), which reflects the concern, once the tyrant was dead, to ensure the continuity of a principate founded on the Augustan principles, to that of Otho and Vitellius (F. PANVINI-ROSATI, 'Aureo unico e inedito di Vitellio', in *Numismatica*, XIV, 1948, pp. 83-7). In particular, on the absence of a senatorial coinage belonging to Otho's reign, the explanation of MOMMSEN, 'Der kaiserliche Oberpontifikat', in *Ztschr. f. Numism.*, I, 1874, pp. 238-44, that the Senate must have waited before issuing its own coins for the conferment on Otho of the position of pontifex maximus (9 March) and that when the Emperor's departure supervened soon afterwards it must have let the matter drop, is not in conflict with the probable secret intention on the part of the Senate to await the outcome of the struggle with Vitellius (*Rom. Imp. Coin.*, I, p. 218). But even this indicates the traditional nature of a relationship. In connection with the uncertainty of the political situation, see F. ARNALDI, 'Nunc pro Othone an pro Vitellio in templa ituros?' (TAC., *Hist.*, I, 50), in *Rend. Acc. Arch. Napoli*, XXVI, 1951, pp. 257-9. For the composition of the Senate, for which the year of crisis represents the beginning of an important renewal, not of structure but in the social background of its members and in the empiricism of the political principles of the transmission of the imperial power, see the articles by M. HAMMOND, 'Composition of the Senate, A.D. 68-235', in *Journ. Rom. St.*, XLVII, 1957, pp. 74-81, and 'The Transmission of the Powers of the Roman Emperor from the Death of Nero in A.D. 68 to that of Alexander Severus in A.D. 235', in *Mem. Am. Ac. Rome*, XXIV, 1956, pp. 61-133 (for the moment under consideration here, pp. 67-78).

As for questions of detail, the chronology, in spite of the scarcity of fixed points in the tradition, does not present serious problems. The decree of Ti. Julius Alexander of 6 July 68 (*O.G.I.S.*, 669), already containing the name of Galba in the form *L. Livius Augustus Sulpicius Galba imperator*, which still wavers between his name as a private citizen (*L. Livius Ocella*, taken from his stepmother Livia Ocellina and added to his own) and his final name as Princeps (*imp. Ser. Sulpicius Galba Caesar Augustus*), indicates the rapidity with which the East declared for him. It would be interesting to know at precisely what points in the first fortnight of January 69 the news reached Rome and the Rhine respectively. It certainly seems strange that on 10 January Galba should know about the refusal of the legions of Germany to swear allegiance (1 January) but not yet about the acclamation of Vitellius (3 January, TAC., *Hist.*, I, 57, 1), especially as people could hardly have taken seriously (as it would appear that they did from SUET., *Galb.*, 16, 2, which seems to link the request of the legions with the acclamation of Otho by the praetorians) the legions' reliance on the Senate and the praetorian guard for the choice of the new Princeps, and the acclamation of the governor could soon be expected. For the chronology of the march of Valens and Caecina and for Otho's departure from Rome on 24 March, see A. PASSERINI, 'Le due battaglie presso Betriacum', in *St. Ant. Class. offerti a E. Ciaceri*, Rome 1940, p. 289. As for the sailing of the fleet from Ostia on 5 March, simultaneously with the *Isidis navigium*, that is, the day of the official opening of the seafaring season, and in connection with the riots mentioned by TAC., *Hist.*, 1, 80–5, and SUET., *Oth.*, 8, 1–2, see E. HOHL, 'Der Prätorianeraufstand unter Otho', in *Klio*, XXXII, 1939, pp. 307–24. HOHL has been criticized by H. HEUBNER, 'Der Prätorianer-tumult vom Jahre 69 n. Chr.', in *Rhein. Mus.*, CI, 1958, pp. 339–53; close to HOHL, on the other hand, is H. DREXLER, 'Zur Geschichte Kaiser Othos bei Tacitus und Plutarch', in *Klio*, XXXVII, 1959, pp. 153–78. For the date of the second battle of Bedriacum, we can deduce that it did not take place before the end of October or the early days of November from the fact that Caecina, deposed from the consulship when it was learnt that he had broken faith and was a prisoner of the troops, was replaced for one day only, 31 October, by Rosius Regulus (TAC., *Hist.*, III, 37; DEGRASSI, *Fasti cons.*, p. 19 f.). Other questions investigated in recent years include the age of Galba at his accession, which is uncertain, for while PLUTARCH, *Galb.*, 8, 1, and SUET., *Galb.*, 23, 1, say that it took place in his 73rd year in 68 – which would put his birth in 5 B.C. – in another place (4, 1) Suetonius gives for the year of his birth the names of the consuls for 3 B.C. – which would make Galba only seventy-one when he became emperor. This appears more probable to W. R. TONGUE, 'The Date of the Birth of the Emperor Galba', summ. in *Trans. Proc. Am. Phil. Ass.*, LXIX, 1938, p. XLIX. For the characterization of Galba in Tacitus, see E. KOESTERMANN, 'Das Charakterbild Galbas bei Tacitus', in *Navicula Chiloniensis (Festschr. Jacoby)*, Leiden 1956, pp. 191–206. Nymphidius Sabinus's bid for the throne seems to be given too much importance by G. MANFRÉ, 'Il. tent. imp. di N.S.', in *Riv. Fil.*, XIX, 1941, pp. 118–20; Manfrè makes Nymphidius the representative of the whole military-provincial world opposed to the Senate. On Verania, the wife of L. Calpurnius Piso Frugi Licinianus, commemorated on the funeral stone (*ILS*, 240) of Verania herself – who died thirty years later – without any mention of his position as co-ruler (this is hardly surprising), see

A. E. GORDON, *Q. Veranius, cit.*, p. 242. The not dishonourable memory that remained of Galba and his activity may be attested (though the reading is not certain) by inscription *AE*, 1948, 3 (cf. *CIL*, VIII, 13 and p. 979) from Leptis Magna, put up by Q. Pomponius Rufus, consul in 95, 'praef. orae. maritimae Hispaniae Citerioris Galliae Narbonensis bello qu [od imp.] Galba (p[ro . . .] gessit' (see G. BARBIERI, 'Il praefectus orae maritimae', in *Riv. Fil.*, XIX, 1941, pp. 268–80). On the repercussions which the general situation caused in Africa (from the proclamation by Clodius Macer to the obscure events connected with Valerius Festus and Calpurnius Piso), see P. ROMANELLI, *St. d. prov. rom. dell'Afr.*, cit., pp. 279–88.

But it is naturally the military campaigns that attract the greatest interest. For the route followed by the Vitellians into Italy (Great St Bernard), I. BERETTA, *La romanizzazione della valle d' Aosta*, Milan and Varese 1954, p. 57 ff. So far as the campaign against the Helvetii is concerned, G. WALSER, 'Das Strafgericht über die Helvetier im Jahre 69 n. Chr.', in *Schweiz. Zeitschr. f. Gesch.*, IV, 1954, pp. 260–70, reduces the revolt of the Helvetii to an episode of the civil war (for *Aventicum*, see D. VAN BERCHEM, 'Aspects de la domination romaine en Suisse', in *Riv. Stor. Svizz.*, 5, 1955, pp. 145–75, espec. pp. 145–57: 'Le statut de la colonie d'Avenches'). For the Othonian legion *XI Claudia P. F.* from Dalmatia, see A. BETZ, *Untersuchungen zur Militärgeschichte der römischen provinz Dalmatien*, Baden by Vienna 1938, pp. 39 f. On the troops recruited among the Gauls, Germans and Batavians and the consequences that followed during the absence of the Vitellian legions engaged in Italy, see K. KRAFT, *Zur Rekrutierung der Alen und Kohorten am Rhein und Donau*, Berne 1951, pp. 37–42. On Antonius Primus, M. TREU, 'M. Antonius Primus in der taciteischen Darstellung', in *Würzburger Jahrb. f. die Altentumswiss.*, III, 1948, pp. 241–62. On Mucianus, M. FORTINA, *Un generale romano del primo secolo dell'impero, C. Licinio Muciano*, Novara 1955. The uncertainties in the account of the battles near Bedriacum denote, rather than a lack of information – which is indeed very precise so far as concerns the characteristics of the topography, vegetation, etc. – a multiplicity of details from eye-witnesses who, as in the case of the Herodotean description of Salamis, had no vision of the strategy as a whole. Plutarch must have gained valuable information from his patron, Mestrius Florus (*Oth.*, 14), who was probably an eye-witness, and from his memories and notes of his visit to the sites, but it is defective for the reason just quoted; and he combines this information with the account also used by Tacitus, which was not exempt from the same

defect, for an official strategic account of the battles can no longer have
existed. Suetonius's father, too, was *tribunus militum* in the XIII legion
(SUET., *Oth.*, 10). A new examination of the tradition about the two
battles of Bedriacum, set against the background of a reconnaissance of
the terrain and of the still fairly clear traces of the division into centuries
of the territory of Cremona, is to be found in the above-mentioned study
by A. PASSERINI, espec. p. 213 f., to which should be added PH.
FABIA, 'La concentration des Othoniens sur le Pô', in *Rev. Ét. Anc.*,
XLIII, 1941, pp. 192–215; K. WELLESLEY, 'Three Historical Puzzles
in Histories III', in *Class. Quart*, N.S. VI, 1956, pp. 207–14, espec.
pp. 207–11; and most recently R. SYME, *Tacitus*, Oxford 1958, pp. 157–
175, 676–84. It is now no longer disputed that Bedriacum was near the
present-day Calvatone; as for the form of the name – *Bedriacum, Bebriacum,
Betriacum* – it seems to me that we should stick to the first, the one found
in the literary tradition. The support lent by PASSERINI, pp. 180 f.,
to the form *Betriacum*, accepted by MOMMSEN (*Ges. Schr.*, IV, p. 356,
n.1), on the grounds of the existence of the name *Betrius*, attested by an
inscription, has been shown to be fallacious by G. FORNI, 'Betriacum,
Betrius o beneficiarius tribuni?', in *Arch. Class.*, V, 1953, pp. 112–15.
PASSERINI and FABIA are convinced of the presence at the first battle
of the whole of Legions VII, XI and XIII (only the XIV being absent)
and of the not very marked numerical inferiority of the Othonians; and in
fact the vague text of TACITUS (*Hist.*, II, 32, 46) does not rule out this
interpretation. As for the tradition that Vespasian was hailed as emperor
for the first time at Aquileia (SUET., *Vesp.*, 6, cf. comm. BRAITHWAITE,
p. 35), this is obviously something invented later to give the army of the
Danube priority in acclaiming the new Princeps. This was realized by
TACITUS, *Hist.*, II, 85. On the date of the acclamation in Judaea, the
difference between TAC., *Hist.*, II, 79, 'quinto Nonas Iulias' (3 July) and
SUET., *Vesp.*, 6, 3, 'quinto Idus Iulias' (11 July) may be a mere manuscript error. As the acclamation at Alexandria occurred on 1 July (TAC.
and SUET. are in agreement here), Suetonius's date is more probable
simply for reasons of time. On precedents in Egypt, see CL. PRÉAUX,
'Le règne de Vitellius en Égypte', in *Mél. Georges Smets*, Brussels 1952,
pp. 571–8. PH. B. SULLIVAN tries to explain the eastern background to
the acclamation of Vespasian in 'A Note on the Flavian Accession'
(*Class. Journ.*, XLIX, 1953–4, pp. 67–70 and 78); he observes that all
the actors in the conspiracy that gave power to V., the chief ones being
Queen Berenice and T. Julius Alexander, were related to one another. On
the reasons for Vespasian's personal occupation of Egypt, the assertion of

CASS. D., LXV, 9, 2, that he wanted to send as much corn as possible to Rome – as opposed to the unanimous explanation given in TAC., *Hist.*, III, 8, 2; 48, 3, SUET., *Vesp.*, 7, 1 and JOSEPH., *B.I.*, IV, 606 (10,5) that he went there to prevent supplies from being sent to Rome – obviously refers to the moment after victory (cf. TAC., *Hist.*, IV, 52, 2). For the events of 18–21 December 69, WEINAND's chronology, in *P.W.*, VI, c. 2640, seems less acceptable than that of L. HOLZAPFEL, in *Klio*, XIII, 1913, pp. 295–304; XV, 1917, pp. 99–103 (death of Sabinus on the 19th, arrival of Antonius in the night of the 19th-20th, death of Vitellius on the 20th, sitting of the Senate on the 21st; cf. G. M. BERSANETTI, *Vespasiano*, Rome 1951, pp. 33, 94). On the date of the arrival of Mucianus, the 22 December of JOSEPH., *B.I.*, IV, 654 (11, 4), seems hardly acceptable (cf. WEINAND, *loc. cit.*, c. 2641); but it cannot have been later than the last days of December or the first days of January (TAC., *Hist.*, IV, 11, 1; cf. 39, 1). The presentation of Domitian to the praetorians by Mucianus (CASS. D., LXV, 22, 2; cf. JOSEPH, *loc. cit.*) is not necessarily to be connected with his acclamation as Caesar, which occurred immediately after the entry of the Flavians into Rome (TAC., *Hist.*, III, 86, 3; IV, 2, 1; SUET., *Dom.*, 1, 3; CASS. D., LXVI, 1, 1; cf. STEIN, in *PIR²*, III, p. 148). For the exceptional appointment of M. Arrecinus Clemens, a senator, as praetorian prefect and for his remaining in the post at the most up to the arrival of Vespasian, see A. PASSERINI, 'M. Arrecino Clemente', in *Alten.*, N.S. XVIII, 1940, pp. 145–63, espec. p. 149 ff.

THE ADVENT OF THE FLAVIANS

In recent years interest in this subject has centred mainly round the religious aspects of the acclamation of Vespasian in the East, but the old problem of the constitutional side of the permanent renewal of the principate in a new family has also attracted attention. The most important and specific references to this question are those dealing with the *lex de imperio Vespasiani* by H. LAST in the *Cambr. Anc. Hist.*, XI, 1936, pp. 404 ff., and M. A. LEVI, 'La legge dell'iscrizione *CIL*, VI, 1930 (Lex de potestate Vespasiani)', in *Athen.*, XXVI, 1938, pp. 85–95, and 'I principii dell'impero di Vespasiono', in *Riv. Fil. Class.*, XVI, 1938, pp. 1–12, according to which it would be a matter of a formulation in terms of constitutional law of rights first exercised by the Princeps on the basis of his own *auctoritas*, a formulation which in Levi's view was effected by the Senate in the particular form of a crystallization of the *potestas*, or *potestates*, of the Princeps, in the absence that had made itself apparent after the end of the Julio-Claudian dynasty, and in the course of the civil war, of the *auctoritas* of the Princeps. It is certainly opportune to lay emphasis on the *auctoritas*, the element rightly underlined in the most recent examinations of the principate (see on this subject A. MAGDELAIN, *Auctoritas principis*; in partic. on the *lex de imp. Vesp.*, p. 90). But to admit that in the absence of the *auctoritas* the Senate wanted to fix the *potestates* of the Princeps, so as to produce, by a sort of compromise, a guarantee for the Senate itself, we need to suppose that at that moment the *auctoritas* of the Senate was superior, or at least equal, to that of the Princeps; and this is dubious in connection with a Senate (one certainly also reduced in numbers) which after the unsuccessful experiment of the superficially senatorial rule of Galba had hastily voted 'Cuncta solita' (TAC., *Hist.*, IV, 3, 1) to Otho, Vitellius and now Vespasian, of whom it could not know whether he was like the others and would last as long as the others. Moreover, the Senate's prestige cannot have been very high after the transferences of loyalty accomplished during the course of the year. Vespasian had won the principate by force of arms, in other words by the most persuasive method of asserting the principate's own *auctoritas* according to the Augustan tradition; in accordance with the same tradition he then sought to reinforce that *auctoritas* by clothing it with *civilitas*. But it cannot be said that at the end of 69, with the troops of the new Augustus bivouacking in Rome, there was any lack of the *auctoritas* of a Princeps. It is significant that Vespasian was the first to date his *imperium* from the first salutation by the troops, not from the senatorial recognition (M. HAMMOND, 'The Transmission of the Powers of the Roman Emperor' etc., in *Mem. Am. Acad. Rome*, XXIV, 1956, p. 76 f.). It seems therefore that the law, so far as we know it, was only a formulation, inscribed on bronze for honorific and commemorative purposes (perhaps at the request of Vespasian himself or of his supporters) and preserved by the family (we do not in fact know of similar documents for other emperors, but if it had been a question of anything special for Vespasian this would not have escaped Tacitus, who on the contrary speaks in his case too of 'cuncta solita'), of the paragraphs constituting precisely the 'cuncta solita', including the customary rights connected with the *auctoritas* of the Princeps, as in January for Otho and in April for Vitellius. This naturally reduces the importance of the document, but it seems a more prudent conclusion than to see in the document the proof of a decisive development in the conception of the principate and of a total transformation 'dei principii costituzionali della monarchia augustea' (LEVI, *art.*

cit., p. 10) – 'principii' that Vespasian's whole work shows on the contrary to have been faithfully preserved. See accounts and bibliography in G. BARBIERI, s.v. *Lex*, in DE RUGGIERO, *Diz. Ep.*, IV, pp. 750–9 (Rome 1957).

The propaganda aspects of Vespasian's assertion of authority have been studied not only by Levi in the opening pages of the second article cited above but also subsequently by J. GAGÉ, 'Vespasien et la mémoire de Galba', in *Rev. Ét. Anc.*, LIV, 1952, pp. 290–315. Gagé pays particular attention to the effort made by Vespasian to ensure a balance between the general support of the West, gained for example by a moderate rehabilitation of Galba and the introduction of the imperial flaminate, and that of the East, which was absolutely predominant at first. So far as the genuineness of Vespasian's eastern religiosity is concerned, too, the most acceptable view, and the one in conformity with the general verdict on his personality, seems to be that it was a matter of political tactics, aimed at destroying the memory of Nero (GAGÉ, p. 292) and acquiring popularity. The subject became extremely topical after the publication, in *Les Papyrus Fouad I. Nos. 1–89*, Cairo 1939, of a papyrus fragment (*Pap. Fouad* no. 8) in which JOUGUET – who devoted several articles to it ('Vespasien acclamé dans l'hippodrome d'Alexandrie', in *Mél Ernout*, Paris 1940, pp. 201–10; 'L'arrivée de Vespasien à Alexandrie', in *Bull. Inst. d'Ég.*, XXIV, 1941–2, pp. 21–32; *La domination romaine en Égypte*, 1947, pp. 44–7) – sees a piece of literary composition, possibly a piece of propaganda, written in the style of an official report, to record the acclamation given to Vespasian on his arrival from Palestine by the people of Alexandria assembled in the hippodrome of Tiberius Alexander. The discussion in progress (the latest contributions are those of W. MÜLLER, 'Zum Edikt des Tiberius Iulius Alexander', in *Festschr. Zucker*, Berlin 1954, pp. 293–7, and, on a new reading of the papyrus, R. MERKELBACH, in *Arch. f. Papyrusforsch*, XVI, 1956, p. 111, no. 1115) on this and subsequent events of the stay at Alexandria (and the relative chronology), on the contacts of Vespasian with priests, wonder-workers, philosophers, on his own wonder-working abilities, on the prophecies in Alexandria and the preceding ones at Mount Carmel, on the cordial relations established with the Greco-pagan element, naturally at loggerheads with the Jewish element hostile to Vespasian because of the war in progress, has produced various detailed observations to be added, so far as concerns the building up by the Greco-Eastern element of the religious *maiestas* of Vespasian, to the chapter on Vespasian in Alexandria in K. SCOTT, *The Imperial Cult under the Flavians*, Stuttgart 1936, pp. 9–19: see S. MORENZ,

'Vespasian, Heiland der Kranken. Persönliche Frömmigkeit im antiken Herrscherkult?', in *Würzb. Jahrb. f. Alt.*, IV, 1949–50, pp. 370–8; CH. PICARD, 'Protohistoire de la thaumaturgie royale', in *Rev. Arch.*, XXXVIII, 1951, pp. 68–9; P. DERCHAIN, 'La visite de Vespasien au Sérapéum d'Alexandrie', in *Latomus*, XII, 1953, pp. 38–52; L. HERR-MANN, 'Basilides', in *Latomus*, XII, 1953, pp. 312–15 (on this Basilides, see the curious deformation in Christian legend, T. S. R. BOASE, 'A Seventeenth-Century Carmelite Legend Based on Tacitus', in *Journ. Warb. & Court. Inst.*, III, 1939–40, pp. 107–18); F. GROSSO, 'La "Vita di Apollonio di Tiana" come fonte storica', in *Acme*, VII, 1954, pp. 391–430. Other interesting details connected with the victory of the Flavian dynasty emerge from some newly known episodes, like the appointment in the field of Ti. Julius Alexander as praetorian prefect, an event which has come to light on a papyrus (E. G. TURNER, *The Hibeh Papyri*, II, London 1955, no. 215, pp. 135–7; cf. the same scholar's 'Tiberius Julius Alexander', in *Journ. Rom. St.*, XLIV, 1954, pp. 54–64; V. BURR, 'Tiberius Julius Alexander', in the series *Antiquitas*, I, 1, Bonn 1955; the latter, not yet aware of Ti. Alexander's prefectship, rejects the idea in an appendix reporting the publication of Turner) and one which indicates, like the earlier appointment of M. Arrecinus Clemens and the subsequent assumption of the post by Titus, the more unprejudiced use of the abilities available and also the relatively exceptional position of the praetorian prefectship under the Flavians, as indeed under Augustus.

A more accurate picture of the scope of the military campaigns still in progress during the Flavian rise to power has been obtained from fresh examination of the archaeological evidence. It seems that we should not speak of a Gallo-German conflict, sometimes exaggerated in connection with the revolt of Julius Civilis and included among the causes of its failure (e.g. HOMO, *Haut-Empire*, p. 357), in face of the establishment of the fact that Gauls and Germans were much intermingled on the Rhine (U. KAHRSTEDT, 'Methodisches zur Geschichte des Mittel- und Niederrheins zwischen Caesar und Vespasian', in *Bonn Jahrb.*, CL, 1950, pp. 63–80; cf. L. A. SPRINGER, 'Rome's Contacts with the Frisians', in *Class. Journ.*, XLVIII, 1952–3, pp. 109–11, and K. KRAFT, *Zur Rekru-tierung*, etc., already cit., pp. 37–42), and that the big towns on the Rhine, Strasbourg, Mainz, Cologne, neither Gallic nor German, were centres of Romanization (J. TOUTAIN, 'L'origine historique des grandes cités rhénanes', in *Mémorial d'un voyage d'études en Rhénanie de la Soc. Nat. d. Antiq. d. France*, Paris 1953, pp. 177–82).

A re-examination of the sources with a view to determining the true relationship between the empire and foreign peoples has also brought some clarifications (G. WALSER, *Rom, das Reich und die fremden Völker*, etc., Baden-Baden 1951, pp. 86–128, cf. K. CHRIST, *Zur röm. Okkupation der Zentralalpen* etc., cit., in *Historia*, VI, 1957, pp. 416–28). Valerius Festus's struggle with the Garamanti, called in as allies by Oea against Leptis (TAC., *Hist.*, IV, 50, 4) is to be connected with the wall round Leptis (R. G. GOODCHILD and J. B. WARD PERKINS, 'The Roman and Byzantine Defences of Leptis Magna', in *Pap. Br. Sch. Rome*, XXI, 1953, pp. 42–73; cf. P. ROMANELLI, *Prov. rom. Afr.*, cit., pp. 288 ff.). On the Jewish war, the most recent critical research has concentrated on seeking echoes and impressions in literature independent of Josephus: L. GRY, 'La ruine du temple par Titus. Quelques traditions juives plus anciennes et primitives à la base de Pesikta Rabbathi XXVI', in *Rev. Bibl.*, LV, 1948, pp. 215–26 (on Hebrew sources other than Josephus hitherto neglected); S. GIET, 'Les épisodes de la guerre juive et l'Apocalypse', in *Rev. des. Sc. Relig.*, XXVI, 1952, pp. 352–62 (on the Christian memories reflected in the Apocalypse and thus dating from the Flavian epoch). Josephus, who denies that Titus gave orders for the temple to be burnt (*B. Iud.*, VI, 241 [4,3]), also seems tendentious in comparison with SULP. SEV., *Chron.*, II, 30, 6–8, which derives from Tacitus. For the date of the fall of Masada and thus of the end of the Jewish war, for which Josephus gives the day (2 May, *B. Iud.*, VII, 401 [9, 1]) but not the year, we have adopted in the main text the year 72, as opposed to the more frequently accepted date of 73 (E. SCHÜRER, *Gesch. d. jüdischen Volkes im Zeitalten J. Christe I*[3&4], Leipzig 1901, p. 639, n. 139 subsequently repeated by everyone). According to Josephus, *B. Iud.*, VII, 410 (10, 1), some of the Sicarii escaped from Palestine and went to Alexandria, where they provoked riots quelled by the prefect Ti. Julius Lupus. Now if these Sicarii moved into Egypt after the fall of Masada, as would appear from the order of the narrative in Josephus, and since the death of Lupus recorded by Josephus himself (434 [10, 4]), can be placed with some probability before 2 May 73 – for the vice-prefect, Caunius Paulinus, who succeeded Lupus and is also named as so doing by Josephus (*ibid.*) may already have been in post, so it seems from *Pap, Oxy.*, X, 1266, at the end of 72 – it follows that the capture of the fortress on the Dead Sea probably occurred in that same year, as had already been maintained, before the papyrus was known, by TILLEMONT, *Hist. des empereurs*, etc., II, p. 999 f. and NIESE, both in the edit. (VI, p. 621) and in the art. 'Zur Chronologie des Josephus', in *Hermes*, XXVIII, 1893, p. 212. On the name *Caunius Paulinus*, proposed in recent years, see R. SYME, in *Journ. Rom.*

St., XLIV, 1954, p. 116 and O. W. REINMUTH, in *P.W.*, Suppl. VIII, c. 529.

THE WORK OF VESPASIAN

The chronological scheme of Vespasian's activities was reconstructed so far as it can be by WEYNAND in *P.W.*, VI, 1909, c. 2623 ff.; only a few details have been subsequently modified. As for the reconstruction of the figure, as well as the activity, of Vespasian, the excellent monograph by G. M. BERSANETTI, *Vespasiano*, Rome 1941, has been joined by L. HOMO's *Vespasien, l'empereur du bon sens*, Paris 1949. From the same angle of complete reconstruction, the commentaries on the principal literary source for Vespasian, Suetonius's 'Life', namely A. W. BRAITH-WAITE, *C. Suetoni Tranquilli Divus Vespasianus*, Oxford 1927, and H. R. GRAF, *Kaiser Vespasian, Untersuchungen zu Suetons Vita Divi Vespasiani*, Stuttgart 1937, are also valuable, especially the first. Individual observations on the human figure of Vespasian, which in any case comes out quite clearly, also take us back to the text of Suetonius: T. L. ZINN, 'A Pun in Suetonius', in *Class. Rev.*, N.S. I, 1951, p. 10, promptly contradicted by A. HUDSON-WILLIAMS, 'Suetonius, Vesp. 22', *ibid.*, II, 1952, p. 72 f. As for the atmosphere in Rome at the beginning of the reign, the moment at which Mucianus made quite clear the limits set to apparent senatorial freedom in the rehabilitation of the part has been pinpointed by R. S. ROGERS, 'A Criminal Trial of A.D. 70 (Tacitus, *Histories*, 4, 44)', in *Trans. Proc. Am. Phil. Ass.*, LXXX, 1949, pp. 347–50, in connection with the sitting of 1 February, on the case of Octavius Sagitta and Antistius Sosianus, who had been banished under Nero, had returned at his death and were now sent back into exile. Another significant point is the consulship of Vespasian and Titus in 70, when they were both absent from Rome (A. E. GORDON, 'Vespasian and Titus as Consuls, A.D. 70', in *Class. Phil.*, L, 1955, pp. 194 ff.). On the opportunist employment of notable but rather colourless personages of the previous régime, such as Tampius Flavianus, Pompeius Silvanus, Aponius Saturninus, see R. SYME, 'Deux proconsulats d'Afrique', in *Rev. Ét. Anc.*, LVIII, 1956, pp. 236–40. On the Stoic opposition in general, which has been the point of departure for occasional writings (B. CROCE, 'Un avversario del "régime totalitario" nell'antichità', *Quad. d. Crit*, II, 1946, no. 4, pp. 25–35, on Helvidius Priscus), but whose scope should not, it would seem, be exaggerated to the point of embracing the whole complex of relations between the Princeps and the Senate, see the recent remarks of F. GROSSO, in *Acme* (*cit.*), pp. 405, 437 and *passim*, and also C. G. STARR, *Civilization and the Caesars*, Ithaca 1954, pp. 134–46. In this connection, and for the concept of freedom under the Flavians, see V. CAPOCCI, 'Il "dialogus de oratoribus", opera giovanile di Tacito', in *Ann. Tac. Lett. Napoli*, II, 1952, pp. 79–136, in whose view not only the action depicted but also the composition of the work should be placed under Vespasian, an opinion which does not stand up to criticism, cf. R. SYME, *Tacitus*, pp. 112–16.

Vespasian's work on the restoration of the finances, the subject of a comprehensive summary by L. HOMO, 'Une leçon d'outre-tombe: Vespasien financier', in *Rev. Ét. Anc.*, XLII, 1940 (Mél. Radet), pp. 453–65, has received further illumination in recent years from epigraphical discoveries, especially discoveries of pillars – to be added to those already known – marking the restitution of public lands: at Tolmetta in Cyrenaica a *cippus* from the first half of 72 (*AE*, 1934, 261); in Tunisia other examples of the *cippi* of the Fossa Regia (*IL Tun.*, 623, 624, 1293) and in Algeria a *cippus* marking the limits of the land of the Cirtensa assigned to the *Nicibes* and the *Suburbures Regiani* (*AE*, 1947, 175); at Canusium a *cippus* of 76 (*AE*, 1945, 85 and 1959, 267; cf. F. CASTAGNOLI, 'Cippo di "restitutio agrorum" presso Canne', in *Rev. Fil.*, LXXVI, 1948, pp. 280–6). But the most interesting discovery is the one concerning the land register of the *Colonia Firma Iulia Secundanorum* (Orange). Above the table of the land register, a record of the first half of 77 commemorates the restitution of the '[loca publ]ica qu[ae Divus Augustus milit. l]eg II Gallicae dederat po[ssessa a priva]tis per aliquod annos' (J. SAUTEL, 'Nouvelles découvertes à Orange en 1950–51. Le cadastre agraire et les frises sculptées,' in *Compt. rend. Ac. Inscr.*, 1951, pp. 236–44; A. PIGANIOL, 'Nouvelles inscriptions d'Orange', *ibid.*, pp. 366–74, after a first summary communication at pp. 89–90). On the *Lex Manciana*, now unanimously attributed to the age of Vespasian, following J. TOUTAIN, 'Culturae Mancianae', in *Mél Martroye*, 1940, pp. 93–100, CH. SAUMAGNE more recently upholds the view, in *Tablettes Albertini*, Paris 1952, pp. 136–42, that the substance and name of the 'law' to which the regulation of 116 or 117 for the tenants of the farm of the *Villa Magna* refers draws its origin from the transference to the provinces of Vespasian's measure on *subseciva*, a transference effected by the proconsul Curtilius Mancia, whose considerable estates – which passed, as Pliny tells us, *Epist.*, VIII, 18, to Domitius Tullus, brother of the son-in-law Domitius Lucanus, and thence to the latter's daughter, Domitia Lucilla, grandmother of the Emperor Marcus Aurelius – constituted by their very extent such an example of provincial land ownership that they still kept alive in the age of Trajan the memory of everything connected with their founder and were models for measures like the ones applied by him (cf. G. TIBILETTI, s.v. *Lex*, in DE RUGGIERO, *Diz Ep.*, IV [1957], p. 768 f.). It seems moreover that just about this time, and in any case before the end of the first century, the division into *centuriae* of present-day Tunisia was carried out (A. CAILLEMER and R. CHEVALLIER, 'Die römische Limitation in Tunesien', in *Germania*, XXXV, 1957, pp. 45–54). The adaptation of part of the *domus aurea* (which would thus be due to Vespasian, contrary to the accepted view, based on *Chron. a.* 354 and HIER., *Chron.*, p. 191 HELM) to convert it into the *horrea piperatoria* on the Via Sacra is connected by H. J. LOANE, 'Vespasian's Spice Market and Tribute in Kind', in *Class. Phil.*, XXXIX, 1944, pp. 10–21, on the basis of the reference by SUET., *Vesp.*, 16, 1, with the search for new sources of revenue, via the trade in spices, which probably came naturally as tribute from the East. On the legislation in the field of private law, in the view of D. DAUBE, 'Did Macedo Murder his Father?', in *Zeitschr. d. Savigny-Stiftung*, Rom. Abt. LXV, 1947, pp. 261–311, the decision of the *s.c. Macedonianum* that loans to the sons of families should no longer be valid, not even after the death of the father, was due to the parricide committed by one Macedo in order to pay his creditor.

On public works in Rome, little fresh is added by the dedication, dating from the end of 78, in *AE*, 1948, 94, and the *fistula aquaria* of *AE*, 1954, 61. The work undertaken to transform the colossal statue of Nero into a statue of Helios and to open the *domus aurea* to the public is referred to, according to A. BOETHIUS, 'Et crescunt media pegmata celsa via (Martial's "De spectaculis" 2, 2)', in *Eranos*, L, 1952, pp. 129–37, in the allusion of Martial's quoted in the title of the article. More interesting is the discussion of the artistic forms of the Flavian era, in connection with the new political climate; K. SCHEFOLD, 'Der Vespasianische Stijl in Pompeji', in *Bull. Veren. Bevord. Kennis Ant. Beschaving*, XXIV–XXVI, 1949–51, pp. 70–5, sees in painting reactionary tendencies as compared with the age of Nero (cf. the same scholar's 'Pompeji unter Vespasian', in *Mitt. deutsch. arch. Inst.*, Rom. Abt. LX–LXI, 1953–4, pp. 107–25), while architecture presents notable novelty and originality (G. LUGLI, 'Nuove forme dell'architettura romana nell'età da Flavi', in *Atti. 3° Convegno, naz. di st. dell'Architett.*, Assisi, 1–4 Oct. 1937, Rome 1939, pp. 95–102). On the amphitheatre at Puteoli, see A. MAIURI, *L'anfiteatro flavio puteolano*, Naples 1955, and for an unspecifiable restoration at Salerno see the fragmentary inscription *AE*, 1951, 200. The favourable attitude to men of science already noted (SUET., 17–18; PHILOSTRAT., *V. Apoll.*, V, 31; for a document confining the immunity already granted to doctors by Augustus, see KEIL, in *Forschungen in Ephesos*, IV, 1, 1932, p. 81) has been illustrated afresh by the inscription at Pergamum found by Wiegand in 1934 and published by R. HERZOG, 'Urkunden zur Hochschulpolitik der römischen Kaiser', in *Sitz.- ber. d. Preuss. Ak. d. Wiss.*, 1935, pp. 967–1010 (*AE*, 1936, 128), containing an edict by Vespasian, of 27 December 74, granting immunity to teachers of rhetoric, followed by a rescript of Domitian, of 93–94, cancelling it because of the greed of these men (cf. N. FESTA, 'Un editto di Vespasiano ed un rescritto di Domiziano. Documenti per la storia della legislazione scholastica nei primi secoli dell'impero romano', in *Bull. Ist. Dir. Rom.*, XLIV, 1936–7, pp. 13–18). On the aims – eminently practical, it seems – of the protection accorded by V. to letters and the arts, see M. S. WOODSIDE, 'Vespasian's Patronage of Education and the Arts', in *Trans. Proc. Am. Phil. Ass.*, LXXIII, 1942, pp. 123–9. Particular aspects of Vespasian's religiosity rather than of any religious policy have attracted attention as a result of the interpretation by M. GUARDUCCI, 'Veleda', in *Rend. Pont. Acc. Arch.*, XXI, 1945–6, pp. 163–76, and 'Nuove osservazioni sull'epigrafe ardeatina di Veleda', *ibid.*, XXIV–XXVI, 1949–51, pp. 75–87, of an inscription from Ardea mentioning the German prophetess Veleda (see also KEIL, 'Ein Spottgedicht auf die gefangene Seherin Veleda', in *Anz. Oesterr. Akad.*, LXXXIV, 1947, pp. 185 ff.; WILHELM, 'Das Gedicht auf Veleda', *ibid.*, LXXXV, 1948, pp. 151 ff., and others cited in Guarducci; but see latterly P. MINGAZZINI, 'Un altro tentativo d'interpretazione dell'iscrizione di Veleda', in *Bull. Comm. Arch.*, LXXIV, 1951–2, pp. 71–6. That Veleda delivered oracles in a sanctuary may be confirmed by the fact that the inscription was found among the ruins of a temple; E STEFANI, 'Ardea [Contrada Casalinaccio]. Resti di un antico tempio scoperto nell'area dello città', in *Not. d. Sc.*, 1954, pp. 6–30). On the restoration of the cult of *Honos* and *Virtus*, in the context of special cultivation (mirrored in the coinage as well) of typical imperial virtues, see M. BIEBER, 'Honos and Virtus', in *Amer. Journ. Arch.*, XLIX, 1945, pp. 25–34. The imperial cult in the traditional Augustan form appears in the oath 'per genium' found in the writing tablets of Herculaneum (G. PUGLIESE CARRATELLI, in *Par. Pass.*, 1948, p. 175 f.). However, a proper temple and altar of Vespasian was put up at Pompeii before 74, on the ruins of a sanctuary of *Genius Augusti* destroyed in the earthquake of 63. (G. NIEBLING, 'Der Tempel und Altar des Vespasian in Pompeji',

in *Forsch. u. Fortschr.*, XXXI, 1957, pp. 23–9). For the introduction
of the flaminate of Augustus into Narbonese Gaul (between Vespasian
and 93–94), see A. AYMARD, 'Du nouveau sur un toulousain et sur
Toulouse à l'époque impériale', in *Bull. soc. arch. du Midi de la France*,
1942–5, pp. 513–28.

As for the reform of the army in general, Mommsen's theory that
Italians were deliberately excluded from the legions has been completely
abandoned. Already contradicted by the continually growing amount of
epigraphical material that has become known, it has been replaced by
wider research into the social conditions that gradually drew the Italian
element away from legionary service (G. E. F. CHILVER, *Cisalpine Gaul*,
Oxford 1941, p. 112 f.; G. FORNI, *Il reclutamento delle legioni da Aug. a
Dioclez.*, Milan 1953, pp. 76 ff.). On the questions of structural reorganization and movement of legions (see table in BRAITHWAITE, *op.
cit.*, p. 42 f.), the most dubious problem is that of Legion *V Alaudae*,
whose survival after 70 and up to 86 or 92 would only be certain if it
could be demonstrated that the legionaries mentioned in the big inscription from Adamklissi belonged to it (*CIL*, III, 14214 = *ILS*, 9107; cf.
RITTERLING, in *P.W.*, XII, c. 1569 f. and in 'Rheinische Legionäre an
der unteren Donau', in *Germania*, IX, 1925, pp. 141 ff.; BRAITHWAITE,
comm. cit., pp. 42 f.; C. PATSCH, 'Der Kampf um den Donauraum unter
Domitian u. Trajan', in *Sitz.-ber. Ak. Wiss. Wien*, 217, I [1937], pp. 3 and
13, cf. *ibid.*, 214, I [1932[, p. 180; the question is left undecided by
R. SYME, in *Cambr. Anc. Hist.*, XI, pp. 133, 171, in 'The Colony of
Cornelius Fuscus: an Episode in the Bellum Neronis', in *Am. Journ. Phil.*,
LVIII, 1937, pp. 16 f. and in 'The First Garrison of Trajan's Dacia', in
Laureae Aquincenses, Budapest 1938, p. 269, and recently by J. COLIN,
'Le Préfet du Prétoire Cornelius Fuscus: un enfant de Pompei,' in
Latomus, XV, 1956, p. 6, n. 2), or else that it was the *V Alaudae*, not the
XXI Rapax (about which there is also a good deal of uncertainty), that was
annihilated by the Sarmatians in 92. In connection with the history of the
legions, even though the point is not directly connected with this period,
it is worth noting that the above-mentioned inscription of the land register
at Orange told us the epithet, *Gallica*, of the II legion. For the reduction
of the praetorian cohorts from the sixteen of Vitellius, see A. PASSERINI,
Le coorti pretorie, Rome 1939, pp. 54–7; his conclusions have been adopted
in the main text. For the duration of the praetorian prefectship of M.
Arrecinus Clemens (only until the return of Vespasian), A. PASSERINI,
'M. Arrecinus Clemens', in *Athen.*, XXVIII, 1940, pp. 155–7. So far as
the *auxilia* are concerned, the most recent discussion of the material is to

be found in K. KRAFT, *Zur Rekrutierung der Alen und Kohorten an Rhein und Donau*, (*Dissertationes Bernenses*, ser. I, 3), Berne 1951, p. 44 f. The progressive transformation of the life of the armies (fixing of the legionary bases in stone camps and *vice versa* more flexibility for tasks requiring mobility through the *vexillationes*; more regular organization of the *auxilia*, etc.) is demonstrated by archaeological discoveries (see only, for example, J. J. HATT, 'Découverte d'un camp romain près de Meinau (Bas-Rhin)', in *Bull. Soc. d. Ant. Fr.*, 1950–1, p. 190, and the same writer's 'Fouilles et découvertes romaines à Strasbourg de 1950 à 1952', in *Cahiers d'Arch. et. d'Hist. d'Alsace*, 1953, no. 133, pp. 73–96, and, for a systematic review, W. SCHLEIERMACHER, 'Römische Archäologie am Rhein 1940 bis 1950', in *Historia*, II, 1953, pp. 94–100; H. V. PETRIKOVITS, *Das römische Rheinland*, *Archäologische Forschungen seit 1945*, Cologne 1960).

So far as Vespasian's attention to the empire is concerned, evidence for a consideration of the general criteria of his policy is provided by the concession of the *ius Latii* to Spain (CH. SAUMAGNE, 'Le statut municipal des provinces sous le haut empire romaine', in *Bull. Soc. d. Ant. d. Fr.*, 1950–1, pp. 126 ff.), by his colonizing activity (J. GOROSTIAGA, 'Flaviobriga, colonia romana, hoy Forua Guernica en Vizcava', in *Helmantica*, V, 1954, espec. p. 15; D. VAN BERCHEM, 'Les colons d'Aventicum', in *Mél. Ch. Gilliard*, Lausanne 1944, pp. 45–6, who reduces to more realistic proportions – precisely through the example of Aventicum, where the previous inhabitants remained as *incolae* alongside the new settlers – the scope of the 'benefit' of the colonial foundation), and by the examination of the careers of senators of provincial origin (I. A. RICHMOND, 'Gnaeus Julius Agricola', in *Journ. of Rom. St.*, XXXIV, 1944, pp. 34–45). For the work of urbanization, in the form of the assignment to already organized Roman communities of native communities with native organizations – an interesting stage on the road to Romanization – see for Pannonia the case of a tribe by the name of the Scordisci; an inscription of theirs found fairly recently (October 1956) at Neu-Slaukamen in Yugoslavia has made known to us a pr(inceps) prae(fectus): A. MÓCSY, 'Zur Geschichte der peregrinen Gemeinden in Pannonien', in *Historia*, VI, 1957, pp. 488–98. Vespasian's concern for the 'immunity' of towns is explicitly attested, in connection with the prohibition of abuses in requisitions for the 'cursus publicus', by the Greek inscription from Hama (Syria) published by R. MOUTERDE and C. MONDÉSERT in *Syria*, XXXIV, 1957, pp. 278–84, and, in connection with the privilege preserved by the *civitates liberae* of receiving payment of taxes and tolls, by

the fragment discovered recently of a decree from Caunus in Caria
(G. E. BEAN, 'Notes and Inscriptions from Caunus', in *Journ. of Hell. St.*,
LXXIV, 1954, pp. 97–104, no. 38). But it is the records of public works
above all that illustrate his concrete activity; here we shall add to that
already noted only the most recently discovered epigraphical evidence of
works carried out by him or dedicated to him, or at any rate of dedications
put up for benefits conferred by him: in Italy, at Brescia, a dedication of
A.D. 74 (*Not. d. Sc.*, 1950, pp. 31 f. = *AE*, 1952, 31); in Spain, at
Tarragona, a dedication *divo Vespasiano* by a private citizen (*AE*, 1930,
146); in Gaul, at Orange, the already cited tablet recording the reorganization of the land register; in Britain, at Wells, four lumps of lead
with Vespasian's name (*AE*, 1959, 107); at Philippi, in Macedonia, a
dedication to Vespasian and Titus dating from 79, probably round about
the day of Vespasian's death (*AE*, 1935, 47); at Appiaria, not far from
Durostorum, in Moesia, an inscription of 76 for the construction of a
military building (*AE*, 1957, 307); at Apamea, a dedication by the *boulē*,
the *demos* and the Romans living there (*M.A.M.A.*, VI, 1939, p. 67, no.
177 = *AE*, 1940, 195); in Syria a milestone from Palmyra, dating from
75 (*Syria*, XIII, 1932, pp. 276 f., cf. *ibid.*, XXII, 1941, p. 174), with the
name of the governor, M. Ulpius Traianus Senior, whose governorship,
usually placed between 76 and 79, must thus have started in 75. But
research has produced particularly plentiful finds in Africa: repairs to the
road from Cirta to Hippo Regius ('ab Alpibus usque ad sinum') are
recorded in *AE*, 1955, 145 (though this could refer to Titus); numerous
dedications – to Vespasian and Titus in the forum at Tebessa (*AE*, 1930,
126), to Vespasian by the *colonia Iulia Tubusuctu*, from late 73 – early 74
(*AE*, 1934, 39), to Vespasian and to Titus by the people of Leptis (*Inscr. of
Rom. Trip.*, 342 = *AE*, 1949, 84, from the first half of 78; *AE*, 1957,
206 from 77–78, on the blocks of an arch) and by the people of Sabrata
(*Inscr. of Rom. Trip.*, 15, between 76 and 79). A dedication from Leptis to
Vespasian has also been seen by H. G. PFLAUM (*Mém. Soc. Ant. d. Fr.*,
LXXXII, 1951, p. 189 = *AE*, 1952, 104) in the inscription CIL, VIII,
7019; and *Inscr. of Rom. Trip.*, no. 300 provides the first complete publica-
cation of inscr. CIL, VIII, 22671, after the discovery of numerous other
fragments; also the dedication of the temple of the Magna Mater at
Leptis, dating from 71–72. Recent epigraphical finds also include the
diploma from Herculaneum, *AE*, 1932, 27 = *CIL*, XVI, 11, dated
7 March 70, for the soldiers of the *II Adiutrix*, which on that day became
'*iusta legio*'.

Changes in provincial administration present some problems. The date of the abolition of the *libertas* and *immunitas* of Greece wavers between the 70 of Philostratus (*V. Apoll.*, V, 41; but see GROSSO, *art. cit.*, pp. 412 f., which however is too subtle) and the 73–74 of St Jerome (*A. Abr.*, 2090). The second date is the more probable one (BRAITHWAITE, pp. 44 f.; E. GROAG, *Die römische Reichsbeamten von Achaia bis auf Diokletian*, Vienna and Leipzig 1939, Ch. 41; on the 'libertas' of Rhodes in particular, see A. MOMIGLIANO, in *Journ. of Rom. St.*, XLI, 1951, pp. 150 f.). The simultaneous return of Sardinia and Corsica to procuratorial government is regarded as certain by P. MELONI, 'L'ammin. della Sard. nel I sec. d. Cr.', in *Ann. Fac. Lett. Cagliari*, XXI, 1953, (St Motzo, I), pp. 117–47, espec. p. 134 ff., and placed towards 73–74 (cf. the same writer's *L'ammin. d. Sard. da Aug. all'invas. vandalica*, Rome 1958, pp. 26 ff.). The alternation between proconsular and procuratorial government subsequently continued until Commodus, though the periods cannot be determined for certain. In Meloni's view the province returned to the Senate towards the end of Trajan's reign and remained under this régime until Commodus or Septimius Severus (or at any rate this is the hypothesis that Meloni prefers). In the view of A. E. ASTIN, 'The Status of Sardinia in the Second Century A.D.', in *Latomus*, XVIII, 1959, pp. 150–3, there was a transfer to the Senate in 110 in exchange for Bithynia, a return to the procuratorial régime under Hadrian, and a new transfer to the Senate under M. Aurelius, in exchange for Baetica. But it seems that the principle of compensation was not always adhered to rigidly.

As for military campaigns, Britain is naturally the centre of interest; see E. BIRLEY, 'Britain under the Flavians: Agricola and his Predecessors', in *Durham Univ. Journal*, 1946, pp. 79–84 (= *Roman Britain and the Roman Army*, Kendal 1953, pp. 10–19), who stresses the importance of the work of Agricola's predecessors and of Vespasian himself under Claudius (but on this see A. MOMIGLIANO, ' "Panegyricus Messalae" and "Panegyricus Vespasiani". Two References to Britain', in *Journ. of Rom. St.*, XL, 1950, pp. 39–42, replied to by BIRLEY, *loc. cit.*, p. 19); see also the same writer's 'The Brigantian Problem and the First Roman Contact with Scotland', in *Roman Britain*, cit., pp. 31–47. On the conquest and settlement of Wales, V. E. NASH-WILLIAMS, 'Wales and the Roman Frontier System', in *The Congress of Roman Frontier Studies 1949*, edited by E. BIRLEY, Durham 1952, pp. 68–73. On the problem of the Brigantes and their queen Cartimandua, a figure no less important than Boudicca but one neglected by Tacitus because she was less relevant to the aims of historico-moral evocation, I. A. RICHMOND, 'Queen Cartimandua', in

Journ. of Rom. St., XLIV, 1954, pp. 43–52, who had earlier also re-examined the politico-military work of Agricola in the *art. cit.* in *Journ. of Rom. St.*, XXXIV, 1944, pp. 34–45. At present it still remains uncertain whether Agricola's governorship began in 77 or 78. However, it should be noted that if we accept the connection already established by MOMMSEN, *Röm. Gesch.*, V⁵, pp. 136 f., n. 1., and confirmed recently by H. NESSELHAUF, 'Tacitus and Domitian', in *Hermes*, LXXX, 1952, p. 237, between the episode of the mutiny and flight of the cohort of Usipi in *Agr.*, 28, and Domitian's German campaign, which belongs to 83 (a coincidence also confirmed by *Agr.*, 26, 1, where there is a reference in the same year to the *IX Hispana* legion as 'maxime invalida'; and in fact a *vexillatio* from this legion took part in the war againt the Chatti, *CIL*, XIV, 3612 = *ILS*, 1025), a connection which puts the episode in the *sixth* year of the war (*Agr.*, 25, 1), and then count backwards, we arrive at 78 rather than 77. Moreover, other reasons suggest that we should accept 84 rather than 83 as the year of Agricola's last campaign and recall (WEYNAND, in *P.W.*, VI, c. 2560; SYME, in *Cambr. Anc. Hist.*, XI, p. 158). On the value to be attached to the accounts given by Tacitus in the *Agricola*, S. N. MILLER, 'The Fifth Campaign of Agricola', in *Journ. of Rom. St.*, XXXVIII, 1948, pp. 15–19, thinks that certain parts of the narrative, such as Chaps. 23–5, were based on Agricola's own notes. He also thinks that the stature of Agricola, neither a great general nor a proud champion of freedom, was heightened by Tacitus more than is believed by F. GROSSO, 'Tendenziosità dell'Agricola', *In mem. A. Beltrami*, *Misc. Philol.*, Genoa 1954, pp. 97–145. A comprehensive evaluation of the work of Agricola is to be found in A. R. BURN, *Agricola and Roman Britain*, London 1953. On the colonization of the region of the Upper Rhine, see latterly H. NESSELHAUF, 'Die Besiedlung der Oberrheinlande in römischer Zeit', in *Badische Fundberichte*, XIX, 1951, pp. 71–85. For the situation in the East and relations with the Parthians at the time of Vespasian, see F. GROSSO, 'M. Ulpio Traiano, governatore di Siria', in *Rend. Ist. Lomb.*, XCI, 1957, pp. 318–42.

THE REIGN OF TITUS

M. FORTINA's recent monograph, *L' imperatore Tito*, Turin 1955, sticks for the most part, as is inevitable in the present state of our knowledge, to the conclusions now commonly accepted (cf. WEYNAND, *P.W.*, VI, cc. 2695–2729). On the year of Titus's birth see also F. GROSSO, *art. cit.*, pp. 433 f. The date 39 (SUET., *Tit.*, 11, as opposed to *Tit.*, 1;

CASS. D., LXVI, 18, 4; EUTROP., VII, 22; PHILOSTR., *V. Apoll.*, VI, 30, vague) is almost certain. The same GROSSO, 'La morte di Tito', in *Antidoron H. H. Paoli oblatum – Miscellanea Philologica*, Genoa 1956, pp. 137–62, in the course of studying the details of Titus's death, especially the rumour that he had been poisoned by Domitian, adduces fresh arguments in support of the view that sees the origin of this rumour in the aristocratic tradition hostile to the last of the Flavians. But any attempt to trace a coherent political line in Titus's activity has to rely too much on conjecture. This is true of the link discovered by J. A. CROOK, 'Titus and Berenice', in *Am. Journ. Phil.*, LXXII, 1951, pp. 162–75, between the presence of Berenice in Rome and political developments. According to Crook, the background was formed on the one hand by the conflict between Titus and Mucianus, as a result of which Berenice, left in the East in 71, came to Rome after Mucianus's death (though the date of this event is also unknown) and on the other by the need for concessions to the aristocratic circle, whose goodwill, affected by the execution of Caecina and the condemnation of Eprius Marcellus in 79, was regained by sending away the queen and confirmed even when, after the death of Vespasian, she returned (on the 'small-scale Cleopatra' of MOMMSEN, *Rom. Gesch.*, V^5, p. 540, see also E. MIREAUX, *La reine Bérénice*, Paris 1951). Equally hypothetical is M. A. LEVI's reconstruction, 'La clemenza di Tito', in *Par. Pass.*, IX, 1954, pp. 288–93. From an examination of the coinage in relation to the Suetonian life, Levi finds in Titus's activity while his father was still alive, and in contrast to the attitude of his father, traces of a policy favourable to the East which gained him, when he came to the throne, the hostility of the aristocratic class; it was precisely this hostility, Levi thinks, which Titus sought to eliminate by the acts which can be grouped under the heading of *clementia*, the ones that subsequently exerted an almost exclusive influence on the tradition. As for details of political events, on the date of the beginning of Titus's *trib. pot.* (1 July 71), see M. HAMMOND, in *Amer. Journ. Arch.*, XV, 1938, p. 34 ff., and on the return of Titus from the East in a cargo ship, an episode already interpreted by the ancients (SUET., *Tit.*, 5, 3) as an indication of his wish to allay any possible anxieties on the part of his father, see J. ROUGÉ, 'Voyages officiels en Méditerranée orientale à la fin de la république et au premier siècle de l'empire', in *Rev. Ét. Anc.*, LV, 1953, pp. 294–300. On the attitude of clemency, H. PRICE, 'Titus, amor et deliciae generis humani', in *Class. Weekly*, XXXIX, 1945–6, pp. 58–61. On the most memorable event of Titus's reign, the eruption of Vesuvius, R. M. HAYWOOD, 'The Strange Death of the Elder Pliny', in *Class.*

Weekly, XLVI, 1952, pp. 1–3; H. C. LIPSCOMB, *ibid.*, under the same title, XLVII, 1954, p. 74, with a reply from Haywood. On the iconography of Titus, H. GOETZE, 'Ein Triumphalbildnis des Titus', in *Festschrift Schweitzer*, Stuttgart 1954, pp. 354–7.

So far as activity at home is concerned, A. GUARINI, 'Sull'origine del testamento dei militari nel diritto romano', in *Rend. Ist. Lomb.*, Cl. Lett., LXXII, 1939, pp. 355–67, followed by S. BOLLA, 'Zum römischen Militärtestament', in *St. Arango-Ruiz*, I, 1953, pp. 273–8 (who finds the political reasons for the measure in the requirements of the army, which changed profoundly in ethnic and social composition during the Flavian period) has attributed to Titus the introduction into Roman law of the privilege of the *testamentum militare*, regarding as an interpolation the report in the *Dig.*, XXIX, 1, 1, of an analogous provisional concession by Caesar (but see L. CHEVALLIER, 'Notes sur le testament militaire', in *Varia*, II, 1956 [Public. de l'Inst. de Dr. Rom. de l'Univ. de Paris, XIV], p. 5). On the military diploma of Titus most recently discovered (*CIL*, XVI, Suppl. no. 158), see A. DEGRASSI, in *Par. Pass.*, 1947, pp. 349–56, who was the first to attribute it to Titus, placing it between 14 January and 11 February 80, contrary to the view of the first editor, who had attributed it to Domitian (D. DETSCHEW, in *Bull. Inst. Arch. Bulgare*, XV, 1946, pp. 86–93). To the already plentiful evidence of work for the empire must be added the most recent finds: *AE*, 1957, 169 (fragment of a dedication to Titus and Domitian, at Verulamium in Britain); *AE*, 1938, 128 (in Spain, first half of 80); *AE*, 1954, 137 (= L. LESCHI, 'Inscriptions latines de Lambèse et de Zama, I. Un nouveau camp de Titus à Lambèse (81 ap. J.C)', in *Libyca*, I, 1953, pp. 189–97), an inscription from the first camp at Lambaesis, put up between 1 July and 13 September 81; *AE*, 1955, 146, a dedication from Hippo Regius; also the dedication from the East, *AE*, 1929, 172 (Varna), *AE*, 1930, 86 (Ephesus, first half of 80), *AE*, 1941, 2 (Karnak in Egypt), and the two characteristic ones from Cyprus, one at Palepaphus, to Titus and Aphrodite Paphia, put up in 79–80 (*AE*, 1950, 5, new reading of *IGRR*, III, 944) and one at Amathus, put up roughly about the same time by the proconsul L. Bruttius Maximus to Aphrodite Cipria and Titus (*AE*, 1950, 122). At Aquileia a veteran commemorates the military awards received 'ab divo Tito' in the Jewish war (*AE*, 1952, 153). On the subject of new interpretations of old evidence, the seductive explanation of *CIL*, VI, 944 = *ILS*, 264 (the inscription from the broken arch in the Circus Maximus) put forward by H. U. INSTINSKY, 'Der Ruhm des Titus', in *Phil.*, XCVII, 1948, p. 370 f., according to which the expression 'omnibus ante se ducibus regibus gentibus aut frustra petitam aut omnino intemptatam delevit' would refer not to the whole previous history of Jerusalem but simply to the course of the Jewish war (*reges* and *gentes* would denote the detachments of the client states and kings), need only be met with the objection that in the war there was only one single previous *dux*, and that was Titus's father, who is moreover named in the inscription itself: 'praeceptis patr[is] consiliisq(ue) et auspiciis'. Finally a papyrus fragment (from the Rendel Harris collection) has restored to us a passage of the so-called *Acts of the Pagan Martyrs* that is to be placed under Titus (C. H. ROBERTS, 'Titus and Alexandria. A New Document', in *Journ. of Rom. St.*, XXXIX, 1949, pp. 79–80; cf. H. A. MUSURILLO, *The Acts of the Pagan Martyrs*, Oxford 1954, pp. 32, 147–9): something rather surprising in view of the fame of Titus's characteristic clemency, even though his relations with the Egyptians, in spite of the hatred of the Jews for him and his father, were not, as his father's were, extremely friendly.

THE FIGURE OF DOMITIAN AND THE CONFLICT WITH THE ARISTOCRACY

In spite of the difficulties deriving from the tradition, a plausible reconstruction of the figure of Domitian has been arrived at, and it does not present the problems left open in the case, for example, of Nero. Thus the most recent treatments, whether in general histories or in the form of monographs (P. E. ARIAS, *Domiziano*, Catania 1945, with a translation of Suetonius's *Life* and a commentary on it), add little to the famous verdict of MOMMSEN, according to whom Domitian was 'one of the most meticulous administrators that the empire had had' (*Röm. Gesch.*, V, p. 90), to the long essay of ST GSELL, *Essai sur le règne de l'empereur Domitian*, Paris 1894, and to the articles of WEYNAND, in *P.W.*, VI (1909) cc. 2451–2596, and CORRADI, in DE RUGGIERO, *Diz. Epigr.*, II (1913–14), pp. 1960–2046.

In the realm of home affairs, the main interest in recent times has centred round Domitian's conflict with the aristocracy and the philosophers, the question at issue being not so much the chronology, which has been fairly well established in the studies cited, as the ideological reasons for the opposition. It does not seem likely that this opposition had already crystallized at the time of the succession in an attempt by the Senate to debate whether or not to accept Domitian (F. GROSSO, 'La morte di Tito', in *Misc. Paoli, cit.*, p. 151). It is clear that the responsibility for the emergence of the conflict with the aristocracy and for the sharpening of the theoretical opposition of the philosophers, which had already existed under Vespasian, falls on Domitian, whose personal assertion of despotism must have gradually made its effects felt. Quite apart from the conjectures of psychopathological research, which has not neglected even Domitian (W. C. HELMBOLD, 'The Complexion of Domitian', in *Class. Journ.*, XLV, 1950, p. 388 f.) and of research, based particularly on the legends on coins, into the recurrence of propaganda motifs (F. M. WOOD, JR., 'Fides Publica: Domitian and the Roman People', in *Trans. Proc. Am. Phil. Ass.*, LXXII, 1941, p. XLV f.; 'Domitian and the Imperial Fortuna', *ibid.*, LXXIII, 1942, p. XXXIV), the chronological examination of events and the analysis of the development of the ideas confirm the crescendo of hostility indicated by the tradition. To deal with the reasons for some of the chronological choices made in the main text in connection with this, it seemed preferable to assign a date between 82 and 83 for the death of T. Flavius Sabinus, to fit in with the report in EUSEB., *Chron.*, p. 190 HELM, of a wholesale banishment of senators, since the downfall of Eusebius's friend Dio of Prusa occurred in 82. No difficulty is raised by the fact that Sabinus had held the consulship (ord. A.D. 82 with Domitian) in spite of the incident of the herald (SUET., *Dom.*, 10, 4), which may only later have proved fatal; and in any case this conjecture is preferable to postulating a new nomination for the consulship, a nomination of which there is no trace but which is rendered necessary by the attribution of Sabinus's death, on the ground indicated, to 87 (*Act. Arv.*, 22 Sept. 87: 'ob detecta scelera nefariorum', which it is possibly better to connect with the downfall of C. Vettulenus Civica Cerialis) or else to 89 or 90 (WEYNAND, *P.W.*, VI, c. 2572). Another event which is uncertain, and to be placed somewhere between 85 and 96, is the condemnation of Sallustius Lucullus, the governor of Britain. 89–90, in connection with the revolt of Saturninus, seems the best date (E. BIRLEY, *Rom. Brit. and the Rom. Army*, pp. 20, 22, proposes 93 on somewhat weak grounds; he cites TAC., *Agr.*, 45). For the war of Saturninus, the reconstruction by RITTERLING (in *Westd. Zeitschr.*, XII, 218 ff.) remains the best from every point of view, including the chronological one (for the definitively ascertained name of Saturninus's conqueror, A. Lappius Maximus Norbanus, as in the *Fasti Ostienses* and *Potentini*, see N. ALFIERI, 'I Fasti consulares de Potentia', in *Athen.*, XXXVI, 1948, p. 121). That the rhetorician Maternus executed in 91 or 92 (CASS. D., LXVII, 12, 5) was Curiatius Maternus, the interlocutor of the *Dialogus de Oratoribus*, may well be so. The *praetextae* written by him on themes such as *Cato* and *Domitius* (*Dial.*, 2, 3) belong to the same order of

ideas as those in the account given by Cassius Dio, and the part assigned
to him by the author in the dialogue fits in: that of pointing to the lack of
political freedom as the cause of the decline of oratory. On the actual
personal relations of Domitian with the aristocracy, there is an examination
of the 'consilium' of JUVEN., Sat., IV, in J. A. CROOK, Consilium
Principis, Cambridge 1955. It looks as if light is thrown on adlectio to the
Senate and on the tone of the Emperor's personal relations with senators
and officials by the codicil of Pap. Berl., 8334, published, with the suggestions of W. SCHUBART and J. STROUX, by H. KORTENBEUTEL,
'Ein Kodizill eines römischen Kaisers', in Abhandl. d. Preuss. Ak. d. Wiss.,
Phil.-hist. Kl., 1939, 13 (pub. in 1940), if the author of the codicil is in
fact Domitian and if it is in fact a question of the appointment to the
Senate of two prefects of Egypt in succession, of a certain . . . Ursus (who
could be the man made consul in 84, acc. to CASS. D., LXVII, 3, 1, at the
request of Julia, though this is denied by A. STEIN, Zu dem kaiserlichen
Ernennungsschreiben in P. Berl. 8334, in Aegyptus, XX, 1940, pp. 51–60, who
distinguishes the various persons called Ursus attested under Domitian)
and of a certain . . . Maximus, identified with the prefect of Egypt in 83,
L. Laberius Maximus. A. PIGANIOL, on the other hand, 'Le codicille
impérial du Papyrus de Berlin 8334', in Compt. rend. Acad. Inscr., 1947,
pp. 376–86, thinks that the codicil deals with the formula of appointment
of the praetorian prefect and that the names of Julius Ursus and Laberius
Maximus should therefore be added to the list of praetorian prefects under
Domitian. For the possibility, based on the Fasti Potentini, that Maximus is
A. Lappius Maximus Norbanus, see A. GARZETTI, 'A. Lappio Massimo pre-
fetto d'Egitto sotto Domiziano?', in Aegyptus, XXXVII, 1957, pp. 65–70.
On the collaboration of individual senators, see E. BIRLEY, 'Senators in
the Emperor's Service', in Proc. Br. Acad., XXXIX, 1953, pp. 197–214,
and on the regularly ordered careers of men of merit under Domitian,
F. OERTEL, 'Zur politischen Haltung des jüngeren Plinius', in Rh. Mus.,
LXXXVIII, 1939, pp. 179–84, who confirms the theory of W. OTTO
('Zur Lebensgeschichte des jüngeren Plinius', in Sitz.-ber. d. Bay. Ak. d.
Wiss., 1919) that Pliny was a conformist under Domitian (cf. A. N.
SHERWIN-WHITE, 'Pliny's Praetorship Again', in Journ. of Rom. St.,
XLVII, 1957, pp. 126–30). So far as other personages are concerned, it is
worth noting the unfavourable verdict (as opposed to GSELL, p. 62) of
A. PASSERINI, 'M. Arrecinus Clemens', in Athen. XXVIII, 1940,
pp. 145–63, on the friend of Domitian and praetorian prefect in 70,
executed, probably for treason, in 93 (in connection with a new inscription
from Pesaro; cf. AE, 1947, 40): and the also unfavourable verdict on

Agricola's behaviour of H. W. TRAUB, 'Agricola's Refusal of a Governorship (TAC., *Agr.*, 42, 3)', in *Class. Phil.*, XLIX, 1954, pp. 255–7.
According to Traub, Agricola was within his rights and acting in accordance with custom when he asked for *excusatio* from a province, but committed an act offensive to the Princeps when he did not ask, in accordance
with usage even in the case of renunciation of a province, for the
salarium; a circumstance turned by Tacitus to his father-in-law's credit
(but see on this and on the general concept of Domitian's principate,
K. V. FRITZ, 'Tacitus, Agricola, Domitian, and the Problem of the
Principate', *ibid.*, LII, 1957, pp. 73–97, espec. pp. 74–7).

The intellectual opposition sprang not only from the uncertainty about
the concept of freedom and the anti-imperial polemic already existing
under Vespasian (CH. WIRSZUBSKI, *Libertas*; A. MOMIGLIANO
'Liberty and Libertas', in *Journ. of Rom. St.*, XLI, 1951, pp. 146–9) but
also from Domitian's concrete relations with philosophers. The problem
presented in the *Dialogus de Oratoribus*, with its fundamental contradiction
(the orator finds the cause of the lamented decline in the art of speaking
in the lack of freedom peculiar to the principate, which is nevertheless
accepted as the best political organization), and also cropping up in the
other works of Tacitus, becomes a commonplace in a vast literature which
sees in Domitian, either openly or by allusion, the typical tyrant. The life
of Apollonius of Tyana by the deutero-Philostratus has in particular
attracted attention, with conclusions which allot to it varying degrees of
historical credibility (F. GROSSO, 'La "Vita di Apoll. di Tiana" come
fonte storica', in *Acme*, VII, 1954, pp. 441–91 allows it a considerable
degree; A. CALDERINI, 'Teoria e pratica politica nella "Vita di Apoll. di
Tiana" ', in *Rend. Ist. Lomb.*, LXXIV, 1940–1, pp. 213–41, with more
probability, allows it rather less), but which spotlight the intellectual
atmosphere to which Dio of Prusa also explicitly bears witness (A. MOMI-
GLIANO, *art. cit.*, 151–3). The points emphasized are not only the limits
of direct opposition to the Princeps but also the wider question (one also
present in Tacitus, as the motive inspiring the *Germania*) of the argument
about the freedom and uprightness of the 'primitives' as opposed to the
servitude of the civilized empire (C. PATSCH, 'Der Kampf um den
Donauraum unter Domitian und Trajan', in *Sitz.-ber. Ak. Wiss. Wien*,
217, 1 (1937), pp. 44–52, on Dio's stay on the Danube and his studies of
the customs of the Dacians). Yet Dio of Prusa, whose works were written,
like those of Tacitus and Pliny, for the society of Trajan's reign, in point
of fact accepts the principate in the form of the functional necessity which
it now represented in the public mind, and the opposition to Domitian is

opposition to the individual tyrant as a person and as a term of comparison with the excellence of Trajan. Epictetus too alludes to Domitian without naming him; his 'tyrant' is evidently Domitian (CH. G. STARR, JR., 'Epictetus and the Tyrant', in *Class. Phil.*, XLIV, 1949, pp. 20-9). But in the field of the search for allusions this is all that can be granted, and it looks as if A. BALLANTI, 'Documenti sull'opposizione intellettuale a Domiziano', in *Ann. Fac. Lett. Napoli*, IV, 1954, pp. 75-95, did not achieve much success in his attempt to attribute to the intellectual opposition to Domitian, though it may have been conducted on a 'wide front' by philosophers, politicians, moralists, rhetoricians, prophets and Christians, a goodly part of the anonymous works in existence: the satire of Sulpicia, the correspondence that goes by the name of Chio of Heraclea, the letters of the Seven Wise Men in the lives of the philosophers by Diogenes Laertius, and the correspondence between Seneca and St Paul! Naturally, even the Apocalypse is said to belong to the years after 93 and to be a document of the opposition to Domitian: of that opposition to the emperor, not to the empire, which would soon give way to 'enlightened conformism' (p. 76, an expression which indubitably deserves to gain wide currency). Observations on the general problem of the spiritual opposition are to be found in the notes to the survey by H. FUCHS, *Der geistige Wederstand gegen Rom in der antiken Welt*, Berlin 1938. For other factors relating to Domitian's autocratic policy, see F. SPERANZA, 'L'inizio e la pubblicazione delle Selve di P. Papinio Stazio', in *Ann. Fac. Lett. Napoli*, I, 1951, pp. 29-33; and 'La data di composizione della prima Selva di Stazio', in *St. Ital. Fil. Class.*, XXV, 1951, pp. 135-48. On the *damnatio memoriae*, see F. VITTINGHOFF, *Der Staatsfeind in der römischen Kaiserzeit, Untersuchungen zur "damnatio memoriae"*, Berlin 1936, p. 104.

THE WORK OF DOMITIAN

Even when it comes simply to a chronological account of the – so to speak – administrative acts of Domitian's reign, we meet once again, in the absence of Tacitus, the usual difficulties, constrained as we are to try to give consecutive dates to the items presented in classified form by Suetonius, to use meagre chronicles like that of Eusebius–St Jerome, to dig out the concrete facts from the hyperboles of contemporary poetry and the denigrations of that of the succeeding age, and to draw inferences from, say, a panegyric of Pliny, with the object of finding a context for the archaeological and epigraphical material, itself not even abundant and by its nature not very revealing. The greatest interest centres round the alleged financial bankruptcy and, in connection with it, or even independently of it, Domitian's building activities. Taking up MOMMSEN's assertion, *loc. cit.*, R. SYME, 'The Imperial Finances under Domitian, Nerva and Trajan', in *Journ. of Rom. St.*, XX, 1930, pp. 55–70, has demonstrated that no crisis existed, and this is now the current opinion, either with some modifications (C. H. V. SUTHERLAND, 'The State of the Imperial Treasury at the Death of Domitian', in *Journ. of Rom. St.*, XXV, 1935, pp. 150–62; T. FRANK, *An Econ. Survey of Anc. Rome*, V, Baltimore 1940, pp. 55 f.) or with hardly any at all (D. M. ROBATHAN, 'Domitian's Midas Touch', in *Trans. Proc. Am. Phil. Ass.*, LXXIII, 1942, pp. 130–44: Domitian's building did not come to a halt even in his last few years). In fact the coinage remained unchanged in value (unlike under Nero) and the confiscations were essentially political in character (F. M. WOOD JR., 'The "Bankruptcy" of Domitian', *ibid.*, LXXIV, 1943, p. xxiv f.). Suetonius's reports on the subject (*Dom.*, 3, 2; 12, 1) refer to a state of affairs confined to the city and the court. The rigorous control and personal interventions in the financial administration (which gave rise, together with the confiscations, to the verdict of 'inopia rapax') are a different matter. On the extent of the Emperor's intervention in the coinage (particularly with the object of controlling propaganda) see L. VOELKEL, 'The Selection of Coin Types During the Reign of the Emperor Domitian', in *St. Robinson*, II, Saint Louis 1953, pp. 243–7. As for building activity in Rome, so far as individual works are concerned (A. M. COLINI, *Stadium Domitiani*, Rome 1943) a special mention must be made of the two friezes consisting of several slabs found in 1937 during the restoration work on the palace of the Cancellaria, behind the tomb of A. Hirtius – the consul who fell in 43 B.C. in the Battle of Modena – with every appearance of having been abandoned in a marble-cutter's storeroom. The definitive publication was produced by F. MAGI, *I rilievi Flavi del palazzo della Cancellaria*, Rome 1945. It has seemed plausible to suppose that the reliefs must have belonged to a monument similar to the *Ara Pacis Augustae*, and were similarly intended to celebrate the *Pax Flavia*, especially as the figures of Vespasian and Domitian are clearly recognizable, the second in particular bearing traces of a curious attempt (only in the first frieze) to transform the features into those, it would seem, of Nerva (certainly as a result of the *damnatio memoriae*). The first relief thus seems to represent an *adventus* of Domitian (possibly that of 83, after the war against the Chatti) and the second the *adventus* of Vespasian in 70. The date of the monument would therefore be 83–85. All these dates (like the theory advanced about the original siting: the temple of *Fortuna Redux*) naturally smack, for the purposes of historical deductions, of the uncertainty characteristic of this kind of evidence, objectively silent and thus capable only of subjective interpretation (see above, p. 574 f.). Subsequent critics have on the whole accepted Magi's attribution to the Flavian era but dissented notably in other respects: H. FUHRMANN, in *Jahrb. d. deutsch. arch. Inst.*, Arch. Anz., LV, 1940, cc. 460–76 (cf. *ibid.*, LVI, 1941, cc. 542–5); P. G. HAMBERG, *Studies in Roman Imperial Art*, Copenhagen 1945, pp. 50–6; J. M. C. TOYNBEE, in *Journ. of Rom. St.*, XXXVII, 1947, pp. 187–91 (cf. *ibid.*, XXXVI, 1946, p. 180) sees in the first frieze the *profectio* of Domitian for the Batavian war in 70; H. LAST, 'On the Flavian Reliefs from the Palazzo della Cancellaria', in *Journ. of Rom. St.*, XXXVIII, 1948, pp. 9–14, underlines the propaganda nature of the scenes depicted, which in themselves can be interpreted as Magi has done, but also in other ways; G. BENDINELLI, *I rilievi domizianei di Pal. d. Canc. in Roma*, Turin 1949, p. 27, considers that the two friezes correspond with each other and that they represent a *profectio* and *reditus* of Domitian (but SUET., *Dom.*, 2, 1 is misunderstood and TAC., *Hist.*, IV, 85–6 is ignored); K. SCHEFOLD, *Orient, Hellas und Rom, in der archäologischen Forschung seit 1939*, Berne 1949, pp. 188–90, 235 f. maintains that they were made for Nerva from the start; and finally A. RUMPF, 'Römische historische Reliefs, I. Die Reliefs von der Cancellaria', in *Bonner Jahrb.*, 155–6, 1955–6, pp. 112–19, opens up the whole question again by bringing the reliefs down to the age of Hadrian. On the attribution to Domitian of the trophies from the Piazza del Campidoglio, following K. LEHMANN-HARTLEBEN, 'Ein Siegesdenkmal Domitians', in *Rh. Mus.*, XXXVIII–XXXIX, 1923–4, p. 185 ff., see MAGI, *op. cit.*, p. 54. It has been suggested that another of Domitian's buildings in Rome, the arch of the Iseo Campense, can be recognized on Alexandrian coins: see B. SESLER, 'Arco di Domiziano all'Iseo Campense in Roma', in *Riv. It. Num.*, LVII, 1955, pp. 88–93. For Flavian sculpture in general, see the survey by CH. PICARD, in *Rev. Ét. Lat.*, XXIX, 1951, pp. 349–73.

On activity in the empire, to cite as usual the most recently discovered evidence, we must mention, in continuation of a concern characteristic of Vespasian, the inscription of 87 published by P. ROMANELLI, in *Épigr.*, I, 1939, p. 111 f. (*Inscr. Rom. Trip.*, 854), dealing with a delimitation of boundaries near Serti, 'inter nationem Muduciuviorum et Zamuciorum'; the cippus *AE*, 1942–3, 35, which bears witness to a restitution made by Hadrian of the boundaries 'inter Suppenses et Vofricenses', first established by Capito Pomponianus under Domitian; the cippus of 88–89 recording the restitution of boundaries to Ptolemais in Cyrenaica (G. CAPUTO, in *Quad. Arch. Libia*, III, 1954, p. 51 = *AE*, 1954, 188); and the cippus marking the area sacred to Artemis at Ephesus (*AE*, 1933, 123). The interesting inscription from Hama (Syria) published by R. MOUTERDE and C. MONDÉSERT, in *Syria*, XXXIV, 1957, pp. 278–84, dealing with abuses in connection with the 'cursus publicus', has given us decisive evidence on criteria of Domitian's provincial administration. As for public works, little evidence has been added to what we possessed already: a water pipe from Ostia (*Not. di. Sc.*, 1953, p. 153 f. = *AE*, 1954, 170); the dedication of an aqueduct at Anazarbus in Cilicia (A.D. 90–91, *AE*, 1954, 10a); a milestone from the road from Carthage to Theveste (L. POINSSOT, 'Note sur un milliaire de la région d'Haïdra', in *Bull. Comm. Tr. Hist.*, 1934–5 [pub. 1940], p. 218 f.); the inscription modified in the early days of Domitian's reign from the camp at Lambaesis, built by Titus (*AE*, 1954, 137); the inscribed fragments of the blocks from the Flavian temple at Leptis (*Inscr. Rom. Trip.*, 348, A.D. 93–94) and from an altar and podium built in 92 in the theatre at Leptis (G. CAPUTO, 'Ara e podio domizanei nella conistra del teatro di Leptis Magna', in *Dioniso*, XII, 1949, pp. 83–91 = *Inscr. Rom. Trip.*, 347). But, as usual, interventions by the Princeps can be inferred from mentions in honorific inscriptions: the dedication (A.D. 86) of the *colonia Flavia Aug. Puteolana* (M. CAGIANO DE AZEVEDO, in *Bull. Mus. Imp. Rom.*, X, 1939, pp. 45–56); the dedication Iovi Optimo Maximo and to the Genius Domitiani found at Colonia in 1950 (M. BOES, 'Eine Weihung an Jupiter und den Genius Domitians', in *Bonner Jahrb.*, CLVIII, 1958, pp. 29–35); the inscriptions from Lindus, *AE*, 1948, 185 and 188, the first a dedication to Domitian, the second mentioning a priest of Domitian; an inscription of the Isaurians which seems to be a dedication to Domitian (*AE*, 1937, 255, cf. 106); the portrayal of Domitian in the temple at Karnak (A. VARILLE, 'Description sommaire du temple d'Arnon-Ré à Karnak', in *Ann. Serv. Ant. d'Ég.*, L, 1950, p. 167 and plates XXXVI–XXXVII) and the probable allusion to him on the walls of the temple of Esné (S. SAUNERON, 'Trajan ou Domitien?', in *Bull. Inst. Franç. Arch. Or.*, LIII, 1953, pp. 49–52); the dedication of the *iuventus civitatis Mactaritanae*, in proconsular Africa (G. C. PICARD, 'Civitas Mactaritana', in *Karthago*, VIII, 1957, pp. 77, 95 = *AE*, 1959, 172). Some new attributions to Domitian derive from better readings and fuller discussions of documents already noted: the inscr. *CIL*, XIV, 2096, at first attributed to the Julio-Claudian period and now assigned by J. COLIN, 'Restitution de l'inscription des sévirs de Lanuvium au Vatican', in *Rev. Phil.*, XXV, 1951, pp. 195–201, to 1 October 81, the day after the comitia for the *trib. pot.* of Domitian, would make an interesting contribution to our knowledge of the start of Domitian's reign; the inscription from Thebes, *IG*, VII, 2495, is now regarded as a dedication to Domitian (B. D. MERITT, in *Hesperia*, XVI, 1947, p. 61 f. = *AE*, 1950, 88); the reading 'oper[ibus itera]tis' proposed by N. VULIČ (*Klio*, XXXV, 1942, p. 178) for *CIL*, III, 13813c = *ILS*, 9373, would indicate concern for the maintenance of the important road linking the camps along the Danube; the aqueduct of Aphrodisias is now attributed to Domitian alone by I. M. R. CORMACK, 'Epigraphic Evidence for the Water Supply of Aphrodisias', in *Ann. Brit. Sch. Ath.*, XLIX, 1954, pp. 9–10.

As for the army under Domitian, S. J. DE LAET, 'La préfecture du prétoire sous le haut empire et le principe de la collégialité,' in *Rev. Belg. Phil. Hist.*, XXII, 1943, pp. 73–95 (espec. 74–90 ff.; cf. the same scholar's 'Cohortes prétoriennes et préfets du prétoire au haut empire', *ibid.*, XXIII, 1944, p. 498 ff.), thinks that collegiality in the command of the praetorian guard was not restored but instituted by Domitian. This can be accepted if it is understood as the definitive fixing – henceforth established *de jure*, no longer just *de facto* – of a usage that had at first oscillated. On the rise in status of the praetorian prefects, who now begin to come normally from the prefectship of Egypt, and no longer *vice versa*, see A. PASSERINI, *Le coorti pretorie*, Rome 1939, p. 285 f. An example of such promotion under Domitian would be provided – if the above-mentioned theory of PIGANIOL (*Compt. rend. Ac. Inscr.*, 1947, pp. 376–86) is on the target – by L. Julius Ursus and L. Laberius Maximus (but they are not included in ENSSLIN's list in *P.W.*, XXII, 2, 1954, c. 2423). For other commands in war of the praetorian prefect, besides that of Cornelius Fuscus, and for the long stays in office even in the first century, cf. DE LAET, 'Les pouvoirs militaires des préfets du prétoire et leur développement progressif', in *Rev. Belg. Phil. Hist.*, XXV, 1946–7, pp. 509–54, espec. 517, 551. The old view of CICHORIUS (*Die römischen Denkmäler in der Dobrudscha, ein Erklärungsversuch*, 1904) that in the inscription at Adamklissi the name of the *praef. praet.* Cornelius Fuscus, who would have come from Pompeii, should be restored, a view frequently rejected (most recently by R. SYME, 'The Colony of Cornelius Fuscus, an Episode in the bellum Neronis', in *Am. Journ. Phil.*, LVIII, 1937, pp. 7–18), has been taken up again by J. COLIN, 'Le Préfet du Prétoire Cornelius Fuscus: un enfant de Pompei', in *Latomus*, XV, 1956, pp. 57–82, espec. 66 ff. The numerous military diplomas of Domitian's reign have been joined by another: R. THOUVENOT, 'Diplome militaire délivré par l'empereur Domitien (Valentia, Banasa, Maroc)', in *Compt. rend. Ac. Inscr.*, 1952, pp. 192–98 (= *CIL*, XVI, Suppl. 159, the oldest military diploma found in Morocco: 9 January 88). The diploma *CIL*, XVI, Suppl. 158, attributed to Domitian by the first editor, D. DETSCHEW, has been assigned to Titus by A. DEGRASSI (see above, p. 644). An interesting inscription is the one from Aquileia published by G. BRUSIN, in *Not. Sc.*, 1951, pp. 1–6 (= *AE*, 1952, 153) of a legionary *evocatus* (the only one to whom there is epigraphical testimony in the first century) of the XV *Apollinaris* legion, discharged by Domitian with a personal bounty of 30,000 sesterces, 'quod ante illum nemo alius accepit', evidently when the legion was already on the Danube. On the moving forward of the Pannonian legions to the Danube between 85 and 101, see G. ALFÖL, 'Die Truppenverteilung der Donaulegionen am Ende des I Jahrhunderts', in *Act. Arch. Ac. Sc. Hung.*, XI, 1959, pp. 113–41.

As for miscellaneous measures, on the rescript of Pergamum repealing the immunity granted to the rhetoricians by Vespasian, see R. HERZOG, in *Sitz.-ber. d. Preuss. Ak. d. Wiss.*, 1935, espec. pp. 1011-1018 (cf. above, p. 637). On Domitian's *congiaria* (A.D. 84, *Fast. Ost.* A.D. 89 and A.D. 93), A. DEGRASSI, *Inscr. It.*, XIII, 1, p. 221; G. BARBIERI, *Diz. Epigr.*, IV, p. 842.

On religious policy, the relationship established by Domitian between the imperial cult and the traditional religion, through the cult of Jupiter in particular, has been illustrated by A. MOMIGLIANO, 'Sodales Flaviales Titiales e culto di Giove', in *Bull. Comm. Arch.*, LXIII, 1935 (pub. 1938), pp. 165–71. On the *Ludi Capitolini*, see I. LANA, 'I ludi capitolini di Domiziano', in *Rev. Fil.*, XXIX, 1951, pp. 145–60. On the homages of poetry to the *dominus et deus*, F. SAUTER, *Der römische Kaiserkult bei Martial und Statius*, Stuttgart and Berlin 1934, espec. pp. 31–40, as well as K. SCOTT, *The Imperial Cult under the Flavians*, Stuttgart and Berlin 1936, pp. 61–75. Finally, on relations with Judaism, E. MARY SMALL-WOOD, 'Domitian's Attitude towards the Jews and Judaism', in *Class. Phil.*, LI, 1956, pp. 1–13, plays down the tradition of persecution. The ecclesiastical tradition about Domitian's persecutions of the Christians is not based on very secure foundations either: J. MOREAU, 'A propos de la persécution de Domitien', in *Nouv. Clio*, V, 1953 (Mél. Carnoy), pp. 121–9; M. GOGUEL, *Jésus et les origines du Christianisme*, Paris 1946, pp. 575–84.

THE WARS WAGED BY DOMITIAN

An admirable reconstruction of the war against the Chatti in 83 is to be found in H. NESSELHAUF, 'Tacitus und Domitian', in *Hermes*, LXXX, 1952, pp. 222–45, as well as a balanced analysis of the reasons for the hostility shown by the tradition, which distorted these foreign events in particular. H. BRAUNERT, 'Zum Chattenkriege Domitians', in *Bonner Jahrb.*, 153, 1953, pp. 97–101, advances the triumph right to the summer of 83 and dates the title *Germanicus* from 83, regarding as trustworthy the evidence of *P. Oxy.*, II, 331, *P. Flor.* III, 361, 12, *IGGR.*, I, 1138, and *RIC*, II, 158, 39, which is usually regarded as inadequate (WEYNAND, *P.W.*, VI, c. 2556). On the *vexillationes* of the army of Britain moved to Germany for the war of 83, DOMASZEWSKI ('Beiträge zur Kaiser-geschichte', IV, in *Phil.*, LXVI, 1907, pp. 164–70) referred the presence in Gaul, attested by *ILS*, 9200, of Velius Rufus in command of *vexillationes* of 9 legions, including the 4 British ones, to the time of Vespasian, and RITTERLING (*Oest. Jahresh.*, 1904, Beibl. p. 23), followed by SYME (*Cambr. Anc. Hist.*, XI, p. 163), referred it to this war and to the after-math up to 85. The latter view is shared by T. D. PRYCE and E. BIRLEY, 'The Fate of Agricola's Northern Conquests', in *Journ. of Rom. St.*, XXVIII, 1938, pp. 141–52 (espec. p. 151). Although we cannot be certain, it seems unlikely that Domitian would have taken detachments from *all* Agricola's legions without the fact being noted by Tacitus as proof of malicious behaviour (see above, p. 642 f.). On the renunciation of the permanent conquest of Caledonia, the traditional view that Domitian deliberately held back from the conquest in favour of more seriously threatened fronts is defended by T. D. PRYCE and E. BIRLEY, *art. cit.*, espec. pp. 142–4, in opposition to G. MACDONALD, ' "Britannia statim omissa" ', in *Journ. of Rom. St.*, XXVII, 1937, pp. 93–8, who thinks that the 'omissa' of TAC., *Hist.*, I, 2, 1 signifies 'left to look after itself' and that the withdrawal took place only under Trajan, towards 104–106. For the permanent establishment as early as the Flavian era of the legionary camps of Deva, Isca and Eburacum and the subsequent civil developments, see E. BIRLEY, 'The Status of Roman Chester', in *Rom. Brit. Rom. Army, cit.*, pp. 64–8. A recent study on the homelands of the Chatti is W. NIEMEYER's *Die Stammessitze der Chatten nach Bodenfunden und antiker Ueberlieferung, insbesondere bei Cl. Ptolemäus*, Kassel and Basle 1955, pp. 10 ff.; on Domitian's wars against the Chatti in general, on the alliance they made with Saturninus and on the constitution of the *limes*, see L. SCHMIDT, *Gesch. d. deutschen Stämme, Die Westgermanen*, II², 1,

Munich 1940, pp. 133–7. On the Germano-Raetian *limes*, the lasting consequence of the war and one of Domitian's most grandiose works in continuation of his father's frontier policy, see the surveys by W. SCHLEIERMACHER, 'Römische Archäologie am Rhein 1940 bis 1950', in *Historia*, II, 1953, pp. 94–100; also H. VON PETRIKOVITS's *Das römische Rheinland, Archäologische Forschungen seit 1945*, Cologne 1960, as well as U. KAHRSTEDT, 'Domitians Politik zwischen Donau und Main', in *Bonner Jahrb.*, 145, 1940, pp. 63–70, on the original project, subsequently abandoned, for a direct line of forts from the Danube to the middle Main; and, on the Lower Rhine frontier, *The Congress of Roman Frontier Studies 1949*, ed. E. BIRLEY, Durham 1952, pp. 41–54. On the development of relations between the people inside the empire and those outside as the physical boundary became more and more firmly fixed, see the surveys of A. ALFÖLDI, 'Rhein u. Donau in der Römerzeit', in *Jahresb. d. Gesellschaft pro Vindonissa*, 1948–9, pp. 3–19; 'Die ethische Grenzscheide am römischen Limes', in *Schweizer Beiträge zur allgemeinen Gesch.*, VIII, 1950, pp. 37–50 (cf. 'The Moral Barrier on Rhine and Danube', in *The Congress of Roman Frontier Studies, cit.*, pp. 1–16). The dating of Domitian's intervention in the conflict between the Chatti and the Cherusci and of the contacts with Cariomerus, king of the latter, mentioned by CASS. D., LXVII, 5, 1 is uncertain, but on the whole the chronology 90–92 suggested by BOISSEVAIN (III, p. 176) seems preferable to that of WEYNAND, c. 2565 (A.D. 85–87) in the context of the diplomatic activity in Germany that also embraces the relations with the Semnones and the Lugii. As for reflections of the German wars in poetry, J. ASBACH, in *Bonner Jahrb.*, LXXXI, 1886, pp. 44 ff. collected all the references to the Germans and to Domitian's expeditions in Latin poetry. See also H. HAAS, 'Die Germanen im Spiegel der römischen Dichtung vor und zur Zeit des Tacitus', in *Gymnasium*, LIV–LV, 1943–4, p. 73 ff., and S. JOHNSON, 'A Note on Martial VI, 82, 4–6', in *Class. Journ.*, XXXVIII, 1942, pp. 31–5 (cf. A. NORDH, 'Historical Exempla in Martial', in *Eranos*, LII, 1954, pp. 224–38).

The most recent general reconstructions of the wars on the Danube were carried out independently of each other (R. SYME, in *Cambr. Anc. Hist.*, XI, 1936, pp. 168–78, C. PATSCH, 'Der Kampf um den Donauraum unter Domitian und Trajan – Beiträge zur Völkerkunde von Südosteuropa V-2', in *Sitz.-ber. d. Akad. d. Wiss. in Wien*, Phil.-hist. Kl. 217, I, 1937, pp. 3–52; cf. the direction to p. 250), and the correspondences between them are therefore significant. For the Dacian war of 85–86, the *terminus ante quem* for Domitian's extended stay in Moesia is the inauguration of the *ludi capitolini* in the summer of 86. Whether or not he had celebrated a triumph depends on how we interpret STAT., *Silv.*, III, 3, 118. But everything is uncertain (WEYNAND, *P.W.*, VI, 2563, thinks he did; SYME, *CAH*, XI, p. 171, thinks not). The triumph may certainly have taken place if the activities and defeat of Fuscus are to be placed in 87, as PATSCH, p. 11, thinks, following E. KÖSTLIN, *Die Donaukriege Domitians*, Diss., Tübingen, 1910, pp. 59, 68. But the same year, 86, seems more acceptable for Fuscus's campaign; better to assume a delay after the defeat (87 would have been spent in preparations for the recovery) than after the successes of 86. As for the cenotaph of Adamklissi in the Dobruja (*ILS*, 9107), it may commemorate those who fell in Fuscus's battle, but probably not them alone; it does not even indicate the site of the battle, since Fuscus fought and was beaten on the far side of the Danube (cf. R. SYME, *art. cit.*, in *Amer. Journ. Phil.*, LVIII, 1937, p. 15): PATSCH (pp. 13–20) thinks the monument may have been built after the victory and peace of 89, at a spot where there must have been fighting on some earlier occasion, with Bastarni or Roxolani (taking advantage of the defeat of Oppius Sabinus?), as would appear from the barbarian types represented, which are different from the Dacians (PATSCH, pp. 20–5). See also J. COLIN, in *Latomus*, XV, 1956, pp. 63–71 and plate IV, with preceding bibliography, and most recently F. B. FLORESCU, 'Monumentul de la Adamklissi (Tropaeum Traiani)', *Acad. Rep. Pop. Rom.*, 1959, who once again attributes the whole monument to Trajan. On the end of the XXI *Rapax* legion, annihilation by the Sarmatians in 92 remains the most likely hypothesis (RITTERLING, *P.W.*, XII, c. 1789), even after the conjectures of J. J. HATT, in *Compt. rend. Ac. Inscr.*, 1949, pp. 40–6, and J. CARCOPINO, 'L'hérédité dynastique chez les Antonins', in *Rev. Ét. Anc.*, LI, 1949, p. 271, about its presence at Strasbourg in 97 (see below, p. 659). The *Bellum Marcomannicum*, mentioned separately from the Quadi and Sarmati (cf. *ILS*, 9200), is attested for the first time by an inscription from Leptis (*Inscr. Rom. Trip.*, 545) containing almost certainly the career of C. *Bruttius Praesens L. Fulvius Rusticus*, cos. II in 139, rewarded as tribune of Legion I *Minervia* 'ab imperatore Augusto (i.e. Domitian) ob bellum Marcomannicum', The title is thus attributed retrospectively from the age of Hadrian. It was not even known that the I *Minervia* or a *vexillatio* from it took part in the war. On the Dacian problem as a whole, see C. DAICOVICIU, *La Transilvania nell'antichità*, Bucharest 1943, espec. p. 65 f., and on the tribes on both sides of the Danube at this time A. ALFÖLDI, 'I Varciani della Pannonia meridionale ed i loro vicini', in *L'Ant. Class.*, XVII, 1948 (Mél. van de Weerd), pp. 13–18;

'Die Roxolanen in der Walachei', in *Berichte VI Intern. Kongress f. Arch.*, Berlin 1939, pp. 528–38. On Domitian's responsibility for the *limes* in the Dobruja, see A. FROVA, 'The Danubian Limes in Bulgaria, and Excavations at Oescus', in *The Congress of Rom. Frontier Studies, cit.*, p. 26. On Domitian's return to Rome in the early days of 94 rather than 93, see HANSLIK, in *Ann. Ép.*, 1941, 11, and W. REIDINGER, *Die Statthalter des ungeteilten Pannonien und Oberpannonien*, Bonn 1956, p. 137.

Attention has been drawn to eastern problems by the publication of the inscription from Baku (*AE*, 1951, 263), the easternmost Latin inscriptions so far known, dating from the years 84–96 and dealing with a centurion of Legion XII *Fulminata*, which had sent a detachment into the territory of the Albanians, probably on work analogous to that attested under Vespasian by the inscription from Harmozica (Tiflis; *ILS*, 8795): L. MORETTI, 'Due note epigraphice', in *Athen.*, XXXIII, 1955, p. 43; F. GROSSO, 'Aspetti della politica orientale di Domiziano, I', in *Epigraphica*, XVI, 1954 but published in 1956, pp. 117–79; II, *ibid.*, XVII, 1955 but published in 1957, pp. 33–78.

On Africa and the defence under Domitian of the land towards the interior gradually conquered and cultivated, see R. G. GOODCHILD, 'Oasis Forts of Legio III Augusta on the Routes to the Fezzan', in *Pap. Br. Sch. Rome*, XXII, 1954, pp. 56–68; J. BARADEZ, *Fossatum Africae*, Paris 1949, pp. 152 f.; P. ROMANELLI, *St. prov. rom Afr. cit.*, pp. 301–8.

THE REIGN OF NERVA

The figure of Nerva as an autocrat in the tradition of the Augustan principate, with a position more effectively independent of the Senate than is commonly accepted, seems to result from the re-examination of the tradition which I carried out in the monograph *Nerva*, Rome 1950, to which the reader is referred for the bibliography and all questions of detail. In fact Nerva's relationship with the Senate as a whole seems to have been simply the usual one of conventional deference, even if this deference was particularly stressed. This remains true whatever deductions may be drawn from an examination of the coinage (GENIUS SENATUS, PROVIDENTIA SENATUS), which can be interpreted within the limits of formal homage, without any need to see in it the Senate's claim, which was in any case not made good, to an effective sharing and division of power with the Princeps (A. ALFÖLDI, 'Insignien und Tracht der römischen Kaiser', in *Röm. Mitt.*, L, 1935, pp. 118 f.).

A new fragment of the *Fasti Ostienses* published by G. BARBIERI, 'Nuovi frammenti di Fasti Ostiensi', in *Studi Romani*, I, 1953, pp. 365–375, allows us to fix other consulships in the year 97 (cf. DEGRASSI, *Fasti Cons.*, p. 288, supplements, together with the review of this book by R. SYME, in *Journ. of Rom. St.*, XLIII, 1953, espec. pp. 150 and 159), and to obtain some indications on Nerva's activity – to confirm, for example, the accuracy of the attribution to him by CASS. D. LXVIII, 2, 4, of the veto on castration, where there was suspicion of confusion with the similar measure of Domitian's – and on the atmosphere of the reign, in connection with the presumably threatening wait by the armies (A. GARZETTI, 'Nerviana', in *Aevum*, XXVII, 1953, pp. 549–53; R. SYME, 'The Consuls of A.D. 97: Addendum', in *Journ. of Rom. St.*, XLIV, 1954, pp. 81 f.; cf. the same scholar's *Tacitus*, cit., pp. 1–18; 627–36). New dedications from Delphi (CH. DUNANT, 'Inscr. de Delphes', in *Bull. Corr. Hell.*, LXXVI, 1952, p. 627 = *AE*, 1953, 50) and from Histria (*SEG.*, XVI, 1959, no. 432). The most controversial question of Nerva's reign – that of financial activity – has been taken up again by G. BIRAGHI, 'Il problema economico del regno di Nerva', in *Par. Pass.*, VI, 1951, pp. 257–73. The same writer ('Di alcuni tipi monetari dell'impero di Nerva', in *Acme*, VI, 1953, pp. 489–96) takes the view that the maintenance of the coin types introduced by Domitian provides confirmation of the continuation of the Flavian policy on the part of Nerva. The institution by Nerva of the *alimentationes* as a state responsibility has recently been called into question by M. HAMMOND, 'A Statue of Trajan represented on the "Anaglypha Traiani"', in *Mem. Am. Acad. Rome*, XXI, 1953, pp. 147–53. The theory mentioned by J. J. HATT, 'Les récentes fouilles de Strasbourg (1947–48), leurs résultats pour la chronologie d'Argentorate', in *Compt. rend. Ac. Inscr.*, 1949, pp. 40–6, of a fire of Strasbourg caused by a legionary revolt (accepted by J. CARCOPINO, in *Rev. Ét. Anc.*, LI, 1949, p. 271; cf. *Nerva*, p. 38, n. 5), was taken up again by the same writer in 'L'incendie d'Argentorate en 96–97 ap. J.-C.; une révolte militaire ignorée dans les champs décumates sous Nerva', in *Compt. rend. Ac. Inscr.*, 1949, pp. 132–6, and in 'Essai de synthèse sur l'histoire et la topographie de Strasbourg romain', in *Misc. Galbrati*, II, Milan 1951, pp. 19–31. According to this theory, under Nerva there would have been five legions on the Upper Rhine, the I *Adiutrix* at Mainz, the VIII *Augusta* at Strasbourg, the XI *Claudia* at Vindonissa, and the XIV *Gemina* and XXI *Rapax* on the *limes*; the XXI would have rebelled and, crossing the *agri decumates*, fallen on Strasbourg, setting fire to everything. Trajan would have hastened from Mainz with the I *Adiutrix* and first defeated, then disbanded (acc. to Carcopino, in 97) the rebellious legion. Hence the probable origin of the epithet *Germanicus* for Nerva and Trajan. This is a pretty bold theory, not only because of the silence of Pliny but also because of the difficulty of accepting the presence of five legions on the Upper Rhine at this time (M. DURRY, 'Le bellum Suebicum de 97 et le Panégyrique de Pline', in *Mémorial d'un voyage d'études de la Soc. d'Antiq. d. Fr. en Rhénanie*, Paris 1953, pp. 197–200), as opposed to the still solid grounds advanced by Ritterling for the end of the XXI *Rapax* in 92 and the transfer to the Danube, not to return, of the I *Adiutrix*, at any rate from 83–85, and of the XIV *Gemina* from 92. In addition, the conception of the *limes* presupposed in Hatt's theory does not seem the most likely one (see NESSELHAUF, in *Hermes*, LXXX, 1952, p. 238) and the suggested origin of the title *Germanicus* is also out of tune with PLIN., *Pan.*, 9, 2 ('eidem, cum Germaniae praesideret, Germanici nomen hinc [from Rome] missum'). On the relations of Casperius Aelianus with Apollonius of Tyana and Nerva, see F. GROSSO, *art. cit.*, in *Acme*, VII, 1954, pp. 470–8.

As for the adoption of Trajan, besides the numerous references in the general studies of the constitutional and ideological development of the principate, for which this adoption unquestionably represents a moment of extreme interest (H. SIBER, 'Das Führeramt des Augustus', in *Abhandl. d. Sachs. Ak. d. Wiss.*, Phil.-hist. Kl. XLIV, 1940, 2, p. 82 f. on the juridical form of the adoption of Trajan; H. U. INSTINSKY, 'Consensus Universorum', in *Hermes*, LXXV, 1940, pp. 265–78, espec. 272 f. on the basis of real legitimacy conferred by the public consensus; L. WICKERT, 'Princeps und Basileus', in *Klio*, XXXVI, 1943, pp. 21 ff., on the question of the hereditary principle and of merit as the prevailing criteria in the succession – on which see also J. CARCOPINO, 'L'hérédité dynastique chez les Antonins', in *Rev. Ét. Anc.*, LI, 1949, pp. 262 ff.; W. ENSSLIN, 'Gottkaiser und Kaiser von Gottes Gnaden', in *Sitz.-ber. d. Bay. Ak. d. Wiss.*, Phil.-hist. Abt., 1943, 6, pp. 31–4, on the religious elements in the calling of Trajan to power; and finally L. WICKERT, 'Der Prinzipat und die Freiheit', in *Symbola Coloniensia I. Kroll oblata*, 1949, pp. 111–41, on the reconciliation of *libertas* and *principatus* under Nerva; cf. H. VOLKMANN's review of my *Nerva*, in *Gnomon*, XXIV, 1952, pp. 115 f.), in recent years scholars have taken up again the historiographical question of the priority of PLIN., *Pan.*, 7–8, or TAC., *Hist.*, I, 15–16 (Galba's speech on the adoption of Piso). The most recent commentaries on the panegyric have declared the problem insoluble (E. MALCOVATI, comm. on *Plinio il Giovani, Il panegyrico di Traiano*, Florence 1952,

p. 28) or effectively non-existent since the two authors wrote contemporaneously and in complete community of thought, depending as they did on the same source (the *A fine Aufidi Bassi* by Pliny the Elder, published by his nephew: M. DURRY, *Pline le Jeune, Panégyrique de Trajan*, Paris 1938, pp. 61–3). The priority of Pliny has been raised again by R. T. BRUÈRE, 'Tacitus and Pliny's Panegyricus', in *Class. Phil.*, XLIX, 1954, pp. 161–79, and that of Tacitus by K. BÜCHNER, 'Tacitus and Plinius über Adoption des römischen Kaisers', in *Rh. Mus.*, XCVIII, 1955, pp. 289–312. Finally H. GOETZE, 'Ein neues Bildnis des Nerva', in *Mitt. deutsch. arch. Inst.*, I, 1948, pp. 139–56, in the course of studying a new bust of Nerva, gives a useful list of all the portraits of him known to us.

THE REIGN OF TRAJAN. SUCCESSION AND ADOPTION. CHRONOLOGICAL PROBLEMS

The reconstruction of the reign of Trajan has always presented considerable problems because of the scarcity and fragmentary nature of the historico-narrative sources, notwithstanding the relative abundance of contemporary literary sources and of epigraphical evidence. On the other hand, the importance of Trajan's figure and of his work has recently stimulated efforts both to produce complete pictures of the reign and to fix details, on the basis of some new dates revealed by epigraphy. The most extensive general reconstruction is that of R. PARIBENI, *Optimus Princeps*, Messina 1926–7, but a stir was caused about the same time, because of the fresh points of view they respectively represented, by the treatments of W. WEBER, 'Trajan und Hadrian', in *Meister der Politik*, Stuttgart 1923, pp. 244 ff. (subsequently reprinted in *Röm. Herrschertum und Reich in II Jahrhundert*, Stuttgart 1937) and B. W. HENDERSON, *Five Roman Emperors*, Cambridge 1927. The former of these was intended to emphasize the despotic character of the reigns of Trajan and Hadrian – a concept just in itself, but exaggerated and obscured by the author with considerations influenced by an excessively psychological approach – while the latter aimed at a more concrete and traditional evaluation of the intentions and achievements of the emperors from Vespasian to Hadrian. The conflict between these two points of view recurs in the chapters on Trajan and Hadrian in the *Cambr. Anc. Hist.*, in which R. P. LONGDEN was responsible for the pages on Trajan (XI, 188–252) and W. WEBER for those on Hadrian (294–324) and the Antonines (325–92). The most recent discussion of the sources and of modern studies of Trajan is to be found in A. PASSERINI, *Il regno di Traiano* (lezione raccolte da M. SODRI),

Milan and Venice 1950. The chapters on Trajan in R. SYMES's *Tacitus*, pp. 30–58, 217–33, 785 ff., are also important. The review *Estudios Clasicos* (III, 1955) dedicated a whole issue to the centenary of Trajan's birth (bibliography compiled by A. MONTENEGRO DUQUE, pp. 25–38). The aspect of the reign which has attracted most attention lately is the Parthian war, on which see below.

As for the succession and the principle of adoption, problems which merge with those of the essence of the Trajanic principate and of the relations between Trajan and the Senate, the part assigned to senatorial initiative is tending to become more and more difficult to pin down. In the view of J. CARCOPINO, 'L'hérédité dynastique chez les Antonins', in *Rev. Ét. Anc.*, LI, 1949, pp. 262–321 (for Trajan in particular see pp. 271–85), the illusions which find their most explicit formulation in Pliny's Panegyric and which were long kept alive by Trajan were subsequently destroyed by the Emperor himself in his last few years. H. NESSELHAUF, 'Die Adoption des römischen Kaisers', in *Hermes*, LXXXIII, 1955, pp. 477–95, sees in the theory of adoption a concept that is genuinely despotic in character; M. HAMMOND, 'The Transmission of the Powers of the Roman Emperor', etc., in *Mem. Amer. Acad. Rome*, XXIV, 1956 (see pp. 86–90 in partic. for Trajan), while recognizing the Senate as the source of the imperial powers, accepts the continuous practical diminution of this reality, already in any case only a formal one. In fact the idea of the emperor's power as a personal and monarchical thing is particularly strong in the meticulous paternalism of Trajan (cf. on the whole problem F. M. DE ROBERTIS, 'Dal potere personale alla competenza dell'officio', in *St. Doc. Hist. Iur.*, VIII, 1942, p. 255–307): the bureaucratic automatism and the depersonalization of power in the functions are different things from the political direction, which was neither more nor less centralized and despotic than before. For the atmosphere of freedom, see CH. G. STARR, *Civilization and the Caesars*, Ithaca 1954, pp. 148–50, and CH. WIRSZUBSKI, *Libertas*. To define a succession of alternations in the relations between Trajan and the Senate is difficult (was there hostility from the Senate over the Dacian war, manifesting itself in Pliny's Panegyric, Ch. 16–17? cf. DURRY, *Comm.*, pp. 13 f.): all one can do is note a general basic cordiality. An attempt at finding polemical motifs of this sort in the coinage is to be found in C. GATTI, 'Motivi costituzionali nelle coniazione traianee', in *Acme*, IX, 1956, pp. 11–25.

The reconstruction of the reign's chronology, in which the coins, though varied and full of allusions to various events, do not give, as they usually do, a great deal of help, because of Trajan's few consulships and the constant omission of the *tribunicia potestas*, has received considerable assistance from epigraphical discoveries. The *Fasti Ostienses* have told us – if we accept G. BABIERI's conjectural reading of a new fragment (in *Studi Romani*, I, 1953, p. 374, cf. *AE*, 1954, 223) – the approximate date of the II *congiarium*, between 14 January and 13 February 103; and in addition the date of Trajan's departure for the second Dacian war (4 June 105). Moreover, the *Fasti Ostienses* and the diploma dated 11 August 106, published by C. DAICOVICIU, 'Neue Mitteilungen aus Dazien', in *Dacia*, VII–VIII, 1937–40, pp. 299–336 (*AE*, 1944, 57 = *CIL*, XVI, Suppl. 160; cf. A. DEGRASSI, 'Nuove iscriz. della Dacia', in *Epigr.*, IV, 1942, pp. 153–6), have fixed to 106 the end of the second Dacian war (as opposed to MOMMSEN in *CIL*, III, 550, who argued for 107). The dates of the inauguration of the baths on the Appian (22 June 109); of Trajan's aqueduct (24 June 109), of the 'Naumachia' (11 November 109), of the forum and Basilica Ulpia (1 January 112) and of the column (12 May 113) are all now certain. It is known that Marciana died in 112, on 29 August, and was deified at once, before the *funus censorium*, which took place on 3 September. On 29 August 112 Matidia received the title of Augusta. The date of the inauguration of the column (12 May 113) gives us a terminus *post quem* for the date of Trajan's departure for the Parthian campaign. The terminus *ante quem* can now only be October 113 (not 114), because the conferment of the title *Optimus*, received by Trajan in Armenia, is now confined within fairly precise limits (10 August–1 September 114: TH. FRANKFORT, *Trajan Optimus*. 'Recherche de chronologie', in *Latomus*, XVI, 1957, pp. 333 f.: cf. *AE*, 1957, 174). The conferment of the title *Parthicus* is fixed with precision by the *Fasti Ostienses* to 20–1 February 116. Many details of the shows given by Trajan in the years 107–109 and 112–113 have also been restored by the *Fasti Ostienses*. These and the *Fasti Potentini* (*Athenaeum*, XXVI, 1948, pp. 110–34), as well as military diplomas, have informed us of many consulships unknown to us before and resolved some problems, like that of the first consulship (A.D. 110) of L. Catilius Severus, previously placed in 115, with consequent difficulties for the identification of his governorship of Armenia. Another interesting point is G. BARBIERI's theory of a third *cos. III* in the year 100 (besides the ones already known, those of Julius Frontinus and Vestricius Spurinna), in connection with a new fragment of the *Fasti Ostienses* (*St. Rom.*, I, 1953, pp. 372 f.). On the consulship in 72 of Trajan's father, see J. MORRIS, 'The Consulate of the Elder Trajan', in *Journ. of Rom. St.*, XLIII, 1953, pp. 79–80. For his governorship of Syria

75–79, as given by a milestone from Palmyra, see above, p. 640. On the iconography of Trajan the elder, see S. STUCCHI, 'Il ritratto di Traianus Pater', in *Studi Calderini-Paribeni*, III, Milan 1956, pp. 527–40. On the question whether, out of deference to tradition, Trajan had begun to date his *tribunicia potestas* from 10 December, see M. HAMMOND, 'The Tribunician Day from Domitian through Antoninus', in *Mem. Am. Acad. Rome*, XIX, 1949, pp. 45–55 (probable, not certain). The fixing of the chronology concerns the campaigns in particular: the reconstructions of C. PATSCH, *Der Kampf um den Donauraum unter Domitian und Trajan*, Vienna 1937, on the Dacian wars (pp. 52–233), of J. GUEY, *Essai sur la guerre parthique de Trajan (114–117)*, Bucharest 1937, espec. pp. 39 ff., and F. A. LEPPER, *Trajan's Parthian War*, Oxford 1948, espec. pp. 28–96, on the Parthian war, are models in this kind of research.

TRAJAN'S ADMINISTRATION

So far as concerns the practical functioning of the republic in accordance with Trajan's will, Chapters 56–79 of Pliny's Panegyric pose various problems, particularly in connection with the system of elections. It is obvious that since Pliny was dealing with things that were well known he did not spread himself on constitutional details and consequently left many points obscure to us. On the other hand, it seems fairly clear that in practice senatorial independence amounted to very little. This observation concerns the Senate as a whole and as an organ of government, not individual senators, many of whom were also the highest officials of the empire and thus employed on practical duties of great importance. But we can see that in the solemn sittings of the Senate everything took place in a ceremonial atmosphere; nor should we give too much weight to the apparent divergences from normal usage in the elections of the supplementary consuls, the praetors, the aediles and the tribunes (*nominatio, commendatio*, vote: here the second and third of the three moments leading up to the *destinatio* are missing; cf. M. DURRY, *Pline le Jeune, Panégyrique de Trajan*, Paris 1938, pp. 241 f.). Apart from these variations on a reality that was always the same, namely the creation or at any rate the approval of the magistrates by the Princeps, the forms were nevertheless respected in the two fundamental Acts of *destinatio* (in the Senate) and *renuntiatio* (before the people), through which *destinatio* became *designatio*: H. SIBER, 'Die Wahlreform des Tiberius', in *Festschr. Koschaker*, I, 1939, pp. 171–217, V, 'Wahlen unter Trajan', pp. 199–210. The problem has been taken up again and thoroughly discussed most recently by M. L. PALADINI,

'Le votazioni del senato romano nell'età di Traiano', in *Athenaeum*, XXXVII, 1959, pp. 3–134; see also the same writer's 'Elezione dei magistrati al tempo di Plinio il Giovane e di Traiano: completamento al Campo Marzio della "destinatio" senatoriale', in *Homm. Herrmann* (Coll. Latomus, XLIV), Brussels 1960 pp. 571–83.

As for senatorial careers and fresh senatorial levies, especially in the provinces, quite a few new documents add interesting particulars to what was known already of the tendency to cosmopolitanism in the aristocracy itself, that is, in the class involved in governing at the highest level. Alongside the royal families of the East, which ended in the common crucible of the senatorial class (for the Herods, see A. H. M. JONES, *The Herods of Judaea*, Oxford 1938, p. 261; the consulship of C. Iulius Alexander Berenicianus has been confirmed by the *Fasti Ostienses* for the year 116), other people in every province founded, via the senatorial career, the noble status of their own family, with the dynastic character typical of the aristocracy of the empire. One among many characteristic examples is the family of the Quintilii, *PIR*, III, pp. 116 f., nos. 19–24, whose history can be followed for almost a century, from the Flavians to Commodus. For Greece, see J. A. O. LARSEN, 'A Thessalian Family under the Principate', in *Class. Phil.*, XLVIII, 1953, pp. 86–95, and for the Romanized families of Caria, L. ROBERT, *La Carie*, II, Paris 1954, p. 383. That the widening of the base of the aristocracy through service to the empire, a process already very much at work under the Flavians, continued under Trajan, with still greater elasticity and liberality, is demonstrated by numerous individual careers. Here are the details of recent discoveries in this field: H. SEYRIG, 'Heliopolitana', in *Bull. Mus. Beyrouth*, I, 1937, p. 80 (= *AE*, 1939, 60) gives the equestrian career, from *praefectus fabrum* to procurator of Belgica, of Sex. Attius Suburanus Aemilianus, Trajan's first praetorian prefect, who quickly became a senator and in 101 was already *cos. suff.* and in 104 *cos. ord.*; ED. FRÉZOULS, 'Inscription de Cyrrhus relative à Q. Marcius Turbo', in *Syria*, XXX, 1953, pp. 247–78 (= *AE*, 1955, 225) discusses the career of Q. Marcius Turbo, Hadrian's praetorian prefect and – another interesting point – moves back to Trajan the institution of the *praefectus vehiculorum*, previously attributed to Hadrian; E. MAREC and H. G. PFLAUM, 'Nouvelle inscription sur la carrière de Suétone, l'historien', in *Compt. rend. Ac. Inscr.*, 1952, pp. 76–85 (= *AE*, 1953, 73) deal with the career of Suetonius – this inscription, too, confirms the view suggested by other evidence that the definitive organization of the equestrian career had already been almost completed under Trajan, though this had normally been regarded

as the work of Hadrian. For other information about the service of provincials, see the inscription from Heraclea ad Salbacum of T. Statilius
Apollinaris, procurator of Lycia, Pamphylia and Cyprus under Hadrian
(BUCKLER and CALDER, *Mon. Asiae. Min. Ant.*, VI, 1939, p. 36, n. 97,
cf. ROBERT, *La Carie*, II, pp. 163 ff., in which there are also interesting
details about T. Statilius Crito, Trajan's doctor, and the family, pp. 223 ff.
with a new inscription, n. 75, = *AE*, 1955, 275); the dedication to
Plotina by a prefect of an ala, C. Iulius Serenus, at Lugdunum Convenarum
(A. AYMARD, 'Note sur des inscriptions de Lugdunum Convenarum',
in *Rev. Ét. Anc.*, XLIII, 1941, pp. 216–39); R. SYME's notes on Vibius
Maximus, prefect of Egypt from 103 to 107, which also deal with the
equestrian career in general and the relations between the two classes
('C. Vibius Maximus, Prefect of Egypt', in *Historia*, VI, 1957, pp. 480–7).
Interesting deductions about Trajan's criteria for employing men are
drawn, though in a different context, by H. BLOCH, in *Bull. Comm. Arch.*,
LXVI, 1938, pp. 184–8 (see below), in connection with M. Rutilius
Lupus, prefect of Egypt, who was, it seems, as is shown by the weight
from Ostia also published by Bloch (*AE*, 1940, 38), the same person as
M. Rutilius Lupus, the proprietor of *figlinae*, the first man to have the
date put on terracotta seals, and thus a technician. The Ostia weight,
certified 'cura M. Rutili Lupi prae(fecti) annonae' and datable between
103 and 111, also shows that the supervision of weights and measures had
already ceased under Trajan to be the function of the *praefectus urbi*. This
reform, too, had been generally regarded as due to Hadrian. To turn to
details, for the uncertainty about the identification of the *Maximus* of
PLIN., *Epist.*, VIII, 24, with *Sex. Quinctilius Valerius Maximus*, an
identification generally accepted, see M. N. TOD, 'The Corrector
Maximus', in *Anat. St. presented to W. H. Buckler*, Manchester 1939,
pp. 333–44. The exceptional grant of a career 'beneficio optimi principis'
to the citizen of Nîmes L. Aemilius Honoratus (*CIL*, XII, 3164) can
hardly be attributed to any emperor but Trajan (but see DESSAU, *ILS*,
1048 and GROAG, *P.I.R.²*, I, no. 350); for Pliny's career see A. N.
SHERWIN-WHITE, 'Pliny's Praetorship Again', in *Journ. of Rom. St.*,
XLVII, 1957, pp. 126–30; on other personalities of the period, see
R. SYME, 'The Friend of Tacitus', *ibid.*, pp. 131–5 (L. Fabius Iustus);
also the same scholar's 'The Jurist Neratius Priscus', in *Hermes*, LXXXV,
1957, pp. 480–93, and the small appendices in *Tacitus*, II, Oxford 1958,
pp. 625 ff.

As for Trajan's public works and the related questions of building
techniques and art in this reign, recent studies have made notable

contributions to our knowledge. We have already mentioned in the main text (p. 333) the theory that Trajan restored the *Aedes Castoris*, a theory based on stylistic considerations (A. VON GERKAN, 'Einiges zur Aedes Castoris in Rom', in *Rom. Mitt.*, LX–LXI, 1953–4, pp. 200–6). Roman building, for which the period of Trajan and Hadrian was one of great development, has been studied by H. BLOCH, 'I bolli laterizi e la storia edilizia Romana. Contributi all'archaeologia e alla storia romana' in *Bull. Comm. Arch.*, LXIV, 1936, pp. 141–225 (the Flavians and Trajan); LXV, 1937, pp. 83–187 (Hadrian); LXVI, 1938, pp. 61–221 (Hadrian, II, and up to the fourth century). See now G. LUGLI, *La tecnica edilizia romana*, Rome 1957 (for Trajan in particular, I, p. 436, 600 ff., etc.). The *Fasti Ostienses* have given us chronological details about Trajan's works in Rome, but the excavations round the forum and the basilica Ulpia (cf. G. LUGLI, *Roma antica, il centro monumentale*, Rome 1946, pp. 278–309) have revealed the substantial complex of Trajanic markets and provided the basis for the accurate mapping of a large tract of the city's topography. The greatest engineer and artist of Trajan's reign was Apollodorus of Damascus, who was probably responsible for the bridge over the Danube, the markets, the forum, the baths, the odeum (CASS. D., LXIX, 4, 1) and other Trajanic buildings, and also for the frieze on the column and the four panels now inserted in the arch of Constantine: see R. BIANCHI BANDINELLI, 'Un problema di arte Romana. Il maestro delle imprese di Traiano', in *Le Arti*, I, 1939, pp. 325–34 (R. PARIBENI, 'Apollodoro di Damasco', in *Rend. Acc. It.*, IV, 1942–3, pp. 124–30, tends to reduce the number of works to be attributed to Apollodorus). The column poses two main problems of interpretation: the first is that of its origin, with which is connected that of the inscription or the base, and the second is that of the significance of the figures, which is bound up with the chronological reconstruction of the Dacian wars. The most recent additions to the vast bibliography on the subject are the following: (*a*) On the problem of origin – J. DEN TEX, 'L'inscription de la colonne Trajane', in *Mededeelingen van het Nederlandsch historisch Institut te Rome*, VII, 1938, pp. 27–34 (proposes 'tant[is op]ibus sit egestus'); S. FERRI, 'Sull'origine della Colonna Traiana', in *Rend. Acc. Lincei*, XV, 1939, pp. 343–56 ('tant[is mol]ibus sit egestus'); L. SCHNITZLER, 'Die Trajanssäule und die mesopotamischen Bildannalen', in *Jahrb. d. deutsch. arch. Inst.*, LXVII, 1952, pp. 43–77 (suggests that the idea came from the East, via Apollodorus, who was certainly the creator of the column). (*b*) On the problem of historical interpretation: I. A. RICHMOND, 'Trajan's Army on Trajan's Column', in *Pap. Br. Sch. Rome*, XIII, 1935, pp. 1–40, maintains that the details of the clothes, arms, etc. derive from original sketches, translated into sculpture by the artist – which would make the historical value of the scenes high (K. LEHMANN-HARTLEBEN, in *Class. Phil.*, XXXIV, 1939, pp. 385 f., has some reservations); and a general study by G. LUGLI, 'Il triplice significato, topografico, storico e funerario della colonna traiana', in *Analele Academiei Romane*, Mem. sect. istor., III, 25, 20, Bucharest 1943–4. For the big frieze – probably commemorating the second Dacian war – in the same monumental precinct of the forum and its immediate surroundings, see M. PALLOTTINO, 'Il grande fregio di Traiano', in *Bull. Comm. Arch.*, LXVI, 1938, pp. 17–56, and, for other fragments possibly belonging to this frieze, G. PICARD, in *Mél. Éc. Fr. Rome*, 1939, pp. 136–50. See too C. PIETRANGELI, 'Rilievo funerario di Villa Medici', in *Bull. Comm. Arch.*, LXXI, 1943–5, pp. 117–22; A. PIGANIOL, 'Note sur un bas-relief de la Villa Médici', in *Homm. Bidez-Cumont*, Brussels 1949, pp. 265–70; and M. CAGIANO DE AZEVEDO, *Le antichità di Villa Medici*, Milan 1951, pp. 54–5. On the subject of the 'plutei di Traiano', the marble bas-relief in the forum, M. HAMMOND, 'A Statue of Trajan' represented on the 'Anaglypha Traiani', in *Mem. Am. Ac. Rome*, XXI, 1953, pp. 125–83, assigns it to the period of Hadrian and from a comparison with coins advances the ingenious theory that the scene of Trajan with the personification of Italy reproduces a piece of statuary dedicated towards 111 in the forum by the Senate and Roman people. A general bibliographic survey of Trajanic art, of which the historical friezes form such a large part, is given by CH. PICARD, 'Chronique de la sculpture étrusco-latine (1940–1950), Les principats de Trajan et d'Hadrien', in *Rev. Ét. Lat.*, XXX, 1952, pp. 318–47 (the surveys for the preceding periods are in the volumes for 1949, p. 234; 1950, p. 299; 1951, pp. 349 ff.). On the inauguration of Trajan's aqueduct, which also ran on the near side of the Tiber (on a *fistula* from Trajan's baths, see A. M. COLINI, in *Bull. Comm. Arch.*, LXVI, 1938, p. 245 = *AE*, 1940, 40) and helped to supply the baths on the Oppian, see H. BLOCH, 'Aqua Traiana', in *Amer. Journ. Arch.*, XLVIII, 1944, pp. 337–41.

Regarding public works, records of interventions and expressions of gratitude in Italy and the provinces, we shall give details here of the essential additions to the bibliography and the new documents of which account has been taken in the main text. On the arch of Trajan at at Beneventum, see A. PIGANIOL, 'Le décor de l'arc de Bénévent', in *Bull. Soc. Ant. de Fr.*, 1945–7, pp. 193 f.; J. SCERRATO, 'Un frammento dell'arco di Traiano a Benevento', in *Arch. Class.*, V, 1953, pp. 215–21;

J. BEAUJEU, *La relig. rom.*, Paris 1955, pp. 431–7 ('La signification de l'Arc. de Bénévent'). An arch at Pozzuoli may have also marked the completion of the road works (A.D. 103) and – in the view of J. KAEHLER, 'Der Trajansbogen in Puteoli', in *St. Robinson*, I, 1951, pp. 430–9 – of the harbour. A new milestone from the Via Traiana, the LXXV, 'A Benevento Brundisium', dating from 109, has come to light at Canne (M. GERVASIO, in *Iapigia*, IX, 1938, p. 401 = *AE*, 1945, 83). In the provinces, the sacred way from Miletus to Didyma has yielded a milestone from the year 100 (TH. WIEGAND, *Milet*, II, 3, Berlin and Leipzig 1934, p. 134 = *AE*, 1937, 258); the road between Philomelion and Caesarea Antiochia, in eastern Phrygia, has yielded another, possibly from A.D. 105 (W. M. CALDER, *Mon. As. Min. Ant. Ant.*, VII, 1956, p. 38, n. 193); yet another has come to light to the west of Palmyra, dating from 108–109 and hence earlier than the Parthian war (D. SCHLUMBERGER, 'Bornes milliaires de la Palmyrène', in *Mel. Dussaud*, II, Paris 1939, pp. 547–55 = *AE*, 1940, 210). A cippus of 102 refers to a delimitation of boundaries in Palmyrene territory (D. SCHLUMBERGER, 'Bornes frontières de la Palmyrène', in *Syria*, XX, 1939, pp. 43–73, espec. 52–61; cf. *AE*, 1939, 178). On the public works in Antioch which the late tradition explicitly attributes to Trajan, see G. DOWNEY, 'The Water Supply of Antioch-on-the-Orontes in Antiquity', in *Ann. Arch. de Syrie*, I, 1951, pp. 171–87, and the criticisms of G. SPANO, 'Il nimfeo del proscinio del teatro di Antiochia su l'Oronte', in *Rend. Acc. Lincei*, VIII, 7, 1952, pp. 144–74 (cf. R. H. CHOWEN, 'The Nature of Hadrian's Theatron at Daphne', in *Amer. Journ. Arch.*, LX, 1956, pp. 275–7). On the canals (including those in Egypt and the region of the Rhine), F. G. MOORE, 'Three Canal Projects, Roman and Byzantine', in *Amer. Journ. Arch.*, LIV 1950, pp. 97–111; the article takes as its point of departure the plan mentioned by PLIN., *Epist.*, X, 41, 61, to link the lake inland from Nicomedia with the sea. On the excavations in the numerous settlements founded in Trajan's reign, see H. V. PETRIKOVITS, 'Die Ausgrabungen in der Colonia Traiana bei Xanten. Die Ausgrabung der Kernsiedlung und der Uferanlagen (1934–36)', in *Bonner Jahrb.*, CLII, 1952, pp. 41–161. On the shores of the Black Sea, inscriptions from buildings at Callatis and Tyras testify to Trajan's attention (T. SAUCIUC-SAVEANU, 'L'empereur Trajan et la mer Noire', in *Revista Istorică Română*, XVI, 1946, pp. 119–28 = *AE*, 1950, 176). The new excavations at Histria have revealed the prosperity of the town, which received a new circle of walls under Domitian or Trajan (G. BORDENACHE, 'Il tempio greco di Histria', in *Par. Pass.*, XIII, 1958, pp. 195–201). As for honorific inscriptions probably recording interventions by the Emperor, in the East, at Güplüpmar, there is a dedication to Trajan by ephebes (G. IACOPI, *Esplorazioni e studi in Paflagonia e Cappadocia*, Rome 1937, pp. 41 f. = *AE*, 1941, 165); a base with dedication, earlier than 102, at Lebadia (J. JANNORAY, 'Nouvelles inscriptions de Lébadée', in *Bull. Corr. Hell.*, LXIV–LXV, 1940–1, pp. 36–59); and another at Athens, dating from between 97 and 102 (N. M. VERDÉLIS, 'Inscriptions de l'agora romaine d'Athènes', *ibid.*, LXXI–LXXII, 1947–8, pp. 39–46 = *AE*, 1950, 34). In Thrace there is a dedication to Trajan in the temple of Asclepios Zulmuzdrienos which is also interesting from the point of view of religious history (D. TSON-TCHEV, *Le sanctuaire thrace près du village de Batkoun*, Sofia 1941, cf. *Wiener Jahresh.*, XXXII, 1940, Beibl., c. 86 f. and *AE*, 1944, 77). In Africa there is a dedication dating from 98 at Sétif (P. MASSIÉRA, 'Inscriptions de Sétif et des environs', in *Bull. Com. Tr. Hist.*, Nov. 1947, pp. XV–XXII = *AE*, 1949, 42); one dating from 106–107 at Msaken (L. POINSSOT, 'Une dédicace à Trajan trouvée à Msaken', *ibid.*, March 1938, pp. VIII–XV = *AE*, 1938, 43); another in Trajan's baths at Acholla (possibly their dedication, G. PICARD, 'Acholla', in *Compt. rend. Ac. Inscr.*, 1947, pp. 557–62, cf. *AE*, 1948, p. 45, and 1949, p. 19 – an important inscription because it resolved the problem of the whereabouts of Acholla = Botria); and there are also the new fragments from Leptis Magna (*Inscr. Rom. Trip.*, 353: arch, A.D. 109–110; 355: dedication in the *forum vetus*, later than 102).

In the field of economic policy and financial administration it is certainly difficult to decide how far one can speak of *dirigisme* in connection with Trajan. In fact the limits of general paternalistic care were not exceeded by the alleged propaganda for a 'return to the land' (for which Dio Chrysostom served as mouthpiece, according to P. MAZON, 'Dion de Pruse et la politique agraire de Trajan', in *Compt. rend. Ac. Inscr.*, 1943, pp. 74 and 85–6); by the practical organization of loans for agriculture, the aim of which was purely to render assistance (*alimenta*, cf. H. U. INSTINSKY, 'Zur Interpretation der Tabula Traiana', in *Wiener Jahresh.*, XXXV, 1943, Beibl., cc. 33–8; P. VEYNE, 'La Table des Ligures Baebiani et l'institution alimentaire de Trajan', in *Mél. Éc. Fr. Rome*, LXIX, 1957, pp. 81–135); or by the regulations for the imperial domains (see the extensive commentary by CH. SAUMAGNE on the inscr. from Henchir-Metlich of 117 – the *lex fundi Villae Magnae* – in the edition by COURTOIS, LESCHI, PERRAT and SAUMAGNE of the *Tablettes Albertini*, Paris 1952, pp. 116–41). For landed property and the conditions obtaining on it and for every problem to do with agriculture in

Italy, see V. A. SIRAGO, *L'Italia agraria sotto Traiano*, Louvain 1958, partic. pp. 3–59 and 275–303 (on the *tabulae alimentariae*). Nor is the development of trade necessarily attributable more to Trajan's planning (some scholars think it was the principal cause of the Parthian campaign; see J. GUEY, *Essai sur la guerre parthique de Trajan*, Bucharest 1937, pp. 20–6) than to the spontaneous increase deriving from the general conditions – which were, of course, improved thanks to Trajan. The fact remains that precisely in Trajan's reign eastern trade did expand considerably, to such an extent as to change relations and conditions of life along the whole frontier system. Palmyra, already incorporated in practice in the empire in the Flavian era – if the recruitment of cohorts of *sagittarii Palmyreni* began towards 95 (G. FORNI, 'Contributo alla storia della Dacia romana', in *Athen.*, XXXVI, 1958, p. 20) – attained its greatest importance at this period and its direct trade extended as far as the Aegean (G. LEVI DELLA VIDA, 'Une bilingue gréco-palmyrènienne à Cos', in *Mel. Dussaud*, II, Paris 1938, pp. 883–6). It was ROSTOVTZEFF, with his *Caravan Cities*, Oxford 1932, who opened the discussion on the subject, with the simultaneous publication of a group of inscriptions ('Inscriptions caravanières de Palmyre', in *Mel. Glotz*, II, pp. 792–811), which were later joined by others (SEYRIG, in *Syria*, XXII, 1941, pp. 223–70). The names of Palmyrene merchants and notables of the second century (M. Ulpius Soados, M. Ulpius Iahrai) are certainly indicative of fairly close relations with Rome in the period of Trajan (E. WILL, 'Marchands et chefs de caravanes à Palmyre', in *Syria*, XXXIV, 1957, pp. 262–77). For the interpretation of the corrupt passage in FRONTO, *Princ. Hist.*, 17, p. 209 NABER = p. 109 VAN DEN HOUT, in the sense that Trajan attended personally to the establishment of the posts of the *portorium* on the Tigris and Euphrates, see DE LAET, *Portorium*, Bruges 1949, p. 339; cf. also H. G. PFLAUM, *Procur. équestres*, Paris 1950, pp. 107–9.

An attempt at a comprehensive reconstruction of the state finances in the time of Trajan is to be found in R. KNAPOWSKI, 'Das Aerarium Saturni oder der Schatz des römischen Volkes. Untersuchung über das römische Finanzwesen zur Zeit Trajans', in *Bull. International de l'Acad. Polonaise des Sc. et des Lettres de Cracovie*, Cl. de Philol., d'Hist. et de Philos. 1938, pp. 125–33 (it is interesting to note that under Trajan there was already a hierarchy of posts, even senatorial ones, based on the remuneration for them). Examples of quite ordinary administrative measures are the so-called *Horothesia Laberii Maximi* of inscription *SEG*, I, 329, published by V. PARVAN and now republished with rectifications and new observations by D. M. PIPPIDI, 'La "Horothesia Laberii Maximi"[1] (Quarante ans après sa découverte)', in *Studii si cercetări de istorie veche*, VII, 1956, pp. 137–58 (cited above, p. 620), and the confirmation of immunity to the doctors of the Museion of Ephesus (J. KEIL, in *Forschungen in Ephesos*, IV, 1, 1932, p. 81; the inscription, dating from Trajan's time, may possibly contain simply a reference to a privilege already in existence, at any rate since the Augustan period, CASS. D., LIII, 30). On the procedure and limits of validity in general of Trajan's measures in regard to the provinces, see E. VOLTERRA, 'L' efficacia delle costituzione imperiali emanate per le provinciè e l'istituto della espositio', in *Studi Besta*, I, Milan 1939, pp. 447–77, an article hingeing on PLIN., *Epist.*, X, 65–6.

On the provinces, the Bithynian inscription copied by RADET and published by L. ROBERT, 'Inscriptions de Bithynie copiées par G. Radet', in *Rev. Ét. Anc.*, XLII, 1940 (Mél. Radet), pp. 302–22 (n. 16, p. 319 = *AE*, 1941, 129), offers some evidence for fixing the boundaries between Asia and Bithynia under Trajan. As for Pliny's governorship of Bithynia, though its duration is known it is not yet possible to decide between the limits autumn 110–spring 112 and autumn 111–spring 113 (D. MAGIE, *Roman Rule in Asia Minor*, II, Princeton, N.J. 1950, p. 1454). According to L. VIDMAN, 'Zur Frage der Vollständigkeit des Briefwechsels des Plinius mit Trajan', in *Listy Filologické* (Prague), V, 1957, pp. 21–30, the correspondence in Book X is more complete than might be thought. On the tendency to employ military garrisons in the interior of provinces – a tendency which we know from the X book of Pliny's letters to have been opposed by Trajan – it is interesting to note the permanent presence of an auxiliary cohort in Macedonia after the Dacian wars (R. K. SHERK, 'Roman Imperial Troops in Macedonia and Achaea', in *Amer. Journ. Phil.*, LXXVIII, 1957, pp. 52–62). A noteworthy group of military diplomas from Trajan's reign has been restored to us recently by excavations: *CIL*, XVI, Suppl. 160 (from Porolissum, Dacia, 11 August 106, cf. above, p. 663); 161 and 162 (from Valentia Banasa, Mauretania, both dated 14 October 109, but for quite different units, THOUVENOT, *AE*, 1936, 70 and 1952, 46. On the first of these, cf. H. NESSELHAUF, 'Zur Militärgeschichte der Provinz Mauretania Tingitana', in *Epigraphica*, XII, 1950, pp. 34–48). Suppl. 163 and 164 (same date, 2 July 110, the first from Porolissum, published by C. DAICOVICIU, in *Dacia*, VII–VIII, 1937–40, p. 333 f. = *AE*, 1944, 58; the second from the neighbourhood of Brigatio, Pannonia). Suppl. 165 (from Valentia Banasa, between 114 and 117, THOUVENOT, *AE*,

1952, 47). What is interesting in connection with the units employed in Dacia by Trajan, though it dates from Hadrian's reign, is the diploma published by C. DAICOVICIU, in *Studii si cercetări de istorie veche*, IV, 1953, pp. 541 ff. and now provided with an ample commentary by G. FORNI in the article cited in *Athen.*, XXXVI, 1958, p. 9 (cf. *CIL*, XVI, Suppl., p. 215, n. 68). The diploma already cited, *CIL*, XVI, Suppl. 160 is also important because it bears witness for the first time to the *civitas* granted to auxiliaries 'ante emerita stipendia'. On the Romanization of the Danubian lands, which reached a decisive point under Trajan, see B. GEROV, 'La romanisation entre le Danube et les Balkans, I: d'Auguste à Hadrien' (Bulg. with French summary), in *Ann. Univ. Sofia*, Fac. hist.-philol., XLV, 4, 1949. The same scholar's 'Nouvelles données sur le début de l'histoire d'Oescus', in *Rev. Phil.*, XXIV, 1950, pp. 146–65, espec. 158 ff., 'Oescus, camp de la XI légion Claudienne pendant le règne de Trajan', shows the camp becoming (in the last years of Trajan's reign) a Latin-speaking town, while the not far distant Nicopolis was Greek, though it characteristically retained a military garrison consisting of a detachment from Legion I *Italica*, stationed at Novae. A good deal of light has now been thrown on Oescus by the excavations (A. FROVA, 'The Danubian Limes in Bulgaria, and Excavations at Oescus' in *The Congress of Roman Frontier Studies 1949*, Durham 1952, pp. 22–30). On the subject of the brief duration in the names of Asian towns of honorifics to Trajan, perhaps simply in connection with his passing through them for the Eastern expedition, in comparison with the numerous foundations in Thrace and Moesia which preserved it tenaciously, see L. ROBERT, *La Carie*, II, Paris 1954, pp. 222–5. On the life of Greeks in general under the Roman dominion, in the conditions particularly attested for Trajan's age (Plutarch, Dio Chrysostom, etc.), see H. BENGTSON, 'Das politische Leben der Griechen in der römischen Kaiserzeit', in *Welt als Geschichte*, X, 1950, pp. 86–97. According to the editor of the inscription from Attaleia (Adalia), E. BOSCH, in *Türk Tarih Kurumu*, Belleten XI, 1947, pp. 88–125, n.19, a settlement of 3000 veterans, under the leadership of a *primus pilus* of Legion III *Cyrenaica* expressly commissioned by Trajan, took place towards 110. This view is based on a connection with coins (STRACK, 120) bearing the image of Ammon. H. G. PFLAUM (cf. *Rev. Ét. Gr.*, LXI, 1948, p. 201) considers it more sensible to place the repopulation of Cyrene ordered by Trajan after the Jewish revolt, and thus towards the end of the reign (in this case the suppression of the revolt at Cyrene too would also have occurred before the end of Trajan, see below; but it still seems difficult to imagine that 3000 soldiers were all discharged together from the same legion, when this legion, the III *Cyrenaica*, was engaged in the war. There is also the additional fact in favour of an earlier dating that the Hadrianic inscriptions – cf. s. APPLEBAUM, in *Journ. of Rom. St.*, XL, 1950, pp. 88–90 – and OROS., VII, 126 mention a city found abandoned by Hadrian, and repopulated and restored by him). For documents on municipal rights from the Flavian period or that of Trajan (use of terms which fade away from the reign of Hadrian onwards), see V. ARANGIO RUIZ and A. VOGLIANO, 'Tre rescritti in tema di diritto municipale', in Athen., XX, 1942, pp. 1–10. As for a supposed enlargement of the *pomerium* as a result of the conquest of Dacia, this theory, deduced from the alleged confirmation that a coin with the inscription '*cos. V*' (103–111) is supposed to lend to SCRIPT. HIST. AUG., *V. Aurel.* 21 (L. LAFFRANCHI, in *Bull. Comm. Arch.*, XLVII, 1919, pp. 35–8) has been rejected for valid reasons by STRACK, *op. cit.*, p. 129 ff. (cf. MATTINGLY, *Coins of the Rom. Emp. in the Br. Mus.*, III, 1936, p. C f.).

For the cultural, intellectual and religious climate of the society of Trajan's day, see G. CARCOPINO, *Daily Life in Ancient Rome*, London 1941. On Pliny the Younger, a typical representative of aristocratic society of the time, E. DE SAINT DENIS, 'Pline le Jeune et l'éducation de la jeunesse', in *Rev. Universitaire* (Paris), LV, 1946, pp. 9–21; H. W. TRAUB, 'Pliny's Treatment of History in Epistolary Form', in *Trans. Proc. Am. Phil. Ass.*, LXXXVI, 1955, pp. 213–32. On Trajan's own standard of culture and on the epigram (*Anth. Pal.*, XI, 418) attributed to him and containing a metrical error, O. WEINREICH, 'Ein Epigramm des Kaisers Traian und sein literarisches Nachleben', in *Antike*, 1941, pp. 229–48. The much-discussed question of the religious feeling of the period has now been surveyed by J. BEAUJEU, in *La religion romaine à l'apogée de l'empire. I: La politique religieuse des Antonins (96–192)*, Paris 1955. Trajan's reign is dealt with in pp. 58–110, where the three basic points of his religion are brought out clearly: an imperial theology, but one without mysticism; deference to the traditional religion, with the usual attitude of political prudence and private scepticism; and benevolent tolerance for foreign religions. On the 'imperial theology', see H. MATTINGLY, 'The Imperial Vota', in *Proc. Brit. Acad.*, XXXIV, 1950, pp. 155–95 and XXXVII, 1953, pp. 219–68. The concept of assimilation to the sun, in the form of 'kosmokrator', is viewed as only a hypothesis by FR. CUMONT, 'Trajan "kosmokrator"?' in *Rev. Ét. Anc.*, XLII, 1940 (Mél. Radet), pp. 408–11, and in any case refers only to the cult in the East. On the attitude to foreign religions, J. FERRON, 'Dédicace latine à Baal-Hammon', in *Byrsa*, III, 1953, pp. 113–19, provides testimony to the peaceful survival of the indigenous cults in Roman Africa. This last heading covers the problem of relations with Christianity (bibliography up to 1955 in BEAUJEU, *op. cit.*, pp. 106–9: up to 1953, on the whole problem of relations between Christianity and the Roman empire, in L. DE REGIBUS *Politica e religione da Augusto a Costantino*, Genoa 1953, pp. 169–86), which for Trajan's reign can almost be reduced to the interpretation of PLIN., *Epist.*, X, 96–7. This document, in connection with which there has also been a question – now settled – of authenticity (but see still, on alleged interpolations, L. HERRMANN, 'Les interpolations de la lettre de Pline sur les Chrétiens', in *Latomus*, XIII, 1954, pp. 343–5), bears witness to a compromise solution – in contradiction with logic, but explicable as a piece of political pragmatism – between the demands of order and security on the one hand and feelings of benevolence and humanitarianism on the other, with local conditions taken into account as well. On the whole scholars have agreed on this position, but there is still controversy about the pre-existence – referred to above (p. 615) – of a precise law on the subject (the *institutum Neronianum*, or some other one). BEAUJEU (p. 107) accepts the existence of this law; DE REGIBUS, followed by A. RONCONI, 'Tacito, Plinio e i Cristiani', in *Studi Paoli*, Florence 1955, pp. 615–28 (and preceded, but more tentatively, by H. GRÉGOIRE, 'Les persécutions dans l'empire romain', in *Mém. Ac. Roy. Belg.*, Cl. Lettr., tom. XLVI, 1950, pp. 25, 144 ff.) rejects it (pp. 65–70, 78), and with good reason. For in fact, if we stick to Pliny's text, it does not seem likely that Trajan could have written 'neque enim in universum aliquid quod quasi certam formam habeat constitui potest' if there had been the possibility of an explicit appeal to a precise law (cf., e.g. *Epist.*, 109). Moreover, and still more strangely, nothing is known of such a law by Pliny, whose enquiries so often centre precisely round the interpretation of a law. Sometimes (*Epist.* 114) he discovers and sends to the imperial chancellery copies of laws it has forgotten. The empirical and discretionary nature of Pliny's operations – he is always concerned to act with equity – is examined from the legal angle by TH. MAYER-MALY, 'Der rechtsgesschichtliche Gehalt der Christenbriefe von Plinius und Trajan', in *St. Doc. Hist. Jur.*, XXII, 1956, pp. 311–28. On obstinacy as an attitude particularly liable to incur punishment, see I. KNOX, 'Pliny and I Peter, A note on I Pet. IV, 14–16 and III, 15', in *Journ. Bibl. Lit.*, LXXII, 1953, pp. 187–9. Finally, on the economic background to the hatred of the Christians, see W. PLANKL, 'Wirtschaftliche Hintergründe der Christenverfolgungen in Bithynien', in *Gymn.*, IX, 1953, pp. 54–6.

On the intellectual and cultural advance of Christianity in the age of Trajan and on the reactions of the traditional culture, L. HOMO, *De la Rome paienne à la Rome chrétienne*, Paris 1950; M. PELLEGRINO, 'La cultura cristiana nei primi secoli', in *Convivium*, NS. I, 1954, pp. 257–70; C. CURTI, 'Luciano e i Cristiani', in *Misc. St. Lett. Crist. Ant.*, Catania 1954, pp. 86–109.

THE WARS OF TRAJAN

Trajan's external activities pose two problems, that of reconstructing the general policy and that of reconstructing the physical sequence of events. The answer to the first of these problems seems to be that Trajan, having inherited a fluid situation on the Danubian front and having discovered that Domitian's kind of settlement (war of 101–102, concluding with the restoration of a client state in Dacia) was unstable, had recourse to the radical and final solution of annexation (war of 105–106), within the limits strictly necessary for the security of the empire. This experience and the prosecution of the Flavian programme of stable and organized defence in the East (Cappadocia–Syria line) may have determined the conduct of the Parthian campaign, which was nevertheless confined by Trajan himself within the limits imposed by circumstances and the means at his disposal. In spite of the enthusiasm of contemporaries, Trajan was not primarily the conquering, warrior emperor, as is evident from what we know about his character and the real nature of his activity, nor was imperialism for its own sake the main element in his policy. Pliny's words, 'non times bella nec provocas' (*Pan.*, 16, 1), best express the idea behind Trajan's foreign policy (for Trajan represented in a statue as the solver of the Parthian problem along traditional Augustan lines, see G. M. A. HANFMANN and C. C. VERMEULE, 'A New Trajan', in *Amer. Journ. Arch.*, LXI, 1957, pp. 223–53). The physical reconstruction of the events presents the usual difficulties that arise from the scarcity and fragmentary nature of the sources, although some recent comprehensive studies have produced, for both the Dacian and Parthian wars, fairly satisfactory solutions. The basic works are those already cited (see above, p. 656): that of C. PATSCH (1937) for the Dacian wars and those of J. GUEY (1937) and F. A. LEPPER (1948) for the Parthian war. All of them now need to be supplemented by the results of subsequent research into various details.

Apart from the two main theatres of war little is known of Trajan's military operations. In Britain something that needs explanation is the disappearance of Legion IX *Hispana*, which is not mentioned any more after 108. Some kind of fighting may have broken out even before the war in progress when Hadrian came to the throne, although the disappearance of the legion, for the decisive reasons advanced by RITTER-LING, *P.W.*, XII, c. 1668 f. – to which can be added the evidence of *CIL*, V, 7159 – could be brought down to Hadrian's reign, and not even its early years (E. BIRLEY, *Roman Britain and the Roman Army*, Kendal 1953, pp. 20–30; 'Britain after Agricola, and the End of the Ninth Legion' = *Durham Univ. Journ.*, 1948, pp. 78–83, on the *bellum Britannicum* of a hitherto unpublished inscription from Cyrene; cf. *AE*, 1951, 88). That the operations on the Rhine and Danube looked like a real *bellum Germanicum* during the reign of Nerva and the first few months of Trajan, so that the centurion and later prefect of a legion of the Tunisian inscription *AE*, 1923, 28 is called 'd(onis) d(onatus) ab. imp. Caes. Traiano Aug. Germanico, bello Germanico', is not contradicted by what we know from other sources (PLIN., *Pan.*, 8, 2, 'adlata erat ex Pannonia laurea . . .'; cf. 9, 23, on the epithet Germanicus assumed both by Nerva and Trajan). As for the preparations and movements of forces for the Dacian wars, the transfer in 101 or 102 at the earliest from the Rhine to the Danube of Legion I *Minervia* (RITTERLING, in *P.W.*, XII, 1925, c. 1426; SYME, 'The First Garrison of Trajan's Dacia', in *Laureae Aquincenses Kuzsinszky dicatae*, I, 1938, p. 273, n. 28) may be disputable in view of *Inscr. Rom. Trip.*, 545, provided that it is not just a matter there of a *vexillatio* (on the caution to be observed in the identification of military units in the figures on the column, see above, p. 664, in connection with I. A. RICHMOND, *Trajan's Army*, etc.). For the Roman roads and fortifications, PATSCH, *op. cit.*, pp. 57–9, and for those of Decebalus, DAICOVICIU, *La Transilvania nell'antichità* Bucharest 1943, p. 74 f. W. ENSSLIN, 'Zu den symmachiarii', in *Klio*, XXXI, 1938, pp. 365–70, is inclined to bring down to the time of Maximinus Thrax the existence of the Asturian *symmachiarii* of inscription *AE*, 1926, 88, which DESSAU assigned to the period of Trajan because of the mention of a *bellum Dacicum* (in *Klio*, XX, 1925, p. 222). So far as the men who made a name for themselves in the war are concerned, the Moor Lusius Quietus – literary references to whom are few and confused and epigraphical references completely absent (which is rather strange in view of the high rank he attained) – has been the centre of a controversy about his country of origin (J. CARCOPINO, 'L'homme de Qwrnyn', in *Istros*, I, 1934, pp. 5–9; A. JORDANESCU, *Lusius Quietus*, Bibliothèque d'Istros, III, Bucharest 1941, p. 86; W. DEN BOER, 'The Native Country of L.Q.', in *Mnem.*,

IV, 1, 1948, pp. 327–37; A. G. ROOS, 'Lusius Quietus again', *ibid.*, IV, 3, 1950, pp. 158–65; W. DEN BOER, 'L. Q. an Ethiopian', *ibid.*, pp. 263–7; A. G. ROOS, 'L. Q., A Reply', *ibid.*, pp. 336–8; W. DEN BOER, 'Lusius Quietus, III', *ibid.*, pp. 339–43). On the conduct of the war, the most noteworthy point in which PATSCH'S reconstruction (followed here in the main text) diverges from earlier ones (particularly that of C. CICHORIUS, *Die Reliefs der Traianssäule*, Berlin 1896–1927, still a fundamental work) consists in its making contemporaneous – in the late autumn of 101 – the action before the Iron Gate and the action in Moesia to repel the diversionary Dacian invasion (pp. 64–7). On the route followed by Trajan to the theatre of war in 105, according to DEGRASSI a departure from Ancona can be ruled out; the arch really dates from 115 (see A. DEGRASSI, 'La via seguita da Traiano nel 105 per recarsi in Dacia', in *Rend. Pont. Acc. Arch.*, XXII, 1946–7, pp. 167–83; cf. PATSCH, *op. cit.*, pp. 95 f.; H. STUART JONES, in *Pap. Br. Sch. Rome*, V, 1940, pp. 444 f.). The same view is taken by CH. PICARD, 'Brundisium. Notes de topographie et d'histoire', in *Rev. Ét. Lat.*, XXXV, 1957, pp. 285–303. For the first military occupation of Dacia, from 107–113, see the above-mentioned article by SYME, and now also the article by G. FORNI, in *Alten.*, XXXVI, 1958, espec. pp. 39–44, and C. DAICOVICIU, 'Dacia capta. Zur Frage der Eroberung und ursprünglichen Organisation Dakiens', in *Klio*, XXXVIII, 1960, pp. 174–84. On the Romanization of Dacia and the fact, easily neglected by historians unfamiliar with the locality (attention is called to this by DAICOVICIU, p. 74), that the Roman colony of Sarmizegetusa did not arise on the site of Decebalus's capital – granted that the latter had a proper capital and not a mere citadel in a system of fortifications resting against the mountains – see V. BUESCU, 'Sarmizegetusa dans la topographie dacoroumaine', in *Rev. Fac. Letr. Lisboa*, XV, 1949, 1. In the view of W. G. FLETCHER, 'The Dacian Cities of Trajan', in *Trans. Proc. Am. Phil. Ass.*, LXXII, 1941, p. XXXI, strategic aims are clearly predominant in Trajan's foundations in Dacia. K. K. KLEIN, *Vallum Traiani*. 'Die Anlage der Trajanswälle in der Dobrudscha und die Goteneinfälle des vierten Jahrhunderts', in *Natalicium C. Jax oblatum*, Innsbruck 1955, pp. 103–9, is mainly concerned with the fourth century, but he touches on the question of the Trajanic origin of the *limes* in the Dobruja. On the civil and social relations between the conquerors and the native inhabitants, see the survey by A. ALFÖLDI, *Daci e Romani in Transilvania*, Budapest 1940.

On Trajan's interest in the East, as a result of the intensification of trade and the development of the new political relations already promoted by the Flavians, some interesting pieces of evidence have come to light. The annexation of Arabia in 105–106 was probably peaceful: coins bear the legend *Arabia adquisita.*, not *capta*, and Trajan did not receive the title *Arabicus* (cf. A. BLANCHET, 'La figure de l'Arabie dans les monnaies de Trajan', in *Compt. rend. Ac. Inscr.*, 1944, pp. 229–37). The step was taken when in the natural process of transition from client kingdom to direct rule – a process at work since the time of Augustus – the hour struck for the old Nabataean kingdom as well. Petra and Bostra, the chief cities, at once became links in a wider system of commercial and strategic communications. The milestones from the road running from Aqaba via Petra to Bostra, bearing the names of Trajan and the governor, C. Claudius Severus, date from 111 at the earliest, but the two letters sent by an Egyptian soldier, Apollinarius, to his father and mother, one of them bearing the date 26 March 107, show that the construction work was already in progress then. Apollinarius says that while the others were breaking stones (obviously for the road) he had been made an assistant secretary to the governor, Claudius Severus, and was getting ready to depart, probably from Petra, for Bostra, the capital of the province (CL. PRÉAUX, 'Une source nouvelle sur l'annexion de l'Arabie par Trajan: les papyrus de Michigan 465 et 466', in *Phoibos*, V, 1950–1 [Mél. Hombert], pp. 123–39; but the deductions about the presence in Arabia and Syria of the Egyptian legions or big detachments from them so many years before the Parthian war are exaggerated). Research into the Arabian-Syrian *limes* and the cities has yielded further information; cf. A. STEIN, 'Une récente exploration en Transjordanie', in *Compt. rend. Ac. Inscr.* 1939, pp. 262–8; R. E. M. WHEELER, 'The Roman Frontier in Mesopotamia', in *The Congress of Roman Frontier Studies 1949*, ed. E. BIRLEY, Durham 1952, pp. 112–29; on the territory of Bostra, A. ALT, 'Das Territorium von Bostra', in *Beiträge zur bibl. Landes – u. Altertumskunde*, LXVIII, 1946–51, pp. 235–45; on Palmyra, see above, p. 671, and on Hatra – the city which, probably under a Sanatruq (whose possible connection with the Arsacid Sanathraces of CASS. D., LXXV, 9, 6, III, p. 218 Boiss. is unknown), repulsed Trajan in 117 and always remained in the Parthian cultural sphere – see H. J. LENZEN, 'Ausgrabungen in Hatra', in *Jahrb. d. Deutsch. arch. Inst.*, LXX, 1955, Arch. Anz. cc. 334–75, and A. MARICQ 'Hatra de Sanatrouq', in *Syria*, XXXII, 1955, pp. 273–88 (who however denies that it was ethnically an Arab city, as opposed to U. KAHRSTEDT, *Artabanos und seine Erben*, Berne 1950, p. 67); cf. the same writer's 'La province d'Assyrie créée par Trajan. A propos de la guerre parthique de Trajan', in *Syria*, XXXVI, 1959, pp. 254–63, for the territorial identification of Assyria, which Kahrstedt regards as none other than classical Babylonia.

For the Parthian war, the above-mentioned works by GUEY and LEPPER give a complete list of the sources and bibliographies up to 1936 and 1948 respectively, together with a discussion of recent trends, particularly on the exploitation of late local sources such as MALALAS (A. VON STAUFFENBERG, *Die römische Kaisergeschichte bei Malalas*, Stuttgart 1931). In *Phoibos*, VIII–IX, 1953–4 and 1954–5, p. 108 f., there is a report of a thesis submitted to the Univ. of Brussels by TH. FRANKFORT, 'Étude sur les guerres orientales de Trajan'; this has not been accessible to me. On individual problems, for the relationships between the Arsacid princes mentioned in the war GUEY's reconstruction has been adopted (*op. cit.*, p. 33; for other details, U. KAHRSTEDT, *op. cit.*, p. 44 f., 66 f.), and for the forces collected for the campaign LEPPER's views have been accepted (*op. cit.*, pp. 174–8). On L. Catilius Severus, the first and only governor of Armenia, the diploma already cited, *CIL*, XVI, 163, giving his supplementary consulship in 110, has enabled us to complete and confirm the knowledge acquired from the conjectures of BOISSEVAIN (on CASS. D., LXXV, 9, 6, cited above) and the reflections of A. MERLIN on an inscription from Thysdrus (in *Rev. Ét. Anc.*, XV, 1913, pp. 268–74). See the same scholar's later article, 'Quelques remarques sur la carrière de L. Catilius Severus, légat de Syrie', in *Mél. Dussaud*, I, Paris 1939, pp. 217–26. The temple begun at Harni for the statue of Trajan in 115, and halted in 117, may be connected with the beginnings of Romanization in Armenia (theory of C. V. TREVER, reported in the bulletin of Soviet researches in the *Amer. Journ. Arch.*, LIV, 1950, p. 427). On the 'empty year' of 115, after the recent acquisitions of chronological data (see above, p. 663), MOMMSEN's view (*Röm. Gesch.*, V, p. 398) that Trajan left Rome in the autumn of 114 is no longer tenable, and LONGDEN's placing (in *Journ. Rom. St.*, XXI, 1931, pp. 1–8; cf. *Cambr. Anc. Hist.*, XI, 1936, pp. 239 ff.) of the Babylonian campaign in 115 is fairly questionable. However, LEPPER's recent theory that the year was occupied with the establishment of the permanent frontier line Chaboras–Singara has also been greeted with considerable reserve (LEPPER, pp. 120 ff.; cf. reviews by A. MOMIGLIANO in *Riv. Stor. Ital.*, LXI, 1949, pp. 124–7; M. I. HENDERSON, in *Journ. of Rom. St.*, XXXIX, 1949, pp. 121–32). The inscription from Dura-Europos published by ROSTOVTZEFF in *Compt. rend. Ac. Inscr.* 1935, pp. 285–90 (= *AE*, 1936, 68–9, cf. *AE*, 1940, 234–5) has given rise to a discussion on the limits and scope of Trajan's renunciation of the idea of annexing all the lands conquered in the campaign of 116 (ROSTOVTZEFF, *loc. cit.*, and 'Kaiser Trajan und Dura', in *Klio*, XXXI, 1938, pp. 285–292, in reply to E. D. GROAG, 'Zu einer Inschrift aus Dura', *ibid.*, XXIX, 1936, pp. 232–6, and A. DEGRASSI, 'Fu Traiano a rinunciare alla Mesopotamia?' in *Rev. Fil.*, LXIV, 1936, pp. 410–11; cf. LEPPER, *op. cit.*, pp. 126–55). For a further confirmation of the date 28 January as the *dies imperii* of Trajan, see J. GUEY, 'Les dates de l'avènement de Trajan et de la Victoria Parthica Maxima', in *Bull. Soc. Ant. Fr.*, 1948–9, pp. 116–18. In the matter of the chronological and factual relationship of the Jewish revolt to the Parthian war, the examination of numerous papyri has enabled us to trace disturbances and riots in Egypt, both in Alexandria and the *chora*, from 115 onwards (edict of the prefect Rutilius Lupus, 13 October 115). The revolt seems to have been suppressed by Q. Marcius Turbo during Trajan's lifetime (A. FUKS, 'The Jewish Revolt in Egypt, A.D. 115–117, in the Light of the Papyri', in *Aegyptus*, XXXIII, 1953 – Scr. Vitelli, IV – pp. 131–58), not only in Egypt but also in Cyrene, if Pflaum's view about the settlement of 3000 veterans of the III *Cyrenaica* at Cyrene (see above, p. 673) is to be adopted. The possibility of a direct and concerted relationship between the Jewish revolt and the Parthian counter-offensive has been considered by M. CANAVESI (M. A. LEVI), *La politica estera di Roma antica*, II, Milan 1942, p. 364; cf. L. MOTTA, 'La tradizione sulla revolta ebraica al tempo di Traiano', in *Aegyptus*, XXXII, 1952 (Scritti Vitelli, III), pp. 477–90. On the fury of the rebels, see A. FUKS, *art. cit.*, pp. 156–8, and S. APPLEBAUM, in *Journ. of Jew. St.*, II, 1951, pp. 177 ff., and on the social background to the conflicts in Egypt (Romans and Greeks, Jews and *fellahin*) see ROSTOVTZEFF, *The Social and Economic History of the Roman Empire*[2], Oxford 1957, pp. 348 and 693 (n. 105). Rostovtzeff thinks the Jews had the support of the *fellahin*, but see A. FUKS, *art. cit.*, p. 153. See also I. CAZZANIGA, 'Torbidi giudaici nell' Egitto Romano nel secondo secolo di Cristo: un papiro della R. Università di Milano', in *Ann. Inst. Phil. Hist. Or. et. Sl.*, V, 1957, (Mél. E. Boisacq., I), pp. 159–67 (but it is not certain that the situation mentioned in the papyrus is to be referred to the reign of Trajan).

HADRIAN.
THE SUCCESSION AND THE PROGRAMME OF THE REIGN

That the contrast seen by the tradition between the reigns of Trajan and Hadrian, a contrast unfavourable to the latter, needs to be toned down is confirmed by a careful examination of the aims and results of Hadrian's activity and by the already striking number of new pieces of epigraphical evidence putting back to Trajan's reign innovations formerly attributed to Hadrian. This fresh evidence reduces the apparent difference in nature between the activities of the two emperors and facilitates the formation of a political judgement on the two reigns. It is now fairly firmly established that basically Hadrian continued the policy of Trajan, systematically completing and consolidating on legal foundations the structures built up empirically. The reduction of Trajan's so-called imperialism to its true proportions, that is, to the realistic policy of defence typical of the Augustan and Flavian tradition (see above, p. 676) also tones down what is apparently the greatest contrast, the contrast in foreign policy. Nevertheless the figure of Hadrian remains difficult to understand completely in its acknowledged complexity and variety, in spite of the – for opposite reasons – too intelligent studies of W. WEBER and B. W. HENDERSON (W. WEBER, *Untersuchungen zur Geschichte des Kaisers Hadrianus*, Leipzig 1907, further developed in *Traian und Hadrian in Meister der Politik*, I², Stuttgart 1923, *Cambr. Anc. Hist.*, XI, 1936, pp. 294–324, and *Rom, Herrschertum u. Reich in zweiter Jahrhundert*, Stuttgart 1937; B. W. HENDERSON, *The Life and Principate of the Emperor Hadrian*, A.D. 76–138, London 1923). These two are the principal monographs on Hadrian, alongside the still excellent collections of material – which only need updating – in the articles in the *Realencyclopädie* (see ROHDEN, I, 1894, cc. 493–520) and the *Dizionario epigrafico* of E. DE RUGGIERO (G. MANCINI and D. VAGLIERI, III, 1911, 600–40). Works of a different sort are B. D'ORGEVAL, *L'empereur Hadrien. Oeuvre législative et administrative*, Paris 1950, and M. YOURCENAR, *Mémoires d'Hadrien*, Paris 1951. See most recently M. HAMMOND, 'The Antonine Monarchy', in *Pap. and Mon. Am. Ac. Rome*, XIX, 1959. Nevertheless Hadrian still retains the acknowledged credit for original theoretical formulations translated into practice with extreme self-denial (perfect administrative organization, policy of peace, etc.). On Hadrian's physical characteristics, see W. S. ANDERSON, 'Juvenal: Evidence on the Years A.D. 117–28', in *Class. Phil.*, L. 1955, p. 255–7 (on Hadrian's famous beard: it appears from Juvenal that wearing a beard did not become common at any rate until 128); J. FINK, 'Die Idee des römischen Herrschertums im Bildnis Hadrians', in *Geistige Welt*, IV, 1951, pp. 153–60 (the portraits of Hadrian represent the fundamental turning-point in the imperial iconography); the same writer has published three new portraits of Hadrian, two at Beirut and one at Klagenfurt (J. FINK, 'Beiträge zum

Bildnis Kaiser Hadrians', in *Jahrb. deutsch. arch. Inst.*, LXX, 1955, Arch. Anz. cc. 69–86).

The discussion about Hadrian's adoption by Trajan is concerned particularly with the form it took (by *testamentum in procinctu*, with the reservation of solemn completion at Rome? Cf. M. HAMMOND, 'The Transmission of the Powers', etc. in *Mem. Am. Ac. Rome*, XXIV, 1956, p. 90). But it is generally accepted that Trajan intended to leave Hadrian as his heir and successor (see most recently J. CARCOPINO, 'L' hérédité dynastique' etc., in *Rev. Ét. Anc.*, LI, 1949, pp. 280–3; M. HAMMOND, *art. cit.*, p. 91 and n. 164 on the Arch of Beneventum, completed after the death of Trajan and to be interpreted as an attempt to legitimize Hadrian's succession; cf. J. BEAUJEU, *La religion romaine etc.*, pp. 431–7; also bibliography and discussion of modern opinions on the whole problem). In Hadrian's career before his accession (analytical examination in L. PERRET, *Essai sur la carrière d'Hadrien jusqu'à son avènement à l'empire* (76–117), Paris 1935) scholars have for the most part looked for factors explaining the succession; what is rightly predominant is the tendency to give full weight to Hadrian's close collaboration with his predecessor and hence to the naturalness of the succession (partic. HENDERSON, *op. cit.*, pp. 34–8; J. CARCOPINO, *art. cit.*, pp. 280–3; M. HAMMOND, *art. cit.*, p. 91). The examination of Hadrian's titles sheds light on his policy (L. PERRET, *La titulature imperiale d'Hadrien*, Paris 1929) and confirms in his case too the development in a straight line of the dynastic-monarchical concept born with the principate and characteristic of it (M. HAMMOND, 'Imperial Elements in the Formula of the Roman Emperors during the first two and a half Centuries of the Empire', in *Mem. Am. Ac. Rome*, XXXV, 1957, pp. 17–64; pp. 28–30 for H. in particular). On the liquidation of the eastern conquests and the alleged somersault in foreign policy, the continuation of an action already decided upon by Trajan seems the simplest hypothesis (J. GUEY, *op. cit.*, pp. 145 f.; see above, p. 680). On the intention to abandon Dacia, see G. FORNI, 'Contributo alla storia della Dacia romana', in *Alten.*, XXXVI, 1958, pp. 46–9. For the rebellion of the Brigantes and the war in Britain, which does not seem to have been the occasion of the disappearance of Legion IX *Hispana*, see E. BIRLEY, 'Britain after Agricola, and the End of the Ninth Legion', in *Rom. Br. and the Rom. Army*, Kendal 1953, pp. 20–30. On the 'plot' and execution of the ex-consuls, the rather too subtle conjectures of A. V. PREMERSTEIN, *Das Attentat der Konsulare auf Hadrian in Jahre 118 n. Chr.* (Beih. Klio 8) Leipzig 1908, have been largely abandoned. Hadrian's responsibility is accepted latterly by J. CARCOPINO, *art. cit.*, p. 284 f.

The connection with previous disagreements between H. and Trajan's staff is probable (Lusius Quietus dismissed, *V. Hadr.*, 5, 8; Celsus and Palma already hostile to him in 112–113, *V. Hadr.*, 4, 3). However, the dating of the command in Upper Moesia of C. Avidius Nigrinus – whose replacement by Q. Marcius Turbo, who had earlier already replaced Lusius Quietus, was in PREMERSTEIN's view (p. 13 ff.) among the immediate causes of the plot – still remains uncertain (112–115, and in Dacia, not Moesia, according to R. SYME, 'The First Garrison of Dacia', in *Laureae Aquincenses*, I, Budapest 1938, p. 279; cf. A. PASSERINI, *Coort. pret.*, p. 298 f., for the precise position held by Turbo). Moreover, even the date of Attianus's and Similis's replacement by Turbo and Clarus cannot be determined precisely. It should be noted that EUSEB., *Chron.*, p. 198 HELM, makes the bellum *contra Sauromatas* end in 120. This, and R. THOUVENOT's deduction ('Encore deux diplômes militaires du Maroc', in *Compt. rend. Ac. Inscr.*, 1949, p. 337) from a military diploma of 28 March 118 (*CIL*, XVI, Suppl. 166), that if Hadrian was discharging troops the disturbances in Mauretania could not yet have begun at this date, so that Marcius Turbo could not have been sent there before the spring of 118, make the following chronology (adopted in the main text) plausible (there is also the further point that there was no need for Marcius Turbo to be sent to the Danube while Hadrian was still there): end of 117–118, Turbo finishes off the operations against the Jews, 118, some time after March, Turbo in Mauretania; end of 118, in command on the Danube; 120, praetorian prefect; 121, best date for the start of Hadrian's journeys. New details on the political background and on personal relations among the aristocrats and between them and the Princeps in the period of transition from Trajan's administration to Hadrian's are to be found in H. G. PFLAUM, 'La chronologie de la carrière de M. Pompeius Macrinus Theophanes, legatus leg. VI Victrix', in *Germania*, XXXVII, 1959, pp. 150–5. As for Hadrian's general programme, its main lines are illustrated right from the start, especially in the celebration of *Pax* and *Aeternitas imperii*, by the coinage, which in comparison with Trajan's shows a tendency to abstraction and the generalization of motifs (H. MATTINGLY, *Coins of the Rom. Emp. in the Br. Mus.*, III, London 1936, pp. CXXIV–CXXX).

HADRIAN'S JOURNEYS

In the reconstruction of the itineraries we have to remember that the records of works or monuments dedicated to H., when identical with the records of other emperors, are not a proof of H's presence in a particular place (we have only to think of the enormous number of similar dedications to H's successor, who never moved from Rome). For the chronology, the tenuous thread preserved by the literary tradition is only partly reinforced by the inscriptions and still less by the coins, owing to the well known absence of numbering in the *tribunicia potestas*. In these circumstances, the story of Hadrian's journeys is still more uncertain than the needs of exposition make it seem in the main text, studded though this is with reservations. This is true particularly for Greece and the East: cf. P. GRAINDOR, *Athènes sous Hadrien*, Cairo 1934; D. MAGIE, *Rom. Rule in Asia Minor*, Princeton, N.J. 1950, pp. 613–22, 1470–1485. A chronological reconstruction with often bold references to the monuments and portraits is to be found in M. WEGNER, *Das römische Herrscherbild, II, 3, Hadrian, Plotina, Marciana, Matidia, Sabina*, Berlin 1936, pp. 53–63 (e.g. Wegner accepts Hadrian's presence at Virunum, in Noricum, in 121 because of the bust found in the theatre). On questions of detail, for Hadrian's first arrival at Athens it seems better to accept autumn 124 (KOLBE, in *Ath. Mitt.*, XLVI, 1921, pp. 112 f., cf. *I.G.*, II–III², 2021, 3287) rather than autumn 125 (see ROHDEN, in *P.W.*, I, c. 507, HENDERSON, pp. 88 f.). For the initiation at Eleusis, see M. GUARDUCCI, 'Adriano e i culti misterici della Grecia', in *Bull. Mus. Imp. Rom.*, XII, 1941, pp. 149–58, and J. H. OLIVER, 'Hadrian's Precedent, the Alleged Initiation of Philip II', in *Amer. Journ. Phil.*, LXXI, 1950, pp. 295–9. Oliver explains the passage in the *V. Hadr.*, 13, 1, which speaks of the previous initiations 'Herculis Philippique', as a corruption of 'Philopappi', the son and colleague as ruler of the Epiphanes of Commagene who had lost his throne in 72 and, settling at Athens, where he died between 114 and 116, had been registered, like H., in the deme of Besa and, again like H., was archon, agonothetes and benefactor. The curious coincidence might have been emphasized and then supplemented in the manuscript tradition by the *lectio facilior* (however, this explanation is opposed, with good arguments, by W. DEN BOER, 'Religion and Literature in Hadrian's Policy', in *Mnem.*, IV, 8, 1955, pp. 128 f.). The second visit to Athens is now universally assigned to the winter of 128–129 (summer 129: MATTINGLY, *Coins etc.*, III, p. XCI), and the third visit to 131–132. The inscription from Epidaurus, *Syll.²*, 842, is decisive in placing the inauguration of the Olympieion and the Panhellenion in 131 (cf. J. A. O. LARSEN, 'Cyrene and the Panhellenion', in *Class. Phil.*, XLVII, 1952, pp. 7–16). For fresh details about H's relations with Greek towns and for the success of the promotion of

Athens as the centre of the Greek world, see J. H. OLIVER, 'Documents Concerning the Emperor Hadrian', in *Hesperia*, X, 1941, pp. 361–70. On the general idea of pan-Hellenic unification see also H. BENGTSON, *Griech. Gesch.*, Munich 1950, p. 507. For the inscription of the senatorial ambassador sent to meet H. in 128 when he was returning from Africa, see A. DEGRASSI, 'P. Cluvius Maximus Paullinus', in *Epigr.*, I, 1939, pp. 307–21. On the visit to Jerusalem, probably made in the spring of 130 when H. was returning from wintering in Gerasa (a hypothesis just as probable as the one, preferred in the main text, that H. wintered at Antioch), W. F. STINESPRING, 'Hadrian in Palestine, 129–130 A.D.', in *Journ. Am. Or. Soc.*, LIX, 939, pp. 360–5. On the subject of the preparations to receive H. in Egypt, to which the *Pap. Leid. inv.* 172 seems to refer, see B. A. GRONINGEN, 'Preparatives to Hadrian's Visit to Egypt', in *St. Calderini – Paribeni*, II, Milan 1956, pp. 253–6, and on the stay in Egypt E. BRECCIA, 'Il viaggio dell'imp. Adriano in Egitto e ciò che resta della città di Antinio', in *Atti. IV Congr. naz. St., Rom.*, Rome 1938, pp. 119–24, and H. I. BELL, 'Antinoopolis: A Hadrianic Foundation in Egypt', in *Journ. Rom. St.*, XXX, 1940, pp. 133–47, quite interesting on H.'s general ideas on the subject of the urbanization of the empire. The idea that in 131 H. went straight from Alexandria to Rome by sea is entertained only by HENDERSON (p. 134).

GOVERNMENT AND ADMINISTRATION.
MEASURES FAVOURING THE EMPIRE

It would be desirable to be able to distinguish those measures taken by the Emperor on the spot. We shall give here the latest information about the most probable and about the epigraphical material of comparatively recent discovery relating to measures and honours – material that is particularly abundant in the East. So far as public works and the expressions of gratitude provoked by them are concerned, there are numerous documents that have come to our knowledge recently or have acquired fresh commentaries, even if this is not explicitly stated. At Rome, two *fistulae aquariae* have come to light, one bearing H.'s name, the other that = Matidia the Elder (C. PIETRANGELI, in *Epigr.*, XIII, 1951, pp. 18 f. of *AE*, 1954, 62 and 63); in Italy there is the splendid amphitheatre at Capua (J. HEURGON, 'Note sur Capoue et les villes campaniennes au IIᵉ siècle de notre ère', in *St. Robinson*, II, 1953, pp. 931–7), and at Heba an important restoration to a building (MINTO, in *Not. Sc.*, 1943, p. 18 = *AE*, 1946, 222); in Lusitania a dedication by the *civitas Aravor(um)*, dating from 119 (*AE*, 1954, 87); at Cyrene the radical restorations, which must have been done at the beginning of the reign and accompanied the resettlement (P. M. FRASER, 'Hadrian and Cyrene, with a note by S. Applebaum', in *Journ. Rom. St.*, XL, 1950, pp. 77–90, with a collection of Hadrianic inscriptions, published and unpublished, from Cyrene, pp. 88–90; M. SMALLWOOD, 'The Hadrianic Inscription from the Caesareum at Cyrene', in *Journ. Rom. St.*, XLII, 1952, pp. 37–8; see also FUHRMANN, in *Jahrb. Deutsch. arch. Inst.*, LVI, 1941, Arch. Anz. c. 704 = *AE*, 1946, 177, for a base dating from 117–118 with a dedication by the *civitas Cyrenensium*, cf. above, pp. 674, 681). The very numerous Athenian inscriptions have been joined by the dedication *AE*, 1947, 17 (see also, for a new reading of the decree of A.D. 124 on olive oil, *SEG*, XV, 1958, no. 108). At Plataea there is a dedication to Hadrian 'Olympio et fundatori' (*AE*, 1937, 8); in Macedonia, at Philippi, a Latin dedication 'Hadriano Olympio et Iunoni Coniugali Sabinae' (*AE*, 1939, 190). Crossing over into Asia, we have to add to the Ephesian inscriptions one referring to the celebrations in honour of a visit by H.; however, it is not dated (*AE*, 1952, 13). On the grandiose temple at Cyzicus, see B. ASHMOLE, 'Cyriac of Ancona and the Temple of Hadrian at Cyzicus', in *Journ. Warb. Court. Inst.*, XIX, 1956, pp. 179–91. For the inscriptions from the wall at Nicaea, referring to the town aqueduct, see *AE*, 1939, 293 and 297. A new dedication from Lebadaea is dated 118, but does not bear any indication – sign of a tendency that was spreading – of the *II trib. pot.*, as if there was a conscious effort not to underline the concept of annual renewability (J. JANNORAY, 'Nouvelles inscriptions de Lébadée', in *Bull. Corr. Hell.*, LXIV-LXV, 1940-1, pp. 36-9). A dedication by the 'Kaisareis Tmolleitai Trokettenoi' to their ancestral gods and Hadrian belongs to 124 (*AE*. 1957, 17). There is a new dedication from Heraclea ad Salbacum in *Mon. As. Min. Ant.*, VI, 92; cf. ROBERT, *La Carie*, II, Paris 1954, n. 51. For the disputed question of the Antioch aqueduct and its *caput* at Daphne, see R. H. CHOWEN, 'The Nature of Hadrian's Theatron at Daphne', in *Amer. Journ. Arch.*, LX, 1956, pp. 275–7 (cf. above, p. 669). A dedication at Palmyra to H. 'Lord of the world and benefactor of the city' (H. SEYRIG, in *Syria*, XX, 1939, p. 312, n. 25), indicates the city's close ties with the empire (see below, p. 689: *cippi*, *AE*, 1939, 179–80). In Egypt, in the Serapeion at Luxor, there is a dedication dated 24 January 126, Hadrian's (*dies*) *natalis* (*AE*, 1952, 159). Some new milestones have also come to light: at Cyrene, dating from 118, recording the restoration of a road 'tum[uitu Iuda]ico eversa et c[orrupta]' (*Pap. Br. Sch. Rome*, XVIII, 1950, pp. 86–8 = *AE*,

1951, 208); and in Galatia, from 119–120 (*AE*, 1946, 178) and 121–122 (*AE*, 1937, 91).

As for personal interventions of an administrative nature, in the spirit of the most direct paternalism, see in general P. J. ALEXANDER, 'Letters and Speeches of the Emperor Hadrian', in *Harv. St. in Class. Phil.*, XLIX, 1938, pp. 141–77. For H.'s participation in local legislation in Greece, see J. H. OLIVER, *The Ruling Power* etc., Philadelphia 1953, pp. 958–63; for the shipowner Erasto's entry into the boulê of Ephesus (*Syll.*³, 838) see D. MAGIE, *Rom. Rule in As. Min.*, pp. 641 and 1505, n. 31; for Hadrian's letters, J. M. R. CORMACK, 'A Letter of Hadrian in Beroea', in *Journ. of Rom. St.*, XXX, 1940, pp. 148–52 (cf. J. H. OLIVER, *Documents*, etc., pp. 369 f., who also deals, pp. 361–3, with a letter of 126 to the Achaean League). Also J. and L. ROBERT, 'Inscriptions de la vallée du Haut-Caïque', in *Hellenica*, VI, 1948, pp. 80–8 (new reading of the three famous letters to the city of Stratonicea). For a new reading of a letter of H.'s dealing with the mineral waters of Prusa and Olympum, already published by L. ROBERT, *Études anatoliennes*, 1937, p. 231 (cf. *Rev. Ét. Gr.*, LV, 1942, p. 357, n. 158), see R. DEMANGEL, 'Une lettre d'Hadrien retrouvée à Brousee', in *Bull. Corr. Hell.*, LXIV–LXV. 1940–1, p. 288 (*AE*, 1948, 52). For the 'normal channels' which H. wished to be fully respected even in relations with the paternalistic administration, see D. MAGIE, *op. cit.*, pp. 613 and 616, on the subject of a petition from the Ephesians on certain financial questions, dated 27 September 120. Hadrian's reply approves the measures taken by a previous proconsul and promises to take the matter up with the present proconsul and to see that he gives them satisfaction. Obviously from the bottom it was possible to go over the proconsul's head and approach the Emperor directly about even the smallest problems, but from the top efforts were made to salve appearances, so strong still in the principate was the sense of form and substance to be superimposed on the most open paternalism. There are numerous fresh inscriptions dealing with the fixing of boundaries: in the East between Nicaea in Bithynia and Dorileus in Asia, by C. Julius Severus, either during his governorship of Asia, 128–131, or during his governorship of Bithynia, 136–138 (*Mon. As. Min. Ant.*, V, 1937, pp. 32–4, n. 60 = *AE*, 1938, 144; cf. L. ROBERT in *Rev. Ét. Anc.*, XLII, 1940, p. 321, n.2); two dedications by the citizens of Abdera, on monuments placed at the limits of the territory recovered through the intervention of H. (*AE*, 1937, 170 and 171; cf. L. ROBERT, *Hellenica*, V, 57, n.8, at *La Carie*, II, p. 225, n.1.); a *cippus* (*AE*, 1940, 44) near the temple of Aezani in Phrygia, dating from 128, for the restitution to the *civitas Aezanitarum* of the old boundaries of the Attalids, effected through the *primus pilus* Septimius Saturninus (A. PASSERINI's theory in *Coort pret.*, p. 348, that in 128 Saturninus was carrying out the functions of *praef. praet.*, does not seem necessary; cf. the case of the *primus pilus* who led 3000 settlers to Cyrene – recorded in the inscription from Adalia cited above, p. 673). There are fresh examples of cippi recording *definitio silvarum*, on the right bank of the Adonis in the Lebanon (*AE*, 1947, 136; 1958, 170). In Syria a cippus dating from December 153 records a restitution by Antoninus Pius, 'ex sententia divi Hadriani', of the 'fines regionis Palmyrenae constitutos a Cretico Silano leg. Aug. pr. pr.' (between A.D. 12 and 17); see D. SCHLUMBERGER, 'Bornes frontières de la Palmyrène', in *Syria*, XX, 1939, pp. 43-73, II, pp. 61-3 = *AE*, 1939, 179. Another cippus (*ibid.*, III, p. 63 f. = *AE*, 1939, 180) refers to the 'fin[es] inter Hadriano[s] Palmyrenos et [He]mesenos'; the Hadrianic epithet for Palmyra suggests a period close to H. and probably a delimitation of boundaries ordered by him. In Africa, where there is much evidence of H.'s attention to the organization of territories and the conditions of the farmers (for the *ara legis Hadrianae* see latterly G. TIBILETTI, in *Diz. Ep.*, IV, p. 769, s.v. *Lex*), three new cippi can be added to those already known. One records the separation of private lands from public land at Cirta (*AE*, 1939, 160); another records the delimitation of the territory of Sigus (*AE*, 1939, 161); and a third commemorates the restitution of the boundaries between the *Suppenses* and the *Vofricenses* (in the neighbourhood of Thagaste) marked out under Domitian and Nerva by the proconsul of Africa, C. Tullius Capito Pomponianus Plotius Firmus (*AE*, 1942-3, 35).

On the norms applied in urbanization, exploitation of Greek qualities and also the extension of Roman citizenship and gradual Romanization, see, for the form of the *polis* promoted in the East and for its functioning, D. MAGIE, *op. cit.*, p. 617 ff., 639-58 (for the typical example of Antinoopolis, see H. I. BELL, *art. cit.*, in *Journ. of Rom. St.*, XXX, 1940, pp. 133-47). For the gradual method represented by the granting of the *Latium* (*maius* and *minus*), A. N. SHERWIN-WHITE, *The Rom. Citizenship*, Oxford 1939, p. 196 ff., and G. VITUCCI, in *Diz. Ep.*, IV, pp. 443-5, s.v. *Latium*. For the *municipia* and *coloniae* in general, see SHERWIN-WHITE, *op. cit.*, and for the numerous foundations in Africa, almost all of them connected with the journey of 128, see L. LESCHI, 'Une inscription nouvelle de Choba (Mauretanie Césarienne)', in *Bull. Arch. Com. Tr. Hist.*, 1946-9 (pub. 1953), pp. 495-7; L. POINSSOT, 'Inscription d'Avitta Bibba', *ibid.*, 1936-7, p. 169; and P. ROMANELLI, *St. d. prov. rom dell'*

Africa, Rome 1959, p. 345 f. At Lysimacheia in Thrace there is a Latin dedication to H. 'Jovi Olympio, conditori col(oniae)'; this was one of the very few colonies founded by H. in the East (*AE*, 1938, 140). For the start under H. of the practice of conferring the title of colony without the actual settlement of colonists, see G. I. LUZZATTO, 'Appunti sul ius Italicum', in *Rev. Int. Dr. Ant.*, III, 1950 (Mél. de Visscher, IV), pp. 79–110. The granting of citizenship to discharged auxiliaries and grants *ad personam* naturally went on, and the rise of eastern notables continued to be sometimes pretty rapid (see the cases of P. Aelius Iuventianus Hermogenes and of his son; inscription from Heraclea ad Salbacum, ROBERT, *La Carie*, II, p. 171, n. 60). On the administration, especially the financial administration, and the administrators, see H. G. PFLAUM, *Essai sur les procurateurs équestres sous le haut empire romain*, Paris 1950, pp. 58–67, and *P.W.*, XXIII, 1, 1957, c. 1251 f. (to this should be added E. MAREC and H. G. PFLAUM, 'Deux carrières équestres d'Hippone', in *Libyca*, I, 1953, pp. 207–14). On customs dues, see, besides DE LAET, *Portorium*, espec. p. 384 ff., H. NESSELHAUF, 'Publicum portorii Illyrici utriusque et ripae Thraciae', in *Epigr.*, I, 1939, pp. 331–8. On H.'s officials and colleagues: G. CH. PICARD, 'Un collaborateur d'Hadrien, Le consulaire Bruttius Praesens', in *Compt. rend. Ac. Inscr.*, 1949, pp. 298–302 (cf. H. G. PFLAUM, art. cited above, p. 684, in *Germania*, XXXVII, 1959, pp. 150–5); L. LESCHI, 'La carrière de Q. Marcius Turbo, préfet du prétoire d'Hadrien', *ibid.*, 1945, pp. 144–62 (on whom see R. SYME, in *Journ. of Rom. St.*, XLIV, 1954, p. 118); EDM. FRÉZOULS, 'Inscription de Cyrrhus relative à Q. Marcius Turbo', in *Syria*, XXX, 1953, pp. 247–78, espec. 260–3; E. MAREC and H. G. PFLAUM, 'Nouvelle inscription sur la carrière de Suétone, l'historien', in *Compt. rend. Ac. Inscr.*, 1952, pp. 76–85; N. LEWIS, 'The Prefects of Egypt in A.D. 119', in *Am. Journ. Phil.*, LXXVI, 1955, pp. 63–9 (The lacuna of about a year in the prefects of Egypt between Q. Rammius Martialis and T. Haterius Nepos – cf. A. STEIN, *Die Präfekten von Ägypten etc.*, pp. 61–5 and O. REINMUTH, in *P.W.*, XXII, 2, c. 2371 – seems to be eliminated by P. Oxy., XX 2265, which shows Nepos already in post on the 20 August 119). Still on the subject of prefects of Egypt, in the above-mentioned inscription from Luxor of 24 January 126 the name of the prefect seems to be erased; according to J. SCHWARTZ, 'Un préfet d'Égypte frappé de "damnatio memoriae" sous le règne d'Hadrien', in *Chron. d'Ég.*, XXVII, 1952, pp. 254–6, the man involved was one C. Vibius Maximus (and thus a fresh prefect to be inserted in the lacuna 124–126 between T. Haterius Nepos and T.

Flavius Titianus, STEIN, *op. cit.*, p. 65), whose *abolitio memoriae* caused through homonymic reasons the retrospective *abolitio* of the prefect C. Vibius Maximus of 103–107, some of whose inscriptions with the name erased were already known (this theory is rejected by R. SYME, 'C. Vibius Maximus, Prefect of Egypt', in *Historia*, VI, 1957, pp. 480–7, espec. p. 485, n. 30).

As for the provinces, the theory that Pannonia as far as Sirmium was included in Italy under Hadrian is not accepted by A. DEGRASSI, *Il confine nord-orientale dell'Italia romana*, Berne 1954, p. 111, n. 60. On the division of Dacia, placed by C. DAICOVICIU (*La Transilvania nell'anti-chità.* Bucharest 1943, p. 80) in 118 or 119, see H. G. PFLAUM, *op. cit.*, pp. 58 f. and G. FORNI, *Contributo etc.*, pp. 49 f. For the extension of Thrace up to the Danube, DE LAET, *Portorium*, p. 201, and NESSELHAUF, *art. cit.*, pp. 333 ff. The *Fasti Ostienses*, by telling us of Tineius Rufus's consulship in 127, confirm that the governor of Judaea was already a man of consular rank even before the war of 132–135 (*Inscr. It.*, XIII, 1, pp. 205, 233).

In the field of the administration of justice the principal question, that of the date of the drafting of the *edictum*, has attracted considerable atten-tion. It still seems better to assign it to the last few years of the reign rather than to the early ones. This view seems to be confirmed by the evidence of the coinage (H. VOGT, 'Hadrians Justizpolitik im Spiegel der römischen Reichsmünzen', in *Festschrift F. Schulz*, II, Weimar 1951, pp. 193–200). It does not exclude a long process of elaboration (MATTINGLY, *Coins in Br. Mus.*, III, p. CXLI), which would explain Eusebius-Jerome's date of 131. As for the codifier of the edict, the fore-names were rectified and the complete name – L. Octavius Cornelius P. Salvius Iulianus Aemilianus – was determined by A. DEGRASSI, 'Note epigraphiche, I: il prenome del giurista Salvio Giuliano e l'omissione del secondo prenome nelle iscrizioni di persone plurinominali', in *Epigr.*, III, 1941, pp. 23–7 (cf. P. DE FRANCISCI, 'Il consolato di Salvio Giuliano', in *St. Doc. Hist. Jur.*, VII, 1941, p. 185). But see also W. KUNKEL, 'Ueber Lebenszeit und Laufbahn des Juristen Julians', in *Iura*, I, 1950, pp. 192–203. A. GUARINO, 'Alla ricerca di Salvio Giuliano', in *Labeo*, V, 1959, pp. 67–78 does not believe that the edict was codified by Salvius Julianus under Hadrian, and he does not identify Salvius Julianus with the personage of *ILS*, 8973 and *AE*, 1959, 286 (but his view has been opposed by B. E. THOMASSON, *Die Statthalter der römischen Provinzen Nordafrikas*, Lund 1960, pp. 81–3). So far as other jurists are concerned, an identification of Gaius has been attempted by

A. KOKOUREK, 'Qui erat Gaius? Indagatio nova quaestionis', in *Atti Congr. Intern. Dir. Rom.*, Bologna and Rome 1933, II, Pavia 1935, pp. 495–526. Kokourek thinks that Gaius was a Syrian, Jew or Egyptian, *servus Caesaris*, under Hadrian, and subsequently employed in the chancellery and a disciple of Julian. On the problem of the origin of the jurists, a problem of considerable significance for social conclusions as well as for measuring the extent of the cultural aspirations of the period in the field of the greatest public interest, see W. KUNKEL, *Herkunft und soziale Stellung der römischen Juristen*, Weimar 1952. On the question – provoked by the controversial passages *Dig.*, 1, 2, 2, 49 and GAI., *Inst.*, 1, 7 – of Hadrian's attitude to the *ius respondendi*, see W. KUNKEL, 'Das Wesen des ius respondendi', in *Zeitschr. Sav. Stift. Rom. Att.*, LXVI, 1948, pp. 423 ff. (pp. 442 f. for H. in particular); A. GUARINO, 'Il ius publice respondendi', in *Rev. Int. Dr. Ant.*, II, 1949 (Mél. de Visscher, I), pp. 401–19; and D. DAUBE, 'Hadrian's Rescript to some Ex-praetors', in *Zeitschr. Sav. Stift.*, Röm. Abt., LXVII, 1950, pp. 511–18. As for particular arrangements, on the subject of the different treatment of the *honestiores* and the *humiliores* in the case of *amotio terminorum*, in contrast with the general tendency, see G. CARDASCIA, 'L'apparition dans le droit des classes d'honestiores et d'humiliores', in *Rev. Dr. Fr. Étr.*, XXVIII, 1950, pp. 305–77, 461–85, espec. pp. 368 f. On Hadrian's policy and the spirit of the age in the juridical field in general, see FR. PRINGSHEIM, 'The Legal Policy and Reforms of Hadrian', in *Journ. of Rom. St.*, XXIV, 1934, pp. 141–53; S. RICCOBONO, 'La definizione del ius al tempo di Adriano', in *Bull. Ist. Dir. Rom. 'V. Scialoia'*, LIII–LIV, 1948, pp. 5–82; and J. CARCOPINO, 'La législation sociale d'Hadrien interprétée à lumière des tablettes latines de l'époque vandale dites Tablettes Albertini', in *Wiss. Zeitschr. der Univ. Leipzig*, V, 1955–6, pp. 403–5. On the assimilation of the imperial edicts into the law, now formally recognized as the end of a process that had started with Augustus, see R. ORESTANO, 'Gli editti imperiale. Contributo alla teoria della loro validità ed efficacia nel diritto romano classico', in *Bull. Ist. Dir. Rom.*, XLIV, 1936–7, pp. 219–331.

In the field of measures for the army and defence, the interesting inscription *AE*, 1955, 238 from Nicopolis, with its surprising data on recruitment, has been studied by J. F. GILLIAM, 'The Veterans and Praefectus Castrorum of the II Traiana in A.D. 157', in *Amer. Journ. Phil.*, LXXVII, 1956, pp. 359–75. However, the inscription reflects an exceptional situation, and a very strange one, inasmuch as it records the presence of numerous westerners and the almost total absence of Egyptians, and it does not invalidate the general results of research into recruitment in the second century (GILLIAM, p. 362 f.). In fact the brick *CIL*, III, 6580 = *ILS*, 2304, listing soldiers enrolled in 168 and discharged in 194, represents the normal recruitment situation for the II *Traiana* (G. FORNI, *Reclutam.*, pp. 95, 204, 219 f.), with Egyptians in a vast majority. On H.'s parsimony in granting military rewards, see E. BIRLEY, *Rom. Br. Rom. Army*, p. 22. However, there are also epigraphical records as well as *V. Hadr.*, 10, 2, 'multos praemiis nonnullos honoribus donans'; and to the inscriptions already known should now be added the one from Elbassan in Albania, *AE*, 1937, 101, about a soldier 'promotus a divo Hadriano in leg. III Gallicam' and decorated 'ob victoriam Iudaicam'. Numerous new fragments of military diplomas granted by H. have joined the considerable number already known, with the peculiarity that, although extending through the whole reign, they almost all come from Mauretania (*CIL*, XVI, Suppl. 166, 169, 170, 171, 173, 176; but the last may date from Antoninus Pius). This peculiarity has been studied in relation to the military history of Mauretania by H. NESSELHAUF, 'Zur Militär-geschichte der Provinz Mauretania Tingitana', in *Epigr.*, XII, 1950, pp. 34–8. One of these diplomas (*CIL*, XVI, 169 = *AE*, 1942–3, 84), by providing for the first time the date (A.D. 122) of the two consuls C. Trebius Maximus-T. Calestrius Tiro, has enabled H. G. PFLAUM, 'Ad CIL, XVI, 81', in *Historia*, II, 1954, p. 364, to give a precise date to another diploma – *CIL*, XVI, 81 – from Vindonissa. As for the others, Dacia furnished the diploma dating from 121 (*CIL*, XVI, 168; cf. *AE*, 1950, 78 and G. FORNI, *art. cit.*, in *Alten.*, XXXVI, 1958, p. 4 ff.) and that of 29 June 120 (*AE*, 1958, 30; cf. G. FORNI, *art. cit.*, pp. 2 ff.). The one possibly to be dated between 127–128 and 134 comes from Mautern in Noricum (*CIL*, XVI, 174; cf. H. THALLER, in *Oesterr. Jahresh.*, XXXIX, 1952, Beibl. 87–96). For the legionary camps in Africa and the consequences of H.'s inspection in 128, see L. LESCHI, 'Le camp de la IIIᵉ légion à Lambèse', in *Bericht über den VI Intern. Kongr. für Archäol.*, Berlin 1949, pp. 565–8, and J. GAGÉ, 'Hadrien et son "viator" sur les champs de manœuvre de Numidie', in *Bull. Fac. Lettr. Strasb.*, XXX, 1951–2, pp. 187–95 and 226. For the camp of Gemellae, built and dedicated by the III *Augusta* in 131, see J. BARADEZ, 'Gemellae, camp d'Hadrien et ville des confins sahariens', in *Compt. rend. Ac. Inscr.*, 1948, pp. 390–5. L. LESCHI, in 'Découvertes épigraphiques dans le camp de Gemellae (El-Kasbat, Algérie)' *ibid.*, 1949, pp. 220–6, published two important inscriptions from the same camp. The first (cf. *AE*, 1950, 58) is a dedication to H. put up by the *cohors I Chalcid. equitata* in 125–126,

TA—Z

naming the commanding officer of the III *Augusta*, Sex. Iulius Maior, and thus informing us of the date of his command in Numidia. The other (cf. *AE*, 1950, 58) is the inscription commemorating the construction of the camp, with the date, 131–132, and the name of the governor L. Varius Ambibulus, whose governorship thus becomes known for the first time. Fresh investigations (J. BARADEZ, 'Deux nouvelles inscriptions dans le praetorium du camp de Gemellae', in *Libyca*, I, 1953, pp. 155–60) disclosed another, almost identical copy (cf. *AE*, 1954, 131) of this last inscription; and on an altar already uncovered once in 1947, but subsequently obscured by the sand again, it was possible to read words inscribed at a later period but on the original monument: 'ara Disciplinae' (cf. *AE*, 1954, 132). There are other inscriptions from Hadrian's reign at Brigetio on the Danube (L. BARKOCZI, *Iscrizioni inedite a Brigetio*, in Hungarian with a summary in Italian, in *Arch. Ertesto*, 3a ser., V–VI, 1944–5, pp. 172–6). For Hadrian's reforms in the army of Upper Germany, see W. SCHLEIERMACHER, 'Zu Hadrians Heeresreform in Obergermanien', in *Germania*, XXV, 1957, pp. 117–20. On the *vallum* in Britain, the problem of the phases of its construction has received its most recent comprehensive treatment in C. E. STEVENS, 'The Building of Hadrian's Wall', in *Archaeologica Aeliana*, 4a ser., XXVI, 1948, pp. 1 ff. There are also interesting references by E. BIRLEY, *Rom. Br. Rom. Army*, p. 29, and by V. E. NASH-WILLIAMS, 'Wales and the Roman Frontier system', in *The Congress of Rom. Frontier Studies 1949*, ed. E. BIRLEY, Durham 1952, pp. 68–73; cf. A. DEMAN, 'L'identification des stations occidentales (à l'ouest de Birdoswald) du Mur d'Hadrien', in *Latomus*, XIII, 1954, pp. 577–89. On inscriptions of the *vallum*, see *Journ. of Rom. St.*, XXVII, 1937, p. 247 (*AE*, 1938, 116), a dedication to H. from the *posta principalis sinistra* of the fort of Halton Chesters, with a mention of legion VI *Victrix* and its commander A. Platorius Nepos; and *Journ. of Rom. St.*, XXXIII, 1943, pp. 78 f. (*AE*, 1947, 123), a new reading of *CIL*, VII, 498.

On the Jewish war, there is a general survey of the relations between the Romans and the Jews in H. ST. J. HART, 'Judaea and Rome. The Official Commentary', in *Journ. Theol. St.*, N.S. III, 1952, pp. 172–98. H. A. MUSURILLO, in *The Acts of the Pagan Martyrs, Acta Alexandrinorum*, Oxford 1954, pp. 49–60, 181–3, 196 ff., examines the *acta Pauli et Antonini*, which certainly date from the Hadrianic period, and the *acta Athenodori*, which probably belong to the same period, and reconstructs the background to the Greco-Jewish riots and the Roman interventions. On the veto on circumcision as alleged cause of the war, see E. M.

SMALLWOOD, 'The Legislation of Hadrian and Ant. Pius against Circumcision', in *Latomus*, XVIII, 1959, pp. 334–47. New inferences about the nature of the Jewish revolt and the leading actors in it have been suggested by the discovery (in 1947) of the Dead Sea scrolls; see – to mention just a few studies that accept a direct relationship – R. DE VAUX, 'Suite aux manuscrits de la Mer Morte', in *Compt. rend. Ac. Inscr.*, 1952, pp. 173–80; A. VINCENT, 'Où en est la question des manuscrits de la Mer Morte? Nouvelles découvertes', in *Rev. des. Sci. Relig.*, XXVI, 1952, pp. 258–64 (espec. p. 263 on Bar-Kozebah). The salutation as *imperator* (Hadrian's second) following on the victory over the Jews is to be placed between the middle of April and December 135; such at any rate is the view of CH. SELTMAN, 'Greek Sculpture and Some Festival Coins', in *Hesperia*, XVII, 1948, pp. 71–85 (espec. p. 85). On the presence of Legion VI *Ferrata* in Palestine even before the war, see B. LÖFSHITZ, 'Sur la date de transfert de la legio VI Ferrata en Palestine', in *Latomus*, XIX, 1960, pp. 109–11. In any case it remains certain that the permanent garrison of two legions under a consular governor dates from the Jewish war.

HADRIANIC CULTURE:
LITERATURE, ART, CUSTOMS, RELIGION AND BELIEFS

On the literary tendencies of the age in general, as represented by the appearance of figures like Fronto and Apuleius, see R. MARACHE, *La critique littéraire de langue latine et le développement du goût archaisant au II siecle de notre ère*, Rennes 1952. For details of Hadrian's literary activity, A. L. HERRMANN, 'La réplique d'Hadrien à Florus', in *Latomus IX*, 1950, pp. 385–7 (correction in the exchange of verses with Florus referred to in *V. Hadr.*, 16). On an episode in the literary life of the period, A. BARIGAZZI, 'Un'orazione pronunziata a Napoli ai tempi de Adriano', in *Alten.*, XXIX, 1951, pp. 3–11 (the speech was probably made by Favorinus of Arelate, in a Naples that was still profoundly Greek in the second century). H.'s hunts, one of the most striking manifestations of the habits of the age, have been thoroughly dealt with by J. AYMARD, *Essai sur les chasses romaines des origines à la fin du siècle des Antonins (Cynegetica)*, Paris 1951 (Bibl. Éc. franc. d' Ath. et de Rome, CLXXI), pp. 173–81, 523–37. But the most durable evidence of the civilization of the period is to be found in the monuments, the numerous remains of which demonstrate the great upsurge and decisive development in figurative art in particular. On H.'s personal involvement and his fame as a connoisseur, see CH. PICARD, in *Rev. Ét. Lat.*, XXX, 1952, p. 347 (cf. P. COLLART, in *Rev. Ét. Anc.* XLIII, 1941, p. 47, on an episode in Egypt); also *idem*, *ibid.*, pp. 347–73: a survey of sculpture in H.'s principate. See also B. M. FELLETTI MAI, in *Enc. Arte Ant.*, I, 1958, pp. 83–8. On the practice of putting on restored monuments the names of the original builders and not that of Hadrian, a practice subsequently regulated by law, cf. *Digest.*, L, 10, 7. On the fact that the stamping of the date and the name of the factory on bricks and tiles begins to be frequent under H., see H. BLOCH, 'The Serapeum of Ostia and the Brick-Stamps of 123 A.D. A New Landmark in the History of Roman Architecture', in *Am. Journ. Arch.*, LXIII, 1959, pp. 225–40. For Hellenistic and eastern influences, E. CONDURACHI, 'Quelques considérations sur la renaissance des arts plastiques à l'époque d'Hadrien', in *Rev. Hist. S.E. Europ.*, XXIII, 1946, pp. 57–70; M. CAGIANO DE AZEVEDO, *La cultura ellenistica a Roma: la scultura*, Milan 1950–1; G. BOTTI and P. ROMANELLI, *Le sculture del Museo Gregoriano Egizio*, Rome 1951 (for Egyptian elements); P. GUSTAF HAMBERG, *Studies in Roman Imperial Art (with special reference to the state reliefs of the second century)*, Uppsala 1945 (on Hadrianic classicism); D. E. STRONG, 'Late Hadrianic Architectural Ornament in Rome', in *Pap. Br. Sch. Rome*, XXI, 1953, pp. 118–51. The unification of styles and of ornamental usages is however, a phenomenon that grows wider and wider: cf. the mosaics of Antioch (D. LEVI, *Antioch Mosaic Pavements*, Princeton, N. J. 1947) and the influence of Roman sculpture on Indian art, even to the extent of the despatch of artists, alluded to by *V. Hadr.*, 21, 14 (A. C. SOPER, 'The Roman Style in Gandhara', in *Am. Journ. Arch.*, LV, 1951, pp. 301–19). It was also an age of transition and development in the portrait, particularly with reference to the imperial iconography (M. WEGNER, *Das Röm. Herrscherbild*, Berlin 1956; R. WEST, 'Der Germanentypus in der röm. Porträtsgestaltung', in *Gymn.*, 1941, pp. 133–46). For the daring forms used in building, see G. A. S. SNIJDER, 'Kaiser Hadrian und der Tempel der Venus und Roma', in *Jahrb. deutsch. arch. Inst.*, LV, 1940, pp. 1–11, on the project of the temple of Venus and Rome and of the criticisms of Apollodorus, who was put to death according to CASS. D., LXIX, 4, though this is contradicted by *V. Hadr.*, 19, 13. To this period, too, belongs, so it would seem, the so-called 'temple of Venus' at Baiae, the main room of a bath building (G. DE ANGELIS D'OSSAT, 'Il "Tempio di Venere" a Baia', in *Bull. Mus. Imp. Rom.*, XII, 1941, pp. 121–32), and possibly the *paedagogium* on the Celian (P. E. ARIAS, in *Not. d. Sc.*, 1939, pp. 86–7). The development and embellishment of the cemetery on the Insula Sacra, inaugurated under Trajan (G. BECATTI, in *Riv. Fil. Istr. Class.*, LXIX, 1941, pp. 70–5, rev. of G. CALZA, *La necropoli del Porto di Roma nell'Isola Sacra*, Rome 1940) certainly took place under Hadrian. The villa at Tibur naturally demands most attention, particularly since the last excavations (H. KÄHLER, in *Enc. Art Ant.*, I, 1958, pp. 74–83) in the Canopus and the Serapeum (S. AURIGEMMA, 'Lavori nel Canopo di Villa Adriana', in *Boll. d'Arte*, XXXIX, 1954, pp. 327–41; XL, 1955, pp. 64–78; A. W. VAN BUREN, 'Recent Finds at Hadrian's Tiburtine Villa', in *Am. Journ. Arch.*, LIX, 1955, pp. 215–17, according to whom the sculptures, copying those of the fifth century, confirm H.'s classical taste). For other sources of inspiration in building, see H. HERTER, 'Die Rundform in Platons Atlantis und ihre Nachwirkung in der Villa Hadriani', in *Rh. Mus.*, XCVI, 1953, pp. 1–20. In the village of Tivoli, the amphitheatre recently brought to light also belongs, it seems, to the Hadrianic period, or at any rate work on it started at that time (D. FACCENNA, 'Tivoli. Prima notizia intorno al rinvenimento dell'anfiteatro romano', in *Not. d. Sc.*, 1948, pp. 278–83).

As for the beliefs people held and the fashion for astronomy and astrology, see J. BABELON, 'Les images des Saisons et du Zodiaque dans l'antiquité, in *Bull. Soc. Ant. d. France*, 1943–4, pp. 367–80; M. GRANT, 'A Capricorn on Hadrian's Coinage', in *Emerita*, XX, 1952, pp. 1–7; this also represents, it would seem, the return to the coinage, for the 150th anniversary of 27 B.C., of an Augustan symbol. On religious policy in general, R. HICKS, 'The Religious Policy of the Emperor Hadrian', in *Trans. Proc. Am. Phil. Ass.*, LXX, 1939, p. XXXVI; W. DEN BOER, 'Religion and Literature in Hadrian's Policy', in *Mnem.*, IV, 8, 1955, pp. 123–44 (espec. on the imperial cult, on which see also J. H. OLIVER, 'The Divi of the Hadrianic Period', in *Harv. Theol. Rev.*, 1949, pp. 35–40, who also discusses the significance of the cult of Antinous); and above all the very large section (more than a third of the whole volume) devoted to H. by J. BEAUJEU, *La religion romaine à l'apogée de l'empire I, La politique religieuse des Antonins* (96–192), Paris 1955, p. 111–278. For details of the various divine incarnations of H. in the East, see also A. E. RAUBITSCHEK, 'Hadrian as the Son of Zeus Eleutherios', in *Am. Journ. Arch.*, XLIX, 1945, pp. 128–33, and A. C. LEVI, 'Hadrian as King of Egypt', in *Num. Chron.*, 1948, pp. 30–8. On the partial refusal of the honours decreed by the Achaean League, J. H. OLIVER, 'Documents' etc., in *Hesp.*, X, 1941, p. 362 (cf. W. DEN BOER, *art. cit.*, p. 133). For the Panhellenion and the concept of politico-religious unification of the Hellenistic East, P. M. FRASER, 'Hadrian and Cyrene', in *Journ. of Rom.*

St., XL, 1950, pp. 77–87; J. H. OLIVER, 'New Evidence on the Attic Panhellenion', in *Hesp.*, XX, 1951, pp. 31–3; J. A. O. LARSEN, 'Cyrene and the Panhellenion', in *Class. Phil.*, XLVII, 1952, pp. 7–16; for the seriousness with which the institution was regarded by the Greeks, J. H. OLIVER, *The Ruling Power*, Philadelphia, Pa. 1953, pp. 891 f. For the religious feelings of the period, F. R. WALTON, 'Religious Thought in the Age of Hadrian', in *Numen*, IV, 1957, pp. 165–70. For relations with Christianity, which continue to be governed in all essentials by the Trajanic attitude, see, besides BEAUJEU, *op. cit.*, p. 272 ff., W. SCHMID, 'The Christian Re-interpretation of the Rescript of Hadrian', in *Maia*, VII, N.S., fasc. I, 1955, pp. 5–13. Schmid thinks that the rescript of H. cited in the Apology of Justin Martyr (69) was a re-interpretation of a document that was really issued, but for another purpose and with a different content. On the other hand, its authenticity is accepted with reservations by M. SORDI, 'I rescritti di Traiano e di Adriano sui cristiani', in *Nuov. St. d. Ch. in Italia*, XIV, 1960, pp. 344–70. For the question of the Dead Sea scrolls, which touches indirectly on Romano-Jewish relations under H., see the bibliographical survey, 1947–56, by CHR. BURCHARD, *Bibliographie zu den Handschriften vom Toten Meer* (*Beihefte zur Zeitschr. f. die Alttestamentliche Wiss.*, LXXVI), Berlin 1957.

HADRIAN'S FAMILY AND THE PROBLEMS OF THE ADOPTIONS OF 136 AND 138

The association of Sabina in the honours paid to H. is common in the East. A new dedication to Sabina Augusta alone (G. PICARD, 'Inscriptions de Tunisie', in *Bull. Arch. Com. Tr. Hist.*, June 1949, pp. XIV–XV = *AE*, 1951, 43) has been found at Mactaris, in proconsular Africa, on a base near the pier of an aqueduct; on it there is also a dedication to L. Aelius Caesar (*ibid.* = *AE*, 1951, 44) with the XXI *trib. pot.* of H. and thus put up in the last few days of December 137. If the inscriptions are contemporaneous, the important consequence would follow that Sabina was still alive at the end of 137. In fact, the date of her death is not indicated at all clearly in the literary sources, nor can it be determined from coins. In particular, it is arbitrary to regard it as having occurred before the adoption of L. Aelius Caesar (J. CARCOPINO, 'L'hérédité dynastique' etc. in *Rev. Ét. Anc.*. LI, 1949, p. 290). Another dedication to L. Aelius Caesar has fairly recently been discovered at Ferentino (*AE*, 1956, 151). Perge, in Pamphylia, has also recently yielded (*AE*, 1958, 77) a dedication to Diva Marciana, which, being situated on the gate of the town, must have referred to a statue in a group comprising the statues of Divus Nerva, Divus Traianus, Diva Matidia and other members of the family. A dedication from Delphi to Matidia (Minor), sister of Sabina (J. JANNORAY, in *Bull. Corr. Hell.*, LXX, 1946, pp. 254–9 = *AE*, 1950, 32), is interesting because of the reference to family relationships: 'daughter of Augusta (*Matidia Maior*), sister of Augusta (*Sabina*), niece of Augusta (*Marciana*), maternal aunt of the emperor Antoninus Pius'. This last tie (already fairly amply attested; see *Diz. Ep.*, I, p. 507) is usually understood as justified by the adoption of Antoninus Pius by H.; when he became the son of H. (and of Sabina), Matidia became his aunt. J. CARCOPINO, *art. cit.*, pp. 313ff. explains the relationship in a different and ingenious way, with the object of finding a relationship with the Ulpii-Aelii which would justify the adoption of M. Annius Verus (M. Aurelius) imposed by H. on Antoninus Pius. Antoninus's wife, Annia Galeria Faustina, says Carcopino, was the daughter of M. Annius Verus, three times consul, and of one Rupilia Faustina, a daughter of Matidia the Elder by another marriage; Rupilia Faustina was therefore the step-sister of Sabina and Matidia the Younger, and the latter was therefore the aunt of Annia Faustina and – became – that of her husband, Antoninus Pius. See the genealogical table in this article, p. 317. The weak link is obviously the second marriage of Matidia the Elder. So far as the central point of Carcopino's theory is concerned, that is, the hypothesis that L. Aelius Caesar was a natural son of Hadrian (the hypothesis is put forward again by CARCOPINO in *Passion et politique chez les Césars*, Paris 1958, pp. 143–222, Ch. V: 'Le bâtard d'Hadrien et l'hérédité dynastique chez les Antonins', and also by P. GRENADE, 'Le règlement successoral d'Hadrien', in *Rev. Ét. Anc.*, LII, 1950, pp. 258–77), its reception has been in general mixed; for it is obvious that such arguments are bold ones and that excessive credit is lent to the clearly inferior material of the *Historia Augusta* (cf. R. SYME, 'Antonine Relatives: Ceionii and Vettulani', in *Alten.*, XXXV, 1957, pp. 306–15, espec. p. 309). E. HOHL, 'Ueber die Glaubwürdigkeit der H.A.,' in *Sitz-ber. d. deutsch. Ak. d. Wiss. zu Berlin*, Kl. f. Gesellschaftswiss., 1955, no. II, 'Darf die Vita Aelii als Geschichtsquelle benutzt werden?' pp. 33–54, shows for example the invalidity of the argument drawn from the citation of Verus as son in the *V. Saturnini:* among other points, this name is attributed to L. Aelius Caesar only in the *Historia Augusta*; it never appears in inscriptions or on coins. On Plautia, the mother of L. Aelius Caesar and the key figure in the whole theory, and on the new deductions about a third marriage of hers to be drawn from a recently discovered inscription from Argos, see

P. CHARNEUX, 'M. Vettulenus Civica Barbarus', in *Bull. Corr. Hell.*, LXXXI, 1957, pp. 121–40, and R. SYME, *art. cit.* It is neither proven nor probable that H. was thinking right from the start of Marcus Aurelius as sole successor and only adopted first L. Ceionius Commodus and then T. Aurelius Antoninus simply to keep the post warm until Marcus Aurelius was more mature (W. HÜTTL, *Antoninus Pius* I, Prague 1936, pp. 41–6).

THE REIGN OF ANTONINUS PIUS

The abundant but scattered materials have been gathered together in a most praiseworthy example of organization and synthesis by W. HÜTTL, *Antoninus Pius*, I, Prague 1936 (*Historisch-politische Darstellung*), and II, Prague 1933 (*Römische Reichsbeamten und Offiziere unter A.P.; Antoninus Pius in den Inschriften seiner Zeit*). We shall mention here only the principal documentary discoveries made since this work was published and some fresh discussions of questions of detail. As for comprehensive reconstructions, since HÜTTL'S book appeared W. WEBER has elaborated his own studies on the Antonines in *Röm. Herrschertum und Reich im zweiten Jahrhundert*, Stuttgart and Berlin 1937 (A.P. : pp. 228–81), and there has been a portrait by L. DE REGIBUS, *Antonino Pio*, Rome 1946; cf. latterly M. HAMMOND, 'The Antonine Monarchy', in *Pap. and Mon. Am. Ac. Rome*, XIX, 1959. Interesting confirmation of the general policy of A.P., particularly in the sense of showing that it was a continuation of Hadrian's policy, has been provided by the work done on coins by P. L. STRACK, *Untersuchungen zur römischen Reichspragen des zweiten Jahrhunderts, III: Die Reichspragung zur Zeit des Antoninus Pius*, Stuttgart 1937, and by H. MATTINGLY, *Coins of the Rom. Emp. in the Br. Mus.*, IV, London 1940, pp. XI–CI. In particular, for reflections in the coinage of the conflict between A.P. and the Senate on the subject of Hadrian's apotheosis, see STRACK, *op. cit.*, p. 4 (the first issue after the succession presents irregularities, it appears) and cf. MATTINGLY, *op. cit.*, p. XI. Aelius Aristides' Roman Oration still provokes much interest both for the purposes of forming a judgement on the general conditions of the age of Hadrian and the Antonines and because of its references to concrete details. There is an edition with an exhaustive commentary by J. H. OLIVER, *The Ruling Power. A Study of the Roman Empire in the Second Century after Christ through the Roman Oration of Aelius Aristides*, Philadelphia 1953 (Transactions of the Amer. Philosophical Society, XLIII, 4, pp. 871–1003). In particular, we have accepted in the main text the date of 143 proposed by OLIVER (pp. 886 f.) for the oration itself. For the title *Pius*, and for the crystallization of the formulas in the imperial title (e.g., *Caesar* for the nominee for the succession) – an indication of an ever more lively tendency to the open expression of a monarchico-dynastic feeling – see M. HAMMOND, 'Imperial Elements in the Formula of the Roman Emperors during the First Two and a Half Centuries of the Empire', in *Mem. Am. Ac. Rome*, XXV, 1957, pp. 17–64. On the members of the imperial family, confirmations and fresh information have been provided by the *Fasti Ostienses* (*Inscr. It.*, XIII, 1, pp. 205–7, 234–7): the date of the marriage of M. Aurelius and Faustina, in the early months of 145, with the distribution of a *congiarium* (the fourth) of 100 denarii; the date of the birth of their first child, 30 November 147; the conferment on 1 December on Faustina of the title of Augusta; and the assumption by M. Aurelius of the *tribunicia potestas*, with his consequent passage to *trib. pot.* II as early as 10 December 147. Previously the three events had always been assigned to 146. The same *Fasti Ostienses*, by the silence they preserve throughout 147, confirm that the 900th anniversary of Rome was celebrated in 148. They also furnish, though only preserved for the three years 145, 146, 147, a modest number of names of fresh personages. Previously we had not known the date of these men's consulships (e.g., Q. Cornelius Quadratus – Fronto's brother – *cos. a. 147*, Salvius Julianus, the jurist, *cos. ord. a. 148*) or even their senatorial rank (as in the case of Claudius Charax, the Pergamene philosopher and historian). We have also learned the date of the death of a senator who had been a distinguished character since Trajan's time, namely Sex. Erucius Clarus, *praef. urbi.* and *cos. ord. II*, in 146. He died while holding this post, in February or March. For other notable men of the reign, see P. CHARNEAUX, 'M. Vettulenus Civica Barbarus', in *Bull. Corr. Hell.*, LXXXI, 1957, pp. 121–40 (he was the step-brother of L. Aelius Caesar); A. MERLIN, 'Un proconsul d'Afrique méconnu, Egrilius Plarianus', in *Compt. rend. Ac. Inscr.*, 1942, pp. 235–42, cf. *AE*, 1942–3, 85 (the combination into one single inscription of fragments from Avitta Bibba thought to belong to two inscriptions produces, it would seem, a new proconsul of Africa, [Q?] Egrilius Plarianus. A man with the same name as his legionary commander; it may be a case of father and son); F. CUMONT, 'Épitaphe d'un fonctionnaire impériale de la Belgique romain', in *Bull. Ac. Roy. Belg.*, Cl. des Lettr. etc., XXXII, 1946, pp. 160–2 (a financial official, *a commentariis prov. Belgicae*). A. STEIN, *Präf. v. Aeg.*, pp. 82 f., inclines to regard the prefect Dinarchus (MALAL., XI, 280) as historical and belonging to the reign of Antoninus Pius.

As for the rule of A.P., what is interesting is the number and total amount of the *congiaria*; for they indicate an evolution in the field of urban relations that is unquestionable, however bad it may have been (FR. PÖSCHL., 'Die Congiarien (liberalitates) des Kaisers Antoninus Pius (nach der Vita in der Historia Augusta und nach den Münzen)', in *Hermes*, LXXVI, 1941, pp. 423–6). For the granting of the privileges in the empire, see J. H. OLIVER, 'A New Letter of Antoninus Pius', in *Am. Journ. Phil.*, LXXIX, 1958, pp. 52–60; also, for A.P. as well as Trajan and Hadrian, J. KEIL, *Forschungen in Ephesos*, IV, 1, p. 81 (immunity for the doctors of Ephesus); and, for the provincial right, S. RICCOBONO JR., *Il Gnomon dell'idios logos*, Palermo 1950 (for the actual date of drafting, L. WENGER, *Die Quellen des römischen Rechts*, Vienna 1953, pp. 462 f., who prefers the period of M. Aurelius). For Ti. Claudius Proculus Cornelianus, 'procu(rator) provin(ciae) Syriae ad rationes putandas', an office known to have been entrusted to senators as well and thus suggesting a deliberate balance between equestrian and senatorial control, see H. G. PFLAUM, in *Libyca*, III, 1955, p. 125. On the normal criteria of provincial administration, G. BARBIERI, 'L'amministrazione delle province Ponto-Bitinia et Licia – Panfilia ner II sec. d. Cr.', in *Riv. Fil.*, LXVI, 1938, pp. 365–70. As for the number of procurators under A.P., the facts given in the text have been extracted from H. G. PFLAUM, in *P.W.*, XXIII, 1, 1957, c. 1252, with the correction necessitated by the discovery of the diploma of 133 (see text, p. 411).

Fresh pieces of testimony to interventions and honours in every part of the empire are extremely numerous. The principal ones discovered since HÜTTL published his book are collected here; and we shall also mention the problems that have provoked fresh discussion. So far as administration and public works are concerned, the most interesting fresh pieces of evidence are those dealing with the boundaries and defences of Thrace. There is an inscription from Teteven in Bulgaria, dating from the years 151–152 (*AE*, 1957, 279) and another from Bizye (Vize, in Turkish Thrace) mentioning the construction of the city's towers, carried out by the local magistrates under the supervision of the governor C. Iulius Commodus, already known to us from work he did in 154–155 in the region of Burgas for the defence of the province (*AE*, 1927, 49; cf. K. BITTEL and A. M. SCHNEIDER, in *Jahrb. d. deutsch arch. Inst.*, LVI, 1941, Anz. cc. 278–80). This is naturally also of interest in connection with the history of the defence of the empire. Evidence of these interventions for work of military importance, work sometimes carried out by the soldiers themselves, has been provided by documents from Africa in particular. First there was the noteworthy discovery of the base of Sulpicius Felix at Sala, in Mauretania Tingitana (*AE*, 1931, 36 and 38;

cf. J. CARCOPINO, *Le Maroc antique*, Paris 1943, pp. 200–28; L. CHATELAIN, *Le Maroc des Romains*, Paris 1944, pp. 91–100), containing the minutes of the resolution passed by the *Salenses* in 144 to confer honours on the commanding officer of an *ala* who had protected them 'ab solitis iniuri(is) pecorumq(ue) iactura', had provided for their security 'municipium infestioribus locis maximo murorum opere minimo sumtu ambiendo' and had also done everything else he could to ensure a secure and ordered local life. Then the recent excavations at Tipasa in Mauretania Caesariensis have revealed the huge scale of the plan for the defence of the province put into effect by A.P.; it was this, as well as energetic military action, that secured the long peace that subsequently reigned in the region (J. BARADEZ, 'Les nouvelles fouilles de Tipasa et les opérations d'Antonin le Pieux en Mauretanie', in *Libyca*, 11, 1954, pp. 89–148). For a milestone of A.P.'s from the road from Auzia to Rapidum, also in Mauretania Caesariensis, see L. LESCHI, 'Route d'Auzia (Aumale) à Rapidum (Masqueray)', in *Bull. Com. Tr. Hist.*, 1936–7, pp. 301–2. On the principal road into Mauretania from Numidia, between Cuicul and Sitifis, L. GALAND, 'Mons, Mopth . . . et Mopti. Fouilles et topographie africaines', in *Mél. Éc. Franç. Rome*, LXI, 1949, pp. 35–91; for granaries built by the troops, also in Mauretania, at Rusuccuru (Tigzirt), see *AE*, 1957, 176; for an unidentifiable piece of work, carried out by a cohort at Medjedel (to the west of Bou-Saada, still in Caesariensis) and dated 148–149, see *AE*, 1938, 51. Other works in Africa: *AE*, 1954, 51, in which the governor M. Valerius Etruscus, in 151–152, dedicates to A.P. the *curia* of Thamugadi (Timgad, in Numidia), 'renovatam et exornatam'; and in the same spot the dedication of the east gate is also to A.P., according to L. LESCHI, in *Bull. Com. Tr. Hist.*, February 1940, pp. XXVII–XXIX = *AE*, 1940, 19. See now, for the whole of the activity in Africa under Antoninus Pius, P. ROMANELLI, *St. d. prov. rom. dell'Afr.*, Rome 1959, pp. 350–65. For building activity in other parts of the empire, H. S. ROBINSON's theory ('The Tower of the Winds and the Roman Marketplace', in *Am. Journ. Arch.*, XLVII, 1943, pp. 291–305) assigns to the age of A.P. the construction in Athens of the *agoranomion*, that is, the market office, in a complex of pre-existing buildings. On A. P.'s building activities at Antioch, confused in the tradition because of the similarity of names with those of Caracalla, G. DOWNEY, 'The Work of Antoninus Pius at Antioch', in *Class. Phil.*, XXXIV, 1939, pp. 369–72. On the vallum in Britain, ANNE S. ROBERTSON, 'The Antonine Wall', in *The Congress of Roman Frontier Studies, 1949*, ed. E. BIRLEY, Durham 1952, pp. 99–111. See BIRLEY's 'The Brigantian Problem, and the

First Roman Contact with Scotland', in *Rom. Br. and Rom. Army, cit.*, pp. 31–47. For a work carried out at Corstopitum (Corbridge) by Legion II *Augusta* in 139, see *AE*, 1936, 75. In Dalmatia (Delminium) the 'coh(ors) VIII vol(untariorum) turrem ad aquam tollendam fecit' towards 145 (*AE*, 1940, 176). At Callatis, in Lower Moesia, a dedication to A.P. dating from 156–157 refers to some piece of work or other (*AE*, 1928, 123, and 1937, 247.) There is also a dedication from Rhodes (G. PUGLIESE CARRATELLI, in *St. Ciaceri*, Naples 1940, pp. 254–60, cf. *AE*, 1948, 199); one from Derbe in Lycaonia (*AE*, 1960, 34); another from Palmyra (H. SEYRIG, 'Antiquités syriennes, XXX: Inscriptions', in *Syria*, XX, 1939, pp. 302–23, n. 26); and finally the inscription recording a work carried out in 150–151 by soldiers under the command of Munatius Felix in the south-eastern desert zone of Egypt (*AE*, 1952, 249).

Fresh military diplomas are also numerous: from Mauretania *CIL*, XVI, Suppl. 181, dating from 156–157; from Valentia Banasa *CIL*, XVI, 182, of the same year; from Volubilis (cf. the article – cited earlier – by H. NESSELHAUF, in *Epigr.*, XII, 1950, pp. 34–48); and the one recently published by R. THOUVENOT, in *Bull. Com. Tr. Hist.*, 1955–6 (pub. 1958), p. 86 f. This last one also comes from Volubilis; in all probability it dates from 160 and it is important because it would seem to confirm, according to H. NESSELHAUF ('Das Bürgerrecht der Soldatenkinder', in *Historia*, VIII, 1959, pp. 434–42), the exemption in favour of the children of decurions of *alae* and centurions of cohorts from the regulation – probably dating from 140 – which excluded the children of auxiliaries from the benefit of citizenship. From Raetia (Straubing) there is *CIL*, XVI, 183, of 156–157, and another from Regensburg (*CIL*, XVI, 187) of uncertain date, somewhere between 150 and 170. From Pannonia we have diplomas *CIL*, XVI, 175, of A.D. 139 (found at Albertfalva, not far from Aquincum, cf. T. NAGY, 'The Military Diploma of Albertfalva', in *Acta Arch. Ac. Scient. Hung.*, VII, 1956, pp. 17–71); *CIL*, XVI, 178, of 19 July 146 (found at Csapdi); and the two based on the same regulation, that of 9 October 148, namely *CIL*, XVI, nos. 179 and 180, both found at Regoli. In addition we have the interesting diploma for the *classiarii* of the fleet based at Misenum, dated 26 November 140 (H. G. PFLAUM, in *Rev. Arch.*, XLI, 1953, p. 68, who does not state where or how it was found; cf. *CIL*, XVI, 177), and the fragments of another, dating from between 156 and 161 and found at Karanis in Egypt (*CIL*, XVI, 184). The military history of the reign of A.P. is also involved in the inscription from Nicopolis (*AE*, 1955, 238) already cited in connection

with Hadrian (see above, p. 692). The exceptional character of the presence of so many Italians among the men discharged from the II *Traiana*
in 157 (if we discount the relative nature of such pieces of evidence) is set
in relief by the composition of the same legion to be inferred from the
discharge of 194 (recruitment of 168) attested by the brick, *CIL*, III,
6580 = *ILS*, 2304 (cf. G. FORNI, *Il reclutamento*, etc., pp. 95, 204, 219
ff.). The names on this second brick are almost all those of Egyptians. In
any case provincial origin was being more and more counterbalanced by
the intensification of Romanization, as can be seen from the names of the
non-Italians in the same inscription from Nicopolis (cf. moreover, even
in Trajan's reign, the names of the six recruits sent by the prefect to the
cohort III *Ituraeorum*, which was in fact an auxiliary cohort, in the papyrus
from Oxyrhynchus, VII, 1022, dating from 103). The inscription from
Nicopolis also seems to show that in the time of A.P. the Egyptian legion
was commanded by the *praefectus castrorum*, that is, that the *praefectus
legionis* had disappeared; this would eliminate for this period the problem
of the relation between the *praefectus castr.* and the *praefecti* of the legions.
Such a change is in any case quite natural with the reduction of the
Egyptian garrison to one single legion (cf. J. F. GILLIAM, 'The Veterans
and Praefectus Castrorum of the II Traiana in A.D. 157', in *Amer. Journ.
Phil.*, LXXVII, 1956, pp. 359–75). For a centurion already decorated by
Hadrian and then *promotus* by A.P. in various legions, see A. BETZ, in
Oesterr. Jahresh., XXXI, 1936, Beibl. cc. 101–8 (cf. *AE*, 1937, 101). On the
Brittones dediticii sent to the German *limes*, and on their conditions of discharge, see H. T. ROWELL, 'The Honesta Missio from the Numeri of the
Roman Imperial Army', in *Yale Class. St.*, VI, 1939, pp. 71–108. On the
same subject of citizenship and elevation in the social classes, the new
inscription from Volubilis about a decurion 'equo publico exornatus a
divo Pio' (*AE*, 1957, 59) is interesting. In the field of foreign affairs, the
journey to Rome of Pharasmanes of Iberia with his wife and child, recorded by CASS. D., LXIX, 15, 3 (BOISS., III, p. 244) and by the
V. Pii, 9, 6, is mentioned in a new fragment of the *Fasti Ostienses*, though
one that cannot be dated (H. NESSELHAUF, 'Ein neues Fragment der
Fasten von Ostia', in *Athen*, XXXVI, 1958, pp. 219–28). On Eastern
policy again see F. CARRATA-THOMES, 'Gli Alani nella politica
orientale di Antonino Pio', in *Ann. Fac. Lett. Torino*, X, 2, 1958.

The new tendencies in the imperial cult are illustrated by some interesting fresh pieces of evidence. While the old formulas (*pro salute*, etc.) still
continue to be used, the dedication of the so-called 'arch of Crescens' at
Cuicul in Numidia (*AE*, 1925, 23–4; 1940, 40) is not to the 'Fortune of

Antoninus' but, as is apparent from new fragments, 'to the Fortuna Augusta, to Antoninus, to Mars, genius of the colony'; see L. LESCHI, 'Inscription de l'arc dit de Crescens à Djemila', in *Bull. Com. Tr. Hist.*, Nov. 1947, pp. VIII–XI(= Années 1946–7–8–9, Paris 1953, pp. 338–342).In connection with the *pietas* particularly reflected in the monumental records of the cult of Hadrian, Marciana and Matidia, see F. CASTAGNOLI, 'Due archi trionfali della Via Fluminia, presso Piazza Sciarra', in *Bull. Comm. Arch.*, LXX, 1942, pp. 57–82, espec. pp. 74–82. In the honours paid to Faustina when she was still alive, the inscription from Corinth, now fragmentary, published by A. WEST in 1931 (*Corinth*, VIII 2, *Latin Inscriptions*, n. 22), can be completed on the basis of the translation of two travellers who saw it intact in the eighteenth century (B. D. MERITT, 'Honours to Faustina at Corinth', in *Class. Phil.*, XLII, 1947, pp. 181–2). For her consecration and the cult, always kept alive, H. MATTINGLY, 'The Consecration of Faustina the Elder and her Daughter', in *Harv. Theol. Rev.*, XLI, 1948, pp. 147–51. Two new dedications 'divae Faustinae' have come to light at Thamugadi (*AE*, 1954, 152) and Naples (*AE*, 1956, 19). There is ample testimony to the cultivation of the worship of the whole imperial family. 'Numini d(omus Augustae)' and to its members, that is, to A.P. and his adoptive sons, is the dedication on the inscribed relief from Ostia, of 160, published by H. FUHRMANN, 'Ein Reliefbildnis des Prinzen L. Aelius Aurelius Commodus aus dem Jahre 160 n. Chr.', in *Jahrb. d. deutsch. arch. Inst.*, LIV, 1939, Arch. Anz., cc. 294–302 (*AE*, 1940, 102). This relief is fragmentary, but must have represented A.P. between his sons. The same iconographical arrangement appears in other monuments and in the record of the arrangement of the statues in temples and public places: at Cillium (proconsular Africa) an inscription (*AE*, 1957, 77) refers to two statues (of A.P. and his son L. Aelius imp. Caesar (?)) and to an 'imago argentea' of Faustina the Younger, presented by some one 'ob honorem aedilitatis'. At Rome an altar dating from 153 is dedicated 'Iovi Optimo Maximo pro salute' of A.P., Marcus Aurelius Caesar and his children (*AE*, 1951, 184). Two others, again at Rome, and again *pro salute* of the same people (A. M. COLINI, in *Epigr.*, I, 1939, pp. 122–5 = *AE*, 1940, 71 and 72) are dedicated one to the Sun and the other to the Moon, 'iussu numinis Iovis Dolochini'; interesting testimony, among other things, to the process of fusion going on in religion. Ostia has also yielded the interesting inscription that lists the gifts for the furnishing of the *statio* of a college for the imperial cult. The *statio* was inaugurated in 143 and further enriched in 154 (G. CALZA, 'Un documento del culto imperiale in una nuova iscrizione Ostiense', in *Epigr.*, I, 1939, pp. 28–36 = *AE*, 1940, 62). Among these gifts are several 'imagines argenteae' of A.P. and of the two adoptive sons (the name *Verissimus Caesar* for M. Aurelius is interesting – it seldom appears in inscriptions; and the name *Aelius Caesar* for the other son is a *unicum* unless it is a question of a bust of his father, L. Aelius Caesar, who died in 138. The other mention, *L. Aelius Commodus*, is regular in form and gives the precise official name, *L. Aelius Aurelius Commodus*, and the consular date). There are also a great many new inscriptions bearing witness to collective religious dedications in the provinces as well. From Capidava in Lower Moesia, there is the series of dedications by veterans 'I.O.M. et Iunoni Reginae pro salute' of A.P. and M. Aurelius (*AE*, 1934, 102, 103, 104) and of A.P. and L. Aurelius (106). From Abritus, also in Moesia, comes the inscription 'Herculi pro salute' of A.P. and M. Aurelius, put up by the 'veterani et c(ives) R(omani) et consistentes Abrito ad c[an(abas)]' (*AE*, 1957, 97). And there are the two altars from Troesmis in Moesia (*AE*, 1957, 266 and 1960, 337); the first lacks the inscription, which was however probably similar to the one on the second and contained the dedication *pro salute* of A.P. and M. Aurelius. The dedication from Volubilis (*AE*, 1942–3, 18), put up 'ob honorem seviratus' by a freedman 'imp. Caes. divo Antonino Pio' is interesting because of the mixed formula it employs.

To turn to problems concerning the affirmation of Christianity: for the ascription to the period of Hadrian (in conformity with the ancient tradition) and not to that of A.P. of the Apology of Aristides of Athens, see J. QUASTEN, *Patrology*, I, *The Beginnings of Patristic Literature*, Utrecht and Brussels 1950, pp. 191 f., and A. OMODEO, *Saggi sul Cristianesimo antico*, Naples 1958, pp. 593–601 (the opposite view is taken by H. E. STIER, with bibliography, in *Reallex. f. Antike u. Christentum*, I, 1942, c. 478). For the shifting to M. Aurelius's reign of the martyrdom of St Polycarp, see H. GRÉGOIRE and P. ORGELS, 'La véritable date du martyre di S. Polycarpe (23 février 177) et le "corpus Polycarpianum"', in *Anal. Boll.*, LXIX, 1951, pp. 1–38; H. I. MARROU, 'La date du martyre de S. Polycarpe', *ibid.*, LXXI, 1953, pp. 5–20 (anni 161–8). This shift is also accepted by J. VOGT, in *Reallex, f. Antike u. Christentum*, II, 1954, c. 1175.

For the history of the law, G. CARDASCIA, 'L'apparition dans le droit des classes d'honestiores et d'humiliores', in *Rev. Dr. Fr. Étr.*, XXVIII, 1950, pp. 305–37; 461–85. In the field of literature and intellectual currents, according to A. PERETTI (*Luciano, un intellettuale greco contro Roma*, Florence 1946), Lucian's *Nigrinus* is a reply to Aelius

Aristides' Roman Oration (for a different view, see OLIVER, *The Ruling Power, cit.*, p. 892, n. 20). For art, see C. WEICKERT, 'Der Beginn der Spätantike', in *Jahrb. d. deutsch arc. Inst.*, LXIII–LXIV, 1948–9, Arch. Anz., cc. 260–6; also the survey of sculpture, seen as characteristic of an era of relative 'enlightened' classicism, by CH. PICARD, 'Chronique de la sculpture étrusco-latine (1940–50)', in *Rev. Ét. Lat.*, XXXI, 1953, pp. 301–94. On Chap. 8, 2 of the *Vita Pii*, containing the list of the buildings erected by A.P., see FR. PÖSCHL. 'Erläuterungen zur Vita Antonini Pii in der Historia Augusta', in *Wien. St.*, LXVI, 1953, pp. 178–81.

MARCUS AURELIUS.
THE PHILOSOPHER EMPEROR. THE FAMILY

Most interest at the moment centres round Marcus Aurelius the philosopher and man of letters; to cite only a few recent monographs and general works, see AD. LEVI, *Storia della filosofia romana*, Florence 1949, pp. 167–84; A. CRESSON, *Marc-Aurèle. Sa vie, son œuvre, avec un exposé de sa philosophie*, Paris 1939; W. GOERLITZ, *Marc Aurel. Kaiser und Philosoph*, Stuttgart 1954. Particular attention has been given to the beginnings and formation of his thought and of his literary style itself in the cultural climate of the time and in the context of the tradition (F. MARTINAZZOLI, *La successio di Marco Aurelio. Struttura e spirito del primo libro dei Pensieri*, Bari 1951, espec. the final chapter, pp. 193–202; G. FUNAIOLI, 'La conquista dell'individuo nel mondo antico', in *Misc. Galbiati*, II, Milan 1951, pp. 1–11; H. R. NEUENSCHWANDER, *Mark Aurels Beziehungen zu Seneca und Poseidonios*, Berne 1951; L. ALFONSI, 'Contributo allo studio delle fonti del pensiero di M. Aurelio', in *Aevum*, XXVIII, 1954, pp. 101–17, with ample bibliography, pp. 102–3; M. VAN DEN HOUT, 'Reminiscences of Fronto in Marcus Aurelius' Book of Meditations', in *Mnem.* IV, 3, 1950, pp. 330–5. There is more about the recent upsurge of interest in M. Aurelius in L. ALFONSI's review of NEUENSCHWANDER's book and in the comment on W. THEILER's *Recordi* (Zurich 1951) in *Aevum*, XXVI, 1952, pp. 579–82. In addition, people have tried to discover the essence of his character (J. A. DE GROOT, 'Karakterstructuur van een Keizer', in *Hermeneus*, XX, 1948, pp. 17–24 and 33–41; R. DAILLY and H. VAN EFFENTERRE, 'Le cas Marc-Aurèle. Essai de psychosomatique historique', in *Rev. Ét. Anc.*, LVI, 1954, pp. 347–65). The man and philosopher undoubtedly prevail over the emperor in modern reconstructions and even those scholars who aim to illuminate his political activity in particular or to examine the concrete historical milieu in which M. Aurelius was formed and lived are influenced in this direction (WEBER, *Röm. Herrschertum und Reich im zweiten Jahrhundert*, Stuttgart and Berlin 1937, pp. 282–350, cf. *Cambr. Anc. Hist.*, XI, 1936, pp. 340–76; A. S. L. FARQUHARSON, *Marcus Aurelius, His Life and His World*, ed. D. A. REES, Oxford 1951, 2nd ed., 1952, who in any case deals only with the period before the accession, producing in particular a penetrating survey of the cultural conditions of the period, pp. 2–8). This has happened partly because the question of the extent of the influence of M. Aurelius's philosophical training on his practical activity has been seen as a problem in itself. In the view of P. NOYEN, 'Marcus Aurelius, the Greatest Practician of Stoicism' in *Ant. Class.*, XXIV, 1955, pp. 372–83, Marcus did in fact practise stoicism in his public and private life, and this conclusion on the fundamental unity of the man as philosopher and emperor is certainly acceptable. The history of the reign of Marcus Aurelius on this basis has still to be written. What would be useful for this would be a preliminary collection of all the material in an analytical work like the one produced by HÜTTL for Antoninus Pius. Only certain aspects of the political activity are examined by F. CARRATA THOMES, *Il regno di Marco Aurelio*, Turin 1953 (cf. the same scholar's 'Per la critica di M. Aurelio', in *Pubbl. Fac. Lett. e. Fil. Univ. Torino*, VII 5, Turin 1955). A. PIGANIOL's 'Marc-Aurèle', in *Les grandes figures*, pub. by S. CHARLÉTY, Paris 1939, and G. SOLERI, *Marc' Aurelio*, Brescia 1947, are only useful profiles. See latterly CH. PARAIN, *Marc-Aurèle*, Paris 1957 (*Portraits d'histoire*).

M. Aurelius's succession does not present any difficulties: see M. HAMMOND, 'The Transmission of the Powers' etc., in *Mem. Am. Ac. Rome*, XXIV, 1956, pp. 98 ff. As for L. Verus, P. LAMBRECHTS' attempt at a rehabilitation, 'L'empereur Lucius Verus. Essai de réhabilitation', in *Ant. Class.*, III, 1934, pp. 173–201, is not convincing. Similarly CARRATA THOMES's view, *op. cit.*, pp. 64–8, that Marcus took Lucius as a colleague in a second period is contradicted not only by the information furnished by the sources but also by the complete absence of any coins of Marcus before the co-regency with Lucius and by the existence of coins of Lucius as well as those of Marcus celebrating the *congiarium* distributed at the succession (MATTINGLY, *Coins of the Rom. Emp. in the Br. Mus.*, IV, 1940, p. CIX). For the honours paid to Antoninus Pius after M. Aurelius's succession, E. HOHL, 'Die angebliche Doppelbestattung des Antoninus Pius', in *Klio*, XXXI, 1938, pp. 169–85 (*contra*, A. PIGANIOL, *Hist. de Rome*[3], Paris 1948, p. 333). For the consolidation of the mystique of power in the names and titles, see M. HAMMOND, 'Imperial Elements in the Formula of the Roman Emperors' etc., in *Mem. Am. Ac. Rome*, XXV, 1957, pp. 17–64 (in particular, *Verissimus Caesar* for M. Aurelius when he was still Caesar – a title known from the literary sources – is now attested epigraphically for the first time in an inscription from Ostia, *AE*, 1940, 62).

So far as M. Aurelius's family is concerned, see on Faustina, J. TOUTAIN, 'Réflexions sur une monnaie romaine', in *Hommages Bidez-Cumont*, Brussels 1949, pp. 331–8. Without completely rejecting the derogatory reports of the *Historia Augusta* and Cassius Dio, Toutain seeks to justify the empress's conduct as that of a queen 'au tempérament ardent et voluptueux'. He finds confirmation of this (but is it possible in something so official?) in the absolute predominance of representations of Venus on her coins. For the worship of *Diva Faustina*, similar in kind and intensity to that given to her mother, see H. MATTINGLY, 'The Consecration of Faustina the Elder and her Daughter', in *Harv. Theol. Rev.*, XLI, 1948, pp. 147–51. On her daughters, see the recent remarks of G. BARBIERI, in *Not. d. Sc.*, 1953, pp. 155 f. and of E. HOHL, 'Kaiser Commodus und Herodian', in *Sitz.-ber. d. deutsch. Ak. d. Wiss. zu Berlin*, Kl. f. Gesellschaftswiss, 1954, I, pp. 5–7. The date 30 November 147 – known from the *Fasti Ostienses* – of the birth of Annia Galeria Aurelia Faustina, who must certainly have been the first-born child for the event to provoke the extraordinary honours voted to her parents (*tribunicia potestas* for Marcus, title of Augusta for Faustina) at a time when after more than two years of marriage there may have been doubts about the couple's fertility, now prevents us from retaining the date 147 (BORGHESI, MOMMSEN) for M. Aurelius Caesar's letter to the people of Smyrna (DITTENBERGER, *Syll.*[3], 851 = *IGR*, IV, 1399). In this letter there is mention of a male child born to M. Aurelius but dying soon afterwards. The letter cannot be moved back to 146 since it contains a reference to the *tribunicia potestas* (though without a figure), which we now know (from the *Fast. Ost.*) to have been conferred on 30 November 147. The year 148 can also be excluded, since the date 28 March contained in the letter rules out the idea of the birth of another child if Anna Galeria Aurelia Faustina was born on the previous 30 November. The date of the letter and consequently the date (a few days earlier) of the birth of the male child for whom the people of Smyrna had commissioned the augurs and received the Emperor's thanks – who was grateful, even though 'things turned out differently' (line 10), since the child died – must therefore lie between 28 March 149 and the year 158 (the date of the *praescriptum*, preserved only in part, of a letter of Antoninus Pius following immediately on the same tablet). No more precise indication is provided by the name, contained in the letter, of the proconsul of Asia, T. Atilius Maximus, who himself is placed in 146–7 simply on the basis of this inscription (MAGIE, *Rom. Rule in Asia Min.*, p. 1584). Nor is any further light shed by the references to the II consulship of M. Aurelius (from 145 to 161) and to the *tribunicia potestas*, used of course without any figure. Thus we also need to shift to 149 – from the usually-accepted 148 (*PIR²*, I, p. 127, no. 707) – the date of birth of Annia Aurelia Galeria Lucilla, the future Lucilla Augusta, whose birthday is known (7 March, *IGR*, I, 1509). The combination of dates suggests that the male child of the letter to the citizens of Smyrna was Lucilla's twin brother; but he can also be placed elsewhere in the numerous progeny of M. Aurelius, whether or not it was the T. Aelius Antoninus of the inscription from Olympia (*ILS*, 8803c) or one of the children of Marcus who died during the lifetime of Antoninus Pius and figure in the inscriptions in Hadrian's mausoleum (*ILS*, 383, 384). On Lucilla Augusta, Verus's widow, betrothed to Pompeianus, and for the problem she presents in connection with the succession of her brother Commodus, see J. AYMARD, 'Lucilla Augusta', in *Rev. Arch.*, XXXV, 1950, pp. 58–66. On Marcus Aurelius's sons-in-law as conflicting factors in the succession, J. KEIL, 'Kaiser Marcus und die Thronfolge', in *Klio*, XXXI, 1938, pp. 293–300, who also publishes (p. 296, cf. *AE*, 1939, 127) the unpublished inscription from Ephesus reported by A. STEIN in *PIR²*, II, p. 141, no. 612. This inscription, by revealing that Ceionia Fabia, the sister of L. Verus, was the mother of M. Peducaeus Plautius Quintillus, one of M. Aurelius's sons-in-law, has disclosed a new link in the dynastic chain. That L. Verus's and Ceionia's uncle, who accompanied Lucilla on her bridal journey in 164, must have been called M. Vettulenus (not M. Ceionius) Civica Barbarus has been demonstrated by R. SYME, 'Antonine Relatives: Ceionii and Vettulani', in *Athen.*, XXXV, 1957, p. 308. There are a number of fresh inscriptions mentioning members of the family. A terracotta seal of Domitia Lucilla Minor, wife of Annius Verus and mother of M. Aurelius, was published in the *Am. Journ. Arch.*, LIX, 1955, p. 162 (*AE*, 1955, 3). Altars of Diva Faustina, M. Aurelius's wife, are recorded at Aquileia and at Iader (Zara), *AE*, 1956, 232 – an interesting piece of testimony, among other things, to the diffusion of the worship of the second deified Faustina, which was quite extensive. A *fistula aquaria* bearing the name of Cornificia, a daughter of M. Aurelia, is described by G. BARBIERI, in *Not. d. Sc.*, 1953, pp. 151–89 (*AE*, 1954, 171).

According to L. ROBERT, *Hellenica*, II, 1946, pp. 37–42, the eighteen texts from Thessalonica mentioning, between 219 and 269, priests and agonotheti of the 'theòs Phoulbos, theòs Aurelios Phoulbos' refer to T. Aurelius Fulvus Antoninus, Commodus's twin brother, who died in 165 at the age of four; previously 'Phoulbos' had been thought to be Antoninus Pius (cf. *AE*, 1948, 221). According to PFLAUM, the inscription (*AE*, 1950, 245) from an architrave at Yalova in Bithynia refers to Crispina Augusta, the wife of Commodus (cf. J. and L. ROBERT, in *Rev. Ét. Gr.*, LXII, 1949, p. 144, no. 183a). Two dedications, one from Athens (*IG*, II², 4780 + *Am. Journ. Arch.*, 1941, p. 540; cf. *AE*, 1947, 10) and another, dating from 168–169, from Pompeiopolis in Paphlagonia (*AE*, 1939, 26) refer to the son-in-law Claudius Severus. The dedications to Verus alone present a certain interest; for example, the one from Ostia, to the 'Genio decurionum Ostiensium' and L. Aelius Aurelius Commodus (i.e., to L. Verus when Antoninus Pius was still alive, *AE*, 1940, 30); the one from Attaleia put up by the boulê and demos, *AE*, 1960, 314; and the one from Hebran in Syria, put up by the soldiers of Legion III *Gallica* when Avidius Cassius was governor and hence after the eastern expedition (*AE*, 1936, 153). On L. Verus, see the theory about his relations with the Athenian aristocracy and the sanctuary of Eleusis in the commentary on the new edition of inscription *IG*, II², 1092, by J. H. OLIVER, 'The Eleusinian Endowment', in *Hesperia*, XXI, 1952, pp. 381–99.

On the iconography of M. Aurelius and L. Verus, see P. SCHAZMANN, 'Buste en or représentant l'empereur Marc-Aurèle trouvé à Avenches en 1939', in *Rev. Suisse d'Art et d'Arch.*, 1940, pp. 69–93, and more recently G. CAPUTO, 'Nuovi ritratti colossali di Marco Aurelio e Lucio Vero', in *Arch. Class.*, X, 1958, pp. 64–8 (from the theatre at Leptis Magna).

MARCUS AURELIUS'S WORK AT HOME

That this seems like a continuation of Antoninus Pius's work is shown by the substantial identity of principles and interests in the legislation (as is attested by what remains of it in the *Digest*) and by the epigraphical remains as a whole, which repeat in type and occasion those of his predecessor. A survey of the legislative activity is provided (in Dutch), with a useful index of the laws of Marcus Aurelius mentioned in the *Digest*, by P. NOYEN, 'Divus Marcus, princeps prudentissimus et iuris religiosissimus', in *Rev. Intern. de Dr. de l'Ant.*, 3 sér., I, 1954, pp. 349–71. For individual laws, see again P. NOYEN, 'Marc-Aurèle et le problème de l'irresponsabilité, in *Nouv. Clio*, VI, 195 (Mél. R. Goossens), pp. 278–

282, and A. GUARINO, 'Di un rescritto dei divi fratres in tema di collatio bonorum', in *Rend. Ist. Lomb.*, LXXIII, 1939–40, pp. 363–82 (who confirms the concept of a pure and simple continuation in private law, without any original innovations by the Princeps). See also, for the even wider affirmation of the different treatment in penal law of the *honestiores* and *humiliores*, the article mentioned above (p. 707) by G. CARDASCIA, 'L'apparition' etc., in *Rev. Dr. Fr. Étr.*, XXVIII, 1950, pp. 305–37. On the important question of the judicial competence of the praetorian prefects, see the new commentary on the famous letter to the magistrates of Saepinum (*CIL*, IX, 2438) by A. PASSERINI, *Coort. pret.*, pp. 251–9. The resumption of the discussion on the *oratio de pretiis gladiatorum minuendis* (*ILS*, 5163, cf. RICCOBONO, *Leges*², p. 294, no. 49), after the better readings proposed by ALVARO D'ORS, 'Observaciones al texto de la or. de pretiis glad. minuendis', in *Emerita*, XVIII, 1950 (but pub. 1952), pp. 311–39, has produced important studies, especially in the field of research into the concrete procedure involved in the formation of the laws: J. STROUX, 'Neues zur Geschäftsordnung des römischen Senates', in *Philologus*, XCVIII, 1954, pp. 150–4; J. H. OLIVER and R. E. A. PALMER, 'Minutes of an Act of the Roman Senate', in *Hesperia*, XXIV, 1955, pp. 320–49 (which must be regarded as the definitive edition of the famous text from Italica and also of the fragments of the similar text from Sardis, *ILS*, 9340; see also J. H. OLIVER, in *Am. Journ. Phil.*, LXXVI, 1955, pp. 189–92). From this point of view the document links up with the *oratio Claudii* of papyrus *BGU*, 611 (*col*. III, ll. 10–22, RICCOBONO, *Leges*², pp. 285 ff.; see above, p. 601), which illuminates the procedure in senatorial discussions and the relationship between the Princeps and the Senate on such occasions. The relationship established by OLIVER and PALMER (cf. A. PIGANIOL, 'Les trinci gaulois, gladiateurs consacrés', in *Rev. Ét. Anc.*, XXII, 1920, pp. 283–90 = *Recherches sur les jeux romains*, Strasbourg 1923, pp. 62–71) between this measure and the episode of the Christian martyrs of Lyon is also convincing. See also, on the subject of games and the limitation of expenditure, with deductions about the economic situation, F. M. DE ROBERTIS, 'Dispensa dal munus venatorium in una costituzione imperiale di recente scoperta', in *Historia*, IX, 1935, pp. 248–60. The article deals with the inscription (which completes *CIL*, VI, 31420) published by R. PARIBENI with the others from the excavations of the imperial fora in *Not. d. Sc.*, 1933, pp. 438–44. The inscription concerns the dispensation claimed by a *magister vici*, on the basis of an imperial *epistula*, from the *munera* of his office, more specifically that of giving a *venatio*. The public importance, indeed indispensability, of games as a manifestation of munificence (this is how J. AYMARD interprets the 'megalopsychia' of the mosaic pavement from Antioch, in 'La Mégalopsychia de Yakto et la magnanimitas de Marc-Aurèle', in *Rev. Ét. Anc.*, LV, 1953, pp. 301–6) is unquestioned in the age of Marcus Aurelius, but the recognition that 'facultates sufficere iniuncto munere possint' is henceforth explicit and is 'a juridical principle introduced by the emperors into the public law via administrative practice' (p. 257). However, the attribution of the document to the period of M. Aurelius is not certain, although ideas of this kind are characteristic of the epoch and the link with the measure concerning gladiators seems natural. For another recent document connected with the growing state control over the organization of shows, see M. SORDI, 'L'epigrafe di un pantomimo recentemente scoperta a Roma', in *Epigr.*, XV, 1953 (but pub. 1955), pp. 104–21, especially the observations on pp. 119 f. For the health of the finances under M. Aurelius, see TH. PEKARY, 'Studien zur römischen Wahrungs- und Finanzgeschichte von 161 bis 235 n. Chr.', in *Historia*, VIII, 1959, pp. 443–89.

So far as the administration of the empire is concerned, the wide employment of competent provincials and their rapid promotion thanks to merit (and to the need for men, especially during the wars) has been confirmed by the *cursus* (the second, that of M. Valerius Maximianus, is magnificent) reflected in two inscriptions found recently at Lambaesis and Diana Veteranorum (H. G. PFLAUM, 'Deux carrières équestres de Lambèse et de Zana', in *Libyca*, III, 1955, pp. 123–54, cf. *AE*, 1956, 123 and 124; for the part played by the Danubian wars, see below, pp. 721 f.). The career of C. Aufidius Victorinus, M. Aurelius's colleague and friend, has been plausibly reconstructed by H. G. PFLAUM, 'La carrière de C. Aufidius Victorinus, condisciple de Marc-Aurèle', in *Compt. rend. Ac. Inscr.*, 1956, pp. 189–200, on the basis of *AE*, 1934, 155 (cf. 1957, 121; 1958, 26). For other personages, see E. CONDURACHI, 'Sur la carrière de Q. Fullius Maximus, gouverneur de Thrace', in *Anuarul Institutului de Studii Clasice* (Sibiu), III, 1936–40, pp. 148–52, and R. THOUVENOT, 'Deuxième table de patronat découverte à Banasa (Maroc)', in *Compt. rend. Ac. Inscr.*, 1947, pp. 485–9; cf. *AE*, 1948, 115. Thouvenot draws attention to a case (in A.D. 162) of the choice as patron of the colony (known as Aurelia Banasa, not Aelia Banasa, as the inscription disclosed) of an ex-governor of the province, the procurator Q. Claudius Ferox Aeronius Montanus (the name also reveals as erroneous the emendation Q. *Apronius Montanus* made in *PIR*^{2}, I, pp. 73, 191, no. 974 to *CIL*, VIII, 21825). For the two important citizens of Thuburbo Maius honoured by the emperor *equo publico*, see inscriptions *AE*, 1941, 36 and 37. For Bithynia, which was put under a governor at the beginning of Marcus Aurelius's reign, see G. BARBIERI, 'L'amministrazione delle province Ponto-Bitinia e Licia-Panfilia nel II sec. d. Cr.', in *Rev. Fil.*, LXVI, 1938, pp. 365–70. The interesting diploma of 21 July 164 (*CIL*, XVI, Suppl., 185) from Palatovo (Bulgaria) confirms among other things that the procuratorial régime established in Dacia Porolissensis under Hadrian was still in force in 164. An interesting example of relations between the periphery and the centre is furnished by the fragments of an inscription in Greek and Latin from Rome commented upon by M. GUARDUCCI in G. MARCHETTI-LONGHI, 'Gli scavi del Largo Argentina', in *Bull. Comm. Arch.*, LXXI, 1943–5, pp. 74–9. The inscription deals with an embassy which came to Rome in 174 from Seleucia in Pieria. The better reading of the letter from Julius Paternus to the emperors (*CIL*, X, 7024) established by G. MANGANARO in *Kôkalos*, V, 1959, pp. 145–58 (= *AE*, 1960, 202) should be borne in mind. Fresh light is cast on the history of the eminent family of the Vedii Antonini of Ephesus, with a reference to L. Verus's stay there, by *AE*, 1959, 13 and 14, found in 1956.

In the case of M. Aurelius, too, new inscriptions are continually being discovered. They refer to public works carried out in the empire, to occasions when it was thought right to pay honour to the Emperor or to members of his family, or simply to acts of homage by private individuals and communities. For the two areas richest in finds – Africa and Asia Minor – see respectively P. ROMANELLI, *St. prov. rom. Afr.*, Rome 1959, pp. 375–80, and D. MAGIE, *Rom. Rule As. Min.*, Princeton, N.J. 1950, pp. 663 f. and 1528–37, espec. p. 1535, n. 11. The only things to be noted in Rome are two new *cippi* from the banks of the Tiber, marking the continuation of work begun by Pius (*AE*, 1951, 182b–c) and an inscription on a lead pipe (*AE*, 1948, 75). From Ostia there is a dedication to M. Aurelius by a college, *AE*, 1940, 66. The dedication to M. Aurelius and L. Verus on a lead tablet (*AE*, 1952, 88), mentioned as having just been discovered at Wells (England) in an old commentary of 1530, has been explained by R. P. WRIGHT, who juxtaposes it to *CIL*, VII, 1211, in *Journ. of Rom. St.*, XLI, 1951, p. 141, n. 7. From Britain, too, comes the dedication by a *vexillatio* of Legion XX *Valeria Victrix*, dating from autumn 163, *AE*, 1947, 128 (new supplements of *CIL*, VII, 473). From Gallatis (Lower Moesia) there is a dedication – on the occasion of the construction of the town walls, carried out at the town's own expense under the direction of the governor, M. Valerius Bradua – [pro salute] of M. Aurelius, Faustina and the children, [d]omusq[ue totiu]s eorum, [pro]que senatu populoque [R(omano et] ordine et [popul]o Callatia[no]rum, *AE*, 1937, 246. From Cocargea (in the region on the far side of the Danube attached to Moesia) comes an altar with a dedication to M. Aurelius (described by M. FLORIANI SQUARCIAPINO in *St. Rom.*, VI, 1958, p. 698; cf. *AE*, 1960, 342). Other new inscriptions are as follows: at Hoghiz (Dacia) an altar of a cohort with a dedication, dating from 177–180, *AE*, 1944, 42; two dedications from the Megarid, dating from 161–169, *SEG*, XIII, 1956, 291 A.B. (already known, *IG*, VII, 77, but B. D. MERITT has suggested a better reading, cf. *Hesperia*, Suppl. VIII, 1949, p. 220); at Chios a dedication to M. Aurelius when he was still Caesar, *AE*, 1957, 264 = *SEG*, XV, 531; at Orkistos (Phrygia) a dedication already known (*CIG*, III, add. 38226²), now better published (*Mon. As. Min. Ant.*, VII, 1956, p. 69, no. 304); at Gerasa (Syria) the dedication of a temple, dating from about 163, *AE*, 1939, 253; from Rouafa (Hedjaz) a dedication to M. Aurelius and L. Verus (between 166 and 169 for the construction of a big temple, probably the most important shrine of the Tamudei, with a probable reference to the reigning governor of Arabia (H. SEYRIG, 'Antiquités syriennes, 66 – Sur trois inscriptions du Hedjaz', in *Syria*, XXXIV, 1957, pp. 259–61). Cyrene has yielded a number of references to M. Aurelius: a dedication of A.D. 161 (*SEG*, IX, 1944, 170); another dedication dating from 176–180 for the restoration of the temple of Apollo (*SEG*, IX, 172); a mention of M. Aurelius and L. Verus in an inscription used a second time (*AE*, 1960, 200); and finally a dedication connected with the great temple of Zeus 'for the Fortune and Victory' of M. Aurelius (*AE*, 1954, 41). From Leptis Magna comes the dedication by a *lib(ertus)* or *lib(rarius)* *verna* to M. Aurelius when he was still Caesar, *AE*, 1957, 231; from Carthage a dedication by the Colonia Concordia Iulia Carthago to M. Aurelius and L. Verus, A.D. 161–162, *AE*, 1949, 27; from Mactar a dedication by the *civitas Mactaritana* to M. Aurelius (*AE*, 1960, 114); at Thuburbo Maius a dedication to M. Aurelius by a private individual, *AE*, 1941, 35; from Lambaesis the three identical dedications, put up between February and December 169, for the construction of the amphitheatre and the inscription, put up between 176 and 180, for a repair to it (L. LESCHI, in *Libyca*, II, 1954, pp. 171–80 and 181–5; cf. *AE*, 1955, 134, 135); and finally from Volubilis the dedication 'pro salute' of the Emperor of a big altar, dating from between 173 and 175. This is also important (see below, pp. 724 and 728) for the history of the movement of the Mauretanian tribes (EDM. FRÉZOULS, 'Inscriptions nouvelles de Volubilis', in

Mel. Éc. Fr. Rome, LXVIII, 1956, pp. 110–14; cf. *AE*, 1957, 202; first reported in *Compt. rend. Ac. Inscr.*, 1952, pp. 396–8 (= *AE*, 1953, 78).

The art, culture, thought and religious feeling of the period provoke continual interest. The column and the historical friezes will be discussed later in connection with the Danubian wars; here we shall only mention, because of its purely historico-artistic character, M. WEGNER, 'Die Kunstgeschichtliche Stellung der Marcussäule', in *Jahrb. d. deutsch. arch. Inst.*, XLVI, 1931, pp. 61–174. In the general field, see the survey of sculpture by CH. PICARD, 'Chronique de la sculpture étrusco-latine (1940–1950)', in *Rev. Ét. Lat.*, XXXI, 1953, pp. 301–94. In Picard's view, the reign of M. Aurelius, like the period of Antoninus before it and that of Commodus after it, represents an era of relatively 'enlightened classicism'. See also the observations of M. PALLOTTINO, 'L'orientamento stilistico della scultura Aureliana', in *Le Arti*, I, 1938, pp. 32–6, and M. CAGIANO DE AZEVEDO, 'Alcune osservazioni sui rilievi storici aureliani', in *Rom. Mitt.*, LX–LXI, 1953–4, pp. 207–10; both are inclined to see a more emphatic change and distance from the classical tradition. For questions of detail, see F. CASTAGNOLI, 'Osservazioni sul medaglione dell'Adventus di M. Aurelio', in *Bull. Comm. Arch.*, LXXI, 1943–5, pp. 137–40 (topographical identification of monuments depicted on a coin of M. Aurelius); S. AURIGEMMA, *L'arco di Marco Aurelio e di Lucio Vero in Tripoli*, Rome 1938 (cf. G. CAPUTO, 'Il consolidamento dell'arco di M. Aurelio in Tripoli', in *Afr. Ital.*, VII, 1940, pp. 46–66); E. HILL, 'Roman Elements in the Settings of the Synagogue Frescoes at Dura', in *Marsyas*, I, 1941, pp. 1–15 (comparison with the column of M. Aurelius). On M. Aurelius's relations with philosophers, see R. PACK, 'Two Sophists and two Emperors', in *Class. Phil.*, XLII, 1947, pp. 17–20 (Pack regards the relationship with Aelius Aristides, whom Marcus met at Smyrna in 176, PHILOSTR., *V. Sophist.*, II, 9, as comparable with the relationship between Julian and Libanius); on modes of thought dear to Marcus, J. O. THOMSON, 'Marcus Aurelius and the Small Earth', in *Journ. of. Rom St.*, XLIII, 1953, pp. 47 f.; on spiritual conflicts and the ever larger presence in them of Christianity, V. STEGEMANN, 'Christentum und Stoizismus im Kampf um die geistigen Lebenswerte im 2. Jahrhundert nach Christus', in *Welt als Geschichte*, 1941, pp. 295–330. On religion, J. BEAUJEU, *La religion romaine à l'apogée de l'empire*, Paris 1955, now summarizes all the problems, pp. 331–68, relating them above all to political developments, particularly in the field of relations with Christianity (pp. 353–8). Greater official persistence in the persecution of Christians, possibly as a local extension of more general norms (such as those of PAUL., *Sent.*, V, 21 and *Dig.*, XLVIII, 29–30), must have been a reality, as seems to be proved by putting EUSEB., *Hist. Eccl.*, IV, 26, 9–10, alongside the texts cited; see J. ZEILLER, 'Sur un passage énigmatique de l'Apologie de Méliton de Sardes', in *Compt. rend. Ac. Inscr.*, 1956, p. 312, and *idem*, 'A propos d'un passage énigmatique de Méliton de Sardes relatif à la persécution contre les chrétiens', in *Rev. Ét. Augustiniennes*, II, 1956, pp. 257–63. The famous miracles of the fire from heaven and the rain, in the campaign against the Quadi, depicted on the column, have been the subject of fresh discussion, particularly in connection with the chronology of the Danubian wars and with the dating of the column itself (see below, p. 720). For the religious aspects of the episode (especially the typical rivalry between traditional religion, Egyptian cults and Christianity to claim the credit), see J. BEAUJEU, *op. cit.*, pp. 342–7; A. OMODEO, *Saggi sul Cristianesimo antico*, Naples 1958, pp. 96–100 (who confines himself, however, to following the old opinion of MOMMSEN, *Ges. Schr.*, IV, pp. 498–513); and, on M. Aurelius's personal attitude, which was rigidly traditionalist, M. SORDI, 'Le monete di Marco Aurelio con Mercurio e la pioggia miracolosa', in *Ann. Ist. It. Num.*, V–VI, 1958–9 (pub. 1960) pp. 41–55. On the martyrs of Lyon, see most recently H. GRÉGOIRE, 'Les persécutions dans l'Empire romain', in *Mém. Ac. Roy. Belg.*, XLVI, 1950, pp. 5–175, in particular pp. 29 f., 95 ff., 140 ff.; P. WUILLEUMIER, *Lyon, métropole des Gaules*, Paris 1953, pp. 22 and 93–7 (who thinks that the persecution was caused by the cult of the Magna Mater and the Phrygian rites); J. VOGT, in *Reallexikon für Antike und Christentum*, II, 1954, cc. 1173–6; J. H. OLIVER and R. E. A. PALMER, *art. cit.*, in *Hesperia*, XXIV, 1955, p. 324, n. 8; F. SCHEIDWEILER, 'Zur Kirchengeschichte des Eusebios von Kaisareia', in *Zeitschr. Neutestam. Wiss.*, XLIX, 1958, pp. 123–9 (on the letters of the communities of Lyon and Vienne).

THE WARS OF MARCUS AURELIUS

Because of its fragmentary state the traditional account of M. Aurelius's military activity presents many problems. The main one is the reconstruction of the chronology of the wars. As for measures concerning the army, the new military diplomas that have come to our knowledge should be mentioned here: the one already mentioned from Palatovo, of 21 July 164 (*CIL*, XVI, Suppl., 185; cf. D. DETSCHEW, in *Klio*, XXX, 1937, p. 187, and *AE*, 1937, 113); the fragments of a diploma of 165 from Valentia Banasa (*CIL*, XVI, Suppl. 186, cf. R. THOUVENOT, in *Publ. d.*

Serv. Ant. Maroc, IX, 1951, p. 170, and *AE*, 1951, p. 69); the fragments of another, from Regensburg, dating from between 150 and 170 (*CIL*, XVI, Suppl.; 187, cf. K. KRAFT, in *Germania*, XXX, 1952, p. 345, and *AE*, 1953, 116); other fragments from Haskowo (Thrace) dating from between 175 and 180 (*CIL*, XVI, Suppl., 188, cf. D. ZONTSCHEW, in *Oest. Jahresh.*, XXXI, 1939, Beibl., p. 149, and *AE*, 1939, 125). There are in addition, not yet collected in *CIL*, XVI, a fragmentary diploma of the year 163 from Brigetio found in 1957 and published by L. BARKOCZI, 'A New Military Diploma from Brigetio', in *Acta Archaeologica Academiae Scientiarum Hungaricae*, IX, 1958, pp. 413–21 (*AE*, 1960, 21); a diploma dated 20 July 164, found at Gilau in Roumania and published by I. I. RUSSU, in *Materiale si Cercetări Archeologice*, II, Bucharest 1956, p. 703 ff.; and finally a third diploma dating from about the same time and discovered recently in the Dacian-Danubian area. This third diploma, dated 21 July 164, was published by G. FORNI, 'Contributo alla storia della Dacia romana', in *Athen.*, XXXVI, 1958, pp. 31–56. For the reconstruction of the period immediately preceding the Danubian wars, the diplomas of 163 and 164, with their evidence of normal discharges and of the positioning of the units, testify to the normality of the situation in these years. On the social background of the movements in the reign of M. Aurelius, which certainly complicated the military situation, see S. SZÂDECZKY-KARDOSS, 'Sur les mouvements sociaux de la Gaule au IIᵉ siècle', in *Acta Antiqua Acad. Scient. Hung.*, III, 1955–6, pp. 235–40, for the areas behind the front in Gaul, and the same scholar's 'Contributions à l'histoire sociale de la Pannonie à l'époque de Marc-Aurèle', *ibid.*, pp. 321–8, for the same areas in Pannonia.

The chronology of L. Verus's eastern expedition is still based on the useful numismatic research of C. H. DODD, 'Chronology of the Eastern Campaigns of the Emperor Lucius Verus', in *Num. Chron.*, IV, ser. XI, 1911, pp, 209–67. An article that is useful for the reconstruction of details, but not for the general evaluation of Verus's operations in the war, is the one – already cited – by P. LAMBRECHTS, 'L'empereur Lucius Verus' etc., in *Ant. Class.*, III, 1934, pp. 173–201. That the 'Victories' of Carthage had formed part of a symbolic monument exalting M. Aurelius and L. Verus for the Parthian victory is a hypothesis advanced by G. CH. PICARD in 'Le monument aux Victoires de Carthage et l'expédition orientale de Lucius Verus', in *Karthago*, I, 1950, pp. 65–94 (cf. *Compt. rend. Ac. Inscr.*, 1950, pp. 262 f.).

The most difficult problem connected with the Danubian wars is that of combining and reconciling the information furnished by the various different kinds of sources: the *Historia Augusta*, CASSIUS DIO, and the scattered and casual references in other authors (GALEN, LUCIAN, PHILOSTRATUS, AMMIANUS MARCELLINUS); the numerous inscriptions; the coins, which can fortunately be dated fairly easily but whose symbolism cannot always be clearly interpreted; and the column. Some of these fragments of information have been satisfactorily integrated; others, though referring to events of primary importance like the invasion of Italy by the Marcomanni, still remain difficult to place. However, research has achieved noteworthy results, particularly in W. ZWIKKER's fundamental study, *Studien zur Markussäule*, I, Amsterdam 1941, by gradually widening its scope to embrace more and more completely every category of source. What has proved specially valuable is the combination of the literary and numismatic evidence by C. H. DODD, in 'Chronology of the Danubian Wars of the Emperor Marcus Antoninus', in *Num. Chron.*, IV, ser. XIII, 1913, pp. 162–99, 276–321, and the combination of the literary, numismatic and archaeological-cum-monumental evidence by J. DOBIÂŠ, in 'Le monnayage de l'empereur Marc-Aurèle', in *Rev. Num.*, IV sér., XXXV, 1932, pp. 127–72.

Study of the column of M. Aurelius has been particularly intense. It has aimed at dating and interpreting the scenes on the column – an aim that coincides with the reconstruction of the Danubian wars. ZWIKKER's book – being a long historical introduction to the study of the column – is in fact a history of M. Aurelius's Danubian wars. It is comprehensive and exhaustive, especially in its extensive consideration of the situation in the German client states on the basis of the density of archaeological finds (pp. 14–34; see also on this subject the earlier monograph by K. KLOSE, *Roms Klientel-Randstaaten am Rhein und an der Donau*, Breslau 1934) and in its penetrating analysis of the causes of war. However, some of Zwikker's conclusions are questionable. The invasion of Italy by the Marcomanni is put too late; cf. A. DEGRASSI, *Il confine nord-orientale dell'Italia romana*, Berne 1954, p. 115, n. 76, and M. PAVAN, 'La provincia romana della Pannonia Superiore', in *Mem. Acc. Linc.*, VIII, 6, 1955, p. 395, n. 9; the dating and details of the institution of the *praetentura Italiae et Alpium* (cf. DEGRASSI, *op. cit.*, pp. 113–25) and of Legions II and III *Italicae* can be criticized; so can the attribution of the death of Furius Victorinus to the plague and the excessive importance ascribed in general to this factor, like a sort of *deus ex machina*, in order to explain various events; and so on. More recent research on the column, favoured by the greater availability of illustrative material (P. ROMANELLI, *La colonna Antonina, Rilievi fotografici eseguiti in occasione dei lavori di protezione antiaerea*, Rome 1942), has settled once for all the chronological limits of the scenes depicted, even if it is still dubious whether it is a question of a continuous narrative or of episodes, though in chronological order, which is naturally demanded by the spiral form of the monument. These limits must be 172 and 175, as accepted in the recent official publication: C. CAPRINO, A. M. COLINI, G. GATTI, M. PALLOTTINO, P. ROMANELLI, *La colonna di Marco Aurelio* (*Studi e Materiali del Museo dell'Impero Romana*, V) Rome 1955. That the scenes begin with the events of 172 is made almost certain not only by the correspondence (DOBIÁŠ, *art. cit.*, p. 128) between the coin of 172 (*Rom. Imp. Coin.*, III, 1930, p. 234, no. 270; cf. *Coins in the Br. Mus.*, IV, 1940, p. CXXXVIII) depicting the crossing of a bridge with the first scene on the column but also by the reconstruction of the war as a whole, which makes it seem fairly probable that the years 170–171 were spent in defensive operations in the provinces and that the war was only carried into enemy territory in 172. It then became a real offensive, in precise correspondence with the scenes on the column. The terminus of 175 is fixed by the absence from the column of Commodus, who took part in the last German war of 177–180 and would have certainly had himself depicted, granted that the column was erected in his reign: this remains a convincing argument, but see J. MORRIS, 'The Dating of the Column of Marcus Aurelius', in *Journ. Warb. & Court. Inst.*, XV, 1952, pp. 33–47, who thinks that the column recounts the campaigns of 173–175 and 177–180. In the view of P. H. HAMBERG, *Studies in Roman Imperial Art. with Special Reference to the State Reliefs of the Second Century*, Copenhagen 1945, espec. pp. 149–61, the column presents 'a free choice of typical, representative scenes' (p. 156). Hamberg thinks that this choice, certainly chronological, was dictated by the very character of Marcus's wars in comparison with Trajan's: 'a series of defensive manœuvres and punitive expeditions against different tribes and in various territories'.

So far as details are concerned, the inscription of Ti. Claudius Proculus Cornelianus published by H. G. PFLAUM, *art. cit.*, in *Libyca*, III, 1955, pp. 123–34 (*AE*, 1956, 123), has revealed that Cn. Iulius Verus participated in the levying of the Italian legions in 165–167, assisted by the aforesaid knight. If the Iulius Verus of the inscription is the same man as the illustrious consular (*cos.* towards 154 and later designated for a second consulship in 180), known particularly for his governorships of Britain and Syria, this weakens the reservations felt (by MOMMSEN, *Staatsr.* II³, p. 850, n. 3; RITTERLING, in *P.W.*, XII, c. 1301) about ascribing to the preparations for the Danubian campaign the recruiting activity of M. Claudius Fronto (*ILS*, 1908). The reason for these reservations was that such operations were the job of someone of praetorian rather than consular rank (M. Claudius Fronto had been an ex-consul at least since 165), and Cn. Iulius Verus was in fact of consular rank. As for the date of M. Aurelius's and L. Verus's departure from Rome, in spite of the difficult obstacle provided by an inscription from Sbeitla (*Inscr. Lat. d'Afr.*, 1–7) which certainly dates from 167 and uses the title *proconsul* for both Augusti, it seems better to accept the testimony of *Fragmentum Vaticanum 195* (BAVIERA, *Auctores*[2], in *Fontes iur, Rom. anteiust.*, II, p. 503) which bears witness that they were still in Rome on 6 January 168. The inscription's inaccuracy – a phenomenon of frequent occurrence in inscriptions of the period – is proved by the assignment to the Emperors of the title *imp.* III although they had received their fourth salutation in 166. However, the error of anticipation (in the case of the title *proconsul*) is certainly stranger than that of lateness. The theory that M. Aurelius returned to Rome in 173–174 is rejected afresh by J. AYMARD, 'L'Adventus de Marc-Aurèle sur l'arc de Constantin', in *Rev. Ét. Anc.*, LII, 1950, pp. 71–6. The connection made by Lucian (*Pseudomantis*, 48) between the story of the lions thrown into the Danube and the invasion of Italy by the barbarians is difficult to sustain (in spite of DOBIÂŠ, *art. cit.*, in *Rev. Num.*, IV sér., XXXV, 1932, pp. 150–3; the most careful photographic examination of the reliefs on the column makes it highly dubious whether the episode can be discerned at all on it; cf, CAPRINO, *Col. di M. Aur.*, pp. 87 f.). On the date of the miraculous rain in the country of the Quadi – a very important point for the whole chronology of the war and for the dating of the column because of the link, which presents many difficulties, with CASS. D., LXXI: 8–10 (partic. 10; 4, for the mention of the VII salutation as Imperator, which certainly took place in 174), see J. GUEY, 'La date de la "pluie miraculeuse" (172 après J. C.) et la Colonne Aurèlienne', in *Mel. Éc. Fr. Rome*, LX, 1948, pp. 105–27 and LXI, 1949, pp. 93–118; *idem*, 'Encore la pluie miraculeuse, mage et dieu', in *Rev. Phil.*, XXII, 1948, pp. 16–62; and M. SORDI, *art. cit.*, p. 54, who goes back to the traditional date of 176. For the connection between the restoration of the walls of Philippopolis and the raid by the Costoboci, see S. LAMBRINO, in *Rev. Istor. Română*, V, 1935, p. 328, and for the threat, extending to Asia Minor, posed by the movements of the barbarians on the far side of the Danube, D. MAGIE, *Rom. Rule As. Min.*, II, p. 1535.

The most important additions to our knowledge of the history of the Danubian wars have come from the inscription already mentioned, *AE*, 1956, 124, of M. Valerius Maximianus (H. G. PFLAUM, 'Du nouveau sur les guerres du Danube à l'époque de Marc-Aurèle, d'après une inscription récemment découverte à Diana Veterorum en Numidie (avec des observations de Piganiol, A., et Grenier, A.)' in *Compt. rend. Ac. Inscr.*, 1956, pp. 19–23). This inscription informs us of the slaying by the hand of Valerius Maximianus, prefect of an *ala*, of Valao, 'dux Naristarum' (on the Naristae and their territory, see L. BARKOCSI, 'Die Naristen zur Zeit der Markomannenkriege', in *Folia Arch.*, IX, 1957, pp. 92–9; J. DOBIÂŠ, 'Expeditio Naristarum', in *Eunomia*, III, 1959, pp. 22–31; H. BENGTSON, 'Neues zur Geschichte der Naristen', in *Historia*, VIII, 1959, pp. 213–21). It also tells us of the employment of Marcomanni, Naristae and Quadi in the expedition against Avidius Cassius (as opposed to CASS. D., LXXI, 27, 1a); of promotion and public career determined by the merits of military service; of the supply system organized on the Danube with a flotilla manned by units from the fleets of Misenum, Ravenna and Britain; and of a screen of African and Moorish cavalry along the north bank (PFLAUM's interpretation, p. 141 f.; his view is not shared by J. DOBIÂŠ, 'Zana: à propos de l'inscription de M. Valerius Maximianus', in *Libyca*, V, 1957, pp. 107–11, presenting the conclusions of the article 'La nouvelle inscription de Zana (Diana Veterorum) et l'inscription romaine gravée sur le rocher de Trencin [*CIL*, III 13439 = DESSAU, *ILS*, 9122], in *Listy Filologické*, V, 1957, pp. 179–96); of the beginning of the phenomenon of brigandage; and it confirms the stay of the Roman troops at Leugarico (previously known as Laugarico, BARBIERI, in *Diz. Ep.*, IV, pp. 476 f.) on the Waag in the winter of 179–180 (DOBIÂŠ, *art. cit.*, p. 109; see also his summary, 'La second spedizione germanica degli imperatori Marco e Commodo alla luce delle iscrizione', in *Atti III Congr. Intern. Epigr. Gr. e Lat.*, [1957], Rome 1959, pp. 3–14). For the units employed in the war, see R. EGGER, 'Ein kleiner Beitrag zur Markus-Säule', in *Anthemon. Scritti di arch. e di ant. class on honore di C. Anti*, Florence 1955, pp. 171–5, a commentary on inscription *SEG*, III, 525, of a soldier of the XV *Apollinaris* recruited in Thrace; it confirms the participation in the war of this legion, normally stationed at that time in Cappadocia. The legion had in fact already been recognized on the column by DOMASZEWSKI. It is still uncertain whether M. Aurelius died at Vindobona (AUR. VICT., *De Caes.*, 16, 14; *Epit. de Caes.*, 16, 12) or Sirmium (TERTULL., *Apolog.*, 25, 5). Probably Tertullian gives an approximate indication (*apud Sirmium*) equivalent to 'in Pannonia' of which Sirmium was the principal town, in a context in which such a piece of information is clearly secondary; Aurelius Victor and the Epitome, on the other hand, are being precise.

On the incursions by the Moors into Baetica, R. THOUVENOT, 'Les incursions des Maures en Bétique sous le règne de Marc-Aurèle', in *Rev. Ét. Anc.*, XLI, 1939, pp. 20–8; for the situation in Mauretania itself and measures taken by the Romans (fortifications, negotiations with the chiefs of local tribes, etc.) to deal with it, in continuation of the work of Antoninus Pius (see above, p. 703), see R. BLOCH, in *Mel. Éc. Fr. Rome*, LVIII, 1941–6, pp. 17–21 (*AE*, 1948, 132). On a restoration of the walls and gates of Tigava Castra (in Mauretania Caesariensis), see R. THOUVENOT, 'Deuxième table de patronat découverte à Banasa (Maroc)', in *Compt. rend. Ac. Inscr.*, 1947, pp. 485–9 (cf. P. ROMANELLI, *St. prov. rom. Afr.*, pp. 366–75), and also the interesting inscriptions, already cited, on the big altar at Volubilis, dating from between 173 and 175 and put up by the procurator Epidius Quadratus 'conlocutus cum Ucmetio principe gentium Macennitum et Baquatium' (*AE*, 1957, 202). This text, together with the similar one referring to Commodus (see below, p. 728) found at the same time and in the very same spot, joins and confirms the one already known, also from Volubilis, *CIL*, VIII, 21826 (on which see MOMMSEN, *Staatsr.* I², p. 319, n. 2). Light has also been shed on the same subject by the reconstruction, mentioned above, of the career of C. Aufidius Victorinus, who seems to have held the command in the campaign in Baetica in 171–172 (H. G. PFLAUM, *Compt. rend. Ac. Inscr.*, 1956, pp. 189–200; cf. P. MELONI, *L'amministrazione della Sardegna*, etc., Rome 1958, pp. 34 and 269, partic. for the related question of the dating of the quaestorship of Septimius Severus in Sardinia, and A. E. ASTIN, 'The Status of Sardinia in the Second Century A.D.', in *Latomus*, XVIII, 1959, pp. 150–3).

That the revolt of Avidius Cassius began in April of 175 and that the usurper fell in July – the three months and six days indicated by CASS. D., LXXI, 27, 3 – is confirmed by the datings from Egypt, which declared promptly for Cassius (the first date known is 6 May, in a papyrus from Philadelphia, *BGU*, VII, 1584, while *ostraca* from Thebes and Eumeria of 28 and 30 July are already dated again by M. Aurelius: R. RÉMONDON, 'Les dates de la révolte de C. Avidius Cassius (P. Fouad inédit., inventaire no. 132)', in *Chron. d'Ég.*, XXVI, 1951, pp. 364–77). For the alleged Maecianus, 'Iuridicus Alexandriae' and adherent of Avidius Cassius and, worse, confused with the jurist Volusius Maecianus – in spite of DESSAU in *PIR*, III, p. 481, no. 657 and *CIL*, 5347 and 5348 – see S. J. DE LAET, 'Note sur deux passages de l'Histoire Auguste (*V. Marci* XXV, 4; *V. Cassii*, VII, 4)', in *Ant. Class.*, XIII, 1944, pp. 127–34. For the serious losses caused in Egypt by the plague, A. E. R. BOAK,

'Egypt and the Plague of Marcus Aurelius', in *Historia*, VIII, 1959, pp. 248–50. We simply do not know if the erasure in *CIL*, VIII, 2348 = 17866, 4208 = 18496, of the name of the unknown commander of Legion III *Augusta* in 167 was connected with the revolt of Avidius Cassius or with other, unknown events. An interesting point, after the discovery of the above-mentioned inscriptions from the amphitheatre at Lambaesis (*AE*, 1955, 134) dating from 169, also with the name of the legion and its commander erased, but legible, is the identification with M. Lucceius Torquatus, a victim of Commodus. The erasure would in that case date from the reign of Commodus (the erasure of the legion certainly dates from 238); see L. LESCHI, 'Autour de l'Amphithéàtre de Lambèse', in *Libyca*, II, 1954, pp. 171–86. A 'unicum' that is hard to explain by the revolt of Avidius Cassius, not supported, it would seem, by Africa, is the erasure of the name of M. Aurelius himself in the inscription from Diana Veteranorum, *CIL*, VIII, 4593, dating from 167. For a suggested emendation to *IG*, V, 44, which would tell us of the participation of some one from Sparta in M. Aurelius's expedition against Avidius Cassius, see A. M. WOODWARD, in *Ann. Br. Sch. Athens*, XLIII, 1948, pp. 219–23 (*AE*, 1950, 10; *SEG*, XI, 1954, no. 486).

THE REIGN OF COMMODUS

For the first time in the history of the principate the account of the events of Commodus's reign is furnished by writers of more or less the same period, which turns the problem of the sources into one of investigating contemporary influences and feelings. The most recent criticism (since J. M. HEER's study, 'Der historische Wert der Vita Commodi in der Sammlung der S.H.A.', in *Philologus*, Supplementband IX, 1904, on the biography of the *Historia Augusta*) has paid more attention to HERODIAN than to CASSIUS DIO and has come to a more balanced verdict on the ancient 'bellelettrist'. See E. HOHL, 'Kaiser Commodus und Herodian', in *Sitz.-ber. d. deutsch Ak. d. Wiss. zu Berlin*, Kl. f. Gesellschaftswiss., 1954, I, who rejects, for example, the romantic story of Maternus's attempt at assassination at Rome, pp. 17 ff., and cuts down the account of the end of the tyrant, particularly the part ascribed to Marcia, pp. 30 f. (cf. E. HOHL, 'Die Ermordung des Commodus', in *Phil. Wochenschr.*, LII, 1932 [Poland Festschr.], p. 191 ff.). F. CASSOLA, 'Sull'attendibilità dello storico Erodiano', in *Atti Acc. Pontan.*, Naples, N.S., VI, 1957, pp. 191–200, takes a more favourable view. The re-examination of the sources and a shrewd selection of the information they provide, taking into account the tendencies they reveal, should provide the basis for a monograph on Commodus, whose reign was fairly important, not so much in itself as because it was a period of transition. See, besides the chapters in the general histories (W. WEBER, in *Cambr. Anc. Hist.*, XI, pp. 376–92, and in *Röm. Herrschertum und Reich im zweiten Jahrhundert*, Stuttgart and Berlin 1937, pp. 351–409, who remains the most original writer on the reign) the profile by R. ANDREOTTI, *Commodo*, Rome 1942; J. CH. TRAUPMAN's *The Life and Reign of Commodus*, diss., Princeton 1956 (microfilm) has not been accessible to me.

On the succession of Commodus, inevitable as being the most natural one, see J. KEIL, 'Kaiser Marcus und die Thronfolge', in *Klio*, XXXI, 1938, pp. 293–300. For the tendency to emphasis in the imperial style (new titles coined by Commodus and never dropped), see M. HAMMOND, 'Imperial Elements in the Formula', etc., in *Mem. Am. Ac. Rome*, XXV, 1957, pp. 17–64. On the formation of the derogatory tradition about Commodus's birth, A. H. KRAPPE, 'La naissance de Commode dans l'Histoire Auguste', in *Rev. Ét. Anc.*, XXXVIII, 1936, pp. 277–84; on his relations with Lucilla and Crispina, J. AYMARD, 'La conjuration de Lucilla', in *Rev. Ét. Anc.*, LVII, 1955, pp. 85–91. Aymard thinks that Lucilla's conspiracy, to be placed towards the middle of 184, was caused by the old Augusta's jealousy of the new Augusta, who just at that time had presented Commodus with a son.

As for the administration of the empire under Commodus, there is no lack of recent attempts at a revaluation of his personal work (see in particular A. E. RAUBITSCHEK, 'Commodus and Athens', in *Hesperia*, Suppl. VIII, 1949 [Studies Shear], pp. 279–90; cf. J. H. OLIVER, 'Three Attic Inscriptions concerning the Emperor Commodus', in *Amer. Journ. Phil.*, LXXI, 1950, pp. 170–9; L. ROBERT, in *Rev. Ét. Gr.*, LXIII, 1950, pp. 151 f.; *AE*, 1952, 4). In fact discoveries of new inscriptions and dedications, on top of the numerous ones already known, are relatively abundant; but while these, like the fragments of letters of C. in the publications cited (almost all earlier than 184) suggest the mere continuation of an official and honorary practice, there remains the weight of literary evidence, which is contemporary and seems to be confirmed by the inscriptions themselves, as in the case of the temples at Corinth, built by others and dedicated by him; cf. *V. Comm.*, 17 (R. L. SCRANTON, 'Two Temples of Commodus at Corinth', in *Hesperia*, XIII, 1944, pp. 315–48, cf. *AE*, 1947, 90 and 91). G. M. BERSANETTI's reconstruction, 'Perenne e Commodo', in *Athen*, XXIX, 1951, pp. 151–70, which takes Perennis's rule as serious and effective, is perfectly acceptable.

For the praetorian prefectship, primarily under Commodus, see A. PASSERINI, *Coort. pret.*, pp. 293 f., 305–11, and L. L. HOWE, *The Praetorian Prefect from Commodus to Diocletian* (A.D. *180–305*), Chicago 1942, who excludes from his list (p. 89) Sex. Baius Prudens, who is accepted by Passerini (pp. 309 f.; he is in fact also excluded from W. ENSSLIN's list in *P.W.*, XXII, 1954, c. 2424). The chronology itself is uncertain (for the fall of Cleander in 190, as opposed to 189 commonly accepted, H. MATTINGLY, *Coins etc.*, IV, 1940, p. CLXVIII). For the prefects of Egypt, A. STEIN, 'Die Praefecten von Aegypten unter Commodus', in *Aegyptus*, XIX, 1939, pp. 215–26, and C. PRÉAUX, 'La préfecture d'Égypte de 187 à 190', in *Chron. d'Ég.*, XXII, 1947, pp. 338–42 (cf. A. STEIN, *Die Präfekten von Aegypten*, etc., Berne 1950, pp. 98–104). As for administrative problems, DOMASZEWSKI's theory ('Der Truppen-sold der Kaiserzeit', in *Neue Heidelberger Jahrbücher*, 1900, pp. 218 ff.) of an increase in military pay under Commodus has now been finally re-jected: A. PASSERINI, 'Gli aumenti del soldo militare da Commodo a Massimino', in *Athen.*, XXIV, 1946, pp. 145–59; *idem*, 'Il papiro berlinese 6866 e il soldo militare al tempo di Commodo', in *Acme*, I, 1948, p. 366, on the subject of a papyrus strengthening PASSERINI's thesis but causing difficulties to R. MARICHAL (*L'occupation romaine de la Basse Égypte. Le statut des Auxilia*, Paris 1945), a supporter of DOMASZEW-SKI's theory (abandoned, however, in 'La solde des armées romaines d'Auguste à Septime Sévère, d'après les P. Gen. Lat. 1 et 4 et le P. Berlin 6866', in *Ann. Inst. Phil. Hist. Orient.*, XIII, 1953 – Mél. I Lévy – pp. 399–421). On the same subject see latterly G. R. WATSON, 'The Pay of the Roman Army, The Auxiliary Forces', in *Historia*, VIII, 1959, pp. 372–8. Meanwhile PASSERINI, 'Sulla pretesa rivoluzione dei prezzi durante il regno di Commodo', in *Studi Luzzatto*, Milan 1949–50, pp. 1–17, had extended the investigation to the field of general economics.

On the new aristocracy in process of formation, an important aspect of this period of transition, see H. U. INSTINSKY, 'Die Herkunft des L. Fabius Cilo', in *Phil.*, XCVI, 1944, p. 293 f. African inscriptions have also given us fresh details of men of the period: for example, M. Asinius Rufinus Sabinianus, of Acholla, who was made a senator through *adlectio inter praetorios* by Commodus and subsequently reached the consul-ship, was absolutely unknown (*AE*, 1954, 58; cf. 1955, 122 and the commentary by G. CH. PICARD, 'Deux sénateurs romains inconnus', in *Karthago*, IV, 1953, pp. 119–35). Then there is the L. Aemilius . . . of a dedication from Tripoli to Commodus (G. CAPUTO, in *Afr. It.*, VII, 1940, pp. 35–9; cf. *AE*, 1942–3, 1); in the view of G. BARBIERI, 'L.

Aemilius Frontinus proconsule d'Asie', in *Epigr.*, III, 1941, pp. 292–301, this was L. Aemilius Frontinus, possibly supplementary consul between 161 and 168 and proconsul of Asia under Commodus. The career of Ti. Claudius Gordianus, commander of Leg. III *Augusta* in 187–188, has been further illuminated by a new inscription (L. LESCHI, 'Inscriptions latines de Lambèse et de Zana, II, La carrière de Ti. Claudius Gordianus' etc., in *Libyca*, I, 1953, pp. 197–200; cf. *AE*, 1954, 138). The African origin of the praetorian prefect Aemilius Laetus – he came from Thaenae – is now known (*AE*, 1949, 38). These details also confirm the even more pronounced pre-eminence of Africa (for the percentage – 15 per cent – of African senators mentioned in the main text, see G. BARBIERI, *Albo senatorio*, Rome 1952, p. 441; for the same percentage in the equestrian procurators, H. G. PFLAUM, *Procurateurs etc.*, p. 184 f.). Moreover, the most important juridical text of the epoch, the *decretum de saltu Burunitano* (RICCOBONO, *Leges*[2], p. 495, no. 103), also refers to Africa. See also the inscriptions from Volubilis (*AE*, 1936, 37), a dedication to Commodus – almost completely erased – on a monument, dating from 181–182, and *AE*, 1953, 79 (cf. 1957, 203) – another altar similar to that of M. Aurelius (see above, p. 724), with a dedication dated 13 October 180 to the 'Genius' of Commodus, by the procurator D. Veturius Macrinus, *'conlocutus cum Canarta principe genti Baquatium'* (EDM. FRÉZOULS, in *Mél. Éc. Fr. Rome*, LXVIII, 1956, pp. 114–18); the inscription in the camp at Lambaesis (*AE*, 1957, 85); the big dedication from the baths at Cuicul, of 183–184 (*AE*, 1935, 45) with the name of the governor, M. Valerius Maximianus, the man with the splendid *cursus* of the inscription from Diana Veteranorum (*AE*, 1956, 124, see above, pp. 714 and 722). A new reading of one of the dedications to *Divus Commodus* promoted by Septimius Severus, with particular success in Africa (*CIL*, VIII, 27374, from Thugga) is proposed by P. W. TOWNSEND, in *Class. Phil.*, XLV, 1950, pp. 248–50; cf. *AE*, 1951, 71. On the destruction and abandonment of towns in Mauretania (including Volubilis), possibly even under Commodus, see the remarks of M. FLORIANI SQUARCIAPINO, in *St. Rom.*, VI, 1958, p. 701. To turn to other parts of the empire: from Rome there is an inscription on a lead pipe (*AE*, 1945, 116) with a mention of the *statio patrimonii* Commodi Aug(uste) n(ostri), similar to many others; at Falerium (Falerone, Piceno) there is a dedication to Commodus dating from 177 and thus from a time when his father was still alive (*AE*, 1960, 255); at Rudiae a dedication for the restoration of the amphitheatre (*AE*, 1958, 179); in Gaul, the destruction of Iuliobona, in Belgica, is connected with the revolt of Maternus by S. SZÁDECZKY-KARDOSS, 'Iuliobon et le soulèvement de Maternus', in *Arch. Ertesitö*, LXXXIII, 1956, pp. 18–24, while J. JEANNIN, 'Tirelire gallo-romaine trouvée à Mandeure (Doubs)', in *Rev. Arch. Est et Centre-Est*, VI, 1955, pp. 299–303, thinks that the destruction of Epomanduodurum occurred at the end of the reign, for reasons unknown. In Upper Germany, there is evidence bearing witness to the condition of the *municipium* of Arae Flaviae (Rottweil am Neckar) in 186; see W. SCHLEIERMACHER, 'Das Datum der Rottweiler Schreibtafel', in *Germania*, XXXIV, 1956, p. 154; see also the same scholar's publication in *Bayerische Vorgeschichtsblätter*, XXI, 1955, pp. 115–122 (*AE*, 1957, 50), of an altar with a dedication by a soldier Leg. *VIII Augusta*, dated 15 July 189, found at Obernburg am Main and interesting for its connection with the *limes*. In Pannonia a new fragment completes the dedication from Carnuntum (*CIL*, III, 11140), not affected by erasure (*AE*, 1937, 77). See also A. ALFÖLDI, *Epigraphica, IV*, in *Arch. Ertesitö*, 3a ser., II, 1941, pp. 30–59, on the epigraphical evidence about the *latrunculi* across the Danube. In Moesia, at Capidava, in the series of dedications 'pro salute' of the Antonines (above, p. 707), there is also the altar for Commodus (with the unusual cognomen *Verus*, *AE*, 1939, 86). Another altar found in recent years at Pliska (Bulgaria) is described by M. FLORIANI SQUARCIAPINO, in *St. Rom.*, VI, 1958, p. 697, who thinks that *CIL*, III, 7516 (*AE*, 1956, 214) is also a dedication to Commodus. In Phrygia, at Nacolia, there is the dedication (unaffected by erasure) by a tax-collector (*Mon. As. Min. Ant.*, V, 1957, pp. 92–3; cf. *AE*, 1938, 145), and at Attaleia the dedication put up between 177 and 180 to Commodus (with the praenomen Lucius), 'sotèr tês oikouménes' (*AE*, 1960, 314). The road from Philadelphia to Gerasa has yielded a milestone of 181 (*AE*, 1938, 131), and a dedication has been found at Gerasa (*AE*, 1935, 82) or at Capitolias (*SEG*, VIII, 1937, no. 91). Egypt has produced two dedications, of 16 June 180, at Karanis (V. B. SCHUMANN, in *Hesperia*, XVI, 1947, pp. 269–71; cf. *AE*, 1949, 92) and 8 January 189 (*AE*, 1938, 60, in the museum at Alexandria). Cyrene has yielded a dedication of 181 for repairs to the temple of Apollo (*SEG*, IX, 1944, 173; cf. above, p. 716) and another from the excavations of the temple of Zeus (*AE*, 1954, 42 and 1960, 261; cf. above).

Commodus's religious policy, coinciding in the last few years of his reign with the only personal political activity we are in a position to see in the entire reign, is now judged more realistically, after a number of too favourable justifications and explanations (partic. by WEBER): see H. MATTINGLY, *Coins. etc.*, IV, 1940, p. CLXXXIII f. for the conclusions to be drawn from an examination of the coinage, and J. BEAUJEU,

La religion etc., Paris 1955, pp. 369–412. The coinage is naturally the source most eloquent on the subject, and new observations on the gradual process, inspired by Greek notions, of the identification of Commodus with Hercules, as it is reflected in the coinage, are to be found in J. BABELON, 'Monnaies et médaillons de l'empereur Commode', in *Bull. Soc. Antiq. d. Fr.*, 1950–1, and 'Commode en Hercule', in *Rev. Num.*, XV, 1953, pp. 23–36. For contemporary reactions expressed with atrocious sarcasm in the coinage itself, see W. DERICHS, 'Eine Spottmünze auf Kaiser Commodus,' in *Rh. Mus.*, XCV, 1952, pp. 48–52, and V. PISANI, 'Noch einmal die Spottmünze auf Commodus', *ibid.*, pp. 286–7. On the imposition on everything of the title *Commodianus* and on the new name of Rome, *Colonia Lucia Aurelia Nova Commodiana* (prob. more accurate than *Col. Lucia Antoniniana Commodiana, Col. Lucia Annia Commodiana* and similar reductions of the abbreviated formula of the coins), see J. AYMARD, 'Commode-Hercule fondateur de Rome', in *Rev. Ét. Lat.*, XIV, 1936, pp. 350–64. On the detail of the *venatio* with ostriches on the sarcophagus of Meleager, see latterly E. HOHL, *Kaiser Commodus und Herodian*, p. 27, and for the extravagances in general J. GAGÉ, 'L'Hercule impérial et l'amazonisme de Rome. A propos des extravagances religieuses de Commode', in *Rev. d'Hist. et de Phil. religieuses*, XXIV, 1954, pp. 342–72. As for relations with Christianity, the martyrdom of Apollonius, exceptional in the reign's atmosphere of tolerance, has been studied most recently by M. SORDI, 'Un senatore cristiano dell'età di Commodo', in *Epigr.*, XVII, 1955 (but pub. 1957), pp. 104–12, who defends St Jerome's view (*De Vir. Ill.*, 42) that Apollonius was a senator, probably to be identified with one Claudius Apollonius of Smyrna.

PART II

ADDENDA TO THE CRITICAL NOTES:

NEW BOOKS AND ARTICLES
1960-1969

TIBERIUS

New documents

1. Inscr. from Rome of a person who was *comes Ti. Caesaris* and was kept uninterruptedly until the reign of Claudius in charge of the imperial libraries (*supra bibliothecas omnes Augustorum ab Ti. Caesare usque ad Ti. Claudium Caesarem*), *AE*, 1960, 26 = VAN BUREN, in *Amer. Journ. Arch.*, LXIII, 1959, p. 384; cf. E. MEYER, 'Augusti', in *Mus. Helv.*, XVI, 1959, pp. 273–4 and XVII, 1960, p. 118 (on the use of *Augusti* to denote successive emperors).
2. Dedication to Tib. in the agora at Athens, *AE*, 1960, 183 = VANDERPOOL, in *Hesperia*, XXVIII, 1959, pp. 86–90.
3. Dedication to Ammon for Tib. and all his family, *AE*, 1960, 279 = SCHWARTZ, in *Rev. Arch.*, 1960, p. 86 f.
4. Oath by the Cypriots for Tiberius from ancient Palaipaphos; an important document which should be placed alongside the *iusiurandum Paphlagonum* for Augustus of 3 B.C., *AE*, 1962, 248 = MITFORD, in *Journ. Rom. St.*, L, 1960, pp. 75–9; cf. KARAGEORGHIS, in *Bull. Corr. Hell.*, LXXXIV, 1960, pp. 272 f.; ROBERT in *Rev. Ét. Gr.*, LXXIV, 1961, pp. 257–8, n. 826.
5. The inscription from the Tiberieum at Caesarea mentioning Pontius Pilatus *praefectus Iudaeae*, found at Caesarea; A. FROVA, in *Rend. Ist. Lomb.*, Cl. Lett., XCV, 1961, pp. 419–34; B. LIFSHITZ, in *Latomus*, XXII, 1963, p. 783 f. (emendation [*proc. Aug., praef*]*ectus Iudaeae*, and supposition that the Tiberieum was dedicated in 31 after the fall of Sejanus); A. DEGRASSI, in *Rend. Acc. Linc.*, Cl. Sc. Mor. XIX, 1964, pp. 59–65 = *Scritti vari di antichità*, III, 1967, pp. 269–275; cf. p. 280, n. 15 (rejects both of Lifshitz's theories); cf. *AE*, 1963, 104 and 1964, 39.

6. Dedication to Tiberius by the new *Augustales* of Brindisi after the fall of Sejanus ([libertate res]tituta publi[ca laetitia]), *AE*, 1965, 113 = DEGRASSI, in *Athen*, XLII, 1964, pp. 299–306 = *Scritte vari*, III, 1967, pp. 277–83.

7. Milestone from Sadara (Saragossa), *AE*, 1965, 67 (better reading *AE*, 1966, 219) = GARCIA Y BELLIDO, in *Arch. Esp. Arq.*, XXXVI, 1963, p. 206.

8. Milestone from Lusitania, *AE*, 1967, 131 = DE ALMEIDA in *Arqueol. Portuguès.*, III, 1956, pp. 111–16.

9. Tib. honoured at Callatis as supreme magistrate of the town, *AE*, 1966, 368 = PIPPIDI, in *Stud. Class.*, VII, 1966, p. 87.

10. Fragment of a speech attributable to Germanicus, in *Pap. Oxy.*, XXV, London 1959, n. 2435.

Monographs

Biographies

W. GOLLUB, *Tiberius*, Munich 1959.

E. KORNEMANN, *Tiberius*, Stuttgart 1960 (pub. by H. H. SCHMITT, French trans. DELALOUÉ, Paris 1962).

Add to the section On the succession of Tiberius (p. 557):

R. SYME, 'Imperator Caesar, a Study in Nomenclature', in *Historia*, VII, 1958, pp. 172–88.

J. BÉRANGER, 'Diagnostic du principat. L'empereur romain, chef de parti', in *Rev. Ét. Lat.*, XXXVII, 1959, pp. 151–70 (the Princeps head of a party, not of body of clients).

——, 'La prévoyance (providentia) impériale et Tacite, Annales I, 8', in *Hermes*, LXXXVIII, 1960, pp. 475–92 (in the phrase *provisis etiam heredum in rem publicam opibus*, the prep. *in* should be taken to mean 'in favour of' not 'against' in considering the hereditary aspect of the succession; since KÖSTERMANN, in his *Kommentar* on Annals I, 1963, p. 95, has – perhaps wrongly – not taken account of this interpretation, the author has returned to the subject in the following study: 'Fortune privée impériale et État', in *Mél. Bonnard*, Génève 1966, pp. 151–60.

J. GAUDEMET, 'Le régime impérial', in *St. Doc. Hist. Iur.*, XXVI, 1960, pp. 282–322, espec. p. 316 ff.

P. GRENADE, *Essai sur les origines du principat. Investiture et renouvellement des pouvoirs impériaux*, Paris 1961 (Bibl. Éc. Franç. Ath. et Rome, CXCVII), pub. after the author's death by P. BOYANCÉ.

D. KIENAST, 'Imperator', in *Ztschr. Sav. Stift.*, LXXVIII, 1961, pp. 403–21 (on republican precedents, esp. in the first cent. B.C., for the *praenomen imperatoris*).

L. LESUISSE, 'La nomination de l'empereur et le titre d'imperator', in *Ant. Class.*, XXX, 1961, pp. 415–28.

——, 'Tacite et la lex de imperio des premiers empereurs romains', in *Les Ét. Class.*, XXXIX, 1961, pp. 157–65.

——, 'L'aspect héréditaire de la succession impérial sous les Julio-Claudiens', *ibid.*, XXX, 1962, pp. 32–50 (emphasizes, like Béranger, private hereditary aspect of the succession).

D. TIMPE, *Untersuchungen zur Kontinuität des frühen Prinzipats*, Wiesbaden 1962 (*Historia* Einzelschr., V; studies the Julio-Claudian successions as a gradual evolution 'von Familienregiment zur Institution').

B. PARSI, *Désignation et investiture de l'empereur romain (Ier et IIe siècle ap. J.-C.)*, Paris 1963 (an attempt to canalize the fact of the succession into a legal procedure).

M. L. PALADINI, 'L'aspetto dell'imperatore-dio presso i Romani', in *Contrib. Ist. Fil. Class., Sez. St. Ant.*, I (Univ. Catt. S. Cuore), Milan 1963, pp. 1–65.

L. POLVERINI, 'L'aspetto sociale del passaggio dalla repubblica al principato', in *Aevum*, XXXVIII, 1964, pp. 241–85, 439–67; XXXIX, 1965, pp. 1–24.

H. U. INSTINSKY, 'Augustus und die Adoption des Tiberius', in *Hermes*, XCIV, 1966, pp. 324–43.

D. C. A. SHOTTER, 'Tiberius and the Spirit of Augustus', in *Gr. & Rom.*, XIII, 1966, pp. 207–12.

L. DUPRAZ, *De l'association de Tibère au principat à la naissance du Christ. Trois études: I, Les avenues militaires de l'association de Tibère au principat; II, L'année de la naissance du Christ; III, Le recensement de P. Sulpicius Quirinus et la création de la province procuratorienne de Judée* (Studia Friburgensia, 43), Fribourg 1966.

K. WELLESLEY, 'The Dies Imperii of Tiberius', in *Journ. Rom. St.*, LVII, 1967, pp. 23–30 (certainly before 4 September 14; the dating from after 17 September due to Tacitus's imprecision).

Z. YAVETZ, *Plebs and Princeps*, Oxford 1969 (on the participation of the urban populace in the affairs of the principate; particularly interesting from p. 103, for relations with Tiberius and the emperors up to Nero).

Add to the section On the rule of Tiberius (p. 563)

(*relations between Tiberius and the nobility*)

G. KAMPFF, 'Three Senate Meetings in the Early Principate', in *Phoenix*,

XVII, 1963, pp. 25–58 (the two sittings of September 14 and one of 23, after the death of Drusus).

M. HAMMOND, 'Res olim dissociabiles, principatus ac libertas. Liberty under the Early Roman Empire', in *Harv. St. Class. Phil.*, LXVII, 1963, pp. 93–113.

J. MORRIS, 'Senate and Emperor', in *Studies Thomson*, Prague 1963, pp. 149–61. (Compared with Tacitus's idealization round the two poles of *principatus* and *libertas*, Cassius Dio's account is preferable. It is more attentive to the real interests involved.)

A. BERGENER, *Die führende Senatorenschicht im frühen Prinzipat (14 bis 68 n. Chr.)*, Bonn 1965.

H. H. PISTOR, *Prinzeps und Patriziat in der Zeit von Augustus bis Commodus*, Diss. Freiburg 1965.

(elections under Tiberius)

W. K. LACEY, 'Nominatio and the Elections under Tiberius', in *Historia*, XII, 1963, pp. 167–76 (proof of Tiberius's wish to make the Senate collaborate actively).

D. C. A. SHOTTER, 'Elections under Tiberius', in *Class. Quart.*, XVI, 1966, pp. 321–32 (comprehensive re-examination).

B. M. LEVICK, 'Imperial Control of the Elections under the Early Principate. Commendatio, suffragatio and "nominatio" ', in *Historia*, XVI, 1967, pp. 207–30 (useless to seek precise rules in the exercise of the Princeps's power in these phases of the electoral procedure).

B. GEROV, 'Epigraphische Beiträge zur Geschichte des mösischen Limes in vorclaudischer Zeit', in *Acta Ant. Ac. Sc. Hung.*, XV, 1967, pp. 85–105 (the lines of defence in Moesia were already clearly defined under Tiberius).

A. J. CHRISTOPHERSON, 'The Provincial Assembly of the Three Gauls in the Julio-Claudian Period , in *Historia*, XVII, 1968, pp. 351–366.

(administration of justice)

M. HORVAT, 'Note intorno allo ius respondendi', in *Synteleia Arangio-Ruiz*, Naples 1964, pp. 710–16.

(religion – emperor worship)

J. BEAUJEU, 'Politique religieuse et propagande numismatique sous le Haut-Empire', in *Mél. Piganiol*, Paris 1966, pp. 1529–40.

Add to the section on Germanicus (p. 572)

J. VAN OOTEGHEM, 'Germanicus en Égypte', in *Les Ét. Class.*, XXVII, 1959, pp. 241–51.

W. F. AKVELD, *Germanicus*, Groningen 1961 (fairly balanced reconstruction).

G. J. D. AALDERS, 'Germanicus und Alexander der Grosse', in *Historia*, X, 1961, pp. 382–4 (the suggested signs of an imitation of Alexander seem to emerge from the fragment of *Pap. Oxy.*, 2435).

C. QUESTA, 'Sul Pap. Oxy'. 2435, in *Riv. Cult. Class. Med.*, III, 1961, pp. 126 f.

S. WEINSTOCK, 'The Posthumous Honours of Germanicus', in *Mél. Piganiol*, Paris 1966, pp. 891–8 (comparison between the honours indicated by the *tabula Hebana* and those mentioned by Tacitus, *Ann.*, II, 83).

B. LEVICK, 'Drusus Caesar and the Adoptions of A.D. 4', in *Latomus*, XXV, 1966, pp. 227–44 (deference of Tiberius to the wishes of Augustus, and parallelism between the careers of Germanicus and Drusus).

E. MEISE, 'Der Sesterz des Drusus mit den Zwillingen und die Nachfolgepläne des Tiberius', in *Jahrb. f. Num. u. Geldgesch.*, XVI, 1966, pp. 7–21 (the coin reflects the fact that Drusus alone and his family were considered for the succession after the death of Germanicus).

M. PANI, 'Osservazioni intorno alla tradizione su Germanico', in *Ann. Fac. Mag. Bari*, V, 1966, pp. 107–20.

G. V. SUMNER, 'Germanicus and Drusus Caesar', in *Latomus*, XXVI, 1967, pp. 413–35 (against the view of Levick).

M. PANI, 'Il circolo di Germanico', in *Ann. Fac. Mag. Bari*, VII, 1968, pp. 109–27 (heightens monarchico-absolutist position of Germanicus and his circle in comparison with Tiberius's concept of an aristocratic principate).

D. C. A. SHOTTER, 'Tacitus, Tiberius and Germanicus', in *Historia*, XVII, 1968, pp. 194–214.

Add to the section The Trials (p. 576)

J. BLEICKEN, 'Senatsgericht und Kaisergericht. Eine Studie zur Entwicklung des Prozessrechts im frühen Prinzipat', in *Abhandl. d. Ak. d. Wiss. Göttingen*, Phil.-hist. Kl., 3 F, LIII, Göttingen 1962.

G. B. TOWNEND, 'The Trial of Aemilia Lepida in A.D. 20', in *Latomus*, XXI, 1962, pp. 484–93.

R. S. ROGERS, 'The Case of Cremutius Cordus', in *Trans. Proc. Amer. Phil. Ass.*, XCVI, 1965, pp. 351–9.

D. C. A. SHOTTER, 'Tiberius' Part in the Trial of Aemilia Lepida', in *Historia*, XV, 1966, pp. 312–17 (the intervention illegal, but the verdict just).

D. C. A. SHOTTER, 'The Trial of Gaius Silius (A.D. 24)', in *Latomus*, XXVI, 1967, pp. 712–16.

W. KIERDORF, 'Die Einleitung des Pizo-prozesses (Tac., *Ann.*, III, 10)', in *Hermes*, XCVII, 1969, pp. 246–51.

PH. Y. FORSYTH, 'A Treason Case of A.D. 37', in *Phoenix*, XXIII, 1969, pp. 204–7 (on the case of Albucilla, mentioned in Tac., *Ann.*, VI, 47–8).

D. C. A. SHOTTER, 'The Trial of Clutorius Priscus', in *Gr. & Rom.*, XVI, 1969, pp. 14–18.

Add to the section Sejanus. The last years of Tiberius (p. 577)

F. DE VISSCHER, 'La caduta di Seiano e il suo macchinatore Macrone', in *Riv. Cult. Class. Med.*, II, 1960, pp. 245–67 (underlines the part played by Macro in engineering the downfall of Sejanus).

R. SEALEY, 'The Political Attachments of L. Aelius Seianus', in *Phoenix*, XV, 1961, pp. 97–114 (renewal of the tendency to give greater importance to the plot of Sejanus, seen as the central figure in a group deriving directly from the entourage of Maecenas).

G. JACOPI, *L'antro di Tiberio a Sperlonga*, Rome 1963 (Ist. St. Rom., Monumenti Romani, IV).

A. BODDINGTON, 'Sejanus, whose Conspiracy?', in *Amer. Journ. Phil.*, LXXXIV, 1963, pp. 1–16 (Sejanus's fall due to a conspiracy by a powerful group of political figures who – it is suggested – forced Tiberius's hand).

F. DE VISSCHER, 'La politique dynastique sous le règne de Tibère', in *Synteleia Arangio-Ruiz*, Naples 1964, pp. 54–65 (on Macro as the representative and defender of Gaius's interests).

G. V. SUMNER, 'The Family Connections of L. Aelius Seianus', in *Phoenix*, XIX, 1965, pp. 134–45 (constructs a new family tree which produces connections with the imperial house).

F. DE VISSCHER, 'Macro, préfet des vigiles et ses cohortes contre la tyrannie de Séjan', in *Mél. Piganiol*, Paris 1966, pp. 761–8 (further emphasis on the part played by Macro in the fall of Sejanus).

T. PEKÁRY, 'Tiberius und der Tempel der Concordia in Rom', in *Röm. Mitt.*, LXXIII–LXXIV, 1966–7, pp. 105–33 (links up with Lambrino's studies of Fulcinius Trio).

H. W. BIRD, 'L. Aelius Seianus and his Political Significance', in *Latomus*, XXVIII, 1969, pp. 61–98 (on the 'groups' allied against Sejanus and also active subsequently).

P. R. FRANKE, 'Eine Damnatio Memoriae des L. Aelius Seianus in

Spanien', in *Arch. Anz.* (Jahrb. d. Deutsch. Arch. Inst., Beibl.), LXXXIII, 1968–9, pp. 480–2 (numismatic evidence).

GAIUS

Add to the section Gaius and his reign (p. 580)

(*biographies – personalia*)

Anastatic reprint Oxford 1965 of J. P. V. D. BALSDON, *The Emperor Gaius (Caligula)*, Oxford 1934.

J. H. OLIVER, 'Lollia Paulina, Memmius Regulus and Caligula', in *Hesperia*, XXXV, 1966, pp. 150–3 (the curious story of the relations between these three people beomes less strange if we accept a supplement to IG^2 4176, which would show that Lollia Paulina was not Memmius Regulus's wife according to Roman usage, but according to Greek egguēsis).

J. LUCAS, 'Un empereur psychopathe. Contribution à la psychologie du Caligula de Suétone', in *Ant. Class.*, XXXVI, 1967, pp. 159–89 (not schizophrenic, but impulsive psychopath).

(*antisemitism*)

J. P. SIJPESTEIJN, 'The Legationes ad Gaium', in *Journ. Jew St.* XV, 1964, pp. 87–96.

M. ADRIANI, 'Note sull'antisemitismo antico', in *St. Mat. St. Rel.*, XXXVI, 1965, pp. 63–98 (for Gaius, pp. 93–8).

E. M. SMALLWOOD, 'Jews and Romans in the Early Empire', in *History Today*, XV, 1965, pp. 232–9, 313–19 (emphasizes Roman 'tolerance', for which, however, Roman authority demanded reciprocation on the part of the Jews).

A. N. SHERWIN-WHITE, *Racial Prejudice in Imperial Rome*, Cambridge 1967 (administration and foreign policy).

H. G. PFLAUM, 'Légats impériaux à l'intérieur de provinces sénatoriales', in *Homm. Grenier* (Coll. Latomus, LVIII), Brussels 1962, pp. 1232–42 (one of the most notorious episodes was the withdrawal of the legion from the proconsul of Africa).

R. W. DAVIES, 'The Abortive Invasion of Britain by Gaius', in *Historia*, XV, 1966, pp. 124–8 (manœuvres not an invasion plan).

F. D'ERCE, 'La tour de Caligula à Boulogne-sur-Mer', in *Rev. Arch.*, NS I, 1966, pp. 89–96 (in connection with the preparations for the British expedition).

P. BICKNELL, 'The Emperor Gaius' Military Activities in A.D. 40', in

Historia, XVII, 1968, pp. 496–505 (explanation of the episode of the shells, in partial disagreement with Davies, see above).

P. R. FRANKE, 'Publius Petronius, Protektor Judäas 39–41 n. Chr. und die Münzprägung Antiochias', in *Arch. Anz.* (Jahrb. d. Deutsch. Arch. Inst., Beibl.), LXXXIII, 1968-9, pp. 474–80.

(*religion*)

E. KÖBERLEIN, *Caligula und die ägyptischen Kulte*, Meisenheim/am/Glan 1962 (Beitr. zur klass. Philol., III).

CLAUDIUS

New documents

1. Dedication to Claudius by the *Civitas Sulbanectium* (Gaul), possibly in gratitude for its promotion to *civitas* in A.D. 48; *AE*, 1960, 149 = PIGANIOL, in *Compt. rend. Ac. Inscr.*, 1959, pp. 450–7.

2. Letter from Claudius to the Thasians, confirming the privileges granted by Augustus and declining the honour of a temple, for the reasons also expressed in the letter to the Alexandrians, *AE*, 1960, 379 = DUNANT-POILLOUX, *Recherches sur l'histoire et les cultes de Thasos*, II, Paris 1958, pp. 66–9; cf. ROBERT, in *Rev. Ét. Gr.*, LXXII, 1959, p. 234, n. 332.

3. New *termini pratorum coh. IIII Gallorum* found in the province of Leon, *AE*, 1961, 345 = *Hispania Antiqua Epigraphica*, VI–VII, 1955–6 (1960), pp. 21–2, n. 1025–42 (cf. *AE*, 1935, 13).

4. Claudius honoured as 'saviour and founder of the world' in a dedication found in Cilicia Trachea, *AE*, 1963, 5 = BEAN-MITFORD, in *Anat. St.*, XII, 1862, p. 197.

5. Dedications from a shrine *Laribus Augustis* at Ostia, dated with the full titles of Claudius corresponding to the year 51, *AE*, 1964, 151; 152; 154 = BLOCH, in *Harv. Theol. Rev.*, LV, 1962, pp. 211–23.

6. Dedication to Claudius from Ossigi in Baetica, *AE*, 1965, 97 = CABEZON, in *Arch. Esp. Arq.*, XXXVII, 1964, p. 142.

7. Milestone of the year 43 from the road between Castulo and Cordoba, found in the neighbourhood of ancient Ossigi, *AE* 1965, 98 = *Arch. Esp. Arq.*, XXXVII, 1964, p. 144.

8. Dedication to Claudius from Dyrrhacium (Durazzo in Albania), dating from 44, *AE* 1966, 390 = CEKA-ANAMALLI, in *Buletin Universitetit Tiranes*, XV, 1961, p. 108.

9. Inscription from a statue of the Emperor Claudius dedicated at Side

(Lycia-Pamphylia) by the corporation of the artists of Dionysus, *AE* 1966, 455 = BEAN, *The Inscriptions of Side*, 1965, p. 47, n. 147.

10. Inscription from Caesarea-Iol (Cherchel), found in 1941 and never published. It is a dedication put up during his proconsulship of Africa by the future emperor Galba, who would thus have demonstrated a fine political sense in the delicate situation created by Gaius some years before when he separated the command of the legion from that of the province; see M. LE GLAY, 'Une dédicace à Vénus offerte à Caesarea (Cherchel) par le futur empereur Galba', in *Mél. Carcopino*, Paris 1966, pp. 629–40.

Add to the section on Claudius: personality, education, family circumstances (p. 586)

Second edition, with a new bibliography 1942–59, of A. MOMIGLIANO, *Claudius: the Emperor and his Achievement*, Cambridge 1962.

D. REBUFFAT-EMMANUEL, 'Un étruscologue victime de son temps, l'empereur Claude', in *Ann. Fac. Lett. Aix*, XLIII, 1967, pp. 209–15 (Nero's philhellenism a counterblast to Claudius's Etruscology).

J. BABELON, 'Numismatique de Britannicus', in *Homm. Herrmann*, Brussels 1960 (Coll. Latomus, XLIV), pp. 124–37 (on the propaganda in favour of Britannicus and its fluctuations).

M. TORELLI, 'Un nuovo attacco fra gli Elogia Tarquinensia', in *Stud. Etr.*, XXXVI, 1968, pp. 467–70 (important re-arrangement of fragments already known).

(On the problem of the identification of Q. Curtius Rufus and of the dating of his work.)

D. KORZENIEWSKI, *Die Zeit des Quintus Curtius Rufus*, diss., Frankfurt, Cologne 1959 (= Bonn 1960). (K. thinks he belonged to the age of Augustus, a view also supported by C. BRADFORD WELLES, in the Loeb edit. of Diodorus, Vol. VIII, 1963, p. 13.)

G. V. SUMNER, 'Curtius Rufus and the Historiae Alexandri', in *Journ. Australasian Universities Language and Literature Assoc.* (New Zealand), 1961, No. 15, pp. 30–9 (composed under Caligula and Claudius; the author is identified with the rhetorician and with the governor of the Upper Rhine).

H. U. INSTINSKY, 'Zur Kontroverse um die Datierung des Curtius Rufus', in *Hermes*, XC, 1962, pp. 379–83. (I. puts Rufus in the period of Vespasian, like J. STROUX, in *Philologus*, LXXXIV, 1929, pp. 233–251.)

R. D. MILNE, 'The Date of Curtius Rufus and the Historiae Alexandri', in *Latomus*, XXV, 1966, pp. 490–507 (work composed under Galba; author identified with the rhetorician).

R. VERDIÉRE, 'Quinte-Curce, écrivain néronien', in *Wien St.*, LXXIX, 1966, pp. 490–509 (age of Nero; the author possibly the governor of the Upper Rhine, then proconsul of Africa; he cannot be the rhetorician).

G. SCHEDA, 'Zur Datierung des Curtius Rufus', in *Historia*, XVIII, 1969, pp. 380–3 (age of Vespasian).

Add to the section on Claudius's work (p. 589)

(freedmen in the Claudian administration)

D. STOCKTON, 'Tacitus, Annals XII, 60. A Note', in *Historia*, X, 1961, pp. 116–20 (Claudius did not grant powers of jurisdiction to his freedmen-private procurators).

P. R. C. WEAVER, 'The Slave and Freedman "cursus" in the Imperial Administration', in *Proc. Cambr. Philol. Soc.*, X, 1964, pp. 74–92 (greater regularity than was thought in the hierarchy and system of promotion).

F. MILLAR, 'Some Evidence on the Meaning of Tacitus, *Annals*, XXI, 60', in *Historia*, XIII, 1964, pp. 180–7 (probably a question of jurisdiction within the imperial domains).

——, 'The Development of Jurisdiction by Imperial Procurators: Further Evidence', in *Historia*, XIV, 1965, pp. 362–7 (addenda to the previous article).

P. R. C. WEAVER, 'Freedmen Procurators in the Imperial Administration', in *Historia*, XIV, 1965, pp. 460–9 (rules which show a certain strictness in the employment of freedmen).

P. A. BRUNT, 'Procuratorial Jurisdiction', in *Latomus*, XXV, 1966, pp. 461–89 (also on TAC., *Ann.*, XII, 60, opposing Millar's interpretation).

TH. DOREY, 'Claudius und seine Ratgeber', in *Altertum*, XII, 1966, pp. 144–55 (tendency to increase the rôle of the aristocracy and reduce that of the freedmen).

G. BOULVERT, 'Servi et liberti du prince', in *Labeo*, XII, 1966, pp. 94–103 (on private reflections of the employment of slaves and freedmen in the administration).

K. WACHTEL, 'Sklaven und Freigelassene in der staatlichen Finanzverwaltung des römischen Kaiserreiches', in *Acta Ant. Ac. Sc. Hung.*, XV, 1967, pp. 341–6 (on the great social prestige of the imperial slaves and freedmen).

F. MILLAR, 'Emperors at Work', in *Journ. Rom. St.*, LVII, 1967, pp. 9–19 (the administration guided personally by the Emperor, on whom his immediate subordinates in the imperial chancellery had no more influence than other advisers; Claudius played a front-rank part).

(conquest of Britain)

G. WEBSTER and D. R. DUDLEY, *The Roman Conquest of Britain A.D. 43–57*, London 1965.

S. FRERE, *Britannia. A History of Roman Britain*, Cambridge 1967.

J. LIVERSIDGE, *Britain in the Roman Empire*, London 1967.

(provincial government)

A. GARCIA Y BELLIDO, 'El exercitus Hispanicus desde Augusto a Vespasiano', in *Arch. Esp. Arq.*, XXXIV, 1961, pp. 114–51 (for the modifications under Claudius; also discusses the *termini pratorum* of cohort *IIII Gallica*, on which see above, *Documents*).

G. TH. SCHWARTZ, *Die Kaiserstadt Aventicum*, Berne 1964.

S. J. DE LAET, 'Claude et la romanisation de la Gaule septentrionale', in *Mél. Piganiol*, Paris 1966, pp. 951–61 (the foundations for rapid Romanization were laid by Claudius; this was his great merit).

G. FAIDER-FEYTMANS, 'L'occupation préclaudienne dans le bassin supérieur de la Haine (Belgique)', in *Mél. Carcopino*, Paris 1966, pp. 341–51 (the absence of noteworthy traces of Romanization earlier than Claudius confirms the view taken in the monograph cited above).

A. PLASSART, 'L'inscription de Delphes mentionnant le proconsul Gallion', in *Rev. Ét. Gr.*, LXXX, 1967, pp. 372–8 (new interpretation of the fragmentary letter of Claudius, *Syll.*, 3801 D).

CH. SAUMAGNE, 'Saint Paul et Félix, procurateur de Judée, in *Mél. Piganiol*, Paris 1966, pp. 1373–86 (argues that the procuratorship of Antonius Felix ended in 54, not towards 60, as is commonly thought, with the consequence that the martyrdom of St Paul should be advanced to 58).

(religious policy)

F. DE VISSCHER, *Le droit des tombeaux romains*, Milan 1963 (on the inscription from Nazareth, pp. 161–96).

G. E. LONGO, 'Sul diritto sepolcrale romano', in *Iura*, XV, 1964, pp. 137–58 (against De Visscher's view)

NERO

New documents

1. Fragment of a letter from Nero to the Thasians (but almost nothing

has been preserved), *AE*, 1960, 379 = DUNANT-POUILLOUX, *Thasos*, II, 1958, p. 75 f.; cf. ROBERT, in *Rev. Ét. Gr.*, LXXII, 1959, p. 234, n. 332.

2. Dedication to Nero, 'new sun, visible god', at Prostanna (Pisidia), *AE*, 1961, 22 = BEAN, in *Anat. St.*, IX, 1959, p. 128.

3. Inscription of Drusus the Elder, re-used in a curious fashion by Nero (M. G. MALATESTA, in *Arch. Class.*, XII, 1960, pp. 222–3), from Sepino. Published for the first time by V. CIANFARANI, 'Vecchie e nuove iscrizioni sepinati', in *Atti III Congr. Intern. Epigr. Gr. e Lat.*, Rome 1959, p. 376 and plate XLVII 2, and atrributed to Nero. Attribution to Drusus by H. G. PFLAUM, in *AE*, 1959, 278, Cf. *AE*, 1962, 37.

4. Milestone from Lusitania, of 58–59, from the road from Emerita to the Asturian mines, found near Caparra (*municipium Caparensium*), *AE*, 1967, 198 = BLASQUEZ, in *Excavaciones arqueolog. en España*, XXXIV, 1965, p. 26.

5. Fragment containing the preamble to a decree mentioning 'hè toû kyríou theoû [Né] ronos despotía', from Chio, *AE*, 1967, 464 = FORREST, in *Ann. Brit. Sch. Ath.*, LXI, 1966, p. 203.

Studies

Biographies

GEORGES-ROUX, *Néron*, Paris 1962.

J. BISHOP, *Nero, the Man and the Legend*, London 1964.

Add to the section Nero. Personality and milieu (p. 605)

(*on the year of Nero's birth*)

W. F. SNYDER, 'Nero's Birthday in Egypt and his Year of Birth', in *Historia*, XIII, 1964, pp. 503–6, (the Egyptian inscription *SEG*, XVIII, 675, rules out the years 35 and 39, and leaves possible the years 36, 37, 38; but the year traditionally accepted, 37, is made sufficiently certain by all the other evidence).

(*on the cultural atmosphere*)

P. J. PHOTIADES, 'A Profile of Seneca', in *Orpheus*, IX, 1962, pp. 53–7.

E. CIZEK, 'Aspects idéologiques dans la littérature latine à l'époque de Néron', in *Stud. Clas.*, IV, 1962, pp. 221–40 (in Rumanian, with French summary: an examination of the first years of Nero's reign through the medium of the works mirroring the political currents, especially the *Apocolocyntosis* and the *De Clementia* of Seneca).

G. C. GIARDINA, 'Per un inquadramento del teatro di Seneca nella cultura e nella società del suo tempo', in *Riv. Cult. Class. Med.*, VI, 1964, pp. 171–89.

A. L. MOTTO, 'Seneca on Trial. The Case of the Opulent Stoic', in *Class. Journ.*, LXI, 1966, pp. 254–8.

W. JUST, 'L. Annaeus Seneca', in *Altertum*, XII, 1966, pp. 223–33.

E. ELORDUY, 'Séneca, preceptor de Néron', in *Est. Clasicos*, XI, 1967, pp. 41–83.

(*Apocolocyntosis*)

M. COFFEY, 'Seneca, *Apocolocyntosis* 1922–1958', in *Lustrum*, VI, 1961, pp. 239–71 (bibliographical survey).

H. MACL. CURRIE, 'The Purpose of the Apocolocyntosis', in *Ant. Class.*, XXXI, 1962, pp. 91–7 (a vendetta against Claudius which demonstrates Seneca's mental instability).

——, '*Apocolocyntosis*. A Suggestion', in *Rh. Mus.*, CV, 1962, pp. 187 F.

B. BALDWIN, 'Executions under Claudius. Seneca's *Ludus de morte Claudii*', in *Phoenix*, XVIII, 1964, pp. 39–48 (not by Seneca; must have been circulated clandestinely in support of Britannicus; later published, but not before 58).

K. KRAFT, 'Der politische Hintergrund von Senecas *Apocolocyntosis*', in *Historia*, XV, 1966, pp. 96–122 (an expression of view in the controversy about claims to the throne; attacks the memory of Claudius, which could be exploited in favour of Britannicus; in the last analysis a philo-Neronian work).

W. JUST, 'Senecas Satire auf die Apotheose des Kaisers Claudius in ihrer politischen Bedeutung', in *Wiss. Ztschr. Univ. Rostock*, XV, 1966, pp. 447–51 (a manœuvre in the fight against Agrippina).

(*Octavia*)

C. J. HERINGTON, 'Octavia praetexta, a Survey', in *Class. Quart.*, XI, 1961, pp. 18–30 (not by Seneca, but written towards A.D. 90).

(*De clementia*)

L. HERMANN, 'Le De clementia de Sénèque et quelques faits historiques', in *Stud. Clas.*, II, 1960, pp. 243–4 (autumn 58 as date of composition).

M. FUHRMANN, 'Die Alleinherrschaft und das Problem der Gerechtigkeit (Seneca, De clementia)', in *Gymnasium*, LXX, 1963, pp. 481–514.

W. RICHTER, 'Das Problem der Datierung von Seneca De clementia', in *Rh. Mus.*, CVIII, 1965, pp. 146–70 (*terminus ante quem* 15 December 55).

(Persius, Lucan, Petronius – the 'quinquennium aureum')

P. GRIMAL, 'L'éloge de Néron au début de la Pharsale: est-il ironique?', in *Rev. Ét. Lat.*, XXXVIII, 1960, pp. 296–305 (the author thinks it is serious).

I. K. HORVATH, 'Perse et Néron', in *Stud. Clas.*, III, 1961, pp. 337–43 (the allusions show a courageous opposition to Nero).

L. THOMPSON, 'Lucan's Apotheosis of Nero', in *Class. Phil.*, LIX, 1964, pp. 147–53 (Lucan's praise sincere; the beginning of Nero's reign was hailed with enthusiasm as a return to the Augustan régime).

O. MURRAY, 'The Quinquennium Neronis and the Stoics', in *Historia*, XIV, 1965, pp. 41–61 (the *quinquennium* invented by Q. Arulenus Rusticus, biographer of Thrasea Paetus, to justify the latter's collaboration with Nero in the early years of the reign).

P. MCCLOSKEY and E. PHINNEY, JR., 'Ptolemaeus Tyrannus: The Typification of Nero in the Pharsalia', in *Hermes*, XCVI, 1968, pp. 80–7 (deals with the condemnation of the corruption of the Hellenizing court and the depraved Princeps).

(Nero's relations with the aristocracy)

D. GILLIS, 'The Portrait of Afranius Burrus in Tacitus' *Annales*', in *Par. Pass.*, 1963, pp. 5–22 (the praetorian prefect viewed sympathetically by Tacitus).

R. S. ROGERS, 'Freedom of Speech in the Empire. Nero', in *Stud. Caldwell*, Chapel Hill, N.C. 1964, pp. 91–8.

L. PETERSEN, 'Der jüngste Iunius Silanus', in *Historia*, XV, 1966, pp. 328–35.

J. BABELON, 'Sur un buste de Corbulon', in *Mél. Carcopino*, Paris 1966, pp. 45–52 (contains a biography of Corbulo).

B. BALDWIN, 'Executions, Trials and Punishments in the Reign of Nero', in *Par. Pass.*, 1967, pp. 425–39 (not a systematic terror; the various events must be seen in the light of personal relationships and family politics, that is, the political habits inherited from the republic and still flourishing in the time of Nero).

Add to the section The Reign of Nero. Internal problems (p. 612)

(numismatic evidence)

C. GATTI, 'La tribunicia potestas nelle monete di Nerone', in *Par. Pass.*, pp. 426–37.

D. W. MACDOWALL, 'The Quality of Nero's Orichalcum', in *Gaz. Num. Suisse*, XVI, 1966, pp. 101–6.

(fire of Rome and persecution of the Christians)

J. BEAUJEU, *L'incendie de Rome en 64 et les chrétiens*, Brussels 1960 (Coll. Latomus, XLIX) (a survey based on the literary evidence).

J. N. SEVENSTER, *Paul und Seneca*, Leiden 1961 (Novum Testamentum, Suppl. IV) (negative conclusion on the correspondence between Seneca and St Paul; ideological confrontation).

CH. SAUMAGNE, 'Tertullian et l'Institutum Neronianum', in *Theol. Ztschr.*, XVII, 1961, pp. 334–55 (denies the existence of any kind of law against Christians as such).

——, 'Les incendiaires de Rome et les lois pénales des Romains', in *Rev. Hist.*, CCXXVII, 1962, pp. 337–60 (fire attributable to a subversive movement and punished in accordance with the normal criminal laws; explanation of the birth of the tradition that the blame was pushed on the Christians).

M. GUARDUCCI, 'La più antica iscrizione col nome dei Cristiani', in *Mél. Kirschbaum* (Röm. Quartalschr. f. christl. Altertumskunde, Freiburg, LVII, 1962), pp. 116–25 (on *CIL*, IV 679, from Pompeii: 'Bovios audit Cristianos sevos osores').

J. CARCOPINO, *Études d'histoire chrétienne*: I, *Les fouilles de Saint Pierre et la tradition*, 2nd ed., Paris 1963; II, *Les reliques de S. Pierre à Rome*, Paris 1965.

E. GRIFFE, 'La persécution des chrétiens de Rome en l'an 64', in *Bull. Litter. Eccles.*, LXV, 1964, pp. 3–16.

CH. SAUMAGNE, 'Tacite et Saint Paul', in *Rev. Hist.*, CCXXXII, 1964, pp. 67–110 (denies that the statements in TAC., *Ann.*, XV, 44, can refer to Christians living in Rome in 64, a year in which the Christians cannot yet have been known: a bold theory which opens the way for that of Köstermann, see below).

W. H. C. FREUD, *Martyrdom and Persecution in the Early Church. A Study of a Conflict from the Maccabees to Donatus*, Oxford 1965.

J. HERRMANN, 'Tertullians Verfahrenrügen und die frühen Märtyrerakten', in *Journ. Jurist. Papyr.*, XV, 1965, pp. 151–6 (on the absence in the 1st and 2nd centuries of a general law against the Christians).

J. E. A. CRAKE, 'Early Christians and Roman Law', in *Phoenix*, XIX, 1965, pp. 61–70 (also maintains that there was no law against Christians before Trajan).

J. MICHELFEIT, 'Das Christenkapitel des Tacitus', in *Gymnasium*, LXXIII, 1966, pp. 514–40.

H. FUCHS and E. KÖSTERMANN, 'Das Christenkapitel des Tacitus', in *Gymnasium*, LXXIV, 1967, p. 251 (bibliographical supplements to the preceding article).

A. FANTOLI and M. AMBROSI, 'Una ipotesi circa il primo viaggio di S. Pietro a Roma', in *Rend. Acc. Lincei*, XXII, 1967, pp. 3–15 (explanation of the origin of the erroneous tradition of a first journey to Rome by St Peter in the reign of Claudius).

S. GAROFALO, 'La tradizione petriana nel primo secolo', in *Stud. Rom.*, XV, 1967, pp. 135–48.

G. SCHEDA, 'Nero und der Brand Roms', in *Historia*, XVI, 1967, pp. 111–15 (explanation of the origin of the legend that Nero sang a *Troiae Halosis*).

E. KÖSTERMANN. 'Ein folgenschwerer Irrtum des Tacitus (*Ann.*, XV, 44, 2)?', in *Historia*, XVI, 1967, pp. 456–69 (Tacitus's accidental substitution of *Christiani* for *Chrestiani* the origin of the story of the first persecution).

M. GUARDUCCI, 'La data del martirio di S. Pietro', in *Par. Pass.*, 1968, pp. 81–117.

R. RENEHAN, 'Christus or Chrestus in Tacitus?', in *Par. Pass.*, 1968, pp. 368–70.

Nero the artist – works of his reign

G. CH. PICARD, *Auguste et Néron. Le secret de l'empire*, Paris 1962 (biography of N. concentrating on a delineation of the aesthete).

M. F. GYLES, 'Nero, qualis artifex?', in *Class. Journ.*, LVII, 1962, pp. 193–200 (takes N. seriously as an artist).

P. M. FRAZER, 'Nero the Artist-Criminal', in *Class. Journ.*, LXII, 1966, pp. 17–20 (sharply opposes the preceding article).

A. BOETHIUS, *The Golden House of Nero. Some Aspects of Roman Architecture*, Ann Arbor, Michigan, 1960 (Jerome Lectures).

G. ZANDER, 'Nuovi studi e ricerche sulla Domus Aurea', in *Palladio*, XV, 1965, pp. 157–9 (on the excavations of 1965).

G. DI VITA-ÉVRARD, 'Les dédicaces de l'amphithéâtre et du cirque de Lepcis', in *Libya Antiqua*, II, 1965, pp. 29–37 (the amphitheatre completed in 56).

M. P. O. MORFORD, 'The Distortion of the Domus Aurea Tradition', in *Eranos*, LXVI, 1968, pp. 158–79 (tradition too heavily influenced by moralistic considerations).

Add to the section on The reign of Nero. The wars and the provinces (p. 618)

(*Britain, the Parthians*)

CHR. M. BULST, 'The Revolt of Queen Boudicca in A.D. 60. Roman Politics and the Iceni', in *Historia*, X, 1961, pp. 496–509.

D. R. DUDLEY and G. WEBSTER, *Rebellion of Boudicca*, London 1962.

M. F. GYLES, 'Effects of Roman Capital Investment in Britain under Nero', in *Stud. Caldwell*, Chapel Hill, N.C. 1964, pp. 99–109 (rather bold application of modern economic theories).

K. H. ZIEGLER, *Die Beziehungen zwischen Rom und dem Partherreich. Ein Beitrag zur Geschichte des Völkerrechts*, Wiesbaden 1964.

H. PETERSEN, 'New Evidence for the Relations between Romans and Parthians', in *Berytus*, XVI, 1966, pp. 61–9 (the existence of an *ala Parthorum* – not consisting of exiles and deserters – in the middle of the first century puts the relations between the empire and the Parthians in a different light).

J. C. OVERBECK, 'Tacitus and Dio on Boudicca's Rebellion', in *Amer. Journ. Phil.*, XC, 1969, pp. 129–45.

S. J. BASTOMSKY, 'The Emperor Nero in Talmudic Legend', in *Jew. Quart. Rev.*, LIX, 1969, pp. 321–5 (on Nero in relation to the Jewish war and on the false Neros).

(revolt against Nero)

M. RAOSS, 'La rivolta di Vindice e il successo di Galba', in *Epigraphica*, XX, 1958 [1960], pp. 46–120; XXII, 1960 [1961], pp. 37–151.

J. BURIAN, 'L. Clodius Macer, dominus minor Africae', in *Klio*, XXXVIII, 1960, pp. 167–73 (emphasis of the separatist aim).

G. B. TOWNEND, 'The Reputation of Verginius Rufus', in *Latomus*, XX, 1961, pp. 337–41 (the writer argues that the less favourable tradition about the behaviour of Verginius Rufus originated with Cluvius Rufus and that traces of it remain in Cassius Dio; the friends of Verginius, from Nerva onwards, obliterated it to the advantage of the more favourable tradition).

J. B. HAINSWORTH, 'Verginius and Vindex', in *Historia*, XI, 1962, pp. 86–96 (Verginius's irresolution caused by the legalistic scruples natural to a senator; important that the battle of Vesontio should be fixed to the end of May or the early days of June 68, and related directly to the end of Nero; M. SCHUSTER's date of 12 June, in *Realencycl.*, VIII, A2, 1958, c. 1537, obviously wrong).

G. CHALON, *L'édit de Tibérius Julius Alexander, Étude historique et exégétique*, Olten-Lausanne 1964 (complete monograph).

MOSTAFA EL ABBADI, 'The Edict of Tiberius Iulius Alexander. Remarks on its Nature and Aim', in *Bull. Inst. Franç. Arch. Or.*, LXV, 1967, pp. 215–26.

D. C. A. SHOTTER, 'Tacitus and Verginius Rufus', in *Class. Quart.*,

XVII, 1967, pp. 370–81 (on the absence of military qualities in Verginius).

J. VAN OOTEGHEM, 'Verginius et Vindex', in *Les Ét. Class.*, XXXVI, 1968, pp. 18–27.

B. R. REESE, 'The Date of Nero's Death', in *Amer. Journ. Phil.*, XC, 1969, pp. 72–4 (11, not 9, June 68).

THE FOUR EMPERORS

Add to the section The year of the four emperors (p. 622)

(civil war)

R. HANSLIK, 'Die Auseinandersetzung zwischen Otho und Vitellius bis zur Schlacht von Bedriacum nach Tacitus', in *Wiener Studien*, LXXIV, 1961, pp. 113–25 (Tacitus's account preferable to Plutarch's).

E. KÖSTERMANN, 'Die erste Schlacht bei Bedriacum 69 n. Chr.', in *Riv. Cult. Class. Med.*, III, 1961, pp. 16–29 (examination of Tacitus's account).

B. F. HARRIS, 'Tacitus on the Death of Otho', in *Class. Journ.*, LVIII, 1962, pp. 73–7 (the passage a literary elaboration of the theme of the expiatory character of Otho's death).

G. B. TOWNEND, 'The Consuls of A.D. 69–70', in *Amer. Journ. Phil.*, LXXXIII, 1962, pp. 113–29.

P. JAL, *La guerre civile à Rome. Étude littéraire et morale*, Paris 1963. (Comprehensive work following a series of articles on various moments and aspects of the Roman civil wars. One of these articles that is important for the argument of this paragraph is 'Le rôle des Barbares dans les guerres civiles de Rome, de Sylla à Vespasien', in *Latomus*, XXI, 1962, pp. 8–48. The war of 69 is in the forefront of the book.)

G. FORNI, 'Bedriacensia', in *Riv. Cult. Class. Med.*, VII, 1965, pp. 467–76 (on various questions posed by the Tacitean account).

H. JUCKER, 'Hispania Clunia Sul. Zu einem Sesterz des Kaisers Galba', in *Gaz. Num. Suisse*, XV, 1965, pp. 94–111 (historical implications of this coin).

A. MÓCSY, 'Tampius Flavianus in Pannonien', in *Arch. Ertesitö*, XCIII, 1966, pp. 203–7.

B. MOUCHOVÁ, 'Ausgewählte Parallelen aus der Lebensbeschreibung Kaisers Otho bei Sueton und den Historien des Tacitus', in *Listy Filologické*, LXXXIX, 1966, pp. 257–61 (comparison of the accounts of Tacitus and Suetonius shows that there is more sympathy for Otho in the second).

A. GARCIA Y BELLIDO, *Nueve studios sobre la legio VII Gemina y su campamento en León*, León 1968. (Historical-archaeological re-examination in depth of the life at Léon of Legion VII, enrolled by Galba in 68. The epithet *Hispana* for this legion is now attested by an unpublished inscription from Brescia, found in 1959, which I mentioned in my commentary on the translation of the works of Tacitus by C. GIUSSANI, Turin, 1968, p. 547, n. 5. This inscription has been published with a commentary by myself, in the proceedings of the International Conference to mark the nineteenth centenary of the formation of Legion VII and of the foundation of the city of León, held at León from 16 to 21 September 1968.)

M. A. LEVI, 'Le conseguenze della crisi del 69 d. C. nell'ambiente cremonese', in *Atti del Centre St. e Docum. sull'Italia rom.*, I, Milan 1969, pp. 215–18.

(Batavian war)

R. CHEVALLIER, 'Rome et la Germanie au Ier siècle de notre ère. Problèmes de colonisation', in *Latomus*, XX, 1961, pp. 33–51, 266–80, subsequently collected in Vol. LIII of the Collection Latomur, Brussels 1961. (Looks at two points in particular: Germany in Roman literature of the first century, and the ties between the army of the Rhine and the native peoples. This second point is of considerable importance in connection with the crisis of 69–70.)

M. E. CARBONNE, 'The First Relief of Castra Vetera in the Revolt of Civilis. A Note on Tacitus, *Histories*, IV 26, 3', in *Phoenix*, XXI, 1967, pp. 296–8 (on the movements of the legions).

THE FLAVIANS

New documents

For the reign of Vespasian

1. Dedication of 77/78 by a governor of Cilicia to Vespasian, Titus and Domitian; from Cilicia Trachea, *AE*, 1963, 11 = BEAN-MITFORD, in *Anat. St.*, XII, 1962, p. 208.

2. A new fragment, found at Bonn, of inscription *CIL*, XIII, 8046, dating from 75, confirms that after 70 the camp at Bonn was built of stone; cf. *AE*, 1963, 48 = KOLBE, in *Bonner Jahrb.*, CLXI, 1961, pp. 93 f.

3. Rectification by A. DEGRASSI to *AE*, 1951, 200 (*Epigraphica II*, in

Mem. Acc. Lincei, Cl. Sc. Mor., ser. VIII, Vol. XI, 1965, pp. 274–6 = *Scritti vari di antichità*, III, 1967, pp. 85–7; cf. *AE*, 1966, 72): the inscription from Salerno belongs to the reign of Vespasian and refers to an unidentifiable restoration.

4. Boundary pillar (cippus) from terrtories in Dalmatia *ex auctoritate Imp. Vespasiani*, from Iader (Zara), *AE*, 1967, 355 = WILKES, in *Epigraph. Stud.*, IV, 1967, pp. 119–21. We thus come to know a fresh governor, though not his complete name.

5. Boundary pillar from the borders of lands belonging to the people of Apollonia (Cyrenaica), *AE*, 1967, 531 = REYNOLDS-GOODCHILD, in *Libya Antiqua*, II, 1965, pp. 103–7. We thus come to know a new proconsul of Crete and Cyrene.

6. New fragment of the *Fasti Ostienses*, of A.D. 74; E. EQUINI, 'Un frammento inedito dei Fasti Ostiensi del 74', in *Epigr.*, XXIX, 1967 (pub. 1968), pp. 11–17.

For the reign of Titus

1. Letter from Titus to the Muniguenses, bronze tablet from Mulva (Munigua), dating from 79; *AE*, 1962, 288 = NESSELHAUF, in *Madr. Mitt.*, I, 1960, pp. 142–54; cf. A. D'ORS, in *Emerita*, XXIX, 1961, pp. 208–18.

2. Milestone from the road *Asturica-Bracara*, of 79, *AE*, 1966, 215 = ALVAREZ, in *Zephirus*, XI, 1060, n. 312; cf. *Hisp. Ant. Epigr.*, n. 2162.

3. At Demetrias dedication to Titus 'néon Apóllona euergéten' by the Magnesians, *AE*, 1967, 460 = THEOCHARES, in *Thessalika*, III, 1960, p. 81, n. 3.

For the reign of Domitian

1. New military diploma, dated 12 May 91, found in Bulgaria, *AE*, 1961, 319 = BATULAROVA, in *Studia Dečev*, 1958, pp. 317 f. On the name of A. Bucius Lappius Maximus, which would give us the new *nomen* Bucius for this well-known person of the Flavian and Trajanic era, cf. J. ASSA, 'Aulus Bucius Lappius Maximus', in *Akte IV Kongr. f. Epigr.* (Vienna 1962), Vienna 1964, pp. 31–9.

2. Fragments of two military diplomas of 91 found in Bulgaria, *AE*, 1962, 264 *bis* = GEROV, in *Klio*, XXXVII, 1959, pp. 210–16.

3. New fragment of the inscription on the monument of Adamklissi, *AE*, 1963, 99 = DORUTIU, in *Dacia*, V, 1961, p. 347.

4. Dedication to Diana and to Domitian in the Nympheum at Ephesus,

AE, 1966, 424a = MILTNER, in *Anz. Oesterr. Ak. Wiss.*, 1959, p. 37 (cf. *AE*, 1961, 35); *Oesterr. Jahresh.*, XLV, 1960, Beibl., cc. 31–5. The XXIII imperial salutation is now attested for the first time.

5. Inscription for the aqueduct, with mention of Domitian and of the proconsul Calvisius Ruso, *AE*, 1966, 424b = MILTNER, in *Oesterr. Jahresh.*, XLV, 1960, Beibl., c. 34.

6. Inscription on a base belonging to a group set up at Ephesus by various towns in the province, in honour of Domitian, *AE*, 1966, 426 = KEIL-MARECH in *Oesterr. Jahresh.*, XLV, 1960, Beibl., cc. 83–4. The erasure of the name after the *abolitio memoriae* has taken place, but the name of Divus Vespasianus (cf. no. 9 below) has not been inscribed instead, as it has in other cases.

7. Another dedication to Diana and to Domitian, at Ephesus, *AE*, 1967, 466 = KNIBBE-EICHLER, in *Anz. Oesterr. Ak. Wiss.*, CII, 1965, p. 103, n. 1; cf. ROBERT, in *Rev. Ét. Gr.*, LXXX, 1967, p. 533, n. 505.

8. Dedication to Domitian of 92/93, at Ephesus, *AE*, 1967, 471 (cf. *AE*, 1961, 193) = MILTNER, in *Anz. Oesterr. Ak. Wiss.*, XCVI, 1959, pp. 37–8; *Oesterr. Jahresh.*, XLIV, 1959, Beibl., cc. 343–6.

9. Dedication to Domitian by the Teans, at Ephesus, *AE*, 1967, 472 = KNIBBE-EICHLER, in *Anz. Oesterr. Ak. Wiss.*, CII, 1965, pp. 103–4, n. 2; cf. ROBERT, in *Rev. Ét. Gr.*, LXXX, 1967, p. 533, n. 506. Domitian's name has been erased and replaced by that of Divus Vespasianus.

10. Fragment with the start of a letter from Domitian, possibly granting the *neocoria* to Ephesus, *AE*, 1967, 473 = KNIBBE-EICHLER, in *Anz. Oesterr. Ak. Wiss.*, CII, 1965, pp. 104–5, n. 4; cf. ROBERT, in *Rev. Ét. Gr.*, pp. 533–4, n. 508.

Studies

Add to the section The advent of the Flavians (p. 629)

(*Lex de imperio Vespasiani*)

L. LESUISSE, 'La clause transitoire de la lex de imperio Vespasiani', in *Rev. Belg. Phil. Hist.*, XL, 1962, pp. 51–75 (on the ratification of the proceedings of the acclamation of 1 July 69).

M. SORDI, 'Cola di Rienzo e le clausole mancanti della lex de imperio Vespasiani', in *Studi Volterra*, II, Milan 1969, pp. 303–11 (Cola di Rienzo was still familiar with the tablet missing from the document).

(Propaganda and political programme)

G. B. TOWNEND, 'Some Flavian Connections', in *Journ. Rom. St.*, LI, 1961, pp. 54–62 (relatives of the Flavii and their rôle in the accession to the throne).

K. H. WATERS, 'The Second Dynasty of Rome', in *Phoenix*, XVII, 1963, pp. 198–218.

A. FERRILL, 'Otho, Vitellius and the Propaganda of Vespasian', in *Class. Journ.*, LX, 1965, pp. 267–9 (no recriminations, so as not to upset the troops incorporated in the Flavian army).

A. GARZETTI, 'L. Cesennio Peto e la rivalutazione flaviana di personaggi neroniani', in *Mél. Piganiol*, Paris 1966, pp. 777–90.

M. TORELLI, 'The Cursus Honorum of M. Hirrius Fronto Neratius Pansa', in *Journ. Rom. St.*, LVIII, 1968, pp. 170–5 (deals with attention paid by Vesp. to entrusting provincial governorships to men possessing the specific competence required).

H. CASTRETIUS, 'Zu den Frauen der Flavier', in *Historia*, XVIII, 1969, pp. 492–502 (on the mother of Julia Titi and Domitia Longina).

Add to the section The work of Vespasian (p. 634)

(The empire)

EDW. ECHOLS, 'The Provincial Urban Cohorts', in *Class. Journ.*, LVII, 1961, pp. 25–8 (on the apparent paradox of urban cohorts stationed in the provinces: under Vespasian the I *Flavia* at Lyon and the XIII at Carthage).

A. PIGANIOL, *Les documents cadastraux de la colonie romaine d'Orange* (*Suppl.* Gallia, XVI), Paris 1962 (splendid collected edition of this important series of documents; three registers can be distinguished, A.B.C.; A belongs to the period of Vespasian, B to a period subsequent to Trajan, C to an uncertain period).

J. REYNOLDS, 'La colonie flavienne d'Avenches', in *Schweiz. Ztschr. f. Gesch.*, XIV, 1964, pp. 387–91 (argues that only the Latin right was granted).

F. GROSSO, 'Il diritto latino ai militari in età Flavia', in *Riv. Cult. Class. Med.*, VII, 1965, pp. 541–60 (in his tendency to the extensive use of the Latin right as an intermediate stage in Romanization, Vespasian granted it widely to non-citizen military personnel, beginning with the sailors of the fleets; cf. also S. PANCIERA, 'Sulla pretesa esclusione dei cittadini romani dalle flotte italiche nei primi due secoli dell'impero', in *Rend. Acc. Lincei*, XIX, 1964, pp. 316–27).

G. CLEMENTE, 'La presunta politica di scambio dei governi provinciali fra imperatore e senato nel I e II secolo', in *Par. Pass.*, 1965, pp. 195–206 (the principle of compensation not to be taken too rigidly; no political rule about it).

H. W. BENARIO, 'C. Paccius Africanus at Sabratha', in *Epigraphica*, XXVIII, 1966, pp. 135–9 (for the importance of the building work in Africa under Vespasian).

T. KOTULA, 'A propos d'une inscription reconstituée de Bulla Regia (Hammam-Darradji). Quelques municipes "mysterieux" de l'Afrique proconsulaire', in *Mél. Éc. Franç. Rome*, LXXIX, 1967, pp. 207–20 (a new examination of inscription *AE*, 1964, 177, suggests the attribution to Vespasian of the formation of the municipium, and this proves the policy of stabilization and civil development which he pursued in Africa).

(*Agricola's campaign in Britain*)

K. BÜCHNER, 'Reicht die Statthalterschaft des Agricola von 77–82 oder von 78–83 n. Chr.?', in *Rhein. Mus.*, CIII, 1960, pp. 172–8 (prefers the earlier dating).

G. FORNI, *Comm. a Tac. Agr.*, Rome 1962, pp. 159 ff. (prefers the later dates).

R. M. OGILVIE and I. RICHMOND, *Cornelii Taciti de vita Agricolae*, Oxford 1967, p. 317 ff. (also prefer 78–84).

Add to the section The reign of Titus (p. 642)

J.R. JONES, 'Vespasian Junior', in *Num. Chron.*, VI, 1966, pp. 61–3 (on bronze coins from Smyrna with the inscription Ouespasianòs Neóteros, to be attributed to Titus).

G. W. CLARKE, 'The Date of the Consecratio of Vespasian', in *Historia*, XV, 1966, pp. 318–27 (cannot be determined).

C. ZIRKLE, 'The Death of Gaius Plinius Secundus, 23–79 A.D.', in *Isis* (Washington), LVIII, 1967, pp. 553–9 (died of a heart attack).

S. J. BASTOMSKY, 'The Death of the Emperor Titus, a Tentative Suggestion', in *Apeiron* (Clayton, Vict.), I, 2, 1967, pp. 22 f. (died from malaria).

I. WEILER, 'Titus und die Zerstörung des Tempels von Jerusalem – Absicht oder Zufall?', in *Klio*, L, 1968, pp. 139–58 (examination of the tradition justifying the act).

Add to section The figure of Domitian and the conflict with the aristocracy (p. 645)

R. S. ROGERS, 'A Group of Domitianic Treason-trials', in *Class. Phil.*,

LV, 1960, pp. 19–23 (reasons for thinking that the famous 'martiri stoici' were not persecuted for ideological reasons but for actual conspiracy and treason).

K. H. WATERS, 'The Character of Domitian', in *Phoenix*, XVIII, 1964, pp. 49–77 (an attempt at rehabilitation).

K. CHRIST, 'Zur Herrscherauffassung und Politik Domitians. Aspekte des modernen Domitianbildes', in *Schweiz. Ztschr. f. Gesch.*, XII, 1962, pp. 187–213 (the figure of Domitian certainly altered by a tendentious tradition; but he can never have been popular).

Add to section The work of Domitian (p. 649)

(*monuments*)

H. BARDON, 'Le goût à l'époque des Flaviens', in *Latomus*, XXI, 1962, pp. 732–48 (some characteristics in the art that are a proof of vitality).

J. BÉRANGER, 'Les Génies du Sénat et du peuple romain et les reliefs flaviens de la Cancelleria', in *Homm. Bayet* (Coll. Latomus, LXX), Brussels 1964, pp. 76–88 (pieces of Domitian's ideological propaganda).

A. BALLAND, 'Une transposition de la grotte de Tibère à Sperlonga; le Ninfeo Bergantino de Castelgandolfo', in *Mél. Éc. Franç. Rome*, LXXIX, pp. 421–502 (imitation of the cave of Sperlonga).

(*provincial government*)

H. W. PLEKET, 'Domitian, the Senate and the Provinces', in *Mnemosyne*, XIV, 1961, pp. 296–315 (Domitian's interest in the provinces, as testified by the inscriptions, enables us to revise our view of Domitian's relations with the Senate).

J. SCHWARTZ, *Les archives de Sarapion et de ses fils. Une exploitation agricole aux environs d'Hermoupolis Magna (de 90 à 133 p. C.)*, Paris 1961 (Inst. Franç. d'Arch. Or., Bibl. d'étude, XXIX).

TH. FRANKFORT, 'Le royaume d'Agrippa II et son annexion par Domitien', in *Homm. Grenier* (Coll. Latomus, LVIII), Brussels 1962, pp. 659–72.

(*religious policy*)

M. SORDI, 'La persecuzione di Domiziano', in *Riv. St. d. Ch. in It.*, XIV, 1960, pp. 1–26 (a real persecution and much more serious than is commonly thought).

S. ROSSI, 'La cosiddetta persecuzione di Domiziano. Esame delle testimonianze', in *Giorn. Ital. Fil.*, XV, 1962, pp. 303–41 (denies its existence).

Add to section The wars waged by Domitian (p. 655)

F. BOBU FLORESEN, *Monementul de la Adamklissi. Tropaeum Traiani*, 2nd ed., Bucharest 1961.

E. DORUTIU, 'Some Observations on the Military General Altar of Adamclisi', in *Dacia*, V, 1961, pp. 345–63.

D. M. PIPPIDI, 'Apropos d'une hypothèse de Patsch rélative à l'histoire de la Mésie au Ier siècle de notre ère', in *Studii si Cerc. Ist. veche*, XII, 1961, pp. 25–34 = 'Sur une hypothèse de Patsch concernant l'histoire de la Mésie au Ier siècle', in *Homm. Grenier* (Coll. Latomus, LVIII), Brussels 1962, pp. 1265–75 (an inscription from Histria, cf. *AE*, 1964, 199ab, suggests that the Dobrudja was never lost by the Romans under Domitian).

I. BERCIU, 'Cornelius Fuscus et le cénotaphe d'Adam-Klissi', in *Apulum*, V, 1964, pp. 259–70 (the dedication is to the Emperor Domitian; the name to be restored is that of Cornelius Fuscus).

E. DORUTIU-BOILÁ, 'Un fragment inconnu de l'inscription du trophée d'Adamclissi', in *Stud. Clas.*, VII, 1965, pp. 209–14 (new reconstruction of the final part of the inscription).

N. GASTAR, 'Les inscriptions votives du monument triomphal d'Adam-clissi', in *Latomus*, XXVIII, 1969, pp. 120–5.

NERVA

New documents

1. Milestone of Pomponius Bassus, from the road Tavium-Amasia, *AE*, 1962, 167 (cf. *AE*, 1961, 127) = *Fasti Arch.*, XIII, 1958, pp. 211 f., No. 3215 = BITTEL, in *Istamb. Mitt.*, VI, 1955, pp. 22–41.

2. Fragment of an amphora with name of Nerva (*imp. Nervae Aug.*), from Porolissum, in Dacia, *AE*, 1962, 212 = *Fast. Arch.*, XIII, 1958, p. 365, No. 5807 (report of the excavations of M. Macrea at Poro-lissum).

3. Base from Histria (Moesia), with a dedication to Nerva and traces of erasure of Domitian's name, *AE*, 1964, 199a,b = PIPPIDI, in *Homm. Grenier*, Brussels 1962, pp. 1265–75.

4. Dedication at Ephesus to the Theón Nérban, *AE*, 1967, 474 = MILTNER, in *Oesterr. Jahresh.*, XLIV, 1959, Beibl., c. 332.

Studies

Add to section The reign of Nerva (p. 658)

A. DEGRASSI, 'Nerva funeraticium plebi urbanae instituit', in *Boll. Ist.*

Dir. Rom., LXIII, 1960, pp. 233–8 (proof of extravagance in the finances).

A. BALIL, 'Sobre los miembros hispanicos del senado romano durante el imperio de Nerva', in *Zephirus*, XI, 1960, pp. 215–24 (on the part played by senators of Spanish origin in the adoption of Trajan).

I. A. F. BRUCE, 'Nerva and the Fiscus Iudaicus', in *Palestine Exploration Quarterly*, XCVI, 1964, pp. 34 f. (the exemption concerned Jews who were Roman citizens and resident in Italy, who had been subject to Domitian's tax).

D. KIENAST, 'Nerva und das Kaisertum Trajans', in *Historia*, XVII, 1968, pp. 51–71.

TRAJAN

New documents

1. Milestone found 12 miles west of Palmyra, A. BOUNNI, 'Une nouvelle borne milliaire de Trajan dans la Palmyrène', in *Ann. arch. de Syrie*, X, 1960, pp. 159–64.

2. Inscription for the *balineum* and the baths of Cyrene, *AE*, 1960, 198 = REYNOLDS, in *Journ. Rom. St.*, XLIX, 1959, pp. 95–101.

3. Dedication to a personage of the Trajanic period, governor of Aquitania, as 'defensor immunitatis perticae Carthaginiensium', *AE*, 1963, 94 = POINSSOT-PIGANIOL, in *Compt. rend. Ac. Inscr.*, 1962, pp. 55–76.

4. Dedication to Trajan, from Mactar (Tunisia), *AE*, 1963, 96 = PICARD, in *Compt. rend. Ac. Inscr.*, 1963, sess. 3 May. An important document for defining the meaning of *pagus* as a vast collection of *civitates stipendiariae*, deriving directly from the Carthaginian organization.

5. Mutilated inscription from Utica, dealing with military reward granted by Trajan '[ob bellu]m Dacicum', *AE*, 1964, 192 = VEYNE, in *Latomus*, XXIII, 1964, pp. 30–41.

6. Dedication to Trajan from Callatis (Moesia) in the name of the 'cives R. consistentes Callatis', *AE*, 1964, 250 = RADULESCU, in *Stud. Clas.*, IV, 1962, p. 275.

7. Cippus with *sententia* on the delimitation of boundaries between two cities of Macedonia, of the year 114, *AE*, 1965, 206 = MACKAY, in *Hesperia*, XXXIV, 1965, p. 249.

8. Boundary post of the *ager* of Cirta, *AE*, 1965, 233 = BERTHIER, in *Libyca*, VIII, 1960, p. 96.

9. Dedication to Trajan by a tribune of the VII cohort of *vigiles*, at Sarsina, *AE*, 1966, 117 = DONATI, *Aemilia tributim discripta*, Faenza 1967, n. 84 = SUSINI, in *Rend. Acc. Lincei*, X, 1955, n. 16.

10. Inscription of 100 A.D., at Mendoya, for the construction of a bridge by the Aquiflavienses, *AE*, 1966, 216 = ALVAREZ, 'Vias romanas de Galicia', in *Zephirus*, XI, 1960, n. 174 = *Hisp. Ant. Epigr.* 2156.

11. Dedication to Trajan, through the governor M. Laberius Maximus, by the 'cives Romani consistentes Sexaginta Pristis' (Moesia), *AE*, 1966, 356 = VELKOV, in *Epigraphica*, XXVII, 1965, pp. 90–109.

12. Fragment of a dedication to Trajan at Mactar (Tunisia), *AE*, 1966, 515 = PICARD, in *Africa*, I, 1966, p. 67, n. 5.

13. Milestone found near Xanten (*Castra Vetera*), *AE*, 1967, 345 = PETRIKOVITS, in *Epigraphische Studien*, IV, Köln 1967, pp. 114–18.

14. Dedication to Diana and Trajan in the Nymphaeum at Ephesus, *AE*, 1967, 467 (cf. *AE*, 1961, p. 46) = MILTNER, in *Oesterr. Jahresh.*, XLIV, 1959, Beibl., cc. 329–31.

15. Another similar dedication, *AE*, 1967, 468 (cf. *AE*, 1961, 46) = MILTNER, in *Oesterr. Jahresh.*, XLIV, 1959, Beibl., cc. 346–8.

16. Another dedication from Ephesus to Trajan, *AE*, 1967, 475 (cf. *AE*, 1961, 46) = MILTNER, in *Oesterr. Jahresh.*, XLIV, 1959, Beibl., cc. 328–9.

17. Military diploma of 24 September 105, found in Syria, which indicates that at this date Trajan had not yet received the V salutation as *imperator*, H. G. PFLAUM, in *Syria*, XLIV, 1967, pp. 339–62.

Studies

Add to section The reign of Trajan. Succession and adoption. Chronological problems (p. 661)

W. H. GROSS, 'M. Ulpius Traianus', in PAULY-WISSOWA, *Realencycl.*, Suppl. X, 1965, cc. 1035–113.

M. L. PALADINI, 'Divinizzazione di Traiano padre', in *Homm. Grenier* (Coll. Latomus, LVIII), Brussels 1962, pp. 1194–206.

TH. FRANKFORT, 'Le retour de Traian aux apparences républicaines', in *Latomus*, XXI, 1962, pp. 134–44 (examination of Trajan's titles to show his respect for republican forms).

J. BÉRANGER, 'La notion du principat sous Trajan et Hadrien', in *Les emper. rom. d'Esp.*, Paris 1965, pp. 27–44.

M. DURRY, 'Sur Trajan père', in *ibid.*, pp. 45–54 (was a more important figure than is commonly thought; his apotheosis was decreed on the departure of the Emperor Trajan for the East).

Add to section Trajan's administration (p. 664)

(*senators and knights as magistrates and officials*)

R. SYME, 'Pliny's Less Successful Friends', in *Historia*, IX, 1960, pp. 362–79 (observations on the senatorial career under the Flavians and reasons that could slow it up).

P. A. BRUNT, 'Charges of Provincial Maladministration under the Early Principate', in *Historia*, X, 1961, pp. 189–227 (the extent of the improvement in administration as compared with the republican period from the point of view of the personal honesty of the governors has probably been exaggerated).

M. L. PALADINI, 'La gratiarum actio dei consoli in Roma attraverso la testimonianza di Plinio il Giovane', in *Historia*, X, 1961, pp. 356–74 (on the origin of the use of the *gratiarum actio*).

H. G. PFLAUM, 'Tendances politiques et administratives au IIe siècle de notre ère', in *Rev. Ét. Lat.*, XLII, 1964, pp. 112–21 (under Trajan the dynamic tendency still prevails as opposed to the Hadrianic stabilization and the immobilism of Antoninus Pius).

J. FITZ, 'Data to the Career of Q. Marcius Turbo', in *Alba Regia*, VI–VII, 1965–6, pp. 201–2 (epigraphical data to distinguish him from the man of the same name under Antoninus Pius, cf. R. SYME, 'The Wrong Marcius Turbo', in *Journ. Rom. St.*, LII, 1962, pp. 87–96).

G. G. TISSONI, 'Sul consilium principis in età traianea', in *St. Doc. Hist. Iur.*, XXXI, 1965, pp. 222–45.

R. ÉTIENNE, 'Les sénateurs espagnols sous Trajan et Hadrien', in *Les empereurs romains d'Espagne*, Paris 1965, pp. 55–85 (an increase of influence confirmed under Trajan; greater detachment under Hadrian).

R. SYME, 'People in Pliny', in *Journ. Rom. St.*, LVIII, 1968, pp. 135–57 (with prosopographical list).

(*public works – the column*)

F. PANVINI ROSATI, 'La colonna sulle monete di Traiano', in *Ann. Ist. It. Num.*, V–VI, 1958–9, pp. 29–40 (there are two series of coins showing the column, symbolizing different things).

G. BECATTI, *La colonna conclide istoriata. Problemi storici, iconografici, stilistici*, Rome 1960.

S. STUCCHI, *Contributo alla conoscenza della topografia, dell'arte e della storia della Colonna Traiana. Il viaggio marittimo di Traiano all'inizio della seconda guerra dacica*, Udine 1960 (starting from Ancona, the author argues, Trajan went by sea to Classe and Aquileia, and from there by land to

Trieste and Senia, entering the Balkan peninsula from this point; the places can be recognized in the scenes on the column).

A. DEGRASSI, 'Aquileia e Trieste nelle scene della Colonna Traiana?', in *Rend. Acc. Arch. Napoli*, XXXVI, 1961, pp. 139–50 = *Scritti vari di antichità*, III, 1967, pp. 173–85 (supports the view already put forward – a completely convincing one – that Trajan started from Brundisium.)

S. STUCCHI, 'Intorno al viaggio di Traiano nel 105 d.C.', in *Röm. Mitt.*, LXXV, 1965, pp. 142–70 (argues strongly for the route Ancona-Classe-Aquileia).

G. LUGLI, 'Date de la fondation du Forum de Trajan', in *Compt. rend. Ac. Inscr.*, 1965, pp. 233–8.

L. ROSSI, 'L'exercitus nella colonna Traiana', in *Epigraphica*, XXVIII, 1966, pp. 150–5 (the documentary interest is concentrated more on the people than on the events).

J. R. RICHARD, 'Les funérailles de Trajan et le triomphe sur les Parthes', in *Rev. Ét. Lat.*, XLIV, 1966, pp. 351–62 (on the question of the base of the column).

——, 'Tombeaux des empereurs et temples des "divi". Notes sur la signification religieuse des sépultures impériales à Rome', in *Rev. Hist. de Relig.*, CLXX, 1966, pp. 127–42.

——, 'Les aspects militaires des funérailles impériales', in *Mél. Éc. Franç. Rome*, LXXVIII, 1966, pp. 313–25.

F. J. HASSEL, *Der Trajansbogen in Benevent*, Mainz 1966.

F. BOBU FLORESEN, *Die Trajanssäule*, 1969.

(finances, alimentationes)

F. C. BOURNE, 'The Roman Alimentary Program and Italian Agriculture', in *Trans. Proc. Amer. Phil. Ass.*, XCI, 1960, pp. 47–75 (aim was public assistance with beneficial influence on agricultural production).

R. P. DUNCAN-JONES, 'The Purpose and Organisation of the Alimenta', in *Pap. Br. Sch. Rome*, XXXII, 1964, pp. 123–46 (sole aim public assistance).

P. VEYNE, 'Les alimenta de Trajan', in *Les. emp. rom. d'Esp.*, Paris 1965, pp. 163–79 (sole aim public assistance, to increase the population).

J. GUEY, 'De l'or des Daces (1924) au livre de Sture Bolin (1958). Guerre et or. Or et monnaie', in *Mél. Carcopino*, Paris 1966, pp. 445–75 (confirms the well known theory of Carcopino).

S. MROZEK, *Les mines d'or de Dacie au IIe siècle. Aspects sociaux et administratifs* (in Polish with French summary), Torun 1966.

P. GARNSEY, 'Trajan's Alimenta: Some Problems', in *Historia*, XVII, 1968, pp. 367–81.

(provinces)

L. VIDMAN, 'Die Mission Plinius' des Jüngeren in Bithynien', in *Klio*, XXXVII, 1959, pp. 217–25 (Trajan's letters the embryo of the future *liber mandatorum*).

——, *Étude sur la correspondance de Pline le Jeune avec Trajan*, Prague 1960.

A. N. SHERWIN-WHITE, 'Trajan's Replies to Pliny. Authorship and Necessity', in *Journ. Rom. St.*, LII, 1962, pp. 114–25.

L. POLVERINI, 'Le città dell'impero nell'epistolario di Plinio', in *Contrib. dell'Ist. Fil. Class. Sez. St. Ant.*, I (Università Cattolica Milano), Milan 1963, pp. 137–236.

E. POPESCU, 'Epigraphische Beiträge zur Geschichte der Stadt Tropaeum Traiani', in *Stud. Clas.*, VI, 1964, pp. 185–203.

D. M. PIPPIDI, 'Ein unbekanntes Bruchstück der Horothesía Laberíou Maxímou hypatikoû (*SEG*, I, 329)', in *Stud. Clas.*, VI, 1964, pp. 311–42.

E. SWOBODA, 'Traian und der pannonische Limes', in *Les emp. rom. d'Esp.*, Paris 1965, pp. 195–208 (Trajan's work on this should not be over-estimated).

J. GAUDEMET, 'La juridiction provincial d'après la correspondance entre Pline et Trajan', in *Rev. Intern. Dr. Ant.*, XI, 1965, pp. 335–53.

M. MACREA, 'Romani e Daci nella provincia Dacia', in *Arch. Class.*, XIX, 1967, pp. 146–69.

——, 'L'organisation de la province de Dacie', in *Dacia*, XI, 1967, pp. 121–41 (revision of the history of the provincial organization in Dacia, from the creation of the province to 169, in the light of the new evidence, especially that of the military diploma mentioned below among the new Hadrianic documents).

(religion – Christianity)

H. BABEL, *Der Briefwechsel zwischen Plinius und Trajan über die Christen in strafrechtlicher Sicht*, Diss. Erlangen 1961.

J. VOGT, 'Zur Religiosität der Christenverfolger im Römischen Reich', in *Sitz ab. d. Heidelberg Ak. d. Wiss.*, 1962, I, Heidelberg 1962.

F. FOURRIER, 'La lettre de Pline à Trajan sur les Chrétiens (X, 97)', in *Recherches de Théologie*, XXXI, 1964, pp. 161–74 (on the juridical form of the questions put to the Christians).

H. WEISS, 'The Pagani among the Contemporaries of the First Christians', in *Journ. Bibl. Liter.*, LXXXVI, 1967, pp. 42–52 (on the moral strength of paganism).

R. FREUDENBERGER, *Das Verhalten der römischen Behörden gegen die Christen im 2. Jahrhundert*, Munich 1967 (admits an ideological aversion and a persecuting spirit in the behaviour of the Roman authorities in their confrontations with Christianity; cf. VOGT above).

E. J. BICKERMAN, 'Trajan, Hadrian and the Christians', in *Riv. Fil. Istr. Class.*, XCVI, 1968, pp. 290–315 (in the form of a long review of the preceding study by Freudenberger, Bickerman rejects its principal thesis and spotlights the emperors' concern to ensure the legality of the trials, which resulted in an advantage for the Christians, thus protected from the irrational impulses of popular passions).

Add to section The wars of Trajan (p. 676)

A. FUKS, 'Aspects of the Jewish Revolt in A.D. 115–17', in *Journ. Rom. St.*, LI, 1961, pp. 98–104.

E. M. SMALLWOOD, 'Palestine *c.* A.D. 115–118', in *Historia*, XI, 1962, pp. 500–10.

R. VULPE, 'Dion Cassius et la Campagne de Trajan en Mésie inférieure', in *Stud. Clas.*, VI, 1964, pp. 205–32.

R. SYME, 'Pliny and the Dacian Wars', in *Latomus*, XXIII, 1964, pp. 750–9.

HADRIAN

New documents

1. Dedication by the *cohors VIII Raetorum* to Hadrian, in Dacia, A.D. 129, *AE*, 1960, 375 = MACREA, in *Omagiu Daicoviciu*, Bucharest 1960, pp. 339–49.
2. Two dedications to Hadrian at Thasos, *AE*, 1960, 379 = DUNANT-POUILLOUX, *Thasos*, II, Paris 1958, pp. 87–8.
3. Dedication of a statue to Hadrian, in Cyprus, *AE*, 1961, 10 = MITFORD, in *Amer. Journ. Arch.*, LXV, 1961, pp. 123–5.
4. Dedication to Hadrian, in Pisidia, *AE*, 1961, 11 = BEAN, in *Anat. St.*, IX, 1959, p. 79.
5. Dedication to Mercury, *pro salute* of the Emp. Hadrian, found at Thuburbo Maius, *AE*, 1961, 71 = DESANGES, in *Cahiers de Tunisie*, 1959, no. 26–7, pp. 275–8.
6. New fragmentary military diploma of Hadrian dating from between 121 and 125, found at Straubing, in the territory of ancient Raetia,

AE, 1961, 173 = RADNÓTI, in *Germania*, XXXIX, 1961, pp. 93–117.

7. Dedication *Divo Hadriano patri imp. Caes. Antonini Aug. Pii*, at *Vina* (Afr. proconsolare), *AE*, 1961, 199 = VEYNE, in *Karthago*, IX, 1958, pp. 91–109.

8. Fragment of a military diploma from *Apulum* (Dacia), A.D. 122/133, *AE*, 1962, 391 = RUSSU, in *Studii si Comunicări* (Alba Julia), 1961, pp. 119–24.

9. New military diploma from Dacia Porolissensis, dated 2 July 133, *AE*, 1962, 255 = DAICOVICIU-PROTASE, in *Journ. Rom. St.*, LI, 1961, pp. 63–70 (this is the important document which already implies the existence under Hadrian of the province of Dacia Porolissensis; for a different reading of the name, which has visibly been corrected, see A. MÓCSY, 'Zum neuen dakischen Militärdiplom', in *Argo*, III, 1964, pp. 73–4).

10. At Claros, on the architrave of the temple, fragment of an inscription with the beginning of Hadrian's titles, *AE*, 1963, 149 = L. ROBERT, in the symposium *L'Histoire et ses méthodes*, one of the volumes in the *Encyclopédie de la Pléiade*, Paris 1961, p. 494; cf. *Rev. Ét. Gr.*, LXXV, 1962, p. 199, n. 283, and the polemical note by CH. PICARD, in *Rev. Arch.*, N.S.I, 1963, pp. 110 f.

11. Dedication *I(ovi) O(ptimo) M(aximo) Heliopolitano pro salute* of the Emp. Hadrian found at Heliopolis (Baalbek), *AE*, 1964, 55 = SEYRIG, in *Bull. du Musée de Beyrouth*, XVI, 1961, p. 111.

12. Fragment of a dedication to Hadrian from *Novae* (Bulgaria), *AE*, 1964, 187 = MAJEWSKI, in *Latomus*, XXII, 1963, p. 503.

16. Two fragmentary dedications to Hadrian, dating from 132, found at Munigua (Baetica), *AE*, 1966, 182 = FERNANDEZ CHICARRO Y DE DIOS, in *Les emp. rom. d'Esp.*, Paris 1965, pp. 305–7.

17. Another dedication by a cohort to Hadr., in Britain, *AE*, 1966, 222 = WRIGHT, in *Journ. Rom. St.*, LVI, 1966, p. 218.

18. Fragment of a dedication to Hadr. (Dacia), *AE*, 1966, 332 = TUDOR, in *St. si Cerc. de Ist. Veche*, XVI, 1965, p. 369, n. 27.

19. Brick stamps bearing Hadrian's name from the aqueduct of *Ratiaria* (Moesia Inferiore), *AE*, 1966, 343 = VELKOV, in *Eirene* (Prague), V, 1966, p. 174.

20. Fragment of a dedication to Hadr., at *Novae* (Moesia Inferiore), *AE*, 1966, 348 = KOLENDO-TRYNKOWSKI, in *Archeologia*, XVI, 1965, p. 122.

21. Dedication to Hadr., in Latin and Greek, found at Histria (Moesia

Inferiore), *AE*, 1966, 358 = PIPPIDI, in *Mél. Michalowski*, Wàrsaw 1966, pp. 619–23.

22. Dedication to Hadr. in the baths at Ephesus, *AE*, 1966, 427 = KEIL-MARESCH, in *Oesterr. Jahresh.*, XLV, 1960, Beibl., cc. 84–5, n. 10.

23. Big marble base, with a handsome dedication dating from 119, at Miletus, *AE*, 1966, 449 = PEKARY, in *Istamb. Mitt.*, XV, 1965, p. 119, n. 2.

24. Record of a work which Hadr. '[*colonis*] *Alerninis* [. . .] *fecit*' at Aleria (Corsica), *AE*, 1967, 279 = EUZENNAT, in *Gallia*, XXV, 1967, p. 434.

25. New military diploma from *Tibiscum* (Dacia), of the year 126, *AE*, 1967, 395 = DAICOVICIU, in *Acta Musei Napocensis*, II, 1965, pp. 135–9.

26. Letter from Hadr. to the city of Prusa ad Olympum, *AE*, 1967, 461 (cf. 1938, 51 and 1948, 52) = DAUX, in *Bull. Corr. Hell.*, XCI, 1967, pp. 476 f.

27. Dedication to Artemis and Hadr. in the temple of Hadr. at Ephesus, *AE*, 1967, 469 = *AE*, 1961, 184 = MILTNER, in *Oesterr. Jahresh.*, XLIV, 1959, Beibl., cc. 265–6.

28. Inscr. mentioning the dedication of the temple of Hadr. at Ephesus, through which the city became 'dìs neokóros', *AE*, 1967, 484 = MILTNER, in *Anz. Oesterr. Ak. d. Wiss.*, XCIV, 1957, pp. 22–5 = *Oesterr. Jahresh.*, XLIV, 1959, Beibl., c. 266, n. 40.

29. Dedication to Hadr. of the year 122, of the *col*(*oni*) *col*(*oniae*) *Iul*(*iae*) *Aug*(*ustae*) *Tubusuctitanae leg*(*ionis*) *VII immun*(*is*), found at Tubusuctu (Mauretania), *AE*, 1967, 641 = MARCILLET-JAUBERT, in *Bull. Arch. Alg.*, I, 1962–5, n. 1.

Studies

Add to section Hadrian. The succession and the programme of the reign (p. 681)

S. PEROWNE, *Hadrian*, London 1960.

J. DOBIAS, 'A propos de l'expeditio Suebica et Sarmatica de l'empereur Hadrien en l'an 118', in *Omagiu Daicoviciu*, Bucharest 1960, pp. 147–53 (collection of the literary, epigraphical and numismatic evidence of a genuine campaign in 118).

G. FLERES, 'Plotina e la successione di Adriano', in *Atti Acc. Peloritana* (Messina), XLVIII, 1951–64, pp. 199–205 (accepts the notoriety of the relations between Plotina and Hadrian as the origin of the tradition of domestic intrigues in the succession).

T. F. CARNEY, 'The Political Legends on Hadrian's Coinage. Policies and Areas', in *Turtle* (Chicago), VI, 1967, pp. 291–303 (for the general programme of government).

Add to section Hadrian's journeys (p. 684)

A. S. BENJAMIN, 'The Altars of Hadrian in Athens and Hadrian's Panhellenic Program', in *Hesperia*, XXXII, 1963, pp. 57–86.

P. V. HILL, 'The Aurei and Denarii of Hadrian from Eastern Mints', in *Num. Chron.*, VI, 1966, pp. 135–43 (the local coinage provides evidence of Hadrian's liberality).

S. FOLLET, 'Hadrien en Égypte et en Judée', in *Rev. Phil.*, XLII, 1968, pp. 54–77.

P. J. SIJPESTEIJN, 'A New Document Concerning Hadrian's Visit to Egypt', in *Historia*, XVIII, 1969, pp. 109–18 (an *ostracon* dealing with the maintenance of the Emperor and his retinue during the visit).

Add to section Government and administration. Measures favouring the empire (p. 686)

(conditions in the empire)

A. GARCIA Y BELLIDO, *Colonia Aelia Augusta Italica*, Madrid 1960.

R. P. DUNCAN-JONES, 'Costs, Outlays and Summae honorariae from Roman Africa', in *Pap. Br. Sch. Rome*, XXX, 1962, pp. 47–115.

——, 'City Population in Roman Africa', in *Journ. Rom. St.*, LIII, 1963, pp. 85–90.

R. SYME, 'Hadrian and Italica', in *Journ. Rom. St.*, LIV, 1964, pp. 142–149.

A. GARCIA Y BELLIDO, 'La Itálica de Hadriano', in *Les emp. rom. d'Esp.*, Paris 1965, pp. 7–26 (received the title of colony and was completely reconstructed).

A. PIGANIOL, 'La politique agraire d'Hadrien', in *Les emp. rom. d'Esp.*, Paris 1965, pp. 135–46 (care for fixing boundaries, and in general attention to agrarian problems throughout the empire).

R. NIERHAUS, 'Zum wirtschaftlichen Aufschwung der Baetica zur Zeit Trajans und Hadrians', in *Les emp. rom. d'Esp.*, Paris 1965, pp. 181–94 (denies any particular favour from Hadr.).

——, 'Hadrians Verhältnis zu Italica', in *Corolla Swoboda*, Graz 1966, pp. 151–68 (same view restricted to Italica).

J. POUILLOUX, 'Une famille de sophistes thessaliens à Delphes au IIᵉ siècle ap.J.C.', in *Rev. Ét. Gr.*, LXXX, 1967, pp. 379–84 (example of the development of the provincial bourgeoisie under Hadrian).

(law and jurists)

A. M. HONORÉ, *Gaius, a Biography*, Oxford 1962.

CH. SAUMAGNE, 'Essai sur une législation agraire; la lex Manciana et le ius Mancianum', in *Cahiers de Tunisie*, X, 1962, pp. 11–114.

H. BELLEN, 'Zur Appellation vom Senat an den Kaiser', in *Ztschr. Sav. Stift.*, LXXIX, 1962, pp. 143–68.

A. GUARINO, 'Salvius Iulianus. Profilo bibliografico', in *Labeo*, X, 1964, pp. 364–426.

A. D'ORS, 'La signification de l'œuvre d'Hadrien dans l'histoire du droit romain', in *Les emp. rom. d'Esp.*, Paris 1965, pp. 147–61.

VARI AUTORI, *Gaio nel suo tempo. Atti del simposio romanistico*, Naples 1966 (Biblioteca di *Labeo*, III).

M. MEINHART, 'Die Datierung des SC Tertullianum, mit einem Beitrag zur Gaiusforschung', in *Ztschr. Sav. Stift.*, LXXXIII, 1966, pp. 100–41.

(army and defence)

E. BIRLEY, *Research on Hadrian's Wall*, Kendal 1961.

T. STANIER, 'The Brigantes and the Ninth Legion', in *Phoenix*, XIX, 1965, pp. 305–13.

P. SALWAY, *The Frontier People of Roman Britain*, Cambridge 1965 (deals particularly with the civilian settlements in the region of Hadrian's and Antoninus Pius's walls).

M. G. JARRETT, 'Aktuelle Probleme der Hadriansmauer', in *Germania*, XLV, 1967, pp. 96–105 (particularly its subsequent fate after Hadrian's reign).

L. ROSSI, 'The Symbolism related to Disciplina on Roman Imperial Coins and Monuments', in *Num. Circular*, LXXV, 1967, pp. 130 f. (deals also with Hadrian, whose programme was typified by the motif of Disciplina).

R. W. DAVIES, 'Fronto, Hadrian and the Roman Army', in *Latomus*, XXVII, 1968, pp. 75–95 (on Hadrian's services in training the army).

Add to section Hadrianic culture: literature, art, customs, religion and beliefs (p. 695)

H. CASTRITIUS, 'Der Phoenix auf den Aurei Hadrians und Tacitus' Annalen VI 28', in *Jahrb. f. Num. u. Geldgesch.*, XIV, 1964, pp. 89–95 (opposes the theory of Mattingly that relation of the coin to the passage in Tacitus can help to date the *Annals*).

R. TURCAN, 'La fondation du temple de Vénus et de Rome', in *Latomus*, XXIII, 1964, pp. 42–55.

P. KERESZTES, 'Law and Arbitrariness in the Persecution of the Christians and Justin's First Apology', in *Vig. Christ.*, XVIII, 1964, pp. 204–14 (cf. the studies of Vogt, Freudenberger and Bickerman, above, in connection with Trajan).

S. ROSSI, 'Il tempo e l'ambientazione del Dialogus di Giustino', in *Giorn. Ital. Fil.*, XVII, 1964, pp. 55–65.

M. GUARDUCCI, 'La religione di Adriano', in *Les. emp. rom. d'Esp.*, Paris 1965, pp. 209–21.

CHR. BURCHARD, *Bibliographie zu den Handschriften vom Toten Meer*, II, 1956–62 (Beih. zur Zeitschr. f. die AlttestamentlicheWiss., LXXXIX), Berlin 1965.

R. SYME, 'Hadrian the Intellectual', in *Les emp. rom. d'Esp.*, Paris 1965, pp. 243–53 (brilliant modernization).

P. KERESZTES, 'Hadrian's Rescript to Minucius Fundanus', in *Latomus*, XXVI, 1967, pp. 54–66 = 'The Emperor Hadrian's Rescript to Minucius Fundanus', in *Phoenix*, XXI, 1967, pp. 120–9.

Add to section Hadrian's family and the problem of the adoptions of 136 and 138 (p. 698)

L. LESUISSE, 'Le titre de Caesar et son évolution au cours de l'histoire de l'empire', in *Les Ét. Class.*, XXIX, 1961, pp. 271–87 (Hadrian's adoptions an important moment in the evolution).

H. G. PFLAUM, 'Le règlement successoral d'Hadrien', in *Hist. Aug. Coll. 1963*, Bonn 1964, pp. 95–121.

J. CARCOPINO, 'Encore la succession d'Hadrien', in *Rev. Ét. Anc.*, LXVII, 1965, pp. 67–79.

I. I. RUSSU, 'Domus divina in Dacia', in *Stud. Clas.*, IX, 1967, pp. 211–218 (Rumanian, with French summary).

ANTONINUS PIUS

New documents

1. Milestone from the road *Emona-Neviodunum*, P. PETRU, in *Act. Arch. Slov.* (Ljubljana), XI–XII, 1960-1, pp. 27–43.

2. Dedication of one of two statues (the other for M. Aurelius), at Aiané, Upper Macedonia, by a 'koinón tôn Elimiotôn' known now for the first time, *AE*, 1961, 268 = PAPAZOGLOU, in *Ziva Antika*, IX, 1959, pp. 163–71, cf. ROBERT, in *Rev. Ét. Gr.*, LXXIII, 1960, p. 166, n. 201.

3. Fragment of a dedication to A.P., found at Colonia, *AE*, 1962, 194 = FREMERSDORF, in *Kölner Jahrb. f. Vor. – u. Frühgesch.*, I, 1955, pp. 24–32, cf. *Fast. Arch.*, XIII, 1958, p. 323, n. 5067.

4. New military diploma, dated 13 December 140, found in Bulgaria, *AE*, 1962, 264 = GEROV, in *Klio*, XXXVII, 1959, pp. 196–216.

5. Inscription from Rome concerning the *expeditio Mauretanica* of 145–147, *AE*, 1962, 279 = LEGLAY, in *Libyca*, VII, 1959, pp. 216–220, cf. *AE*, 1960, 28 = HOWARTH, in *Amer. Journ. Arch.*, LXIV, 1960, pp. 273–6.

6. Dedications to A.P., in Cilicia Trachea, *AE*, 1963, 13 and 14 = BEAN-MITFORD, in *Anat. St.*, XII, 1962, p. 213.

7. Dedication of an altar *I(ovi) O(ptimo) M(aximo) pro salute* of A.P., at Magonza, *AE*, 1965, 239 = VON PFEFFER, in *Mainzer Ztschr.*, LIX, 1964, p. 55.

8. Dedication to A.P. dating from 139, in the baths at Ephesus, *AE*, 1966, 428 = MILTNER, *Oesterr. Jahresh.*, XLV, 1960, Beibl., cc. 58–59.

9. Dedication *I(ovi) O(ptimo) M(aximo) pro salute* of A.P., from the neighbourhood of Astorga (*Asturica*), by a *vexillatio* of Legion VII *Gemina*, celebrating the *natalis aquilae*, *AE*, 1967, 229 = GARCIA Y BELLIDO, in *Arch. Esp. Arq.*, XXXIX, 1966, p. 24.

10. Inscription of A.P. (in the nominative) at Athens, *AE*, 1967, 446 = RAUBITSCHEK, in *Hesperia*, XXXV, 1966, p. 248, n. 9.

11. Interesting decree by the proconsul of Asia for free access to the port of Ephesus, *AE*, 1967, 480, cf. 1962, 244 = KEIL, in *Oesterr. Jahresh.*, Hauptbl., XLIV, 1959, pp. 142–6; cf. ROBERT, in *Rev. Ét. Gr.*, LXXV, 1962, p. 199, n. 284.

12. Dedication to A.P. at Lambaesis, *AE*, 1967, 564 = MARCILLET-JAUBERT, in *Bull. Arch. Alg.*, II, 1966-7, pp. 171–3.

Studies

Add to section The reign of Antonius Pius (p. 700)

R. SYME, 'La Dacie sous Antonin le Pieux', in *Stud. Clas.*, III, 1961, p. 131 (l'inscr. *AE*, 1946, 113 would indicate military operations in Dacia in 142 or 143).

G. MIHAILOV, 'La fortification de la Thrace par Antonin le Pieux et Marc-Aurèle', in *Stud. Urbin.*, XXXV, 1961, pp. 42–56.

J. BEAUJEU, 'La religion de la classe sénatoriale à 1 époque des Antonins', in *Homm. Bayet*, Brussels 1964, pp. 54–75.

J. F. GILLIAM, 'The Romanisation of the Greek East. The Role of the Army', in *Bull. Amer. Soc. of Papyr.*, II, 1965, pp. 65–73 (a phenomenon particulary intense in the age of A.P.).

A. R. BIRLEY, 'The Duration of Provincial Commands under Antoninus Pius', in *Corolla Swoboda*, Graz 1966, pp. 43–53.

H. G. PFLAUM, 'Les prêtres du culte impérial sous le règne d'Antonin le Pieux', in *Compt. rend. Ac. Inscr.*, 1967, pp. 194–209.

R. FREUDENBERGER, 'Christenreskript. Ein umstrittenes Reskript des Antoninus Pius', in *Ztschr. f. Kirchengesch.*, LXXVIII, 1967, pp. 1–14.

W. WILLIAMS, 'Antoninus Pius and the Control of Provincial Embassies,' in *Historia*, XVI, 1967, pp. 470–83 (on the restriction of the expenses of provincial embassies).

MARCUS AURELIUS

New documents

1. Dedication to M. Aurelius in Pisidia, *AE*, 1961, 11 = BEAN, in *Anat. St.*, IX, 1959, p. 79.
2. Base with Greek inscription for a statue of L. Verus, *AE*, 1961, 19 = BEAN, in *Anat. St.*, IX, 1959, p. 110.
3. New military diploma (fragmentary), A.D. 167 or 168, from Eining (Raetia), *AE*, 1961, 174 = RADNOTI, in *Germania*, XXXIX, 1961, pp. 93–117.
4. Inscription of 175–176, with complete title, for restorations on the road Philippopolis-Oescus (*stabula vetustate dilapsa a solo sua pecunia restituit*), *AE*, 1961, 318 = NIKOLOV, in *Studia Dečev*, Sofia 1958, p. 285.
5. Important inscription, re-used in the third century, containing a letter

from M. A. relating to an appointment of a procurator ducenarius, from *Bulla Regia* (proconsular Africa), *AE*, 1962, 183–4, cf. 1960, 167 = *Fasti Archaeologici*, XIII, 1958, pp. 285–6, n. 4404.

6. Fragmentary inscription of L. Verus after his adoption by A.P. and before his succession, found at Tarragona, *AE*, 1962, 188 = SÁNCHEZ REAL, in *Boletin Arqueologico*, LVI, 1956, pp. 51–8.

7. Dedication of works *pro salute et reditu et victoria* of M.A. and his children, between 169 and 172, at Marsala in Sicily, *AE*, 1964, 181 = BARBIERI, in *Kókalos*, VII, 1961, pp. 15 ff.

8. Dedication *invicto deo pro salute* of M.A., at Niš (Yugoslavia), *AE*, 1964, 263 = DUŠANIĆ-PETROVIĆ, in *Ziva Antika*, XII, 1962–3, pp. 365 f.

9. Syriac milestone of M.A. and Commodus, *ab Hamatha pas(suum) mil(ia) XCIII*, *AE*, 1965, 23 = REY-COQUAIS, in *Ann. Arch. de Syrie*, XV, 1965, p. 71.

10. Fragmentary dedication *I(ovi) O(ptimo) M(aximo) pro salute M. Aureli Antonini* . . . (who could be Caracalla), found at Villalis, near León, *AE*, 1965, 66 = GARCIA Y BELLIDO, in *Arch. Esp. Arq.*, XXXVI, 1963, p. 206.

11. Interesting inscription regarding the visit of the Roman governor to Samothrace in 165, in *Hesperia*, XXXIV, 1965, pp. 100 ff., cf. J. H. OLIVER, 'A Roman Governor visits Samothrace', in *Amer. Journ. Phil.*, LXXXVII, 1966, pp. 75–80.

12. Dedication to L. Verus, found at Barcelona, *AE*, 1966, 206 = MARINER BIGORRA, in *Hisp. Ant. Epigr.*, no. 1943.

13. Fragment of a milestone from Moesia, *AE*, 1966, 367 = PIPPIDI, in *St. Clas.*, VIII, 1966, p. 58, n. 21.

14. New milestone from the road from Scitopolis to Neapolis (Syria), of the year 162, with the names of M.A. and L. Verus, *AE*, 1966, 497b = AVI-YONAH, in *Israel Exploration Journ.*, XVI, 1966, pp. 75 f. (Important because it raises the date of the construction of the road, putting it in relation with the Parthian campaign.)

15. Fragment of a dedication to M.A. and L. Verus, from Thysdrus (Procons. Africa), *AE*, 1966, 517 = FOUCHER, in *Africa*, I, 1966, p. 133.

16. Dedication 'autokrátorsi filadélfois' for the victory in the Parthian war, Athens, *AE*, 1967, 447 = RAUBITSCHEK, in *Hesperia*, XXXV, 1966, pp. 250 f., n. 12, cf. ROBERT, in *Rev. Ét. Gr.*, LXXX, 1967, p. 475, n. 187.

17. Inscription from the arch of Leptis Magna, *AE*, 1967, 536 = DI

VITA-ÉVRARD, in *Mél. Arch. Hist. Éc. Franç. Rome*, LXXV, 1960, 2, pp. 389–414.

18. Dedication for the paving of the *platea* of Lambaesis, *AE*, 1967, 565 = MARCILLET-JAUBERT, in *Bull. Arch. Alg.*, II, 1966–7 pp. 171–3.

19. Dedication to M.A. by the city of Traianopolis, in Thrace, in *Arch. Efem.*, 1965 [pub. 1967], *Archaiologiká Chronikà*, pp. 19–20.

Studies

Add to section Marcus Aurelius, the philosopher emperor. The family (p. 708)

T. W. AFRICA, 'The Opium Addiction of Marcus Aurelius', in *Journ. of Hist. of Ideas*, XXII, 1961, pp. 97–102 (suspicion that Marcus Aurelius habitually used narcotics).

G. BARBIERI, 'Nuove iscrizioni di Marsala', in *Kókalos*, VII, 1961, pp. 15–52 (biographical details on Marcus Aurelius and his family).

H. G. PFLAUM, 'Les gendres de Marc-Aurèle', in *Journ. des Sav.*, 1961, pp. 28–41 (cf. *Rev. Ét. Lat.*, XXXIX, 1961, pp. 45–7).

R. RÉMONDON, *La crise de l'empire romain de Marc-Aurèle à Anastase*, Paris 1964 (examination of reign of Marcus Aurelius as the starting point of the crisis).

A. BIRLEY, *Marcus Aurelius*, London 1966.

A. BODSON, *La morale sociale des derniers Stoïciens, Sénèque, Épictète et Marc-Aurèle*, Paris 1967 (Bibl. Fac. Philos, Univ. Liège, CLXXVI).

M. THIRION, 'Faustina Augusta, Mater Castrorum', in *Gaz. Num. Suisse*, XVII, 1967, pp. 41–9 (importance of the title and presence of Faustina on the Pannonian front).

K. P. JOHNE, 'Zu den Siegernamen der Kaiser Marc Aurel und Commodus', in *Klio*, XLVIII, 1967, pp. 177–82 (the epithets of victory were preserved in Egypt after the death of L. Verus; cf. H. G. GUNDEL, 'Einige Giessener Papyrusfragmente', in *Aegyptus*, XLIII, 1963, pp. 393).

Add to section Marcus Aurelius's work at home (p. 712)

(on the legislative activity)

U. LAFFI, 'L'iscrizione di Sepino', in *St. Class. Orient.*, XIV, 1966 pp. 177–200 (re-examination of the letter from the praetorian prefects to the magistrates of Sepino).

J. GUEY, 'De trincos à Princeps', in *Mél. Piganiol*, Paris 1966, pp. 249–66 (confirmation of the plausible correction to the text of the *oratio de pretiis gladiatorum minuendis*, proposed by A. Piganiol).

(administration – public works)

W. SESTON and M. EUZENNAT, 'La citoyenneté romaine au temps de Marc-Aurèle et de Commode d'après la Tabula Banasitana', in *Compt. rend. Ac. Inscr.*, 1961, pp. 317–24 (discussion with observations by A. Piganiol and J. Carcopino).

B. D. MERITT, 'Greek Inscriptions', in *Hesperia*, XXX, 1961, pp. 231–6 (intervention by M. Aurelius and Commodus for the institution of the 'sacra gerusia' at Athens).

P. MINGAZZINI, 'E' mai esistito l'arco di trionfo di Marcaurelio sul Clivo Argentario', in *Röm. Mitt.*, LXX, 1963, pp. 147–55 (the famous reliefs come from another building).

G. DI VITA-ÉVRARD, 'Les dédicaces de l'amphithéâtre et du cirque de Lepcis', in *Libya Antiqua*, II, 1965, pp. 29–37 (the first had been finished by Nero; the second was completed in 162, under Marcus Aurelius).

(Christianity)

M. SORDI, 'I nuovi decreti di Marco Aurelio contro i cristiani', in *St. Rom.*, IX, 1961, pp. 365–78 (the reign of Marcus Aurelius represents an important turning-point in the relations between the Roman state and Christianity, for it was then that the veto on public investigation lapsed, even if not specifically at the expense of the Christians).

——, 'La polemiche intorno al cristianesimo nel II secolo e la loro influenza sugli sviluppi della politica imperiale verso la Chiesa', in *Riv. St. d. Ch. in It.*, XVI, 1962, pp. 1–28 (development of the research heralded in the preceding article on the ideological climate which determined the attitude of the state in its confrontations with Christianity).

J. COLIN, 'Martyrs grecs de Lyon ou martyrs galates? (Eusèbe, Hist. eccl. V, 1)', in *Ant. Class.*, XXXIII, 1964, pp. 108–15 (not martyrs of Lyon, but Galatians, and the persecution took place in Asia Minor).

——, *L'empire des Antonins et les martyrs gaulois de 177*, Bonn 1964.

——, 'Saint Irénée était-il évêque de Lyon?', in *Latomus*, XXIII, 1964, pp. 81–5 (not of Lyon, but of Neoclaudiopolis in Galatian Pontus).

S. ROSSI, 'Ireneo fu vescovo di Lione?' in *Giorn. It. Fil.*, XVII, 1964, pp. 239–54 (refutation of the preceding article by Colin).

S. ROSSI, 'Il cristianesimo della Gallia e i martiri di Lione', in *Giorn. It. Fil.*, 1964, pp. 289–320 (refutation of Colin's theory about the martyrs of Lyon).

J. COLIN, *Les villes libres de l'Orient gréco-romain et l'envoi au supplice par acclamations populaires* (Coll. Latomus, LXXXII), Brussels 1965 (the theory of Eusebius's error is taken up again, pp. 130–2).

F. HALKIN, 'Martyrs de Lyon ou d'Asie mineure?', in *Anal. Boll.*, LXXXIII, 1965, pp. 189 f. (against the theory of Colin).

P. WUILLEUMIER, 'Le martyre chrétien de 177', in *Mél. Carcopino*, Paris 1966, pp. 987–90 (against Colin's theory).

E. DEMOUGEOT, 'A propos des martyrs lyonnais de 177', in *Rev. Ét Anc.*, LXVIII, 1966, pp. 323–31 (against Colin's theory).

P. KERESZTES, 'The Massacre at Lugdunum in 177 A.D.', in *Historia*, XVI, 1967, pp. 75–86 (against Colin's theory).

J. COLIN, 'A propos du jour de supplice des martyrs de Lyon', in *Pallas* (Toulouse), XIV, 1967, pp. 7–8.

L. W. BARNARD, 'The Embassy of Athenagoras', in *Vig. Christ.*, XXI, 1967, pp. 88–92 (interesting on the personal contacts of M.A. with the Christians; between 176 and 180, thinks the author, Athenagoras presented his petition to the Emperor personally).

R. FREUDENBERGER, 'Ein angeblicher Christenbrief Mark Aurels', in *Historia*, XVII, 1968, pp. 251–6 (on the miracle of the rain).

R. MERKELBACH, 'Ein korrupter Satz im Brief Marc Aurels über das Regenwunder im Feldrug gegen die Quaden', in *Act. Ant. Ac. Sc. Hung.*, XVI, 1968, pp. 339–41.

Add to section The wars of Marcus Aurelius (p. 718)

P. OLIVA, 'Zur Bedeutung der Markomannenkriege', in *Altertum*, VI, 1960, pp. 53–61 (start of the big movement of peoples).

J. F. GILLIAM, 'The Plague under Marcus Aurelius', in *Amer. Journ. Phil.*, LXXXII, 1961, pp. 225–51 (reduces to more modest proportions the scope of the scourge, dramatized and exaggerated for Egypt by Boak).

I. BERCIU and A. POPA, 'Marcus Valerius Maximianus legatus Augusti legionis XIII Geminae', in *St. si cercet. ist. veche*, XII, 1961, pp. 93–104.

A. MÓCSY, 'Zu den Verwüstungen der Markommanenkriege in Savaria', in *Arch. Ert.*, XC, 1963, pp. 17–20 (archaeological traces of devastation and disaster).

G. ALFÖLDI, 'Die Valerii in Poetovio', in *Acta Archaeologica* (Ljubljana), XV–XVI, 1964–5, pp. 137–44 (again on the inscription of M. Valerius Maximianus).

G. BARTA, 'Bemerkungen zur Kriegsgeschichte Daziens im II Jahrhundert (167–171)', in *Acta Class. Debrecen*, II, 1966, pp. 81–7 (the situation under M. Claudius Fronto and Sextus Cornelius Clemens).

J. FITZ, 'Der markomannisch-quadische Angriff gegen Aquileia und Opitergium', in *Historia*, XV, 1966, pp. 336–67 (the attack took place between May and July 169).

——, 'Osservazioni prosopografiche alla carriera di M. Macrinius Avitus Catonius Vindex', in *Epigraphica*, XXVIII, 1966, pp. 50–94.

I. G. NAGY, 'Bemerkungen zur Deutung der Stelle SHA Vita Marci 14', in *Act. Ant. Ac. Sc. Hung.*, XVI, 1968, pp. 343–50 (on the date of the incursion into Italy of the Marcomanni and the problems connected with it).

COMMODUS

New documents

1. New inscription of M. Aurelius Cleander, mentioning other personages of Commodus's reign, *AE*, 1961, 280 = MORETTI, in *Riv. Fil. Istr. Class.*, XXXVIII, 1960, pp. 67–74.

2. Dedication to Commodus in Cilicia Trachea, *AE*, 1963, 9 = BEAN-MITFORD, in *Anat. St.*, XII, 1962, p. 204.

3. Important dedication to Commodus, dating from between 185 and 192, put up by the 'polis' Cyrene, which is called 'metropolis of the Hexapolis', *AE*, 1963, 140 = GOODCHILD, in *Quad. d'Arch. della Libia*, IV, 1961, p. 85, cf. MARCADÉ, In *Rev. Ét. Anc.*, LXIV, 1962, pp. 139–42.

4. Dedication *pro salute* of Comm., at Tropaeum Traiani in the Dobrudja, *AE*, 1964, 251 = POPESCU, in *St. Clas.*, VI, 1964, p. 191 f.

5. Dedication in honour of Comm., found at Villalis (León), put up in the year 191 by auxiliaries, 'ob natale aprunculorum', i.e. of the *vexillum* bearing as a symbol the little banners (?), *AE*, 1966, 188 = GARCIA Y BELLIDO, in *Conimbriga*, I, 1959, 34, cf. *Hisp. Ant. Epigr.*, no. 1927.

6. New fragments of the inscription of the *aqua Commodiana* of the town of Thugga (Procons. Afr.), *AE*, 1966, 511 = POINSSOT, in *Mél. Carcopino*, Paris 1966, pp. 771–86.

7. Dedication I(ovi) O(ptimo) M(aximo) *pro salute* of the Emperor Commodus, for the birthday of the eagle of Legion VII *Gemina*, found in the neighbourhood of Astorga (Asturica), *AE*, 1967, 230 = GARCIA Y BELLIDO, in *Arch. Esp. Arq.*, XXXIX, 1966, p. 26.

8. Dedication of a statue in honour of Comm., in Phocis, MICHAUD, in
   Bull. Corr. Hell., XCIII, 1969, pp. 79 f.

Studies

Monographs

F. GROSSO, *La lotta politica al tempo di Commodo* (Memorie Acc. Sc. di
Torino, Cl. Sc. Mor. Stor. Filol,, ser. IV, n. 7), Turin 1964.

Add to section The reign of Commodus (p. 725)

J. FITZ, 'Massnahmen zur militärischen Sicherheit von Pannonia
inferior unter Commodus', in *Klio*, XXXIX, 1961, pp. 199–214.

——, 'A Military History of Pannonia from the Marcoman Wars to the
Death of Alexander Severus', in *Act. Arch. Ac. Sc. Hung.*, XIV, 1962,
pp. 25–112.

P. ROMANELLI, 'Le iscrizioni volubilitane dei Baquati e i rapporti di
Roma con le tribù indigene dell'Africa', in *Homm. Grenier*, Brussels 1962,
pp. 1347–66.

J. GUEY, 'L'aloi du denier romain de 177 à 211 ap. J.C. (étude des-
criptive)', in *Rev. Num.*, IV, 1962, pp. 73–140 (on the monetary crisis).

C. R. WHITTAKER, 'The Revolt of Papirius Dionysius A.D. 190', in
Historia, XIII, 1964, pp. 348–69 (not a mere episode, but a serious
event, evidence of strong and general opposition, which Cleander
underestimated).

M. SORDI, 'L'apologia del martire romano Apollonio come fonte
dell'Apologeticum di Tertulliano e i rapporti fra Tertulliano e Minu-
cio', in *Riv. St. d. Ch. in It.*, XVIII, 1964, pp. 169–88.

C. TIBILETTI, 'Gli Atti di Apollonio e Tertulliano', in *Atti Acc. Sc.
Torino*, XCIX, 1964–5, pp. 295–337 (against M. Sordi's theory).

F. CASSOLA, 'Pertinace durante il principato di Commodo', in *Par.
Pass.*, XX, 1965, 451–77.

H. G. PFLAUM, 'Note de lecture', in *Ztschr. f. Papyruskunde u. Epigr.*, II,
1968, pp. 151–4 (in the final part of pap. Giessen inv. no. 258 it is not
the Emperor Commodus who is named, as supposed by H. J. GUNDEL,
'Einige Giessener Papyrusfragmente', in *Aeg.*, XLIII, 1963, p. 399, but
Gordianus III).

J. GAGÉ, 'L'assassinat de Commode et les "sortes Herculis" ', in *Rev.
Ét. Lat.* XLVI, 1968, pp. 280–303.

PART III

BIBLIOGRAPHY[1]

I. ON THE SOURCES

1. Literary

APULEIUS (*Apologia*, 2nd ed. HELM, Leipzig 1912; repr. Leipzig 1964 with add. by B. DOER).

R. HELM, in *Reallex. f. Ant. u. Christentum*, I, 1950, c. 573 f.

C. MARCHESI, *Della Magia*, Lat. text, trans. and notes, Bologna 1955.

ARISTIDES OF ATHENS, THE APOLOGIST (reconstruction of the text by R. SEEBERG, *Der Apologet Aristides. Der Text seiner uns erhaltenen Schriften nebst einleitende Untersuchungen ueber dieselben*, Erlangen & Leipzig 1894, and by J. GEFFCKEN, *Zwei Griechische Apologeten*, Leipzig & Berlin 1907, pp. 1–96; for other attempts at reconstruction see B. ALTANER, *Patrologia*, 4th Ital. ed. based on the 13th Germ., Turin 1952, p. 73).

G. LAZZATTI, 'Ellenismo e Cristianesimo. Il primo capitolo dell'Apologia di Aristide' (from *La Scuola Cattolica*, Feb. 1938), Venegono 1938.

ARISTIDES (AELIUS) THE RHETORICIAN (ed. OLIVER, see below).

J. H. OLIVER, *The Ruling Power: A Study of the Roman Empire in the Second Century after Christ through the Roman Oration of Aelius Aristides*, Philadelphia, Pa. 1953 (*Trans. of the Amer. Philos. Soc.*, XLIII, 4, pp. 871–1003), with text.

E. D. PHILLIPS, 'Three Greek Writers on the Roman Empire', in *Class. & Med.*, XVIII, 1957, pp. 102–19 (cf. DIO CHRYSOSTOM and PLUTARCH).

M. PAVAN, 'Sul significato storico dell'Encomio di Roma di Elio Aristide', in *Par. Pass.*, XVII, 1962, pp. 81–95.

H. BENGTSON, 'Das Imperium Romanum in griechischer Sicht', in *Gymnasium*, LXXI, 1964, pp. 150–66.

G. BLEICKEN, 'Der Preis des Aelius Aristides auf das römische Weltreich' (*Nachrichte d. Ak. d. Wiss., in Göttingen*, 7), Göttingen 1966.

[1] Monographs and individual studies have been cited and discussed in Part I of the Appendix. Here too we have taken account particularly of works produced since the publication of Volumes X and XI (1934–6) of the *Cambridge Ancient History*, the bibliographical lists of which remain fundamental up to that date.

C. A. BEHR, 'Aelius Aristides' Birth Date Corrected to November 26, 117 A.D.', in *Amer. Journ. Phil.*, XC, 1969, pp. 75–9.

ARRIAN (*Periplus maris Euxini*, ed. ROOS, Leipzig 1928; see now the ed. by G. MARENGHI in *Collana di studi greci diretta da V. De Falco*, XXIX, Naples 1958, and the review by D. M. PIPPIDI, in *Athen.*, XXVI, 1958, pp. 264–8; for the fragments of the *Parthica*, ROOS, pp. 228–31 and JACOBY, *Fr. Gr. Hist.*, IIB, pp. 860–3, no. 156, with commentary and reconstruction in II *Kommentar*, pp. 574–80).
G. MARENGHI, 'Caratteri e intenti del Periplo di Arriano', in *Athen.*, XXXV, 1957, pp. 177–92; *idem*, 'Sulle fonti del Periplo di Arriano', in *St. Ital. Fil. Class.*, XXIX, 1957, pp. 217–23.
F. A. LEPPER, *Trajan's Parthian War*, Oxford 1948, spec. pp. 127–9 (for the fragments of the *Parthica*).

ATHENAGORAS OF ATHENS, THE APOLOGIST (ed. SCHWARTZ, Leipzig 1891).
L. W. BARNARD, 'The Embassy of Athenagoras', in *Vig. Christ.*, XXI, 1967, pp. 88–92.

AURELIUS, VICTOR (*De Caesaribus*, ed. PICHLMAYR, Leipzig 1911; typed ed. with add. by R. GRÜNDEL, Leipzig 1961, repr. 1966).
E. HOHL, 'Die Historia Augusta und die Caesares des Aurelius Victor', in *Historia*, IV, 1955 (Festschr. Ensslin), pp. 220–8.
CH. G. STARR, 'Aurelius Victor, Historian of Empire', in *Amer. Hist. Rev.*, LXI, 1955–6, pp. 574–86.
A. CHASTAGNOL, 'Emprunts de l'Histoire Auguste aux Caesares d'Aurelius Victor', in *Rev. de Phil.*, XLI, 1967, pp. 85–97.

CALPURNIUS SICULUS (as presumed author of the *Laus Pisonis*).
T. *Calpurni Siculi De laude Pisonis et Bucolica et M. Annaei Lucani De laude Caesaris Einsidlensia quae dicuntur carmina*, ed., trans. comm., R. VERDIÉRE, Brussels 1954.

CRITO (T. STATILIUS, Trajan's doctor, fragments of the *Getica* in JACOBY, *Fr. Gr. Hist.*, II, pp. 931 f., no. 200).
W. H. BUCKLER, 'T. Statilius Crito, Traiani Augusti medicus', in *Oesterr. Jahresh.*, XXX, 1936, Beibl., cc. 5–8.
L. ROBERT, *La Carie*, II, Paris 1954, pp. 222 ff.

DIGESTA (ed. MOMMSEN, in KRUEGER, MOMMSEN, SCHOELL and KROLL, *Corpus Iuris Civilis*, I, Berlin 1902).
L. WENGER, *Die Quellen des römischen Rechts*, Vienna 1953, pp. 562 ff.

B. BIONDI, *Il diritto romano* (*St. di Roma*, XX), Bologna 1957, pp. 149–163, with bibliographies.

DIO CASSIUS (ed. BOISSEVAIN, Berlin 1895–1931, 2nd ed. anast. 1955).
W. F. SNYDER, 'On Chronology in the Imperial Books of Cassius Dio's Roman History', in *Klio*, XXXIII, 1940, pp. 39–56.
E. GABBA, 'Sulla storia romana di Cassio Dione', in *Riv. Stor. Ital.*, LXVII, 1955, pp. 289–333.
——, 'Storici greci dell'impero romano da Augusto ai Severi', in *Riv. St. It.*, LXXI, 1959, pp. 361–81.
C. QUESTA, 'Tecnica biografica e tecnica annalistica nei iibri LXII–LXIII di Cassio Dione', in *Stud. Urb.*, XXXI, 1957, pp. 37–53.
G. B. TOWNEND, 'Traces in Dio Cassius of Cluvius, Aufidius and Pliny', in *Hermes*, LXXXIX, 1961, pp. 227–48.
J. BLEICKEN, 'Der politische Standpunkt Dios gegenüber der Monarchie', in *Hermes*, XC, 1962, pp. 444–67.
F. MILLAR, *A Study of Cassius Dio*, Oxford 1964.

DIO CHRYSOSTOM (*Orationes*, ed. DE BUDE, Leipzig 1916–19).
C. VIELMETTI, 'I discorsi bitinici di Dione Chrisostomo', in *St. It. Fil. Class.*, XVIII, 1941, pp. 89–108.
E. D. PHILLIPS, 'Three Greek Writers on the Roman Empire', in *Class. & Med.*, XVIII, 1957, pp. 102–19.

EPITOME DE CAESARIBUS (ed. PICHLMAYR, Leipzig 1911).
M. GALDI, *L'epitome nella letteratura latina*, Naples 1922, pp. 200–11.

EUSEBIUS OF CAESAREA (*Historia Ecclesiastica*, ed. SCHWARTZ and MOMMSEN, with the Latin trans. of RUFINUS, in Vol. II, 1903–9, of the *Werke* of Eusebius, in the *Griechische Christliche Schriftsteller*, and now in the series *Sources Chrétiennes*, with French trans. by G. BARDY, I (1952), II (1955), III (1958); *Chronicon*: vers. of the Armenian trans. (KARST) in Vol. V, 1911, and ed. of the Latin trans. of St Jerome (HELM) in Vol. VII², 1956, of the *Griech. Christl. Schrifst.*).
D. S. WALLACE-HADRILL, 'The Eusebian Chroncile. The Extent and Date of Composition of its Early Editions', in *Journ. Theol. St.*, NS, VI, 1955, pp. 248–53.
——, *Eusebius of Caesarea*, London 1960.
G. LAZZATI, 'Note su Eusebio epitomatore di Atti di martiri', in *St. Calderini-Paribeni*, I, Milan 1956, pp. 377–84.
G. PUCCIONI, 'Il problema delle fonti storiche di S. Girolamo', in *Ann. Sc. Norm. Sup. Pisa*, XXV, 1956, pp. 191–212.

A. DEMPF, 'Eusebios als Historiker', in *Sitzungsb. d. Bay. Ak. d. Wiss.*, 1964, 11, Munich 1964.

EUTROPIUS (*Breviarum ab urbe condita*, ed. RUEHL, Leipzig 1919).
M. GALDI, *L'epitome nella letteratura latina*, Naples 1922, pp. 229–37.

FAVORINUS OF ARELATE (*Opere*, intro., crit. text and comm. by A. BARIGAZZI, Florence 1966.)

FLAVIUS JOSEPHUS (*Bellum Iudaicum, Antiquitates Iudaicae, Contra Apionem, Vita*, ed. NIESE, Berlin 1887–95, 2nd photog. ed. 1955).
G. C. RICHARDS, 'The Composition of Josephus' Antiquities', in *Class. Quart.*, XXXIII, 1939, pp. 36–40.
M. GELZER, 'Die Vita des Josephos', in *Hermes*, LXXX, 1952, pp. 67–90.
D. TIMPE, 'Römische Geschichte bei Flavius Iosephus', in *Historia*, IX, 1960, pp. 474–502.
TH. FRANKFORT, 'La date de l'autobiographie de Flavius Josèphe et des œuvres de Justus de Tibériade', in *Rev. Belg. Phil. Hist.*, XXXIX, 1961, pp. 52–8.

FLORUS (*Oeuvres*, ed. JAL, Paris 1967).
A. GARZETTI, 'Floro e l'età adrianea', in *Athen.*, XLII, 1964, pp. 136–56.
P. JAL, 'Nature et signification politique de l'œuvre de Florus', in *Rev. Ét. Lat.*, XLIII, 1965, pp. 358–83.
W. DEN BOER, 'Florus und die römische Geschichte', in *Mnemosyne*, XVIII, 1965, pp. 366–87.

FRONTINUS (*De aquaeductu urbis Romae*, ed. KROHN, Leipzig 1922; *Stratagemata*, ed. GUNDERMANN, Leipzig 1888).
TH. ASHBY, *The Aqueducts of Ancient Rome*, ed. by I. A. RICHMOND, Oxford 1935, spec. pp. 26–33.
CH. ROSSET, 'Frontin, auteur des Stratagèmes, a-t-il lu le Bellum Gallicum?', in *Rev. Ét. Lat.*, XXXII, 1954, pp. 275–84.

FRONTO (*Epistulae*, ed. M. P. J. VAN DEN HOUT, Leiden 1954).
R. HANSLIK, 'Die Anordnung der Briefsammlung Frontos', in *Comment. Vindob.*, I, 1935, pp. 41–7.
J. HEURGON, 'Fronton de Cirta', in *Rec. Soc. Arch. Constantine*, LXX, 1957–9, pp. 139–53.
F. PORTALUPI, *M. Cornelio Frontone*, Turin 1961.

H. G. PFLAUM, 'Les correspondants de l'orateur M. Cornelius Fronto de Cirta', in *Homm. Bayet.*, Brussels 1964, pp. 544–60.

L. POLVERINI, 'Sull'epistolario di Frontone come fonte storica', in *Seconda miscellanea greca e romana (Studi Ist. It. St. Ant.*, XIX), Rome 1968.

GALEN (ed. KÜHN, 1821–33, complete and partial in *Corpus Medicorum Graecorum*, Leipzig-Berlin 1914–41).

GELLIUS, AULUS (*Noctes Atticae*, ed. HOSIUS, Leipzig 1903).

V. D'AGOSTINO, 'Aulo Gellio e le Notti attiche', in *Riv. St. Class.*, V, 1957, pp. 26–34.

HERODIAN (*Ab excessu divi Marci*, ed. STAVENHAGEN, Leipzig 1922).

E. HOHL, 'Kaiser Commodus und Herodian', in *Sitz.-ber. d. deutsch. Ak. d. Wiss. zu Berlin*, Kl. f. Gesellschaftswiss., 1954, I.

F. CASSOLA, 'Sulla vita e sulla personalità dello storico Erodiano', in *Nuov. Riv. Stor.*, XLI, 1957, pp. 218–28.

——, 'Sull'attendibilità dello storico Erodiano', in *Atti Acc. Pontan.*, Naples, N.S. VI, 1957, pp. 191–200.

——, 'Erodiano e le sue fonti', in *Rend. Acc. Arch. Lett. Belle Arti*, Naples, XXXII, 1957, pp. 165–72.

W. WIDMER, *Kaisertum, Rom und Welt in Herodians Metà Márkon basiléias historía*, Zürich 1967.

HISTORIA AUGUSTA (ed. HOHL, I-II ed. stereot. correctior; add. et corrig. adiecerunt SAMBERGER and SEYFART, Leipzig 1965; for the lists, PETER, Leipzig 1865).

W. HARTKE, 'Geschichte und Politik im spätantiken Rom. Untersuchung über die Scriptores Historiae Augustae', Beiheft *Klio*, XLV, 1940.

——, *Römische Kinderkaiser*, Berlin 1951.

S. MAZZARINO, *Aspetti sociali del quarto secolo*, Rome 1951, pp. 345–73.

J. STRAUB, *Studien zur Historia Augusta*, Berne 1952.

H. STERN, *Date et destinataire de l'Histoire Auguste*, Paris, 1953.

E. HOHL, 'Ueber die Glaubwürdigkeit der Historia Augusta', in *Sitz.-ber. d. deutsch. Ak. d. Wiss. zu Berlin*, 1953, 2.

E. MANNI, 'Recenti studi sulla Historia Augusta', in *Par. Pass.*, VIII, 1953, pp. 71–80.

A. MOMIGLIANO, 'An Unsolved Problem of Historical Forgery. The Scriptores Historiae Augustae', in *Journ. Court. & Warb. Inst.*, XVII, 1954, pp. 22–46.

E. HOHL, 'Ueber das Problem der Historia Augusta', in *Wien. Stud.*, LXXI, 1958, pp. 132–52.

A. BELLEZZA, *Historia Augusta, I: Le edizioni*, Genoa 1959.

——, *Atti del Colloquio Patavino sull'Historia Augusta*, Rome 1963.

——, *Bonner Historia Augusta-Colloquium, 1963*, Bonn 1964; *1964–65*, Bonn 1966.

P. WHITE, 'The Authorship of the Historia Augusta', in *Journ. Rom. St.*, LVII, 1967, pp. 115–33.

A. BELLEZZA, 'La problematica sull'Historia Augusta', in *Maia*, XIX, 1967, pp. 185–9.

R. SYME, *Ammianus and the Historia Augusta*, Oxford 1968.

(*on Marius Maximus, source of the H.A.*) G. BARBIERI, 'Mario Massimo', in *Riv. Fil.*, XXXII, 1954, pp. 36–66.

(*on historical value and on problems of individual lives*) FR. POESCHL, 'Erläuterungen zur Vita Antonini Pii in der Historia Augusta', in *Wien. Stud.*, LXVI, 1953, pp. 178–81.

J. SCHWENDEMANN, *Der historische Wert der Vita Marci bei der Scriptores Historiae Augustae*, Heidelberg 1923.

J. M. HEER, 'Der historische Wert der Vita Commodi in der Sammlung der S.H.A.', in *Philologus*, Supplementband IX, 1904.

T. D. BARNES, 'Hadrian and Lucius Verus', in *Journ. Rom. St.*, LVII, 1967, pp. 65–79.

ITINERARIA (*Periplus maris Erythraei*, ed. MÜLLER, *Geogr. Gr. Min.*, II, 1882, pp. 257–305; *Itineraria Antonini Augusti et Burdigalense* ed. D. CUNTZ, Leipzig 1929; *Ravennatis Anonymi Cosmographia et Guidonis Geographica*, ed. J. SCHNETZ, Leipzig 1940).

D. VAN BERCHEM, 'Les origines de l'Itinéraire d'Antonin et ses rapports avec les édits relatifs à la perception de l'annone', in *Bull. Soc. Ant. d. Fr.*, 1934, pp. 212 f.

JULIAN IMPERATOR (*Convivium* or *Caesares*, ed. HERTLEIN, Leipzig 1875; the *Caesares* are now also in Vol. II, 2 of the *Oeuvres Complètes*, ed. CHR. LACOMBRADE, Paris 1964).

CHR. LACOMBRADE, 'Note sur les Césars de l'empereur Julien', in *Pallas*, XI, 1962, pp. 47–67.

J. F. GILLIAM, 'Titus in Julian's *Caesares*', in *Amer. Journ. Phil.*, LXXXVIII, 1967, pp. 203–8.

JUSTIN, the APOLOGIST (ed. GOODSPEED, in *Die ältesten Apologeten* Göttingen 1914).

R. M. GRANT, 'The Chronology of the Greek Apologists', in *Vig. Christ.*, IX, 1955, pp. 25–33 (also for Quadratus, Aristides, Apollinaris, Melito, Tatian, Athenagoras, Miltiades).

JUVENAL (*Satirae*, ed. IAHN–BUECHELER–LEO, Berlin 1910, 4th edit.).
G. HIGHET, 'The Life of Juvenal', in *Trans. Proc. Am. Phil. Ass.*, LXVIII, 1937, pp. 480–506.
——, *Juvenal the Satirist*, Oxford 1954.
E. LEPORE, 'Un sintomo di coscienza occidentale all'apogeo dell'impero',in *Riv. Stor. It.*, LX, 1948, pp. 193–203.
C. E. LUTZ, 'Any Resemblance . . . is purely Coincidental', in *Class. Journ.*, XLVI, 1950, pp. 115–20.
M. A. LEVI, 'Aspetti sociali della poesia di Giovenale', in *Studi Funaioli*, Rome 1955, pp. 170–80.
N. SCIVOLETTO, 'Plinio il Giovane e Giovenale', in *Giorn. It. Fil.*, X, 1957, pp. 133–46.
A. SERAFINI, *Studio sulle Satire di Giovenale*, Florence 1947.
B. BALDWIN, 'Cover-names and Dead Victims in Juvenal', in *Athen.*, XLV, 1967, pp. 304–12.
W. HEILMANN, 'Zur Komposition der vierten Satire und des ersten Satirenbuches Juvenals', in *Rh. Mus.*, CX, 1967, pp. 358–70.
J. G. GRIFFITH, 'Juvenal Statius and the Flavian Establishment', in *Greece and Rome*, XVI, 1969, pp. 134–50.

LUCAN (*Pharsalia*, ed. HOSIUS, Leipzig 1913; HOUSMAN, Oxford 1926).
E. MALCOVATI, *M. Anneo Lucano*, Milan 1940.
A. MOMIGLIANO, 'Literary Chronology of the Neronian Age', in *Class. Quart.*, XXXVIII, 1944, pp. 96–100 (also for Seneca and Petronio).
A. PUNTONI, 'La composizione del poema lucaneo', in *Rend. Acc. Lincei*, ser. VIII, II, 1947, pp. 101–26.
M. PAVAN, 'L'ideale politico di Lucano', in *Atti Ist. Ven.*, CXIII, 1954–5, pp. 209–22.
J. BRISSET, *Les idées politiques de Lucain*, Paris 1964.
B. M. MARTI, 'Tragic History and Lucan's Pharsalia', in *St. Ullman*, I, Rome 1964, pp. 165–204.
K. F. C. ROSE, 'Problems of Chronology in Lucan's Career', in *Trans. Proc. Amer. Phil. Ass.*, XCVII, 1966, pp. 377–96.

LUCIAN (complete works ed. IACOBITZ, Leipzig 1851, and successive reprints; incomplete, the new Teubner of NILÉN, 1906 onwards; for the opusculum *Quomodo scribenda sit historia*, the ed. with German trans. and comm. by H. HOMEYER, Munich 1965).

P. GABRIELI, 'L'encomio di una favorita imperiale in due opuscoli lucianei', in *Rend. Acc. Lincei*, ser. VI, X, 1934, pp. 29-101 (for Panthea of Smyrna).

M. CASTER, *Lucien et la pensée religieuse de son temps*, Paris 1938.

A. PERETTI, *Un intellettuale greco contro Roma*, Florence 1946.

J. BOMPAIRE, *Lucien écrivain, imitation et création*, Paris 1958 (*Bibl. Éc. Franç. Ath. et Rome*, CXC).

L. VARCL, 'Lucien et les chrétiens', in *St. Class.*, III, 1961, pp. 377–83.

J. SCHWARTZ, *Biographie de Lucien de Samosate*, Coll. Latomus, LXXXIII, Brussels 1965.

MALALAS, JOHANNES (in MIGNE, *Patr. Gr.*, Vol. 97).

A. SCHENK VON STAUFFENBERG, *Die römische Kaisergeschichte bei Malalas. Griechischer Text der Bücher IX–XII und Untersuchungen*, Stuttgart 1931.

R. E. G. DOWNEY, 'References to Inscriptions in the Chronicle of Malalas', in *Trans. Proc. Amer. Phil. Ass.*, LXVI, 1935, pp. 55–72.

MARCUS AURELIUS (ed. SCHENKL, Leipzig 1913; A. S. L. FAR-QUHARSON, *The Meditations of the Emperor Marcus Antoninus*, Oxford 1945, text with trans. and comm.).

K. DÜRR, 'Das erste Buch der Selbstbetrachtungen des Kaisers Marcus Aurelius Antoninus', in *Gymn.*, 1938, pp. 64–82.

MARTIAL (*Epigrammata*, ed. HERAEUS, Leipzig 1925).

F. SAUTER, *Der römische Kaiserkult bei Martial und Statius*, Stuttgart 1934 (*Tübinger Beitr. zur Altertumswiss.*, XXI).

L. PEPE, *Marziale*, Naples 1950.

ORACULA SIBYLLINA (ed. GEFFCKEN, in *Griech. Christl. Schriftst.*, Leipzig 1902; KURFESS, *Sibyllinische Weissagungen*, hrsg. und übers., Munich 1951).

A. KURFESS, 'Sibyllinische Weissagungen, Eine literar-historische Plauderei', in *Theol. Quartalschr.*, CXVII, 1936, pp. 351–66.

A. PERETTI, *La Sibilla Babilonese*, Florence 1942.

OROSIUS (ed. ZANGEMEISTER, Vienna 1889; repr. anast. Hildesheim 1967).

B. LACROIX, *Orose et ses idées*, Paris 1965.

E. CORSINI, *Introduzione alle 'Storie' di Orosio*, Turin 1968.

PAUSANIAS (*Descriptio Graeciae*, ed. SPIRO, I, II, III, Leipzig 1903, I² 1938, stereot.; J. C. FRAZER, *The Description of Greece*, 6 vol. with trans. and comm., London 1898).

G. DAUX, *Pausanias à Delphes*, Paris 1936.

PERSIUS (*Satirae*, ed. IAHN, BUECHELER AND LEO, Berlin 1910, 4th ed.; ed. CLAUSEN, Oxford 1956).

E. V. MARMORALE, *Persio*, 2nd edit., Florence 1956.

F. BALLOTTO, *Cronologia ed evoluzione spirituale nelle Satire di Persio*, Messina 1964.

PETRONIUS (*Satyricon*, ed. ERNOUT, Paris 1931, 2nd ed., crit. text and Ital. trans. by V. CIAFFI, Turin 1967).

E. V. MARMORALE, *Petronio nel suo tempo*, Naples 1937.

G. BAGNANI, *Arbiter of Elegance. A study of the Life and Works of C. Petronius*, Toronto 1954 (The Phoenix Suppl., II).

K. F. C. ROSE, 'The Author of the "Satyricon" ', in *Latomus*, XX, 1961, pp. 821–5.

C. RONCAIOLI, 'Il diminutivo e l'età di Petronio', in *Giorn. I. Fil.*, XIV, 1961, pp. 1–27.

P. MORENO, 'Aspetti di vita economica nel "Satyricon" ', in *Ann. Ist. It. Num.*, IX–XI, 1962–4, pp. 53–73.

G. SANDY, 'Satire in the "Satyricon" ', in *Amer. Journ. Phil.*, XC, 1969, pp. 293–303.

PHILO ALEXANDRINUS (*In Flaccum, Legatio ad Gaium*, in vol. VI, Berlin 1915, by COHN and REITER, of the ed. COHN–WENDLAND–REITER [Weidmann]; *In Flaccum*, ed. with transl. and comm. by H. BOX, Oxford 1939; *Legatio ad Gaium*, ed. with introd., transl. and comm., by E. M. SMALLWOOD, Leiden 1961).

F. GEIGER, *Philon von Alexandreia als sozialer Denker*, Stuttgart 1932 (*Tübinger Beiträge zur Altertumswissenschaft*, XIV).

S. TRACY, *Philo Iudaeus and the Roman Principate*, Williamsport (U.S.A.) 1933.

E. R. GOODENOUGH, *The Politics of Philo Iudaeus. Practice and Theory, with a General Bibliography of Philo*, by H. L. GOODHART and E. H. GOODENOUGH, New Haven, Conn., 1938.

——, *An Introduction to Philo Iudaeus*, New Haven, Conn., 1940 (2nd ed. Oxford 1962).

J. SCHWARTZ, 'Note sur la famille de Philon d'Alexandrie', in *Ann. Inst. Phil. Hist. Or.* (Brussels), XIII, 1953 (Mél. I. LÉVY), pp. 591–602.
J. DANIÉLOU, *Philon d'Alexandrie*, Paris 1958.

PHILOSTRATUS II (*Vita Apollonii*, ed. KAYSER, I, Leipzig 1870; *Vitae sophistarum*, ed. KAYSER, II, Leipzig 1871; CONYBEARE, *The Life of Apollonius of Tyana*, Loeb. Class. Libr. 1912).
A. CALDERINI, 'Teoria e pratica politica nella "Vita di Apollonio di Tiana"', in *Rend. Ist. Lomb.*, LXXIV, 1940–1, pp. 213–41.
F. GROSSO, 'La "Vita di Apollonio di Tiana" come fonte storica', in *Acme*, VII, 1954, pp. 333–532.

PLINY THE ELDER (*Naturalis Historia*, ed. JAN and MAYHOFF, Leipzig 1892–1909).
N. H. WETHERED, *The Mind of the Ancient World. A Consideration of Pliny's Natural History*, London 1937.

PLINY THE YOUNGER (*Epistulae, Panegyricus*, ed. SCHUSTER, Leipzig 1952; 3rd ed. HANSLIK, Leipzig 1958; A. N. SHERWIN-WHITE, *The Letters of Pliny, A Historical and Social Commentary*, Oxford 1966, reiss. 1968 with corrections).
M. HAMMOND, 'Pliny the Younger's Views on Government', in *Harv. St. Class. Phil.*, XLIX, 1938, pp. 115–40.
R. T. BRUÉRE, 'Tacitus and Pliny's Panegyricus', in *Class. Phil.*, XLIX, 1954, pp. 161–79.
M. W. TRAUB, 'Pliny's Treatment of History in Epistolary Form', in *Trans. Proc. Am. Phil. Ass.*, LXXXVI, 1955, pp. 213–32.
A. N. SHERWIN-WHITE, 'Pliny's Praetorship again', in *Journ. Rom. St.*, XLVII, 1957, pp. 126–30.
V. A. SIRAGO, 'La proprietà di Plinio il Giovane', in *Ant. Class.*, XXVI, 1957, pp. 40–58.
L. VIDMAN, *Étude sur la correspondance de Pline le Jeune avec Trajan*, Prague 1960.
K. ZELZER, 'Zur Frage des Charakters der Briefsammlung des jüngeren Plinius', in *Wien. St.*, LXXVII, 1964, pp. 144–61.
R. MARTIN, 'Pline le Jeune et les problèmes économiques de son temps', in *Rev. Ét. Anc.*, LXIX, 1967, pp. 62–97.
D. KUIJPER F.F., 'De honestate Plinii minoris', in *Mnemosyne*, XXI, 1968, pp. 40–70.

PLUTARCH (*Vitae parallelae*, ed. LINDSKOG and ZIEGLER, Leipzig 1914–39; of the new Teubner ed. by ZIEGLER, Vols. I1, I2 and II1 have appeared, and in the Collection des Universités de France, Vols. I–IV (FLACELIÈRE, CHAMBRY and JANEAUX); *Moralia*, ed. BERNARDAKIS, Leipzig 1888–96, and new Teubner ed. by WEGEHAUPT, PATON, SIEVEKING, NACHSTÄDT, POHLENZ, HUBERT and ZIEGLER in progress since 1925).

F. R. B. GODOLPHIN, 'The Source of Plutarch's Thesis in the Lives of Galba and Otho', in *Amer. Journ. Phil.*, LVI, 1935, LVI, 1935, pp. 324–8.

E. D. PHILLIPS, 'Three Greek Writers on the Roman Empire', in *Class. & Med.*, XVIII, 1957, pp. 102–19.

P. SCAZZOSO, 'Plutarco interprete barocco deila romanità', in *Paideia*, XII, 1957, pp. 3–14.

A. GARZETTI, 'Plutarco e le sue "Vite parallele". Rassegna di studi 1934–52', in *Riv. Stor. Ital.*, LXV, 1953, pp. 76–104.

R. FLACELIÈRE, 'Rome et ses empereurs vus par Plutarque', in *Ant. Class.*, XXXII, 1963, pp. 28–47.

C. R. H. BARROW, *Plutarch and His Times*, Bloomington, Ind. 1967.

PTOLEMAEUS, CLAUDIUS (*Geographia*, ed. MULLER and FISCHER (Didot), Paris 1883–1901).

QUINTILIAN (*Institutionis oratoriae libri XII*, ed. RADERMACHER, Leipzig 1907–35; ed. photog. with add., BUCHHEIT, Leipzig 1959; *Declamationes*, ed. RITTER, Leipzig 1884, repr. photog. Stuttgart 1965). V. E. ALFIERI, 'La pedagogia di Quintiliano', in *Athen.*, XLII, 1964, pp. 400–15.

SENECA (*Apocolocyntosis*, ed. WALTZ, Collection Universités de France, Paris 1934; *Epistulae ad Lucilium*, ed. BELTRAMI, Collect. Acc. Lincei, 2nd ed., Rome 1937; *Dialogi*, ed. HERMES, Leipzig 1905; *Naturales Quaestiones*, ed. GERCKE, Leipzig 1907; *De beneficiis, De clementia*, ed. HOSIUS, 4th ed., Leipzig 1914; *Tragoediae*, in partic. *Octavia*, ed. G. VIANSINO, Turin 1955).

C. MARCHESI, *Seneca*, 2nd ed., Messina-Milan 1934.

F. MARTINAZZOLI, *Seneca. Studio sulla morale ellenica nella esperienza romana*, Florence 1945.

I. LANA, *Lucio Anneo Seneca*, Turin 1955.

F. PRÉCHAC, 'Sénèque et l'histoire', in *Rev. Phil.*, IX, 1935, pp. 361–370.

O. REGENBOGEN, 'Seneca als Denker römischer Willenshaltung', in *Antike*, XII, 1936, pp. 107–30.

s. MOTERO DIAZ, 'Historia y politica en la praetexta Octavia', in *De Caliclés a Trajano*, Madrid 1948.

P. GRIMAL, *Sénèque, sa vie, son œuvre*, Paris 1957.

F. GIANCOTTI, *Cronologia dei Dialoghi di Seneca*, Turin 1957.

E. G. SCHMIDT, 'Die Anordnung der Dialoge Senecas', in *Helikon*, I, 1961, pp. 245–63.

I. LANA, *Lucio Anneo Seneca e la posizione degli intellettuali romani di fronte al principato*, Turin 1964.

F. PRÉCHAC, 'Note sur Sénèque et l'histoire', in *Bull. Ass. Budé*, 1966, pp. 465–505.

See also *Note critiche Nerone*, pp. 619 f.)

SILIO ITALICO (*Punica*, ed. BAUER, Leipzig 1890–2).

E. WISTRAND, 'Die Chronologie der Punica des Silius Italicus. Beiträge zur Interpretation der flavischen Literatur', in *St. Gr. et Lat. Gothoburgensia*, IV, Gothenburg 1956.

M. V. ALBRECHT, *Silius Italicus. Freiheit und Gebundenheit römischer Epik*, Amsterdam 1964.

STATIUS (*Silvae*, ed. PHILLIMORE, 2nd ed., Oxford 1918; MARASTONI, 2nd ed., Leipzig 1969).

STRABO (*Geographica*, ed. MEINEKE, 2nd ed. stereot. Leipzig 1915–25; SBORDONE, I–II, Rome 1963).

W. ALY, *Strabon von Amaseia, Untersuchungen über Text, Aufbau und Quellen der Geographika*, Bonn 1957.

G. ANJAC, *Strabon et la science de son temps*, I, Paris 1966.

SUETONIUS (*De vita Caesarum*, ed. IHM, Leipzig 1918, and stereot. Teubner, Stuttgart 1958, repr. 1967).

C. MARCHESI, 'Svetonio, il biografo dei dodici Cesari', in *Voci di antichi*, Rome 1946, pp. 143–57.

W. STEIDLE, *Sueton und die antike Biographie*, Munich 1951 (*Zetemata*, 1).

J. COISSIN, 'Suétone physiognomiste dans les Vies des XII Césars', in *Rev. Ét. Lat.*, XXXI, 1953, pp. 234–56.

G. D'ANNA, *Le idee letterarie di Svetonio*, Florence 1954.

F. GROSSO, 'L'epigrafe di Ippona e la vita di Suetonio, con i fasti dei pontefici di Vulcano a Ostia', in *Rend. Acc. Lincei*, XIV, 1959, pp. 263–96.

G. B. TOWNEND, 'The Hippo Inscription and the Career of Suetonius', in *Historia*, X, 1961, pp. 99–109.

F. DELLA CORTE, *Suetonio, eques Romanus*, 2nd ed., Florence 1967.

Individual biographies

M. J. DU FOUR, *C. Suetonii Tranquilli Vita Tiberii*, Chs. I–XXIII, Diss. Philadelphia, Penn., 1941.

J. A. MAURER, *Commentary on C. Suetonii Tranquilli Vita C. Caligulae Caesaris*, Diss. Philadelphia, Penn., 1949.

N. NELSON, 'The Value of Epigraphic Evidence in the Interpretation of Latin Historical Literature', in *Class. Journ.*, XXXVII, 1942, pp. 281–90 (on the life of Nero).

A. W. BRAITHWAITE, *C. Svetonii Tranquilli Divus Vespasianus*, with an Introduction and Commentary, Oxford 1927.

H. R. GRAF, *Kaiser Vespasian, Untersuchungen zu Suetons Vita Divi Vespasiani*, Stuttgart 1937.

G. LUCK, 'Über Suetons Divus Titus', in *Rh. Mus.*, CVII, 1964, pp. 63–75.

P. E. ARIAS, *Domiziano. Saggio storico con traduzione e commento della 'Vita' di Svetonio*, Catania 1945.

TACITUS (*Annales*, ed. KOESTERMANN, 7th ed., Leipzig 1952; *Historiae*, ed. KOESTERMANN, 8th ed., Leipzig 1957; *Germania, Agricola, Dialogus de oratoribus*, ed. KOESTERMANN, 8th ed., Leipzig 1957 (all three vols. successively repr.); *Annales* I–IV and *Historiae*, ed. Acc. Lincei, ed. respectively by LENCHANTIN DE GUBERNATIS and GIARRATANO, Rome 1940 and 1939; KOESTERMANN has published a new commentary on the *Annals*, of which three vols. have appeared (books 1–3,) Heidelberg 1963–7; HEUBNER has done a commentary on the first two books of the *Histories*, Heidelberg 1963–8; for the *Agricola* see the two commentaries by G. FORNI, Rome 1962, and by R. M. OGILVIE and I. RICHMOND, Oxford 1967; for the *Germania* see the commentary of G. FORNI and F. GALLI, Rome 1964).

C. MARCHESI, *Tacito*, 4th ed., Milan 1955.

E. PARATORE, *Tacito*, Milan-Varese 1951, 2nd ed. Rome 1962 (cf. *idem, Tacitea*, in *Riv. cult. class. e med.*, II, 1960, pp. 62–92).

R. SYME, *Tacitus*, I, II, Oxford 1958.

ST. BORZSÁK, 'P. Cornelius Tacitus', in PAULY-WISSOWA, *Realencycl.*, Suppl. XI, 1968, cc. 373–512.

Personality and ideals

R. SYME, 'Tacitus on Gaul', in *Latomus*, XII, 1953, pp. 25–37.

——, 'How Tacitus came to History', in *Gr. & Rome*, IV, 1957, pp. 160–7.

B. WALKER, *The Annals of Tacitus: A Study in the Writing of History*, Manchester 1952 (2nd ed. 1960).

P. BEGUIN, 'Psychologie et vérité historique. Réflexions sur un récent ouvrage de critique tacitéenne', in *Ant. Class.*, XXIII, 1954, pp. 118–25 (on WALKER).

W. H. ALEXANDER, 'The "psychology" of Tacitus', in *Class. Journ.*, XLVII, 1952, pp. 326–8 (on the exaggerations of psychology, see A. MOMIGLIANO, in *Journ. Rom. St.*, XXXVI, 1946, pp. 225 ff.).

P. BEGUIN, 'La personalité de l'historien dans l'œuvre de Tacite. Son esprit critique et positiviste' in *Ant. Class.*, XXII, 1953, pp. 322–346.

A. SALVATORE, 'Il senso del male in Tacito', in *Ann. Fac. Lett. Napoli*, III, 1953, pp. 21–79.

——, 'L'immoralité des femmes et la décadence de l'empire selon Tacite', in *Les Ét. Class.*, XXII, 1954, pp. 245–69.

W. JENS, 'Libertas bei Tacitus', in *Hermes*, LXXXIV, 1956, pp. 331–352.

V. POESCHL, 'Tacitus und der Untergang des römischen Reiches', in *Wien. Stud.*, LXIX, 1956 (Festschr. LESKY), pp. 310–20.

FR. HAMPL, 'Beiträge zur Beurteilung des Historikers Tacitus', in *Natalicium Jax*, I, Innsbruck 1955, pp. 89–102.

C. W. MENDEL, *Tacitus, the Man and His Work*, New Haven, Conn. 1957.

V. PÖSCHL, 'Der Historiker Tacitus', in *Welt als Gesch.*, XXII, 1962, pp. 1–10.

R. HANSLIK, 'Die Aemterlaufbahn des Tacitus im Lichte der Aemterlaufbahn seiner Zeitgenossen', in *Anz. Oesterr. Ak. Wiss.*, CII, 1965, pp. 47–60.

R. HAEUSSLER, *Tacitus und das historische Bewusstsein* Heidelberg 1965.

A. MICHEL, *Tacite et le destin de l'empire*, Paris 1966.

Mode of composition, sources

H. VOLKMANN, 'Zur Datierung der Annalen des Tacitus', in *Gymn.*, LX, 1953, pp. 236–9.

K. WELLESLEY, 'The Date of Composition of Tacitus, *Annals II*', in *Rh. Mus.*, XCVIII, 1955, pp. 135–49.

L. FERRERO, 'La voce pubblica nel proemio degli Annali di Tacito', in *Riv. Fil.*, XXIV, 1946, pp. 50–86.

J. S. RYBERG, 'Tacitus' Art of Innuendo', in *Trans. Proc. Amer. Phil. Ass.*, LXXIII, 1942, pp. 383–404.

R. S. ROGERS, 'Tacitean Pattern in Narrating Treason Trials', in *Trans. Proc. Amer. Phil. Ass.*, LXXXIII, 1952, pp. 279–311.

——, 'The Tacitean Account of a Neronian Trial', in *St. Robinson*, II, Saint Louis, Miss. 1953, pp. 711–18.

——, 'Treason in the Early Empire', in *Journ. Rom. St.*, XLIX, 1959, pp. 90–4.

H. W. TRAUB, 'Tacitus' Use of Ferocia', in *Trans. Proc. Amer. Phil. Ass.*, LXXXIV, 1953, pp. 250–61.

J. MOGENET, 'La conjuration de Clemens', in *Ant. Class.*, XXIII, 1954, pp. 321–30 (on method of using the sources).

R. SYME, 'Obituaries in Tacitus', in *Amer. Journ. Phil.*, LXXIX, 1958, pp. 18–31.

C. QUESTA, *Studi sulle fonti degli Annales di Tacito*, 2nd ed., Rome 1963.

G. B. TOWNEND, 'Cluvius Rufus in the Histories of Tacitus', in *Amer. Journ. Phil.*, LXXXV, 1964, pp. 337–77.

N. P. MILLER, 'Dramatic Speech in Tacitus', in *Amer. Journ. Phil.*, LXXXV, 1964, pp. 279–96.

H. PARATORE, *De libro IV Annalium Taciti*, Rome, 1967.

M. C. MITTELSTADT, 'Tacitus and Plutarch. Some Interpretative Methods', in *Riv. St. Class.*, XV, 1967, pp. 293–304.

D. C. A. SHOTTER, 'The Starting-dates of Tacitus' Historical Works', in *Class. Quart.*, XVII, 1967, pp. 158–63.

On individual emperors

G. WALSER, *Rom, das Reich und die fremden Völker in der Geschichtsschreibung der frühen Kaiserzeit*, Baden-Baden 1951 (Julio-Claudian period).

FR. KLINGNER, 'Tacitus über Augustus und Tiberius. Interpretationen zum Eingang der Annalen', in *Sitz.-ber. Bay. Ak. d. Wiss.*, 1953, 7, Munich 1954.

A. GARZETTI, 'Sul problema di Tacito e Tiberio (rassegna)', in *Riv. Stor. It.* LXVII, 1955, pp. 70–80.

U. KNOCHE, 'Zur Beurteilung des Kaisers Tiberius durch Tacitus', in *Gymnasium*, LXX, 1963, pp. 211–26.

J. TRESCH, *Die Nerobücher in den Annalen des Tacitus. Tradition und Leistung*, Heidelberg 1965.

E. KOESTERMANN, 'Das Charakterbild Galbas bei Tacitus', in *Navicula Chiloniensis* (Festschr. JACOBY), Leiden 1956, pp. 191–206.

FR. KLINGNER, *Die Geschichte Kaiser Othos bei Tacitus*, Leipzig 1940.

M. DREXLER, 'Zur Geschichte Kaiser Othos bei Tacitus und Plutarch', in *Klio*, XXXVII, 1959, pp. 153–78.

M. FUHRMANN, 'Das Vierkaiserjahr bei Tacitus. Über den Aufbau der Historien I–III', in *Philologus*, CIV, 1960, pp. 250–78.

P. SCHUNK, 'Studien zur Darstellung des Endes von Galba, Otho und Vitellius in den Historien des Tacitus', in *Symb. Osl.*, XXXIX, 1964, pp. 38–82.

A. BRIESSMANN, *Tacitus und das filavische Geschichtsbild* (Hermes Einzelschrift X), Weisbaden 1955.

H. NESSELHAUF, 'Tacitus und Domitian', in *Hermes*, LXXX, 1952, pp. 222–45.

K. VON FRITZ, 'Tacitus, Agricola, Domitian and the Problem of the Principate', in *Class. Phil.*, LII, 1957, pp. 73–97.
(See *Cambr. Anc. Hist.*, X, pp. 963 f.).

TERTULLIAN (*Apologeticum*, ed. HOPPE, in *Corp. Script. Eccl. Lat.*, 69, Vienna 1939; ed. FRASSINETTI, in *Corpus Paravianum* (?), Turin 1965).

C. BECKER, *Tertullians Apologeticum. Werden und Leistung*, Munich 1954 (idem, ed. with trans. and comm., Munich 1952).

P. KERESZTES, 'Tertullian's Apologeticus. A Historical and Literary Study', in *Latomus*, XXV, 1966, pp. 124–33.

VALERIUS FLACCUS (*Argonautica*, ed. KRAMER, Leipzig 1913).

R. PREISWERK, 'Zeitgeschichtliches bei Valerius Flaccus', in *Phil.*, LXXXIX, 1934, pp. 433–42.

VELLEIUS PATERCULUS (*Historia Romana*, ed. STEGMANN DE PRITZWALD, Leipzig 1933).

I. LANA, *Velleio o della propaganda*, Turin 1952.

——, 'Nota Velleiana', in *Riv. Fil.*, XXXII, 1954, pp. 401–7.

M. L. PALADINI, 'Studi su Velleio Patercolo', in *Acme*, VI, 1953, pp. 447–78.

——, 'Ancora a proposito di Velleio Patercolo come fonte storica', in *Acme*, VII, 1954, p. 563.

——, 'Rapporti tra Velleio Patercolo e Valerio Massimo', in *Latomus*, XVI, 1957, pp. 232–51.

J. HELLEGOUARC'H, 'Les buts de l'œuvre historique de Velleius Paterculus', in *Latomus*, XXIII, 1964, pp. 669–84.

2. *Epigraphical*

Corpus Inscriptionum Latinarum (*CIL*), Vols. I–XVI, Berlin, 1863 onwards (cf. *Corporis Inscr. Lat. Supplementa Italica*, I, ad Vol. V, *Galliae Cisalpinae*, ed. H. PAIS, Rome 1884; also the *Supplementi* to Vol. VI, ed.

C. PIETRANGELI, I–II, in *Bull. Comm. Arch.*, LXVIII, 1940, pp. 175–202; LXIX, 1941, pp. 167–92).

Inscriptiones Graecae (IG), Vols. I–XIV (not all published, and some with no ed.), Berlin, 1873 onwards.

H. DESSAU, *Inscriptiones Latinae Selectae (ILS)*, Vols. I–III, Berlin 1892–1916 (photog. reprint 1954–5).

W. DITTENBERGER, *Sylloge Inscriptionum Graecarum*, 3rd ed. ed. F. HILLER VON GAERTRINGEN, (*Syll.³*), I–IV, Leipzig 1915–24 (photog. reprint 1960).

W. DITTENBERGER, *Orientis Graeci Inscriptiones Selectae (OGIS)*, I–II, Leipzig 1903–5 (photog. reprint 1960).

R. CAGNAT, *Inscriptiones Graecae ad res Romanas pertinentes (IGRR)*, I (1911), III (1906), IV (1908–27).

A. E. and J. S. GORDON, *Album of Dated Latin Inscriptions*, Berkeley, Calif., I (1958), II (1964), III (1965).

Inscriptiones Italiae (I. It.), edit. by the Unione Accademica Nazionale, Rome, 1931 onwards.

G. SOTGIU, *Iscrizioni latine della Sardegna*, Padua, I (1961), II (1968).

E. ESPÉRANDIEU, *Inscriptions latines de la Gaule*, I–II, Paris 1928–1929.

P. WUILLEUMIER, *Inscriptions latines des trois Gaules*, Paris 1963.

R. CAGNAT, A. MERLIN and L. CHATELAIN, *Inscriptions Latines d'Afrique*, Paris, 1923.

ST. GSELL, *Inscriptions Latines d'Algérie*: I, Paris 1932; II, 1, Paris 1957 (*inscr. recueillies par St. Gsell, préparées par G. Albertini et J. Zeiller, publiées par H. G. Pflaum, sous la direct. de L. Leschi*).

A. MERLIN, *Inscriptions Latines de la Tunisie*, Paris 1944.

L. CHATELAIN, *Inscriptions Latines du Maroc*, fasc. I, Paris 1942.

J. B. WARD PERKINS and J. M. REYNOLDS, *The Inscriptions of Roman Tripolitania*, Rome 1952 (cf. J. M. REYNOLDS, 'Inscr. of Rom. Trip. A Supplement', in *Pap. Bri. Sch. Rome*, XXIII, 1955, pp. 124–47).

R. G. COLLINGWOOD and R. P. WRIGHT, *The Roman Inscriptions of Britain*, I: *Inscriptions on Stone*, Oxford 1965.

E. HOWALD and E. MEYER, *Die römische Schweiz. Texte und Inschriften*, Zurich 1941.

V. HOFFILLER and B. SARIA, *Antike Inschriften aus Jugoslavien*, I: *Noricum und Pannonia Superior*, Zagreb 1938 (corrections to one by A. and J. SAJEL in the volume *Inscriptiones Latinae quae in Iugoslavia inter annos MCMXL et MCMLX repertae et editae sunt*, Ljubljana 1963, and reprint of the whole vol. 1969).

G. MIHAILOV, *Inscriptiones Graecae in Bulgaria repertae*, I–IV, Sofia 1956–66.

V. V. STRUVE, *Corpus Inscriptionum Regni Bosporani*, Leningrad 1965.

B. LABYSCHEV, *Inscriptiones antiquae orae septentrionalis ponti Euxini Graecae et Latinae*, I², II, IV, St Petersburg 1891, 1901, 1916 (repr, Hildesheim 1965).

E. KALINKA and R. HEBERDEY, *Tituli Asiae Minoris (TAM)*, Vienna 1901–44, 5 fasc.

Monumenta Asiae Minoris Antiqua (MAMA), pub. by the American Society for Archaeological Research in Asia Minor, I–VIII, Manchester 1928–1962.

L. and J. ROBERT, *Hellenica*, I–XIII, Paris 1940–65.

L. JALABERT, R. MOUTERDE and C. MONDÉSERT, *Inscriptions grecques et latines de la Syrie*, I–V, Beirut 1929–59.

(*for updating*) *L'Année Épigraphique (AÉ). Revue des publications épigraphiques relatives a l'antiquité romaine*. Paris, 1888 onwards, ed. by R. CAGNAT, then by A. MERLIN, and now by J. GAGÉ, M. LEGLAY, H. G. PFLAUM, P. WUILLEUMIER.

Supplementum Epigraphicum Graecum (SEG), Leiden, from 1925, ed. first by J. J. E. HONDIUS, now by A. G. WOODHEAD.

For the principal documents

See above, pp. 565 f. (*Tabula Hebana*), pp. 588 f., 602 f. (the *Elogia Tarquiniensia*), p. 591 (*Claudian tablet of Lyon*), p. 604 (*inscription from Nazareth*), p. 621 (*inscription from Acraephiae dealing with Nero's proclamation of the freedom of Greece*), p. 630 (*Lex de imperio Vespasiani*), p. 637 (*inscription mentioning Veleda*), p. 652 (*inscription from Domitian's reign on the cursus publicus*), pp. 342 and 665 (*inscr. of Q. Marcius Turbo*), p. 667 (*inscr. on Trajan's column*), p. 671 f., cf. 620 (*Horothesia Laberii Maximi*), p. 680 (*inscr. from Dura Europos on the Roman withdrawal*), pp. 693 and 704 (*inscr. from Nicopolis about the veterans discharged in 157*), p. 712 (*Aes Italicense and Marmor Sardianum*), pp. 714 and 722 (*inscr. about M. Valerius Maximianus*).

On the *Fasti Ostienses*, L. VIDMAN, *Fasti Ostienses* (Rozpravy Cesko-slovenské Akademie Věd, LXVII, 6), Prague 1957.

On the *Fasti Potentini*, N. ALFIERI, 'I fasti consulares di Potentia', in *Athen.*, XXVI, 1948, pp. 110–34.

For the brick-stamps, H. BLOCH, 'The Roman Brick-stamps not published in volume XVi of the Corpus Inscr. Lat.', in *Harv. St. Class. Phil.*,

LVI-LVII, 1947, and LVIII–LIX, 1948 (cf. *I bolli laterizi* etc., see below, ARTE, p. 739).

3. *Papyrological*

L. MITTEIS and U. WILCKEN, *Grundzüge und Chrestomathie der Papyruskunde*, Leipzig–Berlin 1912.

A. S. HUNT and C. C. EDGAR, *Select Papyri*: I, *Non-literary Papyri, Private Affairs*; II, *Non-literary Papyri, Public Documents*, London–Cambridge, Mass. 1932–4 (Loeb Classical Library).

A. DEISSMANN, *Licht vom Osten, Das Neue Testament und die neuentdeckten Texte der hellenistisch-römischen Welt*, 4th ed., Tübingen 1923.

H. I. BELL, *Jews and Christians in Egypt*, London 1924.

A. C. JOHNSON, *Roman Egypt to the Reign of Diocletian* (*An Economic Survey of Ancient Rome*, II), Baltimore, Md., 1936.

V. TCHERIKOVER, *The Jews in Egypt in the Hellenistic-Roman Age in the Light of the Papyri*, Jerusalem 1945.

H. A. MUSURILLO, *The Acts of the Pagan Martyrs, Acta Alexandrinorum*, Oxford 1954; idem, *Acta Alexandrinorum* (Bibl. Teubneriana), Lipsiae 1961.

V. A. TCHERIKOVER, A. FUKS and M. STERN, *Corpus Papyrorum Iudaicarum*, I, II, III, Cambridge, Mass. 1957, 1960, 1964 (see *Prolegomena*, I, pp. 48–93; in Vol. II important documents such as the letter of Claudius to the Alexandrians and the Acts of the pagan martyrs are now republished).

S. DARIS, *Documenti per la storia dell'esercito romano in Egitto*, Milan 1964.

P. BURETH, *Les titulatures impériales dans les papyrus, les ostraca et les inscriptions d'Égypte* (30 a.C.–284 p.C.), Brussels 1964.

(*For the principal documents.*) See above, p. 591 (*Letter of Claudius to the Alexandrians*), p. 601 (*Pap. BGU, 611*), p. 631 (*Pap. Fouad I, No. 8*), p. 632 (*pap. attesting the praetorian prefectship of Ti. Julius Alexander*), p. 647 (*pap. Berlin. 8334*), pp. 695 and 698 (*manuscripts from the Dead Sea*), p. 727 (*Pap. Berlin. 6866, on pay under Commodus*).

4. *Numismatic*

K. CHRIST, *Antike Numismatik, Einführung und Bibliographie*, Darmstadt 1967.

H. MATTINGLY, *Roman Coins from the Earliest Times to the Fall of the Western Empire*, 2nd ed., London 1960.

H. COHEN, *Description historique des monnaies frappées sous l'empire romain*, 2nd ed. (photog.), Graz 1955–7.

H. MATTINGLY, *Coins of the Roman Empire in the British Museum*, I

(*Augustus to Vitellius*), London 1923; II (*Vespasian to Domitian*), 1930; III (*Nerva to Hadrian*), 1936; IV (*Antoninus Pius to Commodus*), 1940.

H. MATTINGLY, ed. A. SYDENHAM and C. H. V. SUTHERLAND, *The Roman Imperial Coinage*, I (*Augustus to Vitellius*), London 1923, repr. 1948; II (*Vespasian to Hadrian*), 1926; III (*Antoninus Pius to Commodus*), 1930.

H. A. SEABY, *Roman Silver Coins*, II, 1–2: *Tiberius to Domitian. Nerva to Commodus*, London 1955.

G. ELMER, *Verzeichnis der römischen Reichsprägungen von Augustus bis Anastasius*, 2nd ed., Graz 1956.

S. BOLIN, *State and Currency in the Roman Empire to 300 A.D.*, Stockholm 1958.

P. L. STRACK, *Untersuchungen zur römischen Reichsprägung des 2. Jahrhunderts*, I: *Die Reichsprägung zur Zeit des Traian*, Stuttgart 1931; II: *Die Reichspr. zur Zeit des Hadrian*, Stuttgart 1933; III: *Die Reichspr. zur Zeit des Antoninus Pius*, Stuttgart 1937.

M. BERNHART, *Die Münzen der römischen Kaiserzeit*, Munich 1956.

S. M. BOND, 'The Coinage of the Early Roman Empire', in *Greece & Rome*, 2nd ser., IV, 1957, pp. 149–59.

M. GRANT, *From Imperium to Auctoritas. A Historical Study of Aes Coinage in the Roman Empire, 49 B.C.–A.D. 14*, Cambridge 1946.

——, *Roman Anniversary Issues. An Exploratory Study of the Numismatic and Medallic Commemoration of Anniversary Years 49 B.C.–A.D. 375*, Cambridge 1950.

——, 'Aspects of the Principate of Tiberius. Historical Comments on the Colonial Coinage issued outside Spain' (*Num. Notes and Monogr.*, CXVI), New York 1950.

——, 'Roman Coins as Propaganda', in *Archaeology*, V, 1952, pp. 79–85.

——, 'Roman Imperial Money', Edinburgh 1954.

——, 'The Mints of Roman Gold and Silver in the Early Principate', in *Num. Chron.*, 6th ser., XV, 1955, pp. 39–54.

——, *Roman History from Coins. Some Uses of the Imperial Coinage to the Historian*, Cambridge 1958.

J. C. MILNE, *Greek and Roman Coins and the Study of History*, London 1939.

C. H. V. SUTHERLAND, 'The Historical Evidence of Greek and Roman Coins', in *Greece & Rome*, IX, 1940, pp. 65–80.

——, 'The Personality of the Mints under the Julio-Claudian Emperors', in *Amer. Journ. Phil.*, LXVIII, 1947, pp. 47–63.

——, *Coinage in Roman Imperial Policy, 31 B.C.–A.D. 68*, London 1951.

J. M. C. TOYNBEE, 'Roman Medallions, their Scope and Purpose', in *Num. Chron.*, 6th ser., IV, 1944, pp. 27–44.

A. ABAECHERLI-BOYCE, *Festal and Dated Coins of the Roman Empire*, New York 1965.

M. AMIT, 'Propagande de succès et d'euphorie dans l'empire romain', in *Iura*, XVI, 1965, pp. 52–75.

L. ROSSI, 'Le insegne militari nella monetazione imperiale romana da Augusto a Commodo', in *Riv. It. Num.*, LXVII, 1965, pp. 41–81.

See above, p. 571 (propaganda coins of Tiberius), p. 584 (beginning of coining of gold and silver at the Rome mint), p. 613 (Nero's monetary reform), p. 624 (coinage of the civil war, 68–69), pp. 684 and 697 (coins of Hadrian: aeternitas imperii, provinces, armies), p. 730 (coinage of Commodus),

The epigraphical, papyrological and numismatic evidence is collected in the following works:

V. EHRENBERG and A. H. M. JONES, *Documents illustrating the Reigns of Augustus and Tiberius*, 2nd ed., Oxford 1955.

M. P. CHARLESWORTH, *Documents illustrating the reigns of Claudius and Nero*, Cambridge 1951.

E. M. SMALLWOOD, *Documents illustrating the Principates of Gaius, Claudius and Nero*, Cambridge 1967.

M. MCCRUM and A. G. WOODHEAD, *Select Documents of the Principates of the Flavian Emperors*, A.D. 68–96, Cambridge 1961.

E. M. SMALLWOOD, *Documents illustrating the Principates of Nerva, Trajan and Hadrian*, Cambridge 1966.

II. WORKS AND MONOGRAPHS ON THE EMPIRE AT ITS HEIGHT

1. *General works of reference*

PAULY, WISSOWA, KROLL, MITTELHAUS and ZIEGLER, *Real-encyclopädie der classischen Altertumswissenschaft*, 1893 onwards, I–XXIV; I A–IX A 2; Suppl. I–XI.

Der Kleine Pauly, I–III, Stuttgart 1964, 1967, 1969.

The Oxford Classical Dictionary, Oxford 1949.

Enciclopedia Italiana, Rome 1929–49.

CH. DAREMBERG and E. SAGLIO, *Dictionnaire des antiquités grecques et romaines*, 2nd ed., Paris 1875–1918.

E. DE RUGGIERO, *Dizionario epigrafico di antichità romane*, Rome 1894 onwards (lett. A–L).

Guida allo studio dellà civita romana antica, diretta da V. USSANI and F. ARNALDI, I², Naples 1959, II², Naples 1961.

(*for the chronology*)

H. F. CLINTON, *Fasti Romani. The Civil and Literary Chronology of Rome and Constantinople from the Death of Augustus to the Death of Justin II*, Oxford 1845–50.

(*atlases*)

P. FRACCARO, M. BARATTA and L. VISENTIN, *Grande Atlante geografico-storico-fisico-politico-economico*, IV ed., Novara 1938, plates IX–XIX.

H. BENGTSON and V. MILOJČIČ, *Grosser Historischer Weltatlas*, I, *Vorgeschichte und Altertum* (Atlas u. Erläuterungen), 2nd ed., Munich 1954.

H. E. STIER and E. KIRSTEN, *Westermanns Atlas zur Weltgeschichte*, I, *Vorzeit und Altertum*, Braunschweig 1956 (new ed. 1965).

H. H. SCULLARD and A. A. M. VAN DER HEYDEN, *Shorter Atlas of the Classical World*, Amsterdam and New York 1962.

2. General histories

L. S. LE NAIN DE TILLEMONT, *Histoire des empereurs et des autres princes qui ont régné durant les six premiers siècles de l'Église*, Paris 1690–1738.

CH. MERIVALE, *History of the Romans under the Empire*, 2nd ed., London 1875.

L. VON RANKE, *Weltgeschichte*, 3rd ed., Leipzig 1883 (Vols. II 2–IV 2).

V. DURUY, *Histoire des Romains depuis les temps le plus reculés jusqu'à l'invasion des barbares*, 2nd ed., IV (1882), V (1883), VI (1883), pp. 1–27.

T. MOMMSEN, *The Provinces of the Roman Empire from Caesar to Diocletian* (trans. by W. P. Dickson from the final volume of the *Römische Geschichte*), Turin–Rome, n.d.

H. SCHILLER, *Geschichte der römischen Kaiserzeit*, Gotha I 1 (1883), I 2 (1883), II (1887).

H. STUART JONES, *The Roman Empire*, B.C. 29–A.D. 476, London–New York 1908.

J. B. BURY, *History of the Roman Empire from its Foundation to the Death of M. Aurelius*, 6th ed., London 1913.

A. VON DOMASZEWSKI, *Geschichte der römischen Kaiser*, 3rd ed., I–II, Leipzig 1921–2.

G. BLOCH, *L'empire romain. Évolution et decadence*, Paris 1922.

B. NIESE, *Grundriss der römischen Geschichte nebst Quellenkunde*, 5th ed.

revised by E. HOHL (in the *Handbuch der Altertumswissenschaft*), Munich 1923 (for the empire, pp. 276 ff.); now replaced in the collection by H. BENGTSON, *Grundriss der romischen Geschichte mit Quellenkunde*, I, *Republik u. Kaiserzeit bis 284 n.Chr.*, Munich 1967 (for the empire, pp. 249 ff.).

V. CHAPOT, *Le monde romain* (L'évolution de l'humanité, XXII), Paris 1927, 2nd ed., 1938.

H. DESSAU, *Geschichte der römischen Kaiserzeit*, Berlin, I (1924), II 1 (1926), II 2 (1930).

E. ALBERTINI, *L'empire romain* (Peuples et civilisations, Histoire générale, IV), Paris 1929 (4th ed., 1939).

C. BARBAGALLO, *Storia universale*, II, 2: *Roma antica, L'impero*, Turin 1932 (new ed., 1952).

J. WOLF, *Römische Geschichte*, 2: *Die römische Kaiserzeit* (Gesch. der führenden Völker, VII), Freiburg 1932.

L. HOMO, *Le Haut-empire* (Hist. générale Glotz, Hist. romaine, III), Paris 1933 (2nd ed., 1941).

M. ROSTOVTZEFF, *Storia economica e sociale dell'impero romano*, Florence 1933 (3rd ed. revised by the author; 1st Eng. ed., Oxford 1926; 2nd Ger. ed., Leipzig 1930; a 2nd ed. of the 1st Eng. ed., in 2 vols., Oxford 1957, with revisions and addit. bibl. by P. M. FRASER).

A. FERRABINO, *L'Italia Romana*, Milan 1934.

E. T. SALMON, *A History of the Roman World from 30 B.C. to A.D. 138*, London 1944 (Methuen's History of the Greek and Roman World, VI), 6th ed., London 1968.

H. M. D. PARKER, *A History of the Roman World from A.D. 138 to 337*, London 1935 (Methuen's History of the Greek and Roman World, VII), 2nd ed. with revisions and addit. notes by B. H. WARMINGTON, London 1958.

The Cambridge Ancient History, Vol. X, *The Augustan Empire, 44 B.C.–A.D. 70*, edited by S. A. COOK, F. E. ADCOCK, M. P. CHARLESWORTH, Cambridge 1934 (reprinted with corrections 1962).

——, Vol. XI, *The Imperial Peace, A.D. 70–192*, Cambridge 1936 (reprinted with corrections 1956).

R. PARIBENI, *L'Italia imperiale da Ottaviano a Teodosio* (Storia d'Italia, dir. da P. FEDELE, II), Milan 1938.

A. PIGANIOL, *Histoire de Rome* (Clio, III), Paris 1939 (5th ed. 1962).

E. KORNEMANN, *Römische Geschichte*, II, *Die Kaiserzeit* (Kröners Taschenausgabe, 133), Stuttgart 1939 (5 Auflage bearb. von H. BENGTSON, Stuttgart 1963).

A. SOLARI, *L'impero romano*, I (*Unità e universalità di Augusto*), Genoa–Rome, etc. 1940; II (*Conflitto tra senato e provincie, 14–69*), 1941; III *Compromesso costituzionale, 69–193*), 1945; IV (*Impero provinciale. Restaurazione*), 1947.

G. M. COLUMBA, *L'impero romano*, I, *Da Cesare ai Flavii, 45 av. Cr.–96 d. Cr.* (Storia Politica d'Italia del Vallardi), Milan 1944.

A. FERRABINO, *Nuovà Storia di Roma*, III, *Da Cesare a Traiano*, Rome 1947.

A. PASSERINI, *La civilta del mondo antico*, Milan 1948, pp. 143 ff. (repr. with the title *Questioni di storia antica*, Milan 1952).

E. KORNEMANN, *Weltgeschichte des Mittelmeerraumes* (*von Philip II von Makedonien bis Muhammed*), ed. by H. BENGTSON, Munich, I, 1948; II, 1949 (2nd ed., Munich 1967).

A. PASSERINI, *Linee di storia romana in età imperiale*, Varese-Milan 1949 (repr. in *Nuove questioni di storia antica*, Milan 1968).

M. A. LEVI and A. PASSERINI, *Lineamenti di storia romana*, Milan 1951 (2nd ed., 1954).

S. I. KOVALEV, *Storia di Roma* (trans. from the Russian by R. ANGELOZZI), II, Rome 1952.

A. AYMARD and J. AUBOYER, *Rome et son empire* (Histoire générale des civilisations, II), Paris 1954.

L. PARETI, *Storia di Roma e del mondo romano*, IV, *Dal primo triumvirato all'avvento di Vespasiano*, V, *Da Vespasiano a Decio (69–251 d. Cr.*), Turin 1955, 1960.

Dodici Cesari (Quaderni della Radio, XL), Turin 1955: *Cesare e Augusto* (PARIBENI); *Tiberio, Otone, Vitellio* (PARETI); *Gaio* (MAZZARINO); *Claudio e Nerone* (LEVI); *Galba* (DE REGIBUS); *Vespasiano* (FERRABINO); *Tito* (CALDERINI); *Domiziano* (DEGRASSI).

G. GIANNELLI and S. MAZZARINO, *Trattato di storia romana*, II: *L'impero romano* (S. MAZZARINO), Rome 1956.

Historia mundi. Ein Handbuch der Weltgeschichte, ed. by FR. VALJAVEC, IV: *Römisches Weltreich und Christentum*, Berne 1956.

L. DE REGIBUS, *Storia romana*, Genoa 1957, pp. 160 ff.

H. H. SCULLARD, *From the Gracchi to Nero. A History of Rome from 133 B.C. to A.D. 68*, London 1959.

M. GRANT, *Rom. 133 v. Chr. bis 217 n. Chr.*, Zurich 1960.

M. A. LEVI, *L'impero romano* (*Encicl. Class.*, I 2, 2), Turin 1963 (repr. Milan 1967).

H. G. PFLAUM, *Das römische Kaiserreich* (Propyläen Weltgeschichte, IV, pp. 317–428), Berlin 1963 (trad. Ital., Milan 1968, IV, pp. 359–486).

A. GARZETTI, *L'impero romano* (Storia Politica Universale, II 2, pp. 203–336), Novara 1966.

F. MILLAR and others, *Das römische Reich und seine Nachbarn* (Fischer Weltgeschichte, VIII), Frankfurt 1966 (Eng. ed. London 1967; Ital., Milan 1968).

M. A. LEVI, *L'Italia antica*, II, *Dall'unificazione della penisola al suo isolamento*, Milan 1968.

3. *On various aspects of Roman imperial civilization*

(a) *Constitution*

T. MOMMSEN, *Römisches Staatsrecht*, I³, Berlin 1887; II³, Berlin 1887; III, Berlin 1887–8 (photog. repr., Basle 1952, French trans. by P. F. GIRARD, *Le droit publique romain*, nei Vols. I–VII [8 vols. of the] *Manuel des antiquités romaines* by MOMMSEN-MARQUARDT, Paris 1889–96).

J. N. MADVIG, *Die Verfassung und Verwaltung des römischen Staates*, Leipzig 1881.

J. B. MISPOULET, *Les institutions politiques des Romains*, I (*La constitution*), II (*L'administration*), Paris 1882–3.

E. HERZOG, *Geschichte und System des römischen Staatsverfassung*, Leipzig 1884–91.

F. DE MARTINO, *Storia della costituzione romana*, IV 1–2, Naples 1962–5.

A. BOUCHÉ-LECLERCQ, *Manuel des institutions romaines*, Paris 1886.

J. ASBACH, *Römische Kaisertum und Verfassung bis auf Traian*, Cologne 1896.

O. SCHULZ, *Das Wesen des römischen Kaisertums der ersten zwei Jahrhunderte*, Paderborn 1916 (repr. 1968).

E. KORNEMANN, *Doppelprinzipat und Reichsteilung im Imperium Romanum*, Leipzig 1930 (repr. 1968).

M. HAMMOND, *The Augustan Principate in Theory and Practice during the Julio-Claudian Period*, Cambridge, Mass. 1933.

M. HAMMOND, *The Antonine Monarchy* (Papers and Monographs of the Amer. Acad. in Rome, XIX), Rome 1959.

P. DE FRANCISCI, *Arcana Imperii*, Milan, I (1947), II (1948), III 1 and 2 (1948).

E. MEYER, *Römischer Staat und Staatsgedanke*, Zürich 1948 (2nd ed. Zürich and Stuttgart 1961).

U. COLI, 'Regnum', in *St. et doc. hist. et iuris*, XVII, 1951, pp. 1–168.

H. SIBER, *Römisches Verfassungsrecht in geschichtlicher Entwicklung*, Lahr 1952.

H. U. INSTINSKY, *Sicherheit als politisches Problem des Römischen Kaisertums* (Deutsche Beiträge zur Altertumswissenschaft, 3), Baden-Baden 1952.

L. WICKERT, 'Princeps', in *P.W.*, XXII 2, 1954, cc. 2057 ff.

U. VON LÜBTOW, *Das römische Volk. Sein Staat und sein Recht*, Frankfurt am Main 1955, special. pp. 367 ff.

A. H. M. JONES, *Studies in Roman Government and Law*, Oxford 1960.

J. A. O. LARSEN, *Representative Government in Greek and Roman History*, Berkeley, Calif. 1955.

(b) *Administration*

(*central and financial*)

J. MARQUARDT, *Römische Staatsverwaltung*, I², Leipzig 1881 (for the general organization of the empire); cf. French trans. by A. WEISS and P. LOUIS-LUCAS, in Vol. VIII, Paris 1889, of the *Manuel des antiquités romaines* of MOMMSEN and MARQUARDT.

O. HIRSCHFELD, *Die Kaiserlichen Verwaltungsbeamten bis auf Diocletian*, 2nd ed., Berlin 1905.

H. G. PFLAUM, *Les procurateurs équestres sous le haut empire romain*, Paris 1950.

——, *Les carrières procuratoriennes équestres sous le haut empire romain*, I–IV, Paris 1960–1.

G. VITUCCI, *Ricerche sulla praefectura urbi in etá imperiale* (*sec. I–III*), Rome 1956.

A. R. BURN, *The Government of the Roman Empire from Augustus to the Antonines*, London 1952.

J. MARQUARDT, *Römische Staatsverwaltung*, II², Leipzig 1884, pp. 1–316 (*Das Finanzwesen*, rev. by H. DESSAU; cf. French trans. by A. VIGIÉ, in Vol. X – *De l'organisation financière chez les Romains* – of the *Manuel* by MOMMSEN and MARQUARDT, Paris 1888).

D. VAN BERCHEM, *Les distributions de blé et d'argent à la plèbe romaine sous l'empire*, Geneva 1939.

H. G. PFLAUM, 'Essai sur le cursus publicus sous le haut empire romain', in *Mém. présentés á l'Acad. des Inscr. et Belles Lettres*, XIV, 189–391, Paris 1940.

S. J. DE LAET, *Portorium. Étude sur l'organisation douanière chez les Romains surtout à l'époque du haut empire*, Bruges 1949.

G. BARBIERI, 'Liberalitas', in DE RUGGIERO, *Dizionario Epigrafico*, IV, pp. 838–86, Rome 1957–8.

(*provincial and municipal*)

J. MARQUARDT, *Römische Staatsverwaltung*, I², Leipzig 1881 (for the provinces and the municipal administration); cf. French trans. by A. WEISS and P. LOUIS-LUCAS in Vols. VIII and IX of the *Manuel* by MOMMSEN and MARQUARDT, Paris 1889 and 1892).

W. LIEBENAM, *Städteverwaltung im römischen Kaiserreich*, Leipzig 1900.

F. F. ABBOTT and A. C. JOHNSON, *Municipal Administration in the Roman Empire*, Princeton, N.J. 1926.

G. H. STEVENSON, *Roman Provincial Administration, till the Age of the Antonines*, 2nd ed., Oxford 1949.

A. H. M. JONES, *The Cities of the Eastern Roman Provinces*, Oxford 2nd ed. 1971.

——, *The Greek City from Alexander to Justinian*, Oxford 1940.

——, *The Cities of the Roman Empire. Political, Administrative and Judicial Institutions*, in *La ville*, I: *Institutions administratives et judiciaries* (Rec. de la Soc. Jean Bodin, VI), Brussels 1954, pp. 135–76.

F. VITTINGHOFF, 'Römische Stadtrechtsformen der Kaiserzeit', in *Zeitschr. Sav. Stift.*, Rom. Abt., LXVIII, 1951, pp. 435–85.

A. DEGRASSI, 'L'amministrazione delle città', in *Guida allo studio della civiltà romana antica*, I, Naples 1952, pp. 297–329, with bibliography (2nd ed. 1959).

P. ROMANELLI, 'Le provincie e la loro amministrazione', ibid., pp. 331–377, with bibliography on individual provinces.

D. MAGIE, *Roman Rule in Asia Minor*, Princeton, N.J. 1950.

P. ROMANELLI, *Storia delle province romane dell'Africa*, Rome 1959.

J. J. HATT, *Histoire de la Gaule romaine*, Paris 1959.

O. SEEL, *Römertum und Latinität*, Stuttgart 1964 (cf. H. DREXLER, 'Romanità e latinità', in *Maia*, XVIII, 1966, pp. 103–14).

J. DEININGER, *Die Provinziallandtage der römischen Kaiserzeit von Augustus bis zum Ende des dritten Jahrhunderts n. Chr.*, Munich 1965.

U. LAFFI, *Adtributio e contributio. Problemi del sistema politico-amministrativo dello stato romano*, Pisa 1966.

D. NOERR, *Imperium und Polis in der hohen Prinzipatszeit*, Munich 1966. (See also below, Prosopographical Lists, pp. 819 ff.)

(*military*)

J. MARQUARDT, *Römische Staatsverwaltung*, II², Leipzig 1884, pp. 317–608 (*Das Militärwesen*, rev. by A. V. DOMASZEWSKI; cf. French trans. by J. BRISSAUD, in Vol. XI – *De l'organisation militaire chez les Romains*, of the *Manuel* by MOMMSEN and MARQUARDT, Paris 1891).

J. KROMAYER and G. VEITH, *Heerwesen und Kriegführung der Griechen und Römer* (Handbuch der Altertumswissenschaft, IV, 3, 2), Munich 1928, pp. 470 ff. (by E. V. NISCHER), repr. 1963.

H. DELBRÜCK, *Geschichte der Kriegskunst im Rahmen der politischen Geschichte*, 3rd ed., Berlin 1920.

A. PASSERINI, 'Le forze armate', in *Guida allo studio della civiltà romana antica*, I, Naples 1952, pp. 479–534 (2nd ed. 1959 with bibliography brought up to 1958 by E. GABBA).

G. FORNI, 'Esperienze militari nel mondo romano', in *Nuove questioni di storia antica*, Milan 1968, pp. 815–85.

M. MARIN Y PEÑA, *Instituciones militares romanas* (Enciclopedia clasica, 2), Madrid 1956.

M. DURRY, *Les cohortes prétoriennes*, Paris 1938.

A. PASSERINI, *Le coorti pretorie*, Rome 1939.

M. DURRY (trans. J. KORETZKI), *Praetoriae cohortes*, in PAULY–WISSOWA, *Realencyclopädie*, XXII 2 (1954), cc. 1607–34.

M. SPEIDEL, *Die Equites singulares Augusti*, Bonn 1965.

A. V. DOMASZEWSKI, 'Die Rangordnung des römischen Heeres', in *Bonner Jahrb.*, CXVII, Cologne 1909 (2nd ed. revised by B. DOBSON, in *Bonner Jahrb.*, Beih. XIV, Cologne 1967).

H. FREIS, *Die Cohortes Urbanae* (Epigraphische Studien, 2), Beih. der Bonner Jahrb., Bd. 21, Cologne and Graz 1967.

E. RITTERLING, *Legio*, in PAULY–WISSOWA, XII, 1924–5, cc. 1186–1829.

A. PASSERINI, *Legio*, in DE RUGGIERO, *Dizionario Epigrafico*, IV, pp. 549–624 [Rome 1949].

H. M. D. PARKER, *The Roman Legions*, 2nd ed. (with bibliogr. by G. WATSON, brought up to 1957), Cambridge 1958.

G. FORNI, *Il reclutamento delle legioni da Augusto a Diocleziano*, Milan–Rome 1953.

I. SZILAGYI, 'Les variations des centres de prépondérance militaire dans les provinces frontières de l'empire romain', in *Acta Ant. Ac. Scient. Hung.*, II, 1953, pp. 117–223 (lists of the positions of the units in A.D. 6, 20, 46, 75, 107, 140, 215, 275 and at the beginning of the V[th]c.).

G. ALFÖLDI, 'Die Truppenverteilung der Donaulegionen am Ende des I Jahrhunderts', in *Act. Arch. Ac. Scient. Hung.* XI, 1959, pp. 113–41.

J. F. GILLIAM, 'Enrolment in the Roman Imperial Army', in *Symbolae Taubenschlag*, II, Wroclaw 1956, pp. 207–16.

G. L. CHESSMEN, *The Auxilia of the Roman Imperial Army*, Oxford 1914.

W. WAGNER, *Die Dislokation der römischen Auxiliarformationen in den*

Provinzen Noricum, Pannonien, Moesien und Dakien von Augustus bis Gallienus, Berlin 1938.

G. ALFÖLDI, 'Die Auxiliartruppen der Provinz Dalmatien', in *Act. Arch. Ac. Sc. Hung.*, XIV, 1962, pp. 259–96.

K. KRAFT, *Zur Rekrutierung der Alen und Kohorten an Rhein und Donau* (Dissert. Bernenses, ser. I, 3), Berne 1951.

R. SAXER, 'Untersuchungen zu den Vexillationen des römischen Kaiserheeres von Augustus bis Diokletian', in *Bonner Jahrb.*, Beih. XVIII, Cologne 1967.

CHR. COURTOIS, 'Les politiques navales de l'empire romain', in *Rev. Hist.*, ann. 64°, tom. CLXXXIV, 1939, pp. 17–47 and 225–59.

CH. G. STARR, JR., *The Roman Imperial Navy*, Ithaca, N.Y., 1941 (2nd ed., Cambridge 1960).

L. WICKERT, 'Die Flotte der römischen Kaiserzeit', in *Würzburger Jahrbücher f. die Altertumswiss.* IV, 1949–50, pp. 100–25.

D. KIENAST, *Untersuchungen zu den Kriegsflotten der römischen Kaiserzeit,* Bonn 1966.

E. SANDER, 'Zur Rangordnung des römischen Heeres. Die Flotten', in *Historia*, VI, 1957, pp. 347–67.

G. A. ROST, *Vom Seewesen und Seehandel in der Antike, Eine Studie aus maritim-militärischer Sicht,* Amsterdam 1969.

(c) *Economy, society, culture*

(*economy and its reflections in society*)

F. M. HEICHELHEIM, *Wirtschaftsgeschichte des Altertums, vom Palaeolithikum bis zur Völkerwanderung der Germanen, Slaven und Araber,* I–II, Leiden 1938 (definitive Eng. ed., *An Ancient Economic History*, I–II, trans. by J. STEVENS, Leiden 1958–64).

An Economic Survey of Ancient Rome, ed. T. FRANK, II, *Egypt* (JOHNSON), Baltimore, Md. 1936; III, *Britain* (COLLINGWOOD), *Spain* (VAN NOSTRAND), *Sicily* (SCRAMUZZA), *Gaule* (GRENIER), Baltimore, Md. 1937; IV, *Africa* (HAYWOOD), *Syria* (HEICHELHEIM), *Greece* (LARSEN), *Asia Minor* (BROUGHTON), Baltimore, Md. 1938; V, *Rome and Italy of the Empire* (T. FRANK), Baltimore, Md. 1940; VI, *General Index* (BROUGHTON and TAYLOR). Baltimore, Md. 1940 (photog. repr. Paterson, N.J., 1959).

H. J. LOANE, *Industry and Commerce of the City of Rome* (50 B.C.–A.D 200.). Baltimore, Md. 1938.

G. E. F. CHILVER, *Cisalpine Gaul. Social and Economic History from 49 B.C. to the Death of Trajan,* Oxford 1941.

E. GREN, *Kleinasien und der Ostbalkan in der wirtschaftlichen Entwicklung der römischen Kaiserzeit*, Diss. Uppsala 1941 (also printed in the series Uppsala Universitets Arsskrift, 9, Uppsala–Leipzig 1941).

S. J. DE LAET, *Aspects de la vie sociale et économique sous Auguste et Tibère*, Brussels 1944.

U. KAHRSTEDT, *Das Wirtschaftliche Gesicht Griechenlands in der Kaiserzeit* (Dissertationes Berneses, ser. I, fasc. 7), Berne 1954.

——,'Die Wirtschaftliche Lage Grossgriechenlands in der Kaiserzeit' (*Historia*, Einzelschriften, 4), Wiesbaden 1960.

S. PANCIERA, *Vita economica di Aquileia in età romana*, Aquileia 1957.

V. A. SIRAGO, *L'Italia agraria sotto Traiano*, Louvain 1958.

A. PIGANIOL, *Les documents cadastraux de la colonie romaine d'Orange*, Paris 1962.

J. ROUGÉ, *Recherches sur l'organisation du commerce maritime en Méditerranée sous l'empire romain*, Paris 1966.

(*technology*)

R. J. FORBES, *Studies in Ancient Technology*, I–IX, Leiden 1955–64 (with new editions of the individual vols.).

A History of Technology, edited by CH. SINGER, E. J. HOLMYARD, A. R. HALL and TREVOR J. WILLIAMS, II, *The Mediterranean Civilizations and the Middle Ages, c. 700 B.C. to c. A.D. 1500*, Oxford 1956.

(*social characteristics*)

F. M. DE ROBERTIS, *Contributi alla storia delle corporazioni a Roma*, Bari 1934.

——, *Il diritto associativo romano*, Bari 1938.

——, *Il fenomeno associativo nel mondo romano dai collegi della repubblica alle corporazioni del basso impero*, Naples 1955.

L. HARMAND, *Un aspect social et économique du monde romain. Le patronat sur les collectivités publiques, des origines au bas empire*, Paris 1957.

W. M. RAMSAY, *The Social Basis of Roman Power in Asia Minor*, prepared for the press by J. G. C. ANDERSON, Aberdeen, 1941

J. GAGÉ, *Les classes sociales dans l'empire romain*, Paris 1964.

(*citizenship and classes*)

W. KUBITSCHEK, *Imperium Romanum tributim descriptum*, Vindobonae 1889.

A. N. SHERWIN-WHITE, *The Roman Citizenship*, Oxford 1939.

A. STEIN, *Der römische Ritterstand*, Munich 1927.

M. HAMMOND, 'Composition of the Senate A.D. 68–235, in *Journ. Rom. St.*, XLVII, 1957, pp. 74–81 (more on the origin of the senators in L. HAHN, 'Römische Beamte griechischer und orientalischer Abstammung in der Kaiserzeit (von Hadrian bis zur bleibenden Teilung des Reichs)', in *Festgabe zur 400-Jahrfeier des Alten Gymn. Nürnberg*, Nuremberg 1926, pp. 11–64; C. S. WALTON, 'Oriental senators in the Service of Rome: A Study of Imperial Policy down to the Death of Marcus Aurelius', in *Journ. Rom. St.*, XIX, 1929, pp. 38–66).

B. GRENZHEUSER, *Kaiser und Senat in der Zeit von Nero bis Nerva*, diss. Münster 1964.

CH. SAUMAGNE, *Le droit latin et les cités romaines sous l'empire. Essais critiques*, Paris 1965.

H. HILL, 'Nobilitas in the Imperial Period', in *Historia*, XVIII, 1969, pp. 230–50.

(slavery)

E. CICCOTTI, *Il tramonto della schiavitù nel mondo antico*, 2nd ed., Udine 1940.

A. T. GEOGHEGAN, *The Attitude towards Labour in Early Christianity and Ancient Culture*, Washington, D.C. 1945.

W. L. WESTERMANN, *The Slave Systems of Greek and Roman Antiquity* (Mem. Amer. Philos. Soc. XL). Philadelphia, Pa. 1955.

C. A. FORBES, 'The Education and Training of Slaves in Antiquity', in *Trans. Proc. Amer. Phil. Ass.*, LXXVI, 1955, pp. 321–60.

A. M. DUFF, *Freedmen in the Early Roman Empire*, 2nd ed., Cambridge 1958.

M. I. FINLEY (and others), *Slavery in Classical Antiquity*, Cambridge 1960.

J. VOGT, *Sklaverei und Humanität. Studien zur antiken Sklaverei und ihrer Erforschung* (Historia-Einzelschr., VIII), Wiesbaden 1965.

H. CHANTRAINE, *Freigelassen und Sklaven im Dienst des römischen Kaiser. Studien zu ihrer Nomenklatur* (Forschungen zur antiken Sklaverei, I), Wiesbaden 1967.

(civilization and customs)

L. FRIEDLÄNDER, *Darstellungen aus der Sittengeschichte Roms in der Zeit von Augustus bis zum Ausgang der Antonine*, I–IV, 9th–10th ed., Leipzig 1921–1923.

J. CARCOPINO, *La vie quotidienne à Rome à l'apogée de l'empire*, Paris 1939.

U. E. PAOLI, *Vita romana*, 7th ed., Florence 1955.

P. M. DUVAL, *La vie quotidienne en Gaule pendant la paix romaine (I^e–IIIe siècles ap. J.-C.)*, Paris 1952.

R. ETIENNE, *La vie quotidienne a Pompéi*, Paris 1966.

L. HOMO, *Rome impériale et l'urbanisme dans l'antiquité* (L'évolution de l'humanité, XVIII bis), Paris 1951.

A. VON GERKAN, 'Die Einwohnerzahl Roms in der Kaiserzeit', in *Röm. Mitt.*, LV, 1940, pp. 149–95.

J. AYMARD, *Essai sur les chasses romaines des origines à la fin du siècle des Antonins* (*Cynegetica*), Paris 1951 (Bibl. Éc. Fr. d'Ath. et Rome, CLXX).

G. CH. PICARD, *La civilisation de l'Afrique romaine*, Paris 1959.

(*ideas*)

H. FUCHS, *Der geistige Widerstand gegen Rom in der antiken Welt*, Berlin 1938 (2nd ed. 1964).

C. N. COCHRANE, *Christianity and Classical Culture. A Study of Thought and Action from Augustus to Augustine*, Oxford 1940 (2nd ed., New York 1977).

U. KAHRSTEDT, *Kulturgeschichte der römischen Kaiserzeit*, Munich 1944, 2nd ed. Berne 1958.

E. HOWALD, *Die Kultur der Antike*, 2nd ed., Zurich 1948 (special. p. 191 ff.).

C. WIRSZUBSKI, *Libertas as a Political Idea at Rome during the Late Republic and Early Principate*, Cambridge 1950. (Ital. trans. by A. MUSCA, with append. by A. MOMIGLIANO, Bari 1957.)

M. HAMMOND, 'Res olim dissociabiles, principatus ac libertas. Liberty under the Early Roman Empire', in *Harv. St. Class. Phil.*, LXVII, 1963, pp. 93–113.

P. DE FRANCISCI, *Spirito della civiltà romana*, 2nd ed., Rome 1952.

CH. G. STARR, *Civilization and the Caesars. The Intellectual Revolution in the Roman Empire*, Ithaca, N.Y. 1954.

M. L. CLARKE, *The Roman Mind. Studies in the History of Thought from Cicero to Marcus Aurelius*, London 1956.

S. DILL, *Roman Society from Nero to Marcus Aurelius*, New York 1957.

R. MacMULLEN, *Enemies of the Roman Order: Treason, Unrest and Alienation in the Empire*, Cambridge, Mass. 1966.

(*education*)

H. I. MARROU, *Histoire de l'éducation dans l'antiquité*, new ed., Paris 1966.

(d) *Law*

S. HÄNEL, *Corpus legum ab imperatoribus Romanis ante Iustinianum latarum*, Lipsiae 1857.

C. G. BRUNS and O. GRADENWITZ, *Fontes iuris Romani antiqui*, I⁷, *Leges et negotia*, Tübingen 1909 (photog. repr. 1958, 1969).

Fontes iuris Romani anteiustiniani, I², *Leges* (RICCOBONO), Florence 1941; II², *Auctores* (BAVIERA, FERRINI and FURLANI), Florence 1940; III², *Negotia* (ARANGIO and RUIZ), Florence 1943.

W. W. BUCKLAND, *A Text-book of Roman Law from Augustus to Justinian*, 3rd ed. revised by P. STEIN, Cambridge 1963.

G. PUGLIESE CARRATELLI, 'Tabulae Herculanenses', I, in *Par. Pass.*, 1946, pp. 379–85; II, *ibid.*, 1948, pp. 165–84 (cf. V. ARANGIO–RUIZ, *Il processo di Giusta*, pp. 129–51; repub. in *Boll. Ist. Dire. Rom.*, LXII, 1959, pp. 223–45); III, *ibid.*, 1953, pp. 455–63; IV, *ibid.*, 1954, pp. 54–74, in collaboration with V. ARANGIO–RUIZ (cf. 1951, pp. 224–230, M. DELLA CORTE, *Tabelle cerate ercolanesi*); V, *ibid.*, 1955, pp. 448–77, in collaboration with V. ARANGIO–RUIZ; VI, *ibid.*, 1961, pp. 66–73, in collaboration with V. ARANGIO–RUIZ.

P. KRÜGER, *Geschichte der Quellen und Litteratur des romischen Rechts*, Leipzig 1888 (2nd ed., Munich–Leipzig 1912; French trans. by M. BRISSAUD, *Histoire des sources du droit romain*, in Vol. XVI of the *Manuel* by MOMMSEN, MARQUARDT and KRÜGER, Paris 1894).

L. WENGER, *Die Quellen des römischen Rechts*, Vienna 1953.

H. F. JOLOWICZ, *Historical Introduction to the Study of Roman Law*, 2nd ed., Cambridge 1952.

W. KUNKEL, *Römische Rechtsgeschichte. Eine Einführung*, 4th ed., Cologne 1964.

A. BERGER, *Encyclopedic Dictionary of Roman Law* (Trans. Amer. Philos. Soc., XLIII, 2), Philadelphia, Pa., 1953.

F. SCHULZ, *History of Roman Legal Science*, Oxford 1946.

V. ARANGIO-RUIZ, *Storia del diritto romano*, 7th ed., Naples 1957.

——, *Istituzioni di diritto romano*, 13th ed., Naples 1957.

B. BIONDI, *Il diritto romano* (Vol. XX of this *Storia di Roma*), Bologna 1957.

——, *Istituzioni di diritto romano*, Milan 1956.

——, 'Aspetti universali e perenni del pensiero giuridico romano', in *Symb. Taubenschlag*, II, Wroclaw 1956, pp. 177–205.

T. MOMMSEN, *Römisches Strafrecht*, Leipzig 1899 (photog. repr. Graz 1955; French trans. by J. DUQUESNE, *Le droit pénal romain*, in Vols XVII–XVIII–XIX of the *Manuel* by MOMMSEN, MARQUARDT and KRÜGER, Paris 1907).

M. KASER, *Das römische Zivilprozessrecht*, Munich 1966.

R. ORESTANO, 'Gli editti imperiali. Contributo alla teoria della loro validità ed efficacia nel diritto romano classico', in *Bull. Ist. Dir. Rom.,* XLIV, 1936-7, pp. 219-331.

F. M. DE ROBERTIS, *Sulla efficacia normativa delle costituzioni imperiali,* Bari 1941 (Ann. Fac. Giurispr. Bari, IV).

A. H. M. JONES, 'Imperial and Senatorial Jurisdiction in the Early Principate', in *Historia,* III, 1955, pp. 464-88.

P. GARNSEY, 'The Lex Iulia and Appeal under the Empire', in *Journ. Rom. St.,* LVI, 1966, pp. 167-89.

——, 'The Criminal Jurisdiction of Governors', in *Journ. Rom. St.,* LVIII, 1968, pp. 51-9.

D. DAUBE, *Forms of Roman Legislation,* Oxford 1956.

W. KUNKEL, *Herkunft und soziale Stellung der römischen Juristen,* Weimar 1952.

(e) *Religion*

(*traditional and foreign religion and cults – general works*)

J. MARQUARDT, *Römische Staatsverwaltung,* III, *Das Sacralwesen,* 2nd ed. revised by G. WISSOWA, Leipzig 1885 (French trans. by M. BRISSAUD, *Le culte chez les Romains,* in Vols. XII–XIII of the *Manuel* by MARQUARDT and MOMMSEN, Paris 1889-90).

G. WISSOWA, *Religion und Kultus der Römer,* 2nd ed., Munich 1912.

K. LATTE, *Römische Religionsgeschichte,* Munich 1960.

——, *Die Religion der Römer und der Synkretismus der Kaiserzeit,* Tübingen 1927.

P. TACCHI-VENTURI, *Storia delle Religioni,* I, Turin 1934, 5th ed., 1962 (M. GALDI, *La religione dei Romani*); II, Turin 1936, 5th ed., 1962 (S. ROSADINI, *La religione cristiana;* P. FERRARIS, *Il cristianesimo dai tempi apostolici al Concilio di Trento*).

A. GRENIER, *Le génie romain dans la religion, la pensée et l'art,* Paris 1938.

N. TURCHI, *La religione di Roma antica (Storia di Roma,* XVIII), Bologna 1939.

J. CARCOPINO, *Aspects mystiques de la Rome païenne,* Paris 1941.

A. GRENIER, 'Les religions étrusque et romaine', in *Mana, Introduction à l'histoire des religions,* II, 2, Paris 1948.

F. CUMONT, *Lux perpetua,* Paris 1949.

FR. ALTHEIM, *Römische Religionsgeschichte,* II, Baden-Baden 1953.

M. W. H. LEWIS, *The Official Priests of Rome under the Julio-Claudians* (Pap. and Monogr. Am. Ac. Rome, XVI), Rome 1955.

J. BAYET, *Histoire politique et psychologique de la religion romaine,* Paris 1957.

Études préliminaires aux religions orientales dans l'empire romain, pub. by M. J. VERMASEREN, 11 volumes from 1961 to 1969.

(*religious policy of the emperors*)

L. DE REGIBUS, *Politica e religione da Augusto a Costantino*, Genoa 1953.

J. BEAUJEU, *La religion romaine à l'apogée de l'empire*, I: *La politique religieuse des Antonins (96–192)*, Paris 1955.

P. LAMBRECHTS, 'Les empereurs romains et leur politique religieuse', in *Rev. Belg. Phil. Hist.*, XXXV, 1957, pp. 495–511 (see also below, *Cristianesimo e impero*).

(*imperial cult*)

L. ROSS TAYLOR, *The Divinity of the Roman Emperor* (Phil. Mon. of Amer. Phil. Ass., 1), Middletown, Conn. 1931.

K. SCOTT, *The Imperial Cult under the Flavians*, Stuttgart 1936.

D. M. PIPPIDI, *Recherches sur le culte imperial*, Paris 1939.

W. ENSSLIN, 'Gottkaiser und Kaiser von Gottes Gnaden', in *Sitz.-ber. Bay. Ak. d. Wiss.* 1943, 6, Munich 1943.

L. CERFAUX and J. TONDRIAU *Un concurrent du christianisme. Le culte des souverains dans la civilisation greco-romaine*, Paris 1957.

R. ÉTIENNE, *Le culte impérial dans la péninsule iberique d'Auguste à Dioclétieu* (Bibl. Éc. Franç. Ath. et Rome, CXCI), Paris 1958.

F. BOEMER, 'Der Eid beim Genius des Kaisers', in *Athen.*, XLIV, 1966, pp. 77–133.

(*primitive Christianity; general works; sources*)

Reallexikon für Antike und Christentum, ed. by THEODOR KLAUSER, Stuttgart, from 1950 (lett. A-F).

K. PRÜMM, *Religionsgeschichtliches Handbuch, für den Raum der Altchristlichen Umwelt*, Freiburg 1943 (photog. repr. Rome 1954).

F. VAN DER MEER and CHR. MOHRMANN, *Atlas of the Early Christian World*, transl. and edit. by M. F. HEDLUND and H. H. ROWLEY, Manchester–Nijmegen 1958.

C. KIRCH and L. UEDING, *Enchiridion fontium historiae ecclesiasticae antiquae*, 9th ed., Freiburg 1965.

P. BREZZI, *Fonti e studi di storia della chiesa*, I, Milan 1962.

(*Histories of Christianity and of the Church, and monographs*)

H. LIETZMANN, *Geschichte der Alten Kirche*, I: *Die Anfänge*, Berlin and Leipzig 1932 (3rd ed., Berlin 1953); II: *Ecclesia catholica*, Berlin and Leipzig 1936 (2nd ed., Berlin 1953). Trans. B. L. Woolf, London 1937–51.

A. LOISY, *La naissance du christianisme*, Paris 1933.

J. LEBRETON and J. ZEILLER, *L'Église primitive* (*Histoire de l'Église, depuis les origines jusqu'à nos jours*, published under direction of A. FLICHE and V. MARTIN, I), Paris 1934 (2nd ed. 1946).

Handbuch der Kirchengeschichte, ed. by H. JEDIN, I: K. BAUS, *Von der Urgemeinde zur frühchristlichen Grosskirche*, Freiburg 1963.

J. DANIÉLOU and H. MARROU, *Nouvelle histoire de l'Église*, I, *Des origines à Grégoire le Grand*, Paris 1963.

A. SABA, *Storia della Chiesa dalle origini ai nostri giorni*, I, Turin 1938.

A. S. BARNES, *Christianity at Rome in the Apostolic Age. An Attempt at Reconstruction of History*, London 1938.

S. COLOMBO, *Primavera cristiana. Studi e documenti sulla Chiesa antica*, Turin 1939.

G. BARDY, *Les premiers jours de l'Église*, Paris 1941.

——, *La conversion au Christianisme durant les premiers siècles*, Paris 1949.

E. BUONAIUTI, *Storia del cristianesimo*, I: *Evo antico*, Milan 1942–43.

M. GOGUEL, *Jésus et les origines du christianisme*, I: *La naissance du christianisme*, II: *L'Église primitive*, Paris 1946–7 (Bibliothèque historique; del Vol. I new edit. 1955).

——, *Les premiers temps de l'Église*, Neuchatel 1949.

L. TODESCO, *Storia della Chiesa*, I: *I primi 300 anni*, 4th ed. revis. by I. DANIELE, Turin 1947.

K. D. SCHMIDT, *Grundriss der Kirchengeschichte*, I: *Die Geschichte der christlichen Kirche auf dem Boden der hellenistisch-römischen Kultur*, Göttingen 1949.

P. BREZZI, 'La composizione sociale delle comunità cristiane nei primi secoli. Contributo allo studio della crisi della società alla fine del mondo antico', in *St. e Mat. di St. delle Relig.*, XXII, Bologna 1949–50, pp. 22–55.

S. G. F. BRANDON, *The Fall of Jerusalem and the Christian Church. A Study of the Effect of the Jewish Overthrow of A.D. 70 on Christianity*, London 1951.

K. BIHLMEYER, *Kirchengeschichte* (auf Grund des Lehrbuches von F. X. VON FUNK neubearb.), I: *Das Christliche Altertum*, 12th ed. revised by H. TEUCHLE, Paderborn 1951.

F. X. SEPPELT, *Geschichte der Päpste von den Anfängen bis zur Mitte des zwanzigsten Jahrhunderts*, I, 2nd ed.: *Der Aufstieg des Papstum von den Anfängen bis zum Ausgang des sechsten Jahrhunderts*, Munich 1954.

L. GOPPELT, *Christentum und Judentum im ersten und zweiten Jahrhundert. Ein Aufriss der Urgeschichte der Kirche*, Gütersloh 1954.

C. SCHNEIDER, *Geistesgeschichte des antiken Christentums*, Munich 1954.

J. CARCOPINO, *De Pythagore aux Apôtres. Études sur la conversion du monde romain*, Paris 1956.

P. CARRINGTON, *The Early Christian Church*, Cambridge 1957.

A. OMODEO, *Saggi sul Cristianesimo antico. Gesù il Nazoreo. Il Cristianesimo nel secondo secolo*, Naples 1958.

W. JALGER, *Early Christianity and Greek Paideia*, Cambridge, Mass. 1966.

(*apologetica*)

B. ALTANER, *Patrologie*, 13th ed., Freiburg im Breisgau 1951.

J. QUASTEN, *Patrology*, I: *The Beginnings of Patristic Literature*, Utrecht–Antwerp 1950.

G. LAZZATI, *Gli sviluppi della letteratura sui martiri nei primi quattro secoli*, Turin 1956.

(*Christianity and the Empire*)

A. HARNACK, *Kirche und Staat bis zur Grundung des Staatskirche*, 2nd ed., Berlin 1909.

L. HOMO, *Les empereurs romains et le christianisme*, Paris 1931.

O. MARUCCHI, *Pietro e Paolo a Roma*, 4th ed. revised by C. CECCHELLI, Turin 1934.

P. DE LABRIOLLE, *La réaction païenne. Étude sur la polémique antichrétienne du Ier au VIe siècle*, Paris 1934.

P. BREZZI, *Cristianesimo e impero romano tino alla morte di Costantino*, Rome 1942 (2nd ed. 1944).

——, 'L'impero romano e il cristianesimo dalle origini alla metà del V secolo', in *Guida allo studio della civ. rom. ant.*, I, Naples 1952, pp. 229–50.

——, 'Appunti sul problema dei rapporti tra cristianesimo ed impero romano', in *Stud. Rom.*, V, 1957, pp. 660–3.

H. MATTINGLY, *Christianity in the Roman Empire*, Dunedin, Univ. of Otago (New Zealand) 1955.

J. MOREAU, *La pérsecution du christianisme dans l'empire romain* (Mythes et Religions, XXXII), Paris 1956.

M. SORDI, 'I primi rapporti fra lo stato romano e il cristianesimo e l'origine delle persecuzioni', in *Rend. Acc. Lincei*, ser. VIII, Vol. XII, 1957, pp. 58–93 (see above, pp. 753 and 773, and add V. MONACHINO, 'Il fondamento giuridico delle persecuzioni nei primi due secoli', in *Sc. Catt.*, LXXXI, 1953, pp. 3–32).

H. RAHNER, *Kirche und Staat im frühen Christentum*, Munich 1961.

G. BARBERO, *Il pensiero politico cristiano*, I, *Dai Vangeli a Pelagio*, Turin 1962.

H. GRÉGOIRE, *Les persécutions dans l'empire romain*, 2nd ed. (with the collaboration of P. ORGELS, J. MOREAU and A. MARICQ), Brussels 1964.

M. SORDI, *Il cristianesimo e Roma* (Vol. XIX of the *Storia di Roma*), Bologna 1965.

E. GRIFFE, *Les persécutions contre les chrétiens aux Ier et IIe siècles*, Paris 1967.

J. SPEIGL, *Der römische Staat und die Christen, Staat und Kirche von Domitian bis Commodus*, Amsterdam 1969.

T. D. BARNES, 'Legislation against the Christians', in *Journ. Rom. St.*, LVIII, 1968, pp. 32–50.

(f) *Literature*

M. SCHANZ, *Geschichte der römischen Literatur*, II, *Die römische Literatur in der Zeit der Monarchi bis auf Hadrian*, 4th ed., edited by C. HOSIUS, Munich 1935; III, *Die römische Literatur von Hadrian bis auf Constantin (324 n. Chr.)*, 3rd ed., edited by C. HOSIÜS and G. KRÜGER, Munich 1922 (Handbuch der Altertumswissenschaft, VIII, 2–3).

N. TERZAGHI, *Storia della letteratura latina da Tiberio a Giustiniano*, Milan 1934.

H. BARDON, *Les empereurs et les lettres latines d'Auguste à Hadrien*, Paris 1940.

G. DEVOTO, *Storia della lingua di Roma* (Storia di Roma, XXIII), Bologna 1940, 2nd ed., 1944.

A. G. AMATUCCI, *La letteratura di Roma imperiale* (Storia di Roma, XXV), Bologna 1947.

A. ROSTAGNI, *Storia della letteratura latina*, II: *L'impero*, Turin 1957, 3rd ed. 1964, revised by I. LANA.

J. W. DUFF, *A Literary History of Rome in the Silver Age. From Tiberius to Hadrian*, 2nd ed. revised by A. M. DUFF, New York 1960.

M. L. CLARKE, *Rhetoric at Rome. A Historical Survey*. London 1953.

H. BARDON, *La littérature latine inconnue*, II: *L'époque impériale*, Paris 1956.

M. DURRY, 'Les empereurs comme historiens d'Auguste à Hadrien', in *Histoire et historiens dans l'antiquité*, Geneva 1958, pp. 215–45.

J. PALM, *Rom, Römertum und Imperium in der griechischen Literatur der Kaiserzeit*, Lund 1959.

L. FERRERO, *Rerum scriptor. Saggi sulla storiografia romana*, Trieste 1962.

N. SCIVOLETTO, *Studi di letteratura latina imperiale*, Naples 1963.

S. MAZZARINO, *Il pensiero storico classico*, II 2, Bari 1967.

(See also *On the sources*, p. 779 and ff.; and elsewhere.)

(g) *Philosophy*

W. WINDELBAND, *Geschichte der abendländischen Philosophie im Altertum*, 4th ed., revis. by A. GÖDECKMEYER, Munich 1923 (Handbuch der Altertumswissenschaft, V, 1).

FR. UEBERWEG, *Grundriss der Geschichte der Philosophie*, I, *Die Philosophie des Altertums*, edited by K. PRÄCHTER, 13th ed. (photog. reprint of the 12th, 1925), Basle 1953; II, *Die Patristische und Sholastische Philosophie*, hrsg. by B. GEYER, 12th ed. (photog. reprint of the 11th, 1927), Basle 1951.

FR. KLINGNER, *Römische Geisteswelt*, Leipzig 1943 (3rd ed. Munich 1956).

M. POHLENZ, *Die Stoa. Geschichte einer geistigen Bewegung*, I–II, Göttingen 1948–9.

A. LEVI, *Storia della filosofia romana*, Florence 1949.

——, 'La filosofia in Roma', in *Guida allo st. della civ. rom. ant.*, II, Naples 1954, pp. 463–500.

H. MEYER, *Abendländische Weltanschauung*, II, *Vom Urchristentum bis zu Augustinus*, 2nd ed., Paderborn 1953.

A. GRILLI, *Il problema della vita contemplativa nel mondo greco-romano*, Milan 1953.

(h) *Art*

(*in general*)

Enciclopedia dell'arte antica, classica e orientale, I–VII, Rome 1958–66.

Nella *Guida allo st. della civ. rom. ant.*, II, Naples 1954 (2nd ed., 1961), brief summaries with bibliogr. on *Architettura e Ingegneria* (G. GIOVANNONI), *La scultura romana* (A. ADRIANI), *Pittura e mosaico* (D. MUSTILLI), *Le arti minori* (L. LAURENZI), *Scavi di Ostia* (G. CALZA), *di Pompei ed Ercolano* (M. DELLA CORTE), *di Stabiae* (O. ELIA), *di Cirenaica e Tripolitania* (G. CAPUTO), *in Albania* (D. MUSTILLI), *di Rodi* (L. LAURENZI), finally on the *primordi dell'arte cristiana* (C. COSTANTINI), pp. 65–179.

P. DUCATI, *L'arte in Roma dalle origini al secolo VIII* (Storia di Roma, XXVI), Bologna 1938.

D. LEVI, 'L'arte romana. Schizzo della sua evoluzione e sua posizione nella storia dell'arte antica', in *Ann. Sc. Arch. Ital. Atene*, NS, VIII–X, 1946–8 [publ. 1950], pp. 229–303.

G. BECATTI, *Arte e gusto negli scrittori latini*, Florence 1951.

A. HAUSER, *Sozialgeschichte der Kunst und Literatur*, I–II, Munich 1953.

A. FROVA, *L'arte di Roma e del mondo romano* (*Storia Universale dell'Arte*, II 2), Turin 1961.

L. BREGLIA, *L'arte romana nelle monete dell'età imperiale*, Milan 1968.

CH. V. GORDON, *Piecing together the Past. The Interpretation of Archaeological Data*, New York 1956.

L. CREMA, *L'architettura romana*, Turin 1959.

N. L. MACDONALD, *The Architecture of the Roman Empire*, I: *An Introductory Study*, New Haven, Conn. 1965.

(*topography, town planning, monuments*)

S. B. PLATNER and TH. ASHBY, *A Topographical Dictionary of Ancient Rome*, Oxford 1929.

Fontes ad topographiam veteris Urbis Romae pertinentes, colligendos atque edendos curavit I. LUGLI, I (Rome 1952), II (1953), III (1955).

G. CARETTONI, A. M. COLINI, L. COZZA, G. GATTI, *La pianta marmorea di Roma antica. Forma Urbis Romae*, Rome 1960 (cf. H. BLOCH, 'A New Edition of the Marble Plan of Ancient Rome', in *Journ. Rom. St.*, LI, 1961, pp. 143–52).

A. P. FRUTAZ, *Le piante di Roma*, Rome 1962.

G. LUGLI, *I monumenti antichi di Roma e Suburbio*, I (Rome 1931), II (1934), III (1938), Suppl. (1940).

——, *Roma antica, il centro monumentale*, Rome 1946.

——, *Monumenti minori del foro romano*, Rome 1947.

F. CASTAGNOLI, C. CECCHELLI, G. GIOVANNONI and M. ZOCCA, *Topografia e urbanistica di Roma* (*Storia di Roma*, XXII), Rome 1958 (1st Pt., F. CASTAGNOLI, *Roma antica*, pp. 1–186; also reprinted separately, with corrections and additions, Bologna 1969).

G. BECATTI, *La colonna coclide istoriata, problemi storici, iconografici, stilistici*, Rome 1960.

Carta archeologica di Roma (1:2500), plates 1 & 3, Florence 1962 and 1964.

(*building technology*)

H. BLOCH, 'I bolli laterizi e la storia edilizia romana. Contributi all'archeologia e alla storia romana', in *Bull. Comm. Arch.*, LXIV, 1936, pp. 141–225; LXV, 1937, pp. 83–187; LXVI, 1938, pp. 61–221; also collected in the volume with the same title in the collection *Studi e materiali del Museo dell'Impero Romano*, IV, Rome 1947 (repr. Rome 1968).

G. LUGLI, *La tecnica edilizia romana, con particolare riguardo a Roma e Lazio*, Rome 1957.

M. E. BLAKE, *Roman Construction in Italy from Tiberius through the Flavians* (Carnegie Publication), Washington 1959.

(*imperial iconography*)

J. J. BERNOULLI, *Römische Ikonographie*, Leipzig 1882–96.

K. S. MÜLLER, *Cäsaren-Porträts*, Bonn 1914–27.

R. WEST, *Römische Porträtsplastik*, I, Munich 1933; II, 1941.

R. PARIBENI, *Il ritratto nell'arte antica*, Milan 1934.

L. VON MATT and H. KUEHNER, *Die Cäsaren. Eine Geschichte der römischen Herrscher in Bild und Wort*, Würzburg 1964.

W. H. GROSS, 'Augusta. Untersuchungen zur Grundlegung einer Livia-Ikonographie', in *Abhandl. d. Ak. d. Wiss. Göttingen*, Philol.-hist. Kl., 3 F, LII, Göttingen 1962.

L. POLACCO, *Il volto di Tiberio. Saggio di critica iconografica*, Rome 1955.

A. CARANDINI, *Vibia Sabina. Funzione politica, iconografia e il problema del classicismo adrianeo*, Florence 1959.

For individual monuments, see above, pp. 574–6 (*camée de la Ste Chapelle*), pp. 616–17 ff. (*excavations under the Confessio of St Peter in the Vatican*, to which should be added M. GUARDUCCI, *I graffiti sotto la Confessione di S. Pietro in Vaticano*, I, II, III, Vatican City 1958; *idem, La tomba di Pietro. Notizie storiche e nuove scoperte*, Rome 1959), p. 650f. (*Flavian reliefs of the Cancellaria*), p. 667 (*Trajan's column and works by Apollodorus of Damascus*), p. 697 (*Hadrian's villa at Tivoli*), p. 720 (*Column of Marcus Aurelius*).

III. PROSOPOGRAPHICAL LISTS

1. *General*

Prosopographia Imperii Romani, saec. I, II, III, 2nd ed. revised by E. GROAG and A. STEIN, I (A–B), Berlin and Leipzig 1933; II (C), 1936; III (D–F), 1943; IV, 1 (G), Berlin 1952; IV, 2 (H), 1958; IV, 3 (I), 1966 (ed. L. PETERSEN).

2. *Fasti consulares*

J. KLEIN, *Fasti consulares inde a Caesaris nece usque ad imperium Diocletiani*, Leipzig 1881.

W. LIEBENAM, *Fasti consulares imperii Romani*, Bonn 1910.

A. DEGRASSI, *I fasti consolari dell'impero romano, dal 30 av. Cr. al 613 d. Cr.*, Rome 1952.

G. BARBIERI, 'Nota sui consoli del 40, 44 e 45 d. C.', in *Epigr.*, XXIX, 1967, pp. 3–10 (cf. ibid., XXX, 1968, p. 185).

S. DUSANIC, 'On the consules suffecti of A.D. 74–76', in *Epigr.*, XXX, 1968, pp. 59–74.

E. M. SMALLWOOD, 'Consules suffecti of A.D. 55', in *Historia*, XVII, 1968, p. 384.

3. Senate

S. J. DE LAET, *De Samenstelling van den Romeinschen Senaat gedurende de eerste eeuw van het Principaat (28 vóór Chr., 68 na Chr.)*, Antwerp 1941.

K. T. SCHNEIDER, *Zusammensetzung des römischen Senates von Tiberius bis Nero*, diss. Zurich 1942.

B. STECH, *Senatores Romani qui fuerint inde a Vespasiano usque ad Traiani exitum* (Beiheft *Klio*, X), Leipzig 1912 (repr. 1963).

A. GARZETTI, 'Albo senatorio nel regno di Nerva', in append. to *Nerva*, Rome 1950.

P. LAMBRECHTS, *La composition du sénat romain de l'accession au trône d'Hadrien à la mort de Commode (117–192)*, Antwerp, Paris and The Hague 1936.

——, *La composition du sénat romain de Septime Sévère à Dioclétian (193–284)*, Budapest 1937 (Diss. Pannonicae, I, 8).

G. BARBIERI, *L'albo senatorio da Settimio Severo a Carino*, Rome 1952.

R. SYME, *Tacitus*, II, Oxford 1958 (various lists of senators and other personages from the Flavian period to the age of the Antonines, pp. 639 ff.).

A. PELLETIER, 'Les sénateurs d'Afrique proconsulaire d'Auguste à Gallien', in *Latomus*, XXIII, 1964, pp. 511–31.

4. Priests

P. HABEL, *De pontificum Romanorum inde ab Augusto usque ad Aurelianum condicione publica*, Vratislaviae 1888 (pp. 3–44 list of the pont. max. and of the pontifices).

G. HOWE, *Fasti sacerdotum populi Romani publicorum aetatis imperatoriae*, Leipzig 1904.

M. W. HOFFMAN LEWIS, *The Official Priests of Rome under the Julio-Claudians* (Pap. and Mon. Amer. Ac. Rome, XVI), Rome 1955.

H. G. PFLAUM, 'Les sodales Antoniniani de l'époque de Marc-Aurèle', in *Mem. Ac. Inscr. et Belles Lettres*, XV2, Paris 1966.

5. Magistrates and officials of the central government

H. LEVISON, *Fasti praetorii inde ab Octaviani imperii singularis initio usque ad Hadriani exitum*, Bratislava 1892 (praetors).

F. HEILIGENSTÄDT, *Fasti aedilicii inde a Caesaris nece usque ad imperium Alexandri Severi*, Diss. Halle 1910 (aediles).

G. NICCOLINI, *I fasti dei tribuni della plebe*, Milan 1934 (for the imperial age, pp. 364–86).

M. FORTINA, 'Praefecti aerarii Saturni', in *Riv. St. Class.*, IX, 1961, pp. 217–34.

A. E. GORDON, *Quintus Veranius Consul* A.D. *49*, Berkeley and Los Angeles 1952 (Univ. of California Publ. in *Class. Arch.*, II, 5, pp. 231–352; contains a list of the *curatores aedium sacrarum et operum locorumque publicorum* with their subordinates from Augustus to the IV century, pp. 279–304, and a list of the persons honoured with statues or triumphal insignia in the imperial age, pp. 305–30).

H. G. PFLAUM, 'La chronologie de la carrière de L. Caesennius Sospes. Contribution à l'étude des responsables sénatoriaux de la distribution de blé à la plèbe romaine', in *Historia*, II, 1954, pp. 431–50 (list from Aug. to Diocl.).

J. CROOK, *Consilium Principis. Imperial Councils and Counsellors from Augustus to Diocletian*, Cambridge 1955 (list of the *amici* and of the *comites*, pp. 148–90, replacing the list of BANG in FRIEDLÄNDER, *Sittengesch.*, IV[9–10], pp. 56–76; add R. SYME, 'Some Friends of the Caesars', in *Amer. Journ. Phil.*, LXXVII, 1956, pp. 264–73).

G. VITUCCI, *Ricerche sulla praefectura urbi in età imperiale (sec. I–III)*, Rome 1956 (list of *praefecti urbi*, pp. 133ff.).

A. PASSERINI, *Le coorti pretorie*, Rome 1939; M. DURRY, *Les cohortes prétoriennes*, Paris 1939; L. L. HOWE, *The Pretorian Prefect from Commodus to Diocletian* (A.D. *180–305*), Chicago 1942 (praetorian prefects; add W. ENSSLIN, in *P.W.*, XXII 2, 1954, c. 2423 ff.).

CH. G. STARR, JR, *The Roman Imperial Navy, 31* B.C.–A.D. *324*, Ithaca, N.Y. 1941 (pp. 209–14 *Prosopographia praefectorum classium*).

6. Provincial governors

(*general lists*)

S. J. DE LAET, *De Samenstelling* etc. (see above Senate): contains the lists of governors of senatorial rank for all the provinces from 28 to A.D. 68.

W. HÜTTL, *Antoninus Pius*, II, Prague 1933; contains lists of all the provincial governors and officials under Antoninus Pius.

(Sicily, Sardinia and Corsica)

J. KLEIN, *Die Verwaltungsbeamten von Sicilien und Sardinien*, Bonn 1878.

A. HOLM, *Geschichte Siciliens im Alterthum*, III, Leipzig 1898, pp. 513–542: *Römische Beamte in der Provinz Sicilen*.

P. MELONI, *L'amministrazione della Sardegna da Augusto all'invasione vandalica*, Rome 1958 (lists from p. 181).

(Iberian provinces)

M. MARCHETTI, in DE RUGGIERO, *Diz. Ep.*, III, p. 754 ff. (1915–19), s. v. *Hispania* (cf. for Baetica R. THOUVENOT, 'La province romaine de Bétique', Paris 1940 and for Lusitania G. HEUTEN, 'Les gouverneurs de la Lusitanie et leur administration', in *Latomus*, II, 1938, pp. 236–78; v. also above p. 596).

A. BALIL, 'Los proconsules de la Bética', in *Zephirus*, XIII, 1962, pp. 75–89.

——, 'Los gobernadores de la Hispania Tarraconense durante el imperio romano', in *Emerita*, XXXII, 1964, pp. 19–34.

——, 'Funcionarios subalternos en Hispania durante el imperio romano', in *Emerita*, XXXIII, 1965, pp. 297–319; XXXIV, 1966, pp. 305–13.

G. ALFÖLDI, *Fasti Hispanienses. Senatorische Reichsbeamte und Offiziere in den Spanischen Provinzen des römischen Reiches von Augustus bis Diokletian*, 1969.

(Gallic provinces)

J. TOUTAIN, in DE RUGGIERO, *Diz. Ep.*, III, pp. 376 ff. (1905), s. v. *Gallia*.

(Britain)

D. ATKINSON, 'The Governors of Britain from Claudius to Diocletian', in *Journ. Rom. St.*, XII, 1922, pp. 60–73.

E. BIRLEY, 'The Roman Governors of Britain', in append. to G. H. ASKEW, *The Coinage of Roman Britain*, London 1951.

(The Germanies)

E. RITTERLING, *Fasti des römischen Deutschland unter dem Prinzipat*, Vienna 1932.

G. ALFÖLDI, *Die Legionslegaten der römischen Rheinarmeen* (Epigr. Studien 3), Beih. der Bonner Jahrb., Bd. 22, Cologne–Graz 1967.

(Raetia and Noricum)

MARY B. PEAKS, *The General Civil and Military Administration of Noricum and Raetia*, Chicago 1907 (Univ. of Chicago St. in Class. Phil., IV pp. 161–230).

G. WINKLER, 'Die Reichsbeamten von Noricum und ihr Personal bis zum Ende der römischen Herrschaft', in *Sitz.-b. d. Oesterr. Ak. d. Wiss.*, Phil.-hist. Kl., 261, 2, Vienna 1969.

(*Dalmatia*)

A. JAGENTEUFEL, *Die Statthalter der römischen Provinz Dalmatien von Augustus bis Diokletian* (Oesterr. Ak. d. Wiss, Schrift. d. Balkankomm., Antiq. Abt., 12), Vienna 1958.

J. J. WILKES, 'A New Governor of Dalmatia', in *Epigr. Stud.*, IV, 1967, pp. 119–21.

(*Pannonia*)

E. RITTERLING, 'Die Statthalter der pannonischen Provinzen', in *Arch.-epigr. Mitth.*, XX, 1897, pp. 1 ff.

——, 'Die Legati propraetore von Pannonia Inferior seit Traian', in *Arch. Ertesitö*, XLI, 1927, pp. 281 ff.

M. PAVAN, 'La provincia romana della Pannonia Superior', in *Mem. Acc. Linc.*, ser. VIII, Vol. VI, 5, Rome 1955.

W. REIDINGER, 'Die Statthalter des ungeteilten Pannonien und Oberpannoniens von Augustus bis Diokletian' *Antiquitas*, I, 2, Bonn 1956.

J. FITZ, 'Legati legionum Pannoniae superioris', in *Act. Ant. Ac. Sc. Hung.*, IX, 1961, pp. 159–207.

——, 'Legati Augusti pro praetore Pannoniae Inferioris', in *Act. Ant. Ac. Sc. Hung.*, XI, 1963, pp. 245–324.

A. MÓCSY, s.v. 'Pannonia', in *Realencycl.*, Suppl. IX (1962), cc. 588–94.

R. SYME, 'Governors of Pannonia Inferior', in *Historia*, XIV, 1965, pp. 342–61 (governors from 106 to M. Aurelius).

A. DOBO, *Die Verwaltung der römischen Provinz Pannonien von Augustus bis Diocletianus, Die Provinziale Verwaltung*, Amsterdam 1968.

(*Moesia*)

A. STEIN, *Die Legaten von Moesien*, Budapest 1940.

J. FITZ, *Die Laufbahn der Statthalter in der römischen Provinz Moesia inferior*, Weimar 1966.

(*Dacia*)

J. JUNG, *Fasten der Provinz Dacien, mit Beiträgen zur römischen Verwaltungs- geschichte*, Innsbruck 1894.

A. STEIN, *Die Reichsbeamte von Dazien*, Budapest 1944.

D. W. WADE, 'Some Governors of Dacia: a Rearrangement', in *Class. Phil.*, LXIV, 1969, pp. 105–7.

(*Thrace*)

A. STEIN, *Römische Reichsbeamte der Provinz Thracia*, Sarajevo 1920.

——, 'Neues zu römischen Statthaltern von Thrakien', in *Serta Hoffil-leriana*, Zagreb 1940, pp. 211–15.

(*Achaea*)

E. GROAG, 'Die Römischen Reichsbeamte von Achaia bis auf Diokletian', in *Ad. d. Wiss. in Wien, Schrift. d. Balkankomm., Antiq.*, Abt., IX, Vienna and Leipzig 1939.

A. E. RAUBITSCHEK, 'Two Notes on the Fasti of Achaia', in *St Robinson*, II, St Louis 1953, pp. 330–3.

L. MORETTI, 'Un nuovo proconsole d'Acaia?', in *Arch. Class.*, V, 1953, pp. 255–9.

(*Crete and Cyrene*)

R. PARIBENI, in DE RUGGIERO, *Diz. Ep.*, II, 1906, pp. 1269 ff., s.v. *Creta*.

P. ROMANELLI, 'Un nuovo governatore della provincia di Creta e Cirene, P. Pomponio Secondo', in *Quad. Arch. della Libia*, IV, 1961, pp. 97–100.

J. M. REYNOLDS and R. G. GOODCHILD, 'The City Lands of Apollonia in Cyrenaica', in *Libya Antiqua*, II, 1965, pp. 103–7 (for the new proconsul C. Arinius Modestus).

(*provinces of Asia Minor*)

W. H. WADDINGTON, *Fastes de provinces asiatiques*, Paris 1872.

D. MAGIE, *Roman Rule in Asia Minor*, Princeton, N.J. 1950; p. 1579 onwards, complete lists for the provinces of Asia, Bithynia-Pontus, Cappadocia, Cilicia, Galatia, Lycia-Pamphylia; p. 1601, lists of various local magistrates, lists of centres of the worship of Rome, of Rome and Augustus, and of Augustus alone, lists of groups of Roman residents.

W. H. WADDINGTON, 'Supplément aux Fastes de la province d'Asie', in *Bull. Corr. Hell.*, VI, 1882, pp. 285–92 (for Proconsular Asia alone).

V. CHAPOT, *La province romaine proconsulaire d'Asie, depuis ses origines jusqu'à la fin du haut-empire*, Paris 1904 (pp. 305–402, lists of the proconsuls, quaestors, legates, procurators; from p. 403–89, lists of the sacerdotal titles, of the cities where *neocòri* are mentioned, of the Asiarchs, of the *archiereis* and of the *archiereiai*).

——, 'Données nouvelles sur la prosopographie de l'Asie proconsulaire', in *Mél. Martroye*, Paris 1941, pp. 81–92.

R. K. SHERK, *The Legates of Galatia from Augustus to Diocletian*, Baltimore, Md. 1951.

R. SYME, 'Legates of Cilicia under Trajan', in *Historia*, XVIII, 1969, pp. 352–66.

(*Syria*)

H. SEYRIG, 'Antiquités syriennes, Le statut de Palmyre', in *Syria*, XII, 1941, pp. 155 ff.; pp. 174 f. append. with list of the legates between 63 and 137.

(*Arabia*)

H. G. PFLAUM, 'Les gouverneurs de la province romaine d'Arabie de 193 à 305', in *Syria*, 1957, pp. 128–44.

(*Egypt*)

L. CANTARELLI, 'La serie dei prefetti di Egitto, I, Da Ottaviano Augusto a Diocleziano (a. 30 av. Cr. – A.D. 288)', in *Mem. Acc. Linc.*, ser. V, Vol. XII, Rome 1906.

O. W. REINMUTH, *The Prefect of Egypt from Augustus to Diocletian* (Beiheft *Klio*, 21), Leipzig 1935.

——, 'Praefectus Aegypti', in P. W., *Realencyclopädie*, XXII, 2, 1954, cc. 2353–77; Suppl. VIII, 1956, cc. 525–39.

——, 'A Working List of the Prefects of Egypt, 30 B.C. to 299 A.D.', in *Bull. Amer. Soc. of Papyrologists* (Toronto), IV, 1967, pp. 75–128.

A. STEIN, *Die Präfekten von Aegypten in der römischen Kaiserzeit* (Diss. Bern. ser. I, 1), Bern 1950 (see list of documents concerning the prefects of Egypt from Augustus to the fourth century in P. BURETH, 'Documents papyrologiques relatifs aux préfets d'Egypte', in *Bull. Fac. Strasburg*, XXXIII, 1954–5, pp. 135–48.

(*Provinces of Africa*)

R. CAGNAT, *L'armée romaine d'Afrique et l'occupation militaire de l'Afrique sous les empereurs*, Paris 1892 (specially for Numidia after A.D. 38 and the Mauretanias).

A. C. PALLU DE LESSERT, *Fastes des provinces africaines sous la domination romaine*, I–II, Paris 1896–1901.

P. ROMANELLI, 'Iscrizione inedita di Leptis Magna con nuovi contributi ai Fasti della provincia d'Africa', in *Quad. Arch. Libia*, II, 1951, pp. 71–9.

A. MERLIN, 'Additions aux Fastes proconsulaires d'Afrique', in *Mem. Soc. Antiq. d. Fr.*, LXXXIII, 1954, pp. 23 ff.

R. SYME, 'Proconsuls d'Afrique sous Antonin le Pieux', in *Rev. Ét. Anc.*, LXI, 1959, pp. 310–19.

B. E. THOMASSON, *Die Statthalter der römischen Provinzen Nordafrikas von Augustus bis Diocletianus* (Acta Instituti Romani Regni Sueciae, ser. in 8°, IX, 2), Lund 1960; cf. idem, 'Verschiedenes zu den Proconsules Africae', in *Eranos*, LXVII, 1969, pp. 175–91.

G. DI VITA-EVRARD, 'Un nouveau proconsul d'Afrique, parent de Septime Sévère', in *Mél. Éc. Franç. Ath. et Rome*, LXXV, 1960, pp. 389–414.

R. SYME, 'Les proconsuls d'Afrique sous Hadrien', in *Rev. Ét. Anc.*, LXVII, 1965, pp. 342–52.

J. MARCILLET-JAUBERT, 'Contribution aux fastes de Numidie', in *Bull. Arch. Alg.*, II, 1966–7, pp. 159–73.

INDEX OF NAMES
OF PERSONS AND
NOTABLE EVENTS

INDEX OF NAMES OF PLACES AND PEOPLES

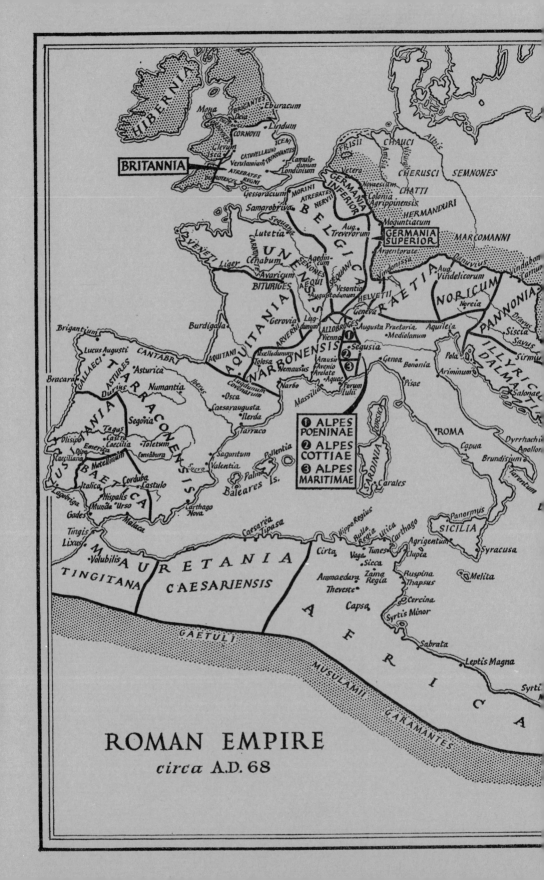

HIBERNIA

Mona
BRIGANTES
Deia •*Eburacum*
CORNOVII
Lindum
Glevum *Isca*
CATUVELLAUNI ICENI
BRITANNIA
Verulamium TRINOVANTES
ATREBATES REGNI *Camulodunum*
DUROTRIGES *Londinium*
Gessoriacum
FRISII CHAUCI
Albis
MORINI
Samarobriva VETERA CHERUSCI SEMNONES
NERVII GERMANIA *Novaesium* CHATTI
Lutetia INFERIOR *Colonia*
BELGICA *Agrippinensis*
VENETI *Liger* *Cenabum* SENONES *Aug.* *Moguntiacum* HERMANDURI
Agedin- *Treverorum*
LUGDUNENSIS *cum* GERMANIA MARCOMANNI
Avaricum EQUI SEQUANI SUPERIOR
BITURIGES *Augustodunum* *Argentorate* NORICUM
Vesontio *Vindonissa* *Aug.*
AQUITANIA *Gerovia* HELVETII RAETIA *Vindelicorum* *Vindobona*
Burdigala ARVERNI *Lug-* *Geneva* *Noreia* PANNONIA
dunum ALLOBROGES *Augusta* *Praetoria* *Aquileia* *Siscia*
AQUITANI *Vienna* ① *Segusia* *Mediolanum* *Sirmium*
Uxellodunum ② *Genoa* *Pola* ILLYRICUM
Tolosa NARBONENSIS ③ *Bononia* *Salonae*
Lugdunum *Arausio* *Ariminum* DALMATIA
Brigantium *Convenarum* *Nemausus* *Avenio*
Lucus Augusti CANTABRI *Osca* *Narbo* *Arelate* *Aquae*
ASTURES *Asturica* *Caesaraugusta* *Massilia* *Forum* CORSICA
Bracara *Durius* *Ilerda* *Julii*
GALLAECI TARRACONENSIS *Numantia*
Segovia ① ALPES
LUSITANIA *Tarraco* POENINAE
Tagus *Castra* *Toletum* ② ALPES *ROMA*
Olisipo *Caecilia* *Consabura* COTTIAE *Capua* *Dyrrhachium*
Emerita SARDINIA ③ ALPES *Apollonia*
Dipo *Metellinum* *Saguntum* MARITIMAE *Brundisium*
Caeciliana BAETICA *Valentia* *Pollentia* *Tarentum*
Corduba *Palma* *Carales*
Italica *Castulo* *Baleares Is.*
Lacobriga *Hispalis* *Munda* *Urso*
Gades *Malaca* *Carthago*
Nova *Panormus*
Tingis *Caesarea* *Hippo Regius* *Utica* SICILIA
Lixus *Tipasa* *Bulla* *Carthago* *Agrigentum*
Volubilis *Regia* *Tunes* *Clupea* *Syracusa*
MAURETANIA *Cirta* *Vaga* *Sicca* *Melita*
TINGITANA CAESARIENSIS *Ammaedara* *Zama* *Ruspina*
Theveste *Regia* *Thapsus*
AFRICA *Cercina*
Capsa *Syrtis Minor*
GAETULI *Sabrata*
Leptis Magna
MUSULAMII GARAMANTES *Syrtis*

ROMAN EMPIRE
circa A.D. 68